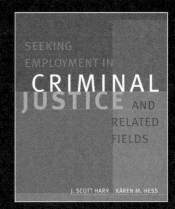

www.wadsworth.com

wadsworth.com is the World Wide Web site for Wadsworth Publishing Company and is your direct source to dozens of online resources.

At *wadsworth.com* you can find out about supplements, demonstration software, and student resources. You can also send e-mail to many of our authors and preview new publications and exciting new technologies.

wadsworth.com
Changing the way the world learns®

CRIMINOLOGY

seventh edition

Larry J. Siegel, Ph.D.
University of Massachusetts—Lowell

Wadsworth
Thomson Learning

Australia • Canada • Denmark • Japan • Mexico • New Zealand • Philippines
Puerto Rico • Singapore • South Africa • Spain • United Kingdom • United States

Executive Editor, Criminal Justice: Sabra Horne
Senior Development Editor: Dan Alpert
Assistant Editor: Shannon Ryan
Editorial Assistant: Ann Tsai
Marketing Manager: Christine Henry
Project Editor: Jennie Redwitz
Print Buyer: Karen Hunt
Permissions Editor: Bob Kauser
Production Service: Cecile Joyner/
　The Cooper Company

Text and Cover Designer: Jeanne Calabrese
Photo Researcher: Linda Rill
Copy Editor: Meg McDonald
Illustrator: Precision Graphics
Indexer: Do Mi Stauber
Compositor: Digital Output
Cover Image: Mark Kostabi, "Conversation Pieces";
　1996 oil on canvas, 24×18 inches
Cover Printer: Phoenix Color Corporation
Printer/Binder: R. R. Donnelley and Sons

Photo credits: page 664

Printed in the United States of America

1 2 3 4 5 6 03 02 01 00 99

**Library of Congress
Cataloging-in-Publication Data**
Siegel, Larry J.
　Criminology/Larry J. Siegel.—7th ed.
　　p. cm.
　Includes bibliographical references and index.
　ISBN 0-534-51696-3
　1. Criminology. 2. Crime—United States.
　I. Title.
　HV6025.S483   1999
364—dc21　　　　　　　　　　　99-25729

Instructor's Edition: ISBN 0-534-51697-1

For more information, contact

Wadsworth/Thomson Learning
10 Davis Drive
Belmont, CA 94002-3098
USA
www.wadsworth.com

International Headquarters
Thomson Learning
290 Harbor Drive, 2nd Floor
Stamford, CT 06902-7477
USA

UK/Europe/Middle East
Thomson Learning
Berkshire House
168-173 High Holborn
London WC1V 7AA
United Kingdom

Asia
Thomson Learning
60 Albert Street #15-01
Albert Complex
Singapore 189969

Canada
Nelson/Thomson Learning
1120 Birchmount Road
Scarborough, Ontario M1K 5G4
Canada

*This book is dedicated to my children,
Julie, Andrew, Eric, and Rachel Siegel,
and to my wife, Therese J. Libby.*

CONTENTS

2 THEORIES OF CRIME CAUSATION

CRIME TYPOLOGIES

4 THE CRIMINAL JUSTICE SYSTEM

PREFACE

On April 20, 1999, a horrific incident took place at Columbine High School in Littleton, Colorado. Two students, Eric Harris, 18, and Dylan Klebold, 17, members of a mysterious group called the "Trenchcoat Mafia," went on a shooting spree that claimed the lives of at least twelve students and one teacher, and wounded twenty-four others, many seriously. Before they could be captured, the boys committed suicide in the school library, leaving authorities to puzzle over the cause of their deadly outburst. In the aftermath of the shooting, national leaders called for strict controls on the distribution of high-powered weapons to minors. Others began to seek a rational explanation for what seemed to be an irrational act. Harris and Klebold lived in affluent homes in suburban Denver. Although they were considered outsiders by the school's more popular students, they had their own close friends and even attended the school prom. How could such a violent outburst be explained? Are there warning signs that point to future violence? Did the boys possess a genetic make-up that made them violence prone?

Events such as the Columbine massacre remind us of the great impact that crime, law, and justice have on the American psyche. The media sustains high interest in notorious killers, serial murderers, drug lords, and sex criminals. It is not surprising then that many Americans are more concerned about crime than almost any other social problem. Most of us are worried about becoming the victims of violent crime, having our houses broken into or our cars stolen. We alter our behavior to limit the risk of victimization and question whether legal punishment alone can control criminal offenders. We watch movies about law firms, clients, fugitives, and stone-cold killers. We are shocked at graphic accounts of drive-by shootings, police brutality, and prison riots.

I have had a life-long interest in crime, law, and justice. Why do people behave the way they do? What causes one person to become violent and anti-social, while another channels his or her energy into work, school, and family? How can the behavior of the "good boy in the high-crime neighborhood"—the "at-risk" kid who successfully resists the "temptation of the streets"—be explained? Conversely, what accounts for the behavior of the multimillionaire who cheats on his or her taxes or engages in fraudulent schemes? The former has nothing yet is able to resist crime; the latter has everything and falls prey to its lure.

I have been able to channel this interest into a career as a teacher of criminology. My goal in writing this text is to help students generate the same interest in criminology that has sustained me during my twenty-four years in college teaching. What could be more important or fascinating than a field of study that deals with such wide-ranging topics as the motivation for mass murder, the association between media violence and interpersonal aggression, the family's influence on drug abuse, and the history of organized crime? Criminology is a dynamic field, changing constantly with the release of major research studies, Supreme Court rulings, and governmental policy. Its dynamism and diversity make it an important and engrossing area of study.

One reason that the study of criminology is so important is that debates continue over the nature and extent of crime and the causes and prevention of criminality. Some view criminals as society's victims who are forced to violate the law because of poverty and the lack of opportunity. Others view aggressive, antisocial behavior as a product of mental and physical abnormalities, present at birth or soon after, which are stable over the life course. Still another view is that crime is a function of the rational choice of greedy, selfish people who can only be deterred though the threat of harsh punishments.

There is also concern about the treatment of known criminals: Should they be punished? Helped? Locked up? Given a second chance? Should crime control policy focus on punishment or rehabilitation? When an American boy Michael Fay was flogged in Singapore in 1994 after being convicted on vandalism charges some commentators openly praised that country's government for its tough stance on crime; a few even voiced the opinion that corporal punishment might work well in this country. Would you like to see a whipping post set up in your town?

Because interest in crime and justice is so great and so timely, this text is designed to review these ongoing issues and cover the field of criminology in an organized and comprehensive manner. It is meant as a broad overview of the field, designed to whet the reader's appetite and encourage further and more in-depth exploration.

TOPIC AREAS

Criminology is divided into four main sections or topic areas. Part 1 provides a framework for studying criminology. The first chapter defines the field and discusses its most basic concepts: the definition of crime, the component areas of criminology, the history of criminology, criminological research methods, and the ethical issues that confront the field. The second chapter covers the criminal law and its functions, processes, defenses, and reform. Chapter 3 covers the nature, extent, and patterns of crime. Chapter 4 is devoted to the concept of victimization, including the nature of victims, theories of victimization, and programs designed to help crime victims.

Part 2 contains six chapters that cover criminological theory: why do people behave the way they do? These views include rational choice (Chapter 5), biology and psychology (Chapter 6), structure and culture (Chapter 7), social process and socialization (Chapter 8), social conflict (Chapter 9), and latent trait and human development (Chapter 10).

Part 3 is devoted to the major forms of criminal behavior. Four chapters cover violent crime, common theft offenses, white-collar and organized crimes, and public order crimes, including sex offenses and substance abuse.

Part 4 focuses on the criminal justice system. Chapter 15 provides an overview of the entire justice process, legal concepts, and justice perspectives. The following chapters cover police, court, and the correctional systems in greater depth.

The text has been carefully structured to cover relevant material in a comprehensive, balanced, and objective fashion.

Features

There have been some exciting new changes in the seventh edition. There are a number of new features, including the division of feature boxes into three new categories: The Criminological Enterprise; Race, Culture, Gender, and Criminology; Policy and Practice in Criminology. Criminological Enterprise boxes focus on important and innovative efforts to conduct research and/or formulate theory in criminology. For example, a Criminological enterprise "Careers in Crack" in Chapter 14 discusses research explaining the rise and fall of the crack epidemic of the 1980s. Race, Culture, Gender, and Criminology features contain detailed analysis of criminological research efforts that focus on issues of gender, race, other cultures or customs. For example, in Chapter 16, the Race, Culture, Gender, and Criminology box deals with the issue of whether race influences the police use of discretion. Policy and Practice in Criminology features describe new programs and policy initiatives that are now being employed in the United States and abroad. For example, in Chapter 5 a program to reduce subway crime based on theoretical principles is discussed in some detail. Each of these boxes now contains an Infotrac College Edition exercise and information that directs students to use this service on the web.

At the end of each chapter is a new feature called "Thinking Like a Criminologist." Each of these features provide students with an interesting hypothetical scenario and/or problem that requires criminological knowledge or reasoning to solve. They can be used to initiate classroom discussion and build problem solving skills. For example, in Chapter 11 students are asked to think how they would respond if the state legislature asked them to prepare a report on statutory rape and address the problem of minor girls impregnated by adult men.

As in previous editions each chapter includes a chapter outline, list of key terms, and discussion questions. Connection boxes scattered throughout the chapters link the material being discussed with relevant information located throughout the text.

WHAT'S NEW IN THIS EDITION

The seventh edition retains many of the same organizational features of the previous edition, but each of the preexisting chapters has undergone considerable revision and reworking.

Chapter 1, "Crime and Criminology," has new information on international crime rates. The section on ethical issues has been expanded.

Chapter 2, "Criminal Law and Its Processes," contains new material on the development of the law, the revisions in the insanity plea, intoxication defenses, exotic criminal defenses such as the "battered woman syndrome," newly emerging stalking laws, and community notification laws.

Chapter 3, "Nature and Extent of Crime," covers crime trends and patterns. A new section takes on the explanation of crime trends: what factors influence the rise and fall in crime rates? The section on race and crime has been expanded.

Chapter 4, "Victims and Victimization," focuses on the nature and extent of victimization, theories of victimization, and the government's response to victimization. New material is included on the costs of victimization and the long-term effects of victimization. There is a feature box on "stalking" of victims.

Chapter 5, "Choice Theory," offers more material on the rational criminal, including the decision to choose crime, situational crime prevention, and routine activities theory. There is a new Criminological Enterprise "In the Drug Business," as well as a Policy and Practice box on reducing crime in the Washington, D.C., subway system.

Chapter 6, "Trait Theories," includes an analysis of the important new book *The Nature Assumption* by Ruth Harris and expanded sections on the media and violence.

In Chapter 7, "Social Structure Theories," recent evidence on poverty trends are presented, including the latest data on race and child poverty. The sections on strain theory have been supplemented, including a new table on community-level sources of strain.

Chapter 8, "Social Process Theories," updates material on control, labeling, and learning theories.

Chapter 9, "Conflict Theory," contains new material on radical feminist theory, left realism, peacemaking, and deconstructionism. It discusses Henry and Barak's Integrative-Constitutive Theory. There are new sections on capitalism and patriarchy, and a new table summarizes the main points of restorative justice.

Chapter 10, "Integrated Theories: Latent Trait and Developmental Theories," has been reworked to reflect changes in these two important theoretical perspectives. There is an analysis of David Rowe's Adaptive Strategy Theory, which links mating habits to crime, as well as updates on life-course-persistent vs. adolescent-limited offenders.

Chapter 11, "Violent Crime," offers new material on mass murder, hate crimes, spouse abuse, and the causes of violence. There is a section on mothers who kill their children, the use of rape as a military terror tactic, statutory rape, and an analysis of important new research on armed robbery.

Chapter 12, "Property Crimes," now contains a section on "'thief takers," organized groups of private police who earned a living by catching wanted thieves in eighteenth-century England and one on train robbery in nineteenth-century America. There is new material on combating auto theft and the nature of confidence games.

Chapter 13, "White-Collar and Organized Crime," includes new material on controlling white-collar crime, including a section on Operation Backbone, a 1997 undercover operation in New York State in which chiropractors were charged for fraudulently over-billing insurance companies. The chapter covers high-tech crimes including Internet abuse.

Chapter 14, "Public Order Crimes," contains new material on controlling prostitution and drug legalization. It covers the recent spate of gay bashing and the tragic Matthew Shepard case. Other topics include child prostitution, streetwalkers in New York, "careers" in crack, and drug use trends.

Chapter 15, "Overview of the Criminal Justice System," has new sections covering the analysis of justice goals and philosophies, and it covers the newly emerging restorative justice view.

Chapter 16, "Police and Law Enforcement," offers new material on problem-oriented and community policing. It has greater coverage on race and police discretion, police violence, and the shooting of police by criminals.

Chapter 17, "The Judiciary Process," presents new material on sentencing practices and the judicial process. It has a new section on truth-in-sentencing laws, international use of the death penalty, and race and sentencing.

Chapter 18, "Corrections," includes updated sections on alternative sanctions, including fines, forfeiture, house arrest, electronic monitoring, and intensive probation supervision. It covers new information on the risk of probation failure and women in prison.

Every attempt has been made to make the presentation of material interesting, balanced, and objective. No single political or theoretical position dominates the text; instead, the many diverse views that are contained within criminology and characterize its interdisciplinary nature are presented. The text includes analysis of the most important scholarly works and scientific research reports, while at the same time, it presents topical information on recent cases and events, such as the brutal dragging death of James Byrd by white supremacists in Jasper, Texas.

ACKNOWLEDGMENTS

Many people helped make this book possible. The reviewers of the seventh and previous editions are listed on page xix. Thanks go to them all. Special thanks must also go to Kathleen Maguire, editor of the *Sourcebook of Criminal Justice,* and the staffs at the Hindelang Research Center in Albany, New York, the Institute for Social Research at the University of Michigan, and the National Criminal Justice Reference Service. Others who helped with material or advice include M. Douglas Anglin, Meda Chesney-Lind, Frank Cullen, Lee Ellis, Chris Eskridge, Charles Faupel, Chuck Fenwick, James A. Fox, David Friedrichs, James Fyfe, Jim Inciardi, Bob

Langworthy, John Laub, Jack Levin, Colin McCauley, Graeme Newman, Spencer Rathus, Bob Regoli, Alphonse Sallett, Marty Schwartz, Darrell Steffensmeier, William Wakefield, Sam Walker, Lorne Yeudall, and Marvin Zalman.

And, of course, my colleagues at Wadsworth Publishing did their usual outstanding job of aiding us in the preparation of the text. Sabra Horne, my wonderful editor, is always there for me with her unbridled enthusiasm and good spirits. Dan Alpert is more than a developmental editor; he is a friend and mentor and someone whose ideas I cherish. Maxine Chuck was patient and thorough in conducting a developmental edit of the book. Shannon Ryan did a superb job coordinating a challenging supplements program. Linda Rill did her usual professional job in photo research, and Cecile Joyner, the production editor, is a joy to work with as usual. I have had the privilege of working with new colleagues on this book, and they were more than up to the task: Christine Henry is a great addition in marketing and Jennie Redwitz is terrific at pulling everything together as production manager.

Larry Siegel
Bedford, New Hampshire

REVIEWERS

Reviewers of the Seventh Edition

William Alex Pridemore
State University of New York—Albany

Gregory B. Talley
Broome Community College

Charles R. Tittle
Washington State University

Janet K. Wilson
University of Central Arkansas

Reviewers of previous editions

M. H. Alsikafi

Alexander Alvarez

Thomas Arvanites

Patricia Atchison

Timothy Austin

Agnes Baro

Bonnie Berry

James Black

Joseph Blake

David Bordua

Stephen Brodt

Thomas Calhoun

Mike Carlie

Mae Conley

Thomas Courtless

Mary Dietz

Edna Erez

Stephen Gibbons

Edward Green

Julia Hall

Marie Henry

Denny Hill

Alfred Himelson

Dennis Hoffman

Gerrold Hotaling

Joseph Jacoby

Casey Jordan

John Martin

Pamela Mayhall

James McKenna

Steven Messner

Linda O'Daniel

Hugh O'Rourke

Nikos Passos

Jim Ruiz

Louis San Marco

Kip Schlegel

Theodore Skotnick

Kevin Thompson

Paul Tracy

Charles Vedder

Joseph Vielbig

Ed Wells

Michael Wiatkowski

Janne Ziembo-Vogl

CONCEPTS OF CRIME, LAW, AND CRIMINOLOGY

How is crime defined? How much crime is there, and what are the trends and patterns in the crime rate? How many people fall victim to crime, and who is likely to become a crime victim? How did our system of criminal law develop, and what are the basic elements of crimes? What is the science of criminology all about? These are some of the core issues that will be addressed in the first four chapters of this text. Chapter 1 introduces students to the field of criminology: its nature, area of study, methodologies, and historical development. Concern about crime and justice has been an important part of the human condition for more than 5,000 years, since the first criminal codes were set down in the Middle East. And while the scientific study of crime—criminology—is considered a modern science, it has existed for more than 200 years.

Chapter 2 introduces students to one of the key components of criminology—the development of criminal law. It discusses the social history of law, the purpose of law, and how law defines crime, and it briefly examines criminal defenses and the reform of the law. The final two chapters of this section review the various sources of crime data to derive a picture of crime in the United States. Chapter 3 focuses on the nature and extent of crime, while Chapter 4 is devoted to victims and victimization. Important, stable patterns in the rates of crime and victimization indicate that these are not random events. The way crime and victimization are organized and patterned profoundly influences how criminologists view the causes of crime.

CHAPTER 1

Crime and Criminology

INTRODUCTION

Seventeen-year-old Luke Woodham was a member of a cultlike group called the Kroth, whose members planned to kill students at Pearl High School in Hattiesburg, Mississippi. Woodham went on a rampage on October 1, 1997, during which he first killed his mother Mary and then shot and killed two classmates and wounded seven others.

At his trial on June 4, 1998, Woodham claimed he was under the spell of demons and was influenced by the cult leader, Grant Boyette. "I remember I woke up that morning and I'd seen demons that I always saw when Grant told me to do something," Woodham told the jury during his trial. "They said I was nothing and I would never be anything if I didn't get to that school and kill those people." He believed Grant had him under a spell. "I just closed my eyes and fought with myself because I didn't want to do any of it," he said. "When I opened my eyes, my mother was laying in her bed."[1]

Woodham said he and Boyette became good friends in January 1997 after Boyette cast a spell from a satanic book that Woodham believed had led to a teenager being run over and killed by a car. "We started a satanic group and through the hate I had in my heart, I used it to try and get vengeance on people and do what he (Boyette) told me to do." He claimed Boyette had directed his activities and had assigned him demons to make sure he followed orders.

Can such outrageous behavior ever be fully explained or understood? Is it a product of a dysfunctional home life? What kind of environment fosters such violent outbursts? Could someone who is "normal" ever commit such a horrible crime? If these actions were the product of mental illness, wouldn't someone as deeply disturbed as Luke Woodham be better off in a hospital than a state prison? If Luke had been sentenced to the death penalty and was then executed for his crime, could this extreme punishment deter others? Research indicates that many habitually aggressive children have been raised in homes in which they are

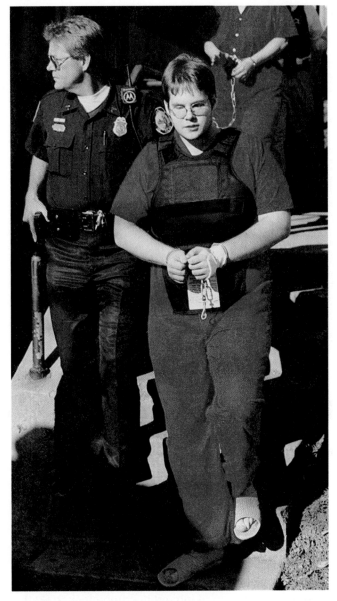

Luke Woodham, shown here after his arrest, went on a killing rampage on October 1, 1997, during which he killed his mother Mary and then attacked students at Pearl High School in Hattiesburg, Mississippi, shooting and killing two classmates and wounding seven others. Can criminologists ever hope to explain such bizarre acts of violence?

physically brutalized by their parents; learned violence then persists into adulthood.[2] Is it possible to overcome a predisposition to violence through the fear of punishment, or are such extreme measures bound to fail?

Crime stories such as these take their toll on the American public, about half of whom report being afraid to walk alone in their own neighborhoods at night.[3] Although females report greater fear of crime than males, both sexes report that they fear being victimized.[4]

THE STUDY OF CRIMINOLOGY

Concern about crime and the need to develop effective measures to control criminal behavior have spurred the development of **criminology** as an academic discipline. This discipline is devoted to developing valid and reliable information that addresses the causes of crime as well as crime patterns and trends. **Criminologists** use scientific methods to study the nature, extent, cause, and control of criminal behavior. Unlike media commentators, whose opinions about crime can be colored by personal experiences, biases, and values, criminologists remain objective as they study crime and its consequences. The field of criminology has gained prominence as an academic area of study due to the constant threat of crime and the social problems it represents.

This text analyzes criminology and its major subareas of inquiry. It focuses on the nature and extent of crime, the causes of crime, crime patterns, and crime control. This chapter introduces and defines criminology: What are its goals? What is its history? How do criminologists define crime? How do they conduct research? What ethical issues face those wishing to conduct criminological research?

WHAT IS CRIMINOLOGY?

Criminology is the scientific approach to studying criminal behavior. In their classic definition, criminologists Edwin Sutherland and Donald Cressey state the following:

> Criminology is the body of knowledge regarding crime as a social phenomenon. It includes within its scope the processes of making laws, of breaking laws, and of reacting toward the breaking of laws. . . . The objective of criminology is the development of a body of general and verified principles and of other types of knowledge regarding this process of law, crime, and treatment.[5]

Sutherland and Cressey's definition includes the most important areas of interest to criminologists: (1) the development of criminal law and its use to define crime; (2) the cause of law violations; (3) the methods used to control criminal behavior. This definition also refers to the term *verified principles,* which implies that the sci-

entific method should be used in studying criminology. Criminologists use objective research methods to pose research questions (hypotheses), gather data, create theories, and test their validity. They also use every method of established social science inquiry, including analysis of existing records, experimental designs, surveys, historical analysis, and content analysis.

Criminology is an **interdisciplinary** science for which relatively few academic centers grant graduate degrees. As a result, many criminologists have also been trained in diverse fields, most commonly sociology, but also criminal justice, political science, psychology, economics, and the natural sciences. Whereas for most of the twentieth century criminology's primary orientation has been sociological, today it can be viewed as an integrated approach to the study of criminal behavior. Although it combines elements of many other fields, the primary interest of its practitioners is understanding the true nature of crime, law, and justice.

A BRIEF HISTORY OF CRIMINOLOGY

The scientific study of crime and criminality is a relatively recent development. Although written criminal codes have existed for thousands of years, these were restricted to defining crime and setting punishments. What motivated people to violate the law remained a matter of conjecture.

CONNECTIONS

Although English common law is the immediate antecedent of our own legal system, the influence of some of the earliest written codes, such as those of the Hebrews and Babylonians, can still be detected. Chapter 2 traces the history of law in some detail.

During the Middle Ages (1200–1600), superstition and fear of satanic possession dominated thinking. People who violated social norms or religious practices were believed to be witches or possessed by demons. The prescribed method for dealing with the possessed was burning at the stake, a practice that survived into the seventeenth century. For example, between 1575 and 1590, Nicholas Remy, head of the Inquisition in the French province of Lorraine, ordered 900 sorcerers and witches burned to death; likewise a contemporary, Peter Binsfield, the bishop of the German city of Trier, ordered the death of 6,500 people. An estimated 100,000 people were prosecuted throughout Europe for witchcraft during the sixteenth and seventeenth centuries. It was also commonly believed that some fami-

During the Middle Ages, superstition and fear of satanic possession dominated thinking. People who violated social norms or religious practices were believed to be witches or possessed by demons. The prescribed method for dealing with the possessed was burning at the stake, a practice that survived into the 17th century. This painting, *The Trial of George Jacobs, August 5, 1692* by J. H. Matteson (1855), depicts the ordeal of Jacobs, a patriarch of Salem, Massachusetts. During the witch craze, he had ridiculed the trials, only to find himself being accused, tried, and executed.

lies produced offspring who were unsound or unstable and that social misfits were inherently damaged by reason of their "inferior blood."[6] It was common practice to use cruel torture to extract confessions, and those convicted of violent or theft crimes suffered extremely harsh penalties, including whipping, branding, maiming, and execution.

Classical Criminology

By the mid-eighteenth century, social philosophers began to rethink the prevailing concepts of law and justice. They argued for a more rational approach to punishment, stressing that the relationship between crimes and their punishment should be balanced and fair. This view was based on the prevailing philosophy of the time called **utilitarianism,** which emphasized that behavior must be useful, purposeful, and reasonable.

Rather than cruel public executions designed to frighten people into obedience or punish those the law failed to deter, reformers called for a more moderate and just approach to penal sanctions. The most famous of these reformers was Cesare Beccaria (1738–1794), whose writings described both a motive for committing crime and methods for its control.

Beccaria believed that people want to achieve pleasure and avoid pain. Therefore, he concluded, crimes must provide some pleasure to the criminal. To deter crime, he believed that one must administer pain in an appropriate amount to counterbalance the pleasure obtained from crime. Beccaria's famous theorem was that in order for punishment not to be in every instance an act of violence of one or many against a private citizen, it must be essentially public, prompt, necessary, the least possible in the given circumstances, proportionate to the crimes, and dictated by the laws.[7]

The writings of Beccaria and his followers form the core of what today is referred to as **classical criminology**. As originally conceived in the eighteenth century, classical criminology theory had several basic elements:

1. In every society, people have free will to choose criminal or lawful solutions to meet their needs or settle their problems.
2. Criminal solutions may be more attractive than lawful ones because they usually require less work for a greater payoff.
3. A person's choice of criminal solutions may be controlled by his or her fear of punishment.
4. The more severe, certain, and swift the punishment, the better able it is to control criminal behavior.

The classical perspective influenced judicial philosophy during much of the late eighteenth and nineteenth centuries. Prisons began to be used as a form of punishment, and sentences were geared proportionately to the seriousness of the crime. Executions were still widely used but slowly began to be employed for only the most serious crimes. The catch phrase was "let the punishment fit the crime."

During the nineteenth century, a new vision of the world challenged the validity of classical theory and presented an innovative way of looking at the causes of crime.

Nineteenth-Century Positivism

Although the classical position guided crime, law, and justice for almost 100 years, during the late nineteenth century, change in the way knowledge was being gathered challenged its dominance. The scientific method was beginning to take hold in Europe. In place of reliance on pure thought and reason, careful observation and analysis of natural phenomena were being undertaken to explain how the world worked. This movement inspired new discoveries in biology, astronomy, and chemistry. If the scientific method could be applied to the study of nature, then why not use it to study human behavior?

Auguste Comte (1798–1857), considered the founder of sociology, applied scientific methods to the study of society. According to Comte, societies pass through stages that can be grouped on the basis of how people try to understand the world in which they live. People in primitive societies believe that inanimate objects have life (for example, the sun is a god); in later social stages, people embrace a rational, scientific view of the world. Comte called this final stage the **positive stage**, and those who followed his writings became known as **positivists**. As we understand it today, **positivism** has two main elements. The first is the belief that human behavior is a function of external forces that are beyond individual control. Some of these forces are social, such as wealth and class, while others are political and histori-

cal, such as war and famine. Other forces are more personal and psychological, such as an individual's brain structure and his or her biological makeup or mental ability. Each of these forces influences human behavior.

The second aspect of positivism is the embrace of the scientific method to solve problems. Positivists rely on strict use of empirical methods to test hypotheses. That is, they believe in factual, firsthand observation and measurement of conditions and events. Positivists would agree that an abstract concept such as "intelligence" exists because it can be measured by an IQ test. They would challenge a concept such as the "soul" because it is a condition that cannot be verified by the scientific method. The positivist tradition was popularized by Charles Darwin (1809–1882), whose work on human evolution encouraged a nineteenth-century "cult of science" that advocated verifying all human activity by scientific principles.

Positivist Criminology The earliest "scientific" studies examining human behavior were biologically oriented. **Physiognomists,** such as J. K. Lavater (1741–1801), studied the facial features of criminals to determine whether the shape of ears, nose, and eyes and the distances between them were associated with antisocial behavior. **Phrenologists,** such as Franz Joseph Gall (1758–1828) and Johann K. Spurzheim (1776–1832), studied the shape of the skull and bumps on the head to determine whether these physical attributes were linked to criminal behavior. Phrenologists believed that external cranial characteristics dictate which areas of the brain control physical activity. Although their primitive techniques and quasi-scientific methods have been thoroughly discredited, these efforts were an early attempt to use a "scientific" method to study crime.

By the early nineteenth century, abnormality in the human mind was being linked to criminal behavior patterns. Phillipe Pinel, one of the founders of French psychiatry, claimed that some people behave abnormally even without being mentally ill. He coined the phrase *manie sans delire* to denote what eventually was referred to as a **psychopathic personality.** In 1812 an American, Benjamin Rush, described patients with an "innate preternatural moral depravity."[8] Another early criminological pioneer, English physician Henry Maudsley (1835–1918), believed that insanity and criminal behavior were strongly linked. He stated, "Crime is a sort of outlet in which their unsound tendencies are discharged; they would go mad if they were not criminals, and they do not go mad because they are criminals."[9] These early research efforts shifted attention to brain functioning and personality as the key to criminal behavior.

Biological Determinism In Italy Cesare Lombroso (1835–1909) studied the cadavers of executed criminals in an effort to scientifically determine whether law violators physically differed from people of conventional values and behavior. Lombroso, known as the "father of criminology," was a physician who served much of his career in the Italian army. That experience gave him ample opportunity to study the physical characteristics of soldiers convicted and executed for criminal offenses. Later he studied inmates at institutes for the criminally insane at Pavia, Pesaro, and Reggio Emilia.[10]

Lombrosian theory can be outlined in a few simple statements.[11] First, Lombroso believed that serious offenders, those who engaged in repeated assault- or theft-related activities, inherited criminal traits. These "born criminals" inherited physical problems that impelled them into a life of crime. This view helped stimulate interest in **criminal anthropology**.[12] Second, Lombroso held that born criminals suffer from **atavistic anomalies**—physically, they are throwbacks to more primitive times when people were savages. For example, criminals were believed to have the enormous jaws and strong canine teeth common to carnivores and savages who devour raw flesh.

Lombroso compared criminals' behavior to that of the mentally ill and those suffering some forms of epilepsy. According to Lombrosian theory, criminogenic traits can be acquired through indirect heredity, from a "degenerate family with frequent cases of insanity, deafness, syphilis, epilepsy, and alcoholism among its members." He believed that direct heredity—being related to a family of criminals—is the second primary cause of crime.

Lombroso's version of criminal anthropology was brought to the United States via articles and textbooks that adopted his ideas. He attracted a circle of followers who expanded upon his vision of biological determinism. His work was actually more popular in the United States than it was in Europe. By the turn of the century, American authors were discussing "the science of penology" and "the science of criminology."[13]

Lombroso's version of strict biological determinism is no longer taken seriously. Today criminologists who suggest that crime has some biological basis also believe that environmental conditions influence human behavior. Hence the term **biosocial theory** has been coined to reflect the assumed link between physical and mental traits, the social environment, and behavior.

The Development of Sociological Criminology

At the same time that biological views were dominating criminology, another group of positivists was developing the field of sociology to scientifically study the major social changes that were taking place in the nineteenth century.

Sociology seemed an ideal perspective from which to study society. After thousands of years of stability, the world was undergoing a population explosion: the population estimated at 600 million in 1700 had risen to 900 million by 1800. People were flocking to cities in ever-increasing numbers. Manchester, England, had 12,000 inhabitants in 1760 and 400,000 in 1850; during the same period, the population of Glasgow, Scotland, rose from 30,000 to 300,000. The development of such machinery as power looms had doomed cottage industries and given rise to a factory system in which large numbers of people toiled for extremely low wages. The spread of agricultural machines increased the food supply while reducing the need for a large rural workforce; the excess farm laborers further swelled the cities' populations. At the same time, political, religious, and social traditions continued to be challenged by the scientific method.

The Foundations of Sociological Criminology

The foundations of sociological criminology can be traced to the work of pioneering sociologists L.A.J. (Adolphe) Quetelet (1796–1874) and (David) Emile Durkheim (1858–1917). Quetelet instigated the use of data and statistics in performing criminological research. Durkheim, considered one of the founders of sociology,[14] defined crime as a normal and necessary social event. These two perspectives have been extremely influential on modern criminology.

L.A.J. (Adolphe) Quetelet L.A.J. (Adolphe) Quetelet (1796–1874) was a Belgian mathematician who began (along with a Frenchman, Andre-Michel Guerry) what is known as the **cartographic school of criminology**.[15] This approach used social statistics that were being developed in Europe in the early nineteenth century. Statistical data provided important demographic information on the population, including density, gender, religious affiliation, and wealth.

Quetelet studied data gathered in France (called the *Comptes generaux de l'administration de la justice*) to investigate the influence of social factors on the propensity to commit crime. In addition to finding a strong influence of age and sex on crime, Quetelet also uncovered evidence that season, climate, population composition, and poverty also were related to criminality. More specifically, he found that crime rates were greatest in the summer, in southern areas, among heterogeneous populations, and among the poor and uneducated. He also found crime rates to be influenced by drinking habits.[16] Quetelet identified many of the relationships between crime and social phenomena that still serve as a basis for criminology today.

Emile Durkheim According to Durkheim's vision of social positivism, crime is part of human nature because it has existed during periods of both poverty and prosperity.[17] Crime is normal because it is virtually impossible to imagine a society in which criminal behavior is totally absent. Such a society would almost demand that all people be and act exactly alike. Durkheim believed that the inevitability of crime is linked to the differences (heterogeneity) within society. Because people are so different from one another and employ such a variety of methods and forms of behavior to meet their needs, it is not surprising that some will resort to criminality. Even if "real" crimes were eliminated, human weaknesses and petty vices would be elevated to the status of crimes. As long as human differences exist, then, crime is inevitable and one of the fundamental conditions of social life.

Crime, argued Durkheim, can be useful and occasionally even healthful for society. He held that the existence of crime paves the way for social change and that the social structure is not rigid or inflexible. Put another way, if crime did not exist, it would mean that everyone behaved the same way and agreed on what is right and wrong. Such universal conformity would stifle creativity and independent thinking. To illustrate this concept, Durkheim offered the example of the Greek philosopher Socrates, who was considered a criminal and put to death for corrupting the morals of youth simply because he expressed ideas that were different than what people believed at that time.

Durkheim reasoned that crime calls attention to social ills. A rising crime rate can signal the need for social change and promote a variety of programs designed to relieve the human suffering that may have caused crime in the first place. For example, national surveys conducted since the 1970s showed that a surprising number of teens were substance abusers. This prompted school systems to develop school-based antidrug programs, which may have helped lower use rates in the teenage population.[18]

In his famous book, *The Division of Labor in Society,* Durkheim described the consequences of the shift from a small, rural society, which he labeled "mechanical," to the more modern "organic" society with a large urban population, division of labor, and personal isolation.[19] From this shift flowed **anomie,** or norm and role confusion, a powerful sociological concept that helps describe the chaos and disarray accompanying the loss of traditional values in modern society. Durkheim's research on suicide indicated that anomic societies maintain high suicide rates; by implication, anomie might cause other forms of deviance as well.

CONNECTIONS

Durkheim's writing and research have profoundly affected criminology and will be discussed further in Chapter 7.

The Chicago School and Beyond

The primacy of sociological positivism was secured by research begun in the early twentieth century by Robert Ezra Park (1864–1944), Ernest W. Burgess (1886–1966), Louis Wirth (1897–1952), and their colleagues in the sociology department at the University of Chicago. The scholars who taught at this program created what is still referred to as the **Chicago School** in honor of their unique style of doing research. These urban sociologists pioneered research on the **social ecology** of the city. Their work inspired a generation of scholars to conclude that social forces operating in urban areas create criminal interactions; some neighborhoods become "natural areas" for crime.[20] These urban neighborhoods maintain such a high level of poverty that critical social institutions, such as the school and the family, break down. The resulting social disorganization reduces the ability of social institutions to control behavior, and the outcome is a high crime rate.

The Chicago School sociologists and their contemporaries focused on the functions of social institutions, such as the school and family, and how their breakdown influenced deviant and antisocial behavior. Criminal behavior, they argued, was not a function of personal traits or characteristics, but rather a reaction to an environment that was inadequate for proper human relations and development. They initiated the ecological study of crime by examining how neighborhood conditions, such as poverty levels, influenced crime rates. Their findings substantiated their belief that crime was a function of where one lived.

During the 1930s and 1940s another group of sociologists, who were strong believers in a social-psychological link to criminological behavior, conducted research to support their beliefs. They concluded that the individual's relationship to important social processes, such as education, family life, and peer relations, was the key to understanding human behavior. For example, they found that children who grow up in homes wracked by conflict, attend inadequate schools, or associate with deviant peers become exposed to procrime forces. One position, championed by the preeminent American criminologist Edwin Sutherland, was that people *learn* criminal attitudes from older, more experienced law violators. Another view, developed by Chicago School sociologist Walter Reckless, was that crime occurs when children develop an inadequate self-image, which renders them incapable of controlling their own misbehavior. Both of these views linked criminality to the failure of **socialization,** the interactions people have with the various individuals, organizations, institutions, and processes of society that help them mature and develop.

By midcentury most criminologists had embraced either the **ecological view** or the **socialization view** of crime. However, these were not the only views of how social institutions influence human behavior. In Europe the writings of another social thinker, Karl Marx (1818–1883), had pushed the understanding of social interaction in another direction and sowed the seeds for a new approach in criminology.[21]

Conflict Criminology

In his Communist Manifesto and other writings, Marx described the oppressive labor conditions prevalent during the rise of industrial capitalism. His observations of the economic structure convinced Marx that the character of every civilization is determined by its mode of production—the way its people develop and produce material goods (materialism). The most important relationship in industrial culture is between the owners of the means of production, the capitalist **bourgeoisie,** and the people who do the actual labor, the **proletariat.** The economic system controls all facets of human life; consequently, people's lives revolve around the means of production. The exploitation of the working class, he believed, would eventually lead to class conflict and the end of the capitalist system.

> CONNECTIONS
>
> Although Marx did not attempt to develop a theory of crime and justice, his writings were applied to legal studies by a few social thinkers, including Ralf Dahrendorf, George Vold, and Willem Bonger. Their attempts to mold a Marxist/conflict criminology will be discussed in some detail in Chapter 9.

Although these writings laid the foundation for a Marxist criminology, decades passed before the impact of Marxist theory was realized. In the United States during the 1960s, social and political upheaval was fueled by the Vietnam War, the development of an antiestablishment counterculture movement, the civil rights movement, and the women's movement. Young sociologists who became interested in applying Marxist principles to the study of crime began to analyze the social conditions in the United States that promoted class conflict and crime. What emerged from this intellectual ferment was a Marxist-based radical criminology that indicted the economic system as producing the conditions that support a high crime rate. The radical tradition has played a significant role in criminology ever since.

Criminology Today

The various schools of criminology developed over 200 years. Although they have evolved, each continues to affect the field. For example, classical theory has evolved into rational choice and deterrence theories. Choice theorists today argue that criminals are rational and use available information to decide if crime is worthwhile; deterrence theory holds that this choice is structured by the fear of punishment. Criminal anthropology has also evolved considerably. Criminologists no longer believe that a single trait or inherited characteristic can explain crime, but some are convinced that biological and psychological traits interact with environmental factors to influence all human behavior, including criminality. Biological and psychological theorists study the association between criminal behavior and such traits as diet, hormonal makeup, personality, and intelligence.

Sociological theories, tracing back to Quetelet and Durkheim, maintain that individuals' lifestyles and living conditions directly control their criminal behavior. Those at the bottom of the social structure cannot achieve success and thus experience anomie, strain, failure, and frustration.

Some sociologists who have added a social-psychological dimension to their views of crime causation find that individuals' learning experiences and socialization directly control their behavior. In some cases, children learn to commit crime by interacting with and modeling their behavior after others they admire, whereas other criminal offenders are people whose life experiences have shattered their social bonds to society.

The writings of Marx and his followers continue to be influential. Many criminologists still view social and political conflict as the root cause of crime. The inherently unfair economic structure of the United States and other advanced capitalist countries is the engine that drives the high crime rate.

Criminology, then, has a rich history that still exerts an important influence on the thinking of its current practitioners. Each of the major perspectives is summarized in Figure 1.1.

> CONNECTIONS
>
> The modern versions of the various schools of criminological thought will be discussed in greater detail throughout the book. Choice theories, the modern offshoot of Beccaria, are reviewed in Chapter 5. Current biological and psychological theories are the topic of Chapter 6. Contemporary theories based on Durkheim's views as well as theories based on the writings of the Chicago School are described in Chapter 7. The social process view is discussed in Chapter 8, while Marxist views are reviewed in Chapter 9. Finally, efforts to integrate a variety of theoretical ideas into a single unified theory are discussed in Chapter 10.

Figure 1.1 Criminology Perspectives

The major perspectives of criminology focus on *individual* (biological, psychological, and choice theories), *social* (structural and process theories), *political and economic* (conflict), and *multiple* (integrated) factors.

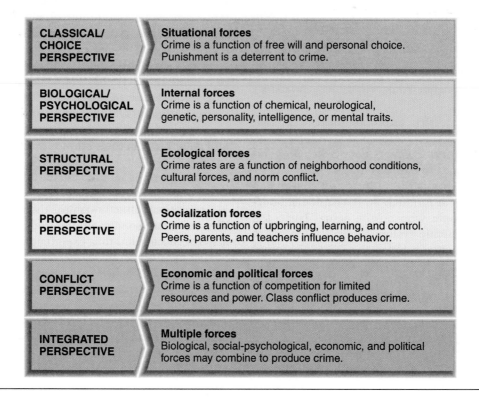

CLASSICAL/ CHOICE PERSPECTIVE	**Situational forces** Crime is a function of free will and personal choice. Punishment is a deterrent to crime.
BIOLOGICAL/ PSYCHOLOGICAL PERSPECTIVE	**Internal forces** Crime is a function of chemical, neurological, genetic, personality, intelligence, or mental traits.
STRUCTURAL PERSPECTIVE	**Ecological forces** Crime rates are a function of neighborhood conditions, cultural forces, and norm conflict.
PROCESS PERSPECTIVE	**Socialization forces** Crime is a function of upbringing, learning, and control. Peers, parents, and teachers influence behavior.
CONFLICT PERSPECTIVE	**Economic and political forces** Crime is a function of competition for limited resources and power. Class conflict produces crime.
INTEGRATED PERSPECTIVE	**Multiple forces** Biological, social-psychological, economic, and political forces may combine to produce crime.

CRIMINOLOGY AND CRIMINAL JUSTICE

In the late 1960s interest in the so-called crime problem gave rise to the development of research projects, such as those conducted by the American Bar Foundation, that were aimed at understanding the way police, courts, and correctional agencies actually operated.[22] Eventually, academic programs devoted to studying the criminal justice system were opened, and courses on the nature and extent of crime, or criminology, were developed.

The Distinction Between Criminology and Criminal Justice

Although the terms criminology and criminal justice are similar and people often confuse the two, there are major differences between these fields of study. Criminology explains the etiology (origin), extent, and nature of crime in society, whereas **criminal justice** refers to the agencies of social control that handle criminal offenders.[23] Whereas criminologists are mainly concerned with identifying the nature, extent, and cause of crime, criminal justice scholars describe, analyze, and

explain the behavior of the agencies of justice—police departments, courts, and correctional facilities—and identify effective methods of crime control.

Because both fields are crime-related, they overlap. Criminologists must be aware of how the agencies of justice operate and how they influence crime and criminals. Criminal justice experts cannot begin to design programs of crime prevention or rehabilitation without understanding something about the nature of crime. It is common, therefore, for criminal justice programs to feature courses on criminology and for criminology courses to evaluate the agencies of justice. The tremendous interest in criminal justice has led to the creation of more than a thousand justice-related academic programs; not surprisingly, these programs are often staffed by criminologists. These two fields not only coexist but help each other grow and develop.

The Distinction Between Criminology and Deviance

Criminology is also sometimes confused with the study of deviant behavior. However, significant distinctions can be made between these disciplines. **Deviant behavior** refers to any action that departs from social norms.[24]

Under this definition, deviant behaviors fall along a broad spectrum, ranging from the most socially harmful, such as rape and murder, to the relatively inoffensive, such as joining a nudist colony.

Crime and deviance are often confused because not all crimes are deviant or unusual acts, and not all deviant acts are illegal or criminal. For example, using recreational drugs such as marijuana may be illegal, but is it deviant? A significant percentage of U.S. youth has used drugs. Therefore, to argue that all crimes are behaviors that depart from the norms of society is probably erroneous. Similarly, many deviant acts are not criminal even though they may be shocking. For example, suppose a passerby observes a person drowning and makes no effort to save that person. Although the general public would probably condemn the person's behavior as callous, immoral, and deviant, no legal action could be taken because citizens are not required by law to effect rescues. In sum, many criminal acts, but not all, fall within the concept of deviance. Similarly, some deviant acts, but not all, are considered crimes.

To understand the nature and purpose of law, criminologists study the process by which crimes are created from behaviors that previously were considered merely deviant. Two issues that involve deviance are of particular interest to criminologists: How do deviant behaviors become crimes? When should crimes be **legalized,** making them immune to state sanction and legal punishment? The first issue involves the historical development of law. Many acts that are legally forbidden today were once considered merely unusual or deviant behavior. For example, the sale and possession of marijuana were legal in this country until 1937, when they were prohibited under federal law. Harry Anslinger, head of the Federal Bureau of Narcotics, spearheaded an extensive lobbying effort in the 1930s that resulted in banning marijuana use. He used magazine articles, public appearances, and public testimony to sway public opinion against using marijuana.[25] In one famous 1937 article, Anslinger told how "an entire family was murdered by a youthful [marijuana] addict in Florida . . . [who] with an axe had killed his father, mother, two brothers, and a sister."[26] Due to Anslinger's efforts, marijuana use was transformed from a deviant act to a crime; previously law-abiding citizens were now defined as criminal offenders.

CONNECTIONS

Some of the drugs considered highly dangerous today were once sold openly and considered medically beneficial. For example, the narcotic drug heroin, now considered extremely addicting and dangerous, was originally named in the mistaken belief that its pain-killing properties would prove "heroic" to medical patients. The history of drug and alcohol abuse will be discussed further in Chapter 14.

Criminologists also consider whether outlawed behaviors have evolved into social norms and, if so, whether they should either be legalized or have their penalties reduced (**decriminalized**). For example, there is still much debate over the legalization of abortion, recreational drugs such as marijuana, and assisted suicide.

A topic that warrants frequent discussion is where to draw the line between behavior that is merely considered deviant and unusual and behavior that is considered criminal. For example, when does sexually oriented material stop being merely suggestive and become pornographic? Can a line be drawn separating sexually oriented materials into two groups, one that is legally acceptable and a second that is considered depraved or obscene? And if such a line can be drawn, who gets to draw it? If an illegal act becomes a norm, should society reevaluate its criminal status and let it become merely an unusual or deviant act? Conversely, if scientists show that a normative act, such as smoking or drinking, poses a serious health hazard, should it be made illegal?

Many recent efforts have been made to control morally questionable behavior and restrict the rights of citizens to freedom of their actions. For example, sexual harassment statutes have attempted to regulate office conduct by placing limits on what in the past had been common, albeit offensive, practices such as telling off-color jokes or hanging suggestive pictures in offices or on bulletin boards.

CONNECTIONS

The regulation of sexual behavior, including pornography, homosexuality, and prostitution, is covered in greater detail in Chapter 14.

In sum, criminologists are concerned with the concept of deviance and its relationship to criminality. The shifting definition of deviant behavior is closely associated with our concepts of crime. The relationships among criminology, criminal justice, and deviance are illustrated in Figure 1.2.

WHAT CRIMINOLOGISTS DO: THE CRIMINOLOGICAL ENTERPRISE

Regardless of their background or training, criminologists are primarily interested in studying crime and criminal behavior. As two noted criminologists, Marvin Wolfgang and Franco Ferracuti, put it, "A criminologist is one whose professional training, occupational role, and pecuniary reward are primarily concentrated on a scientific approach to, and study and analysis of, the phenomenon of crime and criminal behavior."[27]

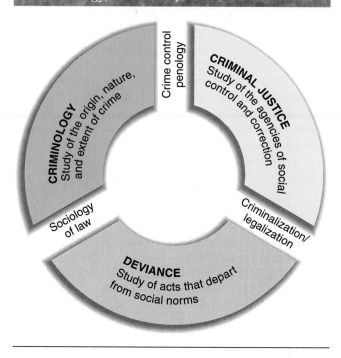

CRIME CONTROL PENOLOGY

CRIMINOLOGY
Study of the origin, nature, and extent of crime

Sociology of law

CRIMINAL JUSTICE
Study of the agencies of social control and correction

Criminalization/legalization

DEVIANCE
Study of acts that depart from social norms

Several subareas of criminology exist within the broader arena of criminology. Taken together, these subareas make up the **criminological enterprise.** Criminologists may specialize in a subarea in the same way that psychologists might specialize in a subfield of psychology, such as child development, perception, personality, psychopathology, or sexuality. Some of the more important criminological specialties are described in the following sections and summarized in Figure 1.3.

Criminal Statistics

The subarea of criminal statistics involves measuring the amount and trends of criminal activity. How much crime occurs annually? Who commits it? When and where does it occur? Which crimes are the most serious?

Criminologists interested in criminal statistics try to create valid and reliable measurements of criminal behavior. For example, they create techniques to access the records of police and court agencies. They develop paper-and-pencil survey instruments and then use them on large samples of citizens to determine the percentage of people who actually commit crime and the number of law violators who escape detection by the justice system. They also develop techniques to identify the victims of crime to establish more accurate indicators of the true number of criminal acts: how many people are victims of crime and what percentage reports crime to police. The study of criminal statistics is one of the most crucial aspects of the criminological

enterprise because without valid and reliable data sources, efforts to conduct research on crime and create criminological theories would be futile.

Sociology of Law

The sociology of law is a subarea of criminology concerned with the role social forces play in shaping criminal law and, concomitantly, the role of criminal law in shaping society. Criminologists study the history of legal thought in an effort to understand how criminal acts, such as theft, rape, and murder, evolved into their present form.

Often criminologists are asked to join the debate when a new law is proposed to banish or control behavior. For example, across the United States a debate has been raging over the legality of art works, films, photographs, and even music that some people find offensive and lewd and others consider harmless. Criminologists help determine the role that the law will take in curbing public access to such media and culture. They help answer questions such as these: Should society curb actions that some people consider immoral but by which no one is actually harmed? How is harm defined? Is a child who reads a pornographic magazine harmed?

Criminologists also actively participate in updating the content of criminal law. In making key decisions, all involved in making laws must take into account that the law must be flexible; it must respond to changing times and conditions. For example, computer fraud, airplane hijacking, theft from automatic teller machines, Internet scams, and illegal tapping of television cable lines are behaviors that did not exist when criminal law was originally conceived. Consequently, the law must be constantly revised to reflect cultural, societal, and technological adaptations of common acts. For example, Dr. Jack Kevorkian has made headlines for helping people to kill themselves by using his "suicide machine." Although some believe that Dr. Kevorkian's actions are criminal, immoral, and socially harmful, national media coverage has made his actions widely known. In response, however, Michigan passed legislation making it a felony to help anyone commit suicide, and in the November 1998 election, Michigan voters defeated an attempt to legalize physician-assisted suicide.[28] After numerous attempts to convict him had failed, on March 26, 1999, Dr. Kevorkian was convicted of murder for helping a man suffering from ALS (Lou Gehrig's Disease) commit suicide. Does his conviction indicate that the public is now opposed to physician-assisted suicide and that efforts to pass enabling legislation will be met with disapproval?

Theory Construction

From the beginning, criminologists have wondered why people engage in criminal acts. Why, when they know

Figure 1.3 The Criminological Enterprise

These subareas constitute the field/discipline of criminology.

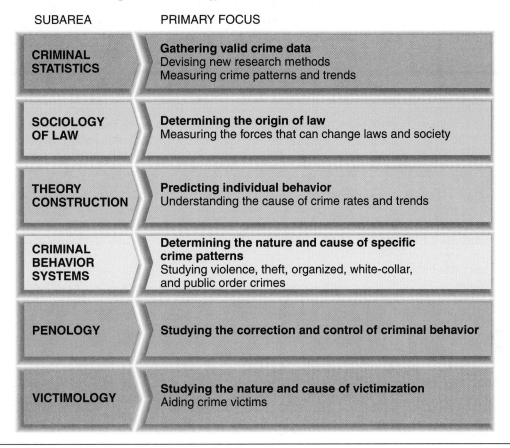

SUBAREA	PRIMARY FOCUS
CRIMINAL STATISTICS	**Gathering valid crime data** / Devising new research methods / Measuring crime patterns and trends
SOCIOLOGY OF LAW	**Determining the origin of law** / Measuring the forces that can change laws and society
THEORY CONSTRUCTION	**Predicting individual behavior** / Understanding the cause of crime rates and trends
CRIMINAL BEHAVIOR SYSTEMS	**Determining the nature and cause of specific crime patterns** / Studying violence, theft, organized, white-collar, and public order crimes
PENOLOGY	**Studying the correction and control of criminal behavior**
VICTIMOLOGY	**Studying the nature and cause of victimization** / Aiding crime victims

their actions can bring harsh punishment and social disapproval, do they steal, rape, and murder? In short, why do people behave the way they do? Does crime have a social or an individual basis? Is it a psychological, biological, social, political, or economic phenomenon? Because criminologists bring their personal beliefs and backgrounds to bear when they study criminal behavior, there are diverse theories of crime causation. Some criminologists who have a psychological orientation view crime as a function of personality, development, social learning, or cognition. Others investigate the biological correlates of antisocial behavior and study the biochemical, genetic, and neurological linkages to crime. Sociologists look at the social forces producing criminal behavior, including neighborhood conditions, poverty, socialization, and group interaction.

Understanding the true cause of crime remains a difficult problem. Criminologists are still unsure why, given similar conditions, one person chooses criminal solutions to his or her problems, while another conforms to accepted social rules of behavior. Understanding crime rates and trends has also proven difficult: Why do rates rise and fall? Why are crime rates higher in some areas or regions than in others? Why are some groups more crime-prone than others? These questions inspire theories that address these issues.

Criminal Behavior Systems

The criminal behavior systems subarea of criminology involves research on specific criminal types and patterns: violent crime, theft crime, public order crime, organized crime, and so on. Numerous attempts have been made to describe and understand particular crime types. For example, Marvin Wolfgang's famous 1958 study, *Patterns in Criminal Homicide,* is considered a landmark analysis of the nature of homicide and the relationship between victim and offender.[29] Edwin Sutherland's analysis of business-related offenses helped coin a new phrase—**white-collar crime**—to describe economic crime activities. The study of criminal behavior also researches the links between different types of crime and criminals. This is known as **crime typology.** Unfortunately, because people often disagree about types of crimes and criminal motivation, no standard exists within the field. Some typologies focus on the criminal,

race, culture, gender, and criminology

The Changing Face of International Crime Rates

People in the United States are justifiably concerned about crime; most people view it as a major social problem. As you may recall, public opinion polls indicate that almost half of all Americans feel it is not safe to walk at night in their own neighborhood. This concern is valid, considering that the United States has traditionally been more crime-prone than other industrialized countries. The United States has led the world with its murder, rape, and robbery rates. For example, police statistics show that the murder rate was 5.7 times higher and the rape rate was about 3 times higher in the United States than in England and Wales.

The United States also imprisons far more people than other countries. The percentage of the population sent to prison and jail in the United States exceeds that of such notoriously punitive countries as Singapore, Romania, and South Africa.

There are a number of explanations for the high U.S. crime rate. Here are some of the suspected reasons:

- Urban areas in which the poorest and wealthiest citizens reside in close proximity
- Racism and discrimination
- Failure of an underfunded educational system
- The troubled American family
- Easy access to handguns
- A culture that defines success in terms of material wealth

Each of these factors may explain the disproportionate amount of violent crime in the United States.

Although the United States may still have a relatively high violence rate compared to many other nations, our crime rates are declining while a disturbing upswing in crime is evident abroad. For example, murder rates have sharply increased in England, Germany, and Sweden. Racial assaults and hate crimes have increased dramatically in Germany and England. Meanwhile, in the United States, some crimes have actually declined to a point where they are lower than in some European nations. The most recent data available indicate that robbery, assault, burglary, and motor vehicle theft rates are actually lower in the United States than they are in England and Wales. One reason is that while robbery rates rose more than 81 percent in England and Wales between 1981 and 1995, they fell 28 percent in the United States. Similarly, assault increased 53 percent in England and Wales but declined 27 percent in the United States; burglary doubled in England and Wales but fell by half in the United States.

England is not alone in experiencing higher crime rates. Russia and the former Soviet republics have experienced an increase in large-scale organized crime gangs, who commonly use violence and intimidation.

In other European nations, violence has been fueled by a dramatic

growth in the number of illegal guns smuggled into these countries from the former Soviet republics. Additionally, unrestricted immigration has brought newcomers who face cultural differences, lack of job prospects, and racism. Social and economic pressures, including unemployment and cutbacks in the social welfare system, have also contributed to increased violence. Especially in the formerly communist countries in Eastern Europe, weak law enforcement institutions, rapid changes in economic laws, deteriorating economic conditions, incomplete reforms, and destabilized social norms have contributed to rising criminality.

Increased criminal activity in Asia is also reported. For example, Japan, a nation that prides itself on low crime rates, has experienced an upsurge in juvenile crime. It is estimated that 45 percent of all crimes are committed by people under 20, about double the percentage in the United States. With so much Japanese crime committed by youths, and with the juvenile crime rate escalating, experts predict an overall increase in future crime rates. Juvenile delinquency is also increasing in Singapore; in fact, it more than doubled during the first half of the 1990s. Ironically, Singapore's crime wave occurred after the government became notorious for its draconian justice policies when in 1993, an American teen, Michael Fay, was flogged after being convicted for vandalism. One

suggesting the existence of offender groups such as professional criminals, psychotic criminals, occasional criminals, and so forth. Others focus on the crimes, clustering them into such categories as property crimes, sex crimes, and so on.

Penology

The study of **penology** involves the correction and control of known criminal offenders. Penologists formulate strategies for crime control and then help implement these policies. Although the field of criminal justice overlaps this area, criminologists have continued their efforts to develop new crime control programs and policies. Some criminologists view penology as involving rehabilitation and treatment. They direct their efforts toward providing behavior alternatives for would-be criminals and treating individuals convicted of law violations. This view portrays the criminal as someone society has failed; someone would think that a nation that applies as severe criminal punishments as Singapore would never experience a crime wave.

Singapore and Japan are not the only Asian nations experiencing an upsurge in crime. Vietnamese authorities report a troubling increase in street crimes like burglary and theft. Many crimes are drug-related: Vietnam has an estimated 200,000 opium addicts, and almost 50,000 acres of land are now growing the poppies from which heroin is produced.

Although it is difficult to obtain accurate crime data from China, the world's largest nation seems to be cracking down on crime. In recent years Chinese courts annually sentenced more than 100,000 street criminals. Death sentences were doled out to 1,000 criminals, and many thousands more were sentenced to life in prison. The current wave of punishment is a response to a significant increase in street crimes, including robberies and drug trafficking.

Violence rates are also increasing in other parts of the Americas. The homicide rate in Jamaica is 32 per 100,000; in Colombia homicide rates are close to 70 per 100,000, about 10 times the U.S. average! As in Asia and Europe, high regional murder rates are tied to the flourishing drug trade.

Rising world crime rates may also be attributed, in part, to a rapid increase in female crime. Countries such as Germany, France, Brazil, and India all report an increase in robberies and drug trafficking involving female offenders. In Italy the 23-year-old daughter of a slain Mafia chieftain took over her father's criminal activities, a development that would have been unheard of only a few years ago. Although some nations (such as Poland, the Philippines, and Argentina) have not experienced rising female crime rates, the trend is global, linked to the growing emancipation of women in developing countries.

Although violence rates are still comparably low overseas, these trends indicate that international crime rates may yet converge.

CRITICAL THINKING

1. Will countries like Japan experience increasing crime as they become more economically dominant?
2. What factors do you think contribute to the high U.S. crime rate?

 INFOTRAC COLLEGE EDITION RESEARCH

To find out about the factors that are causing crime rates to increase in Eastern European countries, see Richard Lotspeich. Crime in the transition economies. *Europe-Asia Studies* June 1995 v47 n4 p. 555 (35)
Tom Fenton. 'Mafia' targets journalists abroad. *Editor & Publisher* July 2, 1994 v127 n27 p15 (2)

Source: Patrick A. Langan and David P. Farrington, *Crime and Justice in the United States and in England and Wales, 1981–96* (Washington, D.C.: Bureau of Justice Statistics, 1998); Michael Zielenziger, "Juvenile Crime Jumps to Record High in Japan," *Boston Globe,* 19 April 1998, A16; John King, "Paradise Lost? Crime in the Caribbean: A Comparison of Barbados and Jamaica," *Caribbean Journal of Criminology and Social Psychology* 2 (1997): 30–44; "With Women's Liberation Comes a Growing Involvement in Crime," *CJ International* 12 (1996): 19; "Crime Crackdown Continues as Statistics Increase," *CJ International* 12 (1996): 8; Sean Malinowski, "Battling an Emerging Crime Problem," *CJ International* 12 (1996): 3–4; "Singapore Says Delinquency Up," *Boston Globe,* 17 February 1996, p. 4; Gunther Kaiser, "Juvenile Delinquency in the Federal Republic of Germany," *International Journal of Comparative and Applied Criminal Justice* 16: (1992): 185–97; Marc Mauer, *Americans Behind Bars: The International Use of Incarceration* (Washington, D.C.: Sentencing Project, 1994); Elizabeth Neuffer, "Violent Crime Rise Fueling Fears in a Changing Europe," *Boston Globe,* 10 April 1994, p. 1.

under social, psychological, or economic stress; and someone who can be helped if society is willing to pay the price. Others argue that crime can be prevented only through a strict policy of social control; they advocate such strict penological measures as the death penalty (**capital punishment**) and **mandatory prison sentences.** Criminologists also help evaluate correctional initiatives to determine if they are effective and how they impact people's lives. Future penological research efforts seem warranted because most criminal offenders continue to commit crime after their release from prison (**recidivate**).

Victimology

Two classic criminological studies, one by Hans von Hentig and another by Stephen Schafer, first identified the critical role of the victim in the criminal process. These authors suggested that victim behavior is often a key determinant of crime and that victim actions may

Victimology has taken on greater importance as more criminologists focus their attention on the victim's role in the criminal event. For example, what effect does victim behavior have on the criminal process? Here Robert Giugliano, one of the victims of Colin Ferguson's shooting rampage on a New York commuter train in December 1993, addresses the media at the close of Ferguson's trial on February 17, 1995. Giugliano holds a picture of Marita Magoto, who was killed in the attack. At his right is Carolyn McCarthy, whose husband was killed and son wounded. Ferguson was sentenced to life in prison for killing 6 people and wounding 19 others. The plight of these victims prompted a public outcry, which sparked reinstatement of the death penalty in New York.

actually precipitate crime. Both von Hentig and Schafer believe that the study of crime is not complete unless the victim's role is considered.[30]

CONNECTIONS

In recent years criminologists have devoted much attention to the victim's role in the criminal process. It has been suggested that lifestyle and behavior may actually increase the risk that a person will become a crime victim. Some suggest that living in a high-crime neighborhood increases risk, whereas others point to problems caused by associating with dangerous peers and companions. For a discussion of victimization risk, see Chapter 4.

Victimologists are particularly interested in the following areas:

• Using victim surveys to measure the nature and extent of criminal behavior, calculating the actual costs of crime to victims

• Creating probabilities of victimization risk
• Studying victim culpability or precipitation of crime
• Designing services for crime victims, such as counseling and compensation programs

Victimology has taken on greater importance as more criminologists focus attention on the victim's role in the criminal event.

HOW CRIMINOLOGISTS VIEW CRIME

Professional criminologists usually align themselves with one of several schools of thought or perspectives in their field. Each perspective maintains its own view of what constitutes criminal behavior and what causes people to engage in criminality. This diversity of thought is not unique to criminology; biologists, psychologists, sociologists, historians, economists, and natural scientists also disagree among themselves about critical issues in their fields. Considering the multidisciplinary nature of the field of criminology, fundamental issues such as the nature and definition of crime itself cause disagreement among criminologists.

A criminologist's choice of orientation or perspective depends, in part, on his or her definition of crime; the beliefs and research orientations of most criminologists are related to this definition. This section discusses the three most common concepts of crime used by criminologists.

The Consensus View of Crime

According to the **consensus view,** crimes are behaviors believed to be repugnant to all elements of society. The **substantive criminal law,** which is the written code that defines crimes and their punishments, reflects the values, beliefs, and opinions of society's mainstream. The term *consensus* implies general agreement among a majority of citizens on what behaviors should be prohibited by criminal law and henceforth be viewed as crimes. Several attempts have been made to create a concise, yet thorough and encompassing, consensus definition of crime. The eminent criminologists Edwin Sutherland and Donald Cressey have taken the popular stance of linking crime with criminal law:

> Criminal behavior is behavior in violation of the criminal law . . . [I]t is not a crime unless it is prohibited by the criminal law [which] is defined conventionally as a body of specific rules regarding human conduct which have been promulgated by political authority, which apply uniformly to all members of the classes to which the rules refer, and which are enforced by punishment administered by the state.[31]

This approach to crime implies that it is a function of the beliefs, morality, and rules established by the existing legal power structure. According to Sutherland and Cressey's statement, criminal law is applied "uniformly to all members of the classes to which the rules refer." This statement reveals the authors' faith in the concept of an "ideal legal system" that deals adequately with all classes and types of people. Whereas laws banning burglary and robbery are directed at controlling the neediest members of society, laws banning insider trading, embezzlement, and corporate price-fixing are aimed at controlling the wealthiest. The reach of criminal law is not restricted to any single element of society.

Most practicing criminologists accept the consensus model of crime. In fact, this model is most often used in criminology texts. Nonetheless, various issues make this definition tenuous, especially the relationship of crime to morality.

The Conflict View of Crime

The **conflict view** depicts society as a collection of diverse groups — such as owners, workers, professionals, and students — who are in constant and continuing conflict. Groups able to assert their political power use the law and the criminal justice system to advance their economic and social position. Criminal laws, therefore, are viewed as acts created to protect the *haves* from the *have-nots*. Conflict criminologists often contrast the harsh penalties exacted on the poor for their "street crimes" (burglary, robbery, and larceny) with the minor penalties the wealthy receive for their white-collar crimes (securities violations and other illegal business practices). Whereas the poor go to prison for minor law violations, the wealthy are given lenient sentences for even the most serious breaches of law.

According to the conflict view, the definition of crime is controlled by wealth, power, and position and not by moral consensus or the fear of social disruption.[32] Crime, according to this definition, is a political concept designed to protect the power and position of the upper classes at the expense of the poor. Even laws prohibiting violent acts, such as armed robbery, rape, and murder, may have political undertones. Banning violent acts ensures domestic tranquillity and guarantees that the anger of the poor and disenfranchised classes will not be directed at their wealthy capitalist exploiters. Rape may be inspired by the capitalist system's devaluation of women, which may increase their vulnerability to sexual assault. The conflict view of crime, then, includes the following in a comprehensive list of "real" crimes:

- Violations of human rights due to racism, sexism, and imperialism
- Unsafe working conditions
- Inadequate child care
- Inadequate opportunities for employment and education and substandard housing and medical care
- Crimes of economic and political domination
- Pollution of the environment
- Price-fixing
- Police brutality
- Assassinations and warmaking
- Violations of human dignity
- Denial of physical needs and necessities, and impediments to self-determination
- Deprivation of adequate food and blocked opportunities to participate in political decision making[33]

Although this list might be criticized as containing vague and subjectively chosen acts, an advocate of the conflict view would counter that consensus law also prohibits crimes that have vague and subjective definitions. Consider substance abuse, gambling, and obscenity. Whereas drugs are illegal, alcohol, which causes far more social harm, is readily available. Gambling is prohibited, but the state sells lottery tickets. Selling of obscene material is illegal, but people can buy magazines featuring sex and nudity, such as *Penthouse* and *Hustler,* at the newsstand.

According to the interactionist view, crimes are outlawed behaviors because society defines them that way and not because they are inherently evil or immoral acts. Here federal agents seize a ship filled with illegal aliens being smuggled into the United States. Are these people criminals who are trying to force their way into our country or brave and courageous freedom lovers who simply want to share in the American Dream? Should they be arrested or welcomed with open arms? Before you answer, think about the Pilgrims coming ashore in Plymouth, Massachusetts. What would have happened to them if the Native Americans had attempted to deport them forcibly? Should the Pilgrims have been considered "illegals"?

The Interactionist View of Crime

The **interactionist view** of crime traces its antecedents to the symbolic interaction school of sociology, first popularized by pioneering sociologists George Herbert Mead, Charles Horton Cooley, and W. I. Thomas.[34] Interactionists hold these beliefs:

1. People act according to their own interpretations of reality, through which they assign meaning to things.
2. They learn the meaning of a thing from the way others react to it, either positively or negatively.
3. They reevaluate and interpret their own behavior according to the meaning and symbols they have learned from others.

According to this perspective, the definition of crime reflects the preferences and opinions of people who hold social power in a particular legal jurisdiction. These people use their influence to impose their definition of right and wrong on the rest of the population. Conversely, criminals are individuals that society labels as outcasts or deviants because they have violated social rules. In a classic statement, sociologist Howard Becker argued, "The deviant is one to whom that label has successfully been applied; deviant behavior is behavior people so label."[35] Crimes are outlawed behaviors because society defines them that way and not because they are inherently evil or immoral acts.

The interactionist view of crime is similar to the conflict perspective in that both suggest that behavior is outlawed when it offends people who maintain the social, economic, and political power necessary to have the law conform to their interests or needs. However, unlike the conflict view, the interactionist perspective does not attribute capitalist economic and political motives to the process of defining crime. Instead, interactionists see criminal law as conforming to the beliefs of "moral crusaders" or **moral entrepreneurs,** who use their influence to shape the legal process as they see fit.[36] Laws against pornography, prostitution, and drugs are believed to be motivated more by moral crusades than by capitalist sensibilities. Consequently, interactionists are concerned with shifting moral and legal standards.

Figure 1.4   The Definition of Crime

The definition of crime affects how criminologists view the cause and control of illegal behavior and shapes their research orientation.

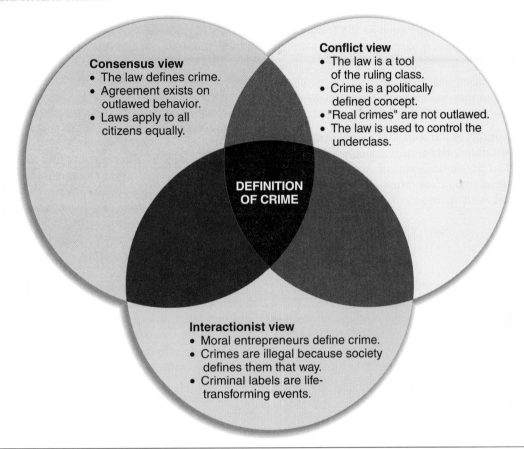

Consensus view
- The law defines crime.
- Agreement exists on outlawed behavior.
- Laws apply to all citizens equally.

Conflict view
- The law is a tool of the ruling class.
- Crime is a politically defined concept.
- "Real crimes" are not outlawed.
- The law is used to control the underclass.

DEFINITION OF CRIME

Interactionist view
- Moral entrepreneurs define crime.
- Crimes are illegal because society defines them that way.
- Criminal labels are life-transforming events.

To the interactionist, crime has no meaning unless people react to it. The one-time criminal, if not caught or labeled, can simply return to a "normal" way of life with little permanent damage. For example, consider the college student who tries marijuana. He does not view himself, nor do others view him, as a criminal or a drug addict. Only when prohibited acts are recognized and sanctioned do they become important, life-transforming events.

CONNECTIONS

Because of the damage caused by the stigma of official criminal justice processing, interactionists believe that society should intervene as little as possible in the lives of law violators lest they be labeled and stigmatized. Labeling theory, discussed in Chapter 8, is based on interactionist views and holds that applying negative labels leads first to a damaged identity and then to a criminal career.

DEFINING CRIME

The consensus view of crime dominated criminological thought until the late 1960s. Criminologists devoted themselves to learning why lawbreakers violated the rules of society. The criminal was viewed as an outlaw who, for one reason or another, flouted the rules defining acceptable conduct and behavior. In the 1960s the interactionist perspective gained prominence. The rapid change in U.S. society made traditional laws and values questionable. Many criminologists were swept along in the social revolution of the 1960s and likewise embraced an ideology suggesting that crimes reflected rules imposed by a conservative majority on nonconforming members of society. At the same time, more radical scholars gravitated toward conflict explanations, which they believed more accurately assessed the social harm caused by crime (see Figure 1.4).

Today each position still has many followers, and criminologists' personal definitions of crime dominate their thinking, research, and attitudes toward their profession. Because of their diverse perspectives, criminologists have taken a variety of approaches in explaining crime's causes and suggesting methods for its control. Considering these differences, it is possible to take elements from each school of thought to formulate an integrated definition of crime such as the following:

> Crime is a violation of societal rules of behavior as interpreted and expressed by a criminal legal code created by people holding social and political power. Individuals who violate these rules are subject to sanctions by state authority, social stigma, and loss of status.

This definition combines the consensus view that criminal law defines crimes, the conflict perspective's emphasis on political power and control, and the interactionist concept of stigma. Thus crime as defined here is a political, social, and economic function of modern life.

CRIMINOLOGY RESEARCH METHODS

Criminologists use a wide variety of research techniques to measure the nature and extent of criminal behavior. To understand and evaluate theories and patterns of criminal behavior, it is important to understand how these data are collected. This understanding also shows how professional criminologists approach various problems and questions in their field.

Survey Research

Survey research can measure the attitudes, beliefs, values, personality traits, and behavior of participants. A great deal of crime measurement is based on analysis of survey data, which is gathered using techniques such as self-report surveys and interviews. Both types of surveys involve **sampling**, which refers to the process of selecting for study a limited number of subjects who represent entire groups sharing similar characteristics, called **populations.** For example, a criminologist might interview a sample of 3,000 prison inmates drawn from the population of more than one million inmates in the United States; in this case the sample represents the entire population of U.S. inmates. Or a sample of burglary incidents could be taken from Miami; here the sample would represent the population of Miami burglaries. The characteristics of people or events in a carefully selected sample should be quite similar to those of the population at large.

One common type of survey simultaneously interviews or questions a diverse sample of subjects, representing a cross section of a community, about research topics under consideration. This method is referred to as **cross-sectional research.** For example, all youths in the tenth grade in a public high school can be surveyed about their substance abuse. Because most youths in the community are currently in school, the survey will contain a sample that represents a cross section of the community: rich and poor, males and females, users and nonusers, and so on.

Self-report surveys ask participants to describe, in detail, their recent and lifetime criminal activity. For example, victimization surveys seek information from people who have been victims of crime. Likewise, **attitude surveys** measure the attitudes, beliefs, and values of different groups, such as prostitutes, students, drug addicts, police officers, judges, or juvenile delinquents.

Pros and Cons of Surveys as Information-Gathering Tools Surveys are among the most widely used methods of criminological study. They are an excellent and cost-effective technique for measuring the characteristics of large numbers of people. Because questions and methods are standardized for all subjects, uniformity is unaffected by the perceptions or biases of the person gathering the data.

Statistical analysis of data gathered from carefully drawn samples enables researchers to generalize their findings from small groups to large populations. Although surveys measure subjects at a single point in their life spans, questions can elicit information on subjects' prior behavior as well as their future goals and aspirations.[37]

Despite their utility, surveys are not foolproof. Because they typically involve a single measurement, they are of limited value in showing how subjects change over time. In addition, surveys have been criticized because they assume that subjects will be honest and forthright. Efforts are usually made to ensure the validity of questionnaire items, but it is difficult to guard against people who either deliberately lie and misrepresent information or are unsure of answers and give mistaken responses. Surveys of delinquents and criminals are especially suspect because they rely on the willingness of a group of people not known for candor about intimate and personal matters. Surveys are also limited when the area to be studied involves the way people interact with one another or other topics an individual may not be able to judge personally, such as how he or she is perceived by significant others. Despite these drawbacks, surveys continue to be an extremely popular method of gathering criminological data.

Cohort Research

Longitudinal research involves observing a group of people who share a like characteristic (**cohort**) over time. For example, researchers might select all girls born in Albany, New York, in 1990 and then follow their behavior patterns for 20 years. The research data might include their school experiences, arrests, hospitalizations, and information about their family life (such as divorces or parental relations). The subjects might be given repeated intelligence and physical exams, and their diets might be monitored. Data could be collected directly from the subjects, or without their knowledge from schools, police, and other sources. If the research is carefully conducted, it may be possible to determine which life experiences, such as growing up in a troubled home or failing at school, typically preceded the onset of crime and delinquency.

Because it is extremely difficult, expensive, and time-consuming to follow a cohort over time, another approach is to take an intact cohort of known offenders and look back into their early life experiences by checking their educational, family, police, and hospital records. This format is known as a **retrospective cohort study.**[38] To carry out cohort studies, criminologists frequently investigate records of social organizations such as hospitals, schools, welfare departments, courts, police departments, and prisons. School records contain data on students' academic performance, attendance, intelligence, disciplinary problems, and teacher ratings. Hospitals record incidents of drug use and suspicious wounds, which may indicate child abuse. Police files contain reports of criminal activity, arrest data, personal information on suspects, victim reports, and actions taken by police officers. Court records allow researchers to compare the personal characteristics of offenders with the outcomes of their court appearances—conviction rates and types of sentences. Prison records contain information on inmates' personal characteristics, adjustment problems, disciplinary records, rehabilitation efforts, and length of sentence served.

CONNECTIONS

Some critical criminological research has been based on cohort studies. Some of the most important research has been conducted by University of Pennsylvania criminologist Marvin Wolfgang and his colleagues. Their findings have been instrumental in developing understanding about the onset and development of a criminal career. Wolfgang's cohort research is discussed in Chapter 3. In addition, other cohort studies are now ongoing. These studies are cited throughout this book.

Aggregate Data Research

Aggregate data can tell us about the effect of social trends and patterns on the crime rate. Criminologists use large government agency and research foundation databases, such as those from the U.S. Census Bureau or Labor Department, state correctional departments, and so on. The most important of these sources is the **Uniform Crime Report (UCR)**, compiled by the Federal

Bureau of Investigation (FBI).[39] The UCR annually reveals the number of crimes reported by citizens to local police departments and the number of arrests made by police agencies in a given year. The UCR is probably the most important source of official crime statistics and is discussed more completely in Chapter 3.

Aggregate data can be used to focus on the social forces that affect crime. For example, to study the relationship between crime and poverty, criminologists use the Census Bureau's data, which provides information about income and the number of people on welfare and single-parent families in an urban area. They then cross-reference this information with official crime statistics from the same locality.

Experimental Research

Sometimes criminologists want to see the direct effect of one factor on another. For example, they may wish to directly test whether watching a violent TV show will cause viewers to act aggressively. This requires experimental research: criminologists manipulate or intervene in the lives of their subjects to see the outcome or effect the intervention has. True experiments usually have three elements: (1) random selection of subjects, (2) a control or comparison group, and (3) an experimental condition. To study the effects of violent TV, a criminologist might have one group of randomly chosen subjects watch an extremely violent and gory film (such as *Scream* or *Psycho*) while another randomly selected group views something more mellow (like *Babe* or *The Parent Trap*). The behavior of both groups would be monitored, and if the subjects who had watched the violent film were significantly more aggressive than those who had watched the nonviolent film, an association between media content and behavior would be supported. The fact that both groups were randomly selected would prevent some preexisting condition from invalidating the results of the experiment.

When it is impossible to randomly select subjects or manipulate conditions, a different type of experiment is used. For example, a criminologist may want to measure the change in driving fatalities and drunk driving arrests brought about by a new state law that mandates jail sentences for persons convicted of driving while intoxicated (DWI). Because police cannot randomly arrest drunk drivers, criminologists need to find an alternative strategy, such as comparing the state's DWI arrest and fatality trends with those of nearby states that have more lenient DWI statutes. Although not a true experiment, this approach would give some indication of the effectiveness of mandatory sentences because the states are comparable *except* for their drunk driving legislation.

Another type of experimental research is referred to as a **time-series design.** Applying this approach to the previous example, criminologists would record statewide

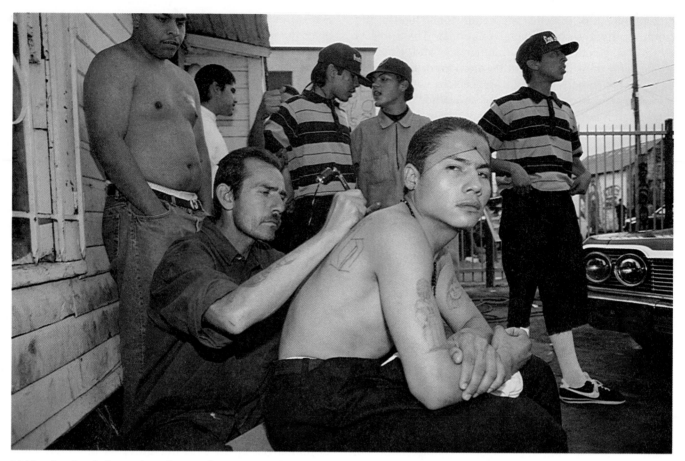

Making first-hand observation of criminals to gain insight into their motives and activities is an important aspect of criminological investigation. These Los Angeles gang members may become research subjects for criminologists who go into the field and participate in group activities. Some observers conduct field studies but remain in the background, observing but not taking part in the ongoing activity.

DWI arrest and fatality data for the months and years before and after passage of the mandatory jail statute. The effectiveness of mandatory jail terms in deterring DWI would be supported if a drop in the arrest and fatality rates coincided with the bill's adoption.

Criminological experiments are relatively rare because they are difficult and expensive to conduct; they involve manipulating subjects' lives, which can cause ethical and legal roadblocks; and they require long follow-up periods to verify results. Nonetheless, they have been an important source of criminological data.

Observational and Interview Research

Sometimes criminologists focus their research on relatively few subjects, interviewing them in depth or observing them as they go about their activities. This research often results in the kind of in-depth data absent in large surveys. For example, a recent study by Claire Sterck-Elifson focused on the lives of middle-class female drug abusers.[40] The 34 interviews she conducted provide insight into a group whose behavior might not be captured in a large survey. Sterck-Elifson found that these women were introduced to cocaine at first "just for fun": "I do drugs," one 34-year-old lawyer told her, "because I like the feeling. I would never let drugs take over my life."[41] Unfortunately, many of these subjects succumbed to the power of drugs and suffered both emotional and financial stress.

Another common criminological method is to observe criminals firsthand in order to gain insight into their motives and activities. This may involve going into the field and participating in group activities, as was done in sociologist William Whyte's famous study of a Boston gang, *Street Corner Society*.[42] Other observers conduct field studies but remain in the background, observing but not being part of the ongoing activity.[43]

Still another type of observation involves bringing subjects into a structured laboratory setting and observing how they react to a predetermined condition or stimulus. This approach is common in experimental studies testing the effect of observational learning on aggressive behavior. For example, experiments such as the one described previously, in which subjects view violent films and their subsequent behavior is monitored, would typically be conducted in a laboratory setting.[44]

Criminology, then, relies on many of the basic research methods common to other fields, including sociology, psychology, and political science. Multiple methods are needed to achieve the goals of criminological inquiry.

ETHICAL ISSUES IN CRIMINOLOGY

A critical issue facing criminology students involves recognizing the field's political and social consequences. All too often criminologists forget the social responsibility they bear as experts in the area of crime and justice. When government agencies request their views of issues, their pronouncements and opinions become the basis for sweeping social policy.

The lives of millions of people can be influenced by criminological research data. Debates over gun control, capital punishment, and mandatory sentences are ongoing and contentious. Whereas some criminologists have successfully argued for social service, treatment, and rehabilitation programs to reduce the crime rate, others consider them a waste of time, suggesting instead that a massive prison construction program coupled with tough criminal sentences can bring the crime rate down. By accepting their roles as experts on law-violating behavior, criminologists place themselves in a position of power; the potential consequences of their actions are enormous. Therefore, they must be both aware of the ethics of their profession and prepared to defend their work in the light of public scrutiny. Major ethical issues include

- What is to be studied.
- Who is to be studied.
- How studies are to be conducted.

Under ideal circumstances, when criminologists choose a subject for study, they are guided by their own scholarly interests, pressing social needs, the availability of accurate data, and other, similar concerns. Nonetheless, in recent years a great influx of government and institutional funding has influenced the direction of criminological inquiry. Major sources of monetary support include the Justice Department's National Institute of Justice and the Office of Juvenile Justice and Delinquency Prevention. Both the National Science Foundation and the National Institute of Mental Health have been prominent sources of government funding. Private foundations, such as the Edna McConnell Clark Foundation, have also played an important role in supporting criminological research.

Although the availability of research money has spurred criminological inquiry, it has also influenced the directions research has taken. Because state and federal governments provide a significant percentage of available research funds, they may also dictate the areas that can be studied. Recently, for example, the federal government has spent millions of dollars funding long-term cohort studies of criminal careers. Consequently, academic research has recently focused on criminal careers. Other areas of inquiry may be ignored because there is not enough funding to pay for the research.

A potential conflict of interest may arise when the institution funding research is itself one of the principal subjects of the research project. For example, governments may be reluctant to fund research on fraud and abuse of power by government officials. They may also influence the criminologists seeking research funding: if criminologists are too critical of the government's efforts to reduce or counteract crime, perhaps they will be barred from receiving further financial help. This situation is even more acute because criminologists typically work for universities or public agencies and are under pressure to bring in a steady flow of research funds or to maintain the continued viability of their agencies. Even when criminologists maintain discretion of choice, the direction of their efforts may not be truly objective.

A second major ethical issue in criminology concerns who will be the subject of inquiries and study. Too often criminologists focus their attention on the poor and minorities while ignoring middle-class criminals committing white-collar crime, organized crime, and government crime. Critics have charged that by "unmasking" the poor and desperate, criminologists have justified any harsh measures taken against them. For example, a few social scientists have suggested that criminals have lower intelligence quotients than the average citizen and that because minority group members have lower than average IQ scores, their crime rates are high.[45] This was the conclusion reached in *The Bell Curve,* a popular but highly controversial book written by Richard Herrnstein and Charles Murray.[46] Although such research is often methodologically unsound, it brings to light the tendency of criminologists to focus on one element of the community while ignoring others. The question that remains is whether it is ethical for criminologists to publish biased or subjective research findings, paving the way for injustice.

In some cases, ethics are once again questioned when subjects are misled about the purpose of research. When white and African-American youngsters are asked to participate in a survey of their behavior or an IQ test, they are rarely told in advance that the data they provide may later be used to prove the existence of significant racial differences in their self-reported crime rates. Should subjects be told what the true purpose of a survey is? Would such disclosures make meaningful research impossible? How far should criminologists go when collecting data? Is it ever permissible to deceive subjects to collect data? These questions and issues will be addressed throughout this text. There are no easy solutions, but asking the questions is an important first step.

SUMMARY

Criminology is the scientific approach to the study of criminal behavior and society's reaction to law violations and violators. It is essentially an interdisciplinary field; many of its practitioners were originally trained as sociologists, psychologists, economists, political scientists, historians, and natural scientists.

Criminology has a rich history with roots in the utilitarian philosophy of Beccaria, the biological positivism of Lombroso, the social theory of Durkheim, and the political philosophy of Marx. A number of fields are related to criminology. In the late 1960s criminal justice programs were created to examine and improve the U.S. system of justice. Today many criminologists work in criminal justice educational programs. Criminology and criminal justice are mutually dedicated to understanding the nature and control of criminal behavior. The study of deviant behavior also overlaps with criminology because many "deviant" acts are violations of criminal law.

The criminological enterprise includes subareas such as criminal statistics, the sociology of law, theory construction, criminal behavior systems, penology, and victimology.

Criminologists believe in one of three perspectives: the consensus view, the conflict view, or the interactionist view. The consensus view holds that crime is illegal behavior defined by existing criminal law, which reflects the values and morals of a majority of citizens. The conflict view states that crime is behavior defined so that economically powerful individuals can retain their control over society. The interactionist view portrays criminal behavior as a relativistic, constantly changing concept that reflects society's current moral values. According to the interactionist view, behavior is labeled as criminal by those in power; criminals are people society chooses to label as outsiders or deviants.

Criminologists use various research methods to gather information that will shed light on criminal behavior. Each type of method, including surveys, longitudinal studies, record studies, experiments, and observations, focuses on a different aspect of the research. Questions about ethical standards arise when information-gathering methods appear biased or exclusionary. These types of issues may cause serious consequences because their findings can significantly impact individuals and groups.

See the book-specific web site at www.cj.wadsworth.com for additional chapter links, discussions, and quizzes.

THINKING LIKE A CRIMINOLOGIST

You have been experimenting with various techniques in order to identify a surefire method to predict violent behavior in delinquents. Your procedure involves brain scans, DNA testing, and blood analysis. Used with samples of incarcerated adolescents, your procedure has been able to distinguish with 80 percent accuracy between youths with a history of violence and those who are exclusively property offenders. Your research indicates that if any youth were tested with your techniques, potentially violence-prone career criminals could be easily identified for special treatment. For example, children in the local school system could be tested, and those identified as violence-prone could be carefully monitored by teachers. Those at risk for future violence could be put into special programs as a precaution.

Some of your colleagues argue that this type of testing is unconstitutional because it violates the subjects' Fifth Amendment right against self-incrimination. There is also the problem of error: some kids may be falsely labeled as violence-prone.

How would you answer your critics? Is it fair or ethical to label people as potentially criminal and violent even though they have not yet exhibited any antisocial behavior? Do the risks of such a procedure outweigh its benefits?

KEY TERMS

criminology
criminologists
interdisciplinary
utilitarianism
classical criminology
positive stage
positivist
positivism
physiognomist
phrenologist
psychopathic personality
criminal anthropology
atavistic anomalies

biosocial theory
cartographic school of criminology
anomie
Chicago School
social ecology
socialization
ecological view
socialization view
bourgeoisie
proletariat
criminal justice
deviant behavior
legalized

decriminalized
criminological enterprise
white-collar crime
crime typology
penology
capital punishment
mandatory prison sentences
recidivate
consensus view
substantive criminal law
conflict view
interactionist view
moral entrepreneurs

sampling
populations
cross-sectional research
self-report surveys

attitude surveys
longitudinal research
cohort
retrospective cohort study

Uniform Crime Report (UCR)
time-series design

NOTES

1. "Teen-Ager Accused of Killing Says He Got Demons' Orders," *New York Times,* 5 June 1998.

2. For a thorough review, see Robin Malinosky-Rummell and David Hansen, "Long-Term Consequences of Childhood Physical Abuse," *Psychological Bulletin* 114 (1993): 68–79.

3. Roper Poll, in Kathleen Maguire, Ann Pastore, and Timothy Flanagan, *Sourcebook of Criminal Justice Statistics 1995* (Washington, D.C.: U.S. Government Printing Office, 1996), p. 153.

4. Elizabeth Perkins, "Gender and Fear of Crime: Evidence from 12 Surveys." Paper presented at the Annual Society of Criminology Meeting, San Diego, Calif., November 1997.

5. Edwin Sutherland and Donald Cressey, *Principles of Criminology,* 6th ed. (Philadelphia: J. B. Lippincott, 1960), p. 3.

6. Eugen Weber, *A Modern History of Europe* (New York: W. W. Norton, 1971), p. 398.

7. Marvin Wolfgang, *Patterns in Criminal Homicide* (Philadelphia: University of Pennsylvania Press, 1958).

8. Described in David Lykken, "Psychopathy, Sociopathy, and Crime," *Society* 34 (1996): 29–38.

9. See Peter Scott, "Henry Maudsley," in *Pioneers in Criminology,* ed. Hermann Mannheim (Montclair, N.J.: Prentice-Hall, 1981).

10. Howard Becker, *Outsiders: Studies in the Sociology of Deviance* (New York: Free Press, 1963), p. 21.

11. Becker, *Outsiders,* p. 9.

12. Nicole Hahn Rafter, "Criminal Anthropology in the United States," *Criminology* 30 (1992): 525–47.

13. Rafter, "Criminal Anthropology," p. 535.

14. See, generally, Robert Nisbet, *The Sociology of Emile Durkheim* (New York: Oxford University Press, 1974).

15. L.A.J. Quetelet, *A Treatise on Man and the Development of His Faculties* (Gainesville, Fla.: Scholars' Facsimiles and Reprints, 1969), pp. 82–96.

16. Quetelet, *A Treatise on Man,* p. 85.

17. Emile Durkheim, *Rules of the Sociological Method,* reprint ed., trans. W. D. Halls (New York: Free Press, 1982).

18. University of Michigan Survey Research Center, "Drug Use by American Young People Begins to Turn Downward," News Release, 18 December 1998, Ann Arbor, Michigan.

19. Emile Durkheim, *The Division of Labor in Society,* reprint ed. (New York: Free Press, 1997).

20. Robert Park and Ernest Burgess, *The City* (Chicago: University of Chicago Press, 1925).

21. Karl Marx and Friedrich Engels, *Capital: A Critique of Political Economy,* trans. E. Aveling (Chicago: Charles Kern, 1906); Karl Marx, *Selected Writings in Sociology and Social Philosophy,* trans. P. B. Bottomore (New York: McGraw-Hill, 1956). For a general discussion of Marxist thought, see Michael Lynch and W. Byron Groves, *A Primer in Radical Criminology* (New York: Harrow and Heston, 1986), pp. 6–26.

22. For a review of the development of criminal justice as a field of study, see Frank Remington, "Development of Criminal Justice as an Academic Field," *Journal of Criminal Justice Education* 1 (1990): 9–20.

23. Marvin Zalman, *A Heuristic Model of Criminology and Criminal Justice* (Chicago: Joint Commission on Criminology Education and Standards, University of Illinois, Chicago Circle, 1981), pp. 9–11.

24. Charles McCaghy, *Deviant Behavior* (New York: MacMillan, 1976), pp. 2–3.

25. Edward Brecher, *Licit and Illicit Drugs* (Boston: Little, Brown, 1972), pp. 413–16.

26. Brecher, *Licit and Illicit Drugs,* p. 414.

27. Marvin Wolfgang and Franco Ferracuti, *The Subculture of Violence* (London: Social Science Paperbacks, 1967), p. 20.

28. Associated Press, "Michigan Senate Acts to Outlaw Aiding Suicides," *Boston Globe,* 20 March 1994, p. 22.

29. Marvin Wolfgang, *Patterns in Criminal Homicide* (Philadelphia: University of Pennsylvania Press, 1958).

30. Hans von Hentig, *The Criminal and His Victim* (New Haven: Yale University Press, 1948); Stephen Schafer, *The Victim and His Criminal* (New York: Random House, 1968).

31. Edwin Sutherland and Donald Cressey, *Criminology,* 8th ed. (Philadelphia: J. B. Lippincott, 1960), p. 8.

32. Eugene Doleschal and Nora Klapmuts, "Toward a New Criminology," *Crime and Delinquency* 5 (1973): 607.

33. Michael Lynch and W. Byron Groves, *A Primer in Radical Criminology* (Albany, N.Y.: Harrow and Heston, 1989).

34. See Herbert Blumer, *Symbolic Interactionism* (Englewood Cliffs, N.J.: Prentice-Hall, 1969).

35. Becker, *Outsiders,* p. 9.

36. Becker, *Outsiders,* p. 9.

37. Michael Gottfredson and Travis Hirschi, "The Methodological Adequacy of Longitudinal Research on Crime," *Criminology* 25 (1987): 581–614.

38. See, generally, David Farrington, Lloyd Ohlin, and James Q. Wilson, *Understanding and Controlling Crime* (New York: Springer-Verlag, 1986), pp. 11–18.

39. The most recent version available at the time of this writing is this: Federal Bureau of Investigation, *Crime in the United States, 1997* (Washington, D.C.: U.S. Government Printing Office, 1998).

40. Claire Sterck-Elifson, "Just for Fun?: Cocaine Use Among Middle-Class Women," *Journal of Drug Issues* 26 (1996): 63–76.

41. Sterck-Elifson, "Just for Fun?", p. 63.

42. William F. Whyte, *Street Corner Society* (Chicago: University of Chicago Press, 1955).

43. Herman Schwendinger and Julia Schwendinger, *Adolescent Subcultures and Delinquency* (New York: Praeger, 1985).

44. For a review of these studies, see L. Rowell Huesmann and Neil Malamuth, eds., "Media Violence and Antisocial Behavior," *Journal of Social Issues* 42 (1986): 31–53.

45. See, for example, Michael Hindelang and Travis Hirschi, "Intelligence and Delinquency: A Revisionist Review," *American Sociological Review* 42 (1977): 471–86.

46. Richard Herrnstein and Charles Murray, *The Bell Curve* (New York: Free Press, 1994).

CHAPTER 2

Criminal Law
and Its Processes

INTRODUCTION

On November 30, 1998, Olympic gymnast Dominique Moceanu obtained a protective order against her father, accusing him of stalking her and threatening to harm her friends. "I am terrified of my father," the 17-year-old Olympic gold medalist told the court. "I believe that all of my father's actions are intended to result in physical harm, bodily injury, or assault to me or my friends." The court order barred Dumitru Moceanu from contacting his daughter except through her attorney. The Moceanus' problems stem from charges that Dominique's earnings had been squandered by her parents on risky investments and a $4 million gym bearing her name.[1] The court order protecting the 17-year-old Ms. Moceanu reflects the recent legal recognition of a new crime category, *stalking,* which involves repeated physical or visual contact, non-consensual communication, or verbal, written, or implied threats sufficient to cause fear in a reasonable person. It also illustrates the role criminal law plays in both defining crime and shaping human behavior. At one time it would have been within Mr. Moceanu's rights to have contact with his young daughter. Now that the law recognizes the dangers of stalking, his behavior is prohibited and outlawed. If he contacts his daughter while the court order is in place, he will suffer arrest.

Olympic gymnast Dominique Moceanu stands with her parents Dumitru and Camelia in a Texas courtroom. The 17-year-old had filed a suit to be considered a legal adult after a financial dispute caused her to run away from home on October 17, 1998.

Criminal law dictates what constitutes a crime and how criminal acts are defined. Having evolved over many generations, today's criminal law incorporates historical traditions, moral beliefs, and social values, as well as political and economic developments and conditions. Criminal law is a living concept, constantly changing to keep pace with society. It governs the form and direction of almost all human interaction. Business practices, family life, education, property transfers, inheritance, and other common forms of social relations must conform to the rules set out by the **legal code,** which are the specific laws that fall within the scope of criminal law. As we examine this topic throughout this chapter, you will begin to see how the law defines behaviors that society labels as "criminal." Consequently, it is important for criminology students to have a basic understanding of the law and its relationship to crime and deviance. This chapter reviews the nature and purpose of the law, charts its history, and discusses its components.

THE ORIGIN OF LAW

We know that crimes and criminal behavior were recognized in many early societies.[2] In preliterate societies, common custom and tradition (**mores** and **folkways**) were the equivalents of law. Each group had its own set of customs, which were created to deal with daily situations. These customs would often be followed long after the reason for their origin was forgotten. In some cases, customs had become such an integral part of the way a culture functioned that eventually they became formal or written law.

The concept of crime was first recognized in the earliest surviving legal codes, which were developed by the Babylonians and the Hebrews and later in legal codes developed by the Romans. King Dungi of Sumer (an area that is part of present-day Iraq) is credited with developing one of the first legal codes in about 2000 B.C. Its content is known today because it was later adopted by Hammurabi (1792–1750 B.C.), the sixth king of Babylon, in his famous set of written laws that today is known as the **Code of Hammurabi.** Preserved on basalt rock columns, the code establishes crimes and their correction. Punishment was based on physical retaliation or **lex talionis** ("an eye for an eye"). The severity of punishment depended on class standing: for assault, slaves would be killed, while freemen might lose a limb.

Judges who were controlled by advisers to the king strictly enforced Babylonian laws. Crimes such as burglary and theft were common in ancient Babylon, and officials responsible for enforcing these laws had to take their duties seriously. Local officials were expected to apprehend criminals. If they failed in their duties, they had to personally replace lost property; if murderers were not caught, the responsible official paid a fine to the deceased's relatives.

CONNECTIONS

Although not exactly an "eye for an eye," efforts are now being made to make punishments fit the crime. Chapter 5's discussion of "just desert" presents the perspective that crime and punishment should be closely aligned. Chapter 17 picks up on this again in discussing determinate sentencing, which shows how the just desert model has been put into practice.

The second of the ancient legal codes still surviving is the Mosaic Code of the Israelites (1200 B.C.). According to tradition, God entered into a covenant or contract with the tribes of Israel in which they agreed to obey his law (the 613 laws of the Old Testament, including the Ten Commandments), as presented to them by Moses, in return for God's special care and protection. The Mosaic Code not only is the foundation of Judeo-Christian moral teachings, but it also is a basis for the U.S. legal system: prohibitions against murder, theft, perjury, and adultery precede, by several thousand years, the same laws found in the U.S. legal system.

Also surviving is the Roman law contained in the **Twelve Tables** (451 B.C.). A special commission of 10 noble Roman men formulated the Twelve Tables in response to pressure from the lower classes, who were referred to as **plebeians.** The plebeians believed that an unwritten code gave arbitrary and unlimited power to the wealthy classes, known as **patricians,** who served as magistrates. The original code was written on bronze plaques, which have been lost, but records of sections, which were memorized by every Roman male, survive. The remaining laws deal with debt, family relations, property, and other daily matters. A sample section of this code is shown in Table 2.1.

Table 2.1 Table VIII of the Twelve Tables: Torts or Delicts
• If any person has sung or composed against another person a song such as was causing slander or insult to another, he shall be clubbed to death.
• If a person has maimed another's limb, let there be retaliation in kind unless he makes agreement for settlement with him.
• Any person who destroys by burning any building or heap of corn deposited alongside a house shall be bound, scourged, and put to death by burning at the stake, provided that he has committed the said misdeed with malice aforethought; but if he shall have committed it by accident, that is, by negligence, it is ordained that he repair the damage, or, if he be too poor to be competent for such punishment, he shall receive a lighter chastisement.

Early Crime, Punishment, and Law in Chaos

The early formal legal codes were lost during the Dark Ages, which lasted for hundreds of years after the fall of Rome (around 500–1000 A.D.). During this period superstition and fear of magic and satanic black arts dominated thinking.

Some attempts were made at regulating the definition and punishment of crime during the early feudal period. Those that still exist feature monetary payments as punishments for crimes. Some early German and Anglo-Saxon societies developed legal systems featuring compensation, called **wergild** (*wer* means worth and refers to what the person, and therefore the crime, was worth), for criminal violations. For example, under the sixth-century legal code of the Salic Franks (a tribe that lived in what today is France), if someone were to kill a freewoman of childbearing age, the murderer was punished by wergild in the amount of 24,000 denars (a form of Frankish currency) to the woman's family. If the woman was past childbearing age, the wergild was reduced to 8,000 denars.

Guilt was determined by two methods, compurgation and ordeal. **Compurgation** involved having the accused person swear an oath of innocence while being backed up by a group of 12 to 25 **oathhelpers,** who would attest to his or her character and claims of innocence. In contrast, **ordeal** was based on the principle of divine intervention and the belief that divine forces would not allow an innocent person to be harmed. Determining guilt by ordeal involved such measures as having the accused place his or her hand in boiling water or hold a hot iron. If the wound healed, the person was found innocent; conversely, if the wound did not heal, the accused was deemed guilty.

Trial by combat was another method for establishing guilt or innocence. Using this method, one could challenge an accuser to a duel, with the outcome determining the legitimacy of the accusation. These measures continued to be used in Europe until the thirteenth century. For example, when William of Normandy (better known as "the Conqueror") assumed the English crown in 1066, the rules of conduct stated the following, in part:

> It was decreed there that if a Frenchman shall charge an Englishman with perjury or murder or theft or homicide or "ran," as the English call open rapine which cannot be denied, the Englishman may defend himself, as he shall prefer, either by the ordeal of hot iron or by wager of battle. But if the Englishman be infirm, let him find another who will take his place. If one of them shall be vanquished, he shall pay a fine of 40 shillings to the king. If an Englishman shall charge a Frenchman and be unwilling to prove his accusation either by ordeal or by wager of battle, I will, nevertheless, that the Frenchman shall acquit himself by a valid oath.[3]

CONNECTIONS

It was possible in trial by combat to have a "champion" fight for you if the combat was obviously one-sided. This evened the odds a bit! The development of the jury trial and the end of the use of ordeal are discussed further in Chapter 17.

Despite such "reforms," the systems of crime, punishment, law, and justice were chaotic. The lords of the great manors, who tried cases according to local custom and rule, controlled the law. Although people generally agreed that such acts as theft, assault, treason, and blasphemy constituted crimes, the penalties were often arbitrary, discretionary, and cruel. Punishments included public flogging, branding, beheading, and

Trial by fire was a common practice during the Middle Ages. Guilt was determined by ordeals, such as having the accused place his or her hand in boiling water or hold a hot iron to see if God would intervene and heal the wounds. This painting illustrates an account given by the twelfth-century historian Godfrey of Viterbo. A count in the court of Holy Roman Emperor Otto the III (890–1002) was accused and executed for adultery with the Empress. Otto forced her to undergo trial by fire. She is shown here holding a piece of red-hot metal that has been heated in the fire at her feet. When her hand is burned, the test "proves" her guilt. Her burning at the stake is shown at the top of the panel.

burning. Peasants who violated the rule of their masters were violently punished, and rebellions were put down with extreme cruelty and loss of lives.

According to a fourteenth-century Norman chronicle, disobedient peasants or those who stole from their masters were treated harshly. Some had their teeth pulled out; others were impaled, with their eyes torn out, hands cut off, and ankles charred; others were burned alive or plunged in boiling lead.[4] Even simple wanderers and vagabonds were viewed as dangerous and were subject to these extreme penalties.

Origins of Common Law

Because the ancient legal codes had been lost during the Dark Ages, the concept of law and crime during this long 500-year period (500–1000 A.D.) was in disarray, often guided by superstition and local custom. After the Norman conquest of England in 1066, **common law** developed, which helped standardize law and justice. Before the Norman conquest, the legal system among the early English (Anglo-Saxons), like that elsewhere in Europe, was decentralized. Each county, also known as a **shire,** was divided into units called **hundreds,** which were groups of 100 families. Each hundred was further divided into groups of 10 families called **tithings.** The **reeve** was the head law enforcement official in the shire. However, within these smaller groups, the tithings were responsible for maintaining order among themselves and dealing with minor disturbances, such as fires, wild animals, and so on. Early law enforcement organized along the lines of the tithing, hundred, and shire.

> CONNECTIONS
>
> The *shire reeve* is embodied today in the county sheriff. For more on the history of law enforcement see Chapter 16.

Petty cases were tried by a court of the hundred group, the **hundred-gemot.** More serious and important cases could be heard by an assemblage of local landholders, known as the **shire-gemot,** or by the local nobleman in a manorial court, sometimes called the **hali-gemot.** If the act concerned any type of spiritual matters, it could be judged by clergy and church officials in courts known as **holy-motes** or **ecclesiastics.** Although the law was becoming more standardized than it had been during past generations, it still varied between counties, hundreds, and tithings.

Compensation for Crime

To a great degree, criminal law was designed to provide equitable solutions to what were previously considered private disputes. Crime before the Norman conquest was viewed as a violation of the victim's personal rights, and compensation therefore was paid directly to the victim and his or her family. In this way medieval criminal law was similar to modern civil law, where victims are compensated for their loss and suffering by the party that harmed them. If payment was not made, the victims' families would attempt to forcibly collect damages or seek revenge. The result could be a blood feud between two families. Crimes warranting these types of feuds included treason, homicide, rape, property theft, **assault** (putting another in fear), and **battery** (wounding another). For acts of **treason,** such as siding with an enemy in a dispute over territory or succession, the punishment was death. Theft before the Norman conquest could result in slavery for the thieves and their families. If caught in the act of fleeing with the stolen goods, the thief could be killed.

For many other acts, including both theft and violence, compensation could be paid to the victim. For example, even a homicide could be settled by paying wergild to the deceased's family unless the crime was carried out by poison or ambush—in which case it was punished by death.

Eventually, wergild was divided so that of the sum (**bot**) paid, part (**wer**) went to the king, and the remainder (**wite**) went to the victim or the deceased's kin (see Figure 2.1). The nobility began to see the value in the wer, and it became the predominant portion of the bot. This arrangement is, in fact, the precursor of the modern criminal fine. A scale of compensation existed for lesser injuries, such as the loss of an arm or an eye. Important persons, such as churchmen and nuns, received greater restitution than the general population, yet they paid more if they were criminal defendants.

> CONNECTIONS
>
> Monetary compensation is used today as a criminal sanction. Criminal forfeiture, used to punish white-collar criminals and organized crime figures, is discussed further in Chapter 13. Today experiments are under way to see whether adjusting fines according to what people earn would work as a deterrent. See the section on day fines in Chapter 18.

The Norman Conquest

In 1066 Edward Confessor, King of England, died without an heir. The kingship was assumed by Harold Godwinson, a son of one of England's great noble families. His rule was soon disputed by William, Duke of Normandy (a province of France). William and his followers invaded and defeated Harold's forces at the famed Battle of Hastings.

Figure 2.1 The Distribution of Wergild

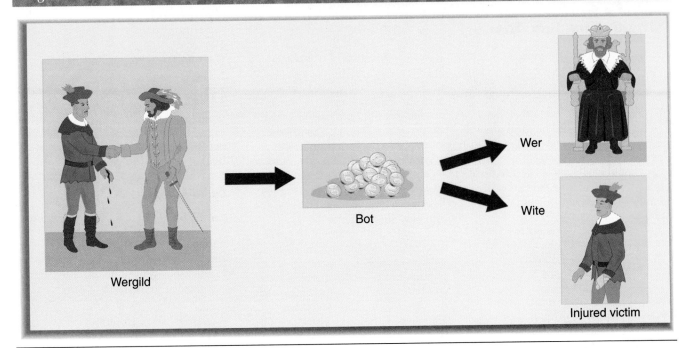

Wergild

Bot

Wer

Wite

Injured victim

After the conquest, William did not immediately change the substance of Anglo-Saxon law. At the outset of William's reign, justice was administered as it had been in previous centuries. The church courts handled acts that might be considered sinful, and the local hundred or **manorial courts** dealt with most secular violations. However, to secure control of the countryside and to ensure military supremacy over his newly won lands, William established royal courts, which dealt with the most serious breaches of the peace.

Because the royal courts could not be present in each community, a system was developed in which they traveled in a circuit throughout the land, holding court in each county several times a year. When court was in session, the royal administrator, or judge, would summon a number of citizens who would, on their oath, tell of the crimes and serious breaches of the peace that had occurred since the judge's last visit. The royal judge then would decide what to do in each case, using local custom and rules of conduct as his guide. If, for example, a local landholder was convicted of theft, he might be executed if those before him had suffered that fate for a similar offense. However, if in previous cases the thief had been forced to make restitution to the victim, then that judgment would be rendered in the present case. This system, known as **stare decisis** (Latin for "to stand by decided cases"), was how the early courts determined the outcome of future cases. Courts were bound to follow the law established in previous cases unless a higher authority, such as the king or the pope, overruled the law.

COMMON LAW

The present English system of law came into existence during the reign of Henry II (1154–1189). Henry also used traveling judges, better known as **circuit judges.** These judges followed a specific route (known as a *circuit*) and heard cases that previously had been under the jurisdiction of local courts. Professional jurists could be found in three central royal courts—The Exchequer, King's Bench, and Common Pleas—and their judges developed a reputation for fairness and the ability to systematize the law across the land. **Juries,** which began to develop about this time, were groups of local landholders whom the judges called not only to decide the facts of cases but also to investigate the crimes, accuse suspected offenders, and even testify at trials. (See the Policy and Practice in Criminology box, "Origin of the Jury Trial.")

Gradually, **royal prosecutors** were established as key players in the court proceedings. These representatives of the Crown submitted evidence and brought witnesses to testify before the jury. Few formal procedures existed at this time, however, and both the judge and the prosecutor felt free to intimidate witnesses and jurors when they considered it necessary. The development of these routine judicial processes heralded the beginnings of common law.

As it is used today, the term *common law* refers to a law applied to all subjects of the land, without regard for geographic or social differences. As best they could, Henry's judges began to apply a national law instead of

Origin of the Jury Trial

In early medieval Europe and England, disputed criminal charges were often decided by an ordeal. In a trial by fire, the accused individuals would have a hot iron placed in their hand, and if the wound did not heal properly, it was considered proof of their guilt. In a trial by combat, the defendant could challenge his accuser to a duel; the accuser had the option of finding an alternate to fight in his place.

Settling trials by ordeal fell out of favor when the Catholic Church, at the Fourth Lateran Council (1215), decreed that priests could no longer participate in trials by ordeal. Without the use of the ordeal in disputed criminal cases, courts both in England and in the rest of Europe were not sure how to proceed.

In England, the Church ban on ordeal meant that a new method of deciding criminal trials needed to be developed. To fill the gap, British justices adapted a method that had long been used to determine real estate taxes. Since the time of William the Conqueror, 12 knights in each district had been called before an "inquest" of the king's justices to give local tax information. Instead of the slow determination of feudal taxes by judges, these "twelve free and lawful men of the neighbourhood" would view the land and testify as to who last had peaceful possession so that an accurate accounting could be made. Since they were available when the king's justices were present on circuit, the Writ of Novel Disseisin, first established in 1166 under Henry II, also required them to settle "claim jumping" disputes over land.

By 1219 the jury (from the Latin term *jurati,* to be sworn) called to decide land cases also began to hear criminal cases. At first jurors were like witnesses, telling the judge what they knew about the case; these courts were known as assise or assize (from the Latin *assideo,* to sit together). By the fourteenth century, jurors had become the deciders of fact. Over the centuries, the English jury came to be seen as a check on the government. The great case that established the principle of jury independence, *Bushell's* case (1670), arose when a London jury acquitted William Penn, a leading Quaker and later the founder of Pennsylvania, of unlawful assembly in connection with his preaching in the street after a Quaker church was padlocked. The jurors were imprisoned by an angry royalist judge. They were freed when British Chief Judge Vaughn held that unless a jury was corrupt, it was free to reach a verdict based on the evidence, or else the jury would be nothing but a useless rubber stamp.

CRITICAL THINKING

1. Do you think that the common-law development of a jury trial is relevant in today's world?
2. Should a jury of one's peers be replaced by professionals who are schooled in the law?

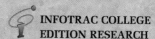

INFOTRAC COLLEGE EDITION RESEARCH

The jury trial continues to be the centerpiece of the legal system. In some ways it is almost like a theater experience. To read more about this, go to Mark I. Bernstein, Laurence R. Milstein. Trial as theater. *Trial,* Oct 1997 33 n10 p64(5)

Source: Marvin Zalman and Larry Siegel, *Criminal Procedure, Constitution and Society* (St. Paul: West Publishing, 1991).

the law that held sway only in local jurisdictions. This attempt was somewhat confused at first because judges and prosecutors had to take into account both local custom and the Norman conquerors' feudal law, which were not always in sync. However, as new situations arose, judges took advantage of legal uncertainty by either inventing new solutions or borrowing from the laws of European countries.

As time went on, judicial decisions began to be written and published. This allowed judicial precedents to be established, and more concrete examples of common-law decisions began to emerge. Together these cases and decisions filtered through the national court system and eventually produced a fixed body of legal rules and principles. This approach to common law, or judge-made law, is defined as **case law.** Judicial decisions were made case by case. Working with customary rules, the judges applied them to new situations as they arose. Legal rules could be merged or expanded and new varieties tried out. If the new rules could be suc-cessfully applied in a number of different cases they would become precedents, which would then be commonly applied in all similar cases. Crimes such as murder, burglary, arson, and rape are common-law crimes — they were initially defined by judges.

Common Law and Statutory Law

Common law was and still is the law of the land in England. In most instances, common law retained traditional Anglo-Saxon concepts. For example, common law originally defined *murder* as the unlawful killing of another human being with malice aforethought.[5] According to this definition, for offenders to be found guilty of murder, they must have (1) planned the crime and (2) intentionally killed the victim out of spite or hatred. However, this general definition proved inadequate to deal with the many situations in which one person took another's life. Over time, to bring the law closer to the realities of human behavior, judges began to differentiate between deaths caused by passion (manslaughter), negligence (involuntary manslaughter), rage (second-degree murder), or cunning (capital or first-degree murder). Using this revised definition, someone who killed another person while committing another crime, such as a robbery, could be convicted of capital murder even though the death was unintentional. Each form of murder warranted a different degree of punishment. Thus common law was a constantly evolving legal code. *Felony Murder*

CONNECTIONS

Common-law practices still guide modern legal codes. For example, murder statutes still retain different degrees of seriousness based on intent. Each degree is correlated with a level of punishment commensurate with its seriousness. The degrees of murder and other defining issues are discussed in Chapter 11.

In some instances, the creation of a new common-law crime can be traced back to a particular case. For example, an unsuccessful attempt to commit an illegal act was not considered a crime under early common law. The modern doctrine that criminal attempts can be punished under law can be traced directly back to 1784 and the case of *Rex v. Scofield*. In that case, Scofield was charged with having put a lit candle and combustible material in a house he was renting with the intention of burning it down; however, the house did not burn. He defended himself by arguing that a failed attempt to break the law could not be considered a criminal offense. In rejecting this argument, the court stated, "The intent may make an act, innocent in itself, criminal; nor is the completion of an act, criminal in itself, necessary to constitute criminality."[6] After *Scofield,* attempts at crime became common-law crimes, and today most U.S. jurisdictions have enacted laws against **criminal attempts,** also known as **inchoate crimes.**

When the situation required it, the English Parliament enacted legislation to supplement the judge-made common law. Violations of these laws are referred to as **statutory crimes.** Statutory laws usually reflect existing social conditions. For example, in 1723 a statutory law known as the Waltham Black Act was created in order to provide the British ruling class a mechanism for protecting its property and position of social power. This act was intended to punish, with death, offenses against rural property, such as poaching small game or arson, if the criminal was armed or disguised.[7] Moreover, the act eroded the rights of the accused; it allowed the death sentence to be carried out without a trial if the accused failed to surrender when ordered to do so. The underlying purpose of the act was Parliament's desire to control the behavior of peasants whose poverty forced them to poach on royal lands.

Other statutory laws dealt with issues of morality, such as gambling, sexual activity, and drug-related offenses. For example, a whole series of statutory laws was created to protect the well-being of British, and later U.S., business enterprise.[8] These laws took into account crimes such as **embezzlement,** which occurs when someone takes others' possessions that have been entrusted to them, such as a bank teller taking bank deposits; and **fraud,** which occurs when someone takes another's possessions through deception.

Common Law and Statutory Law in America

Before the American Revolution, the colonies, then under British rule, were subject to the law handed down by English judges. After the colonies acquired their independence, they adapted and changed English law to fit their needs. State legislatures standardized common-law crimes such as murder, burglary, arson, and rape by putting them into statutory form in criminal codes.

Conversion to statutory law allowed common-law principles to be modified and modernized. An example of this process of modifying common law can be found in the Massachusetts statute defining *arson.* The common-law definition of **arson** is "the malicious burning of the dwelling of another." Massachusetts expanded this definition by passing legislation defining *arson* as "the willful and malicious setting fire to, or burning of, *any building or contents thereof even if they were burned by the owner*"[9] (emphasis added). As in England, whenever common law proved inadequate to deal with changing social and moral issues, the states and Congress supplemented it with legislative statutes, creating new elements in the various state and federal legal codes.

An example of changing statutory law can be found in the history of U.S. drug legislation. Early in the nation's history it was both legal and relatively easy to obtain narcotics such as heroin, opium, and cocaine.[10] Then information about drugs started to reveal trouble. Use of these drugs became habits of the middle class, and public and governmental concern arose over the use of narcotics by immigrants such as the Chinese, who had come to the United States to build railroads and work in mines. Eventually changes in public sentiment resulted in the 1914 passage of the Harrison Act, which outlawed trade in opium and its derivatives. Later, in 1937, pressure from federal law enforcement officials led to passage of the Marijuana Tax Act, which outlawed the sale or possession of that drug. When use of marijuana became widespread among the middle class in the 1960s, several states revised their laws to effectively decriminalize the possession of marijuana. The statutory law began to reflect the views of individual states' legislatures on the use of soft drugs by their citizens. In some states marijuana possession is still punished by many years in prison; in others the punishment is only a small fine.

Common Law in Other Cultures

The British common-law tradition was imposed not only on the American colonies but also on other British overseas jurisdictions, including its African colonies. In some instances this created a dual legal system; for example, African law was divided between traditional tribal law and British common law. Criminologists Edna Erez and Bankole Thompson have described the conflict between traditional tribal law and British common law in the African country of Sierra Leone.[11] According to Erez and Thompson, women in Sierra Leone are still considered the property of their fathers and later their husbands or heads of families. If a woman is raped, the case is usually brought to the **customary courts,** which handle complaints according to traditional tribal customs. If the accused is found guilty of sexual assault, referred to as "woman-damage," he will be forced to pay compensation to the victim's family. Because this is a property issue, the victim's consent is not important; the "damage" involves a trespass or misuse of "someone's property." The victim's story is usually accepted because the tribal custom is that a woman should confess a wrongful sexual act or else suffer divinely imposed ill fate and misfortune. After admitting guilt, the accused typically agrees to compensate either the victim's parents or her husband for the damage he caused. If the defendant refuses to admit guilt or pay damages, the case can be brought under the jurisdiction of the general courts, which use British common law; the maximum penalty can be life in prison. Threat of complaint to the formal justice system is used as an incentive to settle the case according to tribal law and pay monetary penalties rather than face trial, conviction, and imprisonment.

In Sierra Leone, British common law and the traditional tribal customs are often at cross-purposes. Yet the two systems can function together because each helps to maintain group norms.

CLASSIFICATION OF LAW

There are a number of different ways to classify laws. These categories help us understand the nature and purpose of each law. Three of the most important classifications are discussed next.

Crimes and Torts

Law can be divided into two broad categories — criminal law and **civil law.** Civil law is all law other than criminal law, and it includes such legal areas as **prop-erty law,** which governs transfer and ownership of property, and **contract law,** which is the law of personal agreements. Of all the areas of civil law, **tort law,** the law of personal wrongs and damage, is most similar in intent and form to criminal law.

A **tort** is a civil action in which an individual asks to be compensated for personal harm. The harm, which may be either physical or mental, includes such acts as trespassing, assault and battery, invasion of privacy, **libel** (false and injurious writings), and **slander** (false and injurious statements). A tort can occur when someone is injured by the actions of another. As the O. J. Simpson civil trial illustrates, people can be sued for damages even if they have not been found guilty of criminal acts. One justification for this discrepancy is that the standard of evidence for a finding is less in civil cases. In criminal cases, proof must be beyond a reasonable doubt, while in civil cases, proof is a mere preponderance of the evidence. A violation of civil law may also occur when a behavior indirectly causes injury—that is, when it sets off a chain of events that leads to injury or death. In 1990, for example, the families of two youths who had attempted suicide sued the heavy metal rock group Judas Priest and CBS Records because they claimed the group had put the subliminal message "do it" in its albums to effect "mind control" over the band's fans. Although the group was vindicated, the judge ruled that the First Amendment right to free speech, if indeed they had employed privacy-invading mind-control messages, did not protect its recordings.[12]

Because some torts are similar to some criminal acts, a person can possibly be held both criminally and civilly liable for one action. For example, if one man punches another, it is possible for the assailant to be charged by the state with assault and battery—and imprisoned if found guilty—and be sued by the victim in a tort action of assault in which he could be required to pay monetary damages. In a 1993 Massachusetts case, Jennifer Hoult received an award of $500,000 from her father, David, after a federal court accepted her claim that he had raped her at least 3,000 times from the time she was a child of four until she reached age 16. The case is a milestone because the **statute of limitations** (a statute of limitations specifies the amount of time by which action must be taken by the state in a criminal matter) for bringing a tort action in a rape case was three years. However, in the Hoult case, the jury found that because the plaintiff had repressed her memory of the rapes, the statute of limitations did not start running until she had regained her memory through psychological therapy.[13]

Perhaps the most important similarity between criminal law and civil law is that they have a common purpose. Both attempt to control people's behavior by setting limits on what acts are permissible; and both accomplish this through state-imposed sanctions.

The Differences Between Crimes and Torts There are also several differences between criminal law and civil law. The main purpose of criminal law is to give the state the power to protect the public from harm by punishing individuals whose actions threaten the social order. In tort law, the harm or injury is considered a private wrong, and the main concern is to compensate victims for harm that others have inflicted on them.

In a criminal action, the state initiates the legal proceedings by bringing charges and prosecuting the violator. If it is determined that criminal law has been broken, the state can impose punishment such as imprisonment; **probation,** which is community supervision by the court; or a fine payable to the state. In a civil action, however, the injured person must file an action in order to initiate proceedings. In a successful civil action, the injured individual usually receives financial compensation for the harm done.

Another major difference between these types of law is the burden of proof required to establish the defendant's liability. In criminal matters, the defendant's guilt must be proven **beyond a reasonable doubt.** This standard means that the jury must consider all of the evidence presented to them and be entirely satisfied that the party is guilty as charged. If there is any doubt, the jury must find for the defendant by returning a verdict of not guilty. In a civil case, the defendant is required to pay damages if by a **preponderance of the evidence,** the trier of fact (either judge or jury) finds that he or she committed the wrong. According to this doctrine, although both parties may share some blame, the defendant (the target of the civil action) is at fault if he or she contributed more than 50 percent to the cause of the dispute. Establishing guilt by a preponderance of the evidence is easier than establishing it beyond a reasonable doubt.[14] Table 2.2 summarizes the differences and similarities between crimes and torts.

Felonies and Misdemeanors

In addition to being a separate branch of law from civil law, criminal law can be further classified as either felonies or misdemeanors. The distinction is based on seriousness: a **felony** (from the term *felonia,* an act by which a vassal forfeited his fee) is a serious offense, while a **misdemeanor** is a minor or petty crime. Crimes such as murder, rape, and burglary are felonies; crimes such as unarmed assault and battery, petty larceny, and disturbing the peace are misdemeanors.

Most states distinguish between a felony and a misdemeanor on the basis of the punishment that is dispensed to the guilty party. Sentence length and the place of imprisonment will differ significantly. Under this model of classification, a felony is usually defined as a crime punishable by death or imprisonment for more than one year in a **state prison,** which is an institution where felony offenders are held. A misdemeanor

Table 2.2 Comparison of Criminal and Tort Law	
Similarities	
Both criminal and tort law seek to control behavior.	
Both laws impose sanctions.	
Similar areas of legal action exist—for example, personal assault and control of white-collar offenses such as environmental pollution.	
Differences	
CRIMINAL LAW	**TORT LAW**
Crime is a public offense.	Tort is a civil or private wrong.
The sanction associated with criminal law is incarceration or death.	The sanction associated with a tort is monetary damages.
The right of enforcement belongs to the state.	The individual brings the action.
The government ordinarily does not appeal.	Both parties can appeal.
Fines go to the state.	The individual receives compensation for harm done.
The standard of proof is "beyond a reasonable doubt."	Guilt is established by a preponderance of the evidence.

is defined as a crime punished by less than one year in a local county facility that houses convicted misdemeanants, usually called a jail or **house of correction.** Some common-law felonies and misdemeanors are defined in Table 2.3.

Mala in Se and *Mala Prohibitum*

Crimes may also be classified as *mala in se* and *mala prohibitum.* Some illegal acts, referred to as **mala in se** crimes, are rooted in the core values inherent in Western civilization, which are referred to as **natural law.** These values are designed to control such behaviors as inflicting physical harm on another (assault, rape, murder), taking possessions that rightfully belong to another (larceny, burglary, robbery), or harming another person's property (malicious damage, trespass). These have traditionally been considered violations of Western civilization's morals.

Mala prohibitum crimes are statutory crimes, which violate laws that reflect current public opinion and social values. In essence, these crimes are acts that conflict with contemporary standards of morality. Crimes are periodically created to control behaviors that conflict with the way society functions. *Mala prohibitum* offenses include drug use and possession of unlicensed handguns. Whereas it is relatively easy to link

Table 2.3 Common-Law Crimes

Crimes Against the Person	Examples
First-degree murder. Unlawful killing of another human being with malice aforethought and with premeditation and deliberation.	A woman buys some poison and pours it into a cup of coffee her husband is drinking, intending to kill him. The motive—to get the insurance benefits of the victim.
Voluntary manslaughter. Intentional killing committed under extenuating circumstances that mitigate the killing, such as killing in the heat of passion after being provoked.	A husband coming home early from work finds his wife in bed with another man. The husband goes into a rage and shoots and kills both lovers with a gun he keeps by his bedside.
Battery. Unlawful touching of another with intent to cause injury.	A man seeing a stranger sitting in his favorite seat in a cafeteria goes up to that person and pushes him out of the seat.
Assault. Intentional placing of another in fear of receiving an immediate battery.	A student aims an unloaded gun at her professor, who believes the gun is loaded. She says she is going to shoot.
Rape. Unlawful sexual intercourse with a female without her consent.	After a party, a man offers to drive a young female acquaintance home. He takes her to a wooded area and, despite her protests, forces her to have sexual relations with him.
Robbery. Wrongful taking and carrying away of personal property from a person by violence or intimidation.	A man armed with a loaded gun approaches another man on a deserted street and demands his wallet.

Inchoate (Incomplete) Offenses	Examples
Attempt. An intentional act for the purpose of committing a crime that is more than mere preparation or planning of the crime. The crime is not completed, however.	A person intending to kill another person places a bomb in the intended victim's car so that it will detonate when the ignition key is used. The bomb is discovered before the car is started. Attempted murder has been committed.
Conspiracy. Voluntary agreement between two or more persons to achieve an unlawful object or to achieve a lawful object using means forbidden by law.	A drug company sells larger-than-normal quantities of drugs to a doctor, knowing that the doctor is distributing the drugs illegally. The drug company is guilty of conspiracy.

Crimes Against Property	Examples
Burglary. Breaking and entering of a dwelling house of another in the nighttime with the intent to commit a felony.	Intending to steal some jewelry and silver, a young man breaks a window and enters another's house at 10 P.M.
Arson. Intentional burning of a dwelling house of another.	A secretary, angry that her boss did not give her a raise, goes to her boss's house and sets fire to it.
Larceny. Taking and carrying away the personal property of another with the intent to keep and possess the property.	While a woman is shopping, she sees a diamond ring displayed at the jewelry counter. When no one is looking, the woman takes the ring and walks out of the store.

Source: Developed by Therese J. Libby, J.D.

mala in se crimes to an objective concept of morality, it is much more difficult to do so if the acts are *mala prohibitum* because so many average people willingly engage in these behaviors.

FUNCTIONS OF CRIMINAL LAW

Substantive criminal law refers to a written code defining crimes and their punishments. In the United States, state and federal governments have developed their own unique criminal codes. Although all the codes differ, most use comparable terms, and the behaviors they are designed to control are often quite similar. Regardless of which culture or jurisdiction created them or

when, criminal codes have several distinct functions. The most important of these are described next.

Enforcing Social Control

The primary purpose of criminal law is to control the behavior of people within its jurisdiction. Criminal law is a written statement of rules to which people must conform. Every society also maintains unwritten rules of conduct—ordinary customs and conventions referred to as *folkways*—and universally followed behavior is referred to as **norms** and **morals,** or *mores.*

Those in political power rely on criminal law to formally prohibit behaviors believed to either threaten societal well-being or challenge their own authority. For

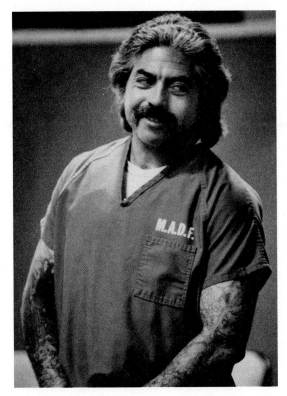

Some illegal acts, referred to as *mala in se* crimes, are rooted in the core values inherent in Western civilization. These "natural laws" are designed to control behaviors that have traditionally been considered a violation of the morals of Western civilization. There is little debate about the seriousness of these acts or their need for control. When Richard Allen Davis was convicted of the abduction and killing of 12-year-old Polly Klaas, the revulsion felt toward his behavior was universal and absolute. During a sentencing hearing, Polly's father Marc Klaas said, "Mr. Davis, when you get to where you're going, say hello to Hitler, to Dahmer, and to Bundy. Good riddance, and the sooner you get there the better we'll all be." Davis was sentenced to death on September 26, 1996.

example, U.S. criminal law incorporates centuries-old prohibitions against the following behaviors harmful to others: taking another person's possessions, physically harming another person, damaging another person's property, and cheating another person out of his or her possessions. Similarly, the law prevents actions that challenge the legitimacy of the government, such as planning its overthrow, collaborating with its enemies, and so on. Although any person can informally punish violations of mores and folkways, control of criminal law is given to those in political power.

Discouraging Revenge

By delegating enforcement to others, criminal law controls an individual's need to seek revenge or vengeance against those who violated his or her rights. By punishing people who infringe on the rights, property, and freedom of others, the law shifts the burden of revenge from the individual to the state. As Oliver Wendell Holmes stated, this prevents "the greater evil of private retribution."[15] Although state retaliation may offend the sensibilities of

many citizens, it is greatly preferable to a system in which people would have to seek justice for themselves.

Expressing Public Opinion and Morality

Criminal law also reflects constantly changing public opinions and moral values. *Mala in se* crimes, such as murder and forcible rape, are almost universally prohibited; however, the prohibition of legislatively created *mala prohibitum* crimes, such as traffic law and gambling violations, changes according to social conditions and attitudes. Criminal law is used to codify these changes. For example, if a state government decides to legalize certain outlawed behaviors, such as gambling or possessing marijuana, it will amend the state's criminal code. The criminal law then has the power to define the boundaries of moral and immoral behavior. Nonetheless, it has proven difficult to legally control public morality because of the problems associated with (1) gauging the will of the majority, (2) respecting the rights of the minority, and (3) enforcing laws that many people consider trivial or self-serving. For example, controlling the sale of pornographic and obscene material has proven to be difficult because (1) it violates people's First Amendment rights to free speech and (2) control efforts devote important resources to eliminating a behavior that many people view as benign.

CONNECTIONS

Although it is generally considered a "victimless" crime, is there actually a victim in the production and sale of pornography? This question is addressed in Chapter 14's discussion of public order crimes.

The power of the law to express norms and values can be viewed in the context of the crime of **vagrancy.** A *vagrant* (whose crime is vagrancy) is a person who goes from place to place without visible means of support and who, although able to work for his or her maintenance, refuses to do so. In a famous 1964 treatise, criminologist William Chambliss links the historical development of vagrancy law to the prevailing economic interests of the ruling class. He argues that the original vagrancy laws were formulated in the fourteenth century after the bubonic plague had killed significant numbers of English peasants, threatening the labor-intensive feudal economy. The first vagrancy laws were aimed at preventing workers from leaving their estates to secure higher wages elsewhere. They punished migration and permissionless travel, thereby mooring peasants to their manors and aiding wealthy landowners by limiting the wages of workers who could not leave their employers to seek higher earnings elsewhere.[16]

In an opposing view of the social conditions that influenced the creation of vagrancy laws, social historian Jeffrey Adler argues that early English vagrancy laws were less concerned with maintaining capitalism than with controlling beggars and relieving the overburdened public relief and welfare systems.[17] Adler suggests that early American vagrancy laws provided town officials with a mechanism to repel the moral threat to the community posed by vagrants, "sabbath breakers," paupers, and the wandering poor. Adler contends that economic demands had little to do with the content of the law.

Deterring Criminal Behavior

Criminal law has a **social control function.** This refers to its ability to control, restrain, and direct human behavior through its ability to punish and correct law violators. The threat of punishment associated with violating the law is designed to prevent crimes before they occur. During the Middle Ages, public executions drove this point home. Today criminal law's impact is felt through news accounts of long prison sentences and an occasional execution.

Karla Faye Tucker was executed despite pleas for clemency and forgiveness. Do well publicized executions such as that of Karla Faye deter would-be killers? Or do they encourage violence by setting the standard of an "eye for an eye"?

Punishing Wrongdoing

The deterrent power of criminal law is tied to the authority it gives the state to sanction or punish offenders. Whereas violations of folkways and mores are controlled informally, breaches of criminal law are left to the jurisdiction of political agencies. Those violating mores and folkways can receive social disapproval, whereas criminal law violators alone are subject to physical coercion and punishment.

Although criminal law is society's instrument of punishment, it need not fulfill a utilitarian purpose to justify its existence. It serves as a barometer of the public's vision of right and wrong. There are firmly entrenched beliefs that some acts are evil and should be punished, regardless of whether their punishment serves any practical purpose. The need for punishment may transcend any practical purpose such as deterrence.[18]

CONNECTIONS

The social control function of criminal law assumes that the threat of punishment will deter crime. This assumption is actually the subject of significant debate: If criminal law can deter crime, then why is there so much crime today? For the answer, see the discussion of general deterrence in Chapter 5.

Maintaining Social Order

All legal systems are designed to support and maintain the boundaries of the social system they serve. In medieval England, the law protected the feudal system by defining an orderly system of property transfer and ownership. Laws in some socialist nations protect the primacy of the state by strictly curtailing profiteering and individual enterprise. Our own capitalist system is also supported and sustained by criminal law. In a sense, the content of criminal law is more a reflection of the needs of those who control the existing economic and political system than a representation of some idealized moral code.

U.S. law, by meting out punishment to those who damage or steal property, promotes the activities needed to sustain an economy based on wealth accumulation. It would be impossible to conduct business through the use of contracts, promissory notes, credit, banking, and so on unless the law protected private capital. Maintaining a legal climate in which capitalism can thrive is an underlying goal of U.S. criminal law.

Criminal law has not always protected commercial enterprise; if one merchant cheated another, it was considered a private matter. This changed in 1473 when, in the *Carrier's Case,* an English court ruled that a merchant who held and transported merchandise for another was guilty of theft if he kept the goods for his own purposes.[19] Before the *Carrier's Case,* the law did not consider it a crime for people to keep something that was voluntarily given them by its rightful owners. Breaking with legal precedent, the British court recognized that the new English mercantile trade system could not be sustained if property rights had to be individually enforced. To this day, substantive criminal law prohibits such business-related acts as **larceny,** fraud, embezzlement, and **commercial theft.** Without the law to protect it, the free enterprise system could not exist.

THE LEGAL DEFINITION OF A CRIME

We occasionally hear in the media about people who admit at trial that they committed the act of which they are accused, yet they are not found guilty of the crime. For example, there was little question that John Hinckley attempted to assassinate President Ronald Reagan in 1981; the act was shown on national TV. Yet Hinckley was not found guilty of the crime because he lacked one of the legal requirements needed to prove his guilt—mental competence. The jury concluded he was not mentally competent at the time of the crime. In most instances, this occurs because state or federal prosecutors have not proven that the defendant's behavior falls within the legal definition of a crime. To ful-

fill the legal definition, all elements of a crime must be proven. For example, in Massachusetts, the common-law crime of burglary in the first degree is defined as follows:

> Whoever breaks and enters a dwelling house in the night-time, with intent to commit a felony, or whoever, after having entered with such intent, breaks into such dwelling house in the nighttime, any person being lawfully therein, and the offender being armed with a dangerous weapon at the time of such breaking or entry, or so arriving himself in such house or making an actual assault on a person lawfully therein, commits the crime of burglary.[20]

Note that burglary in the first degree has the following elements:

- It happens at night.
- It involves breaking, entering, or both.
- It happens at a dwelling house.
- The accused is armed or arms himself or herself after entering the house or actually assaults a person who is lawfully in the house.
- The accused intends to commit a felony.

For the state to prove that a crime occurred and that the defendant committed it, the prosecutor must show that the accused engaged in the guilty act, or **actus reus,** and had the **mens rea,** or criminal intent, to commit the act. The *actus reus* can be either an aggressive act, such as taking someone's money, burning a building, or shooting someone, or a failure to act when there is a legal duty to do so, such as a parent's neglecting to seek medical attention for a sick child. The *mens rea* (guilty mind) refers to an individual's state of mind at the time of the act or, more specifically, the person's intent to commit the crime. For most crimes, both the *actus reus* and the *mens rea* must be present for the act to be considered a crime. For example, if George decides to kill Bob and then takes a gun and shoots Bob, George can be convicted of the crime of murder, because both elements are present. George's shooting of Bob is the *actus reus;* his decision to kill Bob is the *mens rea.* However, if George only thinks about shooting Bob but does nothing about it, the element of *actus reus* is absent, and no crime has been committed. Thoughts of committing an act do not alone constitute a crime. Let us now look more closely at these issues.

Actus Reus

Two different conditions make *actus reus* a criminal act. The first is that, whereas the *actus reus* is the criminal act itself, the action must be voluntary for an act to be considered illegal. The second condition is that a person must act when there is a legal obligation to do so; failure to act is a criminal offense. We will consider both conditions.

If one person shoots another, that certainly could be considered a voluntary act. However, if the shooting occurs while the person holding the gun is sleepwalking or having an epileptic seizure or a heart attack, he or she will not be held criminally liable because the act was not voluntary. But if the individual knew he or she had such a condition and did not take precautions to prevent the act from occurring, then the person could be held responsible for the criminal act. Consider the following: Tom has an epileptic seizure while he is hunting, and his gun goes off and kills Victor. Tom will not be held responsible for Victor's death if this is a freak, unexpected occurrence. However, if Tom knew of his condition and further knew that a seizure could occur at any time, he could be convicted of the crime because it was possible for him to foresee the danger of handling a gun, yet he did nothing about it. The central issue is the voluntary action and whether the individual has control over his or her actions.

In the second type of *actus reus,* three common situations may be judged as a failure to act when there is a legal duty to do so:

1. **The relationship of parties based on status.** These relationships include parent and child and husband and wife. If a husband finds his wife unconscious because she took an overdose of sleeping pills, he is obligated to save her life by seeking medical aid. If he fails to do so and she dies, he can be held responsible for her death.
2. **Imposition by statute.** Some states have passed laws that require a person who observes an automobile accident to stop and help the other parties involved.
3. **A contractual relationship.** These relationships include lifeguard and swimmer, doctor and patient, and baby-sitter or au pair and child. Because lifeguards have been hired to ensure the safety of swimmers, they have a legal duty to come to the aid of drowning persons. If a lifeguard knows a swimmer is in danger and does nothing about it and the swimmer drowns, the lifeguard is legally responsible for the swimmer's death.

The duty to act is a legal, not just a moral, duty. The obligation arises from the relationship between the parties or from explicit legal requirements. For example, a private citizen who sees a person drowning is under no legal obligation to save that person. Although we may find it morally reprehensible, the private citizen could walk away and let the swimmer drown without facing legal sanctions.

In some circumstances of *actus reus,* the use of words is considered criminal. In the crime of **sedition,** the words of disloyalty constitute the *actus reus.* If a person falsely yells "fire" in a crowded theater and people are injured in the rush to exit, that person is held responsible for the injuries because his or her word constitutes an illegal act.

Mens Rea

In most situations, for an act to constitute a crime, it must be done with criminal intent, known as *mens rea. Intent,* in the legal sense, can mean carrying out an act intentionally, knowingly, and willingly. However, the definition also encompasses situations in which recklessness or negligence establishes the required criminal intent. Some crimes require specific intent, and others require general intent. The type of intent needed to establish criminal liability varies depending on how the crime is defined. Most crimes require **general intent,** or an intent to commit the crime. Thus when Ann picks Bill's pocket and takes his wallet, her intent is to steal. **Specific intent,** on the other hand, is an intent to accomplish a specific purpose as an element of the crime. For example, burglary is the breaking and entering of a dwelling house with the intent to commit a felony. The breaking and entering aspect requires general intent; the intent to commit a felony is a specific intent. If Dan breaks into and enters Emily's house because he intends to steal her diamonds, he is guilty of burglary. However, if Dan merely breaks into and enters Emily's house but has no intent to commit a crime once inside, he cannot be convicted of burglary because he lacked specific intent. However, he can still be convicted of breaking and entering.

Criminal intent also exists if the results of an action, although originally unintended, are certain to occur. For example, when Timothy McVeigh planted a bomb in front of the Murrah Federal Building in Oklahoma City, he did not intend to kill any particular person in the building. Yet the law would hold that McVeigh or any other person would be substantially certain that people in the building would be killed in the blast, and McVeigh therefore had the criminal intent to commit murder.

The concept of *mens rea* also encompasses the situation in which a person intends to commit a crime against one person but injures another party instead. For instance, if Sam, intending to kill Larry, shoots at Larry but misses and kills John, Sam is guilty of murdering John even though he did not intend to do so. Under the doctrine of **transferred intent,** the original criminal intent is transferred to the unintended victim.

Mens rea is also found in situations in which harm has resulted because a person has acted negligently or recklessly. **Negligence** involves a person's acting unreasonably under the circumstances. Criminal negligence is often found in situations involving drunken driving. If a drunken driver speeding and zigzagging across lanes hits another vehicle and kills someone, criminal negligence exists. In the case of drunken driving, the law maintains that a reasonable person would not drive a car when drunk and that a drunk driver is unable to control a vehicle. When the intent that underlies an unintentional act results in harm to another, the finding of criminal liability is known as **constructive intent.**

Strict Liability   Both the *actus reus* and the *mens rea* must be present before a person can be convicted of a crime. However, several crimes defined by statute do not require *mens rea*. In these cases, the person accused is guilty simply by doing what the statute prohibits; intent does not enter the picture. These offenses are known as **strict-liability crimes** or *public welfare offenses*. Health and safety regulations, traffic laws, and narcotic control laws are strict-liability statutes. For example, a person stopped for speeding is guilty of breaking the traffic laws regardless of whether he or she intended to go over the speed limit or did it by accident. The underlying purpose of these laws is to protect the public; therefore, intent is not required.[21]

CONNECTIONS

Many white-collar crimes, such as polluting the environment, are considered strict-liability crimes. If a person is found dumping toxic wastes, he or she is guilty of a crime. For an analysis of white-collar law enforcement, see Chapter 13.

CRIMINAL DEFENSES

When people defend themselves against criminal charges, they must refute one or more of the elements of the crime of which they have been accused. A number of different approaches can be taken to create this defense.

First, defendants may deny the *actus reus* by arguing that they were falsely accused and that the real culprit has yet to be identified. Defendants may also claim that although they engaged in the criminal act of which they are accused, they lacked the *mens rea* (intent) needed to be found guilty of the crime. If a person whose mental state is impaired commits a criminal act, it is possible for the person to excuse his or her criminal actions by claiming he or she lacked the capacity to form sufficient intent to be held criminally responsible. Insanity, intoxication, and ignorance are also among the types of excuse defenses.

Another type of defense is **justification.** Here the individual usually admits committing the criminal act but maintains that the act was justified and that he or she should therefore not be held criminally liable. Among the justification defenses are *necessity, duress, self-defense,* and *entrapment.* Persons standing trial for criminal offenses may defend themselves by claiming either that their actions were justified under the circumstances or that their behavior can be excused by their lack of *mens rea.* If either the physical or mental elements of a crime cannot be proven, then the defen-

dant cannot be convicted. We will now examine some of these defenses and justifications in greater detail.

Ignorance or Mistake

Ignorance or mistake can be an excuse if it negates an element of a crime. As a general rule, however, ignorance of the law is no excuse. Some courts have had to accept this excuse in cases where the government failed to make enactment of a new law public. It is also a viable justification when the offender relies on an official statement of the law that is later deemed incorrect. Barring that, even immigrants and other new arrivals to the United States are required to be aware of the content of the law. For example, on October 7, 1998, Chris Ahamefule Iheduru, a Nigerian immigrant, was convicted of sexual assault on the grounds that he had intimate relations with his 14-year-old stepdaughter after signing a contract with the girl to bear him a son (she gave birth to a daughter in September 1998).[22] At trial, Iheduru testified that it is not illegal in his native country to have sex with a juvenile and that he did not know it was against the law in the United States. His ignorance of American law did not shield him from conviction.

There are other cases for which ignorance can be a reasonable excuse. For example, if Andrew purchases stolen merchandise from Eric but is unaware that the material was illegally obtained, he cannot be convicted of receiving stolen merchandise because he had no intent to do so. But if Rachel attempts to purchase marijuana from a drug dealer and mistakenly buys hashish, she can be convicted of a drug charge because she intended to purchase illegal goods; ignorance does not excuse evil intent.[23]

Although ignorance or mistake does not excuse crime when there is evil intent, there is conflict when the evil was purely of moral and not legal consequence. For example, some cases of **statutory rape,** which is a crime that involves sexual relations with underage females (typically younger than 17, although the age of consent varies among state jurisdictions), have been defended on the grounds that the perpetrators were ignorant of their victims' true age. This defense has been allowed in states where sex between unmarried consenting adults is legal. If a reasonable mistake had not been made, no crime would have occurred. However, most states still outlaw sexual relations among unmarried adults. For example, Georgia defines the crime of fornication as follows:

> An unmarried person commits the offense of fornication when he voluntarily has sexual intercourse with another person and, upon conviction thereof, shall be punished as for a misdemeanor. (Code section 16-6-18)

Nonetheless, if the mistake seems unreasonable (for example, if the victim was a preteen), the original charge will stand.[24]

Insanity

Insanity is a defense to criminal prosecution in which the defendant's state of mind negates his or her criminal responsibility. A successful insanity defense results in a verdict of "not guilty by reason of insanity." Insanity, in this case, is a legal category. As used in U.S. courts, it does not necessarily mean that everyone who uses this defense is mentally ill or unbalanced. It means that the defendant's state of mind at the time the crime was committed made it impossible to have the necessary intent to satisfy the legal definition of a crime. Thus a person can be diagnosed as a psychopath or psychotic but still be judged legally sane. It is usually left to **psychiatric testimony,** which is the court testimony of a psychiatric professional, to prove a defendant legally sane.

On Dec. 30, 1994, John Salvi walked into two Planned Parenthood clinics in the Boston area and began shooting with a rifle, killing two receptionists and wounding five others. It was the worst anti-abortion violence in U.S. history. Salvi was tried and convicted of murder, despite the fact that his lawyers claimed he suffered from mental illness. Salvi later hung himself in prison. Should the concept of insanity be abolished if people such as Salvi and serial killer Jeffrey Dahmer (who ate his victims' bodies) are considered legally sane? If their behavior is "sane," what does it take to be considered "insane"?

A person found to be legally insane at the time of trial is placed in the custody of state mental health authorities until diagnosed as sane. Sometimes a person who was sane when he or she committed a crime becomes insane soon afterward. In that instance, the person receives psychiatric care until capable of standing trial and is then tried on the criminal charge because the person actually had *mens rea* at the time the crime was committed. On rare occasions, persons who were legally insane at the time they committed a crime become rational soon afterward. In this case the state can neither try them for the criminal offense nor have them committed to a mental health facility.

The test used to determine whether a person is legally insane varies between jurisdictions. U.S. courts generally use either the *M'Naghten Rule* or the *Substantial Capacity Test.*

The M'Naghten Rule In 1843 an English court established the **M'Naghten Rule,** also known as the *right-wrong test.* Daniel M'Naghten, believing Edward Drummond to be Sir Robert Peel, the prime minister of Great Britain, shot and killed Drummond (Peel's secretary). At his trial for murder, M'Naghten claimed that he could not be held responsible for the murder because his delusions had caused him to act. The jury agreed with M'Naghten and found him not guilty by reason of insanity.

Because the people involved in the case were high-profile, the verdict was not well received. The British House of Lords reviewed the decision and requested the court to clarify the law with respect to insane delusions. The court's response became known as the M'Naghten Rule, which states

> To establish a defense on the ground of insanity, it must be proved that at the time of the committing of the act the party accused was labouring under such a defect of reason from disease of the mind, as not to know the nature and quality of the act he was doing; or, if he did know, that he did not know he was doing what was wrong.[25]

Essentially, the M'Naghten Rule maintains that an individual is insane if he or she is unable to tell the difference between right and wrong or if he does not know what he is doing because of some mental disability. In about half of the states, the M'Naghten rule is the legal test when an issue of insanity is presented. However, over the years, much criticism has arisen concerning M'Naghten. First, great confusion has surfaced over such terms as *disease of the mind* and *know the nature and quality of the act.* These terms have never been properly clarified. Second, critiques, mainly from the mental health profession, have pointed out that the rule is unrealistic and narrow in that it does not cover situations in which people know right from wrong but cannot control their actions.

Table 2.4 Various Insanity Defense Standards

TEST	LEGAL STANDARD BECAUSE OF MENTAL ILLNESS	FINAL BURDEN OF PROOF	WHO BEARS BURDEN OF PROOF
M'Naghten	"didn't know what he was doing or didn't know it was wrong"	Varies, from proof by a balance of probabilities on the defense to proof beyond a reasonable doubt on the prosecutor, depending on state jurisdiction	
Irresistible impulse	"could not control his conduct"		
Substantial capacity	"lacks substantial capacity to appreciate the wrongfulness of his conduct or to control it"	Beyond reasonable doubt	Prosecutor
Present federal law	"lacks capacity to appreciate the wrongfulness of his conduct"	Clear and convincing evidence	Defense

Source: National Institute of Justice, *Crime Study Guide: Insanity Defense* by Norval Morris (Washington, D.C.: U.S. Department of Justice, 1986), 3.

Irresistible Impulse Because of questions regarding M'Naghten, approximately six states have supplemented the rule with another test, known as the **Irresistible Impulse Test.**[26] This test allows the insanity defense to be used for situations in which defendants were unable to control their behavior because of a mental disease. Thus the defendants do not have to prove that they did not know the difference between right and wrong, only that they could not control themselves at the time of the crime. In the event that a jury finds a person acted under an irresistible impulse, he or she would be placed in a mental health facility until considered capable of controlling his or her behavior.

The Substantial Capacity Test The **Substantial Capacity Test,** originally a section of the American Law Institute's Model Penal Code, states

> A person is not responsible for criminal conduct if at the time of such conduct as a result of mental disease or defect he lacks substantial capacity either to appreciate the criminality [wrongfulness] of his conduct or to conform his conduct to the requirement of the law.[27]

The Substantial Capacity Test is essentially a combination of the M'Naghten Rule and the Irresistible Impulse Test. It is, however, broader in its interpretation of insanity, for it requires only a lack of substantial capacity instead of complete impairment as in M'Naghten and the Irresistible Impulse Test. This test also differs in that it uses the term *appreciate* instead of *know,* the term used in M'Naghten. About half the states and the federal government now use variations of the Substantial Capacity Test. See Table 2.4 for more information about insanity defense standards.

Intoxication

Intoxication, which in legal terms is defined as the taking of alcohol or drugs, is generally not considered a defense. Historically, common law punished sober and in-toxicated offenders equally. According to *Reniger v. Fogossa,* an English case from the year 1551:

> [I]f a person that is drunk kills another, this shall be felony, and he shall be hanged for it, and yet he did it through ignorance, for when he was drunk he had no understanding nor memory; but inasmuch as that ignorance was occasioned by his own act and folly, and he might have avoided it, he shall not be privileged thereby. Because the offender created his disability, it could not serve to exculpate.[28]

Generally there are two exceptions to this rule. First, an individual who becomes intoxicated by mistake, through force, or under duress can use involuntary intoxication as a defense. For example, in a Florida case, Victor Brancaccio was convicted in the 1993 beating death of a woman who had criticized his singing.[29] Sentenced to life in prison, Brancaccio was granted a new trial in 1998, when an appeals court ruled that the trial judge erred in not specifically instructing the jury to consider whether at the time of the murder Brancaccio was "involuntarily intoxicated" by either alcohol or the antidepressant Zoloft, or both. The defense lawyers claimed that the antidepressant Victor was taking on doctor's orders mixed with his drinking left him unable to understand the wrongfulness of his acts. Technically, he was incapable of forming intent at the time of his violent attack through no fault of his own.

A second exception is that voluntary intoxication is a defense when specific intent is needed, and it is deemed that the person could not have formed the intent because of his or her intoxicated condition. For example, if a person breaks into and enters another's house but is so drunk that he or she cannot form the intent to commit a felony, the intoxication is a defense against burglary but not against the breaking and entering.

Duress

Duress is a defense to a crime when the defendant commits an illegal act because the defendant or a third

The Insanity Controversy

The insanity defense has been the source of debate and controversy. Many critics of the defense maintain that inquiry into a defendant's psychological makeup is inappropriate at the trial stage; they would prefer that the issue be raised at the sentencing stage, after guilt has been determined. Opponents also charge that criminal responsibility is separate from mental illness and that the two should not be equated. It is a serious mistake, they argue, to consider criminal responsibility as a trait or quality that can be detected by a psychiatric evaluation. Moreover, some criminals avoid punishment because they are erroneously judged by psychiatrists to be mentally ill. Conversely, some people who are found not guilty by reason of insanity because they suffer from a mild personality disturbance are incarcerated as mental patients far longer than they would have been imprisoned if they had been convicted of a criminal offense.

Advocates of the insanity defense say that it serves a unique purpose. Most successful insanity verdicts result in the defendant's being committed to a mental institution until he or she has recovered. The general assumption is that the insanity defense makes it possible to single out for special treatment certain persons who would otherwise be subjected to further penal sanctions following conviction.

The insanity plea was thrust into the spotlight when John Hinckley's unsuccessful attempt to kill President Ronald Reagan was captured by news cameras. Hinckley was found not guilty by reason of insanity. Public outcry against this seeming miscarriage of justice prompted some states to revise their insanity statutes. New Mexico, Georgia, Alaska, Delaware, Michigan, Illinois, and Indiana, among other states, have created the plea of guilty but insane, in which the defendant is required to serve the first part of his or her sentence in a hospital and, once "cured," to be then sent to prison.

In 1984 the federal government revised its criminal code to restrict insanity as a defense solely to individuals who are unable to understand the nature and wrongfulness of their acts; a defendant's irresistible impulse will no longer be considered. This shifted the burden of proof from the prosecutor's need to prove sanity to the defendant's need to prove insanity.

About 11 states have followed the federal government's lead by making significant changes in their insanity defenses, such as shifting the burden of proof from prosecution to defense; three states (Idaho, Montana, and Utah) no longer permit evidence of mental illness as a defense in court, though psychological factors can influence sentencing. On March 28, 1994, the U.S. Supreme Court failed to overturn the Montana law (*Cowan v. Montana*, 93-1264), thereby giving the states the right to abolish the insanity defense if they so choose.

Although such backlash against the insanity plea is intended to close supposed legal loopholes allowing dangerous criminals to go free, the public's fear may be misplaced. It is estimated that the insanity plea is used in fewer than 1 percent of all cases. Moreover, relatively few insanity defense pleas succeed.

Even if the insanity defense is successful, the offender must be placed in a secure psychiatric hospital or the psychiatric ward of a state prison. Because many defendants who successfully plead insanity are nonviolent offenders, their hospital stays may exceed the prison terms they would have received if they had been convicted of the crimes of which they were originally accused.

Despite efforts to ban its use, the insanity plea is probably here to stay. Most crimes require *mens rea,* and unless we are willing to forgo that standard of law, we will be forced to find not guilty those people whose mental state makes it impossible for them to rationally control their behavior.

CRITICAL THINKING

1. Is it fair to excuse the criminal responsibility of someone who acted under an irresistible impulse?
2. Couldn't we argue that all criminals are impulsive people who lack the capacity to control their behavior? If not, why would they commit crimes in the first place? Is it possible that child molesters, for example, are rational people who do not have irresistible impulses?

 INFOTRAC COLLEGE EDITION RESEARCH

To research the impact of the insanity plea on criminal defenses, read: Richard J. Bonnie, Norman G. Poythress, Steven K. Hoge, John Monahan, Marlene Eisenberg. Decision-making in criminal defense: an empirical study of insanity pleas and the impact of doubted client competence. *Journal of Criminal Law and Criminology* Fall 1996 87 n1 p48–62

Source: Daniel N. Robinson, *Wild Beasts and Idle Humours: The Insanity Defense from Antiquity to the Present* (Cambridge, Mass.: Harvard University Press, 1996); Ralph Slovenko, *Psychiatry and Criminal Culpability* (New York: John Wiley & Sons, 1995).

person has been threatened by another with death or serious bodily harm if the act is not performed. However, exceptions to this defense make it tenuous, at best.

For example, if Pete is holding a gun on Jerry and threatens to kill Jerry unless he breaks into and enters Bill's house, Jerry can claim duress as his motivation for the crime of breaking and entering. This defense, however, does not cover defendants who commit a serious crime, such as murder, to save themselves or others. The reason for this exception is that the duress defense is based on the social policy that, when faced with two evils (harm to oneself or violating criminal law), it is better to commit the lesser evil to avoid the threatened harm. In the situation of murder versus threatened harm, however, taking another's life is considered the greater of the two evils.

Necessity

Necessity, as a defense, is applied in situations in which a person must break the law to avoid a greater evil caused by natural physical forces (such as storms, earthquakes, or illness). This defense is available only when committing the crime is the lesser of two evils.

For example, say a person who doesn't have a driver's license drives a car to escape a fire. This is a case of committing an illegal act out of necessity. However, the famous English case of *Regina v. Dudley and Stephens* is a case in point. In that case, three sailors and a cabin boy had been shipwrecked and were floating in the open seas in a lifeboat. After nine days without food and seven without water, two of the sailors, Dudley and Stephens, killed the cabin boy, and the three sailors ate his body and drank his blood. Four days later, the sailors were rescued. The court acknowledged that the cabin boy most likely would have died naturally because he was in the weakest condition, but nevertheless judged the killing unjustified. Therefore, the defense of necessity did not justify the intentional killing of another.[30] (The sailors later were pardoned.)

Self-Defense

Self-defense involves a claim that the defendant's actions were a justified response to the victim's provocative behavior. Self-defense can be used to protect one's person or property. An individual is justified in using force against another to protect himself or herself. When that happens, the person claims to have acted in self-defense and therefore is not guilty of a criminal act. If the defendant was justified in using force, self-defense excuses crimes such as murder, manslaughter, and assault and battery.

However, the law has limited what is reasonable and necessary self-defense. First, defendants must rea-

sonably believe that they are in danger of death or great harm and that it is necessary for them to use force to protect themselves. For example, if Sophia threatens to kill Jan but it is obvious that Sophia is unarmed, Jan is not justified in pulling her gun and shooting Sophia. However, if Sophia, after threatening Jan, reaches into her pocket as if to get a gun and Jan then pulls her gun and shoots Sophia, Jan could claim self-defense even if it is discovered that Sophia was unarmed. In this situation Jan had a reasonable belief that harm was imminent and that it was necessary to shoot first to avoid being shot.

Another condition of self-defense is that the amount of force used must be no greater than that necessary to prevent personal harm. For instance, if Steve punches Ben, Ben could not justifiably hit Steve with an iron rod. Ben could, however, punch Steve back if he believed Steve was going to continue punching.

Some issues arise concerning self-defense in situations in which deadly force may be necessary. For example, does a person have a duty to avoid using deadly force against an attacker by retreating if possible? U.S. courts are split on this issue. The majority of states maintain that the person attacked does not have to retreat, even if he or she can do so safely. This position is based on the policy that a person should not be forced to act in a humiliating or cowardly manner. However, a number of states do require that a person try to retreat, if it is possible to do so safely, before using deadly force. Even in these jurisdictions, people are not required to retreat if attacked in their homes or offices. The rules concerning self-defense also apply to situations involving the defense of a third person. Thus, if a person reasonably believes that another is in danger of bodily harm from an assailant, the person may use the force necessary to prevent the danger.

Using force to defend one's property from trespass or theft is justifiable if the force is reasonable. This means that the use of force should be a last resort after requests to stop interfering with the property or legal actions have failed. Also, the use of deadly force is not considered reasonable when only protection of property is concerned. This is based on the social policy that human life is more important than property.

Entrapment

Entrapment is another defense that excuses a defendant from criminal liability. The entrapment defense is raised when the defendant maintains that law enforcement officers induced him or her to commit a crime. The defendant would not have committed the crime had it not been for trickery, persuasion, or fraud on the officers' part. In other words, if law enforcement officers plan a crime, implant the criminal idea in a person's mind, and pressure that person into doing the act, the person may plead entrapment. This situation is different from that in which an officer simply provides an opportunity for the crime to be committed and the defendant is willing and ready to do the act. For example, if a plainclothes police officer poses as a potential customer and is approached by a prostitute, no entrapment has occurred. However, if the same officer approaches a woman and persuades her to commit an act of prostitution, the defense of entrapment is appropriate.

In an important decision, the U.S. Supreme Court in *Jacobson v. U.S.* ruled that entrapment occurred when a Nebraska man was arrested for ordering pornographic magazines from a company that was really a front for a government sting operation. Jacobson had previously ordered legal sexually oriented material. Government agents, who got his name from the mailing list of the bookstore that had mailed him those materials, sent him repeated offers to buy more. Because the law had changed, it was now illegal to receive the sexually oriented material through the mail. When he responded to the offers and placed an order, he was arrested. After his conviction, Jacobson was able to prove that the government had repeatedly solicited him for 26 months before he placed the order. The Court ruled that the repeated solicitations amounted to entrapment. The fact that Jacobson was predisposed to viewing the material did not mean he was predisposed to breaking the law.[31]

Exotic Defenses

Virginia Kelly, 35, from Jacksonville, Florida, claimed she shot and killed her husband because he abused her. However, her use of the "battered woman's defense" was pierced by prosecutors, who told jurors that she had actually left her husband at one point and moved to South Carolina but wrote him a letter asking him to contact her. When Virginia Kelly returned to Jacksonville, she found her husband was involved with another woman and shot him in a jealous rage.[32] She was convicted of second-degree murder on January 9, 1998, and sentenced to 25 years in prison.

Although Kelly was convicted, it has become common for defense attorneys to defend their clients by raising a variety of new **exotic defenses** based on preexisting conditions or syndromes with which their clients were afflicted. Examples include battered woman syndrome, Vietnam syndrome, child sexual abuse syndrome, Holocaust survivor syndrome, and adopted child syndrome. In using these defenses, attorneys either ask judges to recognize a new excuse for crime or fit these conditions within preexisting defenses. For example, a person who used lethal violence in self-defense might argue that the trauma of serving in Vietnam caused him to overreact to provocation. Or a victim of child abuse may use that experience to mitigate culpability in a

crime, asking a jury, for example, to consider his or her background when making a death penalty decision. In some cases these defenses have succeeded, or nearly so. For instance, in the prominent Menendez brothers case, two brothers were tried for killing their parents. They claimed that their actions were the product of earlier sexual and physical abuse. This defense tactic led to a hung jury, although the brothers were later convicted after a second trial.

Some exotic criminal defenses have been gender-specific. Attorneys have argued that their female clients' behavior was a result of their premenstrual syndrome (PMS) and that male clients were aggressive because of unbalanced testosterone levels. These defenses have achieved relatively little success in the United States.[33] Others contend that prosecuting attorneys can turn the tables and use these defenses against the defendant. For example, some commentators have suggested that courts will ultimately view PMS as an aggravating condition in a crime, prompting harsher penalties.

CHANGING CRIMINAL LAW

Many states and the federal government have recently been examining their substantive criminal law. Because the law partly reflects public opinion and morality regarding various forms of behavior, what was considered criminal 40 years ago may not be considered so today. In some states, crimes such as possession of marijuana have been **decriminalized**—given reduced penalties. Such crimes may be punishable by a fine instead of a prison sentence. Other former criminal offenses, such as vagrancy, have been legalized—all criminal penalties have been removed. And in some jurisdictions, penalties have been toughened, especially for violent crimes such as rape and spousal assault.

In some instances, new criminal laws have been created to conform to emerging social issues. For example, physician-assisted suicide became the subject of national debate when Dr. Jack Kevorkian began practicing what he calls **obitiatry,** helping people take their lives.[34] In an attempt to stop Kevorkian, Michigan banned assisted suicide, reflecting what lawmakers believed to be prevailing public opinion.[35]

Assisted suicide is but one of many emerging social issues that has prompted change in criminal law. More than 25 states have enacted **stalking** statutes, which prohibit and punish acts described typically as "the willful, malicious, and repeated following and harassing of another person."[36] Stalking laws were originally formulated to protect women terrorized by former husbands and boyfriends, although celebrities often are plagued by stalkers as well. In celebrity cases, these laws often apply to stalkers who are strangers or casual acquaintances of their victims.

twinkie defense

CONNECTIONS

Stalking is a relatively new concept in both law and criminology. Chapter 4 discusses the nature and extent of stalking in a Criminological Enterprise box called "Victims of Stalking."

Community notification laws are a response to concern about sexual predators moving into neighborhoods. These are usually referred to as "Megan's Law," named after 7-year-old Megan Kanka of Hamilton Township, New Jersey, who was killed in 1994. Charged with the crime was a convicted sex offender who the Kankas were unaware lived across the street from them. The New Jersey law requires that neighbors in the community be notified if an offender lives near them. In 1996 the federal government passed legislation requiring that the general public be informed of local **pedophiles** (sexual offenders who target children). It was left up to local officials to determine how much public warning was necessary, based on the danger posed by the offender.[37]

Similarly, new laws have been passed to keep the sexually dangerous under control. California's new **sexual predator law** allows authorities to keep some criminals in custody even after their sentences are served. The law, which took effect on January 1, 1996, allows people convicted of sexually violent crimes against two or more victims to be committed to another institution once their prison terms are served. Civil juries may recommend commitment to a mental institution, which would be reviewed every two years. The law has already been upheld by appellate court judges in the state.[38] (**Appellate courts** are those that review trial procedures in order to determine whether their outcomes were influenced by legal mistakes, such as the judge allowing evidence to be considered that violated the defendant's rights.)

The federal government has also revised the U.S. legal code to reflect changing social conditions. For example, the Brady Handgun Control Law of 1993, requiring a five-business-day waiting period before an individual can buy a handgun, reflects concern with gun violence and easy access to handguns. The future direction of U.S. criminal law remains unclear. Certain actions, such as crimes by corporations and political corruption, will be labeled as criminal and given more attention. Other offenses, such as recreational drug use, may be reduced in importance or removed entirely from the criminal law system. In addition, changing technology and its ever-increasing global and local role in our lives will require modifications in criminal law. For example, such technologies as automatic teller machines and cellular phones have already spawned a new generation of criminal acts involving theft of access numbers and cards and software piracy. As the information highway sprawls toward new expanses, the nation's computer network advances, and biotechnology produces new substances, criminal law will be forced to address threats to the public safety that today are unknown.

CONNECTIONS

Chapter 13 contains sections on technological crimes, including the newly emerging area of computer crime. Criminal law must be constantly modified to include areas that only a few years earlier were unknown.

SUMMARY

Substantive criminal law is a set of rules that specifies what behavior society has outlawed. Criminal law can be distinguished from civil law on the basis that the former involves powers given to the state to enforce social rules, whereas the latter controls interactions between private citizens. Criminal law serves several important purposes: it represents public opinion and moral values, it enforces social control, it deters criminal behavior and wrongdoing, it punishes transgressors, and it banishes private retribution.

The criminal law used in U.S. jurisdictions traces its origin to English common law. Common law was formulated during the twelfth and thirteenth centuries, when English royal judges began to use precedents set in previous cases to guide actions in others; this system is called *stare decisis.*

In the U.S. legal system, lawmakers have codified common-law crimes into state and federal penal codes. Today most crimes fall into the category of felony or misdemeanor. Felonies are serious crimes usually punished by a prison term, whereas misdemeanors are minor crimes that carry a fine or a light jail sentence. Common felonies include murder, rape, assault with a deadly weapon, arson, and robbery; misdemeanors include larceny, simple assault, and possession of small amounts of drugs.

Every crime has specific elements. In most instances, these elements include the *actus reus* (guilty act), which is the actual physical part of the crime, like taking money or burning a building. In addition, most crimes also contain a second element, the *mens rea* (guilty mind), which refers to the state of mind of the individual who commits a crime—more specifically, the person's intent to do the act.

At trial, the accused can defend themselves by claiming to have lacked *mens rea* and, therefore, not to be responsible for the criminal actions. One type of defense is excuse for mental reasons such as insanity, intoxication, necessity, or duress. Another defense is justification by reason of self-defense or entrapment. Of all defenses, insanity is perhaps the most controversial. In most states, persons using an insanity defense claim that they did not know what they were doing when they committed a crime or that their mental state did not allow them to tell the difference between right and wrong (the

M'Naghten Rule). Insanity defenses may also include claims that the offender was motivated by an irresistible impulse or lacked the substantial capacity to conform his or her conduct to the criminal law. Regardless of the insanity defense used, critics charge that mental illness is separate from legal responsibility and that the two should not be equated. Supporters counter that the insanity defense allows mentally ill people to avoid penal sanctions.

Criminal law undergoes constant reform. Some acts are being decriminalized—their penalties are being reduced—while laws are being revised to make penalties for other acts more severe. The law must accommodate social and technological change.

 See the book-specific web site at www.cj.wadsworth.com for additional chapter links, discussions, and quizzes.

THINKING LIKE A CRIMINOLOGIST

Congress is considering passing some new laws designed to meet the changing social and economic landscape. They have asked you to appear before the joint legislative committee on criminal code reform in order to identify some of the emerging areas in which legal controls are needed.

One area of concern is whether laws should be passed to control the use of the Internet: for example, regulating the sale of digital information, including data, text, images, sounds, computer programs, software, and databases. The fear is that unscrupulous entrepreneurs may use the

Net to sell undesirable material such as pornography.

Would you advise Congress to control the Net closely? What dangers might be presented by such an attempt at regulation?

KEY TERMS

legal code	juries	vagrancy
mores	royal prosecutors	social control function
folkways	case law	larceny
Code of Hammurabi	criminal attempts	commercial theft
lex talionis	inchoate crimes	*actus reus*
Twelve Tables	statutory crimes	*mens rea*
plebeians	embezzlement	sedition
patricians	fraud	general intent
wergild	arson	specific intent
compurgation	customary courts	transferred intent
oathhelpers	civil law	negligence
ordeal	property law	constructive intent
common law	contract law	strict-liability crimes
shire	tort law	justification
hundreds	tort	statutory rape
tithings	libel	psychiatric testimony
reeve	slander	M'Naghten Rule
hundred-gemot	statute of limitations	Irresistible Impulse Test
shire-gemot	probation	Substantial Capacity Test
hali-gemot	beyond a reasonable doubt	intoxication
holy-motes	preponderance of the evidence	entrapment
ecclesiastics	felony	exotic defenses
assault	misdemeanor	decriminalized
battery	state prison	obitiatry
treason	house of correction	stalking
bot	*mala in se*	community notification laws
wer	natural law	pedophiles
wite	*mala prohibitum*	sexual predator law
manorial courts	substantive criminal law	appellate court
stare decisis	norms	
circuit judges	morals	

NOTES

1. Associated Press, "Gymnast Gets Order Against Her Dad" *USA Today,* 1 December 1998, p.1.

2. The historical material in the following sections was derived from a number of sources. The most important include: Rene Wormser, *The Story of Law,* rev. ed. (New York: Simon and Schuster, 1962); Jackson Spielvogel, *Western Civilization* (St. Paul, Minn.: West Publishing, 1991); Eugen Weber, *A Modern History of Europe* (New York: W. W. Norton, 1971); James Heath, *Eighteenth-Century Penal Theory* (New York: Oxford University Press, 1963); David Jones, *History of Criminology* (Westport, Conn.: Greenwood Press, 1986); Fred Inbau, James Thompson, and James Zagel, *Criminal Law and Its Administration* (Mineola, N.Y.: Foundation Press, 1974); Wayne LaFave and Austin Scott, *Criminal Law,* 2d ed. (St. Paul, Minn.: West Publishing, 1986); and Sanford Kadish and Monrad Paulsen, *Criminal Law and Its Processes* (Boston: Little, Brown, 1975).

3. The Laws of William the Conqueror set down what William, king of the English, established in consultation with his magnates after the conquest of England. This document may be obtained on the Net from the Internet Medieval Sourcebook at [http://www.fordham.edu/halsall/sbook.html]

4. Weber, *A Modern History of Europe,* p. 9.

5. Wayne LaFave and Austin Scott, *Handbook on Criminal Law* (St. Paul, Minn.: West Publishing, 1982), pp. 528–29.

6. Caldwell 397 (1784), cited in LaFave and Scott, *Handbook on Criminal Law,* p. 422.

7. 9 George I, C. 22, 1723, cited in Douglas Hay, "Crime and Justice in Eighteenth and Nineteenth Century England," in *Crime and Justice,* vol. 2, ed. Norval Morris and Michael Tonry (Chicago: University of Chicago Press, 1980), p. 51.

8. Jerome Hall, *Theft, Law, and Society* (Indianapolis: Bobbs-Merrill, 1952); Chapter 1 is generally considered the best source for the history of common-law theft crimes.

9. Mass. Gen. Laws Ann. (West 1982) ch. 266, pp. 1–2.

10. See, generally, Alfred Lindesmith, *The Addict and the Law* (New York: Vintage Books, 1965), chap. 1.

11. Edna Erez and Bankole Thompson, "Rape in Sierra Leone: Conflict Between the Sexes and Conflict of Laws," *International Journal of Comparative and Applied Criminal Justice* 14 (1990): 201–10.

12. William Henry, "Did the Music Say 'Do It'?" *Time,* 30 July 1990, p. 65.

13. Mathew Brelis, "Man Must Pay $500,000 for Raping Daughter," *Boston Globe,* 2 July 1993, p. 1.

14. For example, see *Brinegar v. United States,* 388 U.S. 160 (1949); *Speiser v. Randall,* 357 U.S. 513 (1958); *In re Winship,* 397 U.S. 358 (1970).

15. Oliver Wendell Holmes, *The Common Law,* ed. Mark De Wolf (Boston: Little, Brown, 1881), p. 36.

16. William Chambliss, "A Sociological Analysis of the Law of Vagrancy," *Social Problems* 12 (1964): 67–77; William Chambliss, "On Trashing Marxist Criminology," *Criminology* 27 (1989): 231–39.

17. Jeffrey Adler, "A Historical Analysis of the Law of Vagrancy," *Criminology* 27 (1989): 209–30; Jeffrey Adler, "Vagging the Demons and Scoundrels: Vagrancy and the Growth of St. Louis, 1830–1861," *Journal of Urban History* 13 (1986): 3–30.

18. Todd Clear, *Harm in American Penology: Offenders, Victims and their Communities* (Albany: State University of New York Press, 1994), pp. 73–74.

19. *Carrier's Case,* Y.B. 13 Edw. 4, f. 9, pl. 5 (Star Chamber and Exchequer Chamber, 1473), discussed at length in Jerome Hall, *Theft, Law and Society* (Indianapolis: Bobbs-Merrill, 1952), chap. 1.

20. Mass. Gen. Laws Ann. (West 1983) ch. 266, p. 14.

21. 320 U.S. 277 (1943).

22. Associated Press, "Nigerian Used Stepdaughter, 14, for a Son, Jury Finds," *Boston Globe,* 8 October 1998, p.9.

23. LaFave and Scott, *Handbook on Criminal Law,* p. 356.

24. LaFave and Scott, *Handbook on Criminal Law,* p. 361.

25. 8 Eng. Rep. 718 (1843).

26. Kadish and Paulsen, *Criminal Law and Its Processes,* pp. 215–16.

27. *Model Penal Code* 401 (1952).

28. 75 Eng. Rep. 1 (Ex. Ch. 1551), quoted in Mitchell Keiter, "Just Say No Excuse: The Rise and Fall of the Intoxication Defense," *Journal of Criminal Law and Criminology* 87 (1997): 482–520 at 484.

29. Associated Press, "Florida Murder Revisited: Did Medication Play a Part?" *Boston Globe,* 5 October 1998, p. 6.

30. *Regina v. Dudley and Stephens,* 14 Q.B. 273 (1884).

31. *Jacobson v. U.S.,* 112 S.Ct. 1535, 118 L. Ed. 2d 174 (1992).

32. Vivian Wakefield, "Woman Gets 25 Years for Killing Husband," *Jacksonville Times-Union,* 10 January 1998.

33. Deborah W. Denno, "Gender, Crime, and the Criminal Law Defenses," *Journal of Criminal Law and Criminology* 85 (Summer 1994): 80–180.

34. Marvin Zalman, John Strate, Denis Hunter, and James Sellars, "Michigan Assisted Suicide Three Ring Circus: The Intersection of Law and Politics," *Ohio Northern Law Review* 23 (1997): 112–38.

35. 1992 P.A. 270 as amended by 1993 P.A. 3, M.C. L. ss. 752.1021 to 752.1027.

36. National Institute of Justice, *Project to Develop a Model Anti-Stalking Statute* (Washington, D.C.: National Institute of Justice, 1994).

37. "Clinton Signs Tougher 'Megan's Law,'" *CNN News Service,* 17 May 1996.

38. The Associated Press, "Judge Upholds State's Sexual Predator Law," *Bakersfield Californian,* 2 October 1996.

CHAPTER 3

The Nature and Extent of Crime

INTRODUCTION

The fact that people are wary of crime and take steps to protect themselves from it is certainly not a recent phenomenon. Since the twelfth century, kings of England—Henry I, Richard II, and Charles II—holed up in the Tower of London to protect themselves against rebellious nobles or hostile and dangerous villagers. All across Europe, people of means built forts to protect themselves and their clans from the threat of attack by the local population. Vestiges of this system can be seen on the European landscape in the walled abbeys, manors, and castles that still exist in England, Spain, Italy, and other nations.

It is ironic that 500 years later affluent Americans are flocking to gated communities, which have sprung up around the United States. Millions of Americans have chosen to live in walled and fenced residential space guarded by roving security patrols and hidden cameras. In their 1997 book, *Fortress America,* Edward Blakely and Mary Gail Snyder argue that people flock to these gated communities because they feel vulnerable, unsure of their place and the stability of their neighborhoods in the face of rapid social and economic change. They fear crime and are looking for an environment that provides physical and economic security even if it means living in an area that is walled off like the castles of yore.[1]

Are Americans justified in their fear of crime? Should they, in fact, barricade themselves behind armed guards? Are crime rates rising or falling? Where do most crimes occur? In order to answer these and similar questions, criminologists have devised elaborate methods of crime data collection and analysis. In addition, without accurate data on the nature and extent of crime, it would not be possible to formulate theories that explain the onset of crime or to devise social policies that facilitate its control or elimination. This chapter reviews data collected on criminal offenders in some detail. The data provide a summary of crime patterns and trends. We also examine the concept of criminal careers and discover what available crime data can tell us about the onset, continuation, and termination of criminality. We begin with a discussion of the most important sources of crime data.

THE UNIFORM CRIME REPORT

The Federal Bureau of Investigation's **Uniform Crime Report (UCR)** is the best known and most widely cited source of aggregate criminal statistics.[2] The FBI receives and compiles records from over 17,000 police departments serving a majority of the U.S. population. Its major unit of analysis involves the **index crimes,** or **Part I crimes:** murder and nonnegligent manslaughter, forcible rape, robbery, aggravated assault, burglary, larceny, arson, and motor vehicle theft. Table 3.1 defines these crimes. The FBI tallies and annually publishes the number of reported offenses by city, county, standard metropolitan statistical area, and geographical divisions of the United States. In addition to these statistics, the UCR shows the number and characteristics (age, race, and gender) of individuals who have been arrested for these and all other crimes, except traffic violations (**Part II crimes**).

Collecting the Uniform Crime Report

The methods used to compile the UCR are quite complex. Each month law enforcement agencies report the number of index crimes known to them. These data are collected from records of all crime complaints that victims, officers who discovered the infractions, or other sources reported to these agencies.

Whenever criminal complaints are found through investigation to be unfounded or false, they are eliminated from the actual count. However, the number of actual offenses known is reported to the FBI whether or not anyone is arrested for the crime, the stolen property is recovered, or prosecution ensues.

In addition, each month law enforcement agencies also report how many crimes were **cleared.** Crimes are cleared in two ways: (1) when at least one person is arrested, charged, and turned over to the court for prosecution; or (2) by exceptional means, when some element beyond police control precludes the physical arrest of an offender (for example, the offender leaves the country).

Data on the number of clearances involving the arrest of only juvenile offenders, data on the value of property stolen and recovered in connection with Type I

Table 3.1 Part I Index Crime Offenses

CRIME	DESCRIPTION
Criminal homicide	a. Murder and nonnegligent manslaughter: the willful (nonnegligent) killing of one human being by another. Deaths caused by negligence, attempts to kill, assaults to kill, suicides, accidental deaths, and justifiable homicides are excluded. Justifiable homicides are limited to (1) the killing of a felon by a law enforcement officer in the line of duty and (2) the killing of a felon, during the commission of a felony, by a private citizen. b. Manslaughter by negligence: the killing of another person through gross negligence. Traffic fatalities are excluded. Although manslaughter by negligence is a Part I crime, it is not included in the Crime Index.
Forcible rape	The carnal knowledge of a female forcibly and against her will. Included are rapes by force and attempts or assaults to rape. Statutory offenses (no force used—victim under age of consent) are excluded.
Robbery	The taking or attempting to take anything of value from the care, custody, or control of a person or persons by force or threat of force or violence and/or by putting the victim in fear.
Aggravated assault	An unlawful attack by one person upon another for the purpose of inflicting severe or aggravated bodily injury. This type of assault usually is accompanied by the use of a weapon or by means likely to produce death or great bodily harm. Simple assaults are excluded.
Burglary/breaking or entering	The unlawful entry of a structure to commit a felony or a theft. Attempted forcible entry is included.
Larceny/theft (except motor vehicle theft)	The unlawful taking, carrying, leading, or riding away of property from the possession or constructive possession of another. Examples are thefts of bicycles or automobile accessories, shoplifting, pocket picking, or the stealing of any property or article that is not taken by force and violence or by fraud. Attempted larcenies are included. Embezzlement, con games, forgery, worthless checks, and so on are excluded.
Motor vehicle theft	The theft or attempted theft of a motor vehicle. A motor vehicle is self-propelled and runs on the surface and not on rails. Specifically excluded from this category are motorboats, construction equipment, airplanes, and farming equipment.
Arson	Any willful or malicious burning or attempt to burn, with or without intent to defraud, a dwelling house, public building, motor vehicle or aircraft, personal property of another, or the like.

Source: FBI, Uniform Crime Report, 1997.

offenses, and detailed information pertaining to criminal homicide are also reported. Traditionally, slightly more than 20 percent of all reported index crimes are cleared by arrest each year (see Figure 3.1).

CONNECTIONS

The 20 percent clearance rate is a sore point with police. Despite years of effort, the clearance rate has not changed measurably. This has prompted many police departments to adopt new techniques. See Chapter 16 for more on this topic.

Violent crimes are more likely to be solved than property crimes because police devote more resources to the more serious acts. For these types of crime, witnesses (including the victim) are frequently available to identify offenders, and in many instances the victim and offender were previously acquainted.

The UCR uses three methods to express crime data. First, the number of crimes reported to the police and arrests made are expressed as raw figures (for example, 18,209 murders occurred in 1997). Second, crime rates per 100,000 people are computed. That is, when the UCR indicates that the murder rate was 6.8 in 1997, it means that about 7 people in every 100,000 were murdered between January 1 and December 31 of 1997. This is the equation used:

$$\frac{\text{Number of reported crimes}}{\text{Total U.S. population}} \times 100{,}000 = \frac{\text{Rate per}}{100{,}000}$$

Third, the FBI computes changes in the number and rate of crime over time. For example, murder rates declined 8.1 percent between 1996 and 1997.

Figure 3.1   Crimes Cleared by Arrest, 1997

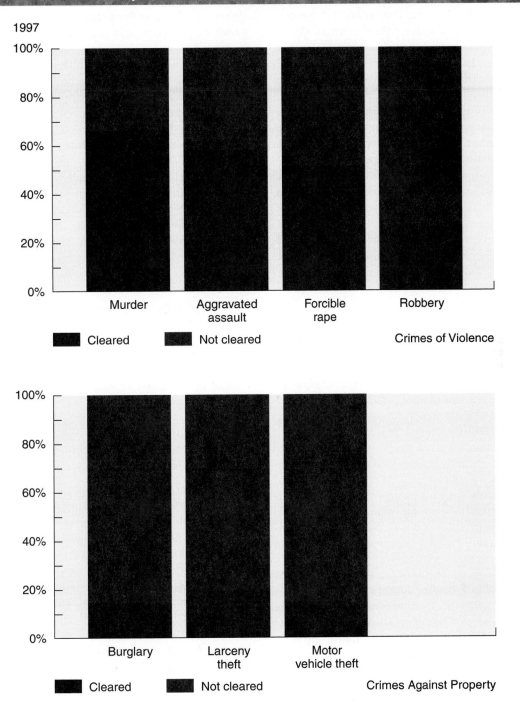

Source: FBI, Uniform Crime Report, 1997, p. 204.

How Accurate Are the Uniform Crime Reports?

Despite criminologists' continued reliance on the UCR, its accuracy has been suspect. The three main areas of concern include reporting practices, law enforcement practices, and methodological problems, which are discussed next.

Reporting Practices   Some criminologists claim that victims of many serious crimes do not report these incidents to police; therefore, these crimes do not become part of the UCR. The reasons for not reporting vary. Some victims do not trust the police or have confidence in their ability to solve crimes. Others do not have property insurance and therefore believe it is useless to report theft. In other cases, victims fear reprisals from an offender's friends or family. According to surveys of crime victims, less than 40 percent of all criminal incidents are reported to the police. Some of these victims justify nonreporting by stating that the incident was "a private matter," that "nothing could be done," or that the victimization was "not important enough."[3] These findings indicate that the UCR data may significantly underrepresent the total number of annual criminal events.

Law Enforcement Practices The way police departments record and report criminal and delinquent activity also affects the validity of UCR statistics. This effect was recognized more than 40 years ago, when between 1948 and 1952, the number of burglaries in New York City rose from 2,726 to 42,491, and larcenies increased from 7,713 to 70,949.[4] These increases related to the change from a precinct-based to a statewide centralized reporting system for crime statistics.[5]

How law enforcement agencies interpret the definitions of index crimes may also affect reporting practices. Some departments may define crimes loosely—for example, reporting a trespass as a burglary or an assault on a woman as an attempted rape—whereas others pay strict attention to FBI guidelines. These reporting practices may help explain interjurisdictional differences in crime.[6] For example, arson may be seriously underreported because many fire departments do not report to the FBI, and those that do define as accidental or spontaneous many fires that may well have been set by arsonists.[7]

Some local police departments make systematic errors in UCR reporting. Some count an arrest only after a formal booking procedure, although the UCR requires arrests to be counted if the suspect is released without a formal charge. One survey of arrests found an error rate of about 10 percent in every Part I offense category.[8] More serious allegations claim that in some cases police officials may deliberately alter reported crimes to improve their department's public image. Police administrators interested in lowering the crime rate may falsify crime reports by, for example, classifying a burglary as a nonreportable trespass.[9]

Ironically, boosting police efficiency and professionalism may actually help *increase* crime rates; as people develop confidence in the police, they may be more motivated to report crime. For example, a recent New York City police program provided special services (such as follow-up visits and education) to a select sample of domestic violence victims.[10] Evaluation of the program showed that households that received the extra attention were more likely to report new incidence of violence than those that received no special services. Although it is possible that the follow-ups encouraged violence, a more realistic assessment is that the interventions increased citizens' confidence in the ability of the police to handle domestic assaults and encouraged greater crime reporting.

Higher crime rates may occur as departments adopt more sophisticated computer technology and hire better-educated, better-trained employees. Crime rates also may be altered based on the way law enforcement agencies process UCR data. As the number of employees assigned to dispatching, record keeping, and criminal incident reporting increases, so too will national crime rates. What appears to be a rising crime rate may be simply an artifact of improved police record-keeping ability.[11]

CONNECTIONS

The number of civilian employees in police departments is increasing. Administrators like hiring civilians because they bring needed skills to specialized tasks such as data collection without needing to be qualified as uniformed officers. See Chapter 16 for more on the changing composition of police departments.

Methodological Problems Methodological issues also contribute to questions pertaining to the UCR's validity. The most frequent issues include the following:

1. No federal crimes are reported.
2. Reports are voluntary and vary in accuracy and completeness.
3. Not all police departments submit reports.
4. The FBI uses estimates in its total crime projections.
5. If an offender commits multiple crimes, only the most serious is recorded. Thus if a narcotics addict rapes, robs, and murders a victim, only the murder is recorded. Consequently, many lesser crimes go unreported.
6. Each act is listed as a single offense for some crimes but not for others. If a man robbed six people in a bar, the offense is listed as one robbery; but if he assaulted or murdered them, it would be listed as six assaults or six murders.
7. Incomplete acts are lumped together with completed ones.
8. Important differences exist between the FBI's definition of certain crimes and those used in a number of states.[12]

The complex scoring procedure means that many serious crimes are not counted. For example, during an armed bank robbery, the offender strikes a teller with the butt of a handgun. The robber runs from the bank

Figure 3.2   Self-Report Survey Questions

PLEASE INDICATE HOW OFTEN IN THE PAST 12 MONTHS YOU DID EACH ACT. (CHECK THE BEST ANSWER.)	Never did act	One time	2-5 times	6-9 times	10+ times
Stole something worth less than $50					
Stole something worth more than $50					
Used cocaine					
Been in a fistfight					
Carried a weapon such as a gun or knife					
Fought someone using a weapon					

and steals an automobile at the curb. Although the offender has technically committed robbery, aggravated assault, and motor vehicle theft, which are three Part I offenses, because robbery is the most serious, it would be the only one recorded in the UCR.[13]

The Future of the Uniform Crime Report

Clearly there must be a more reliable source for crime statistics than the UCR as it stands today. For the past 15 years, the FBI has been implementing some important changes in the Uniform Crime Report. An attempt is being made to provide more detailed information on individual criminal incidents by using a uniform, comprehensive program called the **National Incident-Based Reporting System (NIBRS).** Instead of submitting statements of the kinds of crime that individual citizens reported to the police and summary statements of resulting arrests, the new program will require local police agencies to provide at least a brief account of each incident and arrest within 22 crime patterns, including the incident, victim, and offender information. These expanded crime categories would include numerous additional crimes, such as blackmail, embezzlement, drug offenses, and bribery; this would allow a national database on the nature of crime, victims, and criminals to be developed.[14] Other information to be collected includes statistics gathered by federal law enforcement agencies, as well as data on hate or bias crimes. When this new UCR program is finally implemented and adopted across the nation, it should bring about greater uniformity in cross-jurisdictional reporting and improve the accuracy of official crime data.

SELF-REPORT SURVEYS

The problems associated with official statistics have led many criminologists to seek alternative sources of information in assessing the true extent of crime patterns. In addition, official statistics do not say much about the personality, attitudes, and behavior of individual criminals. They also are of little value in charting the extent of substance abuse in the population because relatively few abusers are arrested. Criminologists have therefore sought additional sources to supplement and expand official data. One frequently employed alternative to official statistics is the **self-report survey.** These surveys allow participants to reveal information about their violations. Most often, self-report surveys are administered to groups of subjects through a mass distribution of questionnaires. Although the surveys might ask for the subjects' names, more commonly the responses remain anonymous. The basic assumption of self-report studies is that anonymity and confidentiality will be assured, which encourages people to accurately describe their illegal activities. Self-reports are viewed as a mechanism to get at the "dark figures of crime," the figures missed by official statistics. Figure 3.2 illustrates some typical self-report items.

The Focus of Self-Reports

Most self-report studies have focused on juvenile delinquency and youth crime, for two reasons.[15] First, the school setting makes it convenient to test thousands of subjects simultaneously because they all have the means to respond to a research questionnaire (pens, desks, and time). Second, because school attendance is universal, a school-based self-report survey represents a cross-section of the community. However, self-reports are not restricted to youth crime. They are also used to examine the offense histories of prison inmates, drug users, and other segments of the population. Along with statistical estimating techniques, they make it possible for criminologists to use their sample data to calculate the number of people in the population who have committed illegal acts and the frequency of their law violations. These reports are particularly useful for assessing the extent of the national substance abuse problem because most drug use goes undetected by police. Also, because most self-report instruments contain items measuring subjects' attitudes, values, personal characteristics, and behaviors, the data obtained from them can be used for various purposes. These include testing theories, measuring attitudes toward crime, and computing the association between crime and important social variables, such as family relations, educational attainment, and income. Self-reports provide a broader picture of the distribution of criminality than official data because they do not depend on apprehension of the offender. They can be used to estimate the number of criminal offenders who have previously been unknown to the police. These respondents represent many criminals who have never figured in official crime statistics, some of whom may even be serious or chronic offenders.[16] Because many criminologists believe that class, gender, and racial bias exists in the criminal justice system, self-reports allow them to evaluate the distribution of criminal behavior across racial, class, and gender lines. They also enable criminologists to determine if official arrest data truly represent the offender population or if they reflect bias, discrimination, and selective enforcement. For example, racial bias may be present if black and white respondents report equal amounts of crime, but official data indicate that minorities are arrested more often than whites. In sum, self-reports provide an appreciable amount of information about offenders that cannot be found in official statistics.

Self-Report Findings In general, self-reports indicate that the number of people who break the law is far greater than the number projected by official statistics. Almost everyone questioned is found to have violated some law.[17] Furthermore, self-reports dispute the notion that criminals and delinquents specialize in one type of crime or another; offenders seem to engage in a "mixed bag" of crime and deviance.[18]

Self-report studies indicate that the most common offenses are truancy, alcohol abuse, use of a false ID, shoplifting or larceny under $50, fighting, marijuana use, and damage to the property of others. It is not unusual for self-reports to find combined substance abuse, theft, violence, and damage rates of more than 50 per-

Table 3.2 Self-Reported Delinquent Activity During the Past 12 Months Among High School Seniors

CRIME CATEGORY	PERCENTAGE ENGAGING IN OFFENSES	
	AT LEAST ONE OFFENSE	MULTIPLE OFFENSES
Serious fight	8%	7%
Gang fight	10%	8%
Hurt someone badly	7%	6%
Used a weapon to steal	2%	2%
Stole less than $50	14%	17%
Stole more than $50	4%	6%
Shoplifted	12%	17%
Did breaking and entering	11%	13%
Committed arson	1.5%	1%
Damaged school property	6%	8%

Source: *Monitoring the Future, 1997* (Ann Arbor, Mich.: Institute for Social Research, 1998).

cent among suburban, rural, and urban high school youths. What is surprising is the consistency of these findings in samples taken around the United States. Table 3.2 contains data from a self-report study called ***Monitoring the Future,*** which researchers at the University of Michigan Institute for Social Research (ISR) conduct annually. This national survey of over 2,500 high school seniors, one of the most important sources of self-report data, shows a widespread yet stable pattern of youth crime since 1978.[19] The ISR survey shows that young people commit a great deal of crime: about 40 percent of high school seniors now report stealing in the last 12 months; almost 20 percent said they were involved in a gang fight, and more than 10 percent injured someone so badly that the victim had to see a doctor; about 30 percent admitted shoplifting; and almost one-quarter engaged in breaking and entering. The facts that so many—at least one-third—of all U.S. high school students engaged in theft and almost 19 percent committed a serious violent act during the past year show that criminal activity is widespread and is not restricted to a few "bad apples."

Are Self-Reports Accurate?

Although self-report data have profoundly affected criminological inquiry, some important methodological issues have been raised about their accuracy. Critics of self-report studies frequently suggest that it is unreasonable to expect people to candidly admit illegal acts. They have nothing to gain, and the ones taking the greatest risk are the ones with official records who may be engaging in the most criminality. On the other hand, some people may exaggerate their criminal acts, forget some of them, or be confused about what is being asked. Some surveys contain an overabundance of trivial offenses, such as shoplifting small amounts of items or using false identification, often lumped together with serious crimes to form a total crime index. Consequently, comparisons between groups can be highly misleading.

Various techniques have been used to verify self-report data.[20] The "known group" method compares incarcerated youths with "normal" groups to see whether the former report more delinquency. Another approach is to use peer informants who can verify the honesty of a subject's answers. Subjects can be tested twice to see if their answers remain stable. Sometimes questions are designed to reveal respondents who are lying on the survey; for example, an item might say, "I have never done anything wrong in my life." It is also possible to compare the answers youths give with their official police records. A typical approach is to ask youths if they have ever been arrested for or convicted of a delinquent act and then check their official records against their self-reported responses. A number of studies using this method have found a remarkable uniformity between self-reported answers and official records.[21] Another method is to correlate self-reported delinquency with official records because youths who self-report crime may be the ones most likely to get arrested or petitioned to court. Research studies indicate a substantial association between official processing and self-reported crime.[22] **Polygraphs,** commonly known as lie detectors, have also been used to verify the responses given on self-report surveys. The results often validate the accuracy of self-report survey data.[23]

In what is probably the most thorough analysis of self-report methodologies, criminologists Michael Hindelang, Travis Hirschi, and Joseph Weis closely reviewed literature concerning the reliability and validity of self-reports. They concluded that the problems of accuracy in self-reports are surmountable; self-reports are more accurate than most criminologists believe; and self-reports and official statistics are quite compatible.[24]

The "Missing Cases"

Although these findings are encouraging, nagging questions still remain about the validity of self-reports. Even if 90 percent of a school population voluntarily participates in a self-report study, researchers can never be sure whether the few who refuse to participate or are absent that day comprise a significant portion of the school's population of persistent high-rate offenders. Research indicates that offenders with the most extensive prior criminality are also the most likely to "be poor historians of their own crime commission rates."[25] It is also unlikely that the most serious chronic offenders in the teenage population are the most willing to cooperate with university-based criminologists administering self-report tests.[26] Institutionalized youths, who are not generally represented in the self-report surveys, are not only more delinquent than the general youth population, but they are also considerably more misbehaving than the most delinquent youths identified in the typical self-report survey.[27] Consequently, self-reports may measure only nonserious, occasional delinquents while ignoring hard-core chronic offenders who may be institutionalized and unavailable for self-reports.

CONNECTIONS

Criminologists suspect that a few high-rate offenders are responsible for a disproportionate share of all serious crime. Results would be badly skewed if even a few of these chronic offenders were absent or refused to participate in a schoolwide self-report survey. For more on chronic offenders, see the sections at the end of this chapter.

Substance Abusers Self-reports of substance abusers are particularly problematic.[28] Criminologists suspect that substance abusers tend to underreport the frequency of their drug use. For example, in studies of juvenile detainees, many children who tested positively for drug use failed to report using any drugs.[29] Although this research involves a sample of incarcerated youth who might be expected to underreport drug use, the findings call into question the validity of self-report surveys. Similar research with adult pretrial detainees also found that self-reports significantly undercounted substance abuse.[30]

As self-reports continue to be used to measure criminal behavior, their accuracy is not assured. The least reliable self-reports are those of two offending populations—chronic offenders and persistent drug abusers. These groups may be among the most frequent and serious criminal offenders.

CONNECTIONS

Self-report data are used as the standard measure of U.S. youthful drug use. When reading the results of national drug use surveys in Chapter 14, keep in mind the limited validity of these self-report surveys.

VICTIM SURVEYS

A third source of crime data is surveys that ask crime victims about their encounters with criminals. Because many victims do not report their experiences to the police, victim surveys are considered a method of getting at the unknown figures of crime. The first national survey of 10,000 households was conducted in 1966 as part of the President's Commission on Law Enforcement and the Administration of Justice. The national survey showed that the number of criminal victimizations in the United States was far higher than previously believed because many victims failed to report crime to the police, fearing retaliation or official indifference. This early research encouraged development of the **National Crime Victimization Survey (NCVS),** which is the current method of assessing victimization in the United States.[31]

The National Crime Victimization Survey

The National Crime Victimization Survey is conducted by the U.S. Bureau of the Census in cooperation with the Bureau of Justice Statistics of the U.S. Department of Justice. In these national surveys, samples of housing units are selected using a complex, **multistage sampling technique.** Each year data are obtained from a nationally representative sample of roughly 45,000 households that includes more than 94,000 persons. They are asked to report on the frequency, characteristics, and consequences of criminal victimization in the United States. The survey is designed to report the likelihood of victimization by rape, sexual assault, robbery, assault, theft, household burglary, and motor vehicle theft for the population as a whole as well as for segments of the population such as women, the elderly, members of various racial groups, city dwellers, and other groups. The total sample is interviewed twice a year about victimizations suffered in the preceding six months. Households remain in the sample for about three years, and new homes rotate into the sample continually. The NCVS reports that the interview completion rate in the national sample is usually more than 90 percent in any given period. Because of the care with which the samples are drawn and the high completion rate, NCVS data are considered a relatively unbiased, valid estimate of all victimizations for the target crimes included in the survey.

CONNECTIONS

Victim surveys not only provide information about criminal incidents that have occurred, but also can describe the individuals who are most at risk of falling victim to crime, where the crime might occur, and when they are most likely to become victimized. Data from recent NCVS surveys will be used in Chapter 4 to draw a portrait of the nature and extent of victimization in the United States.

NCVS Findings The number of crimes accounted for by the NCVS (about 37 million) is considerably larger than the number of crimes reported to the FBI. For example, whereas the UCR shows that about 500,000 robberies occur annually, the NCVS estimates that about 1.1 million actually occur. The reason for such discrepancies is that fewer than half of the violent crimes, fewer than one-third of the personal theft crimes (such as pocket picking), and fewer than half of the household thefts are reported to police. The reasons most often given by victims for not reporting crime include believing that "the police can do nothing about it," that it was a "private matter," or that they did not want to "get involved." Victims seem to report to the police only crimes that involve considerable loss or injury. If we are to believe NCVS findings, the official UCR statistics do not provide an accurate picture of the crime problem because many crimes go unreported to the police.

Is the NCVS Valid?

Like the UCR and self-report surveys, the NCVS may also suffer from some methodological problems. As a result, its findings must be interpreted with caution. Among the potential problems are these:

- Overreporting due to victims' misinterpretation of events. For example, a lost wallet may be reported as stolen, or an open door may be viewed as a burglary attempt.
- Underreporting due to the embarrassment of reporting crime to interviewers, fear of getting in trouble, or simply forgetting an incident.
- Inability to record the personal criminal activity of those interviewed, such as drug use or gambling; murder is also not included for obvious reasons.
- Sampling errors, which produce a group of respondents who do not represent the nation as a whole.
- Inadequate question format that invalidates responses. Some groups, such as adolescents, may be particularly susceptible to error because of question format.[32]

In 1992 the NCVS was redesigned to improve its validity. One important change is that victims are now asked directly if they were raped or sexually assaulted. In the past, rape was indirectly surveyed with the question "Did anything else happen to you?" The straightforward approach makes it easier for the victim to respond and, in turn, for the interviewer to record more accurate information.

Are Crime Statistics Sources Compatible?

Are the various sources of crime statistics compatible? Each has strengths and weaknesses. The FBI survey is carefully tallied and contains data on the number of murders and people arrested, information that the other data sources lack. However, this survey omits the many crimes victims choose not to report to police, and it is subject to the reporting caprices of individual police departments.

The availability of firearms may influence the crime rate, especially the proliferation of weapons in the hands of teens. It is still relatively easy to buy high-powered weapons, and there is evidence that more guns than ever before are finding their way into the hands of young people. Sophisticated automatic weapons, some of which are laser-aimed, have become armament for juvenile gangs and criminal groups.

The NCVS contains unreported crime and important information on the personal characteristics of victims, but the data consist of estimates made from relatively limited samples of the total U.S. population, so that even narrow fluctuations in the rates of some crimes can have a major impact on findings. It also relies on personal recollections that may be inaccurate. The NCVS does not include data on important crime patterns, including murder and drug abuse.

Self-report surveys can provide information on the personal characteristics of offenders, such as their attitudes, values, beliefs, and psychological profiles, that is unavailable from any other source. Yet, at their core, self-reports rely on the honesty of criminal offenders and drug abusers, a population not generally known for accuracy and integrity.

Despite these differences, a number of prominent criminologists have concluded that the data sources are more compatible than was first believed. Although their tallies of crimes are certainly not in synch, the crime patterns and trends they record are often quite similar.[33] For example, all three sources generally agree about the personal characteristics of serious criminals (such as age and gender) and where and when crime occurs (such as urban areas, nighttime, and summer months).

This may be persuasive, but some criminologists still question the compatibility between the data sources and imply that they measure separate concepts (for example, reported crimes, actual crimes, and victimization rates).[34] This ongoing academic debate accentuates the fact that interpreting crime data is often problematic. Because each source of crime data uses a different method to obtain results, differences inevitably will occur among them. These differences must be carefully considered when criminologists interpret data on the nature and trends in crime.[35]

CRIME TRENDS

Crime is not new to this century.[36] Studies have indicated that a gradual increase in the crime rate, especially in violent crime, occurred from 1830 to 1860. Following the Civil War, this rate increased significantly for about 15 years. Then, from 1880 up to the time of the First World War, with the possible exception of the years immediately preceding and following the war, the number of reported crimes decreased. After a period of readjustment, the crime rate steadily declined until the Depression (about 1930), when another crime wave was recorded. Crime rates increased gradually following the 1930s until the 1960s, when the growth rate became much greater. The homicide rate, which had actually declined from the 1930s to the 1960s, also began a sharp increase that continued through the 1970s.

In 1981 the number of index crimes peaked at about 13.4 million and then began a consistent decline until

The Criminological Enterprise

Explaining Crime Trends

Criminologists have identified a variety of social, economic, and demographic factors that influence crime rate trends. Some of the most important factors are discussed here.

Age. Criminologists view change in the population age distribution as having the greatest influence on crime trends: as a general rule, the crime rate follows the proportion of young males in the population. With the "graying" of society in the 1980s and a decline in the birth rate, it is not surprising that the overall crime rate declined between 1990 and 1997. The number of juveniles should be increasing over the next decade, and some criminologists fear that this will signal a return to escalating crime rates.

Economy. There is debate over the effects the economy has on crime rates. Some criminologists believe that a poor economy actually helps to *lower* crime rates. They support this belief by claiming that unemployed parents are at home to supervise children and guard their homes. Because there is less to spend, a poor economy reduces the number of valuables worth stealing. Also, it seems unlikely that law-abiding, middle-aged workers

will suddenly turn to a life of crime if they are laid off during an economic downturn.

Nonetheless, during periods of sustained economic weakness and unemployment, crime rates may eventually rise. A long-term economic recession, such as the one that occurred in the late 1980s, may produce a climate of hopelessness in the nation's largest cities, which saw increased violence rates between 1985 and 1990. Crime rates fell when there was a long-term surge in the economy during the 1990s.

Social malaise. As the level of social problems increases—such as single-parent families, dropout rates, and teen pregnancies—so too do crime rates. The number of single mothers and the dropout rate both declined in the 1990s while crime rates dropped. Social malaise may explain why some cities and regions have higher crime rates than others.

Guns and teens. The availability of firearms may influence the crime rate, especially the proliferation of weapons in the hands of teens. There is evidence that more guns than ever before are finding their way into the hands of young people. Surveys of

high school students indicate that between 6 and 10 percent carry guns at least some of the time. As the number of gun-toting students increases, so too will the seriousness of violent crime as, for example, a schoolyard fight turns into murder.

Gangs. Another factor that affects crime rates is the explosive growth in teenage gangs. Surveys indicate that there may be between 500,000 and 700,000 gang members in the United States. Boys who are members of gangs are far more likely to possess guns than non–gang members; criminal activity increases when kids join gangs.

According to Alfred Blumstein, gangs involved in the urban drug trade recruit juveniles because they work cheaply, are immune from heavy criminal penalties, and are "daring and willing to take risks." Arming themselves for protection, these drug-dealing children present a menace to their communities, which persuades non–gang-affiliated neighborhood adolescents to arm themselves for protection. The result is an arms race that produces an increasing spiral of violence.

The recent decline in the crime rate may be tied to changing gang val-

---

1984, when police recorded 11.1 million crimes. By the following year, however, the crime rate once again began an upward trend, so that by 1991 police recorded about 14.6 million crimes. Both the number and rate of crimes have been declining ever since.

In 1997 about 13.5 million crimes were reported to the police, a decrease of about 2 percent from the preceding year. The overall crime rate declined more than 10 percent between 1993 and 1997. Serious crime rates declined another 7 percent between 1997 and 1998.

Trends in Violent Crime

The violent crimes reported by the FBI include murder, rape, assault, and robbery. In 1997 about 1.6 million violent crimes were reported to police, a rate of around 610 per 100,000 Americans. According to the UCR, violence in the United States has decreased during the 1990s, reversing a long trend of skyrocketing increases

(Figure 3.3). The total number of violent crimes declined 15 percent between 1993 and 1997, and the violence rate dropped 18 percent.

Particularly encouraging has been the decrease in the number and rate of murders. The murder statistics are generally regarded as the most accurate aspect of the UCR. Figure 3.4 illustrates homicide rate trends since 1900. Note how the rate peaked around 1930, then fell, rose dramatically around 1960, and peaked once again in 1991, when the number of murders topped 24,000 for the first time in the nation's history. Since 1993 the murder rate has declined by 28 percent, while the number of murders is down 25 percent. The decline in the violence rate has been both unexpected and welcome. Some major cities, such as New York, report a significant decline of over 50 percent in their murder rates through the 1990s. Preliminary 1998 results indicate that robbery declined 11 percent, murders 8 percent, and forcible rape and aggravated assault 5 percent between 1997 and 1998.

ues. Some streetwise kids have told researchers that they now avoid gangs because of the "younger brother syndrome"—they have watched their older siblings or parents caught in gangs or drugs and want to avoid the same fate.

Drug use. Some experts tie increases in the violent crime rate between 1980 and 1990 to the crack cocaine epidemic, which swept the nation's largest cities, and drug-trafficking gangs, which fought over drug turf. These well-armed gangs did not hesitate to use violence to control territory, intimidate rivals, and increase market share. As the crack epidemic has subsided (users are switching to heroin), so too has the violence in cities such as New York City and other metropolitan areas where the crack epidemic was rampant.

Justice policy. Some law enforcement experts have suggested that a reduction in crime rates may be attributed to aggressive police practices that target "quality of life" crimes such as panhandling, graffiti, petty drug dealing, and loitering. By showing that even the smallest infractions will be dealt with seriously, aggressive police departments may be able to discourage potential criminals from committing more serious crimes.

It is also possible that tough laws targeting drug dealing and repeat offenders with lengthy prison terms can affect crime rates. The fear of punishment may inhibit some would-be criminals. Lengthy sentences also help boost the nation's prison population. Placing a significant number of potentially high-rate offenders behind bars may help stabilize crime rates. Some ex-criminals have told researchers that they stopped committing crime because they perceive higher levels of street enforcement and incarceration rates.

CRITICAL THINKING

1. What social policies might be most effective in getting the crime rate down?
2. Can you identify recent social changes that may be responsible for a decline in crime rates?

 INFOTRAC COLLEGE EDITION RESEARCH

Gang activity may have a big impact on crime rates. To read about the effect, see:

John M. Hagedorn, Jose Torres, Greg Giglio. Cocaine, kicks, and strain: patterns of substance use in Milwaukee gangs. *Contemporary Drug Problems,* Spring 1998 v25 n1 p113–145

Mary E. Pattillo. Sweet mothers and gangbangers: managing crime in a black middle-class neighborhood. *Social Forces,* March 1998 v76 n3 p747(28)

Source: Desmond Ellis and Lori Wright, "Estrangement, Interventions, and Male Violence Toward Female Partners," *Violence and Victims* 12 (1997): 51–68; Richard Rosenfeld, "Changing Relationships Between Men and Women: A Note on the Decline in Intimate Partner Homicide," *Homicide Studies* 1 (1997): 72–83; Bruce Johnson, Andrew Golub, and Jeffrey Fagan, "Careers in Crack, Drug Use, Drug Distribution, and Nondrug Criminality," *Crime and Delinquency* 41 (1995): 275–95; Alfred Blumstein, "Violence by Young People: Why the Deadly Nexus," *National Institute of Justice Journal* 229: 2–9 (1995); Joseph Sheley and James Wright, *In the Line of Fire: Youth, Guns, and Violence in Urban America* (New York: Aldine de Gruyter, 1995); Alan Lizotte, Gregory Howard, Marvin Krohn, and Terence Thornberry, "Patterns of Illegal Gun Carrying Among Young Urban Males," *Valparaiso University Law Review* 31 (1997): 376–94; and Rosemary Gartner, "Family Structure, Welfare Spending, and Child Homicide in Developed Democracies," *Journal of Marriage and the Family* 53 (1991): 231–40.

Trends in Property Crime

The property crimes reported in the UCR include larceny, motor vehicle theft, and arson. In 1997 about 11.5 million property crimes were reported, a rate of about 4,300 per 100,000 population. Unlike the violent crime rate, property crimes did not substantially increase in the 1980s; in fact, between 1981 and 1991, the number of property crimes increased less than 5 percent, compared to a more than 30 percent increase in violent crime. Like violent crime, property crime has declined in recent years. For example, between 1993 and 1997, both burglary and auto theft declined by about 16 percent. Motor vehicle theft declined 10 percent, burglary and arson 7 percent, and larceny 6 percent between 1997 and 1998.

Trends in Self-Reports and Victimization

Self-report results appear to be more stable than the UCR. When the results of recent self-report surveys are compared with various studies conducted over a 20-year period, a uniform pattern emerges. The use of drugs and alcohol increased markedly in the 1970s, leveled off in the 1980s, and then began to increase in the mid-1990s until 1997, when it once again stabilized. Theft, violence, and damage-related crimes seem more stable. Although a self-reported crime wave has not occurred, neither has there been any visible reduction in self-reported criminality.[37]

According to the most recently available NCVS data (1996), about 37 million personal crimes occur each year. Like the UCR, the NCVS also shows that violence rates have undergone a major decline in the 1990s. For example, the 1996 victimization rates (the latest available) are the lowest recorded by the NCVS since its inception in 1973 (see Figure 3.5). In 1996 violent crime rates were 16 percent lower and property crime rates 17 percent lower than they were in 1993. The decreasing victimization trends were experienced about equally for all sex, race, and income groups.

What factors influence crime trends? Criminologists have identified a variety of social, economic, and demographic factors. These factors are discussed in the Criminological Enterprise feature entitled "Explaining Crime Trends."

What the Future Holds

It is always risky to speculate about the future of crime trends because current conditions can change rapidly. But some criminologists have tried to predict future patterns. Darrell Steffensmeier and Miles Harer suggest that violent crime will drop during the late 1990s as the baby boomers pass into middle and old age. They speculate that the property crime rate will at first decline, then level off and begin rising toward the end of the decade as the baby-boomlet kids born in the early 1980s enter their peak crime years. After the year 2000, both property and violent crimes are predicted to increase.[38] Steffensmeier and Harer find that the age structure of society is the single most powerful influence on the crime rate.

In a similar vein, criminologist James A. Fox predicts a significant increase in teen violence if current trends persist. Approximately 40 million U.S. children are under age 10; this is more than we have had for decades. While many come from stable homes, others lack stable families and adequate supervision; these are some of the children who will soon enter their prime crime years. As a result, Fox predicts a wave of youth violence that will be even worse than that of the past 10 years. If current trends persist, the number of juvenile homicides should grow from fewer than 4,000 today to about 9,000 in 2004 (see Figure 3.6).[39] Such predictions are based on population trends and other factors discussed earlier.

Figure 3.3 Crime Rate Trends

After years of steady increase, crime rates declined between 1993 and 1997.

Rate per 1,000 population

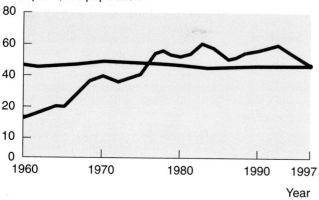

Source: FBI, Uniform Crime Report, 1997.

Figure 3.4 Homicide Rate Trends, 1900–1997

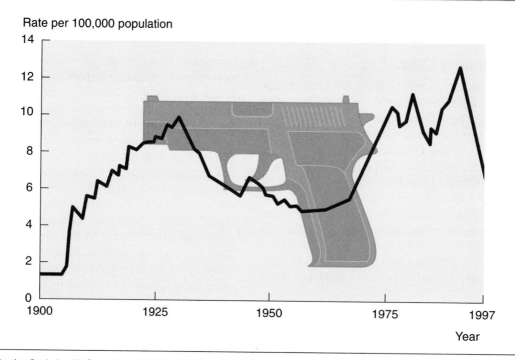

Source: Bureau of Justice Statistics, *Violent Crime in the United States* (Washington, D.C.: Bureau of Justice Statistics, 1992; updated, 1997).

Figure 3.5 Trends in Violent Victimization Rates, 1973–96

Violent victimizations per 1,000 population age 12 or over

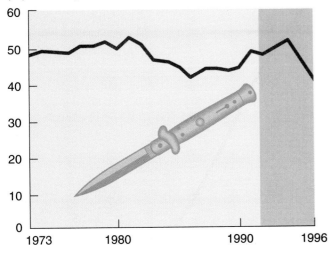

Note: The violent crimes included are rape and sexual assault, robbery, aggravated assault, and simple assault. The light gray area indicates that because of changes made to the victimization survey, data prior to 1992 are adjusted to make them comparable to data collected under the redesigned methodology. Data for 1995 and beyond are based on collection year (see *Criminal Victimization 1996: Changes 1995–96 with Trends 1993–96*).

Source: Michael Maltz and Marianne W. Zawitz, *Displaying Violent Crime Trends Using Estimates from the National Crime Victimization Survey* (Washington, D.C.: Bureau of Justice Statistics, 1998).

CRIME PATTERNS

Criminologists look for stable crime rate patterns to gain insight into the nature of crime. If crime rates are consistently higher at certain times, in certain areas, and among certain groups, this knowledge might help explain the onset or cause of crime. For example, if criminal statistics show that crime rates are consistently higher in poor neighborhoods in large urban areas, then crime may be a function of poverty and neighborhood decline. If, in contrast, crime rates are spread evenly across the social structure, this would provide little evidence that crime has an economic basis; instead, crime might be linked to socialization, personality, intelligence, or some other trait unrelated to class position or income. In this section we examine traits and patterns that may influence the crime rate.

The Ecology of Crime

Patterns in the crime rate seem to be linked to temporal and ecological factors. Some of the most important of these are discussed here.

Day, Season, and Climate Most reported crimes occur during the warm summer months of July and August. During the summer, teenagers, who usually have the highest crime levels, are out of school and have greater opportunity to commit crime. People spend more time outdoors during warm weather, making themselves easier targets. Similarly, homes are left vacant more often during the summer, making them more vulnerable to property crimes. Two exceptions to this trend are murders and robberies, which occur frequently in December and January (although rates are also high during the summer).

Figure 3.6 Forecast of Teen Homicide Offenders

Counts include both known perpetrators and an estimated share of unidentified perpetrators.

Homicides committed by juveniles

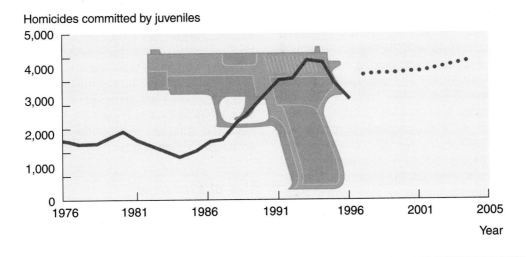

Year

Figure 3.7   The Relationship Between Temperature and Crime

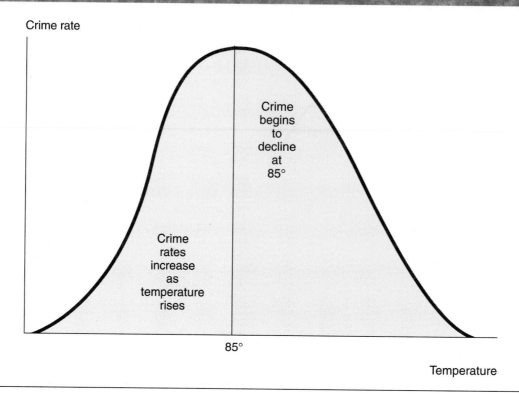

Crime rate

Crime begins to decline at 85°

Crime rates increase as temperature rises

85°

Temperature

Crime rates also may be higher on the first day of the month than at any other time. Government welfare and Social Security checks arrive at this time, and with them come increases in such activities as breaking into mailboxes and accosting recipients on the streets. Also, people may have more disposable income at this time, and the availability of extra money may relate to behaviors associated with crime such as drinking, partying, gambling, and so on.[40]

Temperature   Although weather effects (such as temperature swings) may also impact violent crime rates, laboratory studies suggest that the association between temperature and crime resembles an inverted U-shaped curve. Crime rates increase with rising temperatures and then begin to decline at some point (85 degrees) when it may be too hot for any physical exertion[41] (see Figure 3.7). However, field studies indicate that the rates of some crimes (such as domestic assault), but not all of them (for example, rape), continue to increase as temperatures rise.[42] Research has also shown that a long stretch of highly uncomfortable weather is related to homicide rates, indicating that the stress of long-term exposure to extreme temperatures may prove sufficiently unpleasant as to increase violence rates.[43]

In their study of the relationship of temperature to assault, criminologists Ellen Cohn and James Rotton found evidence of a highly significant effect, especially during the morning and evening hours. They found that a person is four times more likely to be assaulted at midnight when the temperature exceeds 90 degrees than when the temperature is 10 degrees below zero![44]

Population Density   Large urban areas have by far the highest violence rates. Areas with low per-capita crime rates tend to be rural. These findings are also supported by victim data. Exceptions to this trend are low-population resort areas with large transient or seasonal populations—such as Atlantic City, New Jersey, and Nantucket, Massachusetts.

Region   Crime rates vary by region. For many years, southern states had significantly higher rates in almost all crime categories than were found in other regions of the country; this data convinced some criminologists that there was a *southern subculture of violence*. However, as illustrated in Figure 3.8, the western states now have the dubious distinction of having the highest crime and violence rates.

Use of Firearms

Firearms play a dominant role in criminal activity. According to the NCVS, firearms were involved in 20 percent of robberies, 10 percent of assaults, and 6 percent of rapes. In 1997 the UCR reported that almost 70 per-

Note that the southern states have the highest rates.

West 652 4,683

Midwest 526 4,046

Northeast 536 3,197

South 682 4,865

■ Violent crime rate ■ Property crime rate

Source: Federal Bureau of Investigation, *Crime in the United States, 1997* (Washington, D.C.: U.S. Government Printing Office, 1998), p. 9.

cent of all murders involved firearms; most of these weapons were handguns. Many have linked the high incidence of crime in the United States to the widespread availability and use of handguns.[45] An ongoing battle between opposing factions has held either that guns are necessary for self-protection or that the ease with which people are able to get guns is a travesty and leads to unnecessary death and destruction.

Most guns used in crime are obtained illegally. Even if legitimate gun stores were more strictly regulated, this would not inhibit private citizens from selling, bartering, or trading handguns. Unregulated gun fairs and auctions are common throughout the United States; many gun deals are made at gun shows with few questions asked. So many guns are in use that controlling

their ownership or banning their manufacture would have a negligible impact for years to come. Sophisticated automatic weapons, some of which are laser-aimed, have become armament for juvenile gangs and criminal groups. Some police departments, feeling outgunned, have switched from the traditional .38 caliber police special revolver to 9 mm pistols that have 15 rounds. If handguns were banned or outlawed, they would become more valuable; illegal importation of guns might increase as it has for another controlled substance, narcotics. Increasing penalties for gun-related crimes has also met with limited success because judges may be reluctant to alter their sentencing policies to accommodate legislators. Regulating dealers is difficult, and tighter controls on them would only encourage

Gun Control Practices

America is by far the most heavily armed nation on earth.
—Gary Kleck, 1997

Over 200 million guns are in private hands; half of U.S. households possess a gun. An estimated 50 million of these guns are illegal. Handguns are linked to many violent crimes, including 20 percent of all injury deaths (second to autos) and 60 percent of all homicides and suicides. They are also responsible for the deaths of about two-thirds of all police officers who are killed in the line of duty. The association between guns and crime has spurred many Americans to advocate controlling the sale of handguns and banning the cheap mass-produced handguns known as "Saturday night specials." In contrast, gun advocates view control as a threat to personal liberty and call for severe punishment of criminals rather than control of handguns. They argue that the Second Amendment of the U.S. Constitution protects the right to bear arms.

Efforts to control handguns have many different sources. The states and many local jurisdictions have laws banning or restricting sales or possession of guns; some regulate dealers who sell guns. For example, the Federal Gun Control Act of 1968, which is still in effect, prohibits dealers from selling guns to minors, ex-felons, and drug users. In addition, each gun dealer must keep detailed records of who purchases guns. Unfortunately, the resources available to enforce this law are meager.

Another gun control method creates a waiting period before a purchaser can obtain a handgun so that authorities can check the buyer's background. In 1993 Congress passed the **Brady Bill**, which required a weeklong wait (for a background check) before a gun can be sold. The bill was named after former Press Secretary James Brady, who was severely wounded in the 1981 attempted assassination of President Ronald Reagan by John Hinckley. Beginning on No-

vember 30, 1998, the Brady law changed, providing an instant check on whether a prospective buyer is prohibited from purchasing a weapon. Federal law bans gun purchases by people convicted of or under indictment for felony charges, fugitives, the mentally ill, those with dishonorable military discharges, those who have renounced U.S. citizenship, illegal aliens, illegal drug users, and those convicted of domestic violence misdemeanors or who are under domestic violence restraining orders (individual state laws may create other restrictions). The Brady law now requires background approval not just for handgun buyers but also for those who buy long guns and shotguns.

Although gun control advocates see this legislation as a good first step, some question whether such measures will ultimately curb gun violence. Criminologist David McDowall and his colleagues, who prepared a methodologically sophisticated analysis of jurisdictions that have already increased waiting periods, indicate that such measures have little effect on gun violence.

Another approach is to severely punish people caught with unregistered handguns. The most famous attempt to regulate handguns using this method is the Massachusetts **Bartley-Fox Law**, which provides a mandatory one-year prison term for possessing a handgun (outside the home) without a permit. A detailed analysis of violent crime in Boston after the law's passage found that the use of handguns in robberies and murders did decline substantially (in robberies by 35 percent and in murders by 55 percent in a two-year period). However, these optimistic results must be tempered by two facts: rates for similar crimes dropped significantly in comparable cities that did not have gun control laws, and the use of other weapons, such as knives, increased in Boston.

Some jurisdictions have tried to reduce gun violence by adding extra

punishment, such as a mandatory prison sentence for any crime involving a handgun. California's new "10-20-life" law requires an additional 10 years in prison for carrying a gun while committing a violent felony, 20 years if the gun is fired, and if someone is injured, the penalty increases to from 25 years to life in prison. Although it is too early to evaluate the effect of this tough new 1998 law, evaluations of similar efforts are inconclusive.

Even when gun control laws have seemed to succeed in reducing crime, gun advocates refute the findings. There is some evidence that gun control laws can reduce violence rates, but the issue is far from settled.

CRITICAL THINKING

1. Should the sale and possession of handguns be banned?
2. Which of the gun control methods discussed do you feel would be most effective in deterring crime?

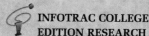 **INFOTRAC COLLEGE EDITION RESEARCH**

One method of reducing gun violence may be to make guns safer. Read more about this plan in:
Krista D. Robinson, Stephen P. Teret, Susan DeFrancesco, Stephen W. Hargarten. Making guns safer. *Issues in Science and Technology* Summer 1998 v14 n4 p37(4)

Source: Associated Press, "All Gun Buyers to Be Checked," *New York Times,* November 30, 1998, p. 1; "Gun Crime Mandatory Sentences Take Effect in California," *Criminal Justice Newsletter* 28 (December 15, 1997); Gary Kleck and Marc Gertz, "Armed Resistance to Crime: The Prevalence and Nature of Self-Defense with a Gun," *Journal of Criminal Law and Criminology* 86 (1995): 150–87; Colin Loftin, David McDowall, Brian Wiersma, and Talbert Cottey, "Effects of Restrictive Licensing of Handguns on Homicide and Suicide in the District of Columbia," *New England Journal of Medicine* 325 (1991): 1615–20; and Gary Kleck, "The Incidence of Gun Violence Among Young People," *Public Perspective* 4 (1993): 3–6.

While crime rates are higher in the United States than in most other Western nations, violence abroad is not unknown. The most catastrophic incident occurred in the village of Dunblane, Scotland, at 3:10 P.M. on July 8, 1996, when heavily armed Horret Campbell walked onto the grounds of St. Luke's Infants School and began to methodically shoot children in this kindergarten class. Sixteen children and their teacher were killed. The Dunblane massacre prompted the passage of legislation to control handguns in Scotland and England, which failed to please some critics who felt there should be an outright ban on the possession of guns.

private sales and bartering. Even if purchased by a legitimate gun enthusiast, weapons can fall into the wrong hands as a result of burglaries and break-ins.

Some experts, like Gary Kleck and Marc Gertz, maintain that handguns may be more of an effective deterrent to crime than gun control advocates are ready to admit. Their research indicates that as many as 400,000 people per year use guns in situations in which they later claim that the guns almost "certainly" saved lives. Even if these estimates are off by a factor of 10, it means that armed citizens may save 40,000 lives annually. Although Kleck and Gertz recognize that guns are involved in homicides, suicides, and accidents, which claim over 30,000 lives per year, they believe that their benefit as a crime prevention device should not be overlooked.[46]

The issue of gun control is discussed in the Policy and Practice in Criminology feature.

Social Class and Crime

A still-unresolved issue in criminological literature is the relationship between social class and crime. Traditionally crime has been thought of as a lower-class phenomenon. After all, people at the lowest rungs of the social structure have the greatest incentive to commit crimes. Those unable to obtain desired goods and services through conventional means may consequently resort to theft and other illegal activities — such as selling narcotics — to obtain them. These activities are referred to as **instrumental crimes.** Those living in poverty are also believed to engage in disproportionate amounts of **expressive crimes,** such as rape and assault, as a means of expressing their rage, frustration, and anger against society. Alcohol and drug abuse, common in impoverished areas, helps fuel violent episodes.[47]

Official statistics indicate that crime rates in inner-city, high-poverty areas are generally higher than those in suburban or wealthier areas. For example, both males and females experience the highest homicide victimization levels in deteriorated inner-city areas.[48] Studies using aggregate police statistics (arrest records) have consistently shown that crime rates in lower-class areas exceed those in wealthier neighborhoods. Another "official" indicator of a class–crime relationship can be obtained through surveys of prison inmates, which consistently show that prisoners were members of the lower class and unemployed or underemployed in the years before their incarceration.

An alternative explanation for these findings is that the relationship between official crime and social class is a function of law enforcement practices, not actual criminal behavior patterns. Police may devote more resources to poor areas, and consequently apprehension rates may be higher there. Similarly, police may be more likely to formally arrest and prosecute lower-class citizens than those in the middle and upper classes, which may account for the lower class's overrepresentation in official statistics and the prison population.

Class and Self-Reports Self-report data have been used extensively to test the class–crime relationship. If people in all social classes self-report similar crime patterns, but only those in the lower class are formally arrested, that would explain higher crime rates in lower-class neighborhoods. However, if lower-class people report greater criminal activity than their middle- and upper-class peers, it would indicate that official statistics accurately represent the crime problem. Surprisingly, early self-report studies conducted in the 1950s, specifically those conducted by James Short and F. Ivan Nye, did not find a direct relationship between social class and youth crime.[49] They found that socioeconomic class was related to official processing by police, courts, and correctional agencies, but not to the actual commission of crimes. In other words, while lower- and middle-class youths self-reported equal amounts of crime, the lower-class youths had a greater chance of getting arrested, convicted, and incarcerated and becoming official delinquents. In addition, factors generally associated with lower-class membership, such as broken homes, were found to be related to institutionalization, but not to admissions of delinquency. Other studies of this period reached similar conclusions.[50]

For more than 20 years after the use of self-reports became widespread, a majority of self-report studies concluded that a class–crime relationship did not exist: if the poor possessed more extensive criminal records than the wealthy, this difference was attributed to **differential law enforcement** and not to class-based behavior differences. That is, police may be more likely to arrest lower-class offenders and treat the affluent more leniently.

In their landmark 1978 study, Charles Tittle, Wayne Villemez, and Douglas Smith reviewed 35 studies containing 363 separate estimates concerning the relationship between class and crime.[51] They concluded that little if any support exists for the contention that crime is primarily a lower-class phenomenon. Consequently, Tittle and his associates argued that official statistics probably reflect class bias in processing lower-class offenders. The Tittle review is usually cited by criminologists as the strongest statement refuting the claim that the lower class is disproportionately criminal. In a subsequent article written with Robert Meier, Tittle once again reviewed existing data on the class–crime relationship and found little evidence of a consistent association between class and crime.[52]

Weighing Evidence for a Class–Crime Relationship Tittle's research has sparked significant debate. Many self-report instruments include trivial offenses such as using a false ID or drinking alcohol. Their inclusion may obscure the true class–crime relationship because affluent youths frequently engage in trivial offenses such as petty larceny, using drugs, and simple assault. Those who support a class–crime relationship suggest that if only serious felony offenses are considered, a significant association can be observed.[53] Studies showing middle- and lower-class youths to be equally delinquent rely on measures weighted toward minor crimes (for example, using a false ID or skipping school); when serious crimes, such as burglary and assault, are compared, lower-class youths are significantly more delinquent.[54]

The Class–Crime Controversy The relationship between class and crime is an important one for criminological theory. If crime is related to social class, then it follows that economic and social factors, such as poverty and neighborhood disorganization, cause criminal behavior.

CONNECTIONS

If class and crime are unrelated, then the causes of crime must be found in factors experienced by members of all social classes—psychological impairment, family conflict, peer pressure, school failure, and so on. Theories that view crime as a function of problems experienced by members of all social classes are reviewed in Chapter 8.

One reason that a true measure of the class–crime relationship has so far eluded criminologists is that the methods now employed to measure social class vary widely. So many different indicators are used that findings are ambiguous. For example, David Brownfield found that some widely used measures of social class, such as father's occupation and education, are only weakly related to self-reported crime, while others, such as unemployment or receiving welfare, are much stronger correlates of criminality.[55]

It is also possible that the association between class and crime is more complex than a simple linear relationship (the poorer you are, the more crime you commit). Age, race, and gender may all influence this connection.[56] For example, Sally Simpson and Lori Elis found that indigent white females are more likely to be offenders than indigent African-American females. They speculate that exclusion from paid labor creates resentment and criminality in those who expect better treatment than they are getting. White females have had their expectations raised by the women's movement; as a result, they envision greater occupational opportunities than do minority females, whose vision is tempered by the economic reality of joblessness in minority neighborhoods.[57] In light of these findings, it is not surprising that the true relationship between class and crime is difficult to determine. The effect may be obscured because its impact varies within and between groups.

Like so many other criminological controversies, the debate over the true relationship between class and crime will most likely persist. The weight of recent evidence seems to suggest that serious, official crime is more prevalent among the lower classes, whereas less serious and self-reported crime is spread more evenly throughout the social structure.[58] Income inequality, poverty, and resource deprivation are all associated with the most serious violent crimes, including homicide and assault.[59] Nonetheless, although crime rates may be higher in lower-class areas, poverty alone cannot explain why a particular individual becomes a chronic violent criminal; if it could, the crime problem would be much worse than it is now.[60]

Age and Crime

There is general agreement that age is inversely related to criminality. Criminologists Travis Hirschi and Michael Gottfredson state, "Age is everywhere correlated with crime. Its effects on crime do not depend on other demographic correlates of crime."[61] Regardless of economic status, marital status, race, sex, and so on, younger people commit crime more often than their older peers; research indicates this relationship has been stable across time periods ranging from 1935 to the present.[62] Official statistics tell us that young people are arrested at a disproportionate rate to their numbers in the population; victim surveys generate similar findings for crimes in which assailant age can be determined. Whereas youths aged 13 to 17 collectively make up about 6 percent of the total U.S. population, they account for about 30 percent of index crime arrests and 18 percent of arrests for all crimes. As a general rule, the peak age for property crime is believed to be 16, and for violence, 18 (see Figure 3.9). In contrast, adults 45 and over, who make up 32 percent of the population, account for only 8 percent of index crime arrests. The elderly are particularly resistant to the temptations of crime; they make up more than 12 percent of the population and less than 1 percent of arrests. Elderly males 65 and over are predominantly arrested for alcohol-related matters (public drunkenness and drunk driving) and elderly females for larceny (shoplifting). The elderly crime rate has remained stable for the past 20 years.[63]

Age and Crime I: Age Does Not Matter The relationship between age and crime is important because many criminological theories fail to adequately explain why the crime rate drops with age, which is referred to as **aging out** or **the desistance phenomenon.** This theoretical failure has been the subject of considerable academic debate. One position, championed by respected criminologists Travis Hirschi and Michael Gottfredson, is that the relationship between age and crime is con-

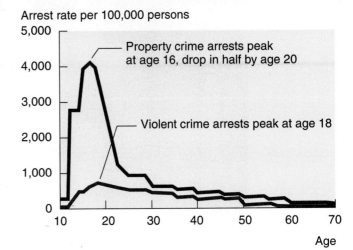

Figure 3.9 The Relationship Between Age and Serious Crime Arrests

Arrest rate per 100,000 persons

Property crime arrests peak at age 16, drop in half by age 20

Violent crime arrests peak at age 18

Source: FBI, Uniform Crime Report, 1997, p. 245.

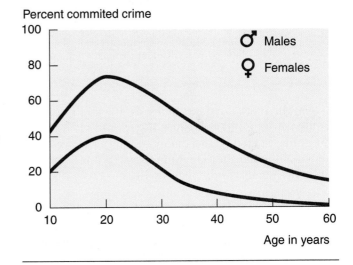

Figure 3.10 Age, Gender, and Crime

Percent commited crime

♂ Males
♀ Females

Age in years

stant, and therefore age is actually irrelevant to the study of crime. Because all people, regardless of their demographic characteristics (race, gender, class, family structure, domicile, work status, and so on), commit less crime as they age, it is not important to consider age as a factor in explaining crime.[64] Even hard-core chronic offenders will commit less crime as they age.[65] Hirschi and Gottfredson find that differences in offense rates for groups (for example, between males and females or between rich and poor) that exist at any point in their respective life cycles will be maintained throughout their lives. As Figure 3.10 illustrates, if

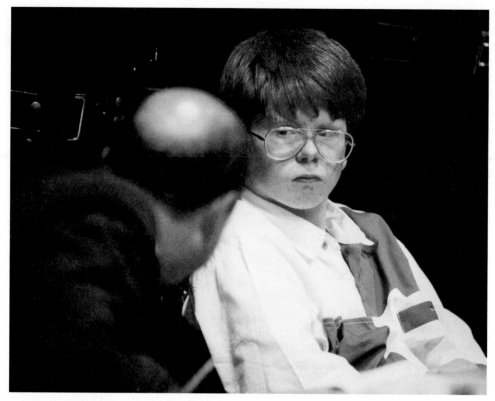

While youths aged 13 to 17, collectively, make up about 6 percent of the total U.S. population, they account for about 30 percent of the index crime arrests and 18 percent of the arrests for all crimes. There have been many shocking cases of very young children who commit violent crimes. Here Eric Smith, aged 14, is seen in court where in 1994 he was found guilty of murdering a preschooler. Smith's lawyer argued unsuccessfully that Smith suffers from a disorder that makes him prone to uncontrollable rage.

15-year-old boys are four times as likely to commit crime as 15-year-old girls, then 50-year-old men will be four times as likely to commit crime as 50-year-old women, although the actual number of crimes committed by both males and females will constantly decline.

CONNECTIONS

Hirschi and Gottfredson have used their views on the age–crime relationship as a basis for their General Theory of Crime. This important theory holds that the factors that produce crime change little after birth and that the association between crime and age is constant. For more on this view, see the sections on the General Theory of Crime in Chapter 10.

Age and Crime II: Age Matters   Those who oppose the Hirschi and Gottfredson view of the age–crime relationship suggest that personal factors (like gender and race) and social factors (like lifestyle, economic situation, and peer relations) significantly impact the age–crime relationship.[66] There are a number of reasons why criminal behavior is not constant. Evolving patterns or cycles of criminal behavior may be keyed to personal characteristics and lifestyle, including gender, race, and class.[67] For example, gender seems to influence the age–crime association; male–female crime ratio differences appear to decline with age.[68] The female homicide rate peaks at age 20 and then continues at a stable but low rate through adulthood; in contrast, the male homicide rate is much higher but begins to drop after age 30.[69]

The likelihood of a long-term criminal career may be determined by the age at which offenses start.[70] People who commit crimes at a very early age (**early onset**) and who establish official criminal records are most likely to become chronic offenders.[71] These "early starters" may accumulate delinquent friends who support their deviant behavior and encourage the continuity of criminal behaviors.[72] Stigma may also play a role. Research shows that preschoolers who are labeled as "troublesome" or "difficult" by their parents are the most likely to become persistent offenders through adolescence,[73] and their criminal behavior is resistant to aging out.

Desistance, or termination of criminal behavior, may also be influenced by criminal specialization; crime types may peak at different ages and follow different trajectories. Crimes that provide significant economic gain, such as gambling, embezzlement, and fraud, are less likely to decline with maturity than high-risk, low-profit offenses such as assault.[74] People who frequently use cocaine and heroin continue to commit criminal acts 10 years or more past the age when non-addicts have terminated their criminal activity.[75]

Two Classes of Criminals?   The population, then, may contain different sets of criminal offenders:

- One or more groups whose criminality declines with age
- Another whose criminal behavior remains constant through maturity[76]

The age–crime pattern may also change; a greater proportion of violent criminal behavior is concentrated among youthful offenders than it was 40 years ago (although the youth violence rate has declined along with the adult rate since 1995).

In sum, whereas some criminologists view the relationship between crime and age as constant, others believe that it varies according to offense and offender. This difference has important implications for criminological research and theory. If age is a constant, then the criminality of any group can be accurately measured at any single point in time. If, on the other hand, the relationship between age and crime varies, it would be necessary to conduct longitudinal studies that follow criminals over their life cycle to fully understand how their age influences their crime patterns.[77] Crime would then be seen as a type of social event that takes on different meanings at different times in a person's life.[78]

Disagreements over this critical issue have produced some of the most spirited debates in recent criminological literature.[79] Right now researchers are examining this issue in the United States, in Sweden, and in Britain. Early results from the Scandinavian study find many general similarities with U.S. research.[80] Clearly more research is required on this important topic.

Why Does Aging Out Occur?   Despite the debate raging over the relationship between age and crime, there is little question that the overall crime rate declines with age. Why does this phenomenon take place? One view is that there is a direct relationship between aging and desistance. Psychologists note that young people, especially the indigent and antisocial, tend to discount the future.[81] They are impatient, and because their future is uncertain, they are unwilling or unable to delay gratification. As they mature, troubled youths are able to develop a long-term life view and resist the need for immediate gratification.[82] Gordon Trasler found that kids view teenage crime as fun. Youths view their petty but risky and exciting crimes as a social activity that provides adventure in an otherwise boring and unsympathetic world. As they grow older, Trasler finds, their life patterns are inconsistent with criminality; delinquents literally grow out of crime.[83]

James Q. Wilson and Richard Herrnstein argue that aging out is a function of the natural history of the human life cycle.[84] Deviance in adolescence is fueled by the need for conventionally unobtainable money and sex and reinforced by close relationships with peers who defy conventional morality. At the same time, teenagers are becoming independent from parents and other adults who enforce conventional standards. They have a new sense of energy and strength and are involved with peers who are similarly vigorous and frustrated.

Adults, on the other hand, develop the ability to delay gratification and forgo the immediate gains that law violations bring. They also start wanting to take responsibility for their behavior and to adhere to conventional mores, such as establishing long-term relationships and starting a family.[85]

Aging out of crime may also be influenced by the success or failure of interpersonal relationships. Children who are labeled antisocial by teachers, police, parents, and neighbors find they may then have little choice but to remain committed to their criminal careers.[86] If, however, youngsters believe that they have little chance of achieving success, money, and happiness through crimes, they are more likely to desist.[87] As they mature, people may be influenced by their adult relationships. For example, people who maintain successful marriages are more likely to desist from antisocial behaviors than those whose marriages fail.[88]

CONNECTIONS

A discussion of how life events influence behavioral choices is presented in more depth in Chapter 10.

Although most people age out of crime, some may find a criminal career a reasonable alternative. Yet even people who actively remain in a criminal career will eventually slow down as they age. Crime is too dangerous, physically taxing, and unrewarding (and punishments too harsh and long-lasting) to become a long-term way of life for most people. The uniformity of maturational change in the crime rate suggests that it must be part of a biological "evolutionary process."[89] By middle age even the most chronic offenders terminate criminal behavior.

Gender and Crime

The three data-gathering criminal statistics tools support the theory that male crime rates are much higher than those of females. Victims report that their assailant was male in more than 80 percent of all violent personal crimes. The Uniform Crime Report arrest statistics indicate that the overall male–female arrest ratio is

Rates for female violence are rising faster than rates for males. One reason may be that ever-increasing numbers of young girls are joining gangs. Here one gang member attacks another on the streets of Los Angeles.

about 3.5 male offenders to 1 female offender; for serious violent crimes, the ratio is closer to 5 males to 1 female. Recent self-report data collected by the Institute for Social Research at the University of Michigan also show that males commit more serious crimes, such as robbery, assault, and burglary, than females. However, although the patterns in self-reports parallel official data, the ratios seem smaller. In other words, males self-report more criminal behavior than females, but not to the degree suggested by official data.

Explaining Gender Differences: Physical Ramifications
Early criminologists pointed to emotional, physical, and psychological differences between males and females to explain the differences in crime rates. Their views maintained that because females were weaker and more passive, they were less likely to commit crimes. The most widely cited evidence was contained in Cesare Lombroso's 1895 book, *The Female Offender*.[90] Lombroso argued that a small group of female criminals lacked "typical" female traits of "piety, maternity, undeveloped intelligence, and weakness."[91] In physical appearance as well as in their emotional makeup, delinquent females appeared closer to men than to other women. Lombroso's theory became known as the **masculinity hypothesis**; in essence, a few "masculine" females were responsible for the handful of crimes women commit.

Another early view of female crime focused on the supposed dynamics of sexual relationships. Female criminals were viewed as either sexually controlling or sexually naive, either manipulating men for profit or being manipulated by them. The female's criminality was often masked because criminal justice authorities were reluctant to take action against a woman.[92] This perspective is described in the **chivalry hypothesis**, which holds that much female criminality is hidden because of our culture's generally protective and benevolent attitudes toward women.[93] In other words, police are less likely to arrest, juries are less likely to convict, and judges are less likely to incarcerate female offenders.

Although these early writings are no longer taken seriously, some criminologists still consider trait differences a key determinant of crime rate differences. For example, some criminologists link antisocial behavior to hormonal influences by arguing that male sex hormones (**androgens**) account for more aggressive male behavior and that gender-related hormonal differences can also explain the gender gap in the crime rate.[94]

CONNECTIONS

Gender differences in the crime rate may be a function of androgen levels because these hormones cause areas of the brain to become less sensitive to environmental stimuli, making males more likely to seek high levels of stimulation and to tolerate more pain in the process. Chapter 6 discusses the biosocial causes of crime and reviews this issue in greater detail.

Explaining Gender Differences: Socialization By mid-century criminologists commonly portrayed gender differences in the crime rate as a function of socialization. Textbooks explained the relatively low female crime rate by citing the fact that in contrast to boys, girls were supervised more closely and protected from competition.[95] The few female criminals were described as troubled individuals, alienated at home, who pursued crime as a means of compensating for their disrupted personal lives.[96] The streets became a "second home" to girls whose physical and emotional adjustment was hampered by a strained home life marked by such conditions as absent fathers, overly competitive mothers, and so on.

Some experts continue to explain gender-based crime differences as a function of socialization. Most girls, they argue, are socialized to be less aggressive than boys and are supervised more closely by parents.[97] Females usually learn to respond to provocation by feeling anxious and depressed, whereas boys are encouraged to retaliate with aggression.[98] Although females get angry as often as males, many have been taught to blame themselves for harboring such negative feelings. Females are therefore much more likely than males to respond to anger with feelings of depression, anxiety, fear, and shame. Whereas females are socialized to fear that their anger will harm valued relationships, males react with "moral outrage" and look to blame others for their discomfort.[99] Overall, women are much more likely to feel distressed than men, experiencing sadness, anxiety, and uneasiness.[100] The relatively few females who commit violent crimes report having home and family relationships that are more troubled than those experienced by male delinquents.[101]

Explaining Gender Differences: Feminist Views In the 1970s several influential works, most notably Freda Adler's *Sisters in Crime*[102] and Rita James Simon's *The Contemporary Woman and Crime,*[103] revolutionized the thinking on the cause of gender differences in the crime rate. Their research, which today is referred to as **liberal feminist theory,** focused attention on the social and economic role of women in society and its relationship to female crime rates. Both Adler and Simon believed that the traditionally lower crime rate for women could be explained by their "second-class" economic and social position. They further contended that as women's social roles changed and their lifestyles became more like those of males, their crime rates would converge.

Criminologists, responding to this research, began to refer to the "new female criminal." The rapid increase in the female crime rate during the 1960s and 1970s, especially in what had traditionally been male-oriented crimes (like burglary and larceny), supported the convergence model presented by Adler and Simon. In addition, self-report studies seem to indicate that

(1) the pattern of female criminality, if not its frequency, is quite similar to that of male criminality; and (2) the factors that predispose male criminals to crime have an equal impact on female criminals.[104] The contributions of Adler and Simon encouraged other criminologists to assess the association between economic issues, gender roles, and criminality.

CONNECTIONS

Critical criminologists view gender inequality as stemming from the unequal power of men and women in a capitalist society and the exploitation of females by fathers and husbands. This perspective, along with radical feminism, is considered more fully in Chapter 9.

Is Convergence Likely? Will the gender differences in the crime rate eventually dissolve? Some criminologists, most notably Darrell Steffensmeier, find that gender-based crime rate differences remain significant and argue that the emancipation of women has had relatively little influence on female crime rates.[105] He disputes that increases in the female arrest rate reflect economic or social change brought about by the women's movement. For one thing, many female criminals come from the socioeconomic class least affected by the women's movement; their crimes seem more a function of economic inequality than women's rights. For another, the offense patterns of women are still quite different from those of men, who still commit a disproportionate share of serious crimes like robbery, burglary, murder, and assault.[106] Steffensmeier and his associates have conducted research in the United States and abroad that fails to find an association between economic development and female crime rates.[107] There is little evidence that nations undergoing economic development also experience increases in the female violence rate.[108]

Perhaps it is too soon for criminologists to write off "the new female criminal." Although male arrest rates are still considerably higher than female rates, female arrest rates seem to be increasing at a faster pace. For example, between 1988 and 1997, male arrests increased 11 percent while female arrests increased almost 40 percent. And more recently, between 1993 and 1997, total male arrests increased 6 percent while female arrests increased almost 19 percent. Importantly, the increase in the arrests of teenage girls between 1993 and 1997 (25 percent) was double the increase in male teenage arrests (11 percent), a finding suggesting that young females are increasing their offense rates at a pace even greater than their older sisters.[109]

It is possible, as Roy Austin claims, that convergence has been delayed by a slower-than-expected change in gender roles; the women's movement has not yet achieved its full impact on social life.[110] One reason is that while expanding their economic role, women have not abandoned their conventional role as family caretaker and home provider; women today are forced to cope with added financial and social burdens. If gender roles were truly equivalent, then crime rates might eventually converge; these changes are still evolving.

Race and Crime

Official crime data indicate that minority group members are involved in a disproportionate share of criminal activity. According to UCR reports, African-Americans make up about 12 percent of the general population, yet they account for about 41 percent of Part I violent crime arrests and 32 percent of property crime arrests. They also are responsible for a disproportionate number of Part II arrests (except for alcohol-related arrests, which detain primarily white offenders).

Self-Report Differences   Another approach to examining this issue is to compare the racial differences in self-report data with those found in official delinquency records. Charges of racial discrimination in the arrest process would be supported if racial differences in self-report data were insignificant. That is, police bias would be suspected if whites and blacks self-reported equal numbers of crimes but minorities were arrested far more often.

Early efforts by noted criminologists Leroy Gould in Seattle, Harwin Voss in Honolulu, and Ronald Akers in seven midwestern states found virtually no relationship between race and self-reported delinquency.[111] These research efforts supported a case for police bias in the arrest decision. Other, more recent self-report studies that use large national samples of youths have also found little evidence of racial disparity in crimes committed. For example, one effort conducted by the Institute for Social Research at the University of Michigan found that if anything, black youths self-report less delinquent behavior and substance abuse than whites.[112] Another nationwide study of youth, conducted by social scientists at the Behavioral Science Institute at Boulder, Colorado, found few interracial differences in crime rates, although black youths were much more likely to be arrested and taken into custody.[113]

These and other self-report studies seem to indicate that the delinquent behavior rates of black and white teenagers are generally similar and that differences in arrest statistics may indicate a differential selection policy by police.[114]

Causes of Racial Disparity   Racial differences in the crime rate remain an extremely sensitive issue. Although official arrest records indicate that African-Americans are arrested at a higher rate than members of other racial groups, some question whether this is a function of crime rate differences, racism by police, or faulty data collection.[115] Research shows that suspects who are poor, minority males are more likely to be formally arrested than suspects who are white, affluent females.[116]

The UCR may reflect discriminatory police practices; however, African-Americans are arrested for a disproportionate amount of violent crime, such as robbery and murder, and it is improbable that police discretion alone could account for these proportions. It is doubtful that police routinely ignore white killers, robbers, and rapists while arresting violent black offenders.

Today many criminologists concede that recorded differences in the black and white violent crime arrest rates cannot be explained away solely by racism or differential treatment within the criminal justice system.[117] To do so would be to ignore the social problems that exist in the nation's inner cities.

How then can racial patterns be explained? Most focus on the impact of economic deprivation, social disorganization, subcultural adaptations, and the legacy of racism and discrimination on personality and behavior.[118] The fact that U.S. culture influences African-American crime rates is underscored by the fact that black violence rates are much lower in other nations—both those that are predominantly white, such as Canada, and those that are predominantly black, such as Nigeria.[119]

One approach has been to trace the black experience in the United States. Some criminologists view black crime as a function of socialization in a society where the black family was torn apart and black culture destroyed in such a way that recovery has proven impossible. Early experiences, beginning with slavery, have left a wound that has been deepened by racism and lack of opportunity.[120] Children of the slave society were thrust into a system of forced dependency and ambivalence and antagonism toward one's self and group. Years of segregation amplified negative self-images, anger, and rage. Neighborhoods and communities of adequately functioning families were then overwhelmed by the most troubled individuals and families.[121]

In his influential book *Criminal Violence, Criminal Justice*, Charles Silberman describes the problem as a function of the black experience in this country—"an experience that differs from that of other ethnic groups."[122] Silberman's provocative argument is that black citizens have learned to be violent because of their treatment in U.S. society. First they were violently uprooted from their African homelands. Then their slavery was maintained by violence. After emancipation, their lower-class position was enforced by violent means, such as intimidation by the Ku Klux Klan. To strike back meant harsh retaliation by the white-controlled law.

In another important work, *All God's Children: The Bosket Family and the American Tradition of Violence,* crime reporter Fox Butterfield chronicles the history of the Boskets, a black family, through five generations.[123] He focuses on Willie Bosket, who is charming, captivating, and brilliant. He is also one of the worst criminals in the New York State penal system. By the time he was in his teens, he had committed over 200 armed robberies and 25 stabbings. Butterfield shows how early struggles in the South, with its violent slave culture, led directly to Willie Bosket's rage and violence on the streets of New York City. Beginning in South Carolina in the 1700s, the Southern slave society was a place where white notions of honor demanded immediate retaliation for the smallest slight. According to Butterfield, contemporary black violence is a tradition inherited from white southern violence. The need for respect has turned into a cultural mandate that can provoke retaliation if even a slight insult is sensed.

To survive and reach cultural and personal fulfillment, African-Americans have developed a set of norms, values, and traditions. In the 1960s many blacks began to adopt the image, first developed in southern folklore and myth, of being "bad" in their personal lives. "After 350 years of fearing whites," Silberman writes, "black Americans have discovered that the fear runs the other way, that whites are intimidated by their very presence; it would be hard to overestimate what an extraordinarily liberating force this discovery is.... 350 years of festering hatred has come spilling out."[124]

> **CONNECTIONS**
>
> According to some criminologists, racism has created isolated subcultures that espouse violence as a way of coping with conflict situations. Exasperation and frustration among minority group members who feel powerless to fit within middle-class society are manifested in aggression. This view is discussed further in Chapter 11's review of the subculture of violence theory.

Economic Disparity Racial differentials in crime rates may also be tied to economic disparity. African-Americans typically have higher unemployment rates and lower incomes than whites. Even during times of economic growth, lower-class African-Americans are left out of the economic mainstream, a fact that meets with a growing sense of frustration and failure.[125] As a result of being shut out of educational and economic opportunities enjoyed by the rest of society, this population may be prone, some believe, to the lure of illegitimate gain and criminality. Young African-American males in the inner city often are resigned to a lifetime of little if any social and economic opportunity. Even when economic data say they are doing better, news accounts of "protests, riots, and acts of civil disobedience" tell them otherwise.[126] African-Americans living in lower-class slums may be disproportionately violent because they are exposed to more violence in their daily lives

than other racial and economic groups. This exposure is a significant risk factor for violent behavior.[127]

Family Dissolution Family dissolution in the minority community is tied to low employment rates among African-American males, which places a strain on marriages. The relatively large number of single female–headed households in these communities may be tied to the high mortality rate among African-American males due in part to their increased risk of early death by disease and violence.[128] When families are weakened or disrupted, their social control is compromised. It is not surprising, then, that divorce and separation rates are significantly associated with homicide rates in the African-American community.[129]

Is Convergence Possible? Considering these overwhelming social problems, is it possible that racial crime rates will soon converge? One argument is that if economic conditions improve in the minority community, then differences in crime rates will eventually disappear.[130] A trend toward residential integration, under way since 1980, may also help reduce crime rate differentials.[131] Despite economic disparity, there are actually few racial differences in attitudes toward crime and justice today. Convergence in crime rates will occur if economic and social obstacles can be removed.

> **CONNECTIONS**
>
> The concept of *relative deprivation* refers to the fact that people compare their success to those with whom they are in immediate contact. Even if conditions improve, they still may feel as if they are falling behind. A sense of relative deprivation, discussed in Chapter 7, may lead to criminal activity.

In sum, the weight of the evidence shows that although there is little difference in the self-reported crime rates of racial groups, African-Americans are more likely to be arrested for serious violent crimes. The causes of minority crime have been linked to poverty, racism, hopelessness, lack of opportunity, and urban problems experienced by all too many African-American citizens.

CRIMINAL CAREERS

Crime data show that most offenders commit a single criminal act, and upon arrest, discontinue their antisocial activity. Others commit a few less serious crimes. A small group of criminal offenders, however, accounts for a majority of all criminal offenses. These persistent offenders are referred to as **career criminals** or **chronic offenders.**

Delinquency in a Birth Cohort

The concept of the chronic or career offender is most closely associated with the research efforts of Marvin Wolfgang, Robert Figlio, and Thorsten Sellin.[132] In their landmark 1972 study, *Delinquency in a Birth Cohort,* Wolfgang, Figlio, and Sellin used official records to follow the criminal careers of a cohort of 9,945 boys born in Philadelphia in 1945 from the time of their birth until they reached 18 years of age in 1963. Official police records were used to identify delinquents. About one-third of the boys (3,475) had some police contact. The remaining two-thirds (6,470) had none. Each delinquent's actions were given a seriousness weight score for every delinquent act.[133] The weighting of delinquent acts allowed the researchers to differentiate, for example, between a simple assault requiring no medical attention for the victim and serious battery in which the victim needed hospitalization. The most well-known discovery of Wolfgang and his associates was that of the so-called chronic offender. The cohort data indicated that 54 percent (1,862) of the sample's delinquent youths were repeat offenders, whereas the remaining 46 percent (1,613) were one-time offenders. However, the repeaters could be further categorized as **nonchronic recidivists** and **chronic recidivists.** The former consisted of 1,235 youths who had been arrested more than once but fewer than five times and who made up 35.6 percent of all delinquents. The latter were a group of 627 boys arrested five times or more, who accounted for 18 percent of the delinquents and 6 percent of the total sample of 9,945.

The chronic offenders (known today as "the chronic 6 percent") were involved in the most dramatic amounts of delinquent behavior: they were responsible for 5,305 offenses, or 51.9 percent of all the offenses committed by the cohort. Even more striking was the involvement of chronic offenders in serious criminal acts. Of the entire sample, they committed 71 percent of the homicides, 73 percent of the rapes, 82 percent of the robberies, and 69 percent of the aggravated assaults.

Wolfgang and his associates found that arrests and court experience did little to deter the chronic offender. In fact, punishment was *inversely* related to chronic offending: the more stringent the sanction chronic offenders received, the more likely they would be to engage in repeated criminal behavior.

Birth Cohort

The subjects who made up Wolfgang's original birth cohort were born in 1945. Wolfgang and his associates selected a new, larger birth cohort, born in Philadelphia in 1958, and followed them until their maturity.[134] The 1958 cohort was larger than the original, having more than 27,000 subjects, including 13,000 males and 14,000 females.

Although the proportion of delinquent youths was about the same as that in the 1945 cohort, those in the larger sample were involved in 20,089 delinquent arrests. Chronic offenders (five or more arrests as juveniles) made up 7.5 percent of the 1958 sample (compared with 6.3 percent in 1945) and 23 percent of all delinquent offenders (compared with 18 percent in 1945). Chronic female delinquency was relatively rare—only 1 percent of the females in the survey were chronic offenders.

Chronic male delinquents continued to commit more than their share of criminal behavior. They accounted for 61 percent of the total offenses and a disproportionate amount of the most serious crimes: 61 percent of the homicides, 76 percent of the rapes, 73 percent of the robberies, and 65 percent of the aggravated assaults. The chronic female offenders were less likely to be involved in serious crimes.

As a group, the 1958 cohort was involved in significantly more serious crimes than the 1945 group. For example, their violent offense rate (149 per 1,000 in the sample) was three times higher than the rate for the 1945 cohort (47 per 1,000 subjects).

The 1945 cohort study determined that chronic offenders dominate the total crime rate and continue their law-violating careers as adults. The second cohort study showed that the chronic offender syndrome could be found in a group of subjects born 13 years after the original cohort sample, and these offenders were even more violent than their older siblings. Finally, the efforts of the justice system seem to have little preventive effect on the behavior of chronic offenders: the more often a person was arrested, the more likely he or she was to be arrested again. For males, 26 percent of the entire group had one violent-offense arrest; of that 26 percent, 34 percent went on to commit a second violent offense, while 43 percent of the three-time offenders went on to a fourth arrest, and so on.

Wolfgang's pioneering effort to identify the chronic career offender has been replicated by a number of other researchers in a variety of locations in the United States.[135] The chronic offender has also been found abroad.[136] The accompanying Race, Culture, Gender, and Criminology feature discusses this issue.

Stability in Crime: From Delinquent to Criminal

Are persistent juvenile offenders likely to continue their criminal careers into adulthood? One study followed a 10 percent sample of the original Pennsylvania cohort (974 subjects) through their adulthood to age 30.[137] Seventy percent of the persistent adult offenders had also been chronic juvenile offenders; they had an 80 percent chance of becoming adult offenders and a 50 percent chance of being arrested four or more times as

Criminal Careers in Europe

While developmental research has been ongoing in the United States, there also have been European efforts to corroborate cohort findings. The Stockholm cohort project (Project Metropolitan) contains 15,117 male and female subjects. Recent analysis of data from this project indicates that criminal career development in Sweden follows many of the same patterns found in U.S. cohorts.

In an important analysis, David Farrington and Rolf Loeber compared samples of boys born in London, England, and Pittsburgh, Pennsylvania, on both their offense patterns and their personal characteristics. The London sample consisted of 411 London boys, most of whom were born in 1953, who were part of a long-term longitudinal study known as the Cambridge Study in Delinquent Development. The study used self-report data as well as in-depth interviews and psychological testing. The boys were interviewed eight times over a period of 24 years, beginning at age 8 and continuing to age 32. The 1,517 Pittsburgh youths were also part of a study that measured children over a long period of time, beginning in 1987, to determine the factors that predict the onset of delinquency.

These researchers found that several factors predicted delinquency in both the U.S. and British samples. The most important were such personal/developmental traits as hyperactivity, impulsivity, and poor concentration ability. A number of family-related factors also seemed to impact later delinquent behavior. In both samples, boys who had antisocial parents, whose mother was relatively young when she gave birth to them, who lived in large and indigent families, and whose parents had either divorced or separated, were the ones most likely to enter a delinquent way of life. Doing poorly in school also was associated with delinquency.

There were also some important differences in the factors that influenced delinquency between the boys in the two samples. In London, if a youth experienced harsh physical punishment from his mother, or if he spent his leisure time outside the home, then he was more prone to delinquency. Youths living in poor housing and having a parent who was convicted of crime also were more likely to get involved in delinquency. However, these factors had less effect on the Pittsburgh youth. In contrast, boys in Pittsburgh were more strongly influenced by their socioeconomic class and family structure than the London boys.

It is not clear why differences exist. Variation in the way data was collected and the variables measured might help explain some of the differences. Also, boys living in different cultures may be affected by social and environmental conditions somewhat differently.

Despite the differences found, these two cross-cultural studies show that the personal and social factors that produce criminal careers are similar in samples of boys taken from two different countries. The data indicate that criminal careers have multiple sources ranging from personality to the environment. Child-rearing and parenting practices also played a role in the boys' behavior in both samples. The findings support the further development of complex, integrated theories of criminal behavior.

CRITICAL THINKING

1. Does the fact that chronic offenders exist in both the United States and Europe indicate that this serious crime problem is not unique to American culture?
2. Chronic offenders in both locations seemed to share abnormal personality traits such as impulsivity; they also lived in dysfunctional families. Does this mean the locus of serious crime can be found in the individual and not in the environment?

 INFOTRAC COLLEGE EDITION RESEARCH

How are European nations dealing with delinquency? Can their techniques be applied to the United States? To research this topic, see: Peggy L. Chown, John H Parham. Can we talk? Mediation in juvenile cases. *The FBI Law Enforcement Bulletin* Nov. 1995 v64, n11, pg 21(5)

Source: David Farrington and Rolf Loeber, "Transatlantic Replicability of Risk Factors in the Development of Delinquency," in Patricia Cohen, Cheryl Slomkowski, and Lee Robins (eds.), *Where and When: The Influence of History and Geography on Aspects of Psychopathology* (Mahwah, N.J.: Lawrence Erlbaum, 1998); Per-Olof Wikstrom, "Age and Crime in a Stockholm Cohort," *Journal of Quantitative Criminology* 6 (1990): 61–82.

adults. In comparison, subjects with no juvenile arrests had only an 18 percent chance of being arrested as an adult. The chronic offenders also continued to engage in the most serious crimes. Although they accounted for only 15 percent of the follow-up sample, the former chronic delinquents were involved in 74 percent of all arrests and 82 percent of all serious crimes, such as homicide, rape, and robbery.

This stability of criminal careers was also detected by Paul Tracy and Kimberly Kempf-Leonard in their follow-up study of all subjects in the second 1958 cohort. By age 26, cohort II subjects were displaying the same behavior patterns as their older peers. Few delinquent offenders (about one-third) and even fewer nondelinquent offenders (10 percent) became adult criminals, a finding that supports desistance. Nonetheless,

The awareness of persistent chronic offenders has led agents of the criminal justice system to focus their attention on offenders whom they believe are likely to repeat their criminal activity. Here a local police officer is handing out information informing residents that a convicted sex offender is living in their neighborhood. Do efforts such as creating criminal history databases that can be accessed by the public or labeling people as potential threats to neighbors violate a person's right to privacy? Is it possible or fair to predict that someone will offend in the future just because they did so in the past?

delinquents with high juvenile offense rates, who started their delinquent careers early and who committed serious violent crimes throughout adolescence, were the most likely to persist as adults.[138]

Continuity of Crime　Research on criminal careers clearly shows that chronic juvenile offenders continue violating the law as adults, a concept referred to as the **continuity of crime.** Children who are found to be disruptive and antisocial as early as age 5 or 6 are the most likely to exhibit stable, long-term patterns of disruptive behavior through adolescence.[139] They have measurable behavior problems in areas such as learning and motor skills, cognitive abilities, family relations, and other areas of social, psychological, and physical functioning.[140] Youthful offenders who persist are more likely to abuse alcohol, get into trouble while in military service, become economically dependent, have lower aspirations, get divorced or separated, and have a weak employment record.[141] They do not specialize in one type of crime; rather, they engage in a variety of criminal acts, including theft, drugs, and violent offenses. Apprehension and punishment seem to have little effect on their offending behavior. A recent study followed the offending careers of nearly 2000 serious, chronic youthful offenders for 10 years after their release from the California Youth Authority. These

chronic delinquents were arrested on 24,615 occasions over the following decade, an average of 22 arrests each. More than 90 percent had been rearrested during the following decade, and their arrests were for an average of 9 property crimes, 4 violent offenses, 3 drug crimes, and 6 other type crimes.[142] This recent research suggests the axiom, "The best predictor of future behavior is past behavior."

Implications of the Chronic Offender Concept

The findings of the cohort studies and the discovery of the chronic offender have revitalized criminological theory. If relatively few offenders become chronic, persistent criminals, then perhaps they possess some individual trait that is responsible for their behavior. Most people exposed to troublesome social conditions, such as poverty, do not become chronic offenders, so it is unlikely that social conditions alone can cause chronic offending. Traditional theories of criminal behavior have failed to distinguish between chronic and occasional offenders. They concentrated more on explaining why people begin to commit crime and paid scant attention to why people stop offending. The discovery of the chronic offender 25 years ago forced criminologists to consider such issues as persistence and desistance in their explanations of crime; more recent theories account for not only the onset of criminality but also its termination.

The chronic offender concept also has raised questions about the treatment of known offenders. If we can identify chronic offenders, what should we do about them? How can chronic offenders be controlled if punishment only escalates the frequency of their criminal activity? The chronic offender has become a central focus of crime control policy. Concern about repeat offenders has been translated into programs at various stages of the justice process. For example, police departments and district attorneys' offices around the nation have set up programs to focus resources on capturing and prosecuting dangerous or repeat offenders.[143]

Even more important has been the effect of the chronic offender concept on sentencing policy. Around the country, legal jurisdictions are developing sentencing policies designed to incapacitate serious offenders for long periods of time without hope of probation or parole. Among the policies spurred by the chronic offender concept are mandatory sentences for violent or drug-related crimes in more than 30 states, commonly known as a **"three strikes and you're out" policy.** Three strikes policies require people convicted of a third felony offense to serve a mandatory life sentence. Whether such policies can reduce crime rates or are merely "get tough" measures designed to placate conservative voters still remains to be seen.

SUMMARY

There are three primary sources of crime statistics: the Uniform Crime Reports based on police data accumulated by the FBI, self-reports from criminal behavior surveys, and victim surveys. They tell us that there is quite a bit of crime in the United States, although the amount of violent crime is decreasing. Each data source has its strengths and weaknesses, and although quite different from one another, they actually agree on the nature of criminal behavior.

The data sources show stable patterns in the crime rate. Ecological patterns show that some areas of the country are more crime-prone than others, that there are seasons and times for crime, and that these patterns are quite stable. There is also evidence of gender and age gaps in the crime rate: men usually commit more crime than women, and young people commit more crime than the elderly. Crime data show that people commit less crime as they age, but the significance and cause of this pattern are still not completely understood.

Similarly, racial and class patterns appear in the crime rate. However, it is still unclear whether these are true differences or a function of discriminatory law enforcement.

One of the most important findings in the crime statistics is the existence of the chronic offender, a repeat criminal responsible for a significant amount of all law violations. Chronic offenders begin their careers early in life and, rather than aging out of crime, persist into adulthood. The discovery of the chronic offender has led to the study of developmental criminology—why people persist, desist, terminate, or escalate their deviant behavior.

 See the book-specific web site at www.cj.wadsworth.com for additional chapter links, discussions, and quizzes.

THINKING LIKE A CRIMINOLOGIST

The planning director for the State Department of Juvenile Justice has asked for your advice on how to reduce the threat of chronic offenders. Some of the more conservative members of her staff seem to believe that these kids need a strict dose of rough justice if they are to be turned away from a life of crime. They believe that juvenile delinquents who are punished harshly are less likely to recidivate than youths who receive lesser punishments, such as community corrections or probation. In addition, they believe that hard-core, violent offenders deserve to be punished; excessive concern for offenders and not their acts ignores the rights of victims and society in general.

The planning director is unsure whether such an approach can reduce the threat of chronic offending. Can tough punishment produce deviant identities that lock kids into a criminal way of life? She is concerned that a strategy stressing punishment will have relatively little impact on chronic offenders and, if anything, may cause escalation in serious criminal behaviors.

She has asked you for your professional advice. On the one hand, the system must be sensitive to the adverse effects of stigma and labeling. On the other hand, the need for control and deterrence must not be ignored. Is it possible to reconcile these two opposing views?

KEY TERMS

Uniform Crime Report (UCR)	cleared	*Monitoring the Future*
index crimes	National Incident-Based Reporting	polygraph
Part I crimes	System (NIBRS)	National Crime Victimization Survey
Part II crimes	self-report survey	(NCVS)

multistage sampling technique
Brady Bill
Bartley-Fox law
instrumental crime
expressive crime
differential law enforcement
aging out

the desistance phenomenon
early onset
desistance
masculinity hypothesis
chivalry hypothesis
androgens
liberal feminist theory

career criminal
chronic offender
nonchronic recidivist
chronic recidivist
continuity of crime
"three strikes and you're out" policy

NOTES

1. Edward J. Blakely and Mary Gail Snyder, *Fortress America: Gated Communities in the United States* (Washington, D.C.: Brookings Institution Press, 1998).

2. Federal Bureau of Investigation, *Crime in the United States, 1997* (Washington, D.C.: U.S. Government Printing Office, 1998). Herein cited in notes as FBI, Uniform Crime Report, and referred to in text as Uniform Crime Report or UCR.

3. Craig Perkins and Patsy Klaus, *Criminal Victimization, 1994* (Washington, D.C.: Bureau of Justice Statistics, 1996). Hereinafter cited as NCVS, 1994.

4. Paul Tappan, *Crime, Justice and Corrections* (New York: McGraw-Hill, 1960).

5. Daniel Bell, *The End of Ideology* (New York: Free Press, 1967), p. 152.

6. Duncan Chappell, Gilbert Geis, Stephen Schafer, and Larry Siegel, "Forcible Rape: A Comparative Study of Offenses Known to the Police in Boston and Los Angeles," in *Studies in the Sociology of Sex*, ed. James Henslin (New York: Appleton Century Crofts, 1971), pp. 169–93.

7. Patrick Jackson, "Assessing the Validity of Official Data on Arson," *Criminology* 26 (1988): 181–95.

8. Lawrence Sherman and Barry Glick, "The Quality of Arrest Statistics," *Police Foundation Reports* 2 (1984): 1–8.

9. David Seidman and Michael Couzens, "Getting the Crime Rate Down: Political Pressure and Crime Reporting," *Law and Society Review* 8 (1974): 457.

10. Robert Davis and Bruce Taylor, "A Proactive Response to Family Violence: The Results of a Randomized Experiment," *Criminology* 35 (1997): 307–33.

11. Robert O'Brien, "Police Productivity and Crime Rates: 1973–1992," *Criminology* 34 (1996): 183–207.

12. Leonard Savitz, "Official Statistics," in *Contemporary Criminology*, ed. Leonard Savitz and Norman Johnston (New York: John Wiley, 1982), pp. 3–15.

13. FBI, *UCR Handbook* (Washington, D.C.: U.S. Government Printing Office, 1998), p. 33.

14. Roger Hood and Richard Sparks, *Key Issues in Criminology* (New York: McGraw-Hill, 1970), p. 72.

15. A pioneering effort in self-report research is A. L. Porterfield, *Youth in Trouble* (Fort Worth, Tex.: Leo Potishman Foundation, 1946); for a review, see Robert Hardt and George Bodine, *Development of Self-Report Instruments in Delinquency Research: A Conference Report* (Syracuse, N.Y.: Syracuse University Youth Development Center, 1965). See also Fred Murphy, Mary Shirley, and Helen Witner, "The Incidence of Hidden Delinquency," *American Journal of Orthopsychology* 16 (1946): 686–96.

16. Franklyn Dunford and Delbert Elliott, "Identifying Career Criminals Using Self-Reported Data," *Journal of Research in Crime and Delinquency* 21 (1983): 57–86.

17. For example, the following studies have noted the great discrepancy between official statistics and self-report studies: Martin Gold, "Undetected Delinquent Behavior," *Journal of Research in Crime and Delinquency* 3 (1966): 27–46; James Short and F. Ivan Nye, "Extent of Undetected Delinquency, Tentative Conclusions," *Journal of Criminal Law, Criminology and Police Science* 49 (1958): 296–302; Michael Hindelang, "Causes of Delinquency: A Partial Replication and Extension," *Social Problems* 20 (1973): 471–87.

18. D. Wayne Osgood, Lloyd Johnston, Patrick O'Malley, and Jerald Bachman, "The Generality of Deviance in Late Adolescence and Early Adulthood," *American Sociological Review* 53 (1988): 81–93.

19. Lloyd Johnston, Patrick O'Malley, and Jerald Bachman, *Monitoring the Future, 1990* (Ann Arbor, Mich.: Institute for Social Research, 1991); Timothy Flanagan and Kathleen Maguire, *Sourcebook of Criminal Justice Statistics, 1989* (Washington, D.C.: U.S. Government Printing Office, 1990), pp. 290–91.

20. See, for example, Spencer Rathus and Larry Siegel, "Crime and Personality Revisited: Effects of MMPI Sets on Self-Report Studies," *Criminology* 18 (1980): 245–51; John Clark and Larry Tifft, "Polygraph and Interview Validation of Self-Reported Deviant Behavior," *American Sociological Review* 31 (1966): 516–23.

21. See, for example, Harwin Voss, "Ethnic Differences in Delinquency in Honolulu," *Journal of Criminal Law, Criminology and Police Science* 54 (1963): 322–27; Maynard Erickson and LaMar Empey, "Court Records, Undetected Delinquency and Decision Making," *Journal of Criminal Law, Criminology and Police Science* 54 (1963): 456–59; H. B. Gibson, Sylvia Morrison, and D. J. West, "The Confession of Known Offenses in Response to a Self-Reported Delinquency Schedule," *British Journal of Criminology* 10 (1970): 277–80; and John Blackmore, "The Relationship Between Self-Reported Delinquency and Official Convictions Amongst Adolescent Boys," *British Journal of Criminology* 14 (1974): 172–76.

22. David Farrington, Rolf Loeber, Magda Stouthamer-Loeber, Welmoet Van Kammen, and Laura Schmidt, "Self-Reported Delinquency and a Combined Delinquency Seriousness Scale Based on Boys, Mothers, and Teachers: Concurrent and Predictive Validity for African-Americans and Caucasians," *Criminology* 34 (1996): 501–25.

23. Clark and Tifft, "Polygraph and Interview Validation of Self-Reported Deviant Behavior."

24. Michael Hindelang, Travis Hirschi, and Joseph Weis, *Measuring Delinquency* (Beverly Hills: Sage, 1981).

25. Leonore Simon, "Validity and Reliability of Violent Juveniles: A Comparison of Juvenile Self-Reports with Adult Self-Reports Incarcerated in Adult Prisons." Paper presented at the American Society of Criminology meeting, Boston, Mass., November 1995, p. 26.

26. Stephen Cernkovich, Peggy Giordano, and Meredith Pugh, "Chronic Offenders: The Missing Cases in Self-Report Delinquency Research," *Journal of Criminal Law and Criminology* 76 (1985): 705–32.

27. Terence Thornberry, Beth Bjerregaard, and William Miles, "The Consequences of Respondent Attrition in Panel Studies: A Simulation Based on the Rochester Youth Development Study," *Journal of Quantitative Criminology* 9 (1993): 127–58.

28. Minu Mathur, Richard Dodder, and Harjit Sandhu, "Inmate Self-Report Data: A Study of Reliability," *Criminal Justice Review* 17 (1992): 258–67.

29. Eric Wish, Thomas Gray, and Eliot Levine, *Recent Drug Use in Female Juvenile Detainees: Estimates from Interviews, Urinalysis and Hair Analysis* (College Park, Md.: Center for Substance Abuse Research, 1996); Thomas Gray and Eric Wish, *Maryland Youth at Risk: A Study of Drug Use in Juvenile Detainees* (College Park, Md.: Center for Substance Abuse Research, 1993).

30. Eric Wish and Christina Polsenberg, "Arrestee Urine Tests and Self-Reports of Drug Use: Which Is More Related to Rearrest?" Paper presented at the annual meeting of the American Society of Criminology, Phoenix, Arizona, November 1993.

31. NCVS, 1992, p. 2.

32. L. Edward Wells and Joseph Rankin, "Juvenile Victimization: Convergent Validation of Alternative Measurements," *Journal of Research in Crime and Delinquency* 32 (1995): 287–307.

33. Alfred Blumstein, Jacqueline Cohen, and Richard Rosenfeld, "Trend and Deviation in Crime Rates: A Comparison of UCR and NCVS Data for Burglary and Robbery," *Criminology* 29 (1991): 237–48. See also Hindelang, Hirschi, and Weis, *Measuring Delinquency*.

34. For a critique, see Scott Menard, "Residual Gains, Reliability, and the UCR–NCVS Relationship: A Comment on Blumstein, Cohen and Rosenfield (1991)," *Criminology* 30 (1992): 105–15.

35. David McDowall and Colin Loftin, "Comparing the UCR and NCVS over Time," *Criminology* 30 (1992): 125–33.

36. Clarence Schrag, *Crime and Justice: American Style* (Washington, D.C.: U.S. Government Printing Office, 1971), p. 17.

37. D. Wayne Osgood, Patrick O'Malley, Jerald Bachman, and Lloyd Johnston, "Time Trends and Age Trends in Arrests and Self-Reported Illegal Behavior," *Criminology* 27 (1989): 389–417.

38. Darrell Steffensmeier and Miles Harer, "Did Crime Rise or Fall During the Reagan Presidency? The Effects of an 'Aging' U.S. Population on the Nation's Crime Rate," *Journal of Research in Crime and Delinquency* 28 (1991): 330–39.

39. James A. Fox, *Trends in Juvenile Violence: A Report to the United States Attorney General on Current and Future Rates of Juvenile Offending* (Boston, Mass.: Northeastern University, 1996).

40. Ellen Cohn, "The Effect of Weather and Temporal Variations on Calls for Police Service," *American Journal of Police* 15 (1996): 23–43.

41. R. A. Baron, "Aggression as a Function of Ambient Temperature and Prior Anger Arousal," *Journal of Personality and Social Psychology* 21 (1972): 183–89.

42. Ellen Cohn, "The Prediction of Police Calls for Service: The Influence of Weather and Temporal Variables on Rape and Domestic Violence," *Journal of Environmental Psychology* 13 (1993): 71–83.

43. Derral Cheatwood, "The Effects of Weather on Homicide," *Journal of Quantitative Criminology* 11 (1995): 51–70.

44. Ellen Cohn and James Rotton, "Assault as a Function of Time and Temperature: A Moderator-Variable Time-Series Analysis." Paper presented at the annual meeting of the American Society of Criminology, Chicago, Ill., November 1996, p. 23.

45. See generally Joseph Sheley and James Wright, *Gun Acquisition and Possession in Selected Juvenile Samples* (Washington, D.C.: National Institute of Justice, 1993).

46. Gary Kleck and Marc Gertz, "Armed Resistance to Crime: The Prevalence and Nature of Self-Defense with a Gun," *Journal of Criminal Law and Criminology* 86 (1995).

47. Robert Nash Parker, "Bringing 'Booze' Back In: The Relationship Between Alcohol and Homicide," *Journal of Research in Crime and Delinquency* 32 (1995): 3–38.

48. Victoria Brewer and M. Dwayne Smith, "Gender Inequality and Rates of Female Homicide Victimization Across U.S. Cities," *Journal of Research in Crime and Delinquency* 32 (1995): 175–190.

49. Short and Nye, "Extent of Undetected Delinquency."

50. Ivan Nye, James Short, and Virgil Olsen, "Socio-economic Status and Delinquent Behavior," *American Journal of Sociology* 63 (1958): 381–89; Robert Dentler and Lawrence Monroe, "Social Correlates of Early Adolescent Theft," *American Sociological Review* 63 (1961): 733–43. See also Terence Thornberry and Margaret Farnworth, "Social Correlates of Criminal Involvement: Further Evidence of the Relationship Between Social Status and Criminal Behavior," *American Sociological Review* 47 (1982): 505–18.

51. Charles Tittle, Wayne Villemez, and Douglas Smith, "The Myth of Social Class and Criminality: An Empirical Assessment of the Empirical Evidence," *American Sociological Review* 43 (1978): 643–56.

52. Charles Tittle and Robert Meier, "Specifying the SES/Delinquency Relationship," *Criminology* 28 (1990): 271–301.

53. Delbert Elliott and Suzanne Ageton, "Reconciling Race and Class Differences in Self-Reported and Official Estimates of Delinquency," *American Sociological Review* 45 (1980): 95–110.

54. See also Delbert Elliott and David Huizinga, "Social Class and Delinquent Behavior in a National Youth Panel: 1976–1980," *Criminology* 21 (1983): 149–77. For a similar view, see John Braithwaite, "The Myth of Social Class and Criminality Reconsidered," *American Sociological Review* 46 (1981): 35–58; Hindelang, Hirschi, and Weis, *Measuring Delinquency*, p. 196.

55. David Brownfield, "Social Class and Violent Behavior," *Criminology* 24 (1986): 421–39.

56. Douglas Smith and Laura Davidson, "Interfacing Indicators and Constructs in Criminological Research: A Note on the Comparability of Self-Report Violence Data for Race and Sex Groups," *Criminology* 24 (1986): 473–88.

57. Sally Simpson and Lori Elis, "Doing Gender: Sorting Out the Case and Crime Conundrum," *Criminology* 33 (1995): 47–81.

58. Judith Blau and Peter Blau, "The Cost of Inequality: Metropolitan Structure and Violent Crime," *American Sociological Review* 147 (1982): 114–29; Richard Block, "Community Environment and Violent Crime," *Criminology* 17 (1979): 46–57; Robert Sampson, "Structural Sources of Variation in Race-Age-Specific Rates of Offending Across Major U.S. Cities," *Criminology* 23 (1985): 647–73.

59. Chin-Chi Hsieh and M. D. Pugh, "Poverty, Income Inequality, and Violent Crime: A Meta-Analysis of Recent Aggregate Data Studies," *Criminal Justice Review* 18 (1993): 182–99.

60. Alan Lizotte, Terence Thornberry, Marvin Krohn, Deborah Chard-Wierschem, and David McDowall, "Neighborhood Context and Delinquency: A Longitudinal Analysis," in *Cross National Longitudinal Research on Human Development and Criminal Behavior*, ed. E. M. Weitekamp and H. J. Kerner (Stavernstr, Netherlands: Kluwer, 1994), pp. 217–27.

61. Travis Hirschi and Michael Gottfredson, "Age and the Explanation of Crime," *American Journal of Sociology* 89 (1983): 552–84, at 581.

62. Darrell Steffensmeier and Cathy Streifel, "Age, Gender, and Crime Across Three Historical Periods: 1935, 1960 and 1985," *Social Forces* 69 (1991): 869–94.

63. For a comprehensive review of crime and the elderly, see Kyle Kercher, "Causes and Correlates of Crime Committed by the Elderly," in *Critical Issues in Aging Policy*, ed. E. Borgatta and R. Montgomery (Beverly Hills: Sage, 1987), pp. 254–306; Darrell Steffensmeier, "The Invention of the 'New' Senior Citizen Criminal," *Research on Aging* 9 (1987): 281–311.

64. Hirschi and Gottfredson, "Age and the Explanation of Crime."

65. Michael Gottfredson and Travis Hirschi, "The True Value of Lambda Would Appear to Be Zero: An Essay on Career Criminals, Criminal Careers, Selective Incapacitation, Cohort Studies and Related Topics," *Criminology* 24 (1986): 213–34; further support for their position can be found in Lawrence Cohen and Kenneth Land, "Age Structure and Crime," *American Sociological Review* 52 (1987): 170–83.

66. Kyle Kercher, "Explaining the Relationship Between Age and Crime: The Biological Versus Sociological Model." Paper presented at the American Society of Criminology meeting, Montreal, Canada, November 1987.

67. Alfred Blumstein, Jacqueline Cohen, and David Farrington, "Criminal Career Research: Its Value for Criminology," *Criminology* 26 (1988): 1–37.

68. Sung Joon Jang and Marvin Krohn, "Developmental Patterns of Sex Differences in Delinquency Among African American Adolescents: A Test of the Sex-Invariance Hypothesis," *Journal of Quantitative Criminology* 11 (1995): 195–220.

69. Candace Kruttschnitt, "Violence by and Against Women: A Comparative and Cross-National Analysis," *Violence and Victims* 8 (1994): 1–28.

70. David Greenberg, "Age, Crime, and Social Explanation," *American Journal of Sociology* 91 (1985): 1–21.

71. Marvin Wolfgang, Robert Figlio, and Thorsten Sellin, *Delinquency in a Birth Cohort* (Chicago: University of Chicago Press, 1972); Lyle Shannon, *Assessing the Relationship of Adult Criminal Careers to Juvenile Careers: A Summary* (Washington, D.C.: U.S. Department of Justice, 1982); D. J. West and David P. Farrington,

The Delinquent Way of Life (London: Hienemann, 1977); Donna Hamparian, Richard Schuster, Simon Dinitz, and John Conrad, The Violent Few (Lexington, Mass.: Lexington Books, 1978).

72. Lening Zhang, William Wieczorek, and John Welte, "The Impact of Age of Onset on Substance Use on Delinquency," Journal of Research in Crime and Delinquency 34 (1997): 253–68.

73. Rolf Loeber, Magda Stouthamer-Loeber, and Stephanie Green, "Age at Onset of Problem Behaviour in Boys and Later Disruptive and Delinquent Behaviours," Criminal Behaviour and Mental Health 1 (1991): 229–46.

74. Darrell Steffensmeier, Emilie Andersen Allan, Miles Harer, and Cathy Streifel, "Age and the Distribution of Crime: Variant or Invariant?" Paper presented at the American Society of Criminology meeting, Montreal, Canada, November 1987.

75. Hilary Saner, Robert MacCoun, and Peter Reuter, "On the Ubiquity of Drug Selling Among Youthful Offenders in Washington, D.C., 1985–1991: Age, Period, or Cohort Effect?" Journal of Quantitative Criminology 11 (1995): 362–73.

76. Arnold Barnett, Alfred Blumstein, and David Farrington, "Probabilistic Models of Youthful Criminal Careers," Criminology 25 (1987): 83–107.

77. Peter Greenwood, "Differences in Criminal Behavior and Court Responses Among Juvenile and Young Adult Defendants," in Crime and Justice, an Annual Review of Research, ed. Michael Tonry and Norval Morris (Chicago: University of Chicago Press, 1986), pp. 151–89.

78. John Hagan and Alberto Palloni, "Crimes as Social Events in the Life Course: Reconceiving a Criminological Controversy," Criminology 26 (1988): 87–101.

79. Travis Hirschi and Michael Gottfredson, "Age and Crime, Logic and Scholarship: Comment on Greenberg," American Journal of Sociology 91 (1985): 22–27; Travis Hirschi and Michael Gottfredson, "All Wise After the Fact Learning Theory, Again: Reply to Baldwin," American Journal of Sociology 90 (1985): 1330–33; John Baldwin, "Thrill and Adventure Seeking and the Age Distribution of Crime: Comment on Hirschi and Gottfredson," American Journal of Sociology 90 (1985): 1326–29.

80. Per-Olof Wikstrom, "Age and Crime in a Stockholm Cohort," Journal of Quantitative Criminology 6 (1990): 61–82.

81. Margo Wilson and Martin Daly, "Life Expectancy, Economic Inequality, Homicide, and Reproductive Timing in Chicago Neighbourhoods," British Journal of Medicine 314 (1997): 1271–74.

82. Edward Mulvey and John LaRosa, "Delinquency Cessation and Adolescent Development: Preliminary Data," American Journal of Orthopsychiatry 56 (1986): 212–24.

83. Gordon Trasler, "Cautions for a Biological Approach to Crime," in The Causes of Crime, New Biological Approaches, ed.

Sarnoff Mednick, Terrie Moffitt, and Susan Stack (Cambridge, England: Cambridge University Press, 1987), pp. 7–25.

84. James Q. Wilson and Richard Herrnstein, Crime and Human Nature (New York: Simon and Schuster, 1985), pp. 126–47.

85. Wilson and Herrnstein, Crime and Human Nature, p. 219.

86. Charles Tittle, "Two Empirical Regularities (Maybe) in Search of an Explanation: Commentary on the Age/Crime Debate," Criminology 26 (1988): 75–85.

87. Neal Shover and Carol Thompson, "Age, Differential Expectations and Crime Desistance," Criminology 30 (1992): 89–105.

88. Erich Labouvie, "Maturing Out of Substance Use: Selection and Self-Correction," Journal of Drug Issues 26 (1996): 457–74.

89. Walter Gove, "The Effect of Age and Gender on Deviant Behavior: A Biopsychosocial Perspective," in Gender and the Life Course, ed. A. Ross (Chicago: Aldine, 1985), p. 131.

90. Cesare Lombroso, The Female Offender (New York: Appleton Publishers, 1920).

91. Lombroso, The Female Offender, p. 122.

92. Otto Pollack, The Criminality of Women (Philadelphia: University of Pennsylvania, 1950).

93. For a review of this issue, see Darrell Steffensmeier, "Assessing the Impact of the Women's Movement on Sex-Based Differences in the Handling of Adult Criminal Defendants," Crime and Delinquency 26 (1980): 344–57.

94. Alan Booth and D. Wayne Osgood, "The Influence of Testosterone on Deviance in Adulthood: Assessing and Explaining the Relationship," Criminology 31 (1993): 93–118.

95. Darrell Steffensmeier and Robert Clark, "Sociocultural Versus Biological/Sexist Explanations of Sex Differences in Crime: A Survey of American Criminology Textbooks, 1918–1965," American Sociologist 15 (1980): 246–55.

96. Gisela Konopka, The Adolescent Girl in Conflict (Englewood Cliffs, N.J.: Prentice-Hall, 1966); Clyde Vedder and Dora Somerville, The Delinquent Girl (Springfield, Ill.: Charles C. Thomas, 1970).

97. Dennis Giever, "An Empirical Assessment of the Core Elements of Gottfredson and Hirschi's General Theory of Crime." Paper presented at the American Society of Criminology meeting, Boston, Mass., November 1995.

98. John Mirowsky and Catherine Ross, "Sex Differences in Distress: Real or Artifact?" American Sociological Review 60 (1995): 449–68.

99. For a review of this issue, see Anne Campbell, Men, Women and Aggression (New York: Basic Books, 1993).

100. Mirowsky and Ross, "Sex Differences in Distress: Real or Artifact?" pp. 460–65.

101. Robert Hoge, D. A. Andrews, and Alan Leschied, "Tests of Three Hypotheses Regarding the Predictors of Delinquency,"

Journal of Abnormal Child Psychology 22 (1994): 547–59.

102. Freda Adler, Sisters in Crime (New York: McGraw-Hill, 1975).

103. Rita James Simon, The Contemporary Woman and Crime (Washington, D.C.: U.S. Government Printing Office, 1975).

104. David Rowe, Alexander Vazsonyi, and Daniel Flannery, "Sex Differences in Crime: Do Mean and Within-Sex Variation Have Similar Causes?" Journal of Research in Crime and Delinquency 32 (1995): 84–100; Michael Hindelang, "Age, Sex, and the Versatility of Delinquency Involvements," Social Forces 14 (1971): 525–34; Martin Gold, Delinquent Behavior in an American City (Belmont, Calif.: Brooks/Cole, 1970); Gary Jensen and Raymond Eve, "Sex Differences in Delinquency: An Examination of Popular Sociological Explanations," Criminology 13 (1976): 427–48.

105. Darrell Steffensmeier and Renee Hoffman Steffensmeier, "Trends in Female Delinquency," Criminology 18 (1980): 62–85; see also Darrell Steffensmeier and Renee Hoffman Steffensmeier, "Crime and the Contemporary Woman: An Analysis of Changing Levels of Female Property Crime, 1960–1975," Social Forces 57 (1978): 566–84; Joseph Weis, "Liberation and Crime: The Invention of the New Female Criminal," Crime and Social Justice 1 (1976): 17–27; Carol Smart, "The New Female Offender: Reality or Myth," British Journal of Criminology 19 (1979): 50–59; Steven Box and Chris Hale, "Liberation/Emancipation, Economic Marginalization or Less Chivalry," Criminology 22 (1984): 473–78.

106. Meda Chesney-Lind, "Female Offenders: Paternalism Reexamined," in Women, the Courts and Equality, ed. Laura Crites and Winifred Hepperle (Newbury Park, Calif.: Sage, 1987), pp. 114–39 at 115.

107. Darrell Steffensmeier, Emilie Allan, and Cathy Streifel, "Development and Female Crime: A Cross-National Test of Alternative Explanations," Social Forces 68 (1989): 262–83.

108. Kruttschnitt, "Violence by and Against Women."

109. UCR, 1997, p. 215.

110. Roy Austin, "Recent Trends in the Male and Female Crime Rate: The Convergence Controversy," Journal of Criminal Justice 21 (1993): 447–66.

111. Leroy Gould, "Who Defines Delinquency: A Comparison of Self-Report and Officially Reported Indices of Delinquency for Three Racial Groups," Social Problems 16 (1969): 325–36; Voss, "Ethnic Differentials in Delinquency in Honolulu"; Ronald Akers, Marvin Krohn, Marcia Radosevich, and Lonn Lanza-Kaduce, "Social Characteristics and Self-Reported Delinquency," in Sociology of Delinquency, ed. Gary Jensen (Beverly Hills: Sage, 1981), pp. 48–62.

112. Institute for Social Research, Monitoring the Future (Ann Arbor, Mich.: ISR, 1992), pp. 102–104.

113. David Huizinga and Delbert Elliott, "Juvenile Offenders: Prevalence, Offender Incidence, and Arrest Rates by Race," *Crime and Delinquency* 33 (1987): 206–23. See also Dale Dannefer and Russell Schutt, "Race and Juvenile Justice Processing in Court and Police Agencies," *American Journal of Sociology* 87 (1982): 1113–32.

114. Paul Tracy, "Race and Class Differences in Official and Self-Reported Delinquency," in *From Boy to Man, from Delinquency to Crime,* ed. Marvin Wolfgang, Terence Thornberry, and Robert Figlio (Chicago: University of Chicago Press, 1987), p. 120.

115. Phillipe Rushton, "Race and Crime: An International Dilemma," *Society* 32 (1995): 37–42; for a rebuttal, see Jerome Neapolitan, "Cross-National Variation in Homicides: Is Race a Factor?" *Criminology* 36 (1998): 139–56.

116. Miriam Sealock and Sally Simpson, "Unraveling Bias in Arrest Decisions: The Role of Juvenile Offender Type-scripts," *Justice Quarterly* 15 (1998): 427–57.

117. Daniel Georges-Abeyie, "Definitional Issues: Race, Ethnicity and Official Crime/Victimization Rates," in *The Criminal Justice System and Blacks,* ed. D. Georges-Abeyie (New York: Clark Boardman, 1984), p. 12; Robert Sampson, "Race and Criminal Violence: A Demographically Disaggregated Analysis of Urban Homicide," *Crime and Delinquency* 31 (1985): 47–82.

118. Barry Sample and Michael Philip, "Perspectives on Race and Crime in Research and Planning," in *The Criminal Justice System and Blacks,* ed. D. Georges-Abeyie (New York: Clark Boardman, 1984), pp. 21–36.

119. Kruttschnitt, "Violence by and Against Women," p. 4.

120. James Comer, "Black Violence and Public Policy," in *American Violence and Public Policy,* ed. Lynn Curtis (New Haven: Yale University Press, 1985), pp. 63–86.

121. Comer, "Black Violence and Public Policy," p. 80.

122. Charles Silberman, *Criminal Violence, Criminal Justice* (New York: Random House, 1979), p. 153.

123. Fox Butterfield, *All God's Children: The Bosket Family and the American Tradition of Violence* (New York: Avon, 1996).

124. Silberman, *Criminal Violence, Criminal Justice,* pp. 153–65.

125. Melvin Thomas, "Race, Class and Personal Income: An Empirical Test of the Declining Significance of Race Thesis, 1968–1988," *Social Problems* 40 (1993): 328–39.

126. Gary LaFree, Kriss Drass, and Patrick O'Day, "Race and Crime in Postwar America: Determinants of African-American and White Rates, 1957–1988," *Criminology* 30 (1992): 157–88.

127. Mallie Paschall, Robert Flewelling, and Susan Ennett, "Racial Differences in Violent Behavior Among Young Adults: Moderating and Confounding Effects," *Journal of Research in Crime and Delinquency* 35 (1998): 148–65.

128. R. Kelly Raley, "A Shortage of Marriageable Men? A Note on the Role of Cohabitation in Black-White Differences in Marriage Rates," *American Sociological Review* 61 (1996): 973–83.

129. Julie Phillips, "Variation in African-American Homicide Rates: An Assessment of Potential Explanations," *Criminology* 35 (1997): 527–59.

130. Roy Austin, "Progress Toward Racial Equality and Reduction of Black Criminal Violence," *Journal of Criminal Justice* 15 (1987): 437–59.

131. Reynolds Farley and William Frey, "Changes in the Segregation of Whites from Blacks During the 1980s: Small Steps Toward a More Integrated Society," *American Sociological Review* 59 (1994): 23–45.

132. Marvin Wolfgang, Robert Figlio, and Thorsten Sellin, *Delinquency in a Birth Cohort* (Chicago: University of Chicago Press, 1972).

133. See Thorsten Sellin and Marvin Wolfgang, *The Measurement of Delinquency* (New York: Wiley, 1964), p. 120.

134. Paul Tracy and Robert Figlio, "Chronic Recidivism in the 1958 Birth Cohort." Paper presented at the American Society of Criminology meeting, Toronto, October 1982; Marvin Wolfgang, "Delinquency in Two Birth Cohorts," in *Perspective Studies of Crime and Delinquency,* ed. Katherine Teilmann Van Dusen and Sarnoff Mednick (Boston: Kluwer-Nijhoff, 1983), pp. 7–17. The following sections rely heavily on these sources.

135. Lyle Shannon, *Criminal Career Opportunity* (New York: Human Sciences Press, 1988).

136. D. J. West and David P. Farrington, *The Delinquent Way of Life* (London: Hienemann, 1977).

137. See, generally, Marvin Wolfgang, Terence Thornberry, and Robert Figlio, eds., *From Boy to Man, from Delinquency to Crime* (Chicago: University of Chicago Press, 1987).

138. Paul Tracy and Kimberly Kempf-Leonard, *Continuity and Discontinuity in Criminal Careers* (New York: Plenum Press, 1996).

139. R. Tremblay, R. Loeber, C. Gagnon, P. Charlebois, S. Larivee, and M. LeBlanc, "Disruptive Boys with Stable and Unstable High Fighting Behavior Patterns During Junior Elementary School," *Journal of Abnormal Child Psychology* 19 (1991): 285–300.

140. Jennifer White, Terrie Moffitt, Felton Earls, Lee Robins, and Phil Silva, "How Early Can We Tell? Predictors of Childhood Conduct Disorder and Adolescent Delinquency," *Criminology* 28 (1990): 507–35.

141. John Laub and Robert Sampson, "Unemployment, Marital Discord, and Deviant Behavior: The Long-Term Correlates of Childhood Misbehavior." Paper presented at the annual meeting of the American Society of Criminology, Baltimore, November 1990; rev. version.

142. Michael Ezell and Amy D'Unger, *Offense Specialization Among Serious Youthful Offenders: A Longitudinal Analysis of a California Youth Authority Sample* (Durham, N.C.: Duke University, 1998): unpublished report.

143. Susan Martin, "Policing Career Criminals: An Examination of an Innovative Crime Control Program," *Journal of Criminal Law and Criminology* 77 (1986): 1159–82.

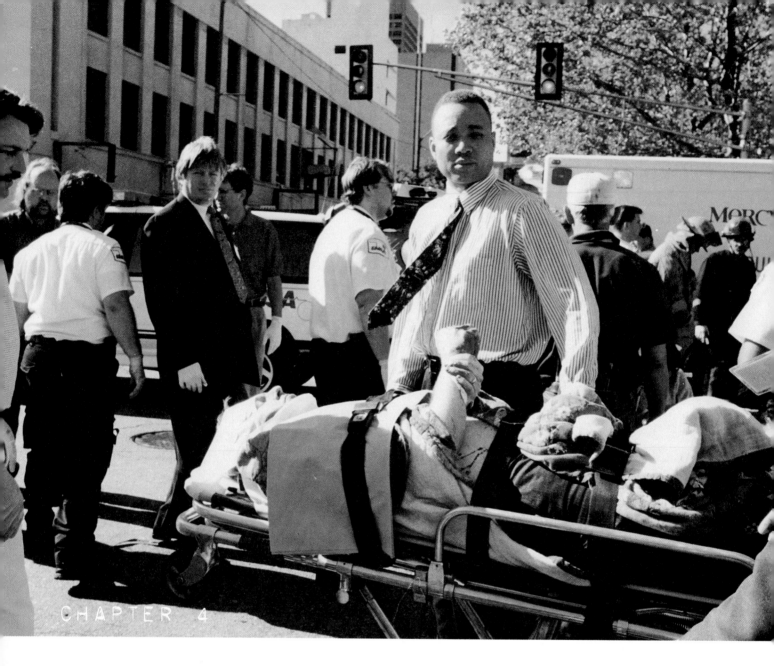

CHAPTER 4

Victims and Victimization

INTRODUCTION

For many years crime victims were not considered an important topic for criminological study. Victims were viewed as the passive recipients of a criminal's anger, greed, or frustration; they were people considered to be in the wrong place at the wrong time. In the late 1960s a number of pioneering studies found that, contrary to popular belief, the victim's function is important in the crime process. Researchers discovered that victims can influence criminal behavior by playing an active role in a criminal incident, such as when an assault victim initially provokes an eventual attacker. Victims can also play an indirect role in a criminal incident, such as when a woman adopts a lifestyle that continually brings her into high-crime areas.

The discovery that victims play an important role in the crime process has prompted the scientific study of victims, or **victimology.** Criminologists who focus their attention on crime victims refer to themselves as **victimologists.** Victim studies began to take on even greater importance during the 1970s and 1980s when crime rates spiraled upward. During this period many Americans experienced injuries from violent crimes and suffered financial loss due to economic crimes.

This chapter examines victims and their relationship to the criminal process. First, using available victim data, we analyze the nature and extent of victimization. We then discuss the relationship between victims and criminal offenders. During this discussion, we look at the various theories of victimization that attempt to explain the victim's role in the crime problem. Finally, we examine how society has responded to the needs of victims, and we determine which special problems they still face.

PROBLEMS OF CRIME VICTIMS

The National Crime Victimization Survey (NCVS) indicates that the annual number of victimizations in the United States is about 37 million incidents.[1] Being the target or a victim of rape, robbery, or assault is a terrible burden and one that can have considerable long-term consequences.[2] In this section we explore some of the effects of these incidents.

Loss

Based on estimates of property taken during larcenies, burglaries, and other reported crimes, the FBI estimates victims lose about $11.5 billion per year. Of that amount, after the crime has been cleared, they recover about $4 billion of their losses.[3]

However, property losses are only a small part of the toll crime takes on victims. In addition, productivity losses are caused by injury, medical costs, and pain and emotional trauma. According to a 1996 study by Urban Institute researchers, the total cost of victimization in terms of property and productivity loss is high, and related medical expenses are $105 billion. The total value of all crime-related costs, including long-term suffering, trauma, and risk of death, amounts to $450 billion annually, or about $1,800 per U.S. citizen.[4] This finding is based on an estimate of about 49 million criminal victimizations per year, a figure that includes crimes such as child abuse, drunk driving, and arson (crimes that are not contained in the NCVS, but that add to the total number of victimizations). To reach these figures the researchers took a civil law approach, which is used to assess costs in damage lawsuits. The researchers assigned a value to each crime type based on **tangible direct costs,** such as property loss, medical bills, and productivity loss, and **indirect costs,** such as long-term psychological pain and suffering (see Table 4.1).

CONNECTIONS

Early common law attached value to the damages caused by criminal acts in an effort to extract wergild. Civil damages for assault and other violent crimes descend from that practice. See Chapter 2 for more information about wergild.

Table 4.1 Costs per Victimization

CRIME	TANGIBLE COSTS	INTANGIBLE COSTS	TOTAL COSTS
Murder	$1,030,000	$1,910,000	$2,940,000
Rape/sexual assault	5,100	81,400	86,500
Robbery/attempt with injury	5,200	13,800	19,000
Assault or attempt	1,550	7,800	9,350
Burglary or attempt	1,100	300	1,400

Source: Ted Miller, Mark Cohen, and Brian Wiersema, *The Extent and Costs of Crime Victimization: A New Look* (Washington, D.C.: National Institute of Justice, 1996), p. 2.

Figure 4.1 The Costs of Heroin Addiction

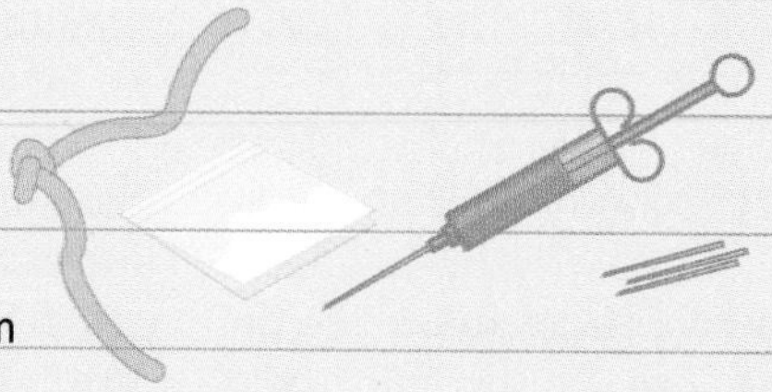

Each heroin addict incurs the following losses annually:

Lost employment earnings	$11,918.12
Value of premature death	$6,909.59
Crime costs	$56,974.91
Costs to the criminal justice system	$30,000.00
Cost of spreading addiction to other users	$29,624.73
Total	**$135,427.35**

Source: George Rengert, *The Geography of Illegal Drugs* (Boulder, Colo.: Westview Press, 1996), p. 5.

In addition to these direct costs to victims, crime also produces social costs that must be paid by nonvictims as well. For example, each heroin addict is estimated to cost society over $135,000 per year (see Figure 4.1); an estimated half-million addicts cost society about $68 billion per year.[5]

Suffering

The problems associated with crime are not restricted to its costs. Victims who suffer serious physical injury often require medical treatment. The suffering endured by crime victims does not end when their attacker leaves the scene of the crime. They may suffer more **victimization** by the justice system.

While the crime is still fresh in their minds, victims may find that the police interrogation following the crime is handled callously, with innuendos or insinuations that they were somehow at fault. Meanwhile, the victim may have difficulty learning what is going on in the case. Property is often kept for a long time as evidence and may never be returned.

Victims may also suffer economic hardship due to wages lost while the victims testify in court. Additionally, time may be wasted when they appear in court only to have the case postponed or dismissed. They may find that authorities are indifferent to their fear of retaliation if they cooperate in the offenders' prosecution. They may also fear testifying in court and being humiliated by defense attorneys.[6]

Long-Term Effects After the incident is over and the justice process has been forgotten, and even after physical traumas and financial losses are well behind them, victims may suffer stress and anxiety. For example, girls who were sexually and physically abused as children are more likely to be suicidal as adults than those who were not abused.[7] Girls who suffer verbal abuse have significantly lower levels of self-esteem as adults.[8] A history of physical and sexual abuse is especially common among homeless women who also display symptoms of mental illness.[9] The long-term emotional trauma suffered by women in the aftermath of spousal assault is also well documented.[10] Spousal abuse victims suffer an extremely high prevalence of depression, **posttraumatic stress disorder** (an emotional disturbance following exposure to stresses outside the range of normal human experience), anxiety disorder, and **obsessive compulsive disorder** (an extreme preoccupation with certain thoughts and compulsive performance of certain behaviors).[11] Symptoms include nightmares, **hyperarousal** (an abnormal level of excitation or activation in a person or animal), and repression of the abuse.[12]

Women are not the only ones who suffer in the aftermath of violence; male victims of violent attacks also suffer postcrime stress disorders. Sexually assaulted males report being emotionally distressed and socially isolated; they are also more likely to have deviant peers and engage in delinquent activities.[13] Viewing themselves from a male frame of reference, these victims express feelings of being weak and helpless. Whereas female victims tend to internalize and place the blame for their victimization on themselves, males are more likely to externalize blame, expressing anger toward their attackers. Consequently, males who are sexually assaulted

The pain and suffering experienced by crime victims does not stop after the criminal act is over. Many go through a fundamental life change, viewing the world more suspiciously and less as a safe, controllable, and meaningful place. Victims are also more likely to suffer psychological stress for extended periods of time. In 1993 tennis great Monica Seles was stabbed in the back by a fan of her rival Steffi Graf. Seles found it difficult to get back on the tour after the incident and remains fearful of further attacks. Her stabbing shows that even the most famous celebrities are not immune from violent victimization.

may feel doubly injured and violated; rather than lashing out at their attackers, they internalize blame.[14]

Some victims may find that the physical wounds received during a criminal incident haunt them for the remainder of their lives. Many violent crime victims are physically disabled due to the serious wounds sustained during episodes of random violence. A growing number suffer paralyzing spinal cord injuries. And if victims have no insurance, the long-term effects of the crime may have devastating financial ramifications as well as the emotional and physical desolation.[15]

Fear

The victim's pain and suffering does not stop after the incident is over. Victims of crime have a heightened sense of fear after their experience. Their fear will be magnified if they believe that their own experience is not a unique event but that they are one small part of a nationwide pattern of crime victimization.

Victims of violent crime are the most deeply affected, fearing a repeat of their attack. There may be a spillover effect in which victims become fearful of other forms of crime they have not yet experienced. For example, people who have been assaulted develop fears that their house will be burglarized.[16] Many go through a fundamental life change, viewing the world more sus-

piciously and less as a safe, controllable, and meaningful place. These people are more likely to suffer psychological stress for extended periods of time.[17]

Antisocial Behavior

In the 1996 film *Never Talk to Strangers,* a psychiatrist played by Rebecca DeMornay suspects that her new boyfriend (Antonio Banderas) is a killer. As the bodies pile up, the audience begins to share her suspicions. But in the film's surprise ending, we learn that DeMornay is the real killer. It seems her personality was irrevocably damaged by the fact that when she was a child, her father sexually abused her and murdered her mother while she looked on.

CONNECTIONS

It is common for Hollywood to depict women as psychopathic serial killers (*Friday the Thirteenth, Black Widow, The Crush*). Despite this depiction, most research shows that women rarely commit multiple murders. Chapter 11 reviews serial murder in some detail.

There is growing evidence that the association between early victimization and later criminality is not merely the fictional subject of Hollywood films; people

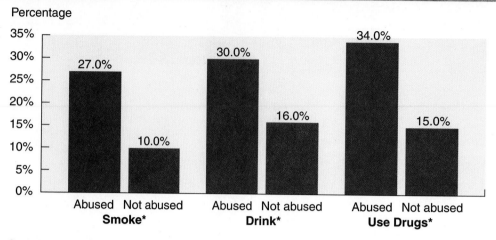

Figure 4.2   Percentage of Male High School Students (Grades 9–12) Reporting Smoking, Drinking, or Using Drugs, by Physical/Sexual Abuse Status

Smoke*: smoked at least several cigarettes in the past week; Drink: drank at least once a month; Use drugs: used illegal drugs at least once in the past month.

Note: The survey was an in-class questionnaire completed by 3,162 boys in grades 5–12 at a nationally representative sample of 265 public, private, and parochial schools from December 1996 to June 1997. The survey included roughly equal samples of adolescent boys in grades 5–8 and 9–12. All responses were weighted to reflect grade, region, race and ethnicity, and gender.

Source: Cathy Schoen et al., *The Health of Adolescent Boys: Commonwealth Fund Survey Findings* (New York: Commonwealth Fund, 1998). Figure prepared by The Center for Substance Abuse Research, University of Maryland, College Park.

who are crime victims also seem more likely to commit crime themselves. For example, an analysis of juvenile court records from a midwestern metropolitan area found that childhood maltreatment significantly predicted future criminality. Being abused or neglected increased the odds of being arrested as a juvenile and also of having at least one alcohol- or drug-related arrest in adulthood. The odds of adult arrest were 39 percent greater for maltreated adolescents than for nonabused adolescents.[18] This outcome is consistent with the fact that males who were physically or sexually abused are much more likely to smoke, drink, and take drugs than are nonabused youth (see Figure 4.2).

Criminologist Cathy Widom has referred to the phenomenon in which child victims later become adult criminals as the **cycle of violence.**[19] Research bears out the cycle of violence hypothesis. It shows that young males are more likely to engage in violent behavior if they were (1) the target of physical abuse and (2) exposed to violent behavior among adults they know or live with. The effect is magnified if weapons were used.[20] The association between victimization and future behavioral difficulties is not limited to males. Research efforts have found that females exposed to family violence may be even more likely to manifest behavioral and adjustment problems as they mature.[21]

Victimization takes many forms, and every form has a different repercussion. Whether the effects are physical, emotional, financial, or all three, the scars are indelible.[22]

THE NATURE OF VICTIMIZATION

How many crime victims are there in the United States, and what are the trends and patterns in victimization? As discussed in the preceding chapter, the NCVS is currently the leading source of information about the nature and extent of victimization. It employs a highly sophisticated and complex sampling methodology to collect data annually from thousands of citizens. Statistical techniques then estimate victimization rates, trends, and patterns that occur in the entire U.S. population. In 1992 the NCVS was redesigned to provide more accurate and valid information; as a consequence of the new system, the number of reported victimizations increased significantly.

According to the revised NCVS, an estimated 37 million criminal events occurred during 1996. As you may recall from Chapter 3, similar to the Uniform Crime Report, the NCVS finds that crime rates have been declining. For example, between 1993 and 1996 the violent crime victimization rate fell 16 percent, and property crime victimization rates dropped 17 percent.

Patterns in the victimization survey findings are stable and repetitive. These patterns are critical social facts because they indicate that victimization is not random, but a function of personal and ecological factors. The stability of these patterns allows judgments to be made about the nature of victimization; policies can then be created in an effort to reduce the victimization rate. Who are victims? Where does victimization take place? What is the relationship between victims and criminals? The NCVS helps to answer these questions. The following sections discuss some of the most important victimization patterns and trends.

The Social Ecology of Victimization

The NCVS data reveal a lot about the ecology of victimization, such as where, when, and how it occurs. Violent crimes are slightly more likely to take place during the daytime or early evening hours, although the more serious forms of these crimes, such as rape and aggravated assaults, typically take place after 6 P.M. Less serious forms of violence, such as unarmed robberies and personal larcenies like purse snatching, are more likely to occur during the daytime. Approximately two-thirds of rapes and sexual assaults occur at night—6 P.M. to 6 A.M.

The most likely site for each crime category tends to be an open, public area, such as a street, a park, or a field, or at a commercial establishment such as a tavern. More than 10 percent of violent incidents usually take place on school grounds. In fact, survey data show that the likelihood of suffering violent crime while on school grounds is increasing. According to the NCVS, the likelihood of victimization increased substantially between 1989 and 1995, and younger students are the most likely candidates for becoming violent crime victims while at school.[23] As Figure 4.3 shows, each year about 15 percent of all youths report being a crime victim while at school.

Neighborhood characteristics influence the chances of victimization. Those living in the central city had significantly higher rates of theft and violence than suburbanites; people living in nonmetropolitan, rural areas had a victimization rate almost half that of city

Figure 4.3   Number of Nonfatal Crimes Against Students Ages 12 Through 18 Occurring at School or Going to or from School per 1,000 Students, by Type of Crime and Selected Student Characteristics

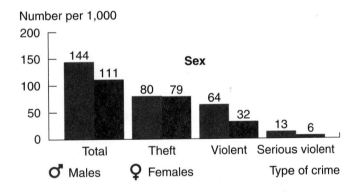

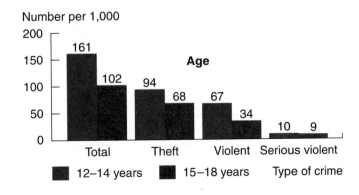

Source: Kathryn A. Chandler, Chris Chapman, Michael R. Rand, and Bruce M. Taylor, *Students' Reports of School Crime: 1989 and 1995* (Washington, D.C.: Bureau of Justice Statistics, 1998), p. 1.

dwellers. The risk of murder for both men and women is significantly higher in disorganized inner-city areas where gangs flourish and drug trafficking is commonplace.[24]

The Victim's Household

Another way to look at the social ecology of victimization is to examine the type of household or dwelling unit most likely to contain victims or to be victimized. What factors are associated with households that contain crime victims?

The NCVS tells us that larger, higher-income, African-American, western, and urban areas are the most vulnerable to crime. In contrast, poor, rural white homes in the Northeast are the least likely to contain crime victims or be the target of theft offenses, such as burglary or larceny. People who own their homes are less vulnerable than renters.

NCVS data indicate that recent population movement and changes may account for current household victimization patterns. U.S. residents have become extremely mobile, moving from urban areas to suburban and rural areas. In addition, family size has been reduced; more people than ever before are living in single-person homes (about 25 percent of households). It is possible that the decline in household victimization rates during the past 15 years can be explained by the fact that smaller households in less populated areas have a lower victimization risk.

Victim Characteristics

Social and demographic characteristics also distinguish victims and nonvictims. The most important of these involve gender, age, social status, and race.

Gender The NCVS provides information on the background characteristics of the victims of crime. As Figure 4.4 shows, gender affects victimization risk. Except for rape and sexual assault, males were more likely than females to suffer violent crime. Men were twice as likely as women to experience aggravated assault and robbery. Women, however, were six times more likely than men to be victims of rape or sexual assault. According to NCVS estimates, about 230,000 women and 40,000 men suffer sexual assault each year.

When men are the victims of violent crime, the perpetrator is described as a stranger; women are much more likely to be attacked by a relative than are men. About two-thirds of all attacks against women are committed by a husband, boyfriend, family member, or acquaintance.[25] In two-thirds of sexual assaults, the victim knew or was acquainted with her or his attacker.

Age On June 4, 1998, in a Dallas, Texas, courtroom, an 11-year-old boy was convicted along with two younger

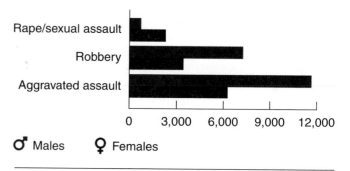

Figure 4.4   Rate of Victimization (by Gender) per 1,000 Persons Age 12 or Older in 1996

Source: Cheryl Ringel, *Criminal Victimization 1996: Changes 1995–96 with Trends 1993–96* (Washington, D.C.: Bureau of Justice Statistics, 1997), p. 4.

boys, ages 7 and 8, of beating and raping a 3-year-old girl. The boys took the girl from a van outside her home and to a neighborhood creek, where she was beaten with a brick and a shoe, stripped, and sexually assaulted. The two younger boys admitted taking part in the attack, but they are too young to face criminal charges under state law. Jurors found the 11-year-old fourth-grader guilty of two counts of sexual assault and one count of injuring a child; he faces a possible 40-year prison sentence.[26]

Although such cases shock the public, victim data reveal that young people face a much greater victimization risk than do older persons. As Figure 4.5 shows, victim risk diminishes rapidly after age 25. The elderly, who are thought of as the helpless targets of predatory criminals, are actually much safer than their grandchildren. People over 65, who make up 14 percent of the population, account for only 1 percent of violent victimizations; teens 12–19, who also make up 14 percent of the population, account for 32 percent of victimizations.

Data gathered in the emergency rooms of the nation's hospitals further confirm that young people have a much greater chance of victimization than the elderly and that more often than not their attackers are people they know or with whom they are acquainted.[27] As Figure 4.6 shows, children under 12 are significantly more likely to be assaulted by people they know or are related to than teens or adults. Teens between 12 and 19 are more likely to be victimized by acquaintances, whereas people over 20 have the highest level of stranger attacks.

The association between age and victimization is undoubtedly tied to the lifestyle shared by young people. Adolescents often stay out late at night, go to public places, and hang out with other kids who have a high risk of criminal involvement. Most adolescents aged 12 to 19 are attacked by offenders in the same age category, whereas a great majority of adults are victim-

Figure 4.5 Correlation Between Age and Victimization

Rate of violent victimization by age (rape, robbery, or assault) in 1996 per 1,000 persons age 12 or older

Age of victim of rape, robbery, or assault

Age	
12–19	
20–24	
25–34	
35–49	
50–64	
65 or older	

(0   20,000   40,000   60,000   80,000   100,000)

Source: Cheryl Ringel, *Criminal Victimization 1996: Changes 1995–96 with Trends 1993–96* (Washington, D.C.: Bureau of Justice Statistics, 1997), p. 4.

Figure 4.6 Relationship Between Age and the Source of Crime-Related Injuries

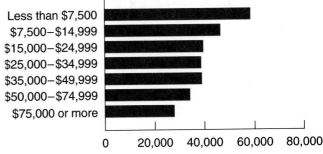

	Under 12	12–19	20 +
Relative	56%	12%	21%
Acquaintance	34%	58%	44%
Stranger	10%	30%	35%

Source: Michael Rand, *Violence-Related Injuries Treated in Hospital Emergency Departments* (Washington, D.C.: Bureau of Justice Statistics, 1997), p. 1.

ized by adult criminals. Teens also face a high victimization risk because they spend a great deal of time in the most dangerous building in the community: the local school!

A recent survey of state correctional inmates underscores the risks faced by young people. About 19 percent of all state inmates surveyed committed a crime against a person under 18 years of age; 20 percent of violent criminals had committed crimes against children. About 7 of 10 offenders with child victims reported that they were imprisoned for a rape or sexual assault. Most of these offenders were older white males with no prior criminal record. They were more likely to have themselves been physically or sexually abused as children than other inmates (though the majority had not suffered such abuse). Nearly a third of their victims had been their own children; only one in seven reported that the victim had been a total stranger.[28]

Social Status The poorest Americans might be expected to be the most likely victims of crime because they live in crime-prone areas: inner-city, urban neighborhoods. The NCVS does, in fact, show that the least affluent (annual incomes of less than $7,500) were by far the most likely to be victims of violent crimes. This association occurs across all gender, racial, and age groups (see Figure 4.7). Although the poor are more likely to suffer violent crimes, the wealthy are more likely targets of personal theft crimes such as pocket picking and purse snatching. Perhaps the affluent, who sport more expensive attire and drive better cars, attract the attention of thieves.

Victim data suggest that thieves choose their targets carefully, selecting those who seem best able to provide

Figure 4.7 Victimization, by Income and Status

Rate of victimization from crimes of violence (rape, robbery, and assault) by household income per 1,000 persons age 12 or older in 1996

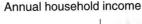

Annual household income

Income	
Less than $7,500	
$7,500–$14,999	
$15,000–$24,999	
$25,000–$34,999	
$35,000–$49,999	
$50,000–$74,999	
$75,000 or more	

(0   20,000   40,000   60,000   80,000)

Source: Cheryl Ringel, *Criminal Victimization 1996: Changes 1995–96 with Trends 1993–96* (Washington, D.C.: Bureau of Justice Statistics, 1997), p. 4.

them with a substantial haul. In contrast, the targets of violence, an expressive crime, are among the nation's poorest people.

Marital Status Marital status also influences victimization risk. Divorced and never-married males and females are victimized by strangers more often than

Though most violent crimes are committed by strangers, relatively few children are actually abducted and killed by strangers. When such a crime occurs, it sends a chill across the entire nation. In Missouri, friends help Rhonda Senter, the mother of 10-year-old murder victim Cassidy Senter, to the gravesite of her daughter. Cassidy was the victim of a serial killer, who in 1993 abducted, molested, and killed another young girl and attempted the abduction of another.

married people or widows and widowers. This association between marital status and victimization is probably influenced by age, gender, and lifestyle.

Many young people who have the highest victim risk are actually too young to have been married. Young single people also go out in public more often and sometimes interact with high-risk peers, increasing their exposure to victimization. In contrast, widows, who are more likely to be older, suffer much lower victimization rates because they interact with older people, are more likely to stay home at night, and avoid public places.

Marital status also influences the nature of victimization within domestic relationships. Married women seem to be at much greater risk of domestic victimization than single people who are living together. A possible cause may be that domestic relationships among single people tend to be less stable and more short-lived, insulating these couples from the pressures and conflicts that come with building longer-term marriages.[29] The rate of domestic violence appears to be declining among both married couples and single cohabitants. One reason is that females now find it easier to get high-paying jobs, to obtain legal divorces, and to receive domestic violence counseling. Financial independence and emotional support allow women to leave a bad marriage before interspousal conflict leads to violence and death. And even if partners stay together in troubled relationships, newly emerging social interventions empower women to end male partner violence.[30]

Race and Ethnicity One of the most important distinctions found in the NCVS data is the racial difference in victimization rates. Blacks are more likely than whites to be victims of violent crime. Robbery—for which blacks are victimized at three times the rate of whites—shows the greatest difference. Additionally, blacks are nearly twice as likely as whites to experience aggravated assault. Young African-American males are also at great risk for homicide victimization. They face a murder risk four or five times greater than that of young African-American females, five to eight times higher than that of young white males, and 16 to 22 times higher than that of young white females.[31]

Ethnic minorities also share a high risk of victimization. For example, Hispanics are twice as likely as non-Hispanics to fall victim to robbery and personal theft. Hispanics are also more likely to suffer completed violent crimes than are non-Hispanics.

Why do these discrepancies exist? Racial and ethnic minorities tend to live in the nation's largest cities in areas beset by alcohol and drug abuse, poverty, racial discrimination, and violence. Forced to live in the nation's most dangerous areas, their lifestyle places them in the most "at risk" population group.

Repeat Victimization Does prior victimization enhance or reduce the chances of future victimization? There may be stable patterns of behavior that encourage victimization, and some people who maintain them may become **chronic victims**—people who are constantly the target of predatory crimes.

Most research efforts in fact show that prior victimization is a strong predictor of future victimization. Individuals who have been crime victims maintain a significantly higher chance of future victimization than people who have remained nonvictims.[32] Households that have experienced victimization in the past are the ones most likely to experience it again in the future.[33]

Repeat victimizations are most likely to occur in areas with high crime rates; they account for a significant portion of all criminal acts. One study found that during a four-year period, 40 percent of all trauma patients in an urban medical center in Ohio were repeat victims.[34] Educational establishments and sports facilities in particular are likely to be repeatedly burglarized in a short time.[35]

What factors predict chronic victimization? Some combination of personal and social factors may encourage victimization. Most repeated victimizations occur soon after a previous crime has occurred, suggesting that repeat victims share some personal characteristic that makes them a magnet for predators.[36] For example, kids who are shy, physically weak, or socially isolated may be prone to being bullied in the schoolyard.[37] David Finkelhor and Nancy Asigian find that three specific types of characteristics increase the potential for victimization:

1. *Target vulnerability:* The victims' physical weakness or psychological distress renders them incapable of resisting or deterring crime and makes them easy targets.
2. *Target gratifiability:* Some victims have some quality, possession, skill, or attribute that an offender wants to obtain, use, have access to, or manipulate. Having attractive possessions such as a leather coat may make one vulnerable to predatory crime.
3. *Target antagonism:* Some characteristics increase risk because they arouse anger, jealousy, or destructive impulses in potential offenders. Being gay or effeminate, for example, may bring on undeserved attacks in the street; being argumentative and alcoholic may provoke barroom assault.[38]

Social, personal, and experiential factors may also interact to enhance chronic victimization. For example, the boy who is bullied at school because he is depressed, shy, and withdrawn may become even more anxious after being victimized. This will likely increase his chances for future victimization.[39] Repeat victimization may also be an offender's rational choice: once an offender learns the weaknesses of victims, he or she may use them over and over again. For example, if an abusive husband finds out that his battered wife will not call police, he repeatedly victimizes her; or if a hate crime is committed and the police do not respond to reported offenses, the perpetrators learn they have little to fear from the law.[40]

CONNECTIONS

The fact that certain people and certain locations are the target of repeat victimizations has prompted law enforcement agencies to select high-risk targets for increased surveillance and patrol. *Hot spot* police tactics have attempted to locate the sites of multiple crimes and allocate forces accordingly. For more on this issue, see the section on hot spots in Chapter 16.

One type of repeat victimization that criminologists now recognize as a real and serious threat is *stalking*, the topic of the following Criminological Enterprise feature.

The Victims and Their Criminals

The NCVS also tells us something about the relationship between victims and criminals:

1. Victims reported that most crimes were committed by a single offender over age 20. About one-quarter of the victims indicated their assailant was a young person under 30 years of age.
2. Crime tends to be intraracial: African-American offenders victimize African-Americans, and caucasians victimize caucasians. However, because the country's population is predominantly white, it stands to reason that criminals of all races will be more likely to target white victims. This conclusion is supported by surveys of prison inmates: whereas 4.7 percent of white inmates report that they attacked African-American victims, black inmates report that 43 percent of their victims were white.[41]
3. Victims reported that substance abuse was involved in about one-third of violent crime incidents. These estimates, if anything, may underestimate the association between substance abuse and crime. Surveys of prison inmates have found that over half of violent inmates report being under the influence of either drugs or alcohol at the time they committed the crime for which they were incarcerated.[42]
4. Although many violent crimes are committed by strangers, the NCVS found that a surprising number of violent crimes were committed by relatives or acquaintances of the victims. In fact, about 40 percent of all violent crimes were committed by people who were described, at least, as being "well known" to the victim.

The Criminological Enterprise

Victims of Stalking

In Wes Craven's popular movies *Scream* and *Scream II*, the heroine Sydney (played by Neve Campbell) is stalked by a mysterious adversary who scares her half to death while killing off most of her peer group. Although obviously extreme even by Hollywood standards, the *Scream* movies focus on this newly recognized form of long-term repeat victimization.

Stalking can be defined as a course of conduct directed at a specific person that involves repeated physical or visual proximity, nonconsensual communication, or verbal, written, or implied threats sufficient to cause fear in a reasonable person. In an effort to better understand this type of crime, the National Violence Against Women Survey collected data from a national sample of 8,000 women and 8,000 men 18 years of age or older.

Survey findings indicated that stalking is a bigger problem than previously thought; it affects about 1.4 million victims annually and is strongly linked to the controlling behavior and physical, emotional, and sexual abuse perpetrated against women by intimate partners. Of those surveyed, 8 percent of women and 2 percent of men said they had been stalked at some point in their lives. The data suggest that 8.2 million females and 2 million males will suffer stalking at some time during their lives. Although stalking episodes usually last one year or less, in a few cases stalking continues for five or more years.

Most victims surveyed knew their stalker. Women were significantly more likely to be stalked by an intimate partner—whether that partner was a current spouse, a former spouse or cohabiting partner, or a date. Only 21 percent of stalkers identified by female victims were strangers. On the other hand, men were significantly more likely to be stalked by a stranger or an acquaintance. In all, about 87 percent of stalkers were men. Women tended to be victimized by lone stalk-

ers, but in 50 percent of male victimizations, the stalker had an accomplice—usually a friend or girlfriend.

Most victims of stalking were between the ages of 18 and 29 when the stalking started. Although there were few racial differences among the survey's stalking victims, Native American women are at significantly greater risk of being stalked than members of any other group.

The survey showed that stalkers behaved in ways that induced fear even though they did not always make credible threats against their victims. The following findings reveal the types of abuse to which stalking victims were subjected:

- Stalkers made overt threats to about 45 percent of victims.
- Stalkers spied on or followed about 75 percent of victims.
- Stalkers vandalized the property of about 30 percent of victims.
- Stalkers threatened to kill or killed the pet(s) of about 10 percent of victims.

The typical female victim thought she had been stalked because her assailant wanted to control her, scare her, or keep her in a relationship. About 60 percent of stalking by intimate partners started before a relationship ended. Men also reported intimidation and control as possible stalker motivations. In fact, there was a clear relationship between stalking and other emotionally controlling and physically abusive behavior. About half of the female stalking victims had been stalked by a current or former marital or cohabiting partner. About 80 percent of these women were, at some point in the relationship, physically assaulted by that partner, and 31 percent were sexually assaulted.

Half of all victims reported their stalking to the police. About one-quarter of the women obtained restraining orders—a far greater proportion than men. Of the cases reported in the survey, the stalkers violated 80 percent of all restraining

orders. About 24 percent of female victims who reported stalking to the police (compared to 19 percent of male victims) said their cases were prosecuted. Of the cases where criminal charges were filed, 54 percent resulted in a conviction. About 63 percent of convictions resulted in jail time.

Although the stalking usually stopped within one to two years, victims experienced its social and psychological consequences long after. About one-third reported they had sought psychological treatment. In addition, one-fifth lost time from work, and 7 percent of those said they never returned to work. When asked why the stalking stopped, about 20 percent of the victims said it was because they moved away, and another 15 percent said it was because of police involvement. Also, stalking of female victims often stopped when the stalker got a new girlfriend or wife.

CRITICAL THINKING

1. How can stalking victims be better protected?
2. Are victims deterred from seeking help because prosecution results from only 24 percent of stalking complaints registered by females and 19 percent by males? Also consider the fact that 80 percent of restraining orders are violated.

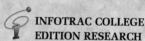

INFOTRAC COLLEGE EDITION RESEARCH

Stalking is now recognized as a serious social problem. To learn more about its social dynamics, read: Robert M. Emerson, Kerry O. Ferris, Carol Brooks Gardner. On being stalked, *Social Problems* August 1998 v45 n3 p289

Source: Adapted from Patricia Tjaden, *The Crime of Stalking: How Big Is the Problem?* (Washington, D.C: National Institute of Justice, 1997).

5. Victimization commonly occurs within families and involves parents, children, and extended family. A shocking example of this is discussed in the following Criminological Enterprise on the murder of parents.

THEORIES OF VICTIMIZATION

For many years criminological theory focused on the actions of the criminal offender; the role of the victim was virtually ignored. When scholars found that the victim was not a passive target in crime, but someone whose behavior can influence his or her own fate, they wanted to know more. One of the first criminologists who discovered that victims were an important part of the crime process was Hans Von Hentig. In the 1940s his writings portrayed the crime victim as someone who "shapes and molds the criminal."[43] The criminal might have been a predator, but the victim may have helped the offender by becoming easy prey. Another pioneering victimologist, Stephen Schafer, focused on the victim's responsibility in the "genesis of crime."[44] Schafer found that some victims may have provoked or encouraged the criminal. These early works helped focus attention on the role of the victim in the crime problem and led to further research efforts that have sharpened the image of the crime victim. Today a number of different theories attempt to explain the cause of victimization; the most important theories are discussed here.

Victim Precipitation Theory

According to the victim precipitation view, some people may actually initiate the confrontation that eventually leads to their injury or death. Victim precipitation can be either active or passive.

Active precipitation occurs when victims act provocatively, use threats or fighting words, or even attack first. This model of victim-precipitated crime was first popularized by Marvin Wolfgang in his 1958 study of criminal homicide. He defined the term *victim precipitation* as follows:

> The term "victim-precipitated" is applied to those criminal homicides in which the victim is a direct, positive precipitator in the crime. The role of the victim is characterized by his having been the first in the homicide drama to use physical force against his subsequent slayer. The victim-precipitated cases are those in which the victim was the first to show and use a deadly weapon, to strike a blow in an altercation—in short, the first to commence the interplay or resort to physical violence.[45]

Examples of a victim-precipitated homicide include the death of an aggressor in a barroom brawl or a wife who kills her husband after he attacks and threatens to kill her. Wolfgang found that 150, or 26 percent, of the 588 homicides in his sample could be classified as victim-precipitated.[46]

Active Precipitation and Rape Nowhere is the concept of victim precipitation more controversial than in the crime of rape. In 1971 Menachem Amir suggested female victims often contribute to their attacks through a relationship with the rapist.[47] Although Amir's findings are controversial, courts have continued to return not guilty verdicts in rape cases if a victim's actions can in any way be construed as consenting to sexual intimacy. **Date rapes,** which may at first start out as romantic though nonintimate relationships and then deteriorate into rape, are rarely treated with the same degree of severity as stranger rapes.[48] As law professor Susan Estrich claims in her book, *Real Rape,*

> . . . the force standard continues to protect, as "seduction," conduct which should be considered criminal. It ensures broad male freedom to "seduce" women who feel themselves to be powerless, vulnerable, and afraid. It effectively guarantees men freedom to intimidate women and exploit their weakness and passivity, so long as they don't "fight" with them, and it makes clear that the responsibility should be placed squarely on the women . . .[49]

Although this legal victimization is publicly condemned, there are still numerous instances of defendants being found not guilty because judges or juries believe that a sexual assault was victim-precipitated. In one nationally publicized case, a Florida defendant was acquitted after jury members concluded his victim "asked for it the way she was dressed." Steven Lord, the 26-year-old defendant, was freed after the jury was told his victim was wearing a lace miniskirt with nothing on underneath and "was advertising for sex." The acquittal came despite the fact that other women testified that they had been raped by Lord.[50]

CONNECTIONS

Efforts to disassociate the casualties of rape from the concept of victim precipitation have resulted in modifications to rape laws. These will be discussed in more detail in Chapter 11.

Passive Precipitation **Passive precipitation** occurs when the victim exhibits some personal characteristic that unknowingly either threatens or encourages the attacker. The crime can occur because of personal conflict—for example, when two people compete over a job, promotion, love interest, or some other scarce and coveted commodity. Although the victim may never have met the attacker or even known of his or her existence, the attacker feels menaced and acts accordingly.[51]

The Criminological Enterprise

Parents Who Get Killed and the Children Who Kill Them

The sensational case of Eric and Lyle Menendez, two wealthy California brothers who killed their parents, captured the attention of the American public in 1994. The boys claimed that they acted in self-defense after years of physical and sexual abuse at their father's hands; both were convicted of murder after two widely followed trials. Their acts are referred to as **parricide,** or the killing of a close relative. Most often this crime involves **patricide,** the killing of a father, or **matricide,** the killing of a mother.

Criminologist Kathleen Heide has extensively researched the nature and extent of family homicides. She finds that the killing of a parent is almost a daily event in the United States, averaging about 300 incidents per year. Although parents are typically killed by adults, about 15 percent of mothers and 25 percent of fathers are killed by juvenile offspring. In addition, about 30 percent of stepmothers and 34 percent of stepfathers are killed by adolescents. These numbers are startling when we consider that only 10 percent of all homicide arrests involve juveniles.

Heide found five conditions that foreshadow parricide:

1. The child who will one day kill his or her parents is raised in a dysfunctional family of substance-abusing parents.
2. The child is severely abused verbally, physically, or sexually.
3. Violence in the family escalates throughout the child's life.
4. The child becomes increasingly vulnerable to stressors in the home environment.
5. Firearms are readily available.

Heide finds that parricide is typically committed by one of three types of offenders:

The severely abused child— An estimated 90 percent of parricide cases involve children who were severely abused by parents. These children were psychologically abused and then witnessed or suffered physical, sexual, and verbal abuse. Their parricide represented an act of desperation—the only

way out of a situation they could no longer endure. This type of crime made national headlines in 1983 when 16-year-old Richard Jahnke and his 17-year-old sister, Deborah, killed their father, an Internal Revenue Service agent, after years of sexual and physical abuse at his hands.

The severely mentally ill child— A few children who kill are suffering from severe **psychosis.** Their personalities are disorganized, perceptions distorted, and communication disjointed. They experience hallucinations and bizarre delusions. Heide tells of the case of Jonathan Cantero, who stabbed his mother 40 times and tried to cut off her left hand to "demonstrate his allegiance to Satan."

The dangerously antisocial child— Some parricidal youths have antisocial or psychopathic personalities. They kill their parents for purely selfish ends, such as obtaining an inheritance or getting money for drugs. Heide relates the case of Michelle White, 14, and her 17-year-old brother, John, Jr., who hired a neighbor to kill their father and then used his credit cards to buy $1,000 worth of video games, televisions, and other merchandise. Their father's corpse lay decaying in the kitchen as they cooked their meals.

Heide found that the typical slain parent or stepparent was a white, non-Hispanic male. The typical slayer was an adult son, and the typical murder weapon was a handgun. Slayings involving multiple offenders and multiple victims were quite rare.

Mothers, more than fathers, tend to be killed by older offspring. Perhaps the mother–child bond is stronger and more enduring, protecting the mother while the child is young. The strength of this bond may tie them together for longer periods, making violence more likely as the child becomes an adult. The number of stepparents killed has trended upward, a pattern of concern consider-

Kathleen Heide, author of *Why Kids Kill Parents: Child Abuse and Adolescent Homicide.*

ing the changing structure of American families. Heide finds that public attitudes toward parricidal youth are changing from horror to sympathy now that there is recognition that most kids who kill are responding to life-threatening physical abuse.

CRITICAL THINKING

1. Should abuse be considered a defense to parricide?
2. How would you handle the case of a 10-year-old who kills his father after an argument?

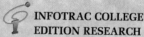

INFOTRAC COLLEGE EDITION RESEARCH

To learn more about parricide, see: Jacques D. Marleau and Thierry Webanck. Parricide and violent crimes: a Canadian study. *Adolescence* Summer 1997 v32 n126 p357

Jean Hellwege. Battered child syndrome is basis for successful clemency petitions. *Trial* April 1995 31 n4 p19

Source: Kathleen Heide, *Why Kids Kill Parents: Child Abuse and Adolescent Homicide* (Columbus, Ohio: Ohio State University Press, 1992); "Parents Who Get Killed and the Children Who Kill Them," *Journal of Interpersonal Violence* 8 (1993): 531–44; "Juvenile Involvement in Multiple Offender and Multiple Victim Parricides," *Journal of Police and Criminal Psychology* 9 (1993): 53–64; and "A Typology of Adolescent Parricide Offenders"; paper presented at the annual meeting of the American Society of Criminology, Baltimore, November 1990.

In another scenario, the victim may belong to a group whose mere presence threatens the attacker's reputation, status, or economic well-being. For example, hate crime violence may be precipitated by immigrant group members arriving in the community to compete for jobs and housing; women in the workforce may threaten insecure and emotionally unstable men and prompt sexual violence. Research indicates that passive precipitation is related to power: if the target group can establish themselves economically or gain political power in the community, their vulnerability will diminish. They are still a potential threat, but they become too formidable a target to attack; they are no longer passive precipitators. For example, research conducted in Canada shows that women employed in the workforce are underrepresented as homicide victims; unemployed women suffer higher homicide victimization rates.[52] By implication, economic power reduces victimization risk.

Whether active or passive, the concept of victim precipitation implies that in some but not all crimes, the victim's actions in some way cause the crime: the crime could not have taken place unless the victim had not acted.

Lifestyle Theories

Some criminologists believe that people may become crime victims because their lifestyle increases their exposure to criminal offenders. Both NCVS and UCR data sources show that victimization risk is increased by such behaviors as staying single, associating with young men, going out in public places late at night, and living in an urban area. Conversely, one's chances of victimization can be reduced by staying home at night, moving to a rural area, staying out of public places, earning more money, and getting married. The basis of this theory is that crime is not a random occurrence, but rather a function of the victims' lifestyle.

According to this view, criminals and victims seem codependent.[53] Crime occurs because potential victims' lifestyle places them in jeopardy: the chances of being attacked are much greater if you frequent New York City's Central Park at 2 A.M. than if you are safe at home in rural North Dakota. Likewise, the chance of an early death by homicide is much greater for Los Angeles gang boys than for their peers who decide to join the church choir.[54]

High-Risk Lifestyles People who have high-risk lifestyles maintain a much greater chance of victimization. For example, one element of the population, teenage males, has an extremely high victimization risk.[55] One reason is that their lifestyle places them at risk both at school and once they leave school grounds. Kids who hang out with their friends and pursue recreational fun may face an elevated risk for victimization, depending on their idea of fun.[56] For example, their friends may give them a false ID so they can go drinking in the neighborhood bar; or they may hang out in taverns at night, which places them at risk because many fights and assaults occur in places that serve liquor.

Even when they go to college, having a high-risk lifestyle continues to place people in jeopardy. Students who spend several nights each week partying and who take recreational drugs are much more likely to suffer violent crime than those who avoid such risky academic lifestyles.[57] Girls who join sororities, become sexually active, and drink excessively face the greatest risk of sexual coercion. These girls are the most likely to associate with sexually aggressive males who routinely use coercive strategies, like getting their dates drunk and threatening them, in order to obtain sex.[58]

Adolescents are not the only ones with high-risk lifestyles. Populations such as the homeless are extremely vulnerable to physical harm because they are constantly exposed to the criminal population in large urban areas and they have no shelter to which they can escape.[59]

The Equivalent Group Hypothesis The **equivalent group hypothesis** holds that the characteristics of criminals and victims are remarkably similar because in reality the two groups are the same. A number of studies have shown that adolescents who engage in delinquent behavior or join gangs also face the greatest risk of victimization. A number of criminologists have found empirical evidence of this reciprocal relationship. For example, Joan McDermott found that young victims of school crime were likely to strike back at other students in order to regain lost possessions or recover their self-respect.[60] In another study, Simon Singer employed data from the Philadelphia cohort (see Chapter 3) and found that the victims of violent assault were those most likely to become offenders themselves.[61] Similarly, Janet Lauritsen, John Laub, and Robert Sampson found a significant association between participation in self-reported delinquent behavior and personal victimization in such crimes as robbery and assault.[62] Gary Jensen and David Brownfield conclude,

> . . . for personal victimizations, those most likely to be the victims of crime are those who have been most involved in crime; and the similarity of victims and offenders reflects that association.[63]

The criminal–victim connection may exist because the conditions that create criminality also predispose people to victimization. Both share similar lifestyle and residence characteristics. Some former criminals may later become targets because they are perceived as vulnerable: criminal offenders are unlikely to call the police, and if they do, who will believe them? Some victims may commit crime out of frustration; others may resort to violence as a means of revenge, self-defense, or social control. Some may have learned antisocial behavior as a consequence of their own victimization experiences, as in the case of abused children.[64] Research by Elise Lake shows that over 85 percent of female offenders have experienced physical and sexual violence both inside and outside the home, at the hands of parents, intimate partners, and strangers.[65]

The Proximity Hypothesis According to the **proximity hypothesis,** the probability of victimization depends more on where one lives than on how one lives. Some people become victims because they are forced to live near criminals and are selected because they share similar backgrounds and circumstances.[66]

According to this theory, victims do not encourage crime; they are simply in the wrong place at the wrong time.[67] For example, people who reside in socially disorganized high-crime areas have the greatest risk of coming into contact with criminal offenders, irrespective of their own behavior or lifestyle. There may be little reason for residents in lower-class areas to alter their lifestyle or take safety precautions because personal behavior choices do not influence the likelihood of victimization.[68] However, people who exhibit high-risk traits, such as unmarried males, increase their chances of victimization if they reside in a high-crime area.[69] Neighborhood crime levels, then, may be more important for determining the chances of victimization than individual characteristics.

The Deviant Place Hypothesis The **deviant place hypothesis** suggests that there are natural areas of crime, places in which crime flourishes regardless of the precautions taken by their residents. According to the proximity hypothesis (just discussed), if lifestyle causes people to live in or near these areas, the likelihood of their experiencing victimization increases.

Rodney Stark has described these areas as poor, densely populated, highly transient neighborhoods in which commercial and residential property exist side by side.[70] The commercial property provides criminals with easy targets for theft crimes, such as shoplifting and larceny. Successful people stay out of these stigmatized areas; they are homes for "demoralized kinds of people" who are easy targets for crime: the homeless, the addicted, the retarded, and the elderly poor.[71]

Sociologist William Julius Wilson has described how people who can afford to leave dangerous areas do so. He suggests that affluent people realize that criminal victimization can be avoided by moving to an area with greater law enforcement and lower crime rates. Because there are significant interracial income differences, white residents are able to flee inner-city high-crime areas, leaving members of racial minorities behind to suffer high victimization rates.[72]

Deviant Place or Deviant Lifestyle? Which has the greatest influence on victimization risk, place of residence or lifestyle? It is likely that both victim lifestyle and domicile interact to produce crime and victimization rates. People who live in more affluent areas and take safety precautions significantly lower their chances of becoming crime victims; the effect of safety precautions is less pronounced in poor areas. Residents of poor areas have a much greater risk of becoming victims because they live in areas with many motivated offenders; to protect themselves, they have to try harder to be safe than the more affluent.[73]

A victim's behavior and habitat are both linked to criminality: people who take chances, who live in high-risk neighborhoods, and who are law violators themselves share the greatest risk of victimization.[74] Victim behavior cannot explain the onset of criminality, but it can influence the occasion of crime. Although criminal motivation may be acquired early in the life cycle, the decision to commit a particular crime may depend on the actions and reactions of potential victims.

Routine Activities Theory

An important attempt to formally describe the conditions that produce victim risk is contained in a series of papers by Lawrence Cohen and Marcus Felson. This perspective is referred to as **routine activities theory.**[75]

Cohen and Felson assume that both the motivation to commit crime and the supply of offenders are constant.[76] Every society will always have some people who are willing to break the law for revenge, greed, or some other motive. The volume and distribution of **predatory crime** (violent crimes against a person and crimes in which an offender attempts to steal an object directly) are closely related to the interaction of three variables that reflect the routine activities of the typical American lifestyle:

1. The availability of **suitable targets,** such as homes containing easily salable goods
2. The absence of **capable guardians,** such as police, homeowners, neighbors, friends, and relatives
3. The presence of **motivated offenders,** such as a large number of unemployed teenagers

The presence of these components increases the likelihood that a predatory crime will take place. Targets are more likely to be victimized if they are poorly guarded and exposed to a large group of motivated offenders such as teenage boys. The interacting components of routine activities theory are illustrated in Figure 4.8.

Cohen and Felson have used the routine activities approach to explain trends in the crime rate since 1960. They argue that the number of adult caretakers at home during the day (guardians) has decreased as a result of increased female participation in the workforce. While mothers are at work and children in day care, homes are left unguarded. Similarly, with the growth of suburbia and the decline of the traditional neighborhood, the

Figure 4.8   Routine Activities Theory: The Interaction of Three Factors

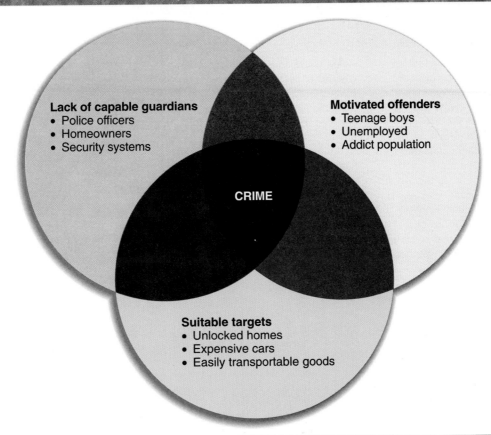

Lack of capable guardians
- Police officers
- Homeowners
- Security systems

Motivated offenders
- Teenage boys
- Unemployed
- Addict population

CRIME

Suitable targets
- Unlocked homes
- Expensive cars
- Easily transportable goods

number of such familiar guardians as family, neighbors, and friends has diminished. At the same time, the volume of easily transportable wealth increased, creating a greater number of available targets. In one study, Cohen and his associates linked burglary rates to the purchase of a commodity easily stolen and disposed of: television sets.[77] Skyrocketing drug use in the 1980s created an excess of motivated offenders, and the rates of some crimes, such as robbery, increased dramatically.

Recent research by Eric Baumer has found that the association between crack use and other forms of crime is a matter of routine activities. When crack use is common in an area, robbery rates increase and burglary rates decline. What accounts for this crime pattern? Crack users need a quick fix of cash to support their habit, making armed robbery the crime of choice. Crack use occurs at night, when addicts have less opportunity to commit residential burglaries (people are at home, and there is little opportunity to sell stolen goods). Robberies are more easily committed at night when streets are less crowded. Crack addicts do not know how to commit commercial burglaries (that is, how to bypass security systems). Also, the prices of black-market jewelry, electronic goods, and guns plummet in crack areas because so many stolen goods are on the market. Consequently, burglary becomes less profitable and less attractive.[78]

Routine Activities and Lifestyle Theories   Routine activities theory and the lifestyle approach have a number of similarities. They both assume that a person's living arrangements can affect victim risk and that people who live in unguarded areas are at the mercy of motivated offenders. These two theories both rely on four basic concepts: (1) proximity to criminals, (2) time of exposure to criminals, (3) target attractiveness, and (4) guardianship.[79]

Considering that these theories are based on the same basic concepts, it follows that they would share predictions, such as these: (1) people who live in high-crime areas who (2) go out late at night (3) carrying valuables such as an expensive watch and (4) engage in risky behavior such as drinking alcohol, (5) without friends or family to watch or help them, increase their victimization risk.[80] For example, young women who drink to excess in bars and frat houses may elevate their risk of date rape because (1) they are easy targets and (2) their attackers can rationalize raping them because they are intoxicated ("she's loose and immoral so I didn't think she'd care"). Intoxication is sometimes seen as making the victim culpable for the crime.[81]

Both views also agree that when a person's lifestyle is altered, he or she may face either additional or reduced exposure to crime. For example, a new public transportation system might put people (such as those

The Criminological Enterprise

Crime and Everyday Life

A core premise of routine activities theory is that all things being equal, the greater the *opportunity* to commit crime, the *higher* the crime and victimization rates. This thesis is cogently presented in a new work by Marcus Felson entitled *Crime and Everyday Life*. Using a routine activities perspective, Felson shows why he believes American crime rates are so high and why U.S. citizens suffer such high rates of victimization.

According to Felson, there are always impulsive, motivated offenders who are willing to take the chance, if conditions are right, of committing crime for profit. Therefore, crime rates are a function of changing social conditions. Crime in the United States grew as the country changed from a nation of small villages and towns to large urban environments. In a village, not only could a thief be easily recognized, but the commodities stolen could be identified long after the crime occurred. Cities provided the critical population mass that allowed predatory criminals to evade apprehension. After the crime, criminals could blend in the crowd, disperse their loot, and then make a quick escape using the public transportation system.

The modern equivalent of the urban center is the shopping mall. Here strangers converge in large numbers and youths loiter. The interior is filled with people, so drug deals can be concealed in the pedestrian flow. Stores have attractively displayed goods that encourage shoplifting and employee pilferage. Substantial numbers of cars are parked in areas that make larceny and car theft virtually undetectable. Cars that carry away

stolen merchandise have an undistinguished appearance; who notices people placing items in a car in a shopping mall lot? Also, shoppers can be attacked in parking lots as people go in isolation to and from their cars.

As American suburbs grew in importance, labor and family life began to be scattered away from the household, decreasing guardianship. The convenience of microwave ovens and automatic dishwashers and increased emphasis on fast food offerings now free adolescents from common household chores. Rather than helping to prepare the family dinner and wash dishes afterward, adolescents are free to meet with their peers and avoid parental control. As car ownership increases, teens have greater access to transportation outside parental control. Greater mobility and access to transportation make it impossible for neighbors to know if a teen belongs in an area or is an intruder planning to commit a crime. As schools become larger and more complex, they also provide ideal sites for crime. The many hallways prevent teachers from knowing who belongs where; spacious school grounds reduce teacher supervision.

Felson finds that these changes in the structure and function of society have been responsible for changes in the crime rates. He concludes that rather than trying to change people, crime prevention strategies must be established in order to reduce the opportunity to commit crime.

CRITICAL THINKING

1. What recent technological changes influence crime rates? The Inter-

Marcus Felson, author of *Crime and Everyday Life*.

net? Video and computer games? Paging systems? Fax machines? Automatic teller systems?
2. Would increased family contact decrease adolescent crime rates, or would it increase the opportunity for child abuse?

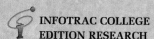

INFOTRAC COLLEGE EDITION RESEARCH

To learn more about routine activities theory, read:
Karen Rodgers and Georgia Roberts, Women's nonspousal multiple victimization: a test of the routine activities theory. *Canadian Journal of Criminology* July 1995 37 n3 p363–91
Carl Keane and Robert Arnold. Examining the relationship between criminal victimization and accidents: a routine activities approach, *The Canadian Review of Sociology and Anthropology* Nov 1996 v33 n4 p457

Source: Marcus Felson, *Crime and Everyday Life: Insights and Implications for Society,* 2nd ed. (Thousand Oaks, Calif.: Pine Forge Press, 1998).

---

who live in the suburbs) at risk for new forms of crime (like subway robbery) committed by offenders (such as inner-city youth) with whom they would have had little contact had their lifestyle not been altered by this new system.[82]

The Criminological Enterprise on crime in everyday life shows how these relationships can be influenced by cultural and structural change.

Is the Routine Activity Approach Valid? Numerous attempts have been made to substantiate the principles of routine activities theory.[83] Homes that are well guarded are the least likely to be burglarized.[84] Rape rates are high in areas where socioeconomic distress results in divorce, unemployment, and overcrowded living conditions; these factors reduce the number of guardians and increase the number of potential offenders.[85] The routine activities view also suggests that lifestyle plays an important role in victimization risk. Those who maintain a high-risk lifestyle by staying out late at night and having frequent activity outside the home also run increased chances of victimization by strangers.[86] Risks increase if people who stay out late use excessive amounts of alcohol, increasing their vulnerability to attack.[87] Not surprisingly, people who stay at home, although safer, are the ones most likely to be killed by family or friends.[88] This empirical support has made routine activities theory the most popular theory of victimization.[89]

However, not all criminologists support the routine activity model. Critics charge that empirical tests of routine activity are often based on false and ambiguous assumptions.[90] For example, according to routine activities theory, the affluent should have a lower victimization risk than the poor because they have the means to purchase security. Yet affluence allows people to increase activity outside the home, and their wealth makes them tempting targets; these factors are also associated with greater risk. Routine activities theory explains why some people become victims, but it fails to explain whether others were first considered and then discarded, and if so, why that decision was made.

Some empirical efforts have not found the relationships predicted by routine activities theory. For example, the risk of property crime victimization has been found to be independent from or unaffected by guardianship; people who take precautions to guard their homes may have equal risk for crime as others who are careless about their home security.[91]

It has also been suggested that routine activities theory places too much emphasis on the victim and overlooks offender differences. Why do offenders choose to commit crime? It is unlikely that all offenders perceive criminal opportunity or apprehension risk in a similar fashion. They are influenced by their peer group and obey cultural norms; routine activities neglects to account for the individual factors that shape criminal choice.[92]

> CONNECTIONS
>
> Despite such criticism, routine activities theory has been and remains an important influence on how both victimization and crime are viewed. Chapter 5 analyzes routine activities theory in conjunction with the rational choice view of crime.

CARING FOR THE VICTIM

National victim surveys indicate that almost every American age 12 and over will one day become the victim of common-law crimes, such as larceny and burglary, and in the aftermath suffer financial problems,

mental stress, and physical hardship.[93] Surveys show that upward of 75 percent of the general public has been victimized by crime at least once in their lives; as many as 25 percent of the victims develop posttraumatic stress syndrome, and their symptoms last for more than a decade after the crime occurred.[94] The long-term effects of sexual victimization can include years of problem avoidance, social withdrawal, and self-criticism.[95]

Helping the victim to cope is the responsibility of all of society. Law enforcement agencies, courts, and correctional and human service systems have come to realize that due process and human rights exist both for the defendant and for the victim of criminal behavior.

The Government's Response

Because of public concern over violent personal crime, President Ronald Reagan created a Task Force on Victims of Crime in 1982.[96] This group was to extensively study crime victimization in the United States and determine how victims of crime could be assisted. It found that crime victims had been transformed into a group of citizens burdened by a justice system that had been designed for their protection. Their participation both as victims and as witnesses was often neglected, and the system seemed to have greater concern for the defendant's rights while ignoring the burdens and suffering of the victim. The task force suggested that a balance be achieved between recognizing the victim's rights and providing the defendant with due process. Its most significant recommendation was that the Sixth Amendment to the U.S. Constitution be augmented by this statement: "In every criminal prosecution, the victim shall have the right to be present and to be heard at all critical stages of the judicial proceedings."[97] Other recommendations included providing witnesses and victims protection from intimidation, requiring restitution in criminal cases, developing guidelines for fair treatment of crime victims and witnesses, and expanding programs of victim compensation.[98] Consequently, the Justice Department provided research funds to create and expand **victim-witness assistance programs,** which identify the needs of victims and witnesses who were involved in a criminal incident. In addition, the Omnibus Victim and Witness Protection Act required the use of victim impact statements at sentencing in federal criminal cases, greater protection for witnesses, more stringent bail laws, and the use of restitution in criminal cases.

In 1984 the Comprehensive Crime Control Act and the Victims of Crime Act authorized federal funding for state victim compensation and assistance projects.[99] With these acts, the federal government began to aid the plight of the victim and make victim assistance an even greater concern of the public and the justice system.

A police officer helps an injured teen in Miami. Americans are becoming increasingly defensive about crime by stocking up on guns, buying security systems, joining street patrols, and demanding greater police protection. However, helping the victim to cope is the responsibility of all of society. Law enforcement agencies, courts, and correctional and human service systems have come to realize that due process and human rights exist both for the defendant and for the victim of criminal behavior.

Victim Service Programs

As a result of the task force's efforts, an estimated 2,000 victim-witness assistance programs have developed around the United States.[100] Victim-witness assistance programs are organized on a variety of governmental levels and serve a variety of clients. We will look at the most prominent forms of victim services operating in the United States.[101]

Victim Compensation   One of the primary goals of victim advocates has been to lobby for legislation creating crime **victim compensation** programs.[102] As a result of such legislation, the victim ordinarily receives compensation from the state to pay for damages associated with the crime. Rarely are two compensation schemes alike, however, and many state programs suffer from lack of both adequate funding and proper organization within the criminal justice system. However, the victim assistance projects seek to help the victim learn about victim compensation services and related programs. Today victim compensation programs exist in almost every state and the federal government. Compensation may be made for medical bills, loss of wages, loss of future earnings, and counseling. In the case of death, the victim's survivors can receive burial expenses and aid for loss of support.[103] Awards are typically in the $100 to $15,000 range. Occasionally programs will provide

emergency assistance to indigent victims until compensation is available. Emergency assistance may come in the form of food vouchers or replacement of prescription medicines.

Court Services   A common victim program service helps victims deal with the criminal justice system. One approach is to prepare victims and witnesses by explaining court procedures: how to be a witness, how bail works, and what to do if the defendant makes a threat. Lack of such knowledge can cause confusion and fear, making some victims reluctant to testify in court procedures. Many victim programs also provide transportation to and from court and counselors, who remain in the courtroom during hearings to explain procedures and provide support. Court escorts are particularly important for elderly and disabled victims, victims of child abuse and assault, and victims who have been intimidated by friends or relatives of the defendant.

Public Education   More than half of all victim programs include public education programs that help familiarize the general public with their services and with other agencies that help crime victims. In some instances, these are primary education programs, which teach methods of dealing with conflict without resorting to violence. For example, school-based programs present information on spousal and dating abuse followed by discussions of how to reduce violent incidents.[104]

Sometimes the educational aspect of victim services can be more immediate and personal. Most programs will help employers to understand the plight of their employee victims. Because victims may miss work or suffer postcrime emotional trauma, they may need to be absent from work for extended periods. If employers are unwilling to give them leave, victims may refuse to participate in the criminal justice process. Explaining the needs of victims to employers is a service provided by more than half of all victim programs.

Crisis Intervention Most victim programs refer victims to specific services to help them recover from their ordeal. Clients are commonly referred to the local network of public and private social service agencies that can provide emergency and long-term assistance with transportation, medical care, shelter, food, and clothing. In addition, more than half of victim programs provide **crisis intervention** to victims, many of whom feel isolated, vulnerable, and in need of immediate services. Some programs counsel at their offices, while others visit victims' homes, the crime scene, or a hospital.

No crimes require more crisis intervention efforts than rape and sexual assault. After years of being ignored by the justice system, increased sensitivity to rape has spurred the opening of crisis centers around the country. These centers typically feature 24-hour-a-day emergency phone lines and information on police, medical, and court procedures. Some provide volunteers to assist the victim as her case is processed through the justice system. The growth of these services, which began with the Washington, D.C., Rape Crisis Center's phone line in 1972, has been so explosive that services are now available in more than 1,000 centers located in almost all major cities and college communities.[105] Most rape programs provide the following services to victims:

1. *Emergency assistance*—including information, referral, and some support, usually provided over the telephone, and available 24 hours a day
2. *Face-to-face crisis intervention or accompaniment*—usually provided in the hospital, police station, courts, or other public locations, also available 24 hours a day
3. *Counseling*—either one-on-one or in groups and for a varying number of sessions, often provided at the center, usually scheduled, and limited to business hours and evenings.[106]

Victim–Offender Reconciliation Programs (VORP) Reconciliation programs are based on the concept of **restorative justice,** which rejects punitive correctional measures and instead suggests that crimes of violence

and theft should be viewed as interpersonal conflicts that need to be settled in the community through non-coercive means. Victim–offender reconciliation programs (VORPs) use mediators to facilitate face-to-face encounters between victims and their attackers. The aim is to engage in direct negotiations that lead to restitution agreements and, possibly, reconciliation between the two parties involved.[107] More than 120 reconciliation programs are currently in operation, and they handle an estimated 16,000 cases per year. Designed at first to handle routine misdemeanors such as petty theft and vandalism, programs now commonly hammer out restitution agreements in more serious incidents like residential burglary and even attempted murder.

CONNECTIONS

The theoretical roots of the restorative justice concept can be found in Chapter 9's discussion of peacemaking criminology.

Victims' Rights

Legal scholar Frank Carrington suggests that crime victims have legal rights that should assure them basic services from the government.[108] According to Carrington, just as the defendant has the right to counsel and a fair trial, society is also obliged to ensure basic rights for law-abiding citizens. These rights range from adequate protection from violent crimes to victim compensation and assistance from the criminal justice system. Here are some suggested changes that might enhance the relationship between the victim and the criminal justice system:

- Liberally using **preventive detention** (pretrial jailing without the right to bail) for dangerous criminals awaiting trial
- Eliminating delays between the arrest and the initial hearing and between the hearing and the trial, which would limit the opportunity an offender has to intimidate victims or witnesses
- Eliminating plea bargaining, or if that proves impossible, allowing victims to participate in the plea negotiations
- Controlling defense attorneys' cross-examination of victims
- Allowing hearsay testimony of police at the preliminary hearing instead of requiring the victim to appear
- Abolishing the **exclusionary rule,** which allows the guilty to go free on technicalities
- Allowing victims to participate in sentencing
- Creating minimum mandatory sentences for crimes
- Prohibiting murderers given life sentences from being freed on parole
- Making criminals serve time for each crime they are convicted of and reducing the use of concurrent

sentences, which allows them to simultaneously serve time for multiple crimes

- Tightening the granting of parole and allowing victims to participate in parole hearings
- Providing full restitution or compensation to victims in all crimes

Some of these suggestions seem reasonable policy alternatives, whereas others, such as repudiating the exclusionary rule, may be impossible to achieve because they violate defendants' due process protection. However, about 14 states have actually incorporated similar language within their legal codes in a "Victims Bill of Rights." Victims are now entitled to find out about the progress of their cases in 22 states and to be present at sentencing hearings in 37 and at parole hearings in 36.[109]

In *Payne v. Tennessee* (90-5721, 1991) the U.S. Supreme Court ruled that juries would be permitted to consider the emotional impact of a victim's murder on surviving family members. *Payne* overruled the standing prohibition against victim statements in death penalty cases (presumably because criminals who killed victims without families would have an advantage at sentencing) and may signal greater judicial sensitivity to the rights of victims.

Assuring victims' rights can involve an eclectic group of advocacy groups, some independent, others government-sponsored, and some self-help. Advocates can be especially helpful when victims need to interact with the agencies of justice. For example, advocates can lobby police departments to keep investigations open as well as request the return of recovered stolen property. They can demand from prosecutors and judges protection from harassment and reprisals by, for example, making "no contact" a condition of bail. They can help victims make statements during sentencing hearings as well as probation and parole revocation procedures. Victim advocates can also interact with news media, making sure that reporting is accurate and that victim privacy is not violated. Victim advocates can be part of an independent agency similar to a legal aid society. If successful, top-notch advocates may eventually open private offices, similar to attorneys, private investigators, or jury consultants.[110]

Self-Protection

Although the general public mostly approves of the police, fear of crime and concern about community safety have prompted many people to become their own "police force," taking an active role in community protection and citizen crime control groups.[111] The more crime in an area, the greater the amount of fear, and the more likely residents will be to engage in self-protective measures.[112] Research indicates that a significant number of crimes may not be reported to police simply because victims prefer to take matters into

Some people practice self-protection techniques and are prepared to fight back when they are attacked by criminals. Research indicates that victims who fight back often frustrate their attackers, but they also face increased odds of being physically harmed during the attack. One way of minimizing harm may be to take self-defense courses and develop good defensive skills.

their own hands.[113] One manifestation of this trend is the concept of **target hardening,** or making one's home and business crime-proof through locks, bars, alarms, and other devices.[114] A national victimization risk survey found that substantial numbers of people have taken specific steps to secure their homes or place of employment.[115] One-third of the households surveyed reported using one or more crime prevention measures, including having a burglar alarm (7 percent), participating in a neighborhood watch program (7 percent), or engraving valuables with an identification number (25 percent). Other commonly used crime prevention techniques include a fence or barricade at the entrance; a doorkeeper, guard, or receptionist in an apartment building; an intercom or phone to gain access to the building; surveillance cameras; window bars; warning signs; and dogs chosen for their ability to guard the house. The use of these measures was inversely proportional to perception of neighborhood safety: people who feared crime were more likely to use crime-prevention techniques.

Although the true relationship is still unclear, there is mounting evidence that people who protect their homes are less likely to be victimized by property crimes.[116] One study conducted in the Philadelphia area found that people who install burglar alarms are less likely to suffer burglary than those who forgo similar preventive measures.[117]

Fighting Back   Some people take self-protection to its ultimate end by preparing to fight back when criminals attack them. How successful are victims when they fight back? Research indicates that victims who fight back often frustrate their attackers but also face increased odds of being physically harmed during the attack.[118] In some cases fighting back decreases the odds of a crime being completed but increases the victim's chances of injury.[119] Resistance may draw the attention of bystanders and make a violent crime physically difficult to complete. It can also cause offenders to escalate their violence. For example, a federal survey found that victims of attempted robbery who fought back were less likely to experience completed crimes than passive victims; however, they were also more likely to be injured during the attack. The victims who escaped both serious injury and property loss were the ones who used the most violent responses to crime, such as a weapon, or the least violent, such as reasoning with their attackers. Those who fought back with their fists or who tried to get help were the most likely to experience both injury and theft.[120]

If unarmed victims are the most likely to be injured when they fight back, are those who use firearms much more successful? Gary Kleck has found that people like to arm themselves when they perceive that violent crime rates are high in their area. Viewing news stories about crime or hearing about crime from coworkers, friends, and family may be a more powerful incentive to buy a gun than actual victimization experiences.[121] People who own guns, Kleck finds, are ready and willing to use them for self-protection. Each year victims use guns for defensive purposes 2.5 million times, a number that is not surprising considering that about one-third of U.S. households contain guns.[122] Kleck has estimated that armed victims kill between 1,500 to 2,800 potential felons each year and wound between 8,700 and 16,000. Kleck's research shows, ironically, that by fighting back, victims kill far more criminals than the estimated 250 to 1,000 killed annually by police.[123] Kleck has found that the risk of collateral injury is relatively rare and that potential victims should be encouraged to fight back.[124] According to Kleck, empirical research studies unanimously show that defensive gun use is associated with both lower rates of crime completion and lower rates of injury to the victim.[125]

CONNECTIONS

Whereas Kleck strongly supports firearm ownership, in Chapter 3, the debate over gun control was discussed in a Policy and Practice in Criminology box. There is some question whether having a handgun can influence crime rates; opponents charge that gun possession brings with it a number of collateral problems, including accidental deaths and the use of stolen guns in other crimes.

Community Organization

Not everyone is capable of buying a handgun or semiautomatic weapon and doing battle with predatory criminals. An alternative approach has been for communities to organize on the neighborhood level against crime. Citizens have been working independently and in cooperation with local police agencies in neighborhood patrol and block watch programs. These programs organize local citizens in urban areas to patrol neighborhoods, watch for suspicious people, help secure the neighborhood, lobby for improvements (such as increased lighting), report crime to police, put out community newsletters, conduct home security surveys, and serve as a source for crime information or tips.[126] Although such programs are welcome additions to police services, there is little evidence that they appreciably affect the crime rate. There is also concern that their effectiveness is spottier in low-income, high-crime areas, which need the most crime prevention assistance.[127] Block watches and neighborhood patrols seem more successful when they are part of general-purpose or multi-issue community groups, rather than when they focus directly on crime problems.[128]

In sum, community crime prevention programs, target hardening, and self-defense measures are flourishing around the United States. They are a response to the fear of crime and the perceived inability of police agencies to ensure community safety. Along with private security, they represent attempts to supplement municipal police agencies and expand the "war on crime" to become a personal, neighborhood, and community concern.

SUMMARY

Criminologists now consider victims and victimization a major focus of study. More than 30 million U.S. citizens suffer from crime each year, and the social and economic costs of crime are in the billions of dollars. Like crime, victimization has stable patterns and trends. Violent crime victims tend to be young, poor, single males living in large cities, although victims come in all ages, sizes, races, and genders. Many victimizations occur in the home, and many victims are the target of relatives and loved ones. In a few cases where children have been the victims of parental abuse, the parents later become the victims of their children. When the crime results in death, this is known as parricide.

Table 4.2 Victimization Theories

THEORY	MAJOR PREMISE	STRENGTHS
Victim precipitation	Victims trigger criminal acts by their provocative behavior. Active precipitation involves fighting words or gestures. Passive precipitation occurs when victims unknowingly threaten their attacker.	Explains multiple victimizations. If people precipitate crime, it follows that they will become repeat victims if their behavior persists over time.
Lifestyle	Victimization risk is increased when people have a high-risk lifestyle. Placing oneself at risk by going out to dangerous places results in increased victimization.	Explains victimization patterns in the social structure. Males, young people, and the poor have high victimization rates because they have a higher-risk lifestyle than females, the elderly, and the affluent.
Equivalent group hypothesis	Criminals and victims are one and the same. Both crime and victimization are part of a high-risk lifestyle.	Shows that the conditions that create criminality also produce high victimization risk. Victims may commit crime out of a need for revenge or frustration.
Proximity hypothesis	People who live in deviant places are at high risk for crime. Victim behavior has little influence over the criminal act.	Places the focus of crime on deviant places. Shows why people with conventional lifestyles become crime victims.
Routine activities	Crime rates can be explained by the availability of suitable targets, the absence of capable guardians, and the presence of motivated offenders.	Can explain crime rates and trends. Shows how victim behavior can influence criminal opportunity. Suggests that victimization risk can be reduced by increasing guardianship and/or reducing target vulnerability.

There are a number of theories of victimization. One view, called victim precipitation, is that victims provoke criminals. More common are lifestyle theories that suggest that victims put themselves in danger by engaging in high-risk activities, such as going out late at night, living in a high-crime area, and associating with high-risk peers. The routine activities theory maintains that a pool of motivated offenders exists and that these offenders will take advantage of unguarded, suitable targets. The major theories of victimization are summarized in Table 4.2.

Numerous programs help victims by providing court services, economic compensation, public education, and crisis intervention. Some people suggest that the U.S. Constitution should be amended to include protection of victims' rights. Rather than depend on the justice system, some victims have attempted to help themselves. In some instances this self-help means community organization for self-protection. In other instances victims have armed themselves and fought back against their attackers. There is evidence that fighting back reduces the number of completed crimes but is also related to victim injury.

 See the book-specific web site at www.cj.wadsworth.com for additional chapter links, discussions, and quizzes.

THINKING LIKE A CRIMINOLOGIST

The director of the state's department of human services has asked you to evaluate a self-report survey of adolescents ages 10 to 18. She has provided you with the following information on physical abuse:

Adolescents experiencing abuse or violence are at high risk of immediate and lasting negative effects on health and well-being. Of the high school students surveyed, an alarming one in five (21 percent) said they had been physically abused. Of the older students, ages 15 to 18, 29 percent said they had been physically abused. Younger students also reported significant rates of abuse: 17 percent responded "yes" when questioned whether they had been physically abused. Although girls were far less likely to report abuse than boys, 12 percent said they had been physically abused. Most abuse occurs at home; it occurs more than once; and the abuser is usually a family member. More than half of those physically abused had tried alcohol and drugs, and 60 percent had admitted to a violent act. Nonabused children were significantly less likely to abuse substances, and only 30 percent indicated they had committed a violent act.

How would you interpret this data? What factors might influence its validity? What is your interpretation of the association between abuse and delinquency?

KEY TERMS

victimology
victimologists
tangible direct costs
indirect costs
victimization
posttraumatic stress disorder
obsessive compulsive disorder
hyperarousal
cycle of violence
chronic victims
stalking
parricide

patricide
matricide
psychosis
victim precipitation
active precipitation
victim-precipitated crime
date rape
passive precipitation
equivalent group hypothesis
deviant place hypothesis
routine activities theory
predatory crime

suitable targets
capable guardians
motivated offenders
proximity hypothesis
victim-witness assistance program
victim compensation
crisis intervention
restorative justice
preventive detention
exclusionary rule
target hardening

NOTES

1. Cheryl Ringel, *Criminal Victimization 1996: Changes 1995–96 with Trends 1993–96* (Washington, D.C.: Bureau of Justice Statistics, 1997).

2. Arthur Lurigio, "Are All Victims Alike? The Adverse, Generalized, and Differential Impact of Crime," *Crime and Delinquency* 33 (1987): 452–67.

3. FBI, *Crime in the United States, 1997* (Washington, D.C.: U.S. Government Printing Office, 1998), p. 210. Hereinafter cited as FBI, Uniform Crime Report, 1997.

4. Ted Miller, Mark Cohen, and Brian Wiersema, *The Extent and Costs of Crime Victimization: A New Look* (Washington, D.C.: National Institute of Justice, 1996).

5. George Rengert, *The Geography of Illegal Drugs* (Boulder, Colo.: Westview Press, 1996), p. 5.

6. Peter Finn, *Victims* (Washington, D.C.: Bureau of Justice Statistics, 1988), p. 1.

7. Michael Wiederman, Randy Sansone, and Lori Sansone, "History of Trauma and Attempted Suicide Among Women in a Primary Care Setting," *Violence and Victims* 13 (1998): 3–11; Susan Leslie Bryant and Lillian Range, "Suicidality in College Women Who Were Sexually and Physically Abused and Physically Punished by Parents," *Violence and Victims* 10 (1995): 195–215.

8. William Downs and Brenda Miller, "Relationships Between Experiences of Parental Violence During Childhood and Women's Self-Esteem," *Violence and Victims* 13 (1998): 63–78.

9. Sally Davies-Netley, Michael Hurlburt, and Richard Hough, "Childhood Abuse as a Precursor to Homelessness for Homeless Women with Severe Mental Illness," *Violence and Victims* 11 (1996): 129–42.

10. See, generally, M. D. Pagelow, *Woman Battering: Victims and Their Experiences* (Beverly Hills, Calif.: Sage, 1981).

11. Dina Vivian and Jean Malone, "Relationship Factors and Depressive Symptomology Associated with Mild and Severe Husband-to-Wife Physical Aggression," *Violence and Victims* 12 (1997): 19–37; Walter Gleason, "Mental Disorders in Battered Women," *Violence and Victims* 8 (1993): 53–66.

12. Daniel Saunders, "Posttraumatic Stress Symptom Profiles of Battered Women: A Comparison of Survivors in Two Settings," *Violence and Victims* 9 (1994): 31–43.

13. Jill Kuhn, Charleanea Arellano, and Ernest Chavez, "Correlates of Sexual Assault in Mexican American and White Non-Hispanic Adolescent Males," *Violence and Victims* 13 (1998): 11–21.

14. Elizabeth Stanko and Kathy Hobdell, "Assault on Men, Masculinity, and Male Victimization," *British Journal of Criminology* 33 (1993): 400–415.

15. James Anderson, Terry Grandison, and Laronistine Dyson, "Victims of Random Violence and the Public Health Implication: A Health Care of Criminal Justice Issue," *Journal of Criminal Justice* 24 (1996): 379–93.

16. Pamela Wilcox Rountree, "A Reexamination of the Crime–Fear Linkage," *Journal of Research in Crime and Delinquency* 35 (1998): 341–72.

17. Robert Davis, Bruce Taylor, and Arthur Lurigio, "Adjusting to Criminal Victimization: The Correlates of Postcrime Distress," *Violence and Victimization* 11 (1996): 21–34.

18. Timothy Ireland and Cathy Spatz Widom, *Childhood Victimization and Risk for Alcohol and Drug Arrests* (Washington, D.C.: National Institute of Justice, 1995).

19. Cathy Spatz Widom, *The Cycle of Violence* (Washington, D.C.: National Institute of Justice, 1992), p. 1.

20. Steve Spaccarelli, J. Douglas Coatsworth, and Blake Sperry Bowden, "Exposure to Serious Family Violence Among Incarcerated Boys: Its Association with Violent Offending and Potential Mediating Variables," *Violence and Victims* 10 (1995): 163–180.

21. Jerome Kolbo, "Risk and Resilience Among Children Exposed to Family Violence," *Violence and Victims* 11 (1996): 113–127.

22. Not all research findings agree that abuse is related to problems in adulthood. For an opposing view, see Bruce Rind, Philip Tromovitch, and Robert Bauserman, "A Meta-Analytic Examination of Assumed Properties of Child Sexual Abuse Using College Samples," *Psychological Bulletin* 124 (1998): 22–53.

23. Kathryn A. Chandler and Chris Chapman, Michael R. Rand and Bruce M. Taylor, "Students' Reports of School Crime: 1989 and 1995" (Washington, D.C: Bureau of Justice Statistics, 1998).

24. M. Dwayne Smith and Victoria Brewer, "A Sex-Specific Analysis of Correlates of Homicide Victimization in United States Cities," *Violence and Victims* 7 (1992): 279–87.

25. Ronet Bachman, *Violence Against Women* (Washington, D.C.: Bureau of Justice Statistics, 1994).

26. Associated Press, "Boy, 11, Faces 40 Years in Sexual Assault Case," *New York Times,* 5 June 1998, p. A17.

27. Michael Rand, *Violence-Related Injuries Treated in Hospital Emergency Departments* (Washington, D.C.: Bureau of Justice Statistics, 1997).

28. Lawrence Greenfeld, *Child Victimizers: Violent Offenders and Their Victims* (Washington, D.C: Bureau of Justice Statistics, 1996).

29. Richard Rosenfeld, "Changing Relationships Between Men and Women: A Note on the Decline in Intimate Partner Homicide," *Homicide Studies* 1 (1997): 72–83.

30. Desmond Ellis and Lori Wright, "Estrangement, Interventions, and Male Violence Toward Female Partners," *Violence and Victims* 12 (1997): 51–68.

31. U.S. Center for Disease Control, "Homicide Among Young Black Males—United States, 1978–1987," *Morbidity and Mortality Weekly Report* 39 (December 7, 1990): 869–73.

32. Janet Lauritsen and Kenna Davis Quinet, "Repeat Victimizations Among Adolescents and Young Adults," *Journal of Quantitative Criminology* 11 (1995): 143–63.

33. Denise Osborn, Dan Ellingworth, Tim Hope, and Alan Trickett, "Are Repeatedly Victimized Households Different?" *Journal of Quantitative Criminology* 12 (1996): 223–45.

34. Terry Buss and Rashid Abdu, "Repeat Victims of Violence in an Urban Trauma Center," *Violence and Victims* 10 (1995): 183–87.

35. Kate Bowers, Alex Hirschfield, and Shane Johnson, "Victimization Revisited: A Case Study of Non-Residential Repeat Burglary on Merseyside," *British Journal of Criminology* 38 (1998): 429–53.

36. Graham Farrell, "Predicting and Preventing Revictimization," in Michael Tonry and David Farrington, eds., *Crime and Justice: An Annual Review of Research,* vol. 20 (Chicago: University of Chicago Press, 1995), pp. 61–126.

37. Farrell, "Predicting and Preventing Revictimization," p. 161.

38. David Finkelhor and Nancy Asigian, "Risk Factors for Youth Victimization: Beyond a Lifestyles/Routine Activities Theory Approach," *Violence and Victimization* 11 (1996): 3–19.

39. Lauritsen and Quinet, "Repeat Victimizations Among Adolescents and Young Adults," p. 161.

40. Graham Farrell, Coretta Phillips, and Ken Pease, "Like Taking Candy: Why Does Repeat Victimization Occur?" *British Journal of Criminology* 35 (1995): 384–99.

41. Christopher Innes and Lawrence Greenfeld, *Violent State Prisoners and Their Victims* (Washington, D.C.: Bureau of Justice Statistics, 1990), p. 4.

42. Innes and Greenfeld, *Violent State Prisoners and Their Victims.*

43. Hans Von Hentig, *The Criminal and His Victim: Studies in the Sociobiology of Crime* (New Haven, Conn.: Yale University Press, 1948), p. 384.

44. Stephen Schafer, *The Victim and His Criminal* (New York: Random House, 1968), p. 152.

45. Marvin Wolfgang, *Patterns of Criminal Homicide* (Philadelphia: University of Pennsylvania Press, 1958).

46. Wolfgang, *Patterns of Criminal Homicide,* p. 252.

47. Menachem Amir, *Patterns in Forcible Rape* (Chicago: University of Chicago Press, 1971).

48. Susan Estrich, *Real Rape* (Cambridge: Harvard University Press, 1987).

49. Estrich, *Real Rape,* p. 69.

50. Associated Press, "Jury Stirs Furor by Citing Dress in Rape Acquittal," *Boston Globe,* 6 October 1989, p. 12.

51. Martin Daly and Margo Wilson, *Homicide* (New York: Aldine de Gruyter, 1988).

52. Rosemary Gartner and Bill McCarthy, "The Social Distribution of Femicide in Urban Canada, 1921–1988," *Law and Society Review* 25 (1991): 287–311.

53. Lawrence Cohen and Marcus Felson, "Social Change and Crime Rate Trends: A Routine Activities Approach," *American Sociological Review* 44 (1979): 588–608; L. Cohen, James Kleugel, and Kenneth Land, "Social Inequality and Predatory Criminal Victimization: An Exposition and Test of a Formal Theory," *American Sociological Review* 46 (1981): 505–24; Steven Messner and Kenneth Tardiff, "The Social Ecology of Urban Homicide: An Application of the Routine Activities Approach," *Criminology* 23 (1985): 241–67.

54. Pamela Lattimore, Richard Linster, and John MacDonald, "Risk of Death Among Serious Young Offenders," *Journal of Research in Crime and Delinquency* 34 (1997): 187–209.

55. See, generally, Gary Gottfredson and Denise Gottfredson, *Victimization in Schools* (New York: Plenum Press, 1985).

56. Gary Jensen and David Brownfield, "Gender, Lifestyles, and Victimization: Beyond Routine Activity Theory," *Violence and Victims* 1 (1986): 85–99.

57. Bonnie Fisher, John Sloan, Francis Cullen, and Chunmeng Lu, "Crime in the Ivory Tower: The Level and Sources of Student Victimization," *Criminology* 36 (1998): 671–710.

58. Kimberly Tyler, Danny Hoyt, and Les Whitbeck, "Coercive Sexual Strategies," *Violence and Victims* 13 (1998): 47–63.

59. Les Whitbeck and Ronald Simons, "A Comparison of Adaptive Strategies and Patterns of Victimization Among Homeless Adolescents and Adults," *Violence and Victims* 8 (1993): 135–51; Kevin Fitzpatrick, Mark La Gory, and Ferris Ritchey, "Criminal Victimization Among the Homeless," *Justice Quarterly* 10 (1993): 353–68.

60. Joan McDermott, "Crime in the School and in the Community: Offenders, Victims and Fearful Youth," *Crime and Delinquency* 29 (1983): 270–83.

61. Simon Singer, "Homogeneous Victim–Offender Populations: A Review and Some Research Implications," *Journal of Criminal Law and Criminology* 72 (1981): 779–99.

62. Janet Lauritsen, John Laub, and Robert Sampson, "Conventional and Delinquent Activities: Implications for the Prevention of Violent Victimization Among Adolescents," *Violence and Victims* 7 (1992): 91–102.

63. Jensen and Brownfield, "Gender, Lifestyles, and Victimization," pp. 85–101.

64. Ross Vasta, "Physical Child Abuse: A Dual Component Analysis," *Developmental Review* 2 (1982): 128–35.

65. Elise Lake, "An Exploration of the Violent Victim Experiences of Female Offenders," *Violence and Victims* 8 (1993): 41–50.

66. Lake, "An Exploration," pp. 41–50.

67. James Garofalo, "Reassessing the Lifestyle Model of Criminal Victimization," in *Positive Criminology,* ed. Michael Gottfredson and Travis Hirschi (Newbury Park, Calif.: Sage Publications, 1987), pp. 23–42.

68. Terance Miethe and David McDowall, "Contextual Effects in Models of Criminal Victimization," *Social Forces* 71 (1993): 741–59.

69. Robert Sampson and Janet Lauritsen, "Deviant Lifestyles, Proximity to Crime and the Offender–Deviant Link in Personal Violence," *Journal of Research in Crime and Delinquency* 27 (1990): 110–39.

70. Rodney Stark, "Deviant Places: A Theory of the Ecology of Crime," *Criminology* 25 (1987): 893–911.

71. Stark, "Deviant Places," p. 902.

72. William Julius Wilson, *The Truly Disadvantaged* (Chicago: University of Chicago Press, 1990); see also Allen Liska and Paul Bellair, "Violent-Crime Rates and Racial Composition: Convergence over Time," *American Journal of Sociology* 101 (1995): 578–610.

73. Pamela Wilcox Rountree, Kenneth Land, and Terance Miethe, "Macro–Micro Integration in the Study of Victimization: A Hierarchical Logistic Model Analysis Across Seattle Neighborhoods." Paper presented at the annual meeting of the American Society of Criminology, Phoenix, Arizona, November 1993.

74. Sampson and Lauritsen, "Deviant Lifestyles."

75. Lawrence Cohen and Marcus Felson, "Social Change and Crime Rate Trends: A Routine Activities Approach," *American Sociological Review* 44 (1979): 588–608.

76. For a review, see James LeBeau and Thomas Castellano, *The Routine Activities Approach: An Inventory and Critique* (Carbondale, Ill.: Center for the Studies of Crime, Delinquency, and Corrections, Southern Illinois University—Carbondale, unpublished, 1987).

77. Lawrence Cohen, Marcus Felson, and Kenneth Land, "Property Crime Rates in the United States: A Macrodynamic Analysis, 1947–1977, with Ex-ante Forecasts for the Mid-1980s," *American Journal of Sociology* 86 (1980): 90–118.

78. Eric Baumer, Janet Lauritsen, Richard Rosenfeld, and Richard Wright, "The Influence of Crack Cocaine on Robbery, Burglary, and Homicide Rates: A Cross-City, Longitudinal Analysis," *Journal of Research in Crime and Delinquency* 35 (1998): 316–40.

79. Terence Miethe and Robert Meier, *Crime and its Social Context: Toward an Integrated Theory of Offenders, Victims, and Situations* (Albany, N.Y.: State University of New York Press, 1994).

80. Richard Felson, "Routine Activities and Involvement in Violence as Actor, Witness, or Target," *Violence and Victimization* 12 (1997): 209–223.

81. Georgina Hammock and Deborah Richardson, "Perceptions of Rape: The Influence of Closeness of Relationship, Intoxication, and Sex of Participant," *Violence and Victimization* 12 (1997): 237–47.

82. Manon Tremblay and Pierre Tremblay, "Social Structure, Interaction Opportunities, and the Direction of Violent Offenses," *Journal of Research in Crime and Delinquency* 35 (1998): 295–315.

83. See also Messner and Tardiff, "The Social Ecology of Urban Homicide"; Philip Cook, "The Demand and Supply of Criminal Opportunities," in *Crime and Justice*, vol. 7, ed. Michael Tonry and Norval Morris (Chicago: University of Chicago Press, 1986), pp. 1–28; and Ronald Clarke and Derek Cornish, "Modeling Offender's Decisions: A Framework for Research and Policy," in *Crime and Justice*, vol. 6, ed. Michael Tonry and Norval Morris (Chicago: University of Chicago Press, 1985), pp. 147–87.

84. James Lynch and David Cantor, "Ecological and Behavioral Influences on Property Victimization at Home: Implications for Opportunity Theory," *Journal of Research in Crime and Delinquency* 29 (1992): 335–62.

85. David Maume, "Inequality and Metropolitan Rape Rates: A Routine Activities Approach," *Justice Quarterly* 6 (1989): 513–27.

86. Terance Miethe, Mark Stafford, and Douglas Stone, "Lifestyle Changes and Risks of Criminal Victimization," *Journal of Quantitative Criminology* 6 (1990): 357–75.

87. James Lasley, "Drinking Routines, Lifestyles, and Predatory Victimization: A Causal Analysis," *Justice Quarterly* 6 (1989): 529–42.

88. Messner and Tardiff, "The Social Ecology of Urban Homicide."

89. Christopher Birkbeck and Gary LaFree, "The Situational Analysis of Crime and Deviance," *Annual Review of Sociology* 19 (1993): 113–37.

90. Birkbeck and LaFree, "The Situational Analysis of Crime and Deviance," 127–28.

91. James Massey, Marvin Krohn, and Lisa Bonati, "Property Crime and the Routine Activities of Individuals," *Journal of Research in Crime and Delinquency* 26 (1989): 378–400, at 396.

92. Leslie Kennedy and Stephen Baron, "Routine Activities and a Subculture of Violence: A Study of Violence on the Street," *Journal of Research in Crime and Delinquency* 30 (1993): 88–112.

93. Patricia Resnick, "Psychological Effects of Victimization: Implications for the Criminal Justice System," *Crime and Delinquency* 33 (1987): 468–78.

94. Dean Kilpatrick, Benjamin Saunders, Lois Veronen, Connie Best, and Judith Von, "Criminal Victimization: Lifetime Prevalence, Reporting to Police, and Psychological Impact," *Crime and Delinquency* 33 (1987): 479–89.

95. Mark Santello and Harold Leitenberg, "Sexual Aggression by an Acquaintance: Methods of Coping and Later Psychological Adjustment," *Violence and Victims* 8 (1993): 91–103.

96. U.S. Department of Justice, *Report of the President's Task Force on Victims of Crime* (Washington, D.C.: U.S. Government Printing Office, 1983).

97. U.S. Department of Justice, *Report of the President's Task Force on Victims of Crime*, p. 115.

98. U.S. Department of Justice, *Report of the President's Task Force on Victims of Crime*, pp. 2–10; and "Review on Victims—Witnesses of Crime," *Massachusetts Lawyers Weekly*, 25 April 1983, p. 26.

99. Robert Davis, *Crime Victims: Learning How to Help Them* (Washington, D.C.: National Institute of Justice, 1987).

100. Peter Finn and Beverly Lee, *Establishing a Victim-Witness Assistance Program* (Washington, D.C.: U.S. Government Printing Office, 1988).

101. This section leans heavily on Albert Roberts, "Delivery of Services to Crime Victims: A National Survey," *American Journal of Orthopsychiatry* 6 (1991): 128–37; see also Albert Roberts, *Helping Crime Victims: Research, Policy, and Practice* (Newbury Park, Calif.: Sage, 1990).

102. Randall Schmidt, "Crime Victim Compensation Legislation: A Comparative Study," *Victimology* 5 (1980): 428–37.

103. Schmidt, "Crime Victim Compensation Legislation."

104. Pater Jaffe, Marlies Sudermann, Deborah Reitzel, and Steve Killip, "An Evaluation of a Secondary School Primary Prevention Program on Violence in Intimate Relationships," *Violence and Victims* 7 (1992): 129–45.

105. Vicki McNickel Rose, "Rape as a Social Problem: A Byproduct of the Feminist Movement," *Social Problems* 25 (1977): 75–89.

106. Janet Gornick, Martha Burt, and Karen Pittman, "Structure and Activities of Rape Crisis Centers in the Early 1980s," *Crime and Delinquency* 31 (1985): 247–68.

107. Andrew Karmen, "Victim–Offender Reconciliation Programs: Pro and Con," *Perspectives of the American Probation and Parole Association* 20 (1996): 11–14.

108. See Frank Carrington, "Victim's Rights Litigation: A Wave of the Future," in *Perspectives on Crime Victims*, ed. Burt Galaway and Joe Hudson (St. Louis: C.V. Mosby Co., 1981).

109. Andrew Karmen, "Toward the Institutionalization of a New Kind of Justice Professional: The Victim Advocate," *The Justice Professional* 9 (1995): 2–15.

110. Karmen, "Toward the Institutionalization of a New Kind of Justice Professional," pp. 9–10.

111. Sara Flaherty and Austin Flaherty, *Victims and Victims' Risk* (New York: Chelsea House, 1998).

112. Pamela Wilcox Rountree and Kenneth Land, "Burglary Victimization, Perceptions of Crime Risk, and Routine Activities: A Multilevel Analysis Across Seattle Neighborhoods and Census Tracts," *Journal of Research in Crime and Delinquency* 33 (1996): 1147–80.

113. Leslie Kennedy, "Going It Alone: Unreported Crime and Individual Self-Help," *Journal of Criminal Justice* 16 (1988): 403–413.

114. Ronald Clarke, "Situational Crime Prevention: Its Theoretical Basis and Practical Scope," in *Annual Review of Criminal Justice Research*, ed. Michael Tonry and Norval Morris (Chicago: University of Chicago Press, 1983).

115. Catherine Whitaker, *Crime Prevention Measures* (Washington, D.C.: Bureau of Justice Statistics, 1986).

116. See generally, Dennis P. Rosenbaum, Arthur J. Lurigio, and Robert C. Davis, *The Prevention of Crime: Social and Situational Strategies* (Belmont, Calif.: Wadsworth, 1998).

117. Andrew Buck, Simon Hakim, and George Rengert, "Burglar Alarms and the Choice Behavior of Burglars," *Journal of Criminal Justice* 21 (1993): 497–507; for an opposing view, see Lynch and Cantor, "Ecological and Behavioral Influences on Property Victimization at Home."

118. Alan Lizotte, "Determinants of Completing Rape and Assault," *Journal of Quantitative Criminology* 2 (1986): 213–17.

119. Polly Marchbanks, Kung-Jong Lui, and James Mercy, "Risk of Injury from Resisting Rape," *American Journal of Epidemiology* 132 (1990): 540–49.

120. Caroline Wolf Harlow, *Robbery Victims* (Washington, D.C.: Bureau of Justice Statistics, 1987).

121. Gary Kleck, "Guns, Collective Security, and Gun Ownership: A Multi-Level Application of the General Social Surveys." Paper presented at the American Society of Criminology meeting, San Diego, Calif., 1997.

122. Gary Kleck, "Guns and Violence: An Interpretive Review of the Field," *Social Pathology* 1 (1995): 12–45, at 17.

123. Kleck, "Guns and Violence."

124. Gary Kleck, "Rape and Resistance," *Social Problems* 37 (1990):149–62.

125. Personal communication with Gary Kleck, January 10, 1997; see also Kleck, "Guns and Violence: An Interpretive Review of the Field."

126. James Garofalo and Maureen McLeod, *Improving the Use and Effectiveness of Neighborhood Watch Programs* (Washington, D.C.: National Institute of Justice, 1988).

127. Peter Finn, *Block Watches Help Crime Victims in Philadelphia* (Washington, D.C.: National Institute of Justice, 1986).

128. Finn, *Block Watches Help Crime Victims in Philadelphia.*

THEORIES OF CRIME CAUSATION

An important goal of the criminological enterprise is to create valid and accurate theories of crime causation. Social scientists have defined theory as sets of statements that explain why and how several concepts are related. For a set of statements to qualify as a theory, we must be able to deduce some conclusions from it that are subject to empirical verification; that is, theories must predict or prohibit certain observable events or conditions.*

Criminologists have sought to collect vital facts about crime and interpret them in a scientifically meaningful fashion. By developing empirically verifiable statements, or hypotheses, and organizing them into theories of crime causation, they hope to identify the causes of crime.

Since the late nineteenth century, criminological theory has pointed to various underlying causes of crime. The earliest theories generally attributed crime to a single underlying cause: atypical body build, genetic abnormality, insanity, physical anomalies, and poverty. Later theories attributed crime causation to multiple factors: poverty, peer influence, school problems, and family dysfunction.

In this section, theories of crime causation are grouped into five chapters. Chapters 5 and 6 focus on theories based on individual traits. They hold that crime is either a free-will choice made by an individual, a function of personal psychological or biological abnormality, or both. Chapters 7 through 9 investigate theories based in sociology and political economy. These theories portray crime as a function of the structure, process, and conflicts of social living. Chapter 10 is devoted to theories that combine or integrate these various concepts into a cohesive, complex view of crime.

*Rodney Stark, *Sociology*, 2nd ed. (Belmont, Calif.: Wadsworth, 1987), 618.

Choice Theory

INTRODUCTION

On October 16, 1998, Arthur Gus Bennett, 45, a former Marine sergeant, was charged with murder, arson, kidnapping, insurance fraud, theft, and sexual assault of a minor.[1] Bennett's case history began in 1994 when he faced a military court-martial on charges of sexually abusing children. When a body was found in his trailer, burned beyond recognition and unidentifiable, it was assumed that he had committed suicide, and his family collected on a $200,000 government life insurance policy. But Bennett was not dead; he had moved with his family to Hurricane, Utah, and changed his name to Joe Benson. His plot unraveled in October 1997 when one of his daughters told police that she had been sexually assaulted by her father. A routine fingerprint check revealed that "Benson" was really Bennett. Police are still unsure whose burned body was found in Bennett's trailer. Arthur Bennett's elaborate plot to avoid prosecution, fraudulently collect insurance money, escape detection, and begin a new life smacks of cold, cunning calculation. His actions suggest that rather than being an unplanned or random act, the decision to commit fraud and possibly murder was a function of *personal choice.*

This view is also held by a number of criminologists who believe that the decision to violate any law — commit a robbery, sell drugs, attack a rival, fill out a false tax return — is made for a variety of personal reasons, including greed, revenge, need, anger, lust, jealousy, thrill-seeking, or vanity. The central issue is that the illegal act is a matter of *rational choice,* which is made after weighing of the potential benefits and consequences of crime. The jealous suitor, for example, concludes that the risk of punishment is worth the satisfaction of punching a rival. The greedy shopper considers the chance of apprehension by store detectives so small that she takes a "five-finger discount" on a new sweater. The drug dealer concludes that the huge profit that he can earn from a single shipment of cocaine far outweighs the possible costs of apprehension. In the final analysis, rational choice theorists believe that people choose crime simply because it is rewarding, satisfying, easy, or fun.

This chapter reviews the philosophical underpinnings of **choice theory,** the view that criminals rationally choose crime, which derives from classical criminology. We then turn to more recent theoretical models that flow from the concept of choice. These models hold that because criminals are rational, their behavior can be controlled or deterred by the fear of punishment; desistance can then be explained by a growing and intense fear of criminal sanctions. These views include *situational crime control, general deterrence theory, specific deterrence theory,* and *incapacitation.* Finally, the chapter briefly reviews how choice theory has influenced criminal justice policy.

THE DEVELOPMENT OF RATIONAL CHOICE THEORY

Rational choice theory has roots in the classical school of criminology developed by the Italian social thinker Cesare Beccaria.[2]

CONNECTIONS

As you may recall from Chapter 1, classical criminology is based on the work of Cesare Beccaria and other utilitarian philosophers. Its core concepts are that (1) people choose all behavior, including criminal behavior; (2) their choices can be controlled by fear of punishment; and (3) the more severe, certain, and swift the punishment, the greater its ability to control criminal behavior.

In keeping with his utilitarian views, Beccaria called for fair and certain punishment to deter crime. Because people are egotistical and self-centered, he believed, they must be motivated by the fear of punishment, which provides a tangible motive for them to obey the law and suppress the "despotic spirit" that resides in every person.[3]

To be effective, Becarria believed, crimes and their punishments must be proportional. Without proportionality people would not be deterred from committing more serious offenses. For example, if both rape and murder were punished by death, a rapist would have little reason to refrain from killing his victim in order to eliminate the potential threat of her contacting the police and giving evidence in court.

Although some have questioned Beccaria's principles and motives, even his harshest critics recognize that he is one of the rare reformers to have an enduring influence on justice policy. He is viewed today as a true criminological success story.[4] Beccaria's ideas and writings have inspired criminologists who believe that criminals choose to commit crime and that crime can be controlled by judicious punishment.

The Classical Theory of Crime

Beccaria's vision powerfully influenced events in the criminal justice system and was widely accepted throughout Europe and the United States.[5] The belief that punishment should fit the crime and that people should be punished proportionately for their criminal activity was thought to be more rational than punishing a criminal according to the whim of a capricious judge or ruler. In Britain philosopher Jeremy Bentham (1748–1833) helped popularize Beccaria's views in his writings on **utilitarianism.** According to this view, actions are evaluated by their tendency to produce advantage, pleasure, and happiness and to avoid or prevent mischief, pain, evil, or unhappiness.[6] Bentham believed that the purpose of all law is to produce and support the total happiness of the community it serves. Because punishment is in itself harmful, its existence is justified only if it promises to prevent greater evil than it creates. Punishment, therefore, has four main objectives:

1. To prevent all criminal offenses
2. When it cannot prevent a crime, to convince the offender to commit a less serious one
3. To ensure that a criminal uses no more force than is necessary
4. To prevent crime as cheaply as possible[7]

The most stunning example of how Beccaria and Bentham's philosophy was embraced in Europe occurred in 1789, when France's postrevolutionary Constituent Assembly adopted these ideas in the Declaration of the Rights of Man:

> [T]he law has the right to prohibit only actions harmful to society.... The law shall inflict only such punishments as are strictly and clearly necessary ... no person shall be punished except by virtue of a law enacted and promulgated previous to the crime and applicable to its terms.

Similarly, a prohibition against cruel and unusual punishment was incorporated in the Eighth Amendment to the U.S. Constitution.

The use of torture and severe punishment was largely abandoned in the nineteenth century. The practice of incarcerating criminals and structuring prison sentences to fit the severity of crime was a reflection of classical criminology. The general theme of gearing punishment to deter crime was widely accepted.

By the end of the nineteenth century, the popularity of the classical approach began to decline, and by the middle of the twentieth century, the perspective was neglected by mainstream criminologists. During this period, positivist criminologists focused on internal and external factors — poverty, IQ, education, home life — that were believed to be the true causes of criminality.

CONNECTIONS

The rise of positivist criminology is discussed in Chapter 1. Positivist theories of criminology, which stress that people are influenced by internal and external forces beyond their control, are analyzed in Chapters 6, 7, 8, and again in Chapter 10.

Because these conditions could not be easily manipulated, the concept of punishing people for behaviors beyond their control seemed both foolish and cruel. Although classical principles still controlled the way police, courts, and correctional agencies operated, most criminologists rejected classical criminology as an explanation of criminal behavior.

Choice Theory Emerges

Beginning in the mid-1970s, the classical approach began to enjoy resurging popularity. The rehabilitation of known criminals, considered a cornerstone of positivist policy, came under attack. According to positivist criminology, if crime was caused by some social or psychological problem, such as poverty, then crime rates could be reduced by providing good jobs and economic opportunities. A number of national surveys (the most well-known being Robert Martinson's "What Works?") failed to find examples of rehabilitation programs that prevented future criminal activity.[8] A well-publicized book, *Beyond Probation* by Charles Murray and Louis Cox, went as far as suggesting that punishment-oriented programs could suppress future criminality much more effectively than those that relied on rehabilitation and treatment efforts.[9] A significant increase in the reported crime rate, as well as serious disturbances in the nation's prisons, frightened the general public. To many criminologists, reviving the classical concepts of social control and punishment made more sense than futilely trying to improve entrenched social conditions or to rehabilitate criminals using ineffective methodologies.[10]

Thinking About Crime Beginning in the late 1970s, a number of criminologists began producing books and monographs expounding the theme that criminals are rational actors who plan their crimes, fear punishment, and deserve to be penalized for their misdeeds. In a 1975 book that came to symbolize renewed interest in classical views, *Thinking About Crime,* political scientist James Q. Wilson debunked the positivist view that crime was a function of external forces, such as poverty, that could be altered by government programs. Instead, he argued, efforts should be made to reduce criminal opportunity by deterring would-be offenders and incarcerating known criminals. Persons who are likely to commit crime, he maintained, lack inhibition against misconduct, value the excitement and thrills of breaking the law, have a low stake in conformity, and are willing to take greater chances than the average person. If they could be convinced that their actions will bring severe punishment, only the totally irrational would be willing to engage in crime.[11] Although incapacitating criminals should not be the sole goal of the justice system, such a policy does have the advantage of restraining offenders and preventing their future criminality without having to figure out how to change their attitudes or nature, a goal that has proven difficult to accomplish. Wilson made this observation:

> Wicked people exist. Nothing avails except to set them apart from innocent people. And many people, neither wicked nor innocent, but watchful, dissembling, and calculating of their chances, ponder our reaction to wickedness as a clue to what they might profitably do.[12]

Here Wilson is saying that unless we react forcefully to crime, those "sitting on the fence" will get a clear message: crime pays.

Responding Forcefully to Crime Coinciding with the publication of Wilson's book was a conservative shift in U.S. public policy, which resulted in Ronald Reagan's election to the presidency in 1980. Political decision makers embraced Wilson's ideas as a means to bring the crime rate down. During the Reagan and Bush presidencies, tough new laws were passed creating mandatory prison sentences for drug offenders, and the nation's prison population skyrocketed. Critics decried the disproportionate number of young minority men being locked up for drug law violations.[13] Despite liberal anguish, these conservative views of crime control have helped shape criminal justice policy for the past two decades.

From these roots, a more contemporary version of classical theory evolved that is based on intelligent thought processes and criminal decision making; today this is referred to as the *rational choice* approach to crime causation.[14]

The Concepts of Rational Choice

According to the **rational choice** approach, law-violating behavior occurs when an offender decides to risk transgressing after considering both personal factors (such as the need for money, revenge, thrills, and entertainment) and situational factors (how well a target is protected and the efficiency of the local police force). Before choosing to commit a crime, the **reasoning criminal** evaluates the risk of apprehension, the seriousness of expected punishment, the potential value of the criminal enterprise, and his or her immediate need for criminal gain.

The decision to commit a specific type of crime, then, is a matter of personal choice based on a weighing of available information. Conversely, the decision to forgo crime may be based on the criminal's perception that the economic benefits are no longer there or the risk of apprehension is too great. For example, studies of residential burglary indicate that criminals will forgo activity if they believe a neighborhood is well patrolled by police.[15] In fact, when police concentrate patrols in a particular area of the city, crime rates tend to increase in adjacent areas that criminals perceive as being safer. This is referred to as **crime displacement.**[16]

Offense and Offender Specifications Rational choice theorists view crime as both offense- and offender-specific.[17] When crime is **offense-specific,** offenders react selectively to the characteristics of particular offenses. The decision of whether to commit burglary, for example, might involve evaluating the target's likely cash yield, the availability of resources, such as a getaway car, and the probability of capture by police.[18]

When crime is **offender-specific,** criminals are not simply driven people who, for one reason or another, engage in random antisocial acts. Before deciding to commit crime, they analyze whether they have the prerequisites for a criminal act, including their skills, motives, needs, and fears. Criminal acts might be ruled out if potential offenders perceive that they can reach a desired personal goal through legitimate means or if they are too afraid of getting caught.[19]

Note the distinction made here between crime and criminality.[20] Crime is an *event;* criminality is a *personal trait.* Criminals do not commit crime all the time; conversely, even the most honest citizens may, on occasion, violate the law. Likewise, some high-risk people lacking opportunity may never commit crime; on the other hand, given enough provocation or opportunity, a low-risk, law-abiding person may commit crime. What conditions promote crime and criminality?

Structuring Criminality A number of personal factors condition people to choose criminality. Perceptions of economic opportunity may influence the choice to commit crime. However, offenders are likely to desist from crime if they believe that (1) their future criminal earnings will be relatively low and that (2) attractive and legal opportunities to generate income are available.[21] In this sense, rational choice is a function of a person's perception of conventional alternatives and opportunities.

Learning and experience may be important elements in structuring the choice of crime.[22] Career criminals may learn the limitations of their powers; they know when to take a chance and when to be cautious. Experienced criminals may turn from a life of crime when they develop a belief that the risk of crime is greater than its potential profit.[23]

Personality and lifestyle also affect criminal choices. People who choose crime over conformity may be more impulsive and have less self-control than other people; they seem unaffected by fear of criminal punishment.[24] They are typically under stress or facing some serious personal problem or condition, which forces them to choose risky behavior.[25]

Structuring Crime According to the rational choice approach, the decision to commit crime, regardless of its substance, is structured by the choices of (1) where it occurs, (2) the characteristics of the target, and (3) the means available for its completion.

1. **Choosing the place of crime:** Criminals often choose where they will commit their crime. Criminologist Bruce Jacobs's interviews with 40 active crack cocaine street dealers in a Midwestern city showed that dealers carefully evaluate the desirability of their sales area before setting up shop.[26] Dealers considered the middle of a long block the best choice because they could see everything in both directions. In particular, police raids could then be spotted before they occurred.[27] Another tactic mentioned in Jacobs's interviews was to entice buyers who seemed suspicious to the dealer either into spaces between apartment buildings or into back lots in order to do drug deals. Although the dealers might lose the tactical edge of being on a public street, they gained a measure of protection because their colleagues could watch over the operation and come to the rescue if the buyer tried to "pull something."[28]

2. **Choosing targets:** Evidence of rational choice may also be found in the way criminals locate their targets. Victimization data indicates that high-income households are the most likely targets of property crimes; in contrast, the wealthy are rarely the victims of violent crimes.[29] Studies of both professional and occasional criminals show that choosing targets is a rational event. Burglars check to make sure that no one is home before they enter a residence. Some call ahead, whereas others ring the doorbell, preparing to claim they had the wrong address if someone answers. Some find out which families have star high school athletes because those that do are sure to be at the weekend game, leaving their houses unguarded.[30] Others seek unlocked doors and avoid the ones with deadbolts; houses with dogs are usually considered off-limits.[31]

Other considerations when choosing targets involve the types of buildings selected. Some robbers avoid freestanding buildings because they can more easily be surrounded by police; others select targets that are known to do a primarily cash business, such as bars,

supermarkets, and restaurants.[32] Burglars also report being sensitive to the activities of their victims. They note that homemakers often develop predictable behavior patterns, which helps them plan their crimes.[33] Burglars seem to prefer "working" between 9 A.M. and 11 A.M. and in mid-afternoon, when parents are either working or dropping off or picking up kids at school. Burglars avoid Saturdays because most families are at home; Sunday morning during church hours is considered a prime time for weekend burglaries.[34]

3. **Learning criminal techniques:** Criminals report learning techniques of crime to help them avoid detection. In his studies of drug dealers, criminologist Bruce Jacobs found that crack dealers learn how to stash crack cocaine in some undisclosed location so that they are not forced to carry large amounts of product on their persons. Other dealers have mastered the trick of conversing while hiding five $20 rocks of cocaine in their mouths.[35] Research conducted by Leanne Fiftal Alarid and her partners found that women drawn into dealing drugs learn the trade in a businesslike manner. One young dealer told them how she learned the techniques of the trade from an older male partner: "He taught me how to 'recon' [reconstitute] cocaine, cutting and repacking a brick from 91 proof to 50 proof, just like a business. He treats me like an equal partner, and many of the friends are business associates. I am a catalyst . . . I even get guys turned on to drugs."[36] Note the business terminology used. This coke dealer could be talking about taking a computer training course at a major corporation! If criminal acts are treated as business decisions, in which profit and loss potential must be carefully calculated, then crime must indeed be a rational event.

In sum, rational choice involves both shaping criminality and structuring crime. Personality, age, status, risk, and opportunity seem to influence the decision to become a criminal; place, target, and techniques help to structure crime.

Rational Choice and Routine Activities

Rational choice theory dovetails with routine activities theory, which you learned about in Chapter 4.[37] Although not identical, these approaches both claim that crime rates are a product of criminal opportunity. They suggest that if the number of guardians increases, the suitability of targets decreases; or reducing the offender population should lower crime rates. Conversely, increased opportunity and reduced guardianship will increase crime rates.

What are the connections between rational choice and routine activities?

Suitable Targets Research indicates that criminal choice is influenced by the perception of target vulnerability. As they go about their daily activities, traveling to school or work, potential criminals may encounter targets of illegal opportunity: an empty carport, an open door, an unlocked car, or a bike left on the street. Corner homes, usually near traffic lights or stop signs, are the ones most likely to be burglarized: stop signs give criminals a legitimate reason to stop their cars and look for an attractive target.[38] Secluded homes, such as those at the end of a cul-de-sac or surrounded by wooded areas, make suitable targets.[39] Thieves also report being concerned about target convenience. They are more apt to choose familiar burglary sites that are located in easily accessible and open areas.[40] Because criminals often go on foot or use public transportation, they are unlikely to travel long distances to commit crimes and are more likely to drift toward the center of a city than move toward outlying areas.[41] Criminals prefer **permeable neighborhoods**—those with a greater than usual number of access streets from traffic arteries into the neighborhood.[42] These areas are chosen for theft and break-ins because they are familiar and well traveled, they appear more open and vulnerable, and they offer more potential escape routes.[43] Communities that organize themselves, restrict traffic, change street patterns, and limit neighborhood entrances and exits have experienced significant declines in property crime.[44] Here we can see the influence of routine activity on criminal choice: the more suitable and accessible the target, the more likely that crime will occur.[45]

Criminals will occasionally commute to distant locations to commit crimes. This **spillover effect** is structured by the criminal's perceptions of the abundance of goods, the physical security of goods, the level of surveillance, and the attractiveness of the area as a potential target; the richer the area, the greater the expected payoff from commuting.[46] Spillover may also be encouraged by changing police strategy that increases the probability of being apprehended on "home turf" and may cause the criminal to shift activities to another area of the city.[47]

Capable Guardians Routine activity also implies that the presence of capable guardians may deter crime. Criminals tend to shy away from victims who are perceived to be armed and potentially dangerous. In a series of interviews with career property offenders, Kenneth Tunnell found that burglars will avoid targets if they feel there are police in the area or if "nosy neighbors" might be suspicious and cause trouble.[48] Evidence is accumulating that predatory criminals are aware of law enforcement capability; communities with the reputation of employing aggressive "crime-fighting" cops are less likely to attract potential offenders than areas perceived to have passive law enforcers.[49] Guardianship can also involve passive or mechanical devices like security fences or burglar alarms. Research indicates that physical security measures can improve guardianship and limit offender access to targets.[50]

Motivated Criminals Routine activities theory predicts that crime rates correspond to the number of motivated criminals in the population, such as teenage males, drug users, and unemployed adults. Rational offenders may be less likely to commit crime if they believe that they can achieve personal goals through legitimate means; job availability reduces crime. In contrast, criminal motivation increases when there is a need to accumulate wealth; a rising cost of living has been associated with increasing criminal motivation.[51] If crime is rational, criminal motivation should be reduced if potential offenders perceive alternatives to crime; in contrast, the perception of blocked legitimate opportunities should increase criminal motivation.

CONNECTIONS

Lack of conventional opportunity is a persistent theme in sociological theories of crime. The frustration caused by a perceived lack of opportunity explains the high crime rates in lower class areas. Chapter 7 discusses strain and cultural deviance theories, which provide alternative explanations of how lack of opportunity is associated with crime.

Tunnell's career criminals said they committed crimes because they considered legitimate opportunities unavailable to people with their limited education and background. As one offender told him,

> I tried to stay away from crime. . . . Nobody would hire me. I was an ex-con and I tried, I really tried to get gainful employment. There was nobody looking to hire me with my record. I went in as a juvenile and came out as an adult and didn't have any legitimate employment résumé to submit. Employment was impossible. So, I started robbing.[52]

Although crime became the choice when legitimate alternatives were absent, the reverse is also true.

Interactive Effects According to the routine activities approach, motivation, opportunity and targets are interactive: the presence of any one factor encourages the others. Motivated criminals will not commit crime unless they have suitable targets available. Motivated offenders must also have the opportunity to commit crime; without opportunity, even the most driven criminals will forgo criminality. The presence of guardians will also deter most offenders, rendering attractive targets off-limits.

Ronald Clarke shows the relationship among opportunity, routine activities, and environmental factors in Figure 5.1. This figure shows that criminal opportunities (like suitable victims and targets) abound in urban environments where facilitators (such as guns and drugs) are readily found. Environmental factors, such as

Research indicates that criminal choice is influenced by the perception of target vulnerability. One form of crime prevention is to make targets less "vulnerable" by installing security measures. The bombing of the World Trade Center in New York City and the Murrah Federal Building in Oklahoma City has heightened awareness of the threat of terrorist bombings, and consequently crime prevention measures have been increased. Sights such as security guards inspecting packages are not uncommon. Here at a federal building in San Francisco, a security guard checks a worker's lunch bag before allowing her to enter.

physical layout and cultural style, may either facilitate or restrict criminal opportunity. Motivated offenders living in these urban "hot spots" continually learn about criminal opportunities from peers, the media, and their own perceptions; such information may either escalate their criminal motivation or warn them of its danger.[53]

Measuring Interaction Efforts to measure the interaction among opportunity, motivation, and crime show that the relationship is significant. For example, kids who are attached to their parents and spend their weekends at home report little in the way of criminal motivation; lack of opportunity may reduce motivation.[54] Adolescents whose family relationships are strained, distant, and unrewarding are more likely to become attached to deviant peers; attachment to deviant peers increases criminal motivation.[55] Adolescents who spend a great deal of time socializing with peers in the absence of authority figures (riding around in cars, going to parties, going out at night for fun) are also most likely to engage in deviant behaviors.[56] In the presence of motivated peers, the lack of structure and guardianship leaves more opportunity for antisocial behavior like substance abuse, crime, and dangerous driving.

Participation in unstructured activities can be associated with crime rates based on gender, age, and status. Teenage boys have the highest crime rates because they are the group most likely to socialize without supervision. Even when adolescents perform what should be "character-building" activities, such as having a part-time job after school, the opportunity to socialize with deviant peers combined with lack of parental supervision increases criminal motivation.[57] As teens mature, unstructured activities gravitate toward bars and night spots, where liberal consumption of alcohol fuels the likelihood that young adults will either get involved in violent acts or become their target.[58]

IS CRIME RATIONAL?

It is relatively easy to show that some crimes are the product of rational, objective thought, especially when they involve an ongoing criminal conspiracy centered on economic gain. When prominent bankers in the savings and loan industry were indicted for criminal fraud, their elaborate financial schemes not only showed signs of rationality but exhibited brilliant, though flawed, fi-

Figure 5.1 The Opportunity Structure for Crime

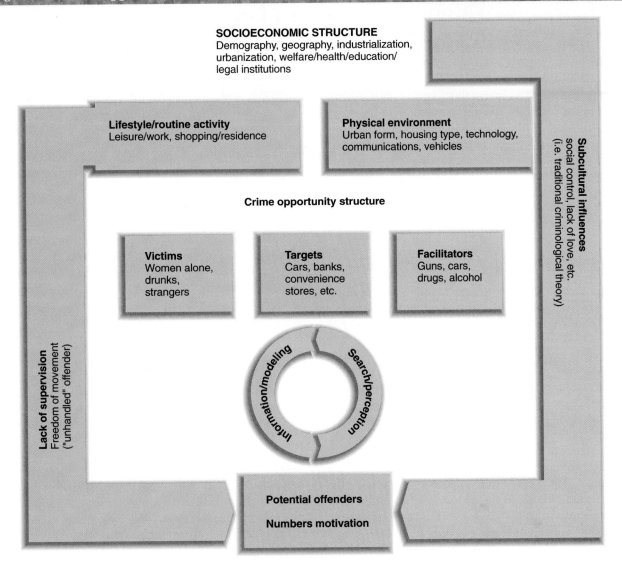

Source: Ronald Clarke, "Situational Crime Prevention," in *Building a Safer Society: Strategic Approaches to Crime Prevention*, vol. 19 of *Crime and Justice, A Review of Research*, ed. Michael Tonry and David Farrington (Chicago: University of Chicago Press, 1995), p. 103. Reprinted by permission.

nancial expertise.[59] The stock market manipulations of Wall Street insiders, such as Ivan Boesky and Michael Milken, and the drug dealings of organized crime bosses demonstrate a reasoned analysis of market conditions, interests, and risks. Even small-time wheeler-dealers, such as the female drug dealer discussed earlier in the chapter, are guided by their rational assessment of the likelihood of apprehension and take pains to avoid detection.

Are Street Crimes Rational?

It is not surprising that ongoing criminal conspiracies involving organized and white-collar crime exhibit rationality; but what about common street crimes such as prostitution and petty theft? These would seem more likely to be random acts of criminal opportunity rather than well-thought-out conspiracies. However, there is evidence that even these "unplanned" street crimes may also be the product of careful risk assessment, including environmental, social, and structural factors. Ronald Clarke and Patricia Harris found that auto thieves are very selective in their choice of targets. If they want to strip cars for parts, they are most likely to choose Volkswagens; if they want to sell the cars or keep them permanently, they choose Mercedes; for temporary use, Buicks are top-ranked.[60] Vehicle selection seems to be based on attractiveness and suitability for a particular purpose; for example, German cars are selected for stripping because they usually have high-quality audio equipment that has good value on the second-hand market. Target selection seems highly rational.

Studies of prostitutes suggest that even these often desperate women make clear choices in their daily activities. For example, sociologist Lisa Maher's interviews with "street-level sex workers" in Brooklyn, New York, showed that prices for sexual services are declining and competition is increasing. An increase in drug use has produced an influx of women new to the street willing to charge little to support their habits. Despite fierce competition, more experienced street workers still resist sex practices that compromise their chances of survival, such as refusing to trade sex for drugs and refusing to service clients they consider too dangerous or distasteful for sex.[61] Their activities show clear signs of rational choice.

Is Drug Use Rational?

Did actor Robert Downey, Jr., make an objective, rational choice to abuse drugs and potentially sabotage his career? Did comedian Chris Farley make a rational choice when he abused alcohol and other drugs to the point that it killed him? Is it possible that drug users and dealers, a group not usually associated with clear thinking, make rational choices? Research does in fact show that from its onset, drug use is controlled by rational decision making. Users report that they begin taking drugs when they believe that the benefits of substance abuse outweigh its costs (for example, they believe that drugs will provide a fun, exciting, thrilling experience). Their entry into substance abuse is facilitated by their perception that valued friends and family members endorse and encourage drug use and abuse substances themselves.[62]

In adulthood, heavy drug users and dealers show signs of rationality and cunning in their daily activity, as is discussed in the Criminological Enterprise feature titled "In the Drug Business." Bruce Jacobs found that these offenders use specific techniques to avoid being apprehended by police. They play what they call the "peep game" before dealing drugs, scoping out the territory to make sure the turf is free from anything out of place that may be a potential threat (like police officers or rival gang members).[63] One crack dealer told Jacobs,

> There was this red Pontiac sittin' on the corner one day with two white guys inside. They was just sittin' there for an hour, not doin' nothin.' Another day, diff'rent people be walkin' up and down the street you don't really recognize. You think they might be kin of someone but then you be askin' around and they (neighbors) ain't never seen them before neither. When ya' see strange things like that, you think somethin' be goin' on (and you don't deal).[64]

Drug dealers told Jacobs that they also carefully consider whether they should deal alone or in groups; large groups draw more attention from the police but

can offer more protection. Drug-dealing gangs and groups can help divert the attention of police: if their drug dealing is noticed by detectives, a dealer can slyly walk away or dispose of evidence while confederates distract the cops.[65]

Patricia Morgan and Karen Ann Joe's three-city (San Francisco, San Diego, and Honolulu) study of female drug abusers also found a great deal of rationality and careful decision making. One dealer who earns $50,000 per year told them,

> I stayed within my goals, basically . . . I don't go around doing stupid things. I don't walk around telling people I have drugs for sale. I don't have people sitting out in front of my house. I don't have traffic in and out of my house . . . I control the people I sell to.[66]

Morgan and Joe found that these female dealers consider drug distribution a positive experience that gives them economic independence, self-esteem, increased ability to function, professional pride, and the ability to maintain control over their lives. These women often seemed more like yuppies opening a boutique than out-of-control addicts:

> I'm a good dealer. I don't cut my drugs, I have high-quality drugs insofar as it's possible to get high-quality drugs. I want to be known as somebody who sells good drugs, but doesn't always have them, as opposed to someone who always has them and sometimes the drugs are good.[67]

Can Violence Be Rational?

Whereas there is evidence that instrumental crimes, such as drug dealing and burglaries, are rational, is it possible that violent acts, through which the offender gains little material benefit, are the product of reasoned decision making?

Evidence confirms that even violent criminals select suitable targets by picking people who are vulnerable and lack adequate defenses. For example, when Richard Wright and Scott Decker interviewed active street robbers in St. Louis, Missouri, their subjects expressed a considerable amount of rational thought in their choice of criminality.[68] One told them why he chose to be a robber:

> I feel more safer doing a robbery because doing a burglary, I got a fear of breaking into somebody's house not knowing who might be up in there. . . . On robbery I can select my victims, I can select my place of business. I can watch and see who all work in there or I can rob a person and pull them around in the alley or push them up in a doorway and rob them.[69]

Other research bears out Wright and Decker's findings. For example, according to research by criminologist Jody Miller, female armed robbers are likely to choose female targets, reasoning that they will be more vulnerable and offer less resistance.[70] When robbing

The Criminological Enterprise

In the Drug Business

According to criminologist George Rengert's study of drug markets, drug dealers face many of the same problems as legitimate retailers. If they are too successful in one location, rivals will be attracted to the area, and stiff competition may drive down prices and cut profits. The dealer can fight back by discounting drugs or increasing quality, but this too will reduce profit margins.

Of course, drug dealing differs from other kinds of retail sales. Police can arrest you and your customers, and it is difficult to collect unpaid bills. Drug markets become stabilized in areas that offer the minimum risk and the maximum sales potential. Whereas dealers like to sell in familiar areas that they can control, many customers are willing to pay higher prices to buy close to home.

Rengert notes that there are a variety of levels or stages of drug marketing:

- **Mutual societies** involve drugs shared among friends at parties or teenage hangouts. Drug distribution here is for casual or recreational use.
- **Periodic markets** are drug sites that provide relatively low incomes because sales can be made only at limited times during the day. For example, a dealer may travel to the site to sell to students on their way home from school. Dealers may establish a number of retail outlets and spend a short amount of time each day at different locations. If an area has enough customers, competitors may set up shop to take advantage of the trade.
- **Fixed-site neighborhoods** are neighborhoods in which demand is so great that dealers will remain in a single location all day. Consumers know where the drug dealerships are in the neighborhood and simply travel there on foot to buy merchandise.
- **Drug marts** are neighborhoods that are so drug-infested that law-abiding citizens have moved out and competing drug dealers have taken over. The drug mart's notoriety, heightened by media coverage, allows dealers to obtain a steady flow of customers who know where to shop.

Here we can see the parallels between drug dealing and commercial sales. Fixed sites seem like a convenience store that stays open 24 hours a day because there are sufficient customers to make a profit. The drug mart seems similar to the shopping mall, which occupies a large area, has numerous retailers under one roof, and attracts customers without the need for advertising. Service stations and fast food restaurants may sprout up around shopping malls to provide for customers' needs. Similarly, drug marts may attract gun dealers, prostitutes, and **fences,** who buy stolen merchandise for cash in order to provide for the "customers" (that is, burglars who "shop" at drug marts). If retail purchases and sales are rational and market-driven, so too are drug sales and purchases.

CRITICAL THINKING

1. If drug dealing is similar to any type of commercial sales, can it be controlled or eliminated in the same way a competitor is put out of business? For example, by driving down the price of goods and offering a much cheaper alternative?
2. If so, what sort of legal alternative could you suggest?

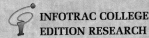 **INFOTRAC COLLEGE EDITION RESEARCH**

For research on drug markets, see: Gordon James Knowles. Dealing crack cocaine: a view from the streets of Honolulu. *The FBI Law Enforcement Bulletin* July 1996 v65 n7 p1(7)

Source: George Rengert, *The Geography of Illegal Drugs* (Boulder, Colo.: Westview Press, 1996).

---

males, women "set them up" in order to catch them off guard; some feign sexual interest or prostitution in order to gain the upper hand.[71]

CONNECTIONS

Wright and Decker found that the armed robbers in their sample displayed a great deal of rationality when choosing the target and place of crime. The motivation for robberies was typically the need for ready cash. The economic basis of the crime shows that it is a need-based act demanding thought and calculation. For more on this study of armed robbery, see Chapter 11's Criminological Enterprise feature titled "Armed Robbers in Action."

Research shows that robbers are likely to choose victims who are vulnerable, have low coercive power, and do not pose any threat.[72] In their survey of violent felons, James Wright and Peter Rossi found that violent offenders avoid victims who may be armed and dangerous. About three-fifths of all felons interviewed were more afraid of armed victims than police; about 40 percent had avoided a victim because they believed the victim was armed; and almost one-third reported that they had been scared off, wounded, or captured by armed victims.[73] It comes as no surprise that criminals fear armed victims, considering that there are an estimated 2.5 million annual incidents of defensive gunshot-inflicted injuries. Cities with higher than average gun-carrying rates generally have lower rates of violent

Miami Beach police inspect the body of Jesus Antonio Tamalio, who committed suicide on September 2, 1997, after shooting his ex-wife and her friend as they stood on line in a local post office. Is it possible that violence is truly rational or are most violent crimes the product of demented people who engage in inexplicable, irrational, and bizarre acts?

crimes, especially unarmed robbery. It follows that if criminals are rational, unarmed robbers will be deterred by the thought of encountering armed victims.[74]

Even serial murderers, outwardly the most irrational of all offenders, tend to pick their targets with care. Most choose victims who are either defenseless or cannot count on police protection: prostitutes, gay men, hitchhikers, children, hospital patients, the elderly, the homeless. Rarely do serial killers target weightlifters, martial arts experts, or any other potentially powerful group.[75] Serial rapists also show rationality in their choice of targets. They travel, on average, three miles from their homes in order to commit their crimes. This indicates that they are careful, for the most part, to avoid victims who might recognize them later.

The desire to avoid detection supersedes the wish to obtain a victim with little effort. Older, more experienced rapists who have extensive criminal histories are willing to travel farther; younger rapists who have less experience committing crimes travel less and are therefore more at risk of detection.[76]

Even in apparently senseless killings among strangers, the conscious motive is typically revenge for a prior dispute or disagreement among the parties involved or their families.[77] Many homicides are motivated by the offenders' desire to avoid retaliation from a victim they assaulted or to avoid future prosecutions by getting rid of witnesses.[78] Although some killings are the result of anger and aggression, others are the result of rational planning.

The Seductions of Crime

Rational choice theory focuses on the opportunity to commit crime and how criminal choices are structured by the social environment. There will always be people willing and able to bypass the law, given the proper conditions and opportunity. Some irrational or mentally disturbed people may commit crime without thought of potential hazard, but it seems likely that immediate or situational variables determine and guide most criminal behavior. People commit crime when they view its outcome as beneficial.[79]

For many, crime is attractive; it brings rewards, excitement, prestige, or other desirable outcomes without lengthy work or effort. Whether it is violent or profit-oriented, crime has an allure that some people cannot resist. Crime may produce a natural "high" and other positive sensations that are instrumental in maintaining and reinforcing criminal behavior.[80] Some law violators describe the "adrenaline rush" that comes from successfully executing illegal activities in dangerous situations. This has been described as **edgework,** the "exhilarating, momentary integration of danger, risk, and skill" that motivates people to try a variety of dangerous criminal and noncriminal behavior.[81]

Sociologist Jack Katz argues that there are, in fact, immediate benefits to criminality, which he labels the **seductions of crime.**[82] These situational inducements directly precede the commission of crime and draw offenders into law violations. For example, someone challenges their authority or moral position, and they vanquish their opponent with a beating; or they want to do something exciting, so they break into and vandalize a school building.

According to Katz, choosing crime can help satisfy personal needs. For some people, shoplifting and vandalism are attractive because getting away with crime is a thrilling (Katz calls this "sneaky thrills") demonstration of personal competence; monetary gain is not their prime motive. Even murder can have an emotional payoff. Killers behave like the avenging gods of mythology, choosing to have life-or-death control over their victims.

Katz finds that situational inducements created from emotional upheaval can also structure the decision to commit crime. When an individual is faced with humiliation, righteousness, arrogance, or ridicule, violent reactions seem a natural response. For example, when someone is rebuked at a party because he or she is disturbing people, the person may respond, "So, I'm acting like a fool, am I?" and attack. Public embarrassment leads to action; the person must "sacrifice" or injure the body of the victim to maintain his or her "honor." A number of research studies have supported Katz's view that situational inducements play an important role in causing adolescent misbehavior.[83] People are most likely to be "seduced" if they fear neither the risk of apprehension nor its social consequences. People who either (1) fear losing the respect of their peers or (2) suffer legal punishment are most likely to forgo the "seductions of crime."[84]

CONNECTIONS

In Chapter 6 we discuss the thrill-seeking aspect of crime as a biological process. This view of crime, called **arousal theory,** holds that thrill seeking is a function of such biological processes as abnormal brain chemistry and brain structure. It is possible that people commit crime because they have a biologically based need to engage in risky behaviors.

ELIMINATING CRIME

If crime is rational and people choose to commit crime, then it follows that crime can be controlled or eradicated by convincing potential offenders that crime is a poor choice that will bring them not rewards, but instead pain, hardship, and deprivation. Evidence shows that jurisdictions with relatively low incarceration rates also experience the highest crime rates.[85] As we have seen, according to rational choice theory, street-smart offenders know which areas offer the least threat and plan their crimes accordingly. A number of potential strategies flow from this premise:

1. *Situational crime prevention* is aimed at convincing would-be criminals to avoid specific targets. It relies on the doctrine that crime can be avoided if motivated offenders are denied access to suitable targets. When people install security systems in their homes or hire security guards, they are broadcasting the message that guardianship is great here, stay away, the potential reward is not worth the risk of apprehension.

2. *General deterrence* strategies are aimed at making potential criminals fear the consequences of crime. The threat of punishment is aimed at convincing rational criminals that crime does not pay.

3. *Specific deterrence* refers to punishing known criminals so severely that they will never be tempted to repeat their offenses. If crime is rational, then painful punishment should reduce its future allure.

4. *Incapacitation strategies* attempt to reduce crime rates by denying motivated offenders the opportunity to commit crime. If, despite the threat of law and punishment, some people still find crime attractive, then the only way to control their behavior is to incarcerate them for extended periods.

The following sections discuss each of these crime reduction or control strategies based on the rationality of criminal behavior.

Situational Crime Prevention

Rational choice theory suggests that because criminal activity is offense-specific, crime prevention, or at least crime reduction, should be achieved through policies that convince potential criminals to desist from criminal activities, delay their actions, or avoid a particular target. Criminal acts will be avoided if (1) potential targets are carefully guarded, (2) the means to commit crime are controlled, and (3) potential offenders are carefully monitored. Desperate people may contemplate crime, but only the truly irrational would attack a well-defended, inaccessible target and risk strict punishment. Crime prevention can be achieved by reducing the opportunities people have to commit particular crimes, a practice known as **situational crime prevention.**

Situational crime prevention was first popularized in the United States in the early 1970s by Oscar Newman, who coined the term **defensible space.** This term signifies that crime can be prevented or displaced through the use of residential architectural designs that reduce criminal opportunity, such as well-lit housing projects that maximize surveillance.[86] C. Ray Jeffery wrote *Crime Prevention Through Environmental Design,*

Ronald Clarke, author of *Situational Crime Prevention,* has written extensively on the strategies and tactics to reduce criminal incidents.

Table 5.1 A Total Community Situational Crime Prevention Model

- Schedule school release uniformly so that there is no doubt when kids belong in school and when they are truant.
- Control truancy.
- Organize after-school activities to keep kids under adult supervision.
- Organize weekend activities with adult supervision.
- Offer school lunches to keep kids in school and away from shopping areas.
- Prohibit cash in schools to reduce kids' opportunity to either be a target or consume drugs or alcohol.
- Keep shopping areas and schools separate.
- Construct housing to maximize guardianship and minimize illegal behavior.
- Encourage neighborhood stability so that residents will be acquainted with one another.
- Encourage privatization of parks and recreation facilities so that people will be responsible for their area's security.

Source: Marcus Felson, "Routine Activities and Crime Prevention," in National Council for Crime Prevention, *Studies on Crime and Crime Prevention, Annual Review,* vol. 1 (Stockholm: Scandinavian University Press, 1992), pp. 30–34.

which extended Newman's concepts and applied them to nonresidential areas, such as schools and factories.[87] According to this view, mechanisms such as security systems, dead-bolt locks, high-intensity street lighting, and neighborhood watch patrols should reduce criminal opportunity.[88] In 1992 Ronald Clarke published *Situational Crime Prevention,* which compiled the best-known strategies and tactics to reduce criminal incidents.[89]

Crime Prevention Strategies

Criminologists have suggested using a number of situational crime prevention efforts that might reduce crime rates. One approach is not to target a specific crime but to create an environment that can reduce the overall crime rate by limiting the access to tempting targets for a highly motivated offender group (like high school students). Notice that this approach is designed not to eliminate a specific crime but to reduce the overall crime rate. Such a strategy might include some or all of the elements contained in Table 5.1.[90]

Targeting Specific Crimes Situational crime prevention can also involve developing tactics to reduce or eliminate a specific crime problem (such as shoplifting in an urban mall or street-level drug dealing). According to criminologists Ronald Clarke and Ross Homel, crime prevention tactics used today generally fall in one of four categories:

- Increase the effort needed to commit crime.
- Increase the risks of committing crime.
- Reduce the rewards for committing crime.
- Induce guilt or shame for committing crime.

These basic techniques and some specific methods that can be used to achieve them are illustrated in Table 5.2.

Some of the tactics to increase effort include *target-hardening techniques* such as putting unbreakable glass on storefronts, locking gates, and fencing yards. Technological advances can make it more difficult to commit crimes; for example, having an owner's photo on credit cards should reduce the use of stolen cards. The development of new products, such as steering locks on cars, can make it more difficult to commit crimes. Empirical evidence indicates that using steering locks has helped reduce car theft in the United States, Britain, and Germany.[91] Installing a locking device on cars that prevents inebriated drivers from starting the vehicle significantly reduces drunk-driving rates.[92] Removing signs from store windows, installing brighter lights, and instituting a pay-first policy can help reduce thefts from gas stations and convenience stores.[93]

Target reduction strategies are designed to reduce the value of crime to the potential criminal. These include making car radios removable so they can be kept at home at night, marking property so that it is more difficult to sell when stolen, and having gender-neutral phone listings to discourage obscene phone calls. Tracking systems, such as those made by the Lojack Corporation, help police locate and return stolen vehicles.

Inducing guilt or shame might include such techniques as setting strict rules to embarrass offenders. For example, publishing "John lists" in the newspaper punishes those arrested for soliciting prostitutes. Facilitating compliance by providing trash bins might shame

Table 5.2 Sixteen Techniques of Situational Prevention

INCREASING PERCEIVED EFFORT	INCREASING PERCEIVED RISKS	REDUCING ANTICIPATED REWARDS	INDUCING GUILT OR SHAME
1. *Target hardening* Slug rejector devices Steering locks Bandit screens 2. *Access control* Parking lot barriers Fenced yards Entry phones 3. *Deflecting offenders* Bus stop placement Tavern location Street closures 4. *Controlling facilitators* Credit card photo Caller ID Gun controls	5. *Entry/exit screening* Automatic ticket gates Baggage screening Merchandise tags 6. *Formal surveillance* Burglar alarms Speed cameras Security guards 7. *Surveillance by employees* Pay phone location Park attendants CCTV systems 8. *Natural surveillance* Defensible space Street lighting Cab driver ID	9. *Target removal* Removable car radio Women's refuges Phone card 10. *Identifying property* Property marking Vehicle licensing Cattle branding 11. *Reducing temptation* Gender-neutral phone lists Off-street parking 12. *Denying benefits* Ink merchandise tags PIN for car radios Graffiti cleaning	13. *Rule setting* Harassment codes Customs declaration Hotel registrations 14. *Strengthening moral condemnation* "Shoplifting is stealing" Roadside speedometers "Bloody idiots drink and drive" 15. *Controlling disinhibitors* Drinking age laws Ignition interlock Server intervention 16. *Facilitating compliance* Improved library checkout Public lavatories Trash bins

Source: Ronald Clarke and Ross Homel, "A Revised Classification of Situational Crime Prevention Techniques," in *Crime Prevention at a Crossroads*, ed. Steven Lab (Cincinnati: Anderson, 1997), p. 4.

chronic litterers into using them. Ronald Clarke shows how caller ID in New Jersey resulted in significant reductions in the number of obscene phone calls. Caller ID displays the telephone number of the party placing the call; the threat of exposure had a deterrent effect on the number of obscene calls reported to police.[94] The Policy and Practice in Criminology feature on page 127 titled "Reducing Subway Crime" describes how these ideas have been implemented to protect passengers on the Washington, D.C., subway system.

Crime Discouragers The success of situational crime prevention may also rest on the behavior of people whose actions directly influence crime prevention. These people are known as **crime discouragers**.[95]

Discouragers can be grouped into three categories: *guardians*, who monitor targets (such as store security guards); *handlers*, who monitor potential offenders (such as parole officers and parents); and *managers*, who monitor places (such as homeowners and doorway attendants). According to this view, crime requires a desirable target without an effective guardian, a motivated offender without an effective handler, and a facilitating place that lacks an attentive manager.[96]

Crime discouragers also have different levels of responsibility, ranging from highly personal involvement, such as the homeowner protecting her house and the parent controlling his children, to the most impersonal general involvement, such as a stranger who stops someone from shoplifting in the mall (see Table 5.3).

Felson suggests that the concept of crime discouragement can be useful in planning situational crime prevention tactics. More effective crime reduction may occur if (1) managers are given better tools to monitor places, (2) guardians are better equipped to protect targets, and (3) handlers are allowed to exert greater control over offenders. For example, a store clerk is in a better position to discourage offenders if armed with a mirror to watch merchandise and a button to summon supervisory help. Handlers become more effective if they are supplied with hidden cameras and eavesdropping devices.

Research indicates that crime discouragers can impact crime rates. An evaluation of a police initiative in Oakland, California, found that an active working partnership with residents and businesspeople who have a stake in maintaining order in their places of work or residences can reduce levels of drug dealing while at the same time increasing civil behavior. Collective action and cooperation in solving problems were effective in controlling crime, whereas individual action (like calling 911) seemed to have little effect.[97]

Displacement, Extinction, Discouragement, and Diffusion Although situational crime prevention seems plausible, it can also produce unforeseen and unwanted consequences. Preventing crime in one location does not address or deter criminal motivation. People who desire the benefits of crime may choose alternative targets, so that crime is not prevented but deflected or displaced.[98]

Table 5.3 Crime Discouragers

TYPES OF SUPERVISORS AND OBJECTS OF SUPERVISION

LEVEL OF RESPONSIBILITY	A. GUARDIANS (monitoring suitable targets)	B. HANDLERS (monitoring likely offenders)	C. MANAGERS (monitoring amenable places)
1. *Personal* (owners, family, friends)	Student keeps eye on own bookbag	Parent makes sure child gets home	Homeowner monitors area near home
2. *Assigned* (employees with specific assignment)	Store clerk monitors jewelry	Principal sends kids back to school	Doorman protects building
3. *Diffuse* (employees with general assignment)	Accountant notes shoplifting	School clerk discourages truancy	Hotel maid impairs trespasser
4. *General* (strangers, other citizens)	Bystander inhibits shoplifting	Stranger questions boys at mall	Customer observes parking structure

Source: Marcus Felson, "Those Who Discourage Crime," in John Eck and David Weisburd, *Crime and Place* (Monsey, N.Y.: Criminal Justice Press, 1995), p. 59. Reprinted by permission.

For example, beefed-up police patrols in one area may shift crimes to a more vulnerable neighborhood.[99] Although crime displacement does not solve the general problem of crime, under some circumstances deflection efforts can partially reduce the frequency of crime or produce less serious offense patterns.[100]

There is also the problem of **extinction**: crime reduction programs may produce a short-term positive effect, but benefits dissipate as criminals adjust to new conditions. They learn to dismantle alarms or avoid patrols; they may try new offenses they had previously avoided. For example, if every residence in a neighborhood has a foolproof burglar alarm system, motivated offenders may turn to armed robbery, a riskier and more violent crime.

Although displacement and extinction may create problems, Ronald Clarke and David Weisburd note a hidden benefit of situational crime prevention: **diffusion of benefits**.[101] Diffusion occurs when (1) efforts to prevent one crime unintentionally prevent another, and (2) crime control efforts in one locale reduce crime in other nontarget areas. Diffusion may be produced by two independent effects. Crime control efforts may deter criminals by causing them to fear apprehension. For example, video cameras set up in a mall to reduce shoplifting can also reduce property damage because would-be vandals fear they are being caught on camera. One recent police program targeting drugs in areas of Jersey City, New Jersey, also reduced public morals crimes.[102]

Another type of diffusion effect is called **discouragement**. If one type of target is limited, would-be lawbreakers may forgo other criminal activity because crime no longer pays. Criminologist Lorraine Green found in her study of the effects of the SMART program (a drug enforcement program in Oakland, California, that enforces municipal codes and nuisance abatement laws) that not only did drug dealing decrease in tar-

geted areas, but improvement was found in surrounding areas as well. She suggests that the program most likely discouraged buyers and sellers who saw familiar hangouts closed. This sign that drug dealing would not be tolerated probably decreased the total number of people involved in drug activity even though they did not operate in the targeted areas.[103] Another example of this effect can be found in evaluations of the Lojack auto protection system, which uses hidden radio transmitters to track stolen cars. Lojack also seems to disrupt the operation of *chop shops,* where stolen vehicles are taken apart for the resale of parts. Police can trace the Lojack signals directly to the chop shop; in Los Angeles alone Lojack has resulted in the breakup of more than 50 chop shops (as of 1998). Car theft rings are afraid to buy stolen cars because they cannot be sure if they contain Lojack.[104] A device designed to protect cars from theft also has the benefit of disrupting the sale of stolen car parts.

General Deterrence

As you have already learned, according to the rational choice view, motivated, rational people will violate the law if left free and unrestricted. The concept of **general deterrence** holds that crime rates are influenced and controlled by the threat of criminal punishment. If people fear being apprehended and punished, they will not risk breaking the law. An inverse relationship should then exist between crime rates and the severity, certainty, and speed of legal sanctions. If, for example, the punishment for a crime is increased and the effectiveness and efficiency of the criminal justice system are improved, then the number of people engaging in that crime should decline. The factors of severity, certainty, and speed of punishment may also influence one another. For example, if a crime—say, robbery—is pun-

Reducing Subway Crime

Washington, D.C.'s, subway system has experienced less crime than expected since it began operations in 1976. One reason is that the system, called "the Metro," employs design characteristics, management practices, and maintenance policies that incorporate principles of situational crime prevention. Here are some of the crime-reducing strategies included:

- High, arched ceilings not only are architecturally sound and aesthetically pleasing, but also create a feeling of openness that reduces passenger fears and provides them with an open view of the station. Long, winding corridors and corners were avoided to reduce shadows and nooks that criminals and panhandlers could occupy.
- Passengers buy multiple-use fare cards in any dollar amount, reducing the time money is exposed to pickpockets and robbers. Fare cards also must be used on entry and exit from the system, reducing the likelihood of fare evasion.
- Metro trains are equipped with graffiti- and vandal-resistant materials to discourage potential offenders. When graffiti artists or vandals do cause damage, mainte-

nance workers clean and repair damaged property promptly.
- No public restrooms, lockers, or excess seats allow potential offenders to loiter. Fast food establishments are prohibited because customers generate litter and provide victims for robbers and pickpockets.
- Rules prohibiting "quality of life" violations, such as smoking or eating on trains are enforced, and all vandalism and graffiti are promptly reported to maintenance personnel to ensure a safe and clean environment.
- Entrance kiosks are continuously staffed while Metro is open. Station attendants are aided by closed-circuit televisions at all unattended entrances, tunnels, and platforms, and they carry two-way radios to report crime and maintenance problems.

Metro's crime rates have been stable and far lower than those experienced in the subway systems in Atlanta, Boston, and Chicago. Applying Metro's design, maintenance, and crime prevention strategies may help new or existing systems reduce subway crime.

CRITICAL THINKING

1. Is it possible that the Metro policies do not actually reduce crime but shift it above ground (crime displacement)? Explain your response.
2. Which methods employed by the Metro system might other government institutions adopt to reduce their own crime problems? For example, which techniques might school systems employ?

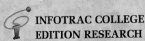

INFOTRAC COLLEGE EDITION RESEARCH

How can theft on subways be deterred? How can terrorist attacks be prevented? For the effects of terrorism on subway crime, read:
Eugene Trivizas, Philip T. Smith. The deterrent effect of terrorist incidents on the rates of luggage theft in railway and underground stations. *British Journal of Criminology,* Wntr 1997 v37 n1 p63(12)

Source: Nancy LaVigne, *Visibility and Vigilance: Metro's Situational Approach to Preventing Subway Crime* (Washington, D.C.: National Institute of Justice, 1997).

---

ished severely, but few robbers are ever caught or punished, the severity of punishment for robbery will probably not deter people from robbing. On the other hand, if the certainty of apprehension and conviction is increased by modern technology, more efficient police work, or some other factor, then even minor punishment might deter the potential robber. Do these factors actually affect the decision to commit crime and, consequently, general crime rates?

Certainty of Punishment   According to **deterrence theory,** if the probability of arrest, conviction, and sanctioning increases, crime rates should decline. Rational offenders will soon realize that the increased likelihood of punishment outweighs any benefit they perceive from committing crimes.

A few research efforts do, in fact, show a direct relationship between crime rates and the certainty of punishment.[105] Research indicates that if police could

make an arrest in at least 30 percent of all reported crimes, the crime rate would significantly decline.[106]

Although these results seem to support the deterrent effect of certain punishment, the relationship between certainty and crime rates is far from settled. There is a great deal of contradictory evidence; in fact, some research efforts have found little relationship between the likelihood of being arrested or imprisoned and corresponding crime rates.[107]

One reason for this ambivalent finding is that the association between certainty of punishment and crime may be time-, crime-, and group-specific. For example, as the number of arrests increases, the number of index crimes reported to police *declines the next day.*[108] It is possible that news of increased and aggressive police activity is rapidly diffused through the population and has an immediate impact that erodes over time. Studies using data collected annually may miss this immediate deterrent effect.

This historical woodcut depicts the execution of King Charles I of England on January 30, 1649. Severe punishments have traditionally been used to deter criminal offenses. The execution of as great a personage as England's king must certainly have had a dramatic impact on the common person. Would severe and public punishments have a similar effect in contemporary society?

Research also finds that deterrence effects may be race-specific. African-American arrest probability influences only African-American offense rates, whereas white arrest probability affects white offending patterns. In large cities, the threat of arrest may be communicated within neighborhoods, many of which are racially segregated. This threat independently affects residents of each racial grouping.[109]

Some research efforts have found a crime-specific deterrent effect. For example, using national data sets measuring crime and arrest rates, criminologist Edwin Zedlewski found that an increased probability of arrest may help lower the burglary rate, whereas larceny rates remain unaffected by law enforcement efforts.[110]

Increasing Police Activity If certainty of apprehension and punishment deters criminal behavior, then increasing the number of police officers on the street should cut the crime rate. Moreover, if these police officers are active, aggressive crime fighters, would-be criminals should be convinced that the risk of apprehension outweighs the benefits they can gain from crime.

There has been some debate whether the mere number of police officers on the street can reduce the crime rate.[111] Numerous studies have failed to show that increasing the number of police officers in a community can lower crime rates.[112] Although these results

are discouraging, the lack of association between police presence and crime rates may be a result of the methodological difficulty in measuring a police–crime association. One problem is that as crime rates increase, communities add police officers. Consequently, the number of officers increases along with the crime rate, making it appear that adding police actually increases community crime rates. However, adding officers may have a long-term deterrent effect.[113]

Some police departments have conducted experiments to determine whether increasing police activities or allocation of services can influence crime rates. Perhaps the most famous experiment was conducted by the Kansas City, Missouri, police department.[114] To evaluate the effectiveness of police patrols, 15 independent police beats or districts were divided into three groups:

1. The first retained a normal police patrol.
2. The second (proactive) was supplied with two to three times the normal amount of patrol forces.
3. The third (reactive) eliminated its preventive patrol entirely, and police officers responded only when summoned by citizens to the scene of a crime.

Surprisingly, these variations in patrol techniques had little effect on the crime patterns in the 15 locales. The presence or absence of patrol forces did not seem to af-

Police crackdowns can target specific neighborhoods or specific offenses, and their duration can range from a few weeks to several years. The following examples illustrate this range. Initial and residual deterrent effects varied, sometimes based on factors outside the scope of the crackdowns themselves.

Drug crackdown, Washington, D.C. A massive police presence—60 police officers per day and a parked police trailer—in the Hanover Place neighborhood open-air drug market provided an effective initial deterrent.

Lynn, Massachusetts, open-air heroin market. A four-year crackdown using four to six officers led to 140 drug arrests in the first 10 months and increased demand for drug treatment.

Operation Clean Sweep, Washington, D.C. The city allocated 100 to 200 officers—many on overtime—to 59 drug markets, making 60 arrests a day. Tactics included roadblocks, observation of open-air markets, "reverse-buy" sell-and-bust by undercover officers, and seizure of cars.

Repeat Call Address Policing (RECAP) Experiment, Minneapolis. A special unit of five police officers attempted to reduce calls for service from 125 residential addresses by increasing their presence with landlords and tenants. This short-term targeting of resources led to a 15 percent drop in calls from these addresses, compared to 125 control addresses.

Nashville, Tennessee, patrol experiment. A sharp increase in moving patrols at speeds under 20 miles per hour in four high-crime neighborhoods netted a measurable decrease in Type 1 index crime during two short crackdowns (11 days and 15 days).

Disorder crackdown in Washington, D.C. Massive publicity accompanied a crackdown on illegal parking and disorder that was attracting street crime to the Georgetown area of the city. Police raised their weekend staffing 30 percent and installed a trailer at a key intersection to book arrestees.

New York City subway crackdown. This massive crackdown involved increasing the number of police officers from 1,200 to 3,100, virtually guaranteeing an officer for every train and every station. Crime fell during the first two years of the crackdown but rose again during the following six years.

Cheshire, England, drunk-driving crackdowns. During two short-term crackdowns, one accompanied by continuing publicity, police increased breathalyzer tests up to sixfold between 10 P.M. and 2 A.M. Significant deterrent effects continued up to six months after the crackdowns ceased.

London prostitution crackdown. Stepped-up arrests of prostitutes, pimps, and brothel keepers—combined with cautions of their customers—succeeded in reducing "curb crawling," with no displacement.

New Zealand drunk-driving crackdowns. Deterrent effects of two short-term crackdowns were felt even before they began because of intensive publicity about the impending crackdowns and stepped-up administration of breathalyzer tests.

Source: Lawrence Sherman, "Police Crackdowns," *NIJ Reports,* March/April 1990, p. 3.

fect residential or business burglaries, auto thefts, larcenies involving auto accessories, robberies, vandalism, or other criminal behavior. Variations in police patrol techniques appeared to have little effect on citizens' attitudes toward the police, their satisfaction with police, or their fear of future criminal behavior.

Other police departments have instituted **crackdowns**—sudden changes in police activity designed to increase the communicated threat or actual certainty of punishment—to lower crime rates. For example, a police task force might target street-level narcotics dealers by using undercover agents and surveillance cameras in known drug-dealing locales. An analysis of 18 police crackdowns by Lawrence Sherman found that while they initially deterred crime, crime rates resumed earlier levels once the crackdown ended. Table 5.4 describes various police crackdowns.[115]

Severity of Punishment and Deterrence The introduction or threat of severe punishment should also bring the crime rate down. Some studies have found that increasing sanction levels can, in fact, control common criminal behaviors. For example, Gary Green has shown that stiffer sanctions stop at least one crime: using an illegal, unauthorized descrambler to obtain pay cable television programs.[116] Green first determined how many people out of a sample of 3,500 in a western town were using a descrambler without paying the local cable company. Threatening letters were sent to the 67 violators, conveying the general message that illegal theft of cable signals would be criminally prosecuted. The letters did not indicate that the subjects' personal violations had been discovered. Green found that about two-thirds of the 67 violators reacted to the threat by desisting and trying to hide their crime by removing the illegal device; a six-month follow-up showed that the intervention had a long-lasting effect. Although Green's research shows that the threat of strict punishment can deter crime, there is little consensus that draconian sanctions alone can reduce criminal activities. Because the likelihood of getting caught for some crimes (like drunk driving) is relatively low, the impact of deterrent measures is negligible over the long term.[117]

Research has also examined the effect of firearm sentencing laws on violent crime rates. These laws provide expanded or mandatory sentences for felonies committed with guns. Although some findings show that these laws can lower crime rates, others question their deterrent effect; there is little evidence that they can cut crime or increase the prison population on a national level.[118]

In sum, it has not been proved that just increasing the punishment for specific crimes can reduce their occurrence.

Capital Punishment It stands to reason that if severity of punishment can deter crime, then fear of the death penalty, the ultimate legal deterrent, should significantly reduce murder rates. Because no one denies its emotional impact, failure of the death penalty to deter violent crime jeopardizes the validity of the entire deterrence concept.

Various studies have tested the assumption that capital punishment deters violent crime. The research can be divided into three types: *immediate impact studies, comparative research,* and *time series analysis.*

1. **Immediate impact:** If capital punishment is a deterrent, the reasoning goes, then its impact should be greatest after a well-publicized execution. Robert Dann began testing this assumption in 1935 when he chose five highly publicized executions of convicted murderers in different years and determined the number of homicides in the 60 days before and after each execution.[119] Each 120-day period had approximately the same number of homicides, as well as the same number of days on which homicides occurred. Dann's study revealed that an average of 4.4 more homicides occurred during the 60 days following an execution than during those preceding it, suggesting that the overall impact of executions might actually *increase* the incidence of homicide.

The fact that executions may actually increase the likelihood of murders being committed is a consequence referred to as the **brutalization effect.** The basis of this theory is that potential criminals may begin to model their behavior after state authorities: if the government can kill its enemies, so can they.[120] The brutalization effect means that after an execution murders may increase, causing even more deaths of innocent victims.[121]

Although many criminologists question the utility of capital punishment, claiming it causes more harm than it prevents, others believe that in the short run, executing criminals can bring the murder rate down.[122] Steven Stack's analysis of 16 well-publicized executions found that they may have saved 480 lives by immediately deterring potential murderers.[123] In sum, a number of criminologists find that executions actually increase murder rates, whereas others argue that their immediate impact lowers murder rates.

2. **Comparative research:** Another type of research compares the murder rates in jurisdictions that have abolished the death penalty with the rates of those that employ the death penalty. Using this approach, Karl Schuessler analyzed 11 states' murder rates between 1930 and 1949 while considering their "execution risk" (the numbers of executions for murder per 1,000 homicides per year). His conclusion: homicide rates and execution risks move independently of each other.[124]

Two pioneering studies, one by Thorsten Sellin (1959) and the other by Walter Reckless (1969), also showed little difference in the murder rates of adjacent states, regardless of their use of the death penalty; capital punishment did not appear to influence the reported rate of homicide.[125] More recent research gives little reason to believe that executions deter homicide.[126] Comparisons of murder rates in jurisdictions having a death penalty statute with those that don't, which also take into account the actual number of people who have been executed, indicate that both having and using a death penalty do not deter violent crime.[127]

The failure to show a deterrent effect of the death penalty is not limited to cross-state comparisons. Research conducted in 14 nations around the world found little evidence that countries with a death penalty have lower violence rates than those without; homicide rates actually decline after capital punishment is abolished, a direct contradiction to its supposed deterrent effect.[128]

3. **Time series analysis:** Econometric statistical analysis has allowed researchers to accurately gauge whether the murder rate changes when death penalty statutes are created or eliminated. The most widely cited study is Isaac Ehrlich's 1975 work, which used national crime and execution data.[129] According to Ehrlich, the perception of execution risk is an important determinant of whether one individual will murder another. As a result of his analysis, Ehrlich concluded that each individual execution per year in the United States would save seven or eight people from being murdered. Ehrlich's research has been widely cited by advocates of the death penalty as empirical proof of the deterrent effect of capital punishment. However, subsequent research that attempted to replicate Ehrlich's analysis showed that his approach was flawed and that capital punishment is no more effective as a deterrent than life imprisonment.[130]

In sum, studies that have attempted to show the deterrent effect of capital punishment on the murder rate indicate that executing convicted criminals has relatively little influence on behavior.[131] Although it is still uncertain why the threat of capital punishment has failed as a deterrent, the cause may lie in the nature of homicide itself. Murder is often an expressive "crime of passion" involving people who knew each other and who may be under the influence of drugs and alcohol; murder is also a by-product of the criminal activity of people who suffer from the burdens of poverty and income inequality.[132] These factors may either prevent or inhibit rational evaluation of the long-term consequences of an immediate violent act.

The failure of the "ultimate deterrent" to deter the "ultimate crime" has been used by critics to question the validity of the general deterrence hypothesis that severe punishment will lower crime rates. In general, there is little direct evidence that severity of punishment alone can reduce or eliminate crime.

Perception and Deterrence A core element of general deterrence theory is that people who believe that they are likely to be caught and severely punished will abstain from crime; this is referred to as **perceptual deterrence.** Deterrence theory would be compromised if perceptions of future punishment had little or no effect on behavior.[133]

Research measuring the association between crime and deterrence has been inconclusive. Some efforts have found that the greater the perceived risk of apprehension, the less likely criminals are willing to risk crime.[134] However, others have found little association between fear of future punishment and criminal activity.[135] One reason that perception of punishment may have less of a deterrent effect than predicted is that among some groups of high-risk offenders, such as teens living in economically depressed neighborhoods, the threat of formal sanctions is irrelevant. Members of these subgroups may not have internalized the norms of society, which hold that getting arrested is wrong. Young people in these areas have less to lose if arrested because their opportunities are few and they have little attachment to social institutions such as school or family. They also may not make connections between their illegal behavior and punishment. In their environment, they see many people committing crimes without getting caught or punished.[136] As a result, they don't learn to fear the consequences of criminal behavior.

When criminal behavior will likely result in apprehension, the deterrent effect is much more prominent than when the possible punishment is severe.[137] For example, people who believe they will be caught and subjected to criminal prosecution seem less willing to engage in a variety of crimes, ranging from tax evasion to burglary.[138] As a result, the perceived risk of punishment may deter some potential and active criminal offenders.

One criticism of perceptual deterrence research is that it usually involves samples of noncriminals, such as college students, and minor crimes, such as smoking marijuana. Experienced offenders, who are more criminally motivated and less committed to moral values, may be less deterred by the perception that they will be punished in the future.[139] Experienced offenders have been found to be the least intimidated by the threat of future punishment.[140] In fact, criminals with the greatest number of prior convictions have the lowest fear of legal sanctions.[141] Perhaps past punishments had been less harsh than they had anticipated. Only the most severe, draconian punishments seem to influence experienced criminals.[142]

In sum, studies measuring the perceptions of punishment agree with studies using aggregate criminal justice data to determine deterrent effects. Certainty of punishment seems to have a greater influence on the choice of crime than severity of punishment. Nonetheless, neither the perception nor the reality of punishment can deter most crimes.

Informal Sanctions Evidence is accumulating that the fear of informal sanctions may have a greater crime-reducing impact than the fear of formal legal punishment.[143] **Informal sanctions** occur when significant others, such as parents, peers, neighbors, and teachers, direct their disapproval, stigma, anger, and indignation toward an offender. If this happens, law violators run the risk of feeling shame, being embarrassed, and suffering a loss of respect.[144] Can the fear of public humiliation deter crime?

Research efforts have in fact established that the threat of informal sanctions can be a more effective deterrent than the threat of formal sanctions.[145] The reason for this is that social control is influenced by the way people perceive negative reactions from interpersonal acquaintances. Legal sanctions may act as a supplement to informal control processes. In other words, a combination of informal and formal social control may have a greater impact on the decision to commit crime than either deterrent measure acting alone.[146] Other studies have also found that people who are committed to conventional moral values or believe crime to be sinful are unlikely to violate the law.[147] For example, British efforts to control drunk driving by shaming offenders produced a moral climate that helped reduce its incidence.[148]

Shame and Humiliation Fear of shame and embarrassment can be a powerful deterrent to crime. Those who fear being rejected by family and peers are reluctant to engage in deviant behavior.[149] These factors manifest themselves in two ways: (1) personal shame over violating the law and (2) the fear of public humiliation if the deviant behavior becomes public knowledge. People who say that their involvement in crime will cause them to feel ashamed are less likely to commit theft, fraud, motor vehicular, and other offenses than people who report they will not feel ashamed.[150]

Anticrime campaigns have been designed to play on this fear of shame; they are most effective when they convince the general public that being accused of crime will make them feel ashamed or embarrassed.[151] For example, spouse abusers report they are more afraid of the social costs of crime (like loss of friends and family disapproval) than they are of legal punishment (such as going to jail). Women are more likely to fear shame and embarrassment than men, a finding that may help explain gender differences in the crime rate.[152]

The effect of informal sanctions may vary according to the cohesiveness of community structure and the type of crime. Informal sanctions may be most effective in highly unified areas where everyone knows one another and the crime cannot be hidden from public view. The threat of informal sanctions seems to have the greatest influence on instrumental crimes, which involve planning, and not on impulsive or expressive criminal behaviors or those associated with substance abuse.[153]

Critique of General Deterrence   Some experts believe that the purpose of the law and justice system is to create a "threat system."[154] That is, the threat of legal punishment should, on the face of it, deter lawbreakers through fear. Nonetheless, as we have already discussed, the relationship between crime rates and deterrent measures is far less than choice theorists might expect. Despite efforts to punish criminals and make them fear crime, there is little evidence that the fear of apprehension and punishment can reduce crime rates. How can this discrepancy be explained?

1. **Rationality:** Deterrence theory assumes a rational offender who weighs the costs and benefits of a criminal act before deciding on a course of action. In many instances, criminals are desperate people who suffer from personality disorders that impair their judgment and render them incapable of making truly rational decisions. As you learned in Chapter 3, a relatively small group of chronic offenders commits a significant percentage of all serious crimes. Some psychologists believe that this select group suffers from an innate or inherited emotional state that renders them both incapable of fearing punishment and less likely to appreciate the consequences of crime.[155] For example, people who are easily aroused sexually also say that they will be more likely to act in a sexually aggressive fashion and not consider the legal consequences of their actions.[156] Their heightened emotional state negates the deterrent effect of the law.

2. **Need:** Many offenders are members of what is referred to as the *underclass*—people cut off from society, lacking the education and skills they need to be in demand in the modern economy.[157] Such desperate people may not be deterred from crime by fear of punishment because, in reality, they perceive few other options for success.

3. **Severity and speed:** As Beccaria's famous equation tells us, the threat of punishment involves not only its severity, but its certainty and speed. Our legal system is not very effective. Only 10 percent of all serious offenses result in apprehension (because half go unreported and police make arrests in about 20 percent of reported crimes). Police routinely do not arrest suspects in personal disputes even when they lead to violence.[158] As apprehended offenders are processed through all the stages of the criminal justice system, the odds of their receiving serious punishment diminish. As a result, some offenders believe that they will not be severely punished for their acts and consequently have little regard for the law's deterrent power.

As you may recall, only offenders who suffer the most severe, draconian sanctions are likely to fear future legal punishment. Criminologist Raymond Paternoster found that adolescents, a group responsible for a disproportionate amount of crime, may be well aware that the juvenile court is generally lenient about imposing meaningful sanctions on even the most serious juvenile offenders.[159] Even those accused of murder are often convicted of lesser offenses and spend relatively short amounts of time behind bars.[160] In making their "rational choice," offenders may be aware that the deterrent effect of the law is minimal.

Specific Deterrence

The general deterrence model focuses on future or potential criminals. In contrast, the theory of **specific** (also called *special* or *particular*) **deterrence** holds that criminal sanctions should be so powerful that known criminals will never repeat their criminal acts. For example, the drunk driver whose sentence is a substantial fine and a week in the county jail should, according to this theory, be convinced that the price to be paid for drinking and driving is too great to consider future violations. Similarly, burglars who spend five years in a tough, maximum-security prison should find their enthusiasm for theft dampened.[161] In principle, punishment works if a connection can be established between the planned action and memories of its consequence; if these recollections are adequately intense, the action will be unlikely to occur again.[162]

Does Specific Deterrence Deter Crime?   At first glance, specific deterrence does not seem to work because a majority of known criminals are not deterred by their punishment. As you have already seen, arrest and punishment seem to have little effect on experienced criminals and may even increase the likelihood that first-time offenders will commit new crimes.[163] Chronic offender research indicates that a stay in a juvenile justice facility does little to deter a persistent delinquent from becoming an adult criminal.[164] It follows that most prison inmates had prior records of arrest and conviction before their current offenses.[165] About two-thirds of all convicted felons are rearrested within three years of their release from prison, and those who have been punished in the past are the most likely to recidivate.[166] Incarceration may sometimes slow down or delay recidivism in the short term, but the overall probability of re-arrest does not change following incarceration.[167]

Research also shows that offenders sentenced to prison do not have lower rates of recidivism than those receiving community sentences for similar crimes. For example, white-collar offenders who receive prison sentences are as likely to recidivate as a matched group of offenders who receive alternative sanctions.[168]

Some research efforts have actually showed that rather than reducing the frequency of crime, punishment increases reoffending rates.[169] Punishment may bring defiance rather than deterrence, or the stigma of apprehension may help lock offenders into a criminal career instead of convincing them to avoid one. However, empirical research indicates that in a few instances, offenders who receive harsher punishments than their peers will be less likely to recidivate, or if they do commit crimes again, they may do so less frequently.[170] But the consensus is that the association between crime and specific deterrent measures remains uncertain at best. The effects of specific deterrence on preventing domestic violence are discussed in the Race, Culture, Gender, and Criminology feature titled "Deterring Domestic Violence."

CONNECTIONS

Theoretically, experiencing punishment should deter future crime. However, punishment stigmatizes people and spoils their identity, a turn of events that may encourage antisocial behavior. The two factors may cancel one another out, helping to explain why punishment does not substantially reduce future criminality. The effects of stigma and negative labels are discussed further in Chapter 8.

Pain Versus Shame If current efforts at specific deterrence are less than successful, should new approaches be attempted? In their two widely discussed works on specific deterrence strategies, criminologists Graeme Newman and John Braithwaite take opposing approaches to reforming criminals. Newman embraces traditional concepts of specific deterrence in his book *Just and Painful*.[171] However, he adds a new wrinkle in his provocative suggestion that society should return to the use of corporal (or physical) punishment. He advocates the use of electric shocks to punish offenders because they are over quickly, they have no lasting effect, and they can easily be adjusted to fit the severity of a crime.

Police officers help a victim of domestic violence escape through a window in her Florida home. Efforts to reduce the incidence of spouse abuse and domestic violence through mandatory arrest policies showcase the specific deterrent effect of legal punishment. Early research efforts conducted by Larry Sherman and Richard Berk in Minneapolis found a specific deterrent effect. However, subsequent efforts failed to replicate the initial findings. While the replications yielded disappointing results, there are indications that specific deterrence policies can, under some circumstances, deter domestic abuse. For example, specific deterrence seems to work better with those who have more to lose, such as a high-paying job.

Deterring Domestic Violence

Is it possible to use a specific deterrence strategy to control domestic violence? Would the memory of a formal police arrest reduce the incidence of spousal abuse? Despite the fact that domestic violence is a prevalent, serious crime, police departments have been accused of rarely arresting suspected perpetrators. Lack of forceful action may contribute to chronic episodes of violence, which obviously is of great concern to women's advocacy groups. Is it possible that prompt, formal action by police agencies might prevent the reoccurrence of this serious crime that threatens and even kills so many women?

In the famous Minneapolis domestic violence study, Lawrence Sherman and Richard Berk had police officers randomly assign treatments to the domestic assault cases they encountered on their beats. One approach was to give some sort of advice and mediation; another was to send the assailant from the home for a period of eight hours; and the third was to arrest the assailant. They found that when police took formal action (arrest), the

chance of recidivism was substantially less than with less punitive measures, such as warning offenders or ordering offenders out of the house for a cooling-off period. A six-month follow-up found that only 10 percent of those who were arrested repeated their violent behavior, while 19 percent of those advised and 24 percent of those sent away repeated their offenses. Sherman and Berk's interviews of 205 victims demonstrated that arrests were somewhat effective in controlling domestic assaults: 19 percent of the women whose attackers had been arrested reported their mates had assaulted them again; in contrast, 37 percent of those whose mates were advised and 33 percent of those whose mates were sent away reported further assaults. Sherman and Berk concluded that a formal arrest was the most effective means of controlling domestic violence, regardless of what happened to the offender in court.

The Minneapolis experiment deeply affected police operations around the nation. Atlanta, Chicago, Dallas, Denver, Detroit, New York,

Miami, San Francisco, and Seattle, among other large cities, adopted policies encouraging arrests in domestic violence cases. A number of states adopted legislation mandating that police either take formal action in domestic abuse cases or explain in writing their failure to act.

Although the findings of the Minneapolis experiment received quick acceptance, government-funded research replicating the experimental design in other locales, including Omaha, Nebraska, and Charlotte, North Carolina, failed to duplicate the original results. In these locales, formal arrest was not a greater deterrent to domestic abuse than warning or advising the assailant. There are also indications that police officers in Minneapolis failed to assign cases randomly, which altered the experimental findings.

In another study, Sherman and his associates found that the duration of custody influenced recidivism. A short-term arrest (custody lasting about three hours) was found to have a different impact, and may actually

---

According to Newman, corporal punishment could be used as an alternative sanction to fill the gap between the severe punishment of prison and the nonpunishment of probation. Electric shocks can be controlled and calibrated to fit the crime. For violent crimes, in which the victim was terrified and humiliated and for which a local community does not wish to incarcerate, violent corporal punishment such as whipping should be considered. In these cases, humiliation of the offender is seen as justifiably deserved. In sum, Newman embraces specific deterrence strategies if they leave no lasting disabilities and are relatively inexpensive, immediate, and individualized. The use of corporal punishment received national attention in 1994 when a young American boy was flogged in Singapore after he pleaded guilty to vandalizing property. The Singapore incident sparked a nationwide debate over the value of corporal punishment; some conservative politicians advocated that such measures should be adopted in the United States.

Reintegrative Shaming   Braithwaite's *Crime, Shame and Reintegration* takes a radically different approach

from Newman.[172] Braithwaite notes that countries such as Japan, in which conviction for crimes brings an inordinate amount of shame, have extremely low crime rates. In Japan, criminal prosecution proceeds only when the normal process of public apology, compensation, and the victim's forgiveness breaks down.

Shame is a powerful tool of informal social control. Citizens in cultures in which crime is not shameful, such as the United States, do not internalize an abhorrence for crime because when they are punished, they view themselves as mere victims of the justice system. Their punishment comes at the hands of neutral strangers, like police and judges, who are being paid to act. In contrast, shaming relies on the victim's participation.[173]

Braithwaite divides the concept of shame into two distinct types. The most common form of shaming typically involves **stigmatization.** This form of shaming involves an ongoing process of degradation in which the offender is branded as an evil person and cast out of society. Shaming can occur at a school disciplinary hearing or a criminal court trial. Bestowing stigma and degradation may have a general deterrent effect: it have been more effective, than an arrest followed by a longer period of detention. However, while initially a deterrent, the effects of a short-term arrest quickly decayed and, in the long run, may escalate the frequency of repeat domestic violence.

Explaining why the initial deterrent effect of arrest decays over time is difficult. It is possible that offenders who are arrested initially fear punishment, but eventually replace fear with anger and violent intent toward their mates when their cases do not result in severe punishment. Many repeat abusers do not fear arrest, believing that formal police action will not cause them harm.

A stronger response, perhaps emphasizing mandatory jail time, might be necessary before the threat of arrest can deter domestic violence. However, the association between severity of postconviction punishment and repeat domestic violence is equally ambivalent. For example, Amy Thistlethwaite and her associates report an inverse association between severity of punishment (such as jail combined with probation) and the likelihood of reoffending; the effect was greatest for those with a stake in conformity (such as those who are employed and live in a good neighborhood). In contrast, Robert Davis and his associates recently reported no association at all between severity of disposition and rearrest for spousal abuse. Men are just as likely to recidivate if their case is dismissed, if they are given probation, or even if they are sent to jail. In sum, domestic violence research indicates that the association between specific deterrence measures and criminality is tenuous at best.

CRITICAL THINKING

1. Why do arrests seem to have little effect on future domestic violence? Could it be that getting arrested increases feelings of strain and hostility and does little to reduce the problems that led to domestic conflict in the first place? Explain how you think this works.
2. What policies would you suggest to reduce the reoccurrence of domestic violence?

 INFOTRAC COLLEGE EDITION RESEARCH

How can domestic violence be effectively treated? One approach is to intervene early, before the problem has led to severe injury or death. To read more about this method, see: Linda Dakis. Dade County's Domestic Violence Plan: an integrated approach. *Trial,* Feb 1995 31 n2 p44(4)

Source: Robert Davis, Barbara Smith, and Laura Nickles, "The Deterrent Effect of Prosecuting Domestic Violence Misdemeanors," *Crime and Delinquency* 44 (1998): 434–42; Amy Thistlethwaite, John Wooldredge, and David Gibbs, "Severity of Dispositions and Domestic Violence Recidivism," *Crime and Delinquency* 44 (1998): 388–98; J. David Hirschel, Ira Hutchison, and Charles Dean, "The Failure of Arrest to Deter Spouse Abuse," *Journal of Research in Crime and Delinquency* 29 (1992): 7–33; Franklyn Dunford, David Huizinga, and Delbert Elliott, "The Role of Arrest in Domestic Assault: The Omaha Experiment," *Criminology* 28 (1990): 183–206; Lawrence Sherman, Janell Schmidt, Dennis Rogan, Patrick Gartin, Ellen Cohn, Dean Collins, and Anthony Bacich, "From Initial Deterrence to Long-Term Escalation: Short-Custody Arrest for Domestic Violence," *Criminology* 29 (1991): 821–50; Lawrence Sherman and Richard Berk, "The Specific Deterrent Effects of Arrest for Domestic Assault," *American Sociological Review* 49 (1984): 261–72; Michael Steinman, "Lowering Recidivism Among Men Who Batter Women," *Journal of Police Science and Administration* 17 (1990):124–31; and Susan Miller and Leeann Iovanni, "Determinants of Perceived Risk of Formal Sanction for Courtship Violence," *Justice Quarterly* 11 (1994): 282–312.

makes people afraid of social rejection and public humiliation. As a specific deterrent, stigma is doomed to failure: people who suffer humiliation at the hands of the justice system "reject their rejectors" by joining a deviant subculture of like-minded people who collectively resist social control.

Braithwaite argues that crime control can be better achieved through a policy of **reintegrative shaming.** Here disapproval is extended to the offenders' evil deeds, while at the same time they are cast as respected people who can be reaccepted by society. A critical element of reintegrative shaming occurs when the offenders begin to understand and recognize their wrongdoing and shame themselves. To be reintegrative, shaming must be brief and controlled and then followed by ceremonies of forgiveness, apology, and repentance.

To prevent crime, Braithwaite charges, society must encourage reintegrative shaming. For example, the women's movement can reduce domestic violence by mounting a crusade to shame spouse abusers.[174] In addition, an effort must be made to create pride in solving problems nonviolently, in caring for others, and in respecting the rights of women.

As discussed earlier, informal social controls may have a greater impact than legal or formal ones. It is not surprising, then, that the fear of personal shame can have a general deterrent effect. It may also be applied to produce specific deterrence. One Australian program brings offenders together with victims so that the offenders can experience shame. Their close family members and peers are also present to help the offender reintegrate.[175] Efforts like these can humanize a system of justice that today relies on repression, rather than forgiveness, as the basis of specific deterrence.

CONNECTIONS

The use of reintegrative shaming has been advocated by criminologists who consider harsh punishment counterproductive. Their thoughts and some of the programs they advocate are discussed in Chapter 9's sections on peacemaking criminology.

Rethinking Deterrence

So far, both specific and general deterrence strategies have not yielded the results predicted by choice theorists. Although a few studies have shown expected effects, there is still little conclusive evidence that formal sanctions can convince would-be criminals to abstain from their intended behavior or convince experienced offenders that crime does not pay.

In an important 1993 article, Mark Stafford and Mark Warr call for the reconceptualization of both specific and general deterrence.[176] They argue that these concepts are not independent but rather are interactive: most people have had experience with the direct effect of punishment (specific deterrence) and the indirect effect of the fear of punishment (general deterrence). In addition, they may have personally experienced **punishment avoidance**—either getting away with crime themselves or knowing about others who have escaped detection. Conversely, they know others who have been severely punished; this is known as **vicarious deterrence.** The total deterrent effect encompasses a combination of personal and vicarious experiences with punishment and its aftermath. The two effects may cancel each other out, explaining, in part, the ambiguity of deterrent effects: an experienced criminal may fear apprehension, but his experiences tell him that the law's bark is worse than its bite. A person with criminal friends may fear punishment less when his or her friends describe how easy it is to get away with crime.

Empirical research shows that people are influenced by both general and specific deterrent effects; these work in concert to influence behavior.[177] For example, people's intentions to drink and drive seem related to both personal and vicarious knowledge of deterrence, as well as experiences with punishment.[178] People who have both experienced punishment and heard about it from others are likely to believe that punishment is a certainty and to be deterred from crime. Stafford and Warr's views may help criminologists better understand the forces that promote deterrence so that the concept can be studied more rationally.

Incapacitation

It stands to reason that if more criminals are sent to prison, the crime rate should go down. Because most people age out of crime, the duration of a criminal career is limited. Placing offenders behind bars during their prime crime years should lessen their lifetime opportunity to commit crime. The shorter the span of opportunity, the fewer offenses they can commit during their lives; hence crime is reduced. This theory, known as the **incapacitation effect,** seems logical, but does it work? The past 20 years have witnessed significant growth in the number and percentage of the population held in prison and jails; today more than 1.6 million Americans are incarcerated. Advocates of incapacitation suggest that this effort has been responsible for the overall stabilization and actual decline in some crime rates in the 1990s.

> ### CONNECTIONS
>
> The rapid rise in the prison population and the corresponding overcrowding in the nation's prison system are discussed further in Chapter 18. In the sections on sentencing in Chapter 17, other reasons for the prison boom are discussed—specifically, the increase in the number of incarcerated drug offenders who are being punished with relatively stiff mandatory sentences.

Others suggest that this association is illusory and that a stable crime rate is actually controlled by such factors as these:

- The size of the teenage population
- The threat of tough new mandatory sentences
- A healthy economy
- Tougher gun laws
- The end of the crack epidemic
- The implementation of tough, aggressive policing strategies in large cities such as New York[179]

What appears to be an incapacitation effect may actually reflect the effect of some other legal phenomenon and not the incarceration of so many criminals. If, for example, the crime rate drops as more people are sent to prison, it would appear that incapacitation works. However, crime rates may really be dropping because potential criminals now fear punishment and are being deterred from crime. What appears to be an incapacitation effect may actually be an effect of general deterrence. In sum, measurement and other methodological problems have made it extremely difficult to assess whether the criminal justice system's efforts to control crime deter potential criminals.[180]

Can Incapacitation Reduce Crime? Research on the direct benefits of incapacitation has been inconclusive. A number of studies have set out to measure the precise effect of incarceration rates on crime rates, and the results have not supported a strict incarceration policy.[181] It has been estimated that if the prison population were cut in half, the crime rate would most likely go up only 4 percent; if prisons were entirely eliminated, crime might increase 8 percent.[182] Looking at this relationship from another perspective, if the average prison sentence were increased 50 percent, the crime rate might be reduced only 4 percent.[183] A few criminologists, however, have found an inverse relationship between incarceration rates and crime rates. In a frequently cited study, Reuel Shinnar and Shlomo Shinnar's research on incapacitation in New York led them to conclude that mandatory prison sentences of five years for violent crime and three for property offenses could reduce the reported crime rate by a factor of four or five.[184] Other research efforts also claim that an incarceration policy can reduce the level of violent crime.[185] There may also be a spillover effect: crime may be reduced in a jurisdiction if neighboring states increase their incarceration rates, thereby reducing the number of criminals who cross state lines to commit their crimes.[186] Most important, as the prison population has increased dramatically in the 1990s, crime rates have fallen. Yet no direct evidence links prison population increases to falling crime rates and other factors (for example, the waning of the crack epidemic) may have an equal if not greater effect.[187]

CONNECTIONS

Chapter 3 discussed some of the factors that may influence crime rate fluctuations, including drug use, handgun availability, age of the population, social and economic change, and so on.

The Logic Behind Incarceration Incarceration as a crime control strategy should work, considering that the criminals who commit crimes are unable to continue from prison or jail. For example, a recent study of 201 heroin abusers in New York City found that if these abusers were incarcerated for one year, they would not have been able to commit their yearly haul of crimes: 1,000 robberies, 4,000 burglaries, 10,000 shopliftings, and more than 3,000 other property crimes.[188]

Nonetheless, evaluations of incarceration strategies reveal their impact may be less than expected. For one thing, there is little evidence that incapacitating criminals will deter them from future criminality and even more reason to believe that they may be more inclined to commit crimes upon release. Prison has few specific deterrent effects; the more prior incarceration experiences inmates have, the more likely they are to recidivate (and return to prison) within 12 months of their release.[189] The short-term crime reduction effect of incapacitating criminals is negated if the prison experience has the long-term effect of escalating frequency of criminal behavior upon release.

Furthermore, the economics of crime suggest that if money can be made from criminal activity, there will always be someone to take the place of the incarcerated offender. New criminals will be recruited and trained, offsetting any benefit accrued by incarceration. Imprisoning established offenders may likewise open new opportunities for competitors who were suppressed by the more experienced criminals. For example, incarcerating organized crime members may open drug markets to new gangs; the flow of narcotics into the country may increase after organized crime leaders are imprisoned.

Another reason that incarceration may not work is that most criminal offenses are committed by teens and very young adult offenders who are unlikely to be sent to prison for a single felony conviction. In addition, incarcerated criminals, aging behind bars, are already past the age where they are likely to commit crime. As a result, a strict incarceration policy may keep people in prison beyond the time they are a threat to society while a new cohort of high-risk adolescents is on the street. It is possible that the most serious criminals are already behind bars and that adding more to the population will have little appreciable effect while adding tremendous costs to the correctional system.[190]

An incapacitation strategy is also terribly expensive. The prison system costs billions of dollars each year. Even if incarceration could reduce the crime rate, the costs would be enormous. Are U.S. taxpayers willing to spend billions more on new prison construction and annual maintenance fees? A strict incarceration policy would result in a growing number of elderly inmates whose maintenance costs, estimated at $69,000 per year, are three times higher than those of younger inmates. By the year 2001 there will be more than 125,000 of these elderly inmates, and by 2005 about 16 percent of the prison population will be over 50.[191]

Selective Incapacitation: Three Strikes and You're Out A more efficient incapacitation model has been suggested that is based on discovering who the chronic career criminals are. The premise for this model is that if a small number of people account for a relatively large percentage of the nation's crime, then an effort to incapacitate these few troublemakers might have a significant payoff. In an often-cited work, Peter Greenwood of the Rand Corporation suggests that **selective incapacitation** could be an effective crime reduction strategy.[192] In his study of over 2,000 inmates serving time for theft in California, Michigan, and Texas, he found that selective incapacitation of chronic offenders could reduce the rate of robbery offenses by 15 percent and the inmate population by 5 percent. According to Greenwood's model, chronic offenders can be distinguished on the basis of their offending patterns and lifestyle (for example, their employment record and history of substance abuse). Once identified, high-risk offenders would be eligible for sentencing enhancements that would substantially increase the time they serve in prison.

Another concept receiving widespread attention is the **three strikes and you're out** policy of giving people convicted of three violent offenses a mandatory life term without parole. Many states already employ habitual offender laws that provide long (or life) sentences for repeat offenders. Criminologists retort that although such strategies are politically compelling, they will not work because

- Most three-time losers are at the verge of aging out of crime anyway.
- Current sentences for violent crimes are already severe.
- An expanding prison population will drive up already high prison costs.
- There would be racial disparity in sentencing.
- The police would be in danger because two-time offenders would violently resist a third arrest, knowing they face a life sentence.[193]
- The prison population probably already contains the highest-frequency criminals.

Those who support a selective incapacitation strategy argue that criminals who are already in prison (high-rate offenders) commit significantly more crimes each year than the average criminal who is on the outside (low-rate offenders). If a broad policy of incarceration were employed, requiring mandatory prison sentences for all those convicted of crimes, more low-rate criminals would be placed behind bars.[194] It would be both costly and nonproductive to incarcerate large groups of people who commit relatively few crimes. It makes more economic sense to focus incarceration efforts on known high-rate offenders by lengthening their sentences.

POLICY IMPLICATIONS OF CHOICE THEORY

From the origins of classical theory to the development of modern rational choice views, the belief that criminals choose to commit crime has influenced the relationship between law, punishment, and crime. Although research on the core principles of choice theory and deterrence theories produces mixed results, these models have had an important impact on crime prevention strategies.

When police patrol in well-marked cars, it is assumed that their presence will deter would-be criminals. When the harsh realities of prison life are portrayed in movies and TV shows, the lesson is not lost on potential criminals. Nowhere is the idea that the threat of punishment can control crime more evident than in the implementation of tough mandatory criminal sentences to control violent crime and drug trafficking.

Despite its questionable deterrent effect, some advocates argue that the death penalty can effectively restrict criminality; at least it ensures that convicted criminals never again get the opportunity to kill. Many observers are dismayed because people who are convicted of murder sometimes kill again when released on parole. One study of 52,000 incarcerated murderers found that 810 had been previously convicted of mur-

der and had killed 821 people following their previous release from prison.[195] About 9 percent of all inmates on death row have had prior convictions for homicide. Death penalty advocates argue that if these criminals had been executed for their first offenses, hundreds of people would be alive today.[196]

Just Desert

The concept of criminal choice has also prompted the creation of justice policies referred to as **just desert.** The just desert position has been most clearly spelled out by criminologist Andrew Von Hirsch in his book *Doing Justice*.[197] Von Hirsch suggests the concept of desert as a theoretical model to guide justice policy. This utilitarian view purports that punishment is needed to preserve the social equity disturbed by crime. Nonetheless, he claims that the severity of punishment should be commensurate with the seriousness of the crime.[198] Von Hirsch's views can be summarized in these three statements:

1. Those who violate others' rights deserve to be punished.
2. We should not deliberately add to human suffering; punishment makes those punished suffer.
3. However, punishment may prevent more misery than it inflicts; this conclusion reestablishes the need for desert-based punishment.[199]

Desert theory is also concerned with the rights of the accused. It alleges that the rights of the person being punished should not be unduly sacrificed for the good of others (as with deterrence). The offender should not be treated as more (or less) **blameworthy** than is warranted by the character of his or her offense. For example, Von Hirsch asks the following question: If two crimes, A and B, are equally serious, but if severe penalties are shown to have a deterrent effect only with respect to A, would it be fair to punish the person who has committed crime A more harshly simply to deter others from committing the crime? Conversely, imposing a light sentence for a serious crime would be unfair because it would treat the offender as less blameworthy than he or she is.

In sum, the just desert model suggests that retribution justifies punishment because people deserve what they get for past deeds. Punishment based on deterrence or incapacitation is wrong because it involves an offender's future actions, which cannot accurately be predicted. Punishment should be the same for all people who commit the same crime. Criminal sentences based on individual needs or characteristics are inherently unfair because all people are equally blameworthy for their misdeeds. The influence of Von Hirsch's views can be seen in sentencing models that give the same punishment to all people who commit the same type of crime.

Table 5.5 Choice Theories

THEORY	MAJOR PREMISE	STRENGTHS
Rational choice	Law-violating behavior occurs after offenders weigh information on their personal needs and the situational factors involved in the difficulty and risk of committing a crime.	Explains why high-risk youths do not constantly engage in delinquency. Relates theory to delinquency control policy. It is not limited by class or other social variables.
Routine activities	Crime and delinquency are functions of the presence of motivated offenders, the availability of suitable targets, and the absence of capable guardians.	Can explain fluctuations in crime and delinquency rates. Shows how victim behavior influences criminal choice.
General deterrence	People will commit crime and delinquency if they perceive that the benefits outweigh the risks. Crime is a function of the severity, certainty, and speed of punishment.	Shows the relationship between crime and punishment. Suggests a real solution to crime.
Specific deterrence	If punishment is severe enough, criminals will not repeat their illegal acts.	Provides a strategy to reduce crime.
Incapacitation	Keeping known criminals out of circulation will reduce crime rates.	Recognizes the role opportunity plays in criminal behavior. Provides solution to chronic offending.

SUMMARY

Choice theories assume that criminals carefully choose whether to commit criminal acts. These theories are summarized in Table 5.5. People are influenced by their fear of the criminal penalties associated with being caught and convicted for law violations. The more severe, certain, and swift the punishment, the more likely it is to control crime. The choice approach is rooted in the classical criminology of Cesare Beccaria and Jeremy Bentham. These eighteenth-century social philosophers argued that punishment should be certain, swift, and severe enough to deter crime.

The growth of positivist criminology, which stressed external causes of crime and rehabilitation of known offenders, reduced the popularity of the classical approach in the twentieth century. However, in the late 1970s the concept of criminal choice once again became an important criminological perspective. Today choice theorists view crime as offense- and offender-specific. Research shows that offenders consider their targets carefully before deciding on a course of action. By implication, crime can be prevented or displaced by convincing potential criminals that the risks of violating the law exceed the benefits.

Deterrence theory holds that if criminals are indeed rational, an inverse relationship should exist between punishment and crime. However, a number of factors confound the relationship. For example, if people do not believe they will be caught, even harsh punishment may not deter crime. Deterrence theory has been criticized on the grounds that it wrongfully assumes that criminals make a rational choice before committing crimes, ignores the intricacies of the criminal jus-

tice system, and does not take into account the social and psychological factors that may influence criminality. Research designed to test the validity of the deterrence concept has not indicated that deterrent measures actually reduce the crime rate.

Specific deterrence theory holds that the crime rate can be reduced if known offenders are punished so severely that they never commit crimes again. However, there is little evidence that harsh punishment actually reduces the crime rate. Incapacitation theory maintains that if deterrence does not work, the best course of action is to incarcerate known offenders for long periods so that they lack criminal opportunity. Research efforts, however, have not proved that increasing the number of people in prison—and increasing prison sentences—will reduce crime rates.

Choice theory has been influential in shaping public policy. Criminal law is designed to deter potential criminals and fairly punish those who have been caught in illegal acts. Some courts have changed sentencing policies to adapt to classical principles, and the U.S. correctional system seems geared toward incapacitation and specific deterrence. The just desert view is that criminal sanctions should be geared precisely to the seriousness of the crime. People should be punished on the basis of whether they deserve to be punished for what they did and not because it may affect or deter their future behavior.

 See the book-specific web site at www.cj.wadsworth. com for additional chapter links, discussions, and quizzes.

The attorney general has recently funded a national survey of state sentencing practices. The table below provides the most important findings from the survey.

The attorney general wants you to make some recommendations about criminal punishment. Is it possible, she asks, that both the length of criminal sentences and the way they are served can impact crime rates? What could be gained by either increasing punishment or requiring inmates to spend more time behind bars before their release? Are we being too lenient or too punitive? As someone who has studied choice theory, how would you interpret this data, and what does it tell you about sentencing patterns? How might crime rates be affected if the way we punished offenders was radically changed?

TYPE OF OFFENSE	AVERAGE SENTENCE	AVERAGE SENTENCE SERVED BEFORE RELEASE	AVERAGE PERCENTAGE OF SENTENCE SERVED
All violent	89 months	43 months	48%
Homicide	149 months	71 months	48%
Rape	117 months	65 months	56%
Kidnapping	104 months	52 months	50%
Robbery	95 months	44 months	6%
Sexual assault	72 months	35 months	49%
Assault	61 months	29 months	48%
Other	60 months	28 months	47%

KEY TERMS

choice theory
classical theory
utilitarianism
rational choice
reasoning criminal
crime displacement
offense- and offender-specific
suitable targets
permeable neighborhood
spillover effect
capable guardians
motivated criminals
mutual society
periodic market

fixed-site neighborhood
drug mart
fence
edgework
seductions of crime
arousal theory
situational crime prevention
defensible space
crime discouragers
extinction
diffusion of benefits
discouragement
general deterrence
deterrence theory

crackdowns
brutalization effect
perceptual deterrence
informal sanctions
specific deterrence
stigmatization
reintegrative shaming
punishment avoidance
vicarious deterrence
incapacitation effect
selective incapacitation
three strikes and you're out
just desert
blameworthy

NOTES

1. Associated Press, "Death Penalty Sought in Nev. Case," *New York Times,* 17 October 1998.

2. Francis Edward Devine, "Cesare Beccaria and the Theoretical Foundations of Modern Penal Jurisprudence," *New England Journal on Prison Law* 7 (1982): 8–21.

3. Devine, "Cesare Beccaria."

4. Graeme Newman and Pietro Marongiu, "Penological Reform and the Myth of Beccaria," *Criminology* 28 (1990): 325–46.

5. Bob Roshier, *Controlling Crime* (Chicago: Lyceum Books, 1989), p. 10.

6. Jeremy Bentham, *A Fragment on Government and an Introduction to the Principle of Morals and Legislation,* ed. Wilfred Harrison (Oxford: Basil Blackwell, 1967).

7. Bentham, *A Fragment on Government,* p. xi.

8. Robert Martinson, "What Works?—Questions and Answers About Prison Reform," *Public Interest* 35 (1974): 22–54.

9. Charles Murray and Louis Cox, *Beyond Probation* (Beverly Hills: Sage, 1979).

10. Ronald Bayer, "Crime, Punishment, and the Decline of Liberal Optimism," *Crime and Delinquency* 27 (1981): 190.

11. James Q. Wilson, *Thinking About Crime,* rev. ed. (New York: Vintage Books, 1983), p. 260.

12. Wilson, *Thinking About Crime,* p. 128.

13. Michael Tonry, *Malign Neglect: Race, Crime and Punishment in America* (New York: Oxford University Press, 1995).

14. See, generally, Derek Cornish and Ronald Clarke, eds. *The Reasoning Criminal: Rational Choice Perspectives on Offending* (New York: Springer Verlag, 1986); Philip Cook, "The Demand and Supply of Criminal Opportunities," in *Crime and Justice,* vol. 7, ed. Michael Tonry and Norval Mor-

ris (Chicago: University of Chicago Press, 1986), pp. 1–28; Ronald Clarke and Derek Cornish, "Modeling Offender's Decisions: A Framework for Research and Policy," in *Crime and Justice,* vol. 6, ed. Michael Tonry and Norval Morris (Chicago: University of Chicago Press, 1985), pp. 147–87; and Morgan Reynolds, *Crime by Choice: An Economic Analysis* (Dallas: Fisher Institute, 1985).

15. George Rengert and John Wasilchick, *Suburban Burglary: A Time and Place for Everything* (Springfield, Ill.: Charles Thomas, 1985).

16. John McIver, "Criminal Mobility: A Review of Empirical Studies," in *Crime Spillover,* ed. Simon Hakim and George Rengert (Beverly Hills: Sage, 1981), pp. 110–21; Carol Kohfeld and John Sprague, "Demography, Police Behavior, and Deterrence," *Criminology* 28 (1990): 111–36.

17. Derek Cornish and Ronald Clarke, "Understanding Crime Displacement: An Application of Rational Choice Theory," *Criminology* 25 (1987): 933–47.

18. Lloyd Phillips and Harold Votey, "The Influence of Police Interventions and Alternative Income Sources on the Dynamic Process of Choosing Crime as a Career," *Journal of Quantitative Criminology* 3 (1987): 251–74.

19. Phillips and Votey, "The Influence of Police Interventions."

20. Michael Gottfredson and Travis Hirschi, *A General Theory of Crime* (Stanford, Calif.: Stanford University Press, 1990).

21. Liliana Pezzin, "Earnings Prospects, Matching Effects, and the Decision to Terminate a Criminal Career," *Journal of Quantitative Criminology* 11 (1995): 29–50.

22. Ronald Akers, "Rational Choice, Deterrence and Social Learning Theory in Criminology: The Path Not Taken," *Journal of Criminal Law and Criminology* 81 (1990): 653–76.

23. Neal Shover, *Aging Criminals* (Beverly Hills, Sage, 1985).

24. Robert Agnew, "Determinism, Indeterminism, and Crime: An Empirical Exploration," *Criminology* 33 (1995): 83–109.

25. Agnew, "Determinism, Indeterminism, and Crime," pp. 103–104.

26. Bruce Jacobs, "Crack Dealers' Apprehension Avoidance Techniques: A Case of Restrictive Deterrence," *Justice Quarterly* 13 (1996): 359–81.

27. Jacobs, "Crack Dealers' Apprehension Avoidance Techniques," p. 367.

28. Jacobs, "Crack Dealers' Apprehension Avoidance Techniques," p. 372.

29. Michael Rand, *Crime and the Nation's Households, 1989* (Washington, D.C.: Bureau of Justice Statistics, 1990), p. 4.

30. Paul Cromwell, James Olson, and D'Aunn Wester Avary, *Breaking and Entering, An Ethnographic Analysis of Burglary* (Newbury Park, Calif.: Sage, 1989), p. 24.

31. Cromwell, Olson, and Avary, *Breaking and Entering,* pp. 30–32.

32. John Gibbs and Peggy Shelly, "Life in the Fast Lane: A Retrospective View by Commercial Thieves," *Journal of Research in Crime and Delinquency* 19 (1982): 229–30.

33. George Rengert and John Wasilchick, *Space, Time, and Crime: Ethnographic Insights into Residential Burglary* (Washington, D.C.: National Institute of Justice, 1989); see also Rengert and Wasilchick, *Suburban Burglary.*

34. Cromwell, Olson, and Avary, *Breaking and Entering.*

35. Jacobs, "Crack Dealers' Apprehension Avoidance Techniques," p. 369.

36. Leanne Fiftal Alarid, James Marquart, Velmer Burton, Francis Cullen, and Steven Cuvelier, "Women's Roles in Serious Offenses: A Study of Adult Felons," *Justice Quarterly* 13 (1996): 431–54 at 448.

37. Ronald Clarke and Marcus Felson, "Introduction: Criminology, Routine Activity and Rational Choice," in *Routine Activity and Rational Choice* (New Brunswick, N.J.: Transaction Publishers, 1993), pp. 1–14.

38. Cromwell, Olson, and Avary, *Breaking and Entering.*

39. Andrew Buck, Simon Hakim, and George Rengert, "Burglar Alarms and the Choice Behavior of Burglars: A Suburban Phenomenon," *Journal of Criminal Justice* 21 (1993): 497–507.

40. Ralph Taylor and Stephen Gottfredson, "Environmental Design, Crime, and Prevention: An Examination of Community Dynamics," in *Communities and Crime,* ed. Albert Reiss and Michael Tonry (Chicago: University of Chicago Press, 1986), pp. 387–416.

41. Michael Costanzo, William Halperin, and Nathan Gale, "Criminal Mobility and the Directional Component in Journeys to Crime," in *Metropolitan Crime Patterns,* ed. Robert Figlio, Simon Hakim, and George Rengert (Monsey, N.Y.: Criminal Justice Press, 1986), pp. 73–95.

42. Garland White, "Neighborhood Permeability and Burglary Rates," *Justice Quarterly* 7 (1990): 57–67.

43. White, "Neighborhood Permeability," p. 65.

44. Patrick Donnelly and Charles Kimble, "Community Organizing, Environmental Change, and Neighborhood Crime," *Crime and Delinquency* 43 (1997): 493–511.

45. James Massey, Marvin Krohn, and Lisa Bonati, "Property Crime and the Routine Activities of Individuals," *Journal of Research in Crime and Delinquency* 26 (1989): 378–400; note, however, that the findings here generally disagree with the routine activities theory.

46. Joseph Deutsch and Gil Epstein, "Changing a Decision Taken Under Uncertainty: The Case of the Criminal's Location Choice," *Urban Studies* 35 (1998): 1335–44.

47. Deutsch and Epstein, "Changing a Decision Taken Under Uncertainty."

48. Kenneth Tunnell, *Choosing Crime* (Chicago: Nelson-Hall, 1992), p. 105.

49. Robert Sampson and Jacqueline Cohen, "Deterrent Effects of the Police on Crime: A Replication and Theoretical Extension," *Law and Society Review* 22 (1988): 163–88.

50. Marcus Felson et al., "Preventing Crime at Newark Subway Stations," *Security Journal* 1 (1990): 137–40.

51. Simha Landau and Daniel Fridman, "The Seasonality of Violent Crime: The Case of Robbery and Homicide in Israel," *Journal of Research in Crime and Delinquency* 30 (1993): 163–91.

52. Tunnell, *Choosing Crime,* p. 67.

53. Ronald Clarke, "Situational Crime Prevention," in Michael Tonry and David Farrington, eds., *Building a Safer Society, Strategic Approaches to Crime Prevention,* vol. 19 of *Crime and Justice, A Review of Research* (Chicago: University of Chicago Press, 1995), 91–151.

54. Mark Warr, "Parents, Peers, and Delinquency," *Social Forces* 72 (1993): 247–64.

55. John Hagan, "Destiny and Drift: Subcultural Preferences, Status Attainments, and the Risks and Rewards of Youth," *American Sociological Review* 56 (1991): 567–82.

56. D. Wayne Osgood, Janet Wilson, Patrick O'Malley, Jerald Bachman, and Lloyd Johnston, "Routine Activities and Individual Deviant Behavior," *American Sociological Review* 61 (1996): 635–55.

57. Matthew Ploeger, "Youth Employment and Delinquency: Reconsidering a Problematic Relationship," *Criminology* 35 (1997): 659–75.

58. Richard Felson, "Routine Activities and Involvement in Violence as Actor, Witness, or Target," *Violence and Victimization* 12 (1997): 209–223.

59. Associated Press, "Thrift Hearings Resume Today in Senate," *Boston Globe,* 2 January 1991, p. 10.

60. Ronald Clarke and Patricia Harris, "Auto Theft and Its Prevention," in Michael Tonry and Norval Morris, eds., *Crime and Justice: An Annual Edition* (Chicago: University of Chicago Press, 1992), pp. 1–54 at 20–21.

61. Lisa Maher, "Hidden in the Light: Occupational Norms Among Crack-Using Street-Level Sex Workers," *Journal of Drug Issues* 26 (1996): 143–73.

62. John Petraitis, Brian Flay, and Todd Miller, "Reviewing Theories of Adolescent Substance Use: Organizing Pieces in the Puzzle," *Psychological Bulletin* 117 (1995): 67–86.

63. Jacobs, "Crack Dealers' Apprehension Avoidance Techniques."

64. Jacobs, "Crack Dealers' Apprehension Avoidance Techniques," p. 367.

65. Jacobs, "Crack Dealers' Apprehension Avoidance Techniques," p. 368.

66. Patricia Morgan and Karen Ann Joe, "Citizens and Outlaws: The Private Lives and Public Lifestyles of Women in the Illicit Drug Economy," *Journal of Drug Issues* 26 (1996): 125–42 at 132.

67. Morgan and Joe, "Citizens and Outlaws," p. 136.

68. Richard Wright and Scott Decker, *Armed Robbers in Action, Stickups and Street Culture* (Boston, Mass.: Northeastern University Press, 1997).

69. Wright and Decker, *Armed Robbers in Action,* p. 52.

70. Jody Miller, "Up It Up: Gender and the Accomplishment of Street Robbery," *Criminology* 36 (1998): 37–67.

71. Miller, "Up It Up," pp. 54–55.

72. Richard Felson and Steven Messner, "To Kill or Not to Kill? Lethal Outcomes in Injurious Attacks," *Criminology* 34 (1996): 519–45 at 541.

73. James Wright and Peter Rossi, *Armed and Considered Dangerous: A Survey of Felons and Their Firearms* (Hawthorne, N.Y.: Aldine De Guyer, 1983), pp. 141–59.

74. Gary Kleck and Marc Gertz, "Carry Guns for Protection: Results from the National Self-Defense Survey," *Journal of Research in Crime and Delinquency* 35 (1998): 193–224.

75. Eric Hickey, *Serial Murderers and Their Victims* (Pacific Grove, Calif.: Brooks/Cole, 1991), p. 84.

76. Janet Warren, Roland Reboussin, Robert Hazlewood, Andrea Cummings, Natalie Gibbs, and Susan Trumbetta, "Crime Scene and Distance Correlates of Serial Rape," *Journal of Quantitative Criminology* (1998).

77. Scott Decker, "Deviant Homicide: A New Look at the Role of Motives and Victim-Offender Relationships," *Journal of Research in Crime and Delinquency* 33 (1996): 427–49.

78. Felson and Messner, "To Kill or Not to Kill?"

79. Christopher Birkbeck and Gary LaFree, "The Situational Analysis of Crime and Deviance," *American Review of Sociology* 19 (1993): 113–37; Karen Heimer and Ross Matsueda, "Role-Taking, Role Commitment, and Delinquency: A Theory of Differential Social Control," *American Sociological Review* 59 (1994): 400–437.

80. Peter Wood, Walter Gove, James Wilson, and John Cochran, "Nonsocial Reinforcement and Habitual Criminal Conduct: An Extension of Learning," *Criminology* 35 (1997): 335–66.

81. Jeff Ferrell, "Criminological Versthen: Inside the Immediacy of Crime," *Justice Quarterly* 14 (1997): 3–23 at 12.

82. Jack Katz, *Seductions of Crime* (New York: Basic Books, 1988).

83. Bill McCarthy and John Hagan, "Mean Streets: The Theoretical Significance of Situational Delinquency Among Homeless Youths," *American Journal of Sociology* 3 (1992): 597–627.

84. Bill McCarthy, "Not Just 'For the Thrill of It': An Instrumentalist Elaboration of Katz's Explanation of Sneaky Thrill Property Crime," *Criminology* 33 (1995): 519–39.

85. George Rengert, "Spatial Justice and Criminal Victimization," *Justice Quarterly* 6 (1989): 543–64.

86. Oscar Newman, *Defensible Space: Crime Prevention Through Urban Design* (New York: Macmillan, 1973).

87. C. Ray Jeffery, *Crime Prevention Through Environmental Design* (Beverly Hills: Sage, 1971).

88. See also Pochara Theerathorn, "Architectural Style, Aesthetic Landscaping, Home Value, and Crime Prevention," *International Journal of Comparative and Applied Criminal Justice* 12 (1988): 269–77.

89. Ronald Clarke, *Situational Crime Prevention: Successful Case Studies* (Albany, N.Y.: Harrow and Heston, 1992).

90. Marcus Felson, "Routine Activities and Crime Prevention," in National Council for Crime Prevention, S*tudies on Crime and Crime Prevention, Annual Review,* vol. 1 (Stockholm: Scandinavian University Press, 1992), pp. 30–34.

91. Barry Webb, "Steering Column Locks and Motor Vehicle Theft: Evaluations for Three Countries," in *Crime Prevention Studies,* ed. Ronald Clarke (Monsey, N.Y.: Criminal Justice Press, 1994), pp. 71–89.

92. Barbara Morse and Delbert Elliott, "Effects of Ignition Interlock Devices on DUI Recidivism: Findings from a Longitudinal Study in Hamilton County, Ohio," *Crime and Delinquency* 38 (1992): 131–57.

93. Nancy LaVigne, "Gasoline Drive-Offs: Designing a Less Convenient Environment," in *Crime Prevention Studies,* vol. 2, ed. Ronald Clarke (New York: Criminal Justice Press, 1994), pp. 91–114.

94. Ronald Clarke, "Deterring Obscene Phone Callers: The New Jersey Experience," *Situational Crime Prevention,* ed. Ronald Clarke (Albany, N.Y.: Harrow and Heston, 1992), pp. 124–32.

95. Marcus Felson, "Those Who Discourage Crime" in John Eck and David Weisburd, eds, *Crime and Place, Crime Prevention Studies,* vol. 4 (New York: Criminal Justice Press, 1995), pp. 53–66; John Eck, *Drug Markets and Drug Places: A Case-Control Study of the Spatial Structure of Illicit Drug Dealing* (Doctoral dissertation, University of Maryland, College Park, 1994).

96. Eck, *Drug Markets and Drug Places,* p. 29.

97. Lorraine Green Mazerolle, Colleen Kadleck, and Jan Roehl, "Controlling Drug and Disorder Problems: The Role of Place Managers," *Criminology* 36 (1998): 371–404.

98. Robert Barr and Ken Pease, "Crime Placement, Displacement, and Deflection," in *Crime and Justice, A Review of Research,* vol. 12, ed. Michael Tonry and Norval Morris (Chicago: University of Chicago Press, 1990), pp. 277–319.

99. Clarke, *Situational Crime Prevention,* p. 27.

100. Clarke, *Situational Crime Prevention,* p. 35.

101. Ronald Clarke and David Weisburd, "Diffusion of Crime Control Benefits: Observations of the Reverse of Displacement," in *Crime Prevention Studies,* vol. 2, ed. Ronald Clarke (New York: Criminal Justice Press, 1994).

102. David Weisburd and Lorraine Green, "Policing Drug Hot Spots: The Jersey City Drug Market Analysis Experiment," *Justice Quarterly* 12 (1995): 711–34.

103. Lorraine Green, "Cleaning Up Drug Hot Spots in Oakland, California: The Displacement and Diffusion Effects," *Justice Quarterly* 12 (1995): 737–54.

104. Ian Ayres and Steven D. Levitt, "Measuring Positive Externalities from Unobservable Victim Precaution: An Empirical Analysis of Lojack," *Quarterly Journal of Economics,* 113 (1998): 43–78.

105. R. Yeaman, *The Deterrent Effectiveness of Criminal Justice Sanction Strategies: Summary Report* (Washington, D.C.: U.S. Government Printing Office, 1972). See, generally, Jack Gibbs, "Crime Punishment and Deterrence," *Social Science Quarterly* 48 (1968): 515–30.

106. Charles Tittle and Alan Rowe, "Certainty of Arrest and Crime Rates: A Further Test of the Deterrence Hypothesis," *Social Forces* 52 (1974): 455–62.

107. Robert Bursik, Harold Grasmick, and Mitchell Chamlin, "The Effect of Longitudinal Arrest Patterns on the Development of Robbery Trends at the Neighborhood Level," *Criminology* 28 (1990): 431–50; Theodore Chiricos and Gordon Waldo, "Punishment and Crime: An Examination of Some Empirical Evidence," *Social Problems* 18 (1970): 200–217.

108. Stewart D'Alessio and Lisa Stolzenberg, "Crime, Arrests, and Pretrial Jail Incarceration: An Examination of the Deterrence Thesis." Paper presented at the American Society of Criminology Meeting, San Diego, Calif., 1997.

109. Jiang Wu and Allen Liska, "The Certainty of Punishment: A Reference Group Effect and Its Functional Form," *Criminology* 31 (1993): 447–64.

110. Edwin Zedlewski, "Deterrence Findings and Data Sources: A Comparison of the Uniform Crime Rates and the National Crime Surveys," *Journal of Research in Crime and Delinquency* 20 (1983): 262–76.

111. David Bayley, *Policing for the Future* (New York: Oxford, 1994).

112. For a review, see Thomas Marvell and Carlisle Moody, "Specification Problems, Police Levels, and Crime Rates," *Criminology* 34 (1996): 609–646.

113. Marvell and Moody, "Specification Problems," p. 632.

114. George Kelling, Tony Pate, Duane Dieckman, and Charles Brown, *The Kansas City Preventive Patrol Experiment: A Summary Report* (Washington, D.C.: Police Foundation, 1974).

115. Lawrence Sherman, "Police Crackdowns," *NIJ Reports* (March/April 1990): 2–6 at 2.

116. Gary Green, "General Deterrence and Television Cable Crime: A Field Experiment in Social Crime," *Criminology* 23 (1986): 629–45.

117. H. Laurence Ross, "Implications of Drinking-and-Driving Law Studies for Deterrence Research," in *Critique and Explanation, Essays in Honor of Gwynne Nettler,* ed. Timothy Hartnagel and Robert Silverman (New Brunswick, N.J.: Transaction Books, 1986), pp. 159–71; H. Laurence Ross, Richard McCleary, and Gary LaFree, "Can Mandatory Jail Laws Deter Drunk Driving? The Arizona Case," *Journal of Criminal Law and Criminology* 81 (1990): 156–67.

118. For a review, see Jeffrey Roth, *Firearms and Violence* (Washington, D.C.: National Institute of Justice, 1994); and Thomas Marvell and Carlisle Moody, "The Impact of Enhanced Prison Terms for Felonies Committed with Guns," *Criminology* 33 (1995): 247–81.

119. Robert Dann, "The Deterrent Effect of Capital Punishment," *Friends Social Service Series* 29 (1935).

120. William Bowers and Glenn Pierce, "Deterrence or Brutalization: What Is the Effect of Executions?" *Crime and Delinquency* 26 (1980): 453–84.

121. John Cochran, Mitchell Chamlin, and Mark Seth, "Deterrence or Brutalization? An Impact Assessment of Oklahoma's Return to Capital Punishment," *Criminology* 32 (1994): 107–34.

122. David Phillips, "The Deterrent Effect of Capital Punishment," *American Journal of Sociology* 86 (1980): 139–48; Hans Zeisel, "A Comment on the 'Deterrent Effect of Capital Punishment' by Phillips," *American Journal of Sociology* 88 (1982): 167–69; see also Sam McFarland, "Is Capital Punishment a Short-Term Deterrent to Homicide? A Study of the Effects of Four Recent American Executions," *Journal of Criminal Law and Criminology* 74 (1984): 1014–32.

123. Steven Stack, "Publicized Executions and Homicide, 1950–1980," *American Sociological Review* 52 (1987): 532–40; for a study challenging Stack's methods, see William Bailey and Ruth Peterson, "Murder and Capital Punishment: A Monthly Time-Series Analysis of Execution Publicity," *American Sociological Review* 54 (1989): 722–43.

124. Karl Schuessler, "The Deterrent Influence of the Death Penalty," *Annals of the Academy of Political and Social Sciences* 284 (1952): 54–62.

125. Thorsten Sellin, *The Death Penalty* (Philadelphia: American Law Institute, 1959); Walter Reckless, "Use of the Death Penalty," *Crime and Delinquency* 15 (1969): 43–51.

126. Richard Lempert, "The Effect of Executions on Homicides: A New Look in an Old Light," *Crime and Delinquency* 29 (1983): 88–115.

127. Derral Cheatwood, "Capital Punishment and the Deterrence of Violent Crime in Comparable Counties," *Criminal Justice Review* 18 (1993): 165–81.

128. Dane Archer, Rosemary Gartner, and Marc Beittel, "Homicide and the Death Penalty: A Cross-National Test of a Deterrence Hypothesis," *Journal of Criminal Law and Criminology* 74 (1983): 991–1014.

129. Isaac Ehrlich, "The Deterrent Effect of Capital Punishment: A Question of Life and Death," *American Economic Review* 65 (1975): 397–417.

130. James Fox and Michael Radelet, "Persistent Flaws in Econometric Studies of the Deterrent Effect of the Death Penalty," *Loyola of Los Angeles Law Review* 23 (1987): 29–44; William B. Bowers and Glenn Pierce, "The Illusion of Deterrence in Isaac Ehrlich's Research on Capital Punishment," *Yale Law Journal* 85 (1975): 187–208.

131. William Bailey, "Disaggregation in Deterrence and Death Penalty Research: The Case of Murder in Chicago," *Journal of Criminal Law and Criminology* 74 (1986): 827–59.

132. Steven Messner and Kenneth Tardiff, "Economic Inequality and Level of Homicide: An Analysis of Urban Neighborhoods," *Criminology* 24 (1986): 297–317.

133. Donald Green, "Past Behavior as a Measure of Actual Future Behavior: An Unresolved Issue in Perceptual Deterrence Research," *Journal of Criminal Law and Criminology* 80 (1989): 781–804.

134. Donna Bishop, "Deterrence: A Panel Analysis," *Justice Quarterly* 1 (1984): 311–28; Julie Horney and Ineke Haen Marshall, "Risk Perceptions Among Serious Offenders: The Role of Crime and Punishment," *Criminology* 30 (1992): 575–94.

135. Wanda Foglia, "Perceptual Deterrence and the Mediating Effect of Internalized Norms Among Inner-City Teenagers," *Journal of Research in Crime and Delinquency* 34 (1997): 414–42; Raymond Paternoster, "Decisions to Participate in and Desist from Four Types of Common Delinquency: Deterrence and the Rational Choice Perspective," *Law and Society Review* 23 (1989): 7–29; Raymond Paternoster, "Examining Three-Wave Deterrence Models: A Question of Temporal Order and Specification," *Journal of Criminal Law and Criminology* 79 (1988): 135–63; Raymond Paternoster, Linda Saltzman, Gordon Waldo, and Theodore Chiricos, "Estimating Perceptual Stability and Deterrent Effects: The Role of Perceived Legal Punishment in the Inhibition of Criminal Involvement," *Journal of Criminal Law and Criminology* 74 (1983): 270–97; M. William Minor and Joseph Harry, "Deterrent and Experiential Effects in Perceptual Deterrence Research: A Replication and Extension," *Journal of Research in Crime and Delinquency* 19 (1982): 190–203; Lonn Lanza-Kaduce, "Perceptual Deterrence and Drinking and Driving Among College Students," *Criminology* 26 (1988): 321–41.

136. Foglia, "Perceptual Deterrence and the Mediating Effect of Internalized Norms Among Inner-City Teenagers," pp. 419–43.

137. Harold Grasmick and Robert Bursik, "Conscience, Significant Others, and Rational Choice: Extending the Deterrence Model," *Law and Society Review* 24 (1990): 837–61.

138. Steven Klepper and Daniel Nagin, "The Deterrent Effect of Perceived Certainty and Severity of Punishment Revisited," *Criminology* 27 (1989): 721–46; Scott Decker, Richard Wright, and Robert Logie, "Perceptual Deterrence Among Active Residential Burglars: A Research Note," *Criminology* 31 (1993): 135–47.

139. Irving Piliavin, Rosemary Gartner, Craig Thornton, and Ross Matsueda, "Crime, Deterrence, and Rational Choice," *American Sociological Review* 51 (1986): 101–119.

140. Eleni Apospori, Geoffrey Alpert, and Raymond Paternoster, "The Effect of Involvement with the Criminal Justice System: A Neglected Dimension of the Relationship Between Experience and Perceptions," *Justice Quarterly* 9 (1992): 379–92.

141. Apospori, Alpert, and Paternoster, "The Effect of Involvement with the Criminal Justice System," p. 390.

142. Eleni Apospori and Geoffrey Alpert, "Research Note: The Role of Differential Experience with the Criminal Justice System in Changes in Perceptions of Severity of Legal Sanctions over Time," *Crime and Delinquency* 39 (1993): 184–94.

143. Foglia, "Perceptual Deterrence and the Mediating Effect of Internalized Norms Among Inner-City Teenagers," pp. 414–42.

144. Harold Grasmick, Robert Bursik, and Karyl Kinsey, "Shame and Embarrassment as Deterrents to Noncompliance with the Law: The Case of an Anti-Littering Campaign." Paper presented at the annual meeting of the American Society of Criminology, Baltimore, November 1990, p. 3.

145. Charles Tittle, *Sanctions and Social Deviance* (New York: Praeger, 1980).

146. For an opposite view, see Steven Burkett and David Ward, "A Note on Perceptual Deterrence, Religiously Based Moral Condemnation, and Social Control," *Criminology* 31 (1993): 119–34.

147. Burkett and Ward, "A Note on Perceptual Deterrence."

148. John Snortum, "Drinking–Driving Compliance in Great Britain: The Role of Law as a 'Threat' and as a 'Moral Eye-Opener,'" *Journal of Criminal Justice* 18 (1990): 479–99.

149. Green, "Past Behavior as a Measure of Actual Future Behavior," p. 803; Matthew Silberman, "Toward a Theory of Criminal Deterrence," *American Sociological Review* 41 (1976): 442–61; Linda Anderson, Theodore Chiricos, and Gordon Waldo, "Formal and Informal Sanctions: A Comparison of Deterrent Effects," *Social Problems* 25 (1977): 103–114. See also Maynard Erickson and Jack Gibbs, "Objective and Perceptual Properties of Legal Punishment and Deterrence Doctrine," *Social Problems* 25 (1978): 253–64; and Daniel Nagin and Raymond Paternoster, "Enduring Individual Differences and Rational Choice Theories of Crime," *Law and Society Review* 27 (1993): 467–85.

150. Grasmick and Bursik, "Conscience, Significant Others, and Rational Choices," p. 854.

151. Grasmick, Bursik, and Kinsey, "Shame and Embarrassment as Deterrents to Noncompliance with the Law"; Harold Grasmick, Robert Bursik, and Bruce Arneklev, "Reduction in Drunk Driving as a Response to Increased Threats of Shame, Embarrassment, and Legal Sanctions," *Criminology* 31 (1993): 41–69.

152. Harold Grasmick, Brenda Sims Blackwell, and Robert Bursik, "Changes in the Sex Patterning of Perceived Threats of Sanctions," *Law and Society Review* 27 (1993): 679–99.

153. Thomas Peete, Trudie Milner, and Michael Welch, "Levels of Social Integration in Group Contexts and the Effects of Informal Sanction Threat on Deviance," *Criminology* 32 (1994): 85–105.

154. Ernest Van Den Haag, "The Criminal Law as a Threat System," *Journal of Criminal Law and Criminology* 73 (1982): 709–85.

155. David Lykken, "Psychopathy, Sociopathy, and Crime," *Society* 34 (1996): 30–38.

156. George Lowenstein, Daniel Nagin, and Raymond Paternoster, "The Effect of Sexual Arousal on Expectations of Sexual Forcefulness," *Journal of Research in Crime and Delinquency* 34 (1997): 443–73.

157. Ken Auletta, *The Under Class* (New York: Random House, 1982).

158. David Klinger, "Policing Spousal Assault," *Journal of Research in Crime and Delinquency* 32 (1995): 308–324.

159. Paternoster, "Decisions to Participate in and Desist from Four Types of Common Delinquency."

160. James Williams and Daniel Rodeheaver, "Processing of Criminal Homicide Cases in a Large Southern City," *Sociology and Social Research* 75 (1991): 80–88.

161. James Q. Wilson, *Thinking About Crime* (New York: Basic Books, 1975).

162. James Q. Wilson and Richard Herrnstein, *Crime and Human Nature* (New York: Simon and Schuster, 1985), p. 494.

163. Christina Dejong, "Survival Analysis and Specific Deterrence: Integrating Theoretical and Empirical Models of Recidivism," *Criminology* 35 (1997): 561–76.

164. Paul Tracy and Kimberly Kempf-Leonard, *Continuity and Discontinuity in Criminal Careers* (New York: Plenum Press, 1996).

165. Lawrence Greenfeld, *Examining Recidivism* (Washington, D.C.: U.S. Government Printing Office, 1985).

166. Allen Beck and Bernard Shipley, *Recidivism of Prisoners Released in 1983* (Washington, D.C.: Bureau of Justice Statistics, 1989).

167. Dejong, "Survival Analysis and Specific Deterrence," p. 573.

168. David Weisburd, Elin Waring, and Ellen Chayet, "Specific Deterrence in a Sample of Offenders Convicted of White-Collar Crimes," *Criminology* 33 (1995): 587–607.

169. Dejong, "Survival Analysis and Specific Deterrence"; Raymond Paternoster and Alex Piquero, "Reconceptualizing Deterrence: An Empirical Test of Personal and Vicarious Experiences," *Journal of Research in Crime and Delinquency* 32 (1995): 251–58.

170. Charles Murray and Louis Cox, *Beyond Probation* (Beverly Hills: Sage, 1979); Perry Shapiro and Harold Votey, "Deterrence and Subjective Probabilities of Arrest: Modeling Individual Decisions to Drink and Drive in Sweden," *Law and Society Review* 18 (1984): 111–49; Douglas Smith and Patrick Gartin, "Specifying Specific Deterrence: The Influence of Arrest on Future Criminal Activity," *American Sociological Review* 54 (1989): 94–105.

171. Graeme Newman, *Just and Painful* (New York: Macmillan, 1983), pp. 139–43.

172. John Braithwaite, *Crime, Shame, and Reintegration* (Melbourne, Australia: Cambridge University Press, 1989).

173. Braithwaite, *Crime, Shame, and Reintegration*, p. 81.

174. For more on this approach, see Jane Mugford and Stephen Mugford, "Shame and Reintegration in the Punishment and Deterrence of Spouse Assault." Paper presented at the annual meeting of the American Society of Criminology, San Francisco, 1991.

175. Mugford and Mugford, "Shame and Reintegration in the Punishment and Deterrence of Spouse Assault."

176. Mark Warr and Mark Stafford, "A Reconceptualization of General and Specific Deterrence," *Journal of Research on Crime and Delinquency* 30 (1993): 123–35.

177. Raymond Paternoster and Alex Piquero, "Reconceptualizing Deterrence: An Empirical Test of Personal and Vicarious Experiences," *Journal of Research in Crime and Delinquency* 32 (1995): 251–58.

178. Alex Piquero and Raymond Paternoster, "An Application of Stafford and Warr's Reconceptualization of Deterrence to Drinking and Driving," *Journal of Research in Crime and Delinquency* 35 (1998): 3–39.

179. Andrew Karmen, "Why Is New York City's Murder Rate Dropping So Sharply?" (John Jay College, New York City: preliminary draft, 1996).

180. See, generally, Raymond Paternoster, "Absolute and Restrictive Deterrence in a Panel of Youth: Explaining the Onset, Persistence/Desistance, and Frequency of Delinquent Offending," *Social Problems* 36 (1989): 289–307; Raymond Paternoster, "The Deterrent Effect of Perceived Severity of Punishment: A Review of the Evidence and Issues," *Justice Quarterly* 42 (1987): 173–217.

181. Isaac Ehrlich, "Participation in Illegitimate Activities: An Economic Analysis," *Journal of Political Economy* 81 (1973): 521–67; Lee Bowker, "Crime and the Use of Prisons in the United States: A Time Series Analysis," *Crime and Delinquency* 27 (1981): 206–12.

182. David Greenberg, "The Incapacitative Effects of Imprisonment: Some Estimates," *Law and Society Review* 9 (1975): 541–80.

183. Greenberg, "The Incapacitative Effects of Imprisonment," p. 558.

184. Reuel Shinnar and Shlomo Shinnar, "The Effects of the Criminal Justice System on the Control of Crime: A Quantitative Approach," *Law and Society Review* 9 (1975): 581–611.

185. Thomas Marvell and Carlisle Moody, "The Impact of Prison Growth on Homicide," *Homicide Studies* 1 (1997): 205–233.

186. Thomas Marvell and Carlisle Moody, "The Impact of Out-of-State Prison Population on State Homicide Rates: Displacement and Free-Rider Effects," *Criminology* 36 (1998): 513–35.

187. For review of this issue, see James Austin and John Irwin, *Does Imprisonment Reduce Crime? A Critique of "Voodoo" Criminology* (San Francisco: National Council of Crime and Delinquency, 1993).

188. David Greenberg and Nancy Larkin, "The Incapacitation of Criminal Opiate Users," *Crime and Delinquency* 44 (1998): 205–228.

189. John Wallerstedt, *Returning to Prison*, Bureau of Justice Statistics Special Report (Washington, D.C.: U.S. Department of Justice, 1984).

190. Jose Canela-Cacho, Alfred Blumstein, and Jacqueline Cohen, "Relationship Between the Offending Frequency of Imprisoned and Free Offenders," *Criminology* 35 (1997): 133–71.

191. Kate King and Patricia Bass, "Southern Prisons and Elderly Inmates: Taking a Look Inside." Paper presented at the American Society of Criminology Meeting, San Diego, Calif., 1997.

192. Peter Greenwood, *Selective Incapacitation* (Santa Monica, Calif.: Rand Corp., 1982).

193. Marc Mauer, testimony before the U.S. Congress, House Judiciary Committee, on "Three Strikes and You're Out," 1 March 1994.

194. Canela-Cacho, Blumstein, and Cohen, "Relationship Between the Offending Frequency of Imprisoned and Free Offenders."

195. Stephen Markman and Paul Cassell, "Protecting the Innocent: A Response to the Bedeau-Radelet Study," *Stanford Law Review* 41 (1988): 121–70 at 153.

196. James Stephan and Tracy Snell, *Capital Punishment, 1994* (Washington, D.C.: Bureau of Justice Statistics, 1996), p. 8.

197. Andrew Von Hirsch, *Doing Justice* (New York: Hill and Wang, 1976).

198. Von Hirsch, *Doing Justice,* pp. 15–16.

199. Von Hirsch, *Doing Justice,* pp. 15–16.

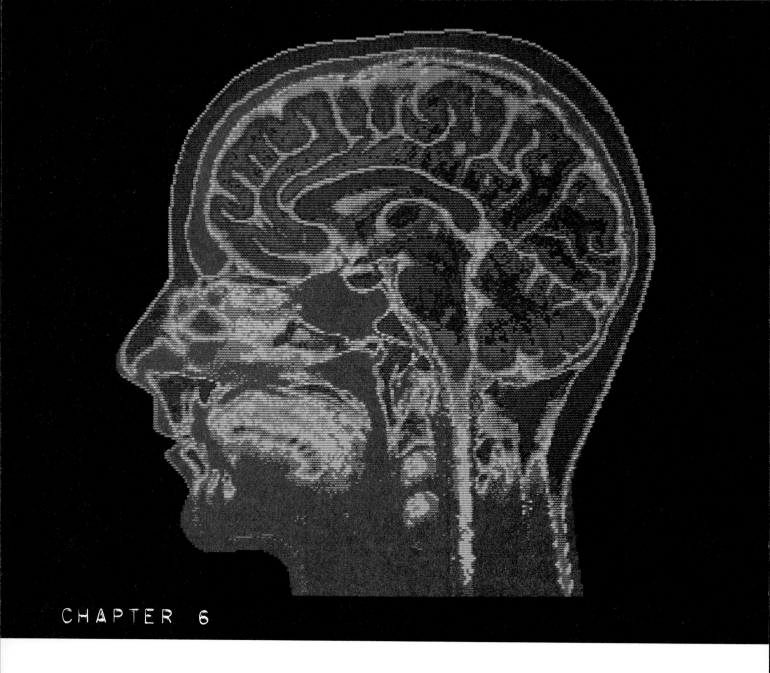

CHAPTER 6

Trait Theories

INTRODUCTION

Russell Eugene Weston, Jr., 41, was a quiet loner who drifted back and forth between a cabin in the Montana mountains and a modest house in rural Illinois.[1] He became an increasingly troubled figure who was hospitalized in 1996 after he wrote threatening letters to government officials. On July 25, 1998, Weston entered the U.S. Capitol building and went on a shooting rampage. Two capitol police officers were slain, and a female tourist was wounded. After his arrest, his parents told officials that their son had been diagnosed by a medical professional as a paranoid schizophrenic. His neighbors portrayed Weston as a withdrawn, introverted loner who had grown increasingly angry and alienated over the years. When invitations went out for a 20-year reunion to the 63 members of his 1974 graduating class at Valmeyer High School, his came back scrawled with obscenities and a warning never to contact him again. "When he was on his medication, he was fine, he would wave and talk," said a neighbor who knew Weston during his youth. "When he was off the medication, he was paranoid; you just didn't know."

One of his former classmates remembered Weston from the seventh grade on, mostly as "one of the forgotten middle kids, kind of on the fat side, not a sports guy, never went out with any girls. Only had a couple of friends." Then around the eleventh grade, "he started getting into the drug scene, smoking marijuana. He and a group of other kids, they all went out to this place in Montana. They wanted to get away, to be free. It was to be some kind of self-sufficient commune. I heard he had a gold claim out there."

Weston's case provides the public with an image of the criminal offender as a deeply disturbed individual who suffers from a variety of mental and physical abnormalities. In fact, he was later found to be mentally ill and incompetent to stand trial. The image of a disturbed, mentally ill offender seems plausible because a generation of Americans has grown up on films and TV shows that portray violent criminals as mentally deranged and physically abnormal.

Beginning with Alfred Hitchcock's film *Psycho*, producers have made millions depicting the ghoulish acts of people who at first seem normal and even friendly but turn out to be demented and dangerous. Lurking out there are crazed baby-sitters (*The Hand That Rocks the Cradle*); frenzied airline passengers (*Turbulence*); deranged roommates (*Single White Female*); psychotic tenants (*Pacific Heights*); demented secretaries (*The Temp*); unhinged police (*Maniac Cop*); irrational fans (*The Fan, Misery*); abnormal girlfriends (*Fatal Attraction*) and boyfriends (*Fear*); unstable husbands (*Sleeping with the Enemy*) and wives (*Black Widow*); loony fathers (*The Stepfather*), mothers (*Friday the 13th Part 1*), and grandmothers (*Hush*); unbalanced crime victims (*I Know What You Did Last Summer*); maniacal children (*The Good Son*); lunatic high school friends (*Scream*) and college classmates (*Scream II*); and nutsy teenaged admirers (*The Crush*). No one can be safe when the psychologists and psychiatrists who

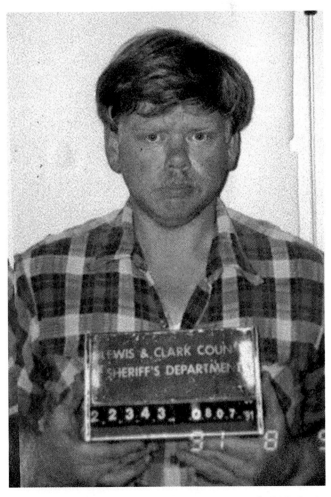

Russell Eugene Weston's violent shooting spree in the U.S. Capitol seemed to be the product of a deranged mind. Can people who go on murderous rampages such as Weston ever be considered "normal" or "sane"?

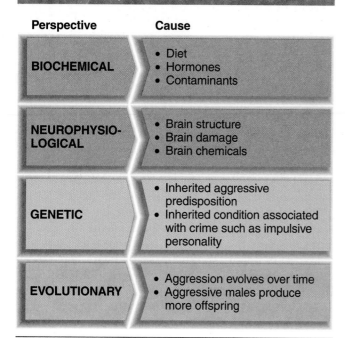

Figure 6.1 Biosocial Perspectives on Criminality

Perspective	Cause
BIOCHEMICAL	• Diet • Hormones • Contaminants
NEUROPHYSIO-LOGICAL	• Brain structure • Brain damage • Brain chemicals
GENETIC	• Inherited aggressive predisposition • Inherited condition associated with crime such as impulsive personality
EVOLUTIONARY	• Aggression evolves over time • Aggressive males produce more offspring

should be treating these disturbed people turn out to be demonic murderers themselves (*Silence of the Lambs, Dressed to Kill,* and *Never Talk to Strangers*). Is it any wonder that we respond to a particularly horrible crime by saying of the perpetrator, "That guy must be crazy" or "She is a monster"?

CONNECTIONS

Some critics have called for strict regulation of movies, videos, and TV shows, believing that viewing them harms their mostly adolescent audience. Does watching aggressive, crazed people cause viewers to act violently themselves? For more on this issue, see the Criminological Enterprise feature on media violence later in this chapter.

The view that criminals have physical or mental traits that make them different and abnormal is not restricted to movie viewers. Since the nineteenth century, criminologists have suggested that biological and psychological traits may influence behavior. They believed that some personal trait must separate the deviant members of society from the nondeviant. These personal differences explain why, when faced with the same life situations, one person commits crime, whereas another obeys the law. All people may be aware of and even fear the sanctioning power of the law, but some are unable to control their urges and passions. This view of crime causation is referred to as **trait theories.**

Trait theories can be divided into two major categories: one that stresses psychological functioning and the other that stresses biological makeup. Although these views often overlap (for example, brain function may have a biological basis), each branch has its unique characteristics and will be discussed separately (see Figure 6.1). First, however, the development of trait theories will be briefly reviewed.

FOUNDATIONS OF BIOLOGICAL TRAIT THEORY

As you may recall, Cesare Lombroso's work on the born criminal was a direct offshoot of applying the scientific method to the study of crime. His identification of primitive, atavistic anomalies was based on what he believed to be sound empirical research using established scientific methods.

CONNECTIONS

Biological explanations of criminal behavior first became popular during the middle part of the nineteenth century with the introduction of positivism—the use of the scientific method and empirical analysis to study behavior. Positivism was discussed earlier in Chapter 1's description of the history of criminology.

Lombroso was not alone in the early development of biological theory. A contemporary of Lombroso, Raffaele Garofalo (1852–1934), shared the belief that certain physical characteristics indicate a criminal nature. For example, Garofalo stated that among criminals, "a lower degree of sensibility to physical pain seems to be demonstrated by the readiness with which prisoners submit to the operation of tattooing."[2] Enrico Ferri (1856–1929), another student of Lombroso, believed that a number of biological, social, and organic factors caused delinquency and crime.[3] Ferri added a social dimension to Lombroso's work and pioneered the view that criminals should not be held personally or morally responsible for their actions because forces outside their control cause criminality.

Advocates of the **inheritance school** traced the activities of several generations of families believed to have an especially large number of criminal members. The most famous of these studies involved the Jukes and the Kallikaks. Richard Dugdale's *The Jukes: A Study in Crime, Pauperism, Disease, and Heredity* (1875) and Arthur Estabrook's *The Jukes* (1915) were two such works.[4] They both studied the fact that members of both these families committed an abnormally large number of property, theft, and violent crimes. Early criminologists who studied them concluded that criminality ran in families and was passed down from one generation to the next.

A later attempt at criminal anthropology, the body build or **somatotype** school, developed more than 50 years ago by William Sheldon, held that criminals manifest distinct physiques that make them susceptible to particular types of delinquent behavior. *Mesomorphs,* for example, have well-developed muscles and an athletic appearance. They are active, aggressive, sometimes violent, and the most likely to become criminals. *Endomorphs* have heavy builds and move slowly. They are known for lethargic behavior that renders them unlikely to commit violent crime and more willing to engage in less strenuous criminal activities such as fencing stolen property. *Ectomorphs* are tall, thin, and less social and more intellectual than the other types.[5]

The work of Lombroso and his contemporaries is now regarded as a historical curiosity, not scientific fact. In fact, their research methodology has been discredited because they did not use control groups from the general population to compare results. Many of the traits they assumed to be inherited are not really genetically determined but could be caused by deprivation in surroundings and diet. Even if most criminals shared some biological traits, they might be products not of heredity but of some environmental condition, such as poor nutrition or health care. It is equally likely that only criminals who suffer from biological abnormality are caught and punished by the justice system. In his later writings, Lombroso admitted that the born criminal was just one of many criminal types. Because of these deficiencies in his theory, the validity of individual-oriented explanations of criminality became questionable, and for a time these theories were disregarded by the criminological mainstream.

Impact of Sociobiology

> What seems no longer tenable at this juncture is any theory of human behavior which ignores biology and relies exclusively on socio-cultural learning.... Most social scientists have been wrong in their dogmatic rejection and blissful ignorance of the biological parameters of our behavior.[6]

Biological explanations of crime fell out of favor in the early twentieth century. During this period criminologists became concerned about the sociological influences on crime, such as the neighborhood, peer group, family life, and social status. The work of biocriminologists was viewed as methodologically unsound and generally invalid by the sociologists who dominated the field and held views that have been referred to as **biophobia**—the belief that no serious consideration should be given to biological factors when attempting to understand human nature.[7]

In the early 1970s, spurred by the publication of *Sociobiology* by criminologist Edmund O. Wilson, biolog-

ical explanations of crime once again emerged.[8] **Sociobiology** differs from earlier theories of behavior in that it stresses that biological and genetic conditions affect how social behaviors are learned and perceived. These perceptions, in turn, are linked to existing environmental structures. Sociobiologists view the gene as the ultimate unit of life that controls all human destiny. Although they believe that environment and experience also impact behavior, their main premise is that most actions are controlled by a person's "biological machine." Most important, people are controlled by the innate need to have their genetic material survive and dominate others. Consequently, they do everything in their power to ensure their own survival and that of others who share their gene pool (relatives, fellow citizens, and so forth). Even when they help others, which is called **reciprocal altruism,** people are motivated by the belief that their actions will be reciprocated and that their gene survival capability will be enhanced.

Sociobiologists view biology, environment, and learning as mutually interdependent factors. Problems in one area can be altered by efforts in another. For example, people suffering from learning disorders can be given special tutoring to improve their reading skills. In this view, then, people are **biosocial** organisms whose personalities and behaviors are influenced by physical as well as environmental conditions. Some criminologists have criticized sociobiology as methodologically unsound and socially dangerous, however, because it suggests that people cannot control their own behavior. It implies, for example, that known criminals are untreatable because the cause of their behavior is innate and instinctual. Nonetheless, the study of sociobiology revived interest in finding a biological basis for crime and delinquency. Consequently, it suggests that if biological (genetic) makeup controls human behavior, it should also determine whether a person chooses law-violating or conventional behavior.

Modern Trait Theories

Trait theorists today do not suggest that a single biological or psychological attribute adequately explains all criminality. Rather, each offender is considered physically and mentally unique; consequently, there must be different explanations for each person's behavior. Some may have inherited criminal tendencies, others may be suffering from neurological problems, and some may have blood chemistry disorders that heighten their antisocial activity. Criminologists who focus on the individual see many explanations for crime because, in fact, there are many differences among criminal offenders.

Social Interaction Trait theorists are not overly concerned with legal definitions of crime; they do not try to explain why people violate particular laws. To them, laws are artificial concepts based on arbitrary boundaries

The Criminological Enterprise

The Nature Assumption

The fact is that children cannot learn how to behave by imitating their parents, because most of the things they see their parents doing—making messes, bossing other people around, driving cars, lighting matches, coming and going as they please, and lots of other things that look like fun to people who are not allowed to do them—are prohibited to children. From the child's point of view, socialization in the early years consists mainly of learning that you're not supposed to behave like your parents.

—Judith Rich Harris in *The Nature Assumption*

Psychologist Judith Rich Harris's highly controversial book *The Nature Assumption* made headlines when it appeared in 1998 because it questioned the cherished belief that parents play an important, if not the most important, role in a child's upbringing. Instead of family influence, Harris claims that genetics and environment determine, to a large extent, how a child turns out. Children's own temperament and peer relations shape their behavior and modify the characteristics they were born with; and interpersonal relations determine the kind of people they will be when they mature.

Harris reasons that parenting skills may be irrelevant to children's future success because researchers have been unable to find any child-rearing method or style that predicts children's accomplishments or failures once they mature and leave home. Besides, most parents don't have a single child-rearing style and may treat each child in the family independently. They are more permissive with their mild-mannered kids and more strict and punitive with those who are temperamental or defiant. Even if every child were treated the same in a family, this would not explain why siblings raised in the same family under relatively similar conditions turn out so differently. Moreover, the way children are raised has little or no influence on children's personalities. Those sent to day care are quite similar to those who remain at home; having working parents seems to have little long-term effect. Family structure also does not seem to matter: adults who grew up in one-parent homes are as likely to be successful as those who were raised in two-parent households.

Harris also questions the abuse–delinquency link. Despite some experts' findings that abused children are more likely to behave antisocially, others have found that most children growing up in troubled or abusive households are noncriminal and do not suffer lasting psychological damage. Conversely, many children who are raised in nurturing homes by caring parents take drugs, join gangs, and are continually involved in antisocial behavior.

Harris finds little or no association between the personality traits of adopted children and their adoptive parents. Nor is there much confluence between the personalities of adopted children and other siblings in the home, as might be expected if home environment strongly influenced personality and development. One reason is that parents' behavior affects children mainly when they are together. When children are alone or playing with other children, parental influence wanes. This, according to Harris, is true whether or not children are adopted.

If parenting has little direct influence on children's long-term development, what does? Harris believes that genetics play the most important role in behavior. But, Harris recognizes,

(for example, speeding is arbitrarily defined as exceeding 65 miles per hour). Instead trait theorists focus on basic human behavior and drives—aggression, violence, and the tendency to act on impulse—that are linked to antisocial behavior patterns. They also recognize that human traits alone do not produce criminality and that crime-producing interactions involve both personal traits (such as intelligence, personality, and chemical and genetic makeup) and environmental factors (such as family life, educational attainment, economic factors, and neighborhood conditions). Physical or mental traits are therefore just some of the environmental, social, and personal factors that account for criminality. Although some people may have a predisposition toward aggression, environmental stimuli can either suppress or trigger antisocial acts.

Even the most committed trait theorists recognize that environmental conditions in disadvantaged inner-city areas may powerfully influence antisocial behavior. As biocriminologists Anthony Walsh and Lee Ellis conclude, "If there is one take-away lesson from studying biological bases of behavior it is that the more we study them the more we realize how important the environment is."[9] The combined influence of heredity and environment is the topic of the Criminological Enterprise feature titled "The Nature Assumption."

Trait theories have gained recent prominence because of what is now known about chronic recidivism and the development of criminal careers. If only a few offenders become persistent repeaters, then what sets them apart from the criminal population may be an abnormal biochemical makeup, brain structure, or genetic constitution.[10] Even if criminals do choose crime, the fact that some repeatedly make that choice could be linked to their physical and mental makeup.

genes alone do not determine behavior. The child's total social environment is the other key influence that helps shape behavior. Kids who act one way at home may be totally different at school or with their peers. Some who are mild-mannered around the house are hell-raisers in the schoolyard, whereas others who bully their siblings are docile with friends. Children may conform to parental expectations at home but leave them behind in their own social environment.

In their own world, the need to conform to peer group values replaces parental influence as the key determinant of behavior. Children know that the peer group is quick to scapegoat anyone who is different, who has different interests, clothes, or accent. Children can be heartless in abusing a kid who is different; conforming then becomes a matter of survival. Children develop their own culture with unique traditions, words, rules, and activities, which often conflict with parental and adult values. What parents encourage their children to pierce their bodies or get tattoos? Parents encourage their children to do the things will make them successful adults, but children are more concerned with becoming successful children! And that often means not behaving like adults. Parents and peers share many social values, such as honesty and loyalty; but

when these values clash, the peer group wins. Peer influence is more important than family environment, and when peer influence is considered, family factors are not significant.

There are exceptions to this pattern. Harris concedes that some kids are square pegs. Some have special skills or an especially close bond to their parents, which enables them to resist peer pressure. But as a general rule, children are more oriented to their peers than their parents.

Those who question Harris's conclusions say that by extending her logic, many favorite social programs are doomed to failure. For example, school antidrug programs are geared to parental values; if peer groups disparage them, they fail. And, by implication, parents who abuse or neglect their children are absolved from blame for their progeny's future problems. If parents are close to their children, Harris claims, it should be because they want to be their companions and friends and not because it will help their life chances. *The Nature Assumption* also contradicts the extensive literature that concludes that parenting matters and that improving the quality of parent–child relationships can significantly impact delinquency. Harris's book will at least reopen the old debate: nature versus nurture, environment versus heredity.

CRITICAL THINKING

1. Harris's views are quite provocative. She suggests that parents should not blame themselves if their children "go bad," nor should they take much credit for their parenting skills if their offspring are overachievers. Is it possible that children growing up with cold, distant parents who show them little interest have the same life chances as kids whose parents are warm, loving, and involved?

2. Do you feel that you are a product of your parents, peers, environment, or all three? Can you trace any specific characteristics to your parents? If so, what are they?

INFOTRAC COLLEGE EDITION RESEARCH

To learn more about how parents influence their children, read:
Susan D. Witt. Parental influence on children's socialization to gender roles. *Adolescence,* 32 (1997): 253.
Mike Males. The influence of parental smoking on youth smoking: is the recent downplaying justified? *Journal of School Health,* August 65 (1995): 228.

Source: Judith Rich Harris, *The Nature Assumption, Why Children Turn Out the Way They Do* (New York: The Free Press, 1998).

BIOLOGICAL TRAIT THEORIES

Rather than viewing the criminal as a person whose behavior is controlled by biological conditions determined at birth, modern biological trait theorists believe that physical, environmental, and social conditions work in concert to produce human behavior. Today criminologists interested in identifying a physical basis of antisocial behavior typically refer to themselves as **biocriminologists,** biosocial criminologists, or biologically oriented criminologists; the terms are used here interchangeably.

Biological trait theory has several core principles.[11] First, it assumes that genetic makeup contributes significantly to human behavior. Further, it contends that not all humans are born with equal potential to learn and achieve; this is referred to as **equipotentiality.** Sociologically oriented criminologists suggest, either explicitly or implicitly, that all people are born equal; they also assert that thereafter behavior is controlled by social forces (parents, schools, neighborhoods, and friends). Biosocial theorists, on the other hand, argue that no two people are alike (with rare exceptions like identical twins) and that the combination of human genetic traits and the environment produces individual behavior patterns.

Learning Potential Another focus of modern biological theory is the importance of brain function, mental processes, and learning. Social behavior, including criminal behavior, is learned, and each individual organism is believed to have a unique potential for learning. The physical and social environments interact to either limit or enhance an organism's capacity for learning. People learn through a process involving the brain and central nervous system. Learning is controlled not by social interactions but by biochemistry and cellular interaction. Learning can take place only when physical changes occur in the brain. There is a significant link, therefore, between behavior patterns and physical or chemical changes that occur in the brain, autonomic nervous system, and central nervous system.[12]

Instinct Some biosocial theorists also believe that learning is influenced by instinctual drives. Developed over the course of human history, instincts are inherited, natural, and unlearned dispositions that activate specific behavior patterns designed to reach certain goals. For example, people are believed to have a drive to possess and control other people and things. Some theft offenses may be motivated by the instinctual need to possess goods and commodities. Rape and other sex crimes may be linked to the primitive instinctual drive males have to possess and control females.[13]

The following sections examine some important schools of thought within biological criminology.[14] First we review the biochemical factors that are believed to affect how proper behavior patterns are learned. Then we consider the relationship of brain function and crime. Next we analyze current ideas about the association between genetic and evolutionary factors and crime. Finally, we evaluate evolutionary views of crime causation.

Biochemical Conditions and Crime

Some trait theorists believe that biochemical conditions, including both those that are genetically predetermined and those that are acquired through diet and environment, influence antisocial behavior. This view of crime received national attention in 1979 when Dan White, who confessed to killing San Francisco Mayor George Moscone and City Councilman Harvey Milk, claimed his behavior was precipitated by an addiction to sugar-laden junk foods.[15] White's successful "Twinkie defense" prompted a California jury to find him guilty of the lesser offense of diminished capacity manslaughter rather than first-degree murder. (White committed suicide after serving his prison sentence.) Some of the biochemical factors that have been linked to criminality are set out in detail here.

Chemical and Mineral Influences Biocriminologists maintain that minimal levels of minerals and chemicals are needed for normal brain functioning and growth, especially in the early years of life. If people with normal needs do not receive the appropriate nutrition, they will suffer from *vitamin deficiency*. If people have genetic conditions that cause greater-than-normal needs for certain chemicals and minerals, they are said to suffer from *vitamin dependency*. People with vitamin deficiency or dependency can manifest many physical, mental, and behavioral problems in-

cluding lower intelligence test scores.[16] Alcoholics often suffer from thiamine deficiency because of their poor diets and consequently are susceptible to the serious, often fatal **Wernicke-Korsakoff disease,** a deadly neurological disorder.[17]

Research conducted over the past decade shows that dietary inadequacy of certain chemicals and minerals, including sodium, potassium, calcium, amino acids, monoamines, and peptides, can lead to depression, mania, cognitive problems, memory loss, and abnormal sexual activity.[18] Research studies examining the relationship between crime and vitamin deficiency and dependency have identified a close link between antisocial behavior and insufficient quantities of some B vitamins and vitamin C. In addition, studies have purported to show that a major proportion of all schizophrenics and children with learning and behavior disorders are dependent on vitamins B3 and B6.[19]

Excessive Sugar Another suspected nutritional influence on behavior is a diet especially high in carbohydrates and sugar.[20] For example, some recent research found that how the brain processed glucose was related to scores on tests measuring reasoning power.[21] In addition, sugar intake levels have been associated with attention span deficiencies.[22]

Diets high in sugar and carbohydrates also have been linked to violence and aggression. Experiments have altered children's diets so that sweet drinks were replaced with fruit juices, table sugar was replaced with honey, and so on. Results indicate that these changes can reduce aggression levels.[23] Biocriminologists who believe in a diet–aggression association claim that every segment of society has violent, aggressive, amoral people whose improper food, vitamin, and mineral intake may cause antisocial behavior. These biocriminologists believe that if diet could be improved, the frequency of violent behavior would be reduced.[24]

Although these results are impressive, a number of biologists have questioned this association, and some recent research efforts have failed to find a link between sugar consumption and violence.[25] In one important study, a group of researchers had 25 preschool children and 23 school-age children described as sensitive to sugar follow a different diet for three consecutive three-week periods. One diet was high in sucrose, the second substituted aspartame (Nutrasweet) as a sweetener, and the third relied on saccharin. Careful measurement of the subjects found little evidence of cognitive or behavioral differences that could be linked to diet. If anything, sugar seemed to calm the children.[26]

In sum, although some research efforts allege a sugar–violence association, others suggest that many people who consume lots of sugar and carbohydrates are not violent or crime-prone. In some cases, in fact, sugar intake has been found to possibly reduce or curtail violent tendencies.[27]

Hypoglycemia Hypoglycemia occurs when blood glucose (sugar) falls below levels necessary for normal and efficient brain functioning. The brain is sensitive to the lack of blood sugar because it is the only organ that obtains its energy solely from the combustion of carbohydrates. Thus, when the brain is deprived of blood sugar, it has no alternative food supply to call upon and its metabolism slows down, impairing its function. Symptoms of hypoglycemia include irritability, anxiety, depression, crying spells, headaches, and confusion.

Research studies have linked hypoglycemia to outbursts of antisocial behavior and violence.[28] Several studies have related assaults and sexual offenses to hypoglycemic reactions.[29] Hypoglycemia has also been connected with a syndrome characterized by aggressive and assaultive behavior, glucose disturbance, and brain dysfunction. Some attempts have been made to measure hypoglycemia using subjects with a known history of criminal activity. Studies of jail and prison inmate populations have found a higher than normal level of hypoglycemia.[30] High levels of reactive hypoglycemia have been found in groups of habitually violent and impulsive offenders.[31]

Hormonal Influences In his 1993 book *The Moral Sense,* criminologist James Q. Wilson concludes that hormones, enzymes, and neurotransmitters may be the key to understanding human behavior. According to Wilson, they help explain gender differences in the crime rate. Males, he writes, are biologically and naturally more aggressive than females, whereas women are more nurturing toward the young.[32] Hormone levels also help explain the aging-out process. Levels of testosterone, the principal male steroid hormone, decline during the life cycle and may explain why violence rates diminish over time.[33]

A number of biosocial theorists are now evaluating the association between violent behavior episodes and hormone levels, and the findings suggest that abnormal levels of male sex hormones (**androgens**) do in fact produce aggressive behavior.[34] Other androgen-related male traits include sensation seeking, impulsivity, dominance, and reduced verbal skills; all of these androgen-related traits are also related to antisocial behavior.[35] A growing body of evidence suggests that hormonal changes are also related to mood and behavior and that adolescents experience more intense mood swings, anxiety, and restlessness than their elders.[36] An association between hormonal activity and antisocial behavior is suggested because rates of both factors peak in adolescence.

One area of concern has been **testosterone,** the most abundant androgen, which controls secondary sex characteristics such as facial hair and voice timbre.[37] Research conducted on both human and animal subjects has found that prenatal exposure to unnaturally high levels of androgens permanently alters behavior. Girls who were unintentionally exposed to elevated amounts of androgens during their fetal development display an unusually high, long-term tendency toward aggression. Conversely, boys who were prenatally exposed to steroids that decrease androgen levels display decreased aggressiveness.[38] In contrast, samples of inmates have shown that testosterone levels were higher in men who committed violent crimes than in other prisoners.[39] Gender differences in the crime rate therefore may be explained by the relative difference in androgens between the two sexes. Females may be biologically protected from deviant behavior in the same way they are immune from some diseases that strike males.[40]

How Hormones Can Influence Behavior Hormones cause areas of the brain to become less sensitive to environmental stimuli. High androgen levels require people to seek excess stimulation and to be willing to tolerate pain in their quest for thrills. Androgens are linked to brain seizures that, under stressful conditions, can result in emotional volatility. Androgens affect the brain structure itself: they influence the left hemisphere of the **neocortex,** the part of the brain that controls sympathetic feelings toward others.[41] Here are some of the hormone-produced physical reactions that have been linked to violence:

1. A lowering of average resting arousal under normal environmental conditions to a point that individuals are motivated to seek unusually high levels of environmental stimulation and are less sensitive to harmful aftereffects resulting from this stimulation
2. A lowering of seizure thresholds in and around the limbic system, increasing the likelihood that stressful environmental factors will trigger strong, impulsive emotional responses
3. A rightward shift in neocortical functioning, resulting in increased reliance on the brain hemisphere that is most closely integrated with the limbic system and is least likely to reason in logical or linguistic forms or to respond to linguistic commands[42]

These effects promote violence and other serious crimes by causing people to seek greater levels of environmental stimulation and to tolerate more punishment, and by increasing impulsivity, emotional volatility, and antisocial emotions.[43]

Although some research studies have been unable to demonstrate hormonal differences in samples of violent and nonviolent offenders, drugs that decrease testosterone levels are now being used to treat male sex offenders.[44] The female hormones estrogen and progesterone have been administered to sex offenders to decrease their sexual potency.[45] The long-term side effects of this treatment and the potential danger are still unknown.[46]

Premenstrual Syndrome Hormonal research has not been limited to male offenders. The suspicion has long

Diana Fishbein, a noted expert on biosocial theory, has conducted research on the biochemical reactions that precede aggressive behavior.

existed that the onset of the menstrual cycle triggers excessive amounts of the female sex hormones, which affects antisocial, aggressive behavior. This condition is commonly referred to as **premenstrual syndrome** or **PMS**.[47] The link between PMS and delinquency was first popularized more than 25 years ago by Katharina Dalton, whose studies of English women indicated that females are more likely to commit suicide and to be aggressive and otherwise antisocial just before or during menstruation.[48]

Although the Dalton research is often cited as evidence of the link between PMS and crime, methodological problems make it impossible to accept her findings at face value; there is still significant debate over any link between PMS and aggression. Some doubters argue that the relationship is spurious; it is equally likely that the psychological and physical stress of aggression brings on menstruation and not vice versa.[49]

Diana Fishbein, a noted expert on biosocial theory, concludes that there is in fact an association between elevated levels of female aggression and menstruation. Research efforts, she argues, show that (1) a significant number of incarcerated females committed their crimes during the premenstrual phase and (2) at least a small percentage of women appear vulnerable to cyclical hormonal changes that make them more prone to anxiety and hostility.[50] The debate is ongoing, but the overwhelming majority of females who suffer anxiety and hostility before and during menstruation do not engage in violent criminal behavior; so any link between PMS and crime is tenuous at best.[51]

Allergies Allergies are unusual or excessive reactions of the body to foreign substances.[52] For example, hay fever is an allergic reaction caused when pollen cells enter the body and are fought or neutralized by the body's natural defenses. The result of the battle is itchy red eyes, sneezing, and swollen sinuses.

Cerebral allergies cause an excessive reaction of the brain, whereas **neuroallergies** affect the nervous system. Neuroallergies and cerebral allergies are believed to cause the allergic person to produce enzymes that attack wholesome foods as if they were dangerous to the body.[53] They may also cause swelling of the brain and produce sensitivity in the central nervous system—conditions linked to mental, emotional, and behavioral problems. Research indicates a connection between allergies and hyperemotionality, depression, aggressiveness, and violent behavior.[54]

Neuroallergy and cerebral allergy problems have also been linked to hyperactivity in children, which may portend antisocial behavior. About 300 foods, including cow's milk, wheat, corn, chocolate, citrus, and eggs, have been identified as allergens. The potential seriousness of the problem has been raised by studies linking the average consumption of one suspected cerebral allergen—corn—to cross-national homicide rates.[55]

Environmental Contaminants Dangerous amounts of copper, cadmium, mercury, and inorganic gases, such as chlorine and nitrogen dioxide, are found in the ecosystem. Research indicates that these environmental contaminants can influence behavior. At high levels, these substances can cause severe illness or death; at more moderate levels, they have been linked to emotional and behavioral disorders.[56] Some studies have linked the ingestion of food dyes and artificial colors and flavors to hostile, impulsive, and otherwise antisocial behavior in youths.[57] Lighting may be another important environmental influence on antisocial behavior: research projects have suggested that radiation from artificial light sources, such as fluorescent tubes and television sets, may produce antisocial, aggressive behavior.[58]

Lead Levels A number of recent research studies have linked lead ingestion to problem behavior. Ingestion of lead may help explain why hyperactive children manifest conduct problems and antisocial behavior.[59] Criminologist Deborah Denno investigated the behavior of more than 900 African-American youths and found that lead poisoning was one of the most significant predictors of male delinquency and persistent adult criminality.[60] Herbert Needleman and his associates also studied the effects of lead poisoning on behavior. They tracked 300 boys from ages 7 to 11 and found that those who had high lead concentrations in their bones were much more likely to report attention problems, delinquency, and aggressiveness.[61] High lead ingestion is also related to lower IQ scores, a factor also linked to aggressive behavior.[62]

Neurophysiological Conditions and Crime

Some researchers focus their attention on **neurophysiology**, or the study of brain activity.[63] They believe that neurological and physical abnormalities are acquired as early as the fetal or perinatal stage or through birth delivery trauma and then control behavior through the life span.[64]

The relationship between neurological dysfunction and crime first received a great deal of attention in 1968 during a tragic incident in Texas. Charles Whitman killed his wife and mother, then barricaded himself in a tower at the University of Texas with a high-powered rifle, where he killed 14 people and wounded 24 others before he was killed by police. An autopsy revealed that Whitman suffered from a malignant infiltrating brain tumor. Whitman had previously experienced uncontrollable urges to kill and had gone to a psychiatrist seeking help for his problems. He kept careful notes documenting his feelings and his inability to control his homicidal urges, and he left instructions for his estate to be given to a mental health foundation so it could study mental problems such as his own.[65]

Since the Whitman case, a great deal of attention has been focused on the association between neurological impairment and crime. Studies conducted in the United States and in other nations have shown a significant relationship between impairment in executive brain functions (like abstract reasoning, problem solving, and motor behavior skills) and aggressive behavior.[66] Research indicates that this relationship can be detected quite early and that children who suffer measurable neurological deficits at birth are more likely to become criminals later in life.[67]

Neurological Impairments and Crime There are numerous ways to measure neurological functioning, including memorization and visual awareness tests, short-term auditory memory tests, and verbal IQ tests. These tests have been found to distinguish criminal offenders from noncriminal control groups.[68]

Traditionally, the most important measure of neurophysiological functioning is the **electroencephalograph (EEG)**. An EEG records the electrical impulses in the brain.[69] It represents a signal composed of various rhythms and transient electrical discharges, commonly called *brain waves*, which can be recorded by electrodes placed on the scalp. The frequency, given in cycles per second, is measured in hertz (Hz) and usually ranges from 0.5 to 30 Hz. Measurements of the EEG reflect the activity of neurons located in the cerebral cortex. The rhythmic nature of this brain activity is determined by mechanisms that involve subcortical structures, primarily the thalamus portion of the brain. EEG studies find that violent criminals have far higher levels of abnormal EEG recordings than nonviolent or one-time offenders.[70] Although about 5 percent of the general population has abnormal EEG readings, about 50 to 60 percent of adolescents with known behavior disorders display abnormal recordings.[71] Behaviors highly correlated with abnormal EEG readings include poor impulse control, inadequate social adaptation, hostility, temper tantrums, and destructiveness.[72] Studies of adults have associated slow and bilateral brain waves with hostile, hypercritical, irritable, nonconforming, and impulsive behavior.[73]

Newer brain scanning techniques using electronic imaging such as *positron emission tomography (PET)*, *brain electrical activity mapping (BEAM)*, and *superconducting interference device (SQUID)* have made it possible to assess which areas of the brain are directly linked to antisocial behavior.[74] Violent criminals have been found to have impairment in the prefrontal lobes, thalamus, medial temporal lobe, and superior parietal and left angular gyrus areas of the brain.[75] A review of existing research by Nathaniel Pallone and James Hennessy finds that chronic violent criminals have far higher levels of brain dysfunction than the general population. Their most striking finding is that the incidence of brain pathology in murderers is 32 times greater than in the general population.[76]

Minimal Brain Dysfunction (MBD) Minimal brain dysfunction (MBD), which is related to abnormal cerebral structure, has been defined as an abruptly appearing, maladaptive behavior that interrupts an individual's lifestyle and life flow. In its most serious form, MBD has been linked to serious antisocial acts, an imbalance in the urge control mechanisms of the brain, and chemical abnormality. Included in the category of minimal brain dysfunction are several abnormal behavior patterns, including dyslexia, visual perception problems, hyperactivity, poor attention span, temper tantrums, and aggressiveness. One type of minimal brain dysfunction is manifested through episodic periods of explosive rage. This form of the disorder is considered an important cause of such behavior as spouse and child abuse, suicide, aggressiveness, and motiveless homicide. One perplexing feature of this syndrome is that people who are afflicted with it often maintain warm, pleasant personalities between episodes of violence. Some studies measuring the presence of minimal brain dysfunction in offender populations have found that up to 60 percent exhibit brain dysfunction on psychological tests.[77] Criminals have been characterized as having dysfunction of the dominant hemisphere of the brain.[78] Researchers using brain wave data have predicted with 95 percent accuracy the recidivism of violent criminals.[79] More sophisticated brain scanning techniques, such as PET, have also shown that brain abnormality is linked to violent crime.[80]

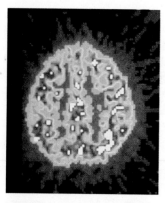

This scan compares a normal brain (left) and an ADHD brain (right). The areas of orange and white demonstrate a higher rate of metabolism, while areas of blue and green represent an abnormally low metabolic rate. Why is ADHD so prevalent in the U.S. today? Some experts believe that our immigrant forebears were risk takers who impulsively left their homelands for a life in the new world. They may have also brought with them a genetic predisposition for ADHD.

Attention Deficit/Hyperactivity Disorder (ADHD) Many parents have noticed that their children do not pay attention to them—they run around and do things in their own way. Sometimes this inattention is a function of age; in other instances it is a symptom of **attention deficit/hyperactivity disorder (ADHD)**, in which a child shows a developmentally inappropriate lack of attention, impulsivity, and hyperactivity. The various symptoms of ADHD are described in Table 6.1. About 3 percent of U.S. children, most often boys, are believed to suffer from this disorder, and it is the most common reason children are referred to mental health clinics. The condition has been associated with poor school performance, grade retention, placement in special needs classes, bullying, stubbornness, and lack of response to discipline.[81] Although the origin of ADHD is still unknown, suspected causes include neurological damage, prenatal stress, and even reactions to food additives and chemical allergies. Recent research has suggested a genetic link.[82] There are also links to family turmoil: mothers of ADHD children are more likely to be divorced or separated, and ADHD children are much more likely to move to new locales than non-ADHD children.[83] It may be possible that emotional turmoil either produces symptoms of ADHD or, if they already exist, causes them to intensify.

Research studies now link ADHD to the onset and sustenance of a delinquent career.[84] Many ADHD children also suffer from **conduct disorder (CD)** and continually engage in aggressive and antisocial behavior in early childhood. The disorders are sustained over the life course: children diagnosed as having ADHD are more likely to be suspended from school and to engage in criminal behavior as adults. This ADHD–crime association is important because symptoms of ADHD seem stable through adolescence into adulthood.[85] Early diagnosis and treatment of children suffering ADHD may

enhance their life chances. Today the most typical treatment is doses of stimulants, such as Ritalin, which ironically help control emotional and behavioral outbursts. The relationship between chronic delinquency and attention disorders may also be mediated by school performance. Kids who are poor readers are the most prone to antisocial behavior; many poor readers also have attention problems.[86] Early school-based intervention programs may benefit those who suffer ADHD.

Other Brain Dysfunctions Other brain dysfunctions have been related to violent crime. Persistent criminality has been linked to dysfunction in the frontal and temporal regions of the brain. These regions are believed to play an important role in regulating and inhibiting human behavior, including formulating plans and controlling intentions; they also regulate complex behaviors.[87] Brain lesions that occur at specific points of the neurological system, such as the auditory system, can permanently affect behavior.[88] Clinical evaluation of depressed and aggressive psychopathic subjects showed a significant number (more than 75 percent) had dysfunction of the temporal and frontal regions of the brain.[89]

Tumors, Injury, and Disease The presence of brain tumors has also been linked to a wide variety of psychological problems, including personality changes, hallucinations, and psychotic episodes.[90] There is evidence that people with tumors are prone to depression, irri-

Table 6.1 Symptoms of Attention Deficit/Hyperactivity Disorder

Lack of Attention
Frequently fails to finish projects
Does not seem to pay attention
Does not sustain interest in play activities
Cannot sustain concentration on schoolwork or related tasks
Is easily distracted

Impulsivity
Frequently acts without thinking
Often "calls out" in class
Does not want to wait his or her turn in lines or games
Shifts from activity to activity
Cannot organize tasks or work
Requires constant supervision

Hyperactivity
Constantly runs around and climbs on things
Shows excessive motor activity while asleep
Cannot sit still; is constantly fidgeting
Does not remain in his or her seat in class
Is constantly on the go like a "motor"

Source: Adapted from American Psychiatric Association, *Diagnostic and Statistical Manual of Mental Disorders,* 4th ed. (Washington, D.C.: American Psychiatric Press, 1994).

Biocriminologist Lee Ellis has found that prenatal exposure of the brain to high levels of androgens can result in a brain structure that is less sensitive to environmental inputs. Ellis has also found that people with high arousal levels are more prone to violent and aggressive behaviors.

tability, temper outbursts, and even homicidal attacks (as in the Whitman case). Clinical case studies of patients suffering from brain tumors indicate that previously docile people may undergo behavior changes so great that they attempt to seriously harm their families and friends. When the tumor is removed, their behavior returns to normal.[91] In addition to brain tumors, head injuries caused by accidents, such as falls or auto crashes, have been linked to personality reversals marked by outbursts of antisocial and violent behavior.[92]

Various central nervous system diseases have also been linked to personality changes. Some of these conditions include cerebral arteriosclerosis, epilepsy, Alzheimer's disease, Korsakoff's syndrome, and Huntington's chorea. Associated symptoms of these diseases are memory deficiency, orientation loss, and affective (emotional) disturbances dominated by rage, anger, and increased irritability.[93]

Brain Chemistry **Neurotransmitters** are chemical compounds that influence or activate brain functions. Those studied in relation to aggression include dopamine, norepinephrine, serotonin, monoamine oxidase, and GABA.[94] Evidence exists that abnormal levels of these chemicals are associated with aggression. For example, several researchers have reported inverse correlations between serotonin concentrates in the blood and impulsive or suicidal behavior.[95] Recent studies of habitually violent Finnish criminals show that low serotonin (5-hydroxytryptamine; 5-HT) levels are associated with poor impulse control and hyperactivity. In addition, a relatively low concentration of 5-hydroxyindoleactic acid (5-HIAA) predicts increased irritability, sensation seeking, and impaired impulse control.[96]

What is the link between brain chemistry and crime? Prenatal exposure of the brain to high levels of androgens can result in a brain structure that is less sensitive to environmental inputs. Affected individuals seek more intense and varied stimulation and are willing to tolerate more adverse consequences than individuals not so affected.[97] Such exposure also shifts brain hemispheric functioning rightward, diminishing cognitive and emotional tendencies. As one result, left-handers are disproportionately represented in the criminal population because the movement of each hand is controlled by the hemisphere of the brain on the opposite side of the body.

It has also been suggested that individuals with a low supply of the enzyme monoamine oxidase (MAO) engage in behaviors linked with violence and property crime, including defiance of punishment, impulsivity, hyperactivity, poor academic performance, sensation seeking and risk taking, and recreational drug use. Abnormal MAO levels may explain both individual and group differences in the crime rate. For example, females have higher MAO levels than males, which may explain gender differences in the crime rate.[98]

The brain and neurological system can produce natural or endogenous opiates that are chemically similar to the narcotics opium and morphine. It has been suggested that the risk and thrills involved in crime cause the neurological system to produce increased amounts of these natural narcotics. The result is an elevated mood state, perceived as an exciting and rewarding experience that positively reinforces crime.[99] In other words, the brain produces its own natural high as a reward for risk-taking behavior. Whereas some people achieve this high by climbing rocks and skydiving, others commit violent crimes.

Because this linkage has been found, it is not uncommon for violence-prone people to be treated with antipsychotic drugs, such as Haldol, Stelazine, Prolixin, and Risperdal, which help control levels of neurotransmitters (such as serotonin or dopamine); these are sometimes referred to as **chemical restraints** or **chemical straitjackets.**

Arousal Theory It has long been suspected that obtaining thrills is a crime motivator. Adolescents may engage in such crimes as shoplifting and vandalism simply because they offer the attraction of "getting away with it"; from this perspective, delinquency is a thrilling demonstration of personal competence.[100]

CONNECTIONS

Jack Katz has written about the "seductions of crime." Perhaps some people are seduced into crime because the experience produces the natural high they crave. Katz's work is discussed in Chapter 5.

According to arousal theory, for a variety of genetic and environmental reasons, some people's brains function differently in response to environmental stimuli. All of us seek to maintain a preferred or optimal level of arousal: too much stimulation leaves us anxious and stressed, whereas too little makes us feel bored and weary. There is, however, variation in the way people's brains process sensory input. Some nearly always feel comfortable with little stimulation, but others require a high degree of environmental input to feel comfortable. The latter group are sensation seekers who look for stimulating activities, which may include aggressive, violent behavior patterns.[101]

Although the factors that determine a person's level of arousal are not fully determined, suspected sources include brain chemistry (such as serotonin levels) and brain structure. Some brains have many more nerve cells with receptor sites for neurotransmitters than others. Another view is that people with low heart rates are more likely to commit crime because they seek stimulation to increase their arousal to normal levels.[102]

Genetics and Crime

Early biological theorists believed that criminality ran in families. Although research on deviant families, such as the Jukes and Kallikaks, is not taken seriously today, modern biosocial theorists are still interested in the role of genetics. If some human behaviors are influenced by heredity, wouldn't that be the case for antisocial tendencies as well? Animals can be bred for aggressive traits: pit bulldogs, fighting bulls, and fighting cocks have been selectively mated to produce superior predators. No similar data exists with regard to people, but a growing body of research is focusing on the genetic factors associated with human behavior.[103] For example, personality traits like extroversion, openness, agreeableness, and conscientiousness may be genetically determined.[104] Data also suggest that human traits associated with criminality have a genetic basis.[105] Personality conditions linked to aggression (such as psychopathy, impulsivity, and neuroticism) and to psychopathology (such as schizophrenia, which is discussed later in this chapter) may be heritable.[106]

This line of reasoning was spotlighted in the 1970s when genetic testing of Richard Speck, the convicted killer of eight Chicago nurses, allegedly found that he had an abnormal XYY chromosomal structure (XY is normal in males). There was much public concern that all people with XYY chromosomes were potential killers and should be closely controlled. Civil libertarians expressed fear that all XYY males could be labeled dangerous and violent regardless of whether they had engaged in violent activities.[107] When it was disclosed that neither Speck nor most violent offenders actually had an extra Y chromosome, interest in the XYY theory dissipated.[108] However, the Speck case drew researchers' attention to looking for a genetic basis of crime.

Researchers have carefully explored the heritability of criminal tendencies by looking at a variety of factors. Some of the most important are described next.

Parental Deviance If criminal tendencies are inherited, then the children of criminal parents should be more likely to become law violators than the offspring of conventional parents. A number of studies have found that parental criminality and deviance do, in fact, powerfully influence delinquent behavior.[109] Some of the most important data on parental deviance were gathered by Donald J. West and David P. Farrington as part of the long-term Cambridge Youth Survey. Directed by Dr. Farrington, this research followed a group of about 1000 males from the time they were 8 until they were in their thirties. The boys in the study were repeatedly interviewed and their school and police records evaluated. These cohort data indicate that a significant number of delinquent youths have criminal fathers.[110] Whereas 8.4 percent of the sons of noncriminal fathers eventually became chronic offenders, about 37 percent of youths with criminal fathers were multiple offenders.[111] In another important analysis, Farrington found that one type of parental deviance, schoolyard aggression or bullying, may be both inter- and intragenerational. Bullies have children who bully others, and these second-generation bullies grow up to father children who are also bullies, in a never-ending cycle.[112]

The cause of intergenerational deviance is still uncertain. It is possible that environmental, genetic, psychological, or child-rearing factors are responsible for the linkage between generations. The link might have also have some biological basis. Research on the sons of alcoholic parents finds that they suffer many neurological impairments related to chronic delinquency.[113] These results may indicate either that prolonged parental alcoholism causes genetic problems related to developmental impairment or that the children of substance-abusing parents are likely to suffer neurological impairment before, during, or after birth.

The quality of family life may be key in determining children's behavior. Criminal parents should be least likely to have close, intimate relationships with their offspring. Research shows that substance-abusing and criminal parents are most likely to use harsh, inconsistent discipline, a factor closely linked to delinquent behavior.[114]

There is, then, no certainty about the relationship between parental and child deviance.[115] Nonetheless, recent evidence indicates that at least part of the association is genetic.[116] The association may also be related to the labeling process and family stigma. Social control agents may be quick to fix a delinquent label on the children of known law violators: the acorn, the reasoning goes, does not fall far from the tree.[117]

Sibling Influence Some evidence exists that sibling relationships may be very influential. Sibling pairs who report warm, mutual relationships and share friends are the most likely to behave similarly; those who maintain a close relationship also have similar rates of drug abuse and delinquency.[118] There are a number of ways to interpret these findings:

- Siblings who live in the same environment are influenced by similar social and economic factors.
- Deviant siblings may grow closer because of shared interests.
- Younger siblings who admire their older siblings may imitate the elders' behavior.

What seems to be a genetic effect may actually be the result of close sibling interaction. The genetic effect of sibling behavior is yet to be determined.

Twin Behavior If, in fact, inherited traits cause criminal behavior, we might expect that twins would be quite similar in their antisocial activities. However, because twins are usually brought up in the same household and exposed to the same social conditions, determining whether their behavior is a result of biological, sociological, or psychological conditions is difficult. Trait theorists have tried to overcome this dilemma by comparing identical, monozygotic (MZ) twins with fraternal, dizygotic (DZ) twins.[119] MZ twins are genetically identical, whereas DZ twins have only half their genes in common. If heredity determines criminal behavior, we should expect that MZ twins would be much more similar in their antisocial activities than DZ twins.

The earliest studies conducted on twin behavior detected a significant relationship between the criminal activities of MZ twins and a much lower association between those of DZ twins. A review of relevant studies conducted between 1929 and 1961 found that 60 percent of MZ twins shared criminal behavior patterns (if one twin was criminal, so was the other), whereas only 30 percent of DZ twins were similarly related.[120] These findings may be viewed as powerful evidence of a genetic basis for criminality.

Other studies have supported these findings. In one well-known work, Danish criminologist Karl Christiansen studied 3,586 male twin pairs and found a 52 percent concordance for MZ pairs and a 22 percent concordance for DZ pairs. This result suggests that the identical MZ twins may share a genetic characteristic that increases the risk of their engaging in criminality.[121] Similarly, criminologists David Rowe and D. Wayne Osgood analyzed the factors that influence self-reported delinquency in a sample of twin pairs and concluded that genetic influences have significant explanatory power.[122] Genetic effects significantly predict problem behaviors in children as young as 3 years old.[123] Although the behavior of some twin pairs seems to be influenced by their environment, others display behavior disturbances that can be explained only by their genetic similarity.[124]

The controversy over the heritability of crime still rages. On the one hand, opponents suggest that available evidence does not conclusively prove that crime is genetically determined. Not all research efforts have found that MZ twin pairs are more closely related in their criminal behavior than DZ or ordinary sibling pairs, and some have found an association that is at best modest.[125] On the other hand, some experts conclude that individuals who share genes are alike in personality regardless of how they are reared; environment, they argue, induces little or no personality resemblance in twin pairs.[126]

Adoption Studies It seems logical that if the behavior of adopted children is more closely aligned to that of their biological parents than to that of their adoptive parents, then the idea of a genetic basis for criminality would be supported. If, on the other hand, adoptees are more closely aligned to the behavior of their adoptive parents than their biological parents, an environmental basis for crime would seem more valid.

Several studies indicate that some relationship exists between biological parents' behavior and the behavior of their children, even when they have had no contact.[127] In what is considered the most significant study in this area, Barry Hutchings and Sarnoff Mednick analyzed 1,145 male adoptees born in Copenhagen, Denmark, between 1927 and 1941. Of these, 185 had criminal records.[128] After following up on 143 of the criminal adoptees and matching them with a control group of 143 noncriminal adoptees, Hutchings and Mednick found that the biological father's criminality strongly predicted the child's criminal behavior. When both the biological and the adoptive fathers were criminal, the probability that the youth would engage in criminal behavior greatly increased: 24.5 percent of the boys whose adoptive and biological fathers were criminals had been convicted of a criminal law violation. Only 13.5 percent of those whose biological and adoptive fathers were not criminals had similar conviction records.[129]

A more recent analysis of Swedish adoptees also found that genetic factors were highly significant, accounting for 59 percent of the variation in petty crime rates. Boys who had criminal parents were significantly more likely to violate the law. Environmental influences and economic status were less important, explaining about 19 percent of the variance in crime. Nonetheless, having a positive environment, such as being adopted into an affluent home, helped inhibit genetic predisposition.[130]

Evaluating Genetic Research   The findings of the twin and adoption studies tentatively support a genetic basis for criminality. However, those who oppose the genes–crime relationship point to inadequate research designs and weak methodologies of supporting research. The newer, better-designed research studies, critics charge, provide less support than earlier, less methodologically sound studies.[131]

The genes–crime relationship is quite controversial because it implies that the propensity to commit crime is present at birth and cannot be altered. It raises moral dilemmas. If in utero genetic testing could detect a gene for violence and a violence gene was found to be present, what could be done as a precautionary measure?

Evolutionary Views of Crime

There are also criminologists who believe that the human traits that produce violence and aggression have been advanced by the long process of human evolution.[132] According to this evolutionary view, the competition for scarce resources has influenced and shaped the human species.[133] Over the course of human existence, people whose personal characteristics allow them to accumulate more than others are the most likely to breed and dominate the species. People have been shaped to engage in actions that promote their well-being and ensure the survival and reproduction of their genetic line. Males who are impulsive risk takers may be able to father more children because they are reckless in their social relationships and have sexual encounters with numerous partners. If, according to evolutionary theories, such behavior patterns are inherited, impulsive behavior becomes intergenerational, passed down from parents to children. It is therefore not surprising that human history has been marked by war, violence, and aggression.

The Evolution of Gender and Crime   Evolutionary concepts that have been linked to the gender differences in violence rates are based loosely on mammalian mating patterns. To ensure survival of the gene pool (and the species), it is beneficial for a male of any species to mate with as many suitable females as possible because each can bear its offspring. In contrast, because of the long period of gestation, females require a secure home and a single, stable, nurturing partner to ensure their survival. Because of these differences in mating patterns, the most aggressive males mate most often and have the greatest number of offspring. There-

fore, over the history of the human species, aggressive males have had the greatest impact on the gene pool. The descendants of these aggressive males now account for the disproportionate amount of male aggression and violence.[134] Crime rate differences between the genders, then, may be less a matter of socialization than inherent differences in mating patterns that have developed over time.[135] Among young men, reckless, life-threatening risk proneness is especially likely to evolve in cultures that force them to find suitable mates to ensure their ability to reproduce. Unless they are aggressive with potential mates and potential rivals for those suitable mates, they will remain childless.[136] High rates of spouse abuse in modern society may be a function of aggressive men seeking to control and possess mates. Men who feel most threatened over the potential of losing mates to rivals are the most likely to engage in sexual violence. Research shows that women in common-law marriages, especially those who are much younger than their husbands, are at greater risk of abuse than older, married women. Abusive males may fear the potential loss of their younger mates, especially if they are not bound by a marriage contract, and may use force for purposes of control and possession.[137]

There are two general evolutionary theories of crime: *r/k selection theory* and *cheater theory*.[138]

• **R/k selection theory** holds that all organisms can be located along a continuum based on their reproductive drives. Those along the r- end reproduce rapidly whenever they can and invest little in their offspring; those along the k- end reproduce slowly and cautiously and take care in raising their offspring. Evolutionary theorists believe that males today lean toward r-selection because they can reproduce faster without the need for investing in their offspring; females are k-selected because they have fewer offspring but devote more care to them. K-oriented people are more cooperative and sensitive to others, whereas r-oriented people are more cunning and deceptive. Males, therefore, tend to exhibit more criminal behavior. In general, people who commit violent crimes seem to exhibit r-selection traits, such as premature birth and early, frequent sexual activity. They are more likely to have been neglected as children and have a short life expectancy.[139]

• **Cheater theory**, the second evolutionary model, suggests that a subpopulation of men has evolved with genes that incline them toward extremely low parental involvement. They are sexually aggressive and use cunning to gain sexual conquests with as many females as possible. Because females would not willingly choose them as mates, they use stealth to gain sexual access, including such tactics as mimicking the behavior of more stable males. They use devious, illegal means to acquire resources they need for sexual domination. Their deceptive reproductive tactics spill over into other endeavors, where their irresponsible, opportunistic behavior supports their antisocial activities. Deceptive reproductive strategies, then, are linked to a deceitful lifestyle.[140]

Psychologist Byron Roth notes that cheater-type males may be especially attractive to younger, less intelligent women who begin having children at a very early age. State-sponsored welfare, claims Roth, removes the need for potential mates to have the resources required of stable providers and family caretakers.[141] With the state meeting their financial needs, these women are attracted to men who are physically attractive and flamboyant. Their fleeting courtship produces children with low IQ scores, aggressive personalities, and little chance of proper socialization in father-absent families. Because the criminal justice system treats them leniently, argues Roth, sexually irresponsible men are free to prey upon young girls. Over time, their offspring will make up an ever-expanding supply of cheaters who are both antisocial and sexually aggressive.

> **CONNECTIONS**
>
> The relationship between evolutionary factors and crime has just begun to be studied. Criminologists are now exploring how social organizations and institutions interact with biological traits to influence personal decision making, including criminal strategies. See Chapter 10's sections on latent trait theories for more about the integration of biological and environmental factors.

Evaluation of the Biological Branch of Trait Theory

Biosocial perspectives on crime have raised some challenging questions. Critics find some of these theories racist and dysfunctional. If there are biological explanations for street crimes such as assault, murder, or rape, the argument goes, and if, as official crime statistics suggest, the poor and minority-group members commit a disproportionate number of such acts, then by implication, biological theory says that members of these groups are biologically different, flawed, or inferior.

> **CONNECTIONS**
>
> Biosocial theory focuses on the violent crimes of the lower classes while ignoring the white-collar crimes of the upper and middle classes. That is, although it may seem logical to believe there is a biological basis to aggression and violence, it is more difficult to explain how insider trading and fraud are biologically related. For the causes of white-collar crime, see Chapter 13.

Biological explanations for the geographic, social, and temporal patterns in the crime rate are also problematic. Is it possible that more people are genetically predisposed to crime in the South and the West than in New England and the Midwest? Furthermore, biological theory seems to divide people into criminals and noncriminals on the basis of their genetic and physical makeup, ignoring self-reports that indicate almost everyone has engaged in some type of illegal activity.

Biosocial theorists counter that their views should not be confused with Lombrosian, deterministic biology. Rather than suggesting that there are born criminals and noncriminals, they maintain that some people carry the potential to be violent or antisocial and that environmental conditions can sometimes trigger antisocial responses.[142] This would explain why some otherwise law-abiding citizens perform a single, seemingly unexplainable antisocial act and, conversely, why some people with long criminal careers often behave conventionally. It also explains geographic and temporal patterns in the crime rate: people who are predisposed to crime may simply have more opportunities to commit illegal acts in the summer in Los Angeles and Atlanta than in the winter in Bedford, New Hampshire, and Minot, North Dakota.

The biosocial view, then, is that behavior is a product of interacting biological and environmental events.[143] Physical impairments may put some people at risk for crime, but when these impairments are linked to social and environmental problems, such as family dysfunction, they trigger criminal acts.[144] For example, Avshalom Caspi and his associates found that girls who reach early physical maturity are most likely to engage in delinquent acts. This finding might suggest a relationship between biological traits (hormonal activity) and crime. However, the Caspi research found that the association may also have an environmental basis. Physically mature girls are likely to have prolonged contact with a crime-prone group: older adolescent boys.[145] Here the combination of biological change, social relationships, and routine opportunities may predict crime rates.

> **CONNECTIONS**
>
> The routine activities approach was discussed in Chapters 4 and 5. Is it possible that a person's daily activities and opportunities to commit crime are structured by his or her biological makeup? This may be an important avenue of research for criminologists to follow.

The most significant criticism of biosocial theory has been the lack of adequate empirical testing. Most research samples are relatively small and nonrepresentative. A great deal of biosocial research is conducted with samples of adjudicated offenders who have been placed in clinical treatment settings. Methodological problems make it impossible to determine whether findings apply only to offenders who have been convicted of crimes and placed in treatment or to all criminals.[146] More research is needed to clarify the relationships proposed by biosocial researchers and to silence critics.

PSYCHOLOGICAL TRAIT THEORIES

The second branch of trait theory focuses on the psychological aspects of crime, including the associations among intelligence, personality, learning, and criminal behavior.

> **CONNECTIONS**
>
> Chapter 1 discussed how some of the early founders of psychiatry tried to understand the criminal mind. Later theories suggested that mental illness and insanity were inherited and that deviants were inherently mentally damaged by their inferior genetic makeup.

In *The English Convict*, Charles Goring (1870–1919) studied the mental characteristics of 3,000 English convicts.[147] He found little difference in the physical characteristics of criminals and noncriminals, but instead uncovered a significant relationship between crime and a condition he referred to as **defective intelligence**, which involves such traits as feeblemindedness, epilepsy, insanity, and defective social instinct.[148] Goring believed that criminal behavior was inherited and could therefore be controlled by regulating the reproduction of families who produced mentally defective children.

Theory of Imitation

Gabriel Tarde (1843–1904) was the forerunner of modern learning theorists. He used a somewhat different psychological approach in his early research.[149] Unlike Goring, who viewed criminals as mentally impaired, Tarde believed people learn from one another through imitation. Tarde proposed three laws of imitation to describe why people engage in crime:

1. Individuals in close, intimate contact imitate each other's behavior.
2. Imitation spreads from the top down; consequently, youngsters imitate older individuals; paupers imitate the rich; peasants imitate royalty; and so on. According to this law, crime among young, poor, or low-status people is really their effort to imitate wealthy, older, high-status people (for example,

through gambling, drunkenness, or accumulation of wealth).

3. Tarde's **law of insertion** dictates that new acts and behaviors are superimposed on old ones and subsequently either reinforce or discourage previous customs. For example, taking drugs may be popular among college students who previously used alcohol. However, students may find that combining both substances provides even greater stimulation, causing both drug and alcohol use to increase. In the case of criminal behavior, a new criminal custom can eliminate an older one — for example, train robbing has been replaced by airplane hijacking.

Tarde's ideas are quite similar to those of modern social learning theorists, who believe that both interpersonal and observed behavior, such as a movie or television, can influence criminality.

Since the pioneering work of people like Pinel, Maudsley, Tarde, and Goring, psychologists, psychiatrists, and other mental health professionals have long played an active role in formulating criminological theory. In their quest to understand and treat all varieties of abnormal mental conditions, psychologists have encountered clients whose behavior falls within categories society has labeled as criminal, deviant, violent, and antisocial.

> **CONNECTIONS**
>
> Chapter 1 discussed the early history of the psychological branch of trait theory, including the work of Maudsley. He believed, you may recall, that insanity and criminal behavior were strongly linked.

This section is organized along the lines of the predominant psychological views most closely associated with the cause of criminal behavior. These perspectives are outlined in Figure 6.2. Some psychologists view antisocial behavior from a **psychoanalytic** or **psychodynamic** perspective: their focus is on early childhood experience and its effect on personality. In contrast, **behaviorists** stress social learning and behavior modeling as the keys to criminality. **Cognitive** theorists analyze human perception and how it affects behavior.

> **CONNECTIONS**
>
> There is also a biological branch of psychology that holds that behavior is controlled by the effect of biochemical, neurological, and genetic influences on the brain. This latter viewpoint is quite similar to the biosocial views just discussed, and a great deal of biosocial research is conducted by people trained as psychologists and psychiatrists.

Figure 6.2 Psychological Perspectives on Criminality

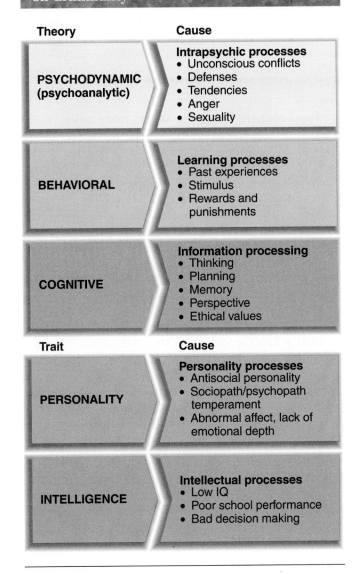

Theory	Cause
PSYCHODYNAMIC (psychoanalytic)	**Intrapsychic processes** • Unconscious conflicts • Defenses • Tendencies • Anger • Sexuality
BEHAVIORAL	**Learning processes** • Past experiences • Stimulus • Rewards and punishments
COGNITIVE	**Information processing** • Thinking • Planning • Memory • Perspective • Ethical values

Trait	Cause
PERSONALITY	**Personality processes** • Antisocial personality • Sociopath/psychopath temperament • Abnormal affect, lack of emotional depth
INTELLIGENCE	**Intellectual processes** • Low IQ • Poor school performance • Bad decision making

Psychodynamic Perspective

Psychodynamic or psychoanalytic psychology was originated by Viennese psychiatrist Sigmund Freud (1856–1939) and has since remained a prominent segment of psychological theory.[150] Freud's vision of psychoanalysis was crafted over 45 years, during which he published 23 volumes that outlined his clinical techniques, the way he interpreted patient behavior and dreams, and his views of human psychological development. Freud believed that we all carry with us residue of the most significant emotional attachments of our childhood, which then guides future interpersonal relationships. To treat people suffering from emotional problems, he developed pychoanalytic therapy, which is based on patient–doctor conversation aimed at relieving mental and emotional distress; it is sometimes called the *talking cure* because it relies on conversation. Psy-

choanalytic therapy is based on the premise that human thought and behavior are controlled by the unconscious portion of our mind and are therefore beyond ordinary conscious control. The psychoanalytic therapist helps people reveal unconscious needs, motivations, wishes, and memories in order to gain conscious control of their lives. Many psychologists still practice Freud's treatment techniques, and they remain a cornerstone of psychological thought and process.

According to Freud's version of psychodynamic theory, the human mind performs three separate functions. The conscious mind is the part of the mind that people are most aware of; it contains sensations and thoughts like hunger, pain, thirst, and desire. The preconscious mind holds elements of experiences that are out of our awareness but that can be brought back to consciousness at any time through memories and experiences. The unconscious part of the mind contains biological desires and urges that cannot readily be experienced as thoughts. Part of the unconscious holds feelings about sex and hostility, which people keep below the surface of consciousness by a process called **repression.**

Psychodynamic theory also says that the human personality has a three-part structure. The **id** is the primitive part of people's mental makeup present at birth. It represents unconscious biological drives for sex, food, and other life-sustaining necessities. The id follows the **pleasure principle:** it requires instant gratification without concern for the rights of others.

The **ego** develops early in life when a child begins to learn that his or her wishes cannot be instantly gratified. The ego is the part of the personality that compensates for the demands of the id by helping the individual guide his or her actions to remain within the boundaries of social convention. The ego is guided by the **reality principle:** it takes into account what is practical and conventional by societal standards.

The **superego** develops as a result of incorporating within the personality the moral standards and values of parents, community, and significant others. It is the moral aspect of people's personalities; it judges their behavior. The superego is divided into two parts: conscience and ego ideal. **Conscience** tells us what is right and wrong; it forces the ego to control the id and directs people into morally acceptable and responsible behaviors, which may not be pleasurable. The **ego ideal** refers to a person's idealized self-image. Table 6.2 summarizes Freud's personality structure.

Psychosexual Stages of Human Development The most basic human drive present at birth is **eros,** the instinct to preserve and create life. Eros is expressed sexually. Consequently, very early in their development humans experience sexuality, which is expressed by seeking pleasure through various parts of the body. During the first year of life a child attains pleasure by sucking and biting; Freud called this the **oral stage.**

Table 6.2   Freud's Model of the Personality Structure

PERSONALITY STRUCTURE	GUIDING PRINCIPLE	DESCRIPTION
Id	Pleasure principle	Unconscious biological drives; requires instant gratification
Ego	Reality principle	Helps the personality refine the demands of the id; helps person adapt to conventions
Superego	The conscience	The moral aspect of personality

During the second and third years of life, the focus of sexual attention is on the elimination of bodily wastes — the **anal stage.** The **phallic stage** occurs during the third year when children focus their attention on their genitals. Males begin to have sexual feelings for their mother (the **Oedipus complex**) and girls for their fathers (the **Electra complex**). **Latency** begins at age six. During this period, feelings of sexuality are repressed until the **genital stage** begins at puberty; this marks the beginning of adult sexuality.

If conflicts are encountered during any of the psychosexual stages of development, a person can become **fixated** at that point. As an adult, the fixated person will exhibit behavior traits characteristic of those encountered during infantile sexual development. For example, an infant who does not receive enough oral gratification during the first year of life is likely as an adult to engage in such oral behavior as smoking, drinking, or drug abuse or to be clinging and dependent in personal relationships. Thus, according to Freud, adult behavioral problems can be traced to problems developed in the earliest years of life.

Psychodynamics of Abnormal Behavior   Psychodynamic theory originally referred to people who experience feelings of mental anguish and are afraid that they are losing control of their personalities as **neurotics.** People who had completely lost control and who were dominated by their primitive id were referred to as **psychotics.** Today these terms have, for the most part, been replaced with various **disorders,** including anxiety disorder, mood disorders, and conduct disorders. The most serious disorder is **schizophrenia,** marked by hearing nonexistent voices, seeing hallucinations, and exhibiting inappropriate responses.

Schizophrenics have illogical, incoherent thought processes and lack insight into their behavior. They may experience delusions and hallucinate. For example, they may see themselves as agents of the devil, avenging angels, or the recipients of messages from an-imals and plants. David Berkowitz, the "Son of Sam" or the "44-calibre killer," a noted serial killer who went on a 1976–1977 rampage, exhibited these traits when he claimed that his killing spree began after he received messages from a neighbor's dog. **Paranoid schizophrenics,** such as U.S. Capitol slayer Russell Eugene Weston, suffer complex behavioral delusions involving wrongdoing or persecution — they think everyone is out to get them.

Psychologists have long linked criminality to abnormal mental states produced by early childhood trauma. For example, Alfred Adler (1870–1937), the founder of individual psychology, coined the term **inferiority complex** to describe people who feel inferior and compensate with a drive for superiority. Controlling others may help reduce personal inadequacies. Erik Erikson (1902–1984) identified the **identity crisis**—a period of serious personal questioning people undertake in an effort to determine their own values and sense of direction. Adolescents undergoing an identity crisis might exhibit out-of-control behavior and experiment with drugs and other forms of deviance.

The psychoanalyst whose work is most closely associated with criminality is August Aichorn.[151] After examining many delinquent youths, Aichorn concluded that societal stress, though damaging, could not alone cause a life of crime unless a predisposition existed that psychologically prepared youths for antisocial acts. This mental state, which he labeled **latent delinquency,** is found in youngsters whose personality requires them to

- Seek immediate gratification (act impulsively).
- Consider satisfying their personal needs more important than relating to others.
- Satisfy instinctual urges without considering right and wrong (that is, they lack guilt).

Psychodynamics of Criminal Behavior   Since Freud's original research, psychoanalysts have continued to view criminals as id-dominated persons who suffer from one or more disorders that render them incapable of controlling impulsive, pleasure-seeking drives.[152] The psychodynamic model of the criminal offender depicts an aggressive, frustrated person dominated by events that occurred early in childhood. Perhaps because they may have suffered unhappy experiences in childhood or had families that could not provide proper love and care, criminals suffer from weak or damaged egos that make them unable to cope with conventional society. Weak egos are associated with immaturity, poor social skills, and excessive dependence on others. People with weak egos may be easily led into crime by antisocial peers and drug abuse. Some offenders have underdeveloped superegos and consequently lack internalized representations of those behaviors that are punished in conventional society. They commit crimes because they have difficulty understanding the consequences of their actions.[153]

Social learning theory maintains that some behavior modeling may be grounded in the images provided by the mass media. Films such as *Scream* (Drew Barrymore is shown here screaming) commonly depict violence graphically. Moreover, violence is often portrayed as an acceptable behavior, especially for the heroes, who never have to face legal consequences for their actions.

Offenders, then, suffer various mood and behavior disorders. They may be histrionic, depressed, antisocial, or narcissistic.[154] They may suffer conduct disorders, which include long histories of antisocial behavior or mood disorders characterized by disturbance in expressed emotions. Among the latter is **bipolar disorder,** in which moods alternate between periods of wild elation and deep depression.[155] Some offenders are driven by an unconscious desire to be punished for prior sins, either real or imaginary. As a result, they may violate the law to gain attention or punish their parents.

Crime therefore is a manifestation of feelings of oppression and people's inability to develop the proper psychological defenses and rationales to keep these feelings under control. Criminality allows troubled people to survive by producing positive psychic results: it helps them feel free and independent, and it gives them the possibility of excitement and the chance to use their skills and imagination. It also promises positive gain; it allows them to blame others for their predicament (for example, the police); and it gives them a chance to rationalize their sense of failure ("If I hadn't gotten into trouble, I could have been a success").[156]

Behavioral Theories

Behavior theory maintains that human actions are developed through learning experiences. Rather than focus on unconscious personality traits or cognitive development patterns produced early in childhood, be-

havior theorists are concerned with actual behaviors in people's daily lives. The major premise of behavior theory is that people alter their behavior according to the reactions it receives from others. Behavior is supported by rewards and extinguished by negative reactions or punishments.

Behaviorist theory is quite complex with many different subareas. The behaviorist views crimes, especially violent acts, as learned responses to life situations that do not necessarily represent abnormality or moral immaturity.

Social Learning Theory **Social learning** is the branch of behavior theory most relevant to criminology.[157] Social learning theorists, most notably Albert Bandura, argue that people are not actually born with the ability to act violently, but that they learn to be aggressive through their life experiences. These experiences include personally observing others acting aggressively to achieve some goal or watching people being rewarded for violent acts on television or in movies. People learn to act aggressively when, as children, they model their behavior after the violent acts of adults. Later in life, these violent behavior patterns persist in social relationships. For example, the boy who sees his father repeatedly strike his mother with impunity is likely to become a battering parent and husband.

Although social learning theorists agree that mental or physical traits may predispose a person toward violence, they believe that a person's violent tendencies are activated by factors in the environment. The specific form of aggressive behavior, the frequency with which it is expressed, the situations in which it is displayed, and the specific targets selected for attack are largely determined by social learning. However, people are self-aware and engage in purposeful learning. Their interpretations of behavior outcomes and situations influence the way they learn from experiences. One adolescent who spends a weekend in jail for drunk driving may find it the most awful experience of her life — one that teaches her never to drink and drive again. Another person, however, may find it an exciting experience about which he can brag to his friends.

Social Learning and Violence Social learning theorists view violence as something learned through a process called **behavior modeling.** In modern society, aggressive acts are usually modeled after three principal sources:

1. Most prominent is family members. Bandura reports that studies of family life show that aggressive children have parents who use similar tactics when dealing with others.
2. A second influence is provided by environmental experiences. People who reside in areas in which violence occurs daily are more likely to act violently than those who dwell in low-crime areas whose norms stress conventional behavior.
3. A third source of behavior modeling is provided by the mass media. Films and television shows commonly depict violence graphically. Moreover, violence is often portrayed as acceptable, especially for heroes who never have to face legal consequences for their actions. For example, David Phillips found the homicide rate increases significantly immediately after a heavyweight championship prize fight.[158] (See the Criminological Enterprise feature titled "The Media and Violence.")

Social learning theorists have tried to determine what triggers violent acts. One position is that a direct, pain-producing physical assault will usually trigger a violent response. Yet the relationship between painful attacks and aggressive responses has been found to be inconsistent. Whether people counterattack depends, in part, on their fighting skill and their perception of the strength of their attackers. Verbal taunts and insults have also been linked to aggressive responses. People who are predisposed to aggression by their learning experiences are likely to view insults from others as a challenge to their social status and to react violently. Still another violence-triggering mechanism is a perceived reduction in one's life conditions. Prime examples of this phenomenon are riots and demonstrations in poverty-stricken ghetto areas. Studies have shown that discontent also produces aggression in the more successful members of lower-class groups, who have

been led to believe they can succeed but then have been thwarted in their aspirations. Although it is still uncertain how this relationship is constructed, it is apparently complex. No matter how deprived some individuals are, they will not resort to violence. People's perceptions of their relative deprivation have different effects on their aggressive responses.

In summary, social learning theorists say that the following four factors may contribute to violent or aggressive behavior:

1. An event that heightens arousal — such as a person's frustrating or provoking another through physical assault or verbal abuse.
2. Aggressive skills — learned aggressive responses picked up from observing others, either personally or through the media.
3. Expected outcomes — the belief that aggression will somehow be rewarded. Rewards can come in the form of reducing tension or anger, gaining some financial reward, building self-esteem, or gaining the praise of others.
4. Consistency of behavior with values — the belief, gained from observing others, that aggression is justified and appropriate, given the circumstances of the current situation.

Cognitive Theory

One area of psychology that has received increasing recognition in recent years has been **cognitive theory.** Psychologists with a cognitive perspective focus on mental processes and how people perceive and mentally represent the world around them and solve problems. The pioneers of this school were Wilhelm Wundt (1832–1920), Edward Titchener (1867–1927), and William James (1842–1920). Today there are several subdisciplines within the cognitive area. The **moral development** branch is concerned with how people morally represent and reason about the world. **Humanistic psychology** stresses self-awareness and getting in touch with feelings. **Information-processing theory** focuses on how people process, store, encode, retrieve, and manipulate information to make decisions and solve problems.

Moral and Intellectual Development Theory The moral and intellectual development branch of cognitive psychology is perhaps the most important for criminological theory. Jean Piaget (1896–1980), the founder of this approach, hypothesized that people's reasoning processes develop in an orderly fashion, beginning at birth and continuing until they are 12 years old and older.[159] At first children respond to the environment in a simple manner, seeking interesting objects and developing their reflexes. By the fourth and final stage, the formal operations stage, they have developed into mature adults who can use logic and abstract thought.

Table 6.3 Kohlberg's Stages of Development

Stage 1: Right is obedience to power and avoidance of punishment.

Stage 2: Right is taking responsibility for oneself, meeting one's own needs, and leaving to others the responsibility for themselves.

Stage 3: Right is being good in the sense of having good motives, having concern for others, and putting oneself in the other person's shoes.

Stage 4: Right is maintaining the rules of a society and serving the welfare of the group or society.

Stage 5: Right is based on recognized individual rights within a society with agreed-upon rules—a social contract.

Stage 6: Right is an assumed obligation to principles applying to all humankind—principles of justice, equality, and respect for human life.

Lawrence Kohlberg, *Stages in the Development of Moral Thought and Action* (New York: Holt, Rinehart and Winston, 1969).

Lawrence Kohlberg first applied the concept of moral development to issues in criminology.[160] He found that people travel through stages of moral development, during which their decisions and judgments on issues of right and wrong are made for different reasons. It is possible that serious offenders have a moral orientation that differs from that of law-abiding citizens. Kohlberg's stages of development are listed in Table 6.3.

Kohlberg classified people according to the stage on this continuum at which their moral development ceased to grow. Kohlberg and his associates conducted studies in which criminals were found to have significantly lower development of their moral judgment than noncriminals of the same social background.[161] Since his pioneering efforts, researchers have continued to show that criminal offenders are more likely to be classified in the lowest levels of moral reasoning (stages 1 and 2), whereas noncriminals have reached a higher stage of moral development (stages 3 and 4).[162]

Recent research indicates that the decision not to commit crimes may be influenced by one's stage of moral development. People at the lowest levels report that they are deterred from crime because of their fear of sanctions. Those in the middle consider the reactions of family and friends. Those at the highest stages refrain from crime because they believe in duty to others and universal rights.[163]

CONNECTIONS

The deterrent effect of informal sanctions and feelings of shame discussed in Chapter 5 may hinge on the level of a person's moral development. The lower one's state of moral development, the less impact informal sanctions may have; with greater moral development, informal sanctions may be better able to control crime.

Moral development theory suggests that people who obey the law simply to avoid punishment or who have outlooks mainly characterized by self-interest are more likely to commit crimes than those who view the law as something that benefits all of society. Higher stages of moral reasoning are associated with sympathy with the rights of others and conventional behaviors, such as honesty, generosity, and nonviolence.

Information Processing When cognitive theorists who study information processing try to explain antisocial behavior, they do so in terms of mental perception and how people use information to understand their environment. When people make decisions, they engage in a sequence of cognitive thought processes.

1. First they encode information so that it can be interpreted.
2. Next they search for a proper response and decide on the most appropriate action.
3. Finally, they act on their decision.[164]

According to this cognitive approach, people who use information properly, who are better conditioned to make reasoned judgments, and who can make quick and reasoned decisions when facing emotion-laden events are best able to avoid antisocial behavior choices.[165] In contrast, violence-prone people may use information incorrectly when they make decisions. One reason is that they may be relying on mental scripts learned in childhood that tell them how to interpret events, what to expect, how they should react, and what the outcome of the interaction should be.[166] Hostile children may have learned improper scripts by observing how others react to events; their own parents' aggressive, inappropriate behavior would have considerable impact. Some may have had early, prolonged exposure to violence (such as child abuse), which increases their sensitivity to slights and maltreatment. Oversensitivity to rejection by their peers is a continuation of sensitivity to rejection by their parents.[167] Violence becomes a stable behavior because the scripts that emphasize aggressive responses are repeatedly rehearsed as the child matures.

To violence-prone kids, people seem more aggressive than they actually are and intend them ill when there is no reason for alarm. According to information-processing theory, as these children mature, they use fewer cues than most people to process information. Some use violence in a calculating fashion as a means of getting what they want; others react in an overly volatile fashion to the slightest provocation. Aggressors are more likely to be vigilant, on edge, or suspicious. When they attack victims, they may believe they are defending themselves, even though they are misreading the situation.[168]

Information-processing theory has been used to explain the occurrence of date rape. Sexually violent

The Criminological Enterprise

The Media and Violence

In 1999 the influence of the media on violence became a topic of renewed interest in the aftermath of the Littleton, Colorado, school shooting. The boys involved had been fascinated by violent films and videogames. A number of national politicians called for strict controls on media violence. Former Senator Robert Dole, a critic of media violence, has said, "Those who work in Hollywood's corporate suites must also be willing to accept their share of blame. Is this how they want to make their livelihoods? Is this their contribution to society?"

Do the media influence behavior? Does broadcast violence cause aggressive behavior in viewers? This has become a hot topic because of persistent violence on television and in films. Critics have called for drastic measures ranging from banning TV violence to putting warning labels on heavy metal music because of fear that listening to hard-rock lyrics produces delinquency.

If there is, in fact, a TV–violence link, the problem is indeed alarming. Systematic TV viewing begins at age 2½ and continues at a high level during the preschool and early school years. It has been estimated that children between the ages of 2 and 5 watch TV for 27.8 hours each week; children aged 6 to 11, 24.3 hours per week; and teens, 23 hours per week. Marketing research indicates that adolescents aged 11 to 14 rent more violent horror movies than any other age group. Children this age use older peers and siblings and apathetic parents to gain access to R-rated films. More than 40 percent of U.S. households now have cable TV, which features violent films and shows. Even children's programming is saturated with violence.

The fact that children watch so much violent TV is not surprising considering the 1995 findings of a well-publicized UCLA study. These researchers found that at least 10 network shows made heavy use of violence. Of the 161 television movies monitored (every one that aired that season), 23 raised concerns about their use of violence, violent themes, violent titles, or inappropriate portrayals of a scene. Of the 118 theatrical films monitored (every one that aired that season), 50 raised concerns about their use of violence.

On-air promotions also reflect a continuing, if not worsening, problem. Some series may contain several scenes of violence, each of which is appropriate within its context. An advertisement for that show, however, may feature only those violent scenes without any of the context. Even some children's programming features "sinister combat" as the theme of the show. The characters are usually happy to fight and frequently do so with little provocation. A University of Pennsylvania study found that children's programming contains an average of 32 violent acts per hour, that 56 percent have violent characters, and that 74 percent have characters who become the victims of violence (though "only 3.3 percent have characters who are actually killed"). In all, the average child views 8,000 TV murders before finishing elementary school.

Numerous anecdotal cases of violence have been linked to TV and films:

- In 1974 a 9-year-old California girl was raped with a bottle by four other girls who said they had watched a similar act in the television movie *Born Innocent,* which depicted life in a girls' reformatory. Her parents' lawsuit against NBC, the network that broadcast the film, was dismissed in court.
- In 1977 Ronald Zamora killed an elderly woman and then pleaded guilty by reason of insanity. His attorney claimed Zamora was addicted to TV violence and could no longer differentiate between reality and fantasy; the jury did not accept the defense and found Zamora guilty as charged.
- At least 43 deaths have been linked to the movie *The Deer Hunter,* which features a scene in which a main character kills himself while playing Russian roulette for money.
- In a famous incident, John Hinckley shot President Ronald Reagan due to his obsession with actress Jodie Foster, which developed after he watched her play a prostitute in the film *Taxi Driver.* Hinckley viewed the film at least 15 times.
- On October 1993 a 5-year-old Ohio boy set a fire that killed his 2-year-old sister. The boy's mother charged that the youth was influenced by the MTV show *Beavis and Butthead,* whose cartoon heroes regularly start fires and chant "fire is good." MTV responded to the public outcry over the incident by moving the show's broadcast time from 7 P.M. to 10:30 P.M.

Psychologists believe that media violence does not in itself *cause* violent behavior; if it did, there would be millions of daily incidents in which viewers imitated the aggression they watched on TV or movies. But most psychologists agree that media violence *contributes* to aggression. There are several explanations for the effects of television and film violence on behavior:

- Media violence can provide aggressive scripts that children store in memory. Repeated exposure to these scripts can increase their retention and change attitudes.
- Children learn from what they observe. In the same way they learn cognitive and social skills from their parents and friends, children learn to be violent by watching television.
- Television violence increases the arousal levels of viewers and makes them more prone to act aggressively. Studies measuring the galvanic skin response of subjects—a physical indication of arousal based on the amount of electricity conducted across the palm of the hand—show that viewing violent television shows increases arousal levels in young children.
- Watching television violence promotes negative attitudes such as suspiciousness and the expectation that the viewer will become involved in violence. Those who watch television frequently view aggression and violence as common, socially acceptable behavior.
- Television violence allows aggressive youths to justify their behav-

ior. Instead of causing violence, television may help violent youths rationalize their behavior as a socially acceptable activity.

- Television violence may disinhibit aggressive behavior, which is normally controlled by other learning processes. **Disinhibition** takes place when adults are viewed as being rewarded for violence and when violence is seen as socially acceptable. This contradicts previous learning experiences in which violent behavior was viewed as wrong.

Such distinguished bodies as the American Psychological Association, the National Institute of Mental Health, and the National Research Council support the TV–violence link. They base their conclusion on research showing that watching TV violence increases levels of violence in laboratory settings as well as in natural settings.

A number of experimental approaches have been used. Some of these include

- Exposing groups of subjects to violent TV shows in a laboratory setting, then monitoring their behavior afterward compared to control groups who viewed nonviolent programming.
- Observing subjects in playgrounds, athletic fields, and residences after they have been exposed to violent television programs.
- Requiring subjects to answer attitude surveys after watching violent TV shows.
- Using aggregate measures of TV viewing; for example, tracking the number of violent TV shows on the air during a given time period and comparing these figures to crime rates during the same period.

Most evaluations of experimental data indicate that watching violence on TV is correlated to aggressive behaviors or at least has a short-term impact on behavior. Subjects who view violent TV shows are likely to exhibit aggressive behavior almost immediately.

A number of critics argue that the evidence simply does not support the claim that watching TV or movies and listening to heavy metal music are related to antisocial behavior. Criminologist Simon Singer found that

teenaged heavy metal fans were no more delinquent than nonlisteners. Candace Kruttschnitt and her associates found that an individual's exposure to violent TV shows is only weakly related to subsequent violent behavior. There is also little evidence that areas with the highest levels of violent TV viewing have above-normal rates of violent crime. Millions of children watch violence every night but do not become violent criminals. If violent TV shows cause interpersonal violence, there should be few ecological and regional patterns in the crime rate, of which there are many. Put another way, how can regional differences in rates of violence be explained when people all across the nation watch the same TV shows and films?

In the end, experiments that show a correlation between aggression and TV fail to link the association with actual criminal behaviors, such as rape or assault. The weight of the experimental results, then, indicates that violent media immediately impact people with a preexisting tendency toward crime and violence.

Considering the evidence, should violent TV shows be curtailed or controlled? One answer would be to have government regulators limit the content of programs or restrict times that violent shows may be aired (presumably, as in the *Beavis and Butthead* case, after adolescent bedtimes). As a consequence of the UCLA survey, the TV industry has joined with the film industry to place advisory warnings (like PG-13) on shows that have objectionable content. Although such practices may help guide some parents, they do little to restrict TV watching when children are home alone (although it may soon be possible to equip television sets with computer chips that prevent the reception of shows designated as having violent themes). Critics charge that such policies run afoul of First Amendment guarantees of free speech; who is to say when a TV show is too violent?

CRITICAL THINKING

1. Should the government control the content of TV shows and limit the amount of broadcast violence? How could the national news be shown if violence were omitted? What

about boxing matches or hockey games?

2. How can we explain the fact that millions of kids watch violent TV shows and remain nonviolent? If there is a TV–violence link, how can we explain the fact that violence rates may have been higher in the "Old West" than they are today? Do you think violent gang kids stay home and watch TV shows?

 INFOTRAC COLLEGE EDITION RESEARCH

For a different take on the effects of viewing TV violence, see:
David Link. Facts about fiction: in defense of TV violence. *Reason,* March 1994 v25 n10 p22.
Mike Males. Who us? Stop blaming kids and TV. *The Progressive,* Oct 1997 v61 n10 p25(3)

Source: UCLA Center for Communication Policy, *Television Violence Monitoring Project* (Los Angeles, 1995); Associated Press, "Hollywood Is Blamed in Token Booth Attack," *Boston Globe,* 28 November 1995, p. 30; Garland White, Janet Katz, and Kathryn Scarborough, "The Impact of Professional Football Games upon Violent Assaults on Women," *Violence and Victims* 7 (1992): 157–71; Simon Singer, "Rethinking Subcultural Theories of Delinquency and the Cultural Resources of Youth" (paper presented at the annual meeting of the American Society of Criminology, Phoenix, Arizona, November 1993); Albert Reiss and Jeffrey Roth, eds., *Understanding and Preventing Violence* (Washington, D.C.: National Academy Press, 1993); Reuters, "Seventy-nine Percent in Survey Link Violence on TV and Crime," *Boston Globe,* 19 December 1993, p. 17; Scott Snyder, "Movies and Juvenile Delinquency: An Overview," *Adolescence* 26 (1991): 121–31; Steven Messner, "Television Violence and Violent Crime: An Aggregate Analysis," *Social Problems* 33 (1986): 218–35; Candace Kruttschnitt, Linda Heath, and David Ward, "Family Violence, Television Viewing Habits, and Other Adolescent Experiences Related to Violent Criminal Behavior," *Criminology* 243 (1986): 235–67; Jonathan Freedman, "Television Violence and Aggression: A Rejoinder," *Psychological Bulletin* 100 (1986): 372–78; Wendy Wood, Frank Wong, and J. Gregory Chachere, "Effects of Media Violence on Viewers' Aggression in Unconstrained Social Interaction," *Psychological Bulletin* 109 (1991): 371–83.

males believe that when their dates refuse sexual advances, the women are really playing games and actually want to be taken forcefully.[169]

Treatment based on how people process information takes into account that people are more likely to respond aggressively to provocation if thoughts intensify the insult or otherwise stir feelings of anger. Cognitive therapists attempt to teach explosive people to control aggressive impulses by viewing social provocations as problems demanding a solution rather than retaliation. Programs are aimed at teaching problem-solving skills that may include self-disclosure, role-playing, listening, following instructions, joining in, and using self-control.[170] Therapeutic interventions designed to make people better problem solvers may involve measures that enhance

- Coping and problem-solving skills.
- Relationships with peers, parents, and other adults.
- Conflict resolution and communication skills, and methods for resisting peer pressure related to drug use and violence.
- Consequential thinking and decision-making abilities.
- Prosocial behaviors, including cooperation with others, self-responsibility, respecting others, and public speaking efficacy.
- Empathy.[171]

Treatment interventions based on learning social skills are relatively new, but there are some indications that this approach can have long-term benefits for reducing criminal behavior.[172]

Crime and Mental Illness

The nation was shocked on March 24, 1998, when a 13-year-old boy, who had vowed to kill all the girls who had broken up with him, and his 11-year-old cousin opened fire on students outside a middle school in Jonesboro, Arkansas, killing four girls and a teacher and wounding 11 other people.[173] The two boys, dressed in camouflage clothing, lay in wait in a wooded area near the school after setting off a fire alarm, forcing students and faculty members outside. Similar school shootings in the past few years have included well-publicized incidents in West Paducah, Kentucky, Pearl, Mississippi, and Littleton, Colorado.

Cases such as these, in which an obviously disturbed person commits an unfathomable violent act, suggest a linkage between mental illness and crime. Although the association appears clear-cut, empirical evidence has been contradictory. Many early research efforts found that offenders who engage in serious, violent crimes suffer from some sort of mental disturbance. Juvenile murderers have been clinically diagnosed as "overtly hostile," "explosive or volatile," "anxious," and "depressed."[174] Studies of adolescent males accused of murder found that 75 percent could be classified as having some mental illness, including schizophrenia.[175] Abusive mothers have been found to have mood and personality disorders and a history of psychiatric diagnoses.[176] Reported substance abuse among the mentally ill is also significantly higher than that of the general population.[177] The diagnosed mentally ill appear in arrest and court statistics at a rate disproportionate to their presence in the population.[178]

Is the Link Valid? Despite this evidence, questions remain as to whether the mentally ill population has a greater inclination toward criminal behavior than the mentally sound. The mentally ill may in fact be more likely to withdraw or harm themselves than to act aggressively toward others.[179] Research shows that after release, prisoners who have prior histories of hospitalization for mental disorders are less likely to be rearrested than those who have never been hospitalized.[180] Research also shows that mentally disordered inmates who recidivate after release appear to do so for the same reasons as the mentally sound: extensive criminal histories, substance abuse, or family dysfunction.[181] Even research that finds a mental illness–crime association indicates that the great majority of known criminals are not mentally ill and that the relationship is at best modest. And if there is a statistically significant association between mental illness and crime, the fact remains that most mentally ill people are not criminals.

Although research efforts only tentatively support the proposition that mental disturbance or illness can cause violent crime, it is still possible that some link exists. Existing data suggest that certain *symptoms* of mental illness are connected to violence: for example, the feeling that others wish the person harm, or that the person's mind is dominated by forces beyond his or her control, or that thoughts are being put into the person's head by others.[182] It is also likely that people suffering from other psychological disorders, such as substance abuse, psychopathy (discussed in the Criminological Enterprise feature titled "The Antisocial Personality"), and neuroticism, rather than mental illnesses such as schizophrenia, are most at risk for chronic criminal behavior.[183] Currently, major assessments and research studies are ongoing; results should soon determine the true link between mental illness and crime.[184]

Personality and Crime

Personality can be defined as the reasonably stable patterns of behavior, including thoughts and emotions, that distinguish one person from another.[185] One's personality reflects a characteristic way of adapting to life's demands and problems. The way we behave is a function of how our personality enables us to interpret life events and make appropriate behavioral choices. Can the cause of crime be linked to personality? This issue has always caused significant debate.[186] Sheldon Glueck and Eleanor Glueck have identified a number of personality traits that they believe characterize antisocial youth:

Self-assertiveness	Sadism
Defiance	Lack of concern for others
Extroversion	Feeling unappreciated
Ambivalence	Distrust of authority
Impulsiveness	Poor personal skills
Narcissism	Mental instability
Suspicion	Hostility
Destructiveness	Resentment[187]

CONNECTIONS

The Glueck research represents the view that antisocial people maintain a distinct set of personal traits that makes them particularly sensitive to environmental stimuli. This view was once dismissed by mainstream criminologists; but Chapter 10's section on life-course theories shows how the Gluecks' views still influence contemporary criminological theory.

Several other research efforts have attempted to identify criminal personality traits.[188] For example, Hans Eysenck associates two personality traits with antisocial behavior: *extraversion-introversion* and *stability-instability*. Extreme introverts are overaroused and avoid sources of stimulation, while in contrast, extreme extroverts are unaroused and seek sensation. Introverts are slow to learn and be conditioned; extroverts are impulsive individuals who lack the ability to examine their own motives and behaviors. Those who are unstable, a condition that Eysenck calls *neuroticism*, are anxious, tense, and emotionally unstable.[189] People who are both neurotic and extroverted lack self-insight and are impulsive and emotionally unstable; they are unlikely to have reasoned judgments of life events. Whereas extroverted neurotics may act self-destructively, for example, by abusing drugs, more stable people will be able to reason that such behavior is ultimately harmful. Eysenck believes that personality is controlled by genetic factors and is heritable.

Sociopathy A number of other personality deficits have been identified in the criminal population. A common theme is that criminals are hyperactive, impulsive individuals with short attention spans (attention deficit disorder), conduct disorders, anxiety disorders, and depression.[190] These traits make them prone to problems ranging from psychopathology to drug abuse, sexual promiscuity, and violence.[191] As a group, people who share these traits are believed to have a character defect referred to as *antisocial, sociopathic,* or *psychopathic personality*. Although these terms are often used interchangeably, some psychologists distinguish between

sociopaths and psychopaths by suggesting that the former are a product of a destructive home environment, whereas the latter are a product of a defect or aberration within themselves.[192]

Research on Personality Because deviant personality has been related to crime and delinquency, numerous attempts have been made to devise accurate measures of personality and determine whether they can predict antisocial behavior. Two types of standardized personality tests have been constructed. *Projective techniques* require a subject to react to an ambiguous picture or shape by describing what it represents or by telling a story about it. The **Rorschach Inkblot Test** and the **Thematic Apperception Test** are examples of two widely used projective tests, which are administered by clinicians trained to interpret responses and categorize them according to established behavioral patterns.

The second method of psychological testing is the *personality inventory,* which requires subjects to agree or disagree with groups of questions in a self-administered survey. One widely used psychological test is the **Minnesota Multiphasic Personality Inventory,** commonly called the **MMPI.** Developed by R. Starke Hathaway and J. Charnley McKinley, the MMPI has subscales that purport to measure many different personality traits, including psychopathic deviation (Pd scale), schizophrenia (Sc), and hypomania (Ma).[193] Elio Monachesi and Hathaway pioneered the use of the MMPI to predict criminal behavior. They concluded that scores on some of the MMPI scales, especially the Pd scale, significantly predict delinquency. In one major effort, they administered the MMPI to a sample of ninth-grade boys and girls in Minneapolis and found that Pd scores had a significant relationship to later delinquent involvement. Other research studies have detected an association between scores on the Pd scale and criminal involvement.[194] Another personality test, the **California Personality Inventory (CPI),** has also been used to distinguish deviants from nondeviant groups.[195]

Despite the time and energy put into using the MMPI and other scales to predict crime and delinquency, the results have proved inconclusive.[196] Although some law violators may have abnormal personality structure, many more have personalities indistinguishable from the norm. Efforts to improve the MMPI have resulted in the MMPI-2, a new scale with, it is hoped, improved validity; current research efforts should determine whether this version can successfully identify the potential for crime and violence.[197]

Are Some People Crime-Prone? Interest in criminal personality characteristics has been increasing. Because the most commonly used tests, such as the CPI and MMPI, have not been uniformly successful in predicting criminality, psychologists have turned to other measures, including the **Multidimensional Personality**

The Criminological Enterprise

The Antisocial Personality

Some violent offenders may have a disturbed character structure commonly called *psychopathy, sociopathy,* or *antisocial personality.* **Psychopaths** exhibit a low level of guilt and anxiety and persistently violate the rights of others. Although they may exhibit superficial charm and above-average intelligence, this often masks a disturbed personality that makes them incapable of forming enduring relationships with others and continually involves them in such deviant behaviors as violence, risk taking, substance abuse, and impulsivity.

From an early age, many psychopaths have had home lives that were filled with frustrations, bitterness, and quarreling. That instability and frustration helps form unreliable, unstable, demanding, and egocentric personalities. Most psychopaths are risk-taking sensation seekers who are constantly involved in antisocial behavior. They are often described as grandiose, egocentric, manipulative, forceful, and coldhearted, with shallow emotions and the inability to feel remorse, empathy with others, or anxiety over their misdeeds.

Hervey Cleckley, a leading authority on psychopathy, describes them as follows:

> [Psychopaths are] chronically antisocial individuals who are always in trouble, profiting neither from experience nor punishment, and maintaining no real loyalties to any person, group, or code. They are frequently callous and hedonistic, showing marked emotional immaturity, with lack of responsibility, lack of judgment and an ability to rationalize their behavior so that it appears warranted, reasonable and justified.

Considering these personality traits, it is not surprising that research shows that people evaluated as psychopaths are significantly more prone to criminal and violent behavior than nonpsychopathic control groups. Psychopaths tend to continue their criminal careers long after other offenders age out of crime. They are continually in trouble with the law and therefore are likely to wind up in penal institutions. Criminologists estimate that 10 percent or more of all prison inmates display psychopathic tendencies.

Although psychologists are still not certain of psychopathy's cause, a number of factors are believed to contribute to its development. Some focus on family experiences, suggesting that the influence of an unstable parent, parental rejection, lack of love during childhood, and inconsistent discipline may be related to psychopathy. Children who lack the opportunity to form an attachment to a mother figure in the first three years of life, who suffer sudden separation from the mother figure, or who see changes in the mother figure are most likely to develop psychopathic personalities.

Psychopathy may also be related to personal experiences. Donald Lynam finds that ADHD children are more likely to suffer from conduct problems in childhood, and as they mature, they fall prey to a serious form of conduct disorder he labels **fledgling psychopathy.** This condition is, in turn, highly associated with chronic offending.

Psychopaths may also suffer from lower-than-normal levels of arousal. Research studies have revealed that psychopaths have lower skin conductance levels and fewer spontaneous responses than normal subjects. This finding may indicate a link between psychopathy and autonomic nervous system (ANS) dysfunction. The ANS mediates physiological activities associated with emotions and is manifested in such measurements as pulse, blood pressure, respiration, muscle tension, papillary size, and electrical activity of the skin (*galvanic skin resistance*).

Another view is that psychopathy is caused by a dysfunction of the limbic inhibitory system manifested through damage to the frontal and temporal lobes of the brain. Consequently, psychopaths may need extra

---

Questionnaire (MPQ), to assess such personality traits as control, aggression, alienation, and well-being. Research by Avshalom Caspi and his associates finds that MPQ scales can produce "robust personality correlates of delinquency" and that these measures are valid across genders, races, and cultures.[198] The Caspi research indicates that adolescent offenders who are crime-prone respond to frustrating events with strong negative emotions, feel stressed and harassed, and are adversarial in their interpersonal relationships. Crime-prone people maintain "negative emotionality"—a tendency to experience aversive affective states such as anger, anxiety, and irritability. They also are predisposed to weak personal constraints and have difficulty controlling impulsive behavior urges. Because they are both impulsive and aggressive, crime-prone people are quick to act against perceived threats.

Evidence that personality traits predict crime and violence suggests that the root cause of crime can be found in the forces that influence early human development. If these results are valid, rather than focus on job creation and neighborhood improvement, crime control efforts might be better focused on helping families raise reasoned, reflective children who enjoy a safe environment.

Intelligence and Crime

Early criminologists maintained that many delinquents and criminals have below-average intelligence and that low IQ causes their criminality. Criminals were be-stimulation to bring them up to comfortable levels (similar to arousal theory). The desire for this stimulation may originate in their physical differences. Psychologists have attempted to treat patients diagnosed as psychopaths by giving them adrenaline, which increases their arousal levels.

Psychologist David Lykken suggests that psychopaths have an inherited "low fear quotient," which inhibits their fear of punishment. All people have a natural fear of certain stimuli, such as spiders, snakes, fires, or strangers. Psychopaths, as a rule, have few fears. Normal socialization processes punish antisocial behavior to inhibit future transgressions. Someone who does not fear punishment is harder to socialize.

Psychopaths may also be less capable of regulating their activities than other people. Nonpsychopaths may become anxious when facing the prospect of committing a criminal act, but psychopaths in the same circumstances feel no such fear. Ogloff and Wong conclude that their reduced anxiety levels result in more impulsive, inappropriate behaviors and in deviant behavior, apprehension, and incarceration.

The antisocial personality concept seems to agree with what is known about chronic offending. In a recent paper, Lawrence Cohen and Bryan Vila argue that chronic offending should be conceived as a continuum of behavior, at the apex of which lie the most dangerous, predatory criminals. As many as 80 percent of these high-end chronic offenders exhibit sociopathic behavior patterns. Although they comprise about 4 percent of the total male population and less than 1 percent of the total female population, they are responsible for half of all serious felony offenses. Although not all high-rate chronic offenders are sociopaths, there are enough to support a strong link between personality dysfunction and long-term criminal careers.

CRITICAL THINKING

1. Should people diagnosed as psychopaths be separated and treated even if they have not yet committed a crime?
2. Should psychopathic murderers be spared the death penalty because they cannot control their behavior?

 INFOTRAC COLLEGE EDITION RESEARCH

To read more about the development of psychopathology, see: John V. Lavigne, Richard Arend, Diane Rosenbaum, Helen J. Binns, Katherine Kaufer Christoffel, Andrew Burns, Andrew Smith. Mental health service use among young children receiving pediatric primary care. *Research Journal of the American Academy of Child and Adolescent Psychiatry*, Nov 1998 v37 n11 p1175. Shirley Feldman, Jaime Waterman, Hans Steiner, Elizabeth Cauffman. Posttraumatic stress disorder among female juvenile offenders. *Journal of*

the American Academy of Child and Adolescent Psychiatry, Nov 1998 v37 n11 p1209(8)

Source: David Lykken, "Psychopathy, Sociopathy, and Crime," *Society* 34 (1996): 30–38; Lawrence Cohen and Bryan Vila, "Self-Control and Social Control: An Exposition of the Gottfredson-Hirschi/Sampson-Laub Debate," *Studies on Crime and Crime Prevention* 5 (1996): 31–58; Donald Lynam, "Early Identification of Chronic Offenders: Who Is the Fledgling Psychopath?" *Psychological Bulletin* 120 (1996): 209–234; James Ogloff and Stephen Wong, "Electrodermal and Cardiovascular Evidence of a Coping Response in Psychopaths," *Criminal Justice and Behavior* 17 (1990): 231–45; Laurie Frost, Terrie Moffitt, and Rob McGee, "Neuropsychological Correlates of Psychopathology in an Unselected Cohort of Young Adolescents," *Journal of Abnormal Psychology* 98 (1989): 307–313; Hervey Cleckley, "Psychopathic States," in *American Handbook of Psychiatry*, ed. S. Aneti (New York: Basic Books, 1959), pp. 567–69; Spencer Rathus and Jeffrey Nevid, *Abnormal Psychology* (Englewood Cliffs, N.J.: Prentice-Hall, 1991), pp. 310–16; Helene Raskin White, Erich Labouvie, and Marsha Bates, "The Relationship Between Sensation Seeking and Delinquency: A Longitudinal Analysis," *Journal of Research in Crime and Delinquency* 22 (1985): 197–211.

lieved to have inherently substandard intelligence and thus seemed naturally inclined to commit more crimes than more intelligent persons. Furthermore, it was thought that if authorities could determine which individuals had low IQs, they might identify potential criminals before they committed socially harmful acts.

Because social scientists had a captive group of subjects in juvenile training schools and penal institutions, they began to measure the correlation between IQ and crime by testing adjudicated offenders. Thus inmates of penal institutions were used as a test group around which numerous theories about intelligence were built, leading ultimately to the nature-versus-nurture controversy that is still raging. These concepts are discussed in some detail in the following sections.

Nature Theory Nature theory argues that intelligence is largely determined genetically, that ancestry determines IQ, and that low intelligence, as demonstrated by low IQ, is linked to criminal behavior. When newly developed IQ tests were administered to inmates of prisons and juvenile training schools in the first decades of the century, the nature position gained support because most of the inmates scored low on the tests. During his studies in 1920, Henry Goddard found that many institutionalized persons were what he considered "feeble-minded"; he concluded that at least half of all juvenile delinquents were mental defectives.[199] In 1926 William Healy and Augusta Bronner tested groups of delinquent boys in Chicago and Boston and found that 37 percent were subnormal in intelligence. They concluded that delinquents were 5 to 10 times more likely to be mentally deficient than normal boys.[200] These and other early studies were embraced as proof that low IQ scores indicated potentially delinquent children and that a correlation existed between innate low intelligence and deviant behavior. IQ tests were believed to measure the inborn genetic makeup of individuals, and many criminologists accepted the idea that individuals with substandard IQs were predisposed toward delinquency and adult criminality.

Nurture Theory The rise of culturally sensitive explanations of human behavior in the 1930s led to the nurture school of intelligence, a theory stating that intelligence must be viewed as partly biological but primarily sociological. Nurture theorists discredited the notion that persons commit crimes because they have low IQs. Instead, they postulated that environmental stimulation from parents, relatives, social contacts, schools, peer groups, and innumerable others create a child's IQ level and that low IQs result from an environment that also encourages delinquent and criminal behavior. Thus, if low IQ scores are recorded among criminals, these scores may reflect the criminals' cultural background, not their mental ability.

Studies challenging the assumption that people automatically commit criminal acts because they have below-average IQs began to appear as early as the 1920s. John Slawson studied 1,543 delinquent boys in New York institutions and compared them with a control group of New York City boys in 1926.[201] Slawson found that although 80 percent of the delinquents achieved lower scores in abstract verbal intelligence, delinquents were about normal in mechanical aptitude and nonverbal intelligence. These results indicated the possibility of cultural bias in portions of the IQ tests. He also found no relationship between the number of arrests, the types of offenses, and IQ.

In 1931 Edwin Sutherland evaluated IQ studies of criminals and delinquents and noted significant variation in the findings, which disproved Goddard's notion that criminals are feebleminded.[202] Goddard attributed discrepancies to testing and scoring methods rather than differences in the mental ability of criminals. However, Sutherland's research all but put an end to the belief that crime was caused by feeblemindedness; the IQ–crime link was almost forgotten in criminological literature.

IQ and Criminality Although the alleged IQ–crime link was dismissed by mainstream criminologists, it once again became an important area of study when respected criminologists Travis Hirschi and Michael Hindelang published a widely read 1977 article linking the two variables.[203] After reexamining existing research data, Hirschi and Hindelang concluded that "the weight of evidence is that IQ is more important than race and social class" for predicting criminal and delinquent involvement. Rejecting the notion that IQ tests are race- and class-biased, they concluded that major differences exist between criminals and noncriminals within similar racial and socioeconomic class categories. They proposed the idea that low IQ increases the likelihood of criminal behavior through its effect on school performance. That is, youths with low IQs do poorly in school, and school failure and academic incompetence are highly related to delinquency and later to adult criminality.

Hirschi and Hindelang's inferences have been supported by both U.S. and international research.[204] Some studies have found a direct IQ–delinquency link among samples of adolescent boys.[205] In their influential book *Crime and Human Nature*, James Q. Wilson and Richard Herrnstein also agreed that the IQ–crime link is indirect: low intelligence leads to poor school performance, which enhances the chances of criminality.[206] They conclude, "A child who chronically loses standing in the competition of the classroom may feel justified in settling the score outside, by violence, theft, and other forms of defiant illegality."[207]

Cross-National Studies The IQ–crime relationship has also been tested in cross-national studies. A significant relationship between low IQ and delinquency has been found among samples of youth in Denmark. Researchers found that Danish children with low IQ tended to become delinquent because their poor verbal ability was a handicap in the school environment.[208] Research by Canadian neural-psychologist Lorne Yeudall and his associates found samples of delinquents possessed IQs about 20 points lower than nondelinquent control groups on one of the standard IQ tests, the **Wechsler Adult Intelligence Scale**.[209] An IQ–crime link was also found in a longitudinal study of Swedish youth; low IQ measured at age 3 significantly predicted later criminality.[210]

IQ and Crime Reconsidered Although the Hirschi and Hindelang research increased interest and research on the association between IQ and crime, the issue is far from settled and is still a matter of debate. A number of recent studies have found that IQ has negligible influence on criminal behavior.[211] Also, a recent evaluation of research on intelligence conducted by the American Psychological Association concluded that the strength of an IQ–crime link was "very low."[212]

In contrast, *The Bell Curve*, Richard Herrnstein and Charles Murray's influential but controversial book on intelligence, firmly advocates an IQ–crime link. Their extensive review of the available literature shows that

Is it nature or nurture? Even if some aspects of intelligence are inherited, there seems little question that those children who are raised in an environment lacking in economic resources and parental support will fail to maximize their intellectual potential. The mother shown here is going to college while on welfare in order to better support herself and child. Is it the responsibility of society to provide resources sufficient to enable all American youth to achieve their rightful share of intellectual development?

adolescents with low IQ are more likely to commit crime, get caught, and be sent to prison. Conversely, at-risk kids with higher IQs seem to be protected from becoming criminals by their superior ability to succeed in school and in social relationships. Herrnstein and Murray conclude that criminal offenders have an average IQ of 92, about 8 points below the mean; chronic offenders score even lower than the average criminal. To those who suggest that the IQ–crime relationship can be explained by the fact that only low-IQ criminals get caught, they counter with data showing little difference in IQ scores between self-reported and official criminals.[213] This means that even criminals whose activities go undetected have lower IQs than the general public; the IQ–crime relationship cannot be explained away by the fact that slow-witted criminals are the ones most likely to be apprehended.

It is unlikely that the IQ–criminality debate will be settled soon. Measurement is beset by many methodological problems. The well-documented criticisms suggesting that IQ tests are race- and class-biased would certainly influence the testing of the criminal population, which is besieged with a multitude of social and economic problems. Even if it can be shown that known offenders have lower IQs than the general population, it is difficult to explain many patterns in the crime rate: Why are there more male than female criminals? Why do crime rates vary by region, time of year, and even weather patterns? Why does aging out occur? IQs do not increase with age, so why should crime rates fall?

SOCIAL POLICY IMPLICATIONS

For most of the twentieth century, biological and psychological views of criminality have influenced crime control and prevention policy. The result has been front-end or primary prevention programs that seek to treat personal problems before they manifest themselves as crime. To this end, there are thousands of family therapy organizations, substance abuse clinics, mental health associations, and so on operating around the United States. Teachers, employers, courts, welfare agencies, and others make referrals to these facilities. These services are based on the premise that if a person's problems can be treated before they become overwhelming, some future crimes will be prevented. Secondary prevention programs provide treatment such as psychological counseling to youths and adults after they have violated the law. Attendance in such programs may be a requirement of a probation order, part of a diversionary sentence, or aftercare at the end of a prison sentence.

Biologically oriented therapy is also being used in the criminal justice system. Programs have altered diets, changed lighting, compensated for learning disabilities, treated allergies, and so on.[214] What is more controversial has been the use of mood-altering chemicals, such as lithium, pemoline, imipramine, phenytoin, and benzodiazepines, to control behavior. Another practice that has elicited concern is the use of psychosurgery (brain surgery) to control antisocial behavior: surgical

Table 6.4 Biological and Psychological Theories

THEORY	MAJOR PREMISE	STRENGTHS
Biosocial		
Biochemical	Crime, especially violence, is a function of diet, vitamin intake, hormonal imbalance, or food allergies.	Explains irrational violence. Shows how the environment interacts with personal traits to influence behavior.
Neurological	Criminals and delinquents often suffer brain impairment, as measured by the EEG. Attention deficit/hyperactivity disorder and minimal brain dysfunction are related to antisocial behavior.	Explains irrational violence. Shows how the environment interacts with personal traits to influence behavior.
Genetic	Criminal traits and predispositions are inherited. The criminality of parents can predict the delinquency of children.	Explains why only a small percentage of youth in a high-crime area become chronic offenders.
Evolutionary	As the human race evolved, traits and characteristics have become ingrained. Some of these traits make people aggressive and predisposed to commit crime.	Explains high violence rates and aggregate gender differences in the crime rate.
Psychological		
Psychodynamic	The development of the unconscious personality early in childhood influences behavior for the rest of a person's life. Criminals have weak egos and damaged personalities.	Explains the onset of crime and why crime and drug abuse cut across class lines.
Behavioral	People commit crime when they model their behavior after others they see being rewarded for the same acts. Behavior is reinforced by rewards and extinguished by punishment.	Explains the role of significant others in the crime process. Shows how family life and media can influence crime and violence.
Cognitive	Individual reasoning processes influence behavior. Reasoning is influenced by the way people perceive their environment and by their moral and intellectual development.	Shows why criminal behavior patterns change over time as people mature and develop their moral reasoning. May explain the aging-out process.

procedures have been used to alter the brain structure of convicted sex offenders in an effort to eliminate or control their sex drives. Results are still preliminary, but some critics argue that these procedures are without scientific merit.[215]

Some criminologists view biologically oriented treatments as a key to solving the problem of the chronic offender. The biological analysis of criminal traits could pave the way for developing preventive measures, regardless of whether criminal traits are inherited or acquired. A number of inherited physical traits that cause disease have been successfully treated with medication after their genetic code has been broken; a similar method may genetically solve crime.[216]

Although such biological treatment is relatively new, it has become common since the 1920s to offer psychological treatment to offenders before, during, and after a criminal conviction. For example, beginning in the 1970s, pretrial programs have sought to divert offenders into nonpunitive rehabilitative programs designed to treat rather than punish them. Based on some type of counseling regimen, diversion programs are commonly used with first or nonviolent offenders. At the trial stage, judges often order psychological profiles of convicted offenders for planning treatment. Should they be kept in the community? Do they need more secure confinement? If correctional confinement is called for, inmates are commonly evaluated at a correctional center to measure their personality traits or disorders. Correctional facilities almost universally require inmates to partake in some form of psychological therapy. Parole decisions may be influenced by the prison psychologist's evaluation of the offender's adjustment.

CONNECTIONS

The law recognizes the psychological aspects of crime when it permits the insanity plea as an excuse for criminal liability or when it allows trial delay because of mental incompetence. See Chapter 2 for more about the insanity defense.

SUMMARY

The earliest positivist criminologists were biologists. Led by Cesare Lombroso, these early researchers believed some people manifested primitive traits that made them born criminals. Today their research is debunked because of poor methodology, testing, and logic. Biological views fell out of favor in the early twentieth century. In the 1970s, spurred by the publication of Edmund O. Wilson's *Sociobiology,* several criminologists again turned to study of the biological basis of criminality. For the most part, the effort has focused on the cause of violent crime. Interest has centered on several areas: (1) biochemical factors, such as diet, allergies, hormonal imbalances, and environmental contaminants (like lead); (2) neurophysiological factors, such as brain disorders, EEG abnormalities, tumors, and head injuries; and (3) genetic factors, such as the XYY syndrome and inherited traits. An evolutionary branch holds that changes in the human condition, which have taken millions of years to evolve, may help explain crime rate differences.

Psychological attempts to explain criminal behavior have historical roots in Maudsley's concept that all criminals are insane or mentally damaged. This position is no longer accepted. Today there are three main psychological perspectives: the psychodynamic view, the cognitive view, and the social learning perspective. The psychodynamic view, created by Sigmund Freud, links aggressive behavior to personality conflicts developed in childhood. According to some psychoanalysts, psychotics are aggressive, unstable people who can easily become involved in crime. Cognitive psychology is concerned with human development and how people perceive the world. Criminality is viewed as a function of improper information processing or moral development. In contrast, behavioral and social learning theorists see criminality as a learned behavior. Children who are exposed to violence and see it rewarded may become violent as adults.

Psychological traits such as personality and intelligence have been linked to criminality. One important area of study has been the psychopath, a person who lacks emotion and concern for others. The controversial issue of the relationship of IQ to criminality has been resurrected once again with the publication of research studies purporting to show that criminals have lower IQs than noncriminals. Psychologists have developed standardized tests with which to measure personality traits. One avenue of research has been to determine whether criminals and noncriminals manifest any differences in their responses to test items.

Table 6.4 summarizes the biological and psychological trait theories that have been discussed in this chapter.

 See the book-specific web site at www.cj.wadsworth. com for additional chapter links, discussions, and quizzes.

THINKING LIKE A CRIMINOLOGIST

The American Psychiatric Association believes that a person should not be held legally responsible for a crime if their behavior meets the following standard developed by legal expert Richard Bonnie:

A person charged with a criminal offense should be found not guilty by reason of insanity if it is shown that as a result of mental disease or mental retardation he was unable to appreciate the wrongfulness of his conduct at the time of the offense.

As used in this standard, the terms *mental disease* or *mental retardation* include only those severely abnormal mental conditions that grossly and demonstrably impair a person's perception or understanding of reality and that are not attributable primarily to the voluntary ingestion of alcohol or other psychoactive substances.

As a criminologist who has expertise in trait theories of crime, do you agree with Bonnie's standard? What modifications, if any, might you make in order to include other categories of offenders who are not excused by this definition?

KEY TERMS

trait theories
inheritance school
somatotype
biophobia
sociobiology
reciprocal altruism
biosocial
biocriminologist
equipotentiality
Wernicke-Korsakoff disease
hypoglycemia
androgens
testosterone

neocortex
premenstrual syndrome (PMS)
cerebral allergies
neuroallergies
neurophysiology
electroencephalograph (EEG)
minimal brain dysfunction (MBD)
attention deficit/hyperactivity disorder (ADHD)
conduct disorder (CD)
neurotransmitters
chemical restraints/straitjackets
arousal theory

r/k selection theory
cheater theory
defective intelligence
law of insertion
psychoanalytic
psychodynamic
behaviorist
cognitive
repression
id
pleasure principle
ego
reality principle

superego	disorder	personality
conscience	schizophrenia	Rorschach Inkblot Test
ego ideal	paranoid schizophrenic	Thematic Apperception Test
eros	inferiority complex	Minnesota Multiphasic Personality
oral stage	identity crisis	Inventory (MMPI)
anal stage	latent delinquency	California Personality Inventory (CPI)
phallic stage	bipolar disorder	Multidimensional Personality
Oedipus complex	social learning	Questionnaire (MPQ)
Electra complex	behavior modeling	psychopathy
latency	cognitive theory	fledgling psychopathy
genital stage	moral development	nature theory
fixate	humanistic psychology	nurture theory
neurotic	information-processing theory	Wechsler Adult Intelligence Scale
psychotic	disinhibition	biologically oriented therapy

NOTES

1. Based on James Brooke, Pam Belluck, and John Kifner, and written by James Brooke, "Man Hospitalized in 1996 for Writing Ominous Letters," *New York Times*, 26 July 1998, p. 1.

2. Raffaele Garofalo, *Criminology*, trans. Robert Miller (Boston: Little, Brown, 1914), p. 92.

3. Enrico Ferri, *Criminal Sociology* (New York: D. Appleton, 1909).

4. See Richard Dugdale, *The Jukes* (New York: Putnam, 1910); and Arthur Estabrook, *The Jukes in 1915* (Washington, D.C.: Carnegie Institute of Washington, 1916).

5. William Sheldon, *Varieties of Delinquent Youth* (New York: Harper Bros., 1949).

6. Pierre van den Bergle, "Bringing the Beast Back in: Toward a Biosocial Theory of Aggression," *American Sociological Review* 39 (1974): 779.

7. Lee Ellis, "A Discipline in Peril: Sociology's Future Hinges on Curing Biophobia," *American Sociologist* 27 (1996): 21–41.

8. Edmund O. Wilson, *Sociobiology* (Cambridge: Harvard University Press, 1975).

9. Anthony Walsh and Lee Ellis, "Shoring Up the Big Three: Improving Criminological Theories with Biosocial Concepts." Paper presented at the annual Society of Criminology Meeting, San Diego, Calif., November, 1997, p. 16.

10. Israel Nachshon, "Neurological Bases of Crime, Psychopathy and Aggression," in *Crime in Biological, Social and Moral Contexts*, ed. Lee Ellis and Harry Hoffman (New York: Praeger, 1990), p. 199. Herein cited as *Crime in Biological Contexts*.

11. See, generally, Lee Ellis, "Introduction: The Nature of the Biosocial Perspective," *Crime in Biological Contexts*, pp. 3–18.

12. See, for example, Tracy Bennett Herbert and Sheldon Cohen, "Depression and Immunity: A Meta-Analytic Review," *Psychological Bulletin* 113 (1993): 472–86.

13. See, generally, Lee Ellis, *Theories of Rape* (New York: Hemisphere Publications, 1989).

14. Leonard Hippchen, "Some Possible Biochemical Aspects of Criminal Behavior," *Journal of Behavioral Ecology* 2 (1981): 1–6; Sarnoff Mednick and Jan Volavka, "Biology and Crime," in *Crime and Justice*, ed. Norval Morris and Michael Tonry (Chicago: University of Chicago Press, 1980), pp. 85–159; Saleem Shah and Loren Roth, "Biological and Psychophysiological Factors in Criminality," in *Handbook of Criminology*, ed. Daniel Glazer (Chicago: Rand McNally, 1974), pp. 125–40.

15. *Time*, 28 May 1979, p. 57.

16. Ulric Neisser et al., "Intelligence: Knowns and Unknowns," *American Psychologist* 51 (1996): 77–101 at 88.

17. Leonard Hippchen, ed., *Ecologic-Biochemical Approaches to Treatment of Delinquents and Criminals* (New York: Von Nostrand Reinhold, 1978), p. 14.

18. Michael Krassner, "Diet and Brain Function," *Nutrition Reviews* 44 (1986): 12–15.

19. Hippchen, *Ecologic-Biochemical Approaches to Treatment of Delinquents and Criminals*.

20. J. Kershner and W. Hawke, "Megavitamins and Learning Disorders: A Controlled Double-Blind Experiment," *Journal of Nutrition* 109 (1979): 819–26.

21. Richard Knox, "Test Shows Smart People's Brains Use Nutrients Better," *Boston Globe*, 16 February 1988, p. 9.

22. Ronald Prinz and David Riddle, "Associations Between Nutrition and Behavior in 5-Year-Old Children," *Nutrition Reviews Supplement* 44 (1986): 151–58.

23. Stephen Schoenthaler and Walter Doraz, "Types of Offenses Which Can Be Reduced in an Institutional Setting Using Nutritional Intervention," *International Journal of Biosocial Research* 4 (1983): 74–84; and Stephen Schoenthaler and Walter Doraz, "Diet and Crime," *International Journal of Biosocial Research* 4 (1983): 74–84. See also A. G. Schauss, "Differential Outcomes Among Probationers Comparing Orthomolecular Approaches to Conventional Casework Counseling" (paper presented at the annual meeting of the American Society of Criminology, Dallas, 9 November 1978); A. Schauss and C. Simonsen, "A Critical Analysis of the Diets of Chronic Juvenile Offenders, Part I," *Journal of Orthomolecular Psychiatry* 8 (1979): 222–26; and A. Hoffer, "Children with Learning and Behavioral Disorders," *Journal of Orthomolecular Psychiatry* 5 (1976): 229.

24. Prinz and Riddle, "Associations Between Nutrition and Behavior in 5-Year-Old Children."

25. H. Bruce Ferguson, Clare Stoddart, and Jovan Simeon, "Double-Blind Challenge Studies of Behavioral and Cognitive Effects of Sucrose-Aspartame Ingestion in Normal Children," *Nutrition Reviews Supplement* 44 (1986): 144–58; Gregory Gray, "Diet, Crime and Delinquency: A Critique," *Nutrition Reviews Supplement* 44 (1986): 89–94.

26. Mark Wolraich, Scott Lindgren, Phyllis Stumbo, Lewis Steginks, Mark Appelbaum, and Mary Kiritsy, "Effects of Diets High in Sucrose or Aspartame on the Behavior and Cognitive Performance of Children," *The New England Journal of Medicine* 330 (1994): 303–306.

27. Dian Gans, "Sucrose and Unusual Childhood Behavior," *Nutrition Today* 26 (1991): 8–14.

28. D. Hill and W. Sargent, "A Case of Matricide," *Lancet* 244 (1943): 526–27.

29. E. Podolsky, "The Chemistry of Murder," *Pakistan Medical Journal* 15 (1964): 9–14.

30. J. A. Yaryura-Tobias and F. Neziroglu, "Violent Behavior, Brain Dysrhythmia and Glucose Dysfunction: A New Syndrome," *Journal of Orthopsychiatry* 4 (1975): 182–88.

31. Matti Virkkunen, "Reactive Hypoglycemic Tendency Among Habitually Violent Offenders," *Nutrition Reviews Supplement* 44 (1986): 94–103.

32. James Q. Wilson, *The Moral Sense* (New York: Free Press, 1993).

33. Walter Gove, "The Effect of Age and Gender on Deviant Behavior: A Biopsychosocial Perspective," in *Gender and the Life*

Course, ed. A. S. Rossi (New York: Aldine, 1985), pp. 115–44.

34. Alan Booth and D. Wayne Osgood, "The Influence of Testosterone on Deviance in Adulthood: Assessing and Explaining the Relationship," *Criminology* 31 (1993): 93–118.

35. Booth and Osgood, "The Influence of Testosterone on Deviance in Adulthood."

36. Christy Miller Buchanan, Jacquelynne Eccles, and Jill Becker, "Are Adolescents the Victims of Raging Hormones? Evidence for Activational Effects of Hormones on Moods and Behavior at Adolescence," *Psychological Bulletin* 111 (1992): 62–107.

37. Booth and Osgood, "The Influence of Testosterone on Deviance in Adulthood."

38. Albert Reiss and Jeffrey Roth, eds., *Understanding and Preventing Violence* (Washington, D.C.: National Academy Press, 1993), p. 118. This report by the National Research Council Panel on the Understanding and Control of Violent Behavior is hereafter cited as *Understanding Violence.*

39. L. E. Kreuz and R. M. Rose, "Assessment of Aggressive Behavior and Plasma Testosterone in a Young Criminal Population," *Psychosomatic Medicine* 34 (1972): 321–32.

40. Walsh, "Genetic and Cytogenetic Intersex Anomalies," *International Journal of Offender Therapy and Comparative Criminology* (in press).

41. Lee Ellis, "Evolutionary and Neurochemical Causes of Sex Differences in Victimizing Behavior: Toward a Unified Theory of Criminal Behavior and Social Stratification," *Social Science Information* 28 (1989): 605–636.

42. For a general review, see Lee Ellis and Phyllis Coontz, "Androgens, Brain Functioning, and Criminality: The Neurohormonal Foundations of Antisociality," in *Crime in Biological Contexts,* pp. 162–93.

43. Ellis and Coontz, "Androgens, Brain Functioning, and Criminality," p. 181.

44. Robert Rubin, "The Neuroendocrinology and Neurochemistry of Antisocial Behavior," in *The Causes of Crime, New Biological Approaches,* ed. Sarnoff Mednick, Terrie Moffitt, and Susan Stack (Cambridge: Cambridge University Press, 1987), pp. 239–62.

45. J. Money, "Influence of Hormones on Psychosexual Differentiation," *Medical Aspects of Nutrition* 30 (1976): 165.

46. Sarnoff Mednick and Jan Volavka, "Biology and Crime," in *Crime and Justice,* ed. Norval Morris and Michael Tonry (Chicago: University of Chicago Press, 1980), pp. 85–159.

47. For a review of this concept, see Anne E. Figert, "The Three Faces of PMS: The Professional, Gendered, and Scientific Structuring of a Psychiatric Disorder," *Social Problems* 42 (1995): 56–72.

48. Katharina Dalton, *The Premenstrual Syndrome* (Springfield, Ill.: Charles C. Thomas, 1971).

49. Julie Horney, "Menstrual Cycles and Criminal Responsibility," *Law and Human Nature* 2 (1978): 25–36.

50. Diana Fishbein, "Selected Studies on the Biology of Antisocial Behavior," in John Conklin, ed., *New Perspectives in Criminology* (Needham Heights, Mass.: Allyn and Bacon, 1996), pp. 26–38.

51. Fishbein, "Selected Studies on the Biology of Antisocial Behavior"; Karen Paige, "Effects of Oral Contraceptives on Affective Fluctuations Associated with the Menstrual Cycle," *Psychosomatic Medicine* 33 (1971): 515–37.

52. H. E. Amos and J. J. P. Drake, "Problems Posed by Food Additives," *Journal of Human Nutrition* 30 (1976): 165.

53. Ray Wunderlich, "Neuroallergy as a Contributing Factor to Social Misfits: Diagnosis and Treatment," in *Ecologic-Biochemical Approaches to Treatment of Delinquents and Criminals,* ed. Leonard Hippchen (New York: Von Nostrand Reinhold, 1978), pp. 229–53.

54. See, for example, Paul Marshall, "Allergy and Depression: A Neurochemical Threshold Model of the Relation Between the Illnesses," *Psychological Bulletin* 113 (1993): 23–39.

55. A. R. Mawson and K. J. Jacobs, "Corn Consumption, Tryptophan, and Cross-National Homicide Rates," *Journal of Orthomolecular Psychiatry* 7 (1978): 227–30.

56. Alexander Schauss, *Diet, Crime and Delinquency* (Berkeley, Calif.: Parker House, 1980).

57. C. Hawley and R. E. Buckley, "Food Dyes and Hyperkinetic Children," *Academy Therapy* 10 (1974): 27–32.

58. John Ott, "The Effects of Light and Radiation on Human Health and Behavior," in *Ecologic-Biochemical Approaches to Treatment of Delinquents and Criminals,* ed. Leonard Hippchen (New York: Von Nostrand Reinhold, 1978), pp. 105–183. See also A. Kreuger and S. Sigel, "Ions in the Air," *Human Nature* (July 1978): 46–47; and Harry Wohlfarth, "The Effect of Color Psychodynamic Environmental Modification on Discipline Incidents in Elementary Schools over One School Year: A Controlled Study," *International Journal of Biosocial Research* 6 (1984): 44–53.

59. Oliver David, Stanley Hoffman, Jeffrey Sverd, Julian Clark, and Kytja Voeller, "Lead and Hyperactivity, Behavior Response to Chelation: A Pilot Study," *American Journal of Psychiatry* 133 (1976): 1155–58.

60. Deborah Denno, "Considering Lead Poisoning as a Criminal Defense," *Fordham Urban Law Journal* 20 (1993): 377–400.

61. Herbert Needleman, Julie Riess, Michael Tobin, Gretchen Biesecker, and Joel Greenhouse, "Bone Lead Levels and Delinquent Behavior," *Journal of the American Medical Association* 275 (1996): 363–69.

62. Neisser et al., "Intelligence: Knowns and Unknowns."

63. Terrie Moffitt, "The Neuropsychology of Juvenile Delinquency: A Critical Review," in *Crime and Justice, An Annual Review,* vol. 12, ed. Norval Morris and Michael Tonry (Chicago: University of Chicago Press, 1990), pp. 99–169.

64. Terrie Moffitt, Donald Lynam, and Phil Silva, "Neuropsychological Tests Predicting Persistent Male Delinquency," *Criminology* 32 (1994): 277–300; Elizabeth Kandel and Sarnoff Mednick, "Perinatal Complications Predict Violent Offending," *Criminology* 29 (1991): 519–29; Sarnoff Mednick, Ricardo Machon, Matti Virrkunen, and Douglas Bonett, "Adult Schizophrenia Following Prenatal Exposure to an Influenza Epidemic," *Archives of General Psychiatry* 44 (1987): 35–46; C. A. Fogel, S. A. Mednick, and N. Michelson, "Hyperactive Behavior and Minor Physical Anomalies," *Acta Psychiatrica Scandinavia* 72 (1985): 551–56.

65. R. Johnson, *Aggression in Man and Animals* (Philadelphia: Saunders, 1972), p. 79.

66. Jean Seguin, Robert Pihl, Philip Harden, Richard Tremblay, and Bernard Boulerice, "Cognitive and Neuropsychological Characteristics of Physically Aggressive Boys," *Journal of Abnormal Psychology* 104 (1995): 614–24; Deborah Denno, "Gender, Crime and the Criminal Law Defenses," *Journal of Criminal Law and Criminology* 85 (1994): 80–180.

67. Adrian Raine, Patricia Brennan, Brigitte Mednick, and Sarnoff Mednick, "High Rates of Violence, Crime, Academic Problems, and Behavioral Problems in Males with Both Early Neuromotor Deficits and Unstable Family Environments," *Archives of General Psychiatry* 53 (1966): 544–49.

68. Deborah Denno, *Biology, Crime and Violence: New Evidence* (Cambridge: Cambridge University Press, 1989).

69. Diana Fishbein and Robert Thatcher, "New Diagnostic Methods in Criminology: Assessing Organic Sources of Behavioral Disorders," *Journal of Research in Crime and Delinquency* 23 (1986): 240–67.

70. Fishbein and Thatcher, "New Diagnostic Methods in Criminology."

71. Lorne Yeudall, "A Neuropsychosocial Perspective of Persistent Juvenile Delinquency and Criminal Behavior." Paper presented at the New York Academy of Sciences, 26 September 1979.

72. R. W. Aind and T. Yamamoto, "Behavior Disorders of Childhood," *Electroencephalography and Clinical Neurophysiology* 21 (1966): 148–56.

73. See, generally, Jan Volavka, "Electroencephalogram Among Criminals," in *The Causes of Crime, New Biological Approaches,* ed. Sarnoff Mednick, Terrie Moffitt, and Susan Stack (Cambridge: Cambridge University Press, 1987), pp. 137–45; and Z. A. Zayed, S. A. Lewis, and R. P. Britain, "An Encephalographic and Psychiatric Study of 32 Insane Murderers," *British Journal of Psychiatry* 115 (1969): 1115–24.

74. Nathaniel Pallone and James Hennessy, "Brain Dysfunction and Criminal Violence," *Society* 35 (1998): 21–27; P. F. Goyer, P. J. Andreason, and W. E. Semple,

"Positronic Emission Tomography and Personality Disorders," *Neuropsychopharmacology* 10 (1994): 21–28.

75. Adrian Raine, Monte Buchsbaum, and Lori LaCasse, "Brain Abnormalities in Murderers Indicated by Positron Emission Tomography," *Biological Psychiatry* 42 (1997): 495–508.

76. Nathaniel Pallone and James Hennessy, "Brain Dysfunction and Criminal Violence," p. 25.

77. D. R. Robin, R. M. Starles, T. J. Kenney, B. J. Reynolds, and F. P. Heald, "Adolescents Who Attempt Suicide," *Journal of Pediatrics* 90 (1977): 636–38.

78. R. R. Monroe, *Brain Dysfunction in Aggressive Criminals* (Lexington, Mass.: D.C. Heath, 1978).

79. L. T. Yeudall, *Childhood Experiences as Causes of Criminal Behavior* (Senate of Canada, Issue no. 1, Thirteenth Parliament, Ottawa, 1977).

80. Raine, Buchsbaum, and LaCasse, "Brain Abnormalities in Murderers Indicated by Positron Emission Tomography."

81. Leonore Simon, "Does Criminal Offender Treatment Work?" *Applied and Preventive Psychology* (Summer 1998); Stephen Faraone et al., "Intellectual Performance and School Failure in Children with Attention Deficit Hyperactivity Disorder and in Their Siblings," *Journal of Abnormal Psychology* 102 (1993): 616–23.

82. Simon, "Does Criminal Offender Treatment Work?"

83. Simon, "Does Criminal Offender Treatment Work?"

84. Terrie Moffitt and Phil Silva, "Self-Reported Delinquency, Neuropsychological Deficit, and History of Attention Deficit Disorder," *Journal of Abnormal Child Psychology* 16 (1988): 553–69.

85. Elizabeth Hart et al., "Developmental Change in Attention-Deficit Hyperactivity Disorder in Boys: A Four-Year Longitudinal Study," *Journal of Consulting and Clinical Psychology* 62 (1994): 472–91.

86. Eugene Maguin, Rolf Loeber, and Paul LeMahieu, "Does the Relationship Between Poor Reading and Delinquency Hold for Males of Different Ages and Ethnic Groups?" *Journal of Emotional and Behavioral Disorders* 1 (1993): 88–100.

87. Yeudall, "A Neuropsychosocial Perspective of Persistent Juvenile Delinquency and Criminal Behavior," p. 4; F. A. Elliott, "Neurological Aspects of Antisocial Behavior," in *The Psychopath: A Comprehensive Study of Antisocial Disorders and Behaviors,* ed. W. H. Reid (New York: Brunner/Mazel, 1978), pp. 146–89.

88. Lorne Yeudall, Orestes Fedora, and Delee Fromm, "A Neuropsychosocial Theory of Persistent Criminality: Implications for Assessment and Treatment," in *Advances in Forensic Psychology and Psychiatry,* ed. Robert Rieber (Norwood, N.J.: Ablex, 1987), pp. 119–91.

89. Yeudall, Fedora, and Fromm, "A Neuropsychosocial Theory of Persistent Criminality," p. 177.

90. Yeudall, Fedora, and Fromm, "A Neuropsychosocial Theory of Persistent Criminality," pp. 24–25.

91. H. K. Kletschka, "Violent Behavior Associated with Brain Tumor," *Minnesota Medicine* 49 (1966): 1853–55.

92. V. E. Krynicki, "Cerebral Dysfunction in Repetitively Assaultive Adolescents," *Journal of Nervous and Mental Disease* 166 (1978): 59–67.

93. C. E. Lyght, ed., *The Merck Manual of Diagnosis and Therapy* (West Point, Fla.: Merck, 1966).

94. *Understanding Violence,* p. 119.

95. M. Virkkunen, M. J. DeJong, J. Bartko, and M. Linnoila, "Psychobiological Concomitants of History of Suicide Attempts Among Violent Offenders and Impulsive Fire Starters," *Archives of General Psychiatry* 46 (1989): 604–606.

96. Matti Virkkunen, David Goldman, and Markku Linnoila, "Serotonin in Alcoholic Violent Offenders," The Ciba Foundation Symposium, *Genetics of Criminal and Antisocial Behavior* (Chichester, England: Wiley, 1995).

97. Lee Ellis, "Left- and Mixed-Handedness and Criminality: Explanations for a Probable Relationship," in *Left-Handedness: Behavioral Implications and Anomalies,* ed. S. Coren (Amsterdam: Elsevier, 1990): 485–507.

98. Lee Ellis, "Monoamine Oxidase and Criminality: Identifying an Apparent Biological Marker for Antisocial Behavior," *Journal of Research in Crime and Delinquency* 28 (1991): 227–51.

99. Walter Gove and Charles Wilmoth, "Risk, Crime and Neurophysiologic Highs: A Consideration of Brain Processes That May Reinforce Delinquent and Criminal Behavior," in *Crime in Biological Contexts,* pp. 261–93.

100. Jack Katz, *Seduction of Crime: Moral and Sensual Attractions of Doing Evil* (New York: Basic Books, 1988), pp. 12–15.

101. Lee Ellis, "Arousal Theory and the Religiosity–Criminality Relationship," in Peter Cordella and Larry Siegel, eds. *Contemporary Criminological Theory* (Boston, Mass.: Northeastern University, 1996), pp. 65–84.

102. Adrian Raine, Peter Venables, and Sarnoff Mednick, "Low Resting Heart Rate at Age 3 Years Predisposes to Aggression at Age 11 Years: Evidence from the Mauritius Child Health Project," *Journal of the American Academy of Adolescent Psychiatry* 36 (1997): 1457–64.

103. For a general view, see Richard Lerner and Terryl Foch, *Biological-Psychosocial Interactions in Early Adolescence* (Hillsdale, N.J.: Lawrence Erlbaum Associates, 1987).

104. Kerry Jang, W. John Livesley, and Philip Vernon, "Heritability of the Big Five Personality Dimensions and Their Facets: A Twin Study," *Journal of Personality* 64 (1996): 577–89.

105. David Rowe, "As the Twig Is Bent: The Myth of Child-Rearing Influences on Personality Development," *Journal of Counseling and Development* 68 (1990): 606–611; David Rowe, Joseph Rogers, and Sylvia Meseck-Bushey, "Sibling Delinquency and the Family Environment: Shared and Unshared Influences," *Child Development* 63 (1992): 59–67.

106. Patricia Brennan, Sarnoff Mednick, and Bjorn Jacobsen, "Assessing the Role of Genetics in Crime Using Adoption Cohorts," *Genetics of Criminal and Antisocial Behavior,* pp. 115–28; Gregory Carey and David DiLalla, "Personality and Psychopathology: Genetic Perspectives," *Journal of Abnormal Psychology* 103 (1994): 32–43.

107. T. R. Sarbin and L. E. Miller, "Demonism Revisited: The XYY Chromosome Anomaly," *Issues in Criminology* 5 (1970): 195–207.

108. Mednick and Volavka, "Biology and Crime," p. 93.

109. For an early review, see Barbara Wooton, *Social Science and Social Pathology* (London: Allen and Unwin, 1959); John Laub and Robert Sampson, "Unraveling Families and Delinquency: A Reanalysis of the Gluecks' Data," *Criminology* 26 (1988): 355–80.

110. D. J. West and D. P. Farrington, eds., "Who Becomes Delinquent?" in *The Delinquent Way of Life* (London: Heinemann, 1977); D. J. West, *Delinquency; Its Roots, Careers, and Prospects* (Cambridge: Harvard University Press, 1982).

111. West, *Delinquency,* p. 114.

112. David Farrington, "Understanding and Preventing Bullying," in Michael Tonry, ed., *Crime and Justice,* vol. 17 (Chicago: University of Chicago Press, 1993), pp. 381–457.

113. Philip Harden and Robert Pihl, "Cognitive Function, Cardiovascular Reactivity, and Behavior in Boys at High Risk for Alcoholism," *Journal of Abnormal Psychology* 104 (1995): 94–103.

114. Laub and Sampson, "Unraveling Families and Delinquency," p. 370.

115. See, generally, Wooton, *Social Science and Social Pathology;* H. Wilson, "Juvenile Delinquency, Parental Criminality, and Social Handicaps," *British Journal of Criminology* 15 (1975): 241–50.

116. David Rowe and David Farrington, "The Familial Transmission of Criminal Convictions," *Criminology* 35 (1997): 177–201.

117. D. P. Farrington, Gwen Gundry, and D. J. West, "The Familial Transmission of Criminality," in Alan Lincoln and Murray Straus, eds., *Crime and the Family* (Springfield, Ill.: Charles C. Thomas, 1985), pp. 193–206.

118. David Rowe and Bill Gulley, "Sibling Effects on Substance Use and Delinquency," *Criminology* 30 (1992): 217–32; see also David Rowe, Joseph Rogers, and Sylvia Meseck-Bushey, "Sibling Delinquency and the Family Environment: Shared and Unshared Influences," *Child Development* 63 (1992): 59–67.

119. Mednick and Volavka, "Biology and Crime," p. 94.

120. Mednick and Volavka, "Biology and Crime," p. 95.

121. See Sarnoff A. Mednick and Karl O. Christiansen, eds., *Biosocial Bases in Criminal Behavior* (New York: Gardner Press, 1977).

122. David Rowe, "Genetic and Environmental Components of Antisocial Behavior: A Study of 265 Twin Pairs," *Criminology* 24 (1986): 513–32; David Rowe and D. Wayne Osgood, "Heredity and Sociological Theories of Delinquency: A Reconsideration," *American Sociological Review* 49 (1984): 526–40.

123. Edwin J. C. G. van den Oord, Frank Verhulst, and Dorret Boomsma, "A Genetic Study of Maternal and Paternal Ratings of Problem Behaviors in 3-Year-Old Twins," *Journal of Abnormal Psychology* 105 (1996): 349–57.

124. Michael Lyons, "A Twin Study of Self-Reported Criminal Behavior," and Judy Silberg, Joanne Meyer, Andrew Pickles, Emily Simonoff, Lindon Eaves, John Hewitt, Hermine Maes, and Michael Rutter, "Heterogeneity Among Juvenile Antisocial Behaviors: Findings from the Virginia Twin Study of Adolescent Behavioral Development," in The Ciba Foundation Symposium, *Genetics of Criminal and Antisocial Behavior* (Chichester, England: Wiley), 1995.

125. Gregory Carey, "Twin Imitation for Antisocial Behavior: Implications for Genetic and Family Environment Research," *Journal of Abnormal Psychology* 101 (1992): 18–25; David Rowe and Joseph Rogers, "The Ohio Twin Project and ADSEX Studies: Behavior Genetic Approaches to Understanding Antisocial Behavior" (paper presented at the American Society of Criminology Meeting, Montreal, Canada, November 1987).

126. David Rowe, *The Limits of Family Influence: Genes, Experiences and Behavior* (New York: Guilford Press, 1995), p. 64.

127. R. J. Cadoret, C. Cain, and R. R. Crowe, "Evidence for a Gene–Environment Interaction in the Development of Adolescent Antisocial Behavior," *Behavior Genetics* 13 (1983): 301–310.

128. Barry Hutchings and Sarnoff A. Mednick, "Criminality in Adoptees and Their Adoptive and Biological Parents: A Pilot Study," in *Biological Bases in Criminal Behavior*, ed. S. A. Mednick and K. O. Christiansen (New York: Gardner Press, 1977).

129. For similar results, see Sarnoff Mednick, Terrie Moffitt, William Gabrielli, and Barry Hutchings, "Genetic Factors in Criminal Behavior: A Review," *Development of Antisocial and Prosocial Behavior* (New York: Academic Press, 1986), pp. 3–50; Sarnoff Mednick, William Gabrielli, and Barry Hutchings, "Genetic Influences in Criminal Behavior: Evidence from an Adoption Cohort," in *Perspective Studies of Crime and Delinquency*, ed. Katherine Teilmann Van Dusen and Sarnoff Mednick (Boston: Kluwer-Nijhoff, 1983), pp. 39–57.

130. Michael Bohman, "Predisposition to Criminality: Swedish Adoption Studies in Retrospect," in *Genetics of Criminal and Antisocial Behavior*, pp. 99–114.

131. Glenn Walters, "A Meta-Analysis of the Gene–Crime Relationship," *Criminology* 30 (1992): 595–613.

132. Lawrence Cohen and Richard Machalek, "A General Theory of Expropriative Crime: An Evolutionary Ecological Approach," *American Journal of Sociology* 94 (1988): 465–501.

133. For a general review, see Martin Daly and Margo Wilson, "Crime and Conflict: Homicide in Evolutionary Psychological Theory," in *Crime and Justice, An Annual Edition*, ed. Michael Tonry (Chicago: University of Chicago Press, 1997), pp. 51–100.

134. Lee Ellis, "The Evolution of Violent Criminal Behavior and Its Nonlegal Equivalent," *Crime in Biological Contexts*, pp. 63–65.

135. David Rowe, Alexander Vazsonyi, and Aurelio Jose Figuerdo, "Mating-Effort in Adolescence: A Conditional of Alternative Strategy," *Personal Individual Differences* 23 (1997): 105–115.

136. Rowe, Vazsonyi, and Figuerdo, "Mating-Effort in Adolescence," p. 71.

137. Margo Wilson, Holly Johnson, and Martin Daly, "Lethal and Nonlethal Violence Against Wives," *Canadian Journal of Criminology* 37 (1995): 331–61.

138. Lee Ellis and Anthony Walsh, "Gene-Based Evolutionary Theories of Criminology," *Criminology* 35 (1997): 229–76.

139. Lee Ellis, "Sex Differences in Criminality: An Explanation Based on the Concept of r/K Selection," *Mankind Quarterly* 30 (1990): 17–37.

140. Ellis and Walsh, "Gene-Based Evolutionary Theories of Criminology."

141. Byron Roth, "Crime and Child Rearing," *Society* 34 (1996): 39–45.

142. Deborah Denno, "Sociological and Human Developmental Explanations of Crime: Conflict or Consensus," *Criminology* 23 (1985): 711–41.

143. Israel Nachshon and Deborah Denno, "Violence and Cerebral Function," in *The Causes of Crime, New Biological Approaches*, ed. Sarnoff Mednick, Terrie Moffitt, and Susan Stack (Cambridge: Cambridge University Press, 1987), pp. 185–217.

144. Adrian Raine, Patricia Brennan, Brigitte Mednick, and Sarnoff Mednick, "High Rates of Violence, Crime, Academic Problems, and Behavioral Problems in Males with Both Early Neuromotor Deficits and Unstable Family Environments," *Archives of General Psychiatry* 53 (1966): 544–49.

145. Avshalom Caspi, Donald Lynam, Terrie Moffitt, and Phil Silva, "Unraveling Girls' Delinquency: Biological, Dispositional, and Contextual Contributions to Adolescent Misbehavior," *Developmental Psychology* 29 (1993): 283–89.

146. Glenn Walters and Thomas White, "Heredity and Crime: Bad Genes or Bad Research," *Criminology* 27 (1989): 455–86 at 478.

147. Charles Goring, *The English Convict: A Statistical Study, 1913* (Montclair, N.J.: Patterson Smith, 1972).

148. Edwin Driver, "Charles Buckman Goring," in *Pioneers in Criminology*, ed. Hermann Mannheim (Montclair, N.J.: Patterson Smith, 1970), p. 440.

149. Gabriel Tarde, *Penal Philosophy*, trans. R. Howell (Boston: Little, Brown, 1912).

150. See, generally, Donn Byrne and Kathryn Kelly, *An Introduction to Personality* (Englewood Cliffs, N.J.: Prentice-Hall, 1981).

151. August Aichorn, *Wayward Youth* (New York: Viking Press, 1935).

152. David Abrahamsen, *Crime and the Human Mind* (New York: Columbia University Press, 1944), p. 137; also see, generally, Fritz Redl and Hans Toch, "The Psychoanalytic Perspective," in *Psychology of Crime and Criminal Justice*, ed. Hans Toch (New York: Holt, Rinehart and Winston, 1979), pp. 193–95.

153. See, generally, D. A. Andrews and James Bonta, *The Psychology of Criminal Conduct* (Cincinnati, Ohio: Anderson, 1994), pp. 72–75.

154. Paige Crosby Ouimette, "Psychopathology and Sexual Aggression in Nonincarcerated Men," *Violence and Victimization* 12 (1997): 389–97.

155. Robert Krueger, Avshalom Caspi, Phil Silva, and Rob McGee, "Personality Traits Are Differentially Linked to Mental Disorders: A Multitrait–Multidiagnosis Study of an Adolescent Birth Cohort," *Journal of Abnormal Psychology* 105 (1996): 299–312.

156. Seymour Halleck, *Psychiatry and the Dilemmas of Crime* (Berkeley: University of California Press, 1971).

157. This discussion is based on three works by Albert Bandura: *Aggression: A Social Learning Analysis* (Englewood Cliffs, N.J.: Prentice-Hall, 1973); *Social Learning Theory* (Englewood Cliffs, N.J.: Prentice-Hall, 1977); and "The Social Learning Perspective: Mechanisms of Aggression," in *Psychology of Crime and Criminal Justice*, ed. Hans Toch (New York: Holt, Rinehart and Winston, 1979), pp. 198–236.

158. David Phillips, "The Impact of Mass Media Violence on U.S. Homicides," *American Sociological Review* 48 (1983): 560–68.

159. See, generally, Jean Piaget, *The Moral Judgment of the Child* (London: Kegan Paul, 1932).

160. Lawrence Kohlberg, *Stages in the Development of Moral Thought and Action* (New York: Holt, Rinehart and Winston, 1969).

161. L. Kohlberg, K. Kauffman, P. Scharf, and J. Hickey, *The Just Community Approach in Corrections: A Manual* (Niantic: Connecticut Department of Corrections, 1973).

162. Scott Henggeler, *Delinquency in Adolescence* (Newbury Park, Calif.: Sage, 1989), p. 26.

163. Carol Veneziano and Louis Veneziano, "The Relationship Between Deterrence and Moral Reasoning," *Criminal Justice Review* 17 (1992): 209–216.

164. K. A. Dodge, "A Social Information Processing Model of Social Competence in Children," in *Minnesota Symposium in Child Psychology,* vol. 18, ed. M. Perlmutter (Hillsdale, N.J.: Erlbaum, 1986), pp. 77–125.

165. Adrian Raine, Peter Venables, and Mark Williams, "Better Autonomic Conditioning and Faster Electrodermal Half-Recovery Time at Age 15 Years as Possible Protective Factors Against Crime at Age 29 Years," *Developmental Psychology* 32 (1996): 624–30.

166. L. Huesman and L. Eron, "Individual Differences and the Trait of Aggression," *European Journal of Personality* 3 (1989): 95–106.

167. Rolf Loeber and Dale Hay, "Key Issues in the Development of Aggression and Violence from Childhood to Early Adulthood," *Annual Review of Psychology* 48 (1997): 371–410.

168. J. E. Lochman, "Self and Peer Perceptions and Attributional Biases of Aggressive and Nonaggressive Boys in Dyadic Interactions," *Journal of Consulting and Clinical Psychology* 55 (1987): 404–410.

169. D. Lipton, E. C. McDonel, and R. McFall, "Heterosocial Perception in Rapists," *Journal of Consulting and Clinical Psychology* 55 (1987): 17–21.

170. *Understanding Violence,* p. 389.

171. Kathleen Cirillo, B. E. Pruitt, Brian Colwell, Paul M. Kingery, Robert S. Hurley, and Danny Ballard, "School Violence: Prevalence and Intervention Strategies for At-Risk Adolescents," *Adolescence* 33 (1998): 319–31.

172. *Understanding Violence,* p. 389.

173. Rick Bragg, "4 Girls and a Teacher Are Shot to Death in an Ambush at a Middle School in Arkansas," *New York Times,* 25 March 1998, p. 1.

174. James Sorrells, "Kids Who Kill," *Crime and Delinquency* 23 (1977): 312–20.

175. Richard Rosner, "Adolescents Accused of Murder and Manslaughter: A Five-Year Descriptive Study," *Bulletin of the American Academy of Psychiatry and the Law* 7 (1979): 342–51.

176. Richard Famularo, Robert Kinscherff, and Terence Fenton, "Psychiatric Diagnoses of Abusive Mothers: A Preliminary Report," *Journal of Nervous and Mental Disease* 180 (1992): 658–60.

177. Richard Wagner, Dawn Taylor, Joy Wright, Alison Sloat, Gwynneth Springett, Sandy Arnold, and Heather Weinberg, "Substance Abuse Among the Mentally Ill," *American Journal of Orthopsychiatry* 64 (1994): 30–38.

178. Bruce Link, Howard Andrews, and Francis Cullen, "The Violent and Illegal Behavior of Mental Patients Reconsidered," *American Sociological Review* 57 (1992): 275–92; Ellen Hochstedler Steury, "Criminal Defendants with Psychiatric Impairment: Prevalence, Probabilities and Rates," *Journal of Criminal Law and Criminology* 84 (1993): 354–74.

179. Marc Hillbrand, John Krystal, Kimberly Sharpe, and Hilliard Foster, "Clinical Predictors of Self-Mutilation in Hospitalized Patients," *Journal of Nervous and Mental Disease* 182 (1994): 9–13.

180. Carmen Cirincione, Henry Steadman, Pamela Clark Robbins, and John Monahan, *Mental Illness as a Factor in Criminality: A Study of Prisoners and Mental Patients* (Delmar, N.Y.: Policy Research Associates, 1991). See also Carmen Cirincione, Henry Steadman, Pamela Clark Robbins, and John Monahan, *Schizophrenia as a Contingent Risk Factor for Criminal Violence* (Delmar, N.Y.: Policy Research Associates, 1991).

181. James Bonta, Moira Law, and Karl Hanson, "The Prediction of Criminal and Violent Recidivism Among Mentally Disordered Offenders: A Meta-Analysis," *Psychological Bulletin* 123 (1998): 123–42.

182. John Monahan, *Mental Illness and Violent Crime* (Washington, D.C.: National Institute of Justice, 1996).

183. Howard Berenbaum and Frank Fujita, "Schizophrenia and Personality: Exploring the Boundaries and Connections Between Vulnerability and Outcome," *Journal of Abnormal Psychology* 103 (1994): 148–58.

184. See Monahan, *Mental Illness and Violent Crime.*

185. See, generally, Walter Mischel, *Introduction to Personality,* 4th ed. (New York: Holt, Rinehart and Winston, 1986).

186. D. A. Andrews and J. Stephen Wormith, "Personality and Crime: Knowledge and Construction in Criminology," *Justice Quarterly* 6 (1989): 289–310; Donald Gibbons, "Comment—Personality and Crime: Non-Issues, Real Issues, and a Theory and Research Agenda," *Justice Quarterly* (1989): 311–24.

187. Sheldon Glueck and Eleanor Glueck, *Unraveling Juvenile Delinquency* (Cambridge: Harvard University Press, 1950).

188. See, generally, Hans Eysenck, *Personality and Crime* (London: Routledge and Kegan Paul, 1977).

189. Hans Eysenck and M. W. Eysenck, *Personality and Individual Differences* (New York: Plenum, 1985).

190. David Farrington, "Psychobiological Factors in the Explanation and Reduction of Delinquency," *Today's Delinquent* (1988): 37–51.

191. Laurie Frost, Terrie Moffitt, and Rob McGee, "Neuropsychological Correlates of Psychopathology in an Unselected Cohort of Young Adolescents," *Journal of Abnormal Psychology* 98 (1989): 307–13.

192. David Lykken, "Psychopathy, Sociopathy, and Crime," *Society* 34 (1996): 30–38.

193. See, generally, R. Starke Hathaway and Elio Monachesi, *Analyzing and Predicting Juvenile Delinquency with the MMPI* (Minneapolis: University of Minnesota Press, 1953).

194. R. Starke Hathaway, Elio Monachesi, and Lawrence Young, "Delinquency Rates and Personality," *Journal of Criminal Law, Criminology, and Police Science* 51 (1960): 443–60; Michael Hindelang and Joseph Weis, "Personality and Self-Reported Delinquency: An Application of Cluster Analysis," *Criminology* 10 (1972): 268; Spencer Rathus and Larry Siegel, "Crime and Personality Revisited," *Criminology* 18 (1980): 245–51.

195. See, generally, Edward Megargee, *The California Psychological Inventory Handbook* (San Francisco: Jossey-Bass, 1972).

196. Karl Schuessler and Donald Cressey, "Personality Characteristics of Criminals," *American Journal of Sociology* 55 (1950): 476–84; Gordon Waldo and Simon Dinitz, "Personality Attributes of the Criminal: An Analysis of Research Studies 1950–1965," *Journal of Research in Crime and Delinquency* 4 (1967): 185–201; David Tennenbaum, "Research Studies of Personality and Criminality," *Journal of Criminal Justice* 5 (1977): 1–19.

197. Edward Helmes and John Reddon, "A Perspective on Developments in Assessing Psychopathology: A Critical Review of the MMPI and MMPI-2," *Psychological Bulletin* 113 (1993): 453–71.

198. Avshalom Caspi, Terrie Moffitt, Phil Silva, Magda Stouthamer-Loeber, Robert Krueger, and Pamela Schmutte, "Are Some People Crime-Prone? Replications of the Personality–Crime Relationship Across Countries, Genders, Races and Methods," *Criminology* 32 (1994): 163–95.

199. Henry Goddard, *Efficiency and Levels of Intelligence* (Princeton, N.J.: Princeton University Press, 1920); Edwin Sutherland, "Mental Deficiency and Crime," in *Social Attitudes,* ed. Kimball Young (New York: Henry Holt, 1931), chap. 15.

200. William Healy and Augusta Bronner, *Delinquency and Criminals: Their Making and Unmaking* (New York: McMillan, 1926).

201. John Slawson, *The Delinquent Boys* (Boston: Budget Press, 1926).

202. Sutherland, "Mental Deficiency and Crime."

203. Travis Hirschi and Michael Hindelang, "Intelligence and Delinquency: A Revisionist Review," *American Sociological Review* 42 (1977): 471–586.

204. Deborah Denno, "Sociological and Human Developmental Explanations of Crime: Conflict or Consensus," *Criminology* 23 (1985): 711–41; Christine Ward and Richard McFall, "Further Validation of the Problem Inventory for Adolescent Girls: Comparing Caucasian and Black Delinquents and Nondelinquents," *Journal of Consulting and Clinical Psychology* 54 (1986): 732–33; L. Hubble and M. Groff, "Magnitude and Direction of WISC-R Verbal Performance IQ Discrepancies Among Adjudicated Male Delinquents," *Journal of Youth and Adolescence* 10 (1981): 179–83; Robert Gordon, "IQ Commensurability of Black–White Differences in Crime and Delinquency" (paper presented at the an-

nual meeting of the American Psychological Association, Washington, D.C., August 1986); Robert Gordon, "Two Illustrations of the IQ-Surrogate Hypothesis: IQ Versus Parental Education and Occupational Status in the Race–IQ–Delinquency Model" (paper presented at the annual meeting of the American Society of Criminology, Montreal, Canada, November 1987).

205. Donald Lynam, Terrie Moffitt, and Magda Stouthamer-Loeber, "Explaining the Relation Between IQ and Delinquency: Class, Race, Test Motivation, School Failure or Self-Control," *Journal of Abnormal Psychology* 102 (1993): 187–96.

206. James Q. Wilson and Richard Herrnstein, *Crime and Human Nature* (New York: Simon and Schuster, 1985), p. 148.

207. Wilson and Herrnstein, *Crime and Human Nature,* p. 171.

208. Terrie Moffitt, William Gabrielli, Sarnoff Mednick, and Fini Schulsinger, "Socioeconomic Status, IQ, and Delinquency," *Journal of Abnormal Psychology* 90 (1981): 152–56. For a similar finding, see Hubble and Groff, "Magnitude and Direction of WISC-R Verbal Performance IQ Discrepancies Among Adjudicated Male Delinquents."

209. Lorne Yeudall, Delee Fromm-Auch, and Priscilla Davies, "Neuropsychological Impairment of Persistent Delinquency," *Journal of Nervous and Mental Diseases* 170 (1982): 257–65.

210. Hakan Stattin and Ingrid Klackenberg-Larsson, "Early Language and Intelligence Development and Their Relationship to Future Criminal Behavior," *Journal of Abnormal Psychology* 102 (1993): 369–78.

211. H. D. Day, J. M. Franklin and D. D. Marshall, "Predictors of Aggression in Hospitalized Adolescents," *Journal of Psychology* 132 (1998): 427–35; Scott Menard and Barbara Morse, "A Structuralist Critique of the IQ–Delinquency Hypothesis: Theory and Evidence," *American Journal of Sociology* 89 (1984): 1347–78; Denno, "Sociological and Human Developmental Explanations of Crime."

212. Neisser et al., "Intelligence: Knowns and Unknowns," 77–101 at 83.

213. Richard Herrnstein and Charles Murray, *The Bell Curve: Intelligence and Class Structure in American Life* (New York: Free Press, 1994).

214. Susan Pease and Craig T. Love, "Optimal Methods and Issues in Nutrition Research in the Correctional Setting," *Nutrition Reviews Supplement* 44 (1986): 122–31.

215. Mark O'Callaghan and Douglas Carroll, "The Role of Psychosurgical Studies in the Control of Antisocial Behavior," in *The Causes of Crime: New Biological Approaches,* ed. Sarnoff Mednick, Terrie Moffitt, and Susan Stack (Cambridge: Cambridge University Press, 1987), pp. 312–28.

216. Mednick, Moffitt, Gabrielli, and Hutchings, "Genetic Factors in Criminal Behavior: A Review," pp. 47–48.

Social Structure Theories

INTRODUCTION

The majority of criminologists believe it would be a mistake to ignore social and environmental factors in trying to understand the cause of criminal behavior.[1] Most criminals are indigent and desperate, not calculating or evil. Most grew up in deteriorated parts of town and lack the social support and economic resources familiar to more affluent members of society. Understanding criminal behavior, then, requires analyzing the influence of these destructive social forces on human behavior.

Sociology has been the primary focus of criminology since the early twentieth century, when sociologists Robert Ezra Park (1864–1944), Ernest W. Burgess (1886–1966), Louis Wirth (1897–1952), and their colleagues taught and conducted criminological research in the sociology department at the University of Chicago. Their work on the social ecology of the city inspired a generation of scholars to conclude that social forces operating in urban areas create criminal interactions. This perspective came to be known as the **Chicago School.**

In 1915 Park called for anthropological methods of description and observation to be applied to urban life.[2] He was concerned about how neighborhood structure developed, how isolated pockets of poverty formed, and what social policies could alleviate urban problems. Later Park and Burgess studied the social ecology of the city and found that some neighborhoods formed natural areas of wealth and affluence, while others suffered poverty and disintegration.[3] Regardless of their race, religion, or ethnicity, the everyday behavior of people living in these areas was controlled by the social and ecological climate.

Over the next 20 years, Chicago School sociologists carried out an ambitious program of research and scholarship on urban topics, including criminal behavior patterns. Works such as Harvey Zorbaugh's *The Gold Coast and the Slum,*[4] Frederick Thrasher's *The Gang,*[5] and Louis Wirth's *The Ghetto*[6] are classic examples of objective, highly descriptive accounts of urban life. Their influence was such that most criminologists have been trained in sociology, and criminology courses are routinely taught in departments of sociology.

SOCIOLOGICAL CRIMINOLOGY

Sociology is concerned with the benefits of positive human interactions and the costs of negative ones. Criminologists focus on how negative human interactions may lead to aggression and antisocial behavior. Accordingly, sociology has been closely tied to criminology since its inception.

Criminologists have long attempted to discover why certain geographic locations are more prone to criminal activity than others. They have examined both violent behavior and theft-related crimes in an effort to understand patterns of criminal behavior. Explanations of crime as an individual-level phenomenon, which have their locus in either destructive personal choices or deviant traits, fail to account for these consistent crime rate patterns. If violence, as some criminologists suggest, is related to chemical or chromosome abnormality, then how can ecological differences in crime rates be explained? It is unlikely that all people with physical anomalies live in one section of town or in one area of the country. There has been a heated national debate over the effects of violent TV shows on adolescent aggression. Yet adolescents in cities and towns with widely disparate crime rates may all watch the same shows and movies; so how can crime rate differences in these areas be explained? If violence has a biological or psychological origin, should it not be distributed more evenly throughout the social structure as opposed to being concentrated in certain areas?

CONNECTIONS

Concern about the ecological distribution of crime, the effect of social change, and the interactive nature of crime itself has made sociology the foundation of modern criminology. This chapter reviews sociological theories that emphasize the relationship between social status and criminal behavior. In Chapter 8 the focus shifts to theories that emphasize socialization and its influence on crime and deviance; Chapter 9 covers theories based on the concept of social conflict.

Sociology is also concerned with social change and the dynamic aspects of human behavior. It follows transformations in cultural norms and institutions and their subsequent effects on individual and group behavior. These concepts are useful today because the changing structure of postmodern society continues to have a tremendous impact on intergroup and interpersonal relationships. There has been a reduction in the influence of the family and an increased emphasis on individuality, independence, and isolation. Weakened family ties have been linked to crime and delinquency.[7] Political unrest and mistrust, economic stress, and family disintegration are social changes that have been found to precede sharp increases in crime rates. Conversely, stabilization of traditional social institutions typically precedes crime rate declines.[8]

Another important social change has been the rapid advance in technology and its influence on the social system. People who lack the requisite social and educational training have found that the road to success through upward occupational mobility is almost impassable. This lack of upward mobility may make drug dealing and other crimes an attractive solution to socially deprived but economically enterprising people.[9]

Sociology's stress on intergroup and interpersonal transactions also promotes it as a source for criminological study. Criminologists believe that understanding the dynamics of interactions between individuals and important social institutions, such as families, peers, schools, jobs, criminal justice agencies, and the like, is important for understanding the cause of crime.[10] The relationship of one social class or group to another or to the power structure that controls the nation's legal and economic system may also be closely related to criminality. It seems logical that people on the lowest rung of the economic ladder will have the greatest incentive to commit crime: they may be either enraged by their lack of economic success or simply financially desperate and disillusioned. In either instance, crime, despite its inherent dangers, may be an attractive alternative to a life of indigence.

Crime is itself an interaction and therefore must be studied with regard to the interactions of all participants in a criminal act. This includes the law violator, the victim, the law enforcers, the lawmakers, and social institutions.

ECONOMIC STRUCTURE
AND CRIME

People in the United States live in a **stratified** society. Social strata are created by unequal distribution of wealth, power, and prestige. **Social classes** are segments of the population whose members have a relatively similar portion of desirable things and who share

attitudes, values, norms, and an identifiable lifestyle. In U.S. society, it is common to identify people as upper-, middle-, and lower-class citizens, with a broad range of economic variations existing within each group. The upper-upper class consists of a small number of exceptionally well-to-do families who maintain enormous financial and social resources. In contrast, the indigent have scant, if any, resources and suffer socially and economically as a result. Although the proportion of indigent Americans has been declining, as of 1998, about 13.3 percent or about 36 million people were still living below the poverty line, which is defined as a little more than $16,000 annually for a family of four and $12,800 for a family of three. Although recent economic growth has restored household incomes and poverty to the levels recorded in 1989 (before the last recession), this improvement may be temporary. Moreover, the government's definition of the poverty line seems quite low. A more realistic figure of an $18,000 annual income per family of three would mean that more than 50 million U.S. citizens live in poverty.[11]

A new shift is being noticed in the distribution of poverty. For the first time, poverty among the elderly has dipped below that of working-class people. Federal programs such as Medicare and Social Security, coupled with private pensions, have improved the lifestyle of retirees. At the same time children have been hit hard: 25 percent of children under 6 now live in poverty, a frightening number considering America's self-image as the richest country on earth. A recent report by Columbia University's Center for Children in Poverty indicates that despite stereotypes, child poverty is rising faster among white suburban families than among African-American urban families. Nonetheless, 6 percent of white children can be described as extremely poor, compared to 50 percent of black children.[12] Another ominous sign is the polarization of the American economy: since 1975, the wealthy have amassed an ever-greater share of total income while the middle class and the poor have seen their economic health decline. The wealthiest fifth of the population now earns 11 times more income than the poorest fifth.[13]

CONNECTIONS

Later in this chapter, the section on relative deprivation ties extremes of poverty and wealth to the crime rate. When the extremely poor and the extremely rich live in close proximity, tensions flare and crime rates increase.

Lower-Class Culture

Lower-class areas are scenes of inadequate housing and health care, disrupted family lives, underemployment, and despair. Members of the lower class also suffer in other ways. They are more prone to depression, less

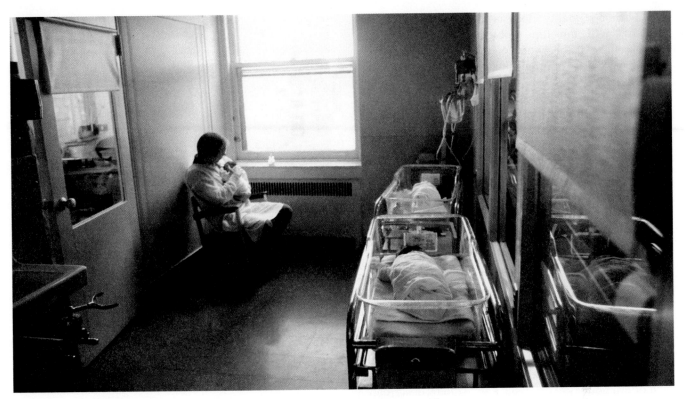

About 25% of children under age six now live in poverty, a frightening statistic considering America's self-image as the "richest country on earth." An estimated 22,000 newborn babies are abandoned each year in hospitals by mothers who are poverty stricken, drug addicted, or homeless. Here a volunteer comforts a crack-addicted baby in an urban hospital ward.

likely to have achievement motivation, and less likely to put off immediate gratification for future gain. For example, they may be less willing to stay in school because the rewards for educational achievement are in the distant future. Some are driven to desperate measures to cope with their economic plight. For example, it is estimated that about 22,000 newborn babies are abandoned in hospitals each year by mothers who are impoverished, addicted to drugs, or homeless.[14]

Members of the lower class are constantly bombarded by advertisements linking material possessions to self-worth, but they are often unable to attain desired goods and services through conventional means. Although they are members of a society that extols material success above any other form, they are unable to satisfactorily compete for such success with members of the upper classes. As a result, they may turn to illegal solutions to their economic plight: they may deal drugs for profit or steal cars and sell them to chop shops; they may even commit armed robberies for desperately needed funds. They may become so depressed that they take alcohol and drugs as a form of self-tranquilization, and because of their poverty, they acquire the drugs and alcohol through illegal channels.

Child Poverty Children are hit especially hard by poverty. Hundreds of studies have documented the as-sociation between family poverty and children's health, achievement, and behavior impairments.[15] Children who grow up in low-income homes are less likely to achieve in school and are less likely to complete their schooling than children with more affluent parents.[16] Poor children are also more likely to suffer from health problems and receive inadequate health care. Unfortunately, the number of children covered by health insurance is declining and will continue to do so for the foreseeable future.[17] Due to the lack of health benefits and without the means to afford medical care, chances are good that health problems afflicting these children may impede their long-term development. Children who live in extreme poverty or who remain poor for multiple years appear to suffer the worst outcomes. The timing of poverty also seems to be relevant. Findings suggest that poverty during early childhood may impact children more than poverty during adolescence or teen years.[18]

In addition to having an increased chance of physical illness, poor children are also much more likely than wealthy children to suffer various social and physical ills, ranging from low birth weight to a limited chance of earning a college degree. The social problems found in lower-class slum areas have been described as an "epidemic" that spreads like a contagious disease, destroying the inner workings that enable neighborhoods to survive; they become "hollowed out."[19] As neighborhood quality decreases, the probability that residents will develop problems sharply increases. Adolescents in the worst neighborhoods share the greatest risk of dropping out of school and becoming teenage parents.

There are significant racial and ethnic differences in the rates of child poverty. As Table 7.1 shows, more than twice as many African-American and Hispanic children are likely to be poor as white and Asian children.

The Underclass In 1966 sociologist Oscar Lewis argued that the crushing lifestyle of slum areas produces a culture of poverty passed from one generation to the next.[20] Apathy, cynicism, helplessness, and mistrust of social institutions, such as schools, government agencies, and the police, mark the **culture of poverty**. This mistrust prevents slum dwellers from taking advantage of the meager opportunities available to them. Lewis's work was the first of a group that described the plight of **at-risk** children and adults. In 1970 Swedish economist Gunnar Myrdal described a worldwide **underclass** that was cut off from society, its members lacking the education and skills needed to be effectively in demand in modern society.[21] In 1982 Ken Auletta described a U.S. underclass in much the same terms.[22]

The burdens of underclass life (discussed in the Race, Culture, Gender, and Criminology feature titled "When Work Disappears") are most often felt by minority group members. Although minority poverty has actually been declining faster than that of non-Hispanic whites, about 26 percent of African-Americans and 27 percent of Hispanic Americans still live in poverty, compared to 8.6 percent of the white population. According to the U.S. Census Bureau, the median 1998 family income for white families was about $37,000, whereas African-Americans and Hispanic families earned about $24,000.[23] Asian and Pacific Islanders were actually the highest-earning U.S. racial/ethnic group in 1998. About 26 percent of black households had no assets, while 8 percent were worth more than $100,000; in contrast, only 10 percent of white households had no assets, and 32 percent were worth more than $100,000. One reason for this discrepancy is home

Sociologist William Julius Wilson is the author of *The Truly Disadvantaged* and *When Work Disappears*. According to Wilson, social breakdown in inner-city areas magnifies the isolation of the underclass from mainstream society and promotes a ghetto culture and behavior.

ownership rates: 42 percent of black and 63 percent of white households were owned by a resident.

Economic disparity will continually haunt members of the underclass and their children. Even if they value education and other middle-class norms, their desperate life circumstances (like high unemployment and non-traditional family structures) may prevent them from developing the skills, habits, and styles that lead first to educational success and later to success in the workplace. Both of these factors have been linked to crime and drug abuse.[24] These problems are exacerbated by the fact that in some jurisdictions, a significant portion—up to half—of all minority males are under criminal justice system control. The costs of crime, such as paying for lawyers and court costs, perpetuate poverty by depriving families and children of this money.[25]

Are the Poor Undeserving?

Despite all our technological success, the fact that a significant percentage of U.S. citizens either are homeless or live in areas of concentrated poverty is an important social problem. The media frequently focus on the distress suffered by homeless and poverty-stricken families. Yet some view impoverished people as somehow responsible for their own fate, the so-called **undeserving poor;** if they tried, the argument goes, they could "improve themselves."[26] This conclusion is baseless. Poverty is becoming more concentrated among minority groups who are forced to live in physically deteriorated inner-city neighborhoods that have lots of crime, poor schools, and excessive mortality.[27] A study by the

Table 7.1	**Race and Child Poverty**	
RACE OR ETHNICITY	**NUMBER IN THOUSANDS**	**PERCENTAGE OF CHILDREN IN GROUP WHO ARE POOR**
Hispanic	4,237	40.0
African-American	4,519	39.9
Asian/Pacific Islander	571	19.5
White	9,044	16.3

Source: Children's Defense Fund, *The State of America's Children, 1998* (Washington, D.C.: Children's Defense Fund, 1998), p. 4.

When Work Disappears

In 1987 William Julius Wilson described the plight of the lowest levels of the underclass, which he labeled the **truly disadvantaged.** Wilson portrayed members of this group as socially isolated people who dwell in inner cities, occupy the bottom rung of the social ladder, and are victims of discrimination. They live in areas in which the basic institutions of society—family, school, and housing—have long since declined. Their decline triggers similar breakdowns in the strengths of inner-city areas, including the loss of community cohesion and the ability of people living in the area to control the flow of drugs and criminal activity. For example, in a more affluent area, neighbors might complain to parents that their children are acting out. In distressed areas, this element of informal social control may be absent because parents are under stress or absent. These effects magnify the isolation of the underclass from mainstream society and promote a ghetto culture and behavior.

Because the truly disadvantaged rarely come into contact with the actual source of their oppression, they direct their anger and aggression at those with whom they are in close contact, such as neighbors, businesspeople, and landlords. Members of this group, plagued by under- or unemployment, begin to lose self-confidence, a feeling supported by the plight of kin and friendship groups who also experience extreme economic marginality. Self-doubt is a neighborhood norm, overwhelming those forced to live in areas of concentrated poverty.

In one of his more recent works, *When Work Disappears,* Wilson assesses the effect of joblessness and underemployment on residents in poor neighborhoods on Chicago's South Side. He argues that for the first time in the twentieth century, most adults in inner-city ghetto neighborhoods are not working during a typical week. He finds that inner-city life is only marginally affected by the surge in the nation's economy, which has been brought about by new industrial growth connected with technological development. Poverty in these inner-city areas is eternal, unchanging, and, if anything, worsening as residents are further shut out of the economic mainstream.

Wilson focuses on the plight of the African-American community, which had enjoyed periods of relative prosperity in the 1950s and 1960s. He suggests that as difficult as life was in the 1940s and 1950s for African-Americans, they at least had a reasonable hope of steady work. Now, because of the globalization of the economy, those opportunities have evaporated. Although past racial segregation limited opportunity, growth in the manufacturing sector fueled upward mobility and provided the foundation of today's African-American middle class. Those opportunities no longer exist as manufacturing plants have moved to inaccessible rural and overseas locations where the cost of doing business is lower. With manufacturing opportunities all but obsolete in the United States, service and retail establishments, which depended on blue-collar spending, have similarly disappeared, leaving behind an economy based on welfare and government support. In fewer than 20 years, formerly active African-American communities have become crime-infested slums.

The hardships faced by residents in Chicago's South Side are not unique to that community. Besides sustaining inner-city poverty, the absence of employment opportunities has torn at the social fabric of the nation's inner-city neighborhoods. Work helps socialize young people, instilling in them such desirable values as hard work, caring, and respect for others. When work becomes scarce, however, the discipline and structure it provides are absent. Communitywide underemployment destroys social cohesion, increasing the presence of neighborhood social problems ranging from drug use to educational failure. Schools in these areas are unable to teach basic skills, and because desirable employment is lacking, few adults serve as role models. In contrast to more affluent suburban households where daily life is organized around job and career demands, children in inner-city areas are not socialized in the workings of the mainstream economy.

Wilson is not optimistic about the job prospects of lower-class African-American males; neither white nor black employers seem particularly inclined to hire poor black men. He is skeptical that private employers will hire the poor as child care providers or in other service tasks even if given tax incentives to do so. Instead, Wilson believes that only a nationwide effort to improve schools, provide day care, and enhance public transportation can turn the inner city around. A public works program modeled after the Depression-era efforts of the Roosevelt administration's Works Project Administration (WPA) may be needed to reverse the damage of inner-city unemployment. People want to work; they must be given the opportunity for legitimate, sustaining employment.

CRITICAL THINKING

1. Is it unrealistic to assume that a government-sponsored public works program can provide needed jobs in this era of budget cutbacks?
2. What are some of the hidden costs of unemployment in a community setting?
3. How would a biocriminologist explain Wilson's findings?

 INFOTRAC COLLEGE EDITION RESEARCH

For more on Wilson's view of poverty, unemployment, and crime, see: Gunnar Almgren, Avery Guest, George Immerwahr, Michael Spittel. Joblessness, family disruption, and violent death in Chicago, 1970–90. *Social Forces,* June 1998 v76 n4 p1465.

William Julius Wilson. Inner-city dislocations. *Society,* Jan–Feb 1998 v35 n2 p270.

Source: William Julius Wilson, *The Truly Disadvantaged* (Chicago: University of Chicago Press, 1987); William Julius Wilson, *When Work Disappears: The World of the Urban Poor* (New York: Alfred Knopf, 1996).

National Research Council on inner-city poverty in the United States concludes that poor people living in areas of extreme poverty are more likely to suffer social ills than poor people living in more affluent communities.[28] People living in urban ghettos suffer higher rates of unemployment, depend more on welfare, and are more likely to live in single-parent households than equally indigent people who reside in more affluent areas. The burden of living in these high-poverty areas, then, goes beyond merely being poor; under these conditions, self-help and upward mobility are highly problematic.

Community effects may particularly damage children. Adolescents residing in areas of concentrated poverty are more likely to suffer in their cognitive development, sexual understanding, school attendance habits, and transition to employment.[29] Lack of education and family instability make them poor candidates for employment or for the eventual formation of their own cohesive families. These findings suggest that the poor of inner-city ghettos confront obstacles far greater than the mere lack of financial resources. The National Research Council's review indicates that the social problems faced by the poor render them unprepared to take advantage of employment opportunities even in tight labor markets.[30] The fact that many of the underclass are African-American children who can expect to spend all their lives in poverty may be the single most important problem facing the nation today.[31]

SOCIAL STRUCTURE THEORIES

Many criminologists view the disadvantaged economic class position as a primary cause of crime. This view is referred to as **social structure theory.** As a group, social structure theories suggest that social and economic forces operating in deteriorated lower-class areas push many of their residents into criminal behavior patterns. These theories consider the existence of unsupervised teenage gangs, high crime rates, and social disorder in slum areas as major social problems.

Lower-class crime is often the violent, destructive product of youth gangs and marginally employed or underemployed young adults. Underemployment means that many working adults earn relatively low wages and have few benefits such as health insurance and retirement programs. Their ability to accumulate capital for home ownership is restricted, and so, consequently, is their stake in society.

Although members of the middle and upper classes also engage in crime, social structure theorists view middle-class and white-collar crime as being of relatively lower frequency, seriousness, and danger to the general public. The real crime problem is essentially a lower-class phenomenon that breeds criminal behavior, begins in youth, and continues into young adulthood.

Most social structure theories focus on children's law-violating behavior. They suggest that the social forces that cause crime begin to affect people while they are relatively young and continue to influence them throughout their lives. Although not all youthful offenders become adult criminals, many begin their training and learn criminal values as members of youth gangs and groups.

Social structure theorists challenge those who suggest that crime expresses psychological imbalance, biological traits, insensitivity to social controls, personal choice, or any other personal trait. They argue that people living in equivalent social environments tend to behave similarly. If the environment did not influence human behavior, then crime rates would be distributed equally across the social structure, which they are not.[32] Because crime rates are higher in lower-class urban centers than in middle-class suburbs, social forces must influence or control behavior.[33] We will examine some specific structure theories that support this perspective.

Branches of Social Structure Theory

There are three independent yet overlapping branches within the social structure perspective—*social disorganization theory, strain theory,* and *cultural deviance theory,* as outlined in Figure 7.1.

Social disorganization theory focuses on the urban conditions that affect crime rates. A *disorganized area* is one in which institutions of social control, such as the family, commercial establishments, and schools, have broken down and can no longer perform their expected or stated functions. Indicators of social disorganization include high unemployment and school dropout rates, deteriorated housing, low income levels, and large numbers of single-parent households. Residents in these areas experience conflict and despair, and as a result, antisocial behavior flourishes.

Strain theory, the second branch of social structure theory, holds that crime is a function of the conflict between people's goals and the means they can use to legally obtain them. Strain theorists argue that although social and economic goals are common to people in all economic strata, the ability to obtain these goals is class-dependent. Most people in the United States desire wealth, material possessions, power, prestige, and other life comforts. Members of the lower class are unable to achieve these symbols of success through conventional means. Consequently, they feel anger, frustration, and resentment, which is referred to as **strain.** Lower-class citizens can either accept their condition and live as socially responsible, if unrewarded, citizens, or they can choose an alternative means of achieving success, such as theft, violence, or drug trafficking.

Cultural deviance theory, the third variation of structural theory, combines elements of both strain and social disorganization theories. According to this view, because of strain and social isolation, a unique lower-

Figure 7.1 The Three Branches of Social Structure Theory

Social disorganization theory focuses on conditions in the environment:
- Deteriorated neighborhoods
- Inadequate social control
- Law-violating gangs and groups
- Conflicting social values

Cultural deviance theory combines the other two:
- Development of subcultures as a result of disorganization and stress
- Subcultural values in opposition to conventional values

CRIME

Strain theory focuses on conflict between goals and means:
- Unequal distribution of wealth and power
- Frustration
- Alternative methods of achievement

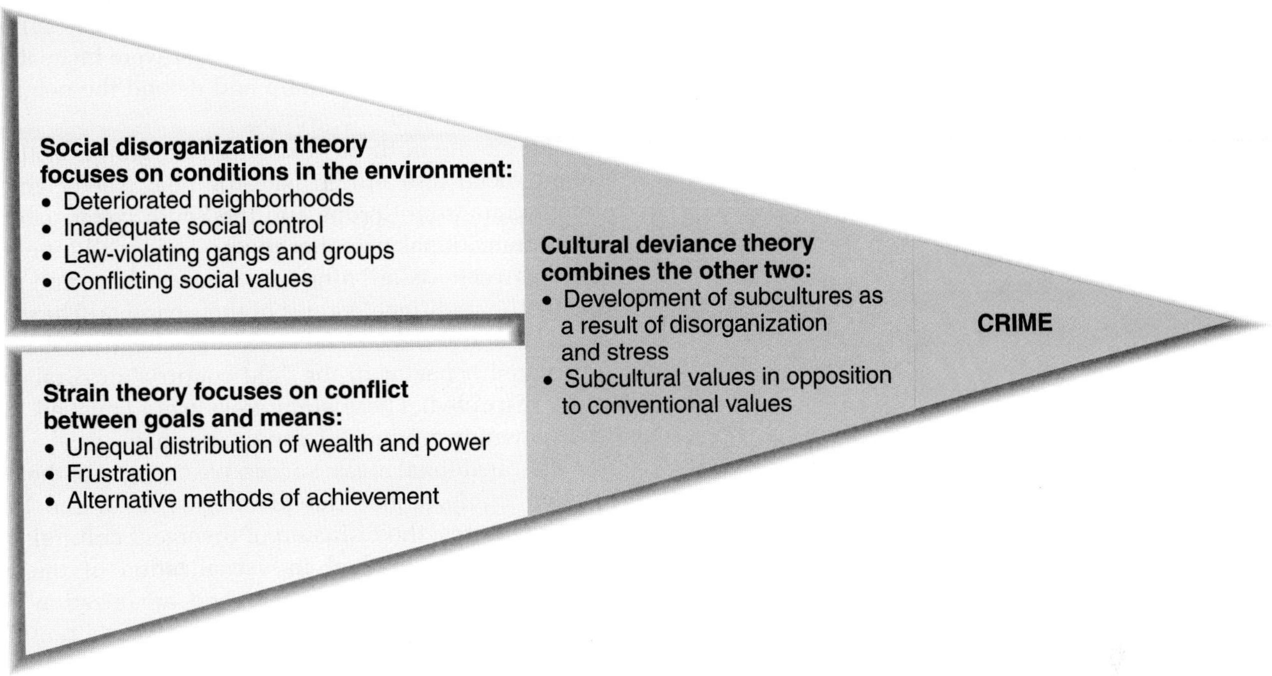

class culture develops in disorganized neighborhoods. These independent **subcultures** maintain unique values and beliefs that conflict with conventional social norms. Criminal behavior is an expression of conformity to lower-class subcultural values and traditions, not a rebellion from conventional society. Subcultural values are handed down from one generation to the next in a process called **cultural transmission.**

Although each of these theories is distinct in critical aspects, each approach has at its core the view that socially isolated people, living in disorganized neighborhoods, are likely to experience crime-producing social forces. Each branch of social structure theory will now be discussed in some detail.

SOCIAL DISORGANIZATION THEORY

Social disorganization theory links crime rates to neighborhood ecological characteristics. Crime rates are elevated in highly transient, mixed-use (where residential and commercial property exist side by side), and changing neighborhoods in which the fabric of social life has become frayed. These localities are unable to provide essential services, such as education, health care, and proper housing, and as a result, they experience significant levels of unemployment, single-parent families, and families on welfare.

Social disorganization theory views crime-ridden neighborhoods as those in which residents are trying to leave at the earliest opportunity. Residents are uninterested in community matters, so the common sources of control—the family, school, business community, social service agencies—are weak and disorganized. Personal relationships are strained because neighbors are constantly moving. Constant resident turnover weakens communications and blocks attempts at solving neighborhood problems or establishing common goals (see Figure 7.2).[34]

The Work of Shaw and McKay

Social disorganization theory was popularized by the work of two Chicago sociologists, Clifford R. Shaw and Henry McKay, who linked life in transitional slum areas to the inclination to commit crime. Shaw and McKay began their pioneering work on Chicago crime during the early 1920s while working as researchers for a state-supported social service agency.[35] They were heavily influenced by the Chicago School sociologists Ernest Burgess and Robert Park, who had pioneered the ecological analysis of urban life.

Shaw and McKay began their analysis during a period in the city's history that was fairly typical of the transition that was taking place in many other urban areas. Chicago had experienced a mid-nineteenth-century population expansion, fueled by a dramatic influx of foreign-born immigrants and, later, migrating

Figure 7.2 Social Disorganization Theory

Poverty
- Development of isolated slums
- Lack of conventional social opportunities
- Racial and ethnic discrimination

Social disorganization
- Breakdown of social institutions and organizations such as school and family
- Lack of informal social control

Breakdown of social control
- Development of gangs, groups
- Peer group replaces family and social institutions

Criminal areas
- Neighborhood becomes crime-prone
- Stable pockets of delinquency develop
- Lack of external support and investment

Cultural transmission
Older youths pass norms (focal concerns) to younger generation, creating stable slum culture

Criminal careers
Most youths "age out" of delinquency, marry, and raise families, but some remain in life of crime

---

opment of the city. They saw that Chicago had developed into distinct neighborhoods (*natural areas*), some affluent and others wracked by extreme poverty. These poverty-ridden **transitional neighborhoods** suffered high rates of population turnover and were incapable of inducing residents to remain and defend the neighborhoods against criminal groups.

Low rents in these areas attracted groups with different racial and ethnic backgrounds. Newly arrived immigrants from Europe and the South congregated in these transitional neighborhoods. Their children were torn between assimilating into a new culture and abiding by the traditional values of their parents. They soon found that informal social control mechanisms that had restrained behavior in the "old country" or rural areas were disrupted. These slum areas were believed to be the spawning grounds of young criminals.

In transitional areas, successive changes in the population composition, the disintegration of the traditional cultures, the diffusion of divergent cultural standards, and the gradual industrialization of the area dissolve neighborhood culture and organization. The continuity of conventional neighborhood traditions and institutions is broken, leaving children feeling displaced and without a strong or definitive set of values.

Concentric Zones   Shaw and McKay identified the areas in Chicago that had excessive crime rates. Using a model of analysis pioneered by Ernest Burgess, they noted that distinct ecological areas had developed in the city, comprising a series of five concentric circles, or zones, and that there were stable and significant differences in interzone crime rates (see Figure 7.3). The areas of heaviest crime concentration appeared to be the transitional inner-city zones, where large numbers of foreign-born citizens had recently settled.[37] The zones farthest from the city's center had correspondingly lower crime rates.

Analysis of these data indicated a surprisingly stable pattern of criminal activity in the five ecological zones over 65 years. Shaw and McKay concluded that in the transitional neighborhoods, multiple cultures and diverse values, both conventional and deviant, coexist. Children growing up in the street culture often find that adults who have adopted a deviant lifestyle (for example, the gambler, pimp, or drug dealer) are the most financially successful people in the neighborhood. Required to choose between conventional and deviant lifestyles, many slum kids opt for the latter. They join other like-minded youths and form law-violating gangs and cliques. The development of teenage law-violating groups is an essential element of youthful misbehavior in slum areas. The values that slum youths adopt often conflict with existing middle-class norms, which demand strict obedience to the legal code. Consequently, a value conflict further separates the delinquent youth and his or her peer group from conventional society; the result is a more solid embrace of deviant goals and

---

southern families. Congregating in the central city, the newcomers occupied the oldest housing areas and therefore faced numerous health and environmental hazards.

Sections of the city started to physically deteriorate. This condition prompted the city's wealthy, established citizens to become concerned about the moral fabric of Chicago society. The belief was widespread that immigrants from Europe and the rural South were crime-prone and morally dissolute. In fact, local groups were created to "save" the children of poor families from moral decadence.[36] It was popular to view crime as the property of inferior racial and ethnic groups.

Transitional Neighborhoods   Shaw and McKay explained crime and delinquency within the context of the changing urban environment and ecological devel-

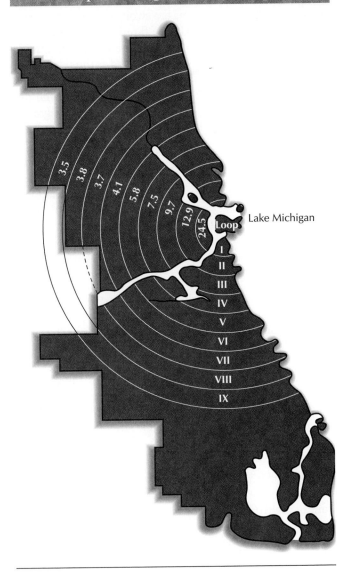

Figure 7.3 Shaw and McKay's Concentric Zones Map of Chicago

3.5
3.8
3.7
4.1
5.8
7.5
9.7
12.9
24.5

Loop

Lake Michigan

I
II
III
IV
V
VI
VII
VIII
IX

Note: Arabic numerals represent the rate of male delinquency.

Source: Clifford R. Shaw et al., *Delinquency Areas* (Chicago: University of Chicago Press, 1929), p. 99. Reprinted with permission. Copyright 1929 by the University of Chicago. All rights reserved.

behavior. To further justify their choice of goals, these youths seek support for their choice by recruiting new members and passing on the delinquent tradition.

Shaw and McKay's statistical analysis confirmed their theoretical suspicions. They found that even though crime rates changed, the highest rates were always in zones I and II (the central city and a transitional area). The areas with the highest crime rates retained high rates even when their ethnic composition changed (the areas Shaw and McKay examined shifted from German and Irish to Italian and Polish).[38]

The Legacy of Shaw and McKay Social disorganization concepts articulated by Shaw and McKay have

remained prominent within criminology for over 75 years. The most important of Shaw and McKay's findings was that crime rates correspond to neighborhood structure and that crime is created by the destructive ecological conditions in urban slums. They contended that criminals are not, as some criminologists of the time believed, biologically inferior, intellectually impaired, or psychologically damaged. Their research supported their belief that crime is a constant fixture in areas of poverty regardless of residents' racial or ethnic identity. Because the basis of their theory was that neighborhood disintegration and slum conditions are the primary causes of criminal behavior, Shaw and McKay paved the way for many community action and treatment programs developed in the last half-century.

CONNECTIONS

Shaw founded a very influential community-based treatment program, the Chicago Area Project, which is discussed later in this chapter. The Chicago Area Project was the forerunner of neighborhood revitalization programs that have been attempted since the 1960s.

Another important feature of Shaw and McKay's work is that it depicted both adult criminality and delinquent gang memberships as normal responses to the adverse social conditions in urban slum areas. Their findings mirror Emile Durkheim's concept that crime can be normal and useful.

CONNECTIONS

As you may recall, Chapter 1 discussed Durkheim's contributions to social theory and the founding of criminology. Durkheim reasoned that crime is beneficial because a rising crime rate can signal the need for social change. Efforts to relieve human suffering might be abandoned if the threat of crime did not remind us of their benefits.

Despite these noteworthy achievements, the validity of Shaw and McKay's findings has been challenged. Some have faulted their assumption that neighborhoods are essentially stable, whereas others have found their definition of social disorganization confusing.[39] The most important criticism, however, concerns their use of police records to calculate neighborhood crime rates. A zone's high crime rate may be a function of the level of local police surveillance, and therefore interzone crime rate differences may be obscured. Numerous studies indicate that police use extensive discretion when arresting people and that social status influences their decisions.[40] It is likely that people in middle-class neighborhoods commit many criminal acts that never show up in official statistics, whereas people in lower-class areas face a far greater chance of arrest and court adjudication.[41] The relationship between ecology and crime rates may therefore reflect police behavior more than criminal behavior.

These criticisms aside, Shaw and McKay's theory provides a valuable contribution to our understanding of the causes of criminal behavior. By introducing a new variable—the ecology of the city—into the study of crime, the authors paved the way for a whole generation of criminologists to study social influences on criminal and delinquent behavior.

The Social Ecology School

During the 1970s criminologists were influenced by several critical analyses of social disorganization theory that challenged its validity.[42] During this period, theories with a social–psychological orientation stressed offender socialization within the family, school, and peer group. These ideas dominated the criminological literature of that time.

CONNECTIONS

If social disorganization causes crime, why are most low-income people law-abiding? To explain this anomaly, some sociologists have devised theoretical models suggesting that individual socialization experiences mediate environmental influences. These theories will be discussed in Chapter 8.

Despite its fall from grace, the social disorganization tradition was kept alive by area studies conducted by Bernard Lander in Baltimore, David Bordua in Detroit, and Roland Chilton in Indianapolis. These studies showed that ecological conditions such as substandard housing, low income, and unrelated people living together predicted a high incidence of delinquency.[43]

In the 1980s a group of criminologists continued studying ecological conditions, reviving concern about the effects of social disorganization.[44] These modern social ecologists developed a purer form of structural theory that emphasizes the association of community deterioration and economic decline to criminality, but places less emphasis on value conflict. The following sections discuss some of the more recent social ecological research.

Community Deterioration   Crime rates and the need for police services are associated with community deterioration: disorder, poverty, alienation, disassociation, and fear of crime.[45] For example, neighborhoods with a high percentage of deserted houses and apartments experience high crime rates; abandoned buildings serve as a "magnet for crime."[46] Areas in which houses are in poor repair, boarded up, and burned out, whose owners are best described as slumlords, are also the location of the highest violence rates and gun crime.[47] These

neighborhoods, in which retail establishments often go bankrupt, are abandoned and deteriorate physically.[48]

The percentage of people living in poverty and the percentage of broken homes are strongly related to neighborhood crime rates.[49] Gangs flourish in deteriorated neighborhoods, adding to the crime rate. Gang homicide rates are associated with such variables as the percentage of the neighborhood living below the poverty line, the lack of mortgage investment in a neighborhood, the unemployment rate, and the influx of new immigrants; these factors are usually found in disorganized areas.[50]

CONNECTIONS

Later in this chapter the gang problem is discussed in some detail. Today there are more than 680,000 gang members in the United States, a constant reminder of the nagging social problems found in inner-city disorganized neighborhoods.

Communities characterized by sparse friendship networks, unsupervised teenage peer groups, and low organizational participation also have the most criminality. This relationship is not unique to the United States; the social disorganization model is robust enough to explain crime rates outside the United States as well.[51] Cross-national research conducted in Scandinavia found a clear link between crime and measures of social disorganization.[52] Likewise, in Great Britain socially disorganized neighborhoods were found to experience more crime and victimization than more stable neighborhoods.

Employment Opportunities   The relationship between unemployment and crime is still unsettled: aggregate crime rates and aggregate unemployment rates seem weakly related. Crime rates sometimes rise during periods of economic prosperity and fall during periods of decline. Yet Shaw and McKay claimed that areas continually wracked by poverty also experience social disorganization.[53] The crime–unemployment association may be place- and time-specific: unemployment may produce crime in particular areas at certain times. Research indicates that neighborhoods with few employment opportunities for youth and adults are the most vulnerable to predatory crime such as armed robbery and muggings.[54] Unemployment destabilizes households, and unstable families are likely to breed children who use violence and aggression to deal with limited opportunity. This lack of opportunity perpetuates higher crime rates, especially when large groups or cohorts of people of the same age compete for relatively scant resources.[55]

Limited employment opportunities also reduce the stabilizing influence of parents and other adults, who may once have counteracted the allure of youth gangs. Sociologist Elijah Anderson's analysis of Philadelphia

Disorganized neighborhoods are often terrorized by rowdy youth, drunks, vagabonds, and loiterers, who leave trash, litter, and graffiti in their wake. Rather than attractive parks and boulevards, they contain abandoned storefronts, burned-out buildings, and littered lots. Pedestrians are harassed by prostitutes and suffer noise, congestion, angry words, dirt, and stench. People try to avoid such neighborhoods knowing if they enter them they face a considerable chance of becoming crime victims.

neighborhood life found that "old heads" (respected neighborhood residents), who at one time played an important role in socializing youth, have been displaced by younger street hustlers and drug dealers. Although the old heads complain that these newcomers may not have earned or worked for their fortune in the old-fashioned way, the old heads admire and envy these kids whose gold chains and luxury cars advertise their wealth amid poverty.[56] So while the old heads may admire the fruits of crime, they disdain the violent manner in which they are acquired.

Community Fear Disorganized neighborhoods suffer social and physical incivilities—rowdy youth, trash and litter, graffiti, abandoned storefronts, burned-out buildings, littered lots, strangers, drunks, vagabonds, loiterers, prostitutes, noise, congestion, angry words, dirt, and stench. The presence of such incivilities makes residents of disorganized areas believe that their neighborhood is dangerous and that they face a considerable chance of becoming crime victims. Therefore, when crime rates are actually high in these disorganized areas, fear levels increase dramatically.[57] Perceptions of crime and victimization produce neighborhood fear.[58]

Fear becomes most pronounced in areas undergoing rapid, unexpected racial and age composition changes, especially when they are out of proportion to the rest of the city.[59] Whites become particularly fearful when they sense that they are becoming a racial minority in their neighborhood; African-Americans seem less affected by

racial change.[60] Although fear experienced by whites may be based on racial stereotypes, it may also be caused by the premonition that they will become less well protected because police do not provide adequate services in a predominantly African-American neighborhood.[61]

Fear can be contagious. People tell others when they have been victimized, thus spreading the word that the neighborhood is getting dangerous and that the chance of future victimization is high.[62] As a result, people dread leaving their homes at night and withdraw from community life. Not surprisingly, people who have already been victimized fear the future more than those who have escaped crime.[63]

CONNECTIONS

Fear of repeat victimization may be both instinctual and accurate. Remember that in Chapter 4 we discussed the fact that some people suffer repeated victimization.

When people live in areas where life expectancies are short, they may alter their behavior out of fear. They may wonder why they should plan for the future when they may never see it. In such areas young boys and girls may psychologically assimilate by taking risks and discounting the future. Teenage birth rates soar, and so do violence rates.[64] For these children, the inevitability of death skews their perspective and how they live.

Fear is a powerful influence. When it grips a neighborhood, business conditions begin to deteriorate, population mobility increases, and a "criminal element" begins to drift into the area.[65] In essence, the existence of fear incites more crime, increasing the chances of victimization and producing even more fear in a never-ending loop.[66]

Siege Mentality A unique aspect of community fear is the development of a **siege mentality,** in which the outside world is considered the enemy out to destroy the neighborhood. Elijah Anderson found that residents in the African-American neighborhoods he studied believed in the existence of a secret plan to eradicate the population by such strategies as permanent unemployment, police brutality, imprisonment, drug distribution, and AIDS.[67] This conspiracy was believed to be hatched by white officials and political leaders and demonstrated by lax law enforcement in poor areas. Residents felt that police cared little about black-on-black crime because it helped reduce the population. Rumors abounded that federal government agencies, such as the CIA, controlled the drug trade and used profits to fund illegal overseas operations. This siege mentality causes mistrust of critical social institutions, including business, government, and schools. To these residents, government officials seem arrogant and haughty. Residents become self-conscious, worry about garnering any respect, and are particularly attuned to anyone who disrespects or "disses" them. For example, in November 1998 Ruth Sherman, a white third-grade teacher in New York City, was removed from the classroom after protests by African-American parents that she used a racially insensitive book in her class. Rumors had circulated throughout the community that the book in question, *Nappy Hair,* was disrespectful of African-Americans. Later it was revealed that the text was actually written by Carolivia Herron, a black writer and scholar, in order to promote diversity and increase children's self-esteem. After years of suffering racism and discrimination, however, many members of the minority community are suspicious of government officials, even teachers, who are viewed as hostile, insensitive, and disrespectful.[68] Because of this feeling of mistrust, when police ignore crime in poor areas or, conversely, when they are violent and corrupt, anger flares, and people take to the streets and react violently.

Population Turnover In our postmodern society, urban areas undergoing rapid structural changes in racial and economic composition also seem to experience the greatest change in crime rates. Recent studies recognize that change, not stability, is the hallmark of inner-city areas. A neighborhood's residents, wealth, density, and purpose are constantly evolving. Even disorganized neighborhoods acquire new identifying features. Some may become multiracial, while others become racially homogeneous. Some areas become stable and family-oriented, while in others, mobile, never-married people predominate.[69]

As areas decline, residents flee to safer, more stable locales. Those who cannot afford to leave for more affluent communities face an increased risk of victimization. Because of racial differences in economic well-being, those left behind are often minority citizens.[70] Those who cannot move find themselves surrounded by new residents. High population turnover can devastate community culture because it thwarts communication and information flow.[71] In response to this turnover, a culture may develop that dictates standards of dress, language, and behavior to neighborhood youth that are opposite those of conventional society. All these factors are likely to increase crime rates.

Community Change Social ecologists have attempted to chart the change that undermines some urban areas. Urban areas seem to have life cycles that begin with building dwellings, followed by a period of decline with marked decreases in socioeconomic status and increases in population density.[72] Later stages in this life cycle include changing racial or ethnic makeup, population thinning, and finally, a renewal stage in which obsolete housing is replaced and upgraded (gentrification). Areas undergoing such change experience increases in their crime rates.[73]

As communities go through cycles, neighborhood deterioration precedes increasing rates of crime and delinquency.[74] Neighborhoods most at risk for increased crime contain large numbers of single-parent families and unrelated people living together, have changed from owner-occupied to renter-occupied units, and have lost semiskilled and unskilled jobs (indicating a growing residue of discouraged workers who are no longer seeking employment).[75] These ecological disruptions strain existing social control mechanisms and inhibit their ability to control crime and delinquency.

Criminologist Robert Bursik has shown that changing lifestyles, including declining economic status, increasing population, and racial shifts, are associated with increased neighborhood crime rates.[76] Areas adjoining neighborhoods undergoing racial change will experience corresponding increases in their own crime rates.[77] This phenomenon may reflect community reaction to perceived racial conflict. In changing neighborhoods, adults may actually encourage young lawbreakers by expressing attitudes that justify violence as a means of protecting their property and way of life by violently resisting newcomers.

Poverty Concentration One aspect of community change may be the concentration of poverty in deteriorated neighborhoods. Although poverty or unemployment may not directly cause crime, areas that are the most deteriorated, even within the context of inner-city poverty, seem to have much higher crime rates than more stable lower-class environments. William Julius Wilson describes how working and middle-class families flee inner-city poverty areas, resulting in a **concentration effect,** in which the most disadvantaged population is consolidated in urban ghettos. As the working and middle classes move out, they take with them their financial and institutional resources and support. Businesses are disinclined to locate in poor areas; banks become reluctant to lend money for new housing or businesses.[78] Areas marked by concentrated poverty become isolated and insulated from the social mainstream and more prone to criminal activity. Gangs also concentrate in these areas, bringing with them a significant increase in criminal activity. For example, the two most dangerous areas in Chicago (Garfield Park and Humboldt Park) had 76 times more gang-related street crime than the two least dangerous areas (Mount Greenwood and Edison Park).[79]

The concentration effect contradicts, in some measure, Shaw and McKay's assumption that crime rates increase in transitional neighborhoods. Today the most crime-prone areas may be stable, homogeneous areas whose residents are trapped in public housing and urban ghettos. Ethnically and racially isolated areas maintain the highest crime rates.[80]

Weak Social Controls　Most people share the common goal of living in a crime-free area. Some communities have the power to regulate the behavior of their residents through the influence of community institutions such as the family and school. Cohesive communities with high levels of social control develop *collective efficacy:* mutual trust, a willingness to intervene in the supervision of children, and the maintenance of public order.[81] Communities with high collective efficacy generally experience low violence rates and low levels of physical and social disorder. In contrast, neighborhoods with low collective efficacy suffer high rates of violence and significant physical and social disorder. Moreover, it is rare to find neighborhoods with high collective efficacy surrounded by communities with low collective efficacy. This suggests that spillover effects extend beyond the geographic boundaries of a single neighborhood.

Socially disorganized neighborhoods find that efforts at social control are weak and attenuated. When community social control efforts are blunted, crime rates increase, further weakening neighborhood cohesiveness. Neighborhoods maintain a variety of agencies and institutions of social control. Some operate on the primary or private level and involve the control placed on people by their peers and families. These sources exert informal control by either awarding or withholding approval, respect, and admiration. Informal control mechanisms include direct criticism, ridicule, ostracism, desertion, or physical punishment.[82] For example, families may exert control by corporal punishment, withholding privileges, or ridiculing lazy or disrespectful children. Communities also use internal networks and local institutions to control crime. Sources of institutional social control include businesses, schools, churches, and social service and volunteer organizations.[83]

Stable neighborhoods can arrange for external sources of social control. The level of policing, an important source of neighborhood stability, may vary between neighborhoods. Police officers patrolling in stable, low-crime areas may have the resources and motivation to respond vigorously to crime, preventing criminal groups from gaining a toehold in the neighborhood.[84] Additionally, community organizations and local leaders may have sufficient political clout to get funding for additional law enforcement personnel. The presence of police sends a message that the area will not tolerate deviant behavior. Criminals and drug dealers avoid such areas and relocate to easier and more appealing targets.[85] In more disorganized areas, on the other hand, police officers are less motivated and their resources are stretched more tightly. These communities cannot mount an effective social control effort because as neighborhood disadvantage increases, informal social control decreases.[86]

The ramifications of having adequate controls are critical. In areas where social control remains high, children are less likely to become involved with deviant peers and engage in problem behaviors.[87] In disorganized areas, however, the population is transient, so interpersonal relationships remain superficial. Social institutions like schools and churches cannot work effectively in a climate of alienation and mistrust. In these areas, the absence of political power brokers limits access to external funding and protection; without outside money, the neighborhood cannot get back on its feet.[88]

Social control is also weakened because unsupervised peer groups and gangs, which flourish in disorganized areas, disrupt the influence of neighborhood control agents.[89] Children who reside in these neighborhoods find that involvement with conventional social institutions, such as schools and afternoon programs, is blocked; they are instead at risk for recruitment into gangs.[90]

Weak social control causes overreliance on formal punishment, such as arrest and prosecution, to control offenders—a situation that helps destabilize neighborhoods by putting many of their residents behind bars.

Social Support/Altruism　Neighborhoods that provide strong social supports for their members help young people cope with life's stressors. Sometimes this is organized on the block level, where neighbors meet face-to-face to deal with problems. Crime rates may be lower on blocks where people preserve their immediate environment by confronting destabilizing forces such as teen gangs and encourage others to do so also.[91] By helping neighbors become more resilient and self-confident, adults in these areas can provide external support systems that enable youths to desist from crime. For example, residents can teach one another that they have moral and social obligations to their fellow citizens; children can learn to be sensitive to the rights of others and respect differences. Residents may form neighborhood associations and self-help groups. In contrast, less altruistic areas stress individualism and self-interest.

Areas that stress caring for fellow citizens are less crime-prone than those that emphasize self-reliance. Even in the cities' poorest areas, if people are generous and caring, their neighborhoods are also relatively crime-free. **Social altruism** (such as contributions given to charity) has been found to be inversely related to crime rates.[92] This relationship can be interpreted in one of two ways: (1) crime rates are lower in altruistic areas because of the overall positive social climate; or (2) well-funded charities in these areas help lower crime rates by providing a secure safety net for at-risk families.

The government can encourage social altruism by providing economic and social support through publicly funded social support and welfare programs. Although welfare programs are often criticized as being government handouts by conservative politicians, there is a significant negative association between the amount of welfare money people receive and crime rates.[93] Government assistance may help people improve their social status by providing them with the financial resources to clothe, feed, and educate their children while at the same time reducing stress, frustration, and anger.

According to the social ecology school, then, social disorganization produces criminality; and the quality of community life, including levels of change, fear, incivility, poverty, and deterioration, directly influences an area's crime rate. It is not some individual property or trait that causes some people to commit crime, but rather the quality and ambience of the community in which they reside. Conversely, in socially altruistic areas, crime rates decrease no matter what the economic situation.

STRAIN THEORIES

Inhabitants of a disorganized inner-city area feel isolated, frustrated, ostracized from the economic mainstream, hopeless, and eventually angry. How do these feelings affect criminal activities?

Criminologists who view crime as a direct result of lower-class frustration and anger are referred to as **strain theorists.** They believe that although most people share similar values and goals, the ability to achieve personal goals is stratified by socioeconomic class.

Strain is limited in affluent areas because educational and vocational opportunities are available. In disorganized areas, strain occurs because legitimate avenues for success are all but closed. To relieve strain, indigent people may either use deviant methods to achieve their goals, such as theft or drug trafficking, or reject socially accepted goals and substitute more deviant goals such as being tough and aggressive (see Figure 7.4).

Anomie

The roots of strain theories can be traced to Emile Durkheim's notion of **anomie** (from the Greek *a nomos,* without norms). According to Durkheim, an anomic society is one in which rules of behavior—norms—have broken down or become inoperative during periods of rapid social change or social crisis such as war or

Figure 7.4 The Basic Components of Strain Theory

Poverty
- Development of isolated slum culture
- Lack of conventional social opportunities
- Racial and ethnic discrimination

Maintenance of conventional rules and norms
Lower-class slum-dwellers remain loyal to conventional values and rules of dominant middle-class culture.

Strain
Lack of opportunity coupled with desire for conventional success produces strain and frustration.

Formation of gangs and groups
Youths form law-violating groups to seek alternative means of achieving success.

Crime and delinquency
Methods of groups—theft, violence, substance abuse—are defined as illegal by dominant culture.

Criminal careers
Most youthful gang members "age out" of crime, but some continue as adult criminals.

famine. An anomic society is not able to control human aspirations and demands. Anomie is most likely to occur in societies that are moving from mechanical to organic solidarity. **Mechanical solidarity** is a characteristic of a preindustrial society, which is held together by traditions, shared values, and unquestioned beliefs. In postindustrial social systems, which are highly developed and dependent on the division of labor, people are connected by their interdependent needs for each others' services and production (**organic solidarity**). The shift in traditions and values creates social turmoil, and established norms begin to erode and lose meaning. If a division occurs between what the population expects and what the economic and productive forces of society can realistically deliver, a crisis situation develops, which can manifest itself in *normlessness* or anomie.

Anomie undermines society's social control function. Every society works to limit people's goals and desires. If a society becomes anomic, it can no longer establish and maintain control over its population's wants and desires. Because people find it difficult to control their appetites, their demands become unlimited. Under these circumstances, obeying legal codes may be strained, and alternative behavior choices, such as crime, may be inevitable.

Theory of Anomie

Durkheim's ideas were applied to criminology by sociologist Robert Merton in his **theory of anomie**.[94] Merton used a modified version of the concept of anomie to fit social, economic, and cultural conditions found in modern U.S. society.[95] He found that two elements of culture interact to produce potentially anomic conditions: culturally defined goals and socially approved means for obtaining them. For example, U.S. society stresses the goals of acquiring wealth, success, and power. Socially permissible means include hard work, education, and thrift.

Merton argues that in the United States, legitimate means to acquire wealth are stratified across class and status lines. Those with little formal education and few economic resources soon find that they are denied the ability to legally acquire wealth—the preeminent success symbol. When socially mandated goals are uniform throughout society and access to legitimate means is bound by class and status, the resulting strain produces anomie among those who are locked out of the legitimate opportunity structure. Consequently, they may develop criminal or delinquent solutions to the problem of attaining goals.

Social Adaptations Merton argues that each person has his or her own concept of society's goals and his or her means to attain them. Whereas some people have inadequate means of attaining success, others who have the means reject societal goals as being unsuited to

Table 7.2 Typology of Individual Modes of Adaptation

MODES OF ADAPTATION	CULTURAL GOALS	INSTITUTIONALIZED MEANS
I. Conformity	+	+
I. Innovation	+	−
II. Ritualism	−	+
V. Retreatism	−	−
V. Rebellion	±	±

Source: Robert Merton, "Social Structure and Anomie," in *Social Theory and Social Structure* (Glencoe, Ill.: Free Press, 1957).

them. Table 7.2 shows Merton's hypothetical relationships among social goals, the means for getting them, and the individual actor.

1. **Conformity.** Conformity occurs when individuals embrace conventional social goals and also have the means to attain them. In a balanced, stable society, this is the most common social adaptation. If a majority of its people did not practice conformity, the society would cease to exist.

2. **Innovation.** Innovation occurs when an individual accepts the goals of society but rejects or is incapable of attaining them through legitimate means. Many people desire material goods and luxuries but lack the financial ability to attain them. The resulting conflict forces them to adopt innovative solutions to their dilemma: they steal, sell drugs, or extort money. Of the five adaptations, innovation is most closely associated with criminal behavior.

If successful, innovation can have serious, long-term social consequences. Criminal success helps convince otherwise law-abiding people that innovative means work better and faster than conventional ones. The prosperous drug dealer's expensive car and flashy clothes send out the message that crime pays. Merton claims, "The process thus enlarges the extent of anomie within the system, so that others, who did not respond in the form of deviant behavior to the relatively slight anomie which they first obtained, come to do so as anomie is spread and is intensified."[96] This explains why crime is initiated and sustained in certain low-income ecological areas.

3. **Ritualism.** Ritualists gain pleasure from practicing traditional ceremonies regardless of whether they have a real purpose or a goal. The strict customs in religious orders, feudal societies, clubs, and college fraternities encourage and appeal to ritualists. Ritualists should have the lowest level of criminal behavior because they have abandoned the success goal, which is at the root of criminal activity.

4. **Retreatism.** Retreatists reject both the goals and the means of society. Merton suggests that people who adjust in this fashion are "in the society but not of it."

Included in this category are "psychotics, psychoneurotics, chronic autists, pariahs, outcasts, vagrants, vagabonds, tramps, chronic drunkards, and drug addicts." Because such people are morally or otherwise incapable of using both legitimate and illegitimate means, they attempt to escape their lack of success by withdrawing—either mentally or physically.

5. **Rebellion.** Rebellion involves substituting an alternative set of goals and means for conventional ones. Revolutionaries who wish to promote radical change in the existing social structure and who call for alternative lifestyles, goals, and beliefs are engaging in rebellion. Rebellion may be a reaction against a corrupt, hated government or an effort to create alternative opportunities and lifestyles within the existing system.

Evaluation of Anomie Theory   According to anomie theory, social inequality leads to perceptions of anomie. To resolve the goals–means conflict and relieve their sense of strain, some people innovate by stealing or extorting money; others retreat into drugs and alcohol; some rebel by joining revolutionary groups; and still others get involved in ritualistic behavior by joining a religious cult. Merton's view of anomie has been one of the most enduring and influential sociological theories of criminality. By linking deviant behavior to the success goals that control social behavior, anomie theory attempts to pinpoint the cause of the conflict that produces personal frustration and consequent criminality. By acknowledging that society unfairly distributes the legitimate means to achieving success, anomie theory helps explain the existence of high-crime areas and the apparent predominance of delinquent and criminal behavior in the lower class. By suggesting that social conditions, not individual personalities, produce crime, Merton greatly influenced the directions taken to reduce and control criminality during the latter half of the twentieth century.

A number of questions are left unanswered by anomie theory.[97] Merton does not explain why people choose to commit certain types of crime. For example, why does one anomic person become a mugger while another deals drugs? Anomie may explain differences in crime rates, but it cannot explain why most young criminals desist from crime as adults. Does this mean that perceptions of anomie dwindle with age? Is anomie short-lived?

Critics have also suggested that people pursue a number of different goals, including educational, athletic, and social success. Juveniles may be more interested in immediate goals, like having an active social life or being a good athlete, than long-term achievements such as monetary success. Achieving these goals is not a matter of social class alone; other factors, including athletic ability, intelligence, personality, and family life, can either hinder or assist goal attainment.[98] Anomie theory also assumes that all people share the same goals and values, which is false.[99] Because of these and other criticisms, the theory of anomie, along with other structural theories, fell into a period of decline for almost 20 years.

Anomie Reconsidered   Like other views of criminality that stress the influence of social structure, strain theories fell out of favor when criminologists turned their attention to social and psychological views of criminality. However, the 1990s have seen a resurgence of interest in strain and anomie. Many Americans may be feeling anomic because of the economic displacement brought on by a shifting economy. The truly disadvantaged in society seem at grave risk of both normlessness and high crime rates. In addition, some researchers have begun to reexamine original concepts such as perceptions of anomie and have found that with more precise, valid measurements, Merton's theory can in fact predict levels of criminal activity.[100] Cross-cultural research efforts have also linked anomic conditions to criminality, indicating that anomie is not unique to U.S. culture.[101]

Criminologists are now producing newer versions of Merton's visionary concepts. Some of these work on the general or macro level; they hold that the success goal integrated within American society influences the nature and extent of the aggregate crime rate. There are also individual or micro-level versions of the theory; these suggest that individuals who experience anomie are more likely to commit crime than those who are immune to feelings of strain or goal conflict. Examples of both of these views are discussed next.

Institutional Anomie Theory

A recent addition to the strain literature has been the publication of *Crime and the American Dream* by Steven Messner and Richard Rosenfeld.[102] Their macro-level version of anomie theory views antisocial behavior as a function of cultural and institutional influences in American society. This is known as the **institutional anomie theory.**

Messner and Rosenfeld agree with Merton's view that the success goal is pervasive in American culture. They refer to this as **the American Dream,** a term that they employ as both a goal and a process. As a goal, the American Dream involves accumulating material goods and wealth via open individual competition. As a process, it involves both being socialized to pursue material success and believing that prosperity is achievable in American culture. Anomic conditions occur because the desire to succeed at any cost drives people apart, weakens the collective sense of community, fosters ambition, and restricts desires to achieve anything that isn't material wealth. Achieving respect, for example, is not sufficient.

The U.S. capitalist system encourages innovation in order to pursue monetary rewards. Businesspeople

According to Messner and Rosenfeld, the relatively high American crime rates can be explained by the interrelationship between culture and institutions. The poor want to be part of the economic mainstream but lack the means to achieve their goals. Some may attempt to use legal methods, such as this curbside auto repair shop being operated in the Hamilton Heights section of New York City. Others become frustrated and angry and choose crime and drug dealing to get ahead.

such as Bill Gates, Warren Buffet, Ross Perot, and Donald Trump are considered national heroes and leaders. What is distinct about American society, according to Messner and Rosenfeld, and what most likely causes the exceedingly high national crime rate, is that anomic conditions have been allowed to "develop to such an extraordinary degree."[103] No alternatives seem to serve the same purpose or the same goal.

Impact of Anomie Why does anomie pervade American culture? According to Messner and Rosenfeld, it is because institutions that might otherwise control the exaggerated emphasis on financial success, such as religious or charitable institutions, have been rendered powerless or obsolete. There are three reasons social institutions have been undermined:

• Noneconomic functions and roles have been devalued. Performance in other institutional settings — the family, school, or community — is assigned a lower priority than the goal of financial success.

• When conflicts emerge, noneconomic roles become subordinate to and must accommodate economic roles. The schedules, routines, and demands of the workplace take priority over those of the home, the school, the community, and other aspects of social life.

• Economic language, standards, and norms penetrate into noneconomic realms. Economic terms become part of the common vernacular: People want to get to the "bottom line." Spouses view themselves as "partners" who "manage" the household. Retired people say they want to "downsize" their household. We "outsource" home repairs instead of doing them ourselves. Corporate leaders run for public office promising to "run the country like a business."

According to Messner and Rosenfeld, the relatively high American crime rates can be explained by the interrelationship between culture and institutions. At the cultural level, the dominance of the American Dream mythology ensures that many people will develop desires for material goods that cannot be satisfied by legitimate means. Anomie becomes a norm, and extralegal means (like crime) become a strategy for attaining material wealth. At the institutional level, the dominance of economic concerns weakens the informal social control exerted by the family, church, and school. These institutions have lost their ability to regulate behavior and have instead become a conduit for promoting material success. For example, schools are evaluated not for imparting knowledge but for their ability to train students to get high-paying jobs. Social conditions reinforce each other: culture determines institutions, and institutional change influences culture. Crime rates may rise in a healthy economy because national prosperity heightens the attractiveness of monetary rewards, encouraging people to gain financial success by any means possible, including illegal ones. In this culture of competition, self-interest prevails and generates amorality, acceptance of inequality, and disdain for the less fortunate.[104]

A recent research effort by criminologists Mitchell Chamlin and John Cochran supports institutional anomie. Chamlin and Cochran use national data, which show that within individual states, poverty rates are associated with crime rates. However, this relationship depends on the strength of institutional controls: areas with high levels of church membership, lower levels of divorce, and high voter turnouts also enjoy lower crime rates. Strong institutional controls (family, church, and polity) may counteract the influence of economic deprivation, a finding that agrees with institutional anomie theory.[105]

The Messner and Rosenfeld version of anomie helps explain why the success goal has reached such prominence in the American culture. The impetus to succeed by any means necessary has become a national icon.

Relative Deprivation Theory

Criminologists have long assumed that income inequality increases both strain and crime rates. Sharp divisions between the rich and poor create envy and mistrust. Societies in which income inequality flourishes, or *inegalitarian societies,* are especially demeaning to the poor. Criminal motivation is fueled by both perceived humiliation and the perceived right to humiliate a victim in return.[106] Psychologists warn that under these circumstances, young males will fear and envy "winners" who are doing well at their expense. If they fail to take risky aggressive tactics, they are surely going to lose out in social competition and have little chance of future success.[107] This is referred to as **relative deprivation.**

The concept of relative deprivation was launched by sociologists Judith Blau and Peter Blau, who combine concepts from anomie theory with those found in social disorganization models.[108] According to the Blaus' view, lower-class people might feel both deprived and embittered when they compare their life circumstances to those of the more affluent. People who feel deprived because of their race or economic class eventually develop a sense of injustice and discontent. The less fortunate begin to distrust the society that has nurtured social inequality and obstructed their chances of progressing by legitimate means. The constant frustration that results from these feelings of inadequacy produces pent-up aggression and hostility, eventually leading to violence and crime. The effect of inequality may be greatest when the impoverished population believes that they are becoming less able to compete in a society where the balance of economic and social power is shifting further toward the already affluent. Under these conditions, the relatively poor are increasingly likely to choose illegitimate life-enhancing activities. Crime rates may then spiral upward even if the relative size of the poor population does not increase.[109]

According to the relative deprivation view, a collective sense of social injustice directly related to income inequality tends to develop in communities or nations in which the poor and wealthy live close to one another. Adolescents raised in inner-city poverty areas, such as those in Boston, New York, Chicago, and Los Angeles, for example, experience frustration as they compare their neighborhood to the most affluent neighborhoods that are located in the same metropolitan area. In the United States, some of these wealthy areas include Beacon Hill in Boston, Park Avenue in New York City, Lake Shore Drive in Chicago, and the Bel Air section of Los Angeles.

Relative deprivation is not unique to American cities. Crime rates are also high in underdeveloped nations that are tourist havens. In the Caribbean, for example, modest living standards become extremely frustrating to residents when affluent tourists arrive each year. This frustration is often accompanied by high levels of property and violent crime.[110]

Relative deprivation is felt most acutely by African-American youths because they consistently suffer racial discrimination and economic deprivation that place them in a lower status than other urban residents.[111] Wage inequality may motivate young males to enter the drug trade, an enterprise that increases the likelihood they will become involved in violent crimes.[112]

Testing Relative Deprivation Theory Earlier we noted that crime rates may actually increase during economic prosperity. This anomaly may be explained in part by the effects of relative deprivation. As the gulf widens between the richest and poorest Americans, crime rates spiral upward.[113] Some research efforts have found that income inequality portends an increase in crime rates.[114] For example, during the 1960s and 1970s, as African-American income levels started to increase, so too did the arrest rates within this population. The increase occurred when African-Americans were enjoying a rapid upgrade in quality of life, income levels, and educational opportunities. How can this anomaly be explained? According to relative deprivation theory, although crime rates increased during this relative affluence and unemployment rates declined, groups whose standard of living was improving, such as African-Americans, still found that they were losing ground in comparison to other groups. It is the *perception* of relative deprivation, not absolute poverty level, that ushers in higher crime rates.[115]

Although some research efforts have failed to find a crime–inequality effect, the most recent evidence supports relative deprivation theory, and it remains an important concept for understanding crime rates.[116]

Is Relative Deprivation Relative?   The theory of relative deprivation holds that people who live in deteriorated urban areas and lack basic human needs resort to such crimes as homicide, robbery, and aggravated assault.[117] These basic needs include proper health care, clothing, and shelter (resource deprivation). Those who live close to others who enjoy the benefits of higher social position will inevitably resort to such crimes as homicide, robbery, and aggravated assault.[118] Is this view restricted to the lower classes, or can it also be applied to affluent communities? In other words, is relative deprivation relative?

Even the most affluent Americans may feel strain when they fail to achieve unlimited goals.[119] That is, no matter what their level of affluence, people may perceive strain because their own goals are so lofty that they can never be achieved. These people, then, tend to suffer when their expected standard of living or economic security declines. Research indicates that when affluent children reside in an economically integrated neighborhood, negative consequences may lead to greater dropout rates and more out-of-wedlock births among prosperous than indigent children.[120]

Some affluent people may feel relatively deprived when they compare their accomplishments to those of their more successful peers. Their method for dealing with their feelings of deprivation may be to use illegal means to satisfy their unrealistic success goals.[121]

CONNECTIONS

Can relative deprivation concepts apply to white-collar crime? Perhaps some of the individuals involved in the savings and loan scandals or Wall Street stock fraud cases felt relatively deprived and socially frustrated when they compared the paltry few millions they had already accumulated with the hundreds of millions held by wealthier people whom they envied. For more on this issue, see Chapter 13's discussions of the savings and loan scandal and also the causes of white-collar crime.

The relative deprivation model helps explain the ambiguous association between crime and the economy. It is possible that crime rates increase during an economic boom because some groups get left out of the job market. In contrast, during a recession, crime rates may fall because everyone is suffering and fewer people feel relatively deprived. However, the bottom line is that crime rates rise when groups feel that they are worse off than other groups. The sense of inadequacy motivates goal attainment by any means possible.

General Strain Theory (GST)

Sociologist Robert Agnew's **general strain theory (GST)** helps identify the micro- or individual-level influences of strain. Whereas Merton tries to explain social class differences in the crime rate, Agnew tries to explain why *individuals* who feel stress and strain are likely to commit crimes. Agnew also attempts to offer a more general explanation of criminal activity among all elements of society rather than restrict his views to lower-class crime.[122]

Multiple Sources of Stress   Agnew suggests that criminality is the direct result of **negative affective states**—the anger, frustration, and adverse emotions that emerge in the wake of destructive social relationships. He finds that negative affective states are produced by a variety of sources of strain (see Figure 7.5):

• **Strain caused by the failure to achieve positively valued goals:** This category of strain, similar to what Merton speaks of in his theory of anomie, is a result of the disjunction between aspirations and expectations. This type of strain occurs when a youth aspires to wealth and fame but, lacking financial and educational resources, assumes that such goals are impossible to achieve.

• **Strain caused by the disjunction of expectations and achievements:** Strain can also be produced by a disjunction between expectations and achievements. When people compare themselves to peers who seem to be doing a lot better financially or socially (such as making more money or getting better grades), even those doing relatively well feel strain. For example, when a high school senior is accepted at a good college but not a prestige school, like some of her friends, she will feel

Sociologist Robert Agnew's general strain theory (GST) shows how both positive and negative stimuli can cause strain, which can lead to anger and aggression.

Figure 7.5 Elements of General Strain Theory (GST)

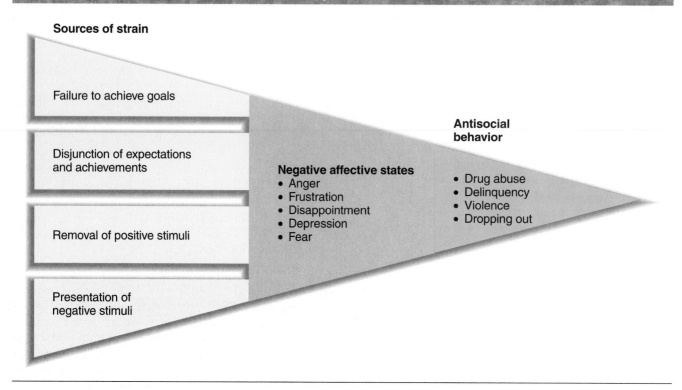

Sources of strain

- Failure to achieve goals
- Disjunction of expectations and achievements
- Removal of positive stimuli
- Presentation of negative stimuli

Negative affective states
- Anger
- Frustration
- Disappointment
- Depression
- Fear

Antisocial behavior
- Drug abuse
- Delinquency
- Violence
- Dropping out

strain. Perhaps she is not being treated fairly because the playing field is tilted against her; "Other kids have connections," she may say. Perceptions of inequity may result in many adverse reactions, ranging from running away from its source to lowering others' benefits through physical attacks or property vandalism.

- **Strain as the removal of positively valued stimuli from the individual:** Strain may occur because of the actual or anticipated loss of positively valued stimuli from the individual.[123] For example, the loss of a girl- or boyfriend can produce strain, as can the death of a loved one, moving to a new neighborhood or school, or the divorce or separation of parents. The loss of positive stimuli may lead to delinquency as the adolescent tries to prevent the loss, retrieve what has been lost, obtain substitutes, or seek revenge against those responsible for the loss.

- **Strain as the presentation of negative stimuli:** Strain may also be caused by negative or noxious stimuli, such as child abuse and neglect, crime victimization, physical punishment, family and peer conflict, school failure, and stressful life events ranging from verbal threats to air pollution. For example, adolescent maltreatment has been linked to delinquency through the rage and anger it generates. Children who are abused at home may take out their rage on younger children at school or become involved in violent delinquency.[124]

Although these sources of strain are independent from one another, they may overlap. For example, if a teacher insults a student, it may be viewed as an unfair application of negative stimuli that interferes with a student's academic aspirations. The greater the intensity and frequency of strain experiences, the greater their impact and the more likely they are to cause delinquency.

According to Agnew, each type of strain increases the likelihood of experiencing such negative emotions as disappointment, depression, fear, and, most importantly, anger. Anger increases perceptions of injury and of being wronged. It produces a desire for revenge, energizes individuals to take action, and lowers inhibitions: violence and aggression seem justified if you have been wronged and are righteously angry. Because it produces these emotions, chronic, repetitive strain can be considered a predisposing factor for delinquency when it creates a hostile, suspicious, aggressive attitude. Individual strain episodes may trigger delinquency, such as when a particularly stressful event ignites a violent reaction.

Coping with Strain Although it may be socially unacceptable, criminality can provide relief and satisfaction for someone living an otherwise stress-filled life. Violent self-protection may increase feelings of self-worth among those who feel inadequate or intellectually insecure; violent responses may also be used in response to negative stimuli. For example, children who report that they hit or strike their parents also report that they had been the targets of parental violence, such as hitting or slapping. Fighting back, then, is a response to strain that the parents are inflicting on their child. The child's violent response to strain may be viewed as a reaction that actually helps remedy a problem.[125]

Not all people who experience strain eventually resort to criminality. Some are able to marshal their emotional, mental, and behavioral resources to cope with the anger and frustration produced by strain. Some defenses are cognitive: individuals may be able to rationalize frustrating circumstances. Not getting the career they desire is "just not that important"; they may be poor, but the "next guy is worse off"; and if things didn't work out, they "got what they deserved." Others seek behavioral solutions: they run away from adverse conditions or seek revenge against those who caused the strain. Some try to regain emotional equilibrium with techniques ranging from physical exercise to drug abuse.

Source of Strain General strain theory acknowledges that the ability to cope with strain varies based on personal experiences. Children who lack economic means are less likely to cope than those who have at their command sufficient financial resources. Personal temperament, prior learning of delinquent attitudes and behaviors, and association with delinquent peers who reinforce anger, among other factors, affect the ability to cope with strain. Coping with strain may also be influenced by the *source* of strain. When individuals identify a target to blame for their problems, they are more likely to retaliate (Joe stole my girl away by lying about me, so I beat him up). When individuals internalize blame, delinquent behavior is less likely (I lost my girlfriend because I was unfaithful; it's all my fault). Sometimes the source of strain is difficult to pinpoint (I feel depressed because my parents got divorced); this type of ambiguous strain is unlikely to produce aggression.[126]

Strain and Criminal Careers How does GST explain both chronic offending and the stability of crime over the life course? GST recognizes that certain people have traits that may make them particularly sensitive to strain. These include an explosive temperament, low tolerance for adversity, poor problem-solving skills, and being overly sensitive or emotional. These traits, linked to aggressive, antisocial behavior, seem to be stable over the life cycle.[127]

CONNECTIONS

As you may recall, Chapter 3's discussion of cohort studies shows that criminal behavior begins early in life and remains stable. Considering that strain-producing interactions are not constant, explaining the stability of chronic offending is an important task for strain theory. Chronic offending is discussed in Chapter 3.

Aggressive people who have these traits are likely to have poor interpersonal skills and to be treated negatively by others; their combative personalities make them feared and disliked. These people are likely to live in families that share similar personality traits. They are also likely to reject conventional peers and join deviant groups. Such individuals are likely to experience a high degree of strain during their lives.

Crime peaks during late adolescence because this is a period of social stress caused by weakening parental supervision and the development of relationships with a diverse peer group. Many kids going through the trauma of family breakup and frequent changes in family structure feel a high degree of strain. They may react by becoming involved in precocious sexuality or by turning to substance abuse to mask the strain. For example, research shows that young girls of any social class are more likely to bear out-of-wedlock children if they experienced an unstable family life.[128]

As they mature, children's expectations increase; some are unable to meet academic and social demands. Adolescents are very concerned about their standing with peers. Teenagers who are deficient in these areas may find they are social outcasts, another source of strain. In adulthood, crime rates drop because these sources of strain are reduced. New sources of self-esteem emerge, and adults seem more likely to align their goals with reality.

Community Sources of Strain GST focuses on individual-level sources of strain; yet there are distinct ecological variations in the crime rate. Some regions, cities, and neighborhoods are more crime-prone than others. Can ecological differences produce negative affective states in large segments of the population that account for these differences? Agnew suggests that there are, in fact, community-level factors that produce feelings of strain. These strain-producing factors are set out in Table 7.3. According to Agnew, communities contribute to strain in several ways:

- They influence the goals people pursue and whether people can meet these goals.
- They influence feelings of relative deprivation and exposure to aversive stimuli, including family conflict, incivility, and economic deprivation.
- They influence the likelihood that angry, strain-filled individuals will interact with one another.

Consequently, not only does GST predict individual deviance, but it can also account for community-level differences in the crime rate.

Evaluating GST Agnew's important work both clarifies the concept of strain and directs future research agendas. It also adds to the body of literature describing how social and life history events influence offending patterns. Because sources of strain vary over the life course, so too do delinquency rates.

Table 7.3 Community-Level Sources of Strain

1. Certain communities prevent residents from achieving desired levels of positively valued goals, such as wealth, respect/status, and justice/fairness.
2. These communities also produce feelings of relative deprivation.
3. Deprived communities maintain levels of economic deprivation, family disruption, child abuse, overcrowding, and incivility that are much higher than surrounding areas. Residents not only experience these traits but witness close friends and family members enduring them; this is *vicarious strain*.
4. These adverse community traits increase the likelihood of negative emotions, including anger and frustration.
5. Residence in these deprived communities increases the likelihood that angry, frustrated individuals will interact with one another, increasing stress levels.
6. Some communities increase the likelihood that angry, frustrated people will commit crime.

Community-Level Reasons Why Strain Produces Crime

1. Blocked opportunity for advancement or creation of new identities in some areas makes legitimate goals impossible to attain.
2. Densely populated communities make it impossible to keep activities and problems private. People may feel pressure to save face by acting tough or committing crimes.
3. Some communities develop subcultures whose members blame others for their misfortunes. This allows people to blame their aggressive illegal acts on others.
4. Residents in deprived areas are less able to develop noncriminal coping strategies for personal problems. They are less able to unite with others to solve their own or communitywide problems.
5. Residents in disorganized areas are less able to gain social support from others. They maintain weakened educational, religious, recreational, and other social institutions.
6. Deprived areas have weakened agencies of both formal and informal social control.
7. Residents of deprived areas are likely to hold values and beliefs conducive to crime.
8. The increased presence of criminal groups heightens the chance strain will lead to crime. Such groups serve as models and also reinforce criminal responses.

Source: Robert Agnew, "A Macro-Strain Theory of Community Differences in Crime Rates." Paper presented at the American Society of Criminology Meeting, San Diego, Calif., 1997.

CONNECTIONS

Explaining continuity and change in offending rates over the life course has become an important goal of criminologists. Chapter 10's analysis of latent trait and developmental theories provides the recent thinking on this topic.

There is also empirical support for GST. Adolescents who score high on self-report test items that measure perceptions of strain (for example, "my classmates do not like me," adults and friends "don't respect my opinions") and negative life events (being a victim of crime, the death of a close friend, serious illness) are also the most likely to engage in crime.[129] Some research efforts show that indicators of strain — family breakup, unemployment, moving, feelings of dissatisfaction with friends and school — are positively related to criminality.[130] For example, middle-class youths who drop out of school are more likely to engage in criminal behavior than lower-class dropouts. Removing the positive stimulus of education may have a greater strain effect on those who are expected to succeed because of their class position than those who already perceive more limited economic opportunities.[131]

As predicted by GST, people who report feelings of stress and anger are more likely to interact with delinquent peers and engage in criminal behaviors.[132] Research shows that persistent drug abusers report feeling a great deal of life stress. They also tend to associate with peers who are substance users.[133] In some cases this interaction may actually help them reduce strain and anxiety: criminality may serve as an effective coping mechanism that helps relieve feelings of anger and resentment. Lashing out at others, for example, may reduce feelings of strain, as might stealing or vandalizing property.[134]

Gender Issues GST fails to adequately explain gender differences in the crime rate. Although females experience as much or more strain, frustration, and anger as males, their crime rate is much lower. Is it possible that there are gender differences in either the relationship between strain and criminality or the ability to cope with the effects of strain? For example, whereas females may experience more strain, males may be more deeply affected by interpersonal stress.[135]

There is evidence that stress influences both males and females equally;[136] however, it leads to much more criminal behavior among males than females. When presented with similar types of strain, males and females respond with a different constellation of negative emotions.[137] Females are socialized to internalize stress, blaming themselves for their problems; males may relieve the same type of strain by striking out at others and deflecting criticism with aggression.[138] Only females who face overwhelming stress may succumb to criminality. Robbin Ogle and her associates suggest that when women experience intense stress, their traditional coping mechanisms may be overwhelmed; in response, they lash out with anger amounting to rage. Women experiencing peaks of stress may be even more likely than men to explode with episodes of extreme uncontrolled violence.[139] Whereas males may resort to criminality in the face of stressors of any magnitude, only extreme levels of strain produce violent reactions from women.

CULTURAL DEVIANCE THEORY

The third branch of social structure theory combines the effects of social disorganization and strain to explain how people living in deteriorated neighborhoods react to social isolation and economic deprivation. Because their lifestyle is draining, frustrating, and dispiriting, members of the lower class create an independent subculture with its own set of rules and values. Whereas middle-class culture stresses hard work, delayed gratification, formal education, and being cautious, the lower-class subculture stresses excitement, toughness, taking risks, fearlessness, immediate gratification, and street smarts.

The lower-class subculture is an attractive alternative because the urban poor find that it is impossible to meet the behavioral demands of middle-class society. Unfortunately, subcultural norms often clash with conventional values. Slum dwellers are forced to violate the law because they obey the rules of the deviant culture with which they are in immediate contact (see Figure 7.6).

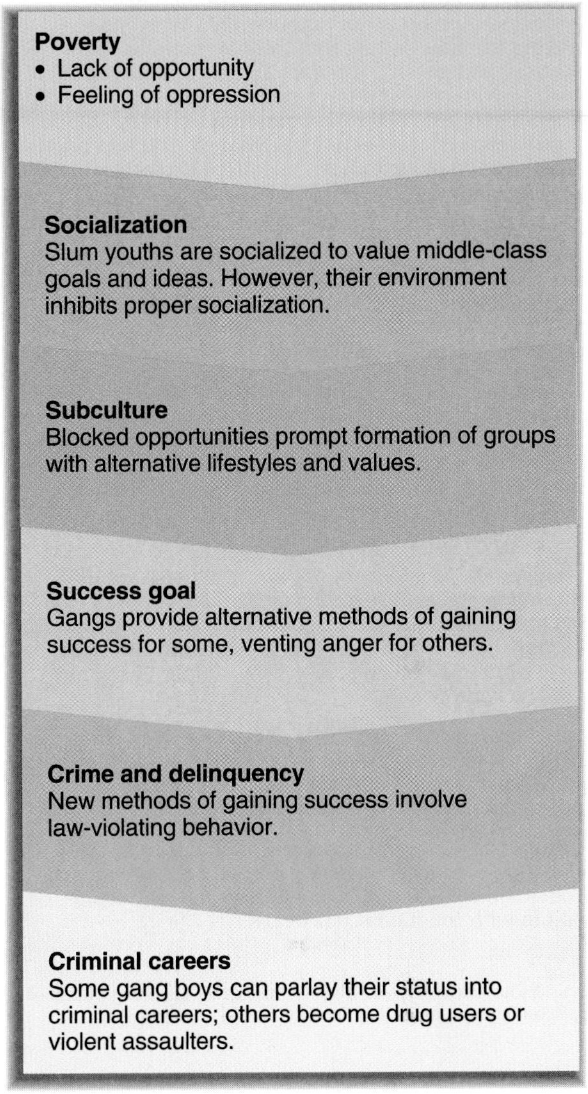

Conduct Norms

The concept that the lower class develops a unique culture in response to strain can be traced to Thorsten Sellin's classic 1938 work, *Culture Conflict and Crime,* a theoretical attempt to link cultural adaptation to criminality.[140] Sellin's main premise is that criminal law expresses the rules of the dominant culture. The content of the law, therefore, may create a clash between conventional, middle-class rules and splinter groups, such as ethnic and racial minorities who are excluded from the social mainstream. These groups maintain their own set of **conduct norms**—rules governing the day-to-day living conditions within these subcultures.[141] Conduct norms can be found in almost any culture and are not the property of any particular group, culture, or political structure.

Complicating matters is the fact that most of us belong to several social groups. In a complex society, people belong to many groups—family, peer, occupational, and religious. A conflict of norms exists when divergent rules of conduct govern a specific life situation.[142] According to Sellin, **culture conflict** occurs when the rules expressed in criminal law clash with the demands of group conduct norms. To make his point, Sellin cited the case of a Sicilian father in New Jersey who killed the 16-year-old boy who seduced his daughter and then expressed surprise at being arrested. He claimed that he had "merely defended his family honor in a traditional way."[143]

Focal Concerns

In his classic 1958 paper, "Lower-Class Culture as a Generating Milieu of Gang Delinquency," Walter Miller identified the unique value system that defines lower-class culture.[144] Conformance to these **focal concerns**

Figure 7.6 Elements of Cultural Deviance Theory

Poverty
- Lack of opportunity
- Feeling of oppression

Socialization
Slum youths are socialized to value middle-class goals and ideas. However, their environment inhibits proper socialization.

Subculture
Blocked opportunities prompt formation of groups with alternative lifestyles and values.

Success goal
Gangs provide alternative methods of gaining success for some, venting anger for others.

Crime and delinquency
New methods of gaining success involve law-violating behavior.

Criminal careers
Some gang boys can parlay their status into criminal careers; others become drug users or violent assaulters.

dominates life among the lower class. Focal concerns do not necessarily represent a rebellion against middle-class values; rather, these values have evolved specifically to fit conditions in slum areas. The major lower-class focal concerns are set out in Table 7.4.[145]

According to Miller, clinging to lower-class focal concerns promotes illegal or violent behavior. Toughness may mean displaying fighting prowess; street smarts may lead to drug deals; excitement may result in drinking, gambling, or drug abuse. This adherence to the prevailing cultural demands of lower-class society causes urban crime. Research, in fact, shows that members of the lower class value toughness and want to show they are courageous in the face of provocation.[146] To illustrate, consider a recent study of violent young men in New York, conducted by sociologist Jeffrey

Table 7.4 Miller's Lower-Class Focal Concerns

Trouble In lower-class communities, people are evaluated by their actual or potential involvement in making trouble. Getting into trouble includes such behavior as fighting, drinking, and sexual misconduct. Dealing with trouble can confer prestige—for example, when a man establishes a reputation for being able to handle himself well in a fight. Not being able to handle trouble, and having to pay the consequences, can make a person look foolish and incompetent.

Toughness Lower-class males want local recognition of their physical and spiritual toughness. They refuse to be sentimental or soft and instead value physical strength, fighting ability, and athletic skill. Those who cannot meet these standards risk getting a reputation for being weak, inept, and effeminate.

Smartness Members of the lower-class culture want to maintain an image of being streetwise and savvy, using their street smarts, and having the ability to outfox and out-con the opponent. Although formal education is not admired, knowing essential survival techniques, such as gambling, conning, and outsmarting the law, is a requirement.

Excitement Members of the lower class search for fun and excitement to enliven an otherwise drab existence. The search for excitement may lead to gambling, fighting, getting drunk, and sexual adventures. In between, the lower-class citizen may simply "hang out" and "be cool."

Fate Lower-class citizens believe their lives are in the hands of strong spiritual forces that guide their destinies. Getting lucky, finding good fortune, and hitting the jackpot are all slum dwellers' daily dreams.

Autonomy Being independent of authority figures, such as the police, teachers, and parents, is required; losing control is an unacceptable weakness, incompatible with toughness.

Source: Walter Miller, "Lower-Class Culture as a Generating Milieu of Gang Delinquency," *Journal of Social Issues* 14 (1958): 5–19.

Fagan. He found that the most compelling function that violence served was to develop status as a tough person. A reputation for toughness helped the young men acquire social power while at the same time insulating them from becoming victims. Violence was also seen as a means to acquire the accoutrements of wealth (like nice clothes, flashy cars, or access to clubs), control or humiliate another person, defy authority, settle drug-related disputes, attain retribution, satisfy the need for thrills or risk taking, and respond to challenges to one's manhood.[147] Lower-class focal concerns seem as relevant today as when they were first identified by Miller more than 40 years ago!

Theory of Delinquent Subcultures

Albert Cohen first articulated the theory of delinquent subculture in his classic 1955 book, *Delinquent Boys*.[148] Cohen's central position was that delinquent behavior of lower-class youths is actually a protest against the norms and values of middle-class U.S. culture. Because social conditions prevent them from achieving success legitimately, lower-class youths experience a form of culture conflict that Cohen labels **status frustration**.[149] As a result, many of them join gangs and engage in behavior that is "non-utilitarian, malicious, and negativistic."[150]

Cohen viewed the delinquent gang as a separate subculture, possessing a value system directly opposed to that of the larger society. He describes the subculture as one that "takes its norms from the larger culture, but turns them upside down. The delinquent's conduct is right by the standards of his subculture precisely because it is wrong by the norms of the larger culture."[151]

According to Cohen, the development of the delinquent subculture is a consequence of socialization practices found in the lower class environment. These children lack the basic skills necessary to achieve social and economic success. They also lack the proper education, and therefore do not have the skills on which to build a knowledge or socialization foundation. He suggests that lower-class parents are incapable of teaching children the necessary techniques for entering the dominant middle-class culture. The consequences of this deprivation include developmental handicaps, poor speech and communication skills, and inability to delay gratification.

Middle-Class Measuring Rods One significant handicap that lower-class children face is the inability to positively impress authority figures, such as teachers, employers, or supervisors. In U.S. society, these positions tend to be held by members of the middle class who have difficulty relating to the lower-class youngster. Cohen calls the standards set by these authority figures **middle-class measuring rods**. The conflict and frustration lower-class youths experience when they fail to meet these standards is a primary cause of delinquency. They may find themselves prejudged by others and not measuring up in the final analysis. For example, teacher ratings may be reviewed and magnified by the periodic updating of records and the informal information exchanges that commonly occur among educators working in the same school. The fact that a lower-class student is deemed substandard, or below the average of what is expected, can have an important impact on his or her future life chances. A school record may be reviewed by juvenile court authorities and by the military; a military record can influence whether someone is qualified for certain jobs. This is just one example of how a person's status and esteem in the community are largely determined by judgments that reflect the traditional values of American society.[152] Negative evaluations become part of a permanent file that follows an individual for the rest of his or her life. When he or she wants to improve, evidence of prior failures is used to discourage advancement.

The Formation of Deviant Subcultures Cohen believes lower-class boys rejected by middle-class decision makers usually join one of three existing subcultures: the *corner boy*, the *college boy*, or the *delinquent boy*. The **corner boy** role is the most common response to middle-class rejection. The corner boy is not a chronic delinquent but may be a truant who engages in petty or status offenses, such as precocious sex and recreational drug abuse. His main loyalty is to his peer group, on which he depends for support, motivation, and interest. His values, therefore, are those of the group with which he is in close contact. The corner boy, well aware of his failure to achieve the standards of the American dream, retreats into the comforting world of his lower-class peers and eventually becomes a stable member of his neighborhood, holding a menial job, marrying, and remaining in the community.

The **college boy** embraces the cultural and social values of the middle class. Rather than scorning middle-class measuring rods, he actively strives to succeed by those standards. Cohen views this type of youth as one who is embarking on an almost hopeless path because he is ill-equipped academically, socially, and linguistically to achieve the rewards of middle-class life.

The **delinquent boy** adopts a set of norms and principles that directly oppose middle-class values. He engages in short-run hedonism, living for today and letting "tomorrow take care of itself."[153] Delinquent boys strive for *group autonomy*. They resist efforts by family, school, or other sources of authority to control their behavior. They may join a gang because it is perceived as autonomous, independent, and the focus of "attraction, loyalty, and solidarity."[154] Frustrated by their inability to succeed, these boys resort to a process Cohen calls **reaction formation**. Symptoms of reaction formation include overly intense responses that seem disproportionate to the stimuli that trigger them. For the delinquent boy, this takes the form of irrational, malicious, and unaccountable hostility to the enemy, which in this case is "the norms of respectable middle-class society."[155] Reaction formation causes delinquent boys to overreact to any perceived threat or slight. They sneer at the college boy's attempts at assimilation and scorn the corner boy's passivity. The delinquent boy is willing to take risks, violate the law, and flout middle-class conventions.

Cohen's work helps explain the factors that promote and sustain a delinquent subculture. By introducing the concepts of status frustration and middle-class measuring rods, Cohen makes it clear that social forces, not individual traits, promote and sustain a delinquent career. By describing the corner boy–college boy–delinquent boy triad, he helps explain why many lower-class youths fail to become chronic offenders: there is more than one social path open to indigent youths.[156] His work skillfully integrates strain and social disorganization theories and has become an enduring element of criminological literature.

Theory of Differential Opportunity

In their classic work *Delinquency and Opportunity*, written almost 40 years ago, Richard Cloward and Lloyd Ohlin combined strain and social disorganization principles to portray a gang-sustaining criminal subculture.[157] Cloward and Ohlin agree with Cohen and find that independent delinquent subcultures exist within society. They consider a delinquent subculture to be one in which certain forms of delinquent activity are essential requirements for performing the dominant roles supported by the subculture.[158]

Youth gangs are an important part of the delinquent subculture. Although not all illegal acts are committed by gang youths, they are the source of the most serious, sustained, and costly criminal behaviors. Delinquent gangs spring up in disorganized areas where youths lack the opportunity to gain success through conventional means. True to strain theory principles, Cloward and Ohlin portray slum kids as individuals who want to conform to middle-class values but lack the means to do so. They state, "Reaching out for socially approved goals under conditions that preclude their legitimate achievement may become a prelude to deviance."[159]

Differential Opportunities The centerpiece of the Cloward and Ohlin theory is the concept of **differential opportunity**. According to this concept, people in all strata of society share the same success goals; however, those in the lower class have limited means of achieving them. People who perceive themselves as failures within conventional society will seek alternative or innovative ways to succeed. People who conclude that there is little hope for legitimate advancement may join like-minded peers to form a gang. Gang members provide the emotional support to handle the shame, fear, or guilt they may develop while engaging in illegal acts; delinquent subcultures then reward these acts that conventional society would punish. The youth who is considered a failure at school and is qualified for only a menial job at a minimum wage can earn thousands of dollars plus the respect of his or her peers by joining a gang and engaging in drug deals or armed robberies.

Cloward and Ohlin recognize that the opportunity for success in both conventional and criminal careers is limited. In stable areas, adolescents may be recruited by professional criminals, drug traffickers, or organized crime groups. Unstable areas, however, cannot support flourishing criminal opportunities. In these socially disorganized neighborhoods, adult role models are absent, and young criminals have few opportunities to join established gangs or learn the fine points of professional crime. Their most important finding, then, is that all opportunities for success, both illegal and conventional, are closed for the most disadvantaged youths.

Because of differential opportunity, kids are likely to join one of three types of gangs.

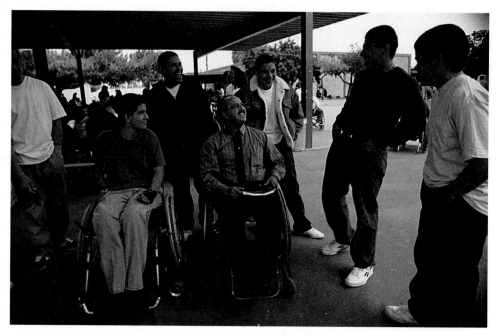

In disorganized areas even criminal opportunities are lacking. Rather than engage in lucrative criminal enterprise some gang boys revert to destructive violence and drive-by shootings. Here a former gang member paralyzed in a shooting counsels teen boys to forego violent acts.

1. **Criminal gangs:** Criminal gangs exist in stable slum areas where close connections among adolescent, young adult, and adult offenders create an environment for successful criminal enterprise.[160] Youths are recruited into established criminal gangs that provide training for a successful criminal career. Gang membership is a learning experience in which the knowledge and skills needed for success in crime are acquired. During this apprenticeship, older, more experienced members of the criminal subculture hold youthful trainees on tight reins, limiting activities that might jeopardize the gang's profits (for example, engaging in nonfunctional, irrational violence). Over time, new recruits learn the techniques and attitudes of the criminal world and how to "cooperate successfully with others in criminal enterprises."[161] To become a fully accepted member of the criminal gang, novices must prove themselves reliable and dependable in their contacts with their criminal associates. They are introduced to the middlemen of the crime business (drug importers, fences, and pawn shop operators) and also to legal connections (crooked police officers and shady lawyers) who can help them gain their freedom in the rare instances when they are apprehended.

2. **Conflict gangs:** Conflict gangs develop in communities unable to provide either legitimate or illegitimate opportunities. These highly disorganized areas are marked by transient residents and physical deterioration. Crime in this area is "individualistic, unorganized, petty, poorly paid, and unprotected."[162] There are no successful adult criminal role models from whom youths can learn criminal skills. When such se-

vere limitations on both criminal and conventional opportunity intensify frustrations of the young, violence is used to gain status. The image of the conflict gang member is the swaggering, tough adolescent who fights with weapons to win respect from rivals and engages in unpredictable and destructive assaults on people and property. Conflict gang members must be ready to fight to protect their own and their gang's integrity and honor. By doing so, they acquire a "rep," which gains admiration from their peers and consequently helps them develop their self-image. Conflict gangs, according to Cloward and Ohlin, "represent a way of securing access to the scarce resources for adolescent pleasure and opportunity in underprivileged areas."[163]

3. **Retreatist gangs:** Retreatists are double failures, unable to gain success through legitimate means and unwilling to do so through illegal ones. Some retreatists have tried crime or violence, but they are too clumsy, weak, or scared to be accepted in criminal or violent gangs. They then retreat into a role on the fringe of society. Members of the retreatist subculture constantly search for ways of getting high—alcohol, pot, heroin, unusual sexual experiences, music. They are always "cool," detached from relationships with the conventional world. To feed their habits, retreatists develop a "hustle"—pimping, conning, selling drugs, or committing petty crimes. Personal status in the retreatist subculture is derived from peer approval.

Analysis of Differential Opportunity Cloward and Ohlin's theory integrates cultural deviance and social disorganization variables and recognizes different modes of criminal adaptation. The fact that criminal cultures can be supportive, rational, and profitable seems to more realistically reflect the actual world of the delinquent than Cohen's original view of purely negativistic, destructive delinquent youths who oppose all social values. Cloward and Ohlin's tripartite model of urban delinquency also relates directly to the treatment and rehabilitation of delinquents. Whereas other social structure theorists portray delinquent youths as having values and attitudes opposite those of middle-class culture, Cloward and Ohlin suggest that many delinquents share the goals and values of the general society but lack the means to obtain success. This position suggests that delinquency can be prevented by giving youths the means for obtaining the success they truly desire without the need to change their basic attitudes and beliefs.

One of the cornerstones of opportunity theory is the activities of teenage gangs, which are even more numerous and active today than they were when Cloward and Ohlin completed their pioneering research.

EVALUATION OF SOCIAL STRUCTURE THEORIES

The social structure approach has significantly influenced both criminological theory and crime prevention strategies. Its core concepts seem to be valid in view of the high rates of crime, delinquency, and gang activity occurring in the deteriorated slum areas of the nation's largest cities. The public's image of the slum includes roaming bands of violent teenage gangs, inner city users, prostitutes, muggers, and similar frightening examples of criminality. All of these are present today in urban areas.

Each branch of the general structural model seems to support and amplify others. Some theorists suggest that these concepts are actually interdependent.[164] Factors that cause strain, such as lack of access to legitimate economic opportunities and economic inequality, also produce social disorganization. Stress leads to alcohol abuse and unprotected sex outside of marriage, resulting in more impaired households, dysfunctional families, urban hostility, and deterioration of informal social controls.

Is the Structural Approach Valid?

Critics of the approach charge that we cannot be sure that lower-class culture, not some other force operating in society, promotes crime. Critics deny that residence in urban areas is sufficient to cause people to violate the law;[165] they say that lower-class crime rates may be an artifact of bias in the criminal justice system. Lower-class areas seem to have higher crime rates because residents are arrested and prosecuted by agents of the justice system who, as members of the middle class, exhibit class bias.[166] Class bias is often coupled with discrimination against minority group members, who have long suffered at the hands of the justice system.

Even if the higher crime rates recorded in lower-class areas are valid, it is still true that most members of the lower class are not criminals. The discovery of the chronic offender indicates that a significant majority of people living in lower-class environments are not criminals and that a relatively small proportion of the population commits most crimes. If social forces alone explain crime, how can we account for the vast number of urban poor who remain honest and law-abiding? Given these circumstances, law violators must be motivated by some individual mental, physical, or social process or trait.[167]

It is also questionable whether a distinct lower-class culture actually exists. Several researchers have found that gang members and other delinquent youths seem to value middle-class concepts, such as sharing, earning money, and respecting the law, as highly as middle-class youths. Criminologists contend that lower-class youths also value education as highly as middle-class students do.[168] Public opinion polls can also be used as evidence that a majority of lower-class citizens maintain middle-class values. National surveys find that people in the lowest income brackets want tougher drug laws, more police protection, and greater control over criminal offenders.[169] These opinions seem similar to conventional middle-class values rather than representative of an independent, deviant subculture. Although this evidence contradicts some of the central ideas of social structure theory, the discovery of stable patterns of lower-class crime, the high crime rates found in disorganized inner-city areas, and the rise of teenage gangs and groups support a close association between crime rates and social class position.

SOCIAL STRUCTURE THEORY AND SOCIAL POLICY

Social structure theory has significantly influenced social policy. If the cause of criminality is viewed as a schism between lower-class individuals and conventional goals, norms, and rules, it seems logical that alternatives to criminal behavior can be provided by giving slum dwellers opportunities to share in the rewards of conventional society.

One approach is to give indigent people direct financial aid through public assistance or **welfare**. Although welfare has been curtailed through the Federal Welfare Reform Act of 1996, research shows that crime rates decrease when families receive supplemental income through public assistance payments.[170]

There are also efforts to reduce crime by improving the community structure in inner-city high-crime areas. Crime prevention efforts based on social structure

Operation Weed and Seed

Operation Weed and Seed is the federal multilevel action plan for revitalizing communities. This plan has four basic elements: law enforcement; community policing; prevention, intervention, and treatment; and neighborhood restoration. The thinking behind the program is that no single approach can reduce crime rates and that social service and law enforcement agencies must cooperate to be effective. The Weed and Seed program has four main components.

Law Enforcement. No social program or community activity can survive in an atmosphere tainted by violent crime and drug abuse. Law enforcement must weed out the most violent offenders by coordinating and integrating the efforts of federal, state, and local law enforcement agencies in targeted high-crime neighborhoods. The law enforcement element consists primarily of suppression activities, including enforcement, adjudication, prosecution, and supervision efforts designed to target, apprehend, and incapacitate violent street criminals who terrorize neighborhoods and account for a disproportionate percentage of

criminal activity. One example of an effective law enforcement strategy is Operation Triggerlock, a Department of Justice initiative that targets violent offenders for federal prosecution to take advantage of tough federal firearms laws. Some suppression activities focus on special enforcement operations such as repeat or violent offender removal programs, intensified narcotics investigations, targeted prosecutions, victim-witness protection, and elimination of narcotics trafficking organizations.

Community Policing. Community policing serves as the bridge between the weeding and seeding components. The community policing element supports intensive law enforcement suppression and containment activities and provides a link to the prevention, intervention, and treatment components, as well as the neighborhood reclamation and restoration components. Local police departments implement community policing strategies in each targeted site. Under community policing, law enforcement works closely with community residents to develop solutions to violent and drug-

related crime. In addition, community policing helps foster a sense of responsibility within the community and stimulates community mobilization. Community policing activities focus on increasing police visibility and developing cooperative relationships between the police and citizenry in the target areas. Techniques such as foot patrols, problem solving, referring victims to support services, and community relations activities increase positive interaction between the police and the community. Special emphasis is placed on addressing the needs of crime victims and minority communities that are disproportionately victimized by crime.

Community mobilization is also important to community policing in crime prevention. Programs that encourage community participation and help prevent crime include neighborhood watches, citizen marches and rallies, prayer services, drug-free zones, and graffiti removal.

Prevention, Intervention, and Treatment. The coordinated efforts of law enforcement and social service agencies, the private sector, and the com-

---

precepts can be traced back to the **Chicago Area Project** supervised by Clifford R. Shaw. This program attempted to organize existing community structures to develop social stability in otherwise disorganized slums. The project sponsored recreation programs for neighborhood children, including summer camping. It campaigned for community improvements in such areas as education, sanitation, traffic safety, resource conservation, and law enforcement. Project members also worked with police and court agencies to supervise and treat gang youth and adult offenders. In a 25-year assessment of the project, Solomon Kobrin found that it was successful in demonstrating the feasibility of creating youth welfare organizations in high-delinquency areas.[171] Kobrin also discovered that the project made a distinct contribution to ending the isolation of urban males from the mainstream of society.

Social structure concepts, especially Cloward and Ohlin's views, were a critical ingredient in the Kennedy and Johnson administrations' War on Poverty, begun in the early 1960s. Rather than organizing existing community structures, as Shaw's Chicago Area Project had

done, this later effort called for an all-out attack on the crime-producing structures of slum areas. The cornerstone of the War on Poverty's crime prevention effort was called **Mobilization for Youth (MFY).** This New York City–based program, funded for over $12 million, was designed to serve multiple purposes, including

- Providing teacher training and education to help educators deal with problem youths.
- Creating work opportunities through a youth job center.
- Organizing neighborhood councils and associations.
- Providing street workers to deal with teen gangs.
- Setting up counseling services and assistance to neighborhood families.

Subsequent War on Poverty programs included the Job Corps; VISTA (the urban Peace Corps); Head Start and Upward Bound (educational enrichment programs); Neighborhood Legal Services; and the largest community organizing effort, the Community Action Program. War on Poverty programs, such as MFY, were sweeping efforts to change the social structure of slum areas.

munity help prevent crime by concentrating a broad array of human services on the target areas to create an environment where crime cannot thrive. Prevention, intervention, and treatment include youth services, school programs, community and social programs, and support groups designed to develop positive community attitudes toward combating narcotics use and trafficking. The Safe Haven, for example, organizes and delivers an array of youth- and adult-oriented human services in a multiservice center setting such as a school. Another program in Durham, North Carolina, attempts to reduce truancy using the following techniques:

- Both parent(s) and student sign a contract with the school to guarantee attendance.
- Police officers patrol school areas.
- Truant officers are given daily information on truants.
- Truant officers actively pursue truant students.
- Parents are informed immediately if their children are truant, and the consequences of their truancy are explained.
- Human service agencies are immediately involved.

- Truant officers follow cases through the court system.
- Student populations are educated about the costs of truancy to their lives.

Neighborhood Restoration. Neighborhood restoration can be achieved only through the coordinated use of federal, state, local, and private-sector resources. This element of Weed and Seed is designed to revitalize distressed neighborhoods and improve quality of life in target communities. The neighborhood restoration element focuses on economic development activities designed to strengthen legitimate community institutions. Resources are dedicated to economic development, provision of economic opportunities for residents, improved housing conditions, enhanced social services, and improved public services in target areas. Programs are developed to improve living conditions by enhancing home security; allowing low-cost physical improvements; developing long-term efforts to renovate and maintain housing; and providing educational, economic, social, recreational, and other vital opportunities. A key feature of this element is fostering self-worth and individual responsibility among community members.

CRITICAL THINKING

1. What steps would you take if you were appointed to head a Weed and Seed program in your own town or a neighboring city?
2. Would aggressive law enforcement tactics turn off residents and defeat the purpose of community restoration? Describe the reaction you would anticipate.

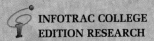

INFOTRAC COLLEGE EDITION RESEARCH

To read more about the techniques needed to redevelop communities, read:

Elmer Johnson. The view from the metropolis. *Brookings Review*, Fall 1998 v16 n4 p12

Mark R. Warren. Community building and political power. *American Behavioral Scientist*, Sept 1998 v42 n1 p78

Source: Information in this section was supplied by Operation Weed and Seed Executive Offices, U.S. Department of Justice, Washington, D.C., 1998; Executive Office for Weed and Seed, *Weed and Seed In-Sites Series* VI: 5 (August/September 1998).

They sought to reduce crime by developing a sense of community pride and solidarity in poverty areas and by providing educational and job opportunities for crime-prone youths.

Unfortunately, the programs failed. Federal and state funding often fell into the hands of middle-class managers and community developers, not the people it was designed to help. Managers were accused of graft and corruption. Some community organizers engineered rent strikes, lawsuits, protests, and the like, which angered government officials and convinced them to end financial backing of such programs. Rather than appeal to the political power structure, program administrators alienated it. Still later, the mood of the country began to

change; the more conservative political climate under the Nixon, Ford, Reagan, and Bush administrations did not favor federal sponsorship of radical change in U.S. cities. Instead, a more selective crime prevention policy was adopted. However, some War on Poverty programs — Head Start, Neighborhood Legal Services, and the Community Action Program — have continued to help people.

Although it may be difficult to revive entire neighborhoods, the federal government continues to sponsor programs that focus on the total community. The Policy and Practice in Criminology feature titled "Operation Weed and Seed" explores this issue in depth.

SUMMARY

Sociology has been the main orientation of criminologists because they know that crime rates vary among elements of the social structure, that society goes through changes that affect crime, and that social interaction relates to criminality. Social

structure theories suggest that people's places in the socioeconomic structure influence their chances of becoming a criminal. Poor people are more likely to commit crimes because they are unable to achieve monetary or social success in any other

Table 7.5 Social Structure Theories

THEORY	MAJOR PREMISE	STRENGTHS
Social Disorganization Theory		
Shaw and McKay's concentric zone theory	Crime is a product of transitional neighborhoods that manifest social disorganization and value conflict.	Identifies why crime rates are highest in slum areas. Points out the factors that produce crime. Suggests programs to help reduce crime.
Social ecology theory	The conflicts and problems of urban social life and communities, including fear, unemployment, deterioration, and siege mentality, influence crime rates.	Accounts for urban crime rates and trends.
Strain Theory		
Anomie theory	People who adopt the goals of society but lack the means to attain them seek alternatives, such as crime.	Points out how competition for success creates conflict and crime. Suggests that social conditions and not personality can account for crime. Can explain middle- and upper-class crime.
General strain theory	Strain has a variety of sources. Strain causes crime in the absence of adequate coping mechanisms.	Identifies the complexities of strain in modern society. Expands on anomie theory. Shows the influence of social events on behavior over the life course.
Institutional anomie theory	Material goals pervade all aspects of American life.	Explains why crime rates are so high in American culture.
Relative deprivation theory	Crime occurs when the wealthy and poor live close to one another.	Explains high crime rates in deteriorated inner-city areas located near more affluent neighborhoods.
Cultural Deviance Theory		
Sellin's culture conflict theory	Obedience to the norms of their lower-class culture puts people in conflict with the norms of the dominant culture.	Identifies the aspects of lower-class life that produce street crime. Adds to Shaw and McKay's analysis. Creates the concept of culture conflict.
Miller's focal concern theory	Citizens who obey the street rules of lower-class life (focal concerns) find themselves in conflict with the dominant culture.	Identifies the core values of lower-class culture and shows their association to crime.
Cohen's theory of delinquent gangs	Status frustration of lower-class boys, created by their failure to achieve middle-class success, causes them to join gangs.	Shows how the conditions of lower-class life produce crime. Explains violence and destructive acts. Identifies conflict of lower class with middle class.
Cloward and Ohlin's theory of opportunity	Blockage of conventional opportunities causes lower-class youths to join criminal, conflict, or retreatist gangs.	Shows that even illegal opportunities are structured in society. Indicates why people become involved in a particular type of criminal activity. Presents a way of preventing crime.

way. Social structure theory has three schools of thought: social disorganization, strain, and cultural deviance theories (summarized in Table 7.5).

Social disorganization theory suggests that slum dwellers violate the law because they live in areas in which social control has broken down. The origin of social disorganization theory can be traced to the work of Clifford R. Shaw and Henry D. McKay. Shaw and McKay concluded that disorganized areas marked by divergent values and transitional populations produce criminality. Modern social ecology theory looks at such issues as community fear, unemployment, siege mentality, and deterioration.

Strain theories comprise the second branch of the social structure approach. They view crime as resulting from the anger people experience over their inability to achieve legitimate social and economic success. Strain theories hold that most people share common values and beliefs, but the ability to achieve them is differentiated throughout the social structure. The best-known strain theory is Robert Merton's theory of anomie, which describes what happens when people have inadequate means to satisfy their goals. Steven Messner and Richard Rosenfeld show that American culture produces strain, and Robert Agnew found that strain has multiple sources.

Cultural deviance theories hold that a unique value system develops in lower-class areas. Lower-class values approve of behaviors such as being tough, never showing fear, and defying authority. People perceiving strain will bond together in their own groups or subcultures for support and recognition. Albert Cohen links the formation of subcultures to the failure of lower-class citizens to achieve recognition from middle-class decision makers, such as teachers, employers, and police officers. Richard Cloward and Lloyd Ohlin have argued that crime results from lower-class people's perception that their opportunity for success is limited. Consequently, youths in low-income areas may join criminal, conflict, or retreatist gangs.

 See the book-specific web site at www.cj.wadsworth. com for additional chapter links, discussions, and quizzes.

THINKING LIKE A CRIMINOLOGIST

You have accepted a position in Washington as an assistant to the undersecretary of urban affairs. The secretary informs you that he wants to initiate a demonstration project in a major city to show that government can reduce poverty, crime, and drug abuse.

The area he has chosen for development is a large inner-city neighborhood in a midwestern city of over 3 million people. It suffers disorganized community structure, poverty, and hopelessness. Predatory delinquent gangs run free and terrorize local merchants and citizens. The school system has failed to provide opportunities and educational experiences sufficient to dampen enthusiasm for gang recruitment. Stores, homes, and public buildings are deteriorated and decayed. Commercial enterprise has fled the area, and civil servants are reluctant to enter the neighborhood. There is an uneasy truce between the varied ethnic and racial groups that populate the area. Residents feel little can be done to bring the neighborhood back to life. Merchants are afraid to open stores, and there is little outside development from major retailers or manufacturers. People who want to start their own businesses find that banks will not lend them money.

One of the biggest problems has been the large housing projects that were developed in the 1960s. These are now overcrowded and deteriorated. Police are actually afraid to enter the buildings unless they arrive with a SWAT team. Each building is controlled by a gang whose members demand tribute from the residents.

You are asked to propose an urban redevelopment program that can revitalize the area and eventually bring down the crime rate. You can bring any public or private element to bear on this overwhelming problem. You can also ask private industry to help in the struggle, promising them tax breaks for their participation. What programs do you feel could break the cycle of urban poverty?

KEY TERMS

Chicago School
stratified
social class
culture of poverty
at-risk
underclass
undeserving poor
truly disadvantaged
social structure theory
social disorganization theory
strain theory
strain
cultural deviance theory
subcultures
cultural transmission

transitional neighborhoods
siege mentality
concentration effect
co-offending
social altruism
strain theorists
anomie
mechanical solidarity
organic solidarity
theory of anomie
institutional anomie theory
the American Dream
relative deprivation
general strain theory (GST)
negative affective states

conduct norms
culture conflict
focal concerns
status frustration
middle-class measuring rods
corner boy
college boy
delinquent boy
reaction formation
differential opportunity
welfare
Chicago Area Project
Mobilization for Youth (MFY)

NOTES

1. Steven Messner and Richard Rosenfeld, *Crime and the American Dream* (Belmont, Calif.: Wadsworth, 1994), p. 11.

2. Robert E. Park, "The City: Suggestions for the Investigation of Behavior in the City Environment," *American Journal of Sociology* 20 (1915): 579–83.

3. Robert Park, Ernest Burgess, and Roderic McKenzie, *The City* (Chicago: University of Chicago Press, 1925).

4. Harvey Zorbaugh, *The Gold Coast and the Slum* (Chicago: University of Chicago Press, 1929).

5. Frederick Thrasher, *The Gang* (Chicago: University of Chicago Press, 1927).

6. Louis Wirth, *The Ghetto* (Chicago: University of Chicago Press, 1928).

7. See, generally, Stephen Cernkovich and Peggy Giordano, "Family Relationships and Delinquency," *Criminology* 25 (1987): 295–321; Paul Howes and Howard Markman, "Marital Quality and Child Functioning: A Longitudinal Investigation," *Child Development* 60 (1989): 1044–51.

8. Gary LaFree, *Losing Legitimacy: Street Crime and the Decline of Social Institu- tions in America* (Boulder, Colo.: Westview Press, 1998).

9. Emilie Andersen Allan and Darrell Steffensmeier, "Youth, Underemployment, and Property Crime: Differential Effects of Job Availability and Job Quality on Juvenile and Young Adult Arrest Rates," *American Sociological Review* 54 (1989): 107–23.

10. Edwin Lemert, *Human Deviance, Social Problems and Social Control* (Englewood Cliffs, N.J.: Prentice-Hall, 1967).

11. Based on William Julius Wilson, "Studying Inner-City Social Dislocations: The

Challenge of Public Agenda Research," *American Sociological Review* 56 (1991): 1–14 at 3.

12. National Center for Children in Poverty, News Release, December 11, 1996.

13. Children's Defense Fund, *The State of America's Children, 1996* (Washington, D.C.: Children's Defense Fund, 1996), p. 3.

14. Jennifer Dixon, "Thousands of Infants Left in Hospitals in '91," *Boston Globe,* 9 November 1993, p. 5.

15. Jeanne Brooks-Gunn and Greg J. Duncan, "The Effects of Poverty on Children," *The Future of Children* 7 (1997): 34–39.

16. Greg Duncan, W. Jean Yeung, Jeanne Brooks-Gunn, and Judith Smith, "How Much Does Childhood Poverty Affect the Life Chances of Children?" *American Sociological Review* 63 (1998): 406–423.

17. Duncan, Yeung, Brooks-Gunn, and Smith, "How Much Does Childhood Poverty Affect the Life Chances of Children?" p. 409.

18. Brooks-Gunn and Duncan, "The Effects of Poverty on Children."

19. Jonathan Crane, "The Epidemic Theory of Ghettos and Neighborhood Effects on Dropping Out and Teenage Childbearing," *American Journal of Sociology* 96 (1991): 1226–59; see also Rodrick Wallace, "Expanding Coupled Shock Fronts of Urban Decay and Criminal Behavior: How U.S. Cities Are Becoming 'Hollowed Out,'" *Journal of Quantitative Criminology* 7 (1991): 333–55.

20. Oscar Lewis, "The Culture of Poverty," *Scientific American* 215 (1966): 19–25.

21. Gunnar Myrdal, *The Challenge of World Poverty* (New York: Vintage Books, 1970).

22. Ken Auletta, *The Under Class* (New York: Random House, 1982).

23. Children's Defense Fund, *The State of America's Children, 1998* (Washington, D.C.: Children's Defense Fund, 1998); U.S. Department of Census Data, *Race and Income* (Washington, D.C.: Census Bureau, 1998).

24. James Ainsworth-Darnell and Douglas Downey, "Assessing the Oppositional Culture Explanation for Racial/Ethnic Differences in School Performances," *American Sociological Review* 63 (1998): 536–53.

25. Eric Lotke, "Hobbling a Generation: Young African-American Men in Washington, D.C.'s Criminal Justice System — Five Years Later," *Crime and Delinquency* 44 (1998): 355–66.

26. Herbert Gans, "Deconstructing the Underclass: The Term's Danger as a Planning Concept," *Journal of the American Planning Association* 56 (1990): 271–77.

27. Douglas Massey and Mitchell Eggers, "The Ecology of Inequality: Minorities and the Concentration of Poverty 1970–1980," *American Journal of Sociology* 95 (1990): 1153–88.

28. Laurence Lynn and Michael G. H. McGeary, eds., *Inner-City Poverty in the United States* (Washington, D.C.: National Academy Press, 1990), p. 3.

29. Lynn and McGeary, *Inner-City Poverty in the United States,* p. 3.

30. Wilson, *The Truly Disadvantaged* (Chicago: University of Chicago Press, 1987).

31. Cynthia Rexroat, *Declining Economic Status of Black Children: Examining the Change* (Washington, D.C.: Joint Center for Political and Economic Studies, 1990), p. 1.

32. David Brownfield, "Social Class and Violent Behavior," *Criminology* 24 (1986): 421–38.

33. See Charles Tittle and Robert Meier, "Specifying the SES/Delinquency Relationship," *Criminology* 28 (1990): 271–95 at 293.

34. See Ruth Kornhauser, *Social Sources of Delinquency* (Chicago: University of Chicago Press, 1978), p. 75.

35. Clifford R. Shaw and Henry D. McKay, *Juvenile Delinquency and Urban Areas,* rev. ed. (Chicago: University of Chicago Press, 1972).

36. Anthony Platt, *The Child Savers: The Invention of Delinquency* (Chicago: University of Chicago Press, 1968).

37. Shaw and McKay, *Juvenile Delinquency and Urban Areas,* p. 52.

38. Shaw and McKay, *Juvenile Delinquency and Urban Areas,* p. 171.

39. For a discussion of these issues, see Robert Bursik, "Social Disorganization and Theories of Crime and Delinquency: Problems and Prospects," *Criminology* 26 (1988): 521–39.

40. Robert Sampson, "Effects of Socioeconomic Context of Official Reaction to Juvenile Delinquency," *American Sociological Review* 51 (1986): 876–85.

41. Jeffrey Fagan, Ellen Slaughter, and Eliot Hartstone, "Blind Justice? The Impact of Race on the Juvenile Justice Process," *Crime and Delinquency* 33 (1987): 224–58; Merry Morash, "Establishment of a Juvenile Police Record," *Criminology* 22 (1984): 97–113.

42. The most well-known of these critiques is Kornhauser, *Social Sources of Delinquency.*

43. Bernard Lander, *Towards an Understanding of Juvenile Delinquency* (New York: Columbia University Press, 1954); David Bordua, "Juvenile Delinquency and 'Anomie': An Attempt at Replication," *Social Problems* 6 (1958): 230–38; Roland Chilton, "Continuities in Delinquency Area Research: A Comparison of Studies in Baltimore, Detroit, and Indianapolis," *American Sociological Review* 29 (1964): 71–73.

44. For a general review, see James Byrne and Robert Sampson, eds., *The Social Ecology of Crime* (New York: Springer Verlag, 1985).

45. See, generally, Bursik, "Social Disorganization and Theories of Crime and Delinquency," pp. 519–51.

46. William Spelman, "Abandoned Buildings: Magnets for Crime?" *Journal of Criminal Justice* 21 (1993): 481–93.

47. Keith Harries and Andrea Powell, "Juvenile Gun Crime and Social Stress: Baltimore, 1980–1990," *Urban Geography* 15 (1994): 45–63.

48. Ellen Kurtz, Barbara Koons, and Ralph Taylor, "Land Use, Physical Deterioration, Resident-Based Control, and Calls for Service on Urban Streetblocks," *Justice Quarterly* 15 (1998): 121–49.

49. Steven Messner and Kenneth Tardiff, "Economic Inequality and Levels of Homicide: An Analysis of Urban Neighborhoods," *Criminology* 24 (1986): 297–317.

50. G. David Curry and Irving Spergel, "Gang Homicide, Delinquency, and Community," *Criminology* 26 (1988): 381–407.

51. Robert Sampson and W. Byron Groves, "Community Structure and Crime: Testing Social Disorganization Theory," *American Journal of Sociology* 94 (1989): 774–802.

52. Per-Olof Wikstrom and Lars Dolmen, "Crime and Crime Trends in Different Urban Environments," *Journal of Quantitative Criminology* 6 (1990): 7–28.

53. Bursik, "Social Disorganization and Theories of Crime and Delinquency," p. 520.

54. Richard McGahey, "Economic Conditions, Organization, and Urban Crime," in *Communities and Crime,* ed. Albert Reiss and Michael Tonry (Chicago: University of Chicago Press, 1986), pp. 231–70.

55. Scott Menard and Delbert Elliott, "Self-Reported Offending, Maturational Reform, and the Easterlin Hypothesis," *Journal of Quantitative Criminology* 6 (1990): 237–68.

56. Elijah Anderson, *Streetwise: Race, Class and Change in an Urban Community* (Chicago: University of Chicago Press, 1990), pp. 243–44.

57. Pamela Wilcox Rountree and Kenneth Land, "Burglary Victimization, Perceptions of Crime Risk, and Routine Activities: A Multilevel Analysis Across Seattle Neighborhoods and Census Tracts," *Journal of Research in Crime and Delinquency* 33 (1996): 147–80.

58. Randy LaGrange, Kenneth Ferraro, and Michael Supancic, "Perceived Risk and Fear of Crime: Role of Social and Physical Incivilities," *Journal of Research in Crime and Delinquency* 29 (1992): 311–34.

59. Ralph Taylor and Jeanette Covington, "Community Structural Change and Fear of Crime," *Social Problems* 40 (1993): 374–92.

60. Ted Chiricos, Michael Hogan, and Marc Gertz, "Racial Composition of Neighborhood and Fear of Crime," *Criminology* 35 (1997): 107–131.

61. Chiricos, Hogan, and Gertz, "Racial Composition of Neighborhood and Fear of Crime," p. 125.

62. Wesley Skogan, "Fear of Crime and Neighborhood Change," in *Communities and Crime,* ed. Albert Reiss and Michael Tonry (Chicago: University of Chicago Press, 1986), pp. 191–232.

63. Stephanie Greenberg, "Fear and Its Relationship to Crime, Neighborhood Deterioration, and Informal Social Control," in *The Social Ecology of Crime*, ed. James Byrne and Robert Sampson (New York: Springer Verlag, 1985), pp. 47–62.

64. Margo Wilson and Martin Daly, "Life Expectancy, Economic Inequality, Homicide, and Reproductive Timing in Chicago Neighborhoods," *BMJ* 314 (1997): 1271–74.

65. Skogan, "Fear of Crime and Neighborhood Change."

66. Skogan, "Fear of Crime and Neighborhood Change."

67. Anderson, *Streetwise: Race, Class and Change in an Urban Community*, p. 245.

68. Lynette Holloway, "Teacher Threatened over Book Weighs Switching Schools," *New York Times*, 27 November 1998, p. 1A.

69. Finn Aage-Esbensen and David Huizinga, "Community Structure and Drug Use: From a Social Disorganization Perspective," *Justice Quarterly* 7 (1990): 691–709.

70. Allen Liska and Paul Bellair, "Violent-Crime Rates and Racial Composition: Convergence over Time," *American Journal of Sociology* 101 (1995): 578–610.

71. Wesley Skogan, *Disorder and Decline: Crime and the Spiral of Decay in American Neighborhoods* (New York: Free Press, 1990), pp. 15–35.

72. Robert Bursik and Harold Grasmick, "Decomposing Trends in Community Careers in Crime." Paper presented at the annual meeting of the American Society of Criminology, Baltimore, November 1990.

73. Ralph Taylor and Jeanette Covington, "Neighborhood Changes in Ecology and Violence," *Criminology* 26 (1988): 553–89.

74. Leo Scheurman and Solomon Kobrin, "Community Careers in Crime," in *Communities and Crime*, ed. Albert Reiss and Michael Tonry (Chicago: University of Chicago Press, 1986), pp. 67–100.

75. Scheurman and Kobrin, "Community Careers in Crime."

76. See, generally, Robert Bursik, "Delinquency Rates as Sources of Ecological Change," in *The Social Ecology of Crime*, ed. James Byrne and Robert Sampson (New York: Springer Verlag, 1985), pp. 63–77.

77. Janet Heitgerd and Robert Bursik, "Extracommunity Dynamics and the Ecology of Delinquency," *American Journal of Sociology* 92 (1987): 775–87.

78. Wilson, *The Truly Disadvantaged*.

79. Carolyn Rebecca Block and Richard Block, *Street Gang Crime in Chicago* (Washington, D.C.: National Institute of Justice, 1993), p. 7.

80. Barbara Warner and Glenn Pierce, "Reexamining Social Disorganization Theory Using Calls to the Police as a Measure of Crime," *Criminology* 31 (1993): 493–519.

81. Felton Earls, *Linking Community Factors and Individual Development* (Washington, D.C: National Institute of Justice, 1998)

82. Donald Black, "Social Control as a Dependent Variable," in *Toward a General Theory of Social Control*, ed. D. Black (Orlando: Academic Press, 1990).

83. Bursik and Grasmick, "The Multiple Layers of Social Disorganization." Paper presented at the annual meeting of the American Society of Criminology, New Orleans, November 1992.

84. David Klinger, "Negotiating Order in Patrol Work: An Ecological Theory of Police Response to Deviance," *Criminology* 35 (1997): 277–306.

85. Rodney Stark, "Deviant Places: A Theory of the Ecology of Crime," *Criminology* 25 (1987): 893–911.

86. Delbert Elliott, William Julius Wilson, David Huizinga, Robert Sampson, Amanda Elliott, and Bruce Rankin, "The Effects of Neighborhood Disadvantage on Adolescent Development," *Journal of Research in Crime and Delinquency* 33 (1996): 389–426.

87. Elliott et al., "The Effects of Neighborhood Disadvantage on Adolescent Development," p. 414.

88. Robert Bursik and Harold Grasmick, "Economic Deprivation and Neighborhood Crime Rates, 1960–1980," *Law and Society Review* 27 (1993): 263–78.

89. Skogan, *Disorder and Decline*.

90. Robert Sampson and W. Byron Groves, "Community Structure and Crime: Testing Social Disorganization Theory," *American Journal of Sociology* 94 (1989): 774–802; Denise Gottfredson, Richard McNeill, and Gary Gottfredson, "Social Area Influences on Delinquency: A Multilevel Analysis," *Journal of Research in Crime and Delinquency* 28 (1991): 197–206.

91. Ralph Taylor, "Social Order and Disorder of Street Blocks and Neighborhoods: Ecology, Microecology, and the Systemic Model of Social Disorganization," *Journal of Research in Crime and Delinquency* 34 (1997): 113–55.

92. Mitchell Chamlin and John Cochran, "Social Altruism and Crime," *Criminology* 35 (1997): 203–227.

93. James DeFronzo, "Welfare and Homicide," *Journal of Research in Crime and Delinquency* 34 (1997): 395–406.

94. Robert Merton, *Social Theory and Social Structure*, enlarged ed. (New York: Free Press, 1968).

95. For an analysis, see Richard Hilbert, "Durkheim and Merton on Anomie: An Unexplored Contrast in Its Derivatives," *Social Problems* 36 (1989): 242–56.

96. Hilbert, "Durkheim and Merton on Anomie," p. 243.

97. Albert Cohen, "The Sociology of the Deviant Act: Anomie Theory and Beyond," *American Sociological Review* 30 (1965): 5–14.

98. Robert Agnew, "The Contribution of Social Psychological Strain Theory to the Explanation of Crime and Delinquency," *Advances in Criminological Theory* (1995): 113–22.

99. These criticisms are articulated in Messner and Rosenfeld, *Crime and the American Dream*, p. 60.

100. Scott Menard, "A Developmental Test of Mertonian Anomie Theory," *Journal of Research in Crime and Delinquency* 32 (1995): 136–74.

101. John Hagan, Hans Merkens, and Klaus Boehnke, "Delinquency and Disdain: Social Capital and Control of Right-Wing Extremism Among East and West Berlin Youth," *American Journal of Sociology* 100 (1995): 1028–52.

102. Steven Messner and Richard Rosenfeld, *Crime and the American Dream* (Belmont, Calif.: Wadsworth, 1994).

103. Steven Messner and Richard Rosenfeld, "An Institutional-Anomie Theory of the Social Distribution of Crime." Paper presented at the annual meeting of the American Society of Criminology, Phoenix, Arizona, November 1993.

104. John Hagan, Gerd Hefler, Gabriele Classen, Klaus Boehnke, and Hans Merkens, "Subterranean Sources of Subcultural Delinquency Beyond the American Dream," *Criminology* 36 (1998): 309–340.

105. Mitchell Chamlin and John Cochran, "Assessing Messner and Rosenfeld's Institutional Anomie Theory: A Partial Test," *Criminology* 33 (1995): 411–29.

106. John Braithwaite, "Poverty Power, White-Collar Crime and the Paradoxes of Criminological Theory," *Australian and New Zealand Journal of Criminology* 24 (1991): 40–58.

107. Margo Wilson and Martin Daly, "Life Expectancy, Economic Inequality, Homicide, and Reproductive Timing in Chicago Neighbourhoods," *British Journal of Medicine* 314 (1997): 1271–74.

108. Judith Blau and Peter Blau, "The Cost of Inequality: Metropolitan Structure and Violent Crime," *American Sociological Review* 147 (1982): 114–29.

109. Tomislav Kovandzic, Lynne Vieraitis, and Mark Yeisley, "The Structural Covariates of Urban Homicide: Reassessing the Impact of Income Inequality and Poverty in the Post-Reagan Era," *Criminology* 36 (1998): 569–600.

110. John King, "Paradise Lost? Crime in the Caribbean: A Comparison of Barbados and Jamaica," *Caribbean Journal of Criminology and Social Psychology* 2 (1997): 30–44.

111. Scott South and Steven Messner, "Structural Determinants of Intergroup Association," *American Journal of Sociology* 91 (1986): 1409–30; Steven Messner and Scott South, "Economic Deprivation, Opportunity Structure, and Robbery Victimization," *Social Forces* 64 (1986): 975–91.

112. Richard Fowles and Mary Merva, "Wage Inequality and Criminal Activity: An Extreme Bounds Analysis for the United States 1975–1990," *Criminology* 34 (1996): 163–82.

113. Gary LaFree and Kriss Drass, "The Effect of Changes in Intraracial Income Inequality and Educational Attainment on Changes in Arrest Rates for African Americans and Whites, 1957 to 1990," *American Sociological Review* 61 (1996): 614–34; Taylor and Covington, "Neighborhood Changes in Ecology and Violence," p. 582; Richard Block, "Community Environment and Violent Crime," *Criminology* 17 (1979): 46–57; Robert Sampson, "Structural Sources of Variation in Race–Age–Specific Rates of Offending Across Major U.S. Cities," *Criminology* 23 (1985): 647–73; Richard Rosenfeld, "Urban Crime Rates: Effects of Inequality, Welfare Dependency, Region and Race," in *The Social Ecology of Crime*, ed. James Byrne and Robert Sampson (New York: Springer Verlag, 1985), pp. 116–30.

114. Fowles and Merva, "Wage Inequality and Criminal Activity"; Ruth Peterson and William Bailey, "Rape and Dimensions of Gender Socioeconomic Inequality in U.S. Metropolitan Areas," *Journal of Research in Crime and Delinquency* 29 (1992): 162–77.

115. Gary LaFree, Kriss Drass, and Patrick O'Day, "Race and Crime in Postwar America: Determinants of African-American and White Rates, 1957–1988," *Criminology* 30 (1992): 157–88.

116. Steven Messner and Reid Golden, "Racial Inequality and Racially Disaggregated Homicide Rates: An Assessment of Alternative Theoretical Explanations" (paper presented at the annual meeting of the American Society of Criminology, Baltimore, November 1990); see also Miles Harer and Darrell Steffensmeier, "The Different Effects of Economic Inequality on Black and White Rates of Violence" (paper presented at the annual meeting of the American Society of Criminology, Chicago, November 1988).

117. Kenneth Land, Patricia McCall, and Lawrence Cohen, "Structural Covariates of Homicide Rates: Are There Any Invariances Across Time and Social Space?" *American Journal of Sociology* 95 (1990): 922–63; Robert Bursik and James Webb, "Community Change and Patterns of Delinquency," *American Journal of Sociology* 88 (1982): 24–42.

118. Land, McCall, and Cohen, "Structural Covariates of Homicide Rates"; Bursik and Webb, "Community Change and Patterns of Delinquency."

119. Robert Agnew, "A Durkheimian Strain Theory of Delinquency." Paper presented at the annual meeting of the American Society of Criminology, Baltimore, November 1990.

120. Jeanne Brooks-Gunn, Greg Duncan, Pamela Klato Klebanov, and Naomi Sealand, "Do Neighborhoods Influence Child and Adolescent Development?" *American Journal of Sociology* 99 (1993): 353–95.

121. Nikos Passas, "Anomie and Relative Deprivation." Paper presented at the annual meeting of the Eastern Sociological Society, Boston, 1987.

122. Robert Agnew, "Foundation for a General Strain Theory of Crime and Delinquency," *Criminology* 30 (1992): 47–87.

123. Agnew, "Foundation for a General Strain Theory of Crime and Delinquency," p. 57.

124. Timothy Brezina, "Adolescent Maltreatment and Delinquency: The Question of Intervening Processes," *Journal of Research in Crime and Delinquency* 35 (1998): 71–99.

125. Timothy Brezina, "The Functions of Aggression: Violent Adaptations to Interpersonal Violence." Paper presented at the American Society of Criminology meeting, San Diego, Calif., 1997.

126. Paul Mazerolle and Alex Piquero, "Linking General Strain with Anger: Investigating the Instrumental, Escapist, and Violent Adaptations to Strain." Paper presented at the American Society of Criminology meeting, Boston, Mass., November 1995.

127. Robert Agnew, "Stability and Change in Crime over the Life Course: A Strain Theory Explanation," in *Advances in Criminological Theory*, vol. 7, *Developmental Theories of Crime and Delinquency*, ed. Terence Thornberry (New Brunswick, N.J.: Transaction Books, 1995), pp. 113–37.

128. Lawrence Wu, "Effects of Family Instability, Income, and Income Instability on the Risk of Premarital Birth," *American Sociological Review* 61 (1996): 386–406.

129. Robert Agnew and Helene Raskin White, "An Empirical Test of General Strain Theory," *Criminology* 30 (1992): 475–99.

130. John Hoffman and Alan Miller, "A Latent Variable Analysis of General Strain Theory," *Journal of Quantitative Criminology* 13 (1997): 111–13; Raymond Paternoster and Paul Mazerolle, "General Strain Theory and Delinquency: A Replication and Extension," *Journal of Research in Crime and Delinquency* 31 (1994): 235–63.

131. G. Roger Jarjoura, "The Conditional Effect of Social Class on the Dropout–Delinquency Relationship," *Journal of Research in Crime and Delinquency* 33 (1996): 232–55.

132. Paul Mazerolle and Alex Piquero, "Violent Responses to Strain: An Examination of Conditioning Influences," *Violence and Victimization* 12 (1997): 323–45; Teresa Lagrange and Robert Silverman, "Perceived Strain and Delinquency Motivation: An Empirical Evaluation of General Strain Theory" (paper presented at the American Society of Criminology meeting, Boston, Mass., November 1995).

133. Thomas Ashby Wills, Donato Vaccaro, Grace McNamara, and A. Elizabeth Hirky, "Escalated Substance Use: A Longitudinal Grouping Analysis from Early to Middle Adolescence," *Journal of Abnormal Psychology* 105 (1996): 166–80.

134. Timothy Brezina, "Adapting to Strain: An Examination of Delinquent Coping Responses," *Criminology* 34 (1996): 39–61.

135. Robert Agnew and Timothy Brezina, "Relational Problems with Peers, Gender and Delinquency," *Youth and Society* 29 (1997): 84–111.

136. John Hoffmann and S. Susan Su, "The Conditional Effects of Stress on Delinquency and Drug Use: A Strain Theory in Assessment of Sex Differences," *Journal of Research in Crime and Delinquency* 34 (1997): 46–78.

137. Lisa Broidy, "The Role of Gender in General Strain Theory." Paper presented at the American Society of Criminology meeting, Boston, Mass., November 1995.

138. Lisa Broidy and Robert Agnew, "Gender and Crime: A General Strain Theory Perspective," *Journal of Research in Crime and Delinquency* 34 (1997): 275–306.

139. Robbin Ogle, Daniel Maier-Katkin, and Thomas Bernard, "A Theory of Homicidal Behavior Among Women," *Criminology* 33 (1995): 173–93.

140. Thorsten Sellin, *Culture Conflict and Crime*, Bulletin no. 41 (New York: Social Science Research Council, 1938).

141. Sellin, *Culture Conflict and Crime*, p. 22.

142. Sellin, *Culture Conflict and Crime*, p. 29.

143. Sellin, *Culture Conflict and Crime*, p. 68.

144. Walter Miller, "Lower-Class Culture as a Generating Milieu of Gang Delinquency," *Journal of Social Issues* 14 (1958): 5–19.

145. Miller, "Lower-Class Culture as a Generating Milieu of Gang Delinquency," pp. 14–17.

146. Fred Markowitz and Richard Felson, "Social-Demographic Attitudes and Violence," *Criminology* 36 (1998): 117–38.

147. Jeffrey Fagan, *Adolescent Violence: A View from the Street*, NIJ Research Preview (Washington, D.C: National Institute of Justice, 1998).

148. Albert Cohen, *Delinquent Boys* (New York: Free Press, 1955).

149. Cohen, *Delinquent Boys*, p. 25.

150. Cohen, *Delinquent Boys*, p. 28.

151. Cohen, *Delinquent Boys*, p. 28.

152. Clarence Schrag, *Crime and Justice American Style* (Washington, D.C.: U.S. Government Printing Office, 1971), p. 74.

153. Cohen, *Delinquent Boys*, p. 30.

154. Cohen, *Delinquent Boys*, p. 31.

155. Cohen, *Delinquent Boys*, p. 133.

156. J. Johnstone, "Social Class, Social Areas, and Delinquency," *Sociology and Social Research* 63 (1978): 49–72; Joseph Harry, "Social Class and Delinquency: One More Time," *Sociological Quarterly* 15 (1974): 294–301.

157. Richard Cloward and Lloyd Ohlin, *Delinquency and Opportunity* (New York: Free Press, 1960).

158. Cloward and Ohlin, *Delinquency and Opportunity*, p. 7.

159. Cloward and Ohlin, *Delinquency and Opportunity*, p. 85.

160. Cloward and Ohlin, *Delinquency and Opportunity*, p. 171.

161. Cloward and Ohlin, *Delinquency and Opportunity,* p. 23.

162. Cloward and Ohlin, *Delinquency and Opportunity,* p. 73.

163. Cloward and Ohlin, *Delinquency and Opportunity,* p. 24.

164. Robert Sampson and William Julius Wilson, "Toward a Theory of Race, Crime, and Urban Inequality," in *Crime and Inequality,* ed. John Hagan and Ruth Peterson (Stanford, Calif.: Stanford University Press, 1995), pp. 37–54.

165. For a general criticism, see Kornhauser, *Social Sources of Delinquency.*

166. Charles Tittle, "Social Class and Criminal Behavior: A Critique of the Theoretical Foundations," *Social Forces* 62 (1983): 334–58.

167. James Q. Wilson and Richard Herrnstein, *Crime and Human Nature* (New York: Simon and Schuster, 1985).

168. Kenneth Polk and F. Lynn Richmond, "Those Who Fail," in *Schools and Delinquency,* ed. Kenneth Polk and Walter Schafer (Englewood Cliffs, N.J.: Prentice-Hall, 1974), p. 67.

169. Kathleen Maguire and Ann Pastore, *Sourcebook of Criminal Justice Statistics, 1996* (Washington, D.C.: U.S. Government Printing Office, 1996), pp. 150–66.

170. James DeFronzo, "Welfare and Burglary," *Crime and Delinquency* 42 (1996): 223–30.

171. Solomon Kobrin, "The Chicago Area Project—25-Year Assessment," *Annals of the American Academy of Political and Social Science* 322 (1959): 20–29.

Social Process Theories

INTRODUCTION

Many criminologists question whether a person's place in the social structure alone can control or predict the onset of criminality. After all, most people in the nation's most deteriorated urban areas obey laws, hold conventional values, and compensate for their lack of social standing and financial success with hard work, frugal living, and planning for the future. On the other hand, self-report studies reveal that many members of the privileged classes steal, use drugs, and commit other crimes.

The National Crime Victimization Survey (NCVS) estimates that about 35 million crimes occur annually. If the average active criminal commits one crime every week, fewer than 2 million people (half being incarcerated at any given time and the other half committing crimes) could account for almost the entire U.S. serious crime problem.[1] Today more than 30 million Americans live in poverty. Even if it is assumed that all criminals come from the lower class (they don't), the great majority of indigent Americans do not commit criminal acts even though they may have a great economic incentive to do so. As discussed in Chapter 7, neighborhood deterioration and disorganization alone cannot explain why one individual embarks on a criminal career while another, living in the same environment, obeys the law, gets an education, and seeks legitimate employment.[2] Relatively few delinquent offenders living in deteriorated areas remain chronic offenders; most desist despite the continuing pressure of social decay. Some other social forces, then, must be at work to explain why most at-risk individuals do not become persistent criminal offenders.

As they pass through the life cycle, most people are influenced by the direction of their familial relationships, peer group associations, educational experiences, and interactions with authority figures, including teachers, employers, and agents of the justice system. If these relationships are positive and supportive, they will be able to succeed within the rules of society.

SOCIALIZATION AND CRIME

To explain these contradictory findings, attention has been focused on social-psychological processes and interactions common to people at all segments of the social structure. **Social process theories** hold that criminality is a function of individual socialization. These theories draw attention to the interactions people have with various organizations, institutions, and processes of society. Most people are influenced by their familial relationships, peer group associations, educational experiences, and interactions with authority figures, including teachers, employers, and agents of the justice system. If these relationships are positive and supportive, people can succeed within the rules of society; if these relationships are dysfunctional and destructive, conventional success may be impossible, and criminal solutions may become a feasible alternative.

Social process theories share one basic concept: all people, regardless of their race, class, or gender, have the potential to become delinquents or criminals. Although members of the lower class may have the added burdens of poverty, racism, poor schools, and disrupted family lives, these social forces can be counteracted by positive peer relations, a supportive family, and educational success. In contrast, even the most affluent members of society may turn to antisocial behavior if their life experiences are intolerable or destructive.

Social process theories have endured because the relationship between social class and crime is still uncertain. Most residents of inner-city areas refrain from criminal activity, and few of those that commit crimes persist into adulthood. If poverty was the sole cause of crime, then indigent adults would be as criminal as indigent teenagers. The association between economic status and crime is problematic because class position alone cannot explain crime rates.[3]

CONNECTIONS

Chapter 3's analysis of the class–crime relationship showed why this is still a hotly debated topic. Although serious criminals may be disproportionately found in lower-class areas, self-report studies show that criminality cuts across class lines. The discussion of drug use in Chapter 14 shows that members of the middle class use and abuse recreational substances; this indicates that many law violators are not necessarily economically motivated.

Criminologists have long studied the critical elements of socialization to determine how they contribute to a burgeoning criminal career. Prominent among these elements are the family, the peer group, school, and church.

Family Relations

Family relationships are considered a major determinant of behavior.[4] In fact, parenting factors, such as the ability to communicate and provide proper discipline, may play a critical role in determining whether people misbehave as children and even later as adults. This is one of the most replicated findings in the criminological literature.[5]

Youths who grow up in a household characterized by conflict and tension, where parents are absent or separated, or where there is a lack of familial love and support are susceptible to crime-promoting forces in the environment.[6] Even children living in high-crime areas will be better able to resist the temptations of the streets if they receive fair discipline, care, and support from parents who provide them with strong, positive role models.[7] Nonetheless, living in a disadvantaged neighborhood places terrific strain on family functioning, especially in single-parent families that are socially isolated from relatives, friends, and neighbors. Children raised within such distressed families are at risk for delinquency.[8]

The relationship between family structure and crime is critical when the high rates of divorce and single parenting are considered. The U.S. Census Bureau estimates that the percentage of children living with both of their biological parents will decline from about 35 percent today to about 29 percent in 2010.[9] Table 8.1 details the living arrangements of America's children.

At one time, growing up in a **broken home** was considered a primary cause of criminal behavior. However, many criminologists today discount the association between family structure and the onset of criminality, claiming that family conflict and discord determine behavior more than family structure.[10] Not

Table 8.1   Profile of Children's Living Arrangements (Children Under Age 18)

- About 48.3 million of the 70.3 million children under age 18 live with two parents (69 percent); 18.9 million live with only one parent (27 percent); and 3.0 million live with neither parent (4 percent).
- Of children living with one parent, 38 percent live with a divorced parent, 35 percent with a never-married parent, 19 percent with a separated parent, 4 percent with a widowed parent, and 4 percent with a parent whose spouse lives elsewhere because of business or some other reason.
- Four million children live in the homes of their grandparents. For 11 percent of them, both parents are also in the household; for 52 percent, one parent is there; and for 37 percent, neither parent is present.
- Most single-parent children live in metropolitan areas (14.5 million), and six in 10 of them (9.2 million) are in cities with populations of 1 million or more.

Source: U.S. Dept. of Commerce, Bureau of the Census, *Children with Single Parents—How They Fare* (Washington, D.C.: U.S. Bureau of the Census, 1997).

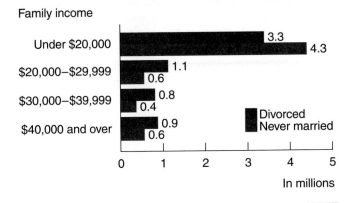

Figure 8.1 Children with Divorced and Never-Married Mothers, by Family Income

Family income

Under $20,000 — 3.3 / 4.3

$20,000–$29,999 — 1.1 / 0.6

$30,000–$39,999 — 0.8 / 0.4

$40,000 and over — 0.9 / 0.6

■ Divorced
■ Never married

0 1 2 3 4 5

In millions

Source: *Children with Single Parents—How They Fare* (Washington: D.C.: U.S. Bureau of the Census, 1997).

children are likely to follow suit. In fact, parental deviance has been linked to children's criminal behavior.

Children growing up in homes where a parent suffers mental impairment are also at risk for delinquency.[18] Children of drug abusers who are as young as 2 exhibit personality defects such as excessive anger and negativity.[19] These and older children are more likely to become persistent substance abusers than the children of nonabusers.[20] John Laub and Robert Sampson support this finding with their own evidence that shows children of parents who engage in criminality and substance abuse are more likely to violate laws than the offspring of law-abiding parents.[21]

CONNECTIONS

Sampson and Laub's research will be discussed more fully in Chapter 10. Although deviant parents may encourage offending, Sampson and Laub believe that life experiences can either encourage crime-prone people to offend or aid them in their return to a conventional lifestyle.

Child Abuse and Crime There is also a suspected link between child abuse, neglect, sexual abuse, and crime.[22] A number of studies show a significant association between child maltreatment and serious self-reported and official delinquency, even when taking into account gender, race, and class.[23] Children who are subjected to even minimal amounts of physical punishment may be more likely to use violence themselves in personal interactions.[24] Whereas nonviolent societies are also ones in which parents rarely punish their children physically, in more violent societies, there are links among corporal punishment, delinquency, anger, spousal abuse, depression, and adult crime.[25]

CONNECTIONS

Chapter 4 noted that victims of abuse may suffer significant social problems and emotional stress related to criminal activity. Process theories recognize the role of family relations in escalating criminal activity.

The effect of the family on delinquency has also been observed in other cultures. Research conducted in 10 European countries shows that the degree to which parents and teachers approve of corporal punishment is related to both the overall homicide rate and the infant homicide rate.[26] Studies of Chinese families show that those who provide firm support inhibit delinquency, whereas families in which one or both parents are deviant are more likely to have children involved in deviant activities.[27]

all experts, though, discount the effects of family structure on crime. Even if single parents can make up for the loss of a second parent, the argument goes, it is simply more difficult to do so, and the chances of failure increase.[11] For example, as Figure 8.1 shows, the family income of children living with divorced or never-married mothers is likely to be under $20,000 per year. Single parents may find it difficult to provide adequate supervision, and children who live with single parents receive less encouragement and less help with schoolwork. Poor school achievement and limited educational aspirations have been associated with delinquent behavior. Also, because they are receiving less attention as a result of having just one parent, these children may be more prone to rebellious acts, such as running away and truancy.[12] Children in two-parent households, on the other hand, are more likely to want to attend college than kids in single-parent homes.[13]

Because their incomes may decrease substantially in the aftermath of marital breakup, some divorced mothers are forced to move to residences in deteriorated neighborhoods. Some of these disorganized neighborhoods may place children at risk of crime and drug abuse.[14] When a mother remarries, it does not seem to mitigate the effects of divorce on her children. Kids living with a stepparent exhibit as many problems as youths in single-parent families and considerably more problems than those who are living with both biological parents.[15]

Other family factors that have predictive value include inconsistent discipline, poor supervision, and the lack of a warm, loving, supportive parent–child relationship.[16] Children who have affectionate ties to their parents report greater levels of self-esteem beginning in adolescence and extending into adulthood; high self-esteem is inversely related to criminal behavior.[17] Conversely, when parents exhibit deviant behavior, their

Educational Experience

The educational process and adolescent school achievement have been linked to criminality. Children who do poorly in school, lack educational motivation, and feel alienated are the most likely to engage in criminal acts.[28] Children who fail in school offend more frequently than those who succeed. These children commit more serious and violent offenses and persist in crime into adulthood.[29]

Schools contribute to criminality by labeling problem youths, which sets them apart from conventional society. One way in which they perpetuate this stigmatization is the *track system,* which identifies some students as college-bound and others as academic underachievers or potential dropouts.[30] Children placed in tracks labeled as advanced placement, college prep, or honors develop positive self-images and achievement motivation, whereas those assigned to lower-level or general courses of study may believe that academic achievement is closed to someone of their limited skills. Research findings over the past two decades indicate that many school dropouts, especially those who have been expelled, face a significant chance of entering a criminal career.[31] In contrast, doing well in school and developing attachments to teachers has been linked to crime resistance.[32]

The association between the educational experience and crime is highlighted by growing evidence that many criminal acts occur on school grounds. Released in 1998, the School Crime Victimization Survey, a joint effort by the Justice Department and the Education Department, showed that 14.6 percent of students aged 12 through 19 reported violent or property victimization at school.[33] One reason for a recent upsurge in school violence may be the number of students who bring weapons to school: by age 15 about 15 percent of students know a student who has brought a gun to school.

Another overview of American school crime, prepared by the Department of Education's National Center for Education Statistics, surveyed principals at 1,234 of the nation's 87,000 public schools.[34] Although only crimes reported to police were included in the survey, the study found that 190,000 weaponless fights occurred each year, along with 116,000 incidents of theft and 98,000 of vandalism. Among more serious crimes, the study found about 4,000 rapes a year, 7,000 robberies, and 11,000 fights or attacks with a weapon.

Peer Relations

Psychologists have long recognized that peer groups powerfully affect human conduct and can dramatically influence decision making and behavior choices.[35] Peer influence on behavior has been recorded in different cultures and may be a universal norm.[36]

Early in children's lives, parents are the primary source of influence and attention. Between the ages of 8 and 14, children begin to seek a stable peer group. If all goes as it should, both the number and variety of friendships increase as children go through adolescence. Soon friends influence decisions more than parents.[37]

By their early teens, children report that their friends give them emotional support when they are feeling badly and that they can confide intimate feelings to peers without worrying about their confidences being betrayed. In later adolescence, peer approval has a major impact on socialization. As they go through adolescence, children form **cliques,** small groups of friends who share activities and confidences. They also belong to **crowds,** loosely organized groups of children who share interests and activities. Whereas clique members share intimate knowledge, crowds are brought together by mutually shared activities like sports, religion, or hobbies. Although bonds in this wider circle of friends may not be intimate, adolescents learn a lot about themselves and their world while navigating through these relationships.[38] Some popular adolescents may be members of a variety of cliques and crowds. The most popular youths, in general, tend to do well in school and are socially astute. In contrast, children who are rejected by their peers are more likely to display aggressive behavior and disrupt group activities through bickering, bullying, or other antisocial behavior.[39] Peer relations, then, are a vital aspect of maturation.

Because of the powerful peer influence on adolescents, they feel persistent pressure to conform to group values. In positive relationships, peers guide each other and help their friends learn to share and cooperate, cope with aggressive impulses, and discuss feelings they would not dare bring up at home. In these relationships, youths can compare their experiences and learn that others have similar concerns and problems. Through these friendships, they realize they are not alone. However, when peers are not positive influences on each other, adolescent criminal activity can begin as a group process.[40]

Although experts have long debated the exact relationship between peer group interaction and delinquency, research shows that adolescents who report inadequate or strained peer relations, and who say they are not popular with the opposite sex, are most likely to become delinquent.[41]

Delinquent peers often exert tremendous influence on behavior, attitudes, and beliefs.[42] In every level of the social structure, youths who fall in with a bad crowd become more susceptible to criminal behavior patterns.[43] Deviant peers provide friendship networks that support delinquency and drug use.[44] Activities such as riding around, staying out late, and partying with deviant peers give these youths the opportunity to commit deviant acts.[45] Because delinquent friends tend to be, as criminologist Mark Warr puts it, "sticky" (once acquired, they are not easily lost), peer influence may continue through the life span.[46]

Some children join more than one deviant group, leading one and being a follower in another. Even when some of these groups are short-lived, being exposed to so many deviant influences in multiple groups may help explain why deviant group membership is highly correlated with personal offending rates.[47] The more antisocial the peer group, the more likely its members will engage in delinquency; nondelinquent friends help moderate delinquency.[48]

As children grow and move forward, friends influence their behavior, and their behavior influences their friends.[49] Antisocial friends guide delinquent careers so they withstand the aging-out process.[50] People who maintain close relations with antisocial peers will sustain their own criminal behavior into their adulthood.

Institutional Involvement and Belief

Logic would dictate that people who hold high moral values and beliefs, who have learned to distinguish right from wrong, and who regularly attend religious services should also eschew crime and other antisocial behaviors. Religion binds people together and forces them to confront the consequences of their behavior. Committing crimes would violate the principles of all organized religions.

An often-cited study by sociologists Travis Hirschi and Rodney Stark found that contrary to expectations, the association between religious attendance or belief and delinquent behavior patterns was negligible.[51] However, some recent research efforts have reached an opposing conclusion: attending religious services significantly reduces crime. Interestingly, this type of participation seems to inhibit crime more than merely having religious beliefs and values.[52] Cross-national research shows that countries with high rates of church membership and attendance have lower crime rates.[53]

CONNECTIONS

Arousal theory would predict that church attendance is inversely correlated with crime rates because criminals need large amounts of stimulation and would not be able to sit through religious services. See Chapter 6 for more about arousal theory.

The Effects of Socialization on Crime

To many criminologists, the elements of socialization described up to this point are the chief determinants of criminal behavior. According to this view, people living in even the most deteriorated urban areas can successfully resist inducements to crime if they have a positive self-image, strong moral values, and support from their parents, peers, teachers, and neighbors. The girl with a positive self-image who is chosen for a college scholar-

ship, has the warm, loving support of her parents, and is viewed as someone "going places" by friends and neighbors is less likely to adopt a criminal way of life than another adolescent who is abused at home, who lives with criminal parents, and whose bond to her school and peer group is shattered because she is labeled a "troublemaker."[54] The boy who has learned criminal behavior from his parents and siblings and joins a neighborhood gang is much more likely to become an adult criminal than his next-door neighbor who idolizes his hardworking, deeply religious parents. Socialization, not social structure, determines life chances. As Figure 8.2 shows, the more social problems encountered during the socialization process, the greater the likelihood that youths will encounter difficulties and obstacles as they mature, such as being unemployed or becoming teenage parents.

Theorists who believe that an individual's socialization determines the likelihood of criminality adopt the **social process approach** to human behavior. The social process approach has several independent branches (see Figure 8.3). The first branch, **social learning theory,** suggests that people learn the techniques and attitudes of crime from close relationships with criminal peers: crime is a learned behavior. The second branch, **social control theory,** maintains that everyone has the potential to become a criminal, but most people are controlled

Figure 8.2 Risk Factors and Social Outcomes

The more damaged a child's relationship with critical social institutions, the more likely he or she will face adverse social outcomes.

Number of risk factors experienced

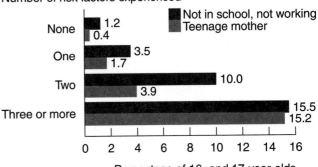

Percentage of 16- and 17-year-olds with adverse outcomes

Risk Factors
- Poverty
- Living on welfare
- Absence of one or both parents
- Unwed mother
- Parent educational failure

Source: *America's Children at Risk* (Washington, D.C.: U.S. Census Bureau, 1997).

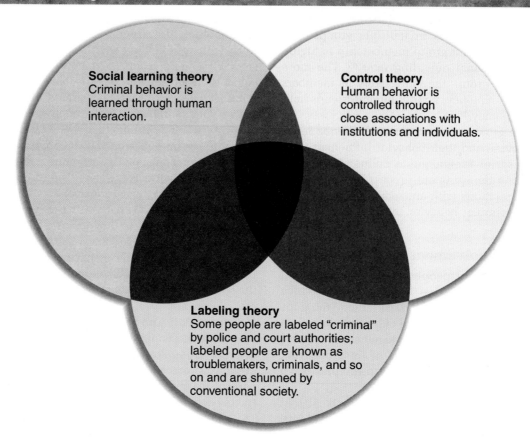

Social learning theory
Criminal behavior is learned through human interaction.

Control theory
Human behavior is controlled through close associations with institutions and individuals.

Labeling theory
Some people are labeled "criminal" by police and court authorities; labeled people are known as troublemakers, criminals, and so on and are shunned by conventional society.

by their bonds to society. Crime occurs when the forces that bind people to society are weakened or broken. The third branch, **social reaction (labeling) theory,** says people become criminals when significant members of society label them as such and they accept those labels as a personal identity.

Put another way, social learning theories assume people are born good and learn to be bad; social control theory assumes people are born bad and must be controlled in order to be good; and social reaction theory assumes that whether good or bad, people are controlled by the reactions of others. Each of these independent branches will be discussed separately.

CONNECTIONS

In the late nineteenth century, Gabriel Tarde's theory of imitation held that criminals imitate superiors they admire and respect. Learning theory also focuses on the influence of significant others. Tarde's work, discussed in Chapter 6, is a precursor to modern learning theories.

SOCIAL LEARNING THEORIES

Social learning theorists believe that crime is a product of learning the norms, values, and behaviors associated with criminal activity. Social learning can involve the actual techniques of crime (how to hot-wire a car or roll a joint) as well as the psychological aspects of criminality (how to deal with the guilt or shame associated with illegal activities). This section briefly reviews the three most prominent forms of social learning theory: *differential association theory, differential reinforcement theory,* and *neutralization theory.*

Differential Association Theory

One of the most prominent social learning theories is Edwin H. Sutherland's **differential association (DA) theory.** Often considered the preeminent U.S. criminologist, Sutherland first put forth his theory in 1939 in his text *Principles of Criminology.*[55] The final version of the theory appeared in 1947. When Sutherland died in 1950, Donald Cressey, his long-time associate, continued his work. Cressey was so successful in explaining

Social learning theorists see crime as a product of learning the norms, values, and behaviors associated with criminal activity. Social learning can involve the actual techniques of crime as well as the psychological aspects of criminality. Parental deviance may thus have a significant influence on children's behavior.

crime are learned as a result of contact with procrime values, attitudes, and definitions and other patterns of criminal behavior.

Principles of Differential Association   The basic principles of differential association are explained as follows:[58]

1. Criminal behavior is learned. This statement differentiates Sutherland's theory from prior attempts to classify criminal behavior as an inherent characteristic of criminals. By suggesting that delinquent and criminal behavior is learned, Sutherland implies that it can be classified in the same manner as any other learned behavior, such as writing, painting, or reading.

2. Criminal behavior is learned as a byproduct of interacting with others. Sutherland says that an individual does not start violating the law simply by living in a crimogenic environment or by manifesting personal characteristics, such as low IQ or family problems, associated with criminality. People actively learn as they interact with other individuals who serve as teachers and guides to crime. Thus criminality cannot occur without the aid of others.

3. Learning criminal behavior occurs within intimate personal groups. People's contacts with their most intimate social companions—family, friends, peers—have the greatest influence on their deviant behavior and attitude development. Relationships with these influential individuals color and control the way individuals interpret everyday events. For example, children who grow up in homes where parents abuse alcohol are more likely to view drinking as socially and physically beneficial.[59] The intimacy of these associations far outweighs the importance of any other form of communication, such as movies or television. Even on rare occasions when violent motion pictures seem to provoke mass criminal episodes, these outbreaks can be more readily explained as a reaction to peer group pressure than as a reaction to the films themselves.

4. Learning criminal behavior involves learning the techniques of committing crime, which are sometimes complicated and sometimes simple. This requires learning the specific direction of motives, drives, rationalizations, and attitudes. Young delinquents learn from their associates the proper way to pick a lock, shoplift, and obtain and use narcotics. In addition, novice criminals learn the proper terminology for their acts and acquire approved reactions to law violations. For example, getting high on marijuana and learning how to smoke a joint are behavior patterns usually acquired from more experienced companions. Moreover, criminals must learn how to react properly to their illegal acts, such as when to defend them, rationalize them, or show remorse for them.

5. The specific direction of motives and drives is learned from perceptions of various aspects of the legal

and popularizing his mentor's efforts that DA theory remains one of the most enduring explanations of criminal behavior.

Sutherland's research on white-collar crime, professional theft, and intelligence led him to dispute the notion that crime was a function of the inadequacy of people in the lower classes.[56] To Sutherland, criminality stemmed neither from individual traits nor from socioeconomic position; instead, he believed it to be a function of a learning process that could affect any individual in any culture. A few ideas are basic to the theory of differential association.[57] Crime is a political construct defined by government authorities who control a particular jurisdiction. In societies wracked by culture conflict, the definition of crime may be inconsistent and consequently rejected by some groups. Put another way, people may vary in their relative attachments to criminal and noncriminal definitions. Acquiring a behavior is a social learning process, not a political or legal process. Skills and motives conducive to

Figure 8.4 Differential Associations

Differential association theory assumes that criminal behavior will occur when the definitions toward crime outweigh the definitions against crime.

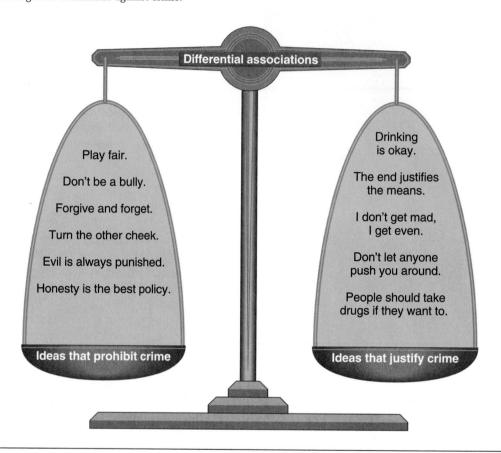

Differential associations

Ideas that prohibit crime

Play fair.

Don't be a bully.

Forgive and forget.

Turn the other cheek.

Evil is always punished.

Honesty is the best policy.

Ideas that justify crime

Drinking is okay.

The end justifies the means.

I don't get mad, I get even.

Don't let anyone push you around.

People should take drugs if they want to.

code as favorable or unfavorable. Because the reaction to social rules and laws is not uniform across society, people constantly meet others who hold different views on the utility of obeying the legal code. Some people they admire may openly disdain or flout the law or ignore its substance. People experience what Sutherland calls *culture conflict* (discussed in Chapter 7) when they are exposed to opposing attitudes toward right and wrong or moral and immoral. The conflict of social attitudes and cultural norms is the basis for the concept of differential association.

6. A person becomes a criminal when he or she perceives more favorable than unfavorable consequences to violating the law (see Figure 8.4). According to Sutherland's theory, individuals become law violators when they are in contact with persons, groups, or events that produce an excess of definitions favorable toward criminality and are isolated from counteracting forces. A definition favorable toward criminality occurs, for example, when a person sees friends sneaking into a theater to avoid paying for a ticket or hears them talking about the virtues of getting high on drugs. A definition unfavorable toward crime occurs when friends or parents demon-

strate their disapproval of crime. Neutral behavior, such as reading a book, is neither positive nor negative with respect to law violation. Cressey argues that neutral behavior is important. For example, when a child is doing something neutral, it prevents him or her from being in contact with those involved in criminal behavior.[60]

7. Differential associations may vary in frequency, duration, priority, and intensity. Whether a person learns to obey the law or to disregard it is influenced by the quality of social interactions. Those of lasting duration have greater influence than those that are brief. Similarly, frequent contacts have greater effect than rare, haphazard contacts. Sutherland did not specify what he meant by *priority*, but Cressey and others have interpreted the term to mean the age of children when they first encounter definitions of criminality. Contacts made early in life probably have more influence than those developed later on. Finally, *intensity* is generally interpreted to mean the importance and prestige attributed to the individual or groups from whom the definitions are learned. For example, the influence of a father, mother, or trusted friend far outweighs the effect of more socially distant figures.

Drug users in Zurich, Switzerland, surrounded by their drug paraphernalia. The principal part of the learning of criminal behavior occurs within intimate personal groups. People's contacts with their most intimate social companions—family, friends, peers—have the greatest influence on their learning of deviant behavior and attitudes.

8. The process of learning criminal behavior by association with criminal and anticriminal patterns involves all of the mechanisms that are involved in any other learning process. Learning criminal behavior patterns is similar to learning nearly all other patterns and is not a matter of mere imitation.

9. Although criminal behavior expresses general needs and values, it is not excused by those general needs and values because noncriminal behavior also expresses the same needs and values. This principle suggests that the motives for criminal behavior cannot logically be the same as those for conventional behavior. Sutherland rules out such motives as desire to accumulate money or social status, personal frustration, or low self-concept as causes of crime because they are just as likely to produce noncriminal behavior, such as getting a better education or working harder on a job. Only learning of deviant norms through contact with an excess of definitions favorable toward criminality produces illegal behavior.

In sum, differential association theory holds that people learn criminal attitudes and behavior during their adolescence from close, trusted friends or relatives. A criminal career develops if learned antisocial values and behaviors are not at least matched or exceeded by conventional attitudes and behaviors. Criminal behavior, then, is learned in a process that is similar to learning any other human behavior.

Testing Differential Association Theory Despite the importance of differential association theory, research devoted to testing its assumptions has been relatively sparse. It has proven difficult to conceptualize the principles of the theory so that they can be empirically tested. For example, social scientists find it difficult to evaluate such vague concepts as "definition favorable toward criminality." It is also difficult to follow people over time, establish precisely when definitions favorable toward criminality begin to outweigh prosocial definitions, and determine if this imbalance produces criminal behavior. Despite these limitations, several notable research efforts have supported the core principles of this theory. For example, differential association seems especially relevant in trying to explain the onset of substance abuse and a career in the drug trade. This requires learning proper techniques and attitudes from an experienced user or dealer.[61] In his interview study of low-level drug dealers, Kenneth Tunnell found that many novices were tutored by a more experienced criminal dealer who helped them connect with buyers and sellers. One told him,

> I had a friend of mine who was an older guy and he introduced me to selling marijuana to make a few dollars. I started selling a little and made a few dollars. For a young guy to be making a hundred dollars or so, it was a lot of money. So I got kind of tied up in that aspect of selling drugs.[62]

Tunnell found that making connections is an important part of the dealer's world. Adolescent drug users are likely to have intimate relationships with a peer friendship network that supports their substance abuse and teaches them how to deal with the drug world.[63]

The Role of Peer Relations Another way to test the validity of DA theory is to show that maintaining deviant friends is associated with delinquent behavior.[64] In a classic work, criminologist James Short surveyed institutionalized youths and found that they had, in fact, maintained close associations with delinquent youths prior to their law-violating acts.[65] Other research efforts support this association with delinquent peers as a precursor of criminal activity.[66] For example, Mark Warr found that antisocial children who maintain delinquent friends over a long duration are much more likely to persist in their delinquent behavior than those without such peer support.[67] Although his research generally supports differential association theory, Warr discovered that recently cultivated friendships had a greater influence on criminality than friends acquired earlier in life, a finding that contradicts differential association theory's emphasis on the priority of criminal influences. Nonetheless, youths who are exposed to antisocial behaviors and learn deviant values from their peers are likely to engage in delinquent behavior themselves.[68]

Differential association theory can also explain the gender difference in crime rates. Males are more likely to socialize with deviant peers than females, and when they do, they are more deeply influenced by peer relations.[69] Females are shielded by their unique moral sense, which makes caring about people and avoiding social harm a top priority. Males, in contrast, are more cavalier toward others and are more interested in their own self-interests; they are therefore more susceptible to the influence of deviant peers.

Attitudes and Crime   One approach to testing the validity of the differential association theory is to challenge or support the assumption that people who have assimilated procrime attitudes are also the most likely to engage in criminal activity.[70] Cross-cultural research has supported this assumption by showing that differential associations are the most significant predictor of delinquent behavior among youths in Hong Kong. Deviant youths may imitate friends' behavior or attempt to keep up appearances by yielding to group pressure.[71]

Alternative Approaches   Evaluating self-reports also tests the validity of differential association theory. Self-reports generally show a correlation between having deviant friends, holding deviant attitudes, and committing deviant acts.[72] Although findings based on self-reports can be persuasive, they must be interpreted with caution. Because subjects are usually asked about their peer relations, learning experiences, perceptions of differential associations, and criminal behaviors simultaneously, it is impossible to determine whether differential associations were the cause or the result of criminal behavior. Youths may learn about crime and then commit criminal acts; but experienced delinquents and criminals may also seek like-minded peers after they engage in antisocial acts. The internalization of deviant attitudes may follow, rather than precede, criminality.[73]

To address critics' concerns, researchers must develop valid measures of differential associations.[74] One possibility is to measure subjects repeatedly over time (longitudinal analysis) to determine if those exposed to excess definitions toward deviance eventually become deviant. Even then, it is difficult to show whether people who continually break the law develop a group of like-minded peers who support their behavior, or "innocent" people are "seduced" into crime by being exposed to the deviant attitudes of criminal peers.[75]

Analysis of Differential Association Theory   Misconceptions about differential association theory have produced unwarranted criticism of its principles and meaning.[76] For example, some criminologists claim that the theory is concerned solely with the number of personal contacts and associations a delinquent has with other criminal or delinquent offenders.[77] If this assumption were true, those most likely to become criminals would be police, judges, and correctional authorities because they constantly associate with criminals. Sutherland stressed excess definitions toward criminality, not mere association with criminals. Although people who work within the juvenile justice system have extensive associations with criminals, this association is more than counterbalanced by their associations with law-abiding citizens.

Another misconception is that definitions toward delinquency are acquired from learning the values of a deviant subculture.[78] According to the **cultural deviance critique,** differential association theory is invalid because it suggests that criminals are people *properly* socialized into a deviant subculture—that is, they are taught criminal norms by significant others. Supporters counter that differential association theory also recognizes that individuals can embrace criminality because they have been *improperly* socialized into the *normative* culture.[79]

Although differential association theory stresses an excess of definitions toward delinquency, it does not specify that delinquents come from the lower class. In fact, this distinguishes Sutherland's work from social structure theories. Outwardly law-abiding, middle-class parents can encourage delinquent behavior by their own drinking, drug use, or family violence. The influence of differential associations may not be affected by social class; deviant learning opportunities can affect youths in all classes.[80]

There are, however, a number of valid criticisms of Sutherland's work. It fails to explain why one youth who is exposed to delinquent definitions eventually succumbs to them, while another, living under the same conditions, avoids criminal entanglements.[81] It also fails to account for the origin of delinquent definitions. How did the first "teacher" learn delinquent attitudes and definitions in order to pass them on? Another criticism of differential association theory is that it assumes criminal and delinquent acts to be rational and systematic. This ignores spontaneous, wanton acts of violence and damage that appear to have little utility or purpose, such as the isolated psychopathic killing that is virtually unsolvable because of the killer's anonymity and lack of delinquent associations.

The most serious criticism of differential association theory concerns the vagueness of its terms, which makes its assumptions difficult to test. For example, what constitutes an excess of definitions toward criminality? How can we determine whether an individual actually has a prodelinquent imbalance of these deviant or criminal definitions? It is simplistic to assume that, by definition, all delinquents have experienced a majority of definitions toward delinquency and all nondelinquents, a minority of them. Unless the theory's terms can be defined more precisely, its validity remains a matter of guesswork.

Despite these criticisms, differential association theory maintains an important place in the study of criminal behavior. For one thing, it consistently explains all types of delinquent and criminal behavior. Unlike social structure theories, it is not limited to explaining a single facet of antisocial activity, like lower-class gang activity. The theory can also account for the extensive delinquent behavior found even in middle- and upper-class areas, where youths may be exposed to a variety of prodelinquent definitions from such sources as overly opportunistic parents and friends. Furthermore, Warr's research, which suggests that delinquent friends are "sticky," indicates that differential associations might be one of the keys to explaining lifelong deviance.

Differential Reinforcement Theory

Differential reinforcement theory (also called *social learning theory*) is another attempt to explain crime as a type of learned behavior. First proposed by Ronald Akers in collaboration with Robert Burgess in 1966, this version of the social learning view employs both differential association concepts and elements of psychological learning theory.

> CONNECTIONS
>
> Psychological learning theories were discussed in Chapter 6. They maintain that human actions are developed through learning experiences. Behavior is supported by rewards and extinguished by negative reactions or punishment. Behavior is constantly shaped by life experiences.

According to Akers, the same process is involved in learning both deviant and conventional behavior. People learn to be neither "all deviant" nor "all conforming," but rather strike a balance between the two opposing poles of behavior. The balance is usually stable, but it can undergo revision over time.[82]

A number of learning processes shape behavior. **Direct conditioning,** also called **differential reinforcement,** occurs when behavior is reinforced by being either rewarded or punished. Punishment of behavior, referred to as **negative reinforcement,** can be distributed by either negative stimuli (punishment) or loss of reward (negative punishment). Whether deviant or criminal behavior has been initiated or persists depends on the degree to which it has been rewarded or punished and the rewards or punishments attached to its alternatives.

According to Akers, people learn to evaluate their own behavior through their interactions with significant others and groups in their lives. These groups control sources and patterns of reinforcement, define behavior as right or wrong, and provide behaviors that can be modeled through observational learning. The more individuals learn to define their behavior as good or at least as justified, rather than as undesirable, the more likely they are to engage in it. For example, adolescents who hook up with drug-abusing peers, who value drugs and alcohol, encourage their use, and provide opportunities to observe people abusing substances, will be encouraged, through this social learning experience, to use drugs themselves.

Akers's theory posits that behavior is principally influenced by "those groups which control individuals' major sources of reinforcement and punishment and expose them to behavioral models and normative definitions."[83] The important groups are the ones with which a person is in differential association—peer and friendship groups, schools, churches, and similar institutions. Within the context of these critical groups, according to Akers, "deviant behavior can be expected to the extent that it has been differentially reinforced over alternative behavior . . . and is defined as desirable or justified."[84] Once people are indoctrinated into crime, their behavior can be reinforced by exposure to deviant behavior models, association with deviant peers, and lack of negative sanctions from parents or peers. The deviant behavior, which was originally executed by imitating someone else's behavior, is sustained by social support. Differential reinforcements may help establish criminal careers and explain persistent criminality.

Testing Differential Reinforcement Theory The principles of differential reinforcement theory have been reviewed empirically by Akers and other criminologists.[85] In an important test of his theory, Akers and his associates surveyed 3,065 male and female adolescents on drug- and alcohol-related activities and their perception of variables related to social learning and differential reinforcement. Items in the scale included the respondents' perceptions of esteemed peers' attitudes toward drug and alcohol abuse, the number of people they admired who used controlled substances, and whether people they admired would reward or punish them for substance abuse. Akers found a strong association between drug and alcohol abuse and social learning variables: those who believed they would be rewarded for deviance by those they respected were the most likely to engage in deviant behavior.[86]

Akers also found that the learning–deviant behavior link is not static. Learning continues within a deviant group as behavior is *both* influenced by, and exerts influence over, group processes. For example, adolescents may learn to smoke because their friends are smoking and therefore approve of this behavior.

Over time, smoking influences friendships and peer group memberships as smokers seek each other out for companionship and support.[87]

Differential reinforcement theory is an important perspective that endeavors to determine the cause of criminal activity. It considers how the content of socialization conditions crime. Because not all socialization is positive, it accounts for negative social reinforcements and experiences producing criminal results. This concurs with research demonstrating that parental deviance is related to adolescent antisocial behavior.[88] Parents may reinforce their children's deviant behavior by supplying negative social reinforcement. Akers's work also fits well with rational choice theory because they both suggest that people learn the techniques and attitudes necessary to commit crime. Criminal knowledge is gained through experience. After considering the outcome of their past experiences, potential offenders decide which criminal acts will be profitable and which dangerous ones should be avoided.[89] Integrating these perspectives, people make rational choices about crime because they have learned to balance risks against the potential for criminal gain.

Neutralization Theory

The **neutralization theory** is identified with the writings of David Matza and his associate Gresham Sykes.[90] Sykes and Matza, like Akers, Burgess, and Sutherland before them, view the process of becoming a criminal as a learning experience. However, whereas Sutherland and Akers dwell on learning techniques, values, and attitudes necessary for performing criminal acts, Sykes and Matza say that most delinquents and criminals hold conventional values and attitudes. The difference, they theorize, is that they master techniques that enable them to neutralize these values and drift back and forth between illegitimate and conventional behavior. One reason this is possible is the subterranean value structure of American society. **Subterranean values** are the morally tinged influences that have become entrenched in the culture but are publicly condemned. They exist side by side with conventional values and, although condemned in public, may be admired or practiced in private. Examples include viewing pornographic films, drinking excessive alcohol, and gambling on sporting events. In American culture it is common to hold both subterranean and conventional values; few people are "all good" or "all bad."

Matza argues that even the most committed criminals and delinquents are not involved in criminality all the time; they also attend schools, family functions, and religious services. Their behavior falls along a continuum between total freedom and total restraint. This process, which he calls **drift,** is movement from one extreme of behavior to another, resulting in behavior that is sometimes unconventional or deviant and at other times constrained and sober.[91] Learning neutralization techniques allows a person to temporarily drift away from conventional behavior and get involved in more subterranean values and behaviors, including crime and drug abuse.[92]

Neutralization Techniques Sykes and Matza suggest that people develop a distinct set of justifications for their law-violating behavior. Sykes and Matza base their theoretical model on several observations:[93]

1. Criminals sometimes voice guilt over their illegal acts. If a stable criminal value system existed in opposition to generally held values and rules, criminals would probably not exhibit remorse for their acts, other than regret at being apprehended.
2. Offenders frequently respect and admire honest, law-abiding persons. Really honest persons are often revered; and if for some reason such persons are accused of misbehavior, the criminal is quick to defend their integrity. Those admired may include entertainers sports figures, priests and other clergy, parents, teachers, and neighbors.
3. Criminals define whom they can victimize. Members of similar ethnic groups, churches, or neighborhoods are often off limits. This practice implies that criminals are aware of the wrongfulness of their acts.
4. Criminals are not immune to the demands of conformity. Most criminals frequently participate in the same social functions as law-abiding people—for example, school, church, and family activities. Because of these factors, Sykes and Matza conclude that criminals neutralize accepted social values by learning standard techniques that allow them to counteract the moral dilemmas posed by illegal behavior.[94]

Their research helped Sykes and Matza identify the following **techniques of neutralization:**

- **Denial of responsibility:** Young offenders sometimes claim their unlawful acts are simply not their fault; criminal acts result from forces beyond their control or are accidents.
- **Denial of injury:** By denying the injury caused by their acts, criminals neutralize illegal behavior. For example, stealing is viewed as borrowing; vandalism is considered mischief that has gotten out of hand. Delinquents may find that their parents and friends support their denial of injury. In fact, they may claim that the behavior was merely a prank, helping affirm the offender's perception that crime can be socially acceptable.
- **Denial of the victim:** Criminals sometimes neutralize wrongdoing by maintaining that the crime victim "had it coming." Vandalism may be directed against a disliked teacher or neighbor; or homosexuals may be beaten up by a gang because their behavior is considered offensive.

Figure 8.5 Techniques of Neutralization

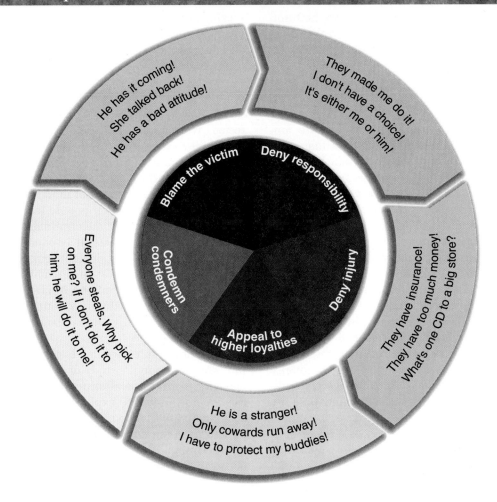

CONNECTIONS

Denial of the victim may help explain hate crimes in which people are victimized simply because they belong to the "wrong" race, religion, or ethnic group or because of their sexual orientation. Hate crimes are discussed in Chapter 11.

Denying the victim may also take the form of ignoring the rights of an absent or unknown victim — for example, stealing from the unseen owner of a department store. It becomes morally acceptable for the criminal to commit crimes such as vandalism when the victims, because of their absence, cannot be sympathized with or respected.

- **Condemnation of the condemners:** An offender views the world as a corrupt place with a dog-eat-dog code. Because police and judges are on the take, teachers show favoritism, and parents take out their frustrations on their kids, it is ironic and un-

fair for these authorities to condemn criminal misconduct. By shifting the blame to others, criminals repress the feeling that their own acts are wrong.

- **Appeal to higher loyalties:** Novice criminals often argue that they are caught in the dilemma of being loyal to their own peer group while attempting to abide by the rules of society. The needs of the group take precedence because group demands are immediate and localized (see Figure 8.5).

In sum, neutralization theory states that people neutralize conventional norms and values by using excuses that allow them to drift into crime.

Testing Neutralization Theory Attempts have been made to verify the assumptions of neutralization theory empirically, but the results have been inconclusive.[95] One area of research has been directed at determining whether law violators really need to neutralize moral constraints. The thinking behind this research is that if criminals hold values in opposition to accepted social norms, then there is really no need to neutralize. So far, the evidence is mixed. Some studies show that law violators approve of criminal behavior such as theft and violence, whereas still others find evidence that even though they may be active participants themselves, criminals voice disapproval of illegal behavior.[96] Some studies indicate that law violators approve of social values such as honesty and fairness; others come to the opposite conclusion.[97]

Although the existing research findings are ambiguous, the weight of the evidence shows that most adolescents generally disapprove of deviant behaviors such as violence, and neutralizations do in fact enable youths to engage in socially disapproved behavior.[98] Equally important is recent evidence showing that, as Matza predicted, people drift in and out of antisocial behavior. Jeffrey Fagan's interviews with 150 young men who had been involved with violent crimes while living in some of New York City's toughest neighborhoods found that many alternated their demeanor between "decent" and "street" codes of behavior, language, and dress. Both orientations lived side by side within the same individuals. The street code's rules for getting and maintaining respect through aggressive behavior forced many "decent" youths to situationally adopt a tough demeanor and perhaps behave violently in order to survive an otherwise hostile and possibly dangerous environment.[99]

The theory of neutralization, then, is a major contribution to the literature of crime and delinquency. It can account for the aging-out process: youths can forgo criminal behavior as adults because they never really rejected the morality of normative society. It helps explain the behavior of the occasional or nonchronic delinquent who is able to successfully age out of crime. If teens are not committed to criminality, as they mature, they simply drift back into conventional behavior patterns. While they are young, justifications and excuses neutralize guilt and enable individuals to continue to feel good about themselves.[100] In contrast, adult criminals may use newly learned techniques to neutralize the wrongfulness of their actions and avoid guilt. For example, research shows that psychotherapists accused of sexually exploiting their clients blame the victims for "seducing them"; some claim little injury was caused by the sexual encounters; others seek scapegoats to blame for their actions.[101]

Are Learning Theories Valid?

Learning theories contribute significantly to our understanding of the onset of criminal behavior. Nonetheless, the general learning model has been criticized. One complaint is that learning theorists fail to account for the origin of criminal definitions. How did the first criminal learn the necessary techniques and definitions? Who came up with the original neutralization technique?

Learning theories also imply that people systematically learn techniques that allow them to be active, successful criminals, but they fail to adequately explain spontaneous, wanton acts of violence, damage, and other expressive crimes that appear to have little utility or purpose. Although principles of differential association can easily explain shoplifting, is it possible that a random shooting is caused by excessive deviant definitions? It is estimated that about 70 percent of all arrestees were under the influence of drugs and alcohol when they committed their crime. Do "crack heads" pause to neutralize their moral inhibitions before mugging a victim? Do drug-involved kids stop to consider what they have learned about moral values?[102]

Little proof exists that people learn the techniques that enable them to become criminals before they actually commit criminal acts. It is equally plausible that people who are already deviant seek others with similar lifestyles. Early onset of deviant behavior is now considered a key determinant of criminal careers. It is difficult to see how extremely young children had the opportunity to learn criminal behavior and attitudes within a peer group setting.

Despite these criticisms, learning theories have an important place in the study of delinquent and criminal behavior. Unlike social structure theories, these theories are not limited to explaining a single facet of antisocial activity; they explain criminality across all class structures. Even corporate executives may be exposed to procriminal definitions and learn to neutralize moral constraints. Learning theories can be applied to a wide assortment of criminal activity.

SOCIAL CONTROL THEORIES

Social control theories maintain that all people have the potential to violate the law and that modern society presents many opportunities for illegal activity. Criminal activities, such as drug abuse and car theft, are often exciting pastimes that hold the promise of immediate reward and gratification.

Considering the attractions of crime, social control theorists question why people obey the rules of society. A choice theorist would respond that it is the fear of punishment; a structural theorist would say that obedience is a function of having access to legitimate opportunities; and a learning theorist would explain that obedience is acquired through contact with law-abiding parents and peers. In contrast, control theorists argue that people obey the law because behavior and passions are controlled by internal and external forces. Some individuals have **self-control**—a strong moral sense that renders them incapable of hurting others and violating social norms. Other people develop a **commitment to conformity,** adhered to because there is a real, present, and logical reason to obey the rules of society.[103] Social

Hirschi maintains that delinquents are not attached to their peers. Even if kids join together to form criminal gangs, within-group relationships are actually strained and remote. Here girl gang members engage in a violent initiation ceremony. Can such violent youths have warm personal relationships?

control theorists say that perhaps individuals believe getting caught at criminal activity will hurt dearly loved parents or jeopardize their chance at college scholarships, or perhaps they fear losing their jobs. In other words, people's behavior, including criminal activity, is controlled by people's attachment and commitment to conventional institutions, individuals, and processes. If that commitment is absent, they are free to violate the law; those who are uncommitted are not deterred by the threat of legal punishment.[104]

Self-Concept and Crime

Early versions of control theory speculated that low self-control was a product of weak self-concept and poor **self-esteem.** Youths who felt good about themselves and maintained a positive attitude were able to resist the temptations of the streets.

As early as 1951, sociologist Albert Reiss described how delinquents had weak egos and lacked the self-control to produce conforming behavior.[105] Scott Briar and Irving Piliavin note that youths who believe criminal activity will damage their self-image and their relationships with others are likely to conform to social rules. In contrast, those less concerned about their social standing are free to violate the law.[106] In his **containment theory,** pioneering control theorist Walter Reckless argued that a strong self-image insulates a youth from the pressures of crimogenic influences in the environment.[107] In studies conducted within the school setting,

Reckless and his colleagues found that nondelinquents are able to maintain a positive self-image in the face of environmental pressures toward delinquency.[108]

Self-Enhancement Theory Sociologist Howard Kaplan also believes that youths with poor self-concepts are likely to engage in delinquent behavior; successful participation in criminality actually helps raise their self-esteem.[109] Kaplan states that adolescents structure their behavior to enhance their self-image and to minimize negative self-attitudes. They conform to social rules, seek membership in **normative** groups (like the high school "in crowd"), and perform conventional tasks as long as their efforts pay off in positive, esteem-enhancing feedback. If they feel threatened, rebuked, or belittled, they may experience **self-rejection** ("I feel I do not have much to be proud of"; "I feel useless at times"). Because of this rejection, they may meet their need for self-esteem by turning to deviant groups made up of youths who have been similarly rejected. Although conventional society may reject them, their new criminal friends give them positive feedback and support. To further enhance their new identity, they may engage in deviant behaviors.[110] Youths who maintain both the lowest self-image and the greatest need for approval are the ones most likely to seek self-enhancement by engaging in criminal activities.

Although low self-esteem does not necessarily lead to criminality, evidence shows that, as Kaplan predicted, associating with antisocial peers can actually raise self-esteem and contribute to self-enhancement. Outcast youths may achieve psychological comfort not necessarily by committing crimes but by maintaining favorable relations with others who are similarly shunned by society.

The focus on self-image sets the stage for subsequent versions of control theories. These rest on the belief that people are controlled by their feelings about themselves and others with whom they share close, intimate relations. Control theory maintains that although all people perceive inducements to crime, some are better able to resist them than others.

Social Control Theory

Social control theory, originally articulated by Travis Hirschi in his influential 1969 book *Causes of Delinquency,* replaced containment theory as the dominant version of control theory.[111] Hirschi links the onset of criminality to the weakening of the ties that bind people to society. Hirschi assumes that all individuals are potential law violators, but most are kept under control because they fear that illegal behavior will damage their relationships with friends, family, neighbors, teachers, and employers. Without these social ties or bonds, and in the absence of sensitivity to and interest in others, a person is free to commit criminal acts. Hirschi does not

view society as containing competing subcultures with unique value systems; most people are aware of the prevailing moral and legal code. He suggests, however, that in all elements of society, people vary in how they respond to conventional social rules and values. Among all ethnic, religious, racial, and social groups, people whose bond to society is weak may fall prey to crimogenic behavior patterns.

Elements of the Social Bond

Hirschi argues that the **social bond** a person maintains with society is divided into four main elements: *attachment, commitment, involvement,* and *belief* (see Figure 8.6).

Attachment   Attachment refers to a person's sensitivity to and interest in others.[112] Psychologists believe that without a sense of attachment, a person becomes a psychopath and loses the ability to relate coherently to the world. Accepting social norms and developing a social conscience depend on attachment to and caring for other human beings.

Hirschi views parents, peers, and schools as the important social institutions with which a person should

Figure 8.6   Elements of the Social Bond

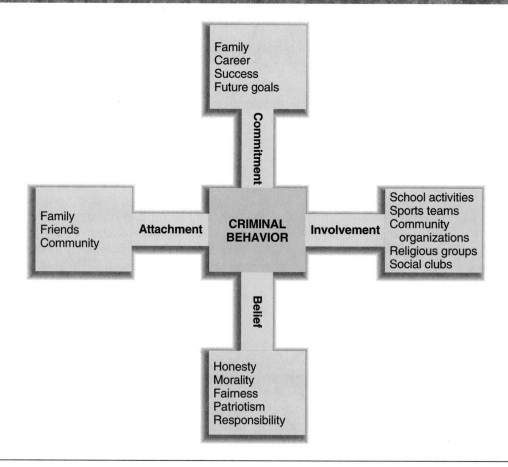

Attachment to the family is a key element of the social bond. Children who maintain strong bonds to supportive parents are the ones least likely to engage in delinquent or criminal behavior. Those whose ties to their parents are weak and attenuated are free to engage in antisocial activities.

maintain ties. Attachment to parents is the most important. Even if a family is shattered by divorce or separation, a child must retain a strong attachment to one or both parents. Without this attachment, it is unlikely that respect for other authorities will develop.

Commitment Commitment involves the time, energy, and effort expended in conventional actions such as getting an education and saving money for the future. If people build a strong commitment to conventional society, they will be less likely to engage in acts that jeopardize their hard-won position. Conversely, the lack of commitment to conventional values may foreshadow a condition in which risk-taking behavior, such as crime, becomes a reasonable behavior alternative.

Involvement Heavy involvement in conventional activities leaves little time for illegal behavior. Hirschi believes that involvement in school, recreation, and family insulates people from the potential lure of criminal behavior. Idleness, on the other hand, enhances that lure.

Belief People who live in the same social setting often share common moral beliefs; they may adhere to such values as sharing, sensitivity to the rights of others, and admiration for the legal code. If these beliefs are absent or weakened, individuals are more likely to participate in antisocial or illegal acts. Hirschi further suggests that the interrelationship of social bond elements controls subsequent behavior. For example, people who feel kinship and sensitivity to parents and friends should be more likely to adopt and work toward legitimate goals.

On the other hand, a person who rejects such social relationships is more likely to lack commitment to conventional goals. Similarly, people who are highly committed to conventional acts and beliefs are more likely to be involved in conventional activities.

Testing Social Control Theory

One of Hirschi's most significant contributions was his attempt to test the principal hypotheses of social control theory. He administered a detailed self-report survey to a sample of over 4,000 junior and senior high school students in Contra Costa County, California.[113] In a detailed analysis of the data, Hirschi found considerable evidence to support the control theory model. Among Hirschi's more important findings are the following:

- Youths who were strongly attached to their parents were less likely to commit criminal acts.
- Commitment to conventional values, such as striving to get a good education and refusing to drink alcohol and "cruise around," was indicative of conventional behavior.
- Youths involved in conventional activity, such as homework, were less likely to engage in criminal behavior.
- Youths involved in unconventional behavior, such as smoking and drinking, were more prone to delinquency.
- Youths who maintained weak, distant relationships with people tended toward delinquency.

- Those who shunned unconventional acts were attached to their peers.
- Delinquents and nondelinquents shared similar beliefs about society.

Hirschi's data gave important support to the validity of social control theory. Even when the statistical significance of his findings was less than he expected, the direction of his research data was notably consistent. Only rarely did his findings contradict the theory's most critical assumptions.

Supporting Research Hirschi's version of social control theory has been corroborated by numerous research studies showing that delinquent youths often feel detached from society.[114] Their relationships within the family, peer group, and school often appear strained, indicating a weakened social bond.[115]

Associations between (1) indicators of attachment, commitment, involvement, and belief and (2) measures of delinquency have tended to be positive and significant.[116] Teens who are attached to their parents are also able to develop the social skills that equip them to both maintain harmonious social ties and escape stresses such as school failure.[117] In contrast, family detachment, including intrafamily conflict, abuse of children, and lack of affection, supervision, and family pride, predicts delinquent conduct.[118] Youths who are detached from the educational experience are at risk of criminality; those committed to school are less likely to engage in delinquent acts.[119]

Other research efforts have shown that holding positive beliefs is inversely related to criminality. Children who participate in religious activities and hold conventional religious beliefs are less likely to abuse alcohol or drugs.[120] Similarly, youths who enjoy conventional leisure activities, such as supervised social activities and noncompetitive sports, are less likely to become delinquent than those who are involved in unconventional leisure activities and unsupervised, peer-oriented social pursuits.[121] Cross-national surveys have also supported the general findings of control theory.[122] For example, one study of Canadian youth found that perception of parental attachment was the strongest predictor of delinquent or law-abiding behavior.

Opposing Views More than 70 published attempts have been made to corroborate social control theory by replicating Hirschi's original survey techniques.[123] Although there has been significant empirical support for Hirschi's work, some question its elements.

- **Friendship:** One significant criticism concerns Hirschi's contention that delinquents are detached loners whose bond to their family and friends has been broken. Some critics question (1) whether delinquents have strained relations with family and peers and (2) whether they may be influenced by close relationships with *de-*viant peers and family members. A number of research efforts show that delinquents are influenced by relationships with deviant peers.[124] Delinquents, however, may not be "lone wolves" whose only personal relationships are exploitative; their friendship patterns seem quite close to those of conventional youth.[125] In fact, some types of offenders, such as drug abusers, may maintain even more intimate relations with their peers than nonabusers.[126]

- **Unequal bond elements:** Hirschi makes little distinction between the importance of each element of the social bond. Yet the evidence suggests that there may be differences. According to Velmer Burton and his associates, adolescents who report high levels of involvement, which Hirschi suggests should reduce delinquency, actually report high levels of criminal behavior. Perhaps kids who are involved in activities outside the home have less contact with parental supervision and greater opportunity to commit crime.[127] When asked, children report that concepts such as *involvement* and *belief* have relatively little influence over behavior patterns.[128]

- **Deviant peers and parents:** Hirschi's conclusion that any form of social attachment is beneficial, even to deviant peers and parents, has also been disputed. Rather than deter delinquency, attachment to deviant peers may support and nurture antisocial behavior. Although his classic study supported the basic principles of control theory, criminologist Michael Hindelang found that attachment to delinquent peers escalated rather than restricted criminality.[129] In a similar fashion, a number of research efforts have found that youths attached to drug-abusing parents are more likely to use drugs themselves.[130] Attachment to deviant family members, peers, and associates may help motivate youths to commit crime and facilitate their antisocial acts.[131]

- **Restricted scope:** There is some question as to whether the theory can explain all modes of criminality (as Hirschi maintains) or is restricted to particular groups or forms of criminality. Marvin Krohn and James Massey surveyed 3,065 junior and senior high school students and found that control variables were better able to explain female than male delinquency and minor delinquency (such as alcohol and marijuana abuse) than more serious criminal acts.[132] Other research efforts substantiate Krohn and Massey's findings that control variables are more predictive of female than male behavior.[133] Perhaps girls are more deeply influenced by the quality of their bond to society.

- **Changing bonds:** Social bonds seem to change over time, a phenomenon ignored by Hirschi. Using samples of 12-, 15-, and 18-year-old boys, Randy LaGrange and Helene Raskin White found age differences in perceptions of social bonds. Children in their midteens are surprisingly likely to be influenced by their parents and teachers; boys in the other two age groups are more deeply influenced by deviant peers.[134] LaGrange and White attribute this finding to the problems of midadolescence, where there is a great need to develop psychological anchors to conformity. So at one age level, weak bonds (to parents) may lead to delinquency, whereas at another, strong bonds (to peers) may lead to delinquency.

• **Crime and social bonds:** The most severe criticism of control theory has been leveled by sociologist Robert Agnew, who claims that Hirschi has miscalculated the direction of the relationship between criminality and a weakened social bond.[135] Hirschi's theory projects that a weakened bond leads to delinquency, but Agnew suggests that the chain of events may flow in the opposite direction: perhaps kids who break the law find that their bonds to parents, schools, and society eventually becomes weak. Other studies have also found that criminal behavior weakens social bonds and not vice versa.[136]

Although these criticisms need to be addressed with further research, the weight of the existing empirical evidence supports control theory. It has emerged as one of the preeminent theories in criminology.[137] For many criminologists, it is perhaps the most important way of understanding the onset of youthful misbehavior.

CONNECTIONS

Although his work has achieved a prominent place in criminological literature, Hirschi, along with Michael Gottfredson, has restructured his concept of control by integrating biosocial, psychological, and rational choice theory ideas into a general theory of crime. Because this theory is essentially integrated, it will be discussed more fully in Chapter 10.

SOCIAL REACTION THEORY

Social reaction theory (commonly called **labeling theory;** the two terms are used interchangeably here) explains how criminal careers are based on destructive social interactions and encounters. Its roots are found in the symbolic interaction theory of sociologists Charles Horton Cooley, George Herbert Mead, and later Herbert Blumer.[138] **Symbolic interaction theory** holds that people communicate via symbols — gestures, signs, words, or images — that stand for or represent something else. People interpret symbolic gestures from others and incorporate them in their self-image. Symbols let people know how well they are doing and whether they are liked or appreciated. How people view reality depends on the content of the messages and situations they encounter, the subjective interpretation of these interactions, and how they shape future behavior. There is no objective reality; people interpret the reactions of others, and this interpretation assigns meaning. Because interpretation changes over time, so does the meaning of concepts and symbols.

Social reaction theory picks up on these concepts of interaction and interpretation.[139] Throughout their lives, people are given a variety of symbolic labels and ways they interact with others. These labels represent a variety of behavior and attitude characteristics; labels help define not just one trait, but the whole person. For example, people labeled "insane" are also assumed to be dangerous, dishonest, unstable, violent, strange, and otherwise unsound. Valued labels, including "smart," "honest," and "hardworking," suggest overall competence. These labels can improve self-image and social standing. Research shows that people who are labeled with one positive trait, such as being physically attractive, are assumed to maintain other positive traits, such as being intelligent and competent.[140] In contrast, negative labels, including "troublemaker," "mentally ill," and "stupid," help stigmatize the recipients of these labels and reduce their self-image.

Both positive and negative labels involve subjective interpretation of behavior: a "troublemaker" is merely someone whom people label as "troublesome." There need not be any objective proof or measure indicating that the person is actually a troublemaker. Although a label may be a function of rumor, innuendo, or unfounded suspicion, its adverse impact can be immense.

If a devalued status is conferred by a significant other — teacher, police officer, parent, or valued peer — the negative label may permanently harm the target. The degree to which a person is perceived as a social deviant may affect his or her treatment at home, at work, at school, and in other social situations. Children may find that their parents consider them a bad influence on younger brothers and sisters. School officials may limit them to classes reserved for people with behavioral problems. Likewise, when adults are labeled as "criminal," "ex-con," or "drug addict," they may find their eligibility for employment severely restricted. If the label is bestowed as the result of conviction for a criminal offense, the labeled person may also be subjected to official sanctions ranging from a mild reprimand to incarceration.

Beyond these immediate results, labeling advocates say that, depending on the visibility of the label and the manner and severity with which it is applied, a person will have an increasing commitment to a deviant career. As one national commission put it, "Thereafter he may be watched; he may be suspect . . . he may be excluded more and more from legitimate opportunities."[141] Labeled persons may find themselves turning to others similarly stigmatized for support and companionship. Isolated from conventional society, they may identify themselves as members of an outcast group and become locked into deviance. Figure 8.7 illustrates this process.

Figure 8.7 The Labeling Process

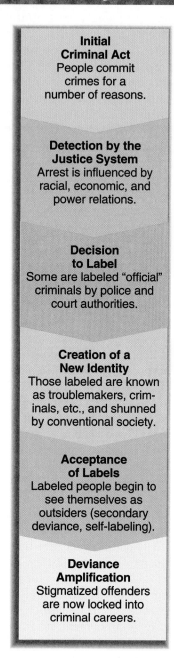

Initial Criminal Act
People commit crimes for a number of reasons.

Detection by the Justice System
Arrest is influenced by racial, economic, and power relations.

Decision to Label
Some are labeled "official" criminals by police and court authorities.

Creation of a New Identity
Those labeled are known as troublemakers, criminals, etc., and shunned by conventional society.

Acceptance of Labels
Labeled people begin to see themselves as outsiders (secondary deviance, self-labeling).

Deviance Amplification
Stigmatized offenders are now locked into criminal careers.

Because the process of acquiring stigma is essentially interactive, labeling theorists blame criminal career formation on the social agencies originally designed for crime control. Often mistrustful of institutions, such as police, courts, and correctional agencies, labeling advocates say that these institutions produce the stigma that harms the people they are trying to help, treat, or correct. Rather than reduce deviant behavior, for which they were designed, such label-bestowing institutions actually help maintain and amplify criminal behavior.

CONNECTIONS

Fear of stigma has prompted efforts to reduce the impact of criminal labels through such programs as pretrial diversion and community treatment. These efforts are reviewed in some detail in Chapter 15. In addition, some criminologists have called for noncoercive "peacemaking" solutions to interpersonal conflict. This peacemaking or restorative justice movement is reviewed in Chapter 9.

Crime and Labeling Theory

Labeling theorists use an interactionist definition of crime. In a defining statement, sociologist Kai Erickson argues, "Deviance is not a property inherent in certain forms of behavior, it is a property conferred upon those forms by the audience which directly or indirectly witnesses them."[142] This definition was amplified by sociologist Edwin Schur, who stated

> Human behavior is deviant to the extent that it comes to be viewed as involving a personally discreditable departure from a group's normative expectation, and it elicits interpersonal and collective reactions that serve to "isolate," "treat," "correct," or "punish" individuals engaged in such behavior.[143]

Crime and deviance, therefore, are defined by the social audience's reaction to people and their behavior and the subsequent effects of that reaction; they are not defined by the moral content of the illegal act itself. In a famous statement, Howard Becker sums up the importance of the audience's reaction:

> Social groups create deviance by making rules whose infractions constitute deviance, and by applying those rules to particular people and labeling them as outsiders. From this point of view, deviance is not a quality of the act a person commits, but rather a consequence of the application by others of rules and sanctions to an "offender." The deviant is one to whom the label has successfully been applied; deviant behavior is behavior that people so label.[144]

In its purest form, social reaction theory argues that such crimes as murder, rape, and assault are only bad or evil because people label them as such. After all, the difference between an excusable act and a criminal one is often a matter of changing legal definition. For example, acts such as abortion, marijuana use, possessing a handgun, and gambling have been legal at some times and places and illegal at others.

Howard Becker refers to people who create rules as **moral entrepreneurs.** An example of a moral entrepreneur today might be a member of an ultra-orthodox religious group who targets the gay lifestyle and campaigns to prevent gays from adopting children or marrying their same-sex partners.[145]

A social reaction theorist views crime as a subjective concept whose definition totally depends on the viewing audience. An act that is considered criminal by one person may be perfectly acceptable behavior to another. Because crime is defined by those in power, the shape of criminal law is defined by the values of those who rule, not an objective standard of moral conduct.

Differential Enforcement

An important principle of social reaction theory is that the law is differentially applied, benefiting those who hold economic and social power and penalizing the powerless. The probability of being brought under the control of legal authority is a function of a person's race, wealth, gender, and social standing. A core concept of social reaction theory is that police officers are more likely to formally arrest males, minority group members, and those in the lower class, and to use their discretionary powers to give beneficial treatment to more favored groups.[146] Minorities and the poor are more likely to be prosecuted for criminal offenses and receive harsher punishment when convicted.[147] Judges may sympathize with white defendants and help them avoid criminal labels, especially if they seem to come from "good families," whereas minority youths are not afforded that luxury.[148]

This evidence is used to support the labeling concept that personal characteristics and social interactions are more important variables in developing criminal careers than merely violating the law. Social reaction theorists also argue that the content of the law reflects power relationships in society. They point to evidence that white-collar crimes (economic crimes that are usually committed by members of the upper class) are most often punished by a relatively small fine and rarely result in prison sentences. This treatment contrasts with long prison sentences given to those convicted of street crimes like burglary or car theft, which are the province of the lower, powerless classes.[149] In sum, a major premise of social reaction theory is that the law is differentially constructed and applied, depending on the offenders. It favors powerful members of society who direct its content and penalizes people whose actions threaten to those in control, such as minority group members and the poor who demand equal rights.[150]

Becoming Labeled

Social reaction theory is not especially concerned with why people originally engage in acts that result in their being labeled.[151] Crime may result from greed, personality, social structure, learning, or control. Regardless of why they commit crime, the less personal power and fewer resources a person has, the greater the chance he or she will be labeled. Race, class, and ethnic differences between those in power and those who are not influence the likelihood of labeling. For example, the poor or minority-group teenager may run a greater chance of being officially processed for criminal acts by police, courts, and correctional agencies than the wealthy white youth. This helps to explain why there are significant racial and economic differences in the crime rate.

Not all labeled people have chosen to engage in label-producing activities, such as crime. Some negative labels (like "mentally ill" and "mentally deficient") are bestowed on people for behaviors over which they have little control. In these categories, the probability of being labeled may depend on how visible that person is in the community, the tolerance of the community for unusual behavior, and the person's own power to combat labels.

Consequences of Labeling

Social reaction theorists are most concerned with two effects of labeling: the creation of stigma and the effect on self-image. Labels are believed to produce **stigma:** the labeled deviant becomes a social outcast who may be prevented from enjoying higher education, well-paying jobs, and other social benefits. Such alienation leads to a low self-image.

Labeling theorists consider public condemnation an important part of the labeling process. It may be accomplished in such ceremonies as a hearing that finds a person to be mentally ill or a trial that convicts an individual of crime. A public record of the deviant acts, such as an arrest or conviction record, causes the denounced person to be ritually separated from a place in the legitimate order and placed outside the world occupied by citizens of good standing. Harold Garfinkle has called transactions that produce irreversible, permanent labels "successful degradation ceremonies."[152]

Changing Self-Image and Lifestyle   Labeling may produce a reevaluation of the self that reflects actual or perceived appraisals made by others. Kids who view themselves as delinquents after being labeled as such are giving an inner voice to their perceptions of how parents, teachers, peers, and neighbors view them. When they believe that others view them as antisocial or troublemakers, they take on attitudes and roles that reflect this assumption. They expect to become suspects and then to be rejected.[153] Tempering or enhancing the effect of this **reflective role-taking** are informal and institutional social control processes. Families, schools, peers, and the social system can either help control children and dissuade them from crime or encourage and sustain deviance. When these groups are dysfunctional, such as when parents use drugs, they encourage, rather than control, antisocial behavior.[154]

Joining Deviant Cliques   Children labeled as deviant may join similarly outcast delinquent peers who facilitate their behavior. Eventually antisocial behavior becomes habitual and automatic.[155] The desire to join deviant cliques and groups may stem from self-rejecting attitudes ("At times, I think I am no good at all") that eventually weaken commitment to conventional values and behaviors. In turn, these children may acquire motives to deviate from social norms. Facilitating this attitude and value transformation is the bond social outcasts form with similarly labeled peers in the form of a deviant subculture.[156] They may join cliques like the "Trenchcoat Mafia" whose members were involved in the 1999 Littleton, Colorado, school massacre. Membership in a deviant subculture often involves conforming to group norms that conflict with those of conventional society.

Deviant behaviors that oppose conventional values can serve a number of different purposes. Some acts are defiant, designed to show contempt for the source of the negative labels. Other acts are planned to distance the transgressor from further contact with the source of criticism (for example, an adolescent runs away from critical parents).[157]

Retrospective Reading   Beyond any immediate results, labels tend to redefine the whole person. For example, the label "ex-con" may create in people's imaginations a whole series of behavior descriptions—tough, mean, dangerous, aggressive, dishonest, sneaky—that may or may not apply to a person who has been in prison. People react to the label description and what it signifies instead of reacting to the actual behavior of the person who bears it. This is referred to as **retrospective reading,** a process in which the past of the labeled person is reviewed and reevaluated to fit his or her current status. For example, boyhood friends of an assassin are interviewed by the media and report that the suspect was withdrawn, suspicious, and negativistic as a youth. According to the retrospective reading, we can now understand what prompted his current behavior; therefore, the label must be accurate.[158]

Dramatization of Evil   Labels become the basis of personal identity. As the negative feedback of law enforcement agencies, parents, friends, teachers, and other figures amplifies the force of the original label, stigmatized offenders may begin to reevaluate their own identities. If they are not really evil or bad, they may ask themselves, why is everyone making such a fuss? Frank Tannenbaum, a social reaction theory pioneer, refers to this process as the **dramatization of evil.** With respect to the consequences of labeling delinquent behavior, Tannenbaum states,

> The process of making the criminal, therefore, is a process of tagging, defining, identifying, making conscious and self-conscious; it becomes a way of stimulating, suggesting and evoking the very traits that are complained of. If the theory of relation of response to stimulus has any meaning, the entire process of dealing with the young delinquent is mischievous insofar as it identifies him to himself or to the environment as a delinquent person. The person becomes the thing he is described as being.[159]

Primary and Secondary Deviance

One of the more well-known views of the labeling process is Edwin Lemert's concept of primary deviance and secondary deviance.[160] According to Lemert, **primary deviance** involves norm violations or crimes that have little influence on the actor and can be quickly forgotten. For example, a college student successfully steals a textbook at the campus bookstore, gets an A in the course, graduates, is admitted to law school, and later becomes a famous judge. Because his shoplifting goes unnoticed, it is a relatively unimportant event that has little bearing on his future life.

In contrast, **secondary deviance** occurs when a deviant event comes to the attention of significant others or social control agents, who apply a negative label. The newly labeled offender then reorganizes his or her behavior and personality around the consequences of the deviant act. The shoplifting student is caught by a security guard and expelled from college. With his law school dreams dashed and future cloudy, his options are limited; people say he lacks character, and he begins to share their opinion. He eventually becomes a drug dealer and winds up in prison (see Figure 8.8).

Secondary deviance involves resocialization into a deviant role. The labeled person is transformed into one who, according to Lemert, "employs his behavior or a role based upon it as a means of defense, attack, or adjustment to the overt and covert problems created by the consequent social reaction to him."[161] Secondary deviance produces a **deviance amplification effect:** offenders feel isolated from the mainstream of society and become locked within their deviant role. They may seek others similarly labeled to form deviant groups.

According to Lemert's theory, if these kids are caught and labeled as "druggies," they may become secondary deviants, taking on an identity associated with their negative label, and enter a life of crime. If their actions go undetected, their behavior remains primary and their drug use remains nothing more than an easily forgotten youthful indiscretion.

Figure 8.8 Primary and Secondary Deviance

Social reaction
Negative label
Degradation ceremonies
Self-labeling
Deviant subculture
Deviance amplification
Secondary deviance
Deviant act

THE LABELING PROCESS

Ever more firmly enmeshed in their deviant role, they are trapped in an escalating cycle of deviance, apprehension, more powerful labels, and identity transformation. Lemert's concept of secondary deviance expresses the core of social reaction theory: deviance is a process in which one's identity is transformed. Efforts to control the offenders, whether by treatment or punishment, simply help lock them in their deviant role.

Research on Social Reaction Theory

Research on social reaction theory can be classified into two distinct categories. The first focuses on the characteristics of offenders who are chosen for labels. The theory predicts that these offenders should be relatively powerless people who are unable to defend themselves against the negative labeling. The second type of research attempts to discover the effects of being labeled. Labeling theorists predict that people who are negatively labeled will view themselves as deviant and commit increasing amounts of crime.

Research on Who Gets Labeled Poor and powerless people are victimized by the law and justice system; labels are not equally distributed across class and racial lines. For example, a report by the National Minority Advisory Council on Criminal Justice argues that although substantive and procedural laws govern almost every aspect of the American criminal justice system, discretionary decision making controls its operation at every level. From the police officer's decision on whom to arrest, to the prosecutor's decisions on whom to charge and for how many and what kinds of charges, to the court's decision on whom to release or whom to permit bail, to the grand jury's decision on indictment, to the judge's decision on sentence length, discretion works to the detriment of minorities.[162] Reviews indicate that race bias adversely influences decisions in many critical areas of the justice system.[163] There is also evidence that those in power try to streamline the labeling process by discounting or ignoring the protestations of innocence made by suspects accused of socially undesirable acts like rape, sex crimes, and child abuse. For example, people are routinely defined as noncredible when they deny accusations of child abuse and are believed only when they confess their guilt. In contrast, victims are believed when they make such accusations but are considered noncredible when they claim the suspect is innocent.[164]

Although these arguments are persuasive, little definitive evidence proves that the justice system is inherently unfair. Procedures such as arrest, prosecution, and sentencing seem to be more often based on legal factors, such as prior record and severity of the crime, than on personal characteristics like class and race.[165] However, the discriminatory practices in labeling may be subtle. For example, in a thorough review of sentencing disparity, Samuel Walker, Cassia Spohn, and Miriam Delone identify what they call **contextual discrimination.** This term refers to judges' practices, in some jurisdictions, of imposing harsher sentences on African-Americans only in some instances, such as when they victimize whites.[166] Judges may also be more likely to impose prison sentences on racial minorities in borderline cases for which whites get probation. According to Walker, Spohn, and Delone, racism is hard to detect but still influences the distribution of criminal sanctions.

The Effects of Labeling Empirical evidence shows that negative labels dramatically influence the self-image of offenders. Considerable evidence indicates that social sanctions lead to self-labeling and deviance amplification.[167]

Family interaction can influence the labeling process. Children negatively labeled by their parents routinely suffer a variety of problems, including antisocial behavior and school failure.[168] This process is important because once they are labeled as troublemakers, adolescents begin to reassess their self-image. Parents who label their kids as troublemakers promote deviance amplification. Labeling alienates parents from their children, and negative labels reduce children's self-image and increase delinquency.[169]

As they mature, children are in danger of receiving repeated, intensive official labeling, which has been shown to produce self-labeling and damage identities.[170] Kids labeled as troublemakers in school are the most likely to drop out; dropping out has been linked to delinquent behavior.[171] Even as adults, the labeling

process can take its toll. Male drug users labeled as addicts by social control agencies eventually become self-labeled and increase their drug use.[172] People arrested in domestic violence cases, especially those with a low stake in conformity (for example, those who are jobless and unmarried) increase offending after being given official labels.[173]

Labeling and Criminal Careers Until recently, scant attention has been paid to the fact that stigma and negative labels may be critical factors in a criminal career.[174] In fact, the definition of a chronic offender is a person who has been arrested and therefore labeled multiple times during his or her offending career.

Empirical evidence supports the fact that labeling plays an important role in persistent offending.[175] Maintaining a damaged identity after official labeling may, along with other negative social reactions from society, produce the cumulative disadvantage that provokes some adolescents into repeating their antisocial behavior.[176] Although labels may not cause adolescents to initiate criminal behaviors, experienced delinquents are significantly more likely to continue offending if they believe that their parents and peers view them in a negative light.[177] Labeling, then, may help sustain criminality over time.

In sum, people who are negatively labeled by parents, schools, and the criminal justice system are likely to commit crime. However, it is still unclear whether this outcome is actually a labeling effect or the product of some other personal and social factors that also caused the labeling to occur.

Is Labeling Theory Valid?

The validity of labeling theory has been debated within criminological circles. Those who criticize it point to its inability to specify the conditions that must exist before an act or individual is labeled deviant; that is, why are some people labeled while others remain "secret deviants?"[178] Critics also charge that social reaction theory fails to explain differences in crime rates: if crime is a function of stigma and labels, why are crime rates higher in some parts of the country at particular times of the year?[179] Labeling also ignores the onset of deviant behavior (that is, it fails to ask why people commit the *initial* deviant act) and does not explain why delinquents and criminals forgo deviance.[180]

In probably the most devastating critique of the theory, Charles Wellford has questioned the general validity of several premises essential to the labeling approach.[181] These premises include the following points:

- Labeling theory claims that deviance is relative; virtually no act is universally considered criminal.

In contrast, Wellford claims that some crimes, such as rape and homicide, are universally sanctioned.

- Labeling theory says that almost all law enforcement is biased against the poor and minorities. Wellford counters that law enforcement officials most often base their arrest decisions on such factors as offense severity and pay less attention to such issues as the race, class, and demeanor of the offender.
- Although labeling may indeed affect offenders' attitudes about themselves, there is little evidence that attitude changes are related to actual behavior changes. Wellford believes that self-labeling is an invalid concept.
- Social reaction theory claims that labels and stigma motivate criminal behavior, whereas Wellford claims that crime is situationally motivated and depends more on ecological and personal conditions than labels and stigma.[182]

Because of these criticisms, a number of criminologists now reject labeling theory. Some charge that it focuses on "nuts, sluts, and perverts" and ignores the root causes of crime.[183]

With the discovery of the chronic offender, it was believed that labeling theory would receive renewed interest as an explanation of this pattern. It seems logical that negative labeling is connected to the onset of persistent offending because the chronic offender is defined as someone who has been repeatedly labeled by the justice system.[184] Although this idea is intriguing, it too has met with criticism.[185] In an in-depth analysis of research on the crime-producing effects of labels, criminologist Charles Tittle found little evidence that stigma produces crime.[186] Tittle claims that many criminal careers occur without labeling; that labeling often comes after, rather than before, chronic offending; and that criminal careers may not follow even when labeling takes place. There is growing evidence that criminal careers begin early in life and that those who go on to a life of crime are burdened with so many social, physical, and psychological problems that negative labeling may be relatively insignificant.[187]

Labeling Reexamined Although criticisms of social reaction theory have reduced its importance in the criminological literature, its use to explain crime and deviance should not be dismissed. Criminologists Raymond Paternoster and Leeann Iovanni have identified other features of the labeling perspective that are important contributions to the study of criminality:[188]

1. The labeling perspective identifies the role played by social control agents in crime causation. Criminal behavior cannot be fully understood if the agencies and individuals empowered to control and treat it are neglected.

2. Labeling theory recognizes that criminality is not a disease or pathological behavior. It focuses attention on the social interactions and reactions that shape individuals and their behavior.

3. Labeling theory distinguishes between criminal acts (primary deviance) and criminal careers (secondary deviance) and shows that these concepts must be interpreted and treated differently.

Labeling theory is also important because of its focus on interaction as well as the situation surrounding the crime. Rather than viewing the criminal as a robotlike creature whose actions are predetermined, it recognizes that crime often results from complex interactions and processes. The decision to commit crime involves actions of a variety of people, including peers, the victim, the police, and other key characters. Labels may expedite crime by guiding the actions of all parties involved in these criminal interactions. Actions deemed innocent when performed by one person are considered provocative when someone who has been labeled as deviant engages in them. Similarly, labeled people may be quick to judge, take offense, or misinterpret others' behavior because of past experience.

AN EVALUATION OF SOCIAL PROCESS THEORY

The branches of social process theory—social learning, social control, and social reaction—are compatible because they all suggest that criminal behavior is part of the socialization process. Criminals are people whose interactions with critically important social institutions and processes—the family, schools, the justice system, peer groups, employers, and neighbors—are troubled. Although some disagree about the relative importance of those influences and the form they take, there is little question that social interactions shape the behavior, beliefs, values, and self-image of the offender. People who have learned deviant social values, find themselves detached from conventional social relationships, or are the subject of stigma and labels from significant others are the most likely to commit crime. These negative influences can influence anyone, beginning in youth and continuing through adulthood. The major strength of the social process view is the vast body of empirical data showing that delinquents and criminals are people who grew up in dysfunctional families, who had troubled childhoods, and who failed at school, at work, and in marriage. Prison data show that these characteristics are typical of inmates.

Although persuasive, these theories do not always account for some of the patterns and fluctuations in the crime rate. If social process theories are valid, for example, people in the West and South must be socialized differently than those in the Midwest and New England because these latter regions have much lower crime rates. How can seasonal crime rate variations be explained if crime is a function of learning or control? How can social processes explain why criminals escalate their activity or why they desist from crime? Once a social bond is broken, how can it be reattached? Once crime is learned, how can it be unlearned?

SOCIAL PROCESS THEORY AND SOCIAL POLICY

Social process theories have had a major influence on social policies since the 1950s. Learning theories have greatly influenced the way criminal offenders are treated. The effect of these theories has been felt mainly by young offenders, who are viewed as being more salvageable than hardened criminals. Advocates of the social learning approach argue that if people become criminal by learning definitions and attitudes toward criminality, they can unlearn them by being exposed to definitions toward conventional behavior. This philosophy has been used in numerous treatment facilities based in part on two early, pioneering efforts: the Highfields Project in New Jersey and the Silverlake Program in Los Angeles. These residential treatment programs, geared toward young male offenders, used group interaction sessions to attack the criminal behavior orientations held by residents while promoting conventional lines of behavior. It is common today for residential and nonresidential programs to offer similar treatment, teaching children and adolescents to refuse drugs, to forgo delinquent behavior, and to stay in school. It is even common for celebrities to return to their old neighborhoods to tell kids to stay in school or off drugs. If learning did not affect behavior, such exercises would be futile.

Control theories have also influenced criminal justice and other social policies. Programs have been developed to increase people's commitment to conventional lines of action. Some work at creating and strengthening bonds early in life before the onset of criminality. The educational system has hosted numerous programs designed to improve basic skills and create an atmosphere in which youths will develop a bond to their schools. The Policy and Practice in Criminology feature on the Head Start program discusses perhaps the largest and most successful attempt to solidify social bonds.

Control theories' focus on the family has played a key role in programs designed to strengthen the bond between parent and child. Others attempt to repair bonds that have been broken and frayed. Examples of this approach are the career, work furlough, and educational opportunity programs being developed in the nation's prisons. These programs are designed to help inmates maintain a stake in society so they will be less willing to resort to criminal activity after their release.

Labeling theorists caution against too much intervention. Rather than ask social agencies to attempt to rehabilitate people having problems with the law, they argue, less is better. Put another way, the more institutions try to help people, the more these people will be stigmatized and labeled. For example, a special education program designed to help problem readers may cause them to label themselves and others as slow or stupid. Similarly, a mental health rehabilitation program created with the best intentions may cause clients to be labeled as crazy or dangerous.

CONNECTIONS

The social reaction perspective has significantly influenced the criminal justice system. In Chapter 15 you will learn more about policies that the criminal justice system has put in place to treat offenders without further enmeshing them in the system or branding them with negative labels.

The influence of labeling theory can be viewed in diversion and restitution programs. **Diversion programs** remove both juvenile and adult offenders from the normal channels of the criminal justice process by placing them in rehabilitation programs. For example, a college student whose drunken driving hurts a pedestrian may, before trial, be placed for six months in an alcohol treatment program. If he successfully completes the program, charges against him will be dismissed; thus he avoids the stigma of a criminal label. Such programs are common throughout the nation. Often they offer counseling, medical advice, and vocational, educational, and family services.

Another popular label-avoiding innovation is **restitution**. Rather than face the stigma of a formal trial, an offender is asked to either pay back the victim of the crime for any loss incurred, or do some useful work in the community in lieu of receiving a court-ordered sentence.

Despite their good intentions, stigma-reducing programs have not met with great success. Critics charge that they substitute one kind of stigma for another—for instance, attending a mental health program in lieu of a criminal trial. In addition, diversion and restitution programs usually screen out violent and repeat offenders. Finally, there is little hard evidence that these alternative programs improve recidivism rates.

Head Start

Head Start is probably the best-known effort to help lower-class youths achieve proper socialization and, in so doing, reduce their potential for future criminality. Head Start programs were instituted in the 1960s as part of the Johnson administration's War on Poverty. Head Start began as a two-month summer program, aimed at embracing the "whole child," for children who were about to enter school. The program offered comprehensive services that helped improve physical health, enhance mental processes, and improve social and emotional development, self-image, and interpersonal relationships. Preschoolers were given an enriched educational environment to develop their learning and cognitive skills. They were allowed to use pegs and pegboards, puzzles, toy animals, dolls, letters and numbers, and other materials that middle-class children take for granted. These opportunities gave these children a leg up in the educational process.

Today there are over 1,300 centers around the nation, including 36,000 classrooms serving 740,000 children and their families, on a budget of more than $3.3 billion annually. Services have been expanded beyond the two-month summer program; more than 13 million children have been served by Head Start since it began. Head Start programs receive 80 percent of their funding from the federal government; the other 20 percent comes from the local community.

Head Start teachers provide a variety of learning experiences appropriate to the child's age and development. These experiences allow the child to read books, understand cultural diversity, express feelings, and play with and relate to their peers. Students are guided in developing gross and fine motor skills and self-confidence. Health care is also an issue; most children enrolled in the program receive comprehensive health screening, physical and dental examinations, and appropriate follow-up. Many programs provide meals to help children receive proper nourishment.

Head Start programs now serve parents in addition to their preschoolers. Some programs allow parents to enroll in classes that cover parenting, literacy, nutrition/weight loss, domestic violence prevention, and other social issues; social services and health, nutrition, and education services are also available.

Considerable controversy has surrounded the success of the Head Start program. In 1970 the Westinghouse Learning Corporation issued a definitive evaluation of the Head Start effort, concluding that there was no evidence of lasting cognitive gains in the participating children. Initial gains seemed to evaporate during the elementary school years, and by the third grade the performance of the Head Start children was no different than their peers.

Although disappointing, this evaluation focused on IQ levels, not improvement in social competence and other survival skills. More recent research has produced dramatically different results. One report found that by age 5, children who experienced the enriched day care offered by Head Start averaged more than 10 points higher on their IQ scores than their peers who did not participate in the program. Other research that carefully compared Head Start children to similar youths who did not attend the program found that the former made significant intellectual gains. Head Start children were less likely to have been retained in a grade or placed in classes for slow learners; they outperformed peers on achievement tests; and they were more likely to graduate from high school. Head Start kids also improved in nonacademic areas: they appear to have better health, immunization rates, nutrition, and enhanced emotional characteristics after leaving the program. Research also shows that the Head Start program can have important psychological benefits for the mothers of participants, such as decreasing depression and anxiety and increasing feelings of life satisfaction. Although findings in some areas may be tentative, they are all in the same direction: Head Start enhances school readiness and has enduring effects on social competence.

If, as many experts believe, there is a close link between school performance, family life, and crime, programs such as Head Start can help some potentially criminal youths avoid problems with the law. By implication, their success indicates that programs that help socialize youngsters can be used to combat urban criminality. Although some problems have been identified in individual centers, the government has shown its faith in Head Start as a socialization agent by planning to expand services in the coming years; total funding could be $8 billion.

CRITICAL THINKING

1. Does a program like Head Start substitute one type of negative label (like special-needs kid) for another (like slow starter)?
2. What benefits do you think children who participate in Head Start will carry with them throughout their childhood and adolescence?

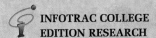 **INFOTRAC COLLEGE EDITION RESEARCH**

What can be done to improve educational achievement in America? See: Robert E. Slavin. Can education reduce social inequity? *Educational Leadership,* Dec 1997 v55 n4 p6 David Bennett. Entrepreneurship: the road to salvation for public schools. *Educational Leadership,* Sept 1994 v52 n1 p76

Source: Edward Zigler and Sally Styfco, "Head Start, Criticisms in a Constructive Context," *American Psychologist* 49 (1994): 127–32; Nancy Kassebaum, "Head Start, Only the Best for America's Children," *American Psychologist* 49 (1994): 123–26; Faith Lamb Parker, Chaya Piorkowski, and Lenore Peay, "Head Start as Social Support for Mothers: The Psychological Benefits of Involvement," *American Journal of Orthopsychiatry* 57 (1987): 220–33.

Table 8.2 Social Process Theories

THEORY	MAJOR PREMISE	STRENGTHS
Social Learning Theories		
Differential association theory	People learn to commit crime from exposure to antisocial definitions.	Explains onset of criminality. Explains the presence of crime in all elements of social structure. Explains why some people in high-crime areas refrain from criminality. Can apply to adults and juveniles.
Differential reinforcement theory	Criminal behavior depends on the person's experiences with rewards for conventional behaviors and punishment for deviant ones. Being rewarded for deviance leads to crime.	Adds psychological learning theory principles to differential association. Links sociological and psychological principles.
Neutralization theory	Youths learn ways of neutralizing moral restraints and periodically drift in and out of criminal behavior patterns.	Explains why many delinquents do not become adult criminals. Explains why youthful law violators can participate in conventional behavior.
Social Control Theories		
Containment theory	Society produces pushes and pulls toward crime. In some people, they are counteracted by internal and external containments, such as a good self-concept and group cohesiveness.	Brings together psychological and sociological principles. Can explain why some people are able to resist the strongest social pressure to commit crime.
Hirschi's control theory	A person's bond to society prevents him or her from violating social rules. If the bond weakens, the person is free to commit crime.	Explains the onset of crime; can apply to both middle- and lower-class crime. Explains its theoretical constructs adequately so they can be measured. Has been empirically tested.
Social Reaction Theory		
Labeling theory	People enter into law-violating careers when they are labeled for their acts and organize their personalities around the labels.	Explains the role of society in creating deviance. Explains why some juvenile offenders do not become adult criminals. Develops concepts of criminal careers.

SUMMARY

Social process theories view criminality as a function of people's interaction with various organizations, institutions, and processes in society. People in all walks of life have the potential to become criminals if they maintain destructive social relationships. Social process theory has three main branches: social learning theory stresses that people learn how to commit crimes; social control theory analyzes the failure of society to control criminal tendencies; and labeling theory maintains that negative labels produce criminal careers. These theories are summarized in Table 8.2.

The social learning branch of social process theory suggests that people learn criminal behaviors much as they learn conventional behavior. Differential association theory, formulated by Edwin Sutherland, holds that criminality is a result of a person's perceiving an excess of definitions in favor of crime over definitions that uphold conventional values. Ronald Akers has reformulated Sutherland's work using psychological learning theory; he calls his approach differential reinforcement theory. Sykes and Matza's theory of neutralization stresses that youths learn behavior rationalizations that enable them to overcome societal values and norms and break the law.

Control theory is the second branch of the social process approach. Control theories maintain that all people have the potential to become criminals, but their bonds to conventional society prevent them from violating the law. Walter Reckless's containment theory suggests that a person's self-concept aids his or her commitment to conventional action. Travis Hirschi describes the social bond as containing elements of belief, commitment, attachment, and involvement. Weakened bonds allow youths to behave antisocially.

Social reaction or labeling theory holds that criminality is promoted by becoming negatively labeled by significant others. Such labels as "criminal," "ex-con," and "junkie" isolate people from society and lock them into lives of crime. Labels create expectations that the labeled person will act in a certain way; labeled people are always watched and suspected. Eventually these people begin to accept their labels as personal identities, locking them further into lives of crime and deviance. Edwin Lemert has said that people who accept labels are involved in secondary deviance. Unfortunately, research on labeling has not supported its major premises. Consequently, critics have charged that it lacks credibility as a description of crime causation.

Social process theories have greatly influenced social policy. They have controlled treatment orientations as well as community action policies.

 See the book-specific web site at www.cj.wadsworth.com for additional chapter links, discussions, and quizzes.

THINKING LIKE A CRIMINOLOGIST

The state legislature is considering a bill that requires the names of people convicted of certain offenses, such as vandalism, soliciting a prostitute, or nonpayment of child support, to be posted in local newspapers under the heading "The Rogues Gallery." Those who favor the bill cite the fact that in Boston men arrested for soliciting prostitutes are forced to clean streets. In Dallas shoplifters are made to stand outside stores with signs stating their misdeeds.[189]

Members of the state Civil Liberties Union have opposed the bill, stating, "It's simply needless humiliation of the individual." They argue that public shaming is inhumane and further alienates criminals who already have little stake in society, further ostracizing them from the mainstream. According to civil liberties attorneys, shaming helps criminals acquire a damaged reputation, which further locks them into criminal behavior patterns.

This "liberal" position is challenged by those who believe that convicted lawbreakers have no right to conceal their crimes from the public. Shaming penalties seem attractive as cost-effective alternatives to imprisonment. These critics ask what could be wrong with requiring a teenage vandal to personally apologize at the school he or she defaced and wear a shirt with a big "V" on it while he or she cleans up the mess. If you do something wrong, they argue, you should have to pay the consequences.

You have been asked to address a legislative committee on the issue of whether shaming could deter crime. What would you say?

KEY TERMS

social process theories	negative reinforcement	labeling theory
broken home	neutralization theory	symbolic interaction theory
cliques	subterranean value	moral entrepreneur
crowds	drift	stigma
social process approach	techniques of neutralization	reflective role-taking
social learning theory	self-control	retrospective reading
social control theory	commitment to conformity	dramatization of evil
social reaction (labeling) theory	self-esteem	primary and secondary deviance
differential association (DA) theory	containment theory	deviance amplification effect
cultural deviance critique	normative	contextual discrimination
differential reinforcement theory	self-rejection	diversion programs
direct conditioning	social bond	restitution
differential reinforcement	social reaction theory	

NOTES

1. Michael Rand, *Criminal Victimization, 1997, Changes 1996–1997, Trends 1993–1997* (Washington, D.C.: Bureau of Justice Statistics, 1998).

2. Alan Lizotte, Terence Thornberry, Marvin Krohn, Deborah Chard-Wierschem, and David McDowall, "Neighborhood Context and Delinquency: A Longitudinal Analysis," in *Cross-National Longitudinal Research on Human Development and Criminal Behavior*, ed. E. M. Weitekamp and H. J. Kerner (Netherlands: Kluwer, 1994), pp. 217–27.

3. Charles Tittle and Robert Meier, "Specifying the SES/Delinquency Relationship," *Criminology* 28 (1990): 271–99 at 274.

4. Sheldon Glueck and Eleanor Glueck, *Unraveling Juvenile Delinquency* (Cambridge: Harvard University Press, 1950); Ashley Weeks, "Predicting Juvenile Delinquency," *American Sociological Review* 8 (1943): 40–46.

5. Denise Kandel, "The Parental and Peer Contexts of Adolescent Deviance: An Algebra of Interpersonal Influences," *Journal of Drug Issues* 26 (1996): 289–315; Ann Goetting, "The Parenting–Crime Connection," *Journal of Primary Prevention* 14 (1994): 167–84.

6. For general reviews of the relationship between families and delinquency, see Alan Jay Lincoln and Murray Straus, *Crime and the Family* (Springfield, Ill.: Charles C. Thomas, 1985); Rolf Loeber and Magda Stouthamer-Loeber, "Family Factors as Correlates and Predictors of Juvenile Conduct Problems and Delinquency," in *Crime and Justice, An Annual Review of Research*, vol. 7, ed. Michael Tonry and Norval Morris (Chicago: University of Chicago Press, 1986), pp. 29–151; Goetting, "The Parenting–Crime Connection."

7. Joseph Weis, Katherine Worsley, and Carol Zeiss, *The Family and Delinquency: Organizing the Conceptual Chaos* (Monograph, Center for Law and Justice, University of Washington, 1982).

8. Susan Stern and Carolyn Smith, "Family Processes and Delinquency in an Ecological Context," *Social Service Review* 37 (1995): 707–731.

9. *Families with Children Under 18 by Type: 1995 to 2010, Series 1, 2, and 3* (Washington, D.C.: U.S. Bureau of the Census, 1996).

10. Lawrence Rosen and Kathleen Neilson, "Broken Homes," in *Contemporary Criminology*, ed. Leonard Savitz and Norman Johnston (New York: Wiley, 1982), pp. 126–32.

11. James Q. Wilson and Richard Herrnstein, *Crime and Human Nature* (New York: Simon and Schuster, 1985), p. 249.

12. L. Edward Wells and Joseph Rankin, "Families and Delinquency: A Meta-Analysis of the Impact of Broken Homes," *Social Problems* 38 (1991): 71–90.

13. Nan Marie Astone and Sara McLanahan, "Family Structure, Parental Practices and High School Completion," *American Sociological Review* 56 (1991): 309–20.

14. Mary Pat Traxler, "The Influence of the Father and Alternative Male Role Models on African-American Boys' Involvement in Antisocial Behavior." Paper presented at the annual meeting of the American Society of Criminology, New Orleans, November 1992.

15. Paul Amato and Bruce Keith, "Parental Divorce and the Well-Being of Children: A Meta-Analysis," *Psychological Bulletin* 110 (1991): 26–46.

16. Joseph Rankin and L. Edward Wells, "The Effect of Parental Attachments and Direct Controls on Delinquency," *Journal of Research in Crime and Delinquency* 27 (1990): 140–65.

17. Robert Roberts and Vern Bengston, "Affective Ties to Parents in Early Adulthood and Self-Esteem Across 20 Years," *Social Psychology Quarterly* 59 (1996): 96–106.

18. Robert Johnson, S. Susan Su, Dean Gerstein, Hee-Choon Shin, and John Hoffman, "Parental Influences on Deviant Behavior in Early Adolescence: A Logistic Response Analysis of Age- and Gender-Differentiated Effects," *Journal of Quantitative Criminology* 11 (1995): 167–92.

19. Judith Brook and Li-Jung Tseng, "Influences of Parental Drug Use, Personality, and Child Rearing on the Toddler's Anger and Negativity," *Genetic, Social and General Psychology Monographs* 122 (1996): 107–128.

20. Thomas Ashby Wills, Donato Vaccaro, Grace McNamara, and A. Elizabeth Hirky, "Escalated Substance Use: A Longitudinal Grouping Analysis from Early to Middle Adolescence," *Journal of Abnormal Psychology* 105 (1996); 166–80.

21. John Laub and Robert Sampson, "Unraveling Families and Delinquency: A Reanalysis of the Gluecks' Data," *Criminology* 26 (1988): 355–80.

22. Richard Famularo, Karen Stone, Richard Barnum, and Robert Wharton, "Alcoholism and Severe Child Maltreatment," *American Journal of Orthopsychiatry* 56 (1987): 481–85; Richard Gelles, "Child Abuse and Violence in Single-Parent Families: Parent Absence and Economic Deprivation," *American Journal of Orthopsychiatry* 59 (1989): 492–501; Cecil Willis and Richard Wells, "The Police and Child Abuse: An Analysis of Police Decisions to Report Illegal Behavior," *Criminology* 26 (1988): 695–716; Carolyn Webster-Stratton, "Comparison of Abusive and Nonabusive Families with Conduct-Disordered Children," *American Journal of Orthopsychiatry* 55 (1985): 59–69.

23. Carolyn Smith and Terence Thornberry, "The Relationship Between Childhood Maltreatment and Adolescent Involvement in Delinquency," *Criminology* 33 (1995): 451–79.

24. Murray Straus, "Discipline and Deviance: Physical Punishment of Children and Violence and Other Crime in Adulthood," *Social Problems* 38 (1991): 101–123.

25. Murray A. Straus, "Spanking and the Making of a Violent Society. The Short- and Long-Term Consequences of Corporal Punishment," *Pediatrics* 98 (1996): 837–43.

26. Straus, "Spanking and the Making of a Violent Society."

27. Lening Zhang and Steven Messner, "Family Deviance and Delinquency in China," *Criminology* 33 (1995): 359–87.

28. *The Forgotten Half: Pathways to Success for America's Youth and Young Families* (Washington, D.C.: William T. Grant Foundation, 1988); Lee Jussim, "Teacher Expectations: Self-Fulfilling Prophecies, Perceptual Biases, and Accuracy," *Journal of Personality and Social Psychology* 57 (1989): 469–80.

29. Eugene Maguin and Rolf Loeber, "Academic Performance and Delinquency," in *Crime and Justice: A Review of Research,* vol. 20, ed. Michael Tonry (Chicago: University of Chicago Press, 1995), pp. 145–264.

30. Jeannie Oakes, *Keeping Track: How Schools Structure Inequality* (New Haven: Yale University Press, 1985); Marc LeBlanc, Evelyne Valliere, and Pierre McDuff, "Adolescents' School Experience and Self-Reported Offending: A Longitudinal Test of Social Control Theory" (paper presented at the annual meeting of the American Society of Criminology, Baltimore, November 1990).

31. G. Roger Jarjoura, "Does Dropping Out of School Enhance Delinquent Involvement? Results from a Large-Scale National Probability Sample," *Criminology* 31 (1993): 149–72; Terence Thornberry, Melaine Moore, and R. L. Christenson, "The Effect of Dropping Out of High School on Subsequent Criminal Behavior," *Criminology* 23 (1985): 3–18.

32. Carolyn Smith, Alan Lizotte, Terence Thornberry, and Marvin Krohn, *Resilient Youth: Identifying Factors That Prevent High-Risk Youth from Engaging in Delinquency and Drug Use* (Albany, N.Y: Rochester Youth Development Study, 1994), pp. 19–21.

33. Kathryn A. Chandler, Chris Chapman, Michael R. Rand, and Bruce M. Taylor, *Students' Reports of School Crime: 1989 and 1995* (Washington, D.C: Bureau of Justice Statistics, 1998).

34. Sheila Heaviside and Shelley Burns, *Violence and Discipline Problems in U.S. Public Schools: 1996–1997* (Washington, D.C.: Department of Education 1998). Herein cited as National Violence Survey,

35. Irving Janis, *Groupthink: Psychological Studies of Policy Decisions and Fiascoes* (Boston: Houghton Mifflin, 1982).

36. Zhang and Messner, "Family Deviance and Delinquency in China."

37. Thomas Berndt, "The Features and Effects of Friendships in Early Adolescence," *Child Development* 53 (1982): 1447–69; Thomas Berndt and T. B. Perry, "Children's Perceptions of Friendships as Supportive Relationships," *Developmental Psychology* 22 (1986): 640–48; Spencer Rathus, *Understanding Child Development* (New York: Holt, Rinehart and Winston, 1988), p. 462.

38. Peggy Giordano, "The Wider Circle of Friends in Adolescence," *American Journal of Sociology* 101 (1995): 661–97.

39. Delbert Elliott, David Huizinga, and Suzanne Ageton, *Explaining Delinquency and Drug Use* (Beverly Hills: Sage, 1985); Helene Raskin White, Robert Padina, and Randy LaGrange, "Longitudinal Predictors of Serious Substance Use and Delinquency," *Criminology* 6 (1987): 715–40.

40. See, generally, John Hagedorn, *People and Folks: Gangs, Crime and the Underclass in a Rustbelt City* (Chicago: Lakeview Press, 1988).

41. Robert Agnew and Timothy Brezina, "Relational Problems with Peers, Gender and Delinquency," *Youth and Society* 29 (1997): 84–111.

42. Scott Menard, "Demographic and Theoretical Variables in the Age-Period Cohort Analysis of Illegal Behavior," *Journal of Research in Crime and Delinquency* 29 (1992): 178–99.

43. Patrick Jackson, "Theories and Findings About Youth Gangs," *Criminal Justice Abstracts* (June 1989): 313–27.

44. Marvin Krohn and Terence Thornberry, "Network Theory: A Model for Understanding Drug Abuse Among African-American and Hispanic Youth," in *Drug Abuse Among Minority Youth: Advances in Research and Methodology,* ed. Mario De La Rosa and Juan-Luis Recio Adrados (Washington, D.C.: U.S. Department of Health and Human Services, 1993).

45. D. Wayne Osgood, Janet Wilson, Patrick O'Malley, Jerald Bachman, and Lloyd Johnston, "Routine Activities and Individual Deviant Behavior," *American Sociological Review* 61 (1996): 635–55.

46. Mark Warr, "Age, Peers, and Delinquency," *Criminology* 31 (1993): 17–40.

47. Mark Warr, "Organization and Instigation in Delinquent Groups," *Criminology* 34 (1996): 11–35.

48. Sara Battin, Karl Hill, Robert Abbott, Richard Catalano, and J. David Hawkins, "The Contribution of Gang Membership to Delinquency Beyond Delinquent Friends," *Criminology* 36 (1998): 93–116.

49. Terence Thornberry, Alan Lizotte, Marvin Krohn, Margaret Farnworth, and Sung Joon Jang, "Delinquent Peers, Beliefs, and Delinquent Behavior: A Longitudinal Test of Interactional Theory," Working Paper no. 6, rev. (Albany, N.Y.: Rochester Youth Development Study, Hindelang Criminal Justice Research Center, 1992), pp. 8–30.

50. Warr, "Age, Peers and Delinquency."

51. Travis Hirschi and Rodney Stark, "Hellfire and Delinquency," *Social Problems* 17 (1969): 202–213.

52. T. David Evans, Francis Cullen, R. Gregory Dunaway, and Velmer Burton, Jr., "Religion and Crime Reexamined: The Impact of Religion, Secular Controls, and Social Ecology on Adult Criminality," *Criminology* 33 (1995): 195–224.

53. Lee Ellis and James Patterson, "Crime and Religion: An International Comparison Among Thirteen Industrial Nations," *Personal Individual Differences* 20 (1996): 761–68.

54. Walter Miller, *Violence by Youth Gangs and Youth Groups as a Crime Problem in Major American Cities* (Washington, D.C.: U.S. Government Printing Office, 1975).

55. Edwin H. Sutherland, *Principles of Criminology* (Philadelphia: Lippincott, 1939).

56. See, for example, Edwin Sutherland, "White-Collar Criminality," *American Sociological Review* 5 (1940): 2–10.

57. This section is adapted from Clarence Schrag, *Crime and Justice: American Style* (Washington, D.C.: U.S. Government Printing Office, 1971), p. 46.

58. See Edwin Sutherland and Donald Cressey, *Criminology*, 8th ed. (Philadelphia: Lippincott, 1970), pp. 77–79.

59. Sandra Brown, Vicki Creamer, and Barbara Stetson, "Adolescent Alcohol Expectancies in Relation to Personal and Parental Drinking Patterns," *Journal of Abnormal Psychology* 96 (1987): 117–21.

60. Sutherland and Cressey, *Criminology*, 8th ed., pp. 77–79.

61. Denise Kandel and Mark Davies, "Friendship Networks, Intimacy, and Illicit Drug Use in Young Adulthood: A Comparison of Two Competing Theories," *Criminology* 29 (1991): 441–67.

62. Kenneth Tunnell, "Inside the Drug Trade: Trafficking from the Dealer's Perspective," *Qualitative Sociology* 16 (1993): 361–81 at 367.

63. Krohn and Thornberry, "Network Theory," pp. 123–24.

64. Douglas Smith, Christy Visher, and G. Roger Jarjoura, "Dimensions of Delinquency: Exploring the Correlates of Participation, Frequency, and Persistence of Delinquent Behavior," *Journal of Research in Crime and Delinquency* 28 (1991): 6–32; Ross Matsueda and Karen Heimer, "Race, Family Structure, and Delinquency: A Test of Differential Association and Social Control Theories," *American Sociological Review* 52 (1987): 826–40; Graham Ousey and David Aday, Jr., "The Interaction Hypothesis: A Test Using Social Control Theory and Social Learning Theory" (paper presented at the American Society of Criminology meeting, Boston, Mass., November 1995).

65. James Short, "Differential Association as a Hypothesis: Problems of Empirical Testing," *Social Problems* 8 (1960): 14–25.

66. Albert Reiss and A. Lewis Rhodes, "The Distribution of Delinquency in the Social Class Structure," *American Sociological Review* 26 (1961): 732.

67. Warr, "Age, Peers, and Delinquency."

68. Matthew Ploeger, "Youth Employment and Delinquency: Reconsidering a Problematic Relationship," *Criminology* 35 (1997): 659–75.

69. Daniel Mears, Matthew Ploeger, and Mark Warr, "Explaining the Gender Gap in Delinquency: Peer Influence and Moral Evaluations of Behavior," *Journal of Research in Crime and Delinquency* 35 (1998): 251–66.

70. Charles Tittle, *Sanctions and Social Deviance* (New York: Praeger, 1980).

71. Yuet-Wah Cheung and Agnes M. C. Ng, "Social Factors in Adolescent Deviant Behavior in Hong Kong: An Integrated Theoretical Approach," *International Journal of Comparative and Applied Criminal Justice* 12 (1988): 27–44.

72. Ploeger, "Youth Employment and Delinquency"; Elton Jackson, Charles Tittle, and Mary Jean Burke, "Offense-Specific Models of the Differential Association Process," *Social Problems* 33 (1986): 335–56; Gerben J. N. Bruinsma, "Differential Association Theory Reconsidered: An Extension and Its Empirical Test," *Journal of Quantitative Criminology* 8 (1992): 29–46.

73. Robert Burgess and Ronald Akers, "A Differential Association–Reinforcement Theory of Criminal Behavior," *Social Problems* 14 (1966): 128–47.

74. Ross Matsueda, "The Current State of Differential Association Theory," *Crime and Delinquency* 34 (1988): 277–306.

75. Burgess and Akers, "A Differential Association–Reinforcement Theory of Criminal Behavior."

76. The most influential critique of differential association is contained in Ruth Kornhauser's *Social Sources of Delinquency* (Chicago: University of Chicago Press, 1978).

77. These misconceptions are derived from Donald Cressey's "Epidemiologies and Individual Conduct: A Case from Criminology," *Pacific Sociological Review* 3 (1960): 47–58.

78. Kornhauser, *Social Sources of Delinquency*; in contrast, see Matsueda, "The Current State of Differential Association Theory."

79. Ronald Akers, "Is Differential Association/Social Learning Cultural Deviance Theory?" *Criminology* 34 (1996): 229–47; for an opposing view, see Travis Hirschi, "Theory Without Ideas: Reply to Akers," *Criminology* 34 (1996): 249–56.

80. Craig Reinerman and Jeffrey Fagan, "Social Organization and Differential Association: A Research Note from a Longitudinal Study of Violent Juvenile Offenders," *Crime and Delinquency* 34 (1988): 307–27.

81. Sue Titus Reed, *Crime and Criminology*, 2d ed. (New York: Holt, Rinehart & Winston, 1979), p. 234.

82. Ronald Akers, *Deviant Behavior: A Social Learning Approach*, 2d ed. (Belmont, Calif.: Wadsworth, 1977).

83. Ronald Akers, Marvin Krohn, Lonn Lonza-Kaduce, and Marcia Radosevich, "Social Learning and Deviant Behavior: A Specific Test of a General Theory," *American Sociological Review* 44 (1979): 638.

84. Akers, Krohn, Lonza-Kaduce, and Radosevich, "Social Learning and Deviant Behavior."

85. Marvin Krohn, William Skinner, James Massey, and Ronald Akers, "Social Learning Theory and Adolescent Cigarette Smoking: A Longitudinal Study," *Social Problems* 32 (1985): 455–71.

86. Akers, Krohn, Lonza-Kaduce, and Radosevich, "Social Learning and Deviant Behavior," pp. 636–55.

87. Ronald Akers and Gang Lee, "A Longitudinal Test of Social Learning Theory: Adolescent Smoking," *Journal of Drug Issues* 26 (1996): 317–43.

88. Gary Jensen and David Brownfield, "Parents and Drugs," *Criminology* 21 (1983): 543–54.

89. Ronald Akers, "Rational Choice, Deterrence, and Social Learning Theory in Criminology: The Path Not Taken," *Journal of Criminal Law and Criminology* 81 (1990): 653–76.

90. Gresham Sykes and David Matza, "Techniques of Neutralization: A Theory of Delinquency," *American Sociological Review* 22 (1957): 664–70; David Matza, *Delinquency and Drift* (New York: John Wiley, 1964).

91. Matza, *Delinquency and Drift*, p. 51.

92. Sykes and Matza, "Techniques of Neutralization"; see also David Matza, "Subterranean Traditions of Youths," *Annals of the American Academy of Political and Social Science* 378 (1961): 116.

93. Sykes and Matza, "Techniques of Neutralization."

94. Sykes and Matza, "Techniques of Neutralization."

95. Ian Shields and George Whitehall, "Neutralization and Delinquency Among Teenagers," *Criminal Justice and Behavior* 21 (1994): 223–35; Robert A. Ball, "An Empirical Exploration of Neutralization Theory," *Criminologica* 4 (1966): 22–32. See also M. William Minor, "The Neutralization of Criminal Offense," *Criminology* 18 (1980): 103–20; and Robert Gordon, James Short, Desmond Cartwright, and Fred Strodtbeck, "Values and Gang Delinquency: A Study of Street Corner Groups," *American Journal of Sociology* 69 (1963): 109–28.

96. Michael Hindelang, "The Commitment of Delinquents to Their Misdeeds: Do Delinquents Drift?" *Social Problems* 17 (1970): 500–509; Robert Regoli and Eric Poole, "The Commitment of Delinquents to Their Misdeeds: A Reexamination," *Journal of Criminal Justice* 6 (1978): 261–69.

97. Larry Siegel, Spencer Rathus, and Carol Ruppert, "Values and Delinquent Youth: An Empirical Reexamination of Theories of Delinquency," *British Journal of Criminology* 13 (1973): 237–44.

98. Robert Agnew, "The Techniques of Neutralization and Violence," *Criminology* 32 (1994): 555–80.

99. Jeffrey Fagan, *Adolescent Violence: A View From the Street*, NIJ Research Preview (Washington, D.C: National Institute of Justice, 1998).

100. John Hamlin, "Misplaced Role of Rational Choice in Neutralization Theory," *Criminology* 26 (1988): 425–38.

101. Mark Pogrebin, Eric Poole, and Amos Martinez, "Accounts of Professional Misdeeds: The Sexual Exploitation of Clients by Psychotherapists," *Deviant Behavior* 13 (1992): 229–52.

102. Eric Wish, *Drug Use Forecasting 1990* (Washington, D.C.: National Institute of Justice, 1991).

103. Scott Briar and Irving Piliavin, "Delinquency: Situational Inducements and Commitment to Conformity," *Social Problems* 13 (1965–1966): 35–45.

104. Lawrence Sherman and Douglas Smith, with Janell Schmidt and Dennis Rogan, "Crime, Punishment, and Stake in Conformity: Legal and Informal Control of Domestic Violence," *American Sociological Review* 57 (1992): 680–90.

105. Albert Reiss, "Delinquency as the Failure of Personal and Social Controls," *American Sociological Review* 16 (1951): 196–207.

106. Briar and Piliavin, "Delinquency: Situational Inducements and Commitment to Conformity."

107. Walter Reckless, *The Crime Problem* (New York: Appleton-Century Crofts, 1967), pp. 469–83.

108. Among the many research reports by Reckless and his colleagues are Frank Scarpitti, Ellen Murray, Simon Dinitz, and Walter Reckless, "The Good Boy in a High Delinquency Area: Four Years Later," *American Sociological Review* 23:555–58 (1960); Walter Reckless, Simon Dinitz, and Ellen Murray, "The Good Boy in a High Delinquency Area," *Journal of Criminal Law, Criminology, and Police Science* 48 (1957): 12–26; Walter Reckless, Simon Dinitz, and Ellen Murray, "Self-Concept as an Insulator Against Delinquency," *American Sociological Review* 21 (1956): 744–46; Walter Reckless and Simon Dinitz, "Pioneering with Self-Concept as a Vulnerability Factor in Delinquency," *Journal of Criminal Law, Criminology, and Police Science* 58 (1967): 515–23; Walter Reckless, Simon Dinitz, and Barbara Kay, "The Self-Component in Potential Delinquency and Potential Non-Delinquency," *American Sociological Review* 22 (1957): 566–70.

109. Howard Kaplan, *Deviant Behavior in Defense of Self* (New York: Academic Press, 1980); Howard Kaplan, "Self-Attitudes and Deviant Response," *Social Forces* 54 (1978): 788–801.

110. Howard Kaplan and Robert Johnson, "Negative Social Sanctions and Juvenile Delinquency: Effects of Labeling in a Model of Deviant Behavior," *Social Science Quarterly* 72 (1991): 98–122; Howard Kaplan, Robert Johnson, and Carol Bailey, "Deviant Peers and Deviant Behavior: Further Elaboration of a Model," *Social Psychology Quarterly* 30 (1987): 277–84.

111. Travis Hirschi, *Causes of Delinquency* (Berkeley: University of California Press, 1969).

112. Hirschi, *Causes of Delinquency*, p. 231.

113. Hirschi, *Causes of Delinquency*, pp. 66–74.

114. Michael Wiatroski, David Griswold, and Mary K. Roberts, "Social Control Theory and Delinquency," *American Sociological Review* 46 (1981): 525–41.

115. Patricia Van Voorhis, Francis Cullen, Richard Mathers, and Connie Chenoweth Garner, "The Impact of Family Structure and Quality on Delinquency: A Comparative Assessment of Structural and Functional Factors," *Criminology* 26 (1988): 235–61.

116. Marc LeBlanc, "Family Dynamics, Adolescent Delinquency, and Adult Criminality." Paper presented at the Society for Life History Research Conference, Keystone, Colorado, October 1990, p. 6.

117. Teresa Lagrange and Robert Silverman, "Perceived Strain and Delinquency Motivation: An Empirical Evaluation of General Strain Theory." Paper presented at the American Society of Criminology meeting, Boston, Mass., November 1995.

118. Patricia Van Voorhis, Francis Cullen, Richard Mathers, and Connie Chenoweth Garner, "The Impact of Family Structure and Quality on Delinquency: A Comparative Assessment of Structural and Functional Factors," *Criminology* 26 (1988): 235–61.

119. Patricia Jenkins, "School Delinquency and the School Social Bond," *Journal of Research in Crime and Delinquency* 34 (1997): 337–67.

120. John Cochran and Ronald Akers, "An Exploration of the Variable Effects of Religiosity on Adolescent Marijuana and Alcohol Use," *Journal of Research in Crime and Delinquency* 26 (1989): 198–225.

121. Robert Agnew and David Peterson, "Leisure and Delinquency," *Social Problems* 36 (1989): 332–48.

122. Marianne Junger and Ineke Haen Marshall, "The Interethnic Generalizability of Social Control Theory: An Empirical Test," *Journal of Research in Crime and Delinquency* 34 (1997): 79–112; Josine Junger-Tas, "An Empirical Test of Social Control Theory," *Journal of Quantitative Criminology* 8 (1992): 18–29.

123. For a review of exciting research, see Kimberly Kempf, "The Empirical Status of Hirschi's Control Theory," in *Advances in Criminological Theory,* ed. Bill Laufer and Freda Adler (New Brunswick, N.J.: Transaction Publishers, 1992), pp. 111–29.

124. Richard Lawrence, "Parents, Peers, School, and Delinquency." Paper presented at the American Society of Criminology meeting, Boston, Mass., November 1995.

125. Peggy Giordano, Stephen Cernkovich, and M. D. Pugh, "Friendships and Delinquency," *American Journal of Sociology* 91 (1986): 1170–1202.

126. Denise Kandel and Mark Davies, "Friendship Networks, Intimacy, and Illicit Drug Use in Young Adulthood: A Comparison of Two Competing Theories," *Criminology* 29 (1991): 441–67.

127. Velmer Burton, Francis Cullen, T. David Evans, R. Gregory Dunaway, Sesha Kethineni, and Gary Payne, "The Impact of Parental Controls on Delinquency," *Journal of Criminal Justice* 23 (1995): 111–126.

128. Kimberly Kempf Leonard and Scott Decker, "The Theory of Social Control: Does It Apply to the Very Young?" *Journal of Criminal Justice* 22 (1994): 89–105.

129. Michael Hindelang, "Causes of Delinquency: A Partial Replication and Extension," *Social Problems* 21 (1973): 471–87.

130. Gary Jensen and David Brownfield, "Parents and Drugs," *Criminology* 21 (1983): 543–54. See also M. Wiatrowski, D. Griswold, and M. Roberts, "Social Control Theory and Delinquency," *American Sociological Review* 46 (1981): 525–41.

131. Leslie Samuelson, Timothy Hartnagel, and Harvey Krahn, "Crime and Social Control Among High School Dropouts," *Journal of Crime and Justice* 18 (1990): 129–61.

132. Marvin Krohn and James Massey, "Social Control and Delinquent Behavior: An Examination of the Elements of the Social Bond," *Sociological Quarterly* 21 (1980): 529–43.

133. Jill Leslie Rosenbaum and James Lasley, "School, Community Context, and Delinquency: Rethinking the Gender Gap," *Justice Quarterly* 7 (1990): 493–513.

134. Randy LaGrange and Helene Raskin White, "Age Differences in Delinquency: A Test of Theory," *Criminology* 23 (1985): 19–45.

135. Robert Agnew, "Social Control Theory and Delinquency: A Longitudinal Test," *Criminology* 23 (1985): 47–61.

136. Alan E. Liska and M. D. Reed, "Ties to Conventional Institutions and Delinquency: Estimating Reciprocal Effects," *American Sociological Review* 50 (1985): 547–60.

137. Michael Wiatrowski, David Griswold, and Mary K. Roberts, "Social Control Theory and Delinquency," *American Sociological Review* 46 (1981): 525–41.

138. George Herbert Mead, *Mind, Self and Society* (Chicago: University of Chicago Press, 1934); George Herbert Mead, *The Philosophy of the Act* (Chicago: University of Chicago Press, 1938); Charles Horton Cooley, *Human Nature and the Social Order* (Schocken: New York, 1964, originally published in 1902); Herbert Blumer, *Symbolic Interactionism: Perspective and Method* (Englewood Cliffs, N.J.: Prentice-Hall, 1969).

139. Bruce Link, Elmer Streuning, Francis Cullen, Patrick Shrout, and Bruce Dohrenwend, "A Modified Labeling Theory Approach to Mental Disorders: An Empirical Assessment," *American Sociological Review* 54 (1989): 400–423.

140. Linda Jackson, John Hunter, and Carole Hodge, "Physical Attractiveness and Intellectual Competence: A Meta-Analytic Review," *Social Psychology Quarterly* 58 (1995): 108–122.

141. President's Commission on Law Enforcement and the Administration of Youth Crime, *Task Force Report: Juvenile Delinquency and Youth* (Washington, D.C.: U.S. Government Printing Office, 1967), p. 43.

142. Kai Erickson, "Notes on the Sociology of Deviance," *Social Problems* 9 (1962): 397–414.

143. Edwin Schur, *Labeling Deviant Behavior* (New York: Harper & Row, 1972), p. 21.

144. Howard Becker, *Outsiders: Studies in the Sociology of Deviance* (New York: Macmillan, 1963), p. 9.

145. Laurie Goodstein, "The Architect of the 'Gay Conversion' Campaign," *New York Times* 13 August 1998, p. A10.

146. Christy Visher, "Gender, Police Arrest Decision, and Notions of Chivalry," *Criminology* 21 (1983): 5–28.

147. Marjorie Zatz, "Race, Ethnicity and Determinate Sentencing," *Criminology* 22 (1984): 147–71.

148. Christina DeJong and Kenneth Jackson, "Putting Race into Context: Race, Juvenile Justice Processing, and Urbanization," *Justice Quarterly* 15 (1998): 487–504.

149. Roland Chilton and Jim Galvin, "Race, Crime, and Criminal Justice," *Crime and Delinquency* 31 (1985): 3–14.

150. Joan Petersilia, "Racial Disparities in the Criminal Justice System: A Summary," *Crime and Delinquency* 31 (1985): 15–34.

151. Walter Gove, *The Labeling of Deviance: Evaluating a Perspective* (New York: John Wiley, 1975), p. 5.

152. Harold Garfinkle, "Conditions of Successful Degradation Ceremonies," *American Journal of Sociology* 61 (1956): 420–24.

153. Karen Heimer and Ross Matsueda, "Role-Taking, Role-Commitment and Delinquency: A Theory of Differential Social Control," *American Sociological Review* 59 (1994): 400–437.

154. Karen Heimer, "Gender, Race, and the Pathways to Delinquency: An Interactionist Explanation," in *Crime and Inequality*, ed. John Hagan and Ruth Peterson (Stanford, Calif.: Stanford University Press, 1995), pp. 32–57.

155. Heimer and Matsueda, "Role-Taking, Role-Commitment and Delinquency."

156. See, for example, Howard Kaplan and Hiroshi Fukurai, "Negative Social Sanctions, Self-Rejection, and Drug Use," *Youth and Society* 23 (1992): 275–98; Howard Kaplan and Robert Johnson, "Negative Social Sanctions and Juvenile Delinquency: Effects of Labeling in a Model of Deviant Behavior," *Social Science Quarterly* 72 (1991): 98–122; Howard Kaplan, Robert Johnson, and Carol Bailey, "Deviant Peers and Deviant Behavior: Further Elaboration of a Model," *Social Psychology Quarterly* 30 (1987): 277–84.

157. Howard Kaplan, *Toward a General Theory of Deviance: Contributions from Perspectives on Deviance and Criminality* (College Station, Tex: Texas A&M University, n.d.).

158. John Lofland, *Deviance and Identity* (Englewood Cliffs, N.J.: Prentice-Hall, 1969).

159. Frank Tannenbaum, *Crime and the Community* (New York: Columbia University Press, 1938), pp. 19–20.

160. Edwin Lemert, *Social Pathology* (New York: McGraw-Hill, 1951).

161. Lemert, *Social Pathology*, p. 75.

162. National Minority Council on Criminal Justice, *The Inequality of Justice* (Washington, D.C.: National Minority Advisory Council on Criminal Justice, 1981), p. 200.

163. Carl Pope and William Feyerherm, "Minority Status and Juvenile Justice Processing," *Criminal Justice Abstracts* 22 (1990): 327–36; see also Carl Pope, "Race and Crime Revisited," *Crime and Delinquency* 25 (1979): 347–57.

164. Leslie Margolin, "Deviance on Record: Techniques for Labeling Child Abusers in Official Documents," *Social Problems* 39 (1992): 58–68.

165. Charles Corley, Stephen Cernkovich, and Peggy Giordano, "Sex and the Likelihood of Sanction," *Journal of Criminal Law and Criminology* 80 (1989): 540–53.

166. Samuel Walker, Cassia Spohn, and Miriam DeLone, *The Color of Justice, Race, Ethnicity and Crime in America* (Belmont, Calif.: Wadsworth, 1996), pp. 145–46.

167. Howard Kaplan and Robert Johnson, "Negative Social Sanctions and Juvenile Delinquency: Effects of Labeling in a Model of Deviant Behavior," *Social Science Quarterly* 72 (1991): 98–122.

168. Ruth Triplett, "The Conflict Perspective, Symbolic Interactionism, and the Status Characteristics Hypothesis," *Justice Quarterly* 10 (1993): 540–58.

169. Ross Matsueda, "Reflected Appraisals, Parental Labeling, and Delinquency: Specifying a Symbolic Interactionist Theory," *American Journal of Sociology* 97 (1992): 1577–1611.

170. Suzanne Ageton and Delbert Elliott, *The Effect of Legal Processing on Self-Concept* (Boulder, Colo.: Institute of Behavioral Science, 1973).

171. Christine Bowditch, "Getting Rid of Troublemakers: High School Disciplinary Procedures and the Production of Dropouts," *Social Problems* 40 (1993): 493–507.

172. Melvin Ray and William Downs, "An Empirical Test of Labeling Theory Using Longitudinal Data," *Journal of Research in Crime and Delinquency* 23 (1986): 169–94.

173. Sherman and Smith, with Schmidt and Rogan, "Crime, Punishment, and Stake in Conformity."

174. Charles Tittle, "Two Empirical Regularities (Maybe) in Search of an Explanation: Commentary on the Age/Crime Debate," *Criminology* 26 (1988): 75–85.

175. Tittle, "Two Empirical Regularities (Maybe) in Search of an Explanation."

176. Robert Sampson and John Laub, "A Life-Course Theory of Cumulative Disadvantage and the Stability of Delinquency," in *Developmental Theories of Crime and Delinquency*, ed. Terence Thornberry (New Brunswick, N.J., 1997): 133–161.

177. Douglas Smith and Robert Brame, "On the Initiation and Continuation of Delinquency," *Criminology* 4 (1994): 607–630.

178. Jack Gibbs, "Conceptions of Deviant Behavior: The Old and the New," *Pacific Sociological Review* 9 (1966): 11–13.

179. Schur, *Labeling Deviant Behavior*, p. 14.

180. Ronald Akers, "Problems in the Sociology of Deviance," *Social Problems* 46 (1968): 463.

181. Charles Wellford, "Labeling Theory and Criminology: An Assessment," *Social Problems* 22 (1975): 335–47.

182. Wellford, "Labeling Theory and Criminology," p. 337.

183. Alexander Liazos, "The Poverty of the Sociology of Deviance: Nuts, Sluts, and Perverts," *Social Problems* 20 (1971): 103–20.

184. Tittle, "Two Empirical Regularities (Maybe) in Search of an Explanation."

185. Paul Lipsett, "The Juvenile Offender's Perception," *Crime and Delinquency* 14 (1968): 49; Jack Foster, Simon Dinitz, and Walter Reckless, "Perception of Stigma Following Public Intervention for Delinquent Behavior," *Social Problems* 20 (1972): 202.

186. Charles Tittle, "Labeling and Crime: An Empirical Evaluation," in *The Labeling of Deviance: Evaluating a Perspective*, ed. Walter Gove (New York: John Wiley, 1975), pp. 157–79.

187. David Farrington, "Early Predictors of Adolescent Aggression and Adult Violence," *Violence and Victims* 4 (1989): 79–100.

188. Raymond Paternoster and Leeann Iovanni, "The Labeling Perspective and Delinquency: An Elaboration of the Theory and an Assessment of the Evidence," *Justice Quarterly* 6 (1989): 358–94.

189. Evan Gahr, "Can Shame Tame Cons?" *Insight on the News*, 31 March 1997, p. 38 (available on InfoTrac).

CHAPTER 9

Conflict Theory

INTRODUCTION

It would be unusual to pick up the morning paper and not see headlines loudly proclaiming renewed strife between the United States and its overseas adversaries, between union negotiators and management attorneys, between citizens and police authorities, or between feminists and reactionary males protecting their turf. The world is filled with conflict. Conflict can be destructive when it leads to war, violence, and death; it can be functional when it results in positive social change. Criminologists who view crime as a function of social conflict and economic rivalry are aligned with a number of schools of thought. These are referred to as *conflict, critical, Marxist,* or *radical* schools of criminology, or one of their affiliated branches, including but not limited to *peacemaking, left realism, radical feminism,* and *postmodernism* (also called *deconstructionism*).

Social conflict theorists try to explain crime within economic and social contexts and to express the connection between social class, crime, and social control.[1] Conflict theorists are concerned with issues such as

- The role government plays in creating a crimogenic environment
- The relationship between personal or group power and the shaping of criminal law
- The prevalence of bias in justice system operations
- The relationship between a capitalist, free-enterprise economy and crime rates

Conflict theorists view crime as the outcome of class struggle. Conflict promotes crime by creating a social atmosphere in which the law is a mechanism for controlling dissatisfied, have-not members of society while the wealthy maintain their power. This is why crimes that are the province of the wealthy, such as illegal corporate activities, are sanctioned much more leniently than those, such as burglary, that are considered lower-class activities.

Karl Marx identified the economic structures in society that control all human relations. Marxian theorists reject the notion that law is designed to maintain a tranquil, fair society and that criminals are malevolent people who wish to trample the rights of others. Conflict theorists consider acts of racism, sexism, imperialism, unsafe working conditions, inadequate child care, substandard housing, pollution of the environment, and warmaking as a tool of foreign policy to be "true crimes." The crimes of the helpless—burglary, robbery, and assault—are more expressions of rage over unjust conditions than actual crimes.[2] By focusing on how the capitalist state uses law to control the lower classes, Marxist thought serves as the basis for all conflict theory. This chapter reviews criminological theories that allege that criminal behavior is a function of conflict, a reaction to the unfair distribution of wealth and power in society. The social conflict perspective has several independent branches. One, generally referred to as **conflict theory,** assumes that intergroup conflict and rivalry cause crime. A second branch focuses on the crime-producing traits of capitalist society. The various schools of thought in this area of scholarship include critical, radical, and Marxist criminology.[3] Other sections are devoted to feminist, new realist, peacemaking, and postmodern thought. The terms "radical" or "Marxist" criminology will be used interchangeably, and where appropriate, distinctions will be made between the various schools of thought they contain. See Figure 9.1.

MARXIST THOUGHT

Karl Marx lived in an era of unrestrained capitalist expansion.[4] The tools of the Industrial Revolution had become regular features of society by 1850. Mechanized factories, the use of coal to drive steam engines, and modern transportation all inspired economic development. Production had shifted from cottage industries to large factories. Industrialists could hire workers on their own terms; as a result, conditions in their factories were terrible. Owners and government agents, who were the agents of capitalists, ruthlessly suppressed trade unions that promised workers salvation from these atrocities.

Marx's early career as a journalist was interrupted by government suppression of the newspaper where he worked because of the paper's liberal editorial policy.

Figure 9.1 The Branches of Social Conflict Theory

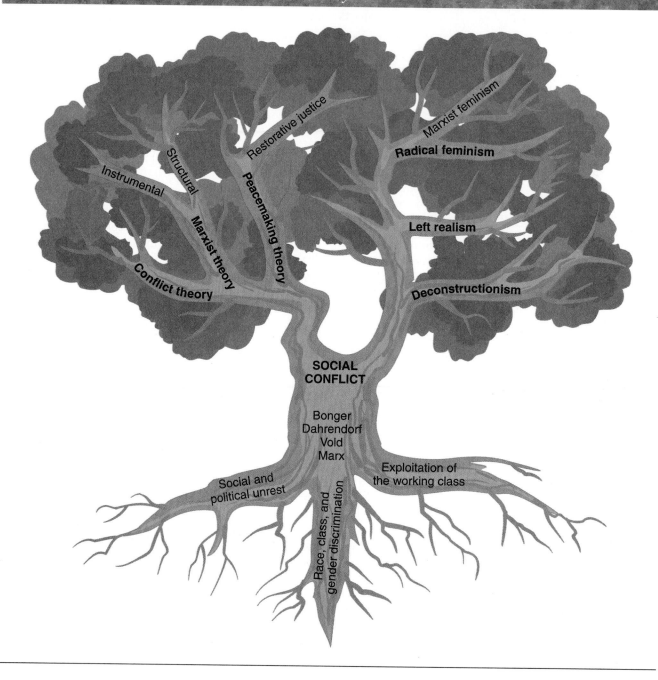

He then moved to Paris, where he met Friedrich Engels (1820–1895), who would become his friend and economic patron. By 1847 Marx and Engels had joined a group of primarily German socialist revolutionaries known as the Communist League.

Productive Forces and Productive Relations

In 1848 Marx issued his famous **communist manifesto.** In this document Marx focused on the economic conditions perpetuated by the capitalist system. He stated that its development had turned workers into a dehumanized mass, existing at the mercy of their capitalist employers. He wrote of the injustice of young children being sent to work in mines and factories from dawn to dusk. He railed against people being beaten down by a system that demanded obedience and cooperation and offered little in return. These oppressive conditions led Marx to conclude that the character of every civilization is determined by its mode of production—the way its people develop and produce material goods (materialism).

Production has two components: (1) **productive forces,** which include such things as technology, energy sources, and material resources; and (2) **productive re-lations,** which are the relationships that exist among the people producing goods and services. The most important relationship in industrial culture is between the owners of the means of production, the **capitalist bourgeoisie,** and the people who do the actual labor, the **proletariat.** Throughout history, society has been organized this way—master–slave, lord–serf, and capitalist–proletarian. According to Marx and Engels, capitalist society develops a rigid class structure with the capitalist bourgeoisie at the top. Next come the working proletariat, who produce goods and services. At the bottom of society are the fringe members who produce nothing and live, parasitically, off the work of others—the **lumpen proletariat.** See Figure 9.2.

In Marxist theory, the term *class* does not refer to an attribute or characteristic of a person or a group; rather, it denotes position in relation to others. Thus it is not necessary to have a particular amount of wealth

or prestige to be a member of the capitalist class; it is more important to have the power to exploit others economically, legally, and socially. The political and economic philosophy of the dominant class influences all aspects of life. Consciously or unconsciously, artists, writers, and teachers bend their work to the whims of the capitalist system. Thus the economic system controls all facets of human life, and people's lives revolve around the means of production. As Marx said,

> In all forms of society, there is one specific kind of production which predominates over the rest, whose relations thus assign rank and influence to the others. It is a general illumination which bathes all the other colours and modifies their particularity. It is a particular ether which determines the specific gravity of every being which has materialized within it.[5]

Marx believed that societies and their structures were not stable and therefore could change through slow evolution or sudden violence. Historically, such change occurs because of contradictions present in a society. These contradictions are antagonism or conflicts between elements in the existing social arrangement that in the long run are incompatible. If these social conflicts are not resolved, they tend to destabilize society, leading to social change.

Surplus Value

How could social change occur in capitalist society? Marx held that the laboring class produces goods that exceed wages in value (the theory of **surplus value**). The excess value goes to capitalists as profit; they use most of it to acquire an ever-expanding capitalist base that relies on advanced technology for efficiency. Because capitalists constantly compete, they must produce goods more efficiently and cheaply. One way is to pay workers the lowest possible wages or to replace them with labor-saving machinery (see Figure 9.3). Soon the supply of efficiently made goods outstrips the ability of the laboring classes to purchase them, a condition that precipitates an economic crisis. During this period of crisis, weaker enterprises fail and are consequently incorporated into ever-expanding, monopolistic megacorporations strong enough to further exploit workers. For example, in the 1980s and 1990s many financial institutions merged, such as Traveler's and Citicorp, BankAmerica and Nationsbank; so did manufacturing enterprises such as Mercedes Benz and Chrysler. This allowed management to control costs, cut excess labor, and reduce the power of workers to demand benefits or wage increases.

Marx believed that the ebb and flow of the capitalist business cycle contained the seeds of its own destruction. He predicted that from its remains would grow a socialist state in which the workers themselves would own the means of production. In his analysis,

Figure 9.2   The Marxist View of Class

The owners of production
Capitalist bourgeoisie

Wages

Profits

The worker
Proletariat

The nonproductive
lumpen proletariat

Figure 9.3 Surplus Value

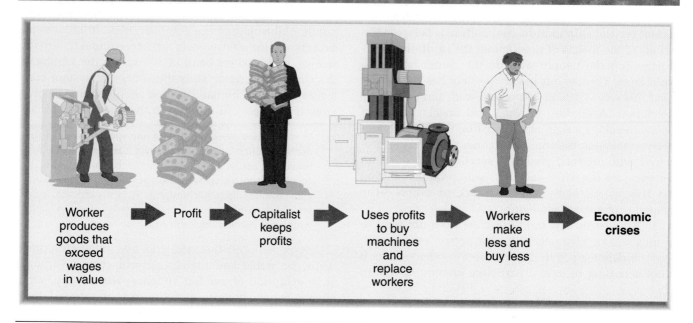

Worker produces goods that exceed wages in value → Profit → Capitalist keeps profits → Uses profits to buy machines and replace workers → Workers make less and buy less → **Economic crises**

Marx used the **dialectic method,** based on the analysis developed by the philosopher Georg Hegel (1770–1831). Hegel argued that for every idea, or thesis, there exists an opposing argument, or **antithesis.** Because neither position can ever be truly accepted, the result is a merger of the two ideas: a synthesis. Marx adapted this analytic method for his study of class struggle. History, argued Marx, is replete with examples of two opposing forces whose conflict promotes social change. When conditions are bad enough, the oppressed will rise up to fight the owners and eventually replace them. Thus, in the end, the capitalist system will destroy itself.

Marx on Crime

Marx did not write a great deal on the subject of crime, but he mentioned it in a variety of passages scattered throughout his writing. He viewed crime as the product of law enforcement policies, akin to a labeling process theory.[6] He also saw a connection between criminality and the inequities found in the capitalist system. He reasoned,

> There must be something rotten in the very core of a social system which increases in wealth without diminishing its misery, and increases in crime even more rapidly than in numbers.[7]

However, his collaborator, Friedrich Engels, spent some time on the subject of crime in his work, *The Condition of the Working Class in England in 1844.*[8] Engels portrayed crime as a function of social demoralization—a collapse of people's humanity reflecting a decline in society. Workers, demoralized by capitalist society, are caught up in a process that leads to crime and violence.

According to Engels, workers are social outcasts, ignored by the structure of capitalist society and treated as brutes.[9] Left to their own devices, working people commit crime because their choice is a slow death of starvation or a speedy one at the hands of the law. The brutality of the capitalist system, he believed, turns workers into animal-like creatures without a will of their own.

DEVELOPING A CONFLICT THEORY OF CRIME

The writings of Karl Marx and Friedrich Engels greatly influenced the development of social conflict thinking. Although Marx himself did not write much on the topic of crime, his views on the relationship between the economic structure and social behavior deeply influenced other thinkers.

Conflict theory was first applied to criminology by three distinguished scholars: Willem Bonger, Ralf Dahrendorf, and George Vold. In some instances, their works share the Marxist view that industrial society is wracked by conflict between the proletariat and the bourgeoisie; in other instances, their writings diverge from Marxist dogma. The writing of each of these pioneers is briefly discussed here.

The Contribution of Willem Bonger

Willem Bonger was born in 1876 in Holland and committed suicide in 1940 rather than submit to Nazi rule. He is famous for his Marxist socialist concepts of crime causation, which were first published in 1916.[10]

Bonger believed that crime is of social, not biological, origin and that, with a few exceptions, crime lies within the boundaries of normal human behavior. According to Bonger, no act is naturally immoral or criminal. He viewed crimes as antisocial acts that reflect current morality, which changes continually along with the social structure. The tension between rapidly changing morality, which is common in modern society, and a comparatively static, predominantly bourgeois criminal, can become great. According to Bonger, the response to crime is applying penalties considered more severe than spontaneous moral condemnation. These penalties are administered by those in political control—that is, by the state. Bonger believed that society is divided into have and have-not groups, not on the basis of innate ability, but because of the system of production. In every society that is divided into a ruling class and an inferior class, penal law serves the will of the ruling class. Even though criminal laws may appear to protect members of both classes, hardly any act is punished that does not injure the interests of the dominant ruling class. Crimes, then, are considered antisocial because they harm those who have the power to control society.

Bonger argued that attempts to control law violations through force are a sign of a weak society. He viewed the capitalist system, characterized by extreme competition, as being held together by force rather than consensus, thus making it a weak system. As a consequence of this force, he claimed that social order is maintained for the benefit of capitalists at the expense of the population as a whole. Although everyone may desire wealth, only the most privileged people, with the most capital, can enjoy luxuries and advantages. Within this society, people care only for their own lives and pleasures, ignoring the plight of the disadvantaged. Because of this dramatic inequity between the haves and have-nots, Bonger claimed, people become egotistical and more capable of crime than if the system were socialist.

The capitalist system makes both the proletariat and the bourgeoisie crime-prone, but only the former are likely to become officially recognized criminals, for two reasons. First, the legal system discriminates against the poor by defending the actions of the wealthy, and second, the proletariat are deprived of the materials that are monopolized by the bourgeoisie.

Upper-class individuals will commit crime if they sense a good opportunity to make a financial gain and if their lack of moral sense enables them to violate social rules. The drive toward success at any price pushes wealthier individuals toward criminality. However, recognized, official crimes are a function of poverty. The relationship can be direct, as when a person steals to survive, or indirect, as when poverty kills the social sentiments between people.

It is not the absolute amount of wealth that affects crime, but its distribution, posits Bonger. If wealth is distributed unequally through the social structure and people are taught to equate economic advantage with superiority, then those who are poor and therefore inferior will be crime-prone. The economic system intensifies any personal disadvantage people have—for example, psychological problems—and increases their propensity to commit crime.

Bonger concluded that almost all crime will disappear if society progresses from competitive capitalism, to monopoly capitalism (in which a relatively few enterprises control the means of production), to having the means of production held in common, to the ultimate state of society, socialism. In other words, Bonger believed that redistributing property according to the maxim "each according to his needs" would be the demise of crime. If this stage of society cannot be reached, a residue of crime will always remain. If socialism can be achieved, however, then remaining crimes will be of the irrational psychopathic type caused by individual mental problems. Bonger's writing continues to be cited often as a source of Marxist thought.

The Contribution of Ralf Dahrendorf

In formulating their views, today's conflict theorists also rely heavily on the writings of pioneering social thinker Ralf Dahrendorf.[11] Dahrendorf believed that modern society is organized into what he called **imperatively coordinated associations.** These associations comprise two groups: those who possess authority and use it for social domination and those who lack authority and are dominated. Because dominating one segment of society (like industry) does not mean dominating another (such as government), society is a plurality of competing interest groups.

In his classic work, *Class and Class Conflict in Industrial Society,* Dahrendorf attempted to show how society has changed since Marx formulated his concepts of class, state, and conflict. Dahrendorf argued that Marx did not foresee the changes that have occurred in the laboring classes. "The working class of today," Dahrendorf stated, "far from being a homogeneous group of equally unskilled and impoverished people, is in fact a stratum differentiated by numerous subtle and not so subtle distinctions."[12] Workers are divided into the *unskilled, semiskilled,* and *skilled;* the interests of one group may not match the needs of the others. Accordingly, Marx's concept of a cohesive proletarian class has proved inaccurate. As a result of his differing perspective, Dahrendorf embraced a non-Marxist conflict orientation. Dahrendorf proposed a **unified conflict theory of human behavior,** which can be summarized as follows:

- Every society is at every point subject to processes of change; social change is everywhere.
- Every society displays at every point dissent and conflict; social conflict is everywhere.

- Every element in a society contributes to its disintegration and change.
- Every society is based on the coercion of some of its members by others.

Dahrendorf did not speak directly to the issue of crime, but his model of conflict serves as a pillar of modern conflict criminology.

The Contribution of George Vold

Although Dahrendorf contributed its theoretical underpinnings, conflict theory was actually adapted to criminology by George Vold.[13] Vold argued that crime can also be explained by social conflict. Laws are created by politically oriented groups who seek government assistance to help them defend their rights and protect their interests. If a group can marshal enough support, a law will be created to curb the interests of some opposition group. According to Vold, the whole political process of lawmaking, lawbreaking, and law enforcement is a direct reflection of deep-rooted conflicts between interest groups. Each competing group desires control over the justice system. Every stage of the process—from passing the law, to prosecuting the case, to developing relationships between inmate and guard and between parole agent and parolee—is marked by conflict. Vold found that criminal acts are a consequence of direct contact between forces struggling to control society. Although their criminal content may mask their political meaning, closer examination of even the most basic violent acts often reveals political undertones.

Vold's model cannot explain all types of crime; it is limited to situations in which rival group loyalties collide. It cannot explain impulsive, irrational acts unrelated to any group's interest. Despite this limitation, Vold found that a great deal of criminal activity results from intergroup clashes.

CONFLICT THEORY

Conflict theory came into criminological prominence during the 1960s. Vold and Dahrendorf had published their influential works in the late 1950s. At the same time, self-report studies began to yield data suggesting that the class–crime correlation found in official crime data was spurious. The self-reports showed that crime and delinquency were much more evenly distributed through the social structure than had been indicated by official statistics, which found more crime in lower-class environments.[14] If this was true, middle-class participation in crime was going unrecorded while the lower class was subjected to discriminatory law enforcement practices.

Criminologists began to view the justice system as a mechanism to control the lower class and maintain the status quo rather than as the means of dispensing evenhanded justice.[15] The publication of important labeling perspective works, such as Lemert's *Social Pathology* and Becker's *Outsiders,* also contributed to the development of the conflict model.[16] Labeling theorists rejected the notion that crime is morally wrong; they called for analysis of the interaction among crime, criminal, victim, and social control agencies. By focusing on social reactions to crime, labeling theorists found that the social context within which crimes occur plays an important role in the criminal process and that agents of social control actually may help produce crime. The criminal's behavior was shaped by the social, political, and legal worlds in which he or she lived.

Some criminologists charged that labeling theory did not go far enough in analyzing the important relationships in society because it was essentially apolitical, satisfied with examining the behavior of social deviants such as drug users and mental patients.[17] As a result, a group of criminologists began to produce scholarship and research directed at

1. Identifying "real" crimes in U.S. society, such as profiteering, sexism, and racism.
2. Evaluating how criminal law is used as a mechanism of social control.
3. Turning the attention of citizens to the inequities in U.S. society.[18]

One of these sociologists, David Greenberg, says that the theme that dominated much of this scholarship was the contention that criminal legislation was determined by the relative power of groups determined to use criminal law to advance their own special interests or to impose their moral preferences on others.[19]

This movement was aided by the widespread social and political upheaval of the late 1960s and early 1970s. These social forces included anti–Vietnam War demonstrations, counterculture movements, and various forms of political protest. Conflict theory flourished within this framework because it provided a systematic basis for challenging the legitimacy of the government's creation and application of law. The federal government agents' crackdown on political dissidents, the prosecution of draft resisters, and the like all seemed designed to maintain control in the hands of political power brokers.

Conflict Criminology

As conflict theory began to influence criminological study, several influential scholars, inspired by the writings of Dahrendorf and Vold, abandoned the criminological mainstream. William Chambliss and Robert Seidman wrote the well-respected treatise *Law, Order and*

According to conflict theory, power is the means by which people shape public opinion to meet their personal interests. Here the family of Castine Deveroux, missing in the Oklahoma City bombing, display their grief in the aftermath of a destructive show of power. Political terrorism and violence may be the product of social conflict.

Power, which documented how the justice system protects the rich and powerful. After closely observing its operations, Chambliss and Seidman concluded,

> In America, it is frequently argued that to have "freedom" is to have a system, which allows one group to make a profit over another. To maintain the existing legal system requires a choice. That choice is between maintaining a legal system that serves to support the existing economic system with its power structure and developing an equitable legal system accompanied by the loss of "personal freedom." But the old question comes back to plague us: Freedom for whom? Is the black man who provides such a ready source of cases for the welfare workers, the mental hospitals, and the prisons "free"? Are the slum dwellers who are arrested night after night for "loitering," "drunkenness," or being "suspicious" free? The freedom protected by the system of law is the freedom of those who can afford it. The law serves their interests, but they are not "society"; they are one element of society. They may in some complex societies even be a majority (though this is very rare), but the myth that the law serves the interests of "society" misrepresents the facts.[20]

Some common objectives of conflict criminology that appear in Chambliss and Seidman's writing include

- Describing how control of the political and economic system affects how criminal justice is administered.
- Showing how definitions of crime favor those who control the justice system.

- Analyzing the role of conflict in contemporary society.

Their scholarship also reflects another major objective of conflict theory: to show how U.S. justice is skewed. Those who deserve to be punished the most (wealthy white-collar criminals whose crimes cost society millions of dollars) are actually punished the least, whereas those whose relatively minor crimes are committed out of economic necessity (petty thieves) receive stricter sanctions.[21]

Power Relations   According to the conflict view, crime is defined by those in power. **Power** refers to the ability of persons and groups to determine and control the behavior of others and to shape public opinion to meet their personal interests. Unequal distribution of power produces conflict, and conflict is rooted in the competition for power. The ability of the powerful majority to control people is exemplified by the relationship between the U.S. justice system and African-Americans. The subtle and not-so-subtle ways the justice system victimizes African-Americans have been well documented.[22] According to this view, poor inner-city youths are driven to commit crimes out of economic desperation. Racial discrimination then results in discretionary decisions by law enforcement officers, who brand them felons, not misdemeanants; they are shunted into criminal courts, not diversion programs.

Busy public defenders often pressure their clients into plea bargains that ensure early criminal records. Health care workers and teachers are quick to report suspected violent acts to the police; this results in frequent, early arrests of minority adults and youths. Police departments routinely search, question, and detain all African-American males in an area if a violent criminal has been described as "looking or sounding black." This is called "racial profiling." By creating the image of pervasive African-American criminality and coupling it with unfair treatment, those in power further alienate this population from the mainstream, perpetuating a class- and race-divided society. Surveys show that African-Americans are much more likely to perceive criminal injustice than white Americans.[23]

The Social Reality of Crime   In his early writings, Richard Quinney embraced a conflict model of crime. He integrated his beliefs about power, society, and criminality into a theory he referred to as the **social reality of crime.** The theory's six propositions are shown in Table 9.1.[24] According to Quinney, criminal definitions (law) represent the interests of those who hold power in society. Where there is conflict between social groups—for example, the wealthy and the poor—those who hold power create laws that benefit themselves and hold rivals in check. This may explain the rather harsh punishments for property crime in the United States; they are designed to help those who are already rich keep their wealth. In contrast, the lenient sanctions attached to corporate crimes are designed to give the already powerful a free hand at economic exploitation.

Quinney wrote that criminal definitions are based on such factors as (1) changing social conditions; (2) emerging interests; (3) increasing demands that political, economic, and religious interests be protected; and (4) changing conceptions of public interest. In the sixth statement on the social reality of crime, Quinney pulls together the ideas he developed in the preceding five: concepts of crime are controlled by the powerful, and the criminal justice system works to secure the needs of the powerful. When people develop behavior patterns that conflict with these needs, the agents of the rich—the justice system—define them as criminals. Because of their reliance on power relations, criminal definitions constantly change to mirror the political organization of society. Law is not an abstract body of rules that represents an absolute moral code; rather, law is an integral part of society, a force that represents a way of life and a method of doing things.

Crime is a function of power relations and an inevitable result of social conflict. Criminals are not simply social misfits, but people who have come up short in the struggle for success and are seeking alternative means of achieving wealth, status, or even survival.[25] Consequently, law violations can be viewed as political or even quasi-revolutionary acts.[26]

Table 9.1   Propositions of the Social Reality of Crime

1. *Definition of crime:* Crime is a definition of human conduct that is created by authorized agents in a politically organized society.
2. *Formulation of criminal definition:* Criminal definitions describe behaviors that conflict with the interests of the segments of society that have the power to shape public policy.
3. *Application of criminal definitions:* Criminal definitions are applied by the segments of society that have the power to shape the enforcement and administration of criminal law.
4. *Development of behavior patterns in relation to criminal definitions:* Behavior patterns are structured in segmentally organized society in relation to criminal definitions, and within this context, persons engage in actions that have relative probabilities of being defined as criminal.
5. *Construction of criminal conceptions:* Conceptions of crime are constructed and diffused in the segments of society by various means of communication.
6. *The social reality of crime:* The social reality of crime is constructed by the formulation and application of criminal definitions, the development of behavior patterns to criminal definitions, and the construction of criminal conceptions.

Source: Richard Quinney, *The Social Reality of Crime* (Boston: Little, Brown, 1970), pp. 15–23.

CONNECTIONS

Quinney has changed his outlook over his long and distinguished career. He now leads the Zen-inspired peacemaking movement, which seeks to remove violence and coercion from the criminal justice system and promotes healing, or restorative justice. See the section on peacemaking later in this chapter.

Norm Resistance   Other criminological writers have made influential contributions to conflict criminology. Austin Turk describes how authority relationships inevitably produce social conflict. Those in society who dominate (the authorities) are in conflict with those who are controlled by, but have little ability to control, the law (the subjects). Conflict is inherent in this superior–subordinate relationship because both groups have their own cultural norms (expressions of ideals and values) and social norms (actual group behaviors). Interaction between authorities and subjects eventually produces **norm resistance,** which is open conflict between the two groups that can take on a number of different forms. The probability of norm resistance is highest under the following conditions:

1. Authorities and subjects are both strongly committed to their cultural norms, which are in opposition to one another.

2. Subjects receive social support from their peers. People with group support resist authority and change.
3. Subjects lack sophistication. People who are sophisticated, who can accurately assess the strengths and weaknesses of their opponents, are better able to avoid conflict with authorities.[27]

Research shows that there is more conflict between authorities and subjects when group sophistication, a key component of Turk's theory, is lacking.[28]

Research on Conflict Theory

Research designed to test conflict theory attempts to show that conflict principles hold up under empirical scrutiny. One method of research is to compare the crime rates of the powerless with those of the elite. Conflict researchers also examine justice system operations to uncover bias and discrimination. In order to identify laws created with the intent of preserving the power of the elite classes at the expense of the poor, they chart the historical development of criminal law. Conflict theorists maintain that social inequality forces people to commit some crimes, such as burglary and larceny, as a means of social and economic survival, whereas other crimes, such as assault, homicide, and drug use, are a means of expressing rage, frustration, and anger. Data show that crime rates vary according to indicators of poverty and need. For example, infant mortality rates have been associated with homicide rates, which shows that a society that cannot care for its young is also prone to social unrest and violence.[29] Crime rates seem strongly related to measures of social inequality such as income level, deteriorated living conditions, and relative economic deprivation.[30]

Another area of conflict-oriented research involves examining the criminal justice system to see if it operates as an instrument of class oppression or as a fair, even-handed social control agency. Some conflict researchers have found evidence of class bias. For example, jurisdictions with significant levels of economic disparity are also the most likely to have large numbers of people killed by police officers. Police may act more forcefully in areas where class conflict creates the perception that extreme forms of social control are needed to maintain order.[31] Criminal courts have also been found to be likely to severely punish members of powerless, disenfranchised groups and to be more lenient with affluent majority group members.[32] When criminals are convicted, both white and black offenders have been found to receive stricter sentences if their personal characteristics (single, young, urban, male) show them to be members of the **dangerous classes.**[33] The unemployed, especially racial minorities, may be perceived as "social dynamite" who present a real threat to society and must be controlled and incapacitated.[34]

Conflict theorists also point to studies showing that the criminal justice system is quick to act when a crime victim is wealthy, white, and male but is disinterested when the victim is poor, black, and female. These studies illustrate how power positions affect justice.[35] Analysis of national population trends and imprisonment rates shows that as the percentage of minority group members increases in a population, the imprisonment rate does likewise.[36] As minority populations increase, the majority may become less tolerant or feel more threatened.

One reason for such displays of discrimination may be the attitudes of decision makers. For example, justice professionals who express racist values (like stating that race-based trait differences exist) are also more punitive, believe that courts should be stricter and that the death penalty is an effective deterrent, and are likely to let race affect their judgments.[37] Critical thinkers argue that there must be a thorough rethinking of the role and purpose of the criminal justice system, giving the powerless a greater voice to express their needs and concerns, if these inequities are to be addressed.[38]

Analysis of Conflict Theory

Conflict theorists attempt to identify the power relations in society and draw attention to their role in promoting criminal behavior. The aim is to describe how class differentials produce an ecology of human behavior that favors the wealthy and powerful over the poor and weak. To believe their view, we must reject the consensus view of crime (Chapter 1), which states that law represents the values of the majority, that legal codes are designed to create a just society, and that by breaking the law, criminals are predators who violate others' rights. To a conflict theorist, criminal law is a weapon employed by the affluent to maintain their dominance in the class struggle. This view is not without its critics. Some criminologists consider the conflict view naive, suggesting instead that crime is a matter of rational choice made by offenders motivated more by greed and selfishness than poverty and hopelessness.[39]

Critics also point to data indicating only a weak relationship between economic factors and crime rates; such data show that crime is less likely to be a function of poverty and class conflict than a product of personal needs, socialization, or some other related factor.[40] For example, Thomas Arvanites found that although race influenced imprisonment, there was little clear evidence that economic factors, such as unemployment rates or poverty levels, influenced crime rates.[41]

Similarly, studies of the criminal justice process, including police discretion, criminal court sentencing, and correctional policy, have not all found indicators of class or race bias, an outcome predicted by conflict theory.[42] For example, socioeconomic status seems unrelated to the length of prison terms assigned by the courts.[43] Evidence of racial bias in sentencing is inconclusive: racial differences in the likelihood of being sent to prison and the length of prison sentences are more often than not insignificant.[44] Evidence that the justice system is not class- and race-biased refutes conflict theory and supports consensus, traditional criminology.

Cross-cultural research indicates that crime rates are not reduced when a free-market system is replaced by a less competitive economic model. One analysis of crime in Tanzania found that when the free enterprise system was replaced by a socialist system, the crime rate actually increased. New crimes, such as theft by public servants and corruption, appeared to increase in response to government policies establishing socialism.[45]

> CONNECTIONS
>
> Racial bias in the criminal justice system is both a highly controversial and important issue. Racial bias in police discretion is covered in Chapter 16, and inequality in sentencing is covered more fully in Chapter 17. Although the direct effect of race is often debated, clear evidence shows that factors *associated* with race affect criminal justice decision making.

Despite its critics, conflict theory has an important niche in criminological literature. However, more radical versions of the general conflict model, such as those discussed next, have become predominant.

MARXIST CRIMINOLOGY

Above all, Marxism is a critique of capitalism.[46]

Marxist criminologists view crime as a function of the capitalist mode of production: capitalism produces haves and have-nots, each engaging in a particular branch of criminality.[47] The mode of production shapes social life. Because economic competitiveness is the essence of capitalism, conflict increases and eventually destabilizes social institutions and the individuals within them.[48]

In a capitalist society, those in political power control the definition of crime and the manner in which the criminal justice system enforces the law.[49] Consequently, the only crimes available to the poor, or proletariat, are the severely sanctioned "street crimes": rape, murder, theft, and mugging. Members of the middle class, or **petit bourgeoisie,** cheat on their taxes and engage in petty corporate crime (employee theft), acts that generate social disapproval but are rarely punished severely. The wealthy bourgeoisie are involved in acts that *should* be described as crimes but are not, such as racism, sexism, and profiteering. Although regulatory laws control illegal business activities, these are rarely enforced, and violations are lightly punished.

> CONNECTIONS
>
> The enforcement of laws against illegal business activities such as price fixing, restraint of trade, environmental crimes, and false advertising is discussed in Chapter 13. Although people are sent to prison for these white-collar offenses, they are still punished more leniently than common-law theft crimes such as burglary and larceny.

Laws regulating corporate crime are actually designed to impress the working class with how fair the justice system is. In reality, the justice system is the equivalent of an army that defends the owners of property in their ongoing struggle against the workers.[50]

The rich are insulated from street crimes because they live in areas far removed from crime. Those who are most powerful use the fear of crime as a tool to maintain their control over society: the poor are controlled through incarceration, and the middle class is diverted from caring about the crimes of the powerful because its members fear the crimes of the powerless.[51] Ironically, they may have more to lose from the economic crimes committed by the rich than the street crimes of the poor. Stock market swindles and savings and loan scams cost the public billions of dollars but are typically settled with fines and probationary sentences.

Because private ownership of property is the true measure of success in capitalism (as opposed to, say, being a worthy person), the state becomes an ally of the wealthy in protecting their property interests. As a result, theft-related crimes are often punished more severely than are acts of violence because while the former may be *interclass,* the latter is typically *intraclass.*

The Development of a Radical Criminology

In 1968 a group of British sociologists formed the National Deviancy Conference (NDC). With about 300 members, this organization sponsored several national symposiums and dialogues. Members came from all walks of life, but at its core was a group of academics who were critical of the positivist criminology being taught in English and U.S. universities. More specifically, they rejected the conservative stance of criminologists and their close financial relationship with government funding agencies. The NDC was not conceived as a Marxist-oriented group; rather, it investigated the concept of deviance from a labeling perspective. It called attention to ways in which social control might actually cause deviance rather than just respond to antisocial behavior. Many conference members became concerned about the political nature of social control. In time, a schism developed within the NDC, with one group clinging to the now-conservative interactionist/labeling perspective, while the second embraced Marxist thought.

In 1973 **radical theory** was given a powerful academic boost when British scholars Ian Taylor, Paul Walton, and Jock Young published *The New Criminology*.[52] This brilliant, thorough, and well-constructed critique of existing concepts in criminology called for the development of new criminological methods of analysis and critique. *The New Criminology* became the standard resource for scholars critical of both the field of criminology and the existing legal process.

While these events were transpiring in Britain, a small group of scholars in the United States began to follow a new radical approach to criminology. The locus of the radical school was the criminology program at the University of California at Berkeley. The most noted Marxist scholars at that institution were Anthony Platt, Paul Takagi, Herman Schwendinger, and Julia Schwendinger. Marxist scholars at other U.S. academic institutions included Richard Quinney (originally a conflict theorist, later a peacemaker), William Chambliss, Steven Spitzer, and Barry Krisberg. The U.S. radicals were influenced by the widespread social ferment during the late 1960s and early 1970s. The war in Vietnam, prison struggles, and the civil rights and feminist movements produced a climate in which criticism of the ruling class seemed a natural by-product. Mainstream, positivist criminology was criticized as being overtly conservative, progovernment, and antihuman. Critical criminologists scoffed when their fellow scholars used statistical analysis of computerized data to describe criminal and delinquent behavior.

Barry Krisberg lamented the social inadequacies of earlier criminologists more than 20 years ago when he wrote, "Many of our scientific heroes of the past, upon rereading, turned out to be racists or, more generally, apologists for social injustice." In response to widespread protests on campuses and throughout society, many of the contemporary giants of social science emerged as defenders of the status quo and vocally dismissed the claims of the oppressed for social justice.[53]

Many of the new Marxist criminologists had enjoyed distinguished careers as positivist criminologists. Some well-known criminologists such as William Chambliss and Richard Quinney shifted their research interests from positivism to social conflict theory to a radical Marxist approach to crime.

Marxists did not enjoy widespread approval at major universities. Rumors that professors were being fired for their political beliefs were common during the 1970s, and the criminology school at Berkeley was eventually closed for what many believe were political reasons. Even today, conflict exists between critical thinkers and mainstream academics. Prestigious Harvard Law School and other law centers have seen conflict, tenure denials, and charges of purges because some professors held critical views of law and society. Although some isolated radicals are tolerated, the majority have been heavily victimized by what has been referred to as "academic McCarthyism."[54]

In the following years, new branches of a radical criminology developed in the United States and abroad. In the early 1980s the left realism school was started by scholars affiliated with the Middlesex Polytechnic and the University of Edinburgh in Great Britain. In the United States, scholars influenced in part by the pioneering work of Dennis Sullivan and Larry Tifft created the peacemaking movement.[55] At the same time, feminist scholars began to critically analyze the relationship between gender, power, and criminality. These movements have coalesced into a rich and complex criminological tradition.

Fundamentals of Marxist Criminology

As a general rule, Marxist criminologists ignore formal theory construction with its heavy emphasis on empirical testing. They scoff at the "objective, value-free" stance of mainstream criminologists and instead advocate a political, ideological basis for criminological scholarship.[56] Crime and criminal justice must be viewed in historical, social, and economic contexts.

Radicals use the conflict definition of crime: crime is a political concept designed to protect the power and position of the upper classes at the expense of the poor. Some, but not all, radicals would include in a list of "real" crimes such acts as violations of human rights due to racism, sexism, and imperialism and other violations of human dignity and physical needs and necessities. Part of the radical agenda, argues criminologist Robert Bohm, is to make the public aware that these behaviors "are crimes just as much as burglary and robbery."[57]

The nature of a society controls the direction of its criminality; criminals are not social misfits, but products of the society and its economic system. "Capitalism," claims Bohm, "as a mode of production, has always produced a relatively high level of crime and violence."[58] According to Michael Lynch and W. Byron Groves, three implications follow from this view:

1. Each society produces its own types and amounts of crime.
2. Each society has its own distinctive ways of dealing with criminal behavior.
3. Each society gets the amount and type of crime that it deserves.[59]

This analysis tells us that criminals are not a group of outsiders who can be controlled by increased law

Women in Hamburg, Germany, search for food in a garbage dump. The conversion of East Germany from communism to capitalism has brought about some of the economic disruption predicted by conflict theorists. It is therefore not surprising that crime and violence have escalated in former socialist republics that have converted to free-market economies.

enforcement. Criminality, instead, is a function of social and economic organization. To control crime and reduce criminality is to end the social conditions that promote crime.

Economic Structure and Surplus Value   Although no single view or theory defines Marxist criminology today, its general theme is the relationship between crime and the ownership and control of private property in a capitalist society.[60] That ownership and control is the principal basis of power in U.S. society.[61] Social conflict is fundamentally related to the historical and social distribution of productive private property. Destructive social conflicts inherent within the capitalist system cannot be resolved unless that system is destroyed or ended.

One important aspect of the capitalist economic system is the effect of surplus value (profit), which can either be reinvested or used to enrich the owners. To increase the rate of surplus value, workers can be made to work harder for less pay, be made more efficient, or be replaced by machines or technology. Therefore, economic growth does not benefit all elements of the population, and in the long run it may produce the same effect as a depression or recession.

As the rate of surplus value increases, more people are displaced from productive relationships, and the size of the marginal population swells. As corporations downsize to increase profits, high-paying labor and managerial jobs are lost to computer-driven machinery.

Displaced workers are forced into service jobs at minimum wage. Many become temporary employees without benefits or a secure position.

As more people are thrust outside the economic mainstream, a condition referred to as **marginalization,** a larger portion of the population is forced to live in areas, known as **structural locations,** conducive to crime. Once people are marginalized, commitment to the system declines, producing another crimogenic force: a weakened bond to society.[62]

The government may be quick to respond during periods of economic decline because those in power assume that poor economic conditions breed crime and social disorder. When unemployment is increasing, public officials assume the worse and devote greater attention to the criminal justice system, perhaps building new prisons to prepare for the coming "crime wave."[63] Empirical research confirms that economic downturns are indeed linked to both crime rate increases and governmental activities such as passing anticrime legislation.[64] For example, as the level of surplus value increases, so too do police expenditures, most likely because of the perceived or real need for the state to control those on the economic margin.[65]

The effect of surplus value is not unique to the United States. Crime and violence have escalated in former socialist republics that have converted to free-market economies. As you may recall, some scholars have criticized conflict theory with the argument that crime rates increase as countries change from capitalism to socialism. Yet evidence shows that an opposite change, from socialism to capitalism, drives crime rates even higher. Both China and the former Soviet Union have experienced an upsurge in gang activity as they embrace market economies; Russia may now have a murder rate higher than that of the United States.[66]

Although these themes can be found throughout Marxist writing, there are actually a number of schools of thought within the radical literature. Some of these different approaches are discussed next.

Instrumental Marxism

One group of Marxists is referred to as **instrumentalists.** They view criminal law and the criminal justice system solely as an instrument for controlling the poor, have-not members of society; the state is the tool of capitalists.

According to the instrumental view, capitalist justice serves the powerful and rich and enables them to impose their morality and standards of behavior on the entire society. Under capitalism, those who wield economic power are able to extend their self-serving definition of illegal or criminal behavior to encompass those who might threaten the status quo or interfere with their quest for ever-increasing profits.[67] For example, the concentration of monetary assets in the nation's largest industrial firms translates into the political power needed to control tax laws to limit the firms' tax liabilities.[68] Some, like Microsoft, have the economic clout to hire top attorneys to defend themselves against governmental antitrust actions, making them almost immune to regulation.

The poor, according to this branch of Marxist theory, may or may not commit more crimes than the rich, but they certainly are arrested and punished more often. Under the capitalist system, the poor are driven to crime because a natural frustration exists in a society in which affluence is well publicized but unattainable. When class conflict becomes unbearable, frustration can spill out in riots, such as the one that occurred in Los Angeles on April 29, 1992, which was described as a "class rebellion of the underprivileged against the privileged."[69]

Because of class conflict, a deep-rooted hostility is generated among members of the lower class toward a social order they are not allowed to shape or participate in.[70] Instrumental Marxists consider it essential to **demystify** law and justice, that is, to unmask its true purpose. They charge that conventional criminology is devoted to identifying the social conditions that cause crime. Criminological theories that focus on family structure, intelligence, peer relations, and school performance keep the lower classes servile by showing why they are more criminal, less intelligent, and more prone to school failure and family problems than the middle class. Demystification involves identifying the destructive intent of capitalist-inspired and -funded criminology. Instrumental Marxists' goal for criminology is to show how capitalist law preserves ruling-class power. The essence of instrumental Marxist theory can be summarized in the following statements:

- U.S. society is based on an advanced capitalist economy.
- The state is organized to serve the interests of the dominant economic class—the capitalist ruling class.
- Criminal law is an instrument of the state and ruling class to perpetuate the existing social and economic order.
- Crime control in capitalist society is accomplished through a variety of institutions and agencies established and administered by a governmental elite, representing ruling-class interests for the purpose of establishing domestic order.
- The contradictions of advanced capitalism—the disjunction between existence and essence—require that the subordinate classes remain oppressed by whatever means necessary, especially through the coercion and violence of the legal system.
- Only with the collapse of capitalist society and the creation of a new society, based on socialist principles, will there be a solution to the crime problem.[71]

Concepts of Instrumental Marxism The writings of a number of other influential instrumental Marxist theorists have helped shape this field of inquiry. According to Herman Schwendinger and Julia Siegel Schwendinger, legal relations in the United States secure an economic infrastructure that centers around a capitalist mode of production. The legal system is designed to guard the position of the owners (bourgeoisie) at the expense of the workers (proletariat). Even common-law crimes, such as murder and rape, are implemented to protect capitalism.

According to the Schwendingers, the laws of the land (such as constitutional laws) are based on the conditions that reproduce the class system as a whole. Laws are aimed at securing the domination of capitalists. Although the legal system may at times secure the interests of the working class, for example, when laws are created that protect collective bargaining, due to the inherent antagonisms built into the capitalist system, all laws generally contradict their stated purpose of producing justice. Legal relations maintain patterns of individualism and selfishness and, in so doing, perpetuate a class system characterized by anarchy, oppression, and crime.[72]

Privilege Barry Krisberg has linked crime to the differentials in privilege that exist in capitalist society.

According to Krisberg, crime is a function of privilege. Crimes are created by the powerful to further their domination. They deflect attention from the violence and social injustice the rich inflict upon the masses to keep them subordinate and oppressed. Krisberg is concerned with how privilege influences criminality. He defines *privilege* as the possession of that which is valued by a particular social group in a given historical period. Privilege includes such rights as life, liberty, and happiness; such traits as intelligence, sensitivity, and humanity; and such material goods as monetary wealth, luxuries, land, and the like. The capitalist system is also concerned with distributing and preserving privilege. Krisberg argues that force—the effective use of violence and coercion—is the major factor in determining which social group ascends to the position of defining and holding privilege.[73]

Other Marxist scholars have called for a review of the role of the professional criminologist. For example, Anthony Platt has charged that criminologists have helped support state repression with their focus on poor and minority-group criminals. He states

> We are just beginning to realize that criminology has serviced domestic repression in the same way that economics, political science, and anthropology have greased the wheels and even manufactured some of the important parts of modern imperialism. Given the ways in which this system has been used to repress and maintain the powerlessness of poor people, people of color, and young people, it is not too farfetched to characterize many criminologists as domestic war criminals.[74]

Platt suggests that criminology must redefine its goals and definitions. He says that criminologists have been constrained by legal definitions of crime, which restricts them to the study and ultimately the control of those legally defined by the ruling class as criminals. Platt believes that a more humanistic definition of crime must reflect the reality of a legal system based on power and privilege. If a human rights definition of crime could be developed, it would free criminologists to examine "imperialism, racism, sexism, capitalism, exploitation, and other political or economic systems which contribute to human misery and deprive people of their potentialities."[75]

Critical criminologist Michael Lynch observes that instrumental Marxist theory may be limited because it is based on incorrect assumptions. It claims that law and justice always operate in the interests of the ruling class; members of the ruling class conspire to control society; and what benefits one member of the ruling class benefits them all. In reality, charges Lynch, some laws benefit the lower classes, and capitalists compete with one another rather than conspire.[76] Because of these deficiencies, some radicals have turned from instrumental theory to embrace structural Marxism.

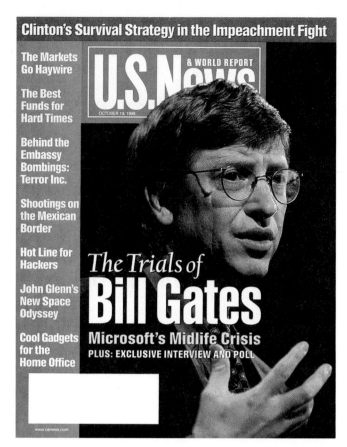

In 1998 and 1999 the Microsoft Corporation was scrutinized by government regulators concerned about its monopolistic practices. This supports the structural Marxist contention that law is not the exclusive domain of the rich, but it is used to maintain the long-term interests of the capitalist system and control members of any class who pose a threat to its existence, for example by gaining monopoly power over fellow capitalists.

Structural Marxism

Structural Marxists disagree with the view that the relationship between law and capitalism is unidirectional, always working for the rich and against the poor.[77] Law is not the exclusive domain of the rich, but rather is used to maintain the long-term interests of the capitalist system and control members of any class who threaten its existence. If law and justice were purely instruments of the capitalist class, why would laws controlling corporate crimes, such as price-fixing, false advertising, and illegal restraint of trade, have been created and enforced? To a structuralist, the law is designed to keep the capitalist system operating efficiently, and anyone, capitalist or proletarian, who rocks the boat is targeted for sanction. For example, antitrust legislation is designed to prevent any single capitalist from dominating the system. If the capital system is to function, no single person can get too powerful at the expense of the economic system as a whole.

There have been a number of attempts to employ these principles in formal theory. Some of these views are discussed in the Criminological Enterprise feature titled "Marxist Theories of Crime."

Research on Marxist Criminology

Marxist criminologists rarely use standard social science methodologies to test their views because many believe the traditional approach of measuring research subjects is antihuman and insensitive.[78] Marxists believe that the research conducted by mainstream liberal and positivist criminologists is designed to unmask weak, powerless members of society so they can be better dealt with by the legal system—a process called **correctionalism.** They are particularly offended by purely empirical studies, such as those designed to show that minority group members have lower IQs than whites or that the inner city is the site of the most serious crime whereas middle-class areas are relatively crime-free.

Empirical research, however, is not considered totally incompatible with Marxist criminology, and there have been some important efforts to quantitatively test its fundamental assumptions.[79] For example, research has shown that the property crime rate reflects a change in the level of surplus value; the capitalist system's emphasis on excessive profits accounts for the need of the working class to commit property crime.[80] Nonetheless, Marxist research tends to be historical and analytical, not quantitative and empirical. Social trends are interpreted with regard to how capitalism has affected human interaction. Marxists investigate both *macro-level issues,* such as how the accumulation of wealth affects crime rates, and *micro-level issues,* such as the effect of criminal interactions on the lives of individuals living in a capitalist society. Of particular importance to Marxist critical thinkers is analyzing the historical development of capitalist social control institutions, such as criminal law, police agencies, courts, and prison systems.

Crime, the Individual, and the State Marxists devote considerable attention to relationships between crime, victims, the criminal, and the state. Two common themes emerge: (1) crime and its control are a function of capitalism, and (2) the justice system is biased against the working class and favors upper-class interests. Marxian analysis of the criminal justice system is designed to identify the often-hidden processes that control people's lives. It takes into account how conditions, processes, and structures evolved into what they are today. One issue considered is the process by which deviant behavior is defined as criminal or delinquent in U.S. society.[81] Another issue is the degree to which class affects the justice system's decision-making process.[82] Also subject to analysis is how power relationships help undermine any benefit the lower class gets from sentencing reforms.[83] In general, Marxist research efforts have yielded evidence linking operations of the justice system to class bias.[84] In addition, some researchers have attempted to show how capitalism intervenes throughout the entire spectrum of crime-related phenomena.

Research by Herman Schwendinger and Julia Schwendinger attempts to show how capitalist social expectations affect women in the aftermath of a rape.[85] The Schwendingers argue that many women who are raped often feel guilty about their role in the rape because they have been raised in a sexist society and have internalized discriminatory norms. The capitalist system has attempted to make women dependent on men by devaluing their labor. For example, a mother's work at home goes unpaid and renders her economically dependent; at the office, women's pay may be lower than men's for doing the same job; even successful women may face the "glass ceiling," which prevents them from attaining top management positions. Because of these enduring limitations, the capitalist system has created a cycle of dependence in which a woman's sense of worth depends on the evaluations of others. Furthermore, negative evaluations, like those created by rape, are likely to be directed inward, creating unwarranted self-recrimination and remorse. Some rape victims may believe they have let down the people they depend on when they are trapped in a rape encounter. A woman's own sense of inadequacy leads to self-blame for the attack and prevents her from focusing on the true culprits: the rapist and the capitalist economic structure that produces rape.

The Schwendingers' research illustrates the Marxian stress on analysis and interpretation of social process and their disdain for quantitative statistical evidence. Critical research of this kind is designed to reinterpret commonly held beliefs about society within the framework of Marxist social and economic ideas.[86] The goal is not to prove statistically that capitalism causes crime but rather to show that it creates an environment in which crime is inevitable. Marxist research is humanistic, situational, descriptive, and analytical rather than statistical, rigid, and methodological.

Historical Analysis A second type of Marxist research focuses on the historical background of commonly held institutional beliefs and practices. One goal is to show how changes in criminal law correspond to the development of the capitalist economy. The second goal is to investigate the development of modern police agencies.

To examine the changes in criminal law, historian Michael Rustigan analyzed historical records to show

The Criminological Enterprise

Marxist Theories of Crime

Radical criminology has been criticized because it offers few formal theories that can be empirically tested. Three of the better-known attempts to articulate a Marxist theory are discussed here.

Integrative-Constitutive Theory

Gregg Barak and Stuart Henry's **integrative-constitutive theory** assumes that crime and its control cannot be separated from the structural and cultural contexts in which it is produced. They define *crime* as the application of harm to others. In our postmodern society, unequal power relations, built upon human differences, provide the conditions that define harm and therefore crime. These power relations often involve pain, conflict, and injury to others. People who are defined as committing criminal acts are at the same time being made unequal or "disrespected"; they are rendered powerless to maintain or express their humanity. In a sense, then, the act of making people "criminals" is a crime. A more realistic or constitutive view of crime would (or should) include current business practices, governmental policies, and unequal social relations.

Much of what occurs in family life (such as sexual harassment, emotional torment, physical beating, and child abuse) is criminal. The emotional torment inflicted on workers by managers who threaten their jobs is extremely harmful and therefore criminal. Government neglect of safety and health regulations is criminal. So is unaffordable housing, which renders so many people homeless. According to constitutive theory, crime must be defined and evaluated in its broadest sense: the amount of harm it inflicts on people.

Crime actually has two aspects: crimes of repression and crimes of reduction. **Crimes of repression** occur when members of a group are prevented from achieving their fullest potential because of racism, sexism, or some other status bias. **Crimes of reduction** occur when the offended parties lose some quality relative to their present standing. The loss can come about through robbery or theft, but they also may be victimized if their dignity is stripped from them when they are taunted by racists.

In order to understand and prevent crime, criminologists must first completely understand what it truly is and the power relations that support its occurrence. This is not easy because each element of harm may have a separate, unique history. Criminologists must focus on the social experiences of different groups (such as African-American females or lower-class white males) and how they interact with one another. Yet charting this interaction is hopelessly complex because each group is itself in constant flux. For example, race-gender-class identities may reinforce criminality in some contexts while helping to neutralize it in others. Criminologists must also understand that they cannot study one group at the expense of another. For example, although gender bias influences females, it also affects males; racism affects majority group members as well as minorities. Crime and its control cannot be understood independently of their cultural and definitional context.

Marxian Theory of Deviance

One of the most highly regarded structural Marxist works is Stephen Spitzer's Marxian theory of deviance. He finds that capitalist law defines as deviant (or criminal) any person who disturbs, hinders, or calls into question any of the following:

- Capitalist modes of appropriating the product of human labor (for example, when the poor steal from the rich)
- The social conditions under which capitalist production takes place (for example, when some people refuse or are unable to perform wage labor)
- Patterns of distribution and consumption in capitalist society (for example, when people use drugs for escape and transcendence rather than sociability and adjustment)
- The process of socialization for productive and nonproductive roles (for example, when youths refuse to be schooled or deny the validity of family life)
- The ideology that supports the functioning of capitalist society (for example, when people advocate alternative forms of social organization)

Among the many important points Spitzer makes is that capitalist societies have special ways of dealing with those who oppose its operation. One mechanism is to normalize formerly deviant or illegal acts by absorbing them into the mainstream of society— for example, through legalizing recreational drugs. Another method is to use **conversion,** which co-opts deviants by making them part of the system; for example, a gang leader may be recruited to work with younger delinquents. Capitalist society also practices **containment,** which segregates deviants into isolated geographic areas so that they can easily be controlled—for example, by creating a ghetto, which further perpetuates the haves and have-nots. Finally, Spitzer believes that capitalist society actively supports some criminal enterprises, such as organized crime, so that they can provide support for groups who

that law reform in nineteenth-century England was largely a response to pressure from the business community to increase punishment for property law violations in order to protect their rapidly increasing wealth.[87] Other research has focused on topics such as how the relationship between convict work and capitalism evolved during the nineteenth century. During this period, prisons became a profitable method of

Figure A Integrated Structural Marxist Theory

Capitalist economic system
- Workplace environment
- Competition

Family relations
- Strain
- Alienation

Adolescent conflict
- Poor schools
- Social maladjustment
- Strain

Deviant peers
- Violence
- Theft

integrates conflict concepts with structural and process factors in a theory of crime that they label **integrated structural theory** (see Figure A). According to Colvin and Pauly, crime is a result of socialization within the family. Coercive family relationships marked by conflict and despair are the forerunner of criminal careers. Family relations and therefore criminality are actually controlled by the marketplace. The quality of one's work experience is shaped by the historical interaction that develops out of competition among capitalists for cheap labor to maximize profits. Wage earners who occupy an inferior position in the economic hierarchy will experience coercive relationships with their supervisors and employers. Negative experiences in the workplace create strain and alienation within the family setting, which in turn may result in inconsistent and overly punitive discipline at home. Juveniles who live in such an environment most likely will become alienated from their parents and, at the same time, will experience adjustment problems in social institutions, especially school. For example, youths growing up in a family headed by parents who are at the bottom of workplace control structures are also the most likely to attend underfunded schools, do poorly on standardized tests, and be placed in slow learning tracks. Each of these factors has been correlated with delinquent behavior.

Negative social relations at home and at school result in feelings of alienation and strain. These feelings are reinforced by association with groups of similarly alienated peers. In some cases peer groups will be oriented toward patterns of violent behavior, while in other instances the groups will enable their members to benefit economically from criminal behavior.

According to integrated structural theory, it is naive to believe that a crime control policy can be formu-

lated without regard for crime's basic root causes. Coercive punishments or misguided treatments cannot be effective unless the core relationships with regard to material production are changed. Those who produce goods must be given a greater opportunity to control the forms of production and be given the power to shape their lives and the lives of their families.

CRITICAL THINKING

1. Considering what these theorists believe about the interlocking relationship between crime and the economic system, what changes would have to be made to reduce or end violence and theft?
2. Do you believe that criminals are forged in the capitalist system? If so, what aspects of that system are most responsible?

 INFOTRAC COLLEGE EDITION RESEARCH

If you are interested in reading more about the Marxist theories discussed here, see:

Sally Simpson and Lori Elis. Is gender subordinate to class? An empirical assessment of Colvin and Pauly's structural Marxist theory of delinquency. *Journal of Criminal Law and Criminology* Fall 1994 85 n2 p453–480
Ronnie Lippens. Critical criminologies and the reconstruction of Utopia. *Social Justice* Spring 1995 v22 n1 p32

Source: Gregg Barak and Stuart Henry, "An Integrative-Constitutive Theory of Crime, Law, and Social Justice," in *Social Justice/ Criminal Justice,* ed. Bruce Arrigo (Belmont, Calif.: West/Wadsworth, 1999), pp. 152–88; Stephen Spitzer, "Toward a Marxian Theory of Deviance," *Social Problems* 22 (1975): 638–51; Mark Colvin and John Pauly, "A Critique of Criminology: Toward an Integrated Structural-Marxist Theory of Delinquency Production," *American Journal of Sociology* 89 (1983): 513–51.

might otherwise become a burden on the state. For example, drug dealers would have no legitimate means of support if their markets were closed, and they and their families might require state welfare assistance. Dealing drugs, which affects only lower-class areas, is tolerated. A "war on drugs" is declared only when drug dealing threatens middle-class neighborhoods.

Integrated Structural Marxist Theory
Conflict theorists Mark Colvin and John Pauly have created a theory that

centralized state control over lower-class criminals, whose labor was exploited by commercial concerns. These criminals were forced to labor in order to pay off wardens and correctional administrators.[88]

Marxists have also found that modern police agencies developed as an antilabor force that provided muscle for industrialists at the turn of the century.[89] Because police often play an active role in putting down labor disputes and controlling political dissidents' activities, their interrelationships with capitalist economics are particularly important to Marxists.[90]

Critique of Marxist Criminology

Marxist criminology has been sharply criticized by some members of the criminological mainstream, who charge that its contribution has "been hot air, heat, but no real light."[91] In turn, radicals have accused mainstream criminologists of being culprits in developing state control over individual lives and selling out their ideals for the chance to receive government funding.

Mainstream criminologists have also attacked the substance of Marxist thought. For example, sociologist Jackson Toby argues that Marxist theory simply rehashes the old tradition of helping the underdog. He likens the ideas behind Marxist criminology to the ideas in such traditional literary works as Robin Hood and Victor Hugo's *Les Miserables,* in which the poor steal from the rich to survive.[92] In reality, Toby claims, most theft is for luxury, not survival. Moreover, he disputes the idea that the crimes committed by the rich are more reprehensible and less understandable than crimes committed by those who live in poverty. Although Toby acknowledges that criminality and immoral behavior occur at every social level, he believes that the relatively disadvantaged contribute disproportionately to crime and delinquency rates.[93]

Other critics, such as criminologist Carl Klockars, charge that Marxists unfairly neglect the capitalist system's efforts to regulate itself (for example, by instituting antitrust regulations) and to create social reforms aimed at helping the poor.[94] They question the logic behind giving poor people more rights as an inducement to control their behavior. They do not feel this is a workable solution to lower-class crime. Klockars also says that Marxists refuse to address the problems and conflicts that exist in socialist countries, such as the gulags and purges of the Soviet Union under Stalin. Similarly, they fail to explain why some highly capitalist countries, such as Japan, have extremely low crime rates. Klockars states that Marxists are too quick to blame capitalism for every human vice without adequate explanation or regard for other social and environmental factors.[95] In so doing, they ignore objective reality and refuse to acknowledge that the members of the lower classes tend to victimize one another. They ignore the plight of the lower classes, who must live in crime-ridden neighborhoods, while they condemn the capitalist system from the security of the "ivory tower."

Marxist scholars respond to their critics by claiming that they rely on "traditional" variables, such as "class" and "poverty," in their analysis of radical thought. Although important, these do not reflect the key issues in the structural and economic process. In fact, like crime, they too may be the outcome of the capitalist system.[96] Marxists also explain that whereas other capitalist nations may have lower crime rates, this does not mean they are crime-free. As an illustration, they point out that even Japan has significant problems with teen prostitution and organized crime.

EMERGING FORMS OF CONFLICT THEORY

Although radical criminologists dispute criticisms, they have also responded by creating new theoretical models that innovatively incorporate Marxist ideas. The following sections discuss in detail some recent forms of radical theory.

Left Realism

Some radical scholars are now addressing the need for the left wing to respond to the increasing power of right-wing conservatives. They are troubled by the emergence of a strict "law and order" philosophy, which has at its centerpiece a policy of punishing juveniles severely in adult court. At the same time, they find the focus of most left-wing scholarship—the abuse of power by the ruling elite—too narrow. It is wrong, they argue, to ignore inner-city gang crime and violence, which often target indigent people.[97] Those who share these concerns are referred to as **left realists.**[98]

Left realism is most often connected to the writings of British scholars John Lea and Jock Young. In their well-respected 1984 work, *What Is to Be Done About Law and Order?,* they reject the utopian views of "idealistic" Marxists who portray street criminals as revolutionaries.[99] They take a more "realistic" approach that street criminals prey on the poor and disenfranchised, thus making the poor doubly abused, first by the capitalist system and then by members of their own class.

Lea and Young's view of crime causation borrows from conventional sociological theory and closely resembles the relative deprivation approach, which posits that experiencing poverty in the midst of plenty creates discontent and breeds crime. As they put it, "The equation is simple: relative deprivation equals discontent; discontent plus lack of political solution equals crime."[100]

Left realists argue that crime victims in all classes need and deserve protection; crime control reflects community needs. They do not view police and the courts as inherently evil tools of capitalism whose tough tactics alienate the lower classes. In fact, they recognize that these institutions offer life-saving public services. The left realists wish, however, that police would reduce their use of force and increase their sensitivity to the public.[101]

Preemptive deterrence is an approach in which community organization efforts eliminate or reduce crime before police forces become necessary. The reasoning behind this is that if the number of marginalized youths (who feel they are not part of society and have nothing to lose by committing crime) could be reduced, then delinquency rates would decline.[102]

To left realists Martin Schwartz and Walter DeKeseredy, street crime is real; the fear of violence among the lower classes has allowed the right wing to seize "law and order" as a political issue.[103] According to Schwartz and DeKeseredy, gangs are not made up of Robin Hoods or revolutionaries who steal from the rich. Most gang kids prey upon members of their own race and class and are happy to keep the proceeds. According to Schwartz and DeKeseredy, gang kids may be the "ultimate capitalists," hustling to obtain the coveted symbols of success.[104]

Although implementing a socialist economy might help eliminate the crime problem, left realists recognize that something must be done to control crime under the existing capitalist system. To create crime control policy, left realists not only welcome radical ideas but also build on the work of strain theorists, social ecologists, and other mainstream views. Community-based efforts seem to hold the most promise of crime control.

Left realism has been critiqued by radical thinkers as legitimizing the existing power structure: by supporting existing definitions of law and justice, it suggests that the "deviant" and not the capitalist system causes society's problems. Critics question whether left realists advocate the very institutions that "currently imprison us and our patterns of thought and action."[105] In rebuttal, left realists would say that it is unrealistic to speak of a socialist state lacking a police force or a system of laws and justice. They believe that the criminal code does, in fact, represent public opinion.

Radical Feminist Theory

Like so many theories in criminology, most of the efforts of radical theorists have been devoted to explaining male criminality.[106] To remedy this theoretical lapse, a number of feminist writers have attempted to explain the cause of crime, gender differences in crime rates, and the exploitation of female victims from a radical feminist perspective. Scholars in this area usually can be described as holding one of two related philosophical orientations: Marxist feminism or radical feminism.

Marxist Feminism The first group of writers can be described as **Marxist feminists,** who view gender inequality as stemming from the unequal power of men and women in a capitalist society. They view gender inequality as a function of female exploitation by fathers and husbands. They suggest that women are considered a commodity worth possessing, like land or money.[107]

Marxist feminists view gender inequality as a function of the exploitation of females by fathers and husbands; women are considered a "commodity" worth possessing, like land or money. The origin of gender differences can be traced to the development of private property and male domination over the laws of inheritance. The abuse of young girls leads them into a life of petty crime, prostitution, and drug abuse.

The origin of gender differences can be traced to the development of private property and male domination of the laws of inheritance, which led to male control over property and power.[108]

A patriarchal system developed in which men's work was valued and women's work was devalued. As capitalism prevailed, the division of labor by gender made women responsible for the unpaid maintenance and reproduction of the current and future labor force, which was derisively called "domestic work." Although this unpaid work done by women is crucial and profitable for capitalists, who reap these free benefits, such labor is exploitative and oppressive for women.[109] Even when women gained the right to work for pay, they were exploited as cheap labor. The dual exploitation of women within the household and in the labor market meant that women would produce far greater surplus value for capitalists than men.

Patriarchy, or male supremacy, has been and continues to be supported by capitalists. This sustains female oppression at home and in the workplace.[110] Although the number of traditional patriarchal families is in steep decline, in those that still exist, a wife's economic dependence ties men more securely to wage-earning jobs, further serving the interests of capitalists by undermining potential rebellion against the system.

Patriarchy and Crime Marxist feminists link criminal behavior patterns to the gender conflict created by the economic and social struggles common in postindustrial societies. James Messerschmidt has made important contributions to understanding the root cause of gender conflict. In his book *Capitalism, Patriarchy, and Crime,* Messerschmidt argues that capitalist society is marked by both patriarchy and class conflict. Capitalists control the labor of workers, while men control women both economically and biologically.[111] This "double marginality" explains why females in a capitalist society commit fewer crimes than males: they are isolated in the family and have fewer opportunities to engage in **elite deviance** (white-collar and economic crimes). They are also denied access to male-dominated street crimes. For example, powerful males will commit white-collar crimes, as will powerful females. However, the female crime rate is restricted because of the patriarchal nature of the capitalist system.[112] Because capitalism renders women powerless, they are forced to commit less serious, nonviolent, self-destructive crimes, such as abusing drugs.

Powerlessness also increases the likelihood that women will become the target of violent acts.[113] When lower-class males are shut out of the economic opportunity structure, they try to build their self-image through acts of machismo; such acts may involve violent abuse of women. This type of reaction accounts for a significant percentage of female victims who are attacked by a spouse or intimate partner.

In his book *Masculinities and Crime,* Messerschmidt expands on these themes.[114] He suggests that in every culture, males try to emulate "ideal" masculine behaviors. In Western culture, this means being authoritative, in charge, combative, and controlling. Failure to adopt these roles leaves men feeling effeminate and unmanly. Their struggle to dominate women in order to prove their manliness is called **doing gender.**

Crime is a vehicle for men to "do gender" because it separates them from the weak and allows them to demonstrate physical bravery. Violence directed toward women is an especially economical way to demonstrate manhood. Would a weak, effeminate male ever attack a woman?

Radical Feminism **Radical feminists** view the cause of female crime as originating with the onset of patriarchy, the subsequent subordination of women, male aggression, and the efforts of men to control females sexually.[115] Radical feminists also focus on the social forces that shape women's lives and experiences to explain female criminality.[116] For example, they attempt to show how the sexual victimization of girls is a function of male socialization because so many young males learn to be aggressive and to exploit women. Males seek out same-sex peer groups for social support; these groups encourage members to exploit and sexually abuse women. On college campuses, peers encourage sexual violence against women who are considered "teasers," "bar pickups," or "loose women." These derogatory labels allow the males to justify their actions; a code of secrecy then protects the aggressors from retribution.[117]

Analyses of national surveys support the radical perspective by showing that about 90 percent of adolescent girls are sexually harassed in school, including one-third who report having been pressured to "do something sexual" and 10 percent who experience sexual violence.[118] Despite the fact that so many young girls are sexual victims, their cries for help are often ignored or demeaned by school officials. When schoolgirls complain about harassment, teachers and school officials sometimes respond by asking the young victim "Did you like it?" or saying, "They [the boys] must be doing it for a reason." Because agents of social control often ignore reports of abuse and harassment, young girls may feel trapped and desperate.

According to the radical feminist view, exploitation triggers the onset of female delinquent and deviant behavior. When female victims run away and abuse substances, they may be reacting to abuse they had suffered at home or at school. Their attempts at survival are labeled as deviant or delinquent behavior.[119] In a sense, the female criminal is a victim herself.

Research shows that a significant number of girls who are sent to hospital emergency rooms to be treated for sexual abuse later report engaging in physical fighting as a teen or as an adult. Many of these abused girls later form romantic attachments with abusive partners. Clearly many girls involved in delinquency, crime, and violence have themselves been the victims of violence in their youth and later as adults.[120]

Radical feminist opinions differ on certain issues. For example, some feminist scholars charge that the movement focuses on the problems and viewpoints of white, middle-class, heterosexual women without taking into account the special interests of lesbians and women of color.[121]

How the Justice System Penalizes Women Radical feminists have indicted the justice system and its patriarchal hierarchy as contributing to the onset of female delinquency. From its inception, the juvenile justice system has viewed most female delinquents as sexually precocious girls who have to be brought under control. Writing about the "girl problem," Ruth Alexander has described how working-class young women desiring autonomy and freedom in the 1920s were considered delinquents and placed in reformatories. Lacking the ability to protect themselves from the authorities, these young girls were considered outlaws in a male-dominated society because they flouted the very narrow rules of appropriate behavior that were applied to females. Girls who rebelled against parental authority or who engaged in sexual behavior deemed inappropriate were incarcerated in order to protect them from a career in prostitution.[122]

In a similar vein, a study of the early Los Angeles Juvenile Court by Mary Odem and Steven Schlossman found that in 1920 so-called delinquency experts identified young female "sex delinquents" as a major social problem that required forceful public response. Civic leaders concerned about immorality mounted a eugenics and social hygiene campaign that identified the "sex delinquent" as a moral and sexual threat to American society and advocated a policy of eugenics or sterilization to prevent these inferior individuals from having children. Los Angeles responded by hiring the first female police officers in the nation to deal with girls under arrest and the first female judges to hear girls' cases in juvenile court; it also established a female detention center and a girls' reformatory.

When Odem and Schlossman evaluated the juvenile court records of delinquent girls who entered the Los Angeles Juvenile Court in 1920, they found that the majority were petitioned for either suspected sexual activity or behavior that placed them at risk of sexual relations. Despite the limited seriousness of these charges, most of the girls were detained before their trials, and while in juvenile hall, all were given a compulsory pelvic exam. Girls adjudged sexually delinquent on the basis of the exam were segregated from the merely incorrigible girls to prevent moral corruption. Those testing positive for venereal disease were usually confined in juvenile hall hospital for one to three months. More than 29 percent of these female adolescents were eventually committed to custodial institutions.[123]

The judicial victimization of female delinquents has continued. A well-known feminist writer, Meda Chesney-Lind, has written extensively about the victimization of female delinquents by agents of the juvenile justice system.[124] She found the following evidence:

- Police in Honolulu were likely to arrest female adolescents for sexual activity and to ignore the same behavior among male delinquents.
- Some 74 percent of the females in her sample were charged with sexual activity or incorrigibility, but only 27 percent of the boys faced the same charges.
- The court ordered physical examinations in over 70 percent of the female cases, but only about 15 percent of the males were forced to undergo this embarrassing procedure.
- Girls were more likely to be sent to a detention facility before trial, and the length of their detention averaged three times that of the boys.
- A higher percentage of females than males were institutionalized for similar delinquent acts.

Chesney-Lind explains her data by suggesting that because female adolescents have a much narrower range of acceptable behavior than male adolescents, any sign of misbehavior in girls is seen as a substantial challenge to authority and to the viability of the double standard of sexual inequality. Female delinquency is viewed as relatively more serious than male delinquency and therefore is more likely to be severely sanctioned.

Power-Control Theory

John Hagan and his associates have created a radical feminist model that uses gender differences to explain the onset of criminality. The most significant statements of these views are contained in a series of scholarly articles and expanded in Hagan's 1989 book, *Structural Criminology*.[125] Hagan's view is that crime and delinquency rates are a function of two factors: (1) class position (power) and (2) family functions (control).[126] The link between these two variables is that within the family, parents reproduce the power relationships they hold in the workplace.

Parents' work experiences and class position influence the criminality of children. A position of dominance at work is equated with control in the household. In paternalistic families, fathers assume the traditional role of breadwinners, while mothers tend to have menial jobs or remain at home to supervise domestic matters. Within the paternalistic home, mothers are expected to control the behavior of their daughters while granting greater freedom to sons. In such a home, the parent–daughter relationship can be viewed as a preparation for the "cult of domesticity," which makes girls' involvement in delinquency unlikely, whereas boys are freer to deviate because they are not subject to maternal control. Consequently, boys exhibit more delinquent behavior than their sisters. On the other hand, in egalitarian families — those in which the husband and wife share similar positions of power at home and in the workplace — daughters gain a kind of freedom that reflects reduced parental control. These families produce daughters whose law-violating behavior mirrors their brothers'. Ironically, these relationships also occur in female-headed households with absent fathers. Similarly, Hagan and his associates found that when fathers and mothers hold equally valued managerial positions, the similarity between the rates of their daughters' and sons' delinquency is greatest. By implication, middle-class girls are the most likely to violate the law because they are less closely controlled than their lower-class counterparts. In homes in which both parents hold positions of power, girls are more likely to have the same expectations of career success as their brothers. Consequently, siblings of both sexes will be socialized to take risks and engage in other behavior related to delinquency.

Power-control theory, then, implies that middle-class youths of both sexes will have higher overall crime rates than their lower-class peers. However, lower-class males may ultimately commit more serious crimes.

Testing Power-Control Theory Power-control theory has received a great deal of attention in the criminological community because it encourages a new approach to the study of criminality, one that includes gender differences, class position, and the structure of the family. Although its basic premises have not yet been thoroughly tested, some critics question its core assumption that power and control variables can explain crime.[127] More specifically, critics fail to replicate the findings that upper-class kids are more likely to deviate than their lower-class peers and that class and power interact to produce delinquency.[128] In response, Hagan and his colleagues suggest that these views are incorrect, and power-control theory can significantly add to our knowledge of the causes of crime.[129]

Despite their assurances, empirical testing may produce further refinement of the theory. For example, Kevin Thompson found few gender-based supervision and behavior differences in worker-, manager-, or owner-dominated households.[130] However, parental supervision practices were quite different in families headed by the chronically unemployed, and these conformed to the power-control model. The Thompson research indicates that the concept of class employed by Hagan may have to be reconsidered: power-control theory may actually explain criminality among the truly disadvantaged, not the working class.

Postmodern Theory

A number of radical thinkers, referred to as **postmodernists,** have embraced **semiotics** (using language elements as signs or symbols beyond their literal meaning) and **deconstructionist analysis** as a method of understanding all human relations, including criminal behavior. These perspectives critically analyze communication and language in legal codes to determine whether they contain language and content that forces racism or sexism to become institutionalized.[131]

Postmodernists rely on semiotics to conduct their research efforts. For example, the term *special needs children* is designed to describe their learning needs, but it may also characterize these children as either mentally challenged, dangerous, or uncontrollable. Many signs or language groupings operate today. For example, sports rely heavily on the use of signs, and becoming a sports expert means learning terminology such as "blitzing the quarterback" and "a hat trick." These terms convey meaning that is far greater than the words themselves and give sports fans familiar with the signs images that would be lost on others.

Postmodernists believe that value-laden language can promote inequities. "Truth," "identity," "justice," and "power" are all concepts whose meaning is derived from the language dictated by those in power.[132] The law, legal skill, and justice are commodities that can be bought and sold like any other service or product.[133] For example, the O. J. Simpson case is vivid proof that the affluent can purchase a different brand of justice than the indigent.[134]

Postmodernists assert that there are different languages and ways of knowing. Those in power can use their own language to define crime and law while excluding or dismissing those who oppose their control,

Restorative justice advocates campaign against punitive measures such as the death penalty and seek nonviolent alternatives to such punishment. Is it possible to reintegrate all offenders back into society, even those who take another's life?

(like prisoners and the poor). By dismissing these oppositional languages, certain versions of how to think, feel, or act are devalued and excluded. This exclusion is the source of conflict in society.[135]

Peacemaking Criminology

One of the newer movements in radical theory is **peacemaking criminology.** To members of the peacemaking movement, the main purpose of criminology is to promote a peaceful, just society. Rather than standing on empirical analysis of data, peacemaking draws its inspiration from religious and philosophical teachings ranging from Quakerism to Zen.

Peacemakers view the efforts of the state to punish and control as crime-encouraging rather than crime-discouraging. These views were first articulated in a series of books with an anarchist theme written by criminologists Larry Tifft and Dennis Sullivan in 1980.[136] In his foreword to Sullivan's book *The Mask of Love,* Larry Tifft writes, "The violent punishing acts of the state and its controlling professions are of the same genre as the violent acts of individuals. In each instance these acts reflect an attempt to monopolize human interaction."[137]

Sullivan recognizes the futility of correcting and punishing criminals in the context of our conflict-ridden society. He comments, "The reality we must grasp is that we live in a culture of severed relationships, where every available institution provides a form of banishment but no place or means for people to become connected, to be responsible to and for each other."[138] Sullivan suggests, then, that mutual aid rather than coercive punishment is the key to a harmonious society. Today advocates of the peacemaking movement, such as Harold Pepinsky and Richard Quinney (who has shifted his theoretical orientation from conflict theory to Marxism and now to peacemaking), try to find humanist solutions to crime and other social problems.[139] Rather than punishment and prison, they advocate such policies as mediation and conflict resolution.

SOCIAL CONFLICT THEORY AND SOCIAL POLICY

At the core of all the varying branches of social conflict theory is the fact that conflict causes crime. If conflict and competition in society could somehow be reduced, crime rates might fall. Some critical theorists believe that this goal can be accomplished only by thoroughly reordering society so that capitalism is destroyed and a socialist state is created. Others call for a more practical application of conflict principles. Nowhere has this been more successful than in applying peacemaking principles in the criminal justice system.

There has been an ongoing effort to reduce the conflict created by the criminal justice system when it harshly punishes offenders, many of whom are powerless social outcasts. Rather than cast them aside, peacemakers have found a way to bring them back to the community. This peacemaking movement has applied nonviolent methods to what is known as **restorative justice.** Springing from both academia and justice system personnel, the restorative approach relies on nonpunitive strategies to prevent and control crime.[140] The principles of restorative justice are outlined in Table 9.2 and are discussed in the Criminological Enterprise feature titled "Restorative Justice."

Table 9.2 Principles of Restorative Justice

1. Crime is fundamentally a violation of people and interpersonal relationships.
    a. Victims and the community have been harmed and need restoration. Victims include the target of the offense, family members, witnesses, and the community at large.
    b. Victims, offenders, and the affected communities are the key stakeholders in justice. The state must investigate crime and ensure safety, but it is not the center of the justice process. Victims are the key, and they must help in the search for restoration, healing, responsibility, and prevention.
2. Violations create obligations and liabilities.
    a. Offenders have the obligation to make things right as much as possible. They must understand the harm they have caused. Their participation should be as voluntary as possible; coercion is to be minimized.
    b. The community's obligations are to victims, to offenders, and to the general welfare of its members. This includes the obligation to reintegrate offenders back into the community and to ensure them the opportunity to make amends.
3. Restorative justice seeks to heal and put right the wrongs.
    a. Victims' needs are the focal concern of the justice process. Safety is a top priority, and victims should be empowered to participate in determining their needs and case outcomes.
    b. The exchange of information between victim and offender should be encouraged; when possible, face-to-face meetings might be undertaken. There should be mutual agreement over imposed outcomes.
    c. Offenders' needs and competencies need to be addressed. Healing and reintegration are emphasized; isolation and removal from the community are restricted.
    d. The justice process belongs to the community; members are encouraged to "do justice." The justice process should be sensitive to community needs and geared toward preventing similar harm in the future. Early interventions are encouraged.
    e. Justice is mindful of the outcomes, intended and unintended, of its responses to crime and victimization. It should monitor case outcome and provide necessary support and opportunity to all involved. The least restrictive intervention should be used, and overt social control should be avoided.

Source: Howard Zehr and Harry Mika, "Fundamental Concepts of Restorative Justice," *Contemporary Justice Review* 1 (1998): 47–55.

The Criminological Enterprise

Restorative Justice

Restorative justice is based on a social rather than a legal view of crime. A system of justice views crime as an injury to personal and community relations rather than as an abstract legal violation against society. For example, when an offender attacks a victim, the injured target is the party with whom justice should be concerned.

Restorative justice can be contrasted with a legalistic view of criminal punishment. According to the legalistic view, *society*, which consists of formal institutions and individuals, is defined as an aggregation of people over which the state has jurisdiction. Legally this aggregation is assumed to possess the social qualities of a group: common meanings and values, sustained interaction, and symbolic bonds. This can be contrasted with the restorative justice view that society, because of its bureaucratic nature, is incapable of manifesting such social qualities. Only in smaller, less formal, and more cohesive social groups, such as families, congregations, residential communities, and the like, are such qualities found. Therefore, the potential for restoring social relations damaged by crime is found not in the state but in social groups.

Without the capacity to restore damaged social relations, society's response to crime has been almost exclusively punitive. The potential of punitive state sanctions, whether they are intended to punish, deter, or induce treatment, demands an adversarial system of justice as insurance against inflicting undeserved punishment. In attempting to ensure equal protection under the law, the procedural design of the adversarial system purposely limits consideration of the unique personal and social qualities of particular crimes. As a result of its preoccupation with protecting individual rights, the adversarial system encourages the accused to deny, justify, or excuse their actions, thereby precluding the acceptance of responsibility. In addition, the central role of trained professionals (prosecution and defense attorneys) in the adversarial process severely limits the possibility of direct exchanges between victim and offender. Because the adversaries are narrowly defined as the "accused" and the "state" (representing both society and the victim), little or no consideration can be given to community concerns and participation.

Restorative justice, a direct response to the inadequacies of the adversarial process, is guided by three essential principles: community ownership of conflict (including crime); material and symbolic reparation for victims and community; and social reintegration of the offender. The process begins by redefining crime in terms of a conflict among the offender, the victim, and affected constituencies (families, schools, workplaces, and so on). Therefore, the resolution must take place within the context in which the conflict originally occurred rather than be transferred to a specialized institution that has no social connection to the community or group from which the conflict originated. By maintaining "ownership" or jurisdiction over the conflict, the community can express its shared outrage about the offense, which is directly communicated to the offender. The victim is given a chance to voice his or her story, and the offender can directly communicate his or her need for social reintegration and treatment.

Restoration turns the justice system into a healing process rather than a distributor of retribution and revenge. Most people involved in offender–victim relationships actually know one another or were related in some way before the crime took place. According to restorative justice advocates, instead of treating one involved party as a victim deserving sympathy and the other as a criminal deserving punishment, it is more productive to address the issues that produced conflict between these people. Rather than take sides and choose whom to isolate and punish, society should try to reconcile the parties involved in conflict.[141]

Restorative programs typically divert the formal court process. Instead, these programs encourage reconciling the conflicts between offenders and victims through victim advocacy, mediation programs, and **sentencing circles,** in which crime victims and their families are brought together with offenders and their families in an effort to formulate a sanction that addresses the needs of each party.[142]

Negotiation, mediation, consensus building, and peacemaking have been part of the dispute resolution process in European and Asian communities for centuries.[143] Native American and Native Canadian people have long used the type of community participation in the adjudication process (for example, sentencing circles, sentencing panels, and elders panels) that restorative justice advocates now embrace.[144] In some Native American communities, people accused of breaking the law will meet with community members, victims, village elders, and agents of the justice system in a sentencing circle. Each member of the circle expresses his or her feelings about the act that was committed and raises questions or concerns. The accused can express regret about his or her actions and a desire

The restoration process depends on a communicative conception of law as a discussion that is cohesive rather than punitive and disruptive. Communicative law encourages people to discuss their main social problems (which are typically manifested in interpersonal conflict). By regularly engaging in such discourse, members of a group keep alive the sense that law unites them rather than separates them. The restoration process involves informal communication among the victim, offender, and community. Although processes differ in structure and style, their discourse generally includes recognition of the injury to personal and social relations, determination and acceptance of responsibility (ideally accompanied by a statement of remorse), commitment to both material and symbolic reparation, and determination of community support and assistance for both victim and offender. The intended result of the process is to repair injuries suffered by the victim and the community while assuring reintegration of the offender.

Although proponents of restorative justice agree as to what constitutes restoration, a clear division exists between those who believe that justice can be achieved within the context of the existing social structure, and those who contend that significant social

structural change must occur in order for the true potential of justice to be realized. The former argue that the social qualities of the group can be recreated within such processes as family group conferencing, victim–offender reconciliation, and sentencing circles. The latter group suggests that such social qualities cannot be effectively recreated; rather, they must already exist.

The effectiveness of restorative justice ultimately depends on the stake a person has in the community (or a particular social group). If a person does not value his or her membership in the group, he or she will be unlikely to accept responsibility, show remorse, or repair the injuries caused by his or her actions. Existing justice programs, such as mediation programs, will be unable to effectively reach persons who are disengaged from all community institutions. Therefore, the relative effectiveness of existing justice programs provides us with a measurement of the need for structural change.

CRITICAL THINKING

1. Can you propose some alternative restorative methods to reduce the crime problem?
2. What might critics say about your ideas, and how would you answer them?

3. Can you think of a recent situation in which the restorative approach could have been an effective alternative to punishment? If so, what was the situation and what happened? How could restorative justice have been applied?
4. Is there an inherent "urge to punish"? If so, how can it be reduced or neutralized? Remember, more than 75 percent of Americans favor the death penalty.

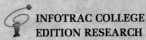
INFOTRAC COLLEGE EDITION RESEARCH

Mediation is a key issue in restorative justice. To learn about both its theoretical base and its practical application, see:

Tag Evers. A healing approach to crime. *The Progressive* Sept 1998 v62 n9 p30(4)
Michael Ornstil. Nailing down mediation agreements. *Trial* June 1996 32 n6 p18

Source: Peter Cordella, *Restorative Justice* (Manchester, N.H.: St. Anselm College, 1997); see also Herbert Bianchi, *Justice as Sanctuary* (Bloomington, Ind.: Indiana University Press, 1994); Nils Christie, "Conflicts as Property," *The British Journal of Criminology* 17 (1977): 1–15; L. Hulsman, "Critical Criminology and the Concept of Crime," *Contemporary Crises* 10 (1986): 63–80.

to change the harmful behavior. People may suggest ways the offender can make things up to the community and those he or she harmed. A treatment program like Alcoholics Anonymous can be suggested, if appropriate. The purpose of this process is to reduce the conflict and harm and restore rather than punish.[145]

SUMMARY

Social conflict theorists view crime as a function of the conflict that exists in society. Social conflict theory is based on the works of Karl Marx as interpreted by Willem Bonger, Ralf Dahrendorf, and George Vold. Conflict theorists suggest that crime in any society is caused by class conflict. Laws are created by those in power to protect their rights and interests.

All criminal acts have political undertones; Richard Quinney has called this concept "the social reality of crime." Unfortunately, research efforts to validate the conflict approach have not produced significant findings. One of conflict theory's most important premises is that the justice system is biased and designed to protect the wealthy. Research has not been unanimous in supporting this point.

Marxist criminology views the competitive nature of the capitalist system as a major cause of crime. The poor commit crimes because of their frustration, anger, and need. The wealthy engage in illegal acts because they are used to competition and because they must do so to keep their positions in society. Marxist scholars such as Quinney, Platt, and Krisberg have attempted to show that the law is designed to protect the wealthy and powerful and to control the poor, have-not members of society. Branches of radical theory include instrumental Marxism and structural Marxism (see Table 9.3 for a summary of these theories).

Research on Marxist theory focuses on how the system of justice was designed and how it operates to further class

Table 9.3 Social Conflict Theories

THEORY	MAJOR PREMISE	STRENGTHS
Conflict theory	Crime is a function of class conflict. Law is defined by people who hold social and political power.	Accounts for class differentials in the crime rate. Shows how class conflict influences behavior.
Marxist theory	The capitalist means of production creates class conflict. Crime is a rebellion of the lower class. The criminal justice system is an agent of class warfare.	Accounts for the associations between economic structure and crime rates.
Instrumental Marxist theory	Criminals are revolutionaries. The real crimes are sexism, racism, and profiteering.	Broadens the definition of crime and demystifies or explains the historical development of law.
Structural Marxist theory	The law is designed to sustain the capitalist economic system.	Explains the existence of white-collar crime and business control laws.
Radical feminist theory	The capital system creates patriarchy, which oppresses women.	Explains gender bias, violence against women, and repression.
Left realism	Crime is a function of relative deprivation; criminals prey on the poor.	Represents a compromise between conflict and traditional criminology.
Deconstructionism	Language controls the meaning and use of the law.	Provides a critical analysis of meaning.
Peacemaking	Peace and humanism can reduce crime; conflict resolution strategies can work.	Offers a new approach to crime control through mediation.

interests. Often this research uses historical analysis to show how the capitalist classes have exerted their control over the police, courts, and correctional agencies. Both Marxist and conflict criminology have been heavily criticized by consensus criminologists. Jackson Toby sees Marxists as sentimental and unwilling to face reality. Carl Klockars suggests Marxists make fundamental errors in their concepts of ownership and class interest.

During the 1990s new forms of conflict theory emerged. Feminist writers draw attention to the influence of patriarchal society on crime; left realism takes a centrist position on crime by showing its rational, destructive nature; peacemaking criminology calls for humanism in criminology; and deconstructionism looks at the symbolic meaning of law and culture.

 See the book-specific web site at www.cj.wadsworth.com for additional chapter links, discussions, and quizzes.

THINKING LIKE A CRIMINOLOGIST

An interim evaluation of Restoration House's New Hope for Families program, a community-based residential treatment program for women with dependent children, shows that 70 percent of women who complete follow-up interviews six months after treatment have maintained abstinence or reduced their drug use. The other 30 percent, however, lapse back into their old habits.

The program relies on restorative justice techniques in which community people meet with the women to discuss the harm drug use can cause and how it can damage both them and their children. The community members show their support and help the women find a niche in the community.

Women who complete the Restoration House program improve their employment, reduce parenting stress, retain custody of their children, and restore their physical, mental, and emotional health. The program focuses not only on reducing drug and alcohol use but also on increasing health, safety, self-sufficiency, and positive attitudes.

As a criminologist, would you consider this program a success? What questions would have to be answered before it gets your approval? How do you think the program should handle women who do not succeed in the program? Are there any other approaches you would try with these women? If so, explain.

KEY TERMS

conflict theory
communist manifesto
productive forces
productive relations
capitalist bourgeoisie

proletariat
lumpen proletariat
surplus value
dialectic method
antithesis

imperatively coordinated associations
unified conflict theory of human behavior
power
social reality of crime
norm resistance

dangerous classes
petit bourgeoisie
radical theory
marginalization
structural location
instrumentalists
demystify
structural Marxist
correctionalism
integrative-constitutive theory

crimes of repression
crimes of reduction
conversion
containment
integrated structural theory
left realism
preemptive deterrence
Marxist feminists
patriarchy
elite deviance

doing gender
radical feminists
postmodernists
semiotics
deconstructionist analysis
peacemaking criminology
restorative justice
sentencing circles

NOTES

1. Michael Lynch, "Rediscovering Criminology: Lessons from the Marxist Tradition," in *Marxist Sociology: Surveys of Contemporary Theory and Research,* ed. Donald McQuarie and Patrick McGuire (New York: General Hall Press, 1994).

2. Michael Lynch and W. Byron Groves, *A Primer in Radical Criminology,* 2d ed. (Albany, N.Y.: Harrow and Heston, 1989), pp. 32–33.

3. Lynch and Groves, *A Primer in Radical Criminology,* p. 4.

4. See, generally, Karl Marx and Friedrich Engels, *Capital: A Critique of Political Economy,* trans. E. Aveling (Chicago: Charles Kern, 1906); and Karl Marx, *Selected Writings in Sociology and Social Philosophy,* trans. P. B. Bottomore (New York: McGraw-Hill, 1956). For a general discussion of Marxist thought, see Lynch and Groves, *A Primer in Radical Criminology,* pp. 6–26.

5. Karl Marx, *Grundrisse: Introduction to the Critique of Political Economy,* trans. Martin Nicolaus (New York: Vintage, 1973), pp. 106–107.

6. Lynch, "Rediscovering Criminology."

7. Karl Marx, "Population, Crime and Pauperism," in Karl Marx and Friedrich Engels, *Ireland and the Irish Question* (Moscow: Progress, 1859, reprinted 1971), p. 92.

8. Friedrich Engels, *The Condition of the Working Class in England in 1844* (London: Allen and Unwin, 1950).

9. Lynch, "Rediscovering Criminology," p. 5.

10. Willem Bonger, *Criminality and Economic Conditions* (1916, abridged ed., Bloomington: Indiana University Press, 1969).

11. Ralf Dahrendorf, *Class and Class Conflict in Industrial Society* (Palo Alto, Calif.: Stanford University Press, 1959).

12. Dahrendorf, *Class and Class Conflict in Industrial Society,* p. 48.

13. George Vold, *Theoretical Criminology* (New York: Oxford University Press, 1958).

14. James Short and F. Ivan Nye, "Extent of Undetected Delinquency: Tentative Conclusions," *Journal of Criminal Law, Criminology, and Police Science* 49 (1958): 296–302.

15. For a general view, see David Friedrichs, "Crime, Deviance, and Criminal Justice: In Search of a Radical Humanistic Perspective," *Humanity and Society* 6 (1982): 200–226.

16. Edwin Lemert, *Social Pathology* (New York: McGraw-Hill, 1951); Howard Becker, *Outsiders: Studies in the Sociology of Deviance* (New York: MacMillan, 1963).

17. Alexander Liazos, "The Poverty of the Sociology of Deviance: Nuts, Sluts, and Perverts," *Social Problems* 20 (1972): 103–120.

18. See, generally, Robert Meier, "The New Criminology: Continuity in Criminological Theory," *Journal of Criminal Law and Criminology* 67 (1977): 461–69.

19. David Greenberg, ed., *Crime and Capitalism* (Palo Alto, Calif.: Mayfield, 1981), p. 3.

20. William Chambliss and Robert Seidman, *Law, Order, and Power* (Reading, Mass.: Addison-Wesley, 1971), p. 503.

21. John Braithwaite, "Retributivism, Punishment, and Privilege," in *Punishment and Privilege,* ed. W. Byron Groves and Graeme Newman (Albany, N.Y.: Harrow and Heston, 1986), pp. 55–66.

22. Daniel Georges-Abeyie, "Race, Ethnicity, and the Spatial Dynamic: Toward a Realistic Study of Black Crime, Crime Victimization, and Criminal Justice Processing of Blacks," *Social Justice* 16 (1989): 35–54.

23. John Hagan and Celesta Albonetti, "Race, Class, and the Perception of Criminal Injustice in America," *American Journal of Sociology* 88 (1982): 329–55.

24. Richard Quinney, *The Social Reality of Crime* (Boston: Little, Brown, 1970), pp. 15–23.

25. Austin Turk, *Criminality and Legal Order* (Chicago: Rand McNally, 1969), p. 58.

26. Lynch and Groves, *A Primer in Radical Criminology,* p. 38.

27. Turk, *Criminality and Legal Order.*

28. Richard Greenleaf and Lonn Lanza-Kaduce, "Sophistication, Organization, and Authority–Subject Conflict: Rediscovering and Unraveling Turk's Theory of Norm Resistance," *Criminology* 33 (1995): 565–85.

29. David McDowall, "Poverty and Homicide in Detroit, 1926–1978," *Victims and Violence* 1 (1986): 23–34; David McDowall and Sandra Norris, "Poverty and Homicide in Baltimore, Cleveland, and Memphis, 1937–1980" (paper presented at the annual meeting of the American Society of Criminology, Montreal, November 1987).

30. Judith Blau and Peter Blau, "The Cost of Inequality: Metropolitan Structure and Violent Crime," *American Sociological Review* 147 (1982): 114–29; Richard Block, "Community Environment and Violent Crime," *Criminology* 17 (1979): 46–57; Robert Sampson, "Structural Sources of Variation in Race-Age-Specific Rates of Offending Across Major U.S. Cities," *Criminology* 23 (1985): 647–73.

31. David Jacobs and David Britt, "Inequality and Police Use of Deadly Force: An Empirical Assessment of a Conflict Hypothesis," *Social Problems* 26 (1979): 403–12.

32. Alan Lizotte, "Extra-Legal Factors in Chicago's Criminal Courts: Testing the Conflict Model of Criminal Justice," *Social Problems* 25 (1978): 564–80.

33. Terance Miethe and Charles Moore, "Racial Differences in Criminal Processing: The Consequences of Model Selection on Conclusions About Differential Treatment," *Sociological Quarterly* 27 (1987): 217–37.

34. Tracy Nobiling, Cassia Spohn, and Miriam DeLone, "A Tale of Two Counties: Unemployment and Sentence Severity," *Justice Quarterly* 15 (1998): 459–85.

35. Nancy Wonders, "Determinate Sentencing: A Feminist and Postmodern Story," *Justice Quarterly* 13 (1996): 610–48; Douglas Smith, Christy Visher, and Laura Davidson, "Equity and Discretionary Justice: The Influence of Race on Police Arrest Decisions," *Journal of Criminal Law and Criminology* 75 (1984): 234–49.

36. Thomas Arvanites, "Increasing Imprisonment: A Function of Crime or Socioeconomic Factors?" *American Journal of Criminal Justice* 17 (1992): 19–38.

37. Michael Leiber. Anne Woodrick, and E. Michele Roudebush, "Religion, Discriminatory Attitudes, and the Orientations of Juvenile Justice Personnel: A Research Note," *Criminology* 33 (1995): 431–47; Michael Leiber and Katherine Jamieson, "Race and Decision Making Within Juvenile Justice: The Importance of Context," *Journal of Quantitative Criminology* 11 (1995): 363–88.

38. Dragan Milovanovic, "Postmodern Criminology: Mapping the Terrain," *Justice Quarterly* 13 (1996): 567–610.

39. Jackson Toby, "The New Criminology Is the Old Sentimentality," *Criminology* 16 (1979): 513–26.

40. Kenneth Land and Marcus Felson, "A General Framework for Building Dynamic Macro Social Indicator Models: An Analysis of Changes in Crime Rates and Police Expenditures," *American Journal of Sociology* 82 (1976): 565–604.

41. Arvanites, "Increasing Imprisonment," p. 34.

42. See generally, William Wilbanks, *The Myth of a Racist Criminal Justice System* (Monterey, Calif.: Brooks/Cole, 1987).

43. Theodore Chiricos and Gordon Waldo, "Socioeconomic Status and Criminal Sentencing: An Empirical Assessment of a Conflict Proposition," *American Sociological Review* 40 (1975): 753–72.

44. Stephen Klein, Joan Petersilia, and Susan Turner, "Race and Imprisonment Decisions in California," *Science* 247 (1990): 812–16.

45. Basil Owomero, "Crime in Tanzania: Contradictions of a Socialist Experiment," *International Journal of Comparative and Applied Criminal Justice* 12 (1988): 177–89.

46. Lynch and Groves, *A Primer in Radical Criminology,* p. 6.

47. This section borrows heavily from Richard Sparks, "A Critique of Marxist Criminology," in *Crime and Justice,* vol. 2, ed. Norval Morris and Michael Tonry (Chicago: University of Chicago Press, 1980), pp. 159–208.

48. Barbara Sims, "Crime, Punishment, and the American Dream: Toward a Marxist Integration," *Journal of Research in Crime and Delinquency* 34 (1997): 5–24.

49. Jeffery Reiman, *The Rich Get Richer and the Poor Get Prison* (New York: Wiley, 1984), pp. 43–44.

50. For a general review of Marxist criminology, see Lynch and Groves, *A Primer in Radical Criminology.*

51. Sims, "Crime, Punishment, and the American Dream."

52. Ian Taylor, Paul Walton, and Jock Young, *The New Criminology: For a Social Theory of Deviance* (London: Routledge and Kegan Paul, 1973).

53. Barry Krisberg, *Crime and Privilege: Toward a New Criminology* (Engelwood Cliffs, N.J.: Prentice-Hall, 1975), p. 167.

54. David Friedrichs, "Critical Criminology and Critical Legal Studies," *Critical Criminologist* 1 (1989): 7.

55. See, for example, Larry Tifft and Dennis Sullivan, *The Struggle to Be Human: Crime, Criminology, and Anarchism* (Orkney Islands, Over-the-Water-Sanday: Cienfuegos Press, 1979); Dennis Sullivan, *The Mask of Love* (Port Washington, N.Y.: Kennikat Press, 1980).

56. R. M. Bohm, "Radical Criminology: An Explication," *Criminology* 19 (1982): 565–89.

57. Robert Bohm, "Radical Criminology: Back to the Basics." Paper presented at the annual meeting of the American Society of Criminology, Phoenix, Arizona, November 1993, p. 2.

58. Bohm, "Radical Criminology: Back to the Basics," p. 4.

59. Lynch and Groves, *A Primer in Radical Criminology,* p. 7.

60. W. Byron Groves and Robert Sampson, "Critical Theory and Criminology," *Social Problems* 33 (1986): 58–80.

61. Gregg Barak, "'Crimes of the Homeless' or the 'Crime of Homelessness': A Self-Reflexive, New-Marxist Analysis of Crime and Social Control." Paper presented at the annual meeting of the American Society of Criminology, Montreal, November 1987.

62. Michael Lynch, "Assessing the State of Radical Criminology: Toward the Year 2000." Paper presented at the annual meeting of the American Society of Criminology, Phoenix, Arizona, November 1993.

63. Steven Box, *Recession, Crime, and Unemployment* (London: MacMillan, 1987).

64. David Barlow, Melissa Hickman-Barlow, and W. Wesley Johnson, "The Political Economy of Criminal Justice Policy: A Time-Series Analysis of Economic Conditions, Crime, and Federal Criminal Justice Legislation, 1948–1987," *Justice Quarterly* 13 (1996): 223–41.

65. Mahesh Nalla, Michael Lynch, and Michael Leiber, "Determinants of Police Growth in Phoenix, 1950–1988," *Justice Quarterly* 14 (1997): 144–63.

66. Bohm, "Radical Criminology: Back to the Basics," p. 5.

67. Gresham Sykes, "The Rise of Critical Criminology," *Journal of Criminal Law and Criminology* 65 (1974): 211.

68. David Jacobs, "Corporate Economic Power and the State: A Longitudinal Assessment of Two Explanations," *American Journal of Sociology* 93 (1988): 852–81.

69. Deanna Alexander, "Victims of the L.A. Riots: A Theoretical Consideration." Paper presented at the annual meeting of the American Society of Criminology, Phoenix, Arizona, November 1993.

70. Richard Quinney, "Crime Control in Capitalist Society," in *Critical Criminology,* ed. Ian Taylor, Paul Walton, and Jock Young (London: Routledge and Kegan Paul, 1975), p. 199.

71. Quinney, "Crime Control in Capitalist Society."

72. Herman Schwendinger and Julia Schwendinger, "Delinquency and Social Reform: A Radical Perspective," in *Juvenile Justice,* ed. Lamar Empey (Charlottesville: University of Virginia Press, 1979), pp. 246–90.

73. Krisberg, *Crime and Privilege.*

74. Elliott Currie, "A Dialogue with Anthony M. Platt," *Issues in Criminology* 8 (1973): 28.

75. Currie, "A Dialogue with Anthony M. Platt," p. 29.

76. Lynch, "Rediscovering Criminology," p. 14.

77. John Hagan, *Structural Criminology* (New Brunswick, N.J.: Rutgers University Press, 1989), pp. 110–19.

78. Roy Bhaskar, "Empiricism," in *A Dictionary of Marxist Thought,* ed. T. Bottomore (Cambridge: Harvard University Press, 1983), pp. 149–50.

79. Byron Groves, "Marxism and Positivism," *Crime and Social Justice* 23 (1985): 129–50; Michael Lynch, "Quantitative Analysis and Marxist Criminology: Some Old Answers to a Dilemma in Marxist Criminology," *Crime and Social Justice* 29 (1987): 110–17.

80. Alan Lizotte, James Mercy, and Eric Monkkonen, "Crime and Police Strength in an Urban Setting: Chicago, 1947–1970," in *Quantitative Criminology,* ed. John Hagan (Beverly Hills: Sage, 1982), pp. 129–48.

81. William Chambliss, "The State, the Law, and the Definition of Behavior as Criminal or Delinquent," in *Handbook of Criminology,* ed. D. Glazer (Chicago: Rand McNally, 1974), pp. 7–44.

82. Timothy Carter and Donald Clelland, "A Neo-Marxian Critique, Formulation, and Test of Juvenile Dispositions as a Function of Social Class," *Social Problems* 27 (1979): 96–108.

83. David Greenberg, "Socio-Economic Status and Criminal Sentences: Is There an Association?" *American Sociological Review* 42 (1977): 174–75; David Greenberg and Drew Humphries, "The Co-optation of Fixed Sentencing Reform," *Crime and Delinquency* 26 (1980): 206–225.

84. Steven Box, *Power, Crime and Mystification* (London: Tavistock, 1984); Gregg Barak, *In Defense of Whom? A Critique of Criminal Justice Reform* (Cincinnati: Anderson Publishing, 1980); for an opposing view, see Franklin Williams, "Conflict Theory and Differential Processing: An Analysis of the Research Literature," in *Radical Criminology: The Coming Crisis,* ed. J. Inciardi (Beverly Hills: Sage, 1980), pp. 213–31.

85. Herman Schwendinger and Julia Schwendinger, *Rape and Inequality* (Newbury Park, Calif., Sage, 1983); Herman Schwendinger and Julia Schwendinger, "Rape Victims and the False Sense of Guilt," *Crime and Social Justice* 13 (1980): 4–17.

86. For more of their work, see Herman Schwendinger and Julia Schwendinger, *Adolescent Subcultures and Delinquency* (New York: Praeger, 1985); Herman Schwendinger and Julia Schwendinger, "The Paradigmatic Crisis in Delinquency Theory," *Crime and Social Justice* 18:

70–78 (1982); Herman Schwendinger and Julia Schwendinger, "The Collective Varieties of Youth," *Crime and Social Justice* 5 (1976): 7–25; Herman Schwendinger and Julia Schwendinger, "Marginal Youth and Social Policy," *Social Problems* 24 (1976): 184–91.

87. Michael Rustigan, "A Reinterpretation of Criminal Law Reform in Nineteenth-Century England," in *Crime and Capitalism,* ed. D. Greenberg (Palo Alto, Calif.: Mayfield, 1981), pp. 255–78.

88. Rosalind Petchesky, "At Hard Labor: Penal Confinement and Production in Nineteenth-Century America," in *Crime and Capitalism,* ed. D. Greenberg (Palo Alto, Calif.: Mayfield, 1981), pp. 341–57; Paul Takagi, "The Walnut Street Jail: A Penal Reform to Centralize the Powers of the State," *Federal Probation* 49 (1975): 18–26.

89. Sidney Harring, "Policing a Class Society: The Expansion of the Urban Police in the Late Nineteenth and Early Twentieth Centuries," in *Crime and Capitalism,* ed. D. Greenberg (Palo Alto, Calif.: Mayfield, 1981), pp. 292–313.

90. Steven Spitzer and Andrew Scull, "Privatization and Capitalist Development: The Case of the Private Police," *Social Problems* 25 (1977): 18–29; Dennis Hoffman, "Cops and Wobblies" (Ph.D. diss., Portland State University, 1977).

91. Jack Gibbs, "An Incorrigible Positivist," *Criminologist* 12 (1987): 2–3.

92. Toby, "The New Criminology Is the Old Sentimentality."

93. Richard Sparks, "A Critique of Marxist Criminology," in *Crime and Justice,* vol. 2, ed. Norval Morris and Michael Tonry (Chicago: University of Chicago Press, 1980), pp. 159–208.

94. Carl Klockars, "The Contemporary Crises of Marxist Criminology," in *Radical Criminology: The Coming Crisis,* ed. J. Inciardi (Beverly Hills: Sage, 1980), pp. 92–123.

95. Klockars, "The Contemporary Crises of Marxist Criminology."

96. Michael Lynch, W. Byron Groves, and Alan Lizotte, "The Rate of Surplus Value and Crime: A Theoretical and Empirical Examination of Marxian Economic Theory and Criminology," *Crime, Law, and Social Change* 1 (1994): 1–11.

97. Anthony Platt, "Criminology in the 1980s: Progressive Alternatives to 'Law and Order,'" *Crime and Social Justice* 21–22 (1985): 191–99.

98. See, generally, Roger Matthews and Jock Young, eds., *Confronting Crime* (London: Sage, 1986); for a thorough review of left realism, see Martin Schwartz and Walter DeKeseredy, "Left Realist Criminology: Strengths, Weaknesses, and the Feminist Critique," *Crime, Law, and Social Change* 15 (1991): 51–72.

99. John Lea and Jock Young, *What Is to Be Done About Law and Order?* (Harmondsworth, England: Penguin, 1984).

100. Lea and Young, *What Is to Be Done About Law and Order?,* p. 88.

101. Richard Kinsey, John Lea, and Jock Young, *Losing the Fight Against Crime* (London: Blackwell, 1986).

102. Martin Schwartz and Walter DeKeseredy, *Contemporary Criminology* (Belmont, Calif.: Wadsworth, 1993), p. 249.

103. Schwartz and DeKeseredy, "Left Realist Criminology."

104. Schwartz and DeKeseredy, "Left Realist Criminology," p. 54.

105. Schwartz and DeKeseredy, "Left Realist Criminology."

106. For a general review of this issue, see Kathleen Daly and Meda Chesney-Lind, "Feminism and Criminology," *Justice Quarterly* 5 (1988): 497–538; Douglas Smith and Raymond Paternoster, "The Gender Gap in Theories of Deviance: Issues and Evidence," *Journal of Research in Crime and Delinquency* 24 (1987): 140–72; and Pat Carlen, "Women, Crime, Feminism, and Realism," *Social Justice* 17 (1990): 106–123.

107. Schwendinger and Schwendinger, *Rape and Inequality.*

108. Daly and Chesney-Lind, "Feminism and Criminology."

109. Janet Saltzman Chafetz, "Feminist Theory and Sociology: Underutilized Contributions for Mainstream Theory," *Annual Review of Sociology* 23 (1997): 97–121.

110. Chafetz, "Feminist Theory and Sociology."

111. James Messerschmidt, *Capitalism, Patriarchy, and Crime* (Totowa, N.J.: Rowman and Littlefield, 1986); for a critique of this work, see Herman Schwendinger and Julia Schwendinger, "The World According to James Messerschmidt," *Social Justice* 15 (1988): 123–45.

112. Kathleen Daly, "Gender and Varieties of White-Collar Crime," *Criminology* 27 (1989): 769–93.

113. Jane Roberts Chapman, "Violence Against Women as a Violation of Human Rights," *Social Justice* 17 (1990): 54–71.

114. James Messerschmidt, *Masculinities and Crime: Critique and Reconceptualization of Theory* (Lanham, Md.: Rowman and Littlefield, 1993).

115. For a review of feminist theory, see Sally Simpson, "Feminist Theory, Crime, and Justice," *Criminology* 27 (1989): 605–32.

116. Suzie Dod Thomas and Nancy Stein, "Criminality, Imprisonment, and Women's Rights in the 1990s," *Social Justice* 17 (1990): 1–5.

117. Walter DeKeseredy and Martin Schwartz, "Male Peer Support and Woman Abuse: An Expansion of DeKeseredy's Model," *Sociological Spectrum* 13 (1993): 393–413.

118. Center for Research on Women, *Secrets in Public: Sexual Harassment in Our Schools* (Wellesley, Mass.: Wellesley College, 1993).

119. Daly and Chesney-Lind, "Feminism and Criminology." See also Drew Humphries and Susan Caringella-MacDonald, "Murdered Mothers, Missing Wives: Reconsidering Female Victimization," *Social Justice* 17 (1990): 71–78.

120. Jane Siegel and Linda Meyer Williams, "Aggressive Behavior Among Women Sexually Abused as Children." Paper presented at the American Society of Criminology meeting, Phoenix, Arizona, 1993. Revised version.

121. Susan Ehrlich Martin and Nancy Jurik, *Doing Justice, Doing Gender* (Thousand Oaks, Calif.: Sage, 1996), p. 27.

122. Ruth Alexander, *The "Girl Problem": Female Sexual Delinquency in New York, 1900–1930* (Ithaca, N.Y.: Cornell University Press, 1995).

123. Mary Odem and Steven Schlossman, "Guardians of Virtue: The Juvenile Court and Female Delinquency in Early 20th-Century Los Angeles," *Crime and Delinquency* 37 (1991): 186–203.

124. Meda Chesney-Lind, "Judicial Enforcement of the Female Sex Role: The Family Court and the Female Delinquent," *Issues in Criminology* 8 (1973): 51–69; see also Meda Chesney-Lind, "Women and Crime: The Female Offender," *Signs: Journal of Women in Culture and Society* 12 (1986): 78–96; Meda Chesney-Lind, "Female Offenders: Paternalism Reexamined," in *Women, the Courts, and Equality,* ed. Laura L. Crites and Winifred L. Hepperle (Newbury Park, Calif.: Sage, 1987): 114–39; Meda Chesney-Lind, "Girls' Crime and a Woman's Place: Toward a Feminist Model of Female Delinquency" (paper presented at a meeting of the American Society of Criminology, Montreal, 1987).

125. Hagan, *Structural Criminology.*

126. John Hagan, A. R. Gillis, and John Simpson, "The Class Structure and Delinquency: Toward a Power-Control Theory of Common Delinquent Behavior," *American Journal of Sociology* 90 (1985): 1151–78; John Hagan, John Simpson, and A. R. Gillis, "Class in the Household: A Power-Control Theory of Gender and Delinquency," *American Journal of Sociology* 92 (1987): 788–816.

127. Gary Jensen, "Power-Control Versus Social-Control Theory: Identifying Crucial Differences for Future Research." Paper presented at the annual meeting of the American Society of Criminology, Baltimore, November 1990.

128. Gary Jensen and Kevin Thompson, "What's Class Got to Do with It? A Further Examination of Power-Control Theory," *American Journal of Sociology* 95 (1990): 1009–23. For some critical research, see Simon Singer and Murray Levine, "Power Control Theory, Gender, and Delinquency: A Partial Replication with Additional Evidence on the Effects of Peers," *Criminology* 26 (1988): 627–48.

129. For a lengthy review, see Hagan, *Structural Criminology.*

130. Kevin Thompson, "Gender and Adolescent Drinking Problems: The Effects of Occupational Structure," *Social Problems* 36 (1989): 30–38.

131. See, generally, Lynch, "Rediscovering Criminology," pp. 27–28.

132. See, generally, Stuart Henry and Dragan Milovanovic, *Constitutive Criminology: Beyond Postmodernism* (London: Sage, 1996).

133. Dragan Milovanovic, *A Primer in the Sociology of Law* (New York: Harrow and Heston, 1988), pp. 127–28.

134. See, generally, Henry and Milovanovic, *Constitutive Criminology.*

135. Bruce Arrigo and Thomas Bernard, "Postmodern Criminology in Relation to Radical and Conflict Criminology," *Critical Criminology* 8 (1997): 39–60.

136. See, for example, Tifft and Sullivan, *The Struggle to Be Human;* and Sullivan, *The Mask of Love.*

137. Larry Tifft, Foreword to Sullivan, *The Mask of Love,* p. 6.

138. Sullivan, *The Mask of Love,* p. 141.

139. Richard Quinney, "The Way of Peace: On Crime, Suffering, and Service," in *Criminology as Peacemaking,* ed. Harold Pepinsky and Richard Quinney (Bloomington: Indiana University Press, 1991), pp. 8–9.

140. Kathleen Daly and Russ Immarigeon, "The Past, Present, and Future of Restorative Justice: Some Critical Reflections," *Contemporary Justice Review* 1 (1998): 21–45.

141. Gene Stephens, "The Future of Policing: From a War Model to a Peace Model," in *The Past, Present and Future of American Criminal Justice,* ed. Brendan Maguire and Polly Radosh (Dix Hills, N.Y.: General Hall, 1996), pp. 77–93.

142. Daly & Immarigeon, "The Past, Present, and Future of Restorative Justice," p. 26.

143. Kay Pranis, "Peacemaking Circles: Restorative Justice in Practice Allows Victims and Offenders to Begin Repairing the Harm," *Corrections Today* 59 (1997): 74.

144. Carol LaPrairie, "The 'New' Justice: Some Implications for Aboriginal Communities," *Canadian Journal of Criminology* 40 (1998): 61–79.

145. Adapted from Kay Pranis, "Peacemaking Circles."

CHAPTER 10

Integrated Theories: Latent Trait and Developmental Theories

INTRODUCTION

Whereas early criminologists readily embraced the theoretical work of their colleagues, modern criminologists have tended to specialize in choice, conflict, labeling, control, or some other kind of theory.[1] As a result, criminological theory ranges from the most radical (Marxist theory) to the most conservative (choice theory) views. The differences among these ideological positions create a gulf that sometimes seems impossible to bridge, especially when advocates dismiss competing viewpoints. Recently, however, to derive more powerful, robust explanations of crime, some criminologists have begun integrating individual factors into complex **multifactor theories,** which attempt to blend seemingly independent concepts into coherent explanations of criminality.

A number of circumstances account for the recent popularity of **integrated theories.** One is practical: the development of large, computerized databases and software that facilitates statistical analysis now makes theory integration practical. Criminologists from an earlier era simply did not have the tools to conduct the sophisticated computations necessary for theory integration.

CONNECTIONS

Later in this chapter the age-graded theory of Robert Sampson and John Laub will be discussed in detail. Sampson and Laub first derived their theory using data that had actually been collected more than 40 years before. Using powerful new statistical tools they were able to identify relationships that were beyond the grasp of the social scientists who originally collected the data, Sheldon and Eleanor Glueck. The computational tools available to social scientists today allow them to identify behavioral patterns that were hidden from earlier researchers.

The other reason for integrated theories' popularity is substantive. Single-factor theories focus on the onset of crime; they tend to divide the world into criminals and noncriminals—those who have a crime-producing condition and those who do not. For example, people who feel anomie become deviant; those who do not remain law-abiding. People with high testosterone levels are violent; people with low levels are not.

The view that people can be classified as either criminals or noncriminals, with this status being stable for life, is now being challenged. Criminologists today are concerned with not only the onset of criminality but its termination as well: why do people age out of or desist from crime? If, for example, criminality is a function of lower intelligence, as some criminologists claim, why do most delinquents fail to become adult criminals? It seems unlikely that intelligence increases as young offenders mature. If the onset of criminality can be explained by low intelligence, then some other factor must explain its termination.

CONNECTIONS

The issues of age and crime desistance were discussed in Chapter 3. As you may recall, crime rates peak in the teenage years and then decline. Explaining this decline has become an important focus of criminology.

It has also become important to chart the natural history of a criminal career. Why do some offenders escalate their criminal activities while others decrease or limit their law violations? Why do some offenders specialize in a particular crime while others become generalists? Why do some criminals reduce criminal activity and then resume it once again? Research now shows that some offenders begin their criminal careers at a very early age, whereas others begin later. How can early- and late-onset criminality be explained?[2] This view of the nature of crime is referred to as **developmental criminology.**

Integrated theories have helped focus on the chronic or persistent offender. Although the concept of chronic offenders, who begin their offending careers as children and persist into adulthood, is now an accepted fact, criminologists are still struggling to understand why this is so. They do not fully understand why, when faced with a similar set of life circumstances, like poverty and family dysfunction, one youth becomes a chronic offender while another may commit an occasional illegal act but later desists from crime. Single-factor theories, such as social structure and social process theories, have trouble explaining why only a relatively few of the many individuals exposed to crimogenic influences in the environment actually become chronic offenders.

> CONNECTIONS
>
> As you may recall from Chapter 3, the Philadelphia cohort studies conducted by Wolfgang and his associates identified the existence of a relatively small group of chronic offenders who committed a significant amount of all serious crimes and persisted in criminal careers into their adulthood.

Figure 10.1 Latent Trait Versus Developmental Theories

Latent Trait Theory

- Master trait
  - Personality
  - Intelligence
  - Genetic makeup
- People do not change, criminal opportunities change; maturity brings fewer opportunities
- Early social control and proper parenting can reduce criminal propensity

- Criminal careers are a passage
- Personal and structural factors influence crime
- Change affects crime
- Personal vs. situational

Developmental Theory

- Multiple traits: social, psychological, economic
- People change over the life course
- Family, job, peers influence behavior

By integrating a variety of ecological, social, psychological, biological, and economic factors into a coherent structure, criminologists are attempting to answer these complex questions.

DEVELOPING COMPLEX THEORIES

The earliest integrated theories were referred to as *multifactor theories.* These theories suggest that social, personal, and economic factors all influence criminal behavior. In addition, multifactor theories combine the influences of variables that have been used in structural, socialization, conflict, choice, and trait theories. The multifactor approach allows criminologists to explain both criminal career formation and desistance from crime. According to this approach, although many youths are at risk of committing crime, relatively few face all the hazards that result in a criminal career, including an impulsive personality, a dysfunctional family, a disorganized neighborhood, deviant friends, and school failure.

Efforts to create multifactor theories are not new. More than 20 years ago, criminologist Daniel Glazer combined elements of differential association with classical criminology and control theory in his **differential anticipation theory.**[3] Glazer asserts, "A person's crime or restraint from crime is determined by the consequences he anticipates from it."[4] According to Glazer, people commit crimes whenever they expect that the gains will exceed the losses (rational choice). This decision (whether or not to commit crime) is tempered by the quality of their social bonds and their relationships with others (control theory), as well as their prior learning experiences (learning theory).

Since Glazer's pioneering efforts, significant attempts have been made to integrate such social process concepts as learning, labeling, and control with structural and other variables. These more recent attempts at creating integrated theories can be divided into two distinct groups: **latent trait** and **developmental theories.** The former hold that criminal behavior is controlled by a "master trait," present at birth or soon after, that remains stable and unchanging throughout a person's lifetime. Developmental theorists view criminality as a dynamic process, influenced by individual characteristics as well as social experiences. Whereas latent trait theorists believe that "people don't change, opportunities do," developmental theorists hope for personal change and growth (see Figure 10.1). Each of these two positions is discussed in detail in the following sections.

LATENT TRAIT THEORIES

In a critical 1990 article, David Rowe, D. Wayne Osgood, and W. Alan Nicewander proposed the concept of **latent traits** to explain the flow of crime over the life cycle. Their model assumes that a number of people in the population have a personal attribute or characteristic that controls their inclination or propensity to commit crimes.[5] This disposition or latent trait may be either present at birth or established early in life, and it remains stable over time. Suspected latent traits include defective intelligence, impulsive personality, genetic abnormalities, the physical-chemical functioning of the brain, and environmental influences on brain function such as drugs, chemicals, and injuries.[6] Those who carry one of these latent traits are in danger of becoming career criminals; those who lack the traits have a much lower risk. Latent traits should affect the behavioral choices of all people equally, regardless of their gender or personal characteristics.[7]

CONNECTIONS

Individual-level factors seem ideally suited for a role in theory integration because, as noted in Chapter 6, even ardent biosocial theorists recognize that they cannot by themselves explain crime rate patterns and changes. Some environmental force must interact with them to control criminality.

Because latent traits are stable, people who are antisocial during adolescence are the most likely to persist in crime. The positive association between past and future criminality detected in the cohort studies of career criminals reflects the presence of this underlying crimogenic trait. That is, if low IQ contributes to delinquency in childhood, it should also cause the same people to offend as adults because intelligence is usually stable over the life span.

Whereas the propensity to commit crime is stable, the opportunity to commit crime fluctuates over time. People age out of crime because as they mature there are simply fewer opportunities to commit crime and greater inducements to remain "straight." They may marry, have children, and obtain jobs. The former delinquents' newfound adult responsibilities leave them little time to hang with their friends, abuse substances, and get into scrapes with the law. For example, assume that a stable latent trait such as low IQ causes some people to commit crime. Teenagers have more opportunity to commit crime than adults, so at every level of intelligence, adolescent crime rates will be higher. As they mature, however, teens with both high and low IQs will commit less crime because their adult responsibilities provide them with fewer criminal opportunities. Because of this assumption, latent trait theories integrate concepts usually associated with trait theories (like personality and temperament) and concepts associated with rational choice theories (like criminal opportunity and suitable targets).

We now turn to two of the most prominent examples of latent trait theory.

Human Nature Theory

Latent trait theorists were encouraged when two prominent social scientists, James Q. Wilson and Richard Herrnstein, published their book *Crime and Human Nature* in 1985.[8] This book and its **human nature theory** argue that personal traits, such as genetic makeup, intelligence, and body build, may outweigh the importance of social variables as predictors of criminal activity.

According to Wilson and Herrnstein, all human behavior, including criminality, is determined by its perceived consequences. A criminal incident occurs when an individual chooses criminal over conventional behavior (referred to as noncrime) after weighing the potential gains and losses of each; crime, then, is a function of rational choice. According to Wilson and Herrnstein, "the larger the ratio of net rewards of crime to the net rewards of noncrime, the greater the tendency to commit the crime."[9]

The rewards for crime can include material gain, sexual gratification, revenge, and peer approval. The unpleasant consequences can include pangs of conscience, victim reprisals, social disapproval, and the threat of legal punishment. Although crime's consequences deter some would-be criminals, their impact may be neutralized by the fact that they are typically distant threats, whereas, in contrast, the rewards of crime are immediate. The rewards for choosing noncrime are also gained in the future: if you "stay clean," someday people will respect you, your self-image and reputation will remain untarnished or improve, and you may achieve happiness and freedom.

Of course, one can never be quite sure of the rewards of either crime or noncrime. The burglar may hope for the "big score" but instead may experience arrest, conviction, and incarceration. Conversely, people who obey the law may find that their honesty does not get them to the place in society they desire.

Choosing Crime or Noncrime The choice between crime and noncrime is quite often difficult. Criminal choices are reinforced by the desire to obtain basic rewards (such as food, clothing, shelter, and sex) or learned goals (such as wealth, power, and status) without having to work and save for them. Even if an individual has been socialized to choose noncrime, crime can be an attractive alternative, especially if any potential negative consequences are uncertain and delayed far into the future. Consider, for example, underage cigarette smoking. It is common because its potentially fatal consequences are distant and uncertain; on the other hand, taking cyanide or arsenic is rare because the effects are immediate and certain (although similar in some other ways).

Integrating Social and Individual Traits Wilson and Herrnstein's model is integrative because it assumes that both biological and psychological traits influence the crime–noncrime choice. They see a close link between a person's decision to choose crime and such biosocial factors as low intelligence, mesomorphic body type, genetic influences (parental criminality), and possessing an autonomic nervous system that responds too quickly to stimuli. Psychological traits, like an impulsive or extroverted personality or generalized hostility, also determine the potential to commit crime.

One of Wilson and Herrnstein's more controversial assertions is that the relationship between crime and intelligence is "robust and significant."[10] Although they are not saying that low intelligence by itself guarantees that a person will become a criminal, they are saying that, all things being equal, those who have lower IQs will be more likely to choose crime over noncrime.

In their theory, Wilson and Herrnstein do not ignore the influence of social factors on criminality. They believe that a turbulent family life, school failure, and membership in a deviant teenage subculture also powerfully influence criminality. According to these theorists, biosocial, psychological, and social conditions, working in concert, affect thought patterns and, eventually, individual behavior patterns. For example, intelligence level is considered an important determinant of criminal behavior; its influence is mediated by a social variable, school performance. A child who chronically loses standing in classroom competition may feel justified in settling the score outside by violence, theft, and other forms of defiant illegality. School failure enhances the rewards for crime by engendering feelings of unfairness. In addition, failure in school predicts, to a substantial degree, failure in the marketplace. For someone who stands to gain little from legitimate work, the rewards of noncrime are relatively weak. Failure in school, therefore, not only enhances the rewards of crime, but it predicts weak rewards for noncrime.[11]

Wilson and Herrnstein do not view harsh punishment as the answer to the crime problem. They argue that the solution can be achieved by strengthening the besieged U.S. family and helping it to orient children toward noncriminal solutions to their problems. The family, regardless of its composition, can help a child cultivate character, conscience, and respect for moral order. Similarly, schools can help by teaching the benefits of accepting personal responsibility and, within limits, helping students understand what constitutes "right conduct."

Wilson and Herrnstein have assembled an impressive array of supporting research in *Crime and Human Nature*. Critics of their work say that much of their evidence suffers from sampling inadequacy, questionable measurement techniques, observer bias, and neglect of sociological dimensions.[12] These criticisms aside, their work presents a dramatic attempt to integrate two of the most prominent theoretical movements in the study of criminality.

General Theory of Crime

Another important work, *A General Theory of Crime,* by Michael Gottfredson and Travis Hirschi, has modi-

fied and redefined some of the principles articulated in Hirschi's social control theory by integrating the concepts of control with those of biosocial, psychological, routine activities, and rational choice theories.[13]

The Act and the Offender In their **general theory of crime (GTC)**, Gottfredson and Hirschi consider the criminal offender and the criminal act as separate concepts (see Figure 10.2). On the one hand, criminal acts, such as robberies or burglaries, are illegal events or deeds that people engage in when they perceive them to be advantageous. For example, burglaries are typically committed by young males looking for cash, liquor, and entertainment; the crime provides "easy, short-term gratification."[14] This aspect of the theory relies on concepts developed first as classical theory and later as rational choice and routine activities theories: crime is rational and predictable; people commit crime when it promises rewards with minimal threat of pain; the threat of punishment can deter crime. If targets are well guarded,

According to Michael Gottfredson (left) and Travis Hirschi, the explanation for individual differences in the tendency to commit criminal acts can be found in a person's level of self-control. People with limited self-control tend to be impulsive; they are insensitive, physical (rather than mental), risk taking, shortsighted, and nonverbal, they have a "here and now" orientation, and they refuse to work for distant goals. They might become involved in the distribution of drugs because their impulsive personalities render them incapable of fearing the sanctioning power of the law.

Figure 10.2   The General Theory of Crime

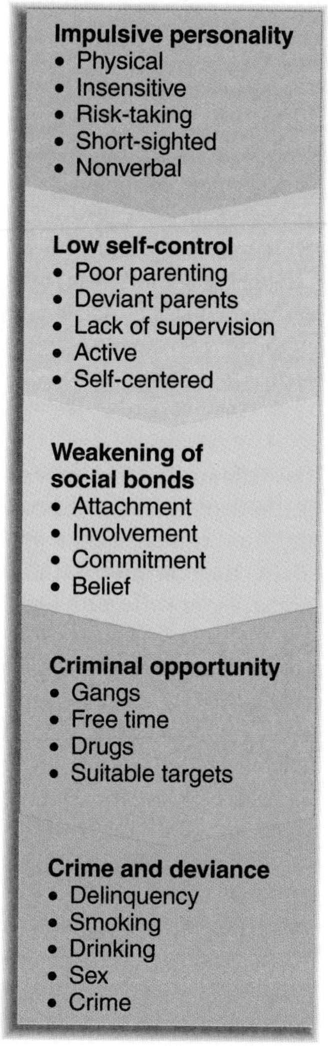

Impulsive personality
- Physical
- Insensitive
- Risk-taking
- Short-sighted
- Nonverbal

Low self-control
- Poor parenting
- Deviant parents
- Lack of supervision
- Active
- Self-centered

Weakening of social bonds
- Attachment
- Involvement
- Commitment
- Belief

Criminal opportunity
- Gangs
- Free time
- Drugs
- Suitable targets

Crime and deviance
- Delinquency
- Smoking
- Drinking
- Sex
- Crime

is the propensity to commit crime; only opportunity changes. The biological and psychological factors that make people impulsive and crime-prone may be inherited or may develop through incompetent or absent parenting. Biosocial theorists recognize that improper parenting can have a long-term impact on human behavior. If a child is not properly socialized, his or her neural pathways are physically affected. Once experiences are ingrained, the brain establishes a pattern of electrochemical activation that remains for life.[15]

What Makes People Crime-Prone?   What, then, causes people to become excessively crime-prone? Gottfredson and Hirschi attribute the tendency to commit crimes to a person's level of self-control. People with limited self-control tend to be impulsive; they are insensitive to other people's feelings, physical (rather than mental), risk takers, shortsighted, and nonverbal.[16] They have a "here and now" orientation and refuse to work for distant goals; they lack diligence, tenacity, and persistence. People lacking self-control tend to be adventuresome, active, physical, and self-centered. As they mature, they often have unstable marriages, jobs, and friendships.[17] People lacking self-control are less likely to feel shame if they engage in deviant acts and are more likely to find them pleasurable.[18] They are also more likely to engage in dangerous behaviors such as drinking, smoking, and reckless driving; all of these behaviors are associated with criminality.[19]

Because those with low self-control enjoy risky, exciting, or thrilling behaviors with immediate gratification, they are more likely to enjoy criminal acts, which require stealth, agility, speed, and power, than conventional acts, which demand long-term study and cognitive and verbal skills. As Gottfredson and Hirschi put it, they derive satisfaction from "money without work, sex without courtship, revenge without court delays."[20] Many of these individuals who have a propensity for committing crime also engage in other behaviors such as smoking, drinking, gambling, and illicit sexuality.[21] Although these acts are not illegal, they too provide immediate, short-term gratification. Table 10.1 lists the elements of self-control.

Gottfredson and Hirschi trace the root cause of poor self-control to inadequate child-rearing practices. Parents who refuse or are unable to monitor a child's behavior, to recognize deviant behavior when it occurs, and to punish that behavior will produce children who lack self-control. Children who are not attached to their parents, who are poorly supervised, and whose parents are criminal or deviant themselves are the most likely to develop poor self-control. In a sense, lack of self-control occurs naturally when steps are not taken to stop its development.[22]

Low self-control develops early in life and remains stable into and through adulthood.[23] Considering the continuity of criminal motivation, Hirschi and Gottfred-

crime rates diminish. Only the truly irrational offender would dare to strike under those circumstances.

On the other hand, criminal offenders are predisposed to commit crimes. They are not robots who commit crime without restraint; their days are also filled with conventional behaviors, such as going to school, parties, concerts, and church. But given the same set of criminal opportunities, such as having a lot of free time for mischief and living in a neighborhood with unguarded homes containing valuable merchandise, crime-prone people have a much higher probability of violating the law than do noncriminals. The propensity to commit crimes remains stable throughout a person's life. Change in the frequency of criminal activity is purely a function of change in criminal opportunity.

By recognizing that there are stable differences in people's propensity to commit crime, the GTC adds a biosocial element to the concept of social control. Individual differences are stable over the life course, and so

Table 10.1 The Elements of Impulsivity: Signs That a Person Has Low Self-Control

- Insensitive
- Physical
- Shortsighted
- Nonverbal
- Here and now orientation
- Unstable social relations
- Enjoys deviant behaviors
- Risk taker
- Refuses to work for distant goals
- Lacks diligence
- Lacks tenacity
- Adventuresome
- Self-centered
- Shameless
- Imprudent
- Lacks cognitive and verbal skills
- Enjoys danger and excitement

son have questioned the utility of the juvenile justice system and of giving more lenient treatment to young delinquent offenders. Why separate youthful and adult offenders legally when the source of their criminality (for example, impulsivity) is essentially the same?[24]

Self-Control and Crime Gottfredson and Hirschi claim that the principles of self-control theory can explain all varieties of criminal behavior and all the social and behavioral correlates of crime. That is, such widely disparate crimes as burglary, robbery, embezzlement, drug dealing, murder, rape, and insider trading all stem from a deficiency of self-control. Likewise, gender, racial, and ecological differences in crime rates can be explained by discrepancies in self-control. Put another way, the male crime rate is higher than the female crime rate because males have lower levels of self-control.

Unlike other theoretical models that explain only narrow segments of criminal behavior (such as theories of teenage gang formation), Gottfredson and Hirschi argue that self-control applies equally to all crimes, ranging from murder to corporate theft. For example, Gottfredson and Hirschi maintain that white-collar crime rates remain low because people who lack self-control rarely attain the positions necessary to commit those crimes. However, the relatively few white-collar criminals lack self-control to the same degree and in the same manner as criminals such as rapists and burglars. Although the criminal activity of individuals with low self-control also declines as those individuals mature, they maintain an offense rate that remains consistently higher than those with strong self-control.

Supporting Evidence for the GTC Following the publication of *A General Theory of Crime,* dozens of research efforts tested the validity of Gottfredson and Hirschi's

theoretical views. One approach involved identifying indicators of impulsiveness and self-control to determine whether scales measuring these factors correlate with measures of criminal activity. A number of studies conducted both in the United States and abroad have successfully showed this type of association.[25] Some of the most important findings are as follows:

- Male and female drunk drivers are impulsive individuals who manifest low self-control.[26]
- Violent recidivists can be distinguished from other offenders on the basis of their impulsive personality structure.[27]
- Incarcerated youths enjoy risk-taking behavior and hold values and attitudes that suggest impulsivity.[28]
- Kids who take drugs and commit crime are impulsive and enjoy engaging in risky behaviors.[29]
- Measures of self-control can predict deviant and antisocial behavior among samples of college students.[30]
- People who commit white-collar and workplace crime have lower levels of self-control than nonoffenders.[31]
- Gang members have lower levels of self-control than the general population; gang members report lower levels of parental management, a factor associated with lower self-control.[32]
- Low self-control shapes perceptions of criminal opportunity and consequently conditions the decision to commit crimes.[33]
- Kids whose problems develop early in life are the most resistant to change in treatment and rehabilitation programs.[34]
- Gender differences in self-control are responsible for crime rate differences. Females who lack self-control are as crime-prone as males with similar personalities.[35]
- Parents who manage their children's behavior increase their self-control, which helps reduce their delinquent activities.[36]

Analyzing the General Theory of Crime Gottfredson and Hirschi's general theory answers many of the questions left unresolved by Hirschi's original single-factor control model. By integrating the concepts of socialization and criminality, Gottfredson and Hirschi help explain why some people who lack self-control can escape criminality, and conversely, why some people who have self-control might not escape criminality. People who are at risk because they have impulsive personalities may forgo criminal careers because there are no criminal opportunities that satisfy their impulsive needs; instead they may find other outlets for their impulsive personalities. In contrast, if the opportunity is strong enough, even people with relatively strong self-control may be tempted to violate the law; the incentives to commit crime may overwhelm self-control.

Integrating criminal propensity and criminal opportunity can explain why some children enter into chronic offending while others living in similar environments are able to resist criminal activity. It can also help us understand why the corporate executive with a spotless record gets caught up in business fraud. Even a successful executive may find self-control inadequate if the potential for illegal gain is large. The driven executive, used to both academic and financial success, may find that the fear of failure can overwhelm self-control. During tough economic times, the impulsive manager who fears dismissal may be tempted to circumvent the law to improve the bottom line.[37]

Although the general theory seems persuasive, several questions and criticisms remain unanswered. Among the most important are the following:

1. **Tautological.** Some critics argue that the theory is tautological or involves circular reasoning: How do we know when people are impulsive? When they commit crimes. Are all criminals impulsive? Of course, or else they would not have broken the law![38]

Gottfredson and Hirschi counter by saying that impulsivity is not itself a propensity to commit crime, but a condition that inhibits people from appreciating the long-term consequences of their behavior. Consequently, if given the opportunity, they are more likely to indulge in criminal acts than their nonimpulsive counterparts.[39] According to Gottfredson and Hirschi, impulsivity and criminality are neither identical nor equivalent. Some impulsive people may channel their reckless energies into noncriminal activity, such as trading on the commodities markets or real estate speculation, and make a legitimate fortune for their efforts.

2. **Personality disorder.** Saying someone lacks self-control implies a personality defect that makes him or her impulsive and rash. The view that criminals have a deviant personality is not new; psychologists have long sought evidence of a "criminal personality."[40] Yet the search for the criminal personality has proven elusive, and there is still no conclusive proof that criminals can be distinguished from noncriminals on the basis of personality alone.

3. **Ecological/individual differences.** The GTC also fails to address individual and ecological patterns in the crime rate. For example, if crime rates are higher in Los Angeles than Albany, New York, can it be assumed that residents of Los Angeles are more impulsive than residents of Albany? There is little evidence of regional differences in impulsivity or self-control. Can these differences be explained solely by variation in criminal opportunity? Few researchers have tried to account for the influence of culture, ecology, economy, and so on. Gottfredson and Hirschi might counter that crime rate differences may reflect criminal opportunity: one area may have more effective law enforcement, more draconian laws, and higher levels of guardianship. In their view, opportunity is controlled by economy and culture.

4. **Racial and gender differences.** Although distinct gender differences in the crime rate exist, there is little evidence that males are more impulsive than females (although females and males differ in many other personality traits).[41] Similarly, Gottfredson and Hirschi explain racial differences in the crime rate as a failure of child-rearing practices in the African-American community.[42] In so doing, they overlook issues of institutional racism, poverty, and relative deprivation, which have been shown to significantly impact crime rate differentials.

5. **Moral beliefs.** The general theory also ignores the moral concept of right and wrong, or "belief," which Hirschi considered a cornerstone in his earlier writings on the social bond.[43] Does this mean that learning and assimilating moral values has little effect on criminality? Belief may be the weakest of the bonds associated with crime, and the general theory may reflect this relationship.[44]

6. **People change.** The general theory assumes that criminal propensity does not change; opportunities change. Is it possible that human personality and behavior patterns remain unaltered over the life course? A number of research efforts show that factors that help control criminal behavior, such as peer relations and school performance, vary over time. Social influences, which are dominant in early adolescence, may fade and be replaced by others in adulthood.[45] For example, maintaining delinquent peers may encourage future criminality; peer relations that develop in adolescence may influence people throughout their lives.[46] As children mature, peer influence continues to grow.[47] Adolescents who spend less time with delinquent friends as they mature also reduce their criminal offending.[48] This finding contradicts the GTC, which suggests the influence of friends should be stable and unchanging.

Research shows that changing life circumstances, such as starting and leaving school, abusing substances, "getting straight," and starting or ending personal relationships, all influence the frequency of offending. For example, people who marry reduce their criminal activity.[49] But getting divorced or becoming widowed elevates offending rates to those of the never-married.[50]

Gottfredson and Hirschi assume that low self-control varies little with age and that low self-control is almost exclusively a product of early childhood rearing; but research shows that self-control may vary with age. As people mature, they may be better able to control their impulsive behavior.[51] These findings contradict the GTC, which assumes that levels of self-control and therefore criminal propensity are constant and independent of personal relationships.

Although these research efforts claim to record change in behavior and personality over time, it is un-

The Criminological Enterprise

Mating Habits and Crime

If impulsivity and lack of self-control are not the key latent traits as Gottfredson and Hirschi suggest, what is? In his **adaptive strategy theory**, evolutionary theorist David Rowe argues that the key latent trait that explains the propensity to commit crime is not impulsivity, but mating habits developed over human history. This argument brings an evolutionary element to latent trait theories.

Rowe agrees that integrating latent traits with social, ecological, and learning variables is the key to understanding both why individuals commit crime and why crime rates vary over time and location. However, according to Rowe, over the course of human existence, humans have devised strategies to make sure they will reproduce and their offspring will thrive. To secure this goal, people are oriented toward either parenting or mating efforts. *Parenting strategies* are those that rely on caring for the young, carefully rearing and protecting them. In contrast, *mating strategies* devote energy to finding mates and protecting them from rivals. Those who favor parenting typically exhibit traits of honesty, nonaggression, empathy, self-control, and

monogamy. Traits associated with mating are deceitfulness, aggression, impulsiveness, and preference for sexual variety: traits that help attract and defend mates.

Crime proneness is related to mating strategies. People who try to maximize their mating potential exhibit strong sex drives, preference for sexual novelty, a lack of strong emotional attachments, lying about one's true emotions, and the use of aggression to deter potential rivals. So although mating may be a normal strategy that has become instinctual in some people, it puts them at risk of pursuing criminal activity. Rowe recognizes that families, peers, and the social milieu also affect how strategies are devised and can enhance or control mating adaptation.

Rowe's theory incorporates elements of r/k selection theory (discussed in Chapter 6), which holds that all organisms can be located along a continuum based on their reproductive drives. Those along the r-end reproduce rapidly whenever they can and invest little in their offspring; those along the k- end reproduce slowly and cautiously and take care in raising their offspring. Males today

lean toward r-selection and are therefore more geared toward violence and aggression.

CRITICAL THINKING

1. If, as Rowe suggests, mating is the key to behavior, what can we do to break the patterns of aggression that have built up?
2. Does this theory mean that little can be done to control or deter violence because it is an inherent human trait?

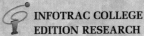 **INFOTRAC COLLEGE EDITION RESEARCH**

Does Rowe's vision of mating habits apply to animal species as well as humans? To find out, read:
Squid sex. *Discover* Oct 1997 v18 n10 p20(1)
Gender-bending bluegills. *Field & Stream* (West ed.), March 1996 v100 n11 p67

Source: David Rowe, "An Adaptive Strategy Theory of Crime and Delinquency," in *Delinquency and Crime*, ed. J. David Hawkins (London: Cambridge University Press, 1996), pp. 268–313.

---

certain whether life changes affect the *propensity* to commit crime or merely the *opportunity*, as Gottfredson and Hirschi would suggest. For example, perhaps single and divorced men have more free time than married fathers who must remain at home and care for children. Also, men who spend less time with their friends as they mature may be spending more with wives and children, who have a stabilizing influence on behavior. Increased levels of offending, then, might be more reflective of criminal opportunity than a change in criminal propensity brought on by the pacifying influence of marriage.

7. **Modest relationship.** Some research results support the proposition that self-control is a causal factor in criminal and other forms of deviant behavior, but that the association is quite modest.[52] This would indicate that other forces influence criminal behavior and that low

self-control alone cannot predict the onset of a criminal or deviant career. Perhaps antisocial behavior is best explained by a condition that either develops subsequent to the development of self-control or is independent of a person's level of impulsivity.[53] This alternative quality, which may be the real stable latent trait, is still unknown. The Criminological Enterprise feature titled "Mating Habits and Crime" discusses one possible alternative.

8. **Cross-cultural differences.** Evidence shows that criminals in other countries do not lack self-control, indicating that the GTC may be culturally limited. For example, Otwin Marenin and Michael Resig actually found equal or higher levels of self-control in Nigerian criminals than in noncriminals.[54] Behavior that may be considered imprudent in one culture may be socially acceptable in another and therefore cannot be viewed as "lack of self-control."[55]

Although questions like these remain, the strength of the general theory lies in its scope and breadth; it attempts to explain all forms of crime and deviance, from lower-class gang delinquency to sexual harassment in the business community.[56] By integrating concepts of criminal choice, criminal opportunity, socialization, and personality, Gottfredson and Hirschi make a plausible argument that all deviant behaviors may originate at the same source. Continued efforts are needed to test the GTC and establish the validity of its core concepts. It remains one of the key developments of modern criminological theory.

DEVELOPMENTAL THEORIES

The second integrated approach that has emerged is developmental theory. According to this view, even as toddlers, people begin relationships and behaviors that will determine their adult life course. At first they must learn to conform to social rules and function effectively in society. Later they are expected to begin thinking about careers, leave their parental homes, find permanent relationships, and eventually marry and begin their own families.[57] These transitions are expected to take place in order, beginning with finishing school, entering the workforce, getting married, and having chil-

dren. Some individuals, however, are incapable of maturing in a reasonable and timely fashion because of family, environmental, or personal problems. In some cases transitions can occur too early—for example, when adolescents engage in precocious sex. In other cases transitions may occur too late, such as when a student fails to graduate on time because of bad grades or too many incompletes. Sometimes disruption of one trajectory can harm another. For example, teenage childbirth will most likely disrupt educational and career development. Because developmental theories focus on the associations between life events and deviant behaviors, they are sometimes referred to as **life-course theories.**

Disruptions in life's major transitions can be destructive and ultimately can promote criminality. Those who are already at risk because of socioeconomic problems or family dysfunction are the most susceptible to these awkward transitions. The cumulative impact of these disruptions sustains criminality from childhood into adulthood.

Because a transition from one stage of life to another can be a bumpy ride, the propensity to commit crimes is neither stable nor constant; it is a developmental process. A positive life experience may help some criminals desist from crime for a while, whereas a negative one may cause them to resume their activi-

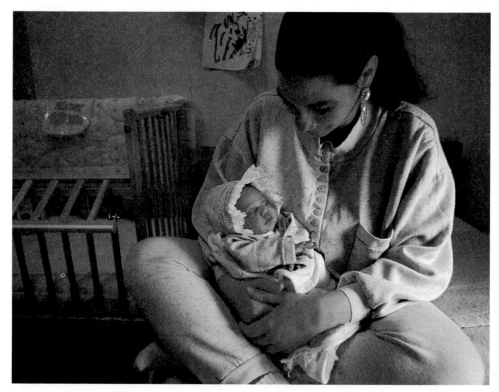

According to developmental theory, having successful life transitions helps inhibit the onset of criminality. Some treatment programs put these views into action. At the La Casita House in New York's South Bronx area, addicted homeless mothers work to get drug clean and develop marketable skills. They are allowed to keep their children with them, which adds to the mother's incentive to get well and prevents family disintegration.

ties. Criminal careers are said to be developmental because people are influenced by the behavior of those around them and, in turn, influence others' behavior. For example, a youth's antisocial behavior may turn his or her more conventional friends against him; their rejection solidifies and escalates his antisocial behavior.

CONNECTIONS

Developmental theories mesh with labeling theory, which was discussed in Chapter 8. However, labeling theory ignores the effect of criminal behavior on those assigning the labels and instead concentrates on the effect of stigma on the development of deviant identities. Developmental theories recognize that the relationship may be reciprocal.

Developmental theories also recognize that as people mature, the factors that influence their behavior change.[58] At first, family relations may be most influential; in later adolescence, school and peer relations predominate; in adulthood, vocational achievement and marital relations may be the most critical influences. For example, some antisocial children who are in trouble throughout their adolescence may manage to find stable work and maintain intact marriages as adults; these life events help them desist from crime. In contrast, the less fortunate adolescents who develop arrest records and get involved with the wrong crowd may find themselves limited to menial jobs and at risk for criminal careers.

CONNECTIONS

Social process theories lay the foundation for assuming that peer, family, educational, and other interactions, which vary over the life course, influence behaviors. See the first few sections of Chapter 8 for a review of these issues. As you may recall from Chapter 3, a great deal of research has been conducted on the relationship of age and crime and the activities of chronic offenders. This scholarship has prompted interest in the life cycle of crime.

Multidimensional Theories Developmental theories are inherently multidimensional, suggesting that criminality has multiple roots, including maladaptive personality traits, educational failure, and family relations. Criminality, according to this view, cannot be attributed to a single cause, nor does it represent a single underlying tendency.[59] People are influenced by different factors as they mature. Consequently, a factor that may have an important influence at one stage of life (like delinquent peers) may have little influence later on.[60]

Developmental theorists conclude that multiple social, personal, and economic factors can influence criminality, and as these factors change over time, so does

criminal involvement.[61] As people make important life transitions—from child to adolescent, from adolescent to adult, from unwed to married—the nature of social interactions changes. Throughout this progression, behavior is altered.

In their **social interactional theory,** Gerald Patterson and his colleagues argue that children whose socialization is ineffective because of improper, maladaptive parenting later build on this improper interactional style and engage in behavior that leads to both peer rejection and academic failure.[62] They then turn to deviant peers, from whom they learn new forms of antisocial behavior. Patterson and his colleagues have found that early childhood family conflicts and lack of a strong bond with parents open the door for social conflict in later adolescence.[63]

The Glueck Research

One of the cornerstones of recent developmental theories lies in renewed interest in the research efforts of Sheldon and Eleanor Glueck. While at Harvard University in the 1930s, the Gluecks popularized research on the life cycle of delinquent careers. In a series of longitudinal research studies, they followed the careers of known delinquents to determine the factors that predicted persistent offending.[64] The Gluecks made extensive use of interviews and records in their elaborate comparisons of delinquents and nondelinquents.[65]

The Gluecks' research focused on early onset of delinquency as a harbinger of a criminal career: "the deeper the roots of childhood maladjustment, the smaller the chance of adult adjustment."[66] They also noted the stability of offending careers: children who are antisocial early in life are the most likely to continue their offending careers into adulthood.

The Gluecks identified a number of personal and social factors related to persistent offending, the most important of which was family relations. This factor was considered in terms of quality of discipline and emotional ties with parents. The adolescent raised in a large, single-parent family of limited economic means and educational achievement was the most vulnerable to delinquency.

The Gluecks did not restrict their analysis to social variables. When they measured such biological and psychological traits as body type, intelligence, and personality, they found that physical and mental factors also played a role in determining behavior. Children with low intelligence, who had a background of mental disease, and who had a powerful (mesomorph) physique were the most likely to become persistent offenders.

The Gluecks' research was virtually ignored for nearly 30 years as the study of crime and delinquency shifted almost exclusively to social and social-psychological factors (like poverty, neighborhood deterioration, and socialization) that formed the nucleus of structural and process theories. The Gluecks' methodology and their integration of biological, psychological, and social factors was heavily criticized by the mainstream sociologists who dominated the field. For many years their work was ignored in criminology texts and overlooked in the academic curriculum.

Developmental Concepts

During the past decade, the Glueck legacy was rediscovered in a series of papers by criminologists Robert Sampson and John Laub. These scholars argued that the Gluecks' careful empirical measurements, which had been cast aside by the criminological community, were actually an ideal platform for studying criminal careers.[67] Sampson and Laub reanalyzed the Glueck data and used it in a series of articles that have gained wide readership. Their work will be discussed in greater detail later in the chapter.

A 1990 review paper (revised in 1998) by Rolf Loeber and Marc LeBlanc was another important event in the development of life-course theory.[68] In their landmark works, Loeber and LeBlanc proposed that criminologists should devote time and effort to understanding some basic questions about the evolution of criminal careers: Why do people begin committing antisocial acts? Why do some stop while others continue? Why do some escalate the severity of their criminality (that is, go from shoplifting to drug dealing to armed robbery) while others deescalate and commit less serious crime as they mature? If some terminate their criminal activity, what, if anything, causes them to begin again? Why do some criminals specialize in certain types of crime, whereas others are generalists engaging in a variety of antisocial behavior? According to Loeber and LeBlanc's developmental view, criminologists must pay attention to how a criminal career unfolds.

A number of key research efforts have also found that crimogenic influences change and develop. In their studies on delinquency prevention, Gerald Patterson and his colleagues at the Oregon Social Learning Center found that poor parental discipline and monitoring was a key to the onset of criminality in early childhood. Then, in middle childhood, social rejection by conventional peers and academic failure sustained antisocial behavior. In later adolescence, commitment to a deviant peer group created a training ground for crime.

Children who are improperly socialized by unskilled parents are the most likely to rebel by wandering the streets with deviant peers.[69] Although the onset of a criminal career is a function of poor parenting skills, its maintenance and support are connected to social relations that emerge later in life.[70] Similar results have been obtained from the Pittsburgh Youth Study, a longitudinal analysis of elementary school–age boys indicating that early onset of delinquency is correlated with social withdrawal, depression, deviant peers, and family

problems, whereas later onset (at age 13 or 14) is geared toward low educational motivation.[71]

From these and similar efforts a view of crime has emerged that incorporates personal change and growth. The factors that produce crime and delinquency at one point in the life cycle may not be relevant at another; as people mature, the social, physical, and environmental influences on their behavior are transformed. Although latent traits may be important, they alone are not enough to control human behavior. People may show a propensity to offend early in their lives, but the nature and frequency of their activities are affected by outside forces beyond their control, such as the likelihood of getting arrested and punished for crime.[72]

The next sections review some of the more important concepts associated with the developmental perspective and discuss some prominent developmental theories.

Problem Behavior Syndrome Most criminological theories portray crime as resulting from, rather than causing, social problems. For example, learning theorists view a troubled home life and deviant friends as precursors of criminality; structural theorists maintain that acquiring deviant cultural values leads to criminality. In contrast, the developmental view is that criminality may best be understood as one of many social problems faced by at-risk youth. These theorists believe that criminality may be part of a **problem behavior syndrome (PBS),** a group of antisocial behaviors that clusters together and typically involves family dysfunction, substance abuse, smoking, precocious sexuality and early pregnancy, educational underachievement, suicide attempts, sensation seeking, and unemployment.[73] People who suffer from one of these conditions typically exhibit many symptoms of the rest.[74] All varieties of criminal behavior, including violence, theft, and drug offenses, may be part of a generalized PBS, indicating that all forms of antisocial behavior have similar developmental patterns (see Table 10.2).[75]

Those who suffer PBS are prone to more difficulties than the general population.[76] They find themselves with a range of personal dilemmas ranging from drug abuse, to being accident-prone, to requiring more health care and hospitalization, to becoming teenage parents. PBS has been linked to personality problems (like rebelliousness and low ego), family problems (like intrafamily conflict and parental mental disorder), and educational failure.[77] Multisite research has shown that PBS is not unique to any single area of the country and that children who suffer PBS, including drug use, delinquency, and precocious sexuality, display symptoms at an early age.[78]

Many examples support the existence of PBS.[79] A survey of Minnesota students in grades 6, 9, and 12 shows that children who experience physical and sexual abuse at the hands of parents or other adults are also likely to have eating disorders (binge eating, purg-

Table 10.2 Problem Behaviors	
Social	• Family dysfunction • Unemployment • Educational underachievement • School misconduct
Personal	• Substance abuse • Suicide attempts • Early sexuality • Sensation seeking • Early parenthood • Accident-prone • Medical problems • Mental disease • Anxiety • Eating disorders (bulimia, anorexia)
Environmental	• High-crime area • Disorganized area • Racism • Exposure to poverty

ing, or anorexia). They are also likely to have increased levels of cigarette smoking, alcohol consumption, stress, anxiety, hard drug use, and suicidal thoughts. These children are likely to have families with histories of alcohol abuse and drug addiction.[80] Other research links family violence to a variety of family and environmental problems that seem to cluster together: low income, single parenthood, residence in isolated ghetto areas, lack of family support or resources, racism, and prolonged exposure to poverty.[81]

In one important research effort that shows the nature of PBS, Helene Raskin White studied a sample of 400 youths measured repeatedly over a six-year cycle and found that behaviors that clustered together included delinquency, substance abuse, school misconduct and underachievement, precocious sexual behavior, violence, suicide, and mental health problems.[82] White found problem behaviors to be stable: subjects who experienced multiple problems at age 15 continued to experience them at age 21. In a subsequent analysis of adolescent misbehavior conducted with Erich Labouvie, White found that PBS might involve one of several clusters of behavior including drug specialists, crime specialists, and generalists who engage in both delinquency and drug abuse. Generalists are the most likely to suffer PBS, displaying higher levels of psychological problems, lack of control, and lower emotional stability.[83]

Problem behaviors, including violence, drug abuse, and theft, may cluster in a number of different ways, affecting people as they mature from adolescence into adulthood.[84] The interconnection of problem behaviors increases the risk of teenage pregnancy, AIDS, and other sources of social distress that require a combination of behaviors (sex, drug use, violence). The fact that youths involved in crime have significantly higher mor-

tality rates than the general population is perhaps the most extreme product of PBS.[85]

Pathways to Crime Developmental theorists recognize that career criminals may travel more than a single road: some may specialize in violence and extortion; some may be involved in theft and fraud; others may engage in a variety of criminal acts. Some offenders may begin their careers early in life, whereas others are late bloomers who begin committing crime when most people desist. Are there different pathways to crime? Using data from a longitudinal cohort study conducted in Pittsburgh, Rolf Loeber and his associates have identified three distinct paths to a criminal career (see Figure 10.3):[86]

1. The **authority conflict pathway** begins at an early age with stubborn behavior. This leads to defiance (doing things one's own way, disobedience) and then to authority avoidance (staying out late, truancy, running away).
2. The **covert pathway** begins with minor, underhanded behavior (lying, shoplifting) that leads to property damage (setting nuisance fires, damaging property). This behavior eventually escalates to more serious forms of criminality, ranging from joyriding, pocket picking, larceny, and fencing to passing bad checks, using stolen credit cards, stealing cars, dealing drugs, and breaking and entering.
3. The **overt pathway** escalates to aggressive acts beginning with aggression (annoying others, bullying), leading to physical (and gang) fighting and then to violence (attacking someone, forced theft).

The Loeber research indicates that each of these paths may lead to a sustained deviant career. Some people enter two and even three paths simultaneously: they are stubborn, lie to teachers and parents, are bullies, and commit petty thefts. These adolescents are the most likely to become persistent offenders as they mature. Although some persistent offenders may specialize in one type of behavior, others engage in varied criminal acts and antisocial behaviors as they mature. For example, they cheat on tests, bully kids in the schoolyard, take drugs, commit burglary, steal a car, and then shoplift from a store.

"Adolescent Limiteds" and "Life-Course Persisters"
In addition to taking different paths to criminality, people may begin their journey at different times: some are precocious, beginning their criminal careers early; others stay out of trouble until their teenage years. Some offenders may peak at an early age, whereas others persist into adulthood. Research shows that there are a number of different classes of criminal careers that seem to reflect changes in the life course (see Table 10.3). Some youth maximize their offending rates at a

Figure 10.3 Loeber's Pathways to Crime

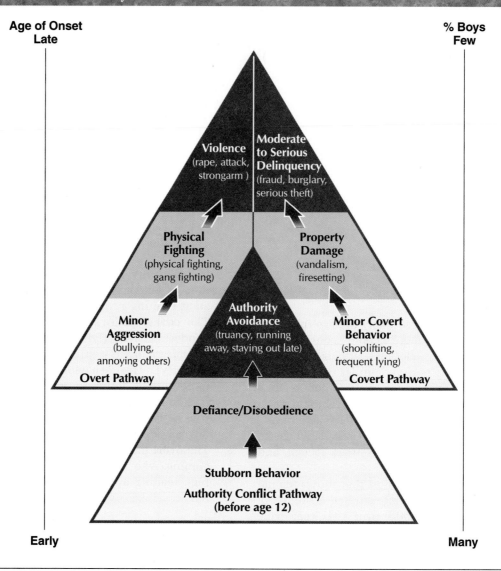

Age of Onset
Late

% Boys
Few

Violence (rape, attack, strongarm)

Moderate to Serious Delinquency (fraud, burglary, serious theft)

Physical Fighting (physical fighting, gang fighting)

Property Damage (vandalism, firesetting)

Minor Aggression (bullying, annoying others)

Authority Avoidance (truancy, running away, staying out late)

Minor Covert Behavior (shoplifting, frequent lying)

Overt Pathway

Covert Pathway

Defiance/Disobedience

Stubborn Behavior

Authority Conflict Pathway
(before age 12)

Early

Many

Source: "Serious and Violent Juvenile Offenders," *Juvenile Justice Bulletin,* May 1998.

relatively early age and then reduce their criminal activity; others persist into their twenties. Some are high-rate offenders, whereas others offend at relatively low rates.[87]

According to psychologist Terrie Moffitt, although the prevalence and frequency of antisocial behavior peak in adolescence and then diminish for most offenders (she labels these **adolescent-limiteds**), a small group of **life-course persisters** offends well into adulthood.[88] Life-course persisters combine family dysfunction with severe neurological problems that predispose them to antisocial behavior patterns. These afflictions can be the result of maternal drug abuse, poor nutrition, or exposure to toxic agents such as lead. Life-course persisters may have lower verbal ability, which

inhibits reasoning skills, learning ability, and school achievement. There may be more than one subset of life-course persisters. One begins acting out during the preschool years; these youths show signs of ADHD and do not outgrow the levels of disobedience typical of the preschool years. The second group shows few symptoms of ADHD but, from an early age, is aggressive, underhanded, and in constant opposition to authority.[89]

During their youth, adolescent-limited delinquents mimic the behavior of these more troubled teens, only to reduce the frequency of their offending as they mature to around age 18.[90] This group tends to focus on a specific type of misbehavior such as drug abuse.

Table 10.3 Different Classes of Criminals

CRIMINAL CLASSES	ONSET	OFFENDING RATE
Adolescent peaked	Early	High
Delinquency maximized ages 15–18	Late	Low
Chronic offender	Early	High
Delinquency maximized ages 17–21	Late	Low

Source: Amy D'Unger, Kenneth Land, Patricia McCall, and Daniel Nagin, "How Many Latent Classes of Delinquent/Criminal Careers? Results from Mixed Poisson Regression Analyses," *American Journal of Sociology* 103 (1998): 1593–1630.

Research has supported Moffitt's model, showing that early-onset delinquents are both more prevalent and more generalized in their delinquent activity and that the patterns predicted by Moffitt can be found in samples of both male and female delinquents.[91] Early-onset delinquents seem to be strongly influenced by individual-level traits like low verbal ability, hyperactivity, and negative or impulsive personality. In contrast, late-adolescent delinquents are more strongly influenced by their delinquent peers. Early-onset delinquents also appear to be more violent than their older peers, who are likely to be involved in nonviolent crimes such as theft.[92]

Evidence shows that children who mature faster have a greater chance of becoming life-course persisters; this is referred to as **pseudomaturity.** The sooner an adolescent engages in substance abuse and sexuality or suffers emotional distress, the more likely he or she will be involved in adult deviance.[93]

Early Versus Late Onset Most developmental theories assume that the seeds of a criminal career are planted early in life and that early onset of deviance strongly predicts later criminality. Research supports this by showing that children who will later become delinquents begin their deviant careers at a very early (preschool) age.[94] Studies of narcotics addicts show that the earlier the onset of substance abuse, the more frequent, varied, and sustained the addict's criminal career.[95]

Continuity Another aspect of developmental theory is the continuity of crime: the best predictor of future criminality is past criminality. Children who are repeatedly in trouble during early adolescence will generally still be antisocial in their middle and late teens and as adults.[96] Early criminal activity is likely to be sustained because these offenders seem to lack the social survival skills necessary to find work or to develop the interpersonal relationships needed to allow them to drop out of crime.[97] The fact that some offenders actually begin their criminal careers in late adolescence, after age 14, is just now being recognized. These late starters are also at high risk for adult criminality.[98]

Why do some people enter a "path to crime" later rather than sooner? Early starters, who begin offending before age 14, experience (1) poor parenting, which leads them into (2) deviant behaviors and then (3) involvement with delinquent groups. In contrast, late starters, who begin offending after age 14, follow a somewhat different path: (1) poor parenting leads to (2) identification with delinquent groups and then to (3) deviant involvement. By implication, adolescents who suffer poor parenting and are at risk for deviant careers can avoid criminality if they can bypass involvement with delinquent peers.[99]

Early- and late-onset offenders may take different paths into crime and are influenced by different life factors. Criminal peers exert a greater influence on the late bloomers than on their more precocious peers. Late starters, then, seem to be influenced by their peer group, a factor that develops and expands as an adolescent matures.[100] There are other differences between the two classes of criminals. Early starters are more likely to be the victims of child abuse than later starters. In addition, criminal punishment seems to have a greater deterrent effect on early starters.[101] It is possible that early starters learn from their experiences and become more cunning criminals, increasing their offending rates while avoiding detection. Because they are more sensitive to the punishment associated with capture, they may be more motivated to find ways to avoid getting caught!

The discovery that people begin their criminal careers at different ages and follow different offense paths and trajectories provides strong support for the life-course view. If all criminals possessed a singular latent trait that made them crime-prone, it would be unlikely that these variations in criminal careers would be observed. It is difficult to explain such concepts as late onset and adolescent-limited behavior from the perspective of latent trait theory. The Race, Culture, Gender, and Criminology feature titled "Violent Female Criminals" explores this issue further.

THEORIES OF CRIMINAL DEVELOPMENT

An ongoing effort has been made to track persistent offenders over their life course.[102] The early data seem to support what is already known about delinquent and criminal career patterns: early onset predicts more lasting crime; there is continuity in crime (juvenile offenders are likely to become adult criminals); and chronic offenders commit a significant portion of all crimes.[103]

Violent Female Criminals

Although considerable research is now being devoted to gender differences in the crime rate, little has been done to chart the life course of one subset of this group: violent female street criminals. To correct this oversight, two studies, one by Deborah Baskin and Ira Sommers and the other by Henry Brownstein, Barry Spunt, Susan Crimmins, and Sandra Langley, have analyzed data based on samples of violent female felons in New York. These data provide considerable insight into formation and maintenance of a criminal career.

Criminal justice scholars Baskin and Sommers used census data, analyses of political and economic changes, and direct observations and interviews to examine the career patterns of violent female offenders. They also looked at the relationships that these women have with their family members and their communities. They provide a detailed account of the criminal careers of 170 women who committed violent street crimes in New York City, describing their entry into criminal activities and their lives as persistent street criminals.

Baskin and Sommers found that about 60 percent of violent female offenders began their criminal careers at a very young age. About half reported regular fighting as early as 10 years old, and about 40 percent reported that they regularly left home carrying a weapon. In contrast, the others reported that they did not start fighting until much later, until they had left school. Because of the clear differential between when these females began their criminal careers, Baskin and Sommers independently analyzed the early- and late-onset offenders.

The women in both groups suffered from severe social and emotional problems. Most were raised in single-parent families and received little parental supervision. Both groups experienced physical and sexual abuse by a parent or guardian and were likely to have witnessed abuse between their guardians. Almost half were raised in households that relied on welfare. More than half had a parent who either was a substance abuser or had been incarcerated sometime during their childhood.

Women in the early-onset group could be distinguished by the severity of their childhood problems. They were most likely to reside in areas with high concentrations of poverty and to have family histories of psychiatric problems requiring hospitalization. They were more likely to be truant, leave school early, and associate with delinquent peers while in school. They also were more likely to be placed in a juvenile detention center.

The major distinction between the groups, however, could be found in the scale and direction of their offending careers. Although both groups used drugs, early-onset women began abusing substances two years ahead of the late-onset group. The women in the early-onset group were involved in a variety of crimes, including serious robberies, assaults, and burglaries, even before they became involved with drugs. In contrast, the women in the late-onset group were involved in mostly nonviolent crimes, such as shoplifting and prostitution, *until* they began taking drugs. The violent offending of the latter group, then, can be attributed to their drug use. In contrast, the violent behavior of the early-onset women was part of a generalized PBS.

A number of research studies support the Baskin and Sommers findings. Helene Raskin White and

---

Based on these findings, a number of systematic theories that account for the onset, continuance, and desistance from crime have been formulated. The following sections discuss a number of developmental theories in some detail.

The Social Development Model (SDM)

In their **social development model (SDM)**, Joseph Weis, Richard Catalano, J. David Hawkins, and their associates have attempted to integrate social control, social learning, and structural models.[104] According to the SDM, a number of community-level risk factors make some people susceptible to developing antisocial behaviors. For example, the quality of the community organization influences the child's risk of developing antisocial behavior. Social control is less effective when the frontline socializing institutions are weak in disorganized areas. In a low-income, disorganized community, for example, families are under great stress; educational facilities are inadequate; there are fewer material goods; and respect for the law is weak. Because crime rates are high, there are more opportunities to violate the law, which puts even greater strain on the agencies of social control.

As children mature within their environment, elements of socialization control their developmental process. Preexisting risk factors are either reinforced or neutralized by socialization. Children are socialized and develop bonds to their families through four distinct interactions and processes:

1. Perceived opportunities for involvement in activities and interactions with others

Stephen Hansell found that girls who begin using alcohol early in life are the most likely to be aggressive and violent in their later years. Although women are less likely to be aggressive than men, early alcohol abuse is a much stronger predictor of female than male violence.

Henry Brownstein and his associates interviewed 215 women convicted of murder. Most of these women told a familiar story: the most violent of these women had histories of juvenile violence, drug abuse, and personal victimization. Out of a sample of 215, they found that

- 65 percent had participated in some violent activity.
- 64 percent claimed to have seriously harmed someone when they were growing up.
- 58 percent had been the victim of serious physical harm.
- 49 percent had been sexually abused.

These women had a long-term commitment to crime beginning in early childhood, which continued through adulthood and culminated in their use of deadly violence. Brownstein also focused on the behavior of 19 women who killed in the context of dealing drugs. Some of these acts were motivated by economic interests, whereas others were motivated

by a relationship to a man (either killing on behalf of a man who controlled them or killing a man who they feared would cause them injury).

The researchers found that there are, in fact, different pathways to crime, and that both involve environmental and serendipitous life circumstances. These conclusions support a developmental view and repudiate the latent trait approach.

CRITICAL THINKING

1. Crime data tell us that women are significantly less violent than men. Are the pathways to chronic offending different among violent females than among males?
2. Do you believe that some conditions present at birth can control future criminal behavior?

 INFOTRAC COLLEGE EDITION RESEARCH

There is a growing body of literature on the violent behavior of female offenders. To read about this phenomenon further, see:
Denise Hien and Nina Hien. Women. Violence with intimates, and substance abuse: relevant theory, empirical findings, and recommendations for future research. *American Journal of Drug and Alcohol Abuse* August 1998 v24 n3 p419

Karen Joe Laidler and Geoffrey Hunt. Violence and social organization in female gangs. *Social Justice* Winter 1997 v24 n4 p148

Source: Deborah Baskin and Ira Sommers, *Casualties of Community Disorder: Women's Careers in Violent Crime* (Boulder, Colo.: Westview Press, 1998); Deborah Baskin and Ira Sommers, "Females' Initiation into Violent Street Crime," *Justice Quarterly* 10 (1993): 559–81; Helene Raskin White and Stephen Hansell, "The Moderating Effects of Gender and Hostility on the Alcohol–Aggression Relationship," *Journal of Research in Crime and Delinquency* 33 (1996): 450–70; Henry Brownstein, Barry Spunt, Susan Crimmins, and Sandra Langley, "Women Who Kill in Drug Market Situations," *Justice Quarterly* 12 (1995): 473–98.

2. The degree of involvement and interaction with parents
3. The children's ability to participate in these interactions
4. The reinforcement (such as feedback) they perceive for their participation

To control the risk of antisocial behavior, a child must maintain **prosocial bonds.** These are developed within the context of family life, which not only provides prosocial opportunities but reinforces them by consistent, positive feedback. Parental attachment affects a child's behavior for life, determining both school experiences and personal beliefs and values. For those with strong family relationships, school will be a meaningful experience marked by academic success and commitment to education. Youths in this category are

likely to develop conventional beliefs and values, become committed to conventional activities, and form attachments to conventional others.

Children's antisocial behavior also depends on the quality of their attachments to parents and other influential relations. If they remain unattached or develop attachments to deviant others, their behavior may become deviant as well. Unlike Hirschi's control theory, which assumes that all attachments are beneficial, the SDM suggests that interaction with antisocial peers and adults promotes participation in delinquency and substance abuse.[105]

As Figure 10.4 shows, the SDM differs from Hirschi's vision of how the social bond develops. Whereas Hirschi maintains that early family attachments are the key determinant of future behavior, the SDM suggests that later involvement in prosocial or

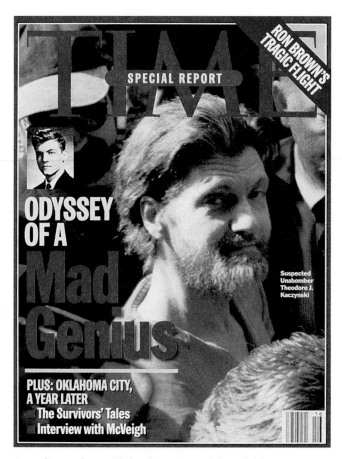

According to the social development model, as children mature, elements of socialization control their developmental process. Pre-existing risk factors are either reinforced or neutralized through socialization. Can irrational behavior such as the actions of political terrorist Theodore Kaczynski, the so-called "Unabomber," be explained in terms of environment and socialization?

antisocial behavior determines the quality of attachments. Adolescents who perceive opportunities and rewards for antisocial behavior will form deep attachments to deviant peers and will become committed to a delinquent way of life. In contrast, those who perceive opportunities for prosocial behavior will take a different path, getting involved in conventional activities and forming attachments to others that share their conventional lifestyle.

The SDM holds that commitment and attachment to conventional institutions, activities, and beliefs insulate youths from the crimogenic influences of their environment. The prosocial path inhibits deviance by strengthening bonds to prosocial others and activities. Without the proper level of bonding, adolescents can succumb to the influence of deviant others.

Many of the core assumptions of the SDM have been tested and verified empirically.[106] The path predicted by the SDM seems an accurate picture of the onset and continuation of delinquency and drug abuse. For example, research indicates that both social learning and control-bonding factors play an important role in pre-

dicting gang membership.[107] Kids who learn deviant attitudes and behaviors and who also have weak ties to conventional institutions are the most likely to engage in criminal behaviors. The SDM has also guided treatment interventions, which promote the development of strong family and school bonds and help kids use these bonds to resist any opportunity or motivation to take drugs and engage in delinquent behaviors. Preliminary evaluations of one program, the Seattle Social Development Project, indicates that SDM-based interventions can help reduce delinquency and drug abuse.[108]

Elliott's Integrated Theory

Another attempt at theory integration, which is similar to the SDM, has been proposed by Delbert Elliott and his colleagues David Huizinga and Suzanne Ageton of the Behavioral Research Institute in Boulder, Colorado.[109] Their view combines the features of strain (Chapter 7), social learning, and control theories into a single theoretical model. According to the Elliott view, illustrated in Figure 10.5, adolescents who live in socially disorganized areas (A) and are improperly socialized at home (B) face a significant risk of perceiving strain (C); perceptions of strain then lead to weakened bonds with conventional groups, activities, and norms (D). Weak conventional bonds and high levels of perceived strain lead some youths to reject conventional social values (E) and seek out and become bonded to deviant peer groups (F). From these delinquent associations come positive reinforcements for delinquent behaviors; delinquent peers provide role models for antisocial behavior (G). Attachment to delinquent groups, when combined with weak bonding to conventional groups and norms, leads to a high level of delinquent behavior and drug abuse (H).

Social Factors Elliott's picture of the teenage delinquent is similar to the one drawn by the SDM with the addition of the concept of strain. Living in a disorganized neighborhood, feeling hopeless, sensing the inability to get ahead, and becoming involved in petty crimes eventually lead to a condition where conventional social values become weak and attenuated. As a result, these children lose interest in school, family, and social order. A deviant peer group becomes an acceptable substitute, amplifying the attitudes and skills that support delinquent tendencies. The result is early experimentation with drugs and delinquency. Although both the SDM and Elliott's integrated theory assume that involvement with delinquent friends increases the risk of criminal involvement, Hirschi's control model disputes this finding.

Testing Integrated Theory Elliott and his colleagues tested their theoretical model with data from a national survey of approximately 1,800 youths, who were inter-

Figure 10.4   The Social Development Model of Antisocial Behavior

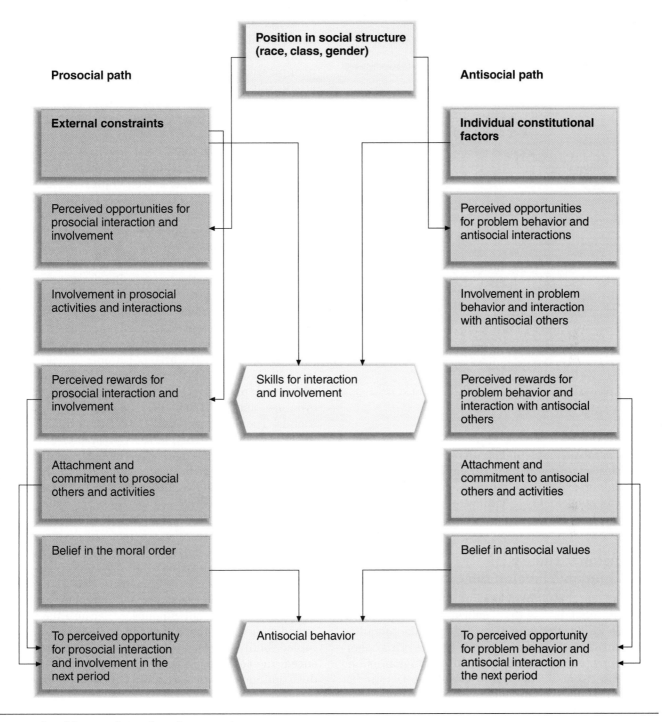

Position in social structure (race, class, gender)

Prosocial path

Antisocial path

External constraints

Individual constitutional factors

Perceived opportunities for prosocial interaction and involvement

Perceived opportunities for problem behavior and antisocial interactions

Involvement in prosocial activities and interactions

Involvement in problem behavior and interaction with antisocial others

Perceived rewards for prosocial interaction and involvement

Skills for interaction and involvement

Perceived rewards for problem behavior and interaction with antisocial others

Attachment and commitment to prosocial others and activities

Attachment and commitment to antisocial others and activities

Belief in the moral order

Belief in antisocial values

To perceived opportunity for prosocial interaction and involvement in the next period

Antisocial behavior

To perceived opportunity for problem behavior and antisocial interaction in the next period

Source: Adapted from Seattle Social Development Project.

viewed annually for three years. With only a few minor exceptions, the results supported Elliott's integrated theory. One difference was that some subjects reported developing strong bonds to delinquent peers even though they did not reject the values of conventional society. Elliott and his colleagues interpreted this finding to mean that youths living in disorganized areas may join law-violating youth groups because conventional groups simply do not exist. Elliott also found that initial experimentation with drugs and delinquency predicted both joining a teenage law-violating peer group and becoming involved with additional delinquency. In a more recent survey, Elliott and his colleagues again tested their theoretical model with data

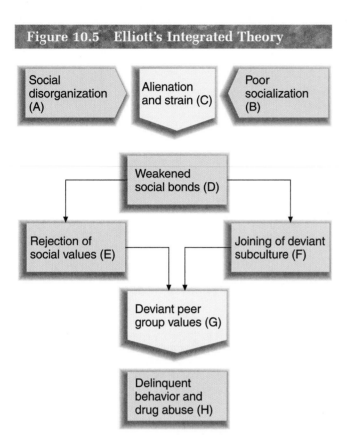

Figure 10.5 Elliott's Integrated Theory

Social disorganization (A)

Alienation and strain (C)

Poor socialization (B)

Weakened social bonds (D)

Rejection of social values (E)

Joining of deviant subculture (F)

Deviant peer group values (G)

Delinquent behavior and drug abuse (H)

from a national survey of more than 1,000 youths, who were interviewed annually for three years.[110] With only a few minor exceptions, these results also supported their integrated theory: bonding to a delinquent peer group escalates involvement in criminal activity.[111]

Farrington's Theory of Delinquent Development

One of the most important longitudinal studies tracking persistent offenders is the Cambridge Study in Delinquent Development, which has followed the offending careers of 411 London boys born in 1953.[112] This cohort study, directed since 1982 by David Farrington, is one of the most serious attempts to isolate the factors that predict lifelong continuity of criminal behavior. The study uses self-report data as well as in-depth interviews and psychological testing. The boys have been interviewed eight times over 24 years, beginning at age 8 and continuing to age 32.[113]

The results of the Cambridge study show that many of the same patterns found in the United States are repeated in a cross-national sample: the existence of chronic offenders, the continuity of offending, and early onset of criminal activity. Each of these patterns leads to persistent criminality.

Farrington found that the traits present in persistent offenders can be observed as early as age 8. The chronic criminal, typically a male, begins as a property offender; is born into a low-income, large family headed by parents who have criminal records; and has delinquent older siblings. The future criminal receives poor parental supervision, including the use of harsh or erratic punishment and child-rearing techniques; his parents are likely to divorce or separate. The chronic offender tends to associate with friends who are also future criminals. By age 8, he exhibits antisocial behavior, including dishonesty and aggressiveness; at school he tends to have low educational achievement and is restless, troublesome, hyperactive, impulsive, and often truant. After leaving school at age 18, the persistent criminal tends to take a relatively well-paid but low-status job and is likely to have an erratic work history and periods of unemployment.

Deviant behavior tends to be versatile rather than specialized. That is, the typical offender not only commits property offenses, such as theft and burglary, but also engages in violence, vandalism, drug use, excessive drinking, drunk driving, smoking, reckless driving, and sexual promiscuity—evidence of a generalized problem behavior syndrome. Chronic offenders are more likely to live away from home and have conflicts with their parents. They wear tattoos, go out most evenings, and enjoy hanging out with groups of their friends. They are much more likely than nonoffenders to get involved in fights, to carry weapons, and to use them in violent encounters. The frequency of offending reaches a peak in the teenage years (about 17 or 18) and then declines in the twenties, when the offenders marry or live with women.

By the time he reaches his thirties, the former delinquent is likely to be separated or divorced from his wife and to be an absent parent. His employment record remains spotty, and he moves often between rental units. His life is still characterized by evenings out, heavy drinking, substance abuse, and more violent behavior than his contemporaries. Because the typical offender provides the same kind of deprived and disrupted family life for his own children that he experienced, the social experiences and conditions that produce delinquency are carried on from one generation to the next.

Nonoffenders and Desisters Farrington has also identified factors that predict the discontinuity of criminal offenses. He found that people who exhibit these factors have backgrounds that put them at risk of becoming offenders; however, either they are able to remain nonoffenders, or they begin a criminal career and then later desist. The factors that protected high-risk youths from beginning criminal careers included

David Farrington's longitudinal research found that the persistent offender was typically a male who began his criminal career as a property offender. Such offenders were born into low-income, large families headed by parents who had criminal records and with delinquent older siblings. The future criminal received poor parental supervision, including the use of harsh or erratic punishment and child-rearing techniques; the parents were likely to have divorced or separated.

- Having a somewhat shy personality.
- Having few friends (at age 8).
- Having nondeviant families.
- Being highly regarded by their mothers.

Shy children with few friends avoided damaging relationships with other adolescent boys (members of a high-risk group) and were therefore able to avoid criminality.

What caused offenders to desist? Holding a relatively good job helped reduce criminal activity. Conversely, unemployment seemed to be related to the escalation of theft offenses; violence and substance abuse were unaffected by unemployment. In a similar vein, getting married also helped diminish criminal activity. However, finding a spouse who was also involved in criminal activity and had a criminal record increased criminal involvement. Physical relocation also helped some offenders desist because they were forced to sever ties with co-offenders. For this reason, leaving the city for a more rural or suburban area was linked to reduced criminal activity.

Although employment, marriage, and relocation helped potential offenders desist, not all desisters found success. At-risk youths who managed to avoid criminal convictions were unlikely to avoid other social problems. Rather than becoming prosperous homeowners with flourishing careers, they tended to live in unkempt homes and have large debts and low-paying jobs. They were also more likely to remain single and live alone. Youths who experienced social isolation at age 8 were also found to experience it at age 32.

Theoretical Modeling Farrington summarized his observations by proposing a theory of criminality based on his long-term data collections. Farrington's theoretical model is outlined here:

1. Childhood factors predict teenage antisocial behavior and adult dysfunction. There is continuity in criminal behavior.
2. Personal and social factors are associated with criminal propensity. Kids who suffer economic deprivation, poor parenting, and antisocial families and have personalities marked by impulsivity, hyperactivity, and attention deficit disorder are the most likely to become delinquent.
3. Adolescents who have crimogenic tendencies are motivated to offend by their desire for material goods, excitement, and status with peers. Boys from less affluent families are unable to achieve these

goals through legitimate means, so they tend to commit offenses.

4. Life events influence behavior. For example, family life is critical to a deviant career. Adolescents exposed to effective child rearing, including consistent discipline and close supervision, tend to build up internal inhibitions against offending in a social learning process. In contrast, this same learning process causes kids raised in antisocial families to model their beliefs and behaviors dysfunctionally.

5. The chance of offending in any particular situation depends on the perceived costs and benefits of crime and noncrime alternatives. The more impulsive boys were more likely to offend because they were less likely to consider possible future consequences (as opposed to immediate benefits).

6. Factors that encourage criminality at one period during the life course may inhibit it in another. Being nervous and withdrawn and having few friends is negatively related to adolescent and teenage offending but is positively related to adult social dysfunction.

7. Adult criminal behavior is predicted by external and internal behaviors. External behaviors include engaging in violence and getting arrested and convicted for crimes. Internal behaviors include psychiatric disorders, substance abuse, nervousness, and social isolation.

Farrington's theory suggests that life experiences shape the direction and flow of behavior choices. People are not controlled by a single, unalterable latent trait. His work is included here as a developmental theory because it is age-graded: although there may be continuity in offending, the factors that predict criminality at one point in the life course may not be the ones that predict criminality at another. Although most adult criminals begin their careers in childhood, life events may help some children forgo criminality as they mature.

Interactional Theory

Terence Thornberry has proposed an age-graded view of crime that he calls **interactional theory** (see Figure 10.6).[114] Thornberry agrees with both Weis and Elliott that the onset of crime can be traced to a deterioration of the social bond during adolescence, marked by weakened attachment to parents, commitment to school, and belief in conventional values. Thornberry's view similarly recognizes the influence of social class and other structural variables: youths growing up in socially disorganized areas also stand the greatest risk of a weakened social bond and subsequent delinquency. The onset of a criminal career is supported by residence in a social setting in which deviant values and attitudes can be learned from and reinforced by delinquent peers.

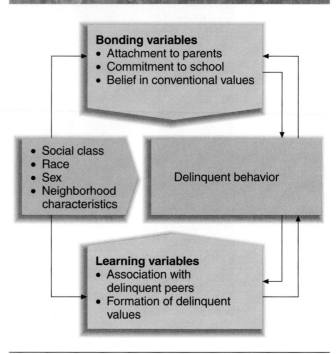

Figure 10.6 Overview of the Interactional Theory of Delinquency

Source: Terence Thornberry, Margaret Farnsworth, Alan Lizotte, and Susan Stern, "A Longitudinal Examination of the Causes and Correlates of Delinquency," working paper No. 1, Rochester Youth Development Study (Albany, N.Y.: Hindelang Criminal Justice Research Center, 1987), p. 11.

Interactional theory also holds that seriously delinquent youths form belief systems that are consistent with their deviant lifestyle. They seek out the company of other kids who share their interests and who are likely to reinforce their beliefs about the world and support their delinquent behavior. According to interactional theory, delinquents find a criminal peer group in the same way that chess buffs look for others who share their passion for the game; hanging out with other chess players helps improve their game. Similarly, deviant peers do not turn an otherwise innocent boy into a delinquent; they support and amplify the behavior of kids who have already accepted a delinquent way of life.[115]

The key idea here is that causal influences are bidirectional. Weak bonds lead kids to develop friendships with deviant peers and get involved in delinquency. Frequent delinquency involvement further weakens bonds and makes it difficult to reestablish conventional ones. Delinquency-promoting factors tend to reinforce one another and sustain a chronic criminal career.

Interactional theory is considered age-graded because it incorporates an element of the **cognitive perspective** in psychology. That is, as people mature, they pass through different stages of reasoning and sophistication.[116] Thornberry applies this concept when he suggests that criminality is a developmental process that takes on different meaning and form as a person matures. According to Thornberry, the causal process is a dynamic one and develops over a person's life.[117] During early adolescence, attachment to the family is the single most important determinant of whether a youth will adjust to conventional society and be shielded from delinquency. By midadolescence the influence of the family is replaced by the "world of friends, school and youth culture."[118] By adulthood, a person's behavioral choices are shaped by his or her place in conventional society and his or her own nuclear family.

Testing Interactional Theory Interactional theory is now being tested by a number of criminologists; most tests involve a panel of Rochester, New York, youths who are being followed through their offending careers.[119] Ample evidence supports the core principles of the theory: crime and social relations are interactional. For example, delinquent behavior has been found to influence the quality of family life; and changes in the quality of family life stimulate delinquency.[120] Kids who take drugs and use alcohol at a very young age are more likely to engage in other high-risk behaviors such as dropping out of school and parenting children out of wedlock. These risky behaviors increase the chances that alcohol and drugs will be used into and during adulthood.[121]

Preliminary results also support interactional theory's explanation of how peer groups influence delinquency.[122] Research indicates that associating with delinquent peers does, in fact, increase delinquent involvement and that the relationship is interactional: as delinquent behavior escalates, kids are more likely to seek out deviant friends, who in turn reinforce delinquent beliefs.[123] In contrast, conventional youths seek equally conforming friends, who then reinforce their prosocial lifestyle. As this process unfolds, antisocial kids will become part of a deviant peer network that reinforces their behavior; conventional youths will be reinforced by their conventional friends.[124] Delinquency has also been related to weakened attachments to family and the educational process; delinquent behavior further weakens the strength of the bonds to family and school.[125] Other researchers have supported an interactional relationship between criminal behavior and moral values (antisocial behavior weakens moral beliefs, and weakened beliefs encourage criminality).[126]

The Rochester data also show that life events can make even high-risk youth resilient to delinquency. Kids who grow up in indigent households that experience unemployment, high mobility, and parental criminality, and who are placed in the care of social service agencies, can resist delinquent involvements if they sustain prosocial life experiences. In later adolescence, kids who are committed to school, develop attachment to teachers, and establish the goal of a college education are best able to resist delinquency. Scoring high on reading and math tests is also associated with prosocial behaviors.[127]

In sum, interactional theory suggests that criminality is part of a dynamic social process and not just an outcome of that process. Although crime is influenced by social forces, it also influences these processes and associations to create behavioral trajectories toward increasing law violations for some people.[128] Interactional theory integrates elements of social disorganization, social control, social learning, and cognitive theories into a powerful model of the development of a criminal career.

Sampson and Laub: Age-Graded Theory

If there are various pathways to crime and delinquency, are there trails back to conformity? In an important 1993 work, *Crime in the Making,* Robert Sampson and John Laub identify the **turning points** in a criminal career.[129] As devotees of the life-course perspective, Sampson and Laub find that the stability of delinquent behavior can be affected by events that occur later in life, even after a chronic delinquent career has been undertaken. They agree with Hirschi and Gottfredson that formal and informal social controls restrict criminality and that crime begins early in life and continues over the life course; they disagree that once this course is set, nothing can impede its progress. Laub and Sampson reanalyzed the data originally collected by the Gluecks more than 40 years ago. Using modern statistical analysis, Laub and Sampson found evidence supporting the developmental view. They state that children who enter delinquent careers are those who have trouble at home and at school and maintain deviant friends; these findings are similar to those from earlier research on delinquent careers.

Turning Points and Social Capital Laub and Sampson's most important contribution is identifying the life events that enable adult offenders to desist from crime (see Figure 10.7). Two critical turning points are marriage and career. For example, adolescents who are at risk for crime can live conventional lives if they can find good jobs or achieve successful careers. Their success may hinge on a lucky break. Even those who have been in trouble with the law may turn from crime if employers are willing to give them a chance despite their records. When they achieve adulthood, adolescents who had significant problems with the law are able to desist from crime if they become attached to a spouse who supports and sustains them even when the spouse knows they had gotten in trouble when they were kids. Happy marriages are life-sustaining, and marital quality improves over time (as people work less and have fewer parental responsibilities).[130] Spending time in marital and family activities also reduces exposure to deviant peers, which in turn reduces the opportunity to become involved in delinquent activities.[131] People who cannot sustain secure marital relations are less likely to desist from crime.

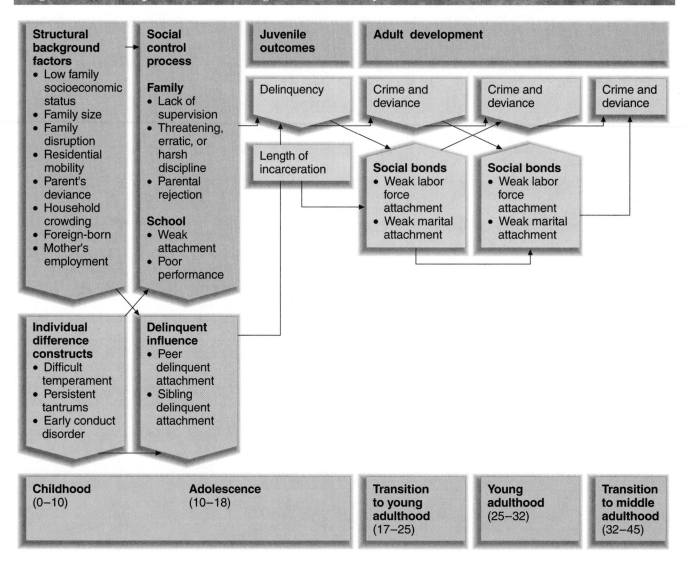

Figure 10.7 Sampson and Laub's Age-Graded Theory

Source: Robert Sampson and John Laub, *Crime in the Making: Pathways and Turning Points Through Life* (Cambridge, Mass.: Harvard University Press, 1993), pp. 244–45.

Sampson and Laub's age-graded theory is also supported by research that shows children who grow up in two-parent families are more likely to later have happier marriages than children who are the product of divorced or never-married parents.[132] This finding suggests the marriage–crime association may be intergenerational: if people with marital problems are more crime-prone, their children will also suffer a greater long-term risk of marital failure and antisocial activity.

Social Capital Social scientists recognize that people build **social capital**—positive relations with individuals and institutions that are life-sustaining. In the same manner that building financial capital improves

the chances for personal success, building social capital supports conventional behavior and inhibits deviant behavior. For example, a successful marriage creates social capital when it improves a person's stature, creates feelings of self-worth, and encourages people to trust the individual. A successful career inhibits crime by creating a stake in conformity; why commit crime when you are doing well at your job? The relationship is reciprocal. If people are chosen to be employees, they return the favor by doing the best job possible; if they are chosen as spouses, they blossom into devoted partners. In contrast, moving to a new city reduces social capital by closing people off from long-term relationships.[133]

While building financial capital improves the chances for personal success, building social capital supports conventional behavior and inhibits deviant behavior. One way of building social capital is to find a high-paying steady job. A successful career inhibits crime by creating a stake in conformity; why commit crime when you are doing well at your job?

Sampson and Laub's research indicates that building social capital and strong social bonds reduces the likelihood of long-term deviance. This finding suggests that, in contrast to latent trait theories, events that occur in later adolescence and adulthood do, in fact, influence the direction of delinquent and criminal careers. Life events can help either terminate or sustain deviant careers. For example, getting arrested and punished may have little direct effect on future criminality, but it can help sustain a criminal career because it reduces the chances of employment and job stability, two factors that are directly related to crime.[134]

Testing Age-Graded Theory Several indicators support the validity of age-graded theory. According to Raymond Paternoster and Robert Brame, youths who exhibit antisocial behavior traits at a very young age are the most likely to persist in delinquency; however, their behavior can be influenced by such dynamic factors as deviant peer relations. This indicates that even if latent traits are related to criminality, these can be influenced by life-course events.[135]

Evidence now shows that once begun, criminal career trajectories can be reversed if life conditions improve, an outcome predicted by age-graded theory.[136] For example, employment status affects behavior: men who are unemployed or underemployed report higher criminal participation rates than employed men. Similarly, men released from prison on parole who obtain jobs are less likely to recidivate than those who lack or lose employment.[137]

Research has been directed at identifying the sources of social capital and determining whether and how it is related to crime. For example, youths who accumulate social capital in childhood (for example, by doing well in school or having a tightly knit family) are also the most likely to maintain steady work as adults; employment may help insulate them from crime.[138] Also, people who maintain a successful marriage in their twenties and become parents are the most likely to mature out of crime.[139] Although it is possible that marriage stabilizes people and helps them build social capital, it is also likely, as Mark Warr suggests, that marriage may discourage crime by reducing contact with criminal peers:

> For many individuals, it seems, marriage marks a transition from heavy peer involvement to a preoccupation with one's spouse . . . that transition is likely to reduce interaction with former friends and accomplices and thereby reduce the opportunities as well as the motivation to engage in crime.[140]

A number of research efforts have supported the Sampson and Laub assumed association between social capital and crime. For example, delinquents who enter the military, serve overseas, and receive veterans' benefits enhance their occupational status (social capital) while reducing criminal involvement.[141] In contrast, research shows that people who are self-centered and present oriented are less likely to accumulate social capital and more prone to commit criminal acts.[142]

Future Research Some important questions still need to be answered: Why do some kids change while others resist? Why do some people enter strong marriages while others fail? What is it about military careers that helps reduce future criminality? Does the connection between military service and desistance suggest universal military service as a crime prevention alternative? Why are some troubled youths able to conform to the requirements of a job or career while others cannot? Is it possible that social capital—family, friends, education, marriage, and employment—aids in the successful recovery from crime?[143]

COMMONALITIES AND DISTINCTIONS BETWEEN LATENT TRAIT AND DEVELOPMENTAL THEORIES

Although the differences between the views presented in this chapter may seem irreconcilable, they in fact share some common ground. They indicate that a criminal career must be understood as a passage along which people travel, that it has a beginning and an end, and that events and life circumstances influence the journey. The factors that affect a criminal career may include structural factors, such as income and status; socialization factors, such as family and peer relations; biological factors, such as size and strength; psychological factors, including intelligence and personality; and opportunity factors, such as free time, inadequate police protection, and a supply of easily stolen merchandise. Developmental theories emphasize the influence of changing interpersonal and structural factors (that is, people change along with the world they live in). Latent trait theories assume that it is not people but criminal opportunities that change (that is, people do not change, but the opportunity to commit crime does).

These perspectives differ in their view of human development. Do people change, as life-course theories suggest, or are they stable, constant, and changeless, as the latent trait view indicates? Does a dominant key control human destiny, or are there multiple influences on human behavior? Are the social and personal factors that influence people stable, or do they change as a person matures? Answers to these questions are what differentiates criminological points of view.

SUMMARY

Recently, criminologists have been combining elements from a number of different theoretical models into integrated theories of crime, which are outlined in Table 10.4.

Latent trait theories hold that some underlying condition present at birth or soon after controls behavior. Suspect traits include low IQ, impulsivity, and personality structure. This underlying trait explains the continuity of offending because once present, it remains with a person throughout his or her life. The latent trait theories developed by Gottfredson and Hirschi and Wilson and Herrnstein both integrate choice theory concepts: people with latent traits choose crime over noncrime. The opportunity for crime mediates their choice.

Developmental theories look at multiple factors derived from a number of different structural and process theories. Examples of this include the social development model and Elliott's integrated theory, which hold that social position controls life events. The SDM finds that living in a disorganized area helps weaken social bonds; Elliott's theory holds that strain leads to weakened bonds. Both theories find that weakened bonds lead to the development of deviant peer group associations.

Life-course theories argue that events that take place over the life course influence criminal choices. The cause of crime constantly changes as people mature. At first, the nuclear family influences behavior; during adolescence, the peer group dominates; in adulthood, marriage and career are critical. There are a variety of pathways to crime: some kids are sneaky, others hostile, and still others defiant. Crime may be part of a variety of social problems, including health, physical, and interpersonal troubles. Important life-course theories have been formulated by Terence Thornberry, David Farrington, and John Laub and Robert Sampson.

 See the book-specific web site at www.cj.wadsworth. com for additional chapter links, discussions, and quizzes.

THINKING LIKE A CRIMINOLOGIST

Luis Francisco is the leader of the Almighty Latin Kings and Queens Nation. He was convicted of murder in 1998 and sentenced to life imprisonment plus 45 years.

Luis Francisco's life has been filled with displacement, poverty, and chronic predatory crime. The son of a prostitute in Havana, at the age of 9 he was sent to prison for robbery. He had trouble in school, and teachers described him as having attention problems; he dropped out in the seventh grade. On his nineteenth birthday in 1980, he immigrated to the United States and soon after became a gang member in Chicago, where he joined the Latin Kings. After moving to the Bronx, he shot and killed his girlfriend in 1981. He fled to Chicago and was not apprehended until 1984. Sentenced to nine years for second-degree manslaughter, Luis Francisco ended up in a New York prison, where he started a New

Table 10.4 Integrated Theories

THEORY	MAJOR PREMISE	STRENGTHS
Latent Trait Theories		
General theory	Crime and criminality are separate concepts. People choose to commit crime when they lack self-control. People lacking in self-control will seize criminal opportunities.	Integrates choice and social control concepts. Identifies the difference between *crime* and *criminality*.
Human nature theory	People choose to commit crime when they are biologically and psychologically impaired.	Shows how physical traits interact with social conditions to produce crime. Can account for noncriminal behavior in high-crime areas. Integrates choice and developmental theories.
Developmental Theories		
Social development model (SDM)	Weak social controls produce crime. A person's place in the structure influences his or her bond to society.	Combines elements of social structural and social process theories. Accounts for variations in the crime rate.
Elliott's integrated theory	Strained and weak social bonds lead youths to associate with and learn from deviant peers.	Combines elements of learning, strain, and control theories.
Farrington's theory of delinquent development	Personal and social factors control the onset and stability of criminal careers.	Makes use of data collected over a 20-year period to substantiate hypothesis.
Interactional theory	Criminals go through lifestyle changes during their offending career.	Combines sociological and psychological theories.
Age-graded theory	As people mature, the factors that influence their propensity to commit crime change. In childhood, family factors are critical; in adulthood, marital and job factors are key.	Shows how crime is a developmental process that shifts in direction over the life course.

York prison chapter of the Latin Kings. As King Blood, Inka, First Supreme Crown, Francisco ruled the 2000 Latin Kings in and out of prison. Disciplinary troubles erupted when some Kings were stealing from the organization. Infuriated, King Blood wrote to his street lieutenants and ordered their termination. Federal authorities, who had been monitoring Francisco's mail, arrested 35 Latin Kings. Thirty-four pled guilty; only Francisco insisted on a trial, where he was found guilty of conspiracy to commit murder.

Explain Luis's behavior patterns from a developmental view. How would a latent trait theorist explain his escalating criminal activities?

KEY TERMS

multifactor theories
integrated theory
developmental criminology
differential anticipation theory
latent trait theory
developmental theory
latent trait
human nature theory
general theory of crime (GTC)

adaptive strategy theory
life-course theory
social interactional theory
integrated structural theory
problem behavior syndrome (PBS)
authority conflict pathway
covert pathway
overt pathway
adolescent-limited

life-course persister
pseudomaturity
social development model (SDM)
prosocial bonds
interactional theory
cognitive perspective
turning points
social capital

NOTES

1. Emilie Andersen Allan, "Theory Is Not a Zero-Sum Game: The Quest for an Integrated Theory." Paper presented at the annual meeting of the American Society of Criminology, Phoenix, Arizona, November 1993.

2. Gerald Patterson and Karen Yoerger, "Developmental Models for Delinquent Behavior," in *Mental Disorder and Crime*, ed. Sheilagh Hodgins (Newbury Park, Calif.: Sage, 1993), pp. 150–59.

3. Daniel Glazer, *Crime in Our Changing Society* (New York: Holt, Rinehart and Winston, 1978).

4. Glazer, *Crime in Our Changing Society*, p. 125.

5. David Rowe, D. Wayne Osgood, and W. Alan Nicewander, "A Latent Trait Approach to Unifying Criminal Careers," *Criminology* 28 (1990): 237–70.

6. Lee Ellis, "Neurohormonal Bases of Varying Tendencies to Learn Delinquent and Criminal Behavior," in *Behavioral Approaches to Crime and Delinquency*, ed.

E. Morris and C. Braukmann (New York: Plenum, 1988), pp. 499–518.

7. David Rowe, Alexander Vazsonyi, and Daniel Flannery, "Sex Differences in Crime: Do Means and Within-Sex Variation Have Similar Causes?" *Journal of Research in Crime and Delinquency* 32 (1995): 84–100.

8. James Q. Wilson and Richard Herrnstein, *Crime and Human Nature* (New York: Simon and Schuster, 1985).

9. Wilson and Herrnstein, *Crime and Human Nature,* p. 44.

10. Wilson and Herrnstein, *Crime and Human Nature,* p. 171.

11. Wilson and Herrnstein, *Crime and Human Nature,* p. 171.

12. Wilson and Herrnstein, *Crime and Human Nature,* p. 528.

13. Michael Gottfredson and Travis Hirschi, *A General Theory of Crime* (Stanford, Calif.: Stanford University Press, 1990).

14. Gottfredson and Hirschi, *A General Theory of Crime,* p. 27.

15. Anthony Walsh and Lee Ellis, "Shoring Up the Big Three: Improving Criminological Theories with Biosocial Concepts." Paper presented at the annual Society of Criminology meeting, San Diego, Calif., November, 1997, p. 15.

16. Gottfredson and Hirschi, *A General Theory of Crime,* p. 90.

17. Gottfredson and Hirschi, *A General Theory of Crime,* p. 89.

18. Alex Piquero and Stephen Tibbetts, "Specifying the Direct and Indirect Effects of Low Self-Control and Situational Factors in Offenders' Decision Making: Toward a More Complete Model of Rational Offending," *Justice Quarterly* 13 (1996): 481–508.

19. David Forde and Leslie Kennedy, "Risky Lifestyles, Routine Activities, and the General Theory of Crime," *Justice Quarterly* 14 (1997): 265–94.

20. Gottfredson and Hirschi, *A General Theory of Crime,* p. 112.

21. Gottfredson and Hirschi, *A General Theory of Crime,* p. 112.

22. Dennis Giever, "An Empirical Assessment of the Core Elements of Gottfredson and Hirschi's General Theory of Crime." Paper presented at the American Society of Criminology meeting, Boston, Mass., November 1995.

23. Robert Agnew, "The Contribution of Social-Psychological Strain Theory to the Explanation of Crime and Delinquency," *Advances in Criminological Theory* 6 (1994).

24. Travis Hirschi and Michael Gottfredson, "Rethinking the Juvenile Justice System," *Crime and Delinquency* 39 (1993): 262–71.

25. David Brownfield and Ann Marie Sorenson, "Self-Control and Juvenile Delinquency: Theoretical Issues and an Empirical Assessment of Selected Elements of a General Theory of Crime," *Deviant Behavior* 14 (1993): 243–64; Harold Grasmick, Charles Tittle, Robert Bursik, and Bruce Arneklev, "Testing the Core Empirical Implications of Gottfredson and Hirschi's General Theory of Crime," *Journal of Research in Crime and Delinquency* 30 (1993): 5–29; John Cochran, Peter Wood, and Bruce Arneklev, "Is the Religiosity–Delinquency Relationship Spurious? A Test of Arousal and Social Control Theories," *Journal of Research in Crime and Delinquency* 31 (1994): 92–123; Marc LeBlanc, Marc Ouimet, and Richard Tremblay, "An Integrative Control Theory of Delinquent Behavior: A Validation 1976–1985," *Psychiatry* 51 (1988): 164–76.

26. Carl Keane, Paul Maxim, and James Teevan, "Drinking and Driving, Self-Control, and Gender: Testing a General Theory of Crime," *Journal of Research in Crime and Delinquency* 30 (1993): 30–46.

27. Judith DeJong, Matti Virkkunen, and Marku Linnoila, "Factors Associated with Recidivism in a Criminal Population," *The Journal of Nervous and Mental Disease* 180 (1992): 543–50.

28. David Cantor, "Drug Involvement and Offending Among Incarcerated Juveniles." Paper presented at the American Society of Criminology meeting, Boston, Mass., November 1995.

29. Brownfield and Sorenson, "Self-Control and Juvenile Delinquency"; Grasmick, Tittle, Bursik, and Arneklev, "Testing the Core Empirical Implications of Gottfredson and Hirschi's General Theory of Crime"; Cochran, Wood, and Arneklev, "Is the Religiosity–Delinquency Relationship Spurious?"

30. Dennis Giever, "Empirical Testing of Gottfredson and Hirschi's General Theory of Crime" (paper presented at the American Society of Criminology meeting, San Diego, Calif., 1997); John Gibbs and Dennis Giever, "Self-Control and Its Manifestations Among University Students: An Empirical Test of Gottfredson and Hirschi's General Theory," *Justice Quarterly* 12 (1995): 231–55.

31. Carey Herbert, "The Implications of Self-Control Theory for Workplace Offending." Paper presented at the American Society of Criminology Meeting, San Diego, Calif., 1997.

32. Dennis Giever, Dana Lynskey, and Danette Monnet, "Gottfredson and Hirschi's General Theory of Crime and Youth Gangs: An Empirical Test on a Sample of Middle School Youth." Paper presented at the American Society of Criminology Meeting, San Diego, Calif., 1997.

33. See for example, Douglas Longshore, Susan Turner, and Judith Stein, "Self-Control in a Criminal Sample: An Examination of Construct Validity," *Criminology* 34 (1996); Grasmick et al., "Testing the Core Empirical Implications of Gottfredson and Hirschi's General Theory of Crime"; Daniel Nagin and Raymond Paternoster, "Enduring Individual Differences and Rational Choice Theories of Crime," *Law and Society Review* 27 (1993): 467–89.

34. Linda Pagani, Richard Tremblay, Frank Vitaro, and Sophie Parent, "Does Preschool Help Prevent Delinquency in Boys with a History of Perinatal Complications?" *Criminology* 36 (1998): 245–68.

35. Velmer Burton, Francis Cullen, T. David Evans, Leanne Fiftal Alarid, and R. Gregory Dunaway, "Gender, Self-Control, and Crime," *Journal of Research in Crime and Delinquency* 35 (1998): 123–47.

36. John Gibbs, Dennis Giever and Jamie Martin, "Parental Management and Self-Control: An Empirical Test of Gottfredson and Hirschi's General Theory," *Journal of Research in Crime and Delinquency* 35 (1998): 40–70.

37. Michael Benson and Elizabeth Moore, "Are White-Collar and Common Offenders the Same? An Empirical and Theoretical Critique of a Recently Proposed General Theory of Crime," *Journal of Research in Crime and Delinquency* 29 (1992): 251–72.

38. Ronald Akers, "Self-Control as a General Theory of Crime," *Journal of Quantitative Criminology* 7 (1991): 201–211.

39. Gottfredson and Hirschi, *A General Theory of Crime,* p. 88.

40. Samuel Yochelson and Clifford Samenow, *The Criminal Personality* (New York: Jason Aronson, 1977).

41. Alan Feingold, "Gender Differences in Personality: A Meta Analysis," *Psychological Bulletin* 116 (1994): 429–56.

42. Gottfredson and Hirschi, *A General Theory of Crime,* p. 153.

43. Ann Marie Sorenson and David Brownfield, "Normative Concepts in Social Control." Paper presented at the annual meeting of the American Society of Criminology, Phoenix, Ariz., November 1993.

44. Brent Benda, "An Examination of Reciprocal Relationship Between Religiosity and Different Forms of Delinquency Within a Theoretical Model," *Journal of Research in Crime and Delinquency* 34 (1997): 163–86.

45. Scott Menard, Delbert Elliott, and Sharon Wofford, "Social Control Theories in Developmental Perspective," *Studies on Crime and Crime Prevention* 2 (1993): 69–87.

46. Delbert Elliott and Scott Menard, "Delinquent Friends and Delinquent Behavior: Temporal and Developmental Patterns," in *Crime and Delinquency: Current Theories,* ed. J. David Hawkins (Cambridge: Cambridge University Press, 1996).

47. Graham Ousey and David Aday, "The Interaction Hypothesis: A Test Using Social Control Theory and Social Learning Theory." Paper presented at the American Society of Criminology Meeting, Boston, Mass., 1995.

48. Ronald Simons, Christine Johnson, Rand Conger, and Glen Elder, "A Test of Latent Trait Versus Life-Course Perspectives on the Stability of Adolescent Antisocial Behavior," *Criminology* 36 (1998): 217–44.

49. Julie Horney, D. Wayne Osgood, and Ineke Haen Marshall, "Criminal Careers in the

Short-Term: Intra-Individual Variability in Crime and Its Relations to Local Life Circumstances," *American Sociological Review* 60 (1995): 655–73.

50. Martin Daly and Margo Wilson, "Killing the Competition," *Human Nature* 1 (1990): 83–109.

51. Charles R. Tittle and Harold G. Grasmick, "Criminal Behavior and Age: A Test of Three Provocative Hypotheses," *Journal of Criminal Law and Criminology* 88 (1997): 309–342.

52. Douglas Longshore, "Self-Control and Criminal Opportunity: A Prospective Test of the General Theory of Crime," *Social Problems* 45 (1998): 102–114.

53. Raymond Paternoster and Robert Brame, "The Structural Similarity of Processes Generating Criminal and Analogous Behaviors," *Criminology* 36 (1998): 633–70.

54. Otwin Marenin and Michael Resig, "*A General Theory of Crime* and Patterns of Crime in Nigeria: An Exploration of Methodological Assumptions," *Journal of Criminal Justice* 23 (1995): 501–518.

55. Bruce Arneklev, Harold Grasmick, Charles Tittle, and Robert Bursik, "Low Self-Control and Imprudent Behavior," *Journal of Quantitative Criminology* 9 (1993): 225–46.

56. Kevin Thompson, "Sexual Harassment and Low Self-Control: An Application of Gottfredson and Hirschi's General Theory of Crime." Paper presented at the annual meeting of the American Society of Criminology, Phoenix, Ariz., November 1993.

57. Marvin Krohn, Alan Lizotte, and Cynthia Perez, "The Interrelationship Between Substance Use and Precocious Transitions to Adult Sexuality," *Journal of Health and Social Behavior* 38 (1997): 87–103 at 88.

58. G. R. Patterson, Barbara DeBaryshe, and Elizabeth Ramsey, "A Developmental Perspective on Antisocial Behavior," *American Psychologist* 44 (1989): 329–35.

59. Joan McCord, "Family Relationships, Juvenile Delinquency, and Adult Criminality," *Criminology* 29 (1991): 397–417.

60. Paul Mazerolle, "Delinquent Definitions and Participation Age: Assessing the Invariance Hypothesis," *Studies on Crime and Crime Prevention* 6 (1997): 151–68.

61. Robert Sampson and John Laub, "Crime and Deviance in the Life Course," *American Review of Sociology* 18 (1992): 63–84.

62. Gerald Patterson, J. B. Reid, and Thomas Dishion, *A Social Interactional Approach: Antisocial Boys* (Eugene, Ore.: Castalia Press, 1992).

63. Francois Poulin, Thomas Dishion, Mike Stoolmiller, and Gerald Patterson, "Modeling Growth in Adolescent Delinquency: The Combined Effect and Developmental Specificity of Parent Bonding and Deviant Peers." Paper presented at the annual meeting of the American Society of Criminology, Chicago, Ill., November, 1996.

64. See, generally, Sheldon Glueck and Eleanor Glueck, *500 Criminal Careers* (New York: Knopf, 1930); Sheldon Glueck and Eleanor Glueck, *One Thousand Juve-*

nile Delinquents (Cambridge: Harvard University Press, 1934); Sheldon Glueck and Eleanor Glueck, *Predicting Delinquency and Crime* (Cambridge: Harvard University Press, 1967), pp. 82–83.

65. Sheldon Glueck and Eleanor Glueck, *Unraveling Juvenile Delinquency* (Cambridge: Harvard University Press, 1950).

66. Glueck and Glueck, *Unraveling Juvenile Delinquency*, p. 48.

67. See, generally, John Laub and Robert Sampson, "The Sutherland–Glueck Debate: On the Sociology of Criminological Knowledge," *American Journal of Sociology* 96 (1991): 1402–40; John Laub and Robert Sampson, "Unraveling Families and Delinquency: A Reanalysis of the Gluecks' Data," *Criminology* 26 (1988): 355–80.

68. Rolf Loeber and Marc LeBlanc, "Toward a Developmental Criminology," in *Crime and Justice,* vol. 12, ed. Norval Morris and Michael Tonry (Chicago: University of Chicago Press, 1990), pp. 375–473; Rolf Loeber and Marc Leblanc, "Developmental Criminology Updated," in *Crime and Justice,* vol. 23, ed. Michael Tonry (Chicago: University of Chicago Press, 1998), pp. 115–198.

69. G. R. Patterson, L. Crosby, and S. Vuchinich, "Predicting Risk for Early Police Arrest," *Journal of Quantitative Criminology* 8 (1992): 335–55.

70. Patterson, DeBaryshe, and Ramsey, "A Developmental Perspective on Antisocial Behavior," pp. 331–33.

71. Rolf Loeber, Magda Stouthamer-Loeber, Welmoet Van Kammen, and David Farrington, "Initiation, Escalation, and Desistance in Juvenile Offending and Their Correlates," *Journal of Criminal Law and Criminology* 82 (1991): 36–82.

72. Raymond Paternoster, Charles Dean, Alex Piquero, Paul Mazerolle, and Robert Brame, "Generality, Continuity, and Change in Offending," *Journal of Quantitative Criminology* 13 (1997): 231–66.

73. Magda Stouthamer-Loeber and Evelyn Wei, "The Precursors of Young Fatherhood and Its Effect on Delinquency of Teenage Males," *Journal of Adolescent Health* 22 (1998): 56–65; Richard Jessor, John Donovan, and Francis Costa, *Beyond Adolescence: Problem Behavior and Young Adult Development* (New York: Cambridge University Press, 1991).

74. Marvin Krohn, Alan Lizotte, and Cynthia Perez, "The Interrelationship Between Substance Use and Precocious Transitions to Adult Sexuality," *Journal of Health and Social Behavior* 38 (1997): 87–103 at 88. Richard Jessor, "Risk Behavior in Adolescence: A Psychosocial Framework for Understanding and Action," in *Adolescents at Risk: Medical and Social Perspectives,* ed. D. E. Rogers and E. Ginzburg (Boulder, Colo.: Westview, 1992).

75. Deborah Capaldi and Gerald Patterson, "Can Violent Offenders Be Distinguished from Frequent Offenders: Prediction from Childhood to Adolescence," *Journal of Research in Crime and Delinquency* 33

(1996): 206–231; D. Wayne Osgood, "The Covariation Among Adolescent Problem Behaviors" (paper presented at the annual meeting of the American Society of Criminology, Baltimore, November 1990).

76. Terence Thornberry, Carolyn Smith, and Gregory Howard, "Risk Factors for Teenage Fatherhood," *Journal of Marriage and the Family* 59 (1997): 505–522; Todd Miller, Timothy Smith, Charles Turner, Margarita Guijarro, and Amanda Hallet, "A Meta-Analytic Review of Research on Hostility and Physical Health," *Psychological Bulletin* 119 (1996): 322–48; Marianne Junger, "Accidents and Crime," in *The Generality of Deviance,* ed. T. Hirschi and M. Gottfredson (New Brunswick, N.J.: Transaction Press, 1993).

77. Robert Johnson, S. Susan Su, Dean Gerstein, Hee-Choon Shin, and John Hoffman, "Parental Influences on Deviant Behavior in Early Adolescence: A Logistic Response Analysis of Age- and Gender-Differentiated Effects," *Journal of Quantitative Criminology* 11 (1995): 167–92; Judith Brooks, Martin Whiteman, and Patricia Cohen, "Stage of Drug Use, Aggression, and Theft/Vandalism," in *Drugs, Crime and Other Deviant Adaptations: Longitudinal Studies,* ed. Howard Kaplan (New York: Plenum Press, 1995), pp. 83–96; Robert Hoge, D. A. Andrews, and Alan Leschied, "Tests of Three Hypotheses Regarding the Predictors of Delinquency," *Journal of Abnormal Child Psychology* 22 (1994): 547–59.

78. David Huizinga, Rolf Loeber, and Terence Thornberry, "Longitudinal Study of Delinquency, Drug Use, Sexual Activity, and Pregnancy Among Children and Youth in Three Cities," *Public Health Reports* 108 (1993): 90–96.

79. For an analysis of more than 30 studies, see Mark Lipsey and James Derzon, "Predictors of Violent or Serious Delinquency in Adolescence and Early Adulthood: A Synthesis of Longitudinal Research," in *Serious and Violent Juvenile Offenders: Risk Factors and Successful Interventions,* ed. Rolf Loeber and David Farrington (Thousand Oaks, Calif.: Sage, 1998).

80. Jeanne Hernandez, "The Concurrence of Eating Disorders with Histories of Child Abuse Among Adolescents." Paper presented at the annual meeting of the American Society of Criminology, Phoenix, Ariz., November 1993.

81. Candace Kruttschnitt, Jane McLeod, and Maude Dornfeld, "The Economic Environment of Child Abuse," *Social Problems* 41 (1994): 299–312.

82. Helene Raskin White, "Early Problem Behavior and Later Drug Problems," *Journal of Research in Crime and Delinquency* 29 (1992): 412–29.

83. Helene Raskin White and Erich Labouvie, "Generality versus Specificity of Problem Behavior: Psychological and Functional Differences," *Journal of Drug Issues* 24 (1994): 55–74.

84. See, generally, Richard Dembo, Linda Williams, Werner Wothke, James Schmeidelr, Alan Getreu, Estrellita Berry, and

Eric Wish, "The Generality of Deviance: Replication of a Structural Model Among High-Risk Youths," *Journal of Research in Crime and Delinquency* 29 (1992): 200–16.

85. Pamela Lattimore, Richard Linster, and John MacDonald, "Risk of Death Among Serious Young Offenders," *Journal of Research in Crime and Delinquency* 34 (1997): 187–209.

86. Rolf Loeber, Phen Wung, Kate Keenan, Bruce Giroux, Magda Stouthamer-Loeber, Wemoet Van Kammen, and Barbara Maughan, "Developmental Pathways in Disruptive Behavior," *Development and Psychopathology* (1993): 12–48.

87. Amy D'Unger, Kenneth Land, Patricia McCall, and Daniel Nagin, " How Many Latent Classes of Delinquent/Criminal Careers? Results from Mixed Poisson Regression Analyses," *American Journal of Sociology* 103 (1998): 1593–1630.

88. Terrie Moffitt, "Natural Histories of Delinquency," in *Cross-National Longitudinal Research on Human Development and Criminal Behavior,* ed. Elmar Weitekamp and Hans-Jurgen Kerner (Dordrecht, Netherlands: Kluwer, 1994), pp. 3–65.

89. Rolf Loeber and Magda Stouthamer-Loeber, "Development of Juvenile Aggression and Violence," *American Psychologist* 53 (1998): 242–59.

90. Terrie Moffitt, "Adolescence-Limited and Life-Course Persistent Antisocial Behavior: A Developmental Taxonomy," *Psychological Review* 100 (1993): 674–701.

91. Paul Mazerole, Robert Brame, Ray Paternoster, Alex Piquero, and Charles Dean, "Onset Age, Persistence, and Offending Versatility: Comparisons Across Sex." Paper presented at the annual Society of Criminology meeting, San Diego, Calif., November, 1997.

92. Dawn Jeglum Bartusch, Donald Lynam, Terrie Moffitt, and Phil Silva, "Is Age Important? Testing a General Versus a Developmental Theory of Antisocial Behavior," *Criminology* 35 (1997): 13–48.

93. Michael Newcomb, "Pseudomaturity Among Adolescents: Construct Validation, Sex Differences, and Associations in Adulthood," *Journal of Drug Issues* 26 (1996): 477–504.

94. R. E. Tremblay and L. C. Masse, "Cognitive Deficits, School Achievement, Disruptive Behavior, and Juvenile Delinquency: A Longitudinal Look at Their Developmental Sequence." Paper presented at the annual meeting of the American Society of Criminology, Phoenix, Ariz., November 1993.

95. David Nurco, Timothy Kinlock, and Mitchell Balter, "The Severity of Preaddiction Criminal Behavior Among Urban, Male Narcotic Addicts and Two Nonaddicted Control Groups," *Journal of Research in Crime and Delinquency* 30 (1993): 293–316.

96. Mark Lipsey and James Derzon, "Predictors of Violent or Serious Delinquency in Adolescence and Early Adulthood: A Synthesis of Longitudinal Research," in *Serious and Violent Juvenile Offenders: Risk Factors and Successful Interventions,* ed. Rolf Loeber and David Farrington (Thousand Oaks, Calif.: Sage, 1998).

97. G. R. Patterson and Karen Yoerger, "Differentiating Outcomes and Histories for Early and Late Onset Arrests." Paper presented at the annual meeting of the American Society of Criminology, Phoenix, Ariz., November 1993.

98. Paul Tracy and Kimberly Kempf-Leonard, *Continuity and Discontinuity in Criminal Careers* (New York: Plenum Press, 1996), p. 208.

99. Ronald Simons, Chyi-In Wu, Rand Conger, and Frederick Lorenz, "Two Routes to Delinquency: Differences Between Early and Later Starters in the Impact of Parenting and Deviant Careers," *Criminology* 32 (1994): 247–75.

100. Paul Mazerolle, "Understanding the Theoretical and Empirical Dimensions of Late Onset to Delinquent Behavior." Paper presented at the annual meeting of the American Society of Criminology, Boston, Mass., November 1995.

101. Charles Dean, Robert Brame, and Alex Piquero, "Criminal Propensities, Discrete Groups of Offenders, and Persistence of Crime," *Criminology* 34 (1966): 547–73.

102. See, for example, the Rochester Youth Development Study, Hindelang Criminal Justice Research Center, 135 Western Avenue, Albany, New York 12222.

103. David Farrington, "The Development of Offending and Antisocial Behavior from Childhood to Adulthood." Paper presented at the Congress on Rethinking Delinquency, University of Minho, Braga, Portugal, July 1992.

104. Joseph Weis and J. David Hawkins, *Reports of the National Juvenile Assessment Centers, Preventing Delinquency* (Washington, D.C.: U.S. Department of Justice, 1981); Joseph Weis and John Sederstrom, *Reports of the National Juvenile Justice Assessment Centers, The Prevention of Serious Delinquency: What to Do* (Washington, D.C.: U.S. Department of Justice, 1981).

105. Julie O'Donnell, J. David Hawkins, and Robert Abbott, "Predicting Serious Delinquency and Substance Use Among Aggressive Boys," *Journal of Consulting and Clinical Psychology* 63 (1995): 529–37.

106. O'Donnell, Hawkins, and Abbott, "Predicting Serious Delinquency and Substance Use Among Aggressive Boys," pp. 534–36; Richard Catalano, Rick Kosterman, J. David Hawkins, Michael Newcomb, and Robert Abbott, "Modeling the Etiology of Adolescent Substance Use: A Test of the Social Development Model," *Journal of Drug Issues* 26 (1996) 429–55.

107. David Brownfield, Kevin Thompson, and Ann Marie Sorenson, "Correlates of Gang Membership: A Test of Strain, Social Learning, and Control-Bonding Theories." Paper presented at the annual meeting of the American Society of Criminology, Chicago, Ill., November, 1996.

108. J. David Hawkins, Richard Catalano, Diane Morrison, Julie O'Donnell, Robert Abbott, and L. Edward Day, "The Seattle Social Development Project," in *The Prevention of Antisocial Behavior in Children,* ed. Joan McCord and Richard Tremblay (New York: Guilford, 1992), pp. 139–60.

109. Delbert Elliott, David Huizinga, and Suzanne Ageton, *Explaining Delinquency and Drug Use* (Beverly Hills: Sage, 1985).

110. Scott Menard and Delbert Elliott, "Delinquent Bonding, Moral Beliefs, and Illegal Behavior: A Three Wave-Panel Model," *Justice Quarterly* 11 (1994): 173–88.

111. Menard and Elliott, "Delinquent Bonding, Moral Beliefs, and Illegal Behavior," p. 184.

112. See, generally, D. J. West and David P. Farrington, *The Delinquent Way of Life* (London: Hienemann, 1977).

113. The material in the following sections is summarized from Farrington, "The Development of Offending and Antisocial Behavior from Childhood to Adulthood"; David Farrington, "Psychobiological Factors in the Explanation and Reduction of Delinquency," *Today's Delinquent* 7 (1988): 44–46; David Farrington, "Childhood Origins of Teenage Antisocial Behaviour and Adult Social Dysfunction," *Journal of the Royal Society of Medicine* 86 (1993): 13–17; David Farrington, "Psychosocial Influences on the Development of Antisocial Personality" (paper presented at the annual meeting of the American Society of Criminology, Phoenix, Ariz., November 1993).

114. Terence Thornberry, "Toward an Interactional Theory of Delinquency," *Criminology* 25 (1987): 863–91.

115. Ross Matsueda and Kathleen Anderson, "The Dynamics of Delinquent Peers and Delinquent Behavior," *Criminology* 36 (1998): 269–308.

116. See, for example, Jean Piaget, *The Grasp of Consciousness* (Cambridge: Harvard University Press, 1976).

117. Thornberry, "Toward an Interactional Theory of Delinquency."

118. Thornberry, "Toward an Interactional Theory of Delinquency," p. 863.

119. This research is known as the Rochester Youth Development Study. Thornberry's colleagues on the project include Alan Lizotte, Margaret Farnworth, Marvin Krohn, and Susan Stern.

120. Sung Joon Jang and Carolyn Smith, "A Test of Reciprocal Causal Relationships Among Parental Supervision, Affective Ties, and Delinquency," *Journal of Research in Crime and Delinquency* 34 (1997): 307–336.

121. Marvin Krohn, Alan Lizotte, and Cynthia Perez, "The Interrelationship Between Substance Use and Precocious Transitions to Adult Sexuality," *Journal of Health and Social Behavior* 38 (1997): 87–103 at 88; Richard Jessor, "Risk Behavior in Adolescence: A Psychosocial Framework for Understanding and Action," in *Adolescents*

at Risk: Medical and Social Perspectives, ed. D. E. Rogers and E. Ginzburg (Boulder, Colo.: Westview, 1992).

122. Terence Thornberry, Alan Lizotte, Marvin Krohn, and Margaret Farnworth, *The Role of Delinquent Peers in the Initiation of Delinquent Behavior*, working paper no. 6, rev., Rochester Youth Development Study (Albany, N.Y.: Hindelang Criminal Justice Research Center, 1993).

123. Terence Thornberry, Alan Lizotte, Marvin Krohn, Margaret Farnworth, and Sung Joon Jang, "Delinquent Peers, Beliefs, and Delinquent Behavior: A Longitudinal Test of Interactional Theory," *Criminology* 32 (1994): 601–37.

124. Terence Thornberry, Alan Lizotte, Marvin Krohn, Margaret Farnworth, and Sung Joon Jang, *Delinquent Peers, Beliefs, and Delinquent Behavior: A Longitudinal Test of Interactional Theory*, working paper no. 6, rev., Rochester Youth Development Study (Albany, N.Y.: Hindelang Criminal Justice Research Center, 1992).

125. Terence Thornberry, Alan Lizotte, Marvin Krohn, Margaret Farnworth, and Sung Joon Jang, "Testing Interactional Theory: An Examination of Reciprocal Causal Relationships among Family, School, and Delinquency," *Journal of Criminal Law and Criminology* 82 (1991): 3–35.

126. Menard and Elliott, "Delinquent Bonding, Moral Beliefs, and Illegal Behavior."

127. Carolyn Smith, Alan Lizotte, Terence Thornberry, and Marvin Krohn, *Resilient Youth: Identifying Factors That Prevent High-Risk Youth from Engaging in Delinquency and Drug Use* (Albany, N.Y.: Rochester Youth Development Study, 1994).

128. Thornberry et al., *Delinquent Peers, Beliefs, and Delinquent Behavior*, pp. 628–29.

129. Robert Sampson and John Laub, *Crime in the Making: Pathways and Turning Points Through Life* (Cambridge: Harvard University Press, 1993); John Laub and Robert Sampson, "Turning Points in the Life Course: Why Change Matters to the Study of Crime" (paper presented at the annual meeting of the American Society of Criminology, New Orleans, November 1992).

130. Terri Orbuch, James House, Richard Mero, and Pamela Webster, "Marital Quality Over the Life Course," *Social Psychology Quarterly* 59 (1996): 162–71; Lee Lillard and Linda Waite, "'Til Death Do Us Part: Marital Disruption and Mortality," *American Journal of Sociology* 100 (1995): 1131–56.

131. Mark Warr, "Life-Course Transitions and Desistance from Crime," *Criminology* 36 (1998): 183–216.

132. Pamela Webster, Terri Orbuch, and James House, "Effects of Childhood Family Background on Adult Marital Quality and Perceived Stability," *American Journal of Sociology* 101 (1995): 404–432.

133. John Hagan, Ross MacMillan, and Blair Wheaton, "New Kid in Town: Social Capital and the Life Course Effects of Family Migration on Children," *American Sociological Review* 61 (1996): 368–85.

134. Sampson and Laub, *Crime in the Making*, p. 249.

135. Raymond Paternoster and Robert Brame, "Multiple Routes to Delinquency? A Test of Developmental and General Theories of Crime," *Criminology* 35 (1997): 49–84.

136. Robert Hoge, D. A. Andrews, and Alan Leschied, "An Investigation of Risk and Protective Factors in a Sample of Youthful Offenders," *Journal of Child Psychology and Psychiatry* 37 (1996): 419–24.

137. Candace Kruttschnitt, Christopher Uggen, and Kelly Shelton, "Individual Variability in Sex Offending and Its Relationship to Informal and Formal Social Controls" (paper presented at the American Society of Criminology meeting, San Diego, Calif., 1997); Mark Collins and Don Weatherburn, "Unemployment and the Dynamics of Offender Populations," *Journal of Quantitative Criminology* 11 (1995): 231–45.

138. Avshalom Caspi, Terrie Moffitt, Bradley Entner Wright, and Phil Silva, "Early Failure in the Labor Market: Childhood and Adolescent Predictors of Unemployment in the Transition to Adulthood," *American Sociological Review* 63 (1998): 424–51.

139. Erich Labouvie, "Maturing Out of Substance Use: Selection and Self-Correction," *Journal of Drug Issues* 26 (1996): 457–74.

140. Mark Warr, "Life-Course Transitions and Desistance from Crime," *Criminology* 36 (1998): 502–535.

141. Robert Sampson and John Laub, "Socioeconomic Achievement in the Life Course of Disadvantaged Men: Military Service as a Turning Point, circa 1940–1965," *American Sociological Review* 61 (1996): 347–67.

142. Daniel Nagin and Raymond Paternoster, "Personal Capital and Social Control: The Deterrence Implications of a Theory of Criminal Offending," *Criminology* 32 (1994): 581–606.

143. Eloise Dunlop and Bruce Johnson, "Family and Human Resources in the Development of a Female Crack-Seller Career: Case Study of a Hidden Population," *Journal of Drug Issues* 26 (1996): 175–98.

CRIME TYPOLOGIES

Regardless of why people commit crime in the first place, their actions are defined by law as falling into particular crime categories, or *typologies*. Criminologists often seek to group individual criminal offenders or behaviors so they may be more easily studied and understood. These are referred to as offender typologies.

In this section, crime patterns are clustered into four typologies: violent crime (Chapter 11); economic crimes involving common theft offenses (Chapter 12); economic crimes involving white-collar criminals or criminal organizations (Chapter 13); and public order crimes, such as prostitution and drug abuse (Chapter 14). This format groups criminal behaviors by their focuses and consequences: bringing physical harm to others; misappropriating other people's property; and violating laws designed to protect public morals.

Typologies can be useful in classifying large numbers of criminal offenses or offenders into easily understood categories. This text has grouped offenses and offenders on the basics of their (1) legal definitions and (2) collective goals, objectives, and consequences.

CHAPTER 11

Violent Crime

INTRODUCTION

On Sunday, June 8, 1998, the broken body of a black man was discovered just outside the East Texas town of Jasper, population 8,000.[1] Authorities determined that James Byrd, Jr., 49, had been dragged to his death from the back of a pickup truck in a rural section of Texas known for racist and Ku Klux Klan activity. An investigation found that Byrd was picked up by three men sometime after midnight and taken to a wooded area, where he was beaten, then chained to the truck and dragged for two miles. The Jasper County district attorney called the killing "probably the most brutal I've ever seen" in 20 years as a prosecutor.

Police quickly identified three suspects, ex-offenders and Klan supporters, whose bodies were covered in racist tattoos. The three had spent time in tough Texas prisons, where for their own protection they had joined inmate gangs segregated by color. Their prison experiences may have intensified preexisting racial prejudice that had been part of their boyhood culture. Two suspects were members of the Confederate Knights of America, a racist group linked to the Klan. Yet this crime was so evil and so widely condemned that Texas Klaverns have denounced it, and a small group of Klansmen applied for a permit to march not in support of the suspects but to disavow any connection with them.[2]

The Jasper killing was a shocking reminder that violence is too common in American life. "Violence is the primal problem of American history," writes social historian David Courtwright, ". . . the dark reverse of its coin of freedom and abundance."[3] Although the violent crime rate has recently declined, people are continually bombarded with news stories featuring grisly accounts of mass murder, child abuse, and serial rape. Unfortunately, these accounts reflect the harsh realities of American life: violence rates in the United States far exceed those in any other industrialized nation.[4]

Many people have personally experienced violence or have a friend who has been victimized. Almost everyone has heard about someone being robbed, beaten, or killed. Riots and mass disturbances have ravaged urban areas; racial attacks plague schools and college campuses; assassination has claimed the lives of political, religious, and social leaders all over the world.[5]

When violence is directed toward strangers, it is **instrumental,** that is, designed to improve the financial or social position of the criminal, such as through an

John William King is escorted from the Jasper County Courthouse after being found guilty of capital murder in the dragging death of James Byrd. Does this killing indicate that America's climate of hate is responsible for its relatively high violence rate? Can executing notorious criminals such as King deter such crimes, or does it serve to further brutalize society?

armed robbery. In contrast, **expressive violence** refers to crimes that vent rage, anger, or frustration. This may have been the case when on April 20, 1999, Eric Harris and Dylan Klebold, two students at Columbine High School in Littleton, Colorado, went on a murderous rampage that left twelve students and one teacher dead and twenty-four other people wounded, before the boys committed suicide. Members of a cult group called the "Trenchcoat Mafia," Harris and Klebold had spent more than a year planning the attack and building home-made bombs. The Littleton incident is an extreme example of expressive violence.

The general public believes that the government should "get tough" about violent crime. Public opinion polls indicate that more than 75 percent of U.S. citizens favor the use of capital punishment for persons convicted of murder, up from 38 percent in 1965.[6] The U.S. Supreme Court has responded by making teenage criminals over the age of 16 eligible for the death penalty.[7] Many people believe that America is becoming even more violent than in the past. But longing for the serenity of the pioneer days may be misplaced: American society has long been stained with violent crime, as is discussed in the Criminological Enterprise feature titled "Violent Land."

What sets off a violent person? Some experts suggest that a small number of inherently violence-prone individuals may themselves have been the victims of physical or psychological abnormalities. Another view is that violence and aggression are inherently human traits that can affect any person at any time. There may be violence-prone subcultures within society whose members value force, routinely carry weapons, and consider violence to have an acceptable place in social interaction.[8]

This chapter surveys the nature and extent of violent crime. First it briefly reviews some hypothetical causes of violence. Then it focuses on specific types of interpersonal violence—rape, assault, homicide, robbery, and domestic violence. Finally, it briefly examines political violence, state-sponsored violence, and terrorism.

THE ROOTS OF VIOLENCE

What causes people to behave violently? There are a number of competing explanations for violent behavior. A few of the most prominent are discussed here and illustrated in Figure 11.1.

Personal Traits

On March 13, 1995, an ex–Boy Scout leader named Thomas Hamilton took four high-powered rifles into the primary school of the peaceful Scottish town of Dunblane and slaughtered 16 children and their teacher. This horrific crime shocked the British Isles into implementing strict controls on all guns.[9]

Bizarre outbursts such as Hamilton's support a link between violence and personal traits. More than 30 years ago, sociologist Laura Bender examined convicted juvenile murderers and concluded that they suffered from abnormal **electroencephalogram** (EEG) readings (based on a device that measures brain activity), learning disabilities, and psychosis.[10] Bender's research is supported by recent studies showing that some murderers suffer from a network of abnormal cortical and subcortical brain processes that may predispose them to violence.[11]

CONNECTIONS

As you may recall from Chapter 6, biosocial theorists link violence to a number of biological irregularities, including but not limited to genetic influences and inheritance, the action of hormones, the functioning of neurotransmitters, brain structure, and diet. Psychologists link violent behavior to observational learning from violent TV shows, traumatic childhood experiences, low intelligence, mental illness, impaired cognitive processes, and abnormal (psychopathic) personality structure.

Psychologist Dorothy Otnow Lewis and her associates found that murderous youths suffer signs of major neurological impairment (such as abnormal EEGs, multiple psychomotor impairment, and severe seizures), low intelligence as measured on standard IQ tests, psychotic close relatives, and psychotic symptoms such as paranoia, illogical thinking, and hallucinations.[12] In

Figure 11.1   Sources of Violence

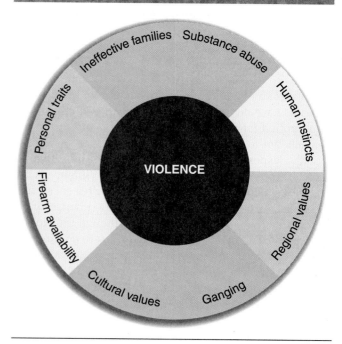

The Criminological Enterprise

Violent Land

David Courtwright, an authority on the sociocultural roots of violence, describes a nineteenth-century American society much more violent than today. According to Courtwright, societies with the highest rates of violent crime have been populations with an overabundance of young males who are "awash with testosterone" and unrestrained by social controls such as marriage and family.

Until the mid-twentieth century, the U.S. population was disproportionately young and male. The male-to-female gender ratio of those who settled here involuntarily—indentured servants and slaves—was more than 2:1. Poor laborers who paid for their passage by signing labor contracts were almost all male; the gender ratio among Chinese laborers was an astounding 27:1. Aside from Ireland, which furnished slightly more female than male immigrants, Europeans who arrived voluntarily were also predominantly male. Because these young men outnumbered women, not all men were able to marry, and those who did not remained unrestrained by the calming influence of family life and parental responsibility.

Cultural factors worsened these population trends. Frontier culture was characterized by racism and preoccupation with personal honor. Some ethnic groups drank heavily and frequented saloons and gambling halls, where petty arguments could become lethal because most patrons carried guns and knives. Violent acts often went unpunished, however, because law enforcement agencies were unable or unwilling to take action. Nowhere were these cultural and population effects felt more acutely than on the western frontier. Here the population was mostly young bachelors who were sensitive about honor, hostile racists, heavy drinkers, morally indifferent, heavily armed, and unchecked by adequate law enforcement. It is not surprising, considering this explosive mix, that 20 percent of the 89,000 miners who arrived in California during the 1849 gold rush were dead within six months. Many died from disease, but others succumbed to drink and violence. Smoking, gambling, and heavy drinking became a cultural imperative, and those who were disinclined to indulge were considered social outcasts.

Over time, gender ratios equalized as more men brought families to the frontier and children of both sexes were born. Many men died, returned home, or drifted elsewhere. By the mid-twentieth century, America's overall male surplus was disappearing, and a balanced population helped bring down the crime rate.

According to Courtwright, rising violence rates in the 1960s and 1970s can be attributed to the fact that men were avoiding, delaying, or terminating marriage. In 1960 Americans spent an average of 62 percent of their lives with spouses and children, an all-time high; in 1980 they spent 43 percent with families, an all-time low. Both the illegitimacy and divorce rates began to spiral upward, guaranteeing that the number of poorly socialized and supervised children would increase dramatically. The inner-city urban ghetto became the "frontier" community of today. Gangs such as the Crips and Bloods in Los Angeles are the modern descendants of the Old West gangs of Jesse James and Butch Cassidy and the Sundance Kid's Hole in the Wall Gang. And although the male-to-female ratio is more balanced than on the western frontier, the presence of unsupervised, poorly socialized males, who have easy access to guns, drugs, and vice, has produced a crime rate of similar proportions. Violence rates have stabilized lately, but they may rise again as the decline in the family remains unchecked.

Courtwright's analysis shows that violence is not a recent development and that demographic and cultural forces determine violent crime rates. It disputes the contention that some artifact of modern life, like violent films and TV, is causing American violence. The factors that predispose societies to violence can be found in demographic and cultural factors that are unique neither to our society nor to our times.

CRITICAL THINKING

1. According to Courtwright, crime rates were exceedingly high in the nineteenth century before TV, movies, and rap videos had been created. What, if anything, does this say about the effect of media on crime?
2. What were some of the other factors that provoked violence? Do you think that these factors still cause violence today?

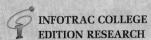 **INFOTRAC COLLEGE EDITION RESEARCH**

If you are interested in reading more about the early history of violence in the West, look up:
Margaret Walsh. New horizons for the American West. *History Today* March 1994 v44 n3 p44(7)

Source: David Courtwright, "Violence in America," *American Heritage* 47 (1996): 36–52, quote at p. 36; David Courtwright, *Violent Land: Single Men and Social Disorder from the Frontier to the Inner City* (Cambridge: Harvard University Press, 1996).

---

her 1998 book *Guilty by Reason of Insanity,* Lewis finds that death row inmates have a history of mental impairment and intellectual dysfunction.[13] Abnormal personality structure, including depression, borderline personality syndrome, and psychopathology, have been associated with various forms of spousal and family abuse.[14] Although this evidence indicates that violent offenders are more prone to psychosis than other people, no single clinical diagnosis can characterize their behavior.[15]

Ineffective Families

In August 1990 residents of Gainesville, Florida, were shocked when five young students were brutally murdered. Newspaper accounts told how the victims, four female University of Florida students and one male Santa Fe Community College student, had been stabbed dozens of times and raped, with their mutilated bodies posed in sexually suggestive positions; one had been beheaded.[16] A 35-year-old drifter named Danny Harold Rolling was arrested and convicted for committing these horrible crimes. On March 24, 1994, after 13 days of testimony, a jury recommended that Rolling be sentenced to death.[17] During the jury phase of the sentencing, Rolling pleaded for mercy and claimed that his behavior was a result of the emotional and physical abuse he had suffered at the hands of his father. His mother, Claudia, a native of Shreveport, Louisiana, submitted a videotape that supported his claim of abuse and ended the tape by stating, "Take me, I'm the one that had to have failed him somewhere."

Much research traces violence to rejecting, ineffective, or abusive parenting.[18] Absent or deviant parents, inconsistent discipline, and lack of supervision have all been linked to persistent violent offending.[19] Although infants demonstrate individual temperaments, who they become may have a lot to do with how they are treated during their early years. Some children are less easy to soothe than others; in some cases, difficult infant temperament has been associated with later aggression and behavioral problems.[20] Parents who fail to set adequate limits or to use proper, consistent discipline reinforce a child's coercive behavior.[21] The effects of inadequate parenting and early rejection may affect violent behavior throughout life.[22]

Abused Children A number of research studies have found that children who are clinically diagnosed as abused later engage in delinquent behaviors, including violence, at a rate significantly greater than that of unabused children.[23] Samples of convicted murderers reveal a high percentage of seriously abused youth.[24] The abuse–violence association has been established in many cases in which parents have been killed by their children; sexual abuse is also a constant factor in father (patricide) and mother (matricide) killings.[25] Dorothy Otnow Lewis found in her study of juvenile death row inmates that all had long histories of intense child abuse.[26]

One of the most outspoken critics of physical punishment of children is Murray Straus of the Family Research Laboratory at the University of New Hampshire. Straus has used survey and record data to show that children who are physically punished by their parents are likely to physically abuse a sibling and later engage in spouse abuse and other forms of criminal violence.[27]

Using actual case studies of violent criminals, sociologist Lonnie Athens found that antisocial careers are often created in a series of stages that begins with brutal episodes during early adolescence:

- The first stage involves the **brutalization process,** during which a young victim begins the process of developing a belligerent, angry demeanor. The brutilization can come at the hands of abusive parents or caretakers. But the brutalization process is broader than parental physical or sexual abuse. It may also result from violent subjugation, personal horrification, and violent coaching by peers, neighbors, and schoolmates. Although most brutalization occurs early in life, some people can be brutalized as they mature.

- Brutalized youth may become belligerent and angry. When confronted at home, school, or on the street, these belligerent youth respond with violent performances of angry, hostile behavior. The success of their violent confrontations provides them with a sense of power and achievement.

- In the **virulency stage,** emerging criminals develop a violent identity that makes them feared; they enjoy intimidating others. To Athens, this process takes violent youths full circle from being the victims of aggression to its initiators; they are now the same person they grew up despising, ready to begin the process with their own children.[28]

Athens recognizes that brutalization alone is not a sufficient condition to cause someone to become a dangerous violent criminal. One must complete the full cycle of the "violentization process"—belligerence, violent performances, and virulency—to become socialized into violence. Many brutalized children do not go on to become violent criminals, and some later reject the fact that they were abused as youths and redefine their early years as normative.

A significant amount of evidence has shown the association between abuse and violent crime, but it is also true that many offenders have not suffered abuse and that many abused youths do not grow up to become persistent adult offenders.[29] The Race, Culture, Gender, and Criminology feature titled "Mothers Who Kill Their Children" discusses one aspect of the abuse–violence link.

Evolutionary Factors/Human Instinct

Perhaps violent responses and emotions are actually inherent in all humans, and the right spark can trigger them. Sigmund Freud believed that human aggression and violence are produced by instinctual drives.[30] Freud maintained that humans possess two opposing instinctual drives that interact to control behavior: **eros,** the life instinct, which drives people toward self-fulfillment and enjoyment; and **thanatos,** the death instinct, which produces self-destruction. Thanatos can be expressed externally (as violence and sadism) or internally (as suicide,

Lyle + Eric Menendanz

race, culture, gender, and criminology

Mothers Who Kill Their Children

It seems inconceivable that a mother would kill her child because the instinct to nurture and protect young children seems to be universal. What would prompt a woman to kill her own child, who is both helpless and dependent on her for care and survival?

To answer this question, Susan Crimmins, Sandra Langley, Henry Brownstein, and Barry Spunt interviewed 42 women in New York state prisons, all of whom had been convicted of manslaughter or murder in the death of their children. The women described a consistent history of social and psychological trauma leading up to their fatal acts. More than two-thirds were characterized as "motherless mothers," who had either absent or abusive mothers themselves. More than one-third reported that their mothers were alcoholics.

About three-fourths of the women had been physically or sexually abused as children. Early childhood experience with abuse was carried over into abusive spousal relations: most of these women (79 percent) had been abused by a partner. Forty-one percent of these women had attempted suicide. All 43 women interviewed experienced more than one incident that damaged their self-image prior to killing their children.

When asked why they killed their children (about three-fourths were biological parents; the others killed foster or adopted children or the children of neighbors or relatives), most reported extreme psychological stress (like depression or schizophrenia). About one-third linked their behavior to alcohol or drug abuse. Isolation in childhood carried over to motherhood, and they felt isolated and alone; they had learned to suffer in silence.

So the link these women shared was a traumatic childhood that was filled with a variety of losses as well as insensitivity to their emotional needs. Social isolation, along with their learned ability to suffer without complaining, reinforced their already poor self-esteem. Lethal violence was connected to their years of social and economic frustration and a prior history of violence to settle disputes in their own families. Because their emotional needs were consistently unmet, their attachments to others were disrupted, and their self-esteem did not develop in a healthy way. Isolated, rejected, and feeling low self-worth, these women were unable to feel empathy with others. Such feelings generated additional rage and despair that later erupted into violent, aggressive behavior.

CRITICAL THINKING

1. What can be done to deal with the issues that produce women who kill their children?
2. Is it possible for government intervention programs to alter the lives of women who have had a long history of trauma and conflict?

 INFOTRAC COLLEGE EDITION RESEARCH

What factors contribute to violent episodes by women? To find out more, read:
Lionel Tiger. Men, women, and aggression: from rage in marriage to violence in the streets—how gender affects the way we act. *Society* March-April 1995 v32 n3 p79A
Ofra Anson, Shifra Sagy. Marital violence: comparing women in violent and nonviolent unions. *Human Relations,* March 1995 v48 n3 p285

Source: Susan Crimmins, Sandra Langley, Henry Brownstein, and Barry Spunt, "Convicted Women Who Have Killed Children: A Self-Psychology Perspective," *Journal of Interpersonal Violence* 12 (1997): 49–69.

---

alcoholism, or other self-destructive habits). Because aggression is instinctual, Freud saw little hope for its treatment.

A number of biologists and anthropologists have also speculated that instinctual violence-promoting traits may be common in the human species. One view is that aggression and violence are the results of instincts inborn in all animals, including human beings. A leading proponent of this view, Konrad Lorenz, developed this theory in his famous book, *On Aggression.*[31] Lorenz argued that aggressive energy is produced by inbred instincts that are independent of environmental forces. In the animal kingdom, aggression usually serves a productive purpose—for example, it leads members of grazing species such as zebras and antelopes to spread out over available territory to ensure an ample food supply and the survival of the fittest. Lorenz found that humans possess some of the same aggressive instincts as animals. But among lower species, aggression is rarely fatal; when a conflict occurs, the winner is determined through a test of skill or endurance. This inhibition against killing members of their own species protects animals from self-extinction. Humans, lacking this inhibition against fatal violence, are capable of killing their own kind in war or as a result of interpersonal conflicts. As technology develops and more lethal weapons are produced, the extinction of the human species becomes a significant possibility.

Evolutionary theories in criminology suggest that violent behavior is predominantly committed by males because over the course of human existence, sexually aggressive males have been the ones most likely to produce children. Their offspring carry genes that support aggression. In all species, the males' competitive success

Are these armed militiamen a product of aggressive male breeding? Or is aggression related to life experiences such as destructive families and hostile living environments?

is determined by their being dangerous and aggressive enough to scare off rivals. Among humans, just the reputation for being dangerous can last a lifetime. This psychologically ingrained need to display virility and toughness comes when young men are at the peak of their physical strength. They are more willing to take risks than at any other point in the life cycle, which factors heavily into their propensity toward violence.[32]

Exposure to Violence

People who are constantly exposed to violence at home, at school, or in the environment may adopt violent methods themselves. Social scientist Felton Earls is now conducting a government-funded longitudinal study of pathways to violence among 8,000 Chicago area youths in 80 different, randomly selected neighborhoods. His research team is asking these youths about their exposure to violence in order to understand how communities control violence and to determine the extent to which exposure to violence predicts future violence.[33] Interviews with youths aged 9 to 15 have revealed, so far, that large numbers of these children in the 80 sample neighborhoods have been victims of or witnesses to violence and that many carry weapons. The researchers found a strong correlation between exposure to violence and self-reports of violent behavior. Between 30 and 40 percent of the children who reported exposure to violence also displayed sig-

nificant violent behavior themselves. The research also shows that girls are involved in violence as much as boys, although the nature of the violence is quite different. Girls are more likely than boys to be victims of sexual violence, and boys are more likely to see or to participate in fights, stabbings, or shootings. Children living in these conditions become **crusted over:** they do not let people inside, nor do they express their feelings. They exploit others and in turn are exploited by those older and stronger; as a result, they develop a sense of hopelessness. They find that parents and teachers focus on their failures and problems, not their achievements. Consequently, they are vulnerable to the lure of delinquent gangs and groups.[34]

Cultural Values

Attempts to explain violent behavior that focus on the individual offender fail to account for the patterns of violence in the United States. Various sources of crime statistics tell us that interpersonal violence is more common in large, urban, inner-city areas than in any other type of community.[35] It is unlikely that violent crime rates would be so high in these socially disorganized areas, however, unless other social forces encouraged violent crime.[36] To explain these disproportionately high violence rates, criminologists Marvin Wolfgang and Franco Ferracuti have suggested that a **subculture of violence** exists.[37]

CONNECTIONS

Delinquent subcultures were discussed in some detail in Chapter 7. Recall that subcultural theorists portray delinquents not as rebels from the normative culture, but rather as people who are in accord with the informal rules and values of their immediate culture. By adhering to cultural norms, they violate the law.

The subculture's norms are separate from society's central, dominant value system. In this subculture, a potent theme of violence influences lifestyles, the socialization process, and interpersonal relationships. Even though the subculture's members share some of the dominant culture's values, they expect that violence will be used to solve social conflicts and dilemmas. In some cultural subgroups, then, violence has become legitimized by custom and norms. It is considered appropriate behavior within culturally defined conflict situations, in which an individual who has been offended by a negative outcome in a dispute seeks reparations through violent means (**disputatiousness**).[38] Whereas Wolfgang and Ferracuti speculated that the subculture of violence was stratified along racial and class lines, more recent research indicates few racial differences in attitudes that support violence; in fact, whites seem to approve more highly of violence as a means of defense or retaliation than do African-Americans.[39]

Ganging   Empirical evidence shows that violence rates are highest in urban areas where subcultural values support teenage gangs, whose members typically embrace the use of violence.[40] Gang boys are more likely to own guns and other weapons than non–gang members. They are also more likely to have peers who are gun owners and more likely to carry guns outside the home.[41]

In a recent study of St. Louis gang boys, criminologist Scott Decker found that violence is a core value of gang membership; it helps boys define what a gang really is, as the following conversation reveals:

> Int: Why do you call the group you belong to a gang?
> Ans: Violence, I guess. There is more violence than a family. With a gang, it's like fighting all the time, killing, shooting.[42]

Decker found that gang violence may be initiated for a variety of reasons:

- It enables new members to show toughness during initiation ceremonies.
- It can be used to retaliate against rivals for actual or perceived grievances.
- It protects ownership, such as when violence erupts when graffiti is defaced by rivals.
- It protects turf from incursions by outsiders.[43]

Research conducted in Chicago by Carolyn Block indicates that gang-related killings have increased significantly in recent years. This finding implies that a growing proportion of urban violence is a product of subcultural clashes.[44]

Regional Values   Some criminologists have suggested that *regional* values promote violence.[45] In a classic study, sociologist Raymond Gastil found a significant relationship between murder rates and residence in the South, a relationship that predates the Civil War. He also found that outside the South, regional homicide rates are related to an influx of southern migration.[46] Gastil attributes high homicide rates to a southern culture that stresses a frontier mentality, mob violence, night riders, personal vengeance, and easily available firearms. Southerners are also thought to place greater emphasis on personal honor, to own more firearms, and to use different child-rearing practices than citizens in other parts of the country.[47] It has been suggested that especially in areas dominated by white populations, southerners behave in the heritage of medieval European knights, ready to defend family and home against any perceived threat.[48]

Not all criminologists agree with the southern subculture concept.[49] Some argue that southern homicide rates are high because of economic and social factors, not any "southern culture of lethal violence."[50] Gastil has responded to his critics by stating that they missed his point—that southern culture promotes violence, not just the approval of violence.[51]

Although the southern subculture view is still debated, Uniform Crime Report data have been used to show that although the southern region has relatively high crime rates, western states today have a higher overall violence rate than southern states.[52] Despite recent evidence that refutes the southern subculture of violence theory, the image of the violent southerner remains, unfortunately, an enduring myth.[53]

Substance Abuse

It has become common to link violence to substance abuse. In fact, substance abuse influences violence in three ways:[54]

1. A **psychopharmacological** relationship may be the direct consequence of ingesting mood-altering substances. Experimental evidence shows that high doses of drugs such as PCP and amphetamines may produce violent, aggressive behavior.[55]
2. Alcohol abuse has long been associated with all forms of violence. A direct alcohol–violence link may occur because drinking reduces cognitive ability, making miscommunication more likely while at the same time limiting the capacity for rational dialogue and compromise.[56]

3. Drug ingestion may also cause **economic compulsive behavior,** in which drug users resort to violence support their habit.

Drug testing of arrestees in major U.S. cities consistently shows that criminals are also drug abusers. Up to 80 percent of all people arrested for violent crimes test positively for drugs.[57] Surveys of prison inmates show that a significant majority report being under the influence of drugs or alcohol when they committed their last criminal offenses.[58]

A bond between violent crime and substance abuse is also forged by the activities of drug-trafficking gangs whose members both sell and use drugs; this is referred to as a **systemic link.** Studies of gangs that sell drugs show that their violent activities may result in a significant proportion of all urban homicides.[59] Most drug-related deaths, in fact, are motivated by drug trafficking and interpersonal conflict that results from drug abuse. Relatively few people are killed by drug users trying to get drug money.[60] With the waning of the crack epidemic, the violence–drug link may be changing as addicts turn to less volatile drugs such as heroin.

Firearm Availability

Although firearm availability does not cause violence, it is certainly a facilitating factor. A petty argument can escalate into a fatal encounter if one party has a handgun. It may not be coincidence that the United States, which has a huge surplus of guns and in which most firearms (80 percent) used in crimes are stolen or obtained through illegal or unregulated transactions, also has one of the world's highest violence rates.[61] Disturbing evidence indicates that more than 80 percent of inmates in juvenile correctional facilities owned a gun just before their confinement, and 55 percent said they carried one almost all the time.[62] The Uniform Crime Reports (UCR) indicate that over half of all murders and 40 percent of all robberies involve firearms.[63]

CONNECTIONS

Although it seems logical that banning the sale and ownership of firearms might help reduce violence, those in favor of gun ownership, as discussed in a feature on gun control in Chapter 3, do not agree. Some experts believe that taking guns away from citizens might endanger them against armed criminals.

Handguns kill two-thirds of all police who die in the line of duty. The presence of firearms in the home also significantly increases the risk of suicide among adolescents, regardless of how carefully the guns are secured or stored.[64] Assaults and violence among family members and other intimates are 12 times more likely to result in death if a handgun is used than if the attacks do not involve firearms.[65]

Each of these factors is believed to influence violent crimes, including both traditional common-law crimes, such as rape, murder, assault, and robbery, and newly recognized problems, such as workplace violence, hate crimes, and political violence. Each of these forms of violent behavior is discussed in some detail later in this chapter.

FORCIBLE RAPE

Rape (from the Latin *rapere,* to take by force) is defined in common law as "the carnal knowledge of a female forcibly and against her will."[66] It is one of the most loathed, misunderstood, and frightening crimes. Under traditional common-law definitions, rape involves nonconsensual sexual intercourse that a male performs against a female whom he is neither married to nor cohabitating with. Sexual acts that are excluded from this definition of rape are usually included in other crime categories; for example:

- A male forcing a female to participate in fellatio, cunnilingus, and, in many states, anal intercourse; these crimes are usually covered by sodomy statutes, which outlaw deviant sexual practices.
- A female or male coercing a male to participate in intercourse or other sexual activity.
- A female coercing another female to participate in sexual activity.
- A male or female coercing sexual intercourse by threatening social, economic, or vocational harm rather than physical injury.[67]

Rape was often viewed as a sexual offense in the traditional criminological literature. It was presented as a crime that involved overwhelming lust driving a man to force his attentions on a woman. Even today, some men view rape as a sexual act, including one Tennessee judge who released an accused rapist after stating that all he needed was a girlfriend and telling the public defender's office to arrange for a dating service. Public outcry led to the release being rescinded.[68]

Criminologists now consider rape a violent, coercive act of aggression, not a forceful expression of sexuality. There has been a national campaign to alert the public to the seriousness of rape, offer help to victims, and change legal definitions to facilitate the prosecution of rape offenders. Such efforts have been only marginally effective in reducing rape rates, but there has been significant progress in overhauling rape laws and developing a vast social service network to aid victims.

History of Rape

Rape has been a recognized crime throughout history. It has been the subject of art, literature, film, and theater. Paintings such as the *Rape of the Sabine Women* by Nicolas Poussin, novels such as *Clarissa* by Samuel Richardson, poems such as *The Rape of Lucrece* by William Shakespeare, and films such as *The Accused* have sexual violence as their central theme.

In early civilization rape was common. Men staked a claim of ownership on women by forcibly abducting and raping them. This practice led to males' solidification of power and their historical domination of women.[69] In fact, in her often-cited book *Against Our Will,* Susan Brownmiller charges that rape was criminalized only after a monetary economy developed during the Middle Ages. Thereafter, the violation of a virgin caused an economic hardship on her family, who expected a significant dowry for her hand in marriage. According to Brownmiller, further proof of the sexist basis of rape law can be seen in Babylonian and Hebraic law. These ancient peoples considered the rape of a virgin to be a crime punishable by death. However, if the victim was married, then both she and her attacker were considered equally to blame. Unless her husband intervened, the victim and her attacker were put to death.

During the Middle Ages, it was common for ambitious men to abduct and rape wealthy women in an effort to force them into marriage. The practice of "heiress stealing" illustrates how feudal law gave little thought or protection to women and equated them with property.[70] Only in the late fifteenth century was forcible sex outlawed, and then only if the victim was of the nobility. Peasant women and married women were not considered rape victims until well into the sixteenth century. The Christian condemnation of sex during this period was also a denunciation of women as evil, having lust in their hearts, and redeemable only by motherhood. A woman who was raped was almost automatically suspected of contributing to her attack.

Rape and the Military Although rape has long been associated with military conquest, the nation was still stunned when in 1996 the national media revealed the presence of a "rape ring" at the Aberdeen Proving Grounds in Maryland. Nearly 20 noncommissioned officers were accused of raping and sexually harassing 19 female trainees. The investigation prompted more than 5,000 female soldiers to call military hot lines to report similar behavior at Army bases around the country. The Army scandal was especially disturbing because it involved drill instructors, who are given almost total control over the lives of young female recruits who depend on them for support, training, and nurturing.[71]

The link between the military and rape is inescapable. Throughout recorded history, rape has been associated with armies and warfare. Soldiers of conquering armies have considered sexual possession of their enemies' women one of the spoils of war. Among the ancient Greeks, rape was socially acceptable within the rules of warfare. During the Crusades, even knights and pilgrims, ostensibly bound by vows of chivalry and Christian piety, took time to rape as they marched toward Constantinople.

The belief that women are part of the spoils of war has continued. During World War II the Japanese army forced as many as 200,000 Korean women into frontline brothels, where they were repeatedly raped. In a 1998 Japanese ruling, the surviving Korean women were awarded the equivalent of $2,300 each in compensation.[72] The systematic rape of Bosnian and Kosovar women by Serbian army officers during the civil war in the former Yugoslavia horrified the world during the 1990s. These crimes seemed particularly atrocious because they seemed part of an official policy of genocide: rape was deliberately used to impregnate Bosnian women with Serbian children.

CONNECTIONS

State-sponsored terrorism, often directed at minority groups who share some personal characteristic such as religion or ethnic background, will be discussed later in this chapter in the sections on political terrorism.

On March 9, 1998, Dragoljub Kunarac, 37, a former Bosnian Serb paramilitary commander, admitted before an international tribunal in the Netherlands that he had raped Muslim women during the Bosnian war in 1992. His confession made him the first person to plead guilty to rape as a war crime.[73] Human rights groups have estimated that over 30,000 women and young girls were sexually abused in the Balkan fighting.

Ethnic Cleansing

Incidence of Rape

According to the most recent UCR data, about 96,122 rapes or attempted rapes were reported to U.S. police in 1997, a rate of 70 per 100,000 females.[74] Although this trend escalated throughout the 1980s, it began a decline in the 1990s, decreasing more than 12 percent between 1993 and 1997.

Population density influences the rape rate. Metropolitan areas today have rape rates significantly higher than rural areas; nonetheless, urban areas have experienced a much greater drop in rape reports than rural areas. The police make arrests in slightly more than half of all reported rape offenses. Of the offenders arrested, about 44 percent were under 25 years of age, 58 percent were white, and 42 percent were minority group members.[75] The racial pattern of rape arrests has been fairly

Teacher Mary La Tourneau began an affair with one of her 13-year-old students. After having his child she was sentenced to prison but given a community sentence with the proviso she have no further contact with the boy. When they were found again together, she was given a 7-year prison sentence for violating the provisions of her release agreement. Later, she gave birth to a second child fathered by the boy. Should Ms. La Tourneau have been sent to prison for her sexual affair with an underage boy who claims to be in love with her?

consistent for some time. Finally, rape is a warm-weather crime—most incidents occur during July and August, with the lowest rates occurring during December, January, and February.

These data must be interpreted with caution, because according to the National Crime Victimization Survey, rape is frequently underreported. For example, in 1997 the NCVS estimates 194,000 rapes and attempted rapes took place, suggesting that fewer than half of such incidents are reported to police.[76] Many people fail to report rapes because they are embarrassed, believe nothing can be done, or blame themselves.

Official data may reflect reporting practices rather than crime trends. The UCR employs a common-law definition of rape (the carnal knowledge of a female forcibly and against her will) that may not agree with current state definitions. The UCR includes in its computations assaults or attempts to commit rape; this interpretation, however, may differ widely from state to state. Finally, multiple rapes committed by serial rapists make the relationship between the number of crimes and the number of offenders problematic.[77]

Because other victim surveys indicate that at least 20 percent of adult women, 15 percent of college-aged women, and 12 percent of adolescent girls have experienced sexual abuse or assault sometime during their lives, it is evident that both official and victimization statistics significantly undercount rape.[78]

Types of Rape

Some rapes are planned, others are spontaneous; some focus on a particular victim, whereas others occur al-

Table 11.1 Varieties of Forcible Rape

Anger rape occurs when sexuality becomes a means of expressing and discharging pent-up anger and rage. The rapist uses far more brutality than would have been necessary if his real objective had been simply to have sex with his victim. His aim is to hurt his victim as much as possible; the sexual aspect of rape may be an afterthought. Often the anger rapist acts on the spur of the moment after an upsetting incident has caused him conflict, irritation, or aggravation. Surprisingly, anger rapes are less psychologically traumatic for the victim than might be expected. Because a woman is usually physically beaten during an anger rape, she is more likely to receive sympathy from her peers, relatives, and the justice system and consequently be immune from any suggestion that she complied with the attack.

Power rape involves an attacker who does not want to harm his victim as much as he wants to possess her sexually. His goal is sexual conquest, and he uses only the amount of force necessary to achieve his objective. The power rapist wants to be in control, to be able to dominate women and have them at his mercy. Yet it is not sexual gratification that drives the power rapist; in fact, he often has a consenting relationship with his wife or girlfriend. Rape is instead a way of putting personal insecurities to rest, asserting heterosexuality, and preserving a sense of manhood. The power rapist's victim usually is a woman equal in age to or younger than the rapist. The lack of physical violence may reduce the support given the victim by family and friends. Therefore, the victim's personal guilt over her rape experience is increased—perhaps, she thinks, she could have done something to get away.

Sadistic rape involves both sexuality and aggression. The sadistic rapist is bound up in ritual—he may torment his victim, bind her, or torture her. Victims are usually related, in the rapist's view, to a personal characteristic that he wants to harm or destroy. The rape experience is intensely exciting to the sadist; he gets satisfaction from abusing, degrading, or humiliating his captive. This type of rape is particularly traumatic for the victim. Victims of such crimes need psychiatric care long after their physical wounds have healed.

Source: A. Nicholas Groth and Jean Birnbaum, *Men Who Rape* (New York: Plenum Press, 1979).

most as an afterthought during the commission of another crime, such as a burglary.[79] Some rapists are one-time offenders, but others engage in multiple or serial rapes. Some serial rapists constantly increase their use of force; others do not. Research by Janet Warren and her associates in 1998 determined that **increasers** (about 25 percent of serial rapists) tend to be white males who attack multiple victims who are typically older than the norm. During these attacks, the rapist uses excessive profanity and takes more time than during typical rapes. Increasers have a limited criminal history for other crimes, a fact suggesting that their behavior is focused almost solely on sexual violence.[80] Some rapists commit **blitz rapes,** in which they attack their victims without warning, whereas others try to "capture" their victims by striking up a conversation or offering them a ride. Others use personal relationships to gain access to their targets.[81]

One of the best-known attempts to classify the personalities of rapists was made by psychologist A. Nicholas Groth, an expert on classifying and treating sex offenders. According to Groth, every rape encounter contains three elements: anger, power, and sexuality.[82] Consequently, rapists can be classified according to one of the dimensions described in Table 11.1. In treating rape offenders, Groth found that about 55 percent were of the power type; about 40 percent, the anger type; and about 5 percent, the sadistic type. Groth's major contribution has been his recognition that rape is generally a crime of violence, not a sexual act. In all of these circumstances, rape involves a violent criminal offense in which a predatory criminal chooses to attack a victim.[83]

Stranger Versus Nonstranger Criminologists usually divide rapes into two broad categories: **stranger-to-stranger rape** and **acquaintance rape.** Whereas the former involves people who had never met before the rape, the latter involves someone known to the victim, including family members and friends. Included within acquaintance rapes are the subcategories of **date rape,** which involves a sexual attack during a courting relationship, and **marital rape,** which is forcible sex between people who are legally married to each other.

It is difficult to estimate the ratio between rapes involving strangers and those in which victim and assailant were in some way acquainted, because women may be more reluctant to report acts involving acquaintances. By some estimates, about 50 percent of rapes involve acquaintances.[84] Stranger rapes are typically more violent than acquaintance rapes; attackers are more likely to carry a weapon, threaten the victim, and harm her physically. Stranger rapes are overrepresented in official statistics because victims who are more viciously harmed are the most likely to contact police.

Date Rape Although official crime data indicate that most rapists and victims were strangers to one another, it is likely that acquaintance rapes constitute the bulk of sexual assaults. One disturbing trend of rape involves people who are in some form of courting relationship. There is no single form of date rape. Some occur on first dates, others after a relationship has been developing; still others occur after the couple has been involved for some time. In long-term or close relationships, the male partner may feel he has invested so much time and money in his partner that he is owed sexual relations or that sexual intimacy is an expression that the involvement is progressing. He may make comparisons to other couples who have dated as long and are sexually active.[85]

Date rape is not unique to the United States. A survey of Canadian college women found that although the overall crime rate in Canada is lower than in the United States, the incidence of date rape is still extremely high.

About one-third of the young women surveyed experienced an episode of physical, verbal, or psychological sexual coercion; 25 percent said they had sexual relations when they did not want to during the past year.[86]

Another disturbing phenomenon is campus **gang rape,** in which a group of men attacks a defenseless or inebriated victim. Well-publicized gang rapes have occurred at the University of New Hampshire, Duke University, Florida State University, Pennsylvania State University, and Bentley College in Massachusetts in the past decade.[87]

Date rape is believed to be frequent on college campuses. It has been estimated that 15 to 20 percent of all college women are victims of rape or attempted rape. One self-report survey conducted on a Midwestern campus found that 100 percent of all rapists knew their victims beforehand.[88] The actual incidence of date rape may be even higher than surveys indicate because many victims blame themselves and do not recognize the incident as a rape, saying, for example, "I should have fought back harder" or "I shouldn't have gotten drunk."[89]

Despite their seriousness and prevalence, fewer than 1 in 10 date rapes may be reported to police. Some victims do not report because they do not view their experiences as a "real rape," which, they believe, involves a strange man "jumping out of the bushes." Other victims are embarrassed and frightened. Some men use a variety of strategies to coerce sex, including getting their dates drunk, threatening them with termination of a relationship, threatening to disclose negative information, making them feel guilty, or uttering false promises (like "we'll get engaged") in order to obtain sex.[90] Coercive sexual encounters have become disturbingly common in our culture. As criminologist Martin Schwartz has stated:

> The conclusion is inescapable that a very substantial minority of women on American college campuses have experienced an event which would fit most states' definitions of felony rape or sexual assault.[91]

Marital Rape In 1978 Greta Rideout filed rape charges against her husband John. This Oregon case grabbed headlines because it was the first in which a husband was prosecuted for raping his wife while sharing a residence with her. John was acquitted, and the couple briefly reconciled; later, continued violent episodes culminated in divorce and a jail term for John.[92]

Traditionally, a legally married husband could not be charged with raping his wife; this was referred to as the **marital exemption.** The origin of this legal doctrine can be traced to the sixteenth-century pronouncement of Matthew Hale, England's chief justice, who wrote

> But the husband cannot be guilty of rape committed by himself upon his lawful wife, for by their mutual matrimonial consent and contract the wife hath given up herself in this kind unto the husband which she cannot retract.[93]

However, research indicates that many women are raped each year by their husbands as part of an overall pattern of spousal abuse, and they deserve the protection of the law. Although popular myth, illustrated by Rhett Butler overcoming the objections of his reluctant bride, Scarlett O'Hara, in the classic film *Gone with the Wind,* says that marital rapes are the result of "healthy male sexuality," the reality is quite the opposite. Many spousal rapes are accompanied by brutal, sadistic beatings and have little to do with normal sexual interests.[94] Not surprisingly, the marital exemption has undergone significant revision. In 1980, only three states had laws against marital rape; today almost every state recognizes marital rape as a crime.[95] Piercing the marital exemption is not unique to U.S. courts; it has also been abolished in Canada, Israel, Scotland, and New Zealand.[96]

Statutory Rape   The term **statutory rape** refers to sexual relations between an underage minor female and an adult male. Although the sex is not forced or coerced, the law says that young girls are incapable of giving informed consent, so the act is legally considered nonconsensual. Typically a state's law will define an age of consent above which there can be no criminal prosecution for sexual relations. Although each state is different, most evaluate the age differences between the parties in order to determine whether an offense has taken place. For example, Indiana law mandates prosecution of men aged 21 or older who have consensual sex with girls younger than 14. In some states, defendants can claim they mistakenly assumed their victims were above the age of consent, whereas in others, "mistake-of-age" defenses are ignored. A recent American Bar Association survey found that prosecution is often difficult in statutory rape cases because the young victims are reluctant to testify. Often parents have given their blessing to the relationships, and juries are reluctant to convict men involved in consensual sex with even young teenaged girls. The ABA report calls for stricter enforcement of these cases, noting that many states are already toughening their laws by raising the age of consent to protect minors from the psychological scars of precocious sexuality with an older predatory partner.[97]

The Causes of Rape

What factors predispose some men to commit rape? Criminologists' responses to this question are almost as varied as the crime itself. However, most explanations can be grouped into a few consistent categories.

Evolutionary/Biological Factors   One explanation for rape focuses on the evolutionary, biological aspects of the male sexual drive. This perspective suggests that rape may be instinctual, developed over the ages as a means of perpetuating the species. In more primitive times, forcible sexual contact may have helped spread genes and maximize offspring. Some believe that these prehistoric drives remain: males still have a natural sexual drive that encourages them to have intimate relations with as many women as possible.[98] The evolutionary view is that the sexual urge corresponds to the unconscious need to preserve the species by spreading one's genes as widely as possible. Men who are sexually aggressive will have a reproductive edge over their more passive peers. In contrast, women are more cautious and want stable partners who seem willing to make a long-term commitment to child rearing. This difference produces sexual tension that causes men to employ forceful copulatory tactics, especially when the chances of punishment are quite low.[99] Rape is bound up with sexuality as well as violence because, according to biosocial theorist Lee Ellis, the act involves the "drive to possess and control others to whom one is sexually attracted."[100]

Male Socialization   In contrast to the evolutionary biological view, some researchers argue that rape is a function of modern male socialization. In her book *The Politics of Rape,* Diana Russell suggests that rape is actually not a deviant act but one that conforms to the qualities regarded as masculine in U.S. society.[101] Russell maintains that from an early age, boys are taught to be aggressive, forceful, tough, and dominating. Men are taught to dominate at the same time that they are led to believe that women want to be dominated. Russell describes the **virility mystique**—the belief that males must separate their sexual feelings from needs for love, respect, and affection. She believes that men are socialized to be the aggressors and expect to be sexually active with many women; consequently, male virginity and sexual inexperience are shameful. Similarly, sexually aggressive women frighten some men and cause them to doubt their own masculinity. Sexual insecurity may lead some men to commit rape to bolster their self-image and masculine identity. Rape, argues Russell, helps keep women in their place.

Hypermasculinity   If rape is an expression of male anger and devaluation of women and not an act motivated by sexual desire, it follows that men who hold so-called macho attitudes will be more likely to engage in sexual violence. **Hypermasculine** men typically have a callous sexual attitude and believe that violence is manly. They perceive danger as exciting and are overly sensitive to insult and ridicule. They are also impulsive, more apt to brag about sexual conquests, and more likely to lose control, especially when using alcohol.[102] These men are quicker to anger and more likely to be sexually aggressive. In fact, the sexually aggressive male may view the female as a legitimate victim of sexual violence.

CONNECTIONS

Recall that Chapter 9 described how the need to prove masculinity helps men justify their abuse of women. Sexually violent men, the argument goes, are viewed as virile and masculine by their peers.

Psychological Abnormality Another view is that rapists suffer from some type of personality disorder or mental illness. Research shows that a significant percentage of incarcerated rapists exhibit psychotic tendencies, and many others have hostile, sadistic feelings toward women.[103]

Social Learning This perspective submits that men learn to commit rapes much as they learn any other behavior. Groth found that 40 percent of the rapists he studied were sexually victimized as adolescents.[104] A growing body of literature links personal sexual trauma with the desire to inflict sexual trauma on others.[105] Watching violent or pornographic films featuring women who are beaten, raped, or tortured has been linked to sexually aggressive behavior in men.[106] In one startling case, a 12-year-old Providence, Rhode Island, boy sexually assaulted a 10-year-old girl on a pool table after watching television trial coverage of a case in which a woman was similarly raped (the incident was made into a film, *The Accused,* starring actress Jodie Foster).[107]

CONNECTIONS

This view will be explored further in Chapter 14 when the issue of pornography and violence is analyzed in greater detail. Most research does not show that watching pornography is directly linked to sexual violence; but there may be a link between sexual aggression and viewing movies with sexual violence as their theme.

Sexual Motivation Most criminologists believe that rape is actually a violent act that is not sexually motivated. Yet it might be premature to dismiss the sexual motive from all rapes.[108] NCVS data reveal that rape victims tend to be young and that rapists prefer younger, presumably more attractive victims. Data show an association between the ages of rapists and their victims, indicating that men choose rape targets of approximately the same age as consensual sex partners. And, despite the fact that younger criminals are usually the most violent, older rapists tend to harm their victims more than younger rapists. This pattern indicates that older criminals may rape for motives of power and control, whereas younger offenders may be seeking sexual gratification and may therefore be less likely to harm their victims.

In sum, criminologists are still at odds over the precise cause of rape, but there is evidence that it is the product of a number of social, cultural, and psychological forces.[109] Although some experts view it as a normal response to an abnormal environment, others view it as the product of a disturbed mind and deviant life experiences.

Rape and the Law

Of all violent crimes, none has created such conflict in the legal system as rape. Even if women choose to report sexual assaults to police, they are often initially reluctant because of the discriminatory provisions built into rape laws. The sexist fashion in which rape victims are treated by police, prosecutors, and court personnel and the legal technicalities that authorize invasion of women's privacy when a rape case is tried in court can devastate the victim. Also, police tend to be hesitant to make arrests and testify in court when the alleged assaults do not yield obvious signs of violence or struggle (presumably showing the victims strenuously resisted the attacks). Police are also loath to testify on the victim's behalf if she had previously known or dated her attacker. Some state laws have made rape so difficult to prove that women believe that the slim chance their attacker will be convicted is not sufficient to warrant their participation in the legal process. However, police and courts are now becoming more sensitive to the plight of rape victims and are just as likely to investigate acquaintance rapes as they are **aggravated rapes** involving multiple offenders, weapons, and victim injuries. In some jurisdictions, the justice system takes all rape cases seriously and does not ignore those in which victim and attacker have had a prior relationship or those that did not involve serious injury.[110]

Proving Rape Proving guilt in a rape case is extremely challenging for prosecutors. First, some male psychiatrists and therapists still maintain that women fantasize that a rape has occurred and therefore may falsely accuse their alleged attackers. Some judges also fear that women may charge men with rape because of jealousy, false marriage proposals, or pregnancy. Although those concerned with protecting the rights of rape victims have campaigned for legal reforms, some well-publicized false rape accusations have hindered change. In one famous 1985 incident, Gary Dotson, convicted of raping a woman in Illinois, served more than six years in prison before his alleged victim recanted her story on national television.[111] In a similar 1996 case, as the Dallas Cowboys were preparing for the playoffs, a young woman accused star players Erik Williams and Michael Irvin of forcible rape only to later admit she had lied about the incident.[112] Irvin's lawyer, Royce West, later argued that the names of the accused should have been withheld before they were charged. If victims' names are not released to the press, he reasoned, why shouldn't the accused be entitled to a similar right of privacy?[113] Such incidents make it more difficult for prosecutors to gain convictions in rape cases.

Suspiciousness   U.S. sexism causes a cultural suspiciousness of women, who are often seen as provocateurs in any sexual encounters with men. Consequently, the burden is shifted to the woman to prove she has not provoked or condoned the rape. Although the law does not recognize it, jurors are sometimes swayed by the insinuation that the rape was victim-precipitated; thus the blame is shifted from rapist to victim. To get a conviction, prosecutors must establish that the act was forced and violent and that no question of voluntary compliance exists. The legal consequences of rape often reflect archaic legal traditions along with inherent male prejudices and suspicions.

Consent   Rape represents a major legal challenge to the criminal justice system for a number of reasons.[114] One issue involves the concept of **consent.** It is essential to prove that the attack was forced and that the victim did not give voluntary consent to her attacker. In a sense, the burden of proof is on the victim to show that her character is beyond question and that she in no way encouraged, enticed, or misled the accused rapist. Proving victim dissent is not a requirement in any other violent crime. For example, robbery victims do not have to prove they did not entice their attackers by flaunting expensive jewelry; yet the defense counsel in a rape case can create reasonable doubt about the woman's credibility. A common defense tactic is to introduce suspicion in the minds of the jury that the woman may have consented to the sexual act and later regretted her decision. Conversely, it is difficult for a prosecuting attorney to establish that a woman's character is so impeccable that the absence of consent is a certainty. Such distinctions are important in rape cases because male jurors may be sympathetic to the accused if the victim is portrayed as unchaste. Simply referring to the woman as "sexually liberated" or promiscuous may be enough to result in exoneration of the accused, even if violence and brutality were used in the attack.[115]

Reform   Because of the difficulty rape victims have in obtaining justice, rape laws have been changing around the country. Efforts for reform include changing the language of statutes, dropping the condition of victim resistance, and changing the requirement of use of force to include the threat of force or injury.[116] Most states and the federal government have developed **shield laws,** which protect women from being questioned about their sexual history unless it directly bears on the case. In some instances these laws are quite restrictive, whereas in others they grant the trial judge considerable discretion to admit prior sexual conduct in evidence if it is deemed relevant for the defense. In an important 1991 case, *Michigan v. Lucas,* the U.S. Supreme Court upheld the validity of shield laws and ruled that excluding evidence of a prior sexual relationship between the parties did not violate the defendant's right to a fair trial.[117]

In addition to requiring evidence that consent was not given, the common law of rape required corroboration that the crime of rape actually took place. This involved the need for independent evidence from police officers, physicians, and witnesses that the accused was actually the person who committed the crime, that sexual penetration took place, and that force was present and consent absent. This requirement shielded rapists from prosecution in cases where the victim delayed reporting the crime or in which physical evidence had been compromised or lost. Corroboration is no longer required except under extraordinary circumstances, such as when the victim is too young to understand the crime, has had a previous sexual relationship with the defendant, or gives a version of events that is improbable and self-contradictory.[118]

The federal government may have given rape victims another source of redress when it passed the Violence Against Women Act in 1994. This statute allows rape victims to sue in federal court on the grounds that sexual violence violates their civil rights; the act's provisions have so far been upheld by appellate courts.[119]

The Limits of Reform   Despite these reform efforts, prosecutors may be influenced in their decision to bring charges by the circumstances of a crime.[120] The victim must still establish her intimate, detailed knowledge of the act for her testimony to be believed in court. This may include searching questions about her assailant's appearance, the location in which the crime took place, and the nature of the physical assault.

A number of states and the federal government have replaced rape laws with the more sexually neutral **crimes of sexual assault.**[121] Sexual assault laws outlaw any type of forcible sex, including homosexual rape.[122] Research shows that the credibility of sexual assault victims is still more likely to be challenged in court than the testimony of assault victims where no sexual contact was involved.[123]

MURDER AND HOMICIDE

Murder is defined in common law as "the unlawful killing of a human being with malice aforethought."[124] It is the most serious of all common-law crimes and the only one that can still be punished by death. Western society's abhorrence of murderers is illustrated by the fact that there is no statute of limitations in murder cases. Whereas state laws limit prosecution of other crimes to a fixed period, usually 7 to 10 years, accused killers can be brought to justice at any time after their crimes were committed. An example of the law's reach in these cases is the murder conviction of George Franklin on January 29, 1990. Franklin's daughter, Eileen Franklin-Lipsker, told legal authorities that in recent psychotherapy sessions she had remembered how her father sexually assaulted and killed her 8-year-old friend. The murder had taken place in 1969, more than 20 years earlier.[125]

To legally prove that a murder has taken place, most state jurisdictions require prosecutors to show that the accused maliciously intended to kill the victim. **Express or actual malice** is the state of mind assumed to exist when someone kills another person in the absence of any apparent provocation. **Implied or constructive malice** is considered to exist when a death results from negligent or unthinking behavior. In these cases, even though the perpetrator did not wish to kill the victim, the killing resulted from an inherently dangerous act and therefore is considered murder. An unusual example of this concept is the attempted murder conviction of Ignacio Perea, an AIDS-infected Miami man who kidnapped and raped an 11-year-old boy. Perea was sentenced to up to 25 years in prison when the jury agreed with the prosecutor's contention that the AIDS virus is a deadly weapon.[126]

Degrees of Murder

There are different levels or degrees of homicide.[127] **First-degree murder** occurs when a person kills another after premeditation and deliberation. **Premeditation** means that the killing was considered beforehand and suggests that it was motivated by more than a simple desire to engage in an act of violence. **Deliberation** means the killing was planned after careful thought rather than carried out on impulse: "To constitute a deliberate and premeditated killing, the slayer must weigh and consider the question of killing and the reasons for and against such a choice; having in mind the consequences, he decides to and does kill."[128] The planning implied by this definition need not be a long process; it may be an almost instantaneous decision to take another's life. Also, a killing accompanying a felony, such as robbery or rape, usually constitutes first-degree murder (**felony murder**).

Second-degree murder requires the killer to have malice aforethought but not premeditation or deliberation. A second-degree murder occurs when a person's wanton disregard for the victim's life and his or her desire to inflict serious bodily harm on the victim results in the victim's death.

Homicide without malice is called **manslaughter** and is usually punished by anywhere between 1 and 15 years in prison. **Voluntary or nonnegligent manslaughter** refers to a killing committed in the heat of passion or during a sudden quarrel that provoked violence. Although intent may be present, malice is not. **Involuntary or negligent manslaughter** refers to a killing that occurs when a person's acts are negligent and without regard for the harm they may cause others. Most involuntary manslaughter cases involve motor vehicle deaths—for example, when a drunk driver kills a pedestrian. However, one can be held criminally liable for the death of another in any instance where disregard of safety kills. For example, on February 16, 1990, Michael Patrick Berry, whose pit bull killed a child who had wandered into his yard, was sentenced to three years and eight months in prison; it was the first U.S. case in which a person was convicted for manslaughter for the actions of a pet.[129]

"Born and Alive" One issue that has received national attention is whether a murder victim can be a fetus that has not yet been delivered; this is referred to as **feticide.** In some instances fetal harm involves a mother whose behavior endangers an unborn child; in other cases feticide results from the harmful action of a third party.

Some states have prosecuted women for endangering or killing their unborn fetuses by their drug or alcohol abuse. Some of these convictions have been overturned because the law applies only to a "human being who has been born and is alive."[130] At least 200 women in 30 states have been arrested and charged in connection with harming (though not necessarily killing) a fetus; appellate courts have almost universally overturned such convictions on the basis that they were without legal merit or were unconstitutional.[131] However, in *Whitner v. State,* the Supreme Court of South Carolina ruled that a women could be held liable for actions during pregnancy that could affect her viable fetus.[132] In holding that a fetus is a "viable person," the court opened the door for a potential homicide prosecution if a mother's action resulted in fetal death.

State laws more commonly allow prosecutions for murder when a third party's actions kill a fetus. Four states (Illinois, Missouri, South Dakota, and West Virginia) extend wrongful death action to the death of any fetus, whereas the remaining states require that the fetus be viable. A viable fetus is able to live outside the mother's body; therefore, the law extends the definition of murder to a fetus that is born alive but dies afterward due to injuries sustained in utero.[133] In a recent Texas case, a man was convicted of manslaughter in the death of a baby who was delivered prematurely after he caused an auto accident while intoxicated. It was one of the first cases to hold that a person can be held criminally liable for harming an unborn child.[134]

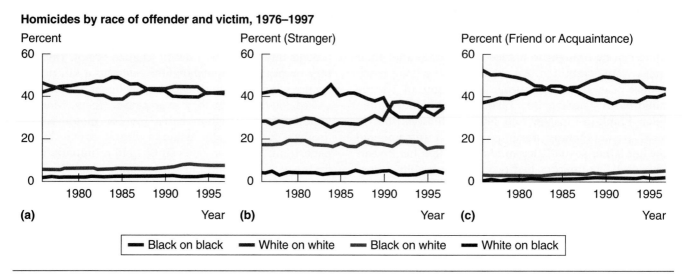

Figure 11.2 Murder Trends by Race of Offenders and Victims

Homicides by race of offender and victim, 1976–1997

(a) Percent — Year

(b) Percent (Stranger) — Year

(c) Percent (Friend or Acquaintance) — Year

■ Black on black   ■ White on white   ■ Black on white   ■ White on black

Source: James Alan Fox and Marianne Zawitz, *Homicide Trends in the United States* (Bureau of Justice Statistics, 1998).

The Nature and Extent of Murder

It is possible to track U.S. murder rate trends from 1900 to the present with the aid of coroners' reports and UCR data. The murder rate peaked in 1933, a time of high unemployment and lawlessness, and then fell until 1958. The homicide rate doubled from the mid 1960s to the late 1970s. In 1980 it peaked again at 10.2 per 100,000 population and subsequently fell to 7.9 per 100,000 in 1985. It rose again in the late 1980s and early 1990s to a peak of 9.8 per 100,000 in 1991. Since then the rate has declined, to 6.8 per 100,000 by 1997. Although this decline is an extremely positive development, more than 18,000 citizens were killed in 1997.

What else do official crime statistics tell us about murder today? Murder victims tend to be males over 18 years of age. There is a disturbing trend for African-Americans to both commit murder and become murder victims (see Figure 11.2). Murder, like rape, tends to be an intraracial crime; about 90 percent of victims are slain by members of their own race. Similarly, people arrested for murder were generally young (under 35) and male (about 90 percent), a pattern that has proven consistent over time.

Today few would deny that some relationship exists between social and ecological factors and murder. This section explores some of the more important issues related to these factors.

Murderous Relations

One factor that has received a great deal of attention from criminologists is the relationship between the murderer and the victim.[135] Most criminologists gener-

ally agree that murders can be separated into those involving strangers, typically stemming from a felony attempt such as a robbery or drug deal, and acquaintance homicides involving disputes between family, friends, and acquaintances.[136] The quality of relationships and interpersonal interactions, then, may influence murder.

CONNECTIONS

Recall from Chapter 4 the discussion of victim precipitation. The argument made by some criminologists is that murder victims help create the "transactions" that lead to their death.

Spousal Relations The rate of homicide among married couples has declined significantly during the past two decades, a finding that can be attributed to the shift away from marriage in modern society. There are, however, significant gender differences in homicide trends among unmarried people. The number of unmarried men killed by their partners has declined (mirroring the overall trend in the murder rate), but the number of women killed by the men they live with has increased dramatically.

It is possible that men kill their spouses or partners because they fear losing control and power. Because unmarried people who live together have a legally and socially more open relationship, males in such relationships may be more likely to feel loss of control and exert their power with violence.[137]

Research indicates that most females who kill their mates do so after suffering repeated violent attacks.[138]

Perhaps the number of males killed by their partners has declined because alternatives to abusive relationships, such as battered women's shelters, are becoming more prevalent around the United States. Regions that provide greater social support for battered women and that have passed legislation to protect abuse victims also have lower rates of female-perpetrated homicide.[139]

Some people kill their mates because they find themselves involved in a love triangle.[140] Interestingly, women who kill out of jealousy aim their aggression at their partners; in contrast, men are more likely to kill their mates' suitors. Love triangles tend to become lethal when the offenders believe they have been lied to or betrayed. Lethal violence is more common when (1) the rival initiated the affair, (2) the killer knew the spouse was already in a steady relationship outside the marriage, and (3) the killer was repeatedly lied to or betrayed.[141]

CONNECTIONS

It is possible that men who perceive loss of face aim their aggression at rivals who are competing with them for a suitable partner. Biosocial theory (Chapter 6) suggests that this behavior is motivated by the male's instinctual need to replenish the species and protect his place in the gene pool. Killing a rival would help a spouse maintain control over a potential mother for his children.

Stranger Relations Over the past decade, the number of stranger homicides has seemed to increase. Under what circumstances do stranger homicides occur? In an often-cited study of homicide rates in nine U.S. cities, criminologists Margaret Zahn and Philip Sagi discovered that stranger homicides are most often felony murders occurring during rapes, robberies, and burglaries. The rest of the homicides are random acts of urban violence that fuel public fear. For example, a homeowner tells a motorist to move his car because it is blocking the driveway, an argument ensues, and the owner gets a pistol and kills the motorist; or consider a young boy who kills a store manager because, he says, "something came into my head to hurt the lady."[142]

How do these murderous relations develop between two people who have never before met? In a well-known study, David Luckenbill studied murder transactions to determine whether particular patterns of behavior are common between the killer and the victim.[143] He found that many homicides follow a sequential pattern. First, the victim makes what the offender considers an offensive move. The offender typically retaliates verbally or physically. An agreement to end things violently is forged with the victim's provocative response. The battle ensues, leaving the victim dead or dying. The offender's escape is shaped by his or her relationship to the victim or the reaction of the audience, if any (see Figure 11.3).

Homicide Networks Some murders may result from wanton violence by a stranger, whereas others may involve social interaction between two or more people who know each other and whose destructive social interaction kills one party.[144] Although on the surface these deaths seem senseless, they often mask a deeper, underlying cause such as revenge, dispute resolution, jealousy, drug deals, racial bias, or threats to identity or status.[145] Perpetrators and victims may be joined together in a homicide network that links victims, suspects, and witnesses. For example, a prior act of violence, motivated by profit or greed, may generate revenge killing, such as when a buyer robs his dealer during a drug transaction.

CONNECTIONS

Later this chapter discusses the life of street robbers in detail. It is common for robbers to choose criminal victims such as drug dealers because they cannot report the crimes to police.

In this type of murder, the instigator of one criminal act becomes the victim in another. Individuals who are most isolated from conventional society and who have the least confidence in the criminal justice system are the most likely to seek street justice. They take the victimization of family and friends seriously and will in turn set up a murderous exchange with the people they hold responsible. If the perpetrator's identity is unknown, then a representative from the same racial or ethnic group can be substituted as a victim, setting off a new round of revenge killings. Violent exchanges become contagious. However, people are much less likely to victimize those they consider close friends than those who are mere acquaintances.[146]

Types of Murders

Other forms of stranger homicides also take a toll on society. **Thrill killing** involves impulsive slaying of a stranger as an act of daring or recklessness. For example, children who throw a boulder from a highway overpass onto an oncoming car may be out for thrills or kicks.[147] Some thrill killings involve relatively stable youths who exhibit few prior symptoms of violence; others are committed by youngsters with long-standing mental or emotional problems.[148]

The FBI records about a thousand **gang killings** each year, and some cities, such as Chicago, may have close to 100 gang-related murders per year.[149] Gang killings involve members of teenage gangs who make

Figure 11.3   Murder Transactions

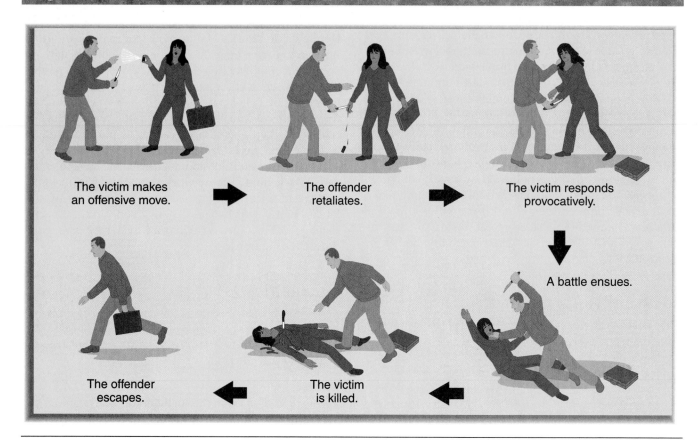

The victim makes an offensive move.

The offender retaliates.

The victim responds provocatively.

A battle ensues.

The offender escapes.

The victim is killed.

violence part of their group activity. Some of these gangs fight over territory or control of the drug trade through drive-by shootings, in which enemies are killed and strangers can be caught in the cross fire.

Cult killings occur when members of religious cults, some of which are devoted to devil worship (**satanism**) and the "black mass," are ordered to kill by their leaders. On some occasions the cult members are ordered to kill peers who are suspected of deviating from the leaders' teachings. Other crimes involve random violence against strangers either as a show of loyalty or because of the misguided belief that they threaten the cult's existence. For example, three Missouri teenagers, all members of a self-styled satanic cult, beat another boy to death with baseball bats and then stuffed his body down a well. The boys planned the crime for months as a human sacrifice for Satan.[150] In another case that occurred in April 1989, police in Matamoros, Mexico, uncovered the grave of a 21-year-old U.S. college student, Mark Kilroy, who had served as a human sacrifice for members of a Mexican drug ring that practiced *palo mayombe,* a form of black magic; killing the youth was believed to bring immunity from bullets and criminal prosecution.[151] Some murders blamed on Satan's influence are carried out not

by members of an organized group but rather by individuals who have visions of the devil telling them to kill. In 1993 a 15-year-old Houston boy, Andrew Merritt, killed his mother after hearing the devil tell him to "kill all the Christians"; law enforcement officials linked Andrew's passion for heavy metal music to the crime.[152]

Serial Murder   Donald Harvey was described as neat, pleasant, outgoing, and remarkably normal by those who knew him best. However, his coworkers in a Cincinnati-area hospital where he worked as a nurse's aide referred to Harvey as the "angel of death" because so many patients died in his ward. Their fears convinced a local TV station to conduct an investigation that resulted in Harvey's arrest and conviction on multiple murder charges. Harvey pleaded guilty to killing at least 21 patients and three other people, and he claims to have killed 28 others, although he cannot remember details of their deaths. Harvey claims that he was a mercy killer; prosecutors described him as a thrill seeker whose behavior was triggered by his sexual ambivalence.[153] He was sentenced to life in prison with possibility of parole in 95 years. Harvey may be the most prolific serial killer in U.S. history, although it is unlikely that the true extent of his activities will ever be known. Donald Harvey's murderous actions fall within a frightening pattern referred to as **serial murder.**

Some serial murderers, such as Theodore Bundy and the Australian race car driver and photographer Christopher Wilder, roam the country killing at random.[154] Other serial killers terrorize a city, such as the Los Angeles–based Night Stalker; the Green River Killer, who is believed to have slain more than four dozen young women in Seattle; and the Hillside Stranglers, Kenneth Bianchi and Angelo Buono, who tortured and killed 10 women in the Los Angeles area.[155] A third type of serial murderer, such as Donald Harvey and Milwaukee cannibal Jeffrey Dahmer, kills so cunningly that many victims are dispatched before the authorities even realize the deaths can be attributed to a single perpetrator.[156] Serial killers operate over a long period and can be distinguished from **mass murderers,** who kill many victims in a single, violent outburst.

Philip Jenkins, who has studied serial killing over the past 50 years, reports an upsurge since the 1960s. In addition, the number of victims per criminal and the ferocity and savagery of the killings also seem to be increasing. Jenkins attributes this increase to a variety of influences ranging from a permissive, drug-abusing culture to a mental health system so overcrowded that potentially dangerous people are released without supervision into an unsuspecting world.[157]

The Criminological Enterprise feature titled "Mass Murder and Serial Killing" further discusses types of serial killers and multiple killers.

Serial Murderers and Their Motivations Research shows that serial killers have long histories of violence, beginning in childhood. They start by targeting other children, siblings, and small animals.[158] They maintain superficial relationships with others, have trouble relating to the opposite sex, and feel guilty about their interest in sex. Despite these common characteristics, there is no single distinct type of serial killer. Some seem to be monsters — like Edmund Kemper, who, in addition to killing six young female hitchhikers in 1972, killed his mother, cut off her head, and used it as a dart board. Others, such as Bianchi, Wilder, and Bundy, were suave ladies' men whose murders surprised even close friends.

Consequently, the cause of serial murder eludes criminologists. Such disparate factors as mental illness, sexual frustration, neurological damage, child abuse and neglect, smothering relationships with mothers (David Berkowitz, the notorious Son of Sam, slept in his parents' bed until he was 10), and childhood anxiety have been suggested as possible causes. However, most experts view serial killers as sociopaths who, from early childhood demonstrate bizarre behavior, such as torturing animals. This behavior extends to the pleasure

that they reap from killing, their ability to ignore or enjoy their victims' suffering, and their propensity for basking in the media limelight when apprehended for their crimes. Wayne Henley, Jr., who along with Dean Corill killed 27 boys in Houston, offered to help prosecutors find the bodies of additional victims so he could break Chicago killer Wayne Gacy's record of 33 murders.[159]

Philip Jenkins's study of serial murder in England contrasts the above findings. He identified one group of offenders who had no apparent personality problems until late in their lives. He found some of the serial killers he studied to be leading normal lives; many were married and respectable and even had careers in the armed services and police force before their murdering sprees.[160]

Ronald Holmes and James DeBurger have also studied serial killers and have devised four categories to describe the different types of killers:

1. *Visionary killers* commit murders in response to some inner voice or vision that demands that some person or category of persons be killed. This type of serial killer is almost always out of touch with reality and is usually considered psychotic.
2. *Mission-oriented killers* want to rid the world of a particular type of undesirable person, such as prostitutes. They are well aware of what they are doing and are in touch with reality.
3. *Hedonistic killers* are thrill-seeking murderers who get excitement and sometimes sexual pleasure from their acts.
4. *Power/control-oriented killers* are murderers who enjoy having complete control over their victims. If they rape or mutilate their victims, the violence is motivated not by sex but by the pleasure of having power over another human being.[161]

Other types of serial killers include the **mysoped,** or **sadistic child killer,** who gains sexual satisfaction from torturing and killing children.[162] The **psychopathic killer** is motivated by a character disorder that causes inability to experience shame, guilt, sorrow, or other normal human emotions; these murderers are concerned solely with their own needs and passions. **Professional hit killers** assassinate complete strangers for economic, political, or ideological reasons; terrorists and organized crime figures fall within this category.[163]

Female Serial Killers An estimated 10 to 15 percent of serial killers are women. A recent study by criminologists Belea Keeney and Kathleen Heide investigated the characteristics of a sample of 14 female serial killers and found some striking differences between the way male and female killers carried out their crimes.[164] Males were much more likely than females to use extreme violence and torture. Whereas males used a "hands-on" approach, including beating, bludgeoning,

The Criminological Enterprise

Mass Murder and Serial Killing

Criminologists Jack Levin and James Alan Fox have written extensively on two of the most frightening aspects of modern violence—mass murder and serial killing. According to Levin and Fox, it is difficult to estimate the number and extent of serial killings; but a reasoned estimate is that up to 20 serial killers are active in a given year, accounting for up to 240 killings or about 1 percent of the total number of homicides.

There are different types of serial killers. Some wander the countryside killing at random; others stay in their hometowns and lure victims to their death. Theodore Bundy, convicted killer of three young women and suspected killer of many others, roamed the country in the 1970s, killing as he went. Wayne Gacy, during the same period, killed over 30 boys and young men without leaving Chicago. Although these men share many characteristics with the general population, one special trait stands out: serial killers are exceptionally skillful in how they present themselves. Based on appearances, they seem beyond suspicion.

Why do serial murderers kill? They kill for fun. They enjoy the thrill, the sexual gratification, and the dominance they achieve over the lives of their victims. The serial killer rarely uses a gun because this method is too quick and would deprive him of his greatest pleasure, exalting in his victim's suffering. Serial killers are not insane, but "more cruel than crazy."

Fox and Levin have their own typology of serial killers, which they describe as follows:

1. *Thrill killers* strive for either sexual sadism or dominance. This is the most common form of serial murderer.
2. *Mission killers* want to reform the world or have a vision that drives them to kill.
3. *Expedience killers* are out for profit or want to protect themselves from a perceived threat.

In contrast to serial killers, mass murderers engage in a single, uncontrollable outburst called **simultaneous killing.** Examples include Charles Whitman, who killed 14 people and wounded 30 others from atop the 307-foot tower on the University of Texas campus on August 1, 1966; James Huberty, who killed 21 people in a McDonald's restaurant in San Ysidro, California, on July 18, 1984; and George Hennard, a deranged Texas man who, on October 16, 1991, smashed his truck through a plate glass window in a cafeteria in Killeen, Texas, got out, and systematically killed 22 people before committing suicide as police closed in.

Fox and Levin define four types of mass murderers:

1. *Revenge killers* seek to get even with individuals or society at large. Their typical target is an estranged wife and "her" children or an employer and "his" employees.
2. *Love killers* are motivated by a warped sense of devotion. They are often despondent people who commit suicide and take others, such as a wife and children, with them.
3. *Profit killers* are usually trying to cover up a crime, eliminate witnesses, and carry out a criminal conspiracy.
4. *Terrorist killers* are trying to send a message. Gang killings tell rivals to watch out; cult killers may actually leave a message behind to warn society about impending doom.

Levin and Fox dispute the notion that all mass murderers and serial killers have some form of biological or psychological problems, such as genetic anomalies or schizophrenia. Even the most sadistic serial murderers are not mentally ill or driven by delusions or hallucinations. Instead, they typically exhibit a sociopathic personality that

and strangling their victims, females were more likely to poison or smother their victims. Men tracked or stalked their victims, but women were more likely to lure victims to their death.

There were also gender-based personality and behavior characteristics. Female killers, somewhat older than their male counterparts, abused both alcohol and drugs; males were not likely to be substance abusers. Women were diagnosed as having histrionic, manic-depressive, borderline, dissociative, and antisocial personality disorders; men were more often diagnosed as having antisocial personalities.

The profile of the female serial killer that emerges is a person who smothers or poisons someone she knows. During childhood she suffered from an abusive relationship in a disrupted family. Female killers' education levels are below average, and if they hold jobs, they are in low-status positions.

Controlling Serial Killers Serial killers come from diverse backgrounds. To date, law enforcement officials have been at a loss to control random killers who leave few clues, constantly move, and have little connection to their victims. Catching serial killers is often a matter of luck. To help local law enforcement officials, the FBI has developed a profiling system to identify potential suspects. In addition, the Justice Department's **Violent Criminal Apprehension Program (VICAP),** a computerized information service, gathers information and matches offense characteristics on violent crimes around the country.[165] This program links crimes to determine if they are the product of a single culprit.

James Alan Fox and Jack Levin, authors of *Overkill: Mass Murder and Serial Killing Exposed,* suggest that serial killers suffer from personality disorders rather than mental illness.

 INFOTRAC COLLEGE EDITION RESEARCH

Serial killers are not new to this century. To read about the history of such gruesome acts, read:
Bernard Capp. Serial killers in 17th-century England. *History Today* March 1996 v46 n3 p21
For more on modern serial killers, see:
Jan Scott. Serial homicide: we need to explore behind the stereotypes and ask why. *British Medical Journal* Jan 6, 1996 v312 n7022 p2
Eugene H. Methvin. The face of evil. *National Review* Jan 23, 1995 v47 n1 p34(7)

Source: James Alan Fox and Jack Levin, *Overkill: Mass Murder and Serial Killing Exposed* (New York: Plenum, 1994); James Allan Fox and Jack Levin, "A Psycho-Social Analysis of Mass Murder," in *Serial and Mass Murder: Theory, Policy, and Research,* ed. Thomas O'Reilly-Fleming and Steven Egger (Toronto: University of Toronto Press, 1993); James Alan Fox and Jack Levin, "Serial Murder: A Survey," in *Serial and Mass Murder: Theory, Policy, and Research,* ed. Thomas O'Reilly-Fleming and Steven Egger (Toronto: University of Toronto Press, 1993); Jack Levin and James Alan Fox, *Mass Murder* (New York: Plenum Press, 1985).

deprives them of pangs of conscience or guilt to guide their behavior. Mass murderers are typically ordinary citizens driven to extreme acts. They experience long-term frustration, blame others for their problems, and then are set off by some catastrophic loss they are unable to cope with or get help for.

So far, police have been successful in capturing simultaneous killers whose outbursts are directed at family members or friends. Serial killers have proven more elusive. The U.S. Justice Department is now coordinating efforts to gather information on unsolved murders in different jurisdictions in order to find patterns linking the crimes. Unfortunately, when a serial murderer is caught, it is often the result of luck — or an informant — not investigative skill.

CRITICAL THINKING

1. Are serial murderers responsible for their actions?
2. Can a mass murderer be legally sane? If not, what should be done with irrational killers?
3. Is it fair to put serial killers and mass murderers to death? Explain your response.

ASSAULT AND BATTERY

Although many people mistakenly believe that the term *assault and battery* refers to a single act, they are actually two separate crimes. **Battery** requires offensive touching, such as slapping, hitting, or punching a victim. **Assault** requires no actual touching but involves either attempted battery or intentionally frightening the victim by word or deed. Although common law originally intended these twin crimes to be misdemeanors, most jurisdictions now upgrade them to felonies either when a weapon is used or when they occur during the commission of a felony (for example, when a person is assaulted during a robbery). In the UCR, the FBI defines *serious assault,* or *aggravated assault,* as "an unlawful attack by one person upon another for the purpose of inflicting severe or aggravated bodily injury"; this definition is similar to the one used in most state jurisdictions.[166]

Under common law, battery required bodily injury, such as broken limbs or wounds. However, under modern law, an assault and battery occurs if the victim suffers a temporarily painful blow, even if no injury results. Battery can also involve offensive touching, such as if a man kisses a woman against her will or puts his hands on her body.

Nature and Patterns of Assault

The pattern of criminal assault is quite similar to that of homicide; one could say that the only difference between the two is that the victim survives.[167] Assaults may be common in our society simply because of common life stresses. Motorists who assault each other have become such a familiar occurrence that the term *road rage* has been coined. There have even been frequent incidents of violent assault among frustrated passengers who lose control while traveling. In 1998 British Airways began issuing printed warnings to abusive passengers, giving notice that continued misbehavior could result in hefty fines and even jail sentences.[168] These warnings were developed after an alarming increase in angry passengers, who punched, kicked, scratched, bit, and head-butted airline workers or one another. For example, in September 1998 an American Airlines flight from New York to Los Angeles made an unscheduled landing in Denver to unload a passenger who had become violent after a bodyguard asked him to stop bothering members of the rock band Hootie and the Blowfish. A few days earlier, a young British woman was sentenced to 15 months in prison for attacking three flight attendants on a British Airways flight from New York to London. The woman had just been denied entry into the United States and appeared to be drunk. When the crew declined to serve her, she became violent, biting a female flight attendant and crushing her leg with a food cart. After being placed in handcuffs, she head-butted two other flight attendants!

In 1997 the FBI recorded about 1 million assaults, a rate of 382 per 100,000 inhabitants. Although the number and rate of assaults have increased over the past 10 years, like other crimes, assault has recently declined (down 13 percent since 1993). People arrested for assault and those identified by victims are usually young, male, and white, although the number of African-Americans arrested for assault (38 percent) is disproportionate to their representation in the population. Assault victims tend to be male, but as Figure 11.4 shows, women also face a significant danger. Assault rates are highest in urban areas, during summer, and in southern and western regions. The most common weapons used in assaults are blunt instruments (33 percent), hands and feet (26 percent), firearms (23 percent), and knives (18 percent).

Emergency Room Data Another way of determining the nature of assault is to review the attributes and extent of injuries people suffer during violent encounters that require them to be treated in local hospital emergency rooms. At last count about 1.4 million people were treated for violence-related injuries, ranging from a nose broken in a fight to a shooting or stabbing during a robbery.[169] About 40 percent of these injuries were quite serious, resulting from rapes and sexual assaults, shootings, and stabbings; about 33 percent of the victims suffered only bruising. About 60 percent of the attacks did not involve a weapon, but guns or knives were used in about 12 percent of the assaults.

Figure 11.4 Violence Against Women

What did women tell NCVS interviewers about their experience with violence?

- Women age 12 or older annually sustain almost 5 million violent victimizations each year. About 75 percent of all lone-offender violence against women and 45 percent of violence involving multiple offenders was perpetrated by offenders whom the victim knew. In 29 percent of all violence against women by a lone offender, the perpetrator was an intimate (husband, ex-husband, boyfriend, or ex-boyfriend).
- Women were about 6 times more likely than men to experience violence committed by an intimate.
- Women annually reported about 500,000 rapes and sexual assaults to interviewers. Friends or acquaintances of the victims committed over half these rapes or sexual assaults. Strangers were responsible for about 1 in 5.
- Women of all races and Hispanic and non-Hispanic women were about equally vulnerable to violence by an intimate.
- Women ages 19 to 29 and women in families with incomes below $10,000 were more likely than other women to be victims of violence by an intimate.
- Among victims of violence committed by an intimate, the victimization rate of women separated from their husbands was about 3 times higher than that of divorced women and about 25 times higher than that of married women. Because the NCVS reflects a respondent's marital status at the time of the interview, which is up to 6 months after the incident, it is possible that separation or divorce followed the violence
- Female victims of violence by an intimate were more often injured by the violence than females victimized by a stranger.

Source: Ronet Bachman and Linda Saltzman, *Violence Against Women: Estimates from the Redesigned Survey* (Washington, D.C.: Bureau of Justice Statistics, 1995), p. 1.

Assault in the Home

Violent attacks in the home are one of the most frightening types of assault. Criminologists recognize that intrafamily violence is an enduring social problem in the United States. One area of intrafamily violence that has received a great deal of media attention is **child abuse**.[170] This term describes any physical or emotional trauma to a child for which no reasonable explanation, such as an accident or ordinary disciplinary practices, can be found.[171]

Child abuse can result from actual physical beatings administered to a child by hands, feet, weapons, belts, sticks, burning, and so on. Another form of abuse results from **neglect**—not providing a child with the care and shelter to which he or she is entitled. It is difficult to estimate the actual number of child abuse cases because many incidents are never reported to the police. Nonetheless, child abuse and neglect appear to be serious social problems. The American Humane Society estimates that 3 million cases of child abuse are reported to authorities each year.[172]

Intrafamily violence is an enduring social problem in the United States. Children who are abused are more likely to be violent and abusive as adults, a process called the "cycle of violence." Here a San Diego, California–based childcare worker on a home visit examines a child of one of his clients. Social service agencies are often overburdened and understaffed, making it difficult for them to effectively deal with abuse cases.

Sexual Abuse Another aspect of the abuse syndrome is **sexual abuse**—the exploitation of children through rape, incest, and molestation by parents or other adults. It is difficult to estimate the incidence of sexual abuse, but a number of attempts have been made to gauge the extent of the problem. In a classic study, Diana Russell's survey of women in the San Francisco area found that 38 percent had experienced intra- or extrafamilial sexual abuse by the time they reached 18.[173] Others have estimated that at least 20 percent of females suffer some form of sexual violence; that is, at least 1 in 5 girls suffers sexual abuse.[174]

As disturbing as these results are, they most likely underestimate the incidence of sexual abuse. It is difficult to get people to respond to questions about youthful sexual abuse, and many victims were too young to understand their abuse or have repressed their memories of the incidents. Children, the most common target, may be inhibited because parents are reluctant to admit abuse occurred. In other cases, threats of injury by the abuser prevent children from reporting these incidents. One study found that 57 percent of children referred to a health clinic because they had sexually transmitted diseases claimed *not* to have been molested despite this irrefutable physical evidence. Parental response significantly influences reporting abuse: kids whose caretakers admitted the possibility of abuse were 3.5 times

more likely to report abuse than those whose parents denied any possibility that their children were victims.[175]

The growing incidence of sexual abuse is of particular concern. Children who have been abused experience a long list of symptoms, including fear, posttraumatic stress disorder, behavior problems, sexualized behavior, and poor self-esteem. The amount of force used during the abuse, its duration, and its frequency are all related to the extent of the long-term effects and the length of time needed for recovery.[176]

Stranger Sexual Abuse Cheryl Amirault LeFave was an aide and driver at the Fell's Acres day care center in Malden, Massachusetts, that her mother, Violet Amirault, had run for more than 20 years. Along with her coworkers, Cheryl Amirault LeFave was accused of taking the center's children, who were between 3 and 5 years old, into a "magic" or "secret" room to molest them. Children told police of being tied naked to a tree, being attacked by a clown, being raped with objects, and being forced to watch the Amiraults kill birds.[177]

The Fell's Acres case is one of many incidents in which children have been victimized by nonrelatives in whose care they have been left. There have been many allegations of sexual impropriety made against religious figures and adults involved in children's activities such as the Boy Scouts.[178] Other day care centers, such as that in California's McMartin preschool case, the Little Rascals Day Care Center in Edenton, North Carolina, and the Wee Care Day Nursery in Maplewood, New Jersey, have also been the sites of sexual abuse accusations.

It is often difficult to prosecute these cases because the children giving testimony are extremely young and make unreliable witnesses. Judges are cautious because they fear that prosecutors may have planted images or made suggestive comments when preparing the children's testimony. Several such convictions have been overturned as questions have mounted over whether interviewers had prodded suggestible children into fabricating stories of abuse. In 1998 Cheryl Amirault LeFave's verdict was overturned when a judge found that prosecutors had tainted the children's testimony.[179]

Causes of Child Abuse Why do parents physically assault their children? Such maltreatment is a highly complex problem with neither a single cause nor a readily available solution. It cuts across ethnic, religious, and socioeconomic lines. Abusive parents cannot be categorized by sex, age, or educational level; they come from all walks of life.[180]

Three factors have been commonly linked to abuse and neglect. First, a cyclical pattern of family violence seems to be perpetuated from one generation to another within families. Evidence indicates that many abused and neglected children grow into adolescence and adulthood with a tendency to engage in violent behavior. The behavior of abusive parents can often be traced to negative experiences in their own childhood — physical abuse, lack of love, emotional neglect, incest, and so on. These parents become unable to separate their own childhood traumas from their relationships with their children; they also often have unrealistic perceptions of the appropriate stages of childhood development. Thus, when their children are unable to act "appropriately"—when they cry, throw food, or strike their parents — the parents may react abusively. According to abuse expert Ruth Inglis, for parents such as these, "the axiom about not being able to love when you have not known love yourself is painfully borne out in their case histories. . . . They spend their days going around the house, ticking away like unexploded bombs. A fussy baby can be the lighted match."[181]

Blended families, which include children living with an unrelated adult such as a stepparent or another unrelated coresident, have also been linked to abuse. For example, children who live with a mother's boyfriend are at much greater risk for abuse than children living with two genetic parents. Some stepparents do not have strong emotional ties to their nongenetic children, nor do they reap emotional benefits from the parent–child relationship. In some ancient or primitive societies, a widow married the brother or another relative of her deceased husband in an effort to provide sur-

viving offspring with a greater share of paternal caring and interest; that option is rarely available today. All too often the genetic parent has to choose between the new mate and the child, sometimes even becoming an accomplice in the exploitation and abuse.[182]

Parents may also become abusive if they are isolated from friends, neighbors, or relatives who can help in times of crisis. Potentially abusive parents are often alienated from society; they have carried the concept of the shrinking nuclear family to its most extreme form and are cut off from ties of kinship and contact with other people in the neighborhood.[183] Many abusive and neglectful parents describe themselves as highly alienated from their families and lacking close relationships with people who could provide support in stressful situations. These people are unable to cope effectively with life crises such as divorce, financial problems, alcohol and drug abuse, or poor housing conditions; so excessive stress leads them to maltreat their children. Statistics show that a high rate of child abuse occurs among the lower economic classes, which has created the misconception that lower-class parents are more abusive than those in the upper classes. However, two conditions may account for this discrepancy. First, low-income people are often subject to greater levels of environmental stress and have fewer resources to deal with it. Second, low-income people are more frequently counted in official statistics.[184] Cases of abuse among poor families are more likely to be dealt with by public agencies and therefore may be more likely to be referred to law enforcement agencies than those involving more affluent parents who can afford private treatment.

Public concern about child abuse has led to the development of programs designed to prevent and deter it. Today laws require doctors, social workers, and other such professionals to report suspicions of child abuse. Some states have created laws that bar abusive parents from the home even before guilt has been determined at trial. Courts have begun to recognize the rights of abused children to collect damages from parents even years after the abuse takes place. In one 1990 case a Colorado court awarded two sisters $2.4 million in damages from a sexually abusive parent more than 20 years after the abuse occurred.[185]

Spousal Abuse On June 23, 1993, John Wayne Bobbitt returned home and according to his wife, Lorena, committed a marital rape. Afterward, while he slept, Lorena used a 12-inch kitchen knife to slice off two-thirds of his penis. In a panic, she drove off and tossed the severed organ into a field. Police officers were able to recover it, and it was reattached in a 9.5-hour operation. The case drew reporters from around the United States; observers at the scene described the media as a "herd of buffaloes," backing into cars and falling in ditches.[186]

John was later tried and acquitted on charges of sexual assault stemming from the alleged rape. Claiming that her actions were a result of the rape and earlier abuse, Lorena was found not guilty, by reason of insanity, on a charge of malicious wounding on January 21, 1994. No longer considered a threat, she was released from Virginia's Central State Hospital on February 28, 1994.[187]

Although one of the most highly publicized cases of the decade, the Bobbitt case is misleading: spouse abuse overwhelmingly involves physical assaults in which wives are injured by husbands.[188] The few cases of **husband battering** typically involve defensive measures taken by previously abused spouses. The presentation of women as violent helps maintain the dominance of men in marital relations.[189]

Spouse abuse has occurred throughout recorded history. Roman men had the legal right to beat their wives for minor acts like attending public games without permission, drinking wine, or walking outdoors with their faces uncovered.[190] More serious transgressions, such as adultery, were punishable by death. During the later stages of the Roman Empire, the practice of wife beating abated; and by the fourth century A.D., excessive violence on the part of husband or wife was grounds for divorce.[191] During the early Middle Ages, there was a separation of love and marriage.[192] The ideal woman was protected, cherished, and loved from afar. In contrast, the wife, with whom marriage had been arranged by family ties, was guarded jealously and could be punished severely for violating her duties. A husband was expected to beat his wife for "misbehaviors" and might himself be punished by neighbors if he failed to do so.[193] Through the later Middle Ages and into modern times (from 1400 to 1900) there was little community objection to a man using force against his wife as long as the assaults did not exceed certain limits, usually construed as death or disfigurement. By the mid-nineteenth century, severe wife beating fell into disfavor, and accused wife beaters were subject to public ridicule. Nonetheless, limited chastisement was still the rule. By the close of the nineteenth century, England and the United States outlawed wife beating. Yet the long history of husbands' domination of their wives made physical coercion hard to control. Until recent times, the subordinate position of women in the family was believed to give husbands the legal and moral obligation to manage their wives' behavior. Even after World War II, English courts found domestic assault a reasonable punishment for a wife who had disobeyed her husband.[194] These ideas form the foundation of men's traditional physical control of women and have led to severe cases of spousal assault.

The Nature and Extent of Spousal Abuse It is difficult to estimate how widespread spousal abuse is today; however, some statistics show the extent of the problem. In their classic study of family violence, Richard Gelles and Murray Straus found that 16 percent of surveyed families had experienced husband–wife assaults.[195] In police departments around the country, 60 to 70 percent of evening calls involve domestic disputes. Nor is violence restricted to marriage: national surveys indicate that between 20 and 40 percent of females experience violence while dating.[196]

Wife abusers share these characteristics:[197]

- *Presence of alcohol.* Excessive alcohol use may turn otherwise docile husbands into wife abusers.
- *Hostility toward dependency.* Some husbands who appear docile and passive may resent their dependence on their wives and react with rage and violence; this reaction has been linked to sexual inadequacy.
- *Excessive brooding.* Obsession with a wife's behavior, however trivial, can result in violent assaults.
- *Social approval.* Some husbands believe that society approves of wife abuse and use these beliefs to justify their violent behavior.
- *Socioeconomic factors.* Men who fail as providers and are under economic stress may take their frustrations out on their wives.
- *Flashes of anger.* Research shows that a significant amount of family violence results from a sudden burst of anger after a verbal dispute.
- *Military service.* Spouse abuse among men who have served in the military service is extremely high. Similarly, those serving in the military are more likely to assault their wives than civilian husbands. The reasons for this phenomenon may be the violence promoted by military training and the close proximity in which military families live to one another.
- *Having been battered children.* Husbands who assault their wives were generally battered as children.

Some people view spousal abuse from an evolutionary standpoint: males are aggressive toward their mates because they have evolved with a high degree of sexual proprietariness. Men fear both losing a valued reproductive resource to a rival and making a paternal investment in a child that is not their own. Violence serves as a coercive social tool to dissuade interest in other males and to lash out in jealousy if threats are not taken seriously (that is, if the woman leaves). This explains why men often kill or injure their ex-wives; threats lose their effectiveness if they are merely a bluff.[198]

Is Spousal Abuse Intergenerational? Although it is generally agreed that child abuse is intergenerational, do the same patterns apply to spousal abuse? There is little conclusive evidence that spouse abusers grew up in homes where spouses were abused; but research indicates that abused children later act abusively toward their own children and spouses.[199] A number of views attempt to explain why this phenomenon occurs:[200]

1. Children learn the roles of parent and spouse through observation, and those who grow up in abusive households believe that harsh parenting and violent behavior are normal.

2. Harsh parenting teaches children that it is often necessary to hit those you love—spouses as well as children.

3. Harsh, incompetent parenting produces children with many behavioral problems including child, spouse, and substance abuse. This variation on problem behavior syndrome suggests that people who have experienced abusive, incompetent parenting are also likely to use drugs, commit crimes, and engage in antisocial behaviors including persistent child and spouse abuse.[201]

The relationship between developing deviant behavior and being the target of physical punishment is constant across race, ethnic origin, and socioeconomic status.[202]

Growing support is being given to battered women. Shelters for assaulted wives are springing up around the country, and laws are being passed to protect a wife's interests. Police departments have made enforcement of domestic abuse laws a top priority. It is essential that this problem be brought to public light and controlled.

ROBBERY

The common-law definition of **robbery** (and the one used by the FBI) is "the taking or attempting to take anything of value from the care, custody or control of a person or persons by force or threat of force or violence and/or by putting the victim in fear."[203] A robbery is considered a violent crime because it involves the use of force to obtain money or goods. Robbery is punished severely because the victim's life is put in jeopardy. In fact, the severity of punishment is based on the amount of force used during the crime, not the value of the items taken.

In 1997 497,950 robberies were reported to police, a rate of 220 per 100,000 population—a decrease of 7 percent in one year. As with other violent crimes, there has been a significant reduction in the robbery rate during the 1990s. Between 1993 and 1997 the rate of robbery declined 27 percent.

The ecological pattern for robbery is similar to that of other violent crimes, with one significant exception: northeastern states have by far the highest robbery rate (260 per 100,000). NCVS data show that robbery is more of a problem than the FBI data indicate. According to the NCVS, about 1.1 million robberies were committed or attempted in 1995. The two data sources agree, however, on the age, race, and sexual makeup of the offenders: they are disproportionately young, male minority group members.

Robbery is most often a street crime; that is, fewer robberies occur in the home than in public places, such as parks, streets, and alleys. The Bureau of Justice Statistics analyzed over 14 million robbery victimizations to provide a more complete picture of the nature and extent of robbery. It found that about two-thirds of victims had property stolen, one-third were injured in the crime, and one-fourth suffered both personal injury and property loss.[204]

Attempts have been made to classify and explain the nature and dynamics of robbery.[205] Among the patterns identified are these:

1. *Robbery of persons who, as part of their employment, are in charge of money or goods.* This category includes robberies in jewelry stores, banks, offices, and other places in which money changes hands.

2. *Robbery in an open area.* These robberies include street muggings, purse snatchings, and other attacks. Street robberies are the most common type, especially in urban areas, where this type of robbery constitutes about 60 percent of reported totals. Street robbery is most closely associated with mugging or **yoking,** which refers to grabbing victims from behind and threatening them with a weapon. Street muggers often target unsavory characters such as drug dealers or pimps who carry large amounts of cash because these victims would find it awkward to report the crime to the police.[206]

3. *Robbery on private premises.* This type of robbery involves breaking into people's homes. FBI records indicate that this type of robbery accounts for about 10 percent of all offenses.

4. *Robbery after a short, preliminary association.* This type of robbery comes after a chance meeting—in a bar, at a party, or after a sexual encounter.

5. *Robbery after a longer association between the victim and offender.* An example of this type of robbery would be an intimate acquaintance robbing his paramour and then fleeing the jurisdiction.

Incidents in patterns 4 and 5 are substantially less common than stranger-to-stranger robberies, which account for more than 75 percent of the total.

Another approach is to characterize types of robbers based on their specialties.[207] Sociologist John Conklin has identified these categories of robbers:

• *Professional robbers* have a long-term commitment to crime as a source of livelihood. This type of robber plans and organizes crimes prior to committing them and seeks money to support a hedonistic lifestyle. Some professionals are exclusively robbers, whereas others engage in additional types of crimes. Professionals are committed to robbing because it is direct, fast, and profitable. They hold no other steady job and plan three or four "big scores" a year to support themselves.

Planning and skill are the trademarks of the professional robber, who usually operates in groups with assigned roles. Professionals usually steal large amounts from commercial establishments. After a score, they may stop for a few weeks until "things cool off."

• *Opportunist robbers* steal to obtain small amounts of money when an accessible target presents itself. They are not committed to robbery but will steal from cab drivers, drunks, the elderly, and other vulnerable persons if they need some extra spending money. Opportunists are usually young minority group members who do not plan their crimes. Although they operate within the milieu of the juvenile gang, they are seldom organized and spend little time discussing weapon use, getaway plans, or other strategies.

• *Addict robbers* steal to support their drug habits. They have a low commitment to robbery because of its danger but a high commitment to theft because it supplies needed funds. The addict is less likely to plan crime or use weapons than the professional robber, but is more cautious than the opportunist. Addicts choose targets that present minimal risk; however, when desperate for funds, they are sometimes careless in selecting the victim and executing the crime. They rarely think in terms of the big score; they just want enough money to get their next fix.

• *Alcoholic robbers* steal for reasons related to their excessive consumption of alcohol. Alcoholic robbers steal (1) when, in a disoriented state, they attempt to get some money to buy liquor or (2) when their condition makes them unemployable and they need funds. Alcoholic robbers have no real commitment to robbery as a way of life. They plan their crimes randomly and give little thought to their victim, circumstance, or escape. For that reason, they are the most likely to be caught.

As these typologies indicate, the typical armed robber is unlikely to be a professional who carefully studies targets while planning a crime. People walking along the street, convenience stores, and gas stations are much more likely robbery targets than banks or other highly secure environments. Robbers, therefore, seem to be diverted by modest defensive measures, such as having more than one clerk in a store or locating stores in strip malls; they are more likely to try an isolated store.[208]

CONNECTIONS

Chapter 5 discussed the rationality of street robbery. Even when robbers are stealing to support a drug habit, their acts do not seem haphazard or irrational. Only the most inebriated might fail to take precautions. The fact that robbery is gender-specific is also evidence that robbers are rational decision makers.

In a recent book, Scott Decker and Richard Wright described their interviews with active robbers in St. Louis, Missouri. Their findings are presented in the Criminological Enterprise feature titled "Armed Robbers in Action."

EMERGING FORMS OF INTERPERSONAL VIOLENCE

Assault, rape, robbery, and murder are traditional forms of interpersonal violence. As more data become available, criminologists have recognized relatively new subcategories within these crime types, such as serial murder and date rape. Additional new categories of interpersonal violence are now receiving attention in criminological literature; the next sections describe two of these forms of violent crime.

Hate Crimes

Hate crimes or **bias crimes** are violent acts directed toward a particular person or members of a group merely because the targets share a discernible racial, ethnic, religious, or gender characteristic.[209] Hate crimes can include the desecration of a house of worship or cemetery, harassment of a minority-group family that has moved into a previously all-white neighborhood, or a racially motivated murder. For example, on August 23, 1989, Yusuf Hawkins, a black youth, was killed in the Bensonhurst section of Brooklyn, New York, because he had wandered into a racially charged white neighborhood.[210]

Hate crimes usually involve convenient, vulnerable targets who are incapable of fighting back. For example, there have been numerous reported incidents of teenagers attacking vagrants and the homeless in an effort to rid their town or neighborhood of people they consider undesirable.[211] Another group targeted for hate crimes is gay men and women: gay bashing has become common in U.S. cities. In the fall of 1998 Matthew Shepard, a gay college student, was kidnapped and severely beaten. He died five days after he was found unconscious on a Wyoming ranch, where he had been left tied to a fence for 18 hours in near freezing temperatures.[212]

Racial and ethnic minorities have also been the targets of attack. In California, Mexican laborers have been attacked and killed; in New Jersey, Indian immigrants have been the targets of racial hatred.[213] Although hate crimes are often mindless attacks directed toward "traditional" minority victims, political and economic trends may cause this form of violence to be redirected. For example, Asians have been attacked by groups who resent the growing economic power of Japan and Korea as well as the commercial success of

The Criminological Enterprise

Armed Robbers in Action

Criminologists Richard Wright and Scott Decker have identified and interviewed a sample of 86 active armed robbers in St. Louis, Missouri. Their sample, primarily young African-American men, helped provide an in-depth view of armed robbery that had been missing from the criminological literature.

Wright and Decker found that most armed robberies are motivated by a pressing need for cash. Many robbers careen from one financial crisis to the next, prompted by their endless quest for stimulation and thrills. Interviewees told of how they partied, gambled, drank, and abused substances until they were broke. Their partying not only provided excitement, but it helped generate a street reputation as a "hip" guy who can "make things happen." Robbers had a "here and now" mentality, which required a constant supply of cash to fuel their appetites. Those interviewed showed little long-range planning or commitment to the future. Because of their street hustler mentality, few if any of the robbers were able to obtain or keep legitimate employment, even if it was available.

Armed robbery also provided a psychic thrill. It was a chance to hurt or humiliate victims, or to get even with someone who may have wronged them in the past. As one robber explained, "This might sound stupid, but I [also] like to see a person get scared, be scared of the pistol. . . . You got power. I come in here with a big old pistol and I ain't playing."

Robbers show evidence of being highly rational offenders. Many choose victims who themselves are involved in illegal behavior, most often drug dealers. Ripping off a dealer kills three birds with one stone, providing both money and drugs while at the same time targeting victims who are quite unlikely to call the police. Another ideal target is a married man who is looking for illicit sexual adventures. He also is disinclined to call the police and bring attention to himself.

Others target noncriminal victims. They like to stay in their own neighborhood, relying on their intimate knowledge of streets and alleys in order to avoid detection. Although some range far afield seeking affluent victims, others believe that residents in the city's poorest areas are more likely to carry cash (wealthy people carry checks and credit cards). Because they realize that the risk of detection and punishment is the same whether the victim is carrying a load of cash or is penniless, experienced robbers use discretion in selecting targets. People whose clothing, jewelry, and demeanor mark them as carrying substantial amounts of cash make suitable targets; people who look like they can fight back are avoided. Some station themselves at cash machines in order to spot targets who are flashing rolls of money.

Robbers have racial, gender, and age preferences in their selection of targets. Some African-American robbers prefer white targets because they believe they are too afraid to fight back. Others concentrate on African-American victims, who are more likely to carry cash than credit cards. As one interviewee revealed, "White guys can be so paranoid [that] they just want to get away. . . . They're not . . . gonna argue with you." Likewise, intoxicated victims in no condition to fight back were a favored target. Some robbers tend to target women because they feel they are easy subjects; however, others avoid them because they believe they will get emotionally upset and bring unwanted attention. Most agree that the elderly are less likely to put up a fuss than younger, stronger targets.

Some robbers choose commercial targets, such as convenience stores or markets, that are cash businesses open late at night. Gas stations are a favorite victim. Security is of little consequence to experienced robbers, who may bring an accomplice to subdue guards.

Once they choose their targets, robbers carefully orchestrate the criminal incidents. They immediately impose their will on their chosen victims, leaving little room for the victims to maneuver and making sure the victims feel threatened enough to offer no resistance. Some approach from behind so they cannot be identified, while others approach the victims head-on, showing that they are tough and bold. By convincing the victims of their impending death, the robber takes control.

CRITICAL THINKING

1. It is unlikely that the threat of punishment can deter robbery (most robbers refuse to think about apprehension and punishment), but Wright and Decker suggest that eliminating cash and relying on debit and credit cards may be the most productive method to reduce the incidence of robbery. Although this seems far-fetched, our society is becoming progressively more cashless; it is now possible to buy both gas and groceries with credit cards. Would a cashless society end the threat of robbery, or would innovative robbers find new targets?

2. Based on what you know about how robbers target victims, how can you better protect yourself from robbery?

 INFOTRAC COLLEGE EDITION RESEARCH

In order to learn more about robbery, see:

Peter J. van Koppen, Robert W. J. Jansen. The road to the robbery: travel patterns in commercial robberies. *British Journal of Criminology* Spring 1998 v38 n2 p230

D. J. Pyle, D. F. Deadman. Crime and the business cycle in post-war Britain. *British Journal of Criminology* Summer 1994 34 n3 p339–357

Source: Richard Wright and Scott Decker, *Armed Robbers in Action, Stickups and Street Culture* (Boston, Mass.: Northeastern University Press, 1997).

Table 11.2 Factors That Produce Hate Crimes

- Poor or uncertain economic conditions
- Racial stereotypes in films and on television
- Hate-filled discourse on talk shows or in political advertisements
- The use of racial code language such as "welfare mothers" and "inner-city thugs"
- An individual's personal experiences with members of particular minority groups
- Scapegoating—blaming of a minority group for the misfortunes of society as a whole

Source: "A Policymaker's Guide to Hate Crimes," Bureau of Justice Assistance Monograph (Washington, D.C.: Bureau of Justice Assistance, 1997).

Asian-Americans.[214] The factors that precipitate hate crimes are discussed in Table 11.2.

The Roots of Hate Why do people commit bias crimes? Research by sociologist Jack McDevitt shows that hate crimes are generally spontaneous incidents motivated by the victims' walking, driving, shopping, or socializing in an area in which their attackers believe they "do not belong."[215] Other factors that motivate bias attacks include a victim moving into an ethnically distinct neighborhood or dating a member of a different race or ethnic group. Although hate crimes are often unplanned, McDevitt finds that most of these crimes are serious incidents that involve assaults and robberies.[216] In their book *Hate Crimes,* McDevitt and Jack Levin say that hate crimes are typically one of three types that reflect different motives:

1. *Thrill-seeking hate crimes.* In the same way some kids like to get together to shoot hoops, hate-mongers join forces to have fun by bashing minorities or destroying property. Inflicting pain on others gives them a sadistic thrill.

2. *Reactive hate crimes.* Perpetrators of these crimes rationalize their behavior as a defensive stand taken against outsiders who they believe are threatening their community or way of life. A gang of teens that attacks a new family in the neighborhood because they are the "wrong" race is committing a reactive hate crime.

3. *Mission hate crimes.* Some disturbed individuals see it as their duty to rid the world of evil. Those on a "mission," like Skinheads, the Ku Klux Klan (KKK), and white supremacist groups, may seek to eliminate people who threaten their religious beliefs because they are members of a different faith or threaten "racial purity" because they are of a different race.[217]

In one study of Boston police records, Levin and McDevitt found that thrill crimes were the most common (58

percent), and most of these (70 percent) involved assault. Reactive crimes (42 percent) also involved assaulting strangers who happened to be in the wrong place at the wrong time. Although there was only one mission-type crime, it was the most violent incident and involved beating two supposedly gay males with baseball bats.[218]

Extent of Hate Crime Information on the extent of hate crimes is just becoming available. There is evidence that the neo-Nazi skinhead movement now contains 70,000 members worldwide in 33 countries. Germany houses about 5,000 skins, and Hungary and the Czech Republic 4,000 each.[219] To some, becoming a skinhead is just a lifestyle that features shaved heads, Doc Marten boots, body piercing, and a love of punk rock and Ska, a music mixture of Caribbean influences, rhythm and blues, and rock. For others, it demonstrates pride in their working-class background. Still others act out their anger toward minorities who, they believe, have cost working-class whites jobs and other opportunities. Indeed, for nearly two decades, antiracist skinheads have been confronting racist skinheads; the two sides have slashed each other's tires, bashed each other over their shaved heads, and even killed rivals.[220]

In the United States the FBI now collects data on hate crimes as part of the Hate Crime Statistics Act of 1990. During 1997 about 8,000 bias-motivated criminal incidents were reported, involving 10,000 hate crime victims.[221] Of the reported incidents, 4,700 were motivated by racial bias; 1,400 by religious bias; 1,100 by sexual orientation bias; and 800 by ethnicity or national origin bias.

Because of the extent and seriousness of the problem, a number of legal jurisdictions have made a special effort to control the spread of hate crimes. Boston maintains the Community Disorders Unit, and the New York City police department formed the Bias Incident Investigating Unit in 1980. When a crime anywhere in the city is suspected of being motivated by bias, the unit initiates an investigation. The unit also assists victims and works with concerned organizations such as the Commission on Human Rights and the Gay and Lesbian Task Force. These agencies deal with noncriminal bias incidents through mediation, education, and other forms of prevention.[222]

Workplace Violence

Paul Calden, a former insurance company employee, walked into a Tampa cafeteria and opened fire on a table at which his former supervisors were dining. Calden shouted, "This is what you all get for firing me!" and began shooting. When he finished, three were dead and two others were wounded.[223] It has become commonplace to read of irate employees or former employees

Figure 11.5   Trends in Workplace Violence

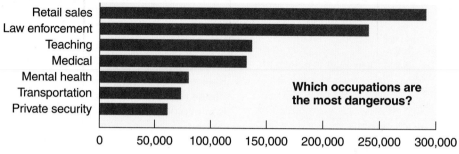

Selected occupations with a larger
number of violent victimizations

Retail sales
Law enforcement
Teaching
Medical
Mental health
Transportation
Private security

**Which occupations are
the most dangerous?**

0   50,000   100,000   150,000   200,000   250,000   300,000

Average annual number of violent victimizations
in the workplace, 1992–1996

- Each year between 1992 and 1996, more than 2 million U.S. residents were victims of a violent crime while they were at work or on duty.

- More than 1,000 workplace homicides occurred annually.

- The most common type of victimization was simple assault, with an estimated 1.5 million occurring each year. U.S. residents also suffered 51,000 rapes and sexual assaults and about 84,000 robberies while they were at work.

- Annually, more than 230,000 police officers became victims of a nonfatal violent crime while they were working or on duty.

- About 40 percent of victims of nonfatal violence in the workplace reported that they knew their offenders.

- Women were more likely than men to be victimized by someone they knew.

- Approximately 12 percent of the nonfatal violent workplace crimes injured the victim. Of those injured, about half received medical treatment.

- Intimates (current and former spouses, boyfriends, and girlfriends) were identified by the victims as the perpetrators of about 1 percent of all workplace violent crime.

Source: Greg Warchol, *Workplace Violence, 1992–1996* (Washington, D.C.: Bureau of Justice Statistics, 1998).

attacking coworkers or sabotaging machinery and production lines. **Workplace violence** is now considered the third leading cause of occupational injury or death.[224]

Who engages in workplace violence? The typical offender is a middle-aged white male who faces termination in a worsening economy. The fear of economic ruin is especially strong in agencies such as the U.S. Postal Service, where long-term employees fear job loss because of automation and reorganization. In contrast, younger workers usually kill while committing a robbery or another felony.

A number of factors precipitate workplace violence. One may simply be the conflict caused by economic restructuring. As corporations cut their staffs due to recent trends such as office automation and company buyouts, long-term employees who had never thought of themselves losing a job are suddenly unemployed. There is often a correlation between sudden, unexpected layoffs and violent reactions.[225] Another trigger may be leadership styles. Some companies, including the U.S. Postal Service, have authoritarian management styles that demand performance, above all else, from employees. Unsympathetic, unsupportive managers may help trigger workplace violence.

Not all workplace violence is triggered by management-induced injustice. In some incidents coworkers have been killed because they refused romantic relationships with the assailants or reported them for sexual harassment. Others have been killed because they got a job the assailant coveted. Irate clients and customers have also killed because of poor service or perceived slights. For example, in one Los Angeles incident, a former patient shot and critically wounded three doctors because his demands for painkillers had gone unheeded.[226]

There are a variety of responses to workplace provocations. Some people take out their anger and aggression by attacking their supervisors in an effort to punish the company that dismissed them; this is a form of murder by proxy.[227] Disgruntled employees may also attack family members or friends, misdirecting the rage and frustration caused by their work situation. Others are content with sabotaging company equipment; computer data banks are particularly vulnerable to tampering. The aggrieved party may do nothing to rectify the situation; this inaction is referred to as **sufferance.** Over time, the unresolved conflict may be compounded by other events that cause an eventual eruption.

The Extent of Workplace Violence   The latest available data show that each year more than 2 million U.S. residents become victims of violent crime while they work. The most common type of victimization is assault, with an estimated 1.5 million simple assaults and 396,000 aggravated assaults reported annually. Each year sees 84,000 robberies, about 51,000 rapes or sexual assaults, and more than 1,000 workplace homicides.[228] As Figure 11.5 shows, retail sales workers have the highest risk of on-the-job injuries, followed by law enforcement officers.

CONNECTIONS

Does the fact that sales clerks and police officers have the highest injury risk support routine activities theory? People in high-risk jobs who are out late at night and, in the case of sales clerks, do business in cash seem to have the greatest risk of injury on the job. See Chapter 5 for more on routine activities and crime.

Can workplace violence be controlled? One approach is to use third parties to mediate disputes.

CONNECTIONS

The restorative justice movement (discussed in Chapter 9) advocates the use of mediation to resolve interpersonal disputes. Restorative justice techniques may work particularly well in the workplace, where disputants know each other and tensions may be simmering over a long period.

This may help control the rising tide of workplace violence. Another idea is for a human resources approach, with aggressive job retraining and continued medical coverage after layoffs; it is also important to use objective, fair hearings to thwart unfair or biased terminations. Perhaps rigorous screening tests can help iden-

tify violence-prone workers so that they can be given anger management training.

POLITICAL VIOLENCE

In addition to interpersonal violence and street crime, violent behavior also involves politically motivated acts, including terrorism. Political crime has been with us throughout history. It is virtually impossible to find a history book of any society that does not record the existence of political criminals, who are defined as "those craftsmen of dreams who possess a gigantic reservoir of creative energy as well as destructive force."[229]

It is often difficult to separate political from interpersonal crimes of violence. For example, if a group robs a bank to obtain funds for its revolutionary struggles, should the act be treated as a political crime or a common bank robbery? In this instance, defining a crime as political depends on the kind of legal response the act evokes from those in power.

To be a political crime, an act must carry with it the intent to disrupt and change the government and must not be merely a common-law crime committed for greed or egotism. Criminologist Stephen Schafer refers to those who violate the law because they believe their actions will ultimately benefit society as **convictional criminals.** They know their actions may be wrong and harmful but believe these actions are necessary to create the changes they fervently desire. "A member of the Second World War Resistance," Schafer argues, "may have condemned violence, yet his own conviction overshadowed any sense of repugnance and induced him to engage in violent crimes in an effort to expel the invader from his Fatherland."[230] In these cases, political violence is not violence for violence's sake; it is violence with a higher, political purpose.

Terrorism

One aspect of political violence that greatly concerns criminologists is terrorism.[231] Because of its complexity, an all-encompassing definition of **terrorism** is difficult to formulate, although most experts agree that it generally involves the illegal use of force against innocent people to achieve a political objective.[232] One national commission defines terrorism as "a tactic or technique by means of which a violent act or the threat thereof is used for the prime purpose of creating overwhelming fear for coercive purposes."[233] In other words, terrorism is usually defined as a type of political crime that emphasizes violence as a mechanism to promote change. Whereas some political criminals may demonstrate, counterfeit, sell secrets, spy, and the like, terrorists systematically murder and destroy or threaten such violence to terrorize individuals, groups, communities, or

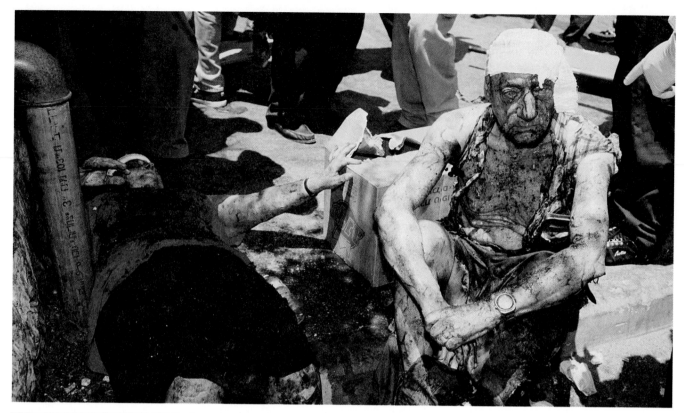

This 1997 terrorist bombing in Jerusalem killed 14 people and wounded 150. Should politically motivated terrorism be considered an act of war? Or is it a violent crime that should be punished in a similar fashion to intentional murders motivated by greed, revenge, or other personal factors?

governments into conceding to the terrorists' political demands.[234] However, it may be erroneous to equate terrorism with political goals because not all terrorist actions are aimed at political change; some terrorists may try to bring about economic or social reform, for example, by attacking women wearing fur coats or sabotaging property during a labor dispute. Terrorism must also be distinguished from conventional warfare because it requires secrecy and clandestine operations to exert social control over large populations.[235]

Terrorists and Guerillas The term *terrorist* is often used interchangeably with guerilla. The latter term, meaning "little war," developed out of the Spanish rebellion against French troops after Napoleon's 1808 invasion of the Iberian peninsula.[236] Terrorists have an urban focus. Operating in small bands, or cadres, of three to five members, they target the property or persons of their enemy, such as members of the ruling class.[237] **Guerillas,** on the other hand, are located in rural areas and attack the military, the police, and government officials. Their organizations can grow quite large and eventually take the form of a conventional military force. However, guerillas can infiltrate urban areas in small bands, while terrorists can make forays into the countryside; consequently, the terms are used interchangeably.[238]

Historical Perspective Acts of terrorism have been known throughout history. The assassination of Julius Caesar on March 15, 44 B.C., is considered an act of terrorism. Terrorism became widespread at the end of the Middle Ages, when political leaders were subject to assassination by their enemies. The word *assassin* was derived from an Arabic term meaning "hashish eater"; it originally referred to members of a drug-using Muslim terrorist organization that carried out plots against prominent Christians and other religious enemies.[239] The literal translation of *assassin* refers to the acts of ritual intoxication undertaken by the warriors before their missions. From A.D. 66 to 73 a Jewish sect known as the Zealots took up arms against the Roman occupation, using daggers to slit the throats of Romans and of Jews who collaborated.[240]

When rulers had absolute power, terrorist acts were viewed as one of the only means of gaining political rights. At times European states encouraged terrorist acts against their enemies. For example, Queen Elizabeth I empowered her naval leaders, including famed captains John Hawkins and Francis Drake, to attack the Spanish fleet. These privateers would have been considered pirates had they not operated with government approval. American privateers attacked the British during the Revolutionary War and the War of 1812 and were considered heroes for their actions against the English Navy.

The term *terrorist* first became popular during the French Revolution. From the fall of the Bastille on July 14, 1789, until July 1794, thousands suspected of counterrevolutionary activity were killed on the guillotine. Here again, the relative nature of political crime is documented: whereas most victims of the French Reign of Terror were revolutionaries who had been denounced by rival factions, thousands of the hated nobility lived in relative tranquility. The end of the terror was signaled by the death of its prime mover, Maximilien Robespierre, on July 28, 1794, as the result of a successful plot to end his rule. He was executed on the same guillotine to which he sent almost 20,000 people.

In the hundred years after the French Revolution, terrorism continued around the world. The Hur Brotherhood in India was made up of religious fanatics who carried out terrorist acts against the ruling class.[241] In Eastern Europe the Internal Macedonian Revolutionary Organization campaigned against the Turkish government, which controlled its homeland (Macedonia became part of the former Yugoslavia). Similarly, the protest of the Union of Death Society, or Black Hand, against the Austro-Hungarian empire's control of Serbia led to the group's assassination of Archduke Franz Ferdinand, which started World War I. The Irish Republican Army, established around 1916, steadily battled British forces from 1919 to 1923, culminating in the Republic of Ireland gaining independence. Between the world wars, right-wing terrorism existed in Germany, Spain, and Italy. Conversely, Russia was the scene of left-wing revolutionary activity, which killed the czar in 1917 and gave birth to the Marxist state.

During World War II, resistance to the occupying German troops was common throughout Europe. The Germans considered the resistance to be terrorists, but the rest of the world considers them heroes. Meanwhile, in Palestine, Jewish terrorist groups—the Haganah, Irgun, and Stern Gang, whose leaders included Menachem Begin, who later became Israel's prime minister—waged war against the British to force them to allow Jewish survivors of the Holocaust to settle in their traditional homeland. Today, of course, many of these alleged terrorists are considered freedom fighters who laid down their lives for a just cause.

Forms of Terrorism

Today the term *terrorism* describes many different behaviors and goals. Some of the more common forms are briefly described here.[242]

Revolutionary Terrorists Revolutionary terrorists use violence to frighten those in power and their supporters. The ultimate goal of these acts is to replace the existing government with a regime that holds acceptable political views. Terrorist actions such as kidnapping, assassi-

nation, and bombing are designed to draw repressive responses from governments trying to defend themselves. These responses help revolutionaries to expose, through the skilled use of media coverage, the governments' inhumane nature. The original reason for the governments' harsh response may be lost as the effect of counterterrorist activities is felt by uninvolved people.[243] Consider, for example, that in Europe, socialist- and Marxist-oriented groups have been pitted against capitalist governments for the past 30 years. During the 1980s the Marxist Baader-Meinhoff group in Germany conducted a series of robberies, bombings, and kidnappings. When east and west Germany were reunified in 1989, terrorist actions were believed over. Yet on April 1, 1991, the Red Army Faction, the successor to Baader-Meinhoff, claimed credit for assassinating Detlev Rohwedder, the head of the government agency charged with rebuilding the East German economy.[244]

In the Middle East, terrorist activities have been linked to the Palestinians' desire to wrest their former homeland from Israel. The leading group, the Palestinian Liberation Organization (PLO), had directed terrorist activities against Israel. Although the PLO has now reached agreement with Israel in preparation for Palestinian political control of the West Bank and the Gaza Strip, splinter groups have broken from the PLO. These groups include the Abu Nidal group, which is the Popular Front for the Liberation of Palestine; Hamas; and the Iranian-backed Hizballah group. These terrorist splinter groups are perpetuating the conflict that Israel and the PLO sought to resolve.[245]

Political Terrorists Political terrorism is directed at people or groups who oppose the terrorists' political ideology or whom the terrorists define as "outsiders" who must be destroyed. U.S. political terrorists tend to be heavily armed groups organized around such themes as white supremacy, militant tax resistance, and religious revisionism. Identified groups have included the Aryan Republican Army, the Aryan Nation, the Posse Comitatus, and the Ku Klux Klan. Some of these groups have formed their own churches. For example, the Church of Jesus Christ Christian claims that Jesus was born an Aryan rather than a Jew, and that white Anglo-Saxons are the true "chosen people." Some groups have conducted common-law crimes such as bank robberies to fund their activities, which might include bombings and other terrorist tactics.[246] Recently right-wing political extremists have engaged in a pattern of uncoordinated violence motivated by hate, rage, and the inability of more coordinated groups to either bring down the government or gain public support.[247] Although unlikely to topple the government, these individualistic acts of terror are difficult to predict or control. On April 19, 1995, 168 people were killed during the Oklahoma City bombing. This is the most severe example of political terrorism in the United States.

Additional examples of political terrorism include the following:

- In April 1996, after an 11-month federal investigation resulted in their indictment on fraud charges, members of the Freemen movement held federal officers at bay in a monthlong standoff before surrendering in Jordan, Montana. The Freemen are one of many right-wing groups who have conducted antigovernment activities. Their peaceful surrender prevented another in a long line of bloody engagements between federal agents and right-wing militants.
- The infamous 1993 standoff in Waco, Texas, between David Koresh, the leader of the Branch Davidian Cult, and federal agents, including the FBI and the Alcohol, Tobacco, and Firearms Department, was yet another incident involving a group of terrorists in conflict with federal agents. This standoff resulted in the fiery deaths of Koresh and his followers.[248]

The list of politically motivated acts of terrorism goes on. Unfortunately, they are likely to continue for generations and centuries to come.

Nationalist Terrorism   Nationalist terrorism promotes the interests of a minority ethnic or religious group that has been persecuted under majority rule. In India, for example, Sikh radicals use violence to recover what they believe to be lost homelands. They assassinated Indian Prime Minister Indira Gandhi on November 6, 1984, in retaliation for the government's storming of their Golden Temple religious shrine (and revolutionary base) in June 1984.[249] Other nationalist terrorist activities include the following:

- Since 1994 fundamentalist Muslims have attacked foreign tourists in Egypt in an effort to sabotage the tourist industry, topple the secular government, and turn Egypt into an Islamic state.[250] On November 17, 1997, over 60 foreign tourists were killed in an attack by Muslim terrorists near the rooms of Luxor in Southern Egypt.
- In Algeria, fundamentalist Muslim groups have waged a decade-long battle against the government. On February 2, 1997, 50 militants armed with axes decapitated 31 people in the city of Medea.[251]

Cause-Based Terrorism   When the American embassies in Kenya and Tanzania were bombed in 1998 in attacks that killed more than 250 people, Osama bin Laden's Al Qaeda movement was quickly identified as the culprit. In a 1997 interview with CNN, bin Laden said his "jihad" or holy war against the United States was started because American forces were still operating in Saudi Arabia. He demanded that the United States end its "aggressive intervention against Muslims

in the whole world." He claimed that his cause was based on Islamic tradition; he believed that it was not permissible for non-Muslims to remain as protectors in Saudi Arabia. He stated that the current Egyptian and Saudi governments were insufficiently devout and therefore suitable targets of his group.[252]

Bin Laden's brand of terrorist activity is one of many conducted by groups that espouse a particular social or religious cause and use violence to address their grievances.[253] For example, antiabortion groups have demonstrated at abortion clinics, and some members have attacked clients, bombed offices, and killed doctors who perform abortions. On October 23, 1998, Dr. Barnett Slepian was shot by a sniper and killed in his Buffalo, New York, home; he was one of a growing number of abortion providers believed to be the victims of terrorists who ironically claim to be "pro-life."[254]

Environmental Terrorism   On October 19, 1998, several suspicious fires were set atop Vail Mountain, a luxurious ski resort in Colorado. Soon after, a militant environmental group, the Earth Liberation Front, claimed that it set the fires to stop a ski operator from expanding into animal habitats (especially that of the mountain lynx). The fires, which cost an estimated $12 million in damages, are the most costly of the over 1,500 terrorist acts committed by environmental terrorists during the past two decades in an effort to slow down developers who they believe are threatening the environment or harming animals. Fires have also been set in government labs where animal research is conducted. Spikes are driven into trees to prevent logging in fragile areas.[255] Members of such groups as the Animal Liberation Front (ALF) and Earth First! take responsibility for these attacks; they have also raided turkey farms before Thanksgiving and rabbit farms before Easter.[256] The Earth Liberation Front has been active for several years in the United States and abroad. In Britain members claim credit for such actions as sabotaging construction equipment and uprooting genetically modified beets. In 1996, near Eugene, Oregon, the Earth Liberation Front name was spraypainted at the scene when someone damaged trucks at a Forest Service ranger station.[257]

State-Sponsored Terrorism   State-sponsored terrorism occurs when a repressive governmental regime forces its citizens into obedience, oppresses minorities, and stifles political dissent.[258] Death squads and the use of government troops to destroy political opposition parties are often associated with Latin American political terrorism.[259] For example, during the 1980s, a paramilitary group known as the Honduran Anti-Communist Liberation Army allegedly kidnapped, tortured, and murdered leftist opposition figures.[260] The Central Intelligence Agency (CIA) is said to have known about the atrocities and futilely warned Honduran security forces to refrain from human rights abuses. Some governments have been accused of using terrorist-type actions to control political dissidents. For example, in the first 18 months of its deployment, members of the Haitian National Police allegedly executed 15 political opponents of the regime.[261]

Much of what we know about state-sponsored terrorism comes from the efforts of human rights groups. London-based Amnesty International maintains that tens of thousands of people continue to become victims of security operations that result in disappearances and executions.[262] Political prisoners are now being tortured in about 100 countries; people have disappeared or are being held in secret detention in about 20; and government-sponsored death squads have been operating in more than 35. Countries known for encouraging violent control of dissidents include Brazil, Colombia, Guatemala, Honduras, Peru Iraq, and the Sudan. When Tupac Amaru rebels seized and held hostages at the Japanese Ambassadors' villa in Peru on December 17, 1996, Amnesty International charged that the action came in response to a decade-long campaign of human rights violations by national security forces and extensive abuses against opposition groups. Between January 1983 and December 1992, Amnesty International documented at least 4,200 cases of people who had disappeared in Peru following detention by the security forces. Thousands more were killed by government forces in extrajudicial executions, including some 500 people in 19 separate massacres.[263]

Nuclear Terrorism State-sponsored terrorism can also be directed at people and governments outside its borders. Nowhere is this threat more disturbing than the possibility that some "outlaw" state such as Libya or North Korea will carry out a nuclear-based attack against a nation it views as the enemy.[264] Although special expertise is needed to build a nuclear bomb, there are enough disaffected scientists available to provide the skills to build an effective device. Raw material such as plutonium-239 is difficult to manufacture, but there are so many existing nuclear bombs in the hands of unstable Eastern European states that nuclear terrorists might be able to purchase what they need to build a bomb. Since 1990 there have been a half-dozen cases involving theft and transportation of nuclear material and other cases involving people who offered to sell agents material not yet in their possession. These are the known cases; it is impossible to know if client states have already purchased enriched uranium or plutonium.

If a nuclear device is planted on U.S. soil, the Department of Energy's Nuclear Emergency Search Team will be responsible for disabling it. This group of scientists and technicians is extensively trained in ways to neutralize devices using robots, video cameras, and other technology. Their job is critical: if the New York Trade Center had been attacked with a low-yield nuclear device rather than chemical explosives, both towers would have collapsed, and as many as 50,000 people would have been killed.

The most extreme form of state-sponsored terrorism occurs when a government seeks to wipe out a minority group within its jurisdiction. This atrocity is referred to as **genocide.** The World War II Holocaust is the most extreme example of genocide to date, but more recent occurrences have taken place in Cambodia, Rwanda, and Bosnia.

Extent of Terrorism

According to the U.S. State Department, Iran, Iraq, Libya, North Korea, and Cuba continue their policy of giving material, logistic, and financial support to groups that commit terrorism. Each year hundreds of attacks take place. Table 11.3 presents information about the number of incidents that occurred during 1996 and 1997. Of the attacks that occurred during that period, approximately one-third were against U.S. targets. The predominant type of attack during 1997 was bombing; most targets were business-related. Most of the bombings consisted of low-level attacks on multinational oil pipelines in Colombia; terrorists there regard the pipelines as a U.S. target.

The following were among the more significant attacks during 1998:

Table 11.3 Comparison of Terrorist Incidents Between 1996 and 1997			
INCIDENTS THAT OCCURRED AS A RESULT OF TERRORISM	**1997**	**1996**	**NUMBER OF +/−**
Overall number of international terrorism acts	296	304	+8
Number of people dead and wounded	221 dead 693 wounded	314 dead 2,912 wounded	−93 dead −2,219 wounded
Number of U.S. citizens dead and wounded	7 dead 21 wounded	23 dead 510 wounded	−16 dead −489 wounded
Assassinations commissioned by the Iraqi government	13	?	

- On November 17, the deadliest terrorist attack ever committed in Egypt occurred when six gunmen entered the Hatsheput Temple in Luxor and for 30 minutes methodically shot and knifed tourists trapped inside the temple's alcoves. Fifty-eight foreign tourists were murdered, along with three Egyptian police officers and one Egyptian tour guide.
- On November 12, four U.S. citizens, employees of Union Texas Petroleum, and their Pakistani driver were shot and killed when the vehicle in which they were riding was attacked one mile from the U.S. Consulate in Karachi.
- On July 30, two suicide bombers attacked a market in Jerusalem. Sixteen persons, including one U.S. citizen, were killed, and 178 others were wounded.
- On September 4, three suicide bombers attacked a pedestrian mall in central Jerusalem, killing seven persons, including a 14-year-old U.S. citizen, and injuring nearly 200 others.

Who Is the Terrorist?

Terrorists engage in criminal activities, such as bombings, shootings, and kidnappings. What motivates these individuals to risk their lives and those of innocent people? One view is that terrorists hold ideological beliefs that prompt their behavior. At first they have heightened perceptions of oppressive conditions—relative deprivation.[265] Once these potential terrorists recognize that these conditions can be changed by an active governmental reform effort that has not happened, they conclude that they must resort to violence to encourage change. The violence need not be aimed at a specific goal. Rather, terror tactics must help set in motion a series of events that enlists others in the cause and leads to long-term change. "Successful" terrorists believe that their "self-sacrifice" outweighs the guilt created by harming innocent people. Terrorism, therefore, requires violence without guilt; the cause justifies the violence.[266] According to Austin Turk, terrorists tend to come from upper- rather than lower-class backgrounds, perhaps because the upper classes can produce people who are more politically sensitive, articulate, and focused in their resentments.[267] Because their position in the class structure gives them the feeling that they can influence or change society, upper-class citizens are more likely to seek confrontations with the authorities. Class differences are also manifested in different approaches to political violence. Lower-class violence often spontaneously expresses dissatisfaction in collective riots and rampages and politically inconsequential acts. Upper-class violence tends to be more calculated and organized, using elaborate strategies of resistance. Revolutionary cells, campaigns of terror and assassination, logistically complex and expensive assaults, and writing and disseminating formal critiques, manifestos, and theories are typical acts of the social elite.

Upper-class political terrorism has been manifested in the **death squads** operating in Latin America and Asia. These vigilantes use violence to intimidate those who oppose the ruling party. One graphic example of these terrorist activities occurred in Sri Lanka on October 5, 1989, when a death squad composed of members of the ruling parties' security forces beheaded 18 suspected members of the antigovernment People's Liberation Front and placed their heads around a pond at a university campus.[268]

Responses to Terrorism

Governments have tried numerous responses to terrorism. Law enforcement agencies have infiltrated terrorist groups and turned members over to police.[269] Rewards are often offered for information leading to the arrest of terrorists. "Democratic" elections have been held to discredit terrorists' complaints that the state is oppressive. Counterterrorism laws have increased penalties and decreased political rights afforded known terrorists.

In the United States, antiterrorist legislation provides jurisdiction over terrorist acts committed abroad against U.S. citizens and gives the United States the right to punish people for killing foreign officials and politically protected persons.[270] On April 24, 1996, President Clinton signed S.735, the "Antiterrorism and Effective Death Penalty Act of 1996," into law. Among its provisions, the legislation bans fund-raising in the United States that supports terrorist organizations. It allows U.S. officials to deport terrorists from American soil without being compelled by the terrorists to divulge classified information; it also bars terrorists from entering the United States.[271] Among its other provisions, it

- Requires plastic explosives to contain chemical markers so that criminals who use them can be tracked down and prosecuted.
- Enables the government to require that chemical taggants be added to some other types of explosives so that police can better trace bombs to the criminals who make them.
- Increases controls over biological and chemical weapons.
- Toughens penalties for a range of terrorist crimes.
- Bans the sale of defense goods and services to countries that are not "cooperating fully" with U.S. antiterrorism efforts.

Some legislative efforts have been directed at punishing specific countries identified with sponsoring or conducting terrorism. For example, The Iran and Libya Sanctions Act of 1996 imposes new sanctions on foreign companies that engage in specified economic transactions with Iran or Libya. It is intended to

- Help deny Iran and Libya revenues that could be used to finance international terrorism.

- Limit the flow of resources necessary to obtain weapons of mass destruction.
- Pressure Libya to comply with U.N. resolutions that, among other things, call for Libya to extradite for trial the accused perpetrators of the Pan Am 103 bombing.

The bill sanctions foreign companies that provide new investments for developing petroleum resources in Iran or Libya. The bill also sanctions foreign companies that violate U.N. prohibitions against trade with Libya in certain goods and services such as arms, oil equipment, and civil aviation services. If a violation occurs, the United States can impose sanctions against the violating company.[272]

Despite these and other antiterrorism statutes, most politically motivated acts are prosecuted as common-law crimes. Political commentators Brent Smith and Gregory Orvis suggest that this underscores the government's effort to highlight the real motivation of domestic terrorism: personal profit.[273] Smith and Orvis state that politically motivated crimes are taken seriously by U.S. prosecutors, who usually charge defendants with multiple criminal violations.

Although the United States has prohibited violence or assassination attempts against suspected terrorists, both federal law enforcement agencies and the U.S. military have specially trained antiterrorist squads. The military, for example, has created the renowned Delta Force. Delta Force activities are generally secret, but it is known that the force was active in Iran (1980), Honduras (1982), Sudan (1983), and during the Grenada invasion (1983); the force was prepared to take action in the hijacking of the ship *Achille Lauro* (1985).

Despite U.S. efforts to control terrorism, any attempts to meet force with force are fraught with danger. Retaliation in kind could provoke increased terrorist activity—either for revenge or to gain the release of captured comrades. Of course, a weak response may be interpreted as a license for terrorists to operate with impunity. The most impressive U.S. antiterrorist action was the bombing of Libya on April 15, 1986, in an attempt to convince its leader, Muammar Gadhafi, to stop sponsoring terrorist organizations. Although this bombing made a dramatic statement, preventing terrorism has so far stymied most governments.

SUMMARY

Although violence occurs throughout the world, the United States is an extremely violent society. Among the various explanations for violent crimes are the availability of firearms, human traits, a subculture of violence that stresses violent solutions to interpersonal problems, and family conflict.

There are many types of interpersonal violent crime. Rape, defined as the carnal knowledge of a female forcibly and against her will, has been known throughout history; but the view of rape has evolved. At present, close to 100,000 rapes are reported to U.S. police each year; the actual number of rapes is probably much higher. Rape is an extremely difficult charge to prove in court. The victim's lack of consent must be proven; therefore, it almost seems that the victim is on trial. Consequently, changes are being made in rape law and procedure.

Murder is defined as killing a human being with malice aforethought. There are different degrees of murder, and punishments vary accordingly. One important characteristic of murder is that the victim and criminal often know each other. This has led some criminologists to believe that murder is partly victim-precipitated. Assault, another serious interpersonal violent crime, often occurs in the home, including child abuse and spouse abuse. It has been estimated that almost 1 million children are abused by their parents each year and that 16 percent of families report husband–wife violence. There also appears to be a trend toward violence between dating couples.

Robbery involves theft by force, usually in a public place. Types of offenders include professional, opportunist, addict, and alcoholic robbers. Robbery is considered a violent crime because it can and often does involve violence.

Political violence is another serious problem throughout the world. Many terrorist groups exist at both the national and international levels. Hundreds of terrorist acts are reported each year in the United States alone. Terrorists may be motivated by criminal gain, psychosis, grievance against the state, or ideology.

 See the book-specific web site at www.cj.wadsworth. com for additional chapter links, discussions, and quizzes.

THINKING LIKE A CRIMINOLOGIST

The state legislature has asked you to prepare a report on statutory rape because of the growing number of underage girls who have been impregnated by adult men. Studies reveal that many teenage pregnancies result from affairs that underage girls have with older men, with age gaps ranging from 7 to 10 years. For example, the typical relationship that is prosecuted in California involves a 13-year-old girl and a 22-year-old male partner. Some outraged parents adamantly support a law that provides state grants to counties to prosecute statutory rape. These grants would allow more vigorous enforcement of the law and could result in the conviction of more than 1,500 offenders annually.

However, some critics suggest that implementing statutory rape laws to punish males who have relationships with minor girls does not solve the problems of teenage pregnancies and out-of-wedlock births. Liberals dislike the idea of using criminal law to solve social problems because it does not provide for the girls and their young children and focuses only on punishing offenders. In contrast, conservatives fear that such laws give the state power to prosecute people for victimless crimes, thereby adding to the government's ability to control people's private lives. Not all cases involve much older men, and critics ask whether we should criminalize the behavior of 17-year-old boys and their 15-year-old girlfriends. As a criminologist with expertise on rape and its effects, what would you recommend regarding implementation of the law?

KEY TERMS

instrumental violence
expressive violence
electroencephalogram (EEG)
brutalization process
virulency stage
eros
thanatos
crusted over
subculture of violence
disputatiousness
psychopharmacological
economic compulsive behavior
systemic link
rape
increaser
blitz rape
stranger-to-stranger rape
acquaintance rape
date rape
marital rape
gang rape
marital exemption
statutory rape
virility mystique

hypermasculine
aggravated rape
consent
shield laws
crimes of sexual assault
express or actual malice
implied or constructive malice
first-degree murder
premeditation
deliberation
felony murder
second-degree murder
manslaughter
voluntary or nonnegligent manslaughter
involuntary or negligent manslaughter
feticide
thrill killing
gang killing
cult killing
satanism
serial murder
mass murderer
mysoped (sadistic child killer)
psychopathic killer

professional hit killer
simultaneous killing
Violent Criminal Apprehension Program (VICAP)
battery
assault
child abuse
neglect
sexual abuse
blended family
husband battering
robbery
yoking
hate crimes
bias crimes
workplace violence
sufferance
convictional criminals
terrorism
guerilla
genocide
death squads

NOTES

1. Carol Marie Cropper, "3 Whites Charged in Brutal Killing of Black," *New York Times,* 10 June 1998.

2. Rick Bragg, "Unfathomable Crime, Unlikely Figure in Jasper, Texas," *New York Times,* 17 June 1998.

3. David Courtwright, "Violence in America," *American Heritage* 47 (1996): 36.

4. Albert Reiss and Jeffrey Roth, *Understanding and Preventing Violence* (Washington, D.C.: National Academy Press, 1993), p. 3.

5. Hans Toch, *Violent Men* (Chicago: Aldine, 1969), p. 1.

6. Kathleen Maguire and Ann Pastore, *Sourcebook of Criminal Justice Statistics, 1997* (Washington, D.C.: U.S. Government Printing Office, 1998), p. 138.

7. *Stanford v. Kentucky,* 109 Supreme Court, 2969 (1989).

8. Robert Nash Parker and Catherine Colony, "Relationships, Homicides, and Weapons: A Detailed Analysis." Paper presented at the annual meeting of the American Society of Criminology, Montreal, November 1987.

9. Stryker McGuire, "The Dunblane Effect," *Newsweek,* 28 October 1996, p. 46.

10. Laura Bender, "Children and Adolescents Who Have Killed," *American Journal of Psychiatry* 116 (1959): 510–16.

11. Adrian Raine, Monte Buchsbaum, and Lori LaCasse, "Brain Abnormalities in Murderers Indicated by Positron Emission Tomography," *Biological Psychiatry* 42 (1997): 495–508.

12. Dorothy Otnow Lewis, Ernest Moy, Lori Jackson, Robert Aaronson, Nicholas Restifo, Susan Serra, and Alexander Simos, "Biopsychosocial Characteristics of Children Who Later Murder," *American Journal of Psychiatry* 142 (1985): 1161–67.

13. Dorothy Otnow Lewis, *Guilty by Reason of Insanity* (New York: Fawcett Columbine, 1998).

14. Amy Holtzworth-Munroe and Gregory Stuart, "Typologies of Male Batterers: Three Subtypes and the Differences Among Them," *Psychological Bulletin* 116 (1994): 476–97.

15. Reiss and Roth, *Understanding and Preventing Violence,* pp. 112–13.

16. Associated Press, "Jury Recommends Death for Florida Killer of Five," *New York Times,* 25 March 1994, p. A14.

17. Associated Press, "Jury Recommends Death for Florida Killer of Five."

18. Robert Marcus and Lewis Gray, Jr., "Close Relationships of Violent and Nonviolent African American Delinquents," *Violence and Victimization* 13 (1998): 31–42.

19. Pamela Lattimore, Christy Visher, and Richard Linster, "Predicting Rearrest for Violence Among Serious Youthful Offenders," *Journal of Research in Crime and Delinquency* 32 (1995): 54–83.

20. Rolf Loeber and Dale Hay, "Key Issues in the Development of Aggression and Violence from Childhood to Early Adulthood," *Annual Review of Psychology* 48 (1997): 371–410.

21. Deborah Capaldi and Gerald Patterson, "Can Violent Offenders Be Distinguished from Frequent Offenders: Prediction from Childhood to Adolescence," *Journal of Research in Crime and Delinquency* 33 (1996): 206–231.

22. Adrian Raine, Patricia Brennan, and Sarnoff Mednick, "Interaction Between Birth Complications and Early Maternal Rejection in Predisposing Individuals to Adult Violence: Specificity to Serious, Early-Onset Violence," *American Journal of Psychiatry* 154 (1997): 1265–71.

23. Robert Scudder, William Blount, Kathleen Heide, and Ira Silverman, "Important Links Between Child Abuse, Neglect, and Delinquency," *International Journal of Offender Therapy* 37 (1993): 315–23.

24. Dorothy Lewis et al., "Neuropsychiatric, Psychoeducational, and Family Characteristics of 14 Juveniles Condemned to Death in the United States," *American Journal of Psychiatry* 145 (1988): 584–88.

25. Charles Patrick Ewing, *When Children Kill* (Lexington, Mass.: Lexington Books, 1990), p. 22.

26. Lewis, *Guilty by Reason of Insanity,* pp. 11–35.

27. Murray Straus, "Discipline and Deviance: Physical Punishment of Children and Violence and Other Crime in Adulthood," *Social Problems* 38 (1991): 133–54.

28. Lonnie Athens, *The Creation of Dangerous Violent Criminals* (Urbana, Ill.: University of Illinois Press, 1992), pp. 27–80.

29. Cathy Spatz Widom, "Child Abuse, Neglect, and Violent Criminal Behavior," *Criminology* 27 (1989): 251–71; Beverly Rivera and Cathy Spatz Widom, "Childhood Victimization and Violent Offending," *Violence and Victims* 5 (1990): 19–34.

30. Sigmund Freud, *Beyond the Pleasure Principle* (London: Inter-Psychoanalytic Press, 1922).

31. Konrad Lorenz, *On Aggression* (New York: Harcourt Brace Jovanovich, 1966).

32. Martin Daly and Margo Wilson, "Evolutionary Psychology of Male Violence," in *Male Violence,* ed. J. Archer (London: Routledge, 1994), pp. 253–88.

33. Felton Earls, *Linking Community Factors and Individual Development* (Washington, D.C: National Institute of Justice, 1998).

34. Michael Greene, "Chronic Exposure to Violence and Poverty: Interventions That Work for Youth," *Crime and Delinquency* 39 (1993): 106–124.

35. Paul Joubert and Craig Forsyth, "A Macro View of Two Decades of Violence in America," *American Journal of Criminal Justice* 13 (1988): 10–25.

36. M. Dwayne Smith and Victoria Brewer, "A Sex-Specific Analysis of Correlates of Homicide Victimization in United States Cities," *Violence and Victims* 7 (1992): 279–85.

37. Marvin Wolfgang and Franco Ferracuti, *The Subculture of Violence* (London: Tavistock, 1967).

38. David Luckenbill and Daniel Doyle, "Structural Position and Violence: Developing a Cultural Explanation," *Criminology* 27 (1989): 419–36.

39. Liqun Cao, Anthony Adams, and Vickie Jensen, "A Test of the Black Subculture of Violence Thesis," *Criminology* 35 (1997): 367–79.

40. Steven Messner, "Regional and Racial Effects on the Urban Homicide Rate: The Subculture of Violence Revisited," *American Journal of Sociology* 88 (1983): 997–1007; Steven Messner and Kenneth Tardiff, "Economic Inequality and Levels of Homicide: An Analysis of Urban Neighborhoods," *Criminology* 24 (1986): 297–317.

41. Beth Bjerregaard and Alan Lizotte, "Gun Ownership and Gang Membership," *Journal of Criminal Law and Criminology* 86 (1995): 37–58.

42. Scott Decker, "Gangs and Violence: The Expressive Character of Collective Involvement" (unpublished manuscript, University of Missouri–St. Louis: 1994), p. 11.

43. Decker, "Gangs and Violence."

44. Carolyn Rebecca Block, "Chicago Homicide from the Sixties to the Nineties: Have Patterns of Lethal Violence Changed?" Paper presented at the annual meeting of the American Society of Criminology, Baltimore, November 1990.

45. See, generally, Kirk Williams and Robert Flewelling, "The Social Production of Criminal Homicide: A Comparative Study of Disaggregated Rates in American Cities," *American Sociological Review* 53 (1988): 421–31.

46. Raymond Gastil, "Homicide and the Regional Culture of Violence," *American Sociological Review* 36 (1971): 12–27.

47. Keith Harries, *Serious Violence: Patterns of Homicide and Assault in America* (Springfield, Ill.: Charles Thomas, 1990).

48. Edem Avakame, "How Different Is Violence in the Home? An Examination of Some Correlates of Stranger and Intimate Homicide," *Criminology* 36 (1998): 601–632.

49. Howard Erlanger, "Is There a Subculture of Violence in the South?" *Journal of Criminal Law and Criminology* 66 (1976): 483–90.

50. Colin Loftin and Robert Hill, "Regional Subculture of Violence: An Examination of the Gastil-Hackney Thesis," *American Sociological Review* 39 (1974): 714–24.

51. Raymond Gastil, "Comments," *Criminology* 16 (1975): 60–64.

52. FBI, *Uniform Crime Report, 1997* (Washington, D.C.: Federal Bureau of Investigation, 1998), pp. 110–24; see also Keith Harries, "Crime and Region: Is the South Still Different?" (paper presented at the annual meeting of the American Society of Criminology, Chicago, November 1996); Gregory Kowalski and Thomas Petee, "Sunbelt Effects on Homicide Rates," *Sociology and Social Research* 76 (1991): 73–79.

53. F. Frederick Hawley and Steven Messner, "The Southern Violence Construct: A Review of Arguments, Evidence, and the Normative Context," *Justice Quarterly* 6 (1989): 481–511.

54. Paul Goldstein, Henry Brownstein, and Patrick Ryan, "Drug-Related Homicide in New York: 1984–1988," *Crime and Delinquency* 38 (1992): 459–76.

55. Reiss and Roth, *Understanding and Preventing Violence,* pp. 193–94.

56. James Collins and Pamela Messerschmidt, "Epidemiology of Alcohol-Related Violence," *Alcohol Health and Research World* 17 (1993): 93–100.

57. Thomas Feucht, *Drug Use Forecasting 1995* (Washington, D.C.: National Institute of Justice, 1996).

58. Christopher Innes, *Profile of State Prison Inmates 1986* (Washington, D.C.: Bureau of Justice Statistics, 1988).

59. Paul Goldstein, Patricia Bellucci, Barry Spunt, and Thomas Miller, "Volume of Cocaine Use and Violence: A Comparison Between Men and Women," *Journal of Drug Issues* 21 (1991): 345–67.

60. Goldstein, Brownstein, and Ryan, "Drug-Related Homicide in New York: 1984–1988," p. 473.

61. Reiss and Roth, *Understanding and Preventing Violence,* p. 19.

62. Joseph Sheley and James Wright, *Gun Acquisition and Possession in Selected Juvenile Samples* (Washington, D.C.: National Institute of Justice, 1993).

63. Federal Bureau of Investigation, *Crime in the United States, 1995* (Washington, D.C: U.S. Government Printing Office, 1996).

64. David Brent, Joshua Perper, Christopher Allman, Grace Moritz, Mary Wartella, and Janice Zelenak, "The Presence and Accessibility of Firearms in the Home and Adolescent Suicides," *Journal of the American Medical Association* 266 (1991): 2989–95.

65. Linda Saltzman, James Mercy, Patrick O'Carroll, Mark Rosenberg, and Philip Rhodes, "Weapon Involvement and Injury Outcomes in Family and Intimate Assaults," *Journal of the American Medical Association* 267 (1992): 3043–47.

66. William Green, *Rape* (Lexington, Mass.: Lexington Books, 1988), p. 5.

67. Susan Randall and Vicki McNickle Rose, "Forcible Rape," in *Major Forms of Crime,* ed. Robert Meyer (Beverly Hills: Sage, 1984), p. 47.

68. Associated Press, "Judge Who Told Rape Suspect to Get a Girlfriend Orders Him into Custody," *Manchester Union Leader,* 19 February 1994, p. 2.

69. Susan Brownmiller, *Against Our Will: Men, Women and Rape* (New York: Simon & Schuster, 1975).

70. Green, *Rape,* p. 6.

71. Gregory Vistica, "Rape in the Ranks," *Newsweek,* 25 November 1996, pp. 29–31.

72. Yuri Kageyama, "Court Orders Japan to Pay Sex Slaves," *Boston Globe,* 28 April 1998, p. A2.

73. Marlise Simons, "Bosnian Serb Pleads Guilty to Rape Charge Before War Crimes Tribunal," *New York Times,* 10 March 1998, p. 8.

74. FBI, *Uniform Crime Report, 1997,* pp. 25–28.

75. FBI, *Uniform Crime Report, 1997,* pp. 25–28.

76. Michael Rand, *Criminal Victimization 1997: Changes 1996–97 with Trends 1993–97* (Washington, D.C.: Bureau of Justice Statistics, 1998).

77. James LeBeau, "Some Problems with Measuring and Describing Rape Presented by the Serial Offender," *Justice Quarterly* 2 (1985): 385–98.

78. Angela Browne, "Violence Against Women: Relevance for Medical Practitioners," *Journal of the American Medical Association* 267 (1992): 3184–89.

79. Mark Warr, "Rape, Burglary and Opportunity," *Journal of Quantitative Criminology* 4 (1988): 275–88.

80. Janet Warren, Roland Reboussin, Robert Hazlewood, Natalie Gibbs, Susan Trumbetta, and Andrea Cummings, "Crime Scene Analysis and the Escalation of Violence in Serial Rape," *Forensic Science International* (1998): 56–62.

81. James LeBeau, "Patterns of Stranger and Serial Rape Offending Factors Distinguishing Apprehended and At-Large Offenders," *Journal of Criminal Law and Delinquency* 78 (1987): 309–26.

82. A. Nicholas Groth and Jean Birnbaum, *Men Who Rape* (New York: Plenum Press, 1979).

83. For another typology, see Raymond Knight, "Validation of a Typology of Rapists," in *Sex Offender Research and Treatment: State-of-the-Art in North America and Europe,* ed. W. L. Marshall and J. Frenken (Beverly Hills, Calif.: Sage, 1997), pp. 58–75.

84. Julie Allison and Lawrence Wrightsman, *Rape: The Misunderstood Crime* (Newbury Park, Calif.: Sage, 1993), p. 51.

85. R. Lance Shotland, "A Model of the Causes of Date Rape in Developing and Close Relationships," in *Close Relationships,* ed. C. Hendrick (Newbury Park, Calif.: Sage, 1989), pp. 247–70.

86. Walter DeKeseredy, Martin Schwartz, and Karen Tait, "Sexual Assault and Stranger Aggression on a Canadian Campus," *Sex Roles* 28 (1993): 263–77.

87. DeKeseredy, Schwartz, and Tait, "Sexual Assault and Stranger Aggression on a Canadian Campus."

88. Thomas Meyer, "Date Rape: A Serious Campus Problem That Few Talk About," *Chronicle of Higher Education* 29 (5 December 1984): 15.

89. Allison and Wrightsman, *Rape: The Misunderstood Crime,* p. 64.

90. Kimberly Tyler, Danny Hoyt, and Les Whitbeck, "Coercive Sexual Strategies," *Violence and Victims* 13 (1998): 47–63.

91. Martin Schwartz, "Humanist Sociology and Date Rape on the College Campus," *Humanity and Society* 15 (1991): 304–16.

92. Allison and Wrightsman, *Rape: The Misunderstood Crime,* pp. 85–87.

93. Cited in Diana Russell, "Wife Rape," in *Acquaintance Rape: The Hidden Crime,* ed. A. Parrot and L. Bechhofer (New York: John Wiley, 1991), pp. 129–39 at 129.

94. David Finkelhor and K. Yllo, *License to Rape: Sexual Abuse of Wives* (New York: Holt, Rinehart and Winston, 1985).

95. Allison and Wrightsman, *Rape: The Misunderstood Crime,* p. 89.

96. Associated Press, "British Court Rejects Precedent, Finds a Man Guilty of Raping Wife," *Boston Globe,* 15 March 1991, p. 68.

97. Sharon Elstein and Roy Davis, *Sexual Relationships Between Adult Males and Young Teen Girls: Exploring the Legal and Social Responses* (Chicago, Ill.: American Bar Association, 1997).

98. Donald Symons, *The Evolution of Human Sexuality* (Oxford: Oxford University Press, 1979).

99. Lee Ellis and Anthony Walsh, "Gene-Based Evolutionary Theories in Criminology," *Criminology* 35 (1997): 229–76.

100. Lee Ellis, "A Synthesized (Biosocial) Theory of Rape," *Journal of Consulting and Clinical Psychology* 39 (1991): 631–42.

101. Diana Russell, *The Politics of Rape* (New York: Stein and Day, 1975).

102. Kala Downs and Steven Gold, "The Role of Blame, Distress, and Anger in the Hypermasculine Man," *Violence and Victims* 12 (1997): 19–36.

103. Paul Gebhard, John Gagnon, Wardell Pomeroy, and Cornelia Christenson, *Sex Offenders: An Analysis of Types* (New York: Harper & Row, 1965), pp. 198–205; Richard Rada, ed., *Clinical Aspects of the Rapist* (New York: Grune & Stratton, 1978), pp. 122–30.

104. A. Nicholas Groth and Jean Birnbaum, *Men Who Rape* (New York: Plenum, 1979), p. 101.

105. See, generally, Edward Donnerstein, Daniel Linz, and Steven Penrod, *The Question of Pornography* (New York: Free Press, 1987); Diana Russell, *Sexual Exploitation* (Beverly Hills: Sage, 1985), pp. 115–16.

106. Neil Malamuth and John Briere, "Sexual Violence in the Media: Indirect Effects on Aggression Against Women," *Journal of Social Issues* 42 (1986): 75–92.

107. Associated Press, "Trial on TV May Have Influenced Boy Facing Sexual-Assault Count," *Omaha World Herald,* 18 April 1984, p. 50.

108. Richard Felson and Marvin Krohn, "Motives for Rape," *Journal of Research in Crime and Delinquency* 27 (1990): 222–42.

109. Larry Baron and Murray Straus, "Four Theories of Rape: A Macrosociological Analysis," *Social Problems* 34 (1987): 467–89.

110. Julie Horney and Cassia Spohn, "The Influence of Blame and Believability Factors on the Processing of Simple Versus Aggravated Rape Cases," *Criminology* 34 (1996): 135–63.

111. "Woman Urges Dotson's Release," *Omaha World Herald,* 25 April 1985, p. 3.

112. Associated Press, "Apology Is Aired for Lie About Rape," *Boston Globe,* 6 September 1990, p. 12.

113. Associated Press, "Protection Urged for Rape Suspects," *Boston Globe,* 13 January 1997, p. A5.

114. Gerald Robin, "Forcible Rape: Institutionalized Sexism in the Criminal Justice System," *Crime and Delinquency* 23 (1977): 136–53.

115. Associated Press, "Jury Stirs Furor by Citing Dress in Rape Acquittal," *Boston Globe,* 6 October 1989, p. 12.

116. Susan Estrich, *Real Rape* (Cambridge: Harvard University Press, 1987), pp. 58–59.

117. *Michigan v. Lucas* 90-149 (1991); Comment, "The Rape Shield Paradox: Complainant Protection Amidst Oscillating Trends of State Judicial Interpretation," *Journal of Criminal Law and Criminology* 78 (1987): 644–98.

118. Andrew Karmen, *Crime Victims* (Pacific Grove, Calif.: Brooks/Cole, 1990), p. 252.

119. "Court Upholds Civil Rights Portion of Violence Against Women Act," *Criminal Justice Newsletter* 28 (Dec. 1, 1997), p. 3.

120. Colleen Fitzpatrick and Philip Reichel, "Conceptions of Rape and Perceptions of Prosecution." Paper presented at the American Society of Criminology meeting, San Diego, Calif., 1997.

121. See, for example, Mich. Comp. Laws Ann. 750.5200-(1); Florida Statutes Annotated, Sec. 794.011; see, generally, Gary LaFree, "Official Reactions to Rape," *American Sociological Review* 45 (1980): 842–54.

122. Martin Schwartz and Todd Clear, "Toward a New Law on Rape," *Crime and Delinquency* 26 (1980): 129–51.

123. Susan Caringella-MacDonald, "The Comparability in Sexual and Nonsexual Assault Case Treatment: Did Statute Change Meet the Objective?" *Crime and Delinquency* 31 (1985): 206–23.

124. Donald Lunde, *Murder and Madness* (San Francisco: San Francisco Book, 1977), p. 3.

125. Amy Dockser Marcus, "Mists of Memory Cloud Some Legal Proceedings," *Wall Street Journal,* 3 December 1990, p. B1.

126. Lisa Baertlein, "HIV Ruled Deadly Weapon in Rape Case," *Boston Globe,* 2 March 1994, p. 3.

127. The legal principles here come from Wayne LaFave and Austin Scott, *Criminal Law* (St. Paul: West Publishing, 1986; updated, 1993). The definitions and discussion of legal principles used in this chapter lean heavily on this work.

128. LaFave and Scott, *Criminal Law.*

129. Reuters, "California Man Gets 3 Years for Pit Bull's Attack on Toddler," *Boston Globe,* 17 February 1990, p. 3.

130. Pauline Arrillaga, "Jurors Give Drunk Driver 16 Years in Fetus's Death," *Manchester Union Leader,* 22 October 1996, p. B20.

131. Center for Reproductive Law and Policy, *Punishing Women for their Behavior During Pregnancy* (New York: Center for Reproductive Law and Policy, 1996), pp. 1–2.

132. *Whitner v. State of South Carolina,* Supreme Court of South Carolina, Opinion Number 24468, July 15, 1996.

133. Janet Kreps, *Feticide and Wrongful Death Laws* (New York: Center For Reproductive Law and Policy, 1996), pp. 1–2.

134. Arrillaga, "Jurors Give Drunk Driver 16 Years in Fetus's Death."

135. See, generally, Marc Reidel and Margaret Zahn, *The Nature and Pattern of American Homicide* (Washington, D.C.: U.S. Government Printing Office, 1985).

136. James L. Williams, "A Discriminant Analysis of Urban Homicide Patterns." Paper presented at the annual meeting of the American Society of Criminology, Baltimore, November 1990.

137. Angela Browne and Kirk Williams, "Gender, Intimacy, and Lethal Violence: Trends from 1976 Through 1987," *Gender and Society* 7 (1993): 78–98.

138. Linda Saltzman and James Mercy, "Assaults Between Intimates: The Range of Relationships Involved," in *Homicide: The Victim/Offender Connection,* ed. Anna Victoria Wilson (Cincinnati: Anderson Publishing, 1993), pp. 65–74.

139. Angela Browne and Kirk Williams, "Exploring the Effect of Resource Availability and the Likelihood of Female-Perpetrated Homicides," *Law and Society Review* 23 (1989): 75–94.

140. Richard Felson, "Anger, Aggression, and Violence in Love Triangles," *Violence and Victimization* 12 (1997): 345–63.

141. Felson, "Anger, Aggression, and Violence in Love Triangles," p. 361.

142. Margaret Zahn and Philip Sagi, "Stranger Homicides in Nine American Cities," *Journal of Criminal Law and Criminology* 78 (1987): 377–97.

143. David Luckenbill, "Criminal Homicide as a Situational Transaction," *Social Problems* 25 (1977): 176–86.

144. Michael Hazlett and Thomas Tomlinson, "Females Involved in Homicides: Victims and Offenders in Two Southern States." Paper presented at the annual meeting of the American Society of Criminology, Montreal, November 1987; rev. 1988.

145. Scott Decker, "Deviant Homicide: A New Look at the Role of Motives and Victim–Offender Relationships," *Journal of Research in Crime and Delinquency* 33 (1996): 427–49.

146. Scott Decker, "Exploring Victim–Offender Relationships in Homicide: The Role of Individual and Event Characteristics," *Justice Quarterly* 10 (1993): 585–613.

147. Associated Press, "Parents Forgive Teenager Convicted of Toddler's Death," *Boston Globe,* 22 January 1987.

148. Charles Ewing, *When Children Kill* (Lexington, Mass.: Lexington Books, 1990), p. 64.

149. Carolyn Rebecca Block and Richard Block, *Street Gang Crime in Chicago* (Washington, D.C.: National Institute of Justice, 1993), p. 2.

150. Cited in Ewing, *When Children Kill,* p. 71.

151. From Foreword/Update to James A. Fox and Jack Levin, *Mass Murder,* 2d ed. (New York: Plenum Press, 1991).

152. Cindy Horswell, "Teen Held in Mom's Shooting Death: 'The Devil Made Me Do It,'" *Houston Chronicle,* 19 May 1993, p. 1.

153. Thomas Palmer, "A Doctor Smelled Arsenic, Leading to Arrest of Serial Killer," *Boston Globe,* 20 August 1987, p. 3.

154. "Police Suspect 'Something Snapped' to Ignite Wilder's Crime Spree," *Omaha World Herald,* 15 April 1984, p. 21A.

155. Mark Starr, "The Random Killers," *Newsweek,* 26 November 1984, pp. 100–106.

156. Thomas Palmer, "Ex-Hospital Aide Admits Killing 24 in Cincinnati," *Boston Globe,* 19 August 1987, p. 3.

157. Philip Jenkins, "A Murder 'Wave'? Trends in American Serial Homicide 1940–1990," *Criminal Justice Review* 17 (1992): 1–18.

158. Ronald Holmes and Stephen Homes, *Murder in America* (Thousand Oaks, Calif.: Sage, 1994), p. 6.

159. Holmes and Homes, *Murder in America,* p. 106.

160. Philip Jenkins, "Serial Murder in England, 1940–1985," *Journal of Criminal Justice* 16 (1988): 1–15 at 9.

161. Ronald Holmes and James DeBurger, *Serial Murder* (Newbury Park, Calif.: Sage, 1988), pp. 58–59.

162. Holmes and Homes, *Murder in America,* pp. 13–14.

163. Holmes and Homes, *Murder in America,* p. 17.

164. Belea Keeney and Kathleen Heide, "Gender Differences in Serial Murderers: A Preliminary Analysis," *Journal of Interpersonal Violence* 9 (1994): 37–56.

165. Jennifer Browdy, "VI-CAP System to Be Operational This Summer," *Law Enforcement News,* 21 May 1984, p. 1.

166. FBI, *Crime in the United States, 1997,* p. 33.

167. Keith Harries, "Homicide and Assault: A Comparative Analysis of Attributes in Dallas Neighborhoods, 1981–1985," *Professional Geographer* 41 (1989): 29–38.

168. Laurence Zuckerman, "The Air-Rage Rage: Taking a Cold Look at a Hot Topic," *New York Times,* 4 October 1998, p. A3.

169. Michael Rand, *Violence-Related Injuries Treated in Hospital Emergency Departments* (Washington, D.C.: Bureau of Justice Statistics, 1997).

170. See, generally, Joel Milner, ed., *Special Issue: Physical Child Abuse, Criminal Justice and Behavior* 18 (1991).

171. See, generally, Ruth S. Kempe and C. Henry Kempe, *Child Abuse* (Cambridge: Harvard University Press, 1978).

172. David Wiese and Deborah Daro, *Current Trends in Child Abuse Reporting and Fatalities: The Results of the 1994 Annual Fifty-State Survey* (Chicago: National Committee to Prevent Child Abuse, 1995).

173. Diana Russell, "The Incidence and Prevalence of Intrafamilial and Extrafamilial Sexual Abuse of Female Children," *Child Abuse and Neglect* 7 (1983): 133–46; see also David Finkelhor, *Sexually Victimized Children* (New York: Free Press, 1979), p. 88.

174. Jeanne Hernandez, "Eating Disorders and Sexual Abuse in Adolescents" (paper presented at the annual meeting of the American Psychosomatic Society, Charleston, S.C., March, 1993); Glenn Wolfner and Richard Gelles, "A Profile of Violence Toward Children: A National Study," *Child Abuse and Neglect* 17 (1993): 197–212.

175. Louanne Lawson and Mark Chaffin, "False Negatives in Sexual Abuse Disclosure Interviews," *Journal of Interpersonal Violence* 7 (1992): 532–42.

176. For a thorough review, see Kathleen Kendall-Tackett, Linda Meyer Williams, and David Finkelhor, "Impact of Sexual Abuse on Children: A Review and Synthesis of Recent Empirical Studies," *Psychological Bulletin* 133 (1993): 164–80.

177. Carey Goldberg, "New Trial Granted in Day-Care Sex-Abuse Case," *New York Times,* 13 June 1998, p. 1.

178. Steve Geissinger, "Boy Scouts Dismissed 1,800 Suspected Molesters from 1971–91," *Boston Globe,* 15 October 1993, p. 3.

179. Goldberg, "New Trial Granted in Day-Care Sex-Abuse Case."

180. Wolfner and Gelles, "A Profile of Violence Toward Children."

181. Ruth Inglis, *Sins of the Fathers: A Study of the Physical and Emotional Abuse of Children* (New York: St. Martin's Press, 1978), p. 68.

182. Martin Daly and Margo Wilson, "Violence Against Step Children," *Current Directions in Psychological Science* 5 (1996): 77–81.

183. Inglis, *Sins of the Fathers,* p. 53.

184. Brandt Steele, "Violence Within the Family," in *Child Abuse and Neglect: The Family and the Community,* ed. R. Helfer and C. H. Kempe (Cambridge, Mass.: Ballinger Publishing, 1976), p. 12.

185. Alison Bass, "Daughter Wins Sex-Abuse Case Against Father," *Boston Globe,* 18 May 1990, p. 17.

186. David Kaplan, "The Unkindest Cut," *Newsweek,* 16 August 1993, p. 56.

187. Associated Press, "Lorena Freed," *Manchester Union Leader,* 1 March 1994, p. 44.

188. Russell Dobash, R. Emerson Dobash, Margo Wilson, and Martin Daly, "The Myth of Sexual Symmetry in Marital Violence," *Social Problems* 39 (1992): 71–86; Martin Schwartz and Walter DeKeseredy, "The Return of the 'Battered Husband Syndrome': Typification of Women as Violent," *Crime, Law, and Social Change* 8 (1993): 11–27.

189. Schwartz and DeKeseredy, "The Return of the 'Battered Husband Syndrome.'"

190. R. Emerson Dobash and Russell Dobash, *Violence Against Wives* (New York: Free Press, 1979).

191. Julia O'Faolain and Laura Martines, eds., *Not in God's Image: Women in History* (Glasgow: Fontana/Collins, 1974).

192. Laurence Stone, "The Rise of the Nuclear Family in Modern England: The Patriarchal Stage," in *The Family in History,* ed. Charles Rosenberg (Philadelphia: University of Pennsylvania Press, 1975), p. 53.

193. Dobash and Dobash, *Violence Against Wives,* p. 46.

194. John Braithwaite, "Inequality and Republican Criminology." Paper presented at the annual meeting of the American Society of Criminology, San Francisco, November 1991, p. 20.

195. Richard Gelles and Murray Straus, "Violence in the American Family," *Journal of Social Issues* 35 (1979): 15–39.

196. Miguel Schwartz, Susan O'Leary, and Kimberly Kendziora, "Dating Aggression Among High School Students," *Violence and Victimization* 12 (1997): 295–307; James Makepeace, "Social Factor and Victim–Offender Differences in Courtship Violence," *Family Relations* 33 (1987): 87–91.

197. Graeme Newman, *Understanding Violence* (New York: Lippincott, 1979), pp. 145–46.

198. Margo Wilson and Martin Daly, "Male Sexual Proprietariness and Violence Against Wives," *Current Directions in Psychological Science* 5 (1996): 2–7.

199. Gerald Hotaling and David Sugarman, "An Analysis of Risk Markers in Husband to Wife Violence," *Violence and Victims* 1 (1986): 101–124.

200. Ronald Simons, Chyi-In Wu, Christine Johnson, and Rand Conger, "A Test of Various Perspectives on the Intergenerational Transmission of Domestic Violence," *Criminology* 33 (1995): 141–71.

201. Simons et al., "A Test of Various Perspectives," pp. 162–163.

202. Murray Straus and Sean Lauer, "Corporal Punishment of Children, Substance Abuse, and Crime in Relation to Race, Culture, and Deterrence." Paper presented at the annual meeting of the American Society of Criminology, New Orleans, November 1992.

203. FBI, *Crime in the United States, 1997,* p. 28.

204. Caroline Wolf Harlow, *Robbery Victims* (Washington, D.C.: Bureau of Justice Statistics, 1989), pp. 1–5.

205. F. H. McClintock and Evelyn Gibson, *Robbery in London* (London: Macmillan, 1961), p. 15.

206. McClintock and Gibson, *Robbery in London,* pp. 54–55.

207. John Conklin, *Robbery and the Criminal Justice System* (New York: Lippincott, 1972), pp. 1–80.

208. James Calder and John Bauer, "Convenience Store Robberies: Security Measures and Store Robbery Incidents," *Journal of Criminal Justice* 20 (1992): 553–66.

209. James Garofalo, "Bias and Non-Bias Crimes in New York City: Preliminary Findings." Paper presented at the annual meeting of the American Society of Criminology, Baltimore, November 1990.

210. Ronald Powers, "Bensonhurst Man Guilty," *Boston Globe,* 18 May 1990, p. 3.

211. "Boy Gets 18 Years in Fatal Park Beating of Transient," *Los Angeles Times,* 24 December 1987, p. 9B.

212. James Brooke, "Gay Student Who Was Kidnapped and Beaten Dies," *New York Times,* 13 October 1998, A1.

213. Ewing, *When Children Kill,* pp. 65–66.

214. Mike McPhee, "In Denver, Attacks Stir Fears of Racism," *Boston Globe,* 10 December 1990, p. 3.

215. Jack McDevitt, "The Study of the Character of Civil Rights Crimes in Massachusetts (1983–1987)." Paper presented at the annual meeting of the American Society of Criminology, Reno, Nevada, November 1989.

216. McDevitt, "The Study of the Character of Civil Rights Crimes in Massachusetts," p. 8.

217. Jack Levin and Jack McDevitt, *Hate Crimes: The Rising Tide of Bigotry and Bloodshed* (New York: Plenum, 1993).

218. Jack Levin and Jack McDevitt, *Hate Crimes: A Study of Offenders' Motivations* (Boston, Mass.: Northeastern University, 1993).

219. "ADL Survey Analyzes Neo-Nazi Skinhead Menace and International Connections," *CJ International* 12 (1996): 7.

220. Don Terry, "Death of Friends Illuminates Chasm Among Skinheads," *New York Times,* 29 August 1998, p. A8.

221. FBI, *Crime in the United States, 1997,* p. 60.

222. Garofalo, "Bias and Non-Bias Crimes in New York City," p. 3.

223. Carl Weiser, "This Is What You Get for Firing Me," *USA Today,* 28 January 1993, p. 3A.

224. James Alan Fox and Jack Levin, "Firing Back: The Growing Threat of Workplace Homicide," *Annals* 536 (1994): 16–30.

225. John King, "Workplace Violence: A Conceptual Framework." Paper presented at the annual meeting of the American Society of Criminology, Phoenix, Arizona, November 1993.

226. Associated Press, "Gunman Wounds 3 Doctors in L.A. Hospital," *Cleveland Plain Dealer,* 9 February 1993, p. 1B.

227. Fox and Levin, "Firing Back," p. 5.

228. Greg Warchol, *Workplace Violence, 1992–96* (Washington, D.C.: Bureau of Justice Statistics, 1998).

229. Stephen Schafer, *The Political Criminal* (New York: Free Press, 1974), p. 1.

230. Schafer, *The Political Criminal,* p. 150.

231. Robert Friedlander, *Terrorism* (Dobbs Ferry, N.Y.: Oceana Publishers, 1979).

232. Walter Laquer, *The Age of Terrorism* (Boston: Little, Brown, 1987), p. 72.

233. National Advisory Commission on Criminal Justice Standards and Goals, *Report of the Task Force on Disorders and Terrorism* (Washington, D.C.: U.S. Government Printing Office, 1976), p. 3.

234. Paul Wilkinson, *Terrorism and the Liberal State* (New York: John Wiley, 1977), p. 49.

235. Jack Gibbs, "Conceptualization of Terrorism," *American Sociological Review* 54 (1989): 329–40 at 330.

236. Friedlander, *Terrorism,* p. 14.

237. Daniel Georges-Abeyie, "Political Crime and Terrorism," in *Crime and Deviance: A Comparative Perspective,* ed. Graeme Newman (Beverly Hills: Sage, 1980), pp. 313–33.

238. Georges-Abeyie, "Political Crime and Terrorism," p. 319.

239. This section relies heavily on Friedlander, *Terrorism,* pp. 8–20.

240. Stephen Engelberg, "Terrorism's New (and Very Old) Face," *New York Times,* 12 September 1998, p. A5.

241. See Friedlander, *Terrorism,* p. 16.

242. For a general view, see Jonathan White, *Terrorism* (Pacific Grove, Calif.: Brooks/Cole, 1991).

243. Jonathan Kaufman, "Trauma of a German Slaying," *Boston Globe,* 3 April 1991, p. 2.

244. Kaufman, "Trauma of a German Slaying."

245. Russell Watson, "An Explosion in the Sky," *Newsweek,* 2 January 1989, pp. 16–19.

246. Reuters, "Five White Separatists Indicted in Robberies," *Boston Globe,* 31 January 1997, p. A8.

247. Michael Barkun, "Leaderless Resistance and Phineas Priests: Strategies of Uncoordinated Violence on the Far Right." Paper presented at the annual Society of Criminology meeting, San Diego, Calif., November 1997.

248. Peter Annin and Mark Hosenball, "A Showdown in Montana," *Newsweek,* 8 April 1996, p. 39.

249. William Smith, "Libya's Ministry of Fear," *Time,* 30 April 1984, pp. 36–38.

250. Reuters, "Nile Tour Boat Is Attacked; Blast Hits Egyptian Resort," *Boston Globe,* 10 April 1993, p. 5.

251. Associated Press, "31 Decapitated South of Algiers," *Boston Globe,* 3 February 1997, p. A5.

252. Engelberg, "Terrorism's New (and Very Old) Face."

253. Bruce Hoffman, *Inside Terrorism* (New York: Columbia University Press, 1998).

254. Joseph Berger, "Murdered Doctor Remembered as Conscientious and Courageous," *New York Times,* 26 October 1998, p. 1.

255. Associated Press, "Colorado Resort Fires Breed Fear of Ecologically Inspired Terrorism," *Boston Globe,* 23 October 1998, p. A21; David Johnston, "Vail Fires Were Arson, Federal Experts Say," *New York Times,* 23 October 1998, p. B1.

256. Charles Hillsinger and Mark Stein, "Militant Vegetarians Tied to Attacks on Livestock Industry," *Boston Globe,* 23 November 1989, p. A34.

257. John Cushman and Evelyn Nieves, "In Colorado Resort Fires, Culprits Defy Easy Labels," *New York Times,* 24 October 1998, p. 3.

258. Ted Robert Gurr, "Political Terrorism in the United States: Historical Antecedents and Contemporary Trends," in *The Politics of Terrorism,* ed. Michael Stohl (New York: Dekker, 1988).

259. Martha Crenshaw, ed., *Terrorism, Legitimacy, and Power* (Middletown, Conn.: Wesleyan University Press, 1983), pp. 1–10.

260. Associated Press, "CIA Knew of Honduran Rights Abuses," *New York Times,* 24 October 1998, p. 2.

261. Reuters, "New Haiti Police Have Executed 15, Rights Group Asserts," *Boston Globe,* 24 January 1997, p. A10.

262. Amnesty International, *Annual Report, 1992* (Washington, D.C.: July 1993).

263. This report on state action in Peru can be obtained on the Amnesty International Web site at http://www.amnesty.org/ailib/aipub/1996/AMR/2460396.htm.

264. Dick Ward, "The Nuclear Terror Threat," *CJ International* 12 (1996): 1–4.

265. Theodore Gurr, *Why Men Rebel* (Princeton, N.J.: Princeton University Press, 1970).

266. M. Cherif Bassiouni, "Terrorism, Law Enforcement, and Mass Media: Perspectives, Problems, and Proposals," *Journal of Criminal Law and Criminology* 72 (1981): 1–51 at 10.

267. Austin Turk, "Political Crime," in *Major Forms of Crime,* ed. R. Meier (Beverly Hills: Sage, 1984), pp. 119–35.

268. Reuters, "18 Beheaded in Sri Lanka; Revenge for Slaying Seen," *Boston Globe,* 6 October 1989, p. 13.

269. Brent Smith and Gregory Orvis, "America's Response to Terrorism: An Empirical Analysis of Federal Intervention Strategies During the 1980s," *Justice Quarterly* 10 (1993): 660–81.

270. 18 USC 113a; 18 USC 51, 1166.

271. U.S. State Department news release, 25 April 1996.

272. Fact Sheet: Iran-Libya Sanctions Act of 1996 (Washington, D.C.: Office of the Press Secretary, The White House, August 5, 1996).

273. Smith and Orvis, "America's Response to Terrorism."

CHAPTER 12

Property Crimes

INTRODUCTION

As a group, **economic crimes** can be defined as acts that violate criminal law and are designed to bring financial reward to an offender. The range and scope of U.S. criminal activity motivated by financial gain are tremendous: self-report studies show that property crime is widespread among the young in every social class. National surveys of criminal behavior indicate that almost 30 million personal and household thefts occur annually; corporate and other white-collar crimes are accepted as commonplace; and political scandals, ranging from Watergate to Whitewater, indicate that even high government officials can be suspected of criminal acts.

Although average citizens may be puzzled and enraged by violent crimes, believing them to be both senseless and cruel, they often view economic crimes with a great deal more ambivalence. Society generally disapproves of crimes involving theft and corruption, but the public seems to tolerate and even admire the "gentleman bandit." Such figures pop up as characters in popular myths and legends—such as the famed English outlaw Robin Hood; Western bank robber Jesse James; and 1930s outlaws Bonnie Parker and Clyde Barrow (the subject of the 1967 award-winning film *Bonnie and Clyde* starring Warren Beatty and Faye Dunaway). They are the semiheroic subjects of books and films, such as *48 Hours* (1982), in which Eddie Murphy plays a thief who helps a police officer (Nick Nolte) catch even more dangerous criminals; and *Heat* (1995), in which Robert DeNiro plays a master thief and Al Pacino the detective who tracks him down. How can such ambivalence toward criminality be explained? If self-report surveys are accurate, almost every U.S. citizen has at some time been involved in economic crime. Even those who would never consider themselves criminals may have at one time engaged in petty theft, cheated on their income tax, stolen a textbook from a college bookstore, or pilfered from their place of employment. Consequently, it may be difficult for people to condemn economic criminals without feeling hypocritical.

People may also be more tolerant of economic crimes because they never seem to seriously hurt anyone—banks are insured, large businesses pass along

While society generally disapproves of crimes involving theft and corruption, the public seems quite tolerant of "gentleman bandits," even to the point of turning them into fictional heroes and heroines. They pop up as characters in popular myths and legends—Robin Hood, Jesse James, Bonnie and Clyde, D. B. Cooper. They are the semiheroic subjects of books and films, such as *48 Hours, Pulp Fiction,* and *Heat.* Robert DeNiro played a master thief in *Heat.*

losses to consumers, stolen cars can be easily replaced and in most cases are insured. The true cost of economic crime often goes unappreciated. Convicted offenders, especially businesspeople who commit white-collar crimes involving millions of dollars, often are punished lightly.

This chapter is the first of two that review the nature and extent of economic crime in the United States. It is divided into two principal sections. The first explains the concept of economic crime and focuses on different types of economic criminals, including the **fence,** who buys and sells stolen merchandise. The chapter then discusses common theft-related offenses, which criminologists often refer to as **street crimes.** These crimes include the major forms of common theft: larceny, embezzlement, and theft by false pretenses. Included within these general offense categories are such common crimes as auto theft, shoplifting, and credit card fraud. Next the chapter discusses a more serious form of theft, **burglary,** which involves forcible entry into a person's home or workplace for the purpose of theft. Finally, the crime of arson is discussed briefly. The following chapter gives attention to white-collar crimes and economic crimes that involve organizations devoted to criminal enterprise.

A BRIEF HISTORY OF THEFT

Theft offenses are frequent. Millions of auto thefts, shoplifting incidents, embezzlements, burglaries, and larcenies are recorded each year. National surveys indicate that between 10 and 15 percent of U.S. residents are victims of theft offenses each year. Theft is not unique to modern times; the theft of personal property has been known throughout recorded history. The Crusades of the eleventh century inspired peasants and downtrodden noblemen to leave the shelter of their estates to prey upon passing pilgrims.[1] Crusaders felt it within their rights to appropriate the possessions of any infidels—Greeks, Jews, or Muslims—they happened to encounter during their travels. By the thirteenth century, returning pilgrims, not content to live as serfs on feudal estates, gathered in the forests of England and the Continent to poach game that was the rightful property of their lord or king and, when possible, to steal from passing strangers. By the fourteenth century, many such highwaymen and poachers were full-time livestock thieves, stealing great numbers of cattle and sheep.[2] The fifteenth and sixteenth centuries brought hostilities between England and France in the Hundred Years' War. Foreign mercenary troops fighting for both sides roamed the countryside; loot and pillage were viewed as a rightful part of their pay. As cities developed and a permanent class of propertyless urban poor[3] was established, theft became more professional.

By the eighteenth century three separate groups of property criminals were active:

- **Skilled thieves** typically worked in the larger cities, such as London and Paris. This group included pickpockets, forgers, and counterfeiters, who operated freely. They congregated in **flash houses**—public meeting places, often taverns, that served as headquarters for gangs. Here deals were made, crimes were plotted, and the sale of stolen goods was negotiated.[4]
- **Smugglers** moved freely in sparsely populated areas and transported goods, such as spirits, gems, gold, and spices, without paying tax or duty.
- **Poachers** typically lived in the country and supplemented their diet and income with game that belonged to a landlord.

By the eighteenth century, professional thieves in the larger cities had banded together into gangs to protect themselves, increase the scope of their activities, and help dispose of stolen goods. Jack Wild, perhaps London's most famous thief, perfected the process of buying and selling stolen goods and gave himself the title of "Thief Taker General of Great Britain and Ireland." Before he was hanged, Wild controlled numerous gangs and dealt harshly with any thief who violated his strict code of conduct.[5] Thief takers are discussed in the Race, Culture, Gender, and Criminology feature titled "Catching Thieves in Eighteenth-Century England."

During this period, individual theft-related crimes began to be defined by common law. The most important of these categories are still used today.

MODERN THIEVES

Of the millions of property and theft-related crimes that occur each year, most are committed by occasional criminals who do not define themselves by a criminal role or view themselves as committed career criminals; other thieves are skilled professional criminals. The following sections review these two orientations toward property crime.

Occasional Criminals

Criminologists suspect that most economic crimes are the work of amateur **occasional criminals,** whose decision to steal is spontaneous and whose acts are unskilled, unplanned, and haphazard. Millions of thefts occur each year, and most are not reported to police agencies. Many of these theft offenses are committed by school-age youths who are unlikely to enter criminal careers and who drift between conventional and criminal behavior. Added to the pool of amateur thieves are the millions of adults whose behavior may occasionally

Catching Thieves in Eighteenth-Century England

By the eighteenth century, the Industrial Revolution had lured thousands from the English countryside to work in the factory towns. The swelling population of urban poor, whose minuscule wages could hardly sustain them, resulted in increased crime rates. In the London area law enforcement was provided by **thief takers**—organized groups of private police who earned a living by catching wanted thieves and collecting rewards for their capture. Between 30 and 40 thief takers were active in London by the mid-eighteenth century.

Most thief takers started as prison turnkeys, constables, court bailiffs, or other minor court officers. They were called "monied police" because they made a living not only from catching and informing on criminals but also from receiving stolen property, stealing, intimidating others, perjuring themselves, and committing blackmail. Typically corrupt, they often relieved their prisoners of money and stolen goods and made additional income by accepting hush money, giving perjured evidence, swearing false oaths, and operating extortion rackets. Petty debtors were especially easy targets for those who combined thief taking with the keeping of alehouses and taverns. The health and safety of incarcerated prisoners was entirely at the whim of the keepers/thief takers,

who were free to charge what their prisoners could pay for board and other necessities. Court bailiffs, who also acted as thief takers, were the most passionately detested legal profiteers. They seized debtors and held them in small lockups, where they forced their victims to pay exorbitant prices for food and lodging.

Thief takers' use of violence was notorious. Among the most infamous violent thief takers was the rascal Jack Wild. He pursued thieves bearing arms and was prepared to maim or kill in order to gain his objectives. Wild was willing to take punishment as well as dish it out: before he was hung in 1725, Wild had two fractures in his skull, and his bald head was covered with silver plates. He had 17 wounds in various parts of his body from swords, daggers, and gunshots, and his throat had been cut in the course of his duties.

Henry Fielding, the famed author of *Tom Jones,* along with Saunders Welch and Sir John Fielding, sought to clean up the thief-taking system. As an appointed city magistrate in 1748, Fielding operated his own group of monied police out of Bow Street in London, directing and deploying them throughout the city and its environs, deciding which cases to investigate and what streets to protect. His agents were carefully instructed

on their legitimate powers and duties. Fielding's "Bow Street Runners" were a marked improvement over the earlier monied police because their administrative structure improved record keeping and investigative procedures. But Fielding's forces were not adequate, and by the nineteenth century state police officers were needed.

CRITICAL THINKING

1. There has been rapid growth in the private security industry. Do you think this reflects a return to the private policing models of the eighteenth century? Why or why not?
2. What are some of the advantages and drawbacks to privatizing police services?

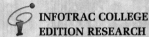

INFOTRAC COLLEGE EDITION RESEARCH

To read more about the history of police, see:
Eric H. Monkkonen. Police forces. *The Reader's Companion to American History* Edition 1991 p847

Source: John L. McMullan, "The New Improved Monied Police: Reform, Crime Control, and the Commodification of Policing in London," *British Journal of Criminology* 36 (1996): 85–108.

violate the law—shoplifters, pilferers, tax cheats—but whose main source of income is conventional and whose self-identity is noncriminal. Added together, their behaviors form the bulk of theft crimes.

According to criminologist John Hepburn, occasional property crime occurs when there is an opportunity or situational inducement to commit crime.[6] Members of the upper class can engage in the more lucrative business-related crimes of price-fixing, bribery, embezzlement, and so on; lower-class individuals are overrepresented in street crime. **Situational inducements** are short-term influences on a person's behavior that increase risk-taking. These include psychological factors, such as financial problems, and social factors, such as peer pressure. According to Hepburn, opportunity and

situational inducements do not cause crime; rather, they are the occasion for crime—hence the term *occasional criminal.*

Opportunities and short-run inducements to commit crime are not randomly situated; some people, typically poor young males, have an ample supply of both. Consequently, the frequency of occasional property crime varies according to age, class, sex, and so on. Occasional offenders are not professional criminals, nor do they make crime their occupation. They do not rely on skills or knowledge to commit their crimes, they do not organize their daily activities around crime, and they are not committed to crime as a way of life.

Occasional criminals, unlike professionals, do not receive informal peer group support for their crimes. In

Millions of theft-related crimes occur each year, and most are not reported to police agencies. Some thieves are involved in fraudulent schemes and scams, such as "con artists" who make their living luring passersby into a rigged "game of chance." The "marks" are reassured that an observant person such as themselves surely cannot lose, but in reality they cannot win.

enced criminals the techniques that will earn the most money with the least risk. Although their numbers are relatively few, professionals engage in crimes that produce the greater losses to society and perhaps cause the more significant social harm.

Professional theft traditionally refers to nonviolent forms of criminal behavior that are undertaken with a high degree of skill for monetary gain and that maximize financial opportunities and minimize the possibilities of apprehension. The most typical forms include pocket picking, burglary, shoplifting, forgery, counterfeiting, extortion, sneak theft, and confidence swindling.[7]

Relatively little is known about the career patterns of professional thieves and criminals. From the literature on crime and delinquency, three patterns emerge:

1. Youths come under the influence of older, experienced criminals who teach them the trade.
2. Juvenile gang members continue their illegal activities when most of their peers have dropped out to marry, raise families, and take conventional jobs.
3. Youths sent to prison for minor offenses learn the techniques of crime from more experienced thieves. For example, Harry King, a professional thief, relates this story about his entry into crime after being placed in a shelter-care home by his recently divorced mother:

> It was while I was at this parental school that I learned that some of the kids had been committed there by the court for stealing bikes. They taught me how to steal and where to steal them and where to sell them. Incidentally, some of the "nicer people" were the ones who bought bikes from the kids. They would dismantle the bike and use the parts: the wheels, chains, handlebars, and so forth.[8]

Here we can see how criminals may be encouraged in their illegal activities by people who are willing to buy stolen merchandise and gain from criminal enterprise.

There is some debate in the criminological literature over who may be defined as a professional criminal. In his classic works, Edwin Sutherland used the term to refer only to thieves who do not use force or physical violence in their crimes and who live solely by their wits and skill.[9] However, some criminologists use the term to refer to any criminal who identifies with a criminal subculture, who makes most of his or her living from crime, and who possesses a degree of skill in his or her chosen trade.[10] Thus one can become a professional safecracker, burglar, car thief, or fence. Some criminologists would not consider drug addicts who steal to support their habit as professionals; they lack skill and therefore are amateur opportunists rather than professional technicians. However, professional criminals who take drugs might still be considered under the general pattern of professional crime. If the sole criterion for being judged a professional criminal is using crime as one's primary source of income, then many drug users have to be placed in the professional category.

fact, they deny any connection to a criminal lifestyle and instead view their transgressions as out of character. They may see their crimes as motivated by necessity. For example, they were only "borrowing" the car the police caught them with; they were going to pay for the merchandise that they stole from the store — eventually. Because of their lack of commitment to a criminal lifestyle, occasional offenders may be the most likely to respond to the general deterrent effect of the law.

Professional Criminals

In contrast to occasional criminals, **professional criminals** make a significant portion of their income from crime. Professionals do not delude themselves with the belief that their acts are impulsive, one-time efforts, nor do they employ elaborate rationalizations to excuse the harmfulness of their actions ("shoplifting doesn't really hurt anyone"). Consequently, professionals pursue their craft with vigor, attempting to learn from older, experi-

Sutherland's Professional Criminal What we know about the lives of professional criminals has come to us through their journals, diaries, and autobiographies and the first-person accounts they have given to criminologists. The best-known account of professional theft is Edwin Sutherland's recording of the life of a professional con artist, Chic Conwell, in Sutherland's classic book, *The Professional Thief.*[11] Conwell and Sutherland's concept of professional theft has two critical dimensions. First, professional thieves engage in limited types of crime, which are described in Figure 12.1.[12]

The second requirement of professional theft is the exclusive use of wits, *front* (a believable demeanor), and talking ability. Manual dexterity and physical force are of little importance. Professionals depend solely on their wit and skill. Thieves who use force or commit crimes that require little expertise are not considered worthy of the title "professional." Their areas of activity include "heavy rackets" such as bank robbery, car theft, burglary, and safecracking. Conwell and Sutherland's criteria for professionalism are weighted heavily toward con games and trickery and give little attention to common street crimes.

Professional thieves must acquire status in their profession. Status is based on their technical skill, financial standing, connections, power, dress, manners, and wide knowledge base. In their world, "thief" is a title worn with pride. Conwell and Sutherland also argue that professional thieves share feelings, sentiments, and behaviors. Of these, none is more important than the code of honor of the underworld: even under the threat of the most severe punishment, a professional thief must never inform (squeal) on his or her colleagues. Sutherland and Conwell view professional theft as an occupation with much the same internal organization as that characterizing such legitimate professions as advertising, teaching, or police work. They conclude

> A person can be a professional thief only if he is recognized and received as such by other professional thieves. Professional theft is a group way of life. One can get into the group and remain in it only by the consent of those previously in the group. Recognition as a professional thief by other professional thieves is the absolutely necessary, universal and definitive characteristic of the professional thief."[13]

Professional thieves have changed their behavior over time in response to crime control technology. As shown in the Criminological Enterprise feature "Transforming Theft," these technology-inspired shifts in criminality began as early as the nineteenth century.

Professional Criminals: The Fence Some experts say that Sutherland's view of the professional thief may be outdated because modern thieves often work alone, are not part of a criminal subculture, and were not tutored by other criminals.[14] However, recent research efforts show that the principles set down by Sutherland still have value for understanding the behavior of one contemporary criminal type—the professional fence, who earns a living solely by buying and reselling stolen merchandise. The fence's critical role in criminal transactions has been recognized since the eighteenth century.[15] Fences purchase stolen items—ranging from diamonds to auto hubcaps—and then resell them to merchants who market them to legitimate customers.[16]

Carl Klockars examined the life of one successful fence who used the alias "Vincent Swaggi." Through 400 hours of listening to and observing Vincent, Klockars found that this highly professional criminal had developed techniques that made him almost immune to prosecution. During a long, profitable career in crime, Vincent spent only four months in prison. He stayed in business, in part, because of his sophisticated knowledge of the law of stolen property. To convict someone of receiving stolen goods, the prosecution must prove that the accused possessed the goods and knew that they had been stolen. Vincent had the skills to make sure that these elements could never be proven. Also helping Vincent stay out of the law's grasp were the close working associations he maintained with society's upper classes, including influential members of the justice system. Vincent helped them purchase stolen items at bargain prices. He also helped authorities recover stolen goods and therefore remained in their good graces. Klockars's work strongly suggests that fences customarily cheat their thief clients and at the same time cooperate with the law.

Sam Goodman, a fence interviewed by sociologist Darrell Steffensmeier, lived in a world similar to Vincent Swaggi's. He also purchased stolen goods from a wide

Figure 12.1 Sutherland's Typology of Professional Thieves

Pickpocket (cannon)

Sneak thief from stores, banks, and offices (heel)

Shoplifter (booster)

Jewel thief who substitutes fake gems for real ones (pennyweighter)

Thief who steals from hotel rooms (hotel prowl)

Confidence game artist (con artist)

Thief in rackets related to confidence games

Forger

Extortionist from those engaging in illegal acts (shakedown artist)

Source: Edwin Sutherland and Chic Conwell, *The Professional Thief* (Chicago: University of Chicago Press, 1937).

The Criminological Enterprise

Transforming Theft: Train Robbers and Safe Crackers

According to Neal Shover, the activities of professional thieves began to be influenced by technology before the twentieth century. For example, train robbery flourished near the end of the nineteenth century because professional robbers considered trains easy pickings. Law enforcement was decentralized, and robbers could escape to a neighboring state to avoid detection. Security arrangements were minimal; robbers could stop, board, and loot trains with little fear of capture. As the threat to trains increased, many technological improvements were initiated to deter would-be robbers:

- Plainclothes officers were placed on trains and rode unobtrusively among the passengers.
- Baggage cars were equipped with ramps and stalls containing fleet horses that could immediately pursue bandits.
- Cars were made with finer precision and strength to make them impregnable.
- Forensic science made it easier to identify robbers, and improved communication made it easier to capture them.
- Federal involvement in train protection extended the ability of law enforcement to go beyond the country and state in which the robbery occurred.

As a result of these innovations, the number of train robberies decreased from 29 in 1900 to 7 in 1905; by 1920 train robbers had all but disappeared.

Safecracking also changed dramatically due to technological improvements in the design of safes. In the early 1900s safes were made of manganese steel because this material was both resistant to drilling and fireproof. The invention and distribution of acetylene torches in the latter part of the nineteenth century made safes constructed of manganese vulnerable and encouraged safecrackers to commit bold crimes. Safe manufacturers fought back by constructing safes with alternating sheets of copper and steel. The copper diffused heat and made the safe resistant to being torched. In response, safecrackers shifted their approach to attack the safes' locking mechanisms: they developed mechanical devices that either dismantled or destroyed locks. Some burglars developed methods of peeling apart the laminated layers of the safe. After World War II, safecrackers began using carbide and then diamond drill bits, which tore through metal. Safe manufacturers responded by lining safes with new metals designed to chip or break drill bits. They also developed sophisticated security systems featuring light beams, which if interrupted would trip an alarm. When thieves learned how to neutralize these alarms, they were supplanted by motion detectors and ultrasonic systems, which fill space with sound waves and set off alarms when they are disturbed. Although these systems can be defeated, it requires expensive electronic gear that most criminals can neither afford nor operate. As a result, the number of safecrackers has declined, and the crime of safecracking is now relatively rare.

CRITICAL THINKING

1. Technology changes the nature and extent of theft crimes. Train robbing and safecracking may be rare today, but using bogus credit cards and stealing from ATM machines have increased. What are some other crime patterns that have been created by technological innovation?
2. What types of crime have technological innovations prevented or deterred?

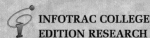 **INFOTRAC COLLEGE EDITION RESEARCH**

To read about the life of an actual train robber, see:
Stephen Fox. Chris Evans could always be relied on to pull a fast one. *Smithsonian* May 1995 v26 n2 p84(8)

Source: Neal Shover, *Great Pretenders: Pursuits and Careers of Persistent Thieves* (Boulder, Colo.: Westview Press, 1996), pp. 50–51.

---

variety of thieves and suppliers, including burglars, drug addicts, shoplifters, dockworkers, and truck drivers. According to Sam, to be successful, a fence must meet the following conditions:

1. *Up-front cash.* All deals are cash transactions, so an adequate supply of ready cash must always be on hand.
2. *Knowledge of dealing.* The fence must be schooled in knowledge of the trade, including developing a "larceny sense," learning to "buy right" at acceptable prices, being able to "cover one's back" and not get caught, finding out how to make the right contacts, and knowing how to "wheel and deal" and how to create opportunities for profit.
3. *Connections with suppliers of stolen goods.* The successful fence must be able to maintain long-term relationships with suppliers of high-value stolen goods who are relatively free of police interference. For example, the warehouse worker who pilfers is a better supplier than the narcotics addict, who is more likely to be apprehended and talk to the police.
4. *Connections with buyers.* The successful fence must have continuing access to buyers of stolen merchandise who are inaccessible to the common thief.
5. *Complicity with law enforcers.* The fence must work out a relationship with law enforcement officials, who invariably find out about the fence's operations.

Steffensmeier found that to stay in business, the fence must either bribe officials with good deals on merchandise and cash payments or act as an informer who helps police recover particularly important merchandise and arrest thieves.

Fences handle a tremendous number of products, such as televisions, cigarettes, stereo equipment, watches, autos, and cameras.[17] In dealing their merchandise, they operate through many legitimate fronts, including art dealers, antique stores, furniture and appliance retailers, remodeling companies, salvage companies, trucking companies, and jewelry stores. When deciding what to pay the thief for goods, the fence uses a complex pricing policy. Professional thieves who steal high-priced items are usually given the highest amounts—about 30 to 50 percent of the wholesale price. For example, furs valued at $5,000 may be bought for $1,200. However, the amateur thief or drug addict who is not in a good bargaining position may receive only 10 cents on the dollar.

Fencing seems to contain many of the elements of professional theft described by Sutherland: fences live by their wits, never engage in violence, depend on their skill in negotiating, maintain community standing based on connections and power, and share the sentiments and behaviors of their colleagues. The only divergence between Sutherland's thief and the fence is the code of honor; the fence seems much more willing to cooperate with authorities than most other professional criminals.

The Nonprofessional Fence Professional fences are the ones who have attracted the attention of criminologists. Yet, like other forms of theft, fencing is not dominated by professional criminals alone; a significant portion of all fencing is performed by amateur or occasional criminals. For example, novice burglars, such as juveniles and drug addicts, often find it so difficult to establish relationships with professional fences that they turn instead to nonprofessionals to unload their stolen goods.[18]

One type of occasional fence is the part-timer who, unlike professional fences, has other sources of income. Part-timers are often legitimate businesspeople who integrate the stolen merchandise into their regular stock. For example, the manager of a local video store who buys stolen VCRs and tapes and rents them along with the legitimate merchandise is a part-time fence. An added benefit of the illegitimate part of this work is the profit made on these stolen items, which is not reported for tax purposes.

Some merchants became actively involved in theft either by specifying the merchandise they want the burglars to steal or by fingering victims. Some businesspeople sell merchandise and then describe the customers' homes and vacation plans to known burglars so that they can steal it back!

Associational fences are amateur fences who barter stolen goods for services. These amateurs typically have legitimate professional dealings with known criminals and include bail bond agents, police officers, and attorneys. One lawyer bragged of getting a $12,000 Rolex watch from one client in exchange for legal services. Bartering for stolen merchandise avoids taxes and becomes a transaction in the underground economy.

Neighborhood hustlers buy and sell stolen property as one of the many ways they make a living. They keep some of the booty for themselves and sell the rest in the neighborhood. These deal makers are familiar figures to neighborhood burglars looking to get some quick cash by selling stolen merchandise.

Amateur receivers can be complete strangers approached in a public place by someone offering a great deal on valuable commodities. It is unlikely that anyone buying a $500 stereo for $200 cash would not suspect that it may have been stolen. Some amateur receivers make a habit of buying suspect merchandise at reasonable prices from a trusted friend, establishing an ongoing relationship. This practice encourages crime because the criminals know that there will always be someone to buy their merchandise. Nonprofessional fences may account for a great deal of criminal receiving.

Criminologists and legal scholars recognize that common theft offenses fall into several categories involving the intentional misappropriation of property for personal gain. In fencing, property is bought from another who illegally possesses the goods. In embezzlement, burglary, and larceny, the property is taken through stealth, whereas in cases of bad checks, fraud, and false pretenses, property is obtained through deception. Some of the major categories of common theft offenses are discussed next.

LARCENY/THEFT

Larceny/theft was one of the earliest common-law crimes created by English judges to define acts in which one person took for his or her own use the property of another.[19] According to common law, **larceny** was defined as "the trespassory taking and carrying away of the personal property of another with intent to steal."[20] Most state jurisdictions have incorporated the common-law crime of larceny in their legal codes. Modern definitions of larceny often include such familiar acts as shoplifting, passing bad checks, and other theft offenses that do not involve using force or threats on the victim or forcibly breaking into a person's home or workplace. (The former is robbery; the latter, burglary.)

When it was originally construed, larceny involved taking property that was in the possession of the rightful owner. For example, it would have been considered larceny for someone to sneak into a farmer's field and steal a cow. Thus the original common-law definition required a "trespass in the taking"; this meant that for an act to be considered larceny, goods must have been

Every year about a million cases of larceny are reported to the FBI. Security forces have been assigned to commercial and residential areas to reduce the incidence of theft. Can such measures be effective, or do they simply displace crimes to other areas of the city?

taken from the physical possession of the rightful owner. In creating this definition of larceny, English judges were more concerned with people disturbing the peace than they were with thefts. They reasoned that if someone tried to steal property from another's possession, the act could eventually lead to a physical confrontation and possibly the death of one party or the other. Consequently, the original definition of larceny did not include crimes in which the thief had taken the property by trickery or deceit. For example, if someone entrusted with another person's property decided to keep it, it was not considered larceny.

The growth of manufacturing and the development of the free enterprise system required greater protection for private property. The pursuit of commercial enterprise often required that one person's legal property be entrusted to a second party; therefore, larceny evolved to include the theft of goods that had come into the thief's possession through legitimate means.

To get around the element of "trespass in the taking," English judges created the concept of **constructive possession.** This legal fiction applies to situations in which persons voluntarily, temporarily give up custody of their property, but still believe that the property is legally theirs. For example, if a person gives a jeweler her watch for repair, she still believes she owns the watch, although she has handed it over to the jeweler. Similarly, when a person misplaces his wallet and someone else finds it and keeps it (although identifica-

tion of the owner can be plainly seen) the concept of constructive possession makes the person who has kept the wallet guilty of larceny.

Larceny Today

Most state jurisdictions have incorporated larceny in their criminal codes. Larceny is usually separated by statute into **petit** (or **petty**) **larceny** and **grand larceny.** The former involves small amounts of money or property; it is punished as a misdemeanor. Grand larceny, involving merchandise of greater value, is a felony punished by a sentence in the state prison. Each state sets its own boundary between grand larceny and petty larceny, but $50 to $100 is not unusual. This distinction often presents a problem for the justice system: it is often difficult to decide whether a particular theft should be considered petty or grand larceny. Car thefts and other larcenies involving high-priced merchandise are easily classified; but if a 10-year-old watch that originally cost $500 is stolen, should its value be based on its original cost, on its current worth (perhaps $50), or on its replacement cost (perhaps $1,000)? As most statutes are worded, the current market value of the property governs its worth. Thus the theft of the watch would be considered petty larceny because its worth today is only $50. However, if a painting originally bought for $25 has a current market value of $5000, its theft would be considered grand larceny.

Larceny/theft is probably the most common crime. Self-report studies indicate that a significant number of youths have engaged in theft. The FBI recorded over 7.7 million acts of larceny in 1997, a rate of over 2,800 per 100,000 persons; larceny rates have remained rather stable for the past five years, declining about 5 percent between 1993 and 1997.[21]

Varieties of Larceny

There are many different varieties of larceny. Some involve small items of little value. Many of these go unreported, especially if the victims are business owners who do not want to take the time to get involved with police; they will simply write off losses as part of doing business. For example, hotel owners estimate that each year guests filch $100 million worth of towels, bathrobes, ashtrays, bedspreads, shower heads, flatware, and even television sets and wall paintings.[22]

Other larcenies involve complex criminal conspiracies from which no one is immune. For example, thieves stole $20.8 million worth of government equipment and supplies and another $10.4 million in personal property from General Services Administration buildings between 1992 and 1997. Nationwide, there were 41,431 reported incidents in that five-year span at 8,200 buildings. Similarly, the Department of Energy reported more than $20 million in property missing from its site in Rocky Flats, Colorado. Missing items included semitrailers, forklifts, cameras, desks, radios, and more than 1,800 pieces of computer equipment.[23]

Shoplifting

Shoplifting is a common form of theft involving the taking of goods from retail stores. Usually shoplifters try to snatch goods — like jewelry, clothes, records, and appliances — when store personnel are otherwise occupied and hide the goods on their bodies. The "five-finger discount" is an extremely common crime, and retailers lose an estimated annual $30 billion to inventory shrinkage; on average, stores small and large lose at least 2 percent of total sales to thieves.[24] Retail security measures add to the already high cost of this crime, all of which is passed on to the consumer. Shoplifting incidents have increased dramatically in the past 20 years, and retailers now expect an annual increase of from 10 to 15 percent. Some studies estimate that about one in every nine shoppers steals from department stores. Moreover, the increasingly popular discount stores, such as K-Mart, Wal-Mart, and Target, have minimal sales help and depend on highly visible merchandise displays to attract purchasers, all of which makes them particularly vulnerable to shoplifters.

The Shoplifter In the early 1960s Mary Owen Cameron conducted a classic study of shoplifting.[25] In her pioneering effort, Cameron found that about 10 percent of all shoplifters were professionals who derived the majority of their income from shoplifting. Sometimes called **boosters** or **heels,** professional shoplifters steal with the intention of reselling stolen merchandise to pawnshops or fences, usually at half the original price.[26]

Cameron found that the majority of shoplifters are amateur pilferers, called **snitches** in thieves' argot. Snitches are otherwise respectable persons who do not conceive of themselves as thieves but systematically steal merchandise for their own use. They are not simply taken by an uncontrollable urge to snatch something that attracts them; they come equipped to steal. Usually snitches who are arrested have never been apprehended before. For the most part, they lack the kinds of criminal experience that suggest extensive association with a criminal subculture.

Criminologists view shoplifters as people who are likely to reform if apprehended. Cameron reasoned that because snitches are not part of a criminal subculture and do not think of themselves as criminals, they are deterred by initial contact with the law. Getting arrested traumatizes them, and they will not risk a second offense.[27] Although this argument seems plausible, some criminologists say that apprehension may in fact have a labeling effect that inhibits deterrence and results in repeated offending.[28]

Controlling Shoplifting One major problem associated with combating shoplifting is that many customers who observe pilferage are reluctant to report it to security agents. Store employees themselves are often reluctant to get involved in apprehending a shoplifter. In fact, fewer than 10 percent of shoplifting incidents are detected by store employees; customers who notice boosters are unwilling to report even serious cases to managers.[29] It is also likely that a store owner's decision to prosecute shoplifters will be based on the value of the goods stolen, the nature of the goods stolen, and the manner in which the theft was realized. For example, shoplifters who plan their crime by using a concealed apparatus, such as a bag pinned to the inside of their clothing, are more apt to be prosecuted than those who impulsively put merchandise into their pockets.[30] The concealment indicates that the crime was premeditated and not a momentary loss of control.

To encourage the arrest of shoplifters, a number of states have passed merchant privilege laws that are designed to protect retailers and their employees from litigation stemming from improper or false arrests of suspected shoplifters.[31] These laws protect but do not immunize merchants from lawsuits. They require that arrests be made on reasonable grounds or probable cause; detention must be short; and store employees or security guards must conduct themselves reasonably.

Prevention Strategies Retail stores are now initiating a number of strategies designed to reduce or eliminate shoplifting. **Target removal strategies** involve displaying dummy or disabled goods while the "real" merchandise is locked up. For example, audio equipment with missing parts is displayed, and only after items are purchased are the necessary components installed. Some stores sell from catalogs while keeping merchandise in stockrooms.

Target hardening strategies involve locking goods into place or having them monitored by electronic systems. Clothing stores may use racks designed to prevent large quantities of garments from being slipped off easily. Store owners also rely on **electronic article surveillance (EAS) systems,** featuring tags with small electronic sensors that trip alarms if not removed by employees before the item leaves the store. Security systems now feature **source tagging,** a process by which manufacturers embed the tag in the packaging or in the product itself. Thieves have trouble removing or defeating such tags, and retailers save on the time and labor needed to attach the tags at their stores.[32]

Situational measures place the most valuable goods in the least vulnerable places, post warning signs to deter potential thieves, and use closed-circuit cameras. Goods may be tagged with devices that activate an alarm if they are taken out of the shop. Figure 12.2 illustrates some additional measures that stores can take to deter shoplifters.

Private Justice   Efforts to control the spread of shoplifting have prompted some commercial enterprises to establish highly sophisticated loss prevention units to combat would-be criminals. Melissa Davis, Richard Lundman, and Ramiro Martinez, Jr., investigated the loss prevention unit in a branch store of a large national retail chain.[33] They uncovered a **private justice system** that works parallel to but independent from the public justice system. Private security officers have many law enforcement powers also granted to municipal police officers, including the powers of arrest, search, and seizure. A merchant's privilege statute immunizes store police from any criminal or civil liability charges stemming from false arrest.

Private police decision making is influenced by state law, allowing stores to recover civil damages from shoplifters. In the 28 states that have implemented this type of legislation, shoplifters may be required to compensate store owners for the value of the goods they attempted to steal, costs incurred because of their illegal acts, and punitive damages. Davis, Lundman, and Martinez found that store detectives use the civil damage route to defray the costs of their operation. The availability of civil damages affects decision making: store owners tend to go after the more affluent shoplifters for civil recovery, and they ship the poor to the public criminal justice system.[34]

Bad Checks

Another form of larceny is cashing bad checks to obtain money or property; the checks are intentionally drawn on a nonexistent or underfunded bank account. In general, for a person to be guilty of passing a bad check, the bank the check is drawn on must refuse payment, and the check casher must fail to make the check good within 10 days after finding out the check was not honored.

Edwin Lemert conducted the best-known study of check forgers more than 40 years ago.[35] Lemert found that the majority of check forgers—he calls them **naive check forgers**—are amateurs who do not believe their actions will hurt anyone. Most naive check forgers come from middle-class backgrounds and have little identification with a criminal subculture. They cash bad checks because of a financial crisis that demands an immediate resolution—perhaps they have lost money at the horse track and have some pressing bills to pay. Lemert refers to this condition as **closure.** Naive check forgers are often socially isolated people who have been unsuccessful in their personal relationships. They are risk-prone when faced with a situation that is unusually stressful for them. The willingness of stores and other commercial establishments to cash checks with a minimum of fuss to promote business encourages the check forger to risk committing a criminal act.

Not all check forgers are amateurs. Lemert found that a few professionals, whom he calls **systematic forgers,** make a substantial living by passing bad checks. It is difficult to estimate the number of such forgeries

---

Figure 12.2   How to Stop Shoplifting

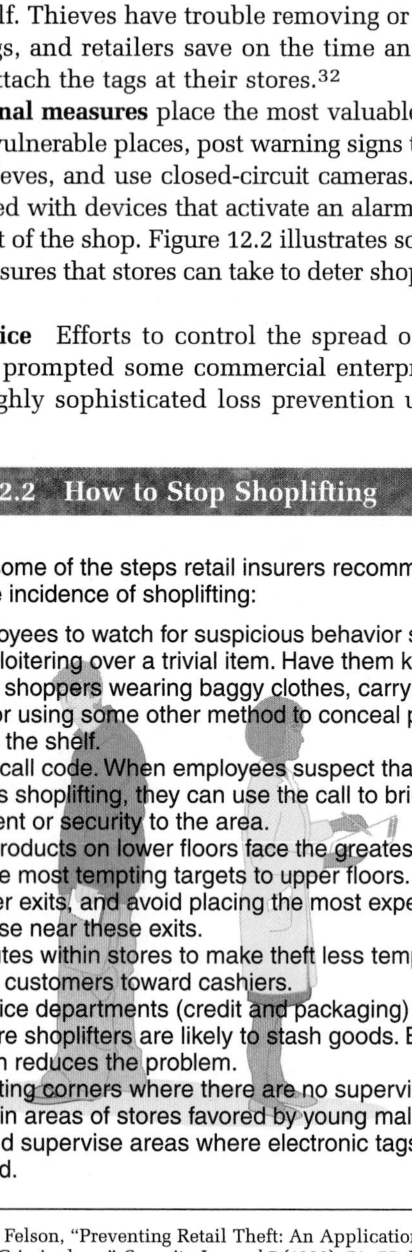

Here are some of the steps retail insurers recommend to reduce the incidence of shoplifting:

- Train employees to watch for suspicious behavior such as a shopper loitering over a trivial item. Have them keep an eye out for shoppers wearing baggy clothes, carrying their own bag, or using some other method to conceal products taken from the shelf.
- Develop a call code. When employees suspect that a customer is shoplifting, they can use the call to bring store management or security to the area.
- Because products on lower floors face the greatest risk, relocate the most tempting targets to upper floors.
- Use smaller exits, and avoid placing the most expensive merchandise near these exits.
- Design routes within stores to make theft less tempting and funnel customers toward cashiers.
- Place service departments (credit and packaging) near areas where shoplifters are likely to stash goods. Extra supervision reduces the problem.
- Avoid creating corners where there are no supervision sight lines in areas of stores favored by young males. Restrict and supervise areas where electronic tags can be removed.

Source: Marcus Felson, "Preventing Retail Theft: An Application of Environmental Criminology," *Security Journal* 7 (1996): 71–75; Marc Brandeberry, "$15 Billion Lost to Shoplifting," *Today's Coverage,* a newsletter of the Grocers Insurance Group, Portland, Oregon, 1997.

---

committed each year or the amounts involved. Stores and banks may choose not to press charges because the effort to collect the money due them is often not worth their while. It is also difficult to separate the true check forger from the neglectful shopper.

Credit Card Theft

The use of stolen credit cards has become a major U.S. problem. It has been estimated that fraud has caused a billion-dollar loss in the credit card industry. Most credit card abuse is the work of amateurs who acquire stolen cards through theft or mugging and then use them for two or three days. However, professional credit card rings may be getting into the act. For example, in Los Angeles, members of a credit card gang got jobs as clerks in several stores, where they collected the names and credit card numbers of customers. Gang members bought plain plastic cards and had the names and numbers of the customers embossed on them. The gang created a fictitious wholesale jewelry company and applied for and received authorization to accept credit cards from customers. The thieves then used the phony cards to charge nonexistent jewelry purchases on the accounts of the people whose names and card numbers they had collected. The banks that issued the original cards honored over $200,000 in payments before the thieves withdrew the money from their business account and left town.[36] To combat losses from credit card theft, in 1971 Congress limited a person's liability to $50 per stolen card. Similarly, some states, such as California, have passed laws making it a misdemeanor to obtain property or services by means of cards that have been stolen, forged, canceled, or revoked, or whose use is for any reason unauthorized.[37]

The problem of credit card misuse is being compounded by thieves who set up bogus Internet sites to trick people into giving them their credit card numbers, which they then use for their own gain. This problem is growing so rapidly that a number of new technologies are being prepared to combat credit card number theft over the Internet. One method incorporates digital signatures into computer operating systems, which can be accessed with a digital key that comes with each computer. Owners of new systems can present three forms of identification to a notary public and trade a notarized copy of their key for a program that will sign files. The basis of the digital signature is a digital certificate, a small block of data that contains a person's "public key." This certificate is signed, in turn, by a certificate authority. The digital certificate acts like a credit card with a hologram and a photograph; it identifies the user to the distant Web site.[38]

Auto Theft

Motor vehicle theft is another common larceny offense. Yet because of its frequency and seriousness, it is treated as a separate category in the Uniform Crime Report (UCR). The FBI recorded almost 1.4 million auto thefts in 1997, accounting for a total loss of more than $7 billion. UCR projections on auto theft are similar to the projections of the National Crime Victim Survey (NCVS), probably because almost every state requires owners to insure their vehicles, and auto theft is one of the most highly reported of all major crimes (75 percent of all auto thefts are reported to police).

A number of attempts have been made to categorize the various forms of auto theft. Typically distinctions are made between theft for temporary personal use, for resale, and for chopping or stripping cars for parts. One of the most detailed of these typologies was developed by Charles McCaghy and his associates after examining data from police and court files in several states.[39] The researchers uncovered five categories of auto theft transactions:

1. *Joyriding:* Many car thefts are motivated by teenagers' desire to acquire the power, prestige, sexual potency, and recognition associated with an automobile. Joyriders steal cars not for profit or gain but to experience, even briefly, the benefits associated with owning an automobile.

2. *Short-term transportation:* Auto theft for short-term transportation is similar to joyriding. It involves the theft of a car simply to go from one place to another. In more serious cases, the thief may drive to another city or state and then steal another car to continue the journey.

3. *Long-term transportation:* Thieves who steal cars for long-term transportation intend to keep the cars for their personal use. Usually older than joyriders and from a lower-class background, these auto thieves may repaint and otherwise disguise cars to avoid detection.

4. *Profit:* Auto theft for profit is motivated by hope for monetary gain. At one extreme are highly organized professionals who resell expensive cars after altering their identification numbers and falsifying their registration papers. At the other end of the scale are amateur auto strippers who steal batteries, tires, and wheel covers to sell them or reequip their own cars.

5. *Commission of another crime:* A few auto thieves steal cars to use in other crimes, such as robberies and thefts. This type of auto thief desires both mobility and anonymity.

At one time joyriding was the predominant motive for auto theft, and most cars were taken by relatively affluent, white, middle-class teenagers looking for excitement.[40] There appears to be a change in this pattern: fewer cars are being taken today, and fewer stolen cars are being recovered. Part of the reason is that there has been an increase in professional car thieves who are linked to chop shops, export rings, or both. Exporting stolen vehicles has become a global problem, and the emergence of capitalism in Eastern Europe has increased the demand for U.S-made cars.[41]

Which Cars Are Taken Most?   Car thieves show signs of rational choice when they select their target. Today luxury cars and sport utility vehicles are in greatest demand. The Toyota Land Cruiser is 23 times more likely to be taken than the average vehicle. Many of the highly desired cars are never recovered because they are immediately shipped abroad, where they command prices three times higher than the U.S. sticker price.[42]

Car models that have been in production for a few years without many design changes stand the greatest risk of theft. These vehicles are popular because their parts are most valued in the secondary market. Luxury cars, on the other hand, typically experience a sharp decline in their theft rate soon after a design change. Enduring models are also in demand because older cars are more likely to be uninsured, so demand for stolen used parts is higher for these vehicles.

CONNECTIONS

Chapter 5 discusses the rational choice view of car theft. As you may recall, cars with expensive radios and parts are more often the target of rational thieves.

Carjacking   You may have read about gunmen approaching a car and forcing the owner to give up the keys; in some cases, people have been killed when they reacted too slowly. This type of auto theft has become so common that it has its own name: **carjacking.**[43] Carjacking is legally considered a type of robbery because it involves theft by force. It accounts for about 2 percent of all car thefts, or 35,000 per year. Carjackings are basically violent. The most recent data indicate that about 24 percent of the victims suffered injuries, about 4 percent of which were considered serious (gunshots, knifings, internal injuries, broken bones and teeth), and about 60 percent of the offenders in carjackings carried handguns.

Both the victims and offenders in carjackings tend to be young black men; about half of the carjackings are typically committed by gangs or groups. These crimes are most likely to occur in the evening, in the central city, and in an open area or parking garage.

Combating Auto Theft   Auto theft is a significant target of situational crime prevention efforts. One approach to theft deterrence has been to increase the risks of apprehension. Information hot lines offer rewards for information leading to the arrest of car thieves. A Michigan-based program, Operation HEAT (Help Eliminate Auto Theft), is credited with recovering over 900 vehicles, worth $11 million, and resulting in the arrest of 647 people. Another approach has been to place fluorescent decals on windows indicating that the car is never used between 1 and 5 A.M.; if police spot a car with the decal being operated during this period, they know it is stolen.[44]

The Lojack system installs a hidden tracking device in cars, which gives off a signal enabling the police to pinpoint its location. Research evaluating the effectiveness of this device finds that it significantly reduces crime.[45] Because car thieves cannot tell that Lojack has been installed, it does not reduce the likelihood that a protected car will be stolen. However, cars with Lojack installed have a much higher recovery rate. There may also be a general deterrent effect: areas with high rates of Lojack use have significantly lower auto theft rates. Ironically, Lojack owners actually accrue a smaller-than-anticipated reward for their foresight because they have to pay for installation and maintenance of the device. Those without it gain because they benefit from a lower auto theft rate without paying any additional cost.

Other prevention efforts involve making it more difficult to steal cars. Publicity campaigns have been directed at encouraging people to lock their cars. Parking lots have been equipped with theft-deterring closed-circuit TV cameras and barriers. Manufacturers have installed more sophisticated steering-column locking devices and other security systems that complicate theft.

A study by the Highway Loss Data Institute (HLDI) found that most car theft prevention methods, especially alarms, have little effect on theft rates. The most effective methods appear to be devices that immobilize a vehicle by cutting off the electrical power needed to start the engine when a theft is detected.[46]

False Pretenses or Fraud

The crime of **false pretenses,** or **fraud,** involves misrepresenting a fact in a way that causes a victim to willingly give his or her property to the wrongdoer, who then keeps it.[47] In 1757 the English Parliament defined false pretenses in order to cover an area of law left untouched by larceny statutes. The first false pretenses law punished people who "knowingly and designedly by false pretense or pretenses, [obtained] from any person or persons, money, goods, wares or merchandise with intent to cheat or defraud any person or persons of the same."[48]

False pretense differs from traditional larceny because the victims willingly give their possessions to the offender, and the crime does not, as does larceny, involve a "trespass in the taking." An example of false pretenses would be an unscrupulous merchant selling someone a chair by claiming it was an antique, knowing all the while that it was a cheap copy. Another example would be a phony healer selling a victim a bottle of colored sugar water as an "elixir" that would cure a disease.

Fraud may also occur when people conspire to cheat a third party or institution — for example, by selling fake IDs, tickets, vouchers, tokens, or licenses that can be used to fraudulently gain services or illegal access. One example of an innovative cheating scheme was instituted by a man named Po Chieng Ma, who conspired to sell answers to the Graduate Management Administration Test (GMATs), the Graduate Record Examinations (GREs), and the Test of English as a Foreign Language (TOEFL) to an estimated 788 customers, each of whom had paid $2,000 to $9,000. People were paid to take the multiple-choice tests in Manhattan and then call California, where the same tests were to be given, with the answers. The answers were passed on to Ma, who, taking advantage of the three-hour time difference, carved the answers in code on the sides of pencils, which were then given to his customers. Ma, who pleaded guilty to conspiracy and obstruction of justice, received a four-year prison term for his efforts. In this case there were many victims, including the testing service, universities, and students who lost places in school because those who inflated their scores through the scheme were admitted instead.[49]

Confidence Games

Confidence games are run by swindlers who aspire to separate a victim from his or her hard-earned money. These con games usually involve getting a **mark** (target) interested in some get-rich-quick scheme, which may have illegal overtones. The criminal's hope is that when victims lose their money, they will be either too embarrassed or too afraid to call the police. There are hundreds of varieties of con games. The classic con is called the **pigeon drop**,[50] in which a package or wallet containing money is "found" by a con man or woman. A passing victim is stopped and asked for advice about what to do because no identification can be found. Another "stranger," who is part of the con, approaches and enters the discussion. The three decide to split the money; but first, to make sure everything is legal, one of the swindlers leaves to consult a lawyer. Upon returning, he or she claims that the lawyer says the money can be split up; first, however, each party must prove he or she has the means to reimburse the original owner, should one show up. The victim then is asked to give some good-faith money for the lawyer to hold. When the victim goes to the lawyer's office to pick up a share of the loot, he or she finds the address bogus and the money gone.

Modern Confidence Games In the 1990s the pigeon drop has been appropriated by corrupt telemarketers who contact people, typically elderly victims, over the phone in order to bilk them out of their savings. The FBI estimates that illicit telephone pitches cost Americans some $40 billion a year.[51] In one scam, a salesman tried to get $500 out of a 78-year-old woman by telling her the money was needed as a deposit to make sure she would get $50,000 cash she had supposedly won in a contest. In another scheme, a Las Vegas–based telephone con game used the name Feed America Inc. to defraud people out of more than $1.3 million by soliciting donations for various causes, including families of those killed in the Oklahoma bombing. With the growth of direct-mail marketing and "900" telephone numbers that charge callers over $2.50 per minute for conversations with what are promised to be beautiful, willing sex partners, a flood of new confidence games may be about to descend on the U.S. public. In all, about 414,000 people were arrested for fraud in 1997, most likely a very small percentage of all swindlers, scam artists, and frauds.

Embezzlement

Embezzlement was mentioned in early Greek culture when, in his writings, Aristotle alluded to theft by road commissioners and other government officials.[52] It was first codified into law by the English Parliament during the sixteenth century to fill a gap in larceny law.[53] Until then, to be guilty of theft, a person had to take goods from the physical possession of another (trespass in the taking). However, as explained earlier, this definition did not cover instances in which one person trusted another and willingly gave that person temporary custody of his or her property. For example, in everyday commerce, store clerks, bank tellers, brokers, and merchants gain lawful possession but not legal ownership of other people's money. **Embezzlement** occurs when someone who is trusted with property fraudulently converts it—that is, keeps it for his or her own use or for the use of others. It can be distinguished from fraud on the basis of when the criminal intent was formed. Most U.S. courts require a serious breach of trust before a person can be convicted of embezzlement. The mere act of moving property without the owner's consent, or damaging it or using it, is not considered embezzlement. However, using it up, selling it, pledging it, giving it away, and holding it against the owner's will are all considered embezzlement.[54]

Although it is impossible to know how many embezzlement incidents occur annually, the FBI found that only 17,400 people were arrested for embezzlement in 1997[55]—probably an extremely small percentage of all embezzlers. However, the number of people arrested for embezzlement has increased 25 percent since 1988, indicating that (1) more employees are willing to steal from their employers, (2) more employers are willing to report instances of embezzlement, or (3) law enforcement officials are more willing to prosecute embezzlers.

BURGLARY

Common law defines the crime of **burglary** as "the breaking and entering of a dwelling house of another in the nighttime with the intent to commit a felony within."[56] Burglary is considered a much more serious crime than larceny/theft because it involves entering another's home, which threatens occupants. Even though at the time of the burglary the home may be unoccupied, the potential for harm to the occupants is so significant that most state jurisdictions punish burglary as a felony. The legal definition of burglary has undergone considerable change since its common-law origins. When first created by English judges during the late Middle Ages, laws against burglary were designed to protect people whose home might be set upon by wandering criminals. Including the phrase "breaking and entering" in the definition protected people from unwarranted intrusions; if an invited guest stole something, it would not be considered a burglary. Similarly, the requirement that the crime be committed at nighttime was added because evening was considered the time when honest people might fall prey to criminals.[57] More recent state laws have changed the requirements of burglary, and most have discarded the necessity of forced entry. Many states now protect all structures, not just dwelling houses. A majority of states have also removed the nighttime element from burglary definitions. States commonly enact laws creating different degrees of burglary: the more serious, heavily punished crimes involve nighttime forced entry into the home, whereas the least serious involve daytime entry into a nonresidential structure by an unarmed offender. Several gradations of the offense may be found between these extremes.

The Nature and Extent of Burglary

The FBI's definition of burglary is not restricted to burglary from a person's home; it includes any unlawful entry of a structure to commit theft or felony. Burglary is further categorized into three subclasses: forcible entry, unlawful entry where no force is used, and attempted forcible entry.

According to the UCR, almost 2.5 million burglaries occurred in 1997. The burglary rate has dropped by more than 16 percent since 1993. As Figure 12.3 shows, both residential and commercial burglaries have undergone steep declines during the 1990s; crimes committed at night have undergone a steeper decline than daytime events. Overall, the average loss for a burglary was about $1,300 per victim, for a total of about $3.3 billion.

The NCVS reports that about 4.8 million residential burglaries occurred in 1997. The difference between the UCR and NCVS is explained by the fact that slightly more than half of all burglary victims reported the incident to police. However, similar to the UCR, the NCVS indicates that the number of burglaries has declined, dropping from 5.8 million in 1992 to 4.8 million in 1997.

According to the NCVS, those most likely to be burglarized are relatively poor Hispanic and African-American families (annual income under $7,500). Owner-occupied and single-family residences had lower burglary rates than renter-occupied and multiple-family dwellings.

Residential Burglary Although some burglars are crude thieves who smash a window and enter a vacant home or structure with minimal preparation, others plan a strategy. Because it involves planning, risk, and skill, burglary has long been associated with professional thieves who carefully learn their craft. For example, Francis Hoheimer, an experienced professional burglar, has described how he learned the craft of burglary from a fellow inmate, Oklahoma Smith, when the two were serving time in the Illinois State Penitentiary. Among Smith's recommendations are these:

> Never wear deodorant or shaving lotion; the strange scent might wake someone up. The more people there are in a house, the safer you are. If someone hears you moving around, they will think it's someone else. . . . If they call, answer in a muffled sleepy voice. . . . Never be afraid of dogs, they can sense fear. Most dogs are friendly, snap your finger, they come right to you.[58]

Despite his elaborate preparations, Hoheimer spent many years in confinement.

Burglars must master the skills of their trade, learning to spot environmental cues that nonprofessionals fail to notice.[59] In an important book called *Burglars on the Job,* Richard Wright and Scott Decker describe the working conditions of active burglars.[60] Most are motivated by the need for cash in order to get high; they want to enjoy the good life, "keeping the party going," without having to work. As Figure 12.4 shows, they approach their job in a rational, businesslike fashion; but their lives are controlled by their culture and environment. Unskilled and uneducated, urban burglars choose crime because there are few conventional opportunities for success.

CONNECTIONS

According to the rational choice approach discussed in Chapter 5, burglars make rational, calculating decisions before committing crimes. If circumstances and culture dictate their activities, their decisions must be considered a matter of choice.

Commercial Burglary Some burglars prefer to victimize commercial property rather than private homes. Of all business establishments, retail stores are the favorite target. They display merchandise so that burglars know exactly what to look for, where it can be found, and, because the prices are displayed, how much they can hope to gain in resale to a fence. Burglars can legitimately enter a retail store during business hours and see what the store contains and where it is stored; they can also check for security alarms and devices. Com-

Figure 12.3 Patterns and Trends

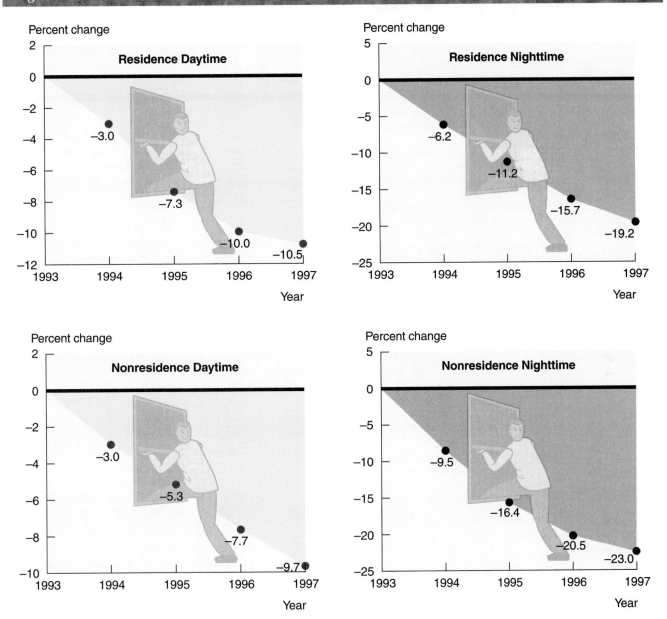

Source: FBI, *Crime in the United States, 1997* (Washington, D.C.: U.S. Government Printing Office, 1998), p. 43.

mercial burglars perceive retail establishments as quick sources of merchandise that can be easily sold.[61]

Other commercial establishments, such as service centers, warehouses, and factories, are less attractive targets because it is more difficult to gain legitimate access to plan the theft. The burglar must use guile to scope out these places, perhaps posing as a delivery person. In addition, the merchandise is more likely to be used or more difficult to fence at a premium price. If burglars choose to attack factories, warehouses, or service centers, the most vulnerable properties are those located far from major roads and away from pedestrian traffic. In remote areas, burglar alarms are less effective

because it takes police longer to respond than on more heavily patrolled thoroughfares, and an alarm is less likely to be heard by a pedestrian who would be able to call for help. Even in the most remote areas, however, burglars are wary of alarms, even if their presence suggests that there is something worth stealing.

Careers in Burglary

Some criminals make burglary their career and continually develop new specialized skills. Neal Shover has studied the careers of professional burglars and uncovered the existence of a particularly successful type—the

Figure 12.4 How Burglars Approach Their "Job"

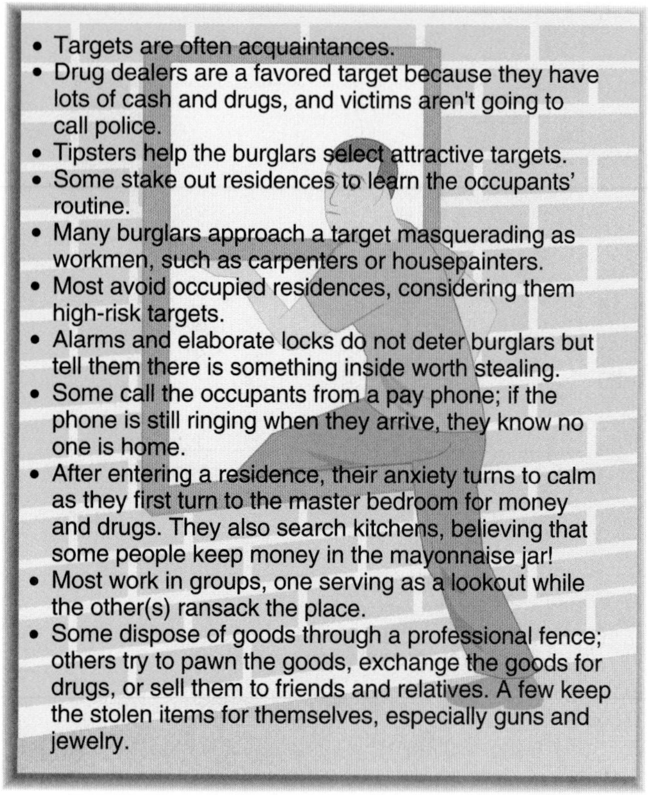

- Targets are often acquaintances.
- Drug dealers are a favored target because they have lots of cash and drugs, and victims aren't going to call police.
- Tipsters help the burglars select attractive targets.
- Some stake out residences to learn the occupants' routine.
- Many burglars approach a target masquerading as workmen, such as carpenters or housepainters.
- Most avoid occupied residences, considering them high-risk targets.
- Alarms and elaborate locks do not deter burglars but tell them there is something inside worth stealing.
- Some call the occupants from a pay phone; if the phone is still ringing when they arrive, they know no one is home.
- After entering a residence, their anxiety turns to calm as they first turn to the master bedroom for money and drugs. They also search kitchens, believing that some people keep money in the mayonnaise jar!
- Most work in groups, one serving as a lookout while the other(s) ransack the place.
- Some dispose of goods through a professional fence; others try to pawn the goods, exchange the goods for drugs, or sell them to friends and relatives. A few keep the stolen items for themselves, especially guns and jewelry.

Source: Richard Wright and Scott Decker, *Burglars on the Job: Streetlife and Residential Break-Ins* (Boston, Mass.: Northeastern University Press, 1994).

good burglar.[62] Professional burglars use this title to characterize colleagues who have distinguished themselves as burglars. Characteristics of the good burglar include technical competence, personal integrity, specialization in burglary, financial success, and the ability to avoid prison sentences. Shover found that to receive recognition as good burglars, novices must develop four key requirements of the trade:

1. They must learn the many skills needed to commit lucrative burglaries. This process may include learning techniques such as gaining entry into homes and apartment houses; selecting targets with high potential payoffs; choosing items with a high resale value; opening safes properly without damaging their contents; and using the proper equipment, including cutting torches, electric saws, explosives, and metal bars.
2. The good burglar must be able to team up to form a criminal gang. Choosing trustworthy companions is essential if the obstacles to completing a successful job—police, alarms, secure safes—are to be overcome.
3. The good burglar must have inside information. Without knowledge of what awaits them inside, burglars can spend a tremendous amount of time and effort on empty safes and jewelry boxes.
4. The good burglar must cultivate fences or buyers for stolen wares. Once the burglar gains access to people who buy and sell stolen goods, he or she must also learn how to successfully sell these goods for a reasonable profit.

CONNECTIONS

Shover finds that the process of becoming a professional burglar is similar to the process described in Sutherland's theory of differential association. For more detail, refer to Chapter 8.

According to Shover, a person becomes a good burglar by learning the techniques of the trade from older, more experienced burglars. During this process, the older burglar teaches the novice how to handle such requirements of the trade as dealing with defense attorneys, bail bond agents, and other agents of the justice system. Apprentices must be known to have the appropriate character before they are accepted for training. Usually the opportunity to learn burglary comes as a reward for being a highly respected juvenile gang member; from knowing someone in the neighborhood who has made a living at burglary; or, more often, from having built a reputation for being solid while serving time in prison. Consequently, the opportunity to become a good burglar is not open to everyone.

The Burglary "Career Ladder" Paul Cromwell, James Olson, and D'Aunn Wester Avary, who interviewed 30 active burglars in Texas, also found that burglars go through stages of career development. They begin as young novices who learn the trade from older, more experienced burglars, frequently siblings or relatives. Novices continue to get this tutoring as long as they can develop their own markets (fences) for stolen goods. After their education is over, novices enter the journeyman stage, characterized by forays in search of lucrative targets and careful planning. At this point they develop reputations as experienced, reliable criminals. They become professional burglars when they have developed advanced skills and organizational abilities that give them the highest esteem among their peers.

The Texas burglars also displayed evidence of rational decision making. Most seemed to carefully evaluate potential costs and benefits before deciding to commit crime. For example, burglars prefer corner houses because they are easily observed and offer the maximum number of escape routes.[63] They look for houses that show evidence of long-term care and wealth. Although people may erect fences and other barriers to deter burglars, these devices may actually attract crime because they are viewed as protecting something worth stealing:

race, culture, gender, and criminology

The Female Burglar

Despite the interest shown in both the careers of residential burglars and female offenders in general, relatively little is known about female burglars. Although most burglars apprehended by police are male, about 9 percent, or 33,000, are female.

To address this issue, Scott Decker, Richard Wright, Allison Redfern Rooney, and Dietrich Smith interviewed 18 females, ranging in age from 15 to 51, who were active residential burglars. For comparison, 87 male burglars were also interviewed.

Decker and his associates found that female burglars had offending patterns quite similar to those of males. In addition to burglary, both groups engaged in other thefts, such as shoplifting and assault. The major difference was that male burglars also stole cars, but females shunned this form of larceny.

Another difference was that whereas females always worked with a partner, about 39 percent of the males said they seldom worked with others. Males also began their offending careers at an earlier age than females. About half of the females interviewed had been involved in fewer than 20 burglaries, whereas only 28 percent of the males reported as few as 20 lifetime burglaries. Because the males started earlier and committed more crimes, it is not surprising that the males had a much greater chance of doing time (26 percent) than females (6 percent).

There were also many similarities between the two groups. A majority of both male and female burglars reported substance abuse problems, including cocaine, heroin, and marijuana use. About 47 percent of the females considered themselves addicts, and 72 percent said they drank alcohol before they committed crimes; males reported less addiction, drug use, and alcohol abuse than females.

Decker and his associates found that the female burglars could be divided into two groups: "accomplices" and "partners." Accomplices committed burglaries because they were caught up in circumstances beyond their control. They felt compelled or pressured to commit crimes because of a relationship with another, more dominant person, typically a boyfriend or husband. Accomplices got into crime because they lacked legitimate employment, were drug dependent, or had alcohol problems. Accomplices exercised little control over their crimes and relied on others for planning and tactics. They commonly acted as lookouts or drivers.

In contrast, partners, who made up two-thirds of the sample, planned and carried out the crimes because they enjoyed both the reward and the excitement of burglary. In planning their crimes, partners displayed many characteristics of the rational criminal: they helped spot targets and planned entries. As one female burglar stated,

> That's one reason why we got so many youngsters in jail today. I see this, so let's go make a hit. No, no, no. If they see this and it looks good, then it's going to be there for a while. So the point is, you have to case it and make sure you know everything. I want to know what time you go to work, the time the children go to school. I know there's no one coming home for lunch. So plan it with somebody else. We'll take the new dishwasher, washing machine, and this other stuff. We just put it in the truck. Do you know when people rent a truck, nobody ever pays that any attention? They think you're moving [but] only if you rent a truck. Now if you bring it out of there and put it in the car, that's a horse of another color.

Once the burglary began, partners carried out all forms of crime-related tasks, including gaining entry, searching the house, carrying loot outside, and disposing of the stolen merchandise.

In conclusion, most female burglars maintain roles and identities similar to those of their male colleagues. Although some gender-based differences are evident, both male and female burglars actively plan crimes for many of the same reasons. The Decker research shows that for most male and female burglars, criminal careers may be a function of economic need and role equality—a finding that supports a feminist view of crime. It also illustrates that repeat criminals use rational choice in planning their activities.

CRITICAL THINKING

1. Does the fact that so many burglars, both male and female, drink and abuse drugs conflict with a rational choice approach to crime?
2. Why are male burglars more likely to be car thieves than females are? Decker and his associates speculate that one reason may be a "strong cultural tradition linking masculinity to driving and car ownership." Can this be so?

 INFOTRAC COLLEGE EDITION RESEARCH

To learn more about the nature of burglary and its prevention and control, see:

Per Stangeland. Other targets or other locations? An analysis of opportunity structures. *British Journal of Criminology* Wntr 38 (1998): 66–76.
Matthew B. Robinson. Burglary revictimization: the time period of heightened risk. *British Journal of Criminology* 38 (1998): 78–88.

Source: Scott Decker, Richard Wright, Allison Redfern, and Dietrich Smith. "A Woman's Place Is in the Home: Females and Residential Burglary." *Justice Quarterly* 10 (1993): 143–63.

---

if there is nothing valuable inside, why go through so much trouble to secure the premises?[64] Cromwell, Olson, and Avary also found that many burglars had serious drug habits and that their criminal activity was, in part, aimed at supporting their substance abuse. The Race, Culture, Gender, and Criminology feature titled "The Female Burglar" describes the activities of both professional and occasional female burglars.

The Criminological Enterprise

What Motivates Juvenile Firesetters?

What motivates young people to commit arson? According to research by sociologist Wayne Wooden, juvenile arsonists can be classified in one of four categories:

1. *The "playing with matches" firesetter:* This is the youngest firestarter, usually between the ages of 4 and 9, who sets fires because parents are careless with matches and lighters. Proper instruction on fire safety can help prevent fires set by these young children.
2. *The "crying for help" firesetter:* This type of firesetter is a 7- to 13-year-old who turns to fire to reduce stress. The source of the stress is family conflict, divorce, death, or abuse. These youngsters have difficulty expressing their feelings of sorrow, rage, or anger and turn to fire as a means of relieving stress or getting back at their antagonists.
3. *The "delinquent" firesetter:* Some youths set fire to school property or surrounding areas to retaliate for some slight experienced at school. These kids may break into the school to vandalize property with friends and later set a fire to cover up their activities.
4. *The "severely disturbed" firesetter:* This youngster is obsessed with fires and often dreams about them in vibrant colors. This is the most disturbed type of juvenile firesetter and the one most likely to set numerous fires with the potential for death and damage.

Table A	Firesetting Groups		
	GROUP 1	**GROUP 2**	**GROUP 3**
Age Range	Under 7	8–12 years	13–18 years
Reason(s) for Firesetting Behavior	Accident or curiosity	Curiosity or psychosocial conflict	History of firestarting behavior, or psychosocial conflict, or intentional criminal behavior

Another research effort by Eileen M. Garry concluded that juvenile firesetters fall into three general groups. The first is made up of children under 7 years of age. Generally, fires started by these children are the result of accidents or curiosity. In the second group of firesetters are children ranging in age from 8 to 12. Although the firesetting of some of these children is motivated by curiosity or experimentation, a greater proportion of their firesetting represents underlying psychosocial conflicts. The third group comprises adolescents between the ages of 13 and 18. These youths tend to have a long history of undetected fire play and firestarting behavior. Their current firesetting episodes are usually the result of either psychosocial conflict and turmoil or intentional criminal behavior. This behavior is summarized in Table A.

CRITICAL THINKING

1. Have you ever been fascinated with fire? Did this ever result in experimenting with matches? If not, what stopped you from acting on your impulses?
2. If you knew of someone who frequently played with matches to the point of concern, how would you handle this situation?

 INFOTRAC COLLEGE EDITION RESEARCH

To read more on the subject of arson, see:

Herschel Prins. Arson: A Review of the Psychiatric Literature. (book reviews) *British Journal of Criminology* Winter 1996 36 n1 p162-163

Source: Wayne Wooden, "Juvenile Firesetters in Cross-Cultural Perspective: How Should Society Respond," in *Official Responses to Problem Juveniles: Some International Reflections,* ed. James Hackler (Onati, Spain: Onati Publications, 1991), pp. 339–48; Eileen M. Garry, *Juvenile Firesetting and Arson* (Washington, D.C.: Office of Juvenile Justice and Delinquency Prevention, 1997).

Repeat Burglary   To what extent do burglars strike the same victim more than once? Research suggests that burglars may in fact return in order to repeat their offenses. One reason is that many burgled items are indispensable (like televisions and VCRs), so it is safe to assume they will quickly be replaced.[65] Graham Farrell, Coretta Phillips, and Ken Pease have articulated why burglars would most likely try to hit the same target more than once:

- It takes less effort to burgle a home or apartment known to be a suitable target than an unknown or unsuitable one.
- The burglar is already aware of the target's layout.
- The ease of entry of the target has probably not changed, and escape routes are known.
- The lack of protective measures and the absence of nosy neighbors, which made the first burglary a success, have probably not changed.

- Goods have been observed that could not be taken out the first time.[66]

CONNECTIONS

Chapter 4 discussed repeat victimization. As you may recall, it is common for particular people and places to be the target of numerous predatory crimes.

ARSON

Arson is the willful, malicious burning of a home, public building, vehicle, or commercial building. Arson is a young man's crime. FBI statistics for 1997 show that juveniles accounted for 46 percent of arson arrests; juveniles are arrested for a greater share of this crime than any other.[67]

There are several motives for arson. Adult arsonists may be motivated by severe emotional turmoil. Some psychologists view fire starting as a function of a disturbed personality and say that arson should be viewed as a mental health problem, not a criminal act.[68] It is alleged that arsonists often experience sexual pleasure from starting fires and then observing their destructive effects. Although some arsonists may be aroused sexually by their activities, there is little evidence that most arsonists are psychosexually motivated.[69] It is equally likely that fires are started by angry people looking for revenge against property owners or by teenagers out to vandalize property.

Juveniles, who are the most prolific firestarters, may get involved in arson for a variety of reasons as they mature. Juvenile firestarting is the topic of the Criminological Enterprise feature titled "What Motivates Juvenile Firestarters?"

Other fires are set by professionals who engage in **arson for profit.** People looking to collect insurance money, but who are afraid or unable to set the fires themselves, hire professional arsonists who know how to set fires yet make the cause seem accidental (like an electrical short). Another form is **arson fraud,** which involves a business owner burning his or her property, or hiring someone to do it, to escape financial problems.[70] Over the years, investigators have found that businesspeople are willing to become involved in arson to collect fire insurance or for various other reasons, such as these:

- Obtaining money during a period of financial crisis
- Getting rid of outdated or slow-moving inventory
- Destroying outmoded machines and technology
- Paying off legal and illegal debt
- Relocating or remodeling a business—for example, a theme restaurant that has not been accepted by customers
- Taking advantage of government funds available for redevelopment
- Applying for government building money, pocketing it without making repairs, and then claiming that fire destroyed the "rehabilitated" building
- Planning bankruptcies to eliminate debts after the merchandise supposedly destroyed was secretly sold before the fire
- Eliminating business competition by burning out rivals
- Employing extortion schemes that demand that victims pay up or the rest of their holdings will be burned
- Solving labor–management problems (this type of arson may be committed by a disgruntled employee)
- Concealing another crime, such as embezzlement

Some recent technological advances may help prove that many alleged arsons were actually accidental fires. There is now evidence of an effect called **flashover,** in which during an ordinary fire, heat and gas at the ceiling of a room can reach 2,000 degrees. This causes clothes and furniture to burst into flame, duplicating the effects of arsonists' gasoline or explosives. It is possible that many suspected arsons are actually the result of flashover.[71]

During the past decade, hundreds of jurisdictions across the nation have established programs to address the growing concern about juvenile firesetting. Housed primarily within the fire service, these programs are designed to identify, evaluate, and treat juvenile firesetters to prevent the recurrence of firesetting behaviors.

SUMMARY

Economic crimes are designed to financially reward the offender. Opportunistic amateurs commit the majority of economic crimes. However, economic crime has also attracted professional criminals. Professionals earn most of their income from crime, view themselves as criminals, and possess skills that aid them in their law-breaking behavior. Edwin Sutherland's classic book *The Professional Thief* is perhaps the most famous portrayal of professional crime. According to Sutherland and his informant, Chic Conwell, professionals live by their wits and never resort to violence. A good example of the professional criminal is the fence who buys and sells stolen merchandise. There are also occasional thieves whose skill level and commitment fall below the professional level.

Common theft offenses include larceny, embezzlement, fraud, and burglary. These are common-law crimes, defined by English judges to meet social needs. Larceny involves taking the legal possessions of another. Petty larceny is typically theft of amounts under $100; grand larceny usually refers to amounts over $100. The crime of false pretenses, or fraud, is similar to larceny in that it involves the theft of goods or money; it differs in that the criminal tricks victims into voluntarily giving up their possessions. Embezzlement is another larceny crime. It involves people taking something that was temporarily entrusted to them, such as bank tellers taking money out of the cash drawer and keeping it for themselves. Most states have codified these common-law crimes in their legal codes. New larceny crimes have also been defined to keep abreast of changing social conditions: passing bad checks, stealing or illegally using credit cards, shoplifting, and stealing automobiles. Burglary, a more serious theft offense, was defined in common law as the "breaking and entering of a dwelling house of another in the nighttime with the intent to commit a felony within." This definition has also evolved over time. Today most states have modified their definitions of burglary to include theft from any structure at any time of day. Because burglary involves planning and risk, it attracts professional thieves. The most competent are known as good burglars. Good burglars have technical competence and personal integrity, specialize in burglary, are financially successful, and avoid prison sentences.

Arson is another serious property crime. Although most arsonists are teenage vandals, there are professional arsonists who specialize in burning commercial buildings for profit.

 See the book-specific web site at www.cj.wadsworth.com for additional chapter links, discussions, and quizzes.

THINKING LIKE A CRIMINOLOGIST

To reduce the risk of loss during the Christmas holidays, the Security Industry Association (SIA) suggests that you don't display presents where they can be seen from a window or doorway, and put gifts in a safe place before leaving the house or taking a trip. Moreover, closing drapes or blinds during even short trips away from home is a good habit.

It is important to trick burglars into believing someone is home. If you are away, the SIA suggests having lights on timers, stopping mail and newspaper delivery, and arranging, if possible, to have the walkways shoveled and have a car parked in the driveway as additional security measures. Other suggestions include installing a good dead bolt lock with at least a one-inch throat into a solid wood or steel door that fits securely into a sturdy frame, keeping doors locked, putting a chain-link fence around a yard, getting a dog, and having police inspect the house for security. Also, buy a weighted safe deposit box to secure items that can't be replaced, and engrave your driver's license number and state of residence on your property to give police a way to contact you if your home is burglarized and the stolen items are later found.

Con artists may take advantage of people's generosity during the holidays by making appeals for nonexistent charities. The SIA suggests that you always ask for identification from solicitors.

As a criminologist, can you come up with any new ideas that the Security Industry Association failed to cover?

KEY TERMS

economic crimes
fence
street crimes
burglary
skilled thieves
flash houses
smuggler
poacher
occasional criminal
thief taker
situational inducement
professional criminal
professional theft
associational fence
neighborhood hustler
amateur receiver

larceny
constructive possession
petit (petty) larceny
grand larceny
shoplifting
boosters
heels
snitches
target removal strategy
target hardening strategy
electronic article surveillance (EAS)
  system
source tagging
situational measures
private justice system
naive check forgers

closure
systematic forgers
carjacking
false pretenses
fraud
confidence games
mark
pigeon drop
embezzlement
burglary
good burglar
arson
arson for profit
arson fraud
flashover

NOTES

1. Andrew McCall, *The Medieval Underworld* (London: Hamish Hamilton, 1979), p. 86.

2. McCall, *The Medieval Underworld*, p. 104.

3. J. J. Tobias, *Crime and Police in England, 1700–1900* (London: Gill and Macmillan, 1979).

4. Tobias, *Crime and Police in England,* p. 9.

5. Marilyn Walsh, *The Fence* (Westport, Conn.: Greenwood Press, 1977), pp. 18–25.

6. John Hepburn, "Occasional Criminals," in *Major Forms of Crime,* ed. Robert Meier (Beverly Hills: Sage, 1984), pp. 73–94.

7. James Inciardi, "Professional Crime," in *Major Forms of Crime,* ed. Robert Meier (Beverly Hills: Sage, 1984), p. 223.

8. Harry King and William Chambliss, *Box Man: A Professional Thief's Journal* (New York: Harper & Row, 1972), p. 24.

9. Edwin Sutherland, "White-Collar Criminality," *American Sociological Review* 5 (1940): 2–10.

10. Gilbert Geis, "Avocational Crime," in *Handbook of Criminology,* ed. D. Glazer (Chicago: Rand McNally, 1974), p. 284.

11. Edwin Sutherland and Chic Conwell, *The Professional Thief* (Chicago: University of Chicago Press, 1937).

12. Sutherland and Conwell, *The Professional Thief,* pp. 197–98.

13. Sutherland and Conwell, *The Professional Thief,* p. 212.

14. See, for example, Edwin Lemert, "The Behavior of the Systematic Check Forger," *Social Problems* 6 (1958): 141–48.

15. Cited in Walsh, *The Fence,* p. 1.

16. Carl Klockars, *The Professional Fence* (New York: Free Press, 1976); Darrell Steffensmeier, *The Fence: In the Shadow of Two Worlds* (Totowa, N.J.: Rowman and Littlefield, 1986); Walsh, *The Fence,* pp. 25–28.

17. Walsh, *The Fence,* p. 34.

18. Paul Cromwell, James Olson, and D'Aunn Avary, "Who Buys Stolen Property? A New Look at Criminal Receiving," *Journal of Crime and Justice* 16 (1993): 75–95.

19. This section depends heavily on a classic book: Wayne La Fave and Austin Scott, *Handbook on Criminal Law* (St. Paul: West Publishing, 1972).

20. La Fave and Scott, *Handbook on Criminal Law,* p. 622.

21. FBI, *Crime in the United States, 1997* (Washington, D.C.: U.S. Government Printing Office, 1998), p. 47.

22. Margaret Loftus, "Gone: One TV," *U.S. News & World Report,* 14 July 1997, p. 61.

23. Timothy W. Maier, "Uncle Sam Gets Rolled," *Insight on the News,* 10 March 1997, p. 13.

24. Jill Jordan Siedfer, "To Catch a Thief, Try This: Peddling High-Tech Solutions to Shoplifting," *U.S. News & World Report,* 23 September 1996, p. 71.

25. Mary Owen Cameron, *The Booster and the Snitch* (New York: Free Press, 1964).

26. Cameron, *The Booster and the Snitch,* p. 57.

27. Lawrence Cohen and Rodney Stark, "Discriminatory Labeling and the Five-Finger Discount: An Empirical Analysis of Differential Shoplifting Dispositions," *Journal of Research on Crime and Delinquency* 11 (1974): 25–35.

28. Lloyd Klemke, "Does Apprehension for Shoplifting Amplify or Terminate Shoplifting Activity?" *Law and Society Review* 12 (1978): 390–403.

29. Erhard Blankenburg, "The Selectivity of Legal Sanctions: An Empirical Investigation of Shoplifting," *Law and Society Review* 11 (1976): 109–29.

30. Michael Hindelang, "Decisions of Shoplifting Victims to Invoke the Criminal Justice Process," *Social Problems* 21 (1974): 580–95.

31. George Keckeisen, *Retail Security Versus the Shoplifter* (Springfield, Ill.: Charles Thomas, 1993), pp. 31–32.

32. Siedfer, "To Catch a Thief, Try This."

33. Melissa Davis, Richard Lundman, and Ramiro Martinez, "Private Corporate Justice: Store Police, Shoplifters, and Civil Recovery," *Social Problems* 38 (1991): 395–408.

34. Davis, Lundman, and Martinez, "Private Corporate Justice," pp. 405–406.

35. Edwin Lemert, "An Isolation and Closure Theory of Naive Check Forgery," *Journal of Criminal Law, Criminology and Police Science* 44 (1953): 297–98.

36. Lemert, "An Isolation and Closure Theory of Naive Check Forgery."

37. La Fave and Scott, *Handbook on Criminal Law,* p. 672.

38. Peter Wayner, "Bogus Web Sites Troll for Credit Card Numbers," *New York Times,* 12 February 1997, p. A18.

39. Charles McCaghy, Peggy Giordano, and Trudy Knicely Henson, "Auto Theft," *Criminology* 15 (1977): 367–81.

40. Donald Gibbons, *Society, Crime and Criminal Careers* (Englewood Cliffs, N.J.: Prentice-Hall, 1977), p. 310.

41. Kim Hazelbaker, "Insurance Industry Analyses and the Prevention of Motor Vehicle Theft," in *Business and Crime Prevention,* ed. Marcus Felson and Ronald Clarke (Monsey, N.Y.: Criminal Justice Press, 1997), pp. 283–93.

42. Hazelbaker, "Insurance Industry Analyses and the Prevention of Motor Vehicle Theft," p. 287.

43. Michael Rand, *Carjacking* (Washington, D.C.: Bureau of Justice Statistics, 1994), p. 1.

44. Ronald Clarke and Patricia Harris, "Auto Theft and Its Prevention," in *Crime and Justice, An Annual Review,* ed. N. Morris and M. Tonry (Chicago: Chicago University Press, 1992).

45. Ian Ayres and Steven D. Levitt, "Measuring Positive Externalities from Unobservable Victim Precaution: An Empirical Analysis of Lojack," *Quarterly Journal of Economics* 113 (1998): 43–78.

46. Hazelbaker, "Insurance Industry Analyses and the Prevention of Motor Vehicle Theft," p. 289.

47. La Fave and Scott, *Handbook on Criminal Law,* p. 655.

48. 30 Geo. III, C.24 (1975).

49. Benjamin Weiser, "4-Year Sentence for Mastermind of Scheme to Cheat on Graduate School Tests," *New York Times,* 3 October 1998, p. 8.

50. As described in Charles McCaghy, *Deviant Behavior* (New York: Macmillan, 1976), pp. 230–31.

51. Susan Gembrowski and Tim Dahlberg, "Over 100 Here Indicted After Telemarketing Fraud Probe Around the U.S.," *San Diego Daily Transcript Online,* 8 December 1995. http://www.sddt.com/files/library/95headlines/DN95_12_08/DN95_12_08_02.html

52. Jerome Hall, *Theft, Law and Society* (Indianapolis: Bobbs-Merrill, 1952), p. 36.

53. La Fave and Scott, *Handbook on Criminal Law,* p. 644.

54. La Fave and Scott, *Handbook on Criminal Law,* p. 649.

55. FBI, *Crime in the United States, 1997,* p. 222.

56. La Fave and Scott, *Handbook on Criminal Law,* p. 708.

57. E. Blackstone, *Commentaries on the Laws of England* (London: 1769), p. 224.

58. Frank Hoheimer, *The Home Invaders: Confessions of a Cat Burglar* (Chicago: Chicago Review, 1975).

59. Richard Wright, Robert Logie, and Scott Decker, "Criminal Expertise and Offender Decision Making: An Experimental Study of the Target Selection Process in Residential Burglary," *Journal of Research in Crime and Delinquency* 32 (1995): 39–53.

60. Richard Wright and Scott Decker, *Burglars on the Job: Streetlife and Residential Break-Ins* (Boston, Mass.: Northeastern University Press, 1994).

61. Simon Hakim and Yochanan Shachmurove, "Spatial and Temporal Patterns of Commercial Burglaries," *The American Journal of Economics and Sociology* 55 (1996): 443–457.

62. See, generally, Neal Shover, "Structures and Careers in Burglary," *Journal of Criminal Law, Criminology and Police Science* 63 (1972): 540–49.

63. Paul Cromwell, James Olson, and D'Aunn Wester Avary, *Breaking and Entering: An Ethnographic Analysis of Burglary* (Newbury Park, Calif.: Sage, 1991), pp. 48–51.

64. See, M. Taylor and C. Nee, "The Role of Cues in Simulated Residential Burglary: A Preliminary Investigation," *British Journal of Criminology* 28 (1988): 398–401; Julia MacDonald and Robert Gifford, "Territorial Cues and Defensible Space Theory: The Burglar's Point of View," *Journal of Environmental Psychology* 9 (1989): 193–205.

65. Roger Litton, "Crime Prevention and the Insurance Industry," in *Business and Crime Prevention,* ed. Marcus Felson and Ronald Clarke (Monsey, N.Y.: Criminal Justice Press, 1997), p. 162.

66. Graham Farrell, Coretta Phillips, and Ken Pease, "Like Taking Candy, Why Does Repeat Victimization Occur?" *British Journal of Criminology* 35 (1995): 384–399 at 391.

67. FBI, *Crime in the United States, 1997,* p. 238.

68. Nancy Webb, George Sakheim, Luz Towns-Miranda, and Charles Wagner, "Collaborative Treatment of Juvenile Firestarters: Assessment and Outreach," *American Journal of Orthopsychiatry* 60 (1990): 305–310.

69. Vernon Quinsey, Terry Chaplin, and Douglas Unfold, "Arsonists and Sexual Arousal to Fire Setting: Correlations Unsupported," *Journal of Behavior Therapy and Experimental Psychiatry* 20 (1989): 203–209.

70. Leigh Edward Somers, *Economic Crimes* (New York: Clark Boardman, 1984), pp. 158–68.

71. Michael Rogers, "The Fire Next Time," *Newsweek,* 26 November 1990, p. 63.

CHAPTER 13

White-Collar and Organized Crime

INTRODUCTION

On December 11, 1998, national newspapers reported that Darlene Gillespie had been convicted of securities fraud. Gillespie had been one of the original Mouseketeers in Walt Disney's *Mickey Mouse Club* in the 1950s and 1960s. Now 57, the former child star was charged with securities fraud, conspiracy, perjury, and obstruction of justice stemming from a scheme hatched by Gillespie and her longtime fiance, Jerry Fraschilla, to buy stock in a high-tech motor-making company called Unique Mobility using bad checks and a made-up identity. They had hoped that run-ups in the stock price would let them profit before their brokers got wise to the deal. The government claimed that Fraschilla and Gillespie bought stock with defaced checks they knew would eventually bounce and conspired to create a fictitious person to buy shares as well.[1]

A complex fraudulent scheme such as the one Gillespie and Fraschilla were charged with takes an enormous amount of planning. Such crimes involve efforts to bend the rules of enterprise and commerce in order to make a profit or gain an illegal advantage over competitors. In this chapter we divide these crimes of illicit **entrepreneurship** into two distinct categories: **white-collar crime** and **organized crime.** The former involves illegal activities of people and institutions whose acknowledged purpose is profit through *legitimate* business transactions. The second category, organized crime, involves illegal activities of people and organizations whose acknowledged purpose is profit through *illegitimate* business enterprise. Organized crime and white-collar crime are linked together here because, as criminologist Dwight Smith argues, **enterprise,** not crime, is the governing characteristic of both phenomena:

> White-collar crime is not simply a dysfunctional aberration. Organized crime is not something ominously alien to the American economic system. Both are made criminal by laws declaring that certain ways of doing business, or certain products of business, are illegal. In other words, criminality is not an inherent characteristic either of certain persons or of certain business activities but rather, an externally imposed evaluation of alternative modes of behavior and action.[2]

According to Smith, business enterprise can be viewed as flowing through a spectrum of acts ranging from the most "saintly" to the most "sinful."[3] Although "sinful" organizational practices may be desirable to many consumers (such as the sale of narcotics) or an efficient way of doing business (such as the dumping of hazardous wastes), society has regulated or outlawed these behaviors. Organized crime and business crimes are the results of a process by which "political, value-based constraints are based on economic activity."[4]

White-collar and organized crime share some striking similarities. Mark Haller has coined the phrase *illegal enterprise crimes* to signify the sale of illegal goods and services to customers who know they are illegal. Haller's analysis also shows the overlap between criminal and business enterprise. For example, he

Darlene Gillespie as she appeared on the Mickey Mouse Club.

compares the Mafia crime family to a chamber of commerce: it is an association of businesspeople who join to further their business careers. Joining a crime syndicate allows one to cultivate contacts and be in a position to take advantage of good deals offered by more experienced players. The criminal group settles disputes between members, who, after all, cannot take their problems to court.[5]

Both of these organizational crimes taint and corrupt the free market system; they involve all phases of illegal entrepreneurial activity. Organized crime involves individuals or groups whose marketing techniques (threat, extortion, smuggling) and product lines (drugs, sex, gambling, loan-sharking) have been outlawed. White-collar crimes include the use of illegal business practices (embezzlement, price-fixing, bribery, and so on) to merchandise what are ordinarily legitimate commercial products.

Surprisingly to some, both forms of crime can involve violence. Although the use of force and coercion by organized crime members has been popularized in the media and therefore comes as no shock, that white-collar crimes may inflict pain and suffering seems more astonishing. Yet experts claim that over 200,000 occupational deaths occur each year and that "corporate violence" annually kills and injures more people than all street crimes combined.[6]

It is also possible to link organized and white-collar crime because some criminal enterprises involve both forms of activity. Organized criminals may seek legitimate enterprises to launder money, diversify their source of income, increase their power and influence, and gain and enhance respectability.[7] Otherwise legitimate businesspeople may turn to organized criminals to help them with economic problems (such as breaking up a strike or dumping hazardous waste products), stifle or threaten competition, and increase their influence. The distinction between organized crime and white-collar criminals may often become blurred.[8]

Some forms of white-collar crime may be more like organized crime than others.[9] Whereas some corporate executives cheat to improve their company's position in the business world, others are motivated purely for personal gain. It is this latter group, people who engage in ongoing criminal conspiracies for their own profit, that most resembles organized crime.[10]

WHITE-COLLAR CRIME

In the late 1930s the distinguished criminologist Edwin Sutherland first used the phrase *white-collar crime* to describe the criminal activities of the rich and powerful. He defined white-collar crime as "a crime committed by a person of respectability and high social status in the course of his occupation."[11] As Sutherland saw

it, white-collar crime involved conspiracies by members of the wealthy classes to use their position in commerce and industry for personal gain without regard to the law. Often these actions were handled by civil courts because injured parties were more concerned with recovering their losses than seeing the offenders punished criminally. Consequently, Sutherland believed that the great majority of white-collar criminals did not become the subject of criminological study. Yet the cost of white-collar crime is probably several times greater than all the crimes that are customarily regarded as the "crime problem." And, in contrast to street crimes, white-collar offenses breed distrust in economic and social institutions, lowering public morale and undermining faith in business and government.[12]

Redefining White-Collar Crime

Although Sutherland's work is considered a milestone in criminological history, his focus was on corporate criminality, including the crimes of the rich and powerful. Modern criminologists have broadened their definition of white-collar crime so that it includes a wide variety of situations.[13] Almost 30 years ago Herbert Edelhertz provided a widely cited reformulation of white-collar crime, describing it as "an illegal act or series of illegal acts committed by nonphysical means and by concealment or guile to obtain money or property or to avoid the payment or loss of money or property or to obtain business or personal advantage."[14] This definition is so broad that it encompasses almost any type of nonviolent property crime, even those with little connection to business enterprise.[15] In contrast, a more recent symposium of experts on white-collar crime formulated the following definition:

> White-collar crime consists of the illegal or unethical acts that violate fiduciary responsibility or public trust, committed by an individual or organization, usually during the course of legitimate occupational activity by persons of high or respectable social status for personal or organizational gain.[16]

While also expanding Sutherland's original concepts, this definition recognizes his focus on crimes of the upper class by limiting white-collar crimes to people with "respectable social status."

Today's definition of white-collar crime typically falls within these extremes; it usually includes individuals who use the marketplace for their criminal activity. Among their numbers are both middle-income Americans and corporate titans.[17] As criminologist Gilbert Geis puts it, "White-collar crimes can be committed by persons in all social classes."[18] Included within recent views of white collar crime are such middle-class acts as income tax evasion, credit card fraud, and bankruptcy fraud. Other white-collar criminals use their positions of trust in business or government to commit crimes. Their activities might include pilfering, soliciting bribes or kickbacks, and embezzlement. Some white-collar criminals set up business for the sole purpose of victimizing the general public. They engage in land swindles (for example, representing swamps as choice building sites), securities theft, medical fraud, and so on.

In addition to acting as individuals, some white-collar criminals become involved in criminal conspiracies designed to improve the market share or profitability of their corporations. This type of white-collar crime, which includes antitrust violations, price-fixing, and false advertising, is known as *corporate crime.* Ronald Kramer and Raymond Michalowski have also identified the concept of *state–corporate crime:* illegal or socially injurious actions resulting from cooperation between governmental and corporate institutions.[19] Kramer and Michalowski charge that the explosion of the *Challenger* space shuttle on January 28, 1986, was the result of a state–corporate crime involving the cooperative and criminally negligent actions of the National Aeronautics and Space Administration and Morton Thiokol, Inc., the shuttle builder.

The White-Collar Crime Problem

It is difficult to estimate the extent and influence of white-collar crime on victims because all too often, those who suffer the consequences of white-collar crime are ignored by victimologists.[20] Some experts place its total monetary value in the hundreds of billions of dollars, far outstripping the expense of any other type of crime. For example, the loss due to employee theft from businesses alone amounts to $90 billion per year.[21] Beyond their monetary cost, white-collar crimes often damage property and kill people. Violations of safety standards, pollution of the environment, and industrial accidents due to negligence can be classified as corporate violence. It is possible that corporate crime annually results in 20 million serious injuries, including 110,000 people who become permanently disabled and 30,000 deaths.[22] White-collar crime also destroys confidence, saps the integrity of commercial life, and has the potential for devastating destruction. Think of the possible results if nuclear regulatory rules are flouted or if toxic wastes are dumped into a community's drinking water supply.[23]

International White-Collar Crime

White-collar crime is not a uniquely U.S. phenomenon. It occurs in other countries, as well, often in the form of corruption by government agents. In China corruption accounts for a high percentage of all cases of economic crime. Despite the fact that the penalty for corruption is death, most of the people involved in corruption and

bribery are state personnel, including some high-ranking officials.[24] In the late 1980s there were no more than 10,000 corruption cases each year; by 1996 there were six times as many. One reason may be the increase in government-sponsored businesses, which now number more than 500,000 and are growing exponentially.[25] China is not alone in experiencing organizational crimes. In Thailand crime and corruption are skyrocketing; top executives of the Bangkok Bank of Commerce are believed to have absconded with billions of depositors' money.[26] U.S. companies are also the targets of white-collar criminals. Agents have been inserted into U.S. companies abroad to steal trade secrets and confidential procedures, including intellectual property such as computer programs and technology. The cost is somewhere between a conservative $50 billion and an astounding $240 billion a year.[27]

Nikos Passas and David Nelken have studied offenses perpetrated against the European Community (EC), an organization set up to bring regularity to the economic activities of its member states, which include England, France, Germany, and most other Western European nations.[28] Passas and Nelken group the crimes into four categories:[29]

1. *Corporate crime,* whereby legitimate companies or organizations, during their usual business, occasionally cheat the EC. A strongly competitive environment may indirectly foster corporate irregularities. This environment may also be created when the illegal activities of competitors create pressure on those who operate legally to consider resorting to similar illegalities.

2. *Government crime* includes illegal acts committed by government officials or with their knowledge and support, as well as those that cover up other persons' crimes. This type falls between corporate crime and occupational crime: it is perpetrated not for one's (direct) personal benefit or monetary gain, but for one's government and political party, the country, the national interest, or the like.

3. *Occupational crime* refers to people who come across an opportunity to make extra money by bending or breaking the rules. They may occasionally commit fraud, but their activities are mainly legal. Conditions under which they might be more likely to engage in illegal activities include financial straits or other business-related problems, which they try to solve by deviating from the rules.

4. *Organized/professional crime* involves people or groups of people whose primary source of income is illegal. They set out to commit fraud; they systematically look for possibilities of making money and profit illicitly. Because EC legislation provides such opportunities and loopholes, and control systems are not uniform and efficient throughout the

EC, there is no reason why criminal enterprises would not enter this market.

Crimes within these categories amount to billions in losses each year. For example, agricultural fraud, which involves tax evasion, deceitful claims, phantom operations, and false or forged documentation, may amount to $8 billion per year.[30]

COMPONENTS OF WHITE-COLLAR CRIME

White-collar crimes today represent a range of behaviors involving individuals acting alone and within the context of a business structure. The victims of white-collar crime can be the general public, the organization that employs the offender, or a competing organization. Numerous attempts have been made to create subcategories or typologies of white-collar criminality.[31] This text adapts a typology created by criminologist Mark Moore to organize the analysis of white-collar crime.[32] Moore's typology contains seven elements, ranging from an individual using a business enterprise to commit theft-related crimes, to an individual using his or her place within a business enterprise for illegal gain, to business enterprises collectively engaging in illegitimate activity. Because no single typology may sufficiently encompass the complex array of acts that the term usually denotes, Moore's typology has been expanded to include newly emerging high-tech crimes such as Internet fraud.[33]

Stings and Swindles

The first category of white-collar crime involves stealing through deception by individuals who have no continuing institutional or business position and whose entire purpose is to bilk people out of their money. Offenses in this category range from fraud involving the door-to-door sale of faulty merchandise to the passing of millions of dollars in counterfeit stock certificates to an established brokerage firm. If caught, white-collar swindlers are usually charged with common-law crimes such as embezzlement or fraud.

> CONNECTIONS
>
> Chapter 12 discussed the crime of fraud in the context of individual-level crimes that involve con games and the like. Although similar, swindles here involve greater organization and are conducted over longer periods than the con games discussed previously.

Swindles can run into millions of dollars. One of the largest to date involved the Equity Funding Corporation of America, whose officers bilked the public out of an estimated $2 billion in 1973. The directors of this firm, a life insurance company, claimed to have 90,000 policyholders. However, more than 60,000 of them existed as fictitious entries in the company's computer banks. Equity sold ownership and management of these bogus policies to reinsurance companies, and corporate officers pocketed the profit.[34]

The collapse of the Bank of Credit and Commerce International (BCCI) was another swindle that cost depositors billions of dollars. BCCI was the world's seventh largest private bank, with assets of about $23 billion. Investigators believe that bank officials made billions in loans to confederates who had no intention of repaying them; BCCI officers also used false accounting methods to defraud depositors. Its officers helped clients, such as Colombian drug cartel leaders and dictators Saddam Hussein and Ferdinand Marcos, launder money, finance terrorist organizations, and smuggle illegal arms. BCCI officers aided drug deals and helped launder drug money so that it could be shifted to legitimate banks. U.S. Drug Enforcement Administration officials were able to compile a list of 379 cases in which BCCI laundered money for narcotics traffickers.[35] After the bank was shut, hundreds of millions of dollars were spent to pay auditors to liquidate the bank's holdings. For example, English liquidators alone were paid $360 million in fees between 1991 and 1994.[36]

Despite the notoriety of the Equity Funding and BCCI cases, investors continue to bite at bogus investment schemes promising quick riches.

Religious Swindles In 1998, 2,100 devout Christians gave Jonathan Strawder and his Sovereign Ministries International between $11 million and $14 million after he promised them not only that they would get huge returns on their investments, but also that with the profits, churches would be built in Kenya and Poland, poor students would have their education paid for, and other Christian ministries would get donations. When Strawder was arrested in Florida, legal authorities found that his fund-raising was a swindle and that he used the money for fancy cars, a yacht, and two apartment buildings in Chicago; most of the money has not yet been recovered.[37]

One of the most cold-blooded swindles is an investment scam that uses religious affiliations to steal from trusting investors. In the most well-known 1989 case, TV evangelist Jim Bakker was convicted of defrauding followers of $3.7 million when he oversold lodging guarantees, called "lifetime partnerships," at his Heritage USA religious retreat while diverting money for his own personal use.[38] Bakker was sentenced to 45 years in prison, a harsh punishment that was later reduced on appeal (Bakker was released from prison in 1996).

The Bakker case is not unique. The North American Securities Administrators Association estimates

Chiseling

Chiseling, the second category of white-collar crime, involves regularly cheating an organization, its consumers, or both. Chiselers may be individuals looking to make quick profits in their own businesses or employees of large organizations who decide to cheat on obligations to clients by doing something contrary to either the law or company policy. Chiseling can involve charging for bogus auto repairs, cheating customers on home repairs, *short-weighting* (intentionally tampering with the accuracy of scales used to weigh products) in supermarkets or dairies, or fraudulently selling securities at inflated prices. In one scheme, some New York City cab drivers routinely tapped the dashboards of their cabs with pens loaded with powerful magnets in order to "zap" their meters and jack up the fares.[41] Chiseling may even involve illegal use of information about company policies that have not been disclosed to the public. The secret information can be sold to speculators or used to make money in the stock market. Use of the information violates the obligation to keep company policy secret.

Corporations engage in large-scale chiseling when they misrepresent products or alter their content. For example, the Beech-Nut Nutrition Corporation paid a $2 million fine for illegally selling a product labeled "apple juice" that was nothing more than sweetened water. Despite enforcement efforts, it is estimated that 10 percent of all fruit juices sold in the United States use illegal additives.[42]

In the best-known case involving a religious swindle, TV evangelist Jim Bakker was convicted of defrauding followers of $3.7 million when he oversold lodging guarantees, called "lifetime partnerships," at his Heritage USA religious retreat.

that swindlers using fake religious identities bilk thousands of people out of $100 million per year.[39] Swindlers take in worshippers of all persuasions: Jews, Baptists, Lutherans, Catholics, Mormons, and Greek Orthodox have all fallen prey to religious swindles. How do religious swindlers operate? Many join close-knit churches and establish a position of trust that enables them to operate without the normal investor skepticism. Some use religious television and radio shows to sell their products. Others place verses from the scriptures on their promotional literature to comfort hesitant investors. For example, between 1993 and 1998, Daniel H. Fletcher set up at least eight business ventures to resell long-distance telephone services, acting as a middleman between consumers and big telephone companies. Using such names as the Church Discount Group, Fletcher is alleged to have cheated hundreds of thousands of consumers, billing customers for at least $20 million while leaving well-established telecommunications companies with unpaid bills of at least $3.8 million. Before he went into hiding, Fletcher's Christian Church Network owed long-distance carrier Sprint millions for services it provided to handle billing the long-distance calls.[40]

Professional Chiseling It is not uncommon for professionals to use their positions to chisel clients. Pharmacists have been known to alter prescriptions or substitute low-cost generic drugs for more expensive name brands. One study found that pharmacists who were business-oriented — and therefore stressed merchandising, inventory turnover, and the pursuit of profit at the expense of professional ethics — were the ones most inclined to chisel customers.[43]

The legal profession has also come under fire because of the unscrupulous behavior of some of its members. In the 1970s the Watergate hearings, which revealed the unethical behavior of high-ranking government attorneys, prompted the American Bar Association to require that all law students take a course in legal ethics. This action is needed because lawyers chisel clients out of millions of dollars each year in such schemes as forging signatures on clients' compensation checks and tapping escrow accounts and other funds for personal investments; one New York lawyer went so far as to slip the name of an imaginary heiress into a client's will and then impersonate the heiress to collect the inheritance.[44] Special funds have been set up by state governments and bar associations to reimburse chiseled clients.[45]

Securities Fraud A great deal of chiseling takes place on the commodity and stock markets, where individuals engage in deceptive practices that are prohibited by federal law (see Table 13.1). Some brokers will use their positions to cheat individual clients, for example by **churning** the client's account by repeated, excessive, and unnecessary buying and selling of stock.[46] Other broker fraud includes *front running,* in which brokers place personal orders ahead of a large customer's order to profit from the market effects of the trade; and *bucketing,* which is skimming customer trading profits by falsifying trade information.[47] Some stock frauds involve conspiracies by financial organizations to cheat their clients. In one 1998 case, employees of Monroe Parker Securities Inc., a. Westchester County, New York, securities firm, were accused of using high-pressure telephone sales tactics to defraud 8,000 investors nationwide of $100 million. In the scheme, brokers at Monroe Parker would persuade a client to open an account by offering blue-chip stocks, like IBM, as the bait. Once a person agreed to open an account, the broker would push stocks in companies in which Monroe Parker owned a majority of shares. The traders pressured clients into buying the "house stocks" at artificially inflated prices. If an investor insisted on selling the house stock, the broker would turn the account over to a colleague, who would start the hard sell all over again.[48]

Table 13.1 Federal Securities Laws

The federal securities laws that control trading in public companies can be found in a number of different statutes, but the two primary sources are the Securities Act of 1933 and the Securities Exchange Act of 1934. These acts prohibit the use of manipulative or deceptive devices, such as mail and wire fraud, making false statements in order to increase market share, conspiracy, and similar acts of unfair market practices. The federal watchdog agency, the Securities and Exchange Commission (SEC), has within its code Rule 10b-5, which articulates general antifraud provisions for securities trading:

It shall be unlawful for any person directly or indirectly, by the use of any means or instrumentality of interstate commerce, or of the mails or of any facility of any national securities exchange,

(a) To employ any device, scheme, or artifice to defraud,

(b) To make any untrue statement of a material fact or to omit to state a material fact necessary in order to make the statements made, in light of the circumstances under which they were made, not misleading, or

(c) To engage in any act, practice, or course of business which operates or would operate as a fraud or deceit upon any person, in connection with the purchase or sale of any security.

Source: Securities Act of 1933, 15 U.S.C. Sec. 77a to 77aa (1982); Securities Exchange Act of 1934, 15 U.S.C. Sec. 78a to 78kk (1982); 17 C.F.R. 240.10b-5 (1987).

Insider Trading Securities chiseling can also involve using one's position of trust to profit from inside business information, referred to as **insider trading.** The information can then be used to buy and sell securities, giving the trader an unfair advantage over the general public, which lacks this inside information.

Insider trading violations can occur in a variety of situations. As originally conceived, it was illegal for corporate employees with direct knowledge of market-sensitive information to use that information for their own benefit—for example, by buying stock in a company that they learn will be taken over by the larger concern for which they work. In recent years, the definition of insider trading has been expanded by federal courts to include employees of financial institutions, such as law or banking firms, who misappropriate confidential information on pending corporate actions to purchase stock or give the information to a third party so that party may buy shares in the company. Courts have ruled that such actions are deceptive and violate security trading codes. In one celebrated 1986 case, R. Foster Winans, the writer of the *Wall Street Journal's* influential "Heard on the Street" column, was convicted on misappropriation of information charges after he wrote favorably about stocks purchased previously by a coconspirator and then sold for profits in which the writer shared. The U.S. Supreme Court upheld the conviction of Winans and his coconspirators on the grounds that their actions fraudulently deprived Winans's employer (the *Wall Street Journal*) of its "property," the information contained in his column; their actions also amounted to a "scheme to defraud" under the Securities and Exchange Act.[49] Winans's case signifies that insider trading can occur even if the offender neither is an employee nor has a fiduciary interest (such as a company's outside accountants would have) in a company whose stock is traded; the Court also found that a "victim" need not lose tangible property for the crime to take place.

Interpretations of what constitutes insider trading vary widely. To many, the "hot tip" is the bread and butter of stock market speculators, and the point when a tip becomes a criminal act is often fuzzy. In the most infamous insider trading cases of the 1980s, billionaires Ivan Boesky and Michael Milken, two of Wall Street's most prominent **arbitrage** experts, were convicted and sentenced to prison. Arbitragers speculate on the stock of companies that are rumored to be targets for takeover by other firms and hope to profit on the difference between current stock prices and the price the acquiring company is willing to pay. Boesky used inside information on such deals as the merger negotiations between International Telephone and Telegraph and Sperry Corporation, Coastal Corporation's takeover of American Natural Resources, and the leveraged buyout of McGraw Edison. Possessing this information allowed Boesky to profit in the millions; he received a three-year prison sentence.

Milken was indicted (with the help of information provided by Ivan Boesky) on 98 counts of security fraud, pleaded guilty to six relatively minor counts, and received a harsh 10-year prison sentence and a billion-dollar fine; Milken's sentence was later reduced because of his cooperation with authorities in other cases.[50]

Individual Exploitation of Institutional Position

Another type of white-collar crime involves individuals' exploiting their power or position in organizations to take advantage of other individuals who have an interest in how that power is used. For example, a fire inspector who demands that the owner of a restaurant pay him to be granted an operating license is abusing his institutional position. In most cases, this type of offense occurs when the victim has a clear right to expect a service and the offender threatens to withhold the service unless an additional payment or bribe is forthcoming.

Exploitation in Government   Throughout U.S. history, various political and governmental figures have been accused of using their positions to profit from bribes and kickbacks.[51] As early as the 1830s, New York's political leaders used their positions to control and profit from the city's police force. In the early nineteenth century, New York City's police chief, George Matsell, was the subject of numerous charges of bribe taking and profiteering. Although his wrongdoing was never proven in court, it was revealed five years after he retired in 1851 that he had "saved" enough on his modest salary to build a 20-room mansion on a 3,000-acre estate. During the Civil War, corruption increased proportionately with the amount of money being spent on the war effort. After the war, the nation's largest cities were controlled by political machines that used their offices to buy and sell political favors. The most notorious of the corrupt politicians was William Marcy "Boss" Tweed, who ruled New York City's Democratic Party (Tammany Hall) from 1857 to 1871.[52] Time and anticorruption campaigns eventually caught up with Tweed, and he died in jail.[53]

The use of political office for economic gain has not subsided. On the local and state levels, scandals commonly emerge in which liquor license board members, food inspectors, and fire inspectors are named as exploiters. A striking example of exploitation made national headlines when on October 6, 1998, San Francisco 49ers co-owner Eddie DeBartolo, Jr., pleaded guilty to concealing an extortion plot by the former governor of Louisiana, Edwin Edwards. According to the authorities, Edwards demanded payments of $400,000 in order to help DeBartolo obtain a license for a riverboat gambling casino. During the hearing, the FBI presented wiretap and other evidence that Edwards and his son, Stephen, had repeatedly sought payments from DeBartolo to ensure that the state gaming board, over

which they had control, would award the license. Edwards had supposedly extracted the money by stating that he must have payment "or there could be problems with the licensing." DeBartolo was sentenced to two years' probation and ordered to pay a $250,000 fine, forfeit the $400,000 he paid to Edwards, and provide up to $350,000 in restitution that can be claimed by anyone injured by the crime.[54] Here a former politician is alleged to have used his still-considerable political clout to demand payment from a businessman desiring to engage in a legitimate business enterprise.

Exploitation in Industry   Exploitation can also occur in private industry. Purchasing agents in large companies often demand a piece of the action for awarding contracts to suppliers and distributors. In one such case, a J.C. Penney employee received $1.4 million from a contractor who eventually did $23 million of business with the company.[55] In another case, a purchasing agent for the American Chiclets division of Warner-Lambert (maker of Dentyne, Chiclets, Trident, and Dynamints) received a $300,000 kickback from the makers of the wire racks on which the gum products are displayed in supermarkets. In 1994 managing agents in some of New York City's most luxurious buildings were convicted on charges that they routinely extorted millions of dollars from maintenance contractors and building suppliers. The contractors recouped the bribes by adding the costs to bills paid by the buildings' owners. More than 65 managing agents pleaded guilty and paid millions in fines. As a result of the investigation, a clause was placed into management contracts requiring that any contractor involved in bribery would forfeit the entire value of the repair, not just the amount of the bribe. Did these fines deter further corruption? Perhaps not: in 1998, the Manhattan District Attorney's office announced an investigation into the practice of building managers to steer repair and maintenance work to particular contractors in exchange for kickbacks totaling millions of dollars.[56]

In some foreign countries, soliciting bribes to do business is a common, even an expected, practice. Not surprisingly, U.S. businesses have complained that stiff penalties for bribery give foreign competitors an edge over them. In European countries, such as Italy and France, giving bribes to secure contracts is perfectly legal; and in West Germany, corporate bribes are actually tax-deductible.[57] Some government officials solicit bribes to allow American firms to do business in their countries.[58]

Influence Peddling and Bribery

Sometimes individuals holding important institutional positions sell power, influence, and information to outsiders who have an interest in influencing or predicting the activities of the institution. Offenses within this category include government employees' taking of kickbacks from contractors in return for awarding them contracts they could not have won on merit or outsiders' bribing of government officials, such as those in the Securities and Exchange Commission, who might sell information about future government activities. Influence peddling may not be directed solely at personal enrichment; it can also involve securing a favored position for one's political party or interest group. Political leaders have been convicted of accepting bribes to rig elections and allow their party to control state politics.[59] One major difference distinguishes influence peddling from the previously discussed exploitation of an institutional position. Exploitation involves forcing victims to pay for services to which they have a clear right. In contrast, influence peddlers and bribe takers use their institutional positions to grant favors and sell information to which their coconspirators are not entitled. In sum, in crimes of institutional exploitation, the victim is the person forced to pay, whereas the victim of influence peddling is the organization compromised by its employees for their own interests.

Influence Peddling in Government   The most widely publicized incident of government bribery was the ABSCAM case. In 1981 FBI agents, working with convicted swindler Melvin Weinberg, posed as wealthy Arabs looking for favorable treatment from high-ranking politicians. The pseudo-Arabs said they wished to obtain U.S. citizenship and receive favorable treatment in business ventures. Several officeholders were indicted, including a U.S. senator from New Jersey, Harrison Williams.[60] Williams was convicted of accepting an interest in an Arab-backed mining venture in return for promising to use his influence to obtain government contracts. He also promised to use his influence to help the "Arab sheik" enter and stay in the United States. At Williams's trial, the prosecution played tapes showing Williams meeting with federal undercover agents, boasting of his influence in the government, and saying he could "with great pleasure talk to the president of the United States" about the business venture; a later tape showed the senator promising to seek immigration help for the bogus sheik and agreeing to take part in the mining operation.

The ABSCAM case is certainly not unique. Senior officials at the Pentagon were found to have received hundreds of thousands of dollars in bribes for ensuring the granting of contracts for military clothing to certain manufacturers. The corruption was so pervasive that the military found it difficult to locate sufficient replacement manufacturers who were not involved in the scandal. In another Pentagon scandal, senior officials were accused of accepting bribes from defense consultants and manufacturers in return for classified information, such as competitors' bids and designs, that would give the consultants and manufacturers an edge in securing government contracts. More than $1 billion worth of contracts were suspended. The scandal touched some of the largest defense contractors in the United States, including Raytheon, Litton Industries, and Lockheed.[61]

In the mid-1980s officials at the Department of Housing and Urban Development (HUD) were involved in a scheme to defraud the government of somewhere between $4 billion and $8 billion. Officials used their power to dispense huge grants to well-connected political figures. Several officials who left the department received huge consulting fees from former associates who still worked for the department. A number of officials were later convicted of taking bribes and defrauding the government, including one woman who siphoned off $5 million from the sale of repossessed homes, the largest individual theft of U.S. government funds in history. Her feat earned her the name "Robin HUD" after she claimed that she gave much of the money to charity; the judge gave her four years in prison.[62]

Federal officials are not the only ones to be accused of influence peddling. It has become all too common for legislators and other state officials to be forced to resign or even jailed for accepting bribes to use their influence. Two West Virginia governors have been jailed on bribery charges since 1960. The Louisiana state insurance commissioner was convicted in 1991 of money laundering, conspiracy, and fraud connected to the collapse of the Champion Insurance Company, which cost policyholders $185 million; the commissioner took $2 million in bribes in return for regulatory favors.[63] And foreign businessmen and officials have also been implicated in corruption. For example, in Italy, the former chairperson of the Montedison agricultural chemical firm admitted making illegal payments to political leaders to secure contracts.[64]

Corruption in the Criminal Justice System   In 1998 New Yorkers awoke to front-page headlines describing police involvement with a midtown brothel. More than 20 officers were alleged to have been patrons of prostitutes working at 335 West 39th Street and a nearby massage parlor; some officers were filmed demanding sex. In the days following the story, 21 officers and one sergeant were stripped of their guns and badges and placed on modified duty. Mayor Rudolph Giuliani described the participating officers as a small group who had invited new officers "who might be interested" to join from time to time. "It was never in any way precinctwide," he said.[65]

Agents of the criminal justice system have also gotten caught up in official corruption, a circumstance that is particularly disturbing because society expects a higher standard of moral integrity from people empowered to uphold the law and judge their fellow citizens. When federal prosecutors mounted Operation Greylord to expose corruption in the Cook County, Illinois, court system, they uncovered examples of judges selling favors to corrupt attorneys for up to $50,000 in under-the-table payments; one culprit received a 15-year prison sentence.

The credibility of the justice process is critically weakened when officials who hold power over other people's reputation and freedom engage in criminal behavior.

Police officers have been particularly vulnerable to charges of corruption. More than 20 years ago, New York Mayor John Lindsay appointed a commission under the direction of Judge Whitman Knapp to investigate allegations of police corruption. The Knapp Commission found that police corruption was pervasive and widespread, ranging from patrol officers' accepting small gratuities from local businesspeople to senior officers receiving payoffs in the thousands of dollars from gamblers and narcotics violators.[66] The commission found that construction firms paid police to ignore violations of city ordinances, such as double parking, obstruction of sidewalks, and noise pollution. Bar owners paid police to allow them to operate after hours or to give free reign to the prostitutes, drug pushers, and gamblers operating on their premises. Drug dealers allowed police to keep money and narcotics confiscated during raids in return for their freedom.

In 1993 New York City empowered the **Mollen Commission** to investigate corruption among city police. The commission found that a relatively small number (compared to the pervasive corruption found earlier by the Knapp Commission) of rogue cops were immersed in a pattern of violence, coercion, theft, and drug dealing. Testifying before the commission to gain a reduced sentence on a narcotics charge, one officer told of shaking down drug dealers, brutalizing innocent citizens, and intimidating fellow officers to force their silence. Protected by the "blue curtain"—the police officer code of secrecy—rogue cops were able to purchase luxury homes and cars with the profits from their illegal thefts, extortion, and drug sales.[67] Even the high visibility given the Mollen Commission has failed to completely eliminate corruption.

Despite the fact that crime is down in New York and the police are being given credit for the improvement, cases of corruption can stain the reputation of the department.

Controlling Police Corruption One approach to controlling corruption is to strengthen the internal administrative review process within police departments. Some departments have adopted an *accountability system* that holds supervisors at each level directly responsible for the illegal behavior of the officers under them; a commander can be forced to resign or be demoted if a member of his or her staff is found guilty of corruption. Outside review boards or special prosecutors have been formed to investigate reported incidents of corruption; outsiders, though, may face the problem of the "blue curtain," which is quickly raised when police officers feel their department is under scrutiny. Anticorruption training and education programs have been instituted for new recruits in the training academy. In 1996 the city

of Philadelphia agreed to implement a set of reforms to combat corruption in order to settle a lawsuit brought by civil rights organizations. Among the measures taken to reduce corruption were the following:

- All citizen complaints must be forwarded for investigation by the internal affairs division.
- Computer files contain all types of complaints and suits against individual officers, which can be easily accessed during investigations.
- Internal affairs is required to give a high priority to any police officer's claim that another officer is corrupt or has used excessive force.
- All incidents in which an officer used more than incidental force must be reported and recorded.
- Officers must be trained to treat citizens without racial bias. A deputy commissioner monitors charges of race discrimination.
- All policies and practices are reviewed to ensure they do not involve or have the potential for race bias.[68]

Although these efforts are important, it will be difficult to eradicate police corruption without changing the social context of policing. Police operations must be made more visible, and the public must be given freer access to police operations. It is also possible that some of the vice-related crimes the police now deal with might be decriminalized or referred to other agencies. Although decriminalization of vice cannot in itself end the problem, it could lower the pressure placed on individual police officers and help relieve their moral dilemmas, such as whether it is really wrong to take money from drug dealers or gamblers.

Influence Peddling in Business Politicians and government officials are not the only ones accused of bribery; business has had its share of scandals. The 1970s witnessed revelations that multinational corporations regularly made payoffs to foreign officials and businesspeople to secure business contracts. Gulf Oil executives admitted paying $4 million to the South Korean ruling party; Burroughs Corporation admitted paying $1.5 million to foreign officials; and Lockheed Aircraft admitted paying $202 million. McDonnell-Douglas Aircraft Corporation was indicted for paying $1 million in bribes to officials of Pakistani International Airlines to secure orders.[69]

In response to these revelations, Congress in 1977 passed the Foreign Corrupt Practices Act (FCPA), which makes it a criminal offense to bribe foreign officials or to make other questionable overseas payments. Violations of the FCPA draw strict penalties for both the defendant company and its officers.[70] Moreover, all fines imposed on corporate officers are paid by them, not absorbed by the company. For example, for violating the antibribery provisions of the FCPA, a domestic corporation can be fined up to $1 million. Company officers, employees, or stockholders who are convicted of bribery may have to serve a prison sentence of up to five years and pay a $10,000 fine. Congressional dissatisfaction with the harshness and ambiguity of the bill has caused numerous revisions to be proposed. Despite the penalties imposed by the FCPA, corporations that deal in foreign trade have continued to give bribes to secure favorable trade agreements.[71] In 1995, for example, several former executives of the Lockheed Aircraft Corporation pleaded guilty to bribery in the sale of transport aircraft to the Egyptian government.[72]

Embezzlement and Employee Fraud

The fourth type of white-collar crime involves individuals' use of their positions to embezzle company funds or appropriate company property for themselves. Here the company or organization that employs the criminal, rather than an outsider, is the victim of white-collar crime.

Blue-Collar Fraud   Employee theft can reach all levels of the organizational structure. Blue-collar employees have been involved in systematic theft of company property, commonly called **pilferage.** The techniques of employee theft are quite varied:

- Piece workers zip up completed garments into their clothing and take them home.
- Cashiers ring up lower prices on single-item purchases and pocket the difference. Some will work with an accomplice and ring up the lower prices as the accomplice goes through the line.
- Clerks do not tag sale merchandise, and then they sell it at its original cost, pocketing the difference.
- Receiving clerks obtain duplicate keys to storage facilities and then return after hours to steal.
- Truck drivers make fictitious purchases of fuel and repairs and then split the gains with truck stop owners. Truckers have been known to cooperate with the receiving staff of department stores to cheat employers. In one instance, truckers would keep 20 cases of goods out of every 100 delivered. The store receiving staff would sign a bill of lading for all 100, and the two groups split the profits after the stolen goods were sold to a fence.
- Some employees simply hide items in garbage pails or incinerators or under trash heaps until they can be retrieved later.[73]

About 35 percent of employees report involvement in pilferage.[74] Employee theft is most accurately explained by factors relevant to the work setting, such as job dissatisfaction and the workers' belief that they are being exploited by employers or supervisors; economic problems play a relatively small role in the decision to pilfer. So although employers attribute employee fraud to economic conditions and declining personal values,

workers themselves say they steal because of strain and conflict. It is difficult to determine the value of goods taken by employees, but it has been estimated that pilferage accounts for 30 to 75 percent of all shrinkage and amounts to losses of up to $10 billion annually.[75]

Management Fraud   Blue-collar workers are not the only employees who commit corporate theft. Management-level fraud is also quite common. Such acts include (1) converting company assets for personal benefit; (2) fraudulently receiving increases in compensation (such as raises or bonuses); (3) fraudulently increasing personal holdings of company stock; (4) retaining one's present position within the company by manipulating accounts; and (5) concealing unacceptable performance from stockholders.[76] There have been a number of well-publicized examples of management fraud. In one recent case, high-ranking employees of the Leslie Fay clothing company were implicated in a fraudulent scheme to overstate company profits. Its accounting reports overstated inventories while the cost of making garments was understated to enhance profits; profits and revenues were also inflated. The false entries resulted in millions being paid to executives because their bonuses were tied to company profits.[77]

Employee fraud seems widespread. A survey of 300 companies by the national accounting firm of KPMG Peat Marwick found that 75 percent reported having fallen prey to employee fraud during the past 12 months; the estimated total loss was $250 million.[78] The most significant cases of management fraud in the nation's history occurred in the savings and loan industry. The Criminological Enterprise feature titled "The Savings and Loan Cases" discusses this scandal.

Client Fraud

A sixth component of white-collar crime is theft by an economic client from an organization that advances credit to its clients or reimburses them for services rendered. These offenses are linked together because they involve cheating an organization (such as a government agency or insurance company) with many individual clients that the organization supports financially (like welfare clients), reimburses for services provided (like health care providers), covers losses of (like insurance policyholders), or extends credit to (like bank clients or taxpayers). Included in this category are insurance fraud, credit card fraud, fraud related to welfare and Medicare programs, and tax evasion. For example, some critics suggest that welfare recipients cheat the federal government out of billions each year.[79] As eligibility for public assistance becomes more limited, recipients are resorting to a number of schemes to maintain their status. Some women collect government checks while working on the side or living illegally with boyfriends or husbands. Some young mothers tell children to answer exam questions incorrectly to be classified as disabled and receive government assistance.[80]

Health Care Fraud Client fraud may be common even among upper-income people.[81] Some physicians have been caught cheating the federal government out of Medicare or Medicaid payments. Abusive practices include such techniques as "ping-ponging" (referring patients to other physicians in the same office), "gang visits" (billing for multiple services), and "steering" (directing patients to particular pharmacies). Doctors who abuse their Medicaid or Medicare patients in this way are liable to civil suits and even criminal penalties. For example, in 1997 the Baptist Medical Center in Kansas City, Missouri, agreed to pay the government $17.5 million to settle claims that it bribed doctors to send it Medicare patients for treatment; the doctors had received over a million dollars in kickbacks.[82]

Medical fraud schemes generally involve billing for services not actually rendered, billing in excessive amounts, setting up kickbacks, and providing false identification on reimbursement forms. Operation Backbone, a 1997 undercover operation in New York State, netted 12 chiropractors and 8 other professionals who were fraudulently overbilling insurance companies. One doctor saw a patient 11 times and billed for 150 office visits; another treated a patient once and sent in 90 claims. One of the chiropractors was secretly videotaped coaching a patient on how to fake injuries when examined by physicians evaluating his insurance claim.[83] In another case a psychiatrist was convicted of submitting false claims by billing an individual counseling session as a family session, which entitled him to higher fees.[84] Doctors involved in these schemes are liable to criminal prosecution under federal and state law.[85]

In addition to individual physicians, some large health care providers have been accused of routinely violating the law in order to obtain millions in illegal payments. In 1998 the federal government filed suit against two of the nation's largest hospital chains, Columbia/HCA Healthcare Corporation (320 hospitals) and Quorum Health Group (250 hospitals), alleging that they routinely overstated expenses in order to bilk Medicare. In its suit the government contended that the companies intentionally misrepresented costs to increase the reimbursement rate or receive payment for costs that were not eligible for reimbursement from governmental health programs. The government alleged that the companies often misreported expenses that were unrelated to patient care, including costs associated with marketing, physician recruitment, and even hospital televisions.[86] For example, one Columbia-owned hospital, Southwest Florida Regional Medical Center in Fort Myers, is alleged to have filed documents with the government in 1991, seeking repayment for a portion of the money it spent while taking care of patients. Southwest claimed $68,000 more in property

taxes than it had been assessed and had paid.[87] It has been estimated that $100 billion spent annually on federal health care is lost to fraudulent practices.[88] Despite the magnitude of this abuse, the state and federal governments have been reluctant to prosecute Medicaid fraud.[89]

In light of these and other health care scandals, the government has attempted to tighten control over the industry. New regulations restrict the opportunity for physicians to commit fraud. For example, in 1993 Congress passed what are known as the Stark Amendments,[90] which prohibit physicians from making a referral to a health care provider that accepts Medicare patients if that physician or a family member holds a financial interest. The Stark laws (named after their sponsor Congressman Pete Stark of California) would prohibit a surgeon from investing in an X-ray lab and then sending all her patients to that lab for X rays. Stricter control may be paying off. Federal efforts to curb fraud and abuse, such as the investigation of Columbia/HCA, have reportedly sent a chill through the hospital industry and are now encouraging greater compliance by health care providers of all types, including doctors, who fear prosecution for submitting false claims.[91] Not coincidentally, as fraud subsides, the growth in the cost of Medicare has been slowing, rising just 1.5 percent between 1997 and 1998—the smallest increase since the beginning of the program in 1965.

Bank Fraud Bank fraud can encompass such diverse schemes as check kiting (Figure 13.1), check forgery, false statements on loan applications, sale of stolen checks, bank credit card fraud, unauthorized use of

Figure 13.1 Check Kiting

Check kiting is a scheme whereby a client with accounts in two or more banks takes advantage of the time required for checks to clear in order to obtain unauthorized use of bank funds. For example, a person has $5,000 on account in a bank and cashes a check for $3,000 from an account in another bank in which he has no funds. The bank cashes the check because he already is a customer. He then closes his account before the check clears or writes checks on his account that total $5,000 and are cleared because he has funds in his account. In some instances the kiter expects a bank to cover a withdrawal before a check is presented to another bank for collection; she simply wants a short-term, interest-free loan. Others have no intention of ever covering the transaction but instead want to take cash out of the system after building accounts to artificially high amounts. Kiting can be a multimillion-dollar offense involving checks written and deposited in banks in two or more states or even in separate countries.

The Criminological Enterprise

The Savings and Loan Cases

For 10 or more years, the owners and managers of some of the nation's largest savings and loan (S&L) banks swindled investors, depositors, and the general public out of billions of dollars. It has been conservatively estimated that over the next 40 years, the cost of rectifying these savings and loan fraud cases could total $500 billion, a number almost too staggering to imagine. It is possible that 1,700 banks, about one-half of the industry, may eventually collapse. Government reports indicate that criminal activity has been a central factor in 70 to 80 percent of all these cases.

How could crimes of this magnitude have been committed? Kitty Calavita, Henry Pontell, and Robert Tillman have looked at the events that created the S&L crisis. At first, problems were created by the industry's efforts to remove federal regulations that had restricted its activities and way of doing business. In 1980, to help the industry recover from money-losing years, the federal government allowed the formerly conservative S&Ls to expand their business operations beyond residential housing loans. Savings banks could now get involved in high-risk commercial real estate lending and corporate or business loans. They

One notorious savings and loan case involved Susan and Jim McDougal, who were Bill Clinton's partners in the so-called "Whitewater" deal. In June 1996 the McDougals were convicted of fraud and conspiracy for dipping into funds at their Arkansas-based savings and loan to bankroll their risky business schemes.

were allowed to compete for deposits with commercial banks by offering high interest rates. The S&Ls made deals with brokerage firms to sell high-interest certificates of deposit, encouraging investors around the nation to pour billions of dollars into banks

they had never seen. Even more damaging, ownership rules were relaxed so that almost anyone could own or operate an S&L, yet the government insured all deposits. Even if crooked owners offered outlandish interest rates to attract deposits and then lent

---

automatic teller machines (ATMs), auto title fraud, and illegal transactions with offshore banks.[92] To be found guilty of bank fraud, one must knowingly execute or attempt to execute a scheme to fraudulently obtain money or property from a financial institution. For example, a car dealer would commit bank fraud by securing loans on titles to cars it no longer owned. A real estate owner would be guilty of bank fraud if he or she obtained a false appraisal on a piece of property with the intention of obtaining a bank loan in excess of the property's real worth. Penalties for bank fraud include a maximum fine of $1,000,000 and up to 30 years in prison.

Tax Evasion   Another important aspect of client fraud is tax evasion. Here the victim is the government that is cheated by one of its clients, the errant taxpayer to

whom it extended credit by allowing the taxpayer to delay paying taxes on money he or she already earned. Tax fraud is a particularly challenging area for criminological study because (1) so many U.S. citizens regularly underreport their income, and (2) it is often difficult to separate honest error from deliberate tax evasion. The basic law on tax evasion is contained in the U.S. Internal Revenue Code, section 7201, which states

> Any person who willfully attempts in any manner to evade or defeat any tax imposed by this title or the payment thereof shall, in addition to other penalties provided by law, be guilty of a felony and, upon conviction thereof, shall be fined not more than $100,000 or imprisoned not more than 5 years, or both, together with the costs of prosecution.

To prove tax fraud, the government must find that the taxpayer either underreported his or her income or them to shady businesspeople, the federal government guaranteed that depositors could not lose money. Why ask questions about whom you were giving your money to and what it was being used for if the government guaranteed the principal? Given this green light, the S&Ls made irresponsible and outright fraudulent loans. Losses began to mushroom. In the first six months of 1988, the industry lost an estimated $7.5 billion.

S&L violations fell into a number of categories. The first was making high-risk investments in violation of law and regulation, including risky loans to commercial real estate developers. Sometimes kickbacks were made to encourage the loans.

A second criminal activity was collective embezzlement (looting). This involved robbing one's own bank by siphoning off funds for personal gain. For example, Erwin Hansen took over Centennial Savings and Loan of California in 1980 and threw a Christmas party that cost $148,000 for 500 friends and guests and included a 10-course, sit-down dinner, roving minstrels, court jesters, and pantomimes. Hansen and his companion, Beverly Haines, traveled extensively around the world in the bank's private airplanes, purchased antique furniture at the S&L's expense, refurbished their home at a cost of over $1 million, and equipped it with a chef. Before it went

bankrupt, the bank bought a fleet of luxury cars and an extensive art collection. As the commissioner of the California Department of Savings and Loans stated in 1987, "The best way to rob a bank is to own one."

Other practices involved outright fraud. Land was sold or "flipped" between conspirators, driving up the assessed valuation. The overpriced land could then be sold to or mortgaged by a friendly bank owned by a co-conspirator for far more than it was worth. One loan broker bought a piece of property in 1979 for $874,000, flipped it, and then sold it two years later to his own S&L for $55 million. Another method was *reciprocal lending,* in which bank insiders would lend each other money that was never paid back and then trade the bad loans back and forth to delay discovery of the fraud. *Linked financing* involved loans based on receipts of deposits in an equivalent amount; the loans were never repaid. Insiders received a finder's fee for attracting deposits, and bank operators got bonuses for increasing business. "S&L," some suggested, stood for "squander and liquidate."

CRITICAL THINKING

1. Should S&L criminals have their personal incomes and homes confiscated by the government?

2. What motivates already wealthy businesspeople to steal?
3. Are white-collar crime and organized crime really the same thing?

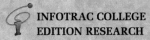

INFOTRAC COLLEGE EDITION RESEARCH

For more on the savings and loan scandal, see:
K. Calavita, R. Tillman, H. N. Pontell. The savings and loan debacle, financial crime, and the state. *Annual Review of Sociology Annual* 1997 v23 p19(20)
Amy Waldman. Move over, Charles Keating. *Washington Monthly* May 1995 v27 n5 p26
Barney Warf, Joseph C. Cox. Spatial dimensions of the savings and loan crisis. *Growth and Change* Spring 1996 v27 n2 p135

Source: Henry Pontell, Kitty Calavita, and Robert Tillman, *Fraud in the Savings and Loan Industry: White-Collar Crime and Government Response* (report to the National Institute of Justice, Washington, D.C., 1994); Robert Tillman and Henry Pontell, "Organizations and Fraud in the Savings and Loan Industry," *Social Forces* 73 (1995): 1439–63; Kitty Calavita and Henry Pontell, "Savings and Loan Fraud as Organized Crime: Toward a Conceptual Typology of Corporate Illegality," *Criminology* 31 (1993): 519–48.

did not report taxable income. No minimum dollar amount is stated before fraud exists, but the government can take legal action when there is a "substantial underpayment of tax." A second element of tax fraud is "willfulness" on the part of the tax evader. In the major case on this issue, willfulness was defined as a "voluntary, intentional violation of a known legal duty and not the careless disregard for the truth."[93] Finally, to prove tax fraud, the government must show that the taxpayer has purposely attempted to evade or defeat a tax payment. If the offender is guilty of passive neglect, the offense is a misdemeanor. **Passive neglect** means simply not paying taxes, not reporting income, or not paying taxes when due. On the other hand, **affirmative tax evasion,** such as keeping double books, making false entries, destroying books or records, concealing assets, or covering up sources of income, constitutes a felony.

Tax evasion is a difficult crime to prosecute. Because legal tax avoidance is a favorite U.S. pastime, it is often hard to prove the difference between the careless, unintentional nonreporting of income and willful fraud. The line between legal and fraudulent behavior is so fine that many people are willing to step over it. In fact, it has been estimated that the "underground economy" may amount to about 33 percent of the nation's production; workers who provide services under the table and off the books range from moonlighting construction workers to "gypsy" cabdrivers (there are an estimated 21,000 gypsy cabs in New York City alone, twice the number of legal ones).[94] The Internal Revenue Service (IRS) estimates that more than $120 billion in taxes go uncollected each year because individuals fail to report all their income; nearly a third of that amount is from self-employed workers, including professionals, laborers, and door-to-door salespeople.[95]

The IRS may be losing its battle against tax cheats. The number of audits it conducts is actually declining. In 1980 it audited about 8 percent of all people whose incomes exceeded $50,000; today the number of audits has declined to 1.8 percent.[96] And despite some well-publicized cases involving the wealthy, such as a $16 million judgment against singer Willie Nelson and the prosecution and conviction of multimillionaire Leona Helmsley, the IRS has been accused of targeting middle-income taxpayers and ignoring the upper classes and large corporations.

Corporate Crime

Yet another component of white-collar crime involves situations in which powerful institutions or their representatives willfully violate the laws that restrain these institutions from doing social harm or require them to do social good. This is also known as **corporate** or **organizational crime.**

Interest in corporate crime first emerged in the early 1900s, when a group of writers, known as the *muckrakers,* targeted the unscrupulous business practices of John D. Rockefeller, Andrew Carnegie, J. P. Morgan, and other corporate business leaders.[97] In a 1907 article, sociologist E. A. Ross described the "criminaloid," a business leader who while enjoying immunity from the law victimized an unsuspecting public.[98] Edwin Sutherland focused theoretical attention on corporate crime when he began his research on the subject in the 1940s; corporate crime was probably what he had in mind when he coined the phrase *white-collar crime.*[99]

Corporate crimes are socially injurious acts committed by people who control companies to further their business interests. The target of their crimes can be the general public, the environment, or even their companies' workers. What makes these crimes unique is that the perpetrator is a legal fiction—a corporation—and not an individual. In reality, it is company employees or owners who commit corporate crimes and who ultimately benefit through career advancement or greater profits. For a corporation to be held criminally liable, the employee committing the crime must be acting within the scope of his employment and must have actual or apparent authority to engage in the particular act in question. **Actual authority** occurs when a corporation knowingly gives authority to an employee; **apparent authority** is satisfied if a third party, like a customer, reasonably believes that the agent has the authority to perform the act in question. Courts have ruled that actual authority may occur even when the illegal behavior is not condoned by the corporation but is nonetheless within the scope of the employee's authority.[100]

Some of the acts included within corporate crime are price-fixing and illegal restraint of trade, false advertising, and the use of company practices that violate environmental protection statutes. The variety of crimes contained within this category is great, and they cause vast damage. The following subsections examine some of the most important offenses.

Illegal Restraint of Trade and Price-Fixing A restraint of trade involves a contract or conspiracy designed to stifle competition, create a monopoly, artificially maintain prices, or otherwise interfere with free market competition. The control of restraint of trade violations has its legal basis in the **Sherman Antitrust Act,** which subjects to criminal or civil sanctions any person "who shall make any contract or engage in any combination or conspiracy" in restraint of interstate commerce.[101] For violations of its provisions, this federal law created criminal penalties of up to three years' imprisonment and $100,000 in fines for individuals and $10 million in fines for corporations.[102] The act outlaws conspiracies between corporations designed to control the marketplace.

In most instances, the act lets the presiding court judge whether corporations have conspired to "unreasonably restrain competition." However, four types of market conditions are considered so inherently anticompetitive that federal courts, through the Sherman Antitrust Act, have defined them as illegal per se, without regard to the facts or circumstances of the case. The first is **division of markets;** here firms divide a region into territories, and each firm agrees not to compete in the others' territories.[103] The second is the **tying arrangement,** in which a corporation requires customers of one of its services to use other services it offers. For example, it would be an illegal restraint of trade if a railroad required that companies doing business with it or supplying it with materials ship all goods they produce on trains owned by the rail line.[104] A third type of absolute Sherman Act violation is **group boycotts,** in which an organization or company boycotts retail stores that do not comply with its rules or desires. Finally, **price-fixing**—a conspiracy to set and control the price of a necessary commodity—is considered an absolute violation of the act.

Of all criminal violations associated with restraint of trade, none, perhaps, is as important as price-fixing, which may take one of four forms.[105] The first is **predation,** in which large firms agree among themselves to bid below market prices to drive out weaker firms. The goal is to reduce competition and permit the remaining firms to raise their prices with relative impunity. A second scheme is **identical bidding:** all competitors agree to submit identical bids for each contract, although they may vary bids from contract to contract. The agreed-on price is well above what would have been expected if collusion had not occurred. Purchasing agents normally use their discretion to choose among bidders; however, identical bidding usually ensures all vendors of getting a share of the market without losing any profitability. **Geographical market sharing** involves dividing the potential market into territories within which

During the nineteenth century, business trusts controlled commerce in the United States. This political cartoon from 1889 suggests that the United States Senate was in the grasp of these powerful cartels. The power of the trusts was curtailed by passage of the Sherman Anti-Trust Act, which made it illegal to conspire to limit open trade.

only one member of the conspiring group is permitted a low bid. The remaining conspirators either refrain from bidding or give artificially high bids. **Rotational bidding** involves a conspiracy in which the opportunity to submit a winning bid for a government or business contract is rotated among institutional bidders. The conspirators meet in advance and determine who will give the low bid. The winning bid is, of course, higher than it should be because the losers have all submitted abnormally high bids. Close coordination among the bidders is essential; therefore, these schemes usually involve only a few large firms.

Despite enforcement efforts, restraint-of-trade conspiracies are quite common. The best-known case involved some of the largest members of the electrical equipment industry.[106] In 1961, 21 corporations, including industry leaders Westinghouse and General Electric, were successfully prosecuted; 45 executives were found guilty of criminal violations of the Sherman Antitrust Act. Company executives met secretly—they referred to their meetings as "choir practice"—to set prices on sales of equipment, allocate markets and territories, and rig bids. At the sentencing, fines amounting to $1,924,500 were levied against the defendants, including $437,500 against General Electric and $372,500 against Westinghouse. Although these fines meant little to the giant corporations, subsequent civil suits cost General Electric $160 million. Even more significant was that seven defendants, all high-ranking executives, were sentenced to jail terms.

Deceptive Pricing Even the largest U.S. corporations commonly use deceptive pricing schemes when they respond to contract solicitations. **Deceptive pricing** occurs when contractors provide the government or other corporations with incomplete or misleading information on how much it will actually cost to fulfill the contracts they are bidding on or use mischarges once the contracts are signed.[107] For example, defense contractors have been prosecuted for charging the government for costs incurred on work they are doing for private firms or shifting the costs on fixed-price contracts to ones in which the government reimburses the contractor for all expenses ("cost-plus" contracts). One well-known example of deceptive pricing occurred when the Lockheed Corporation withheld information that its labor costs would be lower than expected on the C-5 cargo plane. The resulting overcharges were an estimated $150 million. Although the government was able to negotiate a cheaper price for future C-5 orders, it did not demand repayment on the earlier contract. The government prosecutes approximately 100 cases of deceptive pricing in defense work each year, involving 59 percent of the nation's largest contractors.[108]

False Claims and Advertising In 1991 the Food and Drug Administration seized all the Citrus Hill orange juice stored in a Minneapolis warehouse. It seems that the nation's third largest-selling breakfast drink had billed itself as "pure squeezed," "100% pure," and "fresh," despite the fact that it was made from concentrate. The federal agency also objected to the fact that Procter and Gamble, which sells Citrus Hill, claimed, "We pick our oranges at the peak of ripeness, then we hurry to squeeze them before they lose their freshness."[109]

Executives in even the largest corporations sometimes face stockholders' expectations of ever-increasing company profits, which seem to demand that sales be increased at any cost. At times executives respond to this challenge by making claims about their products that cannot be justified by actual performance. However, the line between clever, aggressive sales techniques and fraudulent claims is fine. It is traditional to show a product in its best light, even if that involves resorting to fantasy. It is not fraudulent to show a delivery service vehicle taking off into outer space or to imply that taking one sip of iced tea will make people feel they have just jumped into a swimming pool. However, it is illegal to knowingly and purposely advertise a product as possessing qualities that the manufacturer realizes it does not have.

Charges stemming from false and misleading claims have been common in several U.S. industries. For example, the Federal Trade Commission reviewed and disallowed advertising by the three major U.S. car companies that alleged that new cars got higher gas mileage than buyers actually could expect. The Warner-Lambert drug company was prohibited from claiming that Listerine mouthwash could prevent or cure colds. Sterling Drug was prohibited from claiming that Lysol disinfectant killed germs associated with colds and flu. An administrative judge ruled that the American Home Products Company falsely advertised Anacin as a tension reliever. The list seems endless.[110]

In the pharmaceutical industry, false advertising has a long history.[111] It has been common for medicines to be advertised as cure-alls for previously incurable diseases. Such medicines include alleged cures for cancer and arthritis and drugs advertised to give energy and sexual potency. How can we explain the frequency of false advertising by drug manufacturers? Often the problem arises because several competing companies market similar products, and the key to successful sales is believed to be convincing the public that one of these products is far superior to the rest. Sometimes the intense drive for profits leads to falsification of data and unethical and illegal sales promotions.[112]

It has been difficult for authorities to police such violations of public trust. Often the most serious consequence to the corporation is an order that it refrain from using the advertising or withdraw the advertising claims. Criminal penalties are rarely given for false claims. Recently "900" telephone numbers have been used to advertise products involving sex and companionship, with high fees charged for each phone call. The Federal Trade Commission filed charges against some of these companies for deceptive ad campaigns that promise services they cannot deliver and for overcharging for information calls.[113]

Environmental Crimes Much attention has been paid to intentional or negligent environmental pollution caused by many large corporations. The numerous allegations in this area involve almost every aspect of U.S. business. There are many different types of environmental crimes. Some corporations have endangered the lives of their own workers by maintaining unsafe conditions in their plants and mines. It has been estimated that 21 million workers have been exposed to hazardous materials while on the job. The National Institute of Occupational Safety and Health has estimated that it would cost about $40 million just to alert these workers to the danger of their exposure to hazardous waste and $54 billion to track whether they develop occupationally related disease.[114] Some industries have been hit particularly hard by complaints and allegations. The asbestos industry was inundated with lawsuits after environmental scientists found a close association between

Illegal dumping of pollutants into the water supply is a particularly noxious form of white-collar crime. Here, environmental activist Robert Kennedy, Jr., traces the source of a pollutant at a hospital waste dump site spill.

exposure to asbestos and the development of cancer. Over 250,000 people have filed 12,000 lawsuits against 260 asbestos manufacturers. In all, some insurance company officials estimate that asbestos-related lawsuits could amount to as much as $150 billion. Similarly, some 100,000 cotton mill workers suffer from some form of respiratory disease linked to prolonged exposure to cotton dust. About one-third of the workers are seriously disabled by brown lung disease, an illness similar to emphysema.[115] The control of workers' safety has been the province of the Occupational Safety and Health Administration (OSHA). OSHA sets industry standards for the proper use of such chemicals as benzene, arsenic, lead, and coke. Intentional violation of OSHA standards can result in criminal penalties.

Pollution One type of environmental crime committed by large corporations is the illegal pollution of the environment. Sometimes pollution involves individual acts caused by negligence on the part of the polluter. Two cases stand out. The first involved the leaking of methyl isocyanate from a Union Carbide plant in Bhopal, India, on December 3, 1984. Estimates of the death toll range from 1,400 to 10,000 people; another 60,000 were injured. Union Carbide later reported that the plant had not been operating safely and should have been closed. The firm blamed the negligence, however, on local officials who were running the plant.[116] The second case occurred when the tanker *Exxon Valdez* ran aground on a reef off the coast of Alaska on March 24, 1989, dumping 11 million gallons of crude oil and fouling 700 miles of shoreline. On March 13, 1991, Exxon agreed to pay $1 billion in criminal and civil fines rather than face trial; this is the largest amount paid as a result of environmental pollution to date (a federal judge later refused to accept this amount, and the case is still being settled).[117]

Controlling Environmental Pollution The nature and scope of environmental crimes have prompted the federal government to pass a series of control measures designed to outlaw the worst abuses:[118]

- The Clean Air Act provides sanctions for companies that do not comply with the air quality standards established by the EPA.[119] The act can impose penalties on any person or institution that, for example, knowingly violates EPA plan requirements or emission standards, tampers with EPA monitoring devices, or makes false statements to EPA officials. The Clean Air Act was amended in 1990 to toughen standards for emissions of many air pollutants.
- The Federal Water Pollution Control Act, more commonly called the Clean Water Act, punishes the knowing or negligent discharge of a pollutant into navigable waters.[120] According to the act, a pollutant is any "man-made or man-induced alteration of the chemical, physical, biological, and radiological integrity of the water."
- The Rivers and Harbors Act of 1899 (Refuse Act) punishes any discharge of waste materials that damages natural water quality.[121]
- The Resource Conservation and Recovery Act of 1976 provides criminal penalties for four acts involving the illegal treatment of solid wastes: (1) the knowing transportation of any hazardous waste to a facility that does not have a legal permit for solid waste disposal; (2) the knowing treatment, storage, or disposal of any hazardous waste without a government permit or in violation of the provision of the permit; (3) the deliberate making of any false statement or representation in a report filed in compliance with the act; and (4) the destruction or alteration of records required to be maintained by the act.[122]
- The Toxic Substance Control Act addresses the manufacture, processing, or distributing of chemical mixtures or substances in a manner not in accordance with established testing or manufacturing requirements; commercial use of a chemical substance or mixture that the commercial user knew was manufactured, processed, or distributed in violation of the act's requirements; and noncompliance with the reporting and inspection requirements of the act.[123]
- The Federal Insecticide, Fungicide, and Rodenticide Act regulates the manufacture and distribution of toxic pesticides.[124]
- The Comprehensive Environmental Response, Compensation, and Liability Act, also referred to as the "Superfund," requires the cleanup of hazardous waste at contaminated sites.[125]

Considering the uncertainties of federal budget allocations, there is some question whether these acts can be enforced well enough to effectively deter environmental crime. It is possible that the environmental problem must be solved at the local level.

High-Tech Crime

High-tech crimes are a new breed of white-collar offenses that can be singular or ongoing and typically involve the theft of information, resources, or funds. High-tech crimes cost consumers billions of dollars each year and will most likely increase dramatically in the years to come: What are some of these emerging forms of white-collar crime?

Internet Crimes On October 27, 1998, the SEC announced that it had filed charges against 44 stock promoters for fraudulently recommending more than 235 small companies on the Internet. The alleged fraud occurred when Internet stock newsletters touted investment in small companies without notifying investors that they were being paid by the companies whose shares they were promoting. The promoters not only profited from the fees but were able to sell shares they personally owned when the stock prices jumped due to their involvement. The promoters posted messages on web sites, flooded the Internet with junk e-mail, were paid more than $6.2 million in cash, and were given 1.8 million shares of stock or stock options for their work.[126]

Millions of people use the Internet daily in the United States and Canada alone, and the number entering cyberspace is growing rapidly. Criminal entrepreneurs view this vast pool as a target for high-tech crimes. In a number of highly publicized cases adults have solicited teenagers in Internet "chat rooms." Others have used the Internet to sell and distribute obscene material, prompting some service providers to censor or control sexually explicit material.

Selling pornographic material on the Internet is just one method of its illegal use. Bogus get-rich-quick schemes, weight-loss scams, and investment swindles have been pitched on the Internet. In some cases these fraudulent acts can actually be dangerous to clients. For example, in a 1995 case, a Minnesota woman advertised the health benefits of "germanium" on an Internet provider, claiming that it could cure AIDS, cancer, and other diseases. Germanium products have been banned because they cause irreversible kidney damage.[127]

Controlling Internet Crime Enforcing the law on the Internet can fall to a number of different agencies. The Securities and Exchange Commission, Federal Trade Commission, Secret Service, and state attorney generals' offices have all assigned personnel to be "cyber-cops." In 1996 the federal government passed the Communications Decency Act of 1996, which proscribes the use of a computer to provide minors with "indecent material" as well as the knowing use of a computer to intentionally harass the recipient of communication.[128] Some civil liberty groups consider this law tantamount to censorship, and suits have been filed in federal court requesting clarification of its provisions; so far the Justice Department has suspended enforcement until the cases have been settled.[129]

Computer Crimes Computer-related thefts are a new trend in employee theft and embezzlement. The widespread use of computers to record business transactions has encouraged some people to use them for illegal purposes. Computer crimes generally fall into one of five categories:[130]

1. Theft of services, in which the criminal uses the computer for unauthorized purposes or an unau-

thorized user penetrates the computer system. Included within this category is the theft of processing time and services not entitled to an employee.
2. Use of data in a computer system for personal gain.
3. Unauthorized use of computers employed for various types of financial processing to obtain assets.
4. Theft of property by computer for personal use or conversion to profit.
5. Making the computer itself the subject of a crime—for example, when a virus is placed in it to destroy data.

Although most of these types of crime involve using computers for personal gain, the last category typically involves activities that are motivated more by malice than by profit. When computers themselves are the target, criminals are typically motivated by revenge for some perceived wrong; a need to exhibit their technical prowess and superiority; a wish to highlight the vulnerability of computer security systems; a desire to spy on other peoples' private financial and personal information ("computer voyeurism"); or a philosophy of open access to all systems and programs.[131]

Several common techniques are used by computer criminals. In fact, computer theft has become so common that experts have created their own jargon to describe theft styles and methods:

- *The Trojan horse:* One computer is used to reprogram another for illicit purposes. In one incident, two high school–age computer users reprogrammed the computer at DePaul University, preventing that institution from using its own processing facilities. The youths were convicted of a misdemeanor.
- *The salami slice:* An employee sets up a dummy account in the company's computerized records. A small amount—even a few pennies—is subtracted from customers' accounts and added to the account of the thief. Even if they detect the loss, the customers don't complain, because a few cents is an insignificant amount to them. The pennies picked up here and there eventually amount to thousands of dollars in losses.
- *"Super-zapping":* Most computer programs used in business have built-in antitheft safeguards. However, employees can use a repair or maintenance program to supersede the antitheft program. Some tinkering with the program is required, but the "super-zapper" is soon able to order the system to issue checks to his or her private account.
- *The logic bomb:* A program is secretly attached to the company's computer system. The new program monitors the company's work and waits for a sign of error to appear, some illogic that was designed for the computer to follow. Illogic causes the logic bomb to kick into action and exploit the weakness.

The way the thief exploits the situation depends on his or her original intent—theft of money or defense secrets, sabotage, or the like.

- *Impersonation:* An unauthorized person uses the identity of an authorized computer user to access the computer system.
- *Data leakage:* A person illegally obtains data from a computer system by leaking it out in small amounts.

A different type of computer crime involves installing a virus in a computer system. A **virus** is a program that disrupts or destroys existing programs and networks.[132] All too often this high-tech vandalism is the work of hackers, who consider their efforts to be pranks. In one well-publicized case, a 25-year-old computer whiz named Robert Morris unleashed a program that wrecked a nationwide electronic mail network. His efforts netted him three years' probation, a $10,000 fine, and 400 hours of community service; some critics felt this punishment was too lenient to deter future virus creators.[133]

An accurate accounting of computer crime will probably never be made because so many offenses go unreported. Sometimes company managers refuse to report the crime to police lest they display their incompetence and vulnerability to stockholders and competitors.[134] In other instances, computer crimes go unreported because they involve low-visibility acts such as copying computer software in violation of copyright laws.[135]

Controlling Computer Crime As computer applications become more varied, so will the use of computers for illegal purposes. The growth of computer-related crimes prompted Congress to enact the Counterfeit Active Device and Computer Fraud and Abuse Act (amended in 1986).[136] This statute makes it a felony for a person to illegally enter a computer to gain $5,000, to cause another to lose $5,000, or to access data affecting the national interest. Violating this act can bring up to 10 years in prison and a $10,000 fine. Repeat offenders can receive 20-year prison sentences and $100,000 fines. In 1994 the Computer Abuse Amendments Act was passed to update federal enforcement efforts.[137] This statute addresses six areas of computer-related abuses, including obtaining information related to national defense or financial records, or using a "federal interest computer" to defraud, obtain something of value, or destroy data. The 1994 Act criminalizes "reckless conduct," which means that hackers who plant viruses will now violate federal law.

In addition to the Computer Abuse Act, people who illegally copy software violate the Criminal Copyright Infringement Act, which punishes copying and distribution of software for financial gain or advantage.[138] Computer crime may also be controlled by other federal statutes, including the Electronic Communications Privacy Act of 1986, which prohibits unauthorized interception of computer communications and prohibits obtaining, altering, or preventing authorized access to data through intentional unauthorized access to the stored data.[139] The act is designed to prevent hackers from intercepting computer communications and invading the privacy of computer users.[140]

THE CAUSE OF WHITE-COLLAR CRIME

When Ivan Boesky pleaded guilty to one count of securities fraud, he agreed to pay a civil fine of $100 million, the largest at that time in SEC history. Boesky's fine was later surpassed by Michael Milken's fine of more than $1 billion. How, people asked, can people with so much disposable wealth get involved in a risky scheme to produce even more? There probably are as many explanations for white-collar crime as there are white-collar crimes. Herbert Edelhertz, an expert on white-collar crime, suggests that many offenders feel free to engage in business crime because they can easily rationalize its effects. Some convince themselves that their actions are not really crimes because the acts involved do not resemble street crimes. For example, a banker who uses his position of trust to lend his institution's assets to a company he secretly controls may see himself as a shrewd businessman, not as a criminal. Or a pharmacist who chisels customers on prescription drugs may rationalize her behavior by telling herself that it does not really hurt anyone. Further, some businesspeople feel justified in committing white-collar crimes because they believe that government regulators do not really understand the business world or the problems of competing in the free enterprise system. Even when caught, many white-collar criminals cannot see the error of their ways. For example, one offender who was convicted in the electrical industry price-fixing conspiracy (discussed earlier) categorically denied the illegality of his actions. "We did not fix prices," he said; "I am telling you that all we did was recover costs."[141] Some white-collar criminals believe that everyone violates business laws, so it is not so bad if they do so themselves. Rationalizing greed is a common trait of white-collar criminals.

Greedy or Needy?

Greed is not the only motivation for white-collar crime; need also plays an important role. Executives may tamper with company books because they feel the need to keep or improve their jobs, satisfy their egos, or support their children. Blue-collar workers may pilfer because they need to keep pace with inflation or buy a new car. Kathleen Daly's analysis of convictions in seven federal district courts indicated that many white-collar crimes involve relatively trivial amounts. Women convicted of white-collar crime typically work in lower-echelon positions, and their acts seem motivated more by economic survival than by greed and power.[142]

Even people in the upper echelons of the financial world, such as Ivan Boesky, may carry scars from an earlier needy period in their lives that can be healed only by accumulating ever greater amounts of money. As one of Boesky's associates put it,

> I don't know what his devils were. Maybe he's greedy beyond the wildest imaginings of mere mortals like you and me. And maybe part of what drives the guy is an inherent insecurity that was operative here even after he had arrived. Maybe he never arrived.[143]

A well-known study of embezzlers by Donald Cressey illustrates the important role need plays in white-collar crime.[144] According to Cressey, embezzlement is caused by what he calls a "nonshareable financial problem." This condition may be the result of offenders' living beyond their means, perhaps piling up gambling debts; offenders feel they cannot let anyone know about such financial problems without ruining their reputations. Cressey claims that the door to solving personal financial problems through criminal means is opened by the rationalizations society has developed for white-collar crime: "Some of our most respectable citizens got their start in life by using other people's money temporarily"; "in the real estate business, there is nothing wrong about using deposits before the deal is closed"; "all people steal when they get in a tight spot."[145] Offenders use these and other rationalizations to resolve the conflict they experience over engaging in illegal behavior. Rationalizations allow offenders' financial needs to be met without compromising their values.

There are a number of more formal theories of white-collar crime. The next sections describe two of the more prominent theories.

Corporate Culture Theory The corporate culture view is that some business organizations promote white-collar criminality in the same way that lower-class culture encourages the development of juvenile gangs and street crime. According to the corporate culture view, some business enterprises cause crime by placing excessive demands on employees while at the same time maintaining a business climate tolerant of employee deviance. New employees learn the attitudes and techniques needed to commit white-collar crime from their business peers in a learning process reminiscent of Edwin Sutherland's description of how gang boys learn the techniques of drug dealing and burglary from older youths through differential association.

CONNECTIONS

Chapter 8 discusses differential association and other social process theories.

A number of attempts have been made to use corporate culture and structure to explain white-collar crime. For example, Ronald Kramer argues that business organizations will encourage employee criminality if they encounter serious difficulties in attaining their goals, especially in making profits. Some organizations create cost reduction policies that inspire lawbreaking and corner cutting to become a norm passed on to employees. When new employees balk at violating business laws, they are told informally, "This is the way things are done here, don't worry about it." Kramer finds that a business's organizational environment, including economic, political, cultural, legal, technological, and interorganizational factors, influences the level of white-collar crime. If market conditions are weak, competition intense, law enforcement lax, and managers willing to stress success at any cost, then conditions for corporate crime are maximized.[146]

Kramer's view is analogous to the cultural deviance approach, which suggests that crime occurs when obedience to the cultural norms and values people are in immediate contact with causes them to break the rules of conventional society. However, cultural deviance theory (discussed in Chapter 7) was originally directed at lower-class slum boys, not business executives. Kramer believes that the same crime-producing forces may operate among both socioeconomic groups.

Australian sociologist John Braithwaite has promoted the corporate culture view in his writings on white-collar crime.[147] According to Braithwaite's model, businesspeople in any society may find themselves in a situation where their organization's stated goals cannot be achieved through conventional business practices; they perceive "blocked opportunities." In a capitalist society, up-and-coming young executives may find that their profit ratios are below par; in a socialist society, young bureaucrats panic when their production levels fall short of the five-year plan. Under such stress, entrepreneurs may find that illegitimate opportunities are the only solution to their problems; their careers must be saved at all costs. So when a government official is willing to take a bribe to overlook costly safety violations, the bribe is gratefully offered. Or when insider trading can increase profits, the investment banker leaps at the chance to engage in it. But how can traditionally law-abiding people overcome the ties of conventional law and morality?

Braithwaite believes that organizational crime is a function of the corporate climate. Organizational crime flourishes in corporations that contain an ongoing employee subculture that resists government regulation and socializes new workers in the skills and attitudes necessary to violate the law. For example, junior executives may learn from their seniors how to meet clandestinely with their competitors to fix prices and how to rationalize this as a good, necessary, and inevitable thing. The existence of law-violating subcultures is enhanced when a hostile relationship exists between the organization and the governmental bodies that regulate it. When these agencies are viewed as uncooperative, untrustworthy, and resistant to change, corporations are more likely to develop clandestine, law-violating subcultures. A positive working relationship with their governmental overseers, on the other hand, reduces the need for a secret, law-violating infrastructure. Illegal corporate behavior can exist only in secrecy; public scrutiny brings the shame of a criminal label to people whose social life and community standing rest on their good name and character.

The shame of discovery has an important moderating influence on corporate crime. Its source may be external: the general community, professional or industry peers, or government regulatory agencies. The source of shame and disapproval can also be internal. Many corporations have stated policies that firmly admonish employees to obey the rule of law. For example, it is common for corporations to encourage whistle-blowing by coworkers and to sanction workers who violate the law and cause embarrassment. These organizations are full of "antennas" to pick up irregularities and make it widely known that certain individuals or subunits are responsible for law violations. In a sense, corporations that maintain an excess of definitions unfavorable to violating the law will be less likely to contain deviant subcultures and concomitantly less likely to violate business regulations. In contrast, corporate crime thrives in organizations that isolate people within spheres of responsibility, where lines of communication are blocked or stretched thin, and in which deviant subcultures are allowed to develop with impunity.

Those holding the corporate culture view, such as Braithwaite and Kramer, would view the savings and loan and insider trading scandals as prime examples of what happens when people work in organizations whose cultural values stress profit over fair play, in which government scrutiny is limited and regulators are viewed as the enemy, and in which senior members encourage newcomers to believe that "greed is good."

The Self-Control View Not all criminologists agree with corporate culture theory. Travis Hirschi and Michael Gottfredson take exception to the hypothesis that white-collar crime is a product of corporate culture.[148] If that were true, there would be much more white-collar crime than actually exists, and white-collar criminals would not be embarrassed by their misdeeds, as most seem to be. Instead, Hirschi and Gottfredson maintain, the motives that produce white-collar crimes are the same as those that produce any other criminal behaviors: "the desire for relatively quick, relatively certain benefit, with minimal effort." As you may recall from Chapter 10, Hirschi and Gottfredson's general theory of crime holds that criminals lack self-control; the motivation and pressure to commit white-collar crime are the same as for any other form of crime. White-collar criminals have low self-control and are inclined to follow momentary impulses without considering the long-term costs of such behavior.[149] White-collar crime is relatively rare because, as a matter of course, business executives tend to hire people with self-control, thereby limiting the number of potential white-collar criminals. Hirschi and Gottfredson have collected data showing that the demographic distribution of white-collar crime is similar to other crimes. For example, gender, race, and age ratios are the same for such crimes as embezzlement and fraud as they are for street crimes, such as burglary and robbery.

Do White-Collar Criminals Lack Self-Control? Business executives and corporate executives seem to be people who would have above, rather than below, average self-control. Can Gottfredson and Hirschi's view of white-collar crime be correct?[150] A number of research studies indicate that even white-collar offenders lack self-control.[151] Many are repeat offenders who share several characteristics with street criminals (such as being impulsive and egocentric), although they begin their careers later in life and offend at a slower pace.[152]

Even if the Gottfredson-Hirschi view is accurate, it is possible that white-collar offenders manifest a wide range of self-control and that the actual level of offenders' self-control determines the path they take to crime. Criminologists Michael Benson and Elizabeth Moore found that some executives who commit crime have extremely low self-control and impulsively commit fraud and other crimes to pursue their own self-interest; these are most like common criminals. Others with high self-control pursue "ego gratification in an aggressive and calculating fashion"; they are the products of the "greed is good" philosophy. In the middle are offenders who take advantage of criminal opportunities to satisfy an immediate personal need; here self-control becomes overwhelmed by special problems. Benson and Moore, then, view self-control as a variable, not a constant, that interacts with need and opportunity to produce white-collar crimes.[153]

WHITE-COLLAR LAW ENFORCEMENT SYSTEMS

On the federal level, detection of white-collar crime is primarily in the hands of administrative departments and agencies.[154] Usually the decision to pursue criminal rather than civil violations is based on the seriousness of the case and the perpetrator's intent, actions to conceal the violation, and prior record. Any evidence of criminal activity is then sent to the Department of Justice or the FBI for investigation. Some other federal agencies, such as the Securities and Exchange Commission and the U.S. Postal Service, have their own investigative arms. Usually enforcement is reactive (generated by complaints) rather than proactive (involving ongoing investigations or the monitoring of activities). Investigations are carried out by the various federal agencies and the FBI. The FBI has made enforcement of white-collar criminal law one of its three top priorities (along with combating foreign counterintelligence and organized crime). If criminal prosecution is called for, the case will be handled by attorneys from the criminal, tax, antitrust, and civil rights divisions of the Justice Department. If insufficient evidence is available to warrant a criminal prosecution, the case will be handled civilly or administratively by some other federal agency. For example, the Federal Trade Commission can issue a cease and desist order in antitrust or merchandising fraud cases.

On the state and local levels, enforcement of white-collar criminal law is often disorganized and inefficient. Confusion may exist over the jurisdiction of the state attorney general and local prosecutors. The technical expertise of the federal government is often lacking on the state level. However, local and state law enforcement officials have made progress in a number of areas, such as controlling consumer fraud. The Environmental Crimes Strike Force in Los Angeles County, California, is considered a model for the control of illegal dumping and pollution.[155] The number of state-funded technical assistance offices to help local prosecutors has increased significantly; more than 40 states offer such services.

Local prosecutors pursue white-collar criminals more vigorously if they are part of a team effort involving a network of law enforcement agencies.[156] National surveys of local prosecutors find that many do not consider white-collar crimes particularly serious problems. They are more willing to prosecute cases if the offense causes substantial harm and if other agencies fail to act. Relatively few prosecutors participate in interagency task forces designed to investigate white-collar criminal activity.[157] Benson and his colleagues found that local prosecutors believe that criminal law should be used against corporate offenders and that tougher criminal penalties would improve corporate compliance with the law.

The number of prosecutors who believe that upper-class criminals are not above the law is growing. Although these findings were encouraging, Benson also found that the funds and staff needed for local white-collar prosecutions are often scarce. Crimes considered more serious, such as drug trafficking, usually take precedence over corporate violations. Coordination is

uncommon, and there is relatively little resource sharing. However, concern over the environment may encourage local prosecutors to take action against those who violate state pollution and antidumping laws.[158]

Corporate Policing

White-collar criminal law enforcement is often left to business organizations themselves. Corporations spend hundreds of millions of dollars each year on internal audits that help unearth white-collar offenses. Local chambers of commerce, the insurance industry, and other elements of the business community have mounted campaigns against white-collar crime. Corporate self-enforcement strategies can take a variety of forms:

- Security strategies employ contract security personnel and private police officers who guard merchandise and conduct surveillance in sensitive areas. Passive security measures use badges, passes, key cards, and checkpoints to restrict access to merchandise. Closed-circuit TV and other monitoring devices are used for surveillance.
- Screening and education strategies use preemployment screening and background checks to weed out potential problems. Personality and integrity tests help screen applicants. Stores are teaching employees how to spot theft and the best ways to report problems.
- Whistle-blowing strategies create hot lines by which employees can report theft anonymously without fear of repercussions. Third-party firms sometimes maintain hot lines because employees may be reluctant to report fellow workers to their own employer.[159]

Aiding the investigation of white-collar offenses is a movement toward protecting employees who blow the whistle on their firm's violations. At least five states—Michigan, Connecticut, Maine, California, and New York—have passed laws protecting workers from being fired if they testify about violations.[160] Without such help, the hands of justice are tied.

Controlling White-Collar Crime

The prevailing wisdom is that unlike lower-class street criminals, white-collar criminals are rarely prosecuted and, when convicted, receive relatively light sentences. In years past, it was rare for a corporate or white-collar criminal to receive a serious criminal penalty.[161] For example, physicians who cheat Medicaid are rarely prosecuted, and when they are, judges are reluctant to severely punish them.[162] Marshall Clinard and Peter Yeager's analysis of 477 corporations found that only 1 in 10 serious and 1 in 20 moderate violations resulted in sanctions.[163] In a subsequent analysis, Yeager found that when white-collar statutes are enforced, there is a tendency to penalize small, powerless businesses while treating the market leaders more leniently.[164]

There are a number of reasons for the leniency afforded white-collar criminals. Although white-collar criminals may produce millions of dollars of losses and endanger human life, some judges believe they are not "real criminals" but businesspeople just trying to make a living.[165] As Clinard and Yeager report, businesspeople often seek legal advice and know the loopholes in the law. If caught, they can claim that they had sought legal advice and believed they were in compliance with the law.[166] White-collar criminals are often considered nondangerous offenders because they usually are respectable, older citizens who have families to support. These "pillars of the community" are not seen in the same light as a teenager who breaks into a drugstore to steal a few dollars. Their public humiliation at being caught is usually deemed punishment enough; a prison sentence seems unnecessarily cruel.

Judges and prosecutors may identify with the white-collar criminal based on shared background and world views; they may have engaged in similar types of illegal behavior themselves.[167] Still another factor complicating white-collar crime enforcement is that many legal business and governmental acts seem as morally tinged as those made illegal by government regulation. For example, the Air Force forced a general to step down and punished two others for mismanaging the C-17 cargo plane, which accrued $1.5 billion in cost overruns. Their alleged misconduct included funneling $450 million in payments to the contractor, McDonnell Douglas, that were "premature, improper, and possibly illegal."[168] Despite their questionable morality and ethics, these acts were not treated as crimes. Yet when compared to other business practices made illegal by government regulation, such as price-fixing, the distinctions are hard to see. It may seem unfair to prosecutors and judges to penalize some government and business officials for actions not too different from those applauded in the *Wall Street Journal*.[169]

Finally, some corporate practices that result in death or disfigurement are treated as civil actions in which victims receive monetary damages. The most well-known case involves the A. H. Robins Company's Dalkon Shield intrauterine device, which caused massive trauma to hundreds of thousands of women, including pelvic disease, infertility, and septic abortions, and is suspected in 20 deaths. The outcome of the case was that the company went through bankruptcy and set up a multibillion-dollar trust for the survivors.[170] More recently, a number of drug companies, including Bristol Myers Squibb, set up a similar trust fund to compensate victims who suffered because their products used in breast implant surgery were defective and dangerous. Although these cases involve much more serious injury than, say, insider trading, they are not considered criminal matters.

Compliance Strategies The prevailing wisdom, then, is that many white-collar criminals avoid prosecution, and those that are prosecuted receive lenient punishment. What efforts have been made to bring violators of the public trust to justice? White-collar criminal enforcement typically involves two strategies designed to control organizational deviance: compliance and deterrence.[171]

Compliance strategies aim for law conformity without the necessity of detecting, processing, or penalizing individual violators. At a minimum, they ask for cooperation and self-policing among the business community. Compliance systems attempt to create conformity by giving companies economic incentives to obey the law. They rely on administrative efforts to prevent unwanted conditions before they occur. Compliance systems depend on the threat of economic sanctions or civil penalties (referred to as **economism**) to control corporate violators.

One method of compliance is to set up administrative agencies to oversee business activity. For example, the Securities and Exchange Commission regulates Wall Street activities, and the Food and Drug Administration regulates drugs, cosmetics, medical devices, meats, and other foods. The legislation creating these agencies usually spells out the penalties for violating regulatory standards. This approach has been used to control environmental crimes, for example, by levying heavy fines based on the quantity and quality of pollution released into the environment.[172] For example, after the FMC Corporation was fined $11.8 million in 1998 for violating federal hazardous waste laws at its southeastern Idaho plant, it agreed to spend $158 million over the next four years to upgrade air and hazardous waste treatment operations at the plant, located on the Shoshone-Bannock Indian reservation.[173] It is easier and less costly to be in compliance, the theory goes, than to pay costly fines and risk criminal prosecution for repeat violations. Moreover, the federal government bars people and businesses from receiving government contracts if they have engaged in repeated business law violations.

In sum, compliance strategies attempt to create a marketplace incentive to obey the law; for example, the more a company pollutes, the more costly and unprofitable that pollution becomes. They limit individual blame and punishment, a practice whose deterrent effect seems problematic. Compliance strategies also avoid stigmatizing and shaming businesspeople by focusing on the act, rather than the actor, in white-collar crime.[174]

The Limits of Compliance Although it is difficult to gauge the effectiveness of compliance, research indicates that strict enforcement of regulatory laws can reduce illegal or dangerous business practices. For example, one study found that strict enforcement of

Compliance strategies aim for law conformity by threatening to impose economic sanctions if regulations are violated. Here a federal inspector looks over a pig carcass in a processing plant in San Antonio, Texas. Inspections are aimed at encouraging compliance with federal regulations on meat packing. Critics charge that the economic penalties imposed by compliance strategies are applied only after crimes have occurred, require careful governmental regulation, and often amount to only a slap on the wrist.

penalties under the Occupational and Safety Health Act can significantly reduce workplace injuries.[175] Nonetheless, compliance systems are not applauded by all criminologists. Some experts point out that economic sanctions have limited value in controlling white-collar crime because economic penalties are imposed only after crimes have occurred, require careful governmental regulation, and often amount to only a slap on the wrist.[176] Compliance is particularly difficult to achieve if the federal government adopts a probusiness, antiregulation fiscal policy that encourages economic growth by removing controls over business. Business leaders and their political allies complain that strict regulations create a paperwork nightmare, inhibiting growth and costing jobs. Probusiness political administrations can make regulation difficult by reducing the budgets of oversight agencies, easing restrictions on environmental pollution, and deregulating businesses.[177] Complaints are met with barbs such as "Which is more important, saving trees or saving jobs?" In addition, corporations hit with fines and regulatory fees can pass the costs on to consumers in the form of higher prices or reduced services. Shareholders who had little to do with the crime may see their stock dividends cut or share prices fall.[178]

Compliance strategies are also problematic because overburdened government agencies often find it difficult to monitor violators. For example, in 1998 the Environmental Protection Agency (EPA) reported on the difficulty of regulating water pollution by municipal and industrial dischargers in Alaska and Idaho. Although 33 waste discharge permits had been issued in these states during the past 22 years, 1,000 applications were waiting to be processed, of which 70 percent were over four years old. As a result, large numbers of dischargers were not in compliance with the Clean Water Act or had their permits administratively extended without being subject to current, more stringent discharge requirements. Little formal enforcement action was taken against the most serious violators, which weakened the effectiveness of the program in protecting public health and the environment.[179]

Some criminologists say that the punishment of white-collar crimes should include a retributive component similar to that used in common-law crimes. White-collar crimes, after all, are immoral activities that have harmed social values and deserve commensurate punishment.[180] Corporations can get around economic sanctions by moving their rule-violating activities overseas, where legal controls over injurious corporate activities are lax or nonexistent.[181]

Deterrence Strategies Deterrence strategies involve detecting criminal violations, determining who is responsible, and penalizing the offenders to deter future violations.[182] Punishment warns potential violators who might break rules if other violators had not already been penalized. Deterrence systems are oriented toward apprehending violators and punishing them rather than creating conditions that induce conformity to the law.

Deterrence strategies should work—and they have—because white-collar crime by its nature is a rational act whose perpetrators are extremely sensitive to the threat of criminal sanctions. Perceptions of detection and punishment for white-collar crimes appear to be a powerful deterrent to future law violations.[183] There are numerous instances in which prison sentences for corporate crimes have produced a significant decline in white-collar criminal activity.[184] For example, on February 6, 1998, Christopher Tate, president of Safety Management Institute, Inc. (SMI), pleaded guilty to felony charges of violating the Pennsylvania Solid Waste Management Act. He was sentenced to 10 to 24 months of imprisonment and five years of probation, fined $5,000, and ordered to pay $4,895 in restitution plus the costs of prosecution. As a condition of parole and probation, Tate is prohibited from performing any environmentally related work.[185] Woody Lemons received a 30-year sentence for his role as chairman of the Vernon S&L during that bank's collapse.[186] Corporate executives have even been charged with murder because of the actions of their companies, as is discussed in the Criminological Enterprise feature titled "Can Corporations Commit Murder?"[187]

Although deterrence strategies may prove effective, federal agencies have been reluctant to throw corporate executives in jail. For example, the courts have not hesitated to enforce the Sherman Antitrust Act in civil actions, but they have limited application of the criminal sanctions. Similarly, the government seeks criminal indictments in corporate violations only in "instances of outrageous conduct of undoubted illegality," such as price-fixing.[188] The government has also been lenient with companies and individuals that cooperate voluntarily after an investigation has begun; leniency is not given as part of a confession or plea arrangement. Those who comply with the leniency policy are charged criminally for the activity reported.[189]

Is the Tide Turning? Despite years of neglect, there is growing evidence that white-collar crime deterrence strategies have become normative. The government's willingness to use deterrence policies is underscored by the extremely large fines now being handed out for white-collar violations. For example, before the fall of 1995, the largest criminal fine levied against an antitrust criminal defendant was $6 million. But in 1996 Archer Daniels Midland Company (ADM) agreed to pay a $100 million criminal fine for conspiring to suppress and eliminate competition in the lysine market from June 1992 through June 27, 1995, and for conspiring to suppress and eliminate competition in the citric acid market from January 1993 through June 27, 1995.[190]

Deterrence policies are now being aided because the federal government has created sentencing guidelines that control punishment for convicted criminals. Prosecutors can now control the length and type of sentence through their handling of the charging process. The guidelines also create mandatory minimum prison sentences that must be served for some crimes; judicial clemency can no longer be counted on.[191] This new get-tough deterrence approach appears to be affecting all classes of white-collar criminals. Although many people believe that affluent corporate executives usually avoid serious punishment, public displeasure with such highly publicized white-collar crimes as the S&L scandal, the HUD fraud, and the BCCI case may be producing a backlash that is resulting in more frequent use of prison sentences.[192] Some commentators now argue that the government may actually be going overboard in its efforts to punish white-collar criminals, especially for crimes that are the result of negligent business practices rather than intentional criminal conspiracy.[193] And because white-collar crime is rarely a one-time event, the identification of white-collar criminals is certainly less difficult than it is for street criminals.[194]

ORGANIZED CRIME

The second branch of organizational criminality involves **organized crime**—the ongoing criminal enterprise groups whose ultimate purpose is personal economic gain through illegitimate means. Here a structured enterprise system is set up to continually supply consumers with merchandise and services banned by criminal law but for which a ready market exists: prostitution, pornography, gambling, and narcotics. The system may resemble a legitimate business run by an ambitious chief executive officer, his or her assistants, staff attorneys, and accountants, with thorough, efficient accounts receivable and complaint departments.[195]

Because of its secrecy, power, and fabulous wealth, a great mystique has grown up about organized crime. Its legendary leaders—Al Capone, Meyer Lansky, Lucky Luciano—have been the subjects of books and films. The famous *Godfather* films popularized and humanized organized crime figures; the media often glamorize organized crime figures.[196] Most citizens believe that organized criminals are capable of taking over legitimate business enterprises if given the opportunity. Almost everyone is familiar with such terms as *mob, underworld, Mafia, wise guys, syndicate,* or *La Cosa Nostra,* which refer to organized crime. Although most of us have neither met nor seen members of organized crime families, we feel sure that they exist, and we fear them. This section briefly defines organized crime, reviews its history, and discusses its economic effect and control.

The Criminological Enterprise

Can Corporations Commit Murder?

One of the most controversial issues surrounding the punishment of white-collar criminals involves prosecuting corporate executives who work for companies that manufacture products believed to have killed workers or consumers. Are the executives guilty of manslaughter or even murder?

Federal Law

The Occupational Safety and Health Act (OSH) makes employers criminally liable if their willful violation of a safety rule causes the death of an employee. For example, in one case corporate officers of a Massachusetts asbestos firm were indicted when they made false statements to Occupational Safety and Health Administration (OSHA) officials about the safety of worker respirators when in reality the safety and fit of the devices had not been tested. Although OSHA officials can bring criminal charges, critics maintain that they rarely do, preferring to punish even serious crimes with fines. For example, they negotiated a $10 million fine with IMC Fertilizer and Angus Chemical following a 1991 plant explosion that killed eight workers. They also fined Firestone Tire Company $7.5 million in 1994 after determining that the company had violated OSHA standards by failing to properly use locks and lockout procedures when servicing equipment, resulting in the death of a maintenance worker.

State Enforcement

States may also bring criminal charges for deaths. More than 20 years ago, a local prosecutor failed in an attempt to convict Ford Motor Company executives on charges of homicide in crashes involving Pintos, as a result of deaths due to known dangers in the car's design. The Pinto had a gas tank that burst into flame when involved in a low-velocity, rear-end collision. Although the design defect could have been corrected for about $20 per car, the company failed to take prompt action. When three people were killed in crashes, an Indiana prosecutor brought murder charges

against Ford executives. However, they were acquitted because the jury did not find sufficient evidence that they intended the deaths to occur.

The question of whether corporate executives could be successfully prosecuted for murder was answered on June 16, 1985, when an Illinois judge found three officials of the Film Recovery Systems Corporation guilty of murder in the death of a worker. The employee died after inhaling cyanide under "totally unsafe" work conditions. During the trial, evidence was presented showing that employees were not warned that they were working with dangerous substances, that company officials ignored complaints of illness, and that safety precautions had been deliberately ignored. The murder convictions were later overturned on appeal.

The Pinto and Film Recovery cases opened the door for prosecuting corporate executives on violent crime charges stemming from unsafe products or working conditions. There is little question that corporate liability may be increasing. As Nancy Frank points out, a number of states have adopted the concept of unintended murder in their legal codes. This means that persons can be charged and convicted of murder if their acts, although essentially unintended, are imminently dangerous to another or have a strong probability of causing death or great bodily harm. This legal theory would include corporate executives who knew about the dangers of their products but chose to do nothing either because correction would lower profits or because they simply did not care about consumers or workers.

A case illustrating this legal doctrine involved the fire on September 3, 1991, at Imperial Food Products, Inc., a North Carolina chicken processing plant. The fire, which claimed 25 lives, was deadly because the plant had no sprinkler system, windows, or escape routes. Company executives had *locked* exit doors to prevent employee pilferage. Emmett Roe, the firm's owner, was convicted of involuntary manslaughter and received a

19-year prison sentence. In this case and others around the country, local prosecutors are taking the initiative to prosecute corporate executives as violent criminals.

CRITICAL THINKING

1. If Ford executives knew they had a dangerous car, should they have been found guilty of murder, even though the deaths were the result of collisions?
2. Is it fair to blame a single executive for the activities of a company that has thousands of employees?

 INFOTRAC COLLEGE EDITION RESEARCH

To learn more about work-related dangers, read:
Barbra Marcus, Sarah Minifie, Raj Natarajan, Joseph D. Wilson. Employment-related crimes (Twelfth Survey of White Collar Crime). *American Criminal Law Review* Wntr 1997 34 n2 p457–490
Anton Foek. Sweatshop Barbie: Exploitation of Third World labor. *The Humanist* Jan-Feb 1997 v57 n1 p9
Dana Wilkie. The uphill struggle for workplace health. *State Legislatures* June 1997 v23 n6 p27

Source: David B. Darden, Susannah Merritt, and Robyn J. Greenburg, "Employment-Related Crimes," *American Criminal Law Review* 35 (1998): 561–96; Occupational Safety and Health Act, 29 U.S.C. sections 651–678 (1994); John Wright, Francis Cullen, and Michael Blankenship, "The Social Construction of Corporate Violence: Media Coverage of the Imperial Food Products Fire" (paper presented at the annual meeting of the American Society of Criminology, Phoenix, Arizona, November 1993); Nancy Frank, "Unintended Murder and Corporate Risk-Taking: Defining the Concept of Justifiability," *Journal of Criminal Justice* 16 (1988): 17–24; Francis Cullen, William Maakestad, and Gray Cavender, "The Ford Pinto Case and Beyond: Corporate Crime, Moral Boundaries, and the Criminal Sanction," in *Corporations as Criminals,* ed. Ellen Hochstedler (Beverly Hills: Sage, 1984), pp. 107–130.

Characteristics of Organized Crime

A precise description of the characteristics of organized crime is difficult to formulate, but here are some of its general traits:[197]

- Organized crime is a conspiratorial activity, involving the coordination of numerous persons in the planning and execution of illegal acts or in the pursuit of a legitimate objective by unlawful means (for example, threatening a legitimate business to get a stake in it). Organized crime involves continuous commitment by primary members, although individuals with specialized skills may be brought in as needed. Organized crime is usually structured along hierarchical lines—a chieftain supported by close advisers, lower subordinates, and so on.
- Organized crime has economic gain as its primary goal, although power and status may also be motivating factors. Economic gain is achieved through maintenance of a near-monopoly on illegal goods and services, including drugs, gambling, pornography, and prostitution.
- Organized crime activities are not limited to providing illicit services. They include such sophisticated activities as laundering illegal money through legitimate businesses, land fraud, and computer crimes.
- Organized crime employs predatory tactics, such as intimidation, violence, and corruption. It appeals to greed to accomplish its objectives and preserve its gains.
- By experience, custom, and practice, organized crime's conspiratorial groups are usually very quick and effective in controlling and disciplining their members, associates, and victims. The individuals involved know that any deviation from the rules of the organization will evoke a prompt response from the other participants. This response may range from a reduction in rank and responsibility to a death sentence.
- Organized crime is not synonymous with the Mafia, the most experienced, most diversified, and possibly best-disciplined of these groups. The Mafia is actually a common stereotype of organized crime. Although several families in the organization called the Mafia are important components of organized crime activities, they do not hold a monopoly on underworld activities.
- Organized crime does not include terrorists dedicated to political change. Although violent acts are a major tactic of organized crime, the use of violence does not mean that a group is part of a confederacy of organized criminals.

Activities of Organized Crime

What are the main activities of organized crime? The traditional sources of income are derived from providing illicit materials and using force to enter into and maximize profits in legitimate businesses.[198] Annual gross income from criminal activity is at least $50 billion, more than 1 percent of the gross national product; some estimates put gross earnings as high as $90 billion, outranking most major industries in the United States.[199] Most organized crime income comes from narcotics distribution (over $30 billion annually), loan-sharking (lending money at illegal rates—$7 billion), and prostitution ($3 billion). However, additional billions come from gambling, theft rings, and other illegal enterprises. For example, the Attorney General's Commission on Pornography has concluded that organized crime figures exert substantial influence and control over the pornography industry.[200] Organized criminals have infiltrated labor unions, taking control of their pension funds and dues. Alan Block has described mob control of the New York waterfront and its influence on the use of union funds to buy insurance, health care, and so on from mob-controlled companies.[201] Hijacking of shipments and cargo theft are other sources of income. One study found that the annual losses due to theft of air cargo amount to $400 million; rail cargo, $600 million; trucking, $1.2 billion; and maritime shipments, $300 million.[202] Underworld figures fence high-value items and maintain international sales territories. In recent years they have branched into computer crime and other white-collar activities.

Organized crime figures have also kept up with the information age by using computers and the Internet to sell illegal material such as pornography. For example, when customers called local escort services for dates with either male or female sex workers in Las Vegas, they found the nude dancers and entertainers who arrived at their hotel rooms had been dispatched by another company. The reason? Their calls were being diverted by sophisticated computer programs to the lines of rival companies affiliated with organized crime. On October 9, 1998, six men believed to be part of the Gambino crime family were arrested for their part in pressuring a computer expert to provide the technical know-how for their plot.[203]

Organized Crime and Legitimate Enterprise Outside of criminal enterprises, additional billions are earned by organized crime figures who force or buy their way into legitimate businesses and use them both for profit and as a means of siphoning off (laundering) otherwise unaccountable profits. Merry Morash claims that mob control of legitimate enterprise today is influenced by market conditions. Businesses most likely to be affected are low-technology (such as garbage collection), have uniform products, and operate in rigid markets where price increases will not reduce demand. In addition, industries most affected by labor pressure are highly susceptible to takeovers because a mob-controlled work stoppage would destroy a product or interfere with meeting deadlines. Morash lists five ways in which organized criminals today become involved in legitimate enterprise: (1) business activity that supports illegal enterprises (for example, providing a front); (2) predatory or parasitic exploitation (for example, demanding protection money); (3) organization of monopolies or cartels to limit competition; (4) unfair advantages gained by such practices as manipulating labor unions and corrupting public officials; and (5) illegal manipulation of legal vehicles, particularly stocks and bonds.[204]

These traits show how organized crime is more like a business enterprise than a confederation of criminals seeking merely to enhance their power. Nowhere has this relationship been more visible than in the 1985 scandal that rocked the prestigious First National Bank of Boston. Federal prosecutors charged that the bank made unreported cash shipments of $1.2 million. It received $529,000 in small bills and sent $690,000 in bills of $100 or more. The bank was fined $500,000 for violating a law that requires that banks report any cash transaction of $10,000 or more. The bank's transaction came under scrutiny during an FBI investigation of the Angiulo crime family, which bought more than $41.7 million in cashier's checks from the bank.[205] The First National scandal illustrates that organized crime today involves a cooperative relationship between big business, politicians, and racketeers. The relationship is an expensive one: it has been estimated that organized crime activities stifle competition, resulting in the annual loss of 400,000 jobs and $18 billion in productivity; and because organized crime's profits go unreported, the rest of the population pays an extra $6.5 billion in taxes each year.[206]

The Concept of Organized Crime

The term *organized crime* conjures up images of strong men in dark suits, machine gun–toting bodyguards, rituals of allegiance to secret organizations, professional "gangland" killings, and meetings of "family" leaders who chart the course of crime much as the board members at General Motors decide on the country's transportation needs. These images have become part of what criminologists refer to as the **alien conspiracy theory** concept of organized crime. This is the belief, adhered to by the federal government and many respected criminologists, that organized crime is a direct offshoot of a criminal society—the **Mafia**—that first originated in Italy and Sicily and now controls racketeering in major U.S. cities. A major premise of the alien conspiracy theory is that the Mafia is centrally coordinated by a national committee that settles disputes, dictates policy, and assigns territory.[207] Not all criminologists believe in this narrow concept of organized crime, and many view the alien conspiracy theory as a figment of the media's imagination.[208] Their view depicts organized crime as a group of ethnically diverse gangs or groups who compete for profit in the sale of illegal goods and services or who use force and violence to extort money from legitimate enterprises. These groups are not bound by a central national organization but act independently on their own turf. We will now examine each of these two perspectives in some detail.

Alien Conspiracy Theory: La Cosa Nostra According to the alien conspiracy theory, organized crime is made up of a national syndicate of 25 or so Italian-dominated crime families that call themselves **La Cosa Nostra.** The major families have a total membership of about 1,700 "made men," who have been inducted into organized crime families, and another 17,000 "associates," who are criminally involved with syndicate members.[209] The families control crime in distinct geographic areas. New York City, the most important organized crime area, alone contains five families—the Gambino, Columbo, Lucchese, Bonnano, and Genovese families—named after their founding "godfathers"; in contrast, Chicago contains a single mob organization called the "outfit," which also influences racketeering in such cities as Milwaukee, Kansas City, and Phoenix. The families are believed to be ruled by a "commission" made up of the heads of the five New York families and bosses from Detroit, Buffalo, Chicago, and Philadelphia, which settles personal problems and jurisdictional conflicts and enforces rules that allow members to gain huge profits through the manufacture and sale of illegal goods and services (see Figure 13.2).[210]

Development of a National Syndicate How did this concept of a national crime cartel develop? The first organized gangs comprised Irish immigrants who made their home in the slum districts of New York City.[211] The Forty Thieves, considered the first New York gang with a definite, acknowledged leadership, were muggers, thieves, and pickpockets on the lower east side of Manhattan from the 1820s to just before the Civil War. Around 1890, Italian immigrants began forming gangs modeled after the Sicilian crime organization known as the Mafia; these gangs were called the Black Hand. In 1900 Johnny Torrio, a leader of New York's Five Points gang, moved to Chicago and helped his uncle, Big Jim Colosimo, organize the dominant gang in the Chicago area. Other gangs also flourished in Chicago, including those of Hymie Weiss and Bugs Moran. A later leader was the infamous Al "Scarface" Capone. The turning point of organized crime was the onset of Prohibition and the Volstead Act. This created a multimillion-dollar bootlegging industry overnight. Gangs vied for a share of the business, and bloody wars for control of rackets and profits became common. However, the problems of supplying liquor to thousands of illegal

Figure 13.2   Traditional Organization of the Mafia "Family"

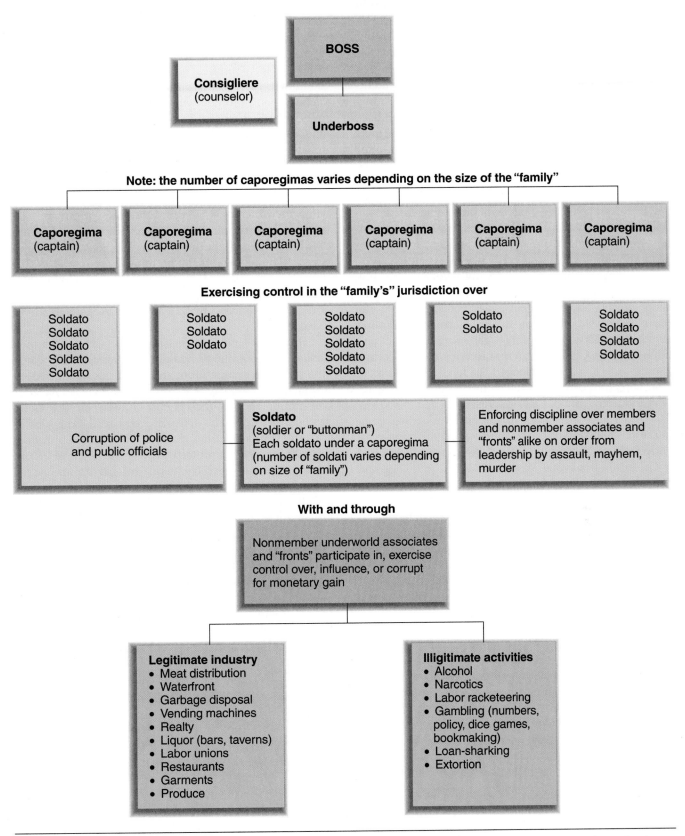

Source: U.S. Senate, Permanent Subcommittee on Investigations, Committee on Government Affairs, *Hearings on Organized Crime and Use of Violence,* 96th Cong., 2d Sess., April 1980, p. 117.

drinking establishments (speakeasies) required organization and an end to open warfare.

In the late 1920s, several events helped create the structure of organized crime. First, Johnny Torrio became leader of the Unione Siciliano, an ethnic self-help group that had begun as a legitimate enterprise but had been taken over by racketeers. This helped bring together the Chicago and New York crime groups; and because Torrio was Italian, it also spurred the beginnings of détente between Italians and Sicilians, who had been at odds with one another. Also during the 1920s, more than 500 members of Sicilian gangs fled to the United States to avoid prosecution; these new arrivals included future gang leaders Carlo Gambino, Joseph Profaci, Stefano Maggadino, and Joseph Bonnano.[212]

In December 1925, gang leaders from across the nation met in Cleveland to discuss strategies for mediating their differences nonviolently and for maximizing profits. A similar meeting took place in Atlantic City in 1929 and was attended by 20 gang leaders, including Lucky Luciano, Al Capone, and Dutch Schultz. Despite such efforts, however, gang wars continued into the 1930s. In 1934, according to some accounts, another meeting in New York, called by Johnny Torrio and Lucky Luciano, led to the formation of a national crime commission and acknowledged the territorial claims of 24 crime families around the country. This was considered the beginning of La Cosa Nostra.

Under the leadership of the national crime commission, organized crime began to expand in a more orderly fashion. Benjamin "Bugsy" Siegel was dispatched to California to oversee West Coast operations. The end of Prohibition required a new source of profits, and narcotics sales became the mainstay of gangland business. Al Polizzi, a Cleveland crime boss, formed a news service that provided information on horse racing, thereby helping create a national network of gang-dominated bookmakers. After World War II, organized crime families began using their vast profits from liquor, gambling, and narcotics to buy into legitimate businesses, such as entertainment, legal gambling in Cuba and Las Vegas, hotel chains, jukebox concerns, restaurants, and taverns. By paying off politicians, police, and judges and by using blackmail and coercion, organized criminals became almost immune to prosecution. The machine gun–toting gangster had given way to the businessman-racketeer. In the 1950s cooperation among gangland figures reached its zenith. Gang control over unions became widespread, and many legitimate businesses made payoffs to promote labor peace. New gang organizations arose in Los Angeles, Kansas City, and Dallas.

Post-1950 Developments In 1950 the Senate Special Committee to Investigate Organized Crime in Interstate Commerce, better known as the Kefauver Committee (after its chairman), was formed to look into organized crime. It reported the existence of a national crime car-

tel whose members cooperated to make a profit and engaged in joint ventures to eliminate enemies. The Kefauver Committee also made public the syndicate's enforcement arm, Murder Inc., which, under the leadership of Albert Anastasia, disposed of enemies for a price. The committee also found that corruption and bribery of local political officials were widespread. This theme was revived by the Senate Subcommittee on Investigations, better known as the McClellan Committee, in its investigation of the role organized crime played in labor racketeering. The committee and its chief counsel, Robert Kennedy, uncovered a close relationship between gang activity and the Teamsters Union, then led by Jimmy Hoffa. Hoffa's disappearance and assumed death has been linked to his gangland connections. Later investigations by the committee produced the testimony of Joseph Valachi, former underworld "soldier," who detailed the inner workings of La Cosa Nostra. The leaders of the national crime cartel at this time were Frank Costello, Vito Genovese, Carlo Gambino, Joseph Bonnano, and Joseph Profaci, all of New York; Sam Giancana of Chicago; and Angelo Bruno of Philadelphia.

During the next 15 years, gang activity expanded further into legitimate businesses. Nonetheless, gangland jealousy, competition, and questions of succession produced an occasional flare-up of violence. The most well-publicized conflict occurred between the Gallo brothers of Brooklyn—Albert, Larry, and Crazy Joe—and the Profaci crime family. The feud continued through the 1960s, uninterrupted by the death of Joseph Profaci and the new leadership of his group by Joe Colombo. Eventually, Colombo was severely injured by a Gallo-hired assassin, and in return, Joey Gallo was killed in a New York restaurant, Umberto's Clam House. Gallo's death once again brought peace in the underworld. Emerging as the most powerful syndicate boss was Carlo Gambino, who held this position until his death by natural causes in 1976.

In sum, the alien conspiracy theory sees organized crime as being run by an ordered group of ethnocentric (primarily of Italian origin) criminal syndicates, maintaining unified leadership and shared values. These syndicates communicate closely with other groups and obey the decisions of a national commission charged with settling disputes and creating crime policy.

The Mafia Myth Some scholars charge that this version of organized crime is fanciful. They argue that the alien conspiracy theory is too heavily influenced by media accounts and by the testimony of a single person, mobster Joseph Valachi, before the McClellan Committee. Valachi's description of La Cosa Nostra was relied upon by conspiracy theorists as an accurate portrayal of mob activities. Yet critics question its authenticity and direction. For example, criminologist Jay Albanese compared Valachi's statements to those of another mob informer, Jimmy Frantianno, and found major discrepancies with respect to the location and size of organized criminal activity.[213]

The challenges to the alien conspiracy theory have produced alternative views of organized crime. For example, Philip Jenkins and Gary Potter studied organized crime in Philadelphia and found little evidence that this supposed "Mafia stronghold" was controlled by an Italian-dominated crime family.[214] Sociologist Alan Block has argued that organized crime is both a loosely constructed social system and a social world that reflects the existing U.S. system, not a tightly organized national criminal syndicate. The system is composed of "relationships binding professional criminals, politicians, law enforcers, and various entrepreneurs."[215] In contrast, the social world of organized crime is often chaotic because of the constant power struggle between competing groups. Block rejects the idea that an all-powerful organized crime commission exists and instead views the world of professional criminals as one shaped by the political economy. He finds that independent crime organizations can be characterized as either *enterprise syndicates* or *power syndicates.* The former are involved in providing services and include madams, drug distributors, bookmakers, and so on. These are "workers in the world of illegal enterprise." They have set positions in an illegal enterprise system, with special tasks to perform if the enterprise is to function. In contrast, power syndicates perform no set task except to extort or terrorize. Their leaders can operate against legitimate business or against fellow criminals who operate enterprise syndicates. Through coercion, buyouts, and other similar means, power syndicates graft themselves onto enterprise systems, legal businesses, trade unions, and so on. Block's view of organized crime is revisionist because it portrays mob activity as a quasi-economic enterprise system swayed by social forces, not a tightly knit, unified cartel dominated by ethnic minorities carrying out European traditions. His world of organized crime is dominated by business leaders, politicians, and union leaders who work hand in hand with criminals. Moreover, the violent, chaotic social world of power syndicates does not lend itself to a tightly controlled syndicate.

Organized Crime Groups

Even such devoted alien conspiracy advocates as the U.S. Justice Department now view organized crime as a loose confederation of ethnic and regional crime groups, bound together by a commonality of economic and political objectives.[216] Some of these groups are located in fixed geographical areas. For example, the so-called Dixie Mafia operates in the South. Chicano crime families are found in areas with significant Hispanic populations, such as California and Arizona. White-ethnic crime organizations are found across the nation.

Some Italian and Cuban groups operate internationally. Some have preserved their past identity, whereas others are constantly changing organizations.

One important recent change in organized crime is the interweaving of ethnic groups into the traditional structure. African-American, Hispanic, and Asian racketeers now compete with the more traditional groups, overseeing the distribution of drugs, prostitution, and gambling in a symbiotic relationship with old-line racketeers. Since 1970 Russian and Eastern groups have been operating on U.S. soil. As many as 2,500 Russian immigrants are believed to be involved in criminal activity, primarily in Russian enclaves in New York City. Beyond extortion from immigrants, Russian organized crime groups have cooperated with Mafia families in narcotics trafficking, fencing stolen property, money laundering, and other traditional organized crime schemes.[217] As the traditional organized crime families drift into legitimate businesses, the distribution of contraband on the street is handled by newcomers, characterized by Francis Ianni as "urban social bandits."[218]

Have these newly emerging groups achieved the same level of control as traditional crime families? Some experts argue that minority gangs will have a tough time developing the network of organized corruption that involves working with government officials and unions, which traditional crime families enjoyed.[219]

As law enforcement pressure has been put on traditional organized crime figures, other groups have filled the vacuum. For example, the Hell's Angels motorcycle club is now believed to be one of the leading distributors of narcotics in the United States. Similarly, Chinese criminal gangs have taken over the dominant role in New York City's heroin market from the traditional Italian-run syndicates.[220]

In sum, most experts now agree that it is simplistic to view organized crime in the United States as a national syndicate that controls all illegitimate rackets in an orderly fashion. This view seems to ignore the variety of gangs and groups, their membership, and their relationship to the outside world.[221] Mafia-type groups may play a major role in organized crime, but they are by no means the only ones that can be considered organized criminals.[222]

Organized Crime Abroad Other countries also confront organized criminal gangs. The Cali and Medellin drug cartels in Colombia are world-famous for both their vast drug trafficking profits and their unflinching use of violence to achieve their objectives. When Pablo Escobar, the head of the Medellin cartel, was captured and killed by police and soldiers on December 2, 1993, experts predicted that drug smuggling would *increase* as the cocaine trade shifted to the control of the smoother and more businesslike Cali cartel.[223]

Drug-dealing gangs are not the only form of organized crime abroad. Japan has a long history of organized criminal activity by *Yakuza* gangs. In 1993 officials of the Kirin Brewery, Japan's largest beer maker, resigned after allegations were made that they paid over 33 million yen in *sokaiya*—extortion money—to racketeers who threatened their business.[224] In China organized gangs use violence to enforce contracts between companies, serving as an alternative to the legal system. They also help smuggle many of the 100,000 mainland Chinese who enter the United States each year. For example, in June 1993 a Chinese ship foundered off the coast of New York, and 10 illegal immigrants drowned.[225]

Russia has been beset by organized crime activity since the breakup of the Soviet Union. There are an estimated 3,000 criminal gangs active in Russia. Bloody shoot-outs have become common as gangs attempt to stake out territory and extort businesses. In one incident, an auto dealership was attacked and two security guards killed when the owner failed to pay "protection money."[226]

Computer and communications technology has fostered international cooperation among crime cartels. For example, East European and Russian gangs sell arms seized from the former Soviet Army to members of the Sicilian Mafia; Japanese and Italian mob members have met in Paris; and drug money from South America is laundered in Canada and England.[227]

Controlling Organized Crime

George Vold has argued that the development of organized crime parallels early capitalist enterprises. Organized crime employs ruthless monopolistic tactics to maximize profits; it is also secretive, protective of its operations, and defensive against any outside intrusion.[228] Consequently, controlling its activities is extremely difficult.

Federal and state governments actually did little to combat organized crime until fairly recently. One of the first measures aimed directly at organized crime was the Interstate and Foreign Travel or Transportation in Aid of Racketeering Enterprises Act (Travel Act).[229] The Travel Act prohibits travel in interstate commerce or use of interstate facilities with the intent to promote, manage, establish, carry on, or facilitate an unlawful activity; it also prohibits the actual or attempted engagement in these activities. In 1970 Congress passed the Organized Crime Control Act. Title IX of the act, probably its most effective measure, has been called the **Racketeer Influenced and Corrupt Organization Act (RICO)**.[230]

RICO did not create new categories of crimes but rather new categories of offenses in racketeering activity, which it defined as involvement in two or more acts prohibited by 24 existing federal and 8 state statutes. The offenses listed in RICO include state-defined crimes, such as murder, kidnapping, gambling, arson, robbery, bribery, extortion, and narcotic violations; and federally defined crimes, such as bribery, counterfeiting, trans-

mission of gambling information, prostitution, and mail fraud. RICO is designed to limit patterns of organized criminal activity by prohibiting involvement in acts intended to

- Derive income from racketeering or the unlawful collection of debts and use or invest such income.
- Acquire through racketeering an interest in or control over any enterprise engaged in interstate or foreign commerce.
- Conduct business through a pattern of racketeering.
- Conspire to use racketeering as a means of making income, collecting loans, or conducting business.

An individual convicted under RICO is subject to 20 years in prison and a $25,000 fine. Additionally, the accused must forfeit to the U.S. government any interest in a business in violation of RICO. These penalties are much more potent than simple conviction and imprisonment. To enforce these policy initiatives, the federal government created the Strike Force Program. This program, operating in 18 cities, brings together various state and federal law enforcement officers and prosecutors to work as a team against racketeering. Several states, including New York, Illinois, New Jersey, and New Mexico, have created their own special investigative teams devoted to organized criminal activity.

These efforts began to pay off more than a decade ago when, in April 1985, a New York–based strike force successfully obtained indictments against members of the Lucchese, Genovese, and Bonnano families.[231] The investigation also uncovered evidence to support the national crime cartel concept. Similar sweeps were conducted in Boston, Chicago, and Miami during the remainder of the decade. From 1985 to 1987 many major organized crime figures were indicted, convicted, and imprisoned, including Gennaro Angiulo, second in command in New England, who received a 45-year sentence. Tony Salerno, Tony Corallo, Carmine Persico, and Gennaro Langella of the New York families each got 100 years in prison; and Nicodemo Scarfo of Philadelphia got 14 years for extortion. The arrest and imprisonment of John Gotti, the so-called "Dapper Don," illustrated the decline of white-ethnic organized crime families and their replacement by emerging groups.

The Future of Organized Crime

Indications exist that the traditional organized crime syndicates are in decline. Law enforcement officials in Philadelphia, New Jersey, New England, New Orleans, Kansas City, Detroit, and Milwaukee all report that years of federal and state interventions have severely eroded the Mafia organizations in their areas.[232] What has caused this alleged erosion of Mafia power? First, a number of the reigning family heads are quite old, in their 70s and 80s, prompting some law enforcement officials to dub them "the Geritol gang."[233] A younger generation of mob leaders is stepping in to take control of the families, and they seem to lack the skill and leadership of the older bosses. In addition, active government enforcement policies have halved what the estimated made membership was 20 years ago; a number of the highest-ranking leaders have been imprisoned. Additional pressure comes from newly emerging ethnic gangs that want to muscle in on traditional syndicate activities, such as drug sales and gambling. For example, Chinese Triad gangs have been active in New York and California in the drug trade, loan-sharking, and labor racketeering. Other ethnic crime groups include black and Colombian drug cartels and the Sicilian Mafia, which operates independently of U.S. groups.

Although most street gangs are too disorganized to become stable crime groups, there are some large gangs such as Chicago's Gangster Disciples whose structure, activities, and relationships are now becoming similar to traditional organized gangs. This African-American gang is actively involved in politics in order to gain power and support. Members meet regularly, commit crime as a group, and maintain ongoing relationships with other street gangs and also with prison-based gangs. The Gangster Disciples have extensive ownership of legitimate private businesses and dealings with other businessmen. They offer "protection" against rival gangs and supply stolen merchandise to customers and employees.[234]

The Mafia has also been hurt by changing values in U.S. society. White, ethnic inner-city neighborhoods, which were the locus of Mafia power, have been shrinking as families move to the suburbs. Organized crime groups have consequently lost their political and social base of operations. In addition, the code of silence that protected Mafia leaders is now broken regularly by younger members who turn informer rather than face prison terms. It is also possible that their success has hurt organized crime families: younger members are better educated than their forebears and are equipped to seek their fortunes through legitimate enterprise.[235]

Jay Albanese, a leading expert on organized crime, predicts that pressure by the federal government will encourage organized crime figures to engage in safer activities, such as credit card and airline ticket counterfeiting and illicit toxic waste disposal. Instead of running illegal enterprises, established families may be content with financing younger entrepreneurs and channeling or laundering profits through their legitimate business enterprises. There may be greater effort among organized criminals in the future to infiltrate legitimate business enterprises to obtain access to money for financing and the means to launder illicitly obtained cash. Labor unions and the construction industry have been favorite targets in the past.[236]

Although these actions are considered a major blow to Italian-dominated organized crime cartels, they are unlikely to stifle criminal entrepreneurship. As long as vast profits can be made from selling narcotics, producing pornography, or taking illegal bets, many groups stand ready to fill the gaps and reap the profits of providing illegal goods and services. It is likely that the New York and Chicago mobs, with a combined total of almost 1,500 made members, will continue to ply their trade. For example, in 1998 Michael Blutrich and Lyle Pfeffer, owners of the Scores nightclub in New York City, told how for years after they opened their midtown club, the Mafia demanded payments. Mobsters opened discussions by slamming guns on the table, threatened to blow up Scores if payoffs weren't made, and mockingly promised to eliminate any "rats" who exposed them.[237] Members of the Gambino family demanded about $200,000 a year in profits from the coat-check room and valet parking, an additional $1,000 a week in cash, and the right to choose the club's bouncers. The gang leaders included John A. Gotti, 34—the son of John J. Gotti, 58, the family's imprisoned boss.

SUMMAR Y

White-collar and organized criminals are similar because they both use ongoing illegal business enterprises to make personal profits. There are various types of white-collar crime. Stings and swindles involve the use of deception to bilk people out of their money. Chiseling customers, businesses, or the government regularly is a second common type of white-collar crime. Surprisingly, many professionals engage in chiseling offenses. Other white-collar criminals use their positions in business and the marketplace to commit economic crimes. Their crimes include exploitation of position in a company or the government to secure illegal payments; embezzlement and employee pilferage and fraud; client fraud; and influence peddling and bribery. Further, corporate officers sometimes violate the law to improve the position and profitability of their businesses. Their crimes include price-fixing, false advertising, and environmental offenses.

So far, little has been done to combat white-collar crimes. Most offenders do not view themselves as criminals and therefore do not seem to be deterred by criminal statutes. Although thousands of white-collar criminals are prosecuted each year, their numbers are insignificant compared with the magnitude of the problem. The government has used various law enforcement strategies to combat white-collar crime. Some involve deterrence, which uses punishment to frighten potential abusers. Others involve economism or compliance strategies, which create economic incentives to obey the law.

The demand for illegal goods and services has produced a symbiotic relationship between the public and an organized criminal network. Although criminal gangs have existed since the early nineteenth century, their power and size were spurred by the Volstead Act and Prohibition in the 1920s. Organized crime supplies alcohol, gambling, drugs, prostitutes, and pornography to the public. It is immune from prosecution because of public apathy and because of its own strong political connections. Organized criminals used to be white ethnics—Jews, Italians, and Irish—but today African-Americans, Hispanics, and other groups have become included in organized crime activities. The old-line "families" are now more likely to use their criminal wealth and power to buy into legitimate businesses.

There is debate over the control of organized crime. Some experts believe a national crime cartel controls all activities.

Others view organized crime as a group of disorganized, competing gangs dedicated to extortion or to providing illegal goods and services. Efforts to control organized crime have been stepped up. The federal government has used antiracketeering statutes to arrest syndicate leaders. But as long as huge profits can be made, illegal enterprises should continue to flourish.

See the book-specific web site at www.cj.wadsworth.com for additional chapter links, discussions, and quizzes.

THINKING LIKE A CRIMINOLOGIST

People who commit computer crime are found in every segment of society. They range in age from 10 to 60, and their skill level runs from novice to professional. They are otherwise average people, not super-criminals possessing unique abilities and talents. Any person of any age with even a little skill is a potential computer criminal. Most studies indicate that employees represent the greatest threat to computers. Almost 90 percent of computer crimes against businesses are inside jobs. Ironically, as advances continue in remote data processing, the threat from external sources will probably increase. With the networking of systems and the adoption of more user-friendly software, the sociological profile of the computer offender may change. For example, computer criminals may soon be members of organized crime syndicates. They will use computer systems to monitor law enforcement activities. To become a made man in the twenty-first-century organized crime family, the recruit will have to develop knowledge of the equipment used for audio surveillance of law enforcement communications: computers with sound card or microphone, modems, and software programs for the remote operation of the systems.

Which theories of criminal behavior best explain the actions of computer criminals, and which ones fail to account for computer crime?

KEY TERMS

entrepreneurship
white-collar crime
organized crime
enterprise
churning
insider trading
arbitrage
Mollen Commission
pilferage
passive neglect
affirmative tax evasion
corporate crime

organizational crime
actual authority
apparent authority
Sherman Antitrust Act
division of markets
tying arrangement
group boycott
price-fixing
predation
identical bidding
geographical market sharing
rotational bidding

deceptive pricing
virus
compliance
economism
deterrence
organized crime
alien conspiracy theory
Mafia
La Cosa Nostra
Racketeer Influenced and Corrupt
 Organization Act (RICO)
forfeiture

NOTES

1. Todd S. Purdum, "Ex-Mousketeer Darlene on Trial for Securities Fraud," *New York Times,* 9 December 1998, p. B1.

2. Dwight Smith, "White-Collar Crime, Organized Crime and the Business Establishment: Resolving a Crisis in Criminological Theory," in *White Collar and Economic Crime: A Multidisciplinary and Crossnational Perspective,* ed. P. Wickman and T. Dailey (Lexington, Mass.: Lexington Books, 1982), p. 53.

3. See, generally, Dwight Smith, Jr., "Organized Crime and Entrepreneurship," *International Journal of Criminology and Penology* 6 (1978): 161–77; Dwight C.

Smith, Jr., "Paragons, Pariahs, and Pirates: A Spectrum-Based Theory of Enterprise," *Crime and Delinquency* 26 (1980): 358–86; Dwight C. Smith, Jr., and Richard S. Alba, "Organized Crime and American Life," *Society* 16 (1979): 32–38.

4. Smith, "White-Collar Crime, Organized Crime and the Business Establishment," p. 33.

5. Mark Haller, "Illegal Enterprise: A Theoretical and Historical Interpretation," *Criminology* 28 (1990): 207–35.

6. Nancy Frank and Michael Lynch, *Corporate Crime, Corporate Violence* (Albany, N.Y.: Harrow and Heston, 1992), p. 7.

7. Nikos Passas and David Nelken, "The Thin Line Between Legitimate and Criminal Enterprises: Subsidy Frauds in the European Community," *Crime, Law and Social Change* 19 (1993): 223–43.

8. Passas and Nelken, "The Thin Line Between Legitimate and Criminal Enterprises," p. 238.

9. For a thorough review see David Friedrichs, *Trusted Criminals* (Belmont, Calif.: Wadsworth, 1996).

10. Kitty Calavita and Henry Pontell, "Savings and Loan Fraud as Organized Crime: Toward a Conceptual Typology of Corporate Illegality," *Criminology* 31 (1993): 519–48.

136. Comprehensive Crime Control Act of 1984, Pub. L. No. 98-473, 2101-03, 98 Stat. 1837, 2190 (1984), adding 18 USC 1030 (1984). Amended by Pub. L. No. 99-474, 100 Stat. 1213 (1986) codified at 18 U.S.C. 1030 (Supp. V 1987).

137. 18 U.S.C. section 1030 (1994).

138. Copyright Infringement Act 17 U.S.C. section 506(a) 1994.

139. 18 U.S.C. 2510–2520 (1988 and Supp. II 1990).

140. Project, Eighth Survey of White Collar Crime, *American Criminal Law Review,* 30 (1993): 501.

141. Herbert Edelhertz and Charles Rogovin, eds., *A National Strategy for Containing White-Collar Crime* (Lexington, Mass.: Lexington Books, 1980), Appendix A, pp. 122–23.

142. Kathleen Daly, "Gender and Varieties of White-Collar Crime," *Criminology* 27 (1989): 769–93.

143. Quoted in Metz and Miller, "Boesky's Rise and Fall Illustrate a Compulsion to Profit by Getting Inside Track on Market," p. 28.

144. Donald Cressey, *Other People's Money: A Study of the Social Psychology of Embezzlement* (Glencoe, Ill.: Free Press, 1973).

145. Cressey, *Other People's Money,* p. 96.

146. Ronald Kramer, "Corporate Crime: An Organizational Perspective," in *White Collar and Economic Crime: A Multidisciplinary and Crossnational Perspective,* ed. P. Wickman and T. Dailey (Lexington, Mass.: Lexington Books, 1982), pp. 75–94.

147. John Braithwaite, "Toward a Theory of Organizational Crime." Paper presented at the annual meeting of the American Society of Criminology, Montreal, November 1987.

148. Travis Hirschi and Michael Gottfredson, "Causes of White-Collar Crime," *Criminology* 25 (1987): 949–74.

149. Michael Gottfredson and Travis Hirschi, *A General Theory of Crime* (Stanford, Calif.: Stanford University Press, 1990), p. 191.

150. For an opposing view, see Darrell Steffensmeier, "On the Causes of 'White-Collar' Crime: An Assessment of Hirschi and Gottfredson's Claims," *Criminology* 27 (1989): 345–59.

151. Carey Herbert, "The Implications of Self-Control Theory for Workplace Offending." Paper presented at the American Society of Criminology Meeting, San Diego, Calif., 1997.

152. David Weisburd, Ellen Chayet, and Elin Waring, "White-Collar and Criminal Careers: Some Preliminary Findings," *Crime and Delinquency* 36 (1990): 342–55.

153. Michael Benson and Elizabeth Moore, "Are White-Collar and Common Offenders the Same? An Empirical and Theoretical Critique of a Recently Proposed General Theory of Crime," *Journal of Research in Crime and Delinquency* 29 (1992): 251–72.

154. This section relies heavily on Daniel Skoler, "White-Collar Crime and the Criminal Justice System: Problems and Challenges," in *A National Strategy for Containing White-Collar Crime,* ed. Herbert Edelhertz and Charles Rogovin (Lexington, Mass.: Lexington Books, 1980), pp. 57–76.

155. Theodore Hammett and Joel Epstein, *Prosecuting Environmental Crime: Los Angeles County* (Washington, D.C.: National Institute of Justice, 1993).

156. Michael Benson, Francis Cullen, and William Maakestad, "Local Prosecutors and Corporate Crime," *Crime and Delinquency* 36 (1990): 356–72.

157. Benson, Cullen, and Maakestad, "Local Prosecutors and Corporate Crime," pp. 369–70.

158. Benson, Cullen, and Maakestad, "Local Prosecutors and Corporate Crime," p. 371.

159. Traub, "Battling Employee Crime: A Review of Corporate Strategies and Programs," pp. 248–252.

160. Alan Otten, "States Begin to Protect Employees Who Blow Whistle on Their Firms," *Wall Street Journal,* 31 December 1984, p. 11.

161. David Simon and D. Stanley Eitzen, *Elite Deviance* (Boston: Allyn and Bacon, 1982), p. 28.

162. Paul Jesilow, Henry Pontell, and Gilbert Geis, "Physician Immunity from Prosecution and Punishment for Medical Program Fraud," in *Punishments and Privilege,* ed. W. Byron Groves and Graeme Newman (New York: Harrow and Heston, 1987), pp. 7–22.

163. Clinard and Yeager, *Corporate Crime,* p. 124.

164. Peter Yeager, "Structural Bias in Regulatory Law Enforcement: The Case of the U.S. Environmental Protection Agency," *Social Problems* 34 (1987): 330–44.

165. Geis, "Avocational Crime," p. 390.

166. Clinard and Yeager, *Corporate Crime,* p. 288.

167. See, generally, Stanton Wheeler, David Weisburd, Elin Waring, and Nancy Bode, "White-Collar Crimes and Criminals," *American Criminal Law Review* 25 (1988): 331–57.

168. Susanne Schafer, "One General Fired, Two Punished for Mismanaging C-17 Plane," *Boston Globe,* 1 May 1993, p. 3.

169. Paul Blustein, "Disputes Arise over Value of Laws on Insider Trading," *Wall Street Journal,* 17 November 1986, p. 28.

170. Paul Barrett, "For Many Dalkon Shield Claimants Settlement Won't End the Trauma," *Wall Street Journal,* 9 March 1988, p. 29.

171. This section relies heavily on Albert Reiss, Jr., "Selecting Strategies of Social Control over Organizational Life," in *Enforcing Regulation,* ed. Keith Hawkins and John M. Thomas (Boston: Klowver Publications, 1984), pp. 25–37.

172. John Braithwaite, "The Limits of Economism in Controlling Harmful Corporate Conduct," *Law and Society Review* 16 (1981–1982): 481–504.

173. Associated Press, "Idaho Plant to Pay $11.8M Fine," *New York Times,* 17 October 1998, p. C2.

174. Michael Benson, "Emotions and Adjudication: Status Degradation Among White-Collar Criminals," *Justice Quarterly* 7 (1990): 515–28; John Braithwaite, *Crime, Shame and Reintegration* (Sydney: Cambridge University Press, 1989).

175. Wayne Gray and John Scholz, "Does Regulatory Enforcement Work? A Panel Analysis of OSHA Enforcement," *Law and Society Review* 27 (1993): 177–91.

176. John Braithwaite and Gilbert Geis, "On Theory and Action for Corporate Crime Control," *Crime and Delinquency* 28 (1982): 292–314.

177. Frank Pearce and Steve Tombs, "Hazards, Law and Class: Contextualizing the Regulation of Corporate Crime," *Social and Legal Studies* 6 (1997): 79–107.

178. Frank and Lynch, *Corporate Crime, Corporate Violence,* pp. 33–34.

179. Environmental Protection Agency Report, *Region 10's Wastewater Permit Program Needs Improvement to Protect Water Quality in Alaska and Idaho,* Report number E1HWF7-10-0012-8100076 (Washington, D.C., Environmental Protection Agency, March 1998).

180. Kip Schlegel, "Desert, Retribution and Corporate Criminality," *Justice Quarterly* 5 (1988): 615–34.

181. Raymond Michalowski and Ronald Kramer, "The Space Between Laws: The Problem of Corporate Crime in a Transnational Context," *Social Problems* 34 (1987): 34–53.

182. Michalowski and Kramer, "The Space Between Laws."

183. Steven Klepper and Daniel Nagin, "The Deterrent Effect of Perceived Certainty and Severity of Punishment Revisited," *Criminology* 27 (1989): 721–46.

184. Geis, "White-Collar and Corporate Crime," p. 154.

185. Associated Press, "Company President Sentenced to 10 to 24 Months Imprisonment Conviction," *New York Times,* 2 February 1998, p. C1.

186. "The Follies Go on," *Time,* 15 April 1991, p. 45.

187. Bill Richards and Alex Kotlowitz, "Judge Finds Three Corporate Officials Guilty of Murder in Cyanide Death of Worker," *Wall Street Journal,* 17 June 1985, p. 2.

188. Christopher M. Brown and Nikhil S. Singhvi, "Antitrust Violations," *American Criminal Law Review* 35 (1998): 467–501.

189. Howard Adler, "Current Trends in Criminal Antitrust Enforcement," *Business Crimes Bulletin* (April 1996): 1.

190. Department of Justice, Antitrust Division, News Release, October 15, 1996; Kurt Eichenwald, "Archer Daniels Agrees to Big Fine for Price-Fixing," *New York Times,* 15 October 1996, p. A1.

191. Robert Bennett, "Foreword," Eighth Survey of White Collar Crime, *American Criminal Law Review* 30 (1993).

192. David Weisburd, Elin Waring, and Stanton Wheeler, "Class, Status, and the Punishment of White-Collar Criminals," *Law and Social Inquiry* 15 (1990): 223–43.

193. Mark Cohen, "Environmental Crime and Punishment: Legal/Economic Theory and Empirical Evidence on Enforcement of Federal Environmental Statutes," *Journal of Criminal Law and Criminology* 82 (1992): 1054–1109.

194. Pearce and Tombs, "Hazards, Law and Class: Contextualizing the Regulation of Corporate Crime," p. 92.

195. See, generally, President's Commission on Organized Crime, Report to the President and the Attorney General, *The Impact: Organized Crime Today* (Washington, D.C.: U.S. Government Printing Office, 1986). Herein cited as *Organized Crime Today.*

196. Frederick Martens and Michele Cunningham-Niederer, "Media Magic, Mafia Mania," *Federal Probation* 49 (1985): 60–68.

197. *Organized Crime Today,* pp. 7–8.

198. Alan Block and William Chambliss, *Organizing Crime* (New York: Elsevier, 1981).

199. *Organized Crime Today,* p. 462.

200. Attorney General's Commission on Pornography, *Final Report* (Washington, D.C.: U.S. Government Printing Office, 1986), p. 1053.

201. Alan Block, *East Side/West Side* (New Brunswick, N.J.: Transaction Books, 1983), pp. VII, 10–11.

202. G. R. Blakey and M. Goldsmith, "Criminal Redistribution of Stolen Property: The Need for Law Reform," *Michigan Law Review* 81 (August 1976): 45–46.

203. The Associated Press, "Mob Seen in Las Vegas Sex Trade," *New York Times,* 17 October 1998, p. A7.

204. Merry Morash, "Organized Crime," in *Major Forms of Crime,* ed. Robert Meier (Beverly Hills: Sage, 1984), p. 198.

205. Stephen Koepp, "Dirty Cash and Tarnished Vaults," *Time,* 25 February 1985, p. 65.

206. Roy Rowan, "The 50 Biggest Mafia Bosses," *Fortune,* 10 November 1986, p. 24.

207. Donald Cressey, *Theft of the Nation* (New York: Harper and Row, 1969).

208. Dwight Smith, *The Mafia Mystique* (New York: Basic Books, 1975).

209. *Organized Crime Today,* p. 489.

210. Robert Rhodes, *Organized Crime: Crime Control versus Civil Liberties* (New York: Random House, 1984).

211. This section borrows heavily from Browning and Gerassi, *The American Way of Crime,* pp. 288–472; and August Bequai, *Organized Crime* (Lexington, Mass.: Lexington Books, 1979).

212. *Organized Crime Today,* p. 52.

213. Jay Albanese, "God and the Mafia Revisited: From Valachi to Frantianno." Paper presented at the annual meeting of the American Society of Criminology, Toronto, 1982.

214. Philip Jenkins and Gary Potter, "The Politics and Mythology of Organized Crime: A Philadelphia Case Study," *Journal of Criminal Justice* 15 (1987): 473–84.

215. Block, *East Side/West Side.*

216. *Organized Crime Today,* p. 11.

217. Omar Bartos, "Growth of Russian Organized Crime Poses Serious Threat," *CJ International* 11 (1995): 8–9.

218. Francis Ianni, *Black Mafia: Ethnic Succession in Organized Crime* (New York: Pocket Books, 1975).

219. Robert Kelly and Rufus Schatzberg, "Types of Minority Organized Crime: Some Considerations." Paper presented at the annual meeting of the American Society of Criminology, Montreal, November 1987.

220. Peter Kerr, "Chinese Now Dominate New York Heroin Trade," *New York Times,* 9 August 1987, p. 1.

221. Jenkins and Potter, "The Politics and Mythology of Organized Crime."

222. William Chambliss, *On the Take* (Bloomington: Indiana University Press, 1978).

223. Russell Watson, "Death on the Spot," *Newsweek,* 13 December 1993, pp. 18–20.

224. Yumiko Ono, "Top Kirin Brewery Executives Resign Amid Reports of Paying off Racketeers," *Wall Street Journal,* 19 July 1993, p. A6.

225. Michael Elliott, "Global Mafia," *Newsweek,* 13 December 1993, pp. 22–29.

226. Associated Press, "Gangland Violence Rises and Startles in Moscow," *Boston Globe,* 22 July 1993, p. 44.

227. Associated Press, "Gangland Violence Rises and Startles in Moscow."

228. George Vold, *Theoretical Criminology,* 2d ed., rev. Thomas Bernard (New York: Oxford University Press, 1979).

229. 18 U.S.C. 1952 (1976).

230. Pub. L. No. 91-452, Title IX, 84 Stat. 922 (1970) (codified at 18 U.S.C. 1961–68, 1976).

231. Ed Magnuson, "Hard Days for the Mafia," *Time,* 4 March 1985.

232. Selwyn Raab, "A Battered and Ailing Mafia Is Losing Its Grip on America," *New York Times,* 22 October 1990, p. 1.

233. Raab, "A Battered and Ailing Mafia Is Losing Its Grip on America."

234. Scott Decker, Tim Bynum, and Deborah Weisel, "A Tale of Two Cities: Gangs and Organized Crime Groups," *Justice Quarterly* 15 (1998): 395–425.

235. Raab, "A Battered and Ailing Mafia Is Losing Its Grip on America," p. B7.

236. Jay Albanese, *Organized Crime in America,* 2d ed. (Cincinnati: Anderson, 1989), p. 68.

237. Selwyn Raab, "Strip Club Partners, Now Ruined, Blame Greed and the Mob," *New York Times,* 30 August 1998.

CHAPTER 14

Public Order Crimes

INTRODUCTION

In 1998 grand juries in Alabama and Tennessee indicted the Barnes and Noble book chain for selling obscene material. The point of controversy was two books, Jock Sturges's *Radiant Identities* and David Hamilton's *The Age of Innocence,* both of which contain photographs of nude children. Protests were organized in 35 states to dissuade the chain from carrying the books. Barnes and Noble refused to comply, arguing that the photographs are not obscene. The books themselves are of high quality, and the photographs attempt to have artistic merit. Sturges countered that his attackers instruct "people in shame by suggesting that there is something about the human body that is inherently gross."[1] Although most state laws strictly restrict or prohibit pictures of children that show them in sexual poses or expose their genitalia, prosecutors are reluctant to take action. After all, many of the great works of Western art depict nude males and females, some quite young. Should the paintings of Leonardo Da Vinci or the sculpture of Michelangelo be considered kiddie porn?

Societies have long banned or limited behaviors that are believed to run contrary to social norms, customs, and values. These behaviors are often referred to as **public order crimes** or **victimless crimes,** although this latter term can be misleading.[2] Public order crimes involve acts that interfere with the operations of society and the ability of people to function efficiently. Put another way, whereas such common-law crimes as rape or robbery are considered inherently wrong and damaging, other behaviors are outlawed because they conflict with social policy, prevailing moral rules, and current public opinion. Statutes designed to uphold public order usually prohibit the manufacture and distribution of morally questionable goods and services such as erotic material, commercial sex, and mood-altering drugs. They may also ban acts that a few people holding political power consider morally tinged, such as homosexual contact. Statutes like these are controversial in part because millions of otherwise law-abiding citizens often engage in these outlawed activities and consequently become criminal. These statutes are also controversial because they selectively prohibit desired goods, services, and behaviors; in other words, they outlaw sin and vice.

This chapter covers these public order crimes; it first briefly discusses the relationship between law and morality. Next the chapter addresses public order crimes of a sexual nature: pornography, prostitution, deviant sex, and homosexual acts. The chapter concludes by focusing on the abuse of drugs and alcohol.

LAW AND MORALITY

Legislation of moral issues has continually frustrated lawmakers. There is little debate that the purpose of criminal law is to protect society and reduce social harm. When a store is robbed or a child assaulted, it is relatively easy to see and condemn the harm done the victim. It is, however, more difficult to sympathize with or even identify the victims of immoral acts, such as pornography or prostitution, where the parties involved may be willing participants; if there is no victim, can there be a crime? Should acts be made illegal merely because they violate prevailing moral standards? If so, who defines morality?

Consider the case of Heidi Fleiss, the wealthy young California woman arrested in 1993 for running the most exclusive call-girl ring in Los Angeles. Fearing that she would reveal names, a number of prominent movie executives and entertainers issued unsolicited statements denying that they were patrons of Fleiss's ring; other well-known stars admitted to being her clients. Some of her employees claimed that it was common for them to earn between $10,000 and $50,000 per month.[3] Fleiss was convicted and sent to jail.

Should Fleiss have been punished? Her clients wanted to hire call girls and willingly purchased their services. It hardly seems possible that these clients were crime victims. What of Fleiss's alleged employees? They willingly engaged in sexual activity for money, and their income was far higher than they would have earned in legitimate jobs. Although "immoral," should Fleiss, her employees, and her clients be considered criminals?

To answer this question we might first consider whether there is actually a victim in so-called victimless crimes. Some participants may have been coerced into their acts; they are therefore its victims. Opponents of pornography, such as Andrea Dworkin, charge that women involved in adult films, far from being highly

Even if public order crimes do not actually harm their participants, then perhaps society as a whole should be considered the victim of these crimes. Is the community harmed when an adult bookstore opens or a brothel is established? Does this signal that a neighborhood is in decline? Does it teach children that deviance is to be tolerated and profited from?

Debating Morality

Some scholars argue that acts like pornography, prostitution, and drug use erode the moral fabric of society and therefore should be prohibited and punished. They are crimes, according to the great legal scholar Morris Cohen, because "it is one of the functions of the criminal law to give expression to the collective feeling of revulsion toward certain acts, even when they are not very dangerous."[6] In his classic statement on the function of morality in the law, Sir Patrick Devlin states,

> Without shared ideas on politics, morals, and ethics no society can exist. . . . If men and women try to create a society in which there is no fundamental agreement about good and evil, they will fail; if having based it on common agreement, the agreement goes, the society will disintegrate. For society is not something that is kept together physically; it is held by the invisible bonds of common thought. If the bonds were too far relaxed, the members would drift apart. A common morality is part of the bondage. The bondage is part of the price of society; and mankind, which needs society, must pay its price.[7]

According to this view, so-called victimless crimes are prohibited because one of the functions of criminal law is to express a shared sense of public morality.[8]

Some argue that basing criminal definitions on moral beliefs is an impossible task: Who defines morality? Are we not punishing differences rather than social harm? Are photographs of nude children by famed photographer Robert Mapplethorpe art or obscenity? As U.S. Supreme Court Justice William O. Douglas so succinctly put it, "What may be trash to me may be prized by others."[9]

Cultural clashes may ensue when behavior that is considered normative in one society is deplored by those living in another. For example, the United Nations estimates that 130 million African women have undergone genital mutilation and that each year more than 2 million girls undergo the procedure, some of them in infancy.[10] The surgery is done to ensure virginity, remove sexual sensation, and render the women suitable for marriage. Critics of this practice, led by American author Alice Walker (*The Color Purple*), consider the procedure mutilation and torture; others argue that this ancient custom should be left to the discretion of the indigenous people who consider it part of their culture. "Torture," counters Walker, "is not culture." Can an outsider define the morality of another culture?[11] Because of outside pressure, several African nations south

Michelangelo's statue of David is one of the most important and beloved pieces of Western art. Is it possible that some might consider the unclothed David obscene or prurient? If so, should children be prevented from viewing the statue? Should it be covered up? If David's nudity is not offensive or sexually suggestive, then what does it take to make a statue or photo "pornographic"?

paid stars, are "dehumanized—turned into objects and commodities."[4] Research on prostitution shows that many young runaways and abandoned children are coerced into a life on the streets, where they are cruelly treated and held as virtual captives.[5]

of the Sahara have now instituted bans that are enforced with fines and jail terms. The procedure is barred in Senegal, Egypt, Burkina Faso, the Central African Republic, Djibouti, Ghana, Guinea, and Togo. Other countries, among them Uganda, discourage it. In North Africa, the Egyptian Supreme Court upheld a ban on the practice and also ruled it had no place in Islam.[12]

Some influential legal scholars have questioned the propriety of legislating morals. H. L. A. Hart states,

> It is fatally easy to confuse the democratic principle that power should be in the hands of the majority with the utterly different claim that the majority, with power in their hands, need respect no limits. Certainly there is a special risk in a democracy that the majority may dictate how all should live.[13]

Joseph Gussfield argues that the purpose of outlawing immoral acts is to show the moral superiority of those who condemn the acts over those who partake of them. The legislation of morality "enhances the social status of groups carrying the affirmed culture and degrades groups carrying that which is condemned as deviant."[14]

Criminal or Immoral?   Acts that most of us deem highly immoral are not criminal. There is no law against lust, gluttony, avarice, spite, or envy, although they are considered some of the "seven deadly sins." Nor is it a crime in most jurisdictions to ignore the pleas of a drowning person, even though such callous behavior is quite immoral.

Violations of conventional morality may also be tolerated because they serve a useful social function. For example, watching sexually explicit films can provide excitement and release tension that might otherwise be satisfied in more harmful, violent acts.[15] Immoral behavior may be condoned because it provides ancillary benefits to legitimate enterprises: illegal betting on football games draws people to watch TV at the neighborhood bar; people go to legitimate massage parlors or hire escort services because they believe employees will engage in sex for profit on the side.[16]

Some acts also seem both well-intentioned and moral but are still considered criminal: it is a crime (euthanasia) to kill a loved one who is suffering from an incurable disease to spare him or her further pain; stealing a rich person's money to feed a poor family is considered larceny; marrying many women (polygamy) is considered a crime (bigamy) even though it may conform to religious beliefs.[17] As legal experts Wayne LaFave and Austin Scott, Jr., state, "A good motive will not normally prevent what is otherwise criminal from being a crime."[18]

Social Harm   It might be possible to settle this argument by saying that immoral acts can be distinguished from crimes on the basis of the social harm they cause: acts that harm the public usually are outlawed. Yet this perspective does not always hold sway. Some acts that cause enormous amounts of social harm are perfectly legal: all of us are aware of the illness and death associated with the consumption of tobacco and alcohol, but they remain legal to produce and sell; manufacturers continue to sell sports cars and motorcycles that can accelerate to over 100 m.p.h., but the legal speed limit is usually 65. More people die each year from alcohol-, tobacco-, and auto-related deaths than from all illegal drugs combined. Should drugs be legalized and fast cars outlawed?

Even if an act was outlawed simply because it caused social harm, it might prove difficult or impossible to enforce the law unless the public was united in its disapproval. For example, assisted suicide may be against the law because many people believe it causes social harm. Prosecutors often fail to gain convictions in assisted suicide cases because many people view it as a humanitarian act. Dr. Jack Kevorkian's conviction in 1999 may help reverse that trend.

Moral Crusaders   In the early West, "Vigilance Committees" were set up in San Francisco and other boom towns to pursue cattle rustlers and stage coach robbers and to dissuade undesirables from moving in. These vigilantes held a strict standard of morality that, when they caught their prey, resulted in sure and swift justice.

The avenging vigilante has remained part of popular culture. Fictional "do gooders" who take it on themselves to enforce the law, battle evil, and personally deal with those whom they consider immoral have become enmeshed in the public psyche. From the Lone Ranger to Batman, the righteous **vigilante** is expected to go on **moral crusades** without any authorization from legal authorities. The assumption that it is okay to take matters in your own hands if the cause is right and the target is immoral is not lost on the younger generation. Gang boys sometimes take on the street identity of Batman or Superman so they can battle their rivals with impunity.

Fictional characters are not the only ones who take it upon themselves to fight for moral decency; members of special interest groups are also ready to do battle. Popular targets of moral crusaders are abortion clinics, pornographers, gun dealers, and logging companies. For example, on March 21, 1993, Baylor University regents voted against allowing nude modeling in art classes after school administrators were swamped with phone calls objecting to "nudity in the classroom."[19] In 1996 Key West, Florida, prohibited nude body painting at the town's annual Fantasy Fest, a raucous Mardi Gras–like festival. The Monroe County Christian Coalition had launched an all-out offensive against Fantasy Fest, calling it "depravity and debauchery," and the city commission responded by curbing some of the more outrageous activities.[20]

The Baylor and Key West incidents illustrate the pressure that can be placed on governing boards by moral crusaders (whom Howard Becker calls **moral entrepreneurs**). These rule creators, argues Becker, operate with an absolute certainty that their way is right and that any means are justified to get their way; "the crusader is fervent and righteous, often self-righteous."[21] Today moral crusaders take on such issues as prayer in school, the right to legal abortions, and the distribution of sexually explicit books and magazines.

Moral crusades are often directed against people clearly defined as evil by one segment of the population, even though they may be admired by others. For example, antismut campaigns may attempt to ban the books of a popular author from the school library or prevent a controversial figure from speaking at the local college. One way for moral crusaders to accomplish their goal is to prove to all who will listen that some unseen or hidden trait makes their target truly evil and unworthy of a public audience. This polarization of good and evil creates a climate where those categorized as "good" are deified while the "bad" are demonized. Categorizing people as all good or all bad influences the nature of social control; crime control policies influenced by exaggerated or one-sided moral judgments may be overly punitive and ineffective.[22] For example, the death penalty is justified if murderers are "bad guys"—unrepentant monsters who commit serial murders and mutilate their victims. If, instead, murderers were viewed as "good guys" who had been damaged (as victims of child abuse and neglect), then the death penalty would be considered inappropriate.

The public order crimes discussed in this chapter are divided into two broad areas. The first relates to what conventional society considers deviant sexual practices: homosexual acts, paraphilias, prostitution, and pornography. The second area concerns the use of substances that have been outlawed or controlled because of the alleged harm they cause: drugs and alcohol.

HOMOSEXUALITY

In October 1998 Matthew Shepard, an openly gay University of Wyoming student, was kidnapped, beaten, and left to die while tied to a fence. A passerby thought at first that his slumped, discolored body was a scarecrow. His death brought cries of outrage from national leaders. Then media stories revealed that while Shepard lay comatose, a Colorado State University homecoming parade passed within a few blocks from his hospital bed. Propped on a fraternity float was a discolored, straw-haired scarecrow, labeled in black spray paint "I'm Gay."[23]

Unfortunately, as the Shepard case proves, hate crimes that target gay men and lesbians are all too common, as is insensitivity toward the homosexual lifestyle.

It may be surprising that a section on homosexuality is still included in a criminology text, but even as a new millennium arrives, homosexuals not only face archaic legal restrictions but are targeted for so many violent hate crimes that a specific term, **gay bashing,** has been coined to describe violent acts directed at people because of their sexual orientation.

Homosexuality (the word derives from the Greek *homos,* meaning "same") refers to erotic interest in members of one's own sex. However, engaging in homosexual behavior does not necessarily mean one is a homosexual. People may engage in homosexuality because heterosexual partners are unavailable (for example, in the armed services). Some may have sex forced on them by aggressive homosexuals, a condition common in prisons. Some adolescents may experiment with partners of the same sex although their sexual affiliation is heterosexual.[24] Finally, it is possible to be a homosexual but not to engage in sexual conduct with members of the same sex. To avoid this confusion, it might be helpful to adopt the definition of a homosexual as one "who is motivated in adult life by a definite preferential erotic attraction to members of the same sex and who usually (but not necessarily) engages in overt sexual relations with them."[25]

Homosexual behavior has existed in most societies. Records of it can be found in prehistoric art and hieroglyphics. In their review of the literature on 76 preliterate societies, anthropologists C. S. Ford and F. A. Beach found that male homosexuality was viewed as normal in 49 of these societies and female homosexuality in 17. Some cultures include homosexual experiences as part of their manhood rituals.[26] Even when homosexuality was banned or sanctioned, it still persisted.[27]

In the United States, estimates show that 3 to 16 percent of the male population and 2 to 6 percent of the female population are exclusively homosexual, although many more may have had homosexual experiences sometime in their lives.[28] These numbers have been the subject of fierce debate, and the percentage of the population that is exclusively gay is still not known with certainty.

Attitudes Toward Homosexuality

Throughout much of Western history, homosexuals have been subject to discrimination, sanction, and violence. The Bible implies that God destroyed the ancient cities of Sodom and Gomorrah because of their residents' deviant behavior, presumably homosexuality; Sodom is the source of the term **sodomy** (deviant intercourse). The Bible expressly forbids homosexuality—in Leviticus in the Old Testament; Paul's Epistles, Romans, and Corinthians in the New Testament—and this prohibition has been the basis for repressing homosexual behavior.[29] Gays were brutalized and killed by the ancient Hebrews, a practice continued by the

Investigators examine the area in Wyoming where Matthew Shepard was left to die, tied to a fence in the freezing cold. How can children be educated about the evil of gender and race hatred? Is violence ingrained in humankind, or can something be done to reduce bias crimes?

Christians who ruled Western Europe. Laws providing the death penalty for homosexuals existed until 1791 in France, until 1861 in England, and until 1889 in Scotland. Until the Revolution, some American colonies punished homosexuality with death. In Hitler's Germany, 50,000 homosexuals were put in concentration camps; up to 400,000 more from occupied countries were killed. Negative feelings about the homosexual lifestyle are, however, not a historical oddity. In 1996 conservative Christian groups began a national campaign aimed at counteracting legislative victories won by gay rights groups in the area of discrimination and civil rights.[30] Some groups have taken out ads in local newspapers showing "former homosexuals" who "overcame" their sexual orientation through prayer and the help of Christian "ex-gay ministries."

Today many reasons are given for an extremely negative overreaction to homosexuals referred to as *homophobia*.[31] The cause of antigay feelings is uncertain. Ultraconservative religious leaders believe that the Bible condemns same-sex relations and that this behavior is therefore a sin. Some are ignorant about the lifestyle of gays and fear that homosexuality is a contagious disease or that homosexuals will seduce their children.[32] Others develop a deep-rooted hatred of gays because they are insecure about their own sexual identity. Research shows that males who express homophobic attitudes are also likely to become aroused by erotic images of homosexual behavior. Homophobia, then, may be associated with homosexual arousal that the homophobe is either unaware of or denies.[33]

There are constant reminders of antigay sentiments. For example, in 1998 the California State Supreme Court upheld the right of the Boy Scouts to reject gays; Maine voters repealed a law protecting gays from discrimination; and the Presbyterian Church in Atlanta banned sexually active gays from its pulpits.[34]

> CONNECTIONS
>
> As you may recall from Chapter 11, gay men and women are still subject to thousands of incidents of violence and other hate crimes each year.

Homosexuality and the Law

Homosexuality, considered a legal and moral crime throughout most of Western history, is no longer a crime in the United States. In the case of *Robinson v. California,* the U.S. Supreme Court determined that people could not be criminally prosecuted because of their status (such as drug addict or homosexual).[35] Despite this protection, most states and the federal government criminalize the lifestyle and activities of homosexuals. For example, no state or locality allows same-sex marriages, and homosexuals cannot obtain a marriage license to legitimize their relationship. Twenty-six states have banned same-sex marriages, and in 1996 Congress passed the Defense of Marriage Law, which declared that states are not obligated to recognize single-sex marriages performed in other states.[36]

Despite long-standing biases, it is illegal to deprive gay men and women of due process of law. In a 1996 Colorado case, *Romer v. Evans,* the U.S. Supreme Court said that gay people cannot be stripped of legal protection and made "strangers to the law."[37] Nonetheless, the Supreme Court let stand a Cincinnati city charter amendment barring protective legislation for gay people;[38] this amendment prevented homosexuals from obtaining special civil protections such as affirmative action.

Oral and anal sex and all other forms of intercourse that are not heterosexual and genital are banned in about half the states under statutes prohibiting sodomy, deviant sexuality, or buggery. Maximum penalties range from three years to life in prison, with 10 years being the most common sentence.[39] In 1986 the Supreme Court in *Bowers v. Hardwick* upheld a Georgia statute making it a crime to engage in consensual sodomy, even within one's own home.[40] The Court disregarded Bowers's claim that homosexuals have a fundamental right to engage in sexual activity and that consensual, voluntary sex between adults in the home was a private matter that should not be controlled by law. If all sex within the home were a private matter, Justice Byron White argued for the majority, then such crimes as incest and adultery could not be prosecuted. Citing the historical legal prohibitions against homosexual sodomy, the Court distinguished between the right of gay couples to engage in the sexual behavior of their choice and the sexual privacy the law affords married heterosexual couples. Ironically, the Georgia statute, which provides a 20-year prison sentence, is not directed solely toward homosexuals but refers to a "person" in its prohibition of sodomy.[41] Prestigious legal bodies such as the American Law Institute (ALI) have called for the abolition of statutes prohibiting homosexual sex unless force or coercion is used.[42] About 25 states, including Illinois, Connecticut, and Nebraska, have adopted the ALI's Model Penal Code policy of legalizing any private, consensual sexual behavior between adults;[43] however, the remaining states still treat sodomy as a felony. Consider the Massachusetts statute:

> GENERAL LAWS OF MASSACHUSETTS
> Chapter 272: Section 34. Crime against nature.
> Section 34. Whoever commits the abominable and detestable crime against nature, either with mankind or with a beast, shall be punished by imprisonment in the state prison for not more than twenty years. *Felony*

Although the U.S. Civil Service Commission found in 1975 that homosexuals could not be barred from federal employment, gays are still considered security risks and are not allowed to work in high-security jobs; it was not until December 1993 that the FBI lifted its ban on hiring homosexuals.[44] The military bans openly gay people from serving but has compromised with a "don't ask, don't tell" policy: the military does not ask about sexual orientation; gay people can serve as long as their sexuality remains secret. In 1996 the U.S. Supreme Court tacitly approved the "don't ask" policy by declining to hear a case brought by Navy Lieutenant Paul Thomasson, who was discharged in 1994 for openly declaring himself homosexual.[45] However, in January

1998 a federal judge barred the U.S. Navy from dismissing Chief Petty Officer Timothy McVeigh, who had posted sexually oriented material on the Internet. The judge ruled that the Navy had violated McVeigh's privacy when it asked America Online to divulge his identity; in so doing the Navy violated the spirit of the "don't ask, don't tell" policy.[46] Gays have also lost custody of their children because of their sexual orientation, although more courts are now refusing to consider a gay lifestyle alone as evidence of parental unfitness.[47]

Is the Tide Turning?   Although the unenlightened may still hold negative attitudes toward gays, there seems to be a long overdue increase in social tolerance. A 1998 survey published by the National Gay and Lesbian Task Force shows that strong majorities of Americans now support gays in the military and equality in employment, housing, inheritance rights, and social security benefits for same-sex couples. In addition, disapproval of same-sex relationships dropped a substantial 19 points from a peak of 75 percent in 1987 to about 56 percent today. The report also shows the percentage of people opposed to same-sex marriage (and those opposed to adoption by gay and lesbian couples) to be in decline.[48] Changing public attitudes are reflected in legal change. In 1998, more than 20 years after one of the country's first gay rights ordinances was repealed in Miami, Florida, the Miami–Dade County commission voted again to ban discrimination based on sexual orientation. As of 1998, 11 states, 27 counties, and 136 cities had passed antidiscrimination laws protecting gays.[49] Ironically, in November 1998, by a vote of 6–1, the Georgia

Supreme Court struck down the state's 182-year-old sodomy law that was the basis for the *Bowers v. Hardwick* decision. The court ruled that the law violated the right to privacy guaranteed by the state's constitution. "We cannot think of any other activity that reasonable persons would rank as more private and more deserving of protection from governmental interference than consensual, private, adult sexual activity," said Chief Justice Robert Benham in his majority opinion.[50]

PARAPHILIAS

In October 1996 over 250,000 Belgians took to the streets to protest what they considered the government's inept handling of a case involving the deaths of four children allegedly killed by a pedophile ring led by convicted rapist Marc Dutroix. Two of the victims (8-year-old girls) had been imprisoned and molested for months in Dutroix's home. They starved to death when he was arrested and sent to jail on an unrelated charge. Other children had been kidnapped, raped, tortured, and allegedly sold into sexual slavery by the ring that many believe enjoyed high-level protection from prosecution.[51]

The case of pedophile Marc Dutroix is an extreme example of sexual abnormality referred to as *paraphilia*. From the Greek *para,* "to the side of," and *philos,* "loving," **paraphilias** are bizarre or abnormal sexual practices involving recurrent sexual urges focused on (1) nonhuman objects (like underwear, shoes, or leather), (2) humiliation or the experience of receiving or giving pain (in sadomasochism or bondage), or

Demonstrators in Belgium protest the killing of young girls by pedophile Marc Dutroix. The Belgian public was shocked to learn that the police had failed to discover two young girls Dutroix held captive in his basement even though they had him under arrest. The girls starved to death in a crime that shocked an entire nation.

Figure 14.1 The Nature of Sexual Offenses: Victims and Criminals

Sexual offenders serving time in state prisons indicate that two-thirds had victims under the age of 18, and 58 percent of those—or nearly 4 in 10 imprisoned violent sex offenders—said their victims were age 12 or younger.

Although most violent sex offenses involve males assaulting female victims, females account for a small percentage of known offenders, and males account for a small percentage of victims. In a very small fraction of sexual assaults, victim and offender are of the same sex.

Victim and offender are likely to have had a prior relationship as family members, intimates, or acquaintances. Victims of sexual offenses report that in nearly three out of four incidents, the offender was not a stranger. Based on police-recorded incident data, in 90 percent of the incidents involving children younger than 12, the child knew the offender; two-thirds of the victims aged 18 to 29 had prior relationships with their attackers. The FBI's UCR arrest data, court conviction data, and prison admissions data all point to a sex offender who is older than other violent offenders, generally in his early thirties, and more likely to be white than other violent offenders.

Source: Lawrence A. Greenfield, *Sex Offenses and Offenders: An Analysis of Data on Rape and Sexual Assault* (Washington, D.C.: Bureau of Justice Statistics, 1997).

(3) children or others who cannot grant consent.[52] Some paraphilias, such as wearing clothes normally worn by the opposite sex (transvestite fetishism), can be engaged in by adults in the privacy of their homes and do not involve a third party; these are usually out of the law's reach. Others, however, risk social harm and are subject to criminal penalties. This group of outlawed sexual behavior includes

- *Asphyxiophilia (autoerotic asphyxia)*—by means of a noose, ligature, plastic bag, mask, volatile chemicals, or chest compression, attempting partial asphyxia and oxygen deprivation to the brain to enhance sexual gratification. Almost all cases of hypoxyphilia involve males.
- *Frotteurism*—rubbing against or touching a nonconsenting person in a crowd, elevator, or other public area.
- *Voyeurism*—obtaining sexual pleasure from spying on a stranger while he or she disrobes or engages in sexual behavior with another.
- *Exhibitionism*—deriving sexual pleasure from exposing the genitals to surprise or shock a stranger.
- *Sadomasochism*—deriving pleasure from receiving pain or inflicting pain on another.

- *Pedophilia*—attaining sexual pleasure through sexual activity with prepubescent children. Research indicates that over 20 percent of males report sexual attraction to at least one child, although the rate of sexual fantasies and the potential for sexual contacts are much lower.[53]

Paraphilias that involve unwilling or underage victims are illegal. Most state criminal codes also ban indecent exposure and voyeurism. Others prosecute paraphilias under common-law assault and battery or sodomy statutes. In their extreme, paraphilias can lead to sexual assaults in which the victims suffer severe harm (Figure 14.1).

PROSTITUTION

Prostitution has been known for thousands of years. The term derives from the Latin *prostituere,* which means "to cause to stand in front of." The prostitute is viewed as publicly offering his or her body for sale. The earliest record of prostitution appears in ancient Mesopotamia, where priests engaged in sex to promote fertility in the community. All women were required to do temple duty, and passing strangers were expected to make donations to the temple after enjoying its services.[54]

Modern commercial sex appears to have its roots in ancient Greece, where Solon established licensed brothels in 500 B.C. The earnings of Greek prostitutes helped pay for the temple of Aphrodite. Famous men openly went to prostitutes to enjoy intellectual, aesthetic, and sexual stimulation; prostitutes, however, were prevented from marrying.[55]

Although some early Christian religious leaders, such as St. Augustine and St. Thomas Aquinas, tolerated prostitution as a necessary evil, this tolerance disappeared after the reformation. Martin Luther advocated abolishing prostitution on moral grounds, and Lutheran doctrine depicted prostitutes as emissaries of the devil who were sent to destroy the faith.[56]

During the early nineteenth century prostitution was tied to the rise of English breweries: saloons controlled by the companies employed prostitutes to attract patrons and encourage them to drink. This relationship was repeated in major U.S. cities, such as Chicago, until breweries were forbidden to own the outlets that distributed their product.

Today there are many variations of prostitution, but in general, **prostitution** can be defined as the granting of nonmarital sexual access, established by mutual agreement of the prostitutes, their clients, and their employers, for remuneration. This definition is sexually neutral because prostitutes can be straight or gay and male or female. A recent analysis has amplified the definition of prostitution by describing the conditions usually present in a commercial sexual transaction:

- *Activity that has sexual significance for the customer:* This includes the entire range of sexual behavior, from sexual intercourse to exhibitionism, sadomasochism, oral sex, and so on.
- *Economic transaction:* Something of economic value, not necessarily money, is exchanged for the activity.
- *Emotional indifference:* The sexual exchange is simply for economic consideration. Although the participants may know one another, their interaction has nothing to do with affection for one another.[57]

Incidence of Prostitution

It is difficult to assess the number of prostitutes operating in the United States. Fifty years ago, about two-thirds of non–college-educated men and one-quarter of college-educated men had visited a prostitute.[58] It is likely that the number of men who hire prostitutes has declined sharply; the number of arrests for prostitution has remained stable for the past two decades while the population has increased.[59]

How can these changes be accounted for? Changing sexual mores, brought about by the so-called sexual revolution, have liberalized sexuality. Men are less likely to use prostitutes because legitimate alternatives for sexuality are more open to them. In addition, the prevalence of sexually transmitted diseases has caused many men to avoid visiting prostitutes for fear of irreversible health hazards. Many prostitutes take intravenous drugs. About 47 percent of males and 85 percent of females arrested for prostitution test positively for drug abuse; almost 7 percent test positively for the HTLV-I virus, which has been linked to leukemia and multiple sclerosis.[60]

Despite such changes, the Uniform Crime Reports (UCR) indicate that about 100,000 prostitution arrests are made annually, with the gender ratio being about 3:4 female.[61] More alarming is the fact that about 1,000 arrests are of minors under 18. In 1997 about 145 recorded arrests were of children age 15 and under; 29 were kids under 12, including 12 who were under 10 years of age. Arguments that criminal law should not interfere with sexual transactions because no one is harmed are undermined by these disturbing statistics.

Types of Prostitutes

Several different types of prostitutes operate in the United States.

Streetwalkers Prostitutes who work the streets in plain sight of police, citizens, and customers are referred to as *hustlers, hookers,* or *streetwalkers.* Although glamorized by the Julia Roberts character in the film *Pretty Woman* (who winds up with multimillionaire Richard Gere), streetwalkers are considered the least attractive, lowest paid, most vulnerable men and women in the profession. Streetwalkers wear bright clothing, makeup, and jewelry to attract customers; they take their customers to hotels. The term *hooker,* however, is not derived from the ability of streetwalkers to hook clients on their charms. It actually stems from the popular name given women who followed Union General "Fighting Joe" Hooker's army during the Civil War.[62] Because streetwalkers must openly display their occupation, they are likely to be involved with the police. Studies indicate they are most likely to be impoverished members of ethnic or racial minorities. Many are young runaways who gravitate to major cities to find a new, exciting life and escape from sexual and physical abuse at home.[63] Of all prostitutes, streetwalkers have the highest incidence of drug abuse and larceny arrests, and they are the toughest.[64]

Bar Girls *B-girls,* as they are also called, spend their time in bars, drinking and waiting to be picked up by customers. Although alcoholism may be a problem, B-girls usually work out an arrangement with the bartender so they are served diluted drinks or water colored with dye or tea, for which the customer is charged an exorbitant price. In some bars, the B-girl is given a credit for each drink she gets the customer to buy. It is common to find B-girls in towns with military bases and large transient populations, such as San Diego.[65]

Brothel Prostitutes Also called *bordellos, cathouses, sporting houses,* and *houses of ill repute,* **brothels** flourished in the nineteenth and early twentieth centuries. They were large establishments, usually run by madams, that housed several prostitutes. A **madam** is a woman who employs prostitutes, supervises their behavior, and receives a fee for her services; her cut is usually 40 to 60 percent of the prostitutes' earnings. The madam's role may include recruiting women into prostitution and socializing them in the trade.[66] The madam, often a retired prostitute, is the senior administrator and owner. She makes arrangements for opening the place, attracts prostitutes and customers, works out understandings with police authorities, and pacifies neighbors.[67] The madam is part psychologist, part parent figure, and part business entrepreneur.

Some brothels and their madams have received national notoriety. Polly Adler wrote a highly publicized autobiography of her life as a madam called *A House Is Not a Home.* Sally Stanford maintained a succession of luxuriously furnished brothels in San Francisco. Stanford never made a secret of her profession; she actually listed her phone number in the city directory. In 1962 and 1970 she ran for the San Francisco City Council. In 1984 socialite Sydney Biddle Barrows was arrested by New York police for operating a $1 million-per-year prostitution ring out of a bordello on West Seventy-Fourth Street.[68] Descended from a socially prominent family who traced their line to the Mayflower, Barrows ranked her 20 women on looks and personality from A ($125 per hour) to C ($400 per hour) and kept 60 percent of their take. Her book of clients was described by police as a mini *Who's Who.*

Brothels declined in importance following World War II. The closing of the last brothel in Texas is chronicled in the play and movie *The Best Little Whorehouse in Texas.* Today the most well-known brothels exist in Nevada, where prostitution is legal outside large population centers. Such houses as "Mustang Ranch," "Miss Kitty's," and "Pink Pussycat" service customers who drive out from Reno and Las Vegas.

Call Girls   The aristocrats of prostitution are **call girls.** They charge customers up to $1,500 per night and may net over $100,000 per year. Some gain clients through employment in escort services, while others develop independent customer lists. Many call girls come from middle-class backgrounds and service upper-class customers. Attempting to dispel the notion that their service is simply sex for money, they concentrate on making their clients feel important and attractive. Working exclusively via telephone "dates," call girls get their clients by word of mouth or by making arrangements with bellhops, cab drivers, and so on. They either entertain clients in their own apartments or visit clients' hotels and apartments. Upon retiring, a call girl can sell her datebook listing client names and sexual preferences for thousands of dollars. Despite the lucrative nature of their business, call girls suffer considerable risk by being alone and unprotected with strangers. They often request the business cards of their clients to make sure they are dealing with "upstanding citizens."

Escort Services/Call Houses   Some escort services are fronts for prostitution rings. Both male and female sex workers can be sent out after the client calls an ad in the yellow pages. In Las Vegas, 134 pages in the phone book are dedicated to such services.[69] A relatively new phenomenon, *call houses,* combines elements of the brothel and call-girl rings: a madam receives a call from a prospective customer, and if she finds the client acceptable, she arranges a meeting between the caller and a prostitute in her service. The madam maintains a list of prostitutes who are on call rather than living together in a house. The call house insulates the madam from arrest because she never meets the client or receives direct payment.[70]

Circuit Travelers   Prostitutes known as *circuit travelers* move around in groups of two or three to lumber, labor, and agricultural camps. They ask the foremen for permission to ply their trade, service the whole crew in an evening, and then move on. Some circuit travelers seek clients at truck stops and rest areas.

Sometimes young girls are forced to become circuit travelers by unscrupulous pimps. In 1998 16 people were charged with enslaving at least 20 women, some as young as 14, and forcing them to work for months as prostitutes in agricultural migrant camps in Florida and South Carolina. The young women were lured from Mexico with offers of jobs in landscaping, health care, housecleaning, and restaurants. During their captivity the young women were raped, beaten, and forced to have abortions. Those who tried to escape were tracked down, brought back, beaten, and raped. One woman was locked in a closet for 15 days, officials said. Some women who became pregnant were forced to have abortions and then return to work within weeks. One pregnant woman was kicked in the abdomen and had a miscarriage. Their captors, known as "ticketeros," forced them to work six days a week under the threat of violence and for little pay; the women were paid $3 for each sexual act, but the ticketeros charged $20.[71]

Rap Booth Prostitutes   A phenomenon in commercial sex, *rap booths* are located in the adult entertainment zones of such cities as New York and San Francisco.[72] The prostitute and her customer occupy booths that are separated by a glass wall. They talk via telephone for as long as the customer is willing to pay. The more money he spends, the more she engages in sexual banter and disrobing. There is no actual touching, and sex is through masturbation, with the prostitute serving as a masturbation aid similar in function to a pornographic magazine.

Skeezers: Bartering Sex for Drugs   With the prevalence of drug abuse and the introduction of crack cocaine to the street culture in the mid-1980s, a new form of prostitution, trading sex for drugs, became common. Surveys conducted in New York and Chicago have found that a significant portion of female prostitutes have substance abuse problems, and more than half claim that prostitution is how they support their drug habits; on the street, women who barter drugs for sex are called **skeezers.** Not all drug-addicted prostitutes barter sex for drugs, but those that do report more frequent drug abuse and sexual activity than other prostitutes.

There is some question of the impact bartering sex for drugs has on prostitutes. The prevailing wisdom is that those who engage in the practice are victims who are often the target of violent attacks and rapes. However, when interviewed by Paul Goldstein and his associates, barterers viewed themselves as being engaged in economic transactions in which they are treated fairly.[73] In contrast to widely held beliefs, these prostitutes are not drug slaves or victims who have no control over their lives. Many believe that bartering gives them the benefit of the deal—valuable drugs for a few minutes of sexual service. According to sociologists Lisa Maher and Kathleen Daly, although the crack trade has done little to improve the relative position of female offenders, trading crack for sex actually lowers wages of experienced street workers because it encourages intense competition from novices; violence and victimization may also increase.[74]

Other Varieties Some "working girls" are based in **massage parlors**. Although it is unusual for a masseuse to offer all the services of prostitution, oral sex and manual stimulation are common. Most localities have attempted to limit commercial sex in massage parlors by passing ordinances specifying that the masseuse keep certain parts of her body covered and limiting the areas of the body that can be massaged. Photography studios and model and escort services sometimes are covers for commercial sex. Some photo studios allow customers to put body paint on models before the photo sessions start. Stag party girls service all-male parties and groups by putting on shows and having sex with participants. In years past, many hotels had live-in prostitutes. Today's hotel prostitute makes a deal with the bell captain or manager to refer customers to her for a fee; some second-rate hotels still have resident prostitutes.

Becoming a Prostitute

Why does someone turn to prostitution? Both male and female prostitutes often come from troubled homes marked by extreme conflict and hostility and from poor urban areas or rural communities. Divorce, separation, or death splits the family; most prostitutes grew up in homes with absent fathers.[75] Many prostitutes were initiated into sex by family members at ages as young as 10 to 12 years; they have long histories of sexual exploitation and abuse.[76] The early experiences with sex help teach them that their bodies have value and that sexual encounters can be used to obtain affection, power, or money.

Lower-class girls who get into "the life" report conflict with school authorities, poor grades, and an overly regimented school experience.[77] Drug abuse, including heroin and cocaine addiction, is often a factor in the prostitute's life.[78] Other personal characteristics found among samples of prostitutes include

- Growing up in a slum neighborhood.
- Being born out of wedlock or into a broken home.
- Dropping out of school.
- Fantasizing about money and success.
- Being a member of a "loose crowd."
- Seeing prostitutes in the neighborhood.
- Having unfortunate experiences with a husband or boyfriend.
- Having trouble keeping a job.[79]

However, there is no actual evidence that people become prostitutes because of psychological problems or personality disturbances. Money, drugs, and survival seem to be greater motivations.

Research indicates that few girls are forced into prostitution by a pimp. Pimps may convince girls by flattery, support, promises, and affection, but relatively few kidnap or coerce kids into prostitution. There is more evidence that friends or relatives introduce kids into prostitution. Most report entering prostitution voluntarily because they disliked the discipline of conventional work.[80] The socialization view argues that sex in our society is a commodity that can be purchased. Women who are socialized to view themselves as sex objects may easily step over the line of propriety and accept money for their favors.[81] These women view their bodies as salable commodities, and most prostitution does in fact pay better than other occupations available to women with limited education.

Pimps A pimp derives part or all of his livelihood from the earnings of a prostitute. The pimp helps steer customers to the prostitute, watches for and deals with police, posts bail, and protects his prostitutes from unruly customers.[82] To the prostitute, the pimp is a surrogate father, husband, and lover. She may sell her body to customers, but she reserves her care and affection for her pimp. Pimps can pick up established "working girls" or they can "turn out" young girls who have never been in "the life." Occasionally they pick up young runaways, buy them clothes and jewelry, and turn them into **baby pros.**

What attracts men to the life of the pimp? One view is that many pimps originally worked on the fringes of prostitution as bellhops, elevator operators, or barmen and subsequently drifted into the profession. An opposing view is that pimps began as young men seduced by older prostitutes who taught them how to succeed in "the life," how to behave, and how to control women.[83]

The role of the pimp is changing. The decline of the brothel, the development of independent prostitutes, and the control of prostitution by organized crime has decreased the number of full-time pimps.[84] Many prostitutes are drug-dependent, and in some areas, drug dealers have replaced pimps as the controlling force in prostitution. Even the cost of sex is drug-dependent, rather than being controlled by a pimp, with the going rate for sexual services geared to the cost of a rock of crack.[85] When a prostitute has a pimp, the relationship is often short-lived and unstable. Pimps may be more reluctant to work with young prostitutes today because they face severe legal penalties if caught running juveniles and also because they consider juveniles unstable and untrustworthy.[86]

Legalize Prostitution?

Prostitution is illegal in all states except Nevada (except in the counties in which Las Vegas and Reno are located). Typically prostitution is considered a misde-

Prostitutes ply their trade legally in Amsterdam. If prostitution was legalized and regulated, would young girls entering the "trade" be protected from harm? Or would it encourage greater participation in what is essentially a degrading and dangerous occupation?

meanor, punishable by a fine or a short jail sentence. The federal **Mann Act** (passed in 1925) prohibits bringing women into the country or transporting them across state lines for the purposes of prostitution. Often called the "white slave act," it carries a $5,000 fine, five years in prison, or both.

Feminists have staked out conflicting views of prostitution. One position is that women must become emancipated from male oppression and reach sexual equality. The *sexual equality* view considers the prostitute a victim of male dominance. In patriarchal societies, male power is predicated on female subjugation, and prostitution is a clear example of this gender exploitation.[87] In contrast, for some feminists, the fight for equality depends on controlling all attempts by men or women to impose their will on women. The *free choice* view is that prostitution, if freely chosen, expresses women's equality and is not a symptom of subjugation.[88]

Advocates of both positions argue that the penalties for prostitution should be reduced (decriminalized); neither side advocates outright legalization. Decriminalization would relieve already desperate women of the additional burden of severe legal punishment. In contrast, legalization might be coupled with regulation by male-dominated justice agencies. For example, required medical examinations would mean increased male control over women's bodies. Although both sides advocate change in the criminal status of prostitution, few communities, except San Francisco, have openly

debated or voted on its legalization. Should prostitution be legalized? Before answering this question, read the Criminological Enterprise feature titled "Victimless Crimes."

PORNOGRAPHY

The term **pornography** derives from the Greek *porne,* meaning "prostitute," and *graphein,* meaning "to write." In the heart of many major cities are stores that display and sell books, magazines, and films depicting every imaginable explicit sex act. Suburban video stores also rent and sell sexually explicit tapes, which make up 15 to 30 percent of the home rental market. The purpose of this material is to provide sexual titillation and excitement for paying customers. Although material depicting nudity and sex is typically legal, protected by the First Amendment's provision limiting the governmental control of speech, most criminal codes prohibit the production, display, and sale of obscene material.

Obscenity, derived from the Latin *caenum* for "filth," is defined by Webster's dictionary as "deeply offensive to morality or decency . . . designed to incite to lust or depravity."[89] The problem of controlling pornography centers on this definition of obscenity. Police and law enforcement officials can legally seize only material that is judged obscene. "But who," critics ask, "is to judge what is obscene?" At one time, such novels as

The Criminological Enterprise

Victimless Crimes: Streetwalkers in New York City

Since April 1989 a mobile van paid for privately has contacted prostitutes throughout the five boroughs of New York City to provide a variety of services: HIV testing and counseling, condom distribution, bleach kits for cleaning needles, and HIV prevention information. Human service specialist Adele Weiner has collected data on close to 2000 streetwalkers who have been given aid; the information covers their personal characteristics, demographics, family and living arrangements, sex and drug practices, HIV status, and health history. These data provide important insight into the lives of urban prostitutes.

Personal Characteristics of Prostitutes

The women had worked an average of almost five years as streetwalkers. About half were African-American, more than one-quarter Hispanic, and the rest non-Hispanic white women. Although the average age was nearly 30, almost half had not completed high school, while about one-third were graduates; some (less than 20 percent) had education beyond high school.

More than two-thirds of the women had at least one child, most of whom lived with relatives or in foster care; about 20 percent had children living with them. Almost 20 percent of the women were homeless; many others lived in hotel rooms or other inadequate shelter.

These prostitutes revealed a startling array of personal, medical, and social problems. They had an extensive history of STDs: 35 percent tested positive for HIV, 27 reported a history of gonorrhea, and 18 percent said they had syphilis. If anything, the history of STDs was underreported because some of the women did not know or remember if they had been infected.

The women also had a long history of illegal drug usage. About two-thirds were crack users, half used alcohol, 40 percent used marijuana and cocaine, and about 25 percent either injected or snorted heroin. Of those who used IV drugs, less than 20 percent reported cleaning their needles, and the same number shared needles with other substance abusers. About a third of the women had lovers with histories of IV drug use, and few practiced safe sex. It is not surprising, then, that so many of the streetwalkers tested positive for HIV; those that did were likely to be homeless drug users who engaged in dangerous sexual practices.

Is This a Victimless Crime?

Being a prostitute makes a woman vulnerable to the loss of social services, removal of her children and termination of parental rights, expulsion from social support systems such as family or church, rape or other violence, and arrest. The stigma associated with being a prostitute may make

it impossible for these women to return to more legitimate lifestyles. They have nothing left to lose yet find it extremely difficult to reach out for help. Is prostitution a victimless crime?

CRITICAL THINKING

1. These data give little support to the *Pretty Woman* myth that street sex workers control their lives and can hope to meet and marry a sympathetic client. Considering this evidence, plus the rising incidence of child prostitution, should heavier penalties be attached to soliciting a prostitute or hiring one who is underage?

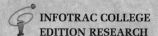

INFOTRAC COLLEGE EDITION RESEARCH

For more on the problems faced by prostitutes and the efforts being made to help them cope with their problems, see:

Dylan Foley, AIDS education for teen prostitutes. *The Progressive* Feb 1996 v60 n2 p19(1)

Barbara Lynn Kail, Deena Watson, Scott Ray. Needle-using practices within the sex industry. *American Journal of Drug and Alcohol Abuse* May 1995 v21 n2 p241(15)

Source: Adele Weiner, "Understanding the Social Needs of Streetwalking Prostitutes," *Social Work* 41 (1996): 97–106.

Tropic of Cancer by Henry Miller, *Ulysses* by James Joyce, and *Lady Chatterley's Lover* by D. H. Lawrence were prohibited because they were considered obscene; today they are considered works of great literary value. Thus what is obscene today may be considered socially acceptable at a future time. After all, *Playboy* and *Penthouse* magazines, sold openly on most college campuses, display nude models in all kinds of sexually explicit poses. Allowing individual judgments on what is obscene makes the Constitution's guarantee of free speech unworkable. Could not antiobscenity statutes also be used to control political and social dissent? The uncertainty surrounding this issue is illustrated by Supreme Court Justice Potter Stewart's famous 1964

statement on how he defined obscenity: "I know it when I see it." Because of this legal and moral ambiguity, the sex trade is booming around the United States. Table 14.1 illustrates the various components in the industry.

The Dangers of Pornography

Opponents of pornography argue that it degrades both the people who are photographed and members of the public who are sometimes forced to see obscene material. Pornographers exploit their models, who often include underage children. The Attorney General's Commission on Pornography, set up by the Reagan ad-

Table 14.1   Sources, Estimated Revenue, and Services of the Sex-for-Profit Industry

SOURCE	ESTIMATED ANNUAL REVENUE	SERVICES/EXAMPLES
Cable, satellite, pay-per-view television	$150 million	Playboy, Adam & Eve, Spice channels; pay-per-view movies
Magazines	$1 billion	*Penthouse, Playboy, Hustler;* thousands of selected titles
Adult videos	$3.1 billion, including $300 million in rentals	An estimated 30 percent of the entire video market
CD-rom	$300 million	Sexually oriented interactive games and films; 150 new titles each year
Phone sex	$1 billion	Typical company has 25 employees, grosses $2 million per year
Internet sex	$100 million	Personals, live interaction strip shows, pictures
Strip clubs	$3 billion	2200 in the United States; becoming more upscale
Private dancing	$250 million	Dancers on call serve as independent contractors
Escort services	$1 billion	Girls on call summoned by beepers; typical service employs 50 people and grosses $4 million

Source: Anthony Flint, "Selling Sex in the 90's," *Boston Globe,* 1 December 1996, p. A36.

ministration to review the sale and distribution of sexually explicit material, concluded that many performers and models are victims of physical and psychological coercion.[90] The kiddie porn industry is estimated to amount to over $1 billion of a total $2.5 billion spent annually on pornography. Each year over a million children are believed to be used in pornography or prostitution, many of them runaways whose plight is exploited by adults.[91]

Child Pornography Rings   How does child pornography get made and distributed? Many of the hard-core pictures that find their way into the hands of collectors are the work of *pornography rings* —adults who join together to exploit children and adolescents for sex. Ann Wolbert Burgess studied 55 child pornography rings and found that they typically contain between 3 and 11 children, predominantly males, some of nursery school age. The adults who control the ring use positions of trust to recruit the children and then continue to exploit them through a combination of material and psychological rewards. Burgess found different types of child pornography rings. *Solo sex rings* involve several children and a single adult, usually male, who uses a position of trust (counselor, teacher, Boy Scout leader) to recruit children into sexual activity. *Transition rings* are impromptu groups set up to sell and trade photos and sex. *Syndicated rings* have well-structured organizations that recruit children and create extensive networks of customers who desire sexual services.[92] Sexual exploitation by these rings can devastate the child victims. Burgess found that children suffer physical problems ranging from headaches and loss of appetite to genital soreness, vomiting, and urinary tract infections. Psychological problems in-

clude mood swings, withdrawal, edginess, and nervousness. Exploited children are prone to such acting-out behavior as setting fires and becoming sexually focused in the use of language, dress, and mannerisms. In cases of extreme, prolonged victimization, children may lock onto the sex group's behavior and become prone to further victimization or even become victimizers themselves.

Does Pornography Cause Violence?

An issue critical to the debate over pornography is whether viewing it produces sexual violence or assaultive behavior. This debate was given added interest when serial killer Ted Bundy claimed his murderous rampage was fueled by reading pornography.

Some evidence exists that viewing sexually explicit material actually has little effect on behavior. In 1970 the National Commission on Obscenity and Pornography reviewed all available material on the effects of pornography and authorized independent research projects. The commission found no clear relationship between pornography and violence, and it recommended that federal, state, and local legislation should not interfere with the rights of adults who wish to read, obtain, or view explicit sexual materials.[93] Almost 20 years later, the highly controversial Attorney General's Commission on Pornography, sponsored by the conservative Reagan administration, called for legal attacks on hard-core pornography and condemned all sexually related material—but also found little evidence that obscenity causes antisocial behavior.[94]

How might we account for this surprisingly insignificant association? Some explanation may be found in Danish sociologist Berl Kutchinsky's widely cited research showing that the rate of sex offenses actually declined shortly after pornography was decriminalized in Denmark in 1967.[95] He attributed this trend to the fact that viewing erotic material may act as a safety valve for those whose impulses might otherwise lead them to violence. Convicted rapists and sex offenders report less exposure to pornography than a control group of nonoffenders.[96]

Viewing prurient material may have the unintended side effect of satisfying erotic impulses that otherwise might result in more sexually aggressive behavior. This issue is far from settled. A number of criminologists believe that the positive relationship between pornography consumption and rape rates in various countries, including the United States, is evidence that obscenity may powerfully influence criminality.[97] Nonetheless, the weight of the evidence shows little relationship between violence and pornography per se.

Violent Pornography, Violent Crime Although there is little or no documentation of a correlation between pornography and violent crime, there is stronger evidence that people exposed to material that portrays violence, sadism, and women enjoying being raped and degraded are likely to be sexually aggressive toward female victims.[98] The Attorney General's Commission on Pornography concluded in 1986 that a causal link can be drawn between exposure to violent sexually explicit material and sexual violence. After reviewing the literature on the subject, the commission found that although the behavioral effects of sexually nonviolent and nondegrading pornography are insignificant, exposure to sexually violent and degrading materials

- Leads to a greater acceptance of rape myths and violence against women.
- Has more pronounced effects when the victim is shown enjoying the use of force or violence.
- Is arousing for rapists and for some males in the general population.
- Has resulted in sexual aggression against women in controlled laboratory settings.[99]

Laboratory experiments conducted by a number of leading authorities have found that men exposed to violent pornography are more likely to act aggressively toward women.[100] The evidence suggests that violence and sexual aggression are not linked to erotic or pornographic films per se but that erotic films depicting violence, rape, brutality, and aggression may evoke similar feelings in viewers. This finding is especially distressing because it is common for adult books and films to have sexually violent themes such as rape, bondage, and mutilation.[101]

Pornography and the Law

All states and the federal government prohibit the sale and production of pornographic material. Child pornography is usually a separate legal category that involves either (1) the creation or reproduction of materials depicting minors engaged in actual or simulated sexual activity ("sexual exploitation of minors") or (2) the publication or distribution of obscene, indecent, or harmful materials to minors.[102] Under existing federal law trafficking in obscenity (18 U.S.C. Sec. 1462, 1464, 1466), child pornography (18 U.S.C. Sec. 2252), harassment (18 U.S.C. Sec. 875(c)), illegal solicitation or luring of minors (18 U.S.C. Sec. 2423(b)), and threatening to injure someone (18 U.S.C. Sec. 875(c)) are all felonies punished by long prison sentences.

Punishing Obscenity Despite the fact that state and federal law control the production and sale of obscene materials, punishing pornographers often creates moral and legal dilemmas. The problems were highlighted by two 1990 incidents. The first was a posthumous exhibition featuring the works of gay photographer Robert Mapplethorpe. The exhibition was heavily criticized by conservative politicians because it contained images of nude children and men in homoerotic poses and because it had received federal funding. When Cincinnati's Contemporary Arts Center mounted the show, obscenity charges were brought against its director; he was later found not guilty. The actions taken against the Mapplethorpe exhibit brought waves of protest from artists and performers as well as civil libertarians, who fear governmental control over art, music, and theater. Then on June 8, 1990, an undercover detective walked into a record shop in Fort Lauderdale, Florida, and bought a copy of *As Nasty as They Wanna Be,* the hit album of the rap group 2 Live Crew. He and six fellow officers then arrested store owner Charles Freeman on the charge of distributing obscene material. This was the first arrest following a federal judge's decision that the group's songs (such as "Me So Horny") contained lyrics having a sexual content that violated local community standards of decency and were therefore obscene.[103] To many, these incidents represented an exercise of criminal law that was a direct attack on the First Amendment's guarantee of free speech. Should free expression be controlled if it offends some people's sense of decency?

The First Amendment of the U.S. Constitution protects free speech and prohibits police agencies from limiting the public's right of free expression. However, the Supreme Court held in the twin cases of *Roth v. United States* and *Alberts v. California* that the First Amendment protects all "ideas with even the slightest redeeming social importance — unorthodox ideas, controversial ideas, even ideas hateful to the prevailing climate of opinion . . . but implicit in the history of the First Amendment is the rejection of obscenity as utterly without redeeming social importance."[104] In the 1966 case of *Memoirs v. Massachusetts,* the Supreme Court again required that for a work to be considered obscene, it must be shown to be "utterly without redeeming social value."[105] These decisions left unclear how obscenity is defined. If a highly erotic movie tells a "moral tale," must it be judged legal even if 95 percent of its content is objectionable? A spate of movies made after the *Roth* decision alleged that they were educational or told a moral tale, so they could not be said to lack redeeming social importance. Many state obscenity cases were appealed to federal courts so judges could decide whether the films totally lacked redeeming social importance. To rectify the situation, the Supreme Court redefined its concept of obscenity in the case of *Miller v. California*:

> The basic guidelines for the trier of fact must be (a) whether the average person applying contemporary community standards would find that the work taken as a whole appeals to the prurient interest; (b) whether the work depicts or describes, in a patently offensive way, sexual conduct specifically defined by the applicable state law, and (c) whether the work, taken as a whole, lacks serious literary, artistic, political or scientific value.[106]

To convict a person of obscenity under the *Miller* doctrine, the state or local jurisdiction must specifically define obscene conduct in its statute, and the pornographer must engage in that behavior. The Court gave some examples of what is considered obscene: "patently offensive representations or descriptions of masturbation, excretory functions and lewd exhibition of the genitals." In subsequent cases the Court overruled convictions for "offensive" or "immoral" behavior; these are not considered obscene. The *Miller* doctrine has been criticized for not spelling out how community standards are to be determined.[107] Obviously a plebiscite cannot be held to determine the community's attitude for every trial concerning the sale of pornography. Works that are considered obscene in Omaha might be considered routine in New York, but how can we be sure? To resolve this dilemma, the Supreme Court articulated in *Pope v. Illinois* a reasonableness doctrine: a work is obscene if a reasonable person applying objective (national) standards would find the material lacking in any social value.[108] Although *Pope* should help clarify the legal definition of obscenity, the issue is far from settled. Justice John Paul Stevens in his dissent offered one interesting alternative: the First Amendment protects material "if some reasonable persons could [find] serious literary[,] artistic, political or scientific value" in it.[109] Stevens believes that if anyone could find merit in a work, it should be protected by law. Do you?

Controlling Sex for Profit

Sex for profit predates Western civilization. Considering its longevity, there seems to be little evidence that it can be controlled or eliminated by legal means alone. Recent reports indicate that the sex business is currently booming and now amounts to $10 billion per year.[110] The Attorney General's Commission on Pornography advocated a strict law enforcement policy to control obscenity, urging that "the prosecution of obscene materials that portray sexual violence be treated as a matter of special urgency."[111] Since then, there has been a concerted effort by the federal government to prosecute adult movie distributors. Law enforcement has been so fervent that industry members have filed suit claiming they are the victims of a "moral crusade" by right-wing zealots.[112]

Although politically appealing, law enforcement crusades may not necessarily obtain the desired effect. A get-tough policy could make sex-related goods and services scarce, driving up prices and making their sale even more desirable and profitable. Going after national distributors may help decentralize the adult movie and photo business and encourage local rings to expand their activities, for example, by making and marketing videos as well as still photos or distributing them through computer networks.

An alternative approach has been to restrict the sale of pornography within acceptable boundaries. For example, municipal governments have tolerated or even established adult entertainment zones in which obscene material can be openly sold. In the case of *Young v. American Mini Theaters,* the Supreme Court permitted a zoning ordinance that restricted theaters showing erotic movies to one area of the city, even though it did not find that any of the movies shown were obscene.[113] The state, therefore, has the right to regulate adult films as long as the public has the right to view them. Some jurisdictions have responded by limiting the sale of sexually explicit material in residential areas and restricting the number of adult stores that can operate in a particular area. For example, New York City has enacted zoning that seeks to break up the concentration of peep shows, topless bars, and X-rated businesses in several neighborhoods, particularly in Times Square.[114] The law forbids sex-oriented businesses within 500 feet of residential zones, schools, churches, or day care centers. Sex shops cannot be located within 500 feet of each other, so concentrated "red light" districts must be dispersed. Rather than close their doors, sex shops got around the law by adding products like luggage, cameras, T-shirts, and classic films. The courts have upheld the law, ruling that stores can stay in business if no more than 40 percent of their floor space and inventory are dedicated to adult entertainment.[115]

Ironically, zoning statutes may not be needed as skyrocketing downtown real estate prices make sex clubs and stores relatively unprofitable. Land that was used for adult movie houses has been redeveloped into high-priced condominiums and office buildings. The number of striptease clubs in Boston's Combat Zone shrank from 22 in 1977 to 5 within 10 years as the area was redeveloped.[116] New York's Times Square area has been redeveloped as land values skyrocket and Disney theme stores replace strip joints.

The threat of governmental regulation may also convince some participants in the sex-for-profit industry to police themselves. Although some forms of sexually explicit material and activities are tolerated by local law enforcement agencies, others bring prompt legal control. For example, child pornography usually spurs otherwise complacent governmental agencies into swift action. Efforts to control this problem have been supported by the courts. The landmark *New York v. Ferber* case indicates the Supreme Court's willingness to allow the states to control child pornography.[117] In this case, Paul Ferber, a Manhattan bookstore owner, was sentenced to 45 days in jail for violating a New York statute banning material that portrays children engaged in sexually explicit, although not necessarily obscene, conduct. He challenged the law as a violation of free speech. By unanimously upholding Ferber's conviction, the Supreme Court found that kiddie porn damages the children it exploits and therefore can be legally banned. In his opinion Justice Byron White said, "It has been found that sexually exploited children are unable to develop healthy affectionate relationships in later life, have sexual dysfunction and have a tendency to become sexual abusers as adults." The Court also found that the films were an invasion of the child's privacy that the child could not control. Fear of governmental control may already have influenced the content of nationally distributed adult magazines.

Criminologists have uncovered a correlation between rape rates and the circulation rates of national adult magazines.[118] The federal government has consequently asked the states to toughen their laws governing the distribution of sex-related material. Some mainstream sex magazines may have altered their content rather than risk provoking public officials.

Technological Change   A 1993 letter to advice columnist Ann Landers gave this cry for help:

Dear Ann Landers,
. . . several months ago, I caught my husband making calls to a 900-sex number. After a week of denial, he admitted that for several years he had been hooked on porn magazines, porn movies, peep shows, strippers, and phone sex. This addiction can start early in life. With my husband it began at age 12 with just one simple, "harmless" magazine. By the time he was 19, it had become completely out of control. . . . For years my husband hated himself, and it affected his entire life.[119]

A 1998 letter asking Ann for help updates the problem:

Dear Ann Landers,
My husband and I have had a fabulous marriage. We have two wonderful children, ages 22 and 25. . . . Here's

the problem. Phil has become obsessed with porn on the Internet. . . . Recently, when I returned from an evening out, I noticed Phil appeared quite nervous and upset. I looked at the computer, and sure enough, he had been looking at some unbelievably raunchy stuff. He said he was sincere when he promised to give it up, but he just couldn't stay away from it. I now believe he is obsessed and self-destructive.[120]

Technological change will provide the greatest challenge to those seeking to control the sex-for-profit industry. Adult movie theaters are closing as people are able to buy or rent tapes in their local video stores and play them in the privacy of their homes.[121] Adult CD-ROMs are now a staple of the computer industry. Internet sex services include live, interactive stripping and sexual activities.[122] The government has moved to control the broadcast of obscene films via satellite and other technological innovations. On February 15, 1991, Home Dish Only Satellite Networks, Inc., was fined $150,000 for broadcasting pornographic movies to its 30,000 clients throughout the United States; it was the first prosecution of the illegal use of satellites to broadcast obscene films.[123]

To control the spread of Internet pornography, Congress passed the Communications Decency Act (CDA), which made all Internet service providers, commercial on-line services, bulletin board systems, and electronic mail providers criminally liable whenever their services are used to transmit any material considered "obscene, lewd, lascivious, filthy, or indecent" (S 314, 1996). These acts were punishable by fines of up to $100,000 and two years in prison. Civil libertarians decried this effort to regulate Internet content, and the American Civil Liberties Union (ACLU) filed suit questioning the constitutionality of the CDA on the grounds that it violated the First Amendment right to free speech. In *Reno v. ACLU* (1997) the Supreme Court upheld the ACLU's claim, ruling that the CDA unconstitutionally restricted free speech.[124] In a landmark 7–2 decision written by Justice Stevens, the Court ruled that the CDA places an "unacceptably heavy burden on protected speech" that "threatens to torch a large segment of the Internet community." Despite this setback, lawmakers are seeking other means of controlling Internet pornography.[125] The defeat of the CDA does not mean that efforts at regulating the content of the Internet have ended. For example, a more recent law, the Child Online Protection Act (H.R. 3783), would ban web postings of material deemed "harmful to minors." The act, signed into law by President Clinton in October 1998, will not take effect while it is undergoing legal challenges.[126]

Despite these efforts, the popularity of pornography on the Internet, in CD-ROMs, and in satellite broadcasts may overwhelm law enforcement efforts and spur the growth of sex-related materials.

SUBSTANCE ABUSE

The problem of substance abuse stretches across the United States. Large urban areas are beset by drug-dealing gangs, drug users who engage in crime to support their habits, and alcohol-related violence. Rural areas are important staging centers for the shipment of drugs across the country and are often the production sites for synthetic drugs and marijuana farming.[127] Nor is the United States alone in experiencing a problem with substance abuse. In Australia 19 percent of youths in detention centers and 40 percent of adult prisoners report having used heroin at least once; in Canada, cocaine and crack are considered serious urban problems; South Africa reports increased cocaine and heroin abuse; Thailand has a serious heroin and methamphetamine problem; and British police have found a major increase in heroin abuse.[128]

Another indication of the concern about drugs has been the increasing number of drug-related arrests: from less than half a million in 1977 to about 1.6 million in 1997. Similarly, the proportion of prison inmates incarcerated for drug offenses has increased by 300 percent since 1986.[129] Clearly the justice system views drug abuse as a major problem and is taking what decision makers regard as decisive measures to control it.

Despite the scope of the drug problem, some still view it as another type of victimless public order crime. There is great debate over the legalization of drugs and the control of alcohol. Some consider drug use a private matter and drug control another example of government intrusion into people's private lives. Furthermore, legalization could reduce the profit of selling illegal substances and drive suppliers out of the market.[130] Others see these substances as dangerous, believing that the criminal activity of users makes the term *victimless* nonsensical. Still another position is that the possession and use of all drugs and alcohol should be legalized but that the sale and distribution of drugs should be heavily penalized. This would punish those profiting from drugs and would enable users to be helped without fear of criminal punishment.

When Did Drug Use Begin?

The use of chemical substances to change reality and provide stimulation, relief, or relaxation has gone on for thousands of years. Mesopotamian writings indicate that opium was used 4,000 years ago—it was known as the "plant of joy."[131] The ancient Greeks knew and understood the problem of drug use. At the time of the Crusades, the Arabs were using marijuana. In the Western Hemisphere, natives of Mexico and South America chewed coca leaves and used "magic mushrooms" in their religious ceremonies.[132] Drug use was also accepted in Europe well into the twentieth century.

Recently uncovered pharmacy records circa 1900 to 1920 showed sales of cocaine and heroin solutions to members of the British royal family; records from 1912 show that Winston Churchill, then a member of Parliament, was sold a cocaine solution while staying in Scotland.[133]

In the early years of the United States, opium and its derivatives were easily obtained. Opium-based drugs were used in various patent medicine cure-alls. Morphine was used extensively to relieve the pain of wounded soldiers in the Civil War. By the turn of the century, an estimated 1 million U.S. citizens were opiate users.[134]

Several factors precipitated the current U.S. stringent drug laws. The rural religious creeds of the nineteenth century—for example, those of the Methodists, Presbyterians, and Baptists—emphasized individual human toil and self-sufficiency while designating the use of intoxicating substances as an unwholesome surrender to the evils of urban morality. Religious leaders were thoroughly opposed to the use and sale of narcotics. The medical literature of the late 1800s began to designate the use of morphine and opium as a vice, a habit, an appetite, and a disease. Nineteenth- and early twentieth-century police literature described drug users as habitual criminals. Moral crusaders in the nineteenth century defined drug use as evil and directed the local and national outlawing of the sale and possession of drugs. Some well-publicized research efforts categorized drug use as highly dangerous.[135] Drug use was also associated with the foreign immigrants who were recruited to work in factories and mines and brought with them their national drug habits. Early antidrug legislation appears to be tied to prejudice against immigrating ethnic minorities.[136]

After the Spanish-American War of 1898, the United States inherited Spain's opium monopoly in the Philippines. Concern over this international situation, along with the domestic issues just outlined, led the U.S. government to participate in the First International Drug Conference, held in Shanghai in 1908, and a second one at The Hague in 1912. Participants in these two conferences were asked to strongly oppose free trade in drugs. The international pressure, coupled with a growing national concern, led to the passage of the antidrug laws discussed here.

Alcohol and Its Prohibition

The history of alcohol and the law in the United States has also been controversial and dramatic. At the turn of the century, a drive was mustered to prohibit the sale of alcohol. This **temperance movement** was fueled by the belief that the purity of the U.S. agrarian culture was being destroyed by the growth of the city. Urbanism was viewed as a threat to the lifestyle of the majority of the nation's population, then living on farms and in villages. The forces behind the temperance movement were such lobbying groups as the Anti-Saloon League led by Carrie Nation, the Women's Temperance Union, and the Protestant clergy of the Baptist, Methodist, and Congregationalist faiths.[137] They viewed the growing city, filled with newly arriving Irish, Italian, and Eastern European immigrants, as centers of degradation and wickedness. The propensity of these ethnic people to drink heavily was viewed as the main force behind their degenerate lifestyle. The eventual prohibition of the sale of alcoholic beverages brought about by ratification of the Eighteenth Amendment in 1919 was viewed as a triumph of the morality of middle- and upper-class Americans over the threat posed to their culture by the "new Americans."[138]

Prohibition failed. It was enforced by the Volstead Act, which defined intoxicating beverages as those containing one-half of 1 percent, or more, alcohol.[139] What doomed Prohibition? One factor was the use of organized crime to supply illicit liquor. Also, the law made it illegal only to sell alcohol, not to purchase it; this factor cut into the law's deterrent capability. Finally, despite the work of Elliot Ness and his "Untouchables," law enforcement agencies were inadequate, and officials were likely to be corrupted by wealthy bootleggers.[140] Eventually, in 1933, the Twenty-First Amendment to the Constitution repealed Prohibition, signaling the end of the "noble experiment."

Commonly Abused Drugs

A wide variety of drugs are sold and used by drug abusers. Some are addicting, others not. Some provide hallucinations; others cause a depressing, relaxing stupor; and a few give an immediate, exhilarating uplift. This section discusses some of the most widely used illegal drugs.[141]

Anesthetics *Anesthetic drugs* are used as nervous system depressants. Local anesthetics block nervous system transmissions; general anesthetics act on the brain to produce a generalized loss of sensation, stupor, or unconsciousness (called *narcosis*). The most widely abused anesthetic drug is phencyclidine (PCP), known on the street as "angel dust." PCP can be sprayed on marijuana or other plant leaves and smoked, or it can be drunk or injected; the last two methods are extremely hazardous. Originally developed as an animal tranquilizer, PCP causes hallucinations and a spaced-out feeling. The effects of PCP can last up to two days; the danger of overdose is extremely high.

Volatile Liquids *Volatile liquids* are liquids that are easily vaporized. Some substance abusers inhale vapors from lighter fluid, paint thinner, cleaning fluid, and model airplane glue to reach a drowsy, dizzy state some-

times accompanied by hallucinations. The psychological effect produced by inhaling these substances is a short-term sense of excitement and euphoria followed by a period of disorientation, slurred speech, and drowsiness. Amyl nitrate is a commonly used volatile liquid that is sold in capsules ("poppers") that are broken and inhaled. Poppers allegedly increase sensation and are sometimes used during sexual activity to prolong and intensify the experience. Some youths use "fry" sticks — marijuana joints or cigars that have been soaked in embalming fluid; sometimes, unbeknownst to users, the fry sticks come laced with PCP. Smoking fry is thought to produce hallucinations, paranoia, and disorientation.[142]

Barbiturates The hypnotic-sedative drugs —*barbiturates*— depress the central nervous system into a sleeplike condition. On the illegal market, barbiturates are called "goofballs" or "downers" or are known by the color of the capsules —"reds" (Seconal), "blue dragons" (Amytal), and "rainbows" (Tuinal). Barbiturates can be prescribed by doctors as sleeping pills. In the illegal market, they are used to create relaxed, sociable, and good-humored feelings. However, if dosages get too high, users become irritable and obnoxious and finally slump off into sleep. Barbiturates are probably the major cause of drug overdose deaths.

Tranquilizers *Tranquilizers* relieve uncomfortable emotional feelings by reducing levels of anxiety; they ease tension and promote a state of relaxation. The major tranquilizers are used to control the behavior of the mentally ill who are suffering from psychoses, aggressiveness, and agitation. They are known by their brand names — Ampazine, Thorazine, Pacatal, Sparine, and so on. The minor tranquilizers are used by the average citizen to combat anxiety, tension, fast heart rate, and headaches. The most common are Valium, Librium, Miltown, and Equanil. These mild tranquilizers are easily obtained by prescription. However, increased dosages can lead to addiction, and withdrawal can be painful and hazardous.

Amphetamines *Amphetamines* ("uppers," "beans," "pep pills") are synthetic drugs that stimulate action in the central nervous system. They produce an intense physical reaction: mood elevation and increased blood pressure, breathing rate, and bodily activity. Amphetamines also produce psychological effects, such as increased confidence, euphoria, fearlessness, talkativeness, impulsive behavior, and loss of appetite. The commonly used amphetamines are Benzedrine ("bennies"), Dexedrine ("dex"), Dexamyl, Bephetamine ("whites"), and Methedrine ("meth," "speed," "crystal meth," "ice"). Methedrine is probably the most widely used and most dangerous amphetamine. Some people swallow it; heavy users inject it for a quick rush. Long-

Marijuana is produced from the leaves of *Cannabis sativa,* a hemp plant grown throughout the world. Here a marijuana crop is being destroyed by drug agents. Despite such efforts, marijuana remains widely used by teens and young adults.

term heavy use can result in exhaustion, anxiety, prolonged depression, and hallucinations.

Cannabis (Marijuana) Commonly called "pot," "grass," "ganja," "maryjane," "dope," and a variety of other names, *marijuana* is produced from the leaves of *Cannabis sativa,* a plant grown throughout the world. *Hashish* (hash) is a concentrated form of cannabis made from unadulterated resin from the female plant. Smoking large amounts of pot or hash can cause drastic distortion in auditory and visual perception, even producing hallucinatory effects. Small doses produce an early excitement ("high") that gives way to a sedated effect and drowsiness. Pot use is also related to decreased physical activity, overestimation in time and space, and increased food consumption. When the user is alone, marijuana produces a quiet, dreamy state. In a group, it is common for users to become giddy and lose perspective. Although marijuana is nonaddicting, its long-term effects have been the subject of much debate.

Hallucinogens *Hallucinogens* are drugs, either natural or synthetic, that produce vivid distortions of the senses without greatly disturbing the viewer's consciousness. Some produce hallucinations, and others cause psychotic behavior in otherwise normal people. One common hallucinogen is mescaline, named after the Mescalero Apaches who first used it. Mescaline occurs naturally in the peyote, a small cactus that grows in Mexico and the southwestern United States. After initial discomfort, mescaline produces vivid hallucinations in all ranges of colors and geometric patterns, a feeling of depersonalization, and out-of-body sensations. A synthetic and highly dangerous form of mescaline used for a brief period in the 1960s was called STP. However, the danger of this drug made its use short-lived. A second group of hallucinogens consists of alkaloid compounds, which occur in nature or can be made in the laboratory. They include such familiar hallucinogens as DMT, morning glory seeds, and psilocybin. These compounds can be transformed into D-lysergic acid diethylamide-25, commonly called LSD. This powerful substance (800 times more potent than mescaline) stimulates cerebral sensory centers to produce visual hallucinations in all ranges of colors, to intensify hearing, and to increase sensitivity. Users often report a scrambling of sensations; they may "hear colors" and "smell music." Users also report feeling euphoric and mentally superior, although to an observer they appear disoriented and confused. Unfortunately, anxiety and panic (a "bad trip") may occur during the LSD experience, and overdoses can produce psychotic episodes, flashbacks, and even death.

Cocaine *Cocaine* is an alkaloid derivative of the coca leaf first isolated in 1860 by Albert Niemann of Gottingen, Germany. When originally discovered, it was considered a medicinal breakthrough that could relieve fatigue, depression, and various other symptoms. Its discovery was embraced by no less a luminary than Sigmund Freud, who used it himself and prescribed it for his friends, patients, and relatives. It quickly became a staple of popular patent medicines. When pharmacist John Styth Pemberton first brewed his new soft drink in 1886, he added cocaine to act as a "brain tonic" and called the drink Coca-Cola; this secret ingredient was taken out in 1906.[143] After its addictive qualities and dangerous side effects became apparent, cocaine's use was controlled by the Pure Food and Drug Act of 1906. Until the 1970s cocaine remained an underground drug—the property of artists, jazz musicians, beatniks, and sometimes even jet-setters.

Cocaine, or coke, is the most powerful natural stimulant. Its use produces euphoria, laughter, restlessness, and excitement. Overdoses can cause delirium, increased reflexes, violent manic behavior, and possible respiratory failure. Cocaine can be sniffed, or "snorted," into the nostrils or injected. The immediate feeling of euphoria ("rush") is short-lived, and heavy users may snort coke as often as every 10 minutes. Mixing cocaine and heroin, called "speedballing," is a highly dangerous practice.

Cocaine Derivatives: Freebase and Crack A great deal of public attention has been focused on cocaine use and the popularity of new, more potent forms of cocaine, such as freebase and crack. **Freebase** is a chemical produced from street cocaine by treating it with a liquid to remove the hydrochloric acid with which pure cocaine is bonded during manufacture. The free cocaine, or cocaine base (hence the term *freebase*) is then dissolved in a solvent, usually ether, that crystallizes the purified cocaine. The resulting crystals are crushed and smoked in a special glass pipe; the high produced is more immediate and powerful than snorting street-strength coke. Unfortunately for the user, freebase is dangerous to make because it involves highly flammable products such as ether; it is an expensive habit; and it is highly addictive.

Despite the publicity, crack is not a new substance and has been on the street for more than 15 years. **Crack,** like freebase, is processed street cocaine. Its manufacture involves using ammonia or baking soda to remove the hydrochlorides and create a crystalline form of cocaine base that can then be smoked.[144] However, unlike freebase, crack is not a pure form of cocaine and contains both remnants of hydrochloride and additional residue from the baking soda (sodium bicarbonate). In fact, crack gets its name from the fact that the sodium bicarbonate often emits a crackling sound when the substance is smoked. Research by Thomas Mieczkowski indicates that today, smoking crack is the preferred method of cocaine ingestion among persistent users.[145] Also referred to as "rock," "gravel," and "roxanne," crack apparently was introduced and gained popularity on both coasts simultaneously. It is relatively cheap and provides a powerful high; users rapidly become psychologically addicted to crack. An even more powerful form of the drug is "space-base"—crack doused with LSD, heroin, or PCP. The Criminological Enterprise feature titled "Careers in Crack" details the nature of the crack epidemic that hit the country in the 1980s.

Narcotics *Narcotic drugs* produce insensibility to pain (analgesia) and free the mind of anxiety and emotion (sedation). Users experience a rush of euphoria, relief from fear and apprehension, release of tension, and elevation of spirits. After experiencing this uplifting mood for a short period, users become apathetic and drowsy and nod off. Narcotics can be injected under the skin or in a muscle. Experienced users inject the drugs directly into the bloodstream (mainlining), which provides an immediate "fix." The most common narcotics are derivatives of opium, a drug produced from the opium poppy. The Chinese popularized the habit of smoking or chewing opium extract to produce euphoric feelings. Morphine (from Morpheus, the Greek god of dreams), a derivative of opium, is about 10 times as strong and is used legally by physicians to relieve pain. It was first popularized as a pain reliever during the Civil War, but its addictive qualities soon became evident. Heroin was first produced as a painkilling alternative to morphine in 1875 because, although 25 times more powerful, it was considered nonaddicting by its creator Heinrich Dreser. (The drug's name derives from the fact it was considered a "hero" because of its painkilling ability when it was first isolated.)[146] Heroin today is the most commonly used narcotic in the United States. Due to its strength, dealers cut it with neutral substances, such as sugar (lactose); street heroin is often only 1 to 4 percent pure. Because users can rapidly build up a tolerance to the drug, they constantly need larger doses to feel an effect. They may also change the method of ingestion to get the desired kick. At first, heroin is usually sniffed or snorted; as tolerance builds, it is injected beneath the skin (skin-popped) and then shot directly into a vein. Through the process, the user becomes an **addict**—a person with an overpowering physical and psychological need to continue taking a particular substance or drug by any means possible. If addicts cannot get enough heroin, they suffer withdrawal symptoms. These include irritability, emotional depression, extreme nervousness, abdominal pain, and nausea. Although it is difficult to obtain accurate data, there may be anywhere between 300,000 and 700,000 practicing heroin addicts and another 2 million to 3 million people who have tried heroin at least once in their lives.[147] Heroin abuse is generally considered a lower-class phenomenon, although a fair number of middle- and upper-class users exist. Even physicians are known to have serious narcotic abuse problems.[148] The popularity of heroin in

The Criminological Enterprise

Careers in Crack

In the 1980s thousands of people selling crack suddenly appeared on the streets of New York City. The media proclaimed that a crack epidemic was sweeping the nation: in 1986 *Time* and *Newsweek* published five cover stories on crack, and more than 1,000 articles appeared in the national news media. Rumors sprang up about the drug: women were driven to prostitution to support their habits; juveniles were being enticed into the crack trade; crack dealers were becoming wealthy; the drug was instantly addicting. Although these rumors captured the public's imagination, little scientific evidence documented the nature and extent of crack usage. The federal government funded the Careers in Crack Project to interview known addicts and systematically analyze how crack affects users, those around them, and the communities in which they live.

Based on more than 1,000 interviews conducted in New York City, investigators found that in contrast to public myth, many crack users were experienced substance abusers who began using crack in their late twenties. Introduced to the drug socially at parties, their initiation into crack abuse was little different from their involvement with other drugs; users found crack no more addicting than powdered cocaine or heroin. However, once introduced to the drug, users' consumption of crack far exceeded that of any other drug: many reported having used crack four or more times per day, spending more than $1000 per month.

Crack and Crime

By 1988 crack had become the most frequently sold and lucrative drug in the street markets of New York. However, crack use did not appear to increase the frequency of users' non-

drug crimes. For example, crack use was not associated with the initiation of violent behaviors such as assault or armed robbery. Although some women increased the frequency of their prostitution to obtain drug money, few initiated careers in prostitution because of crack. Women involved with crack did, however, become more involved in hard drug use, drug sales, and nondrug crime than had been the case with heroin or cocaine use. Where crack seemed to affect crime was the increase in violent behavior associated with its marketing: drug suppliers often used violence to establish power and collect money owed them in drug deals.

The crack epidemic appears to have gone through several distinct phases, beginning in New York around 1982 when cocaine snorters sought purer forms of the drug to increase their highs. Freebase was too complicated and expensive to produce; crack provided a better "bang for the buck." Once crack caught on in 1984, it spread rapidly among hard drug users. By 1987 most of the at-risk population had started using crack, and expansion faded. Popularity began to wane in 1989 when, not coincidentally, state and local criminal justice agencies aimed their drug control strategies at crack users and dealers. Surveys conducted in 1996 shows that crack use was in substantial decline in cities on both coasts, including New Orleans, Los Angeles, Philadelphia, and Washington, D.C. In a few locations within the interior of the country (Atlanta, Denver and St. Louis) the crack epidemic seems to be as strong as ever.

Nonetheless, there are still many hard-core users, especially young people who reached maturity during the height of the epidemic. Crack addiction, like all substance abuse, is likely

to persist in some form as long as unemployment, inequality, and lack of treatment and opportunity plague the inner cities of America.

CRITICAL THINKING

1. Can increased police presence and severe sanctions reduce drug use in the inner city? That is, can a general deterrent reduce or end drug use?
2. Is it fair to punish crack smokers more heavily than cocaine snorters? Consider that the former are more often African-American and the latter white.

 INFOTRAC COLLEGE EDITION RESEARCH

To read more about crack cocaine and the efforts being made to help users, see:

Nabila El-Bassel, Louisa Gilbert, Robert F. Schilling, Andre Ivanoff, Debra Borne, Steven F. Safyer. Correlates of crack abuse among drug-using incarcerated women: psychological trauma, social support, and coping behavior. *American Journal of Drug and Alcohol Abuse* Feb 1996 v22 n1 p41(16)

Harvey A. Siegal, Russel S. Falck, Robert G. Carlson, Jichuan Wang, Ahmmed M. Rahman. Health services research among crack-cocaine users. *American Behavioral Scientist* May 1998 v41 n8 p1063(16)

Source: Andrew Lang Golub and Bruce Johnson, "Crack's Decline: Some Surprises Across U.S. Cities," *National Institute of Justice Research in Brief* (1997): 1–3; Bruce Johnson, Andrew Lang Golub, and Jeffrey Fagan, "Careers in Crack, Drug Use, Drug Distribution, and Nondrug Criminality," *Crime and Delinquency* 41 (1995): 275–95.

---

the 1990s has been linked to its relatively low cost, ready supply, and the effect of government efforts to control other substances such as crack cocaine; the drug of choice seems to be shifting from crack to

heroin. Other opium derivatives used by drug abusers include codeine, Dilaudid, Percodan, and Prinadol. It is also possible to create synthetic narcotics in the laboratory. Synthetics include Demerol, Methadone, Nalline, and Darvon. Although it is less likely that a user will become addicted to synthetic narcotics, it is still possible, and withdrawal symptoms are similar to those experienced by users of natural narcotics.

Steroids *Anabolic steroids* are used to gain muscle bulk and strength for athletics and body building. Black market sales of these drugs now approach $1 billion annually. Although not physically addicting, steroid use can be an obsession among people who desire athletic success. Long-term users may spend up to $400 a week on steroids and may support their habit by dealing the drug.

Steroids are dangerous because of the significant health problems associated with long-term use: liver ailments, tumors, hepatitis, kidney problems, sexual dysfunction, hypertension, and mental problems such as depression. Steroid use runs in cycles, and other drugs, such as Clomid, Teslac, and Halotestin, which carry their own dangerous side effects, are used to curb the need for high dosages. Finally, steroid users often share needles, which puts them at high risk for contracting the AIDS virus.

Designer Drugs **Designer drugs** are chemical substances, made and distributed in relatively small batches, that alter mood. Their chemical characteristics place them somewhere within the broad families of drugs just described. Because they are chemically unique, they escape federal regulation until their danger is recognized and they are added to the schedule of controlled substances. Popular today is MDMA or "ecstasy," which combines an amphetaminelike rush with hallucinogenic experiences; the hallucinogens DMT and 2c-B or "Nexus"; and steroid substitute GHB, which causes drowsiness.

Alcohol Although the purchase and sale of alcohol are legal today in most U.S. jurisdictions, excessive alcohol consumption is considered a major substance abuse problem. The cost of alcohol abuse is quite high. Alcohol may be a factor in nearly half of all U.S. murders, suicides, and accidental deaths.[149] Alcohol-related deaths number 100,000 a year, far more than those related to all other illegal drugs combined. The economic cost of the nation's drinking problem is equally staggering. An estimated $117 billion is lost each year, including $18 billion from premature deaths, $66 billion in reduced work effort, and $13 billion for treatment efforts.[150]

Alcohol has long been considered a "gateway" drug that precedes involvement in more serious forms of abuse. According to this view, abusers escalate the seriousness of their substance abuse, beginning with alcohol and then following with marijuana and more serious drugs as the need for a more powerful high intensifies. Although the "gateway" concept is still debated, there is little disagreement that serious drug users also are heavily involved with alcohol.[151]

Considering these problems, why do so many people drink alcohol to excess? Drinkers report that alcohol reduces tension, diverts worries, enhances pleasure, improves social skills, and transforms experiences for the better.[152] These reactions may follow the limited use of alcohol, but higher doses act as a sedative and depressant. Long-term use has been linked with depression and numerous physical ailments ranging from heart disease to cirrhosis of the liver (although some research links moderate drinking to a reduction in the probability of heart attack).[153] And whereas many people think that drinking stirs their romantic urges, the weight of the scientific evidence indicates that alcohol decreases sexual response.[154]

The Extent of Substance Abuse

Despite continuing efforts at control, the use of mood-altering substances persists in the United States. What is the extent of the substance abuse problem today? Despite media attention given to the incidence of drug abuse, there is actually significant controversy over the nature and extent of drug use. The media assume that drug use is a pervasive, growing menace that threatens to destroy the American way of life. This view is countered by national surveys showing that drug use is now less common than it was two decades ago.

A number of national surveys attempt to chart trends in drug abuse in the general population. One important source of information on drug use is the annual self-report survey of drug abuse among high school students conducted by the Institute of Social Research (ISR) at the University of Michigan.[155] This survey is based on the self-report responses of about 17,000 high school seniors, 15,500 tenth-graders, and 18,800 eighth-graders in hundreds of schools around the United States.

As Figure 14.2 shows, drug use declined from a high point around 1980 until 1990, when it began to increase. In 1998 drug use declined slightly, reversing this decade-long trend. Marijuana, the most widely used of the illicit drugs, accounted for most of the increase in overall illicit drug use during the 1990s, and it now accounts for much of the observed decrease. All three grades showed a gradual decrease in marijuana use in the prior 12 months. Even though marijuana use is decreasing, it is still widespread: nearly a quarter (22 percent) of all eighth-graders said they had tried marijuana, and about half (49 percent) of all seniors said they had done so.[156]

Table 14.2 shows the percentage of students who have used drugs at least once. Although drug and alcohol use has stabilized, more than half of all seniors, almost 45 percent of sophomores, and 30 percent of

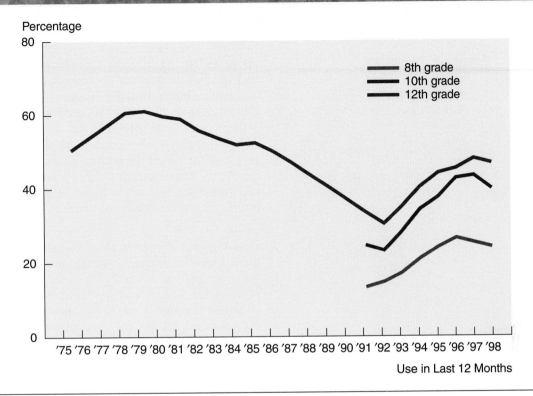

Source: *Monitoring the Future Study* (University of Michigan, 1998).

Table 14.2   Trends in Lifetime Prevalence of Use of Various Drugs for Eighth-, Tenth-, and Twelfth-Graders (*entries are percentages*)

ANY ILLICIT DRUG	LIFETIME								1997–1998 CHANGE
	1991	1992	1993	1994	1995	1996	1997	1998	
8th grade	18.7	20.6	22.5	25.7	28.5	31.2	29.4	29.0	−0.4
10th grade	30.6	29.8	32.8	37.4	40.9	45.4	47.3	44.9	−2.4
12th grade	44.1	40.7	42.9	45.6	48.4	50.8	54.3	54.1	−0.2

Source: *Monitoring the Future Study* (University of Michigan, 1998).

eighth-graders claim to have abused substances at some time. More than half of all high school seniors are users, including 12 percent who have taken LSD and about 9 percent who have tried cocaine. About one-third are "blitz" drinkers, having had the equivalent of five or more drinks in a row.

The National Household Survey of Drug Abuse, conducted by the Department of Health and Human Services' National Institute on Drug Abuse (NIDA), interviews approximately 10,000 people at home each year.[157] The 1997 household survey found that an estimated 13.9 million Americans were current users of il-

licit drugs (Figure 14.3). Like the ISR survey, the household survey indicates that drug use increased substantially between 1991 and 1996 before finally stabilizing in 1997. For example, marijuana use among youths aged 12 to 17 increased from 37 to 83 per thousand potential new users between 1991 and 1996; for young adults aged 18 to 25, marijuana usage increased from 34 to 54 per thousand during the same period. However, there are still far fewer recreational drug users today than 20 years ago, when 25 million Americans used drugs. As Figure 14.4 shows, young people seem to be the most at risk of substance abuse.

Figure 14.3 Types of Drugs Used by Illicit Drug Users: 1997

13.9 million illicit drug users

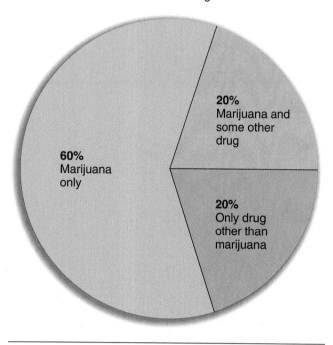

60% Marijuana only

20% Marijuana and some other drug

20% Only drug other than marijuana

Source: National Institute on Drug Abuse (NIDA), *National Household Survey 1997.*

Despite the recent stabilization in drug use, an estimated 1.5 million Americans still use cocaine regularly. Heroin use has also increased since 1992, and today the Household Survey estimates that 325,000 people (0.2 percent of the population) are users. The most serious problem, according to the household survey, is alcohol abuse. In 1997 111 million Americans aged 12 and older had used alcohol in the past month. About 32 million engaged in binge drinking, meaning they drank five or more drinks on one occasion in the past month; and 11 million were heavy drinkers, meaning they had five or more drinks on one occasion on five or more days in the past month. About 11 million current drinkers fall in the 12 to 20 age group. Of this group, 4.8 million, or more than 40 percent, engaged in binge drinking, including 2 million heavy drinkers.

How Can the Trends in Drug Use Be Explained? Although general usage is lower than it was 20 years ago, the drug problem has not gone away. Why has drug use remained a major social problem? When drug use declined in the 1980s, one reason may have been changing perceptions about the harmfulness of drugs, such as cocaine and marijuana; as people come to view these drugs as harmful, they tend to use them less. Because of widespread publicity linking drug use, needle sharing, and the AIDS virus, people began to see drug taking as

Figure 14.4 Past Month Use of Any Illicit Drug by Age, 1997

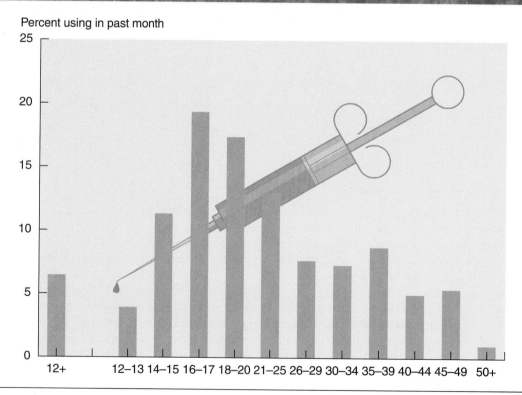

Percent using in past month

Source: National Institute on Drug Abuse (NIDA), *National Household Survey 1997.*

dangerous and risky. In the 1990s the perceived risk of drugs has declined. For example, the ISR reports that 79 percent of high school seniors in 1991 thought they ran a great risk if they were regular marijuana users; today only about 58 percent view regular marijuana use as risky.

In addition, when drug use declined, youths reported greater disapproval of drug use among their friends, and peer pressure may help account for lower use rates. In the 1990s the number of youths disapproving of drugs has declined (although a majority still disapproves); with lower disapproval has come increased usage.

It also appears that it is easier to obtain drugs, especially for younger adolescents. For example, the ISR survey found that in 1992 about 40 percent of eighth-graders said it was easy to obtain pot; today about 50 percent say that it is easy to get that drug, an increase of 25 percent. Finally, parents may now be unwilling or reluctant to educate their children about the dangers of substance abuse because as baby boomers they were drug abusers themselves in the 1960s and 1970s.

It should come as no surprise that young people who perceive little peer rejection for drug use, who consider drugs risk-free and easily available, and whose parents either ignore or condone drug use will consider substance abuse. Although drug use has finally stabilized, it remains to be seen whether this welcome trend will continue into the next millennium.

Are the Surveys Accurate? The ISR survey is methodologically sophisticated, but it relies on self-report evidence that is subject to error. Drug users may boastfully overinflate the extent of their substance abuse, underreport out of fear, or simply be unaware or forgetful. About 20 percent of the ISR survey respondents say they would not provide or are not sure if they provide honest answers.

Another problem is that these national surveys overlook important segments of the drug-using population. For example, the NIDA survey misses people who are homeless, in prison, in drug rehabilitation clinics, or in AIDS clinics and those (about 20 percent of the people contacted) who refuse to participate in the interview. The ISR survey omits kids who are institutionalized, who are absent on the day the survey is administered, who refuse to answer target questions such as their racial background, and who have dropped out of school; research indicates that dropouts may, in fact, be the most frequent users of dangerous drugs.[158] The surveys also rely on accurate self-reporting by drug users, a group whose recall and dependability may both be questionable. A number of studies indicate that serious abusers underreport drug use in surveys.[159]

These surveys also use statistical estimating methods to project national use trends from relatively small

There are many views as to why people take drugs, and no one theory has proven an adequate explanation of all forms of substance abuse. Recent research efforts show that drug users suffer a variety of family and socialization difficulties, have addiction-prone personalities, and are generally at risk for many other social problems; drug use seems to be part of a "problem behavior syndrome."

samples. Sometimes this can result in misleading conclusions. For example, in one year (1991) the Household Survey estimated that 148,000 of the total 701,000 heroin users were aged 79 and 32 percent of the users were over 60! This estimate was based on the responses of eight heroin users who were over 60.[160] Although these weaknesses are troubling, the surveys are administered yearly, in a consistent fashion, so that the effects of over- and underreporting and missing subjects should have a consistent effect in every survey year. The surveys have attempted to improve their methodologies to increase validity. For example, the ISR survey now includes eighth- and tenth-graders in an attempt to survey youths before they drop out of school.

AIDS and Drug Use

Drug use is closely tied to the threat of AIDS.[161] Since monitoring of the spread of AIDS began in 1981, about one-fourth of all adult AIDS cases reported to the Centers for Disease Control in Atlanta have occurred among intravenous (IV) drug users. It is now estimated that as many as one-third of all IV drug users are AIDS carriers.[162]

One reason for the AIDS–drug use relationship is the widespread habit of needle sharing among IV users. For example, a recent study of Los Angeles drug "shooting galleries" conducted by researcher Douglas Longshore found that about one-quarter of users shoot drugs in these abandoned buildings, private apartments, or other sites, where for a small entry fee injection equipment can be borrowed or rented.[163] Most users (72 percent) shared needles, and although some tried to use bleach as a disinfectant, the majority ignored this safety precaution. Asking for or bringing bleach ruined the moment because it reminded the addicts of the risk of AIDS; others were too high to be bothered. As one user told Longshore,

> After I started shooting coke, all hell broke loose, no holds barred, couldn't be bothered to get bleach. That was out of the question. Literally picking needles up that I had no idea who had used . . . I was just out of my mind insane. [HIV] wasn't a consideration. It was more like, I hope this is going to be okay. You just aren't in your right mind anymore.[164]

AIDS is spread through the transfer of blood or other body fluids, and the sharing of HIV-contaminated needles is the primary mechanism for AIDS transmission among drug users. Needle sharing has been encouraged by efforts to control drugs by outlawing the over-the-counter sale of hypodermic needles. Consequently, some jurisdictions have developed outreach programs to help these drug users; others have made an effort to teach users how to clean their needles and syringes; a few states have gone so far as to give addicts sterile needles.[165]

Drug users also have a significant exposure to AIDS because they have multiple sex partners, some of whom may engage in prostitution to support a drug habit. And although research shows that women do not initiate careers in prostitution to support drug habits, prostitutes who acquire a drug habit appear to increase the frequency of their sexual activities.[166] Thus members of the drug culture can be exposed to AIDS even if they do not inject drugs or share needles.[167]

The threat of AIDS may be changing the behavior of recreational and middle-class users, but drug use may still be increasing among the poor, high school dropouts, and other disadvantaged groups. If that pattern is correct, then the recently observed decline in substance abuse may be restricted to one segment of the at-risk population, while another is continuing to use drugs at ever-increasing rates.

The Causes of Substance Abuse

What causes people to abuse substances? Although there are many different views on the cause of drug use, most can be characterized as seeing the onset of an addictive career as either an environmental or a personal matter.

Subcultural View Those who view drug abuse as having an environmental basis concentrate on lower-class addiction. Because a disproportionate number of drug abusers are poor, the onset of drug use can be tied to such factors as racial prejudice, devalued identities, low self-esteem, poor socioeconomic status, and the high level of mistrust, negativism, and defiance found in impoverished areas.

Residing in a deteriorated inner-city slum area is often correlated with entry into a drug subculture. Youths living in these depressed areas, where feelings of alienation and hopelessness run high, often meet established drug users, who teach them that narcotics provide an answer to their feelings of personal inadequacy and stress.[168] The youths may join peers to learn the techniques of drug use and receive social support for their habit. Research shows that peer influence is a significant predictor of drug careers that actually grows stronger as people mature.[169] Shared feelings and a sense of intimacy lead the youths to become fully enmeshed in what has been described as the "drug-use subculture."[170]

Those who can take advantage of educational or vocational opportunities can forgo the drug culture and succeed in the legitimate economic structure. However, upward mobility is available to only a few because of the deterioration of the manufacturing economy. The indigent, especially among minority group members, are much more likely to abuse substances than the upwardly mobile. This phenomenon takes on even greater importance considering the recent polarization of some minority communities into distinct groups of relatively affluent abstainers and desperately poor abusers.[171]

Psychodynamic View Not all drug abusers reside in lower-class slum areas; the problem of middle-class substance abuse is very real. Consequently, some experts have linked substance abuse to personality disturbance and emotional problems that can strike people in any economic class. Psychodynamic explanations of substance abuse suggest that drugs help youths control or express unconscious needs and impulses. Drinking alcohol may reflect an oral fixation that is associated with other nonfunctional behaviors, such as dependence and depression.[172] A young teen may resort to drug abuse to remain dependent on an overprotective mother, to reduce the emotional turmoil of adolescence, or to cope with troubling impulses.[173]

Research on the psychological characteristics of drug abusers does in fact reveal the presence of a significant degree of personal pathology. Studies have found that addicts suffer personality disorders characterized by a weak ego, low frustration tolerance, anxiety, and fantasies of omnipotence. Many addicts exhibit psychopathic or sociopathic behavior characteristics, forming what is called an *addiction-prone personality*.[174] Personality testing of known users suggests that a significant percentage suffer from psychotic disorders, including various levels of schizophrenia. These views have been substantiated by research involving a sample of over 20,291 people in five large U.S. cities. The results of this first large-scale study on the personality characteristics of abusers indicate a significant association between mental illness and drug abuse: about 53 percent of drug abusers and 37 percent of alcohol abusers have at least one serious mental illness. Conversely, 29 percent of the diagnosed mentally ill people in the survey have substance abuse problems.[175]

Genetic Factors It is also possible that substance abuse may have a genetic basis. For example, the biological children of alcoholics reared by nonalcoholic adoptive parents develop alcohol problems more often than the biological children of the adoptive parents.[176] In a similar vein, a number of studies comparing alcoholism among identical twins and fraternal twins have found that the degree of concordance (both siblings behaving identically) is twice as high among the identical twin groups. These inferences are still inconclusive because identical twins are more likely to be treated similarly than fraternal twins and are therefore more likely to be influenced by environmental conditions.

Taken as a group, studies of the genetic basis of substance abuse suggest that people whose parents were alcoholic or drug dependent have a greater chance of developing a problem than children of nonabusers. Nonetheless, most children of abusing parents do not become drug dependent themselves, suggesting that even if drug abuse is heritable, environment and socialization must play some role in the onset of abuse.[177]

Social Learning Social psychologists suggest that drug abuse may also result from observing parental drug use. Parental drug abuse begins to have a damaging effect on children as young as 2 years old, especially when parents manifest drug-related personality problems such as depression or poor impulse control.[178] Children whose parents abuse drugs are more likely to have persistent abuse problems than the children of nonabusers.[179]

People who learn that drugs provide pleasurable sensations may be the most likely to experiment with illegal substances; a habit may develop if the user experiences lower anxiety, fear, and tension levels.[180] Having a history of family drug and alcohol abuse has been found to be a characteristic of violent teenage sexual abusers.[181] Heroin abusers report an unhappy childhood that included harsh physical punishment and parental neglect and rejection.[182]

Drug Gateways According to the social learning view, drug involvement begins with smoking and drinking alcohol at an early age, which progresses to experimentation with marijuana and hashish and finally to cocaine and even heroin. Although most recreational users do not progress to "hard stuff," few addicts begin their involvement with narcotics without first experimenting with recreational drugs. By implication, if teen smoking and drinking could be reduced, the gateway to hard drugs would be narrowed.

A number of research efforts have confirmed the **gateway model.** For example, James Inciardi, Ruth Horowitz, and Anne Pottieger found a clear pattern of adult involvement in adolescent drug abuse. Kids on crack started their careers with early experimentation with alcohol at age 7, began getting drunk at age 8, had alcohol with an adult present by age 9, and became regular drinkers by the time they were 11 years old.[183] Drinking with an adult present, presumably a parent, was a significant precursor of future substance abuse and delinquency. "Adults who gave children alcohol," they argue, "were also giving them a head start in a delinquent career."[184]

Problem Behavior Syndrome (PBS) For many people, substance abuse is just one of many problem behaviors. Longitudinal studies show that drug abusers are maladjusted, alienated, and emotionally distressed and that their drug use is one among many social problems.[185] Having a deviant lifestyle begins early in life and is punctuated with criminal relationships, family history of substance abuse, educational failure, and alienation. People who abuse drugs lack commitment to religious values, disdain education, and spend most of their time in peer activities. A recent meta-analysis of PBS research conducted by John Donovan found robust support for the interconnection of problem drinking and drug abuse, delinquency, precocious sexual behavior, school failure, family conflict, and other similar social problems.[186]

Rational Choice Not all people who abuse drugs do so because of personal pathology. Some may use drugs and alcohol because they want to enjoy their effects: get high, relax, improve creativity, escape reality, and increase sexual responsiveness. Research indicates that adolescent alcohol abusers believe that getting high will make them powerful, increase their sexual performance, and facilitate their social behavior; they care little about negative future consequences.[187] Claire Sterck-Elifson's research on middle-class drug-abusing women shows that most were introduced by friends in the context of "just having some fun."[188]

Substance abuse, then, may be a function of the rational but mistaken belief that drugs can benefit the user. The decision to use drugs involves evaluations of personal consequences (such as addiction, disease, and legal punishment) and the expected benefits of drug use (such as peer approval, positive affective states, heightened awareness, and relaxation). Adolescents may begin using drugs because they believe their peers expect them to do so.[189]

Is There a Single "Cause" of Drug Abuse? There are many different views of why people take drugs, and no one theory has proved adequate to explain all forms of substance abuse. Recent research efforts show that drug users suffer a variety of family and socialization difficulties, have addiction-prone personalities, and are generally at risk for many other social problems.[190] And although it is popular to believe that addicts progress along a continuum of using ever more potent substances from so-called gateway drugs, that view may also be misleading. Research by Andrew Golub and Bruce Johnson shows that many hard-core drug abusers have never smoked or used alcohol. Examining a sample of more than 130,000 hard drug–using arrestees, Golub and Johnson found that the proportion who used marijuana before trying heroin and cocaine shifted significantly over time. The pathways may be different at various times and in different locales.[191]

In sum, there may be no single cause of substance abuse. People may try and continue to use illegal substances for a variety of reasons. As James Inciardi points out,

> There are as many reasons people use drugs as there are individuals who use drugs. For some, it may be a function of family disorganization, or cultural learning, or maladjusted personality, or an "addiction-prone" personality. . . . For others, heroin use may be no more than a normal response to the world in which they live.[192]

Types of Drug Users

The general public often groups all drug users together without recognizing that there are many varieties, ranging from adolescent recreational drug users to adults who run large smuggling operations.[193]

Adolescents Who Distribute Small Amounts of Drugs Many adolescents begin their involvement in the drug trade by using and distributing small amounts of drugs; they do not commit any other serious criminal acts. Kenneth Tunnell found in his interviews with low-level drug dealers that many started out as "stash dealers" who sold drugs to maintain a consistent access to drugs for their own consumption.[194]

Most of these petty dealers occasionally sell marijuana, crack, and PCP to support their own drug use. Their customers are almost always personal acquaintances, including friends and relatives. Deals are arranged over the phone, in school, or in public hang-

outs and meeting places; however, the actual distribution takes place in more private areas, such as at home or in cars. Petty dealers do not consider themselves seriously involved in drugs. They are insulated from the legal system because their activities rarely result in apprehension and sanction.

Adolescents Who Frequently Sell Drugs A small number of adolescents, most often multiple-drug users or heroin or cocaine users, are high-rate dealers who bridge the gap between adult drug distributors and the adolescent user. Although many are daily users, they are not "strung-out junkies" and maintain many normal adolescent roles, such as going to school and socializing with friends. Frequent dealers often have adults who "front" for them—that is, loan them drugs to sell without up-front cash. The teenagers then distribute the drugs to friends and acquaintances, returning most of the proceeds to the supplier while keeping a commission for themselves. They may also keep drugs for their own personal use, and in fact, some consider their drug dealing a way of getting high for free. Frequent dealers are more likely to sell drugs in public and can be seen in known drug user hangouts in parks, schools, or other public places. Deals are irregular, so the chances of apprehension are slight.

Teenage Drug Dealers Who Commit Other Delinquent Acts A more serious type of drug-involved youth comprises those who use and distribute multiple substances and also commit both property and violent crimes. Although these youngsters make up about 2 percent of the teenage population, they commit 40 percent of the robberies and assaults and about 60 percent of all teenage felony thefts and drug sales. There is little gender or racial difference among these youths: girls are as likely as boys to become high-rate, persistent, drug-involved offenders; white youths as likely as black youths; and middle-class adolescents raised outside cities as likely as lower-class city children.

These youths are frequently hired by older dealers to act as street-level drug runners. Each member of a crew of 3 to 12 boys will handle small quantities of drugs, perhaps three bags of heroin, which are received on consignment and sold on the street; the supplier receives 50 to 70 percent of the drug's street value. The crew members also act as lookouts, recruiters, and guards. They may be recreational drug users themselves, but crew members refrain from using addictive drugs, such as heroin; some major suppliers will only hire drug-free kids to make street deals. Between drug sales, the young dealers commit robberies, burglaries, and other thefts. Although these youths may be part of street gangs, their drug-dealing actions are often independent of gang activity; some gangs are drug-oriented, but the majority are not involved in drug trafficking.[195]

Adolescents Who Cycle in and out of the Justice System Some drug-involved youths are failures at both dealing and crime. They do not have the savvy to join gangs or groups and instead begin committing unplanned, opportunistic crimes that increase their chances of arrest. They are heavy drug users, which both increases apprehension risk and decreases their value for organized drug distribution networks. Drug-involved "losers" can earn a living steering customers to a seller in a "copping" area, "touting" drug availability for a dealer, or acting as lookouts. However, they are not considered trustworthy or deft enough to handle drugs or money. They may bungle other criminal acts, which solidifies their reputation as undesirable. Although these persistent offenders get involved in drugs at a very young age, they receive little attention from the justice system until they have developed an extensive arrest record. By then, they are approaching the end of their minority and will either spontaneously desist or become so deeply entrenched in the drug–crime subculture that little can be done to treat or deter their illegal activities.

Drug-Involved Youths Who Continue to Commit Crimes as Adults Although about two-thirds of substance-abusing youths continue to use drugs after they reach adulthood, about half desist from other criminal activities. Those who persist in both substance abuse and crime as adults have the following characteristics:

- They come from poor families.
- They have other criminals in the family.
- They do poorly in school.
- They started using drugs and committing other delinquent acts at a relatively young age.
- They used multiple types of drugs and committed crimes frequently.
- They have few opportunities in late adolescence to participate in legitimate, rewarding adult activities.

Some evidence also exists that these drug-using persisters have low nonverbal IQs and poor physical coordination. Nonetheless, little scientific evidence indicates why some drug-abusing kids drop out of crime while others remain active into their adulthood.

Outwardly Respectable Adults Who Are Top-Level Dealers A few outwardly respectable adult dealers sell large quantities of drugs to support themselves in high-class lifestyles. Outwardly respectable dealers often seem indistinguishable from other young professionals. However, they are rarely drawn from the highest professional circles, such as those of physicians or attorneys, nor are they likely to have worked their way up from lower-class origins. Upscale dealers seem to drift into dealing from many different walks of life. Frequently they are drawn from professions and occupations that are unstable, have irregular working hours, and accept drug abuse. Former graduate students, musicians, performing artists, and barkeepers are among those who are likely to fit the profile of the adult who begins dealing drugs in his or her 20s. Some use their business skills and drug profits to get into legitimate enterprise or illegal scams. Others drop out of the drug trade because they are the victims of violent crime committed by competitors or disgruntled customers; a few wind up in jail or prison.

Smugglers *Smugglers* import drugs into the United States. They are generally men, middle-aged or older, who have strong organizational skills, established connections, capital to invest, and a willingness to take large business risks. Smugglers are a loosely organized, competitive group of individual entrepreneurs. There is a constant flow in and out of the business as some sources become the target of law enforcement activities, new drug sources become available, older smugglers become dealers, and former dealers become smugglers.

Adult Predatory Drug Users Who Are Frequently Arrested Many users who begin abusing substances in early adolescence continue in drugs and crime in their adulthood. Getting arrested, doing time, using multiple drugs, and committing predatory crimes are a way of life for them. They have few skills, did poorly in school, and have long criminal records. The threat of conviction and punishment has little effect on their criminal activities. These "losers" have friends and relatives involved in drugs and crime. They specialize in robberies, burglaries, thefts, and drug sales. They filter in and out of the justice system and begin committing crimes as soon as they are released. In some populations, at least one-third of adult males are involved in drug trafficking and other criminal acts well into their adulthood.[196]

If they make a "big score," perhaps through a successful drug deal, they may significantly increase their drug use. Their increased narcotics consumption then destabilizes their lifestyle, destroying family and career ties. When their finances dry up, they may become *street junkies,* people whose traditional lifestyle has been destroyed, who turn to petty crime to maintain an adequate supply of drugs. Cut off from a stable source of quality heroin, not knowing from where their next fixes or the money to pay for them will come, looking for any opportunity to make a buck, getting sick or "jonesing," being pathetically unkempt and unable to maintain even the most primitive routines of health or hygiene, street junkies live a very difficult existence. Because they are unreliable and likely to become police informants, street junkies pay the highest prices for the poorest quality heroin; lack of availability increases their need to commit habit-supporting crimes.[197]

Adult Predatory Drug Users Who Are Rarely Arrested
Some drug users are "winners." They commit hundreds of crimes each year but are rarely arrested. On the streets, they are known for their calculated violence. Their crimes are carefully planned and coordinated. They often work with partners and use lookouts to carry out the parts of their crimes that have the highest risk of apprehension. These "winners" are more likely to use recreational drugs, such as coke and pot, than the more addicting heroin or opiates. Some become high-frequency users and risk apprehension and punishment. But for the lucky few, their criminal careers can stretch for up to 15 years without interruption by the justice system.

These users are sometimes referred to as *stabilized junkies* who have learned the skills needed to purchase and process larger amounts of heroin. Their addiction enables them to maintain normal lifestyles, although they may turn to drug dealing to create contacts with drug suppliers. They are employable, but earning legitimate income does little to reduce their drug use or dealing activities.[198]

Less Predatory Drug-Involved Adult Offenders Most adult drug users are petty criminals who avoid violent crime. These *occasional users* are people just beginning their addiction, who use small amounts of narcotics, and whose habits can be supported by income from conventional jobs; narcotics have relatively little influence on their lifestyles.[199] They are typically high school graduates and have regular employment that supports their drug use. They usually commit petty thefts or pass bad checks. They stay on the periphery of the drug trade by engaging in such acts as helping addicts shoot up, bagging drugs for dealers, operating shooting galleries, renting needles and syringes, and selling small amounts of drugs. These petty criminal drug users do not have the stomach for a life of hard crime and drug dealing. They violate the law in proportion to the amount and cost of the drugs they are using. Pot smokers have a significantly lower frequency of theft violations than daily heroin users, whose habit is considerably more costly.

Women Who Are Drug-Involved Offenders Women who are drug-involved offenders constitute a separate type of substance abuser. Although women are far less likely than men to use addictive drugs, female offenders are just as likely to be involved in drugs as male offenders. Female drug users are not usually violent criminals but are often involved in prostitution and low-level drug dealing; a few become top-level dealers. Female abusers are quite often mothers. Because they share needles, they are at high risk of contracting AIDS, and many pass the HIV virus to their newborn children. Female addicts are offered fewer services than men because treatment programs are geared toward males. Their children are often malnourished, mistreated, and exposed to a highly criminal population. Some are sold to pornographers and become involved in the sex-for-profit trade; others grow up to become criminals themselves.

The causes of female drug abuse are quite complex. For example, Karen Joe's study of female Asian Pacific–American drug abusers found that from early childhood these women lived in an environment of heated conflict, economic marginality, and parental substance abuse. They were first introduced to drugs by male relatives and school peers. They drifted into using drugs while interacting with their intimate partners and extended kin.[200]

Drugs and Crime

One of the main reasons for the criminalization of particular substances is the significant association believed to exist between drug abuse and crime. Research suggests that many criminal offenders have extensive experience with drug use and that drug users commit an enormous amount of crime. Alcohol abuse has also been linked to criminality.[201] Research shows that almost 4 in 10 violent crimes involve alcohol, according to the crime victims, as do 4 in 10 fatal motor vehicle accidents. And about 4 in 10 criminal offenders report that they were using alcohol at the time of their offenses.[202] This pattern is not unique to the United States. Research conducted in five English communities (Sunderland, Nottingham, Cambridge, London, and Manchester) found that about 61 percent of arrestees tested positively for at least one drug, a finding comparable to arrestees in the United States. Marijuana proved to be the drug of choice in England; American criminals prefer cocaine. When alcohol was included, about 75 percent of the samples tested positive for some substance.[203]

Substance abuse appears to be an important precipitating factor in domestic assault, armed robbery, and homicide cases.[204] Table 14.3 shows the findings of a study of 136 domestic violence cases reported to the authorities. Note that 94 percent of those arrested used substances before the assault; almost half the victims were users also.

Although the drug–crime connection is powerful, the relationship is still uncertain because many users had a history of criminal activity *before* the onset of their substance abuse.[205] Nonetheless, if drug use does not turn otherwise law-abiding citizens into criminals, it certainly amplifies the extent of their criminal activities.[206] And as addiction levels increase, so do the frequency and seriousness of criminality.[207]

Two approaches have been used to study the relationship between drugs and crime. One has been to survey known addicts to assess the extent of their law violations; the other has been to survey known criminals to see if they were or are drug users. These are discussed separately next.

SUBSTANCE	PERCENTAGE OF ASSAILANTS USING SUBSTANCE PRIOR TO ASSAULT	PERCENTAGE OF VICTIMS USING SUBSTANCE PRIOR TO ASSAULT
Table 14.3 Substance Use by Assailants and Victims Prior to Domestic Assault (as Reported by Participants and/or Family Members) (n=136)		
Cocaine and alcohol	47% ⎫ 67%	8% ⎫ 15%
Cocaine, marijuana, and alcohol	20% ⎭	7% ⎭
Alcohol alone	17%	14%
Marijuana and alcohol	8%	6%
Other drugs/combinations	2%	8%
Any alcohol or other drug use	94%	43%

Source: Daniel Brookoff, "Drug Use and Domestic Violence," National Institute of Justice Research in Progress Seminar Series (prepared by the Center for Substance Abuse Research, January 27, 1997).

User Surveys Numerous studies have examined the criminal activity of drug users. As a group, they show that people who take drugs have extensive involvement in crime.[208] Youths who abuse alcohol are also the most likely to engage in violence; adults with long histories of drinking are also more likely to report violent offending patterns.[209] One often-cited study of this type was conducted by sociologist James Inciardi. After interviewing 356 addicts in Miami, Inciardi found that they reported 118,134 criminal offenses during a 12-month period; of these, 27,464 were index crimes.[210] If this behavior is typical, the country's estimated 300,000–700,000 heroin users could be responsible for a significant amount of all criminal behavior. Another survey of 671 known California addicts found persuasive evidence of a link between drug use and property crime; the amount and value of crime increased proportionately with the frequency of the subjects' drug involvement.[211]

Surveys of Known Criminals The second method used to link drugs and crime involves testing known criminals to determine the extent of their substance abuse. The most recent survey of prison inmates disclosed that many (80 percent) are lifelong substance abusers. More than one-third claim to have been under the influence of drugs when they committed their last offense, including about 14 percent who were under the influence of crack and 6 percent who were using heroin; about 62 percent claimed to have regularly used a major drug, such as heroin, cocaine, PCP, or LSD, before their arrest.[212] These data support the view that a strong association exists between substance abuse and serious crime.

Another important source of data on the drug abuse–crime connection is the federally sponsored Arrestee Drug Abuse Monitoring Program (ADAM).[213] All male arrestees in 23 major cities and females in 21 cities around the country are tested for drug use.[214] The most recent ADAM data show that drug use among arrestees,

including use of crack cocaine, has declined somewhat. Nonetheless, at every site, a majority of male arrestees test positive for at least 1 of 10 drugs, most commonly cocaine or marijuana. Drug abuse is common for arrestees in cities such as Chicago, Denver, Atlanta, and Los Angeles. Most sites report overall drug use rates of 50 percent or greater among female arrestees, and in some cities such as Detroit and Philadelphia, female arrestees are more likely to test positive than males.

Recent national drug surveys have found that cocaine and crack use has diminished but that marijuana use is on the rise. Heroin use may also be in decline. Arrest data show that most frequent users are older offenders who started their heroin abuse decades ago. There is reason to believe that heroin use is declining among adolescents, possibly because it has acquired an extremely negative street image among inner-city youth. Most youths know that heroin is addictive and destructive to health and that needle sharing leads to HIV. Research conducted in New York City shows that most youths avoid heroin, shun users and dealers, and wish to avoid becoming addicts.[215]

The Drug–Crime Connection It is of course possible that most criminals are not actually drug users but that police are more likely to apprehend muddle-headed substance abusers than clear-thinking abstainers. A second, and probably more plausible, interpretation is that most criminals are in fact substance abusers. Drug use interferes with maturation and socialization. Drug abusers are more likely to drop out of school, be underemployed, engage in premarital sex, and become unmarried parents. These factors have been linked to a weakening of the social bond that leads to antisocial behaviors.[216] Typically, as Table 14.4 shows, the drug–crime relationship may be explained in one of three possible ways.

In a recent study, Jeffrey Fagan interviewed 150 young New York City men who had a history of violent behavior in order to find out more about the drug–crime

Table 14.4 Summary of Drug–Crime Relationship

DRUGS AND CRIME RELATIONSHIP	DEFINITION	EXAMPLES
Drug-defined offenses	Violations of laws prohibiting or regulating the possession, use, distribution, or manufacture of illegal drugs	Drug possession or use; marijuana cultivation; methamphetamine production; cocaine, heroin, or marijuana sales
Drug-related offenses	Offenses in which a drug's pharmacologic effects contribute; offenses motivated by the user's need for money to support continued use; and offenses connected to drug distribution itself	Violent behavior resulting from drug effects; stealing to get money to buy drugs; violence against rival drug dealers
Drug-using lifestyle	Drug use and crime are common aspects of a deviant lifestyle. The likelihood and frequency of involvement in illegal activity is increased because drug users may not participate in the legitimate economy and are exposed to situations that encourage crime.	A life orientation with an emphasis on short-term goals supported by illegal activities; opportunities to offend resulting from contacts with offenders and illegal markets; criminal skills learned from other offenders

Source: White House Office of National Drug Control Policy, *Fact Sheet: Drug-Related Crime* (Washington, D.C., 1997).

connection. The Criminological Enterprise feature titled "How Substance Abuse Provokes Violence" tells what Fagan found about how drug use relates to criminality.

In sum, research testing both the criminality of known narcotics users and the narcotics use of known criminals produces a very strong association between drug use and crime. Even if the crime rate of drug users were actually half that reported in the research literature, users would be responsible for a significant portion of the total criminal activity in the United States.

Drugs and the Law

The federal government first initiated legal action to curtail the use of some drugs early in the twentieth century.[217] In 1906 the Pure Food and Drug Act required manufacturers to list the amounts of habit-forming drugs in products on the labels but did not restrict their use. However, the act prohibited the importation and sale of opiates except for medicinal purposes. In 1914 the Harrison Narcotics Act restricted importation, manufacture, sale, and dispensing of narcotics. It defined *narcotic* as any drug that produces sleep and relieves pain, such as heroin, morphine, and opium. The act was revised in 1922 to allow importation of opium and coca (cocaine) leaves for qualified medical practitioners. The Marijuana Tax Act of 1937 required registration and payment of a tax by all persons who imported, sold, or manufactured marijuana. Because marijuana was classified as a narcotic, those registering would also be subject to criminal penalty.

In later years, other federal laws were passed to clarify existing drug statutes and revise penalties. For example, the Boggs Act of 1951 provided mandatory sentences for violating federal drug laws. The Durham-Humphrey Act of 1951 made it illegal to dispense barbiturates and amphetamines without a prescription.

The Narcotic Control Act of 1956 increased penalties for drug offenders. In 1965 the Drug Abuse Control Act set up stringent guidelines for the legal use and sale of mood-modifying drugs, such as barbiturates, amphetamines, LSD, and any other "dangerous drugs," except narcotics prescribed by doctors and pharmacists. Illegal possession was punished as a misdemeanor and manufacture or sale as a felony. And in 1970 the Comprehensive Drug Abuse Prevention and Control Act set up unified categories of illegal drugs and associated penalties with their sale, manufacture, or possession. The law gave the U.S. attorney general discretion to decide in which category to place any new drug.

Since then, various federal laws have attempted to increase penalties imposed on drug smugglers and limit the manufacture and sale of newly developed substances. For example, the 1984 Controlled Substances Act set new, stringent penalties for drug dealers and created five categories of narcotic and nonnarcotic substances subject to federal laws.[218] The Anti–Drug Abuse Act of 1986 again set new standards for minimum and maximum sentences for drug offenders, increased penalties for most offenses, and created a new drug penalty classification for large-scale offenses (such as trafficking in more than one kilogram of heroin), for which the penalty for a first offense was 10 years to life in prison.[219] With then-President George Bush's endorsement, Congress passed the Anti–Drug Abuse Act of 1988, which created a coordinated national drug policy under a "drug czar," set treatment and prevention priorities, and, symbolizing the government's hard-line stance against drug dealing, imposed the death penalty for drug-related killings.[220]

For the most part, state laws mirror federal statutes. Some, such as New York's, apply extremely heavy penalties for selling or distributing dangerous drugs, involving long prison sentences of up to 25 years.

The Criminological Enterprise

How Substance Abuse Provokes Violence

Jeffrey Fagan and his fellow researchers at Columbia University's Center for Violence Research and Prevention are conducting a multistage study on adolescent violence in order to construct a situational framework for understanding violent behavior. The research design includes three samples of young men, ages 16 to 24, with histories of involvement in violent activities and currently (or, if incarcerated, formerly) residing in two of New York City's neighborhoods with the highest rates of youth homicide—East New York (Brooklyn) and Mott Haven (South Bronx). The criminal justice sample includes young men convicted on gun-related charges and incarcerated in the Rikers Island Correctional Facility and facilities under the auspices of the New York State Division for Youth Facilities. The second sample consists of victims of violence identified in the emergency rooms of two hospitals, one near each of the two neighborhoods. The community sample consists of young men who are involved in violence but have avoided both the criminal justice system and the emergency room.

The study has found that alcohol and drugs can influence social interactions in two ways that may lead to violence. First, alcohol can shape the dynamics, decisions, and strategies in a violent or near-violent episode. That is, interactions in which one or both individuals have been drinking will turn out differently than those in which one or both are sober. Second, the context in which drinking occurs independently affects how violent or near-violent events unfold. The young men reported that intoxication increased the likelihood that a person's language would become provocative and boastful, turning minor disputes into violent encounters. Alcohol exaggerated the sense of outrage over perceived transgressions of personal codes, resulting in violence to exert control or exact retribution. Some drinkers acted on bystanders' provocations to fight more seriously; others felt invincible and started fights that they then lost. In addition, certain bars were frequent scenes of violence, regardless of who was present or how much alcohol had been consumed; being in the wrong place at the wrong time resulted in injuries, including gunshot wounds, to a number of respondents.

Interestingly, the effects of drugs on violence were much less clear. Marijuana made some subjects less prone to violence, whereas other users sought out victims to exploit or dominate. Another type of user became paranoid and either avoided human contact or became hostile and prone to defensive violence. Yet, if a fight broke out, even the most relaxed, "mellow" individual would immediately snap out of his stupor to defend himself.

Not all of the young men who were interviewed blamed their violent behavior on alcohol or drugs. A number of young men used alcohol or drugs *after* violent events as a form of self-medication. And some youths, even under the influence of alcohol, were able to walk away from violence.

Researchers repeatedly heard stories of "graceful," strategic retreats from violence. However, making a careful, controlled exit in a threatening situation takes verbal skills and mental agility, two cognitive abilities that not everyone possesses.

CRITICAL THINKING

1. The Fagan research shows how substance abuse can facilitate violent episodes. Interestingly, alcohol seems to have a greater influence on violent behavior than other drugs. Some drugs, like marijuana, may even help regulate violence if they provide a sense of euphoria that reduces conflict. Could this be used as an argument for drug legalization?

 INFOTRAC COLLEGE EDITION RESEARCH

Treating alcohol abusers is a major social goal. To research current treatment programs, see:

Deborah Pappas, Chudley E. Werch, Joan M. Carlson. Recruitment and retention in an alcohol prevention program of two inner-city middle schools. *Journal of School Health* August 1998 v68 n6 p231(6)

John P. Allen. Project MATCH: a clarification. *Behavioral Health Management* July-August 1998 v18 n4 p42(2)

Source: Jeffrey Fagan, *Adolescent Violence: A View From the Street*, NIJ Research Preview (Washington, D.C.: National Institute of Justice, 1998).

Controlling Alcohol State legislatures have also acted to control alcohol-related crimes. One of the more serious problems of widespread drinking is the alarming number of highway fatalities linked to drunk driving. In an average week nearly 500 people die in alcohol-related accidents, and 20,000 are injured. That amounts yearly to 25,000 deaths, or about half of all auto fatalities. Spurred by such groups as Mothers Against Drunk Drivers, state legislatures are beginning to create more stringent penalties for drunk driving. For example, Florida has enacted legislation creating a minimum fine of $250, 50 hours of community service, and six months' loss of license for a first offense; a second offense brings a $500 fine and 10 days in jail. In Quincy, Massachusetts, judges have agreed to put every drunk-driving offender in jail for three days.[221] In California a drunk driver faces a maximum of six months in jail, a $500 fine, the suspension of his or her operator's license for six months, and impoundment of the vehicle. As a minimum penalty, a first offender could get (1) four days in jail, a $375 fine, and loss of license for six months or (2) three years' probation, a $375 fine, and either two days in jail or restricted driving privileges for 90 days.[222] In New York persons arrested for drunk driving now risk having their automobiles seized by the government under the state's new Civil Forfeiture Law. Originally designed to combat drug trafficking and racketeering, the new law allows state prosecutors to confiscate cars involved in felony drunk-driving cases, sell them at auction, and give the proceeds to the victims of the crime; Texas enacted a similar law in 1984.[223] More than 30 jurisdictions have passed laws providing severe penalties for drunk drivers, including mandatory jail sentences.

A study conducted by the federal government's National Institute of Justice in such cities as Seattle, Minneapolis, and Cincinnati found that such measures significantly reduced traffic fatalities in the target areas studied.[224] However, there is a price to pay for get-tough policies. In California arrest rates and court workloads increased dramatically, and the use of plea bargaining, which first decreased, eventually rose and reduced the impact of legal reform.[225] Similarly, corrections facilities have become overloaded, prompting the building of expensive new ones to exclusively house drunk-driving offenders.

Alcoholics are a serious problem because treatment efforts to help chronic sufferers have not proved successful.[226] Severe punishments have little effect on their future behavior.[227] In addition, chronic alcoholics are arrested over and over again for public drunkenness and are therefore a burden on the justice system. To remedy this situation, a federal court in 1966 ruled that chronic alcoholism may be used as a defense to crime.[228] However, in a subsequent case, *Powell v. Texas,* the Supreme Court ruled that a chronic alcoholic could be convicted under state public drunkenness laws.[229] Nonetheless, the narrowness of the 5–4 decision allowed those states desiring to excuse chronic alcoholics from criminal responsibility to do so. Thus the trend has been to treat arrested alcoholics in detoxification centers under civil order rather than haul them through the justice system.

Drug Control Strategies

Substance abuse remains a major social problem in the United States. Politicians looking for a safe campaign issue can take advantage of the public's fear of drug addiction by calling for a war on drugs. These wars have been declared even when drug usage is stable or in decline.[230] Can these efforts pay off? Can illegal drug use be eliminated or controlled?

A number of different drug control strategies have been tried with varying degrees of success. Some aim to deter drug use by stopping the flow of drugs into the country, apprehending and punishing dealers, and cracking down on street-level drug deals. Others focus

on preventing drug use by educating potential users to the dangers of substance abuse (convincing them to "say no to drugs") and by organizing community groups to work with the at-risk population in their area. Still another approach is to treat known users so they can control their addictions. Some of these efforts are discussed here.

Source Control One approach to drug control is to deter the sale and importation of drugs through the systematic apprehension of large-volume drug dealers, coupled with the enforcement of strict drug laws that carry heavy penalties. This approach is designed to capture and punish known international drug dealers and deter those who are considering entering the drug trade. A major effort has been made to cut off supplies of drugs by destroying overseas crops and arresting members of drug cartels in Central and South America, Asia, and the Middle East, where many drugs are grown and manufactured. The federal government has been in the vanguard of encouraging exporting nations to step up efforts to destroy drug crops and prosecute dealers. Three South American nations, Peru, Bolivia, and Colombia, have agreed with the United States to coordinate control efforts. However, translating words into deeds is a formidable task. Drug lords are willing and able to fight back through intimidation, violence, and corruption when necessary. The Colombian drug cartels do not hesitate to use violence and assassination to protect their interests.

The amount of narcotics grown each year is so vast that even if three-quarters of the opium crop were destroyed, the U.S. market would still require only 10 percent of the remainder to sustain the drug trade. An estimated 24,000 tons of marijuana, 337,000 tons of coca leaf, and 4,000 tons of opium are produced annually.[231] Even if the amount of illegal drugs produced each year were radically reduced, it likely would have little effect on American consumption. Drug users in the United States are able and willing to pay more for drugs than anyone else in the world. Even if the supply were reduced, whatever drugs there were would find their way to the United States.

Adding to control problems is the fact that the drug trade is an important source of foreign revenue, and destroying the drug trade undermines the economies of Third World nations. More than one million people in Peru, Bolivia, Colombia, Thailand, Laos, and other developing nations depend on the cultivating and processing of illegal substances. The federal government estimates that U.S. citizens spend over $40 billion annually on illegal drugs, and much of this money is funneled overseas. Even if the government of one nation were willing to cooperate in vigorous drug suppression efforts, suppliers in other nations, eager to cash in on the seller's market, would be encouraged to turn more acreage over to coca or poppy production. The United

States has little influence in some key drug-producing areas such as Vietnam, Cambodia, and Mayanmar (formerly Burma).[232]

The drug cartels' power and wealth make them formidable opponents. For example, throughout the 1990s the U.S. government repeatedly tried to prosecute a Mexican national, Rafael Munoz Talavera, who was accused of running a cartel that smuggled tons of cocaine into California. One of Talavera's alleged warehouses was the location of the largest single drug bust in U.S. history. But despite two trials and one conviction, Talavera remained free after a successful appeal. Investigators charge that officials in the Mexican criminal justice system may have taken bribes from Talavera so that damaging evidence was never presented at his trials.[233] In 1997 Mexico's government announced that it had arrested General Jesus Guttierrez Rebello, its top antinarcotics enforcer, for his suspected links to drug traffickers.[234]

Eradication efforts in one country may encourage crop development in another. For example, the Bolivian government's voluntary coca eradication program surpassed its annual target in 1996, kept cultivation levels from significantly expanding, and reduced potential coca leaf production by 12 percent. Unfortunately, this decline was more than offset by a 32 percent increase in both coca cultivation and potential coca leaf production in Colombia, despite an aggressive aerial eradication program by Colombian enforcement authorities. Colombian coca cultivation has nearly tripled since 1987, and source control efforts have convinced the Colombian drug cartels of the importance of controlling all facets of cocaine production at home.[235]

Interdiction Strategies Law enforcement efforts have also been directed at intercepting drug supplies as they enter the country. Border patrols and military personnel using sophisticated hardware have been involved in massive interdiction efforts; many impressive multimillion-dollar seizures have been made. Yet the U.S. borders are so vast and unprotected that meaningful interdiction is impossible. And even if all importation were shut down, home-grown marijuana and laboratory-made drugs, such as "ice," LSD, and PCP, could become the drugs of choice. Even now, their easy availability and relatively low cost are increasing their popularity among the at-risk population.

Law Enforcement Strategies Local, state, and federal law enforcement agencies have been actively fighting against drugs. One approach is to direct efforts at large-scale drug rings. The long-term consequence has been to decentralize drug dealing and encourage young independent dealers to become major suppliers. Ironically, it has proven easier for federal agents to infiltrate and prosecute traditional organized crime groups than to take on drug-dealing gangs. Consequently, some nontraditional groups have broken into the drug trade. For example, the

Hell's Angels motorcycle club has become one of the primary distributors of cocaine and amphetamines in the United States.[236] Police can also target, intimidate, and arrest street-level dealers and users in an effort to make drug use so much of a hassle that consumption is cut back and the crime rate reduced. Approaches that have been tried include *reverse stings,* in which undercover agents pose as dealers to arrest users who approach them for a buy. Police have attacked fortified crack houses with heavy equipment to breach their defenses. They have used racketeering laws to seize the assets of known dealers. Special task forces of local and state police have used undercover operations and drug sweeps to discourage both dealers and users.[237]

Although some street-level enforcement efforts have succeeded, others are considered failures. Drug sweeps have clogged courts and correctional facilities with petty offenders while draining police resources. There are also suspicions that a displacement effect occurs: stepped-up efforts to curb drug dealing in one area or city simply encourage dealers to seek out friendlier territory.[238]

Punishment Strategies Even if law enforcement efforts cannot produce a general deterrent effect, the courts may achieve the required result by severely punishing known drug dealers and traffickers. A number of initiatives have made the prosecution and punishment of drug offenders a top priority. State prosecutors have expanded their investigations into drug importation and distribution and created special prosecutors to focus on drug dealers. The fact that drugs such as crack are considered a serious problem may have convinced judges and prosecutors to expedite substance abuse cases. One study of court processing in New York found that cases involving crack had a higher probability of pretrial detention, felony indictment, and incarceration sentences than other criminal cases.[239] Some states, such as New Jersey and Pennsylvania, report that these efforts have resulted in sharp increases in the number of convictions for drug-related offenses.[240] Once convicted, drug dealers can get very long sentences. Research by the federal government shows that the average sentence for drug offenders sent to federal prison is about six years.[241] However, these efforts often have their downside. Defense attorneys consider delay tactics sound legal maneuvering in drug-related cases. Courts are so backlogged that prosecutors are anxious to plea-bargain. The consequence of this legal maneuvering is that about 25 percent of people convicted on federal drug charges are granted probation or some other form of community release.[242] Even so, prisons have become jammed with inmates, many of whom were involved in drug-related cases. Many drug offenders sent to prison do not serve their entire sentences because they are released in an effort to relieve prison overcrowding. The average prison stay is about two years, or about one-third of the original sentence.[243] It is unlikely that the public would approve of a drug control strategy that locks up large numbers of traffickers; research indicates that the public already believes that drug trafficking penalties are too harsh (while supporting the level of punishment for other crimes).[244]

Community Strategies Another type of drug control effort relies on the involvement of local community groups to lead the fight against drugs. Representatives of various local government agencies, churches, civic organizations, and similar institutions are being brought together to create drug prevention and awareness programs.

Citizen-sponsored programs attempt to restore a sense of community in drug-infested areas, reduce fear, and promote conventional norms and values.[245] According to a survey by Saul Weingart, these efforts can be classified into one of four distinct categories.[246] The first involves law enforcement–type efforts, which may include block watches, cooperative police–community efforts, and citizen patrols. Some of these citizen groups are nonconfrontational: they simply observe or photograph dealers, write down their license plate numbers, and then notify police. On occasion, telephone hot lines have been set up to take anonymous tips on drug activity. Other groups engage in confrontational tactics that may even include citizens' arrests. Some of these community-based efforts are home-grown, whereas others attract outside organizations, such as the Guardian Angels or Black Muslims. Area residents have gone as far as contracting with private security firms to conduct neighborhood patrols.

Another tactic is to use the civil justice system to harass offenders. Landlords have been sued for owning properties that house drug dealers; neighborhood groups have scrutinized drug houses for building code violations. Information acquired from these various sources is turned over to local authorities, such as police and housing agencies, for more formal action.

There are also community-based treatment efforts in which citizen volunteers participate in self-help support programs, such as Narcotics Anonymous or Cocaine Anonymous, which have more than 1,000 chapters nationally. Other programs provide youths with martial arts training, dancing, and social events as an alternative to the drug life.

Weingart found that the fourth drug prevention effort is designed to enhance the quality of life, improve interpersonal relationships, and upgrade the neighborhood's physical environment. Activities might include the creation of drug-free school zones (which encourage police to keep drug dealers away from the vicinity of schools). Consciousness-raising efforts include demonstrations and marches to publicize the drug problem and build solidarity among participants. Politicians have been lobbied to get better police protection or tougher laws passed; New York City residents even sent bags filled with crack collected from street corners to the mayor and police commissioner to protest drug dealing. Residents have cleaned up streets, fixed broken street lights, and planted gardens in empty lots to broadcast the message that they have local pride and do not want drug dealers in their neighborhoods.

Community crime prevention efforts seem appealing, but there is little conclusive evidence that they are an effective drug control strategy. Some surveys indicate that most residents do not participate in programs. There is also evidence that community programs work better in stable, middle-income areas than in those that are crime-ridden and disorganized.[247] Although these findings are discouraging, some studies do find that on occasion deteriorated areas can sustain successful anti-drug programs.[248] Future evaluations of community control efforts should determine whether they can work in the most economically depressed areas.

Drug Education and Prevention Strategies *Prevention strategies* are aimed at convincing youths not to get involved in drug abuse; heavy reliance is placed on educational programs that teach kids to say no to drugs. The most widely used program is Drug Abuse Resistance Education (DARE), an elementary school course designed to give students the skills for resisting peer pressure to experiment with tobacco, drugs, and alcohol. It is unique because it employs uniformed police officers to carry the antidrug message to the students before they enter junior high school. The program has five major focus areas:

- Providing accurate information about tobacco, alcohol, and drugs
- Teaching students techniques to resist peer pressure
- Teaching students respect for the law and law enforcers
- Giving students ideas for alternatives to drug use
- Building the self-esteem of students

DARE is based on the concept that young students need specific analytical and social skills to resist peer pressure and refuse drugs. More than 10,000 communities in 49 counties now use the DARE program, and more than 20 million students attend its seminars. DARE is quite expensive to implement; the average cost per full-time police officer–trainer is over $90,000.[249] However, evaluations show that the program does little to reduce drug use or convince abusers that drugs are harmful.[250] Although there are indications that DARE may be effective with some subsets of the population, such as female and Hispanic students, overall success appears problematic at best.[251] One problem may be that typically little distinction is made between the types of students who are enrolled in the program, so that classrooms may contain some youths who are receptive to the DARE message and others who are openly hostile.[252] A number of prominent locations, including Seattle and Spokane, Washington, have recently dropped the DARE program because community and law enforcement officials were skeptical about its drug-reducing capability.[253]

Drug education programs still hold promise as an effective means of reducing the onset of drug abuse. Even though the DARE evaluation reveals less success than was hoped for, evaluations of other similar programs (Project Alert) prove that prevention strategies can reduce the onset of drug use and cigarette smoking among students.[254] On February 25, 1997, President Bill Clinton announced that antidrug education initiatives will be a major segment of his administration's drug control policy.[255] Part of the strategy will be an aggressive antidrug advertising campaign broadcast on television during prime time.

Drug-Testing Programs Drug testing of private employees, government workers, and criminal offenders is believed to deter substance abuse. In the workplace, employees are tested to enhance on-the-job safety and productivity. In some industries, such as mining and transportation, drug testing is considered essential because abuse can pose a threat to the public.[256] Business leaders have been enlisted in the fight against drugs. Mandatory drug-testing programs in government and industry are common: more than 40 percent of the country's largest companies, including IBM and AT&T, have drug-testing programs. The federal government requires employee testing in regulated industries such as nuclear energy and defense contracting. About 4 million transportation workers are subject to testing.

Drug testing is also common in government and criminal justice agencies. About 30 percent of local police departments test applicants, and 16 percent routinely test field officers. However, larger jurisdictions serving populations over 250,000 are much more likely to test applicants (84 percent) and field officers (75 percent). Drug testing is also part of the federal government's Drug-Free Workplace Program, which has the goal of improving productivity and safety. Employees most likely to be tested include presidential appointees, law enforcement officers, and people in positions of national security.

Criminal defendants are now routinely tested at all stages of the justice system, from arrest to parole. The goal is to reduce criminal behavior by detecting current users and curbing their abuse. Can such programs reduce criminal activity? Two evaluations of pretrial drug-testing programs found little evidence that monitoring defendants' drug use influenced their behavior.[257]

Treatment Strategies A number of approaches are taken to treat known users, getting them clean of drugs and alcohol and thereby reducing the at-risk population. One approach rests on the assumption that users have low self-esteem and treatment efforts must focus on building a sense of self. For example, users have

been placed in worthwhile programs of outdoor activities and wilderness training to create self-reliance and a sense of accomplishment.[258] More intensive efforts use group therapy approaches relying on group leaders who have been substance abusers; through such sessions users get the skills and support to help them reject social pressure to use drugs. These programs are based on the Alcoholics Anonymous approach, which holds that users must find within themselves the strength to stay clean and that peer support from those who understand their experiences can help them achieve a drug-free life.

There are also residential programs for the more heavily involved, and a large network of drug treatment centers has been developed. Some detoxification units use medical procedures to wean patients from the more addicting drugs to others, such as methadone, that can be more easily regulated. Methadone is a drug similar to heroin, and addicts can be treated at clinics where they receive methadone under controlled conditions. However, methadone programs have been undermined because some users sell their methadone in the black market, and others supplement their dosages with illegally obtained heroin.

Other therapeutic programs attempt to deal with the psychological causes of drug use. Hypnosis, aversion therapy (getting users to associate drugs with unpleasant sensations, such as nausea), counseling, biofeedback, and other techniques are often used.

The long-term effects of treatment on drug abuse are still uncertain. Critics charge that a stay in a residential program can help stigmatize people as addicts even if they never used hard drugs; and in treatment they may be introduced to hard-core users with whom they will associate after release. Users do not often enter these programs voluntarily and have little motivation to change.[259] And even those who could be helped soon learn that there are simply more users who need treatment than there are beds in treatment facilities. Many facilities are restricted to users whose health insurance will pay for short-term residential care; when their insurance coverage ends, patients are often released, even though their treatment is incomplete.

Supporters of treatment argue that many addicts are helped by intensive in- and outpatient treatment. As one District of Columbia program shows, clients who complete treatment programs are less likely to use drugs than those who drop out.[260] Although such data support treatment strategies, it is also possible that completers are motivated individuals who would have stopped using drugs even if they had not been treated.

Employment Programs Research indicates that drug abusers who obtain and keep employment will end or reduce the incidence of their substance abuse.[261] Not surprisingly, then, there have been a number of efforts to provide vocational rehabilitation for drug abusers.

One approach is the supported work program, which typically involves job-site training, ongoing assessment, and job-site intervention. Rather than teach work skills in a classroom, support programs rely on helping drug abusers deal with real work settings. Other programs provide training to overcome the barriers to employment, including help with motivation, education, experience, the job market, job-seeking skills, and personal issues. For example, female abusers may be unaware of child care resources that would enable them to seek employment opportunities while caring for their children. Another approach is to help addicts improve their interviewing skills so that once a job opportunity can be identified they are equipped to convince potential employers of their commitment and reliability.

A recent analysis of job programs by Jerome Platt found that relatively few programs exist, and those that do have shortcomings that either limit their implementation or raise questions about their utility and effectiveness. Platt argues that the substance of employment programs must be shaped by a comprehensive approach to the employment problems of drug abusers that recognizes how societal attitudes and job market forces affect the success of employment programs.[262]

Legalization Despite the massive effort to control drugs through prevention, deterrence, education, and treatment strategies, the fight against substance abuse has not proved successful. It is difficult to get people out of the drug culture because of the enormous profits involved in the drug trade: 500 kilos of coca leaves worth $4,000 to a grower yields about 8 kilos of street cocaine valued at about $300,000. A drug dealer who can move 100 pounds of coke into the United States can make $1 million in one shipment. An estimated 60 tons of cocaine are imported into the country each year with a street value of $17 billion.[263] It has also proved difficult to control drugs by convincing known users to quit; few treatment efforts have been successful. The so-called war on drugs is expensive, costing more than $500 billion over the past 20 years — money that could have been spent on education and economic development. Drug enforcement now costs federal, state, and local governments more than $30 billion per year.[264]

Considering these problems, some commentators have called for the legalization or decriminalization of restricted drugs. Legalization is warranted, according to Ethan Nadelmann, because the use of mood-altering substances is customary in almost all human societies; people have always wanted, and will find ways of obtaining, psychoactive drugs.[265] Banning drugs creates networks of manufacturers and distributors, many of whom use violence as part of their standard operating procedures. Although some believe that drug use is immoral, Nadelmann questions whether it is any worse

Nonpunitive treatment approaches have been used to control substance abuse. One type of drug control effort relies on the involvement of local community groups to lead the fight against drugs. Representatives of various local government agencies, churches, civic organizations, and similar institutions are being brought together to create drug prevention awareness programs. Another type of effort provides treatment facilities and counseling for known users. Here a client awaits admission to a methadone clinic.

than the unrestricted use of alcohol and cigarettes, both of which are addicting and unhealthful. Far more people die each year because they abuse these legal substances than are killed in drug wars or from abusing illegal substances.[266]

Nadelmann also states that just as Prohibition failed to stop the flow of alcohol in the 1920s while it increased the power of organized crime, the policy of prohibiting drugs is similarly doomed to failure. When drugs were legal and freely available earlier in this century, the proportion of Americans using drugs was not much greater than today; most users led normal lives, most likely because of the legal status of their drug use.[267]

If drugs were legalized, the argument goes, price and distribution could be controlled by the government. This would reduce addicts' cash requirements, so crime rates would drop because users would no longer need the same cash flow to support their habits. Drug-related deaths would decline because government control would reduce needle sharing and the spread of AIDS. Legalization would also destroy the drug-importing cartels and gangs. Because drugs would be bought and sold openly, the government would reap a tax windfall both from taxes on the sale of drugs and from income taxes paid by drug dealers on profits that have been part of the hidden economy. Of course, drug distribution would be regulated, like alcohol, keeping drugs away from adolescents, public servants such as police and airline pilots, and known felons. Those who favor legalization point to the Netherlands as a country that has legalized drugs and remains relatively crime-free.[268]

The Consequences of Legalization This approach might have the short-term effect of reducing the association between drug use and crime, but it might also have grave social consequences. According to David Courtwright, legalization would increase the nation's rate of drug usage, creating an even larger group of nonproductive, drug-dependent people who must be cared for by the rest of society.[269] If drugs were legalized and

freely available, drug users might significantly increase their daily intake. In countries like Iran and Thailand, where drugs are cheap and readily available, the rate of narcotics use is quite high. Historically, the availability of cheap narcotics has preceded drug use epidemics, as was the case when British and American merchants sold opium in nineteenth-century China.

Courtwright also says that efforts to control legal use would backfire. If juveniles, criminals, and members of other at-risk groups were forbidden to buy drugs, who would be the customers? Noncriminal, nonabusing middle-aged adults? And would not those prohibited from legally buying drugs create an underground market almost as vast as the current one? If the government tried to raise money by taxing legal drugs, as it now does with liquor and cigarettes, that might encourage drug smuggling to avoid tax payments; these "illegal" drugs might then fall into the hands of adolescents.

The problems of alcoholism should serve as a warning of what can happen when controlled substances are made readily available. For example, because women may more easily become dependent on crack than men, the number of drug-dependent babies could begin to match or exceed the number who are delivered with fetal alcohol syndrome.[270] Drunk-driving fatalities, which today number about 25,000 per year, might be matched by deaths due to driving under the influence of pot or crack. And although distribution would be regulated, it is likely that adolescents would have the same opportunity to obtain potent drugs as they now have to obtain alcoholic beverages.

Decriminalization or legalization of controlled substances is unlikely in the near term, but further study is warranted. What effect would a policy of partial decriminalization (for example, legalizing small amounts of marijuana) have on drug use rates? Would a get-tough policy help to "widen the net" of the justice system and actually deepen some youths' involvement in substance abuse? Can society provide alternatives to drugs that will reduce teenage drug dependency?[271] The answers to these questions have proven elusive.

SUMMARY

Public order crimes are acts considered illegal because they conflict with social policy, accepted moral rules, and public opinion. There is usually great debate over public order crimes. Some charge that they are not really crimes at all and that it is foolish to legislate morality. Others view such morally tinged acts as prostitution, gambling, and drug abuse as harmful and therefore subject to public control. Many public order crimes are sex-related. Although homosexuality is not a crime, homosexual acts are subject to legal control. Some states still follow the archaic custom of legislating long prison terms for consensual homosexual sex.

Prostitution is another sex-related public order crime. Although prostitution has been practiced for thousands of years

and is legal in some areas, most states outlaw commercial sex. There are a variety of prostitutes, including streetwalkers, B-girls, and call girls. Studies indicate that prostitutes came from poor, troubled families and have abusive parents. However, there is little evidence that prostitutes are emotionally disturbed, addicted to drugs, or sexually abnormal. Although prostitution is illegal, some cities have set up adult entertainment areas where commercial sex is tolerated by law enforcement agents.

Pornography involves the sale of sexually explicit material intended to sexually excite paying customers. The depiction of sex and nudity is not illegal, but it does violate the law when it is judged obscene. *Obscene material* is a legal term that today is defined as material offensive to community standards. Thus each local jurisdiction must decide what pornographic material is obscene. A growing problem is the exploitation of children in obscene materials (kiddie porn). The Supreme Court has ruled that local communities can pass statutes outlawing any sexually explicit material. There is no hard evidence that pornography is related to crime or aggression, but data suggest that sexual material with a violent theme is related to sexual violence by those who view it.

Substance abuse is another type of public order crime. Most states and the federal government outlaw a wide variety of drugs they consider harmful, including narcotics, amphetamines, barbiturates, cocaine, hallucinogens, and marijuana. One of the main reasons for the continued ban on drugs is their relationship to crime. Numerous studies have found that drug addicts commit enormous amounts of property crime.

Alcohol is another commonly abused substance. Although alcohol is legal to possess, it too has been linked to crime. Drunk driving and deaths caused by drunk drivers are growing national problems. There are many different strategies to control substance abuse, ranging from source control to treatment. So far, no single method seems effective. Although legalization is debated, the fact that so many people already take drugs and the association of drug abuse with crime make legalization unlikely in the near term.

See the book-specific web site at www.cj.wadsworth.com for additional chapter links, discussions, and quizzes.

THINKING LIKE A CRIMINOLOGIST

According to data from a 1997 national school survey, high school boys who have been physically or sexually abused are at least twice as likely as nonabused boys to drink, smoke, or use drugs. The survey was an in-class questionnaire completed by 3,162 boys in grades 5–12 at a nationally representative sample of 265 public, private, and parochial schools from December 1996 to June 1997. The survey included roughly equal samples of adolescent boys in grades 5–8 and 9–12. All responses were weighted to reflect grade, region, race and ethnicity, and gender.

Thirteen percent of boys in grades 9–12 said that they had been physically or sexually abused. Thirty percent of abused boys reported that they drank frequently, and 34 percent reported that they had used drugs in the past month, compared to 16 percent and 15 percent, respectively, of nonabused boys. Abused boys were also nearly three times more likely to smoke frequently (27 percent versus 10 percent).

As a criminologist, what would be your interpretation of these data? What is the association between child abuse and substance abuse?

KEY TERMS

public order crime
victimless crime
vigilante
moral crusades
moral entrepreneurs
gay bashing
homosexuality
sodomy
paraphilias

prostitution
brothels
madams
call girls
skeezers
massage parlors
baby pros
Mann Act
pornography

obscenity
temperance movement
freebase
crack
addict
designer drugs
gateway model

NOTES

1. Malcolm Jones, Jr., "Can Art Photography Be Kiddie Porn?" *Newsweek,* 9 March 1998, p. 58.

2. Edwin Schur, *Crimes Without Victims* (Englewood Cliffs, N.J.: Prentice-Hall, 1965).

3. Charles Fleming and Michele Ingrassia, "The Heidi Chronicles," *Newsweek,* 16 August 1993, p. 51.

4. Andrea Dworkin, quoted in "Where Do We Stand on Pornography," *Ms.* (January–February 1994), p. 34.

5. Jennifer Williard, *Juvenile Prostitution* (Washington, D.C.: National Victim Resource Center, 1991).

6. Morris Cohen, "Moral Aspects of the Criminal Law," *Yale Law Journal* 49 (1940): 1017.

7. Sir Patrick Devlin, *The Enforcement of Morals* (New York: Oxford University Press, 1959), p. 20.

8. See Joel Feinberg, *Social Philosophy* (Englewood Cliffs, N.J.: Prentice-Hall, 1973), chap. 2, 3.

9. *United States v. 12 200-ft Reels of Super 8mm Film,* 413 U.S. 123 (1973) at 137.

10. Barbara Crossette, "Senegal Bans Cutting of Genitals of Girls," *New York Times,* 18 January 1999, p. A11.

11. David Kaplan, "Is It Torture or Tradition?" *Newsweek,* 20 December 1993, p. 124.

12. Crossette, "Senegal Bans Cutting of Genitals of Girls."

13. H. L. A. Hart, "Immorality and Treason," *Listener* 62 (1959): 163.

14. Joseph Gussfield, "On Legislating Morals: The Symbolic Process of Designating Deviancy," *California Law Review* 56 (1968): 58–59.

15. E. Hatfield, S. Sprecher, and J. Traupman, "Men and Women's Reactions to Sexually Explicit Films: A Serendipitous Finding," *Archives of Sexual Behavior* 6 (1978): 583–92.

16. Henry Lesieur and Joseph Sheley, "Illegal Appended Enterprises: Selling the Lines," *Social Problems* 34 (1987): 249–60.

17. Wayne LaFave and Austin Scott, Jr., *Criminal Law* (St. Paul: West Publishing, 1986), p. 12.

18. LaFave and Scott, *Criminal Law*.

19. "Baylor U. Cancels Art Class on Nudes," *Boston Globe*, 22 March 1993, p. 21.

20. Reuters, "In Key West, Body Paint No Longer Counts as Clothes," *Boston Globe*, 22 October 1996, p. A14.

21. Howard Becker, *Outsiders* (New York: Macmillan, 1963), pp. 13–14.

22. Daniel Claster, *Bad Guys and Good Guys: Moral Polarization and Crime* (Westport, Conn: Greenwood Press, 1992), pp. 28–29.

23. James Brooke, "Gay Leaders Say Student's Death Just Tip of the Iceberg," *New York Times*, 14 October 1998, p. A1.

24. Albert Reiss, "The Social Integration of Queers and Peers," *Social Problems* 9 (1961): 102–20.

25. Judd Marmor, "The Multiple Roots of Homosexual Behavior," in *Homosexual Behavior*, ed. J. Marmor (New York: Basic Books, 1980), p. 5.

26. J. Money, "Sin, Sickness, or Status? Homosexual Gender Identity and Psychoneuroendocrinology," *American Psychologist* 42 (1987): 384–99.

27. C. S. Ford and F. A. Beach, *Patterns of Sexual Behavior* (New York: Harper & Bros., 1951).

28. A. Kinsey, W. Pomeroy, and C. Martin, *Sexual Behavior in the Human Male* (Philadelphia: W. B. Saunders, 1948); A. Kinsey, W. Pomeroy, and C. Martin, *Sexual Behavior in the Human Female* (Philadelphia: W. B. Saunders, 1953); Morton Hunt, *Sexual Behavior in the 1970's* (New York: Dell Books, 1974), p. 317.

29. J. McNeil, *The Church and the Homosexual* (Kansas City, Mo.: Sheed, Andrews, and McNeel, 1976).

30. Laurie Goodstein, "The Architect of the 'Gay Conversion' Campaign," *New York Times*, 13 August 1998, p. A10.

31. Marmor, "The Multiple Roots of Homosexual Behavior," pp. 18–19.

32. Marmor, "The Multiple Roots of Homosexual Behavior," p. 19.

33. Henry Adams, Lester Wright, and Bethany Lohr, "Is Homophobia Associated with Homosexual Arousal?" *Journal of Abnormal Psychology* 105 (1996): 440–45.

34. Elsa Arnett, "Efforts Grow to Cap Gay-Rights Gains," *Boston Globe*, 12 April 1998, p. A10.

35. 376 U.S. 660; 82 S.Ct. 1417; 8 L.Ed.2d 758 (1962).

36. Arnett, "Efforts Grow to Cap Gay-Rights Gains."

37. *Romer v. Evans*, 517 U.S. 620 (1996).

38. *Equality Foundation of Greater Cincinnati v. City of Cincinnati*, No. 97–1795, 1998.

39. F. Inbau, J. Thompson, and J. Zagel, *Criminal Law and Its Administration* (Mineola, N.Y.: Foundation Press, 1974), p. 287.

40. *Bowers v. Hardwick*, 106 S.Ct. 2841 (1986); reh. den. 107 S.Ct. 29 (1986).

41. Georgia Code Ann. 16–6–2 (1984).

42. American Law Institute, Model Penal Code, Section 207.5.

43. Gary Caplan, "Fourteenth Amendment— The Supreme Court Limits the Right to Privacy," *Journal of Criminal Law and Criminology* 77 (1986): 894–930.

44. Carolyn Skorneck, "Reno Orders FBI to End Hiring Bias Against Gays," *Boston Globe*, 4 December 1993, p. 3.

45. John Biskupic, "Justice Let Stand 'Don't Ask, Don't Tell' Policy," *Boston Globe*, 22 October 1996, p. A6.

46. Michael Joseph Gross, "A Problem with Privacy, and with Openness," *Boston Globe*, 15 February 1998, p. C3.

47. Associated Press, "Court Gives Sons Back to Gay Father," *Boston Globe*, 16 October 1996, p. A5.

48. National Gay and Lesbian Task Force, "Eye on Equality: Pride and Public Opinion" (press release, 5 July 1998).

49. Mireya Navarro, "Miami Restores Gay Rights Law," *New York Times*, 2 December 1998, p. B1.

50. American Civil Liberties Union Press Release, November 23, 1998.

51. Reuters, "Belgians Promise to Clean Up Courts," *Boston Globe*, 22 October 1996, p. A17.

52. See, generally, Spencer Rathus and Jeffery Nevid, *Abnormal Psychology* (Englewood Cliffs, N.J.: Prentice-Hall, 1991), pp. 373–411.

53. Kathy Smiljanich and John Briere, "Self-Reported Sexual Interest in Children: Sex Differences and Psychosocial Correlates in a University Sample," *Violence and Victims* 11 (1996): 39–50.

54. See, generally, V. Bullogh, *Sexual Variance in Society and History* (Chicago: University of Chicago Press, 1958), pp. 143–44.

55. Spencer Rathus, *Human Sexuality* (New York: Holt, Rinehart and Winston, 1983), p. 463.

56. Annette Jolin, "On the Backs of Working Prostitutes: Feminist Theory and Prostitution Policy," *Crime and Delinquency* 40 (1994): 60–83.

57. Charles McCaghy, *Deviant Behavior* (New York: Macmillan, 1976), pp. 348–49.

58. Cited in McCaghy, *Deviant Behavior*.

59. FBI, *Crime in the United States, 1997*, p. 222.

60. Michael Waldholz, "HTLV-I Virus Found in Blood of Prostitutes," *Wall Street Journal*, 5 January 1990, p. B2.

61. FBI, *Crime in the United States, 1992*, p. 172.

62. Charles Winick and Paul Kinsie, *The Lively Commerce* (Chicago: Quadrangle Books, 1971), p. 58.

63. Mark-David Janus, Barbara Scanlon, and Virginia Price, "Youth Prostitution," in *Child Pornography and Sex Rings*, ed. Ann Wolbert Burgess (Lexington, Mass.: Lexington Books, 1989), pp. 127–46.

64. Jennifer James, "Prostitutes and Prostitution," in *Deviants: Voluntary Action in a Hostile World*, ed. E. Sagarin and F. Montanino (New York: Scott, Foresman, 1977), p. 384.

65. Winick and Kinsie, *The Lively Commerce*, pp. 172–73.

66. Paul Goldstein, "Occupational Mobility in the World of Prostitution: Becoming a Madam," *Deviant Behavior* 4 (1983): 267–79.

67. Goldstein, "Occupational Mobility in the World of Prostitution," p. 267.

68. Alessandra Stanley, "Case of the Classy Madam," *Time*, 29 October 1984, p. 39.

69. The Associated Press, "Mob Seen in Las Vegas Sex Trade," *New York Times*, 17 October 1998, p. A7.

70. Goldstein, "Occupational Mobility in the World of Prostitution," pp. 267–70.

71. Mireya Navarro, "Group Forced Illegal Aliens into Prostitution, U.S. Says," *New York Times*, 24 April 1998, p. A10.

72. Described in Rathus, *Human Sexuality*, p. 468.

73. Paul Goldstein, Lawrence Ouellet, and Michael Fendrich, "From Bag Brides to Skeezers: A Historical Perspective on Sex-for-Drugs Behavior," *Journal of Psychoactive Drugs* 24 (1992): 349–61.

74. Lisa Maher and Kathleen Daly, "Women in the Street-Level Drug Economy: Continuity or Change?," *Criminology* 34 (1996): 465–91.

75. D. Kelly Weisberg, *Children of the Night: A Study of Adolescent Prostitution* (Lexington, Mass.: Lexington Books, 1985), pp. 44–55.

76. Gerald Hotaling and David Finkelhor, *The Sexual Exploitation of Missing Children* (Washington, D.C.: U.S. Department of Justice, 1988).

77. N. Jackman, Richard O'Toole, and Gilbert Geis, "The Self-Image of the Prostitute," in *Sexual Deviance*, ed. J. Gagnon and W. Simon (New York: Harper and Row, 1967), pp. 152–53.

78. Weisberg, *Children of the Night*, p. 98.

79. Winick and Kinsie, *The Lively Commerce*, p. 51.

80. Paul Gebhard, "Misconceptions about Female Prostitutes," *Medical Aspects of Human Sexuality* 3 (July 1969): 28–30.

81. James, "Prostitutes and Prostitution," pp. 388–89.

82. Winick and Kinsie, *The Lively Commerce*, p. 109.

83. James, "Prostitutes and Prostitution," p. 419.

84. Winick and Kinsie, *The Lively Commerce,* p. 120.

85. Goldstein, Ouellet, and Fendrich, "From Bag Brides to Skeezers," p. 359.

86. Dorothy Bracey, *"Baby Pros": Preliminary Profiles of Juvenile Prostitutes* (New York: JohnJay Press, 1979).

87. Andrea Dworkin, *Pornography* (New York: Dutton, 1989).

88. Jolin, "On the Backs of Working Prostitutes," pp. 76–77.

89. *Merriam-Webster Dictionary* (New York: Pocket Books, 1974), p. 484.

90. Attorney General's Commission, *Report on Pornography, Final Report* (Washington, D.C.: U.S. Government Printing Office, 1986), pp. 837–901. Hereinafter cited as Pornography Commission.

91. John Hurst, "Children — A Big Profit Item for the Smut Peddlers," *Los Angeles Times,* 26 May 1977, cited in *Take Back the Night,* ed. Laura Lederer (New York: William Morrow, 1980), pp. 77–78.

92. Albert Belanger et al. "Typology of Sex Rings Exploiting Children," in *Child Pornography and Sex Rings,* ed. Ann Wolbert Burgess (Lexington, Mass.: Lexington Books, 1984), pp. 51–81.

93. *The Report of the Commission on Obscenity and Pornography* (Washington, D.C.: U.S. Government Printing Office, 1970).

94. Pornography Commission, pp. 837–902.

95. Berl Kutchinsky, "The Effect of Easy Availability of Pornography on the Incidence of Sex Crimes," *Journal of Social Issues* 29 (1973): 95–112.

96. Michael Goldstein, "Exposure to Erotic Stimuli and Sexual Deviance," *Journal of Social Issues* 29 (1973): 197–219.

97. John Court, "Sex and Violence: A Ripple Effect," *Pornography and Aggression,* ed. Neal Malamuth and Edward Donnerstein (Orlando, Fla.: Academic Press, 1984).

98. See Edward Donnerstein, Daniel Linz, and Steven Penrod, *The Question of Pornography* (New York: Free Press, 1987).

99. Pornography Commission, pp. 901–1037.

100. Edward Donnerstein, "Pornography and Violence Against Women," *Annals of the New York Academy of Science* 347 (1980): 277–88; E. Donnerstein and J. Hallam, "Facilitating Effects of Erotica on Aggression Against Women," *Journal of Personality and Social Psychology* 36 (1977): 1270–77; Seymour Fishbach and Neil Malamuth, "Sex and Aggression: Proving the Link," *Psychology Today* 12 (1978): 111–22.

101. Don Smith, "Sexual Aggression in American Pornography: The Stereotype of Rape." Paper presented at the annual meeting of the American Sociological Association, 1976.

102. State Laws on Obscenity, Child Pornography, and Harassment: http://www.itaa.org/porn1.htm

103. Tracy Fields, "Florida Vendor Booked for Rap Record Sale," *Boston Globe,* 9 June 1990, p. 1; Richard Lacayo, "The Rap Against a Rap Group," *Time,* 25 June 1990, p. 18.

104. 354 U.S. 476; 77 S.Ct. 1304 (1957).

105. 383 U.S. 413 (1966).

106. 413 U.S. 15 (1973).

107. R. George Wright, "Defining Obscenity: The Criterion of Value," *New England Law Review* 22 (1987): 315–41.

108. *Pope v. Illinois,* 107 S.Ct. 1918 (1987).

109. *Pope v. Illinois,* at 1927 (J. Stevens dissenting).

110. Anthony Flint, "Skin Trade Spreading Across U.S.," *Boston Globe,* 1 December 1996, pp. 1, 36–37.

111. Pornography Commission, pp. 376–77.

112. Bob Cohn, "The Trials of Adam and Eve," *Newsweek,* 7 January 1991, p. 48.

113. 427 U.S. 50 (1976).

114. Thomas J. Lueck, "At Sex Shops, Fear That Ruling Means the End Is Near," *New York Times,* February 25, 1998, p.1.

115. David Rohde, "In Giuliani's Crackdown on Porn Shops, Court Ruling Is a Setback," *New York Times,* 29 August 1998, p. A11.

116. Kevin Cullen, "The Bad Old Days Are Over," *Boston Globe,* 23 December 1987, p. 33.

117. 50 L.W. 5077 (1982).

118. Joseph Scott, "Violence and Erotic Material — The Relationship Between Adult Entertainment and Rape." Paper presented at the annual meeting of the American Association for the Advancement of Science, Los Angeles, 1985.

119. Ann Landers, "Pornography Can Be an Addiction," *Boston Globe,* 19 July 1993, p. 36.

120. Ann Landers, "Husband Is Obsessed with Internet Porn," *Boston Globe,* 22 May 1998, p. D12.

121. Scott, "Violence and Erotic Material."

122. Flint, "Skin Trade Spreading Across U.S."

123. Associated Press, "N.Y. Firm Fined for Broadcasting Pornographic Films by Satellite," *Boston Globe,* 16 February 1991, p. 12.

124. ACLU, *Reno v. ACLU,* No. 96–511.

125. ACLU, "Supreme Court Rules: Cyberspace Will be Free! ACLU Hails Victory in Internet Censorship Challenge" (news release, 26 June 1997).

126. ACLU, "*ACLU v. Reno,* Round 2: Broad Coalition Files Challenge to New Federal Net Censorship Law" (news release, 22 October 1998).

127. Ralph Weisheit, "Studying Drugs in Rural Areas: Notes from the Field," *Journal of Research in Crime and Delinquency* 30 (1993): 213–32.

128. "British Officials Report Skyrocketing Heroin Use," *Alcoholism & Drug Abuse Weekly* 10 (August 17, 1998): 7; National Institute on Drug Abuse, Community Epidemiology Work Group, *Epidemiological Trends in Drug Abuse,* Advance Report (Washington, D.C.: National Institute on Drug Abuse, 1997).

129. See, generally, Marianne Zawitz, ed., *Drugs, Crime and the Justice System* (Washington, D.C.: U.S. Government Printing Office, 1992). Herein cited as *Drugs.*

130. Arnold Trebach, *The Heroin Solution* (New Haven, Conn.: Yale University Press, 1982).

131. James Inciardi, *The War on Drugs* (Palo Alto, Calif.: Mayfield, 1986), p. 2.

132. See, generally, David Pittman, "Drug Addiction and Crime," in *Handbook of Criminology,* ed. D. Glazer (Chicago: Rand McNally, 1974), pp. 209–232; Board of Directors, National Council on Crime and Delinquency, "Drug Addiction: A Medical, Not a Law Enforcement, Problem," *Crime and Delinquency* 20 (1974): 4–9.

133. Associated Press, "Records Detail Royals' Turn-of-Century Drug Use," *Boston Globe,* 29 August 1993, p. 13.

134. See Edwin Brecher, *Licit and Illicit Drugs* (Boston: Little, Brown, 1972).

135. James Inciardi, *Reflections on Crime* (New York: Holt, Rinehart and Winston, 1978), p. 15.

136. William Bates and Betty Crowther, "Drug Abuse," in *Deviants: Voluntary Actors in a Hostile World,* ed. E. Sagarin and F. Montanino (New York: Foresman and Co., 1977), p. 269.

137. Inciardi, *Reflections on Crime,* pp. 8–10. See also A. Greeley, William McCready, and Gary Theisen, *Ethnic Drinking Subcultures* (New York: Praeger, 1980).

138. Joseph Gusfield, *Symbolic Crusade* (Urbana: University of Illinois Press, 1963), chap. 3.

139. McCaghy, *Deviant Behavior,* p. 280.

140. McCaghy, *Deviant Behavior..*

141. This section relies heavily on the descriptions in Kenneth Jones, Louis Shainberg, and Curtin Byer, *Drugs and Alcohol* (New York: Harper & Row, 1979), pp. 57–114.

142. Center for Substance Abuse Research, "Youth Are Unaware that 'Fry' May Contain PCP" (press release, 11 May 1998).

143. Rathus and Nevid, *Abnormal Psychology,* p. 344.

144. Jeffrey Fagan and Ko-Lin Chin, "Initiation into Crack and Powdered Cocaine: A Tale of Two Epidemics," *Contemporary Drug Problems* 16 (1989): 579–617.

145. Thomas Mieczkowski, "The Damage Done: Cocaine Methods in Detroit," *International Journal of Comparative and Applied Criminal Justice* 12 (1988): 261–67.

146. Rathus and Nevid, *Abnormal Psychology,* p. 342.

147. These numbers are open to debate. See Inciardi, *The War on Drugs,* pp. 70–71; Jerome Platt and Christina Platt, *Heroin Addiction* (New York: Wiley, 1976), p. 324.

148. Charles Winick, "Physician Narcotics Addicts," *Social Problems* 9 (1961): 174–86.

149. Data in this section come from U.S. Department of Health and Human Services, *The Household Survey on Drug Abuse, 1997* (Washington, D.C.: Department of Health and Human Services, 1998).

150. Associated Press, "Alcohol Deaths Stopped Declining," *Boston Globe,* 27 January 1991, p. 8.

151. Mary Ellen Mackesy-Amiti, Michael Fendrich, and Paul Goldstein, "Sequence of Drug Use Among Serious Drug Users: Typical vs. Atypical Progression, "*Drug and Alcohol Dependence* 45 (1997): 185–96.

152. D. J. Rohsenow, "Drinking Habits and Expectancies About Alcohol's Effects for Self versus Others," *Journal of Consulting and Clinical Psychology* 51 (1983): 752–56.

153. G. Kolata, "Study Backs Heart Benefits in Light Drinking," *New York Times,* 3 August 1988, p. A24.

154. Spencer Rathus, *Psychology,* 4th ed. (New York: Holt, Rinehart and Winston, 1990), p. 161.

155. The annual survey is conducted by Lloyd Johnston, Jerald Bachman, and Patrick O'Malley of the Institute of Social Research, University of Michigan, Ann Arbor, Michigan.

156. *Monitoring the Future Study* press release, 18 December 1998.

157. Data in this section come from Department of Health and Human Services, *The Household Survey on Drug Abuse, 1997* (Washington, D.C.: Department of Health and Human Services, 1998).

158. Eric Wish, *Drug Use Forecasting Program, Annual Report 1990* (Washington, D.C.: National Institute of Justice, 1990).

159. Thomas Gray and Eric Wish, *Maryland Youth at Risk: A Study of Drug Use in Juvenile Detainees* (College Park, Md.: Center for Substance Abuse Research, 1993); Eric Wish and Christina Polsenberg, "Arrestee Urine Tests and Self-Reports of Drug Use: Which Is More Related to Rearrest?" (paper presented at the annual meeting of the American Society of Criminology, Phoenix, Arizona, November 1993).

160. Thomas Mieczkowski, "The Prevalence of Drug Use in the United States," in *Crime and Justice, A Review of Research,* vol. 20, ed. Michael Tonry (Chicago: University of Chicago Press, 1996), 349–414 at 376.

161. See, generally, Mark Blumberg, ed., *AIDS, The Impact on the Criminal Justice System* (Columbus, Ohio: Merrill Publishing, 1990).

162. Scott Decker and Richard Rosenfeld, "Intravenous Drug Use and the AIDS Epidemic: Findings for a Twenty-City Sample of Arrestees." Paper presented at the annual meeting of the American Society of Criminology, Baltimore, November 1990.

163. Douglas Longshore, "Prevalence and Circumstances of Drug Injection at Los Angeles Shooting Galleries," *Crime and Delinquency* 42 (1996): 21–35.

164. Longshore, "Prevalance and Circumstances of Drug Injection," p. 30.

165. Mark Blumberg, "AIDS and the Criminal Justice System: An Overview," in *AIDS, The Impact on the Criminal Justice System,* ed. Mark Blumberg (Columbus, Ohio: Merrill Publishing, 1990), p. 11.

166. Bruce Johnson, Andrew Golub, and Jeffrey Fagan, "Careers in Crack, Drug Use, Drug Distribution, and Nondrug Criminality," *Crime and Delinquency* 41 (1995): 275–95.

167. Johnson, Golub, and Fagan, "Careers in Crack, Drug Use, Drug Distribution, and Nondrug Criminality."

168. C. Bowden, "Determinants of Initial Use of Opioids," *Comprehensive Psychiatry* 12 (1971): 136–40.

169. Marvin Krohn, Alan Lizotte, Terence Thornberry, Carolyn Smith, and David McDowall, "Reciprocal Causal Relationships Among Drug Use, Peers, and Beliefs: A Five-Wave Panel Model," *Journal of Drug Issues* 26 (1996): 205–428.

170. R. Cloward and L. Ohlin, *Delinquency and Opportunity: A Theory of Delinquent Gangs* (Glencoe, Ill.: Free Press, 1960).

171. Kellie Barr, Michael Farrell, Grace Barnes and John Welte, "Race, Class, and Gender Differences in Substance Abuse: Evidence of Middle-Class/Underclass Polarization among Black Males," *Social Problems* 40 (1993): 314–26.

172. Rathus and Nevid, *Abnormal Psychology,* p. 361.

173. Rathus, *Psychology,* p. 158.

174. Platt and Platt, *Heroin Addiction,* p. 127.

175. Alison Bass, "Mental Ills, Drug Abuse Linked," *Boston Globe,* 21 November 1990, p. 3.

176. D. W. Goodwin, "Alcoholism and Genetics," *Archives of General Psychiatry* 42 (1985): 171–74.

177. For a thorough review of this issue, see John Petraitis, Brian Flay, and Todd Miller, "Reviewing Theories of Adolescent Substance Use: Organizing Pieces in the Puzzle," *Psychological Bulletin* 117 (1995): 67–86.

178. Judith Brooks and Li-Jung Tseng, "Influences of Parental Drug Use, Personality, and Child Rearing on the Toddler's Anger and Negativity," *Genetic, Social and General Psychology Monographs* 122 (1996): 107–128.

179. Thomas Ashby Wills, Donato Vaccaro, Grace McNamara, and A. Elizabeth Hirky, "Escalated Substance Use: A Longitudinal Grouping Analysis from Early to Middle Adolescence," *Journal of Abnormal Psychology* 105 (1996): 166–80.

180. Denise Kandel and Mark Davies, "Friendship Networks, Intimacy, and Illicit Drug Use in Young Adulthood: A Comparison of Two Competing Theories," *Criminology* 29 (1991): 441–71.

181. J. S. Mio, G. Nanjundappa, D. E. Verlur, and M. D. DeRios, "Drug Abuse and the Adolescent Sex Offender: A Preliminary Analysis," *Journal of Psychoactive Drugs* 18 (1986): 65–72.

182. D. Baer and J. Corrado, "Heroin Addict Relationships with Parents During Childhood and Early Adolescent Years," *Journal of Genetic Psychology* 124 (1974): 99–103.

183. James Inciardi, Ruth Horowitz, and Anne Pottieger, *Street Kids, Street Drugs, Street Crime: An Examination of Drug Use and Serious Delinquency in Miami* (Belmont, Calif.: Wadsworth, 1993), p. 43.

184. Inciardi, Horowitz, and Pottieger, *Street Kids, Street Drugs, Street Crime.*

185. John Wallace and Jerald Bachman, "Explaining Racial/Ethnic Differences in Adolescent Drug Use: The Impact of Background and Lifestyle," *Social Problems* 38 (1991): 333–57.

186. John Donovan, "Problem-Behavior Theory and the Explanation of Adolescent Marijuana Use," *Journal of Drug Issues* 26 (1996): 379–404.

187. A. Christiansen, G. T. Smith, P. V. Roehling, and M. S. Goldman, "Using Alcohol Expectancies to Predict Adolescent Drinking Behavior After One Year," *Journal of Counseling and Clinical Psychology* 57 (1989): 93–99.

188. Claire Sterck-Elifson, "Just for Fun?: Cocaine Use Among Middle-Class Women," *Journal of Drug Issues* 26 (1996): 63–76 at 69.

189. Icek Ajzen, *Attitudes, Personality and Behavior* (Homewood, Ill.: Dorsey Press, 1988).

190. Judith Brook, Martin Whiteman, Elinor Balka, and Beatrix Hamburg, "African-American and Puerto Rican Drug Use: Personality, Familial, and Other Environmental Risk Factors," *Genetic, Social, and General Psychology Monographs* 118 (1992): 419–38.

191. Andrew Golub and Bruce Johnson, "The Multiple Paths Through Alcohol, Tobacco and Marijuana to Hard Drug Use Among Arrestees." Paper presented at the annual Society of Criminology meeting, San Diego, Calif., November 1997.

192. Inciardi, *The War on Drugs,* p. 60.

193. These lifestyles are described in Marcia Chaiken and Bruce Johnson, *Characteristics of Different Types of Drug-Involved Offenders* (Washington, D.C.: National Institute of Justice, 1988).

194. Kenneth Tunnell, "Inside the Drug Trade: Trafficking from the Dealer's Perspective," *Qualitative Sociology* 16 (1993): 361–81.

195. Carolyn Rebecca Block, Antigone Christakos, Ayad Jacob, and Roger Przybylski, *Street Gangs and Crime* (Chicago: Illinois Criminal Justice Information Authority, 1996).

196. Hilary Saner, Robert MacCoun, and Peter Reuter, "On the Ubiquity of Drug Selling Among Youthful Offenders in Washington, DC., 1985–1991: Age, Period, or Cohort Effect?" *Journal of Quantitative Criminology* 11 (1995): 362–73.

197. Charles Faupel and Carl Klockars, "Drugs–Crime Connections: Elaborations from the Life Histories of Hard-Core Heroin Addicts," *Social Problems* 34 (1987): 54–68.

198. Charles Faupel, "Heroin Use, Crime and Unemployment Status," *Journal of Drug Issues* 18 (1988) 467–79.

199. Faupel and Klockars, "Drugs–Crime Connections."

200. Karen Joe, "The Lives and Times of Asian-Pacific American Women Drug Users: An Ethnographic Study of Their Methamphetamine Use," *Journal of Drug Issues* 26 (1996): 199–218.

201. Marvin Dawkins, "Drug Use and Violent Crime Among Adolescents," *Adolescence* 32 (1997): 395–406.

202. U.S. Department of Justice, "Four in Ten Criminal Offenders Report Alcohol as a Factor in Violence" (press release, 5 April 1998).

203. Arrestee Drug Abuse Monitoring Program, *1997 Drug Use Forecasting, Annual Report on Adult and Juvenile Arrestees* (Washington, D.C.: National Institute of Justice, 1998); Center for Substance Abuse Research Report, 7 September 1998.

204. Eric Baumer, Janet Lauritsen, Richard Rosenfeld, and Richard Wright, "The Influence of Crack Cocaine on Robbery, Burglary, and Homicide Rates: A Cross-City, Longitudinal Analysis," *Journal of Research in Crime and Delinquency* 35 (1998): 316–40; Carolyn Rebecca Block and Antigone Christakos, "Intimate Partner Homicide in Chicago over 29 Years," *Crime and Delinquency* 41 (1995): 496–526.

205. George Speckart and M. Douglas Anglin, "Narcotics Use and Crime: An Overview of Recent Research Advances," *Contemporary Drug Problems* 13 (1986): 741–69; Faupel and Klockars, "Drugs–Crime Connections."

206. M. Douglas Anglin, Elizabeth Piper Deschenes, and George Speckart, "The Effect of Legal Supervision on Narcotic Addiction and Criminal Behavior." Paper presented at the annual meeting of the American Society of Criminology, Montreal, November 1987, p. 2.

207. Speckart and Anglin, "Narcotics Use and Crime: An Overview of Recent Research Advances," p. 752.

208. Speckart and Anglin, "Narcotics Use and Crime: An Overview of Recent Research Advances," p. 752.

209. Robert Peralta, "The Relationship Between Alcohol and Violence in an Adolescent Population: An Analysis of the *Monitoring the Future Survey*" (paper presented at the annual Society of Criminology meeting, San Diego, Calif., November, 1997); Helene Raskin White and Stephen Hansell, "The Moderating Effects of Gender and Hostility on the Alcohol–Aggression Relationship," *Journal of Research in Crime and Delinquency* 33 (1996): 450–70; D. Wayne Osgood, "Drugs, Alcohol, and Adolescent Violence" (paper pre-

sented at the annual meeting of the American Society of Criminology, Miami 1994).

210. James Inciardi, "Heroin Use and Street Crime," *Crime and Delinquency* 25 (1979): 335–46. See also W. McGlothlin, M. Anglin, and B. Wilson, "Narcotic Addiction and Crime," *Criminology* 16 (1978): 293–311.

211. M. Douglas Anglin and George Speckart, "Narcotics Use and Crime: A Multisample, Multimethod Analysis," *Criminology* 26 (1988): 197–235.

212. Allen Beck, Darrell Gilliard, Lawrence Greenfeld, Caroline Harlow, Thomas Hester, Lewis Jankowski, Tracy Snell, James Stephen, and Danielle Morton, *Survey of State Prison Inmates, 1991* (Washington, D.C.: Bureau of Justice Statistics, 1993). The survey of prison inmates is conducted by the Bureau of Justice Statistics every five to seven years.

213. ADAM replaces the Drug Use Forecasting Program, which had a 10-year run as the national indicator of drug use by arrestees.

214. *1997 Drug Use Forecasting: Annual Report on Adult and Juvenile Arrestees* (Washington, D.C.: National Institute of Justice, 1998).

215. Bruce Johnson, George Thomas, and Andrew Golub, "Trends in Heroin Use Among Manhattan Arrestees from the Heroin and Crack Era," in *Heroin in the Age of Crack-Cocaine,* ed. James Inciardi and Lana Harrison (Thousand Oaks, Calif.: Sage, 1998), 108–130.

216. Paul Goldstein, "The Drugs–Violence Nexus: A Tripartite Conceptual Framework," *Journal of Drug Issues* 15 (1985): 493–506; Marvin Krohn, Alan Lizotte, and Cynthia Perez, "The Interrelationship Between Substance Use and Precocious Transitions to Adult Sexuality," *Journal of Health and Social Behavior* 38 (1997): 87–103 at 88; Richard Jessor, "Risk Behavior in Adolescence: A Psychosocial Framework for Understanding and Action," in *Adolescents at Risk: Medical and Social Perspectives,* ed. D. E. Rogers and E. Ginzburg (Boulder, Colo.: Westview, 1992).

217. See Kenneth Jones, Louis Shainberg, and Carter Byer, *Drugs and Alcohol* (New York: Harper & Row, 1979) pp. 137–146.

218. Controlled Substance Act, 21 U.S.C. 848 (1984).

219. Anti–Drug Abuse Act of 1986, Pub. L. No. 99-570, U.S.C. 841 (1986).

220. Anti–Drug Abuse Act of 1988, Pub. L. No. 100-690; 21 U.S.C. 1501; Subtitle A—Death Penalty, Sec. 7001, Amending the Controlled Substances Abuse Act, 21 U.S.C. 848.

221. Bennett Beach, "Is the Party Finally Over?" *Time,* 26 April 1982, p. 58.

222. "New Drunken Driver Law Shows Results in California," *Omaha World Herald,* 26 May 1982, p. 34.

223. Faye Silas, "Gimme the Keys," *ABA Journal* 71 (1985): 36.

224. Fred Heinzelmann, *Jailing Drunk Drivers* (Washington, D.C.: National Institute of Justice, 1984).

225. Rodney Kingsworth and Michael Jungsten, "Driving Under the Influence: The Impact of Legislative Reform on Court Sentencing Practices," *Crime and Delinquency* 34 (1988): 3–28.

226. Jones, Shainberg, and Byer, *Drugs and Alcohol,* pp. 190–93.

227. Gerald Wheeler and Rodney Hissong, "Effects of Criminal Sanctions on Drunk Drivers: Beyond Incarceration," *Crime and Delinquency* 34 (1988): 29–42.

228. *Easter v. District of Columbia,* 361 F.2d 50 (D.C. Cir. 1966).

229. 392 U.S. 514 (1968).

230. Eric Jensen, Jurg Gerber, and Ginna Babcock, "The New War on Drugs: Grass Roots Movement or Political Construction?" *Journal of Drug Issues* 21 (1991): 651–67.

231. Marianne Zawitz, ed., *Drugs, Crime and the Justice System* (Washington, D.C.: U.S. Government Printing Office, 1992), p. 36.

232. George Rengert, *The Geography of Illegal Drugs* (Boulder, Colo.: Westview Press, 1996), p. 2.

233. Sam Dillon and Craig Pyes, "Alleged Drug Kingpin Benefits from Mexico's Inept Justice System," *New York Times,* 15 April 1998, pp. A1–14 at A14.

234. Christopher Wren, "U.S. Is Certifying Mexico as an Ally in Fighting Drugs," *New York Times,* 1 March 1997, p. 1; Diego Ribadneira, "In Escobar Death, No Curb in Drugs Seen," *Boston Globe,* 4 December 1993, p. 2.

235. Bureau for International Narcotics and Law Enforcement Affairs, *International Narcotics Control Strategy Report, 1996* (Washington, D.C.: U.S. Department of State, 1997).

236. Walter Shapiro, "Going After the Hell's Angels," *Newsweek,* 13 May 1985, p. 41.

237. David Hayeslip, "Local-Level Drug Enforcement: New Strategies," *NIJ Reports* (March/April 1989): 1.

238. Mark Moore, *Drug Trafficking* (Washington, D.C.: National Institute of Justice, 1988).

239. Steven Belenko, Jeffrey Fagan, and Ko-Lin Chin, "Criminal Justice Responses to Crack," *Journal of Research in Crime and Delinquency* 28 (1991): 55–74.

240. *FY 1988 Report on Drug Control* (Washington, D.C.: National Institute of Justice, 1989), p. 103.

241. Carol Kaplan, *Sentencing and Time Served* (Washington, D.C.: Bureau of Justice Statistics, 1987).

242. Kaplan, *Sentencing and Time Served,* p. 2.

243. Patrick Langan and Jodi Brown, *Felony Sentences in the United States, 1994* (Washington, D.C.: Bureau of Justice Statistics, 1997).

244. Peter Rossi, Richard Berk, and Alec Campbell, "Just Punishments: Guideline

Sentences and Normative Consensus," *Journal of Quantitative Criminology* 13 (1997): 267–83.

245. Robert Davis, Arthur Lurigio, and Dennis Rosenbaum, eds., *Drugs and the Community* (Springfield, Ill.: Charles Thomas, 1993), pp. xii–xv.

246. Saul Weingart, "A Typology of Community Responses to Drugs," in *Drugs and the Community,* ed. Robert Davis, Arthur Lurigio, and Dennis Rosenbaum (Springfield, Ill.: Charles Thomas, 1993), pp. 85–105.

247. Davis, Lurigio, and Rosenbaum, *Drugs and the Community,* pp. xii–xiii.

248. Bureau of Justice Statistics, *Drugs, Crime and the Justice System* (Washington, D.C.: Bureau of Justice Statistics, 1992), pp. 109–112.

249. Earl Wyson, Richard Aniskiewicz, and David Wright, "Truth and DARE: Tracking Drug Education to Graduation as Symbolic Politics," *Social Problems* 41 (1994): 448–71.

250. Wyson, Aniskiewicz, and Wright, "Truth and DARE."

251. Dennis Rosenbaum, Robert Flewelling, Susan Bailey, Chris Ringwalt, and Deanna Wilkinson, "Cops in the Classroom: A Longitudinal Evaluation of Drug Abuse Resistance Education (DARE)," *Journal of Research in Crime and Delinquency* 31 (1994): 3–31.

252. Wyson, Aniskiewicz, and Wright, "Truth and DARE," p. 466.

253. Los Angeles Times, "Seattle Rethinks Drug Education," *Boston Globe,* 1 December 1996, p. A9.

254. Phyllis Ellickson and Robert Bell, "Challenges to Social Experiments: A Drug Prevention Example," *Journal of Research in Crime and Delinquency* 29 (1992): 79–101; Phyllis Ellickson and Robert Bell, "Drug Prevention in Junior High: A Multi-Site Longitudinal Test," *Science* 247 (1990): 1299–1305.

255. Robert Jackson, "Clinton Targets Youth in New Drug Plan," *Boston Globe,* 26 February 1997, p. A3.

256. Zawitz, *Drugs, Crime, and the Justice System,* pp. 115–22.

257. John Goldkamp and Peter Jones, "Pretrial Drug-Testing Experiments in Milwaukee and Prince George's County: The Context of Implementation," *Journal of Research in Crime and Delinquency* 29 (1992): 430–65; Chester Britt, Michael Gottfredson, and John Goldkamp, "Drug Testing and Pretrial Misconduct: An Experiment on the Specific Deterrent Effects of Drug Monitoring Defendants on Pretrial Release," *Journal of Research in Crime and Delinquency* 29 (1992): 62–78.

258. See, generally, Peter Greenwood and Franklin Zimring, *One More Chance* (Santa Monica, Calif.: Rand Corporation, 1985).

259. Eli Ginzberg, Howard Berliner, and Miriam Ostrow, *Young People at Risk: Is Prevention Possible?* (Boulder, Colo.: Westview Press, 1988), p. 99.

260. National Evaluation Data and Technical Assistance Center, "The District of Columbia's Drug Treatment Initiative (DCI)," (Washington, D.C., February 1998).

261. The following section is based on material found in Jerome Platt, "Vocational Rehabilitation of Drug Abusers," *Psychological Bulletin* 117 (1995): 416–33.

262. Platt, "Vocational Rehabilitation of Drug Abusers," p. 428.

263. Robert Taylor and Gary Cohen, "War Against Narcotics by U.S. Government Isn't Slowing Influx," *Wall Street Journal,* 27 November 1984, p. 1.

264. Ernest Drucker, "Drug Prohibition and Public Health: 25 Years of Evidence," *Public Health Reports* 114 (1999): 14–15.

265. Ethan Nadelmann, "America's Drug Problem," *Bulletin of the American Academy of Arts and Sciences* 65 (1991): 24–40.

266. Nadelmann, "America's Drug Problem," p. 24.

267. Ethan Nadelmann, "Should We Legalize Drugs? History Answers Yes," *American Heritage* (February/March 1993): 41–56.

268. See, generally, Ralph Weisheit, *Drugs, Crime and the Criminal Justice System* (Cincinnati: Anderson, 1990).

269. David Courtwright, "Should We Legalize Drugs? History Answers No," *American Heritage* (February/March 1993): 43–56.

270. James Inciardi and Duane McBride, "Legalizing Drugs: A Gormless, Naive Idea," *Criminologist* 15 (1990): 1–4.

271. Kathryn Ann Farr, "Revitalizing the Drug Decriminalization Debate," *Crime and Delinquency* 36 (1990): 223–37.

4

THE CRIMINAL JUSTICE SYSTEM

The text's final section reviews the agencies and the process of justice designed to exert social control over criminal offenders. Chapter 15 provides an overview of the justice system and describes its major institutions and processes; Chapter 16 looks at the police; Chapters 17 and 18 analyze the court and correctional systems.

This vast array of people and institutions is beset by conflicting goals and values. Some view the justice system as a mammoth agency of social control; others see it as a great social agency dispensing therapy to those who cannot fit within the boundaries of society.

Consequently, a major goal of justice system policymakers is to formulate and disseminate effective models of crime prevention and control. Efforts are now being undertaken at all levels of the justice system to improve information flow, experiment with new program concepts, and evaluate current operating procedures.

Many important links within the system allow the agencies of justice to be studied on a cross-national level. For example, all agencies must obey the rule of law, and most use a common framework of operations in such everyday events as arrest, detention, bail, and trial. However, the system fails to communicate effectively on what works, what doesn't, and why.

These chapters provide a good foundation for studying the justice system and its links to criminological thought.

CHAPTER 15

Overview
of the Criminal
Justice System

INTRODUCTION

During his lifetime, Michael Riggs had been convicted eight times in California for such offenses as car theft and robbery. In 1996 he was once again in trouble, this time for shoplifting a $20 bottle of vitamins. Riggs was sentenced to a term of twenty-five years to life under California's "three strikes" law, which mandates a life sentence for anyone convicted of a third offense. The law enables a trial judge to treat a defendant's third offense, even a petty crime such as shoplifting, as if it were a felony for purposes of applying the law's mandatory sentencing provisions. Riggs must serve a minimum of 20.8 years before parole eligibility. Without the "three strikes" law he would ordinarily have earned a maximum sentence of six months; if he had been convicted of murder he would have had to serve only 17 years. Riggs appealed his conviction to the Supreme Court in 1999, but the justices refused to rule on the case, letting his sentence stand.[1]

The Riggs case symbolizes the dilemmas faced by the component agencies of the criminal justice system—police, courts, and corrections—that have been established to apprehend, adjudicate, sanction, and treat criminal offenders. These governmental institutions are charged by law with dispensing fair, equal justice to all who come before them. In carrying out this task, the justice system faces an overwhelming burden: maintaining the rule of law in a society beset by racial and social injustice and conflict; deterring crime; and treating both offenders and victims in a just, evenhanded manner.

Not all experts view these objectives as the clear goals of the justice system. Social critics argue that the true purpose of the justice process is actually symbolic: it has been crafted to graphically represent society's outrage over criminal acts.[2] Aided by the news media, justice officials make reassuring statements designed to convince the public that something is being done to punish their "enemy"; the system is aimed at reassuring a frightened, vengeful public that "something is being done" about crime.[3] Justice has become a media event, a spectacle that can be broadcast. When popular opinion, fueled by the media, demands revenge, politicians establish get-tough measures like mandatory sentences for drug offenders and the death penalty for murder. Is Michael Riggs's life sentence for shoplifting the result of society's need for revenge? The facts of the case reveal that Riggs was homeless, hungry, a sub-

stance abuser, and extremely depressed after the death of his young son. Did this troubled person deserve a life sentence for shoplifting?

Questions are still being asked about the general direction the justice system should take, how the problem of crime control should be approached, and what is the most effective method of dealing with known criminal offenders. Criminal justice is far from a unified field. Practitioners, academics, and commentators alike have expressed irreconcilable differences concerning its goals, purpose, and direction. This lack of consensus is particularly vexing because of the multitude of problems facing the justice system. The agencies of justice attempt to eradicate such seemingly diverse social problems as substance abuse, gang violence, and environmental pollution while at the same time respecting individual liberties and civil rights. It is also assumed that the justice system's agencies can efficiently carry out multiple diverse tasks and that its representatives know law, psychology, and social welfare.

This chapter reviews the various components and processes of criminal justice and then discusses the legal constraints on criminal justice agencies. Some of the philosophical concepts that dominate the system will be mentioned and explained.

ORIGINS OF CRIMINAL JUSTICE

The need to deal effectively with crime is an old problem.[4] Guerilla activity was common before, during, and after the Revolutionary War. Bands supporting the British (Tories) and the American revolutionaries savagely attacked each other using hit-and-run tactics, burning, and looting. Early settlers, who were disproportionately young and male, typically laborers who paid for their passage with work contracts, were heavy drinkers who often settled disputes with guns or knives.[5]

CONNECTIONS

As you may recall, Chapter 11's Criminological Enterprise feature titled "Violent Land" discussed historian David Courtwright's views on how cultural factors worsened the already high crime rates among the settlers and immigrants.

The struggle over slavery during the mid-nineteenth century begat decades of conflict, crime, and violence, including the Civil War. After the war, night riders and Ku Klux Klan members were active in the South, using vigilante methods to maintain the status quo and terrorize former slaves. The violence also spilled over into bloody local feuds in the hill country of southern Appalachia. Factional hatred, magnified by the lack of formal law enforcement and grinding poverty, gave rise to violent attacks and family feuding. Some former Union and Confederate soldiers, heading west with the dream of finding gold or starting a cattle ranch, resorted to theft and robbery. Train robbery was popularized by the Reno Brothers of Indiana and bank robbery by the James-Younger gang of Missouri.

The Civil War generated not only criminal gangs but also widespread business crime. The great robber barons bribed government officials and intrigued to corner markets and obtain concessions for railroads, favorable land deals, and mining and mineral rights on government land. The administration of President Ulysses Grant was tainted by numerous corruption scandals.

Crime and Justice in the Twentieth Century

From 1900 to 1935, the nation experienced a sustained increase in criminal activity. This period was dominated by Depression-era outlaws who became mythic figures. Charles "Pretty Boy" Floyd was a folk hero among the sharecroppers of Eastern Oklahoma, and the nation eagerly followed the exploits of its premier bank robber, John Dillinger, until he was killed in front of a Chicago movie house. The infamous "Ma" Barker and her sons Lloyd, Herman, Fred, and Arthur are credited with killing more than 10 people, while Bonnie Parker and Clyde Barrow killed more than 13 before they were slain in a shootout with federal agents.

While these relatively small, mobile outlaw gangs were operating in the Midwest, more organized gangs flourished in the nation's largest cities. The first criminal gangs formed before the Civil War in urban slums such as the Five Points and Bowery neighborhoods in New York City. Although they sported colorful names, such as the Plug Uglies, the Hudson Dusters, and the Dead Rabbits, they engaged in mayhem, murder, and extortion. These gangs were the forerunners of the organized crime families that developed in New York and spread to Philadelphia, Chicago, New Orleans, and other major urban areas.

To protect itself from this ongoing assault, the public began in the mid-nineteenth century to support development of a great array of government agencies whose stated purposes are to control and prevent crime; identify, apprehend, and bring to trial those who violate the law; and devise effective methods of criminal correction. These agencies today make up what is commonly referred to as the *criminal justice system,* and it is to their nature and development we now turn our attention.

Early Origins of American Justice

Until fairly recently, there was little recognition that the agencies of criminal justice worked in concert or formed a system.[6] As the nineteenth century began, there was little formal justice; each legal jurisdiction developed its own methods to deal with criminal offenses, and such familiar institutions as local police departments and state prisons had not been created. Although firmly entrenched in our culture, common criminal justice agencies have existed for only 150 years or so. At first these institutions operated independently, with little recognition that their functions could be coordinated or have common ground. In fact, it was not until 1919 that a unified criminal justice system received recognition. In that year the **Chicago Crime Commission,** a professional association funded by private contributions, was created. This organization acts as a citizens' advocacy group and keeps track of the ongoing activities of local justice agencies.

The pioneering work of the Chicago group was soon copied in a number of other jurisdictions. In 1922 the Cleveland Crime Commission analyzed local criminal justice policy and uncovered the widespread use of discretion, plea bargaining, and other practices unknown to the public. Some commentators view the Cleveland survey as the first to treat criminal justice as a people-processing system, a view still widely held today. Similar projects were conducted by the Missouri Crime Survey (1926) and the Illinois Crime Survey (1929).

In 1931, President Herbert Hoover appointed the National Commission of Law Observance and Enforcement, commonly known today as the **Wickersham Commission.** This national study group analyzed the American justice system in detail and helped usher in the era of treatment and rehabilitation. It showed the complex rules and regulations that govern the system and exposed how difficult it was for justice personnel to keep track of its legal and administrative complexity.

The Modern Era of Justice

The modern era of criminal justice study began with a series of explorations of the criminal justice process conducted under the auspices of the American Bar Foundation. These research studies produced field data that were later incorporated into classic books, including *Arrest* by Wayne LaFave and *Conviction* by Donald Newman, which focused on the decision-making process in criminal justice.[7] As a group, the Bar Foundation studies brought to light some of the hidden or low-visibility processes that were at the heart of justice system operations. They showed how informal decision making and the use of personal discretion were essential ingredients of the justice process.

Another milestone occurred in 1967, when the President's Commission on Law Enforcement and the Administration of Justice (the Crime Commission), which had been appointed by President Lyndon Johnson, published its final report, titled *The Challenge of Crime in a Free Society*.[8] This group of practitioners, educators, and attorneys had been charged with creating a comprehensive view of the criminal justice process and offering recommendations for its reform. Concomitantly, Congress passed the Safe Streets and Crime Control Act of 1968, providing federal funds for state and local crime control efforts. This act helped launch a massive campaign to restructure the justice system by funding the Law Enforcement Assistance Administration (LEAA), an agency that provided hundreds of millions of dollars in aid to local and state justice agencies. Federal intervention through the LEAA ushered in a new era in research and development in criminal justice and established the concept that its component agencies actually make up a system.[9] Since that time, other national groups and agencies, including the American Bar Association and the National Advisory Commission on Criminal Justice Standards and Goals, have also explored the American criminal justice system in depth, reinforcing the systems concept.[10]

As a result of these efforts, the concept of a unified system of criminal justice is now generally recognized. Nearly every federal, state, and local crime control program now uses the term *criminal justice system* in one way or another. Rather than viewing police, court, and correctional agencies as thousands of independent institutions, it has become common to view them as components in a large, integrated, people-processing system that manages law violators from the time of their arrest through trial, punishment, and release.

WHAT IS THE CRIMINAL JUSTICE SYSTEM?

Criminal justice refers to the agencies of government charged with enforcing law, adjudicating crime, and correcting criminal conduct. The criminal justice system is essentially an instrument of **social control:** society considers some behaviors so dangerous and destructive that it either strictly controls their occurrence or outlaws them outright. It is the job of the agencies of justice to prevent these behaviors by apprehending and punishing transgressors or deterring their future occurrence. Although society maintains other forms of social control, such as the family, school, and church, they are designed to deal with moral, not legal, misbehavior. Only the criminal justice system has the power to control crime and punish criminals. The contemporary U.S. criminal justice system is huge, costing taxpayers about $100 billion per year, including more than $40 billion for police, $20 billion for the court and legal system, and $30 billion for corrections; these costs are on the rise, increasing more than 160 percent in the past 15 years.[11]

The justice system today employs close to 2 million people, including over 850,000 in law enforcement and 370,000 in corrections. It consists of over 55,000 public agencies, including approximately 17,000 police agencies, nearly 17,000 courts, over 8,000 prosecutorial agencies, about 6,000 correctional institutions, and over 3,500 probation and parole departments. There are also capital costs. State jurisdictions are now conducting a massive correctional building campaign, adding tens of thousands of prison cells. It costs about $70,000 to build a prison cell and about $25,000 dollars per year to keep an inmate in prison; juvenile institutions cost about $30,000 per year per resident. And beyond the direct costs of funding police, courts, and corrections, many more additional crime-related expenses are incurred by federal, state, and local governments. For example, federal drug control efforts now cost an additional $14 billion per year.[12]

The system is so big because it must process, treat, and care for millions of people each year. Although the crime rate has declined in the 1990s, about 15 million people are still being arrested each year, including almost 3 million for serious felony offenses.[13] In addition, about 1.5 million juveniles are handled by the juvenile courts.[14] State courts today convict over 870,000 adults of felonies.[15]

Considering the enormous number of people processed each year it comes as no surprise that the correctional system population is at an all-time high. More than 5 million people are now under the control of the correctional system, with about 1.7 million men and women in the nation's jails and prisons. About 4 million adult men and women are being supervised in the community while on probation or parole, a number that has been increasing by more than 3 percent each year since 1990.[16]

The major components of this immense system—the police, courts, and correctional agencies—are described in this section. What are there duties? What are the major stages in the formal criminal justice process, and how are decisions made at these critical junctures? What is the informal justice process, and how does it operate? These important questions are addressed next.

Police and Law Enforcement

Approximately 17,000 law enforcement agencies operate in the United States. Most are municipal, general-purpose police forces, numbering about 12,000 in all. In addition, local jurisdictions maintain over 1,000 special

There are more than 1,000 special police units, including park rangers, harbor police, transit police, and campus security agencies at local universities. Here Coast Guard agents are seizing 9,000 pounds of cocaine aboard a boat in a harbor.

police units, including park rangers, harbor police, transit police, and campus security agencies at local universities. At the county level there are approximately 3,000 **sheriff's departments,** which, depending on the jurisdiction, provide police protection in unincorporated areas of the county; perform judicial functions, such as serving subpoenas; and maintain the county jail and detention facilities. Every state except Hawaii maintains a state police force. The federal government has its own law enforcement agencies, including the FBI and the Secret Service. All told, approximately 900,000 people work in federal, state, county, and local law enforcement agencies.[17]

Since their origin in early nineteenth-century Britain, law enforcement agencies have been charged with peacekeeping, deterring potential criminals, and apprehending law violators.[18] The traditional police role involved maintaining order through patrolling public streets and highways, responding to calls for assistance, investigating crimes, and identifying criminal suspects. The police role has gradually expanded to include a variety of human service functions, including preventing youth crime and diverting juvenile offenders from the criminal justice system, resolving family conflicts, facilitating the movement of people and vehicles, preserving civil order during emergencies, providing emergency medical care, and improving police–community relations.[19]

Police are the most visible agents of the justice process. Their reactions to victims and offenders are carefully scrutinized in the news media. On numerous occasions police have been criticized for being too harsh or too lenient, too violent or too passive. Police control of such groups as minority citizens, youths, political dissidents, protesters, and union workers has been publicly debated. Compounding the problem is the tremendous discretion afforded police officers, who determine when a domestic dispute becomes disorderly conduct or criminal assault, whether it is appropriate to arrest juveniles or refer them to a social agency, and when to assume that probable cause exists to arrest a suspect for a crime.[20] At the same time, police agencies have been criticized for such problems as internal corruption, inefficiency, lack of effectiveness, brutality, and discriminatory hiring.[21] Widely publicized cases of police brutality, such as the Rodney King beating in Los Angeles, have prompted calls for the investigation and prosecution of police officers. Consequently, at all levels of government, police have traditionally been defensive toward and suspicious of the public, resistant to change, and secretive in their activities.

The Criminal Courts

There are approximately 25,000 court-related agencies in the United States. These include more than 16,000 criminal courts; about 13,000 try misdemeanor cases, 3,235 are felony courts, and 207 are appellate courts. There are also slightly over 8,000 federal, state, and local prosecutors' offices, which represent the government in criminal and civil trials and appeals. Over half of these offices are municipal, about one-third are county, and the remainder are state and federally affiliated. In addition, some 1,000 public defender offices, which dispense free legal aid to indigent defendants, operate around the country. About 320,000 people work in the various courts and prosecutors' and public defenders' offices in the United States.

The **criminal courts** are considered by many to be the core element in the administration of criminal justice. In the purest sense of justice, the courts determine the criminal liability of defendants. Ideally they are expected to convict and sentence those found guilty of crimes while ensuring that the innocent are freed without any consequence or burden. The courts are formally required to seek the truth, obtain justice, and maintain the integrity of the government's rule of law.

Once the truth has been determined, criminal courts sentence defendants that are found guilty. Whatever sentence is ordered by the court may not only rehabilitate the offender but also deter others from crime. Once sentencing is accomplished, the corrections component of criminal justice begins to function.

Hypothetically, during the entire criminal court process the rights of the individual are protected at all times. These rights, determined by federal and state constitutional mandates, statutes, and case law, form the foundation for protecting the accused. They include such basic concepts as the right to an attorney, the right to a jury trial, and the right to a speedy trial. Under the Fifth and Fourteenth Amendments of the U.S. Constitution, defendants also have the right to **due process** and the right to be treated with **fundamental fairness.** Under the protective umbrella of due process are included the rights to be present at trial, to be notified of the charges, to have an opportunity to confront hostile witnesses, and to have favorable witnesses appear. Such practices are an integral part of a system and process that seek to balance the interests of the individual and the state.

Unfortunately, the ideal conditions of objectivity, fairness, and equal rights under which the nation's courts should operate are rarely achieved. Although some well-publicized defendants, such as O. J. Simpson, receive their full share of rights and privileges, a significant number are herded through the court system with a minimum of interest or care. Court dockets are too crowded and funds too scarce to grant each defendant the full share of justice. Consequently, a system known as **plea bargaining** has developed: defendants are asked to plead guilty as charged in return for consideration of leniency or mercy.[22] Such "bargain justice" is estimated to occur in more than 90 percent of all criminal trials. Although the criminal court system is founded on the concept of equality before the law, poor and wealthy citizens receive unquestionably different treatment when they are accused of crimes.

Corrections

About 9,000 agencies are devoted to the correction and treatment of convicted offenders. Approximately 3,500 are adult and juvenile probation and parole agencies supervising offenders in the community. There are also about 5,700 residential correctional facilities, consisting of 3,500 jails, 800 prisons, and 1,100 juvenile institutions.

After conviction and sentencing, the offender enters this correctional system. Correctional agencies administer the postjudicatory care given to offenders, which, depending on the seriousness of the crimes and the individual needs of offenders, can range from casual monitoring in the community to solitary confinement in a maximum-security prison.

The most common correctional treatment, **probation,** is a legal disposition that allows the convicted offender to remain in the community, subject to conditions imposed by court order under the supervision of a probation officer. This lets the offender continue working and avoid the crippling effects of incarceration.

A person given a sentence involving incarceration ordinarily is confined to a correctional institution for a specified period. Different types of institutions are used to hold offenders. **Jails** or houses of correction hold offenders convicted of misdemeanors and those awaiting trial or involved in other proceedings, such as grand jury deliberations, arraignments, or preliminary hearings. Many of these institutions for short-term detention are administered by county governments, and consequently, little is done to treat inmates because the personnel and institutions lack the qualifications, services, and resources.

State and federally operated facilities that receive felony offenders sentenced by the criminal courts are called **prisons** or **penitentiaries.** They may be minimum-, medium-, or maximum-security institutions. Prison facilities vary throughout the country. Some have high walls, cells, and large, heterogeneous inmate populations; others offer much freedom, good correctional programs, and small, homogeneous populations.

Most new inmates are first sent to a reception and classification center, where they are given diagnostic evaluations and assigned to institutions that meet their individual needs as much as possible within the system's resources. The diagnostic process in the reception center may range from a physical examination and a single interview to an extensive series of psychiatric tests, orientation sessions, and numerous personal interviews.

Classification is a way of evaluating inmates and assigning them to appropriate placements and activities within the state institutional system.

Because the gap between what correctional programs promise to deliver and their actual performance is often significant, many jurisdictions have instituted community-based correctional facilities. Theses programs emphasize the use of small neighborhood residential centers, halfway houses, prerelease centers, and work release and home furlough programs. Experts believe that only a small percentage of prison inmates require maximum security and that most can be more effectively rehabilitated in community-based facilities. Rather than totally confining offenders in an impersonal, harsh prison, such programs offer them the opportunity to maintain normal family and social relationships while providing rehabilitative services and resources at lower cost to taxpayers.

The last segment of the corrections system, **parole,** is a process whereby an inmate is selected for early release and serves the remainder of the sentence in the community under the supervision of a parole officer. The main purpose of parole is to help the ex-inmate bridge the gap between institutional confinement and a positive adjustment within the community. All parolees must adhere to a set of rules of behavior while they are "on the outside." If these rules are violated, the parole privilege can be terminated (*revoked*), and the parolee will be sent back to the institution to serve the remainder of the sentence.

Other ways an offender may be released from an institution include mandatory release upon completion of the sentence and the *pardon,* a form of executive clemency.

An independent juvenile justice handles minors who violate the law. This system is described in the Policy and Practice in Criminology feature titled "The Juvenile Justice System."

THE PROCESS OF JUSTICE

In addition to viewing the criminal justice system as a collection of agencies, it is possible to see it as a series of decision points through which offenders flow. This process, illustrated in Figure 15.1, begins with initial contact with police and ends with the offenders' reentry into society. At any point in the process, a decision may be made to drop further proceedings and allow the accused back into society without further penalty.

In a classic statement, political scientist Herbert Packer described this process as follows:

> The image that comes to mind is an assembly line conveyor belt down which moves an endless stream of cases, never stopping, carrying them to workers who stand at fixed stations and who perform on each case as it comes by the same small but essential operation that brings it

one step closer to being a finished product, or to exchange the metaphor for the reality, a closed file. The criminal process is seen as a screening process in which each successive stage—pre-arrest investigation, arrest, post-arrest investigation, preparation for trial, or entry of plea, conviction, disposition—involves a series of routinized operations whose success is gauged primarily by their tendency to pass the case along to a successful conclusion. [23]

Although each jurisdiction is somewhat different, a comprehensive view of the processing of a felony offender would probably contain the following decision points:

1. *Initial contact.* The initial contact an offender has with the justice system is usually with police. Police officers may observe a criminal act during their patrol of city streets, parks, or highways. They may also find out about a crime through a citizen or victim complaint. Similarly, an informer can alert them about criminal activity in return for financial or other consideration. Sometimes political officials, such as the mayor or city council, ask police to look into ongoing criminal activity, such as gambling, and during their subsequent investigations police officers encounter an illegal act.

2. *Investigation.* Regardless of whether the police observe, hear of, or receive a complaint about a crime, they may investigate to gather sufficient facts, or evidence, to identify the perpetrator, justify an arrest, and bring the offender to trial. An investigation may take a few minutes, as when patrol officers see a burglary in progress and apprehend the burglar at the scene of the crime. An investigation may also take years to complete and involve numerous investigators. For example, when federal agents tracked and captured Theodore Kaczinski (known as the Unabomber) in 1996, it completed an investigation that had lasted more than a decade.

3. *Arrest.* An **arrest** occurs when the police take a person into custody for allegedly committing a criminal act. An arrest is legal when all of the following conditions exist: (a) the officer believes there is sufficient evidence (**probable cause**) that a crime is being or has been committed and that the suspect committed the crime; (b) the officer deprives the individual of freedom; and (c) the suspect believes that he or she is in the custody of a police officer and cannot voluntarily leave. The police officer is not required to use the word *arrest* or any similar word to initiate an arrest; nor does the officer first have to bring the suspect to the police station. For all practical purposes, a person who has been deprived of liberty is under arrest. Arrests can be made at the scene of a crime or after a warrant is issued by a magistrate.

4. *Custody.* After arrest, the suspect remains in police custody. The person may be taken to the police station to be fingerprinted and photographed and to have personal information recorded—a procedure popularly referred to as *booking.* Witnesses may be brought in to

Figure 15.1 The Critical Stages in the Justice Process

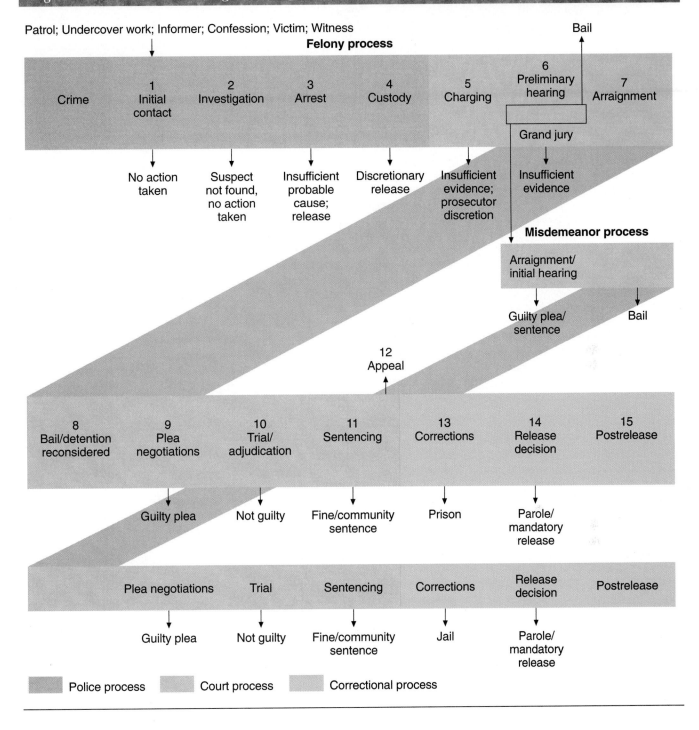

Patrol; Undercover work; Informer; Confession; Victim; Witness

Felony process

view the suspect (in a **lineup**), and further evidence may be gathered on the case. Suspects may be interrogated by police officers to get their side of the story, they may be asked to sign a confession of guilt, or they may be asked to identify others involved in the crime. The law allows suspects to have their lawyers present when police conduct in-custody interrogations.

5. *Complaint/charging.* After police turn the evidence in a case over to the prosecutor, who represents the state at any criminal proceedings, a decision will be made whether to file a complaint, information, or bill of indictment with the court having jurisdiction over the case. **Complaints** are used in misdemeanors; **information** and **indictment** are employed in felonies.

The Juvenile Justice System

Independent of but interrelated with the adult criminal justice system, the juvenile justice system deals with juveniles who commit crimes (*delinquents*) and those who are incorrigible, truants, runaways, or unmanageable (*status offenders*).

The policy of treating juveniles who commit criminal acts separately from adults is relatively new. Until the late nineteenth century, youthful criminals were tried in adult courts and punished in adult institutions. However, nineteenth-century reformers, today known as "child savers," lobbied to separate young offenders from serious adult criminals. Their efforts were rewarded when the first separate juvenile court was set up in Chicago in 1899. Over the next 20 years, most other states created separate juvenile court and correctional systems.

At first the juvenile system was based on the philosophy of *parens patriae.* This meant that the state was acting in the best interests of children in trouble who could not care for themselves. Under the *parens patriae* doctrine, delinquents and status offenders (sometimes called "wayward minors" or "children in need of supervision") were tried in informal juvenile court hearings without the benefit of counsel or other procedural rights. The juvenile correctional system, designed for treatment rather than punishment, was usually located in small institutions referred to as *schools* or *camps.* (The first juvenile reform school opened in 1847 in Massachusetts.) After the separate juvenile justice system developed, almost all incarcerated youths were maintained in separate juvenile institutions that stressed individualized treatment, education, and counseling.

Critics charged that the juvenile justice system's reliance on informal procedure often violated a child's constitutional rights to due process of law. It seemed unfair to place a minor child, tried without benefit of an attorney or other legal safeguards granted adult defendants, in a remote incarceration facility. In the 1960s the Supreme Court revolutionized the juvenile justice system when, in a series of cases—the most important being *In re Gault*—it granted procedural and due process rights to juveniles at trial. The Court recognized that many youths were receiving long sentences without the benefit of counsel and other Fifth and Sixth Amendment rights and that many institutions did not carry out their treatment role. Consequently, the juvenile justice process became similar to the adult process.

In the 1970s, because of the stigma placed on youths by the "delinquent" label, efforts ware made to remove or divert youths from the official justice process and place them in alternative, community-based treatment programs. One state, Massachusetts, even closed its secure correctional facilities and placed all youths, no matter how serious their crimes, in community programs.

Today concern over juvenile violence has caused some critics to question the juvenile justice system's treatment philosophy. Some states, such as New York, have liberalized their procedures for trying serious juvenile offenders in the adult system, consequently making them eligible for incarceration in adult prisons. The general trend has been to remove as many nonviolent and status offenders as possible from secure placements in juvenile institutions and at the same time to lengthen the sentences of serious offenders or to move such offenders to the adult system. Kids who are *waived* to the adult system face long prison sentences and even the death penalty. Today an estimated 27,000 juveniles are tried in criminal court by prosecutors' offices each year.

Some of the similarities and differences between the adult and juvenile justice systems are listed in Table A. Although there are many similarities between rights and privileges in both systems, there are some important differences. Juveniles can be taken into custody and incarcerated for acts (status offenses) made illegal because of their age, such as being truant from school or running away from home. They do not have the right to a jury trial, and juvenile hearings are closed to the public. However, juveniles who are waived to the adult court can be put in prisons and are even subject to the death penalty. These differences reflect the effort to protect adolescents from the stigma of a criminal label. Note that juveniles are never arrested or convicted; they are taken into custody and adjudicated.

The juvenile justice system is a vast enterprise. Juvenile courts process more than 1.5 million delinquents each year, an increase of more than 40 percent since 1985. About 320,000 youths are annually placed in juvenile detention centers awaiting trial. Each year about 265,000 delinquent youths are placed on probation and another 150,000 are placed in some form of secure treatment center. An additional 125,000 status offenders are handled by the court, 11,000 of whom are placed out of their homes. The heavy influx of youths into the system has created crowding problems in detention and other residential facilities.

CRITICAL THINKING

1. A 14-year-old boy commits a grisly murder. Should he be tried as an adult even though he is so young, or does his crime warrant punitive action?

Table A Similarities and Differences Between Juvenile and Adult Justice Systems

SIMILARITIES

Police officers, judges, and correctional personnel use discretion in decision making in both the adult and the juvenile systems.

The right to receive *Miranda* warnings applies to juveniles as well as to adults.

Juveniles and adults are protected from prejudicial lineups or other identification procedures.

Similar procedural safeguards protect juveniles and adults when they admit guilt.

Prosecutors and defense attorneys play equally critical roles in juvenile and adult advocacy.

Juveniles and adults have the right to counsel at most key stages of the court process.

Pretrial motions are available in juvenile and criminal court proceedings.

Negotiations and plea bargaining exist for juvenile and adult offenders.

Children and adults have the right to a hearing and an appeal.

The standard of evidence in juvenile delinquency adjudications, as in adult criminal trials, is proof beyond a reasonable doubt.

Juveniles and adults can be placed on probation by the court.

Both juveniles and adults can be placed in pretrial detention facilities.

Juveniles and adults can be kept in detention without bail if they are considered dangerous.

After trial, juveniles and adults can be placed in community treatment programs.

DIFFERENCES

The primary purpose of juvenile procedures is protection and treatment. With adults, the aim is to punish the guilty.

Age determines the jurisdiction of the juvenile court. The nature of the offense determines jurisdiction in the adult system.

Juveniles can be apprehended for acts that would not be criminal if they were committed by an adult (status offenses).

Juvenile proceedings are not considered criminal; adult proceedings are.

Juvenile court procedures are generally informal and private. Those of adult courts are more formal and are open to the public.

Courts cannot release identifying information about a juvenile to the media, but they must release information about an adult.

Parents are highly involved in the juvenile process but not in the adult process.

The standard of arrest is more stringent for adults than for juveniles.

Juveniles are released into parental custody. Adults are generally given the opportunity for bail.

Juveniles have no constitutional right to a jury trial. Adults have this right.

Juveniles can be searched in school without probable cause or a warrant.

A juvenile's record is sealed when the age of majority is reached. The record of an adult is permanent.

A juvenile court cannot sentence juveniles to county jails or state prisons; these are reserved for adults.

There is no death penalty in the juvenile justice system. However, the U.S. Supreme Court has declared that the Eighth Amendment does not prohibit the death penalty for crimes committed by juveniles ages 16 and 17.

---

2. What actions would you take if you could reorganize the juvenile justice system? Would you remove all nonviolent offenders from the system and have them treated by social service agencies? Would you worry that juvenile justice processing might stigmatize young offenders and enmesh them in crime?

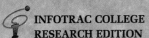

INFOTRAC COLLEGE RESEARCH EDITION

What is the future of the juvenile justice system? To find out, read:

Judge David B. Mitchell. Congress needs to consult profession before enacting juvenile justice reform. *Corrections Today* 60 (1998): 20–23.

Jeffrey M. Jenson, Matthew O. Howard. Youth crime, public policy, and practice in the juvenile justice system: recent trends and needed reforms. *Social Work* 43 (1998): 324–335.

Barry C. Feld. Abolish the juvenile court: youthfulness, criminal responsibility, and sentencing policy. *Journal of Criminal Law and Criminology* 88 (1997): 68–136.

Source: Larry Siegel and Joseph Senna, *Juvenile Delinquency* (Belmont, Calif.: Wadsworth/West, 2000); Carol J. DeFrances and Greg W. Steadman, *Prosecutors in State Courts, 1996* (Washington, D.C.: Bureau of Justice Statistics, 1998); Jeffrey Butts, *Offenders in Juvenile Court, 1994* (Washington, D.C.: Office of Juvenile Justice and Delinquency Prevention, 1996).

Each is a charging document asking the court to bring a case forward to be tried.

CONNECTIONS

The decision of whether to charge an offender with a criminal offense is a complex one that involves judges, prosecutors, defense attorneys, and the accused. The process of charging will be discussed further in Chapter 17.

6. *Preliminary hearing—grand jury.* Because it is a tremendous personal and financial burden to stand trial for a serious felony crime, the U.S. Constitution provides that the state must first prove to an impartial hearing board that there is probable cause that the accused committed the crime and, therefore, that there is sufficient reason to try the person as charged. In about half the states and in the federal system, the decision of whether to bring a suspect to trial (indictment) is made by a group of citizens brought together to form a **grand jury.** The grand jury considers the case in a closed hearing, in which only the prosecutor presents evidence. In the remaining states, an information is filed before an impartial lower-court judge, who decides whether the case should go forward. This is known as a **preliminary hearing** or **probable cause hearing.** The defendant may appear at a preliminary hearing and dispute the prosecutor's charges. During either procedure, if the prosecution's evidence is accepted as factual and sufficient, the suspect is called to stand trial for the crime. These procedures are not used for misdemeanors because of their lesser importance and seriousness.

7. *Arraignment.* An **arraignment** brings the accused before the court that will actually try the case. There defendants are read the formal charges and informed of their constitutional rights (such as the right to legal counsel), have their bail considered, and have the trial date set.

8. *Bail or detention.* If the bail decision has not been considered previously, it is evaluated at arraignment. **Bail** is a money bond, the amount of which is set by judicial authority; it is intended to ensure the presence of suspects at trial while allowing them their freedom until that time. Suspects who do not show up for trial forfeit their bail. Suspects who cannot afford bail or whose cases are so serious that a judge refuses them bail (usually restricted to capital cases) must remain in detention until trial. In most instances, this means an extended stay in the county jail. Many jurisdictions allow defendants awaiting trial to be released on their own recognizance, without bail, if they are stable members of the community.

9. *Plea bargaining.* After arraignment, it is common for the prosecutor to meet with the defendant and his or her attorney to discuss a possible guilty plea arrangement. If a bargain can be struck, the accused pleads guilty as charged, thus ending the criminal trial process. In return for the plea, the prosecutor may reduce charges, request a lenient sentence, or grant the defendant some other consideration.

10. *Adjudication.* If a plea bargain cannot be arranged, a criminal trial takes place. This involves a full-scale inquiry into the facts of the case before a judge, a jury, or both. The defendant can be found guilty or not guilty, or the jury can fail to reach a decision (**hung jury**), thereby leaving the case unresolved and open for a possible retrial.

11. *Disposition.* After a criminal trial, a defendant who is found guilty as charged is sentenced by the presiding judge. **Disposition** usually involves a fine, a term of community supervision (probation), a period of incarceration in a penal institution, or some combination of these penalties. In the most serious capital cases, it is possible to sentence the offender to death. Dispositions are usually made after a presentencing investigation is conducted by the court's probation staff. After disposition, the defendant may appeal the conviction to a higher court.

12. *Postconviction remedies.* After conviction, if the defendant believes he or she was not treated fairly by the justice system, the individual may appeal the conviction. An appellate court reviews trial procedures in order to determine whether an error was made. It considers such questions as whether evidence was used properly, whether the judge conducted the trial in an approved fashion, whether the jury was representative, and whether the attorneys in the case acted appropriately. If the court rules that the appeal has merit, it can hold that the defendant be given a new trial or, in some instances, order his or her outright release. Outright release can be ordered when the state prosecuted the case in violation of the double jeopardy clause of the U.S. Constitution or when it violated the defendant's right to a speedy trial.

13. *Correctional treatment.* Offenders who are found guilty and are formally sentenced come under the jurisdiction of correctional authorities. They may serve a term of community supervision under control of the county probation department; they may have a term in a community correctional center; or they may be incarcerated in a large penal institution.

14. *Release.* At the end of the correctional sentence, the offender is released into the community. Most incarcerated offenders are granted parole before the expiration of the maximum term given them by the court and therefore finish their prison sentences in the community under supervision of the parole department. Offenders sentenced to community supervision, if successful, simply finish their terms and resume their lives unsupervised by court authorities.

15. *Postrelease/aftercare.* After termination of correctional treatment, the offender must successfully re-

After termination of correctional treatment, the offender must make a successful return to the community. This adjustment is usually aided by corrections department staff members who attempt to counsel the offender through the period of reentry into society. The offender may be asked to spend some time in a community correctional center, such as the one shown here, which acts as a bridge between a secure treatment facility and absolute freedom.

turn to the community. This adjustment is usually aided by corrections department staff members, who attempt to counsel the offender through the period of reentry into society. The offender may be asked to spend some time in a community correctional center, which acts as a bridge between a secure treatment facility and absolute freedom. Offenders may find that their conviction has cost them some personal privileges, such as the right to hold certain kinds of jobs. These privileges may be returned by court order once the offenders have proven their trustworthiness and willingness to adjust to society's rules. Successful completion of the postrelease period marks the end of the criminal justice process.

Going Through the System

At every stage of the process, a decision is made by an agency of criminal justice whether to send the case farther down the line or "kick it" from the system (see Table 15.1). For example, an investigation is pursued for a few days, and if a suspect is not identified, the case is dropped. A prosecutor decides not to charge a person in police custody because he or she believes there is insufficient evidence to sustain a finding of guilt. A grand jury fails to hand down indictments because it finds that the prosecutor presented insufficient evidence. A jury fails to convict the accused because it doubts his or her guilt. A parole board decides to release one inmate but denies another's request for early

Table 15.1 The Interrelationship of the Criminal Justice System and the Criminal Justice Process	
THE SYSTEM: AGENCIES OF CRIME CONTROL	**THE PROCESS**
1. Police	1. Contact
	2. Investigation
	3. Arrest
	4. Custody
2. Prosecution and defense	5. Complaint/charging
	6. Grand jury/preliminary hearing
	7. Arraignment
	8. Bail/detention
	9. Plea negotiations
3. Court	10. Adjudication
	11. Disposition
	12. Appeal/postconviction remedies
4. Corrections	13. Correction
	14. Release
	15. Postrelease

release. These decisions transform the identity of the individual passing through the system from an accused to a defendant, convicted criminal, inmate, and ex-con. Conversely, if decision makers take no action, people accused of crime can return to their daily lives with minimal interference in their lives or identities. Their friends and neighbors may not even know that they were once the subject of criminal investigation. Decision making and discretion mark each stage of the system.

The "Wedding Cake" Model

The traditional model of the criminal justice process depicts it as a uniform series of decision points through which cases flow, each characterized by uniform procedures and rights. Yet many experts view this model as fanciful; they argue that the justice system is a political entity that actually works much more subjectively. Some cases receive the full attention of the law, but most are settled with a minimum of legal and procedural due process.

Samuel Walker, a justice historian, suggests that the criminal justice process is best conceived of as a four-layer cake, depicted in Figure 15.2.[24] The relatively small first layer of Walker's model is made up of the celebrated cases involving the famous, wealthy, or powerful, such as O. J. Simpson, Mike Tyson, Ivan Boesky, and William Kennedy Smith, or the not-so-powerful who victimize a famous person, such as Sirhan Sirhan (Robert Kennedy's assassin) and John Hinckley (President Ronald Reagan's would-be assassin). Also included within this category are unknown criminals whose cases become celebrated either because they are brought before the Supreme Court for some procedural irregularity, such as those of Ernesto Miranda and Clarence Gideon, or because they involve media events, such as the case of British nanny Louise Woodward, accused of killing the baby she was hired to care for.

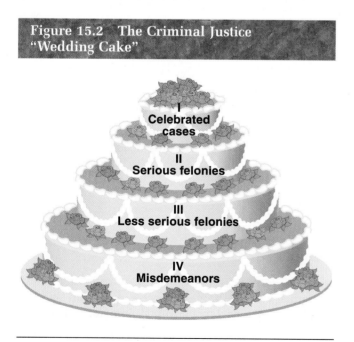

Figure 15.2   The Criminal Justice "Wedding Cake"

I
Celebrated cases

II
Serious felonies

III
Less serious felonies

IV
Misdemeanors

Source: Based on Samuel Walker, *Sense and Nonsense about Crime* (Monterey, Calif.: Brooks/Cole, 1985).

People in the first layer of the criminal justice wedding cake receive a great deal of public attention, and their cases usually involve the full panoply of criminal justice procedures, including famous defense attorneys, jury trials, and elaborate appeals. Because the public hears so much about these cases, they believe them to be a norm; but they do not represent how the system really operates.

The second and third layers of the cake are made up of serious felonies encountered daily in urban jurisdictions, such as robberies, burglaries, rapes, and homicides. Those that fall in the second layer do so by virtue of their seriousness, the prior record of the defendant, and the defendant's relationship to the victim. For example, police treat a burglary in which thousands of dollars are stolen differently than a simple break-in that netted the criminal a stereo.[25] Similarly, an assault on an affluent merchant is perceived by criminal justice decision makers as more serious than the punching of a friend during a fraternity beer party. The more serious second-layer crimes are likely to be prosecuted to the fullest extent of the law, and if convicted, these offenders receive lengthy prison sentences. In contrast, felonies relegated to the third layer because the amount of money taken is relatively small or the damage done trivial usually receive an outright dismissal, a plea bargain, a reduction in charges, or a probationary sentence.

The fourth layer of the cake is made up of the millions of misdemeanors, such as disorderly conduct, shoplifting, public drunkenness, passing bad checks, and minor assault. These are handled by the lower criminal courts in assembly-line fashion. Few defendants insist on exercising their constitutional rights because the delay would cost them valuable time and money. Because the typical penalty is a small fine, everyone wants to get the case over with. Malcolm Feeley's study of the lower court in New Haven, Connecticut, found that in a sense, the experience of going to court is the real punishment in a misdemeanor case; few (4.9 percent) of the cases involved any jail time.[26]

Is There a Criminal Justice Wedding Cake?   The wedding cake model is an intriguing alternative to the traditional criminal justice flow chart. According to Walker's view, the outcome of cases in the criminal justice system is a function of how they are evaluated by decision makers. Within each layer, there is a high degree of consistency; regardless of the size of the jurisdiction, high-profile cases get serious treatment that differs markedly from the attention and time given to run-of-the-mill felonies.

Support for the wedding cake model comes from research showing that the criminal justice system acts like a funnel in which a great majority of cases are screened out before trial. As Figure 15.3 shows, at each stage of the system cases are dismissed, and relatively few reach trial. Those that do are more likely to be handled with a

Figure 15.3   The Criminal Justice "Funnel"

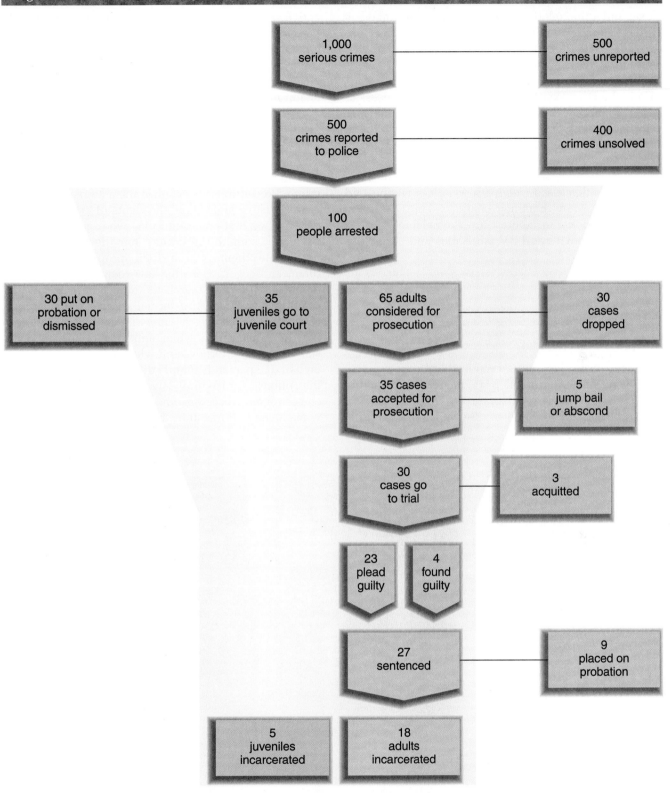

Source: Brian Reaves and Pheny Smith, *Felony Defendants in Large Urban Counties, 1992* (Washington, D.C.: Bureau of Justice Statistics, 1995).

plea bargain than with a criminal trial. The funnel indicates that the justice system does not treat all felonies alike; only the relatively few serious cases make it through to the end of the formal process.[27]

The Walker model helps us realize that public opinion about criminal justice is often formed on the basis of what happens in a few celebrated cases. In fact, criminal justice experts commonly view the process as being dominated by judges, prosecutors, and defense attorneys who work in concert to get cases processed; this spirit of cooperation is referred to as the *courtroom work group.* The tired assistant district attorney, irritable judge, and overworked public defender who get together to settle cases involving lower-class victims and offenders are now common characters in TV shows, films, and books. In contrast are the celebrated cases that inspire movies and TV miniseries and attract top criminal lawyers.

CRIMINAL JUSTICE AND THE RULE OF LAW

For many years U.S. courts exercised little control over the operations of criminal justice agencies, believing that their actions were not an area of judicial concern. This policy is referred to as the *hands-off doctrine.*

However, in the 1960s, under the guidance of Chief Justice Earl Warren, the U.S. Supreme Court became more active in the affairs of the justice system. Today each component of the justice system is closely supervised by state and federal courts. In this section we review the influence of the rule of law on criminal justice agencies and discuss how it affects daily operations and decision making.

Procedural Laws

The law of criminal procedure guarantees citizens certain rights and privileges when they are accused of crime. Procedural laws control the actions of the agencies of justice and define the rights of criminal defendants. They first come into play when people are suspected of committing crimes and the police wish to investigate them, search their property, interrogate them, and so on. Here the law dictates, for example, whether police can search the homes of or interrogate unwilling suspects. If a formal charge is filed, procedural laws guide pretrial and trial activities; for example, they determine when and if people can obtain state-financed attorneys and when they can be released on bail. If a person is found guilty of committing a criminal offense, procedural laws guide the posttrial and correctional processes; for example, they determine when a conviction can be appealed.

Because the makeup of the Supreme Court changes under various presidential administrations and procedural laws are subject to different interpretations, Court decision making remains fluid. Here Chief Justice William Rehnquist is seen conferring with fellow justices Sandra Day O'Connor (right) and Ruth Bader Ginsburg (left).

Procedural laws have several different sources. Most important are the first 10 amendments of the U.S. Constitution, ratified in 1791 and generally called the **Bill of Rights.** The original Constitution, ratified in 1788, structured government and set out the rights and duties of its executive, legislative, and judicial branches. However, aware of the abuses people had been subjected to by royal decree in England and its colonies, the framers of the Constitution wanted to ensure that the national government could not usurp the personal rights of citizens. Therefore, the Bill of Rights guaranteed, among other things, the right of the people to practice the religion of their choice, have freedom of speech and press, be secure in their homes from unwarranted intrusion by government agents, and be protected against cruel punishments, such as torture.

The guarantees of freedom contained in the Bill of Rights initially applied only to the federal government and did not affect the individual states. In 1868 the Fourteenth Amendment made the first 10 amendments to the Constitution binding on the state governments. However, it has remained the duty of state and federal court systems to interpret constitutional law and develop a body of case law that spells out the exact procedural rights to which a person is entitled. For example, the Sixth Amendment states that a person has the right to be represented by legal counsel at a criminal trial. This right once had little meaning because many criminal defendants were indigent and could not afford to pay for their legal defense. Then, in 1963, the U.S. Supreme Court interpreted the Sixth Amendment to mean that all people accused of felonies had the right to counsel; if they could not afford an attorney, the state had to provide the funds to hire one for them. Thus it is the U.S. Supreme Court that interprets the Constitution and sets out the procedural laws that must be followed by the lower federal and state courts. If the Supreme Court has not ruled on a procedural issue, then the lower courts are free to interpret the Constitution as they see fit.

In 1953 Earl Warren became the chief justice of the U.S. Supreme Court; under his leadership, the Supreme Court became quite active in justice issues. The Warren Court granted many new rights to those accused of crimes and imposed specific guidelines on the policies of police, courts, and correctional services to ensure that due process of law would be maintained. Under Warren's successors, first Warren Berger and current Chief Justice William Rehnquist, the Court has moved somewhat more cautiously in granting additional rights; and in some areas, such as capital punishment and prisoners' rights, the Court has reversed the trend toward liberalism established by the Warren Court. Of the criminal justice issues the courts handle, few are as important and have as much influence on the justice system as the concepts of *due process* and the *exclusionary rule.* Therefore, these legal issues will be reviewed here in some detail.

Due Process

The concept of *due process* is mentioned in the Fifth (where it is applied to the federal government) and Fourteenth (where it is applied to the states) Amendments of the U.S. Constitution. It is usually divided into substantive and procedural areas. The substantive aspects generally determine whether a statute is fair, reasonable, and appropriate use of legal power. The concept of substantive due process was used extensively in the 1930s and 1940s to invalidate minimum-wage standards, price-fixing, and employment restriction statutes. Today it is used more sparingly; for example, it may be employed to hold that criminal statutes dealing with disorderly conduct, capital punishment, or a ban on pornography may be unconstitutional because they are arbitrary, vague, or unreasonable.

Much more important today are the procedural aspects of due process, which are the rules and procedures in the legal system designed to protect individual rights. The objectives of due process help define the term even more explicitly. Due process seeks to ensure that no person will be deprived of life, liberty, or property without notice of charges, assistance from legal counsel, a hearing, and an opportunity to confront accusers. Basically, due process is intended to guarantee that functional fairness exists in each individual case. This doctrine of fairness as expressed in due process of the law is guaranteed under both the Fifth and Fourteenth Amendments.

Abstract definitions are only one aspect of due process. Much more significant are the procedures that give meaning to due process in the everyday practices of the criminal justice system. In this regard, due process provides numerous procedural safeguards for the offender; some of the most important are listed in Table 15.2.

Exactly what constitutes due process in a specific case depends on the facts of the case, the federal and state constitutional and statutory provisions, previous

Table 15.2 Important Elements of Procedural Due Process

- Notice of charges
- A formal hearing
- The right to counsel or other representation
- The opportunity to respond to charges in a timely manner
- The opportunity to confront and cross-examine witnesses and accusers
- The privilege to be free from self-incrimination
- The opportunity to present one's own witnesses
- A decision made on the basis of substantial evidence and facts produced at an open and impartial hearing
- A written statement of the reasons for the decision
- An appellate review procedure
- Freedom from illegal searches and seizures

court decisions, and the ideas and principles that society considers important.[28] Justice Felix Frankfurter emphasized this point in *Rochin v. California* (1952) when he wrote,

> Due process of law requires an evaluation based on a disinterested inquiry, pursued in the spirit of science on a balanced order or facts, exactly and clearly stated, on the detached consideration of conflicting claims . . . on a judgement not ad hoc and episodic but duly mindful of reconciling the needs both of continuity and of change in a progressive society.[29]

Both the elements and the definition of due process seem to be flexible and constantly changing. For example, due process at one time did not require a formal hearing for parole revocation, but today it does. Before 1968 juvenile offenders did not have the right to an attorney at their adjudication; counsel is now required in the juvenile court system. Thus the interpretations of due process of law reflect what society deems fair and just at a particular time and in a particular place. The degree of loss suffered by the individual (victim or offender) balanced against the state's interest also determines which and how many due process requirements are ordinarily applied. When the accused person's freedom is at stake in the criminal justice system, all applicable due process rights are usually granted; in other cases due process may be modified.

Changing Concepts of Due Process   In recent years the concept of due process as applied by the courts seems to be changing. The balance of fairness is shifting away from the criminal, and emphasis is instead being placed on the needs of the states to protect their citizens. The rights of both those accused of crime and those convicted of crime have been curtailed. For example, police have been given a freer hand in questioning suspects, searching for evidence, and obtaining search warrants. In a 1991 case, *Arizona v. Fulminante,* the U.S. Supreme Court ruled that convictions would not be automatically overturned even if it is shown that police officers used coercion to obtain confessions. The Court ruled that it is possible that a coerced confession could be "harmless error" if there were other evidence sufficient to convict the suspect.[30] In a 1996 case, *Whren, et al., v. United States,* the Supreme Court ruled that police are allowed to stop motorists for traffic violations even if their real motive is to search the vehicle for drugs.[31] The *Whren* case makes it easier for police to stop and search suspicious vehicles. Similarly, the Court has allowed the resumption of the death penalty with fewer judicial restraints. In *McCleskey v. Zant,* the Court limited the ability of death row inmates to appeal their cases to federal courts, paving the way for faster turnover in capital punishment cases.[32]

These and similar cases give weight to the charge that the Supreme Court has shifted the balance of due process away from the criminal offender and embraced a crime control emphasis. The Court may be responding to recent victim surveys, which indicate that more than half of all Americans believe the justice system favors defendants' rights over the rights of crime victims.[33] However, the basic concept of due process has a secure place in our legal system. Freedom from self-incrimination, the right to legal representation at all stages of the justice system, a fair hearing and trial, and sentencing review are immutable rights. Although courts continue to redefine rights, they do so in the spirit of granting fairness to the criminal defendant without sacrificing the public interest.

In this context, the focus has turned to the exclusionary rule, considered by some to be a cornerstone of individual freedom and by others to be a serious impediment to public safety.

The Exclusionary Rule

If constitutional rights are to be anything more than pious pronouncements, some measurable consequence must be attached to their violation. It would be intolerable if, for example, the guarantee against unreasonable search and seizure could be violated without practical consequences.[34]

The foundation of the **exclusionary rule** is contained in the Fourth Amendment of the Constitution, which states,

> The right of the people to be secure in their persons, houses, papers, and effects, against unreasonable searches and seizures, shall not be violated and no warrant shall issue, but upon probable cause, supported by oath or affirmation, and particularly describing the place to be searched, and the persons or things to be seized.

The primary function of the Fourth Amendment is to protect the individual against an illegal arrest and prevent illegal searches and seizures of a person's possessions. This means that police must follow certain guidelines in searching for and seizing evidence. As a rule, they must have a proper search warrant that is obtained from a court officer after evidence is presented that a crime has occurred and there is probable cause to believe that the person or place to be searched is involved in it; the police cannot act arbitrarily.

Over the years, the Supreme Court has articulated exceptions to the search warrant rule. In other words, there are times, such as when a suspect volunteers to be searched, that a warrant need not be obtained. The standard as stated in the Fourth Amendment is that of reasonableness, and the Supreme Court has gone to great lengths to explain and interpret what this means. In doing so, the Court has balanced the individual's right to privacy, protected by the Fourth Amendment, with the right of the public to be protected against crime. Consequently, a large body of case law describes how searches are to be conducted, when police can seize evidence, when search warrants are needed, and so on.

The Fourth Amendment clearly states that an individual's right against unreasonable searches and seizures is to be protected. However, for many years, evidence obtained in violation of the Fourth Amendment was admitted in criminal trials even though it should have been considered illegal. In 1914 the Supreme Court rectified this injustice in the case of *Weeks v. United States.*[35] The defendant, Weeks, was accused of the federal violation of using the mails for illegal purposes. The evidence on which he was convicted was acquired through a search of his room without a valid search warrant. The Supreme Court ruled that in a federal criminal trial, evidence acquired through an unreasonable search and seizure must be excluded; it can be neither mentioned nor used at trial. Thus the exclusionary rule was established.

The ruling in *Weeks* applied only to the federal government. The states were still free to admit evidence obtained by unreasonable searches and seizures. It was not until 1961, in the case of *Mapp v. Ohio,* that the Supreme Court applied the exclusionary rule to the states.[36] Thus, for the first time, the Supreme Court required that state law enforcement employees follow federal constitutional standards.

The exclusionary rule has been one of the most controversial aspects of justice system legal control. Its opponents argue that it permits the guilty to go free if the police err in handling a case. The rights of honest citizens and society as a whole are threatened because of arbitrary court rulings. The rule weakens the power of the justice system to deter crime because victims and witnesses are reluctant to come forward for fear that an obviously guilty defendant will be released on a technicality.

Those who favor the exclusionary rule believe that it is one of the cornerstones of our freedom and that it protects us from becoming a police state in which law enforcement agents are free to use any means at their disposal to investigate crime. Without the exclusionary rule, houses could be broken into, phones tapped, people searched, and cars stopped—with impunity. The exclusionary rule separates our society from those "evil" totalitarian regimes that we read about in the newspapers.

In sum, the exclusionary rule means that evidence judged to be improperly obtained by police through illegal interrogation of suspects or searches of their persons and property cannot be used (or even mentioned) against them in a court of law. It is as if the evidence did not exist.

Shaping the Rule   Over the past 20 years, the Court has created some important exceptions to the exclusionary rule. In *Illinois v. Gates,* the Supreme Court allowed the use of a search warrant that had been obtained upon consideration of information contained in an anonymous letter to police; prior to *Gates,* warrants had to be based on verifiable information.[37] In a 1998 case, *Knowles v. Iowa,* a police officer stopped a car and gave the driver (Knowles) a speeding ticket. The officer then conducted a full search of the car without either Knowles's consent or probable cause that a crime had occurred. Working on a hunch, the officer found marijuana and a "pot pipe" and arrested Knowles, who was later found guilty on drug charges. The Supreme Court overturned the conviction on the grounds that searching a car that has been stopped for a traffic violation is unreasonable because there is little evidence that the driver presents a danger to the officer or that the car contains evidence of a crime. Although Knowles did in fact have drugs in his possession, his conviction was overturned because the officer's actions violated the exclusionary rule.[38]

Does the Rule Matter?   There seems little doubt that the nation's courts are now granting the police and other agencies of justice greater leeway in conducting their business, even if it means restricting the rights of criminal suspects. But how much will these measures actually affect the justice system? Studies indicate that exclusionary rule violations occur rather infrequently:[39] only 1 to 2 percent of all criminal cases are rejected because police made a technical legal error resulting in the invocation of the exclusionary rule. Only in narcotics-related offenses were a significant number of cases terminated because of exclusionary rule violations, and the percentages were smaller than might be expected—under 3 percent in the jurisdictions surveyed. Police appear more apt to illegally seize evidence in narcotics cases because there is usually no victim or complaining party to help them obtain proper search warrants. The legal "cost" of the exclusionary rule appears to be slight.[40]

Although abolishing or severely limiting the exclusionary rule might have relatively little effect on the justice system, the rule itself is of great symbolic value. It stands for the right to privacy and the primacy of the individual over the state. Even if relatively few cases are thrown out of court on exclusionary rule violations, knowing of its existence places law enforcement agents on notice: obey constitutional limitations and respect the individual's right to privacy, or pay the consequences in court. The exclusionary rule must be evaluated not by those few cases that come under public scrutiny but by the millions of others in which police power is limited by the rule's influence.

In the following chapters the effect of the law on the individual components of the justice system is reviewed in greater detail.

CONCEPTS OF JUSTICE

Many justice system operations are controlled by the rule of law, but they are also influenced by the various philosophies or viewpoints held by its practitioners and policymakers. These, in turn, have been influenced by criminological theory and research. Knowledge about crime, its causes, and its control has significantly affected perceptions of how criminal justice should be managed.

Not surprisingly, many competing views of justice exist simultaneously in our culture. Those in favor of one position or another try to win public opinion to their side, hoping to influence legislative, judicial, or administrative decision making. Over the years, different philosophical viewpoints tend to predominate, only to fall into disfavor as programs based on their principles fail to prove effective.

This section briefly discusses the most important concepts of criminal justice.

Crime Control Model

Those espousing the crime control model believe that the overriding purpose of the justice system is to protect the public, deter criminal behavior, and incapacitate known criminals. Those who embrace its principles view the justice system as a barrier between destructive criminal elements and conventional society. Speedy, efficient justice, unencumbered by legal red tape and followed by punishment designed to fit the crime, is the goal of advocates of the crime control model. Its disciples promote such policies as increasing the size of police forces, maximizing the use of discretion, building more prisons, using the death penalty, and reducing legal controls on the justice system. They point to evidence showing that as many as 30,000 violent criminals, 62,000 drunk drivers, 46,000 drug dealers, and several hundred thousand other criminals go free *every year* in cases dropped because police believe they had violated the suspects' *Miranda* rights.[41] They lobby for the abolition of the exclusionary rule and the *Miranda* decision and applaud when the Supreme Court hands down rulings that increase police power in cases like *Ohio v. Robinette* (1996), which held that police do not have to tell motorists they have stopped for a traffic violation that they are actually free to go before asking permission to search the car.[42]

The crime control philosophy emphasizes protecting society and compensating victims. The criminal is responsible for his or her actions, has broken faith with society, and has chosen to violate the law for reasons of

anger, greed, revenge, and so forth. Therefore, money spent should be directed not at making criminals more comfortable but on increasing the efficiency of police to apprehend them and the courts to effectively try them. As David Garland suggests, criminal punishment has only a limited ability to change the wicked; instead it can enforce cultural values and express the conviction that crime will not be tolerated. Punishment symbolizes the legitimate social order and the power societies have to regulate behavior and punish those who break social rules.[43]

Crime Control Policies The crime control philosophy has become a dominant force in American justice. Fear of crime in the 1960s and 1970s was coupled with a growing skepticism about the effectiveness of rehabilitation efforts. A number of important reviews claimed that treatment and rehabilitation efforts directed at known criminals just did not work.[44] The lack of clear evidence that criminals can be successfully treated has produced a climate in which conservative, hard-line solutions to the crime problem are being sought. The results of this swing can be seen in such phenomena as the increasing use of the death penalty, erosion of the exclusionary rule, prison overcrowding, and attacks on the insanity defense. In the past few years a number of states, including Tennessee, Utah, Iowa, Ohio, and West Virginia, have changed their juvenile codes, making it easier to try juveniles as adults. Other states have expanded their control over ex-offenders, such as by requiring registration of sex offenders. New York has passed a death penalty statute, and other states, including Delaware and South Dakota, have expanded the circumstances under which a person could be eligible for the death penalty.[45]

Can such measures deter crime? There is some evidence that strict crime control measures can in fact have a deterrent effect.[46] For example, research indicates that people arrested for domestic violence violations who receive more severe sentences (like jail) are less likely to repeat their offenses than those who receive more lenient treatment (like probation).[47] In a similar fashion, a 1997 study by the National Center for Policy Analysis uncovered a direct correlation between the probability of imprisonment for a particular crime and a subsequent decline in the rate of that crime.[48]

The probability of going to prison for murder increased 17 percent between 1993 and 1997, and the murder rate dropped 23 percent during that period; robbery declined 21 percent as the probability of prison increased 14 percent. These data support the crime control model.

Justice Model

According to the justice model, it is futile to rehabilitate criminals because treatment programs both are ineffective and deny people equal protection under the law.[49] It is unfair if two people commit the same crime but receive different sentences because only one is receptive to treatment. The consequence is a sense of injustice in the criminal justice system.

Beyond these problems, justice model advocates question the crime control perspective's reliance on deterrence: is it fair to punish or incarcerate based on predictions of what offenders will do in the future or on whether others will be deterred by their punishment? Justice model advocates also are concerned with unfairness in the system, such as racism and discrimination, that causes sentencing disparity and unequal treatment before the law.[50]

As an alternative, the justice model calls for fairness in criminal procedure. This would require **determinate sentencing,** in which all offenders in a particular crime category would receive the same sentence. Prisons would be viewed as places of just, evenhanded punishment, not rehabilitation. Parole would be abolished to avoid the discretionary unfairness associated with that mechanism of early release.

The justice model has had an important influence on criminal justice policy. Some states have adopted flat sentencing statutes and have limited the use of parole. There is a trend toward giving prison sentences because people deserve punishment rather than because the sentences will deter or rehabilitate them. Such measures as sentencing guidelines, which are aimed at reducing sentencing disparity, are a direct offshoot of the justice model.

Due Process Model

In *The Limits of the Criminal Sanction,* Herbert Packer contrasted the crime control model with an opposing view that he referred to as the *due process model.*[51] According to Packer, the due process model combines elements of liberal/positivist criminology with the legal concept of procedural fairness for the accused. Those who adhere to due process principles believe in individualized justice, treatment, and rehabilitation of offenders. If discretion exists in the criminal justice system, it should be used to evaluate the treatment needs of offenders. Most important, the civil rights of the accused should be protected at all costs. This requires practices such as strict scrutiny of police search and interrogation procedures, review of sentencing policies, and development of prisoners' rights.

Advocates of the due process model have demanded that competent defense counsel, jury trials, and other procedural safeguards be offered to every criminal defendant. They have also called for making public the operations of the justice system and placing controls over its discretionary power.

The photo above is of Edward Harvey Stokes, a convicted sex offender who admits to having abused over 200 boys. Fear of sexual predators such as Stokes has prompted the federal government to announce plans for a computerized registry of sex offenders. State jurisdictions are following suit. In the photo on the right, Massachusetts Public Safety Director Kathleen O'Toole announces the state's new sex offender registry information line. Is the posting of the names and pictures of former sex offenders a violation of their right to privacy? If you think not, then would you also require that neighbors be warned when people convicted of tax evasion, larceny, or fraud move into the area so that they can lock up their valuables?

Due process advocates view themselves as protectors of civil rights; they view overzealous cops as violators of basic constitutional rights. Similarly, they are skeptical about the intentions of meddling social workers, whose treatments often entail greater confinement and penalties than punishment does. Their concern is magnified by data showing that the poor and minority group members are often maltreated in the criminal justice system. In some jurisdictions, such as Washington, D.C., almost half of the African-American young men are under control of the justice system. Is it possible that this reflects racism, discrimination, and a violation of their civil rights?[52]

Due process exists to protect citizens—from both those who wish to punish them and those who wish to treat them without regard for legal and civil rights. Due process model advocates worry about the government's expanding ability to use computers in order to intrude into people's private lives. For example, in 1996 the federal government announced plans for a computerized registry of sex offenders; there are plans for nationwide computer-based mug shot and fingerprint systems. Background and fingerprint checks on employees in sensitive areas like airports will soon become routine. These measures can harm privacy and civil liberties, although research shows that they may have relatively little impact on controlling crime.[53]

Advocates of the due process orientation are quick to point out that the justice system remains an adversary process that pits the forces of an all-powerful state against those of a solitary individual accused of crime. If an overwhelming concern for justice and fairness did not exist, the defendant who lacked resources could easily be overwhelmed. They point to miscarriages of justice like the case of Jeffrey Blake, who went to prison for a double murder in 1991 and spent seven years behind bars before his conviction was overturned in 1998. The prosecution's star witness conceded that he lied on the stand, forcing Blake to spend a quarter of his life in prison for a crime he did not commit.[54] His wrongful conviction would have been even more tragic if he had been executed for his alleged crime. The Institute for Law and Justice, a Virginia-based research firm, found that at least 28 cases of sexual assault have been overturned because DNA evidence proved that the convicted men could not have committed the crimes; the inmates averaged seven years in prison before their release.[55] Because such mistakes can happen, even the most apparently guilty offender deserves all the protection the justice system can offer.

The due process orientation has not fared well in recent years. The movement to grant greater civil rights protections to criminal defendants has been undermined by Supreme Court decisions expanding police ability to search and seize evidence and to question suspects. Similarly, the movement between 1960 and 1980 to grant prison inmates an ever-increasing share of constitutional protections has been curtailed. There is growing evidence that the desire to protect the public has overshadowed concerns for the rights of criminal defendants. Although the most important legal rights won by criminal defendants in the 1960s and 1970s remain untouched (for example, the right to have a fair and impartial jury of one's peers), there was little urgency to increase the scope of civil rights in the more conservative 1990s.

Rehabilitation Model

The rehabilitation model embraces the notion that given the proper care and treatment, criminals can be changed into productive, law-abiding citizens. Influenced by positivist criminology, the rehabilitation school suggests that people commit crimes through no fault of their own. Instead, criminals themselves are the victims of social injustice, poverty, and racism; their acts are a response to a society that has betrayed them. And because of their disturbed and impoverished upbringing, they may be suffering psychological problems and personality disturbances that further enhance their crime-committing capabilities. Although the general public wants protection from crime, the argument goes, it also favors programs designed to help unfortunate people who commit crime because of emotional or social problems.[56]

To deal effectively with crime, its root causes must be attacked. Funds must be devoted to equalizing access to conventional means of success. This requires supporting such programs as public assistance, educational opportunity, and job training. If individuals run afoul of the law, efforts should be made to treat them, not punish them, by emphasizing counseling and psychological care in community-based treatment programs. Whenever possible, offenders should be placed on probation in halfway houses or in other rehabilitation-oriented programs.

This view of the justice system portrays it as a method for dispensing "treatment" to needy "patients." Also known as the "medical model," it portrays offenders as people who, because they have failed to exercise self-control, need the help of the state. The medical model rejects the crime control philosophy on the ground that it ignores the needs of offenders, who are people whom society has failed to help. The popularity of the medical model reached its zenith in the 1950s and 1960s; enthusiasm for it waned in the conservative, crime control–oriented 1970s, 1980s, and 1990s.

Yet rehabilitation still retains its enthusiasts. In contrast to literature reviews that find that treatment has little or no effect on known offenders, competing analyses find that a number of programs can have an important influence on offenders.[57] Programs that teach interpersonal skills and use individual counseling and behavioral modification techniques have produced positive results both in the community and within correctional institutions.[58] And many people express preferences for programs that are treatment oriented, such as early childhood intervention and services for at-risk children, over strict punishment and incarceration policies.[59]

CONNECTIONS

The rehabilitation model is linked to social structure and social process theories because it assumes that if lifestyle and socialization could be improved, crime rates would decline. See Chapters 7 and 8 for more on these theories.

Nonintervention Model

In the late 1960s and 1970s both the rehabilitation ideal and the due process movement were viewed suspiciously by experts concerned by the stigmatization of offenders. Regardless of the purpose, the more the government intervenes in the lives of people, the greater the harm done to their future behavior patterns. Once arrested and labeled, the offender is placed at a disadvantage at home, at school, and in the job market.[60] Rather than deter crime, the stigma of a criminal label erodes social capital and jeopardizes future success and achievement.

CONNECTIONS

In Chapter 10, Sampson and Laub's age-graded theory of crime analyzed how the reduction of social capital was a forerunner of future criminality. In contrast, people who develop social capital can desist from crime as they mature.

Noninterventionist philosophy was influenced by Edwin Lemert's concept of *judicious nonintervention*[61] and Edwin Schur's 1973 book, *Radical Nonintervention*.[62] These called for limiting government intrusion into the lives of people, especially minors, who run afoul of the law. They advocated *deinstitutionalization* of nonserious offenders, *diversion* from formal court processes into informal treatment programs, and *decriminalization* of nonserious offenses, such as possessing small amounts of marijuana. Under this concept, the justice system should interact as little as possible with offenders. Police, courts, and correctional agencies would concentrate their efforts on diverting law violators out of the formal justice system, thereby helping them avoid the stigma of formal labels like "delinquent" or "ex-con." Programs instituted under

this model include mediation (instead of trial), diversion (instead of formal processing), and community-based corrections (instead of secure corrections).

Nonintervention advocates are also skeptical about the creation of laws that criminalize acts that previously were legal, thus expanding the reach of justice and creating new classes of offenders. For example, it has become popular to expand control over youthful offenders by creating local curfew laws that make it a crime for young people to be out at night after a certain hour, such as 11 P.M. An adolescent who formerly was a night owl is now a criminal![63]

There are many examples of nonintervention ideas in practice. For example, the juvenile justice system has made a major effort to remove youths from adult jails and reduce the use of pretrial detention. Mediation programs have proven successful alternatives to the formal trial process.[64] In the adult system, pretrial release programs (alternatives to bail) are now the norm instead of an experimental innovation. And, although the prison population is rising, probation and community treatment have become the most common forms of criminal sanction.

CONNECTIONS

New forms of probation and incarceration featuring boot camps, house arrest, and the electronic monitoring of offenders may be the next major form of corrections, as is discussed in Chapter 18.

There has also been criticism of the noninterventionist philosophy. There is little evidence that alternative programs actually reduce recidivism rates. Some critics charge that alternative programs result in **widening the net**.[65] This term refers to the process by which efforts to remove people from the justice system actually enmesh them further within it by ordering them to spend more time in treatment than they would have had to spend in the formal legal process.

In the future, the nonintervention philosophy will be aided by the rising cost of justice. Although low-impact, nonintrusive programs may work no better than prison, they are certainly cheaper; program costs may receive greater consideration than program effectiveness.

Restorative Justice Perspective

A number of liberal and left-oriented scholars have devised the concept of restorative justice. They believe that the true purpose of the criminal justice system is to promote a peaceful, just society; they advocate peacemaking, not punishment.[66]

The restorative justice perspective draws its inspiration from religious and philosophical teachings ranging from Quakerism to Zen. Advocates of restorative justice say that state efforts to punish and control encourage crime. The violent punishing acts of the state, they claim, are not dissimilar from the violent acts of individuals.[67] Whereas crime control advocates associate lower crime rates with increased punishment, restorative justice advocates counter that studies show that punitive methods of correction (like jail) are no more effective than more humanitarian efforts (like probation with treatment).[68] Therefore, mutual aid rather than coercive punishment is the key to a harmonious society. Without the capacity to restore damaged social relations, society's response to crime has been almost exclusively punitive.

Restorative justice is guided by three essential principles: community "ownership" of conflict (including crime); material and symbolic reparation for crime victims; and social reintegration of the offender. Maintaining ownership, or jurisdiction, over the conflict means that the conflict between criminal and victim should be resolved in the community in which it originated, not in some faraway prison. The victim should be given a chance to voice his or her story, and the offender should help compensate the victim financially or by providing some service. The goal is to enable the offender to appreciate the damage caused, to make amends, and to be reintegrated back into society.

Restorative justice programs are geared to these principles. The ability of police officers to mediate disputes rather than resort to formal arrest has long been recognized; it is an essential element of community policing.[69] Mediation and conflict resolution programs are now common. Financial and community service restitution programs as an alternative to imprisonment have been in operation for more than two decades.

Although restorative justice has become an important perspective in recent years, questions are now being raised about its effectiveness. Is it possible that restoration programs actually help widen the net, helping to label clients as criminal or deviant? Might clients be coerced into programs to escape harsher forms of punishment? What happens to clients who fail to meet the terms of a restorative justice program: will they be incarcerated or similarly punished? And finally, can restorative justice programs actually reduce or control crime rates? So far, restorative justice programs do not provide a blueprint for crime control; they rely on untested principles and beliefs.[70]

CONNECTIONS

Restorative justice concepts were discussed in Chapter 9. Growing out of conflict and Marxist theory, restorative justice recognizes the coercive aspects of justice. See the Criminological Enterprise feature titled "Restorative Justice" in Chapter 9.

CONCEPTS OF JUSTICE TODAY

The various philosophies of justice compete today for dominance in the criminal justice system (see Figure 15.4). Each has supporters who lobby diligently for their positions. At the time of this writing, it seems that the crime control and justice models have captured the support of legislators and the general public. There is a growing emphasis on protecting the public by increasing criminal sentences and swelling prison populations. Yet advocates of the rehabilitation model claim that the recent imprisonment binge may be a false panacea. For example, in his 1998 book *Crime and Punishment in America,* liberal scholar Elliott Currie concedes that the crime rate has declined as the incarceration rate has increased.[71] Nonetheless, he claims that the association may be misleading because the crime rate is undergoing a natural revision from the abnormally high, unprecedented increases brought about by the crack cocaine epidemic in the 1980s. He claims that punitive, incarceration-based models of justice are doomed to fail in the long run. Most offenders eventually return to society, and if the justice system neglects to successfully help inmates achieve a productive lifestyle, a steadily increasing cohort of ex-offenders with limited life chances will be on the street. Their chances of success in the legitimate world have, if anything, been severely diminished by their prison experiences. Punishment may produce short-term reductions in the crime rate, but only rehabilitation and treatment can produce long-term gains.

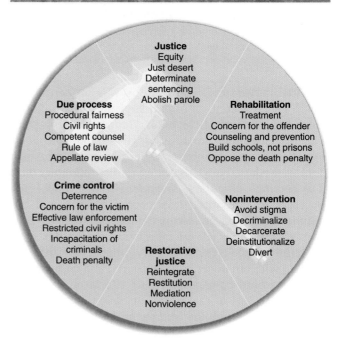

Figure 15.4   Perspectives on Justice: Key Concerns and Concepts

So despite the demand for punishing serious, chronic offenders, the door to treatment for nonviolent, nonchronic offenders has not been closed. The number of noninterventionist and restorative justice programs featuring restitution and nonpunitive sanctions is growing. As the cost of justice skyrockets and the correctional system becomes increasingly overcrowded, alternatives such as house arrest, electronic monitoring, intensive probation supervision, and other cost-effective programs have come to the forefront.

In sum, there are a number of competing views on the core values of criminal justice. These have influenced everyday policy in the justice system.

SUMMARY

Criminal justice refers to the formal processes and institutions that have been established to apprehend, try, punish, and treat law violators. The major components of the criminal justice system are the police, courts, and correctional agencies. Police maintain public order, deter crime, and apprehend law violators. The courts determine the criminal liability of accused offenders brought before them and dispense sanctions to those found guilty of crime. Corrections agencies provide postjudicatory care to offenders who are sentenced by the courts to confinement or community supervision. Dissatisfaction with traditional forms of corrections has spurred the development of community-based facilities and work-release and work-furlough programs. There are about 55,000 justice-related agencies in the United States. About 20,000 of them are police-related, 25,000 are court-related, and 9,000 are correctional agencies. They employ over 1 million people and cost taxpayers about $75 billion per year.

Justice can also be conceived of as a process through which offenders flow. The justice process begins with initial contact by a police agency and proceeds through investigation and custody, trial stages, and correctional system processing. At any stage of the process, the offender can be excused because a lack of evidence exists, the case is trivial, or a decision maker simply decides to discontinue interest in the case.

Procedures, policies, and practices employed within the criminal justice system are scrutinized by the courts to make sure they do not violate the guidelines in the first 10 amendments to the Constitution. If a violation occurs, the defendant can appeal the case and seek to overturn the conviction. Among the rights that must be honored are freedom from illegal searches and seizures and treatment with overall fairness and due process.

Several different philosophies or perspectives dominate the justice process. One is the crime control model, which asserts that the goals of justice are protection of the public and incapacitation of known offenders. In contrast, the due process model emphasizes liberal principles, such as legal rights and procedural fairness for the offender. The rehabilitation model views the justice system as a wise and caring parent; the noninterventionist perspective calls for minimal interference in offenders' lives; the justice model calls for fair, equal treatment for all offenders. The restorative justice model attempts nonpunitive, humane solutions to the conflict inherent in crime and victimization.

 See the book-specific web site at www.cj.wadsworth.com for additional chapter links, discussions, and quizzes.

THINKING LIKE A CRIMINOLOGIST

You have been appointed as the assistant to the president's drug czar, who is in charge of coordinating the nation's drug control policy. She has asked you to develop a plan to reduce drug abuse by 25 percent within three years. You realize that multiple perspectives of justice exist and that the agencies of the criminal justice system can use a number of strategies to reduce drug trafficking and the use of drugs. It might be possible to control the drug trade through a strict crime control effort, for example, by using law enforcement officers to cut off supplies of drugs by destroying crops and arresting members of drug cartels in drug-producing countries. Border patrols and military personnel using sophisticated hardware could also prevent drugs from entering the country. According to the justice model, if drug violations were punished with criminal sentences commensurate with their harm, then the rational drug trafficker might look for a new line of employment. The adoption of mandatory sentences for drug crimes to ensure that all offenders receive similar punishment for their acts might reduce crime. The rehabilitation model suggests that strategies should be aimed at reducing the desire to use drugs and increasing incentives for users to eliminate substance abuse. A noninterventionist strategy calls for the legalization of drugs so distribution could be controlled by the government. Crime rates would be cut because drug users would no longer need the same cash flow to support their habit.

Considering these different approaches, how would you shape drug control strategies?

KEY TERMS

Chicago Crime Commission	criminal court	jail
Wickersham Commission	due process	prison
criminal justice	fundamental fairness	penitentiary
social control	plea bargaining	parole
sheriff's department	probation	arrest

probable cause

lineup

complaint

information

indictment

grand jury

preliminary hearing

probable cause hearing

arraignment

bail

hung jury

disposition

Bill of Rights

exclusionary rule

determinate sentencing

widening the net

NOTES

1. *Riggs vs. California*, No. 98–5021 (1999).

2. David Anderson, *Crime and the Politics of Hysteria: How the Willie Horton Story Changed American Justice* (New York: Random House, 1995).

3. Bonnie Berry, *Social Rage: Emotion and Cultural Conflict* (Garland Press, 1998).

4. This section leans heavily on Ted Robert Gurr, "Historical Trends in Violent Crime: A Critical Review of the Evidence," in *Crime and Justice: An Annual Review of Research,* vol. 3, ed. Michael Tonry and Norval Morris (Chicago: University of Chicago Press, 1981); Richard Maxwell Brown, "Historical Patterns of American Violence," in *Violence in America: Historical and Comparative Perspectives,* ed. Hugh Davis Graham and Ted Robert Gurr (Beverly Hills, Calif.: Sage Publications, 1979).

5. David Courtwright, "Violence in America," *American Heritage* 47 (1996): 36–52, quote p. 36; David Courtwright, *Violent Land: Single Men and Social Disorder from the Frontier to the Inner City* (Cambridge, Mass.: Harvard University Press, 1996).

6. This section leans heavily on Samuel Walker, *Popular Justice* (New York: Oxford University Press, 1980).

7. For a detailed analysis of this work, see Samuel Walker, "Origins of the Contemporary Criminal Justice Paradigm: The American Bar Foundation Survey, 1953–1969," *Justice Quarterly* 9 (1992): 47–76.

8. President's Commission on Law Enforcement and the Administration of Justice, *The Challenge of Crime in a Free Society* (Washington, D.C.: U.S. Government Printing Office, 1967).

9. See Public Law 90-351, Title I—Omnibus Crime Control Safe Streets Act of 1968, 90th Congress, June 19, 1968.

10. American Bar Association, *Project on Standards for Criminal Justice* (New York: Institute of Judicial Administration, 1968–1973); National Advisory Commission on Criminal Justice Standards and Goals, *A National Strategy to Reduce Crime* (Washington, D.C.: U.S. Government Printing Office, 1973).

11. Kathleen Maguire and Ann Pastore, eds., *Sourcebook of Criminal Justice Statistics, 1995* (Washington, D.C.: U.S. Government Printing Office, 1996), p. 3.

12. Maguire and Pastore, *Sourcebook of Criminal Justice Statistics, 1995,* p. 16.

13. Federal Bureau of Investigation, *Crime in the United States, 1995* (Washington, D.C.: U.S. Government Printing Office, 1996), p. 208.

14. Jeffrey Butts, *Offenders in Juvenile Court, 1994* (Washington, D.C: Office of Juvenile Justice and Delinquency Prevention, 1996).

15. Patrick A. Langan and Jodi M. Brown, *Felony Sentences in State Courts, 1994* (Washington, D.C: Bureau of Justice Statistics, 1997).

16. U.S. Department of Justice, "Nation's Probation and Parole Population Reached New High Last Year" (press release, 16 August 1998).

17. Brian Reaves, *Census of State and Local Law Enforcement Agencies, 1992* (Washington, D.C.: Bureau of Justice Statistics, 1993); Sue Lindgren, *Justice Expenditure and Employment* (Washington, D.C.: Bureau of Justice Statistics, 1990).

18. See Albert Reiss, *Police and the Public* (New Haven: Yale University Press, 1972).

19. American Bar Association, *Standards Relating to the Urban Police Function* (New York: Institute of Judicial Administration, 1973), Standard 2.2, p. 9.

20. Kenneth L. Davis, *Police Discretion* (St. Paul: West Publishing, 1975).

21. See Peter Manning and John Van Maanen, eds., *Policing: A View from the Streets* (Santa Monica, Calif.: Goodyear Publishing, 1978).

22. See Donald Newman, *Conviction: The Determination of Guilt or Innocence without Trial* (Boston: Little, Brown, 1966).

23. Herbert L. Packer, *The Limits of the Criminal Sanction* (Stanford, Calif.: Stanford University Press, 1968), p. 159.

24. Samuel Walker, *Sense and Nonsense About Crime and Drugs,* 3d ed. (Belmont, Calif.: Wadsworth, 1994).

25. Steven Brandl, "The Impact of Case Characteristics on Detectives' Decision Making," *Justice Quarterly* 10 (1993): 395–415.

26. Malcolm Feeley, *The Process Is the Punishment* (New York: Russell Sage Foundation, 1979).

27. Barbara Boland, Catherine Conly, Paul Mahanna, Lynn Warner, and Ronald Sones, *The Prosecution of Felony Arrests, 1987* (Washington, D.C.: Bureau of Justice Statistics, 1990), p. 3.

28. See Joseph J. Senna, "Changes in Due Process of Law," *Social Work* 19 (1974): 319.

29. *Rochin v. California,* 342 U.S. 165 (1952).

30. *Arizona v. Fulminante,* 48 Cr.L. 2105 (1991).

31. *Whren, et al., v. U.S.,* No. 95-5841 (1996).

32. *McCleskey v. Zant,* 49 Cr.L. 2029 (1991).

33. "Survey: Americans Think System Favors Defendants over Victims," *Criminal Justice Newsletter* 22 (1991): 5.

34. D. H. Oaks, "Studying the Exclusionary Rule in Search and Seizure," *University of Chicago Law Review* 37 (1970): 756.

35. *Weeks v. United States,* 323 U.S. 383 (1914).

36. *Mapp v. Ohio,* 367 U.S. 643 (1961).

37. *Illinois v. Gates,* 462 U.S. 213 (1983).

38. *Knowles v. Iowa,* No. 97-7597 (1998).

39. Walker, *Sense and Nonsense About Crime and Drugs,* pp. 126–28.

40. Craig Uchida and Timothy Bynum, "Search Warrants, Motions to Suppress and 'Lost Cases': The Effects of the Exclusionary Rule in Seven Jurisdictions," *Journal of Criminal Law and Criminology* 81 (1991): 1034–66.

41. Paul Cassell, "How Many Criminals Has *Miranda* Set Free?" *Wall Street Journal,* 1 March 1995, p. A15.

42. *Ohio v. Robinette,* 95-891 (1996).

43. David Garland, *Punishment and Modern Society* (Chicago: University of Chicago Press, 1990).

44. The most often-cited of these is Douglas Lipton, Robert Martinson, and Judith Wilks, *The Effectiveness of Correctional Treatment: A Survey of Treatment Evaluation Studies* (New York: Praeger, 1975).

45. "Many State Legislatures Focused on Crime in 1995, Study Finds," *Criminal Justice Newsletter* 27 (January 1996), pp. 1–2.

46. Daniel Nagin, "Criminal Deterrence Research: A Review of the Evidence and a Research Agenda for the Outset of the 21st Century," in *Crime and Justice: An Annual Review,* ed. Michael Tonry (Chicago: University of Chicago Press, 1997), pp. 126–58.

47. Amy Thistlewaite, John Wooldredge, and David Gibbs, "Severity of Dispositions and Domestic Violence Recidivism," *Crime and Delinquency* 44 (1998): 388–98.

48. *Crime and Punishment in America: 1997 Update,* National Center for Policy Analysis, Dallas, Texas, 1997.

49. David Fogel, *. . . We Are the Living Proof* (Cincinnati: Anderson, 1975). See also

David Fogel, *Justice as Fairness* (Cincinnati: Anderson, 1980).

50. Travis Pratt, "Race and Sentencing: A Meta-Analysis of Conflicting Empirical Research Results," *Journal of Criminal Justice* 26 (1998): 513–25.

51. Packer, *The Limits of the Criminal Sanction.*

52. Eric Lotke, "Hobbling a Generation: Young African-American Men in Washington, D.C.'s Criminal Justice System—Five Years Later," *Crime and Delinquency* 44 (1998): 355–66.

53. Anthony Petrosino and Carolyn Petrosino, "The Public Safety Potential of Megan's Law in Massachusetts: An Assessment from a Sample of Criminal Sexual Psychopaths," *Crime and Delinquency* 43 (1999): 140–58; "New Laws Said to Raise Demands on Justice Information Systems," *Criminal Justice Newsletter* 27 (17 September 1996), pp. 3–4.

54. Jim Yardley, "Convicted in Murder Case, Man Cleared 7 Years Later," *New York Times,* 29 October 1998.

55. "DNA Testing Has Exonerated 28 Prison Inmates, Study Finds," *Criminal Justice Newsletter,* 17 June 1996, p. 2.

56. Richard McCorkle, "Research Note: Punish and Rehabilitate? Public Attitudes Toward Six Common Crimes," *Crime and Delinquency* 39 (1993): 240–52.

57. For example, see D. A. Andrews, Ivan Zinger, R. D. Hoge, James Bonta, Paul Gendreau, and Francis Cullen, "Does Correctional Treatment Work? A Clinically-Relevant and Psychologically-Informed Meta-Analysis," *Criminology* 28 (1990): 369–404; Carol Garrett, "Effects of Residential Treatment on Adjudicated Delinquents: A Meta-Analysis," *Journal of Research in Crime and Delinquency* 22 (1985): 287–308.

58. Mark Lipsey and David Wilson, "Effective Intervention for Serious Juvenile Offenders: A Synthesis of Research," in *Serious and Violent Juvenile Offenders: Risk Factors and Successful Interventions,* ed. Rolf Loeber and David Farrington (Thousand Oaks, Calif.: Sage, 1998), pp. 39–53.

59. Francis Cullen, John Paul Wright, Shayna Brown, Melissa Moon, Michael Blankenship, and Brandon Applegate, "Public Support for Early Intervention Programs: Implications for a Progressive Policy Agenda," *Crime and Delinquency* 44 (1998): 187–204.

60. Shawn Bushway, "The Impact of an Arrest on the Job Stability of Young White American Men," *Journal of Research in Crime and Delinquency* 35 (1998): 454–79.

61. Edwin M. Lemert, "The Juvenile Court—Quest and Realities," in President's Commission on Law Enforcement and the Administration of Justice, *Task Force Report: Juvenile Delinquency and Youth Crime* (Washington, D.C.: U.S. Government Printing Office, 1967).

62. Edwin Schur, *Radical Nonintervention* (Englewood Cliffs, N.J.: Prentice-Hall, 1973).

63. Craig Hemmens and Katherine Bennett, "Juvenile Curfews and the Courts: Judicial Response to a Not-So-New Crime Control Strategy," *Crime and Delinquency* 45 (1999): 99–121.

64. Mark Umbreit and Robert Coates, "Cross-Site Analysis of Victim–Offender Mediation in Four States," *Crime and Delinquency* 39 (1993): 565–85.

65. James Austin and Barry Krisberg, "The Unmet Promise of Alternatives to Incarceration," *Crime and Delinquency* 28 (1982): 3–19; for an alternative view, see Arnold Binder and Gilbert Geis, "Ad Populum Argumentation in Criminology: Juvenile Diversion as Rhetoric," *Criminology* 30 (1984): 309–33.

66. Herbert Bianchi, *Justice as Sanctuary* (Bloomington: Indiana University Press, 1994); Nils Christie, "Conflicts as Property," *The British Journal of Criminology* 17 (1977) 1–15; L. Hulsman, "Critical Criminology and the Concept of Crime," *Contemporary Crises* 10 (1986): 63–80.

67. Larry Tifft, Foreword, to Dennis Sullivan, *The Mask of Love* (Port Washington, N.Y.: Kennikat Press, 1980), p. 6.

68. Robert Davis, Barbara Smith, and Laura Nickles, "The Deterrent Effect of Prosecuting Domestic Violence Misdemeanors," *Crime and Delinquency* 44 (1998): 434–42.

69. Christopher Cooper, "Patrol Police Officer Conflict Resolution Processes," *Journal of Criminal Justice* 25 (1997): 87–101.

70. Sharon Levrant, Francis Cullen, Betsy Fulton, and John Wozniak, "Reconsidering Restorative Justice: The Corruption of Benevolence Revisited," *Crime and Delinquency* 45 (1999): 3–27.

71. Elliott Currie, *Crime and Punishment in America* (New York: Henry Holt, 1998). See also Elliott Currie, *Confronting Crime: An American Challenge* (New York: Pantheon, 1985); Elliott Currie, *Reckoning, Drugs, the Cities, and the American Future* (New York: Hill and Wang, 1993).

CHAPTER 16

Police and Law Enforcement

INTRODUCTION

On a warm August morning in 1997, Sammy Velez, a transvestite with a crack habit, took advantage of the rush-hour commotion near Penn Station to snatch a purse. Tripping in his high-heeled boots, he couldn't make a clean getaway, so he threw the purse back. Two New York police officers were soon in pursuit. They chased Velez in and out of traffic until he stumbled and fell. Velez curled up on the ground at the feet of the officers and raised his arms to protect a body weakened by AIDS and weighing barely 100 pounds. In the ensuing struggle, Velez's left eyeball was ruptured, and his collarbone and many facial bones were fractured. Velez later told authorities that he was pummeled by the officers, kicked in the face until his eye dangled from its socket. The officers denied beating him; they suggested he hurt himself when he fell. The city of New York paid Velez $75,000 to settle his claim that police used excessive force in blinding his left eye for a botched purse snatching. But neither the New York police department nor the individual officers were held liable; the check came out of the city's general fund. The officers were not disciplined, although one was denied the medal he had sought for dodging traffic to make the arrest. In 1997 New York paid out $27.3 million in claims; the number of police brutality claims has tripled over the past decade.[1]

The Velez case highlights the critical, controversial role police play in the justice system and the need to develop a professional, competent police force. Police are the **gatekeepers** of the criminal justice process. They initiate contact with law violators and decide whether to formally arrest them and start their journey through the criminal justice system, settle the issue informally (such as by issuing a warning), or simply take no action at all. The strategic position of law enforcement officers, their visibility and contact with the public, and their use of weapons and arrest power have kept them in the forefront of public thought for most of the twentieth century.

In the late 1960s and early 1970s, great issue was taken with the political and social roles of the police. Critics viewed police agencies as biased organizations that harassed minority citizens, controlled political dissidents, and generally seemed out of touch with the changing times. The major issues appeared to be controlling the abuse of police power and making police agencies more responsible to public control. During this period, major efforts were undertaken in the nation's largest cities to curb police power.

Since the mid-1970s, the relationship between police and the public has changed. Police departments have become more sensitive to their public image. Programs have been created to improve relations between police and the community and to help police officers on the beat to be more sensitive to the needs of the public and to cope more effectively with the stress of their jobs.[2]

Nonetheless, as the Velez beating illustrates, city police departments continue to be the subject of public scrutiny. There is continuing concern over police use of force and treatment of citizens. The **Mollen Commission** and other police investigations showed that corruption was still rampant in New York City and that the rogue cops of the 1990s are even more brazen and violent than the corrupt cops found by the Knapp Commission 20 years earlier.

CONNECTIONS

As you may recall, the work of the **Knapp Commission** and the Mollen Commission, which investigated police corruption in New York, was discussed in Chapter 13's section on influence peddling and bribery. The police officers investigated by these commissions used an important institutional position to sell power, influence, and information to outsiders. As a result of these and similar investigations, police review boards, designed to allow community members to oversee police policies and operations and investigate citizen complaints, were set up in such cities as Philadelphia, New York, and Detroit.

Despite these investigations, New York, Philadelphia, and other large cities have continued to experience police corruption. Even in smaller cities, police procedures have been questioned because there may be overenforcement in minority communities.[3] Minority citizens are more adversely affected than whites when well-publicized incidents of police misconduct occur, and the effects are longer lasting.[4]

Although critical of police, people are more concerned than ever with increasing their effectiveness: the public wants its police agencies to control the law-violating members of society. The role of police is being reconsidered. Are they strictly crime fighters, or are they a multifaceted social service agency that includes law enforcement as only one part of its daily activities? Compounding the problem is the fact that police behavior is now more visible than ever before because it is commonly captured on video; when police make the local news, these real accounts of the use of force can have an extremely negative impact on public perceptions of police behavior.[5]

This chapter reviews the function and role of police in U.S. society. First the history of police is briefly discussed. Then the role and structure of police agencies is reviewed. Finally, some of the critical issues facing the police in society are analyzed.

HISTORY OF POLICE

As with criminal law, the origin of U.S. police agencies can be traced back to early English society.[6] Before the Norman conquest, there was no regular English police force. Every man living in the villages scattered throughout the countryside was responsible for aiding his neighbors and protecting the settlement from thieves and marauders. This was known as the **pledge system.** People were grouped into a collective of 10 families called a *tithing* and entrusted with policing their own minor problems. Ten tithings were grouped into a *hundred,* whose affairs were supervised by a *constable* appointed by the local nobleman. The constable, who might be considered the first real police officer, dealt with more serious breaches of the law.[7]

Later the hundreds were grouped into *shires* resembling the counties of today. The *shire reeve* was appointed by the crown to supervise a certain territory and assure the local nobleman that order would be kept. The shire reeve, forerunner of today's sheriff, soon began to pursue and apprehend law violators as part of his duties.

In the thirteenth century, during the reign of King Edward I, the **watch system** was created to help protect property in England's larger cities and towns. Watchmen patrolled at night and helped protect against robberies, fires, and disturbances. They reported to the area constable, who became the primary metropolitan law enforcement agent. In larger cities such as London, the watchmen were organized within church parishes; those applying for the job were usually members of the parish they protected.

In 1326 the office of **justice of the peace** was created to assist the shire reeve in controlling the county. Eventually the justices took on judicial functions in addition to their primary duty as peacekeeper. A system developed in which the local constable became the operational assistant to the justice of the peace, supervising

the night watchmen, investigating offenses, serving summonses, executing warrants, and securing prisoners. This working format helped delineate the relationship between police and the judiciary that endured intact for 500 years.

At first the position of constable was an honorary one given to a respected person in the village or parish for one year. Often these men were wealthy merchants who had little time for their duties. It was common for them to hire assistants to help them fulfill their obligations, thereby creating another element of a paid police force. Thus, by the seventeenth century, the justice of the peace, the constable, his assistants, and the night watch formed the nucleus of the local metropolitan justice system. (The sheriff's duties lay outside the cities and towns.)

The London Police

At the end of the eighteenth century, the Industrial Revolution lured thousands from the English countryside to work in the larger factory towns. The swelling population of urban poor, whose minuscule wages could hardly sustain them, heightened the need for police protection. In response to pressure from established citizens, the government passed statutes creating new police offices in London. These offices employed three justices of the peace who were each authorized to hire six paid constables. Law enforcement began to be more centralized and professional. However, many parishes still maintained their own foot patrols, horse patrols, and private investigators.

In 1829 **Sir Robert Peel,** England's home secretary, guided through Parliament an "Act for Improving the Police In and Near the Metropolis." The act established the first organized police force in London. Composed of over a thousand men, the London police force was structured along military lines. Its members wore a distinctive uniform and were led by two magistrates, who were later given the title of commissioner. However, the ultimate responsibility for the police fell to the home secretary and consequently the Parliament.

The London experiment proved so successful that the metropolitan police soon began helping outlying areas that requested law enforcement assistance. Another act of Parliament allowed justices of the peace to establish local police forces; by 1856 every borough and county in England was required to form its own police force.

Policing the American Colonies

Law enforcement in colonial America paralleled the British model. In the colonies, the county sheriff became the most important law enforcement agent.[8] In addition to peacekeeping and crime fighting, these sheriffs collected taxes, supervised elections, and handled a great deal of other legal business. The colonial sheriff did not patrol or seek out crime; instead he reacted to citizens' complaints and investigated crimes that had already occurred. His salary was related to his effectiveness. Sheriffs were paid by the fee system: they were given a fixed amount for every arrest made, subpoena served, or court appearance made. Unfortunately, their tax-collecting chores were more lucrative than crime fighting, so law enforcement was not one of their primary concerns.

In the cities, law enforcement was the province of the town marshal, who was aided, often unwillingly, by a variety of constables, night watchmen, police justices, and city council members. However, local governments had little administrative power, and criminal law enforcement was largely an individual or community responsibility. Individual initiative was encouraged by the practice of offering rewards for the capture of felons.[9] If trouble arose, citizens might be called on to form a posse to chase offenders or break up an angry mob.

As the size of cities grew, it became exceedingly difficult for local leaders to organize citizens' groups. Moreover, the early nineteenth century was an era of widespread urban unrest and mob violence. Local leaders began to realize that a more structured police function was needed to control demonstrators and keep the peace.

Early American Police Agencies

The modern police department was born out of urban mob violence, which wracked the nation's cities in the nineteenth century. Boston created the nation's first formal police department in 1838. New York formed its police department in 1844; Philadelphia, in 1854. The new police departments replaced the night watch system and relegated constables and sheriffs to serving court orders and running the jail.

At first the urban police departments inherited the functions of the older institutions they replaced. For example, Boston police were charged with maintaining public health until 1853; New York police were responsible for street sweeping until 1881.

Politics dominated the departments and determined the recruitment of new officers and promotion of supervisors. An individual with the right connections could be hired despite a lack of qualifications. In New York City during the 1880s, potential police recruits had to be connected to a local politician and pay $300 to be hired as officers; promotions to captain required a payment of $15,000.[10] "In addition to the pervasive brutality and corruption," writes one justice historian, Samuel Walker, "the police did little to effectively prevent crime or provide public services. Officers were primarily tools of local politicians; they were not impartial and professional public servants."[11]

At mid-nineteenth century, the detective bureau was set up as part of the Boston police. Until then, thief

African Americans have served on police forces since the mid-nineteenth century. Thirty years after the Civil War, the streets of Lawrence, Kansas, were patrolled by African American policeman Sam Jeans, shown here. A Republican mayor appointed the first black police officer in Chicago in 1872; by 1884, there were 23 African American officers serving in that city.

taking had been the province of amateur bounty hunters, who hired themselves out to victims. When professional police departments replaced bounty hunters, the close working relationships that developed between police detectives and their underworld informants produced many scandals and, consequently, high personnel turnover.

Police during the nineteenth century were generally incompetent, corrupt, and disliked by the people they served. The police role was only minimally directed at law enforcement. Its primary function was serving as the enforcement arm of the reigning political power, protecting private property, and keeping control of the ever-rising numbers of foreign immigrants.

Reform Movements

Police agencies evolved slowly through the latter half of the nineteenth century. Uniforms were introduced in 1853 in New York. Technological innovations, such as linking precincts to central headquarters by telegraph, appeared in the late 1850s; somewhat later, call boxes allowed patrol officers on the beat to communicate with their commanders. Nonpolice functions, such as care of the streets, began to be abandoned after the Civil War.

Despite any steps they may have made toward improvement, big-city police were not respected by the public, successful in their role as crime stoppers, or involved in progressive activities. The control of police departments by local politicians impeded effective law enforcement and fostered graft and corruption.

In an effort to prevent police corruption, civil leaders in some jurisdictions created police administrative boards to reduce the control over police exercised by local officials. These tribunals were given the responsibility for appointing police administrators and controlling police affairs. In many instances these measures failed because the private citizens appointed to the review boards lacked expertise in the intricacies of police work.

Another reform movement was the takeover of some big-city police agencies by state legislators. Although police budgets were paid through local taxes, control of police was usurped by rural politicians in the state capitals. It was not until the first decades of the twentieth century that cities regained control of their police forces.

The Boston police strike of 1914 heightened interest in police reform. The strike was brought about by dissatisfaction with the status of police officers in society. While other professions were unionizing and increasing their standard of living, police salaries lagged behind. The Boston police officers' organization, the Boston Social Club, voted to become a union affiliated with the American Federation of Labor. The officers struck on September 9, 1914. Rioting and looting broke out, resulting in Governor Calvin Coolidge's mobilization of the state militia to take over the city. Public support turned against the police, and the strike was broken. Eventually, all the striking officers were fired and replaced by new recruits. The Boston police strike ended police unionism for decades and solidified power in the hands of a reactionary, autocratic police administration.

In the aftermath of the strike, local, state, and national crime commissions began to investigate the extent of crime and the ability of the justice system to effectively deal with it. The **Wickersham Commission** was created by President Herbert Hoover to study police issues on a national scale. In its 1931 report the commission identified many of the problems of policing, including a weak command structure and overly complex job requirements.[12]

With the onset of the Great Depression, justice reform became a less important issue than economic revival, and for many years there was little change in the nature of policing.

The Advent of Professionalism

The onset of police professionalism might be traced to the 1920s and the influence of **August Vollmer.**[13] While serving as police chief of Berkeley, California, Vollmer instituted university training as an important part of his development of young officers. He also helped develop the School of Criminology at the University of California at Berkeley, which became the model for justice-related programs around the country.

Vollmer's disciples included O. W. Wilson, who pioneered the use of advanced training for officers when he took over and reformed the Wichita, Kansas, police department in 1923. Wilson also was instrumental in applying modern management and administrative techniques to policing. His text, *Police Administration,* became the single most influential work on the subject. Wilson eventually became dean of the Criminology School at Berkeley and ended his career in Chicago, where Mayor Richard J. Daley asked him to take over and reform the Chicago police department in 1960.

One important aspect of professionalism was the technological breakthroughs that significantly increased and expanded the scope of police operations. The first innovation came in the area of communications, when telegraph police boxes were installed in 1867; an officer could turn a key in a box and his location and number would automatically register at headquarters. The Detroit police department outfitted some of its patrol officers with bicycles in 1897. By 1913 the motorcycle was employed by departments in the eastern part of the country. The first police car was used in Akron, Ohio, in 1910; the police wagon became popular in Cincinnati in 1912.

In the early 1960s police professionalism was interpreted as being a tough, highly trained, rule-oriented law enforcement department organized along militaristic lines. The urban unrest of the late 1960s changed the course of police department development. Efforts were made to promote understanding between police and the community, reduce police brutality, and recognize the stresses of police work. Efforts have also been made to add members of minority groups and women to police departments. With increasing professionalism, the ideal police officer came to be viewed as a product of the computer age, skilled in using the most advanced techniques to fight crime.[14]

Despite technological and professional achievements, the effectiveness of police is still questioned, and their ability to control crime is still considered problematic. Critics argue that plans to increase police professionalism place too much emphasis on hardware and not enough on police–citizen cooperation. As a result, there has been an ongoing effort to make police "user friendly" by decentralizing police departments and making them responsive to community needs. Some police experts, such as David Bayley, believe that the police have made many notable strides over the past three decades, some of the most important of which are listed in Table 16.1.

CONNECTIONS

Later in this chapter the community policing model is discussed in some detail. This is an attempt by police administrators to make police departments more responsive to neighborhood-level problems.

It is likely that police agencies will undergo considerable change during the coming decades. The Criminological Enterprise feature titled "Law Enforcement in the Twenty-First Century" discusses some of the innovations and changes that are beginning to take place.

LAW ENFORCEMENT AGENCIES TODAY

Law enforcement duties are distributed across local, county, state, and federal jurisdictions. This section discusses the role of federal, state, and county agencies. The remainder of the chapter focuses on local police.

Federal Law Enforcement

The federal government maintains about 50 organizations that are involved in law enforcement. Some of the most important of these are discussed here.

The Federal Bureau of Investigation   In 1870 the U.S. Department of Justice became involved in actual policing when the attorney general hired investigators to enforce the Mann Act (which prohibited prostitution across state lines). In 1908 this group of investigators was formally made a distinct branch of the government, the Bureau of Investigation; in the 1930s the agency was reorganized into the Federal Bureau of Investigation under the direction of J. Edgar Hoover.

Today's FBI is not a police agency but an investigative agency, with jurisdiction over all matters in which the United States is, or may be, an interested party. It limits its jurisdiction to federal laws, including all federal statutes not specifically assigned to other agencies. These include statutes dealing with espionage, sabotage, treason, civil rights violations, the murder and assault of federal officers, mail fraud, robbery and burglary of federally insured banks, kidnapping, and interstate transportation of stolen vehicles and property.

The FBI offers important services to local law enforcement agencies. Its identification division, established in 1924, collects and maintains a vast fingerprint file that can be used by local police agencies. Its sophisticated crime laboratory, established in 1932, aids local police in testing and identifying evidence, such as hairs, fibers, blood, tire tracks, and drugs. The Uniform Crime Report is another service of the FBI. Finally, the FBI's National Crime Information Center is a computerized network linked to local police departments by terminals. Through it, information on stolen vehicles, wanted persons, stolen guns, and so on is made readily available to local law enforcement agencies.

Other Federal Agencies   The U.S. government's interest in drug trafficking can be traced back to 1914, when the Harrison Act established federal jurisdiction over the supply and use of narcotics. Several drug enforcement units, including the Bureau of Narcotics and Dangerous Drugs, were originally charged with enforcing drug laws. However, in 1973 these agencies were combined to form the Drug Enforcement Administration (DEA). Agents of the DEA help local and state authorities investigate illegal drug use and carry out independent surveillance and enforcement activities to control the importation of narcotics.

Federal law enforcement agencies under the direction of the Justice Department include the U.S. marshals, the Immigration and Naturalization Service, and the Organized Crime and Racketeering Unit. The U.S. marshals are court officers who help implement federal court rulings, transport prisoners, and enforce court orders. The Immigration and Naturalization Service

The Criminological Enterprise

Law Enforcement in the Twenty-First Century

What changes can we expect in U.S. police agencies in the twenty-first century? What are the trends in policing? Where is police work heading? It is likely that police departments will continue to reshape their role, deemphasizing crime fighting and stressing community organization and revitalization. The number of minority and female police officers should continue to grow. Departments are also increasing their use of civilian employees, thereby freeing sworn officers for law enforcement tasks.

Another change that police agencies will continue to emphasize is the decentralization of command through the creation of specialized units, substations, and direct response teams. Although decentralization does not automatically ensure greater citizen cooperation, it is believed to increase sensitivity to citizen needs, create special knowledge of and commitment to the area served, and foster heightened community trust in the police.

Police departments will become increasingly proactive and focus their attention on solving particular community problems, including vagrancy, disorderly conduct, vandalism, and public drunkenness; these so-called lifestyle crimes are believed to create community disorder. There is also a growing trend for urban departments to create paramilitary-type units to deal with future, though as yet undefined, terrorist threats. Police agencies will have to deal with new categories of high-tech crimes ranging from theft of information and data to electronic counterfeiting. Police officers now trained to prevent burglaries may someday have to learn to work with forensic labs that can identify suspects who steal genetically engineered cultures from biomedical labs. Police agencies are already dealing with Internet crimes ranging from fraud to pornography. Law enforcement officers today use several strategies to deal with on-line child pornography; some officers pose as children in chat rooms to expose offenders; others have created child porn web sites to sting purveyors of kiddie porn.

Figure A   Computerized Mapping in Crime Control

A section of a San Diego Police Department Crime Analysis Unit DMAP shows narcotics arrests (each ★ indicates a narcotics arrest).

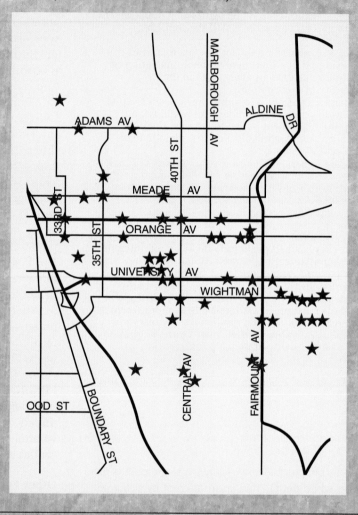

Source: Thomas Rich, *The Use of Computerized Mapping in Crime Control and Prevention Programs* (Washington, D.C.: National Institute of Justice, 1995).

Criminal investigation will be enhanced by the application of sophisticated electronic gadgetry: computers, cellular phones, and digital communication devices. It is now recognized that there are geographic "hot spots" where a majority of predatory crimes are concentrated. Computer mapping programs that translate addresses into map coordinates now allow departments to identify problem areas for particular crimes. Computer maps allow police to identify the location, time of day, and linkage among criminal events and concentrate their forces accordingly (see Figure A).

Fingerprint Analysis

The use of computerized fingerprint systems is growing around the United States. Using mathematical models, Automated Fingerprint Identification Systems (AFIS) can classify fingerprints and identify up to 250 characteristics (minutiae) of the print. These automated systems use high-speed silicon chips to plot each point of minutiae and count the number of ridge lines between that point and its four nearest neighbors, which substantially improves speed and accuracy over earlier systems. Some police departments, such as that in Washington, D.C., report that computerized print systems are allowing them to make over 100 identifications a month from fingerprints taken at crime scenes. AFIS files have been regionalized. For example, the western identification network serves Alaska, California, Idaho, Nevada, Oregon, Utah, Washington, and Wyoming. New methods of fingerprint analysis will soon be available. For example, the FBI plans to create an integrated automated fingerprint identification system that will allow local departments to scan fingerprints, send them electronically to a national depository, and receive identification and criminal history of suspects.

DNA Profiling

DNA profiling involves scientifically matching the genetic material from hair, blood, and other bodily tissues and fluids found at a crime scene with samples taken from known suspects. The use of DNA in criminal trials received a boost in 1997 when the FBI announced that DNA evidence has become so precise that experts no longer have to supply statistical estimates of accuracy while testifying at trial; they can now state in court that there exists "a reasonable degree of scientific certainty" that evidence came from a single suspect.

The FBI has implemented a combined DNA index system (CODIS). This computerized database allows DNA taken at a crime scene to be searched electronically to find matches against samples taken from convicted offenders and crime scenes. One database allows suspects to be identified; the second allows investigators to establish links between crimes. So far there have been more than 100 instances in which offenders have been linked to unsolved cases and more than 130 instances in which two or more cases have been linked to a single assailant. Timothy Spencer, known as the "South Side Strangler," was executed in Virginia on 27 April 1994; this was the first time a person was convicted and executed almost entirely on the basis of DNA evidence. The use of DNA evidence should become commonplace in the twenty-first century.

Improving Communications

Police departments are now tapping into new communications technologies to improve their effectiveness. Some departments are already using cellular phones to facilitate communications with victims and witnesses. Departments that cover wide geographical areas and maintain independent precincts and substations are experimenting with teleconferencing systems that provide both audio and video linkages. In Fairfax, Virginia, police routinely use fax machines to send information to hundreds of local businesses in a matter of minutes. A fax might detail a recent robbery and describe the suspect or notify business owners of the next scheduled crime prevention meeting. Some agencies use electronic bulletin boards to link officers in an active online system, enabling them to communicate faster and more easily. The Searcy, Arizona, police department now operates a computer bulletin board system (BBS) as an information gateway to the public in order to give citizens access to law enforcement–related information.

Police agencies may use advanced communications gear to track stolen vehicles. Car owners will be able to buy transmitters that emit a signal to a satellite or other listening device; the signal can then be monitored and tracked by specially equipped patrol cars. This system is now being tested. Finally, some departments are linking advanced communications systems that allow patrol officers to personally access remote law enforcement data files without having to go through dispatch personnel at central headquarters. Communications will also change rapidly as mobile data terminals (MDTS) become common. Officers will enter reports directly into the department's mainframe. Digital dictation systems will let officers transmit reports by cellular phones; the reports will be stored until data entry operators type the reports directly into the departmental information system.

CRITICAL THINKING

1. Do you believe that the increased sophistication of police technology presents a threat to civil liberties?
2. If the police are able to identify people by DNA testing, should all citizens be forced to submit tissue samples so that their genetic code can be stored on police computers? Would this be an unreasonable intrusion into people's lives, or are such measures justifiable considering the potential for crime control?

 INFOTRAC COLLEGE EDITION RESEARCH

To read more about the application of DNA testing to crime control, see: Ryan McDonald. Juries and crime labs: correcting the weak links in the DNA chain. *American Journal of Law & Medicine* 24 (Summer-Fall 1998): 345–363.
DNA profiling advancement. *The FBI Law Enforcement Bulletin* 67 (Feb 1998), p.24.

Source: Peter B. Kraska and Victor E. Kappeler, "Militarizing American Police: The Rise and Normalization of Paramilitary Units," *Social Problems* 44 (1997): 1–18; Kim Waggoner, "Focus on Crime Prevention: Creative Solutions to Traditional Problems," *FBI Law Enforcement Bulletin* 66 (1997): 8–10; Tim Webb, "Community Policing Online," *FBI Law Enforcement Bulletin* 66 (1997): 6–9; Kevin Sack, "DNA Tests Free 2 Men Convicted in '83 Rape," *New York Times,* 4 December 1997, p. A20; David L. Carter and Andra J. Katz, "Computer Crime: An Emerging Challenge for Law Enforcement," *The FBI Law Enforcement Bulletin* 65 (1996): 1–8; David E. Kaplan, "New Cybercop Tricks to Fight Child Porn: Police Struggle Against an Online Onslaught," *U.S. News & World Report* 122 (May 26, 1997): 29; Larry Coutorie, "The Future of High-Technology Crime: A Parallel Delphi Study," *Journal of Criminal Justice* 23 (1995): 13–27; Noreen Purcell, L. Thomas Winfree, and G. Larry Mays, "DNA (Deoxyribonucleic Acid) Evidence and Criminal Trials: An Exploratory Survey of Factors Associated with the Use of 'Genetic Fingerprinting' in Felony Prosecutions," *Journal of Criminal Justice* 22 (1994): 145–73; Associated Press, "Under New Policy, FBI Examiners Testify to Absolute DNA Matches," *Criminal Justice Newsletter* 28 (15 October 1997), pp. 1–2.

administers immigration laws, deports illegal aliens, and naturalizes aliens lawfully present in the United States. This service also patrols borders to prevent aliens from entering the United States illegally.

The Treasury Department maintains the Alcohol, Tobacco, and Firearms (ATF) Bureau, which has jurisdiction over the sales and distribution of firearms, explosives, alcohol, and tobacco products. The ATF made national headlines with its 1993 tragic confrontation and shootout with the Branch Davidian cult in Waco, Texas. Fighting started when ATF agents attempted to serve a warrant issued because cult members were believed to possess illegal automatic weapons.

The Internal Revenue Service, established in 1862, enforces violations of income, excise, stamp, and other tax laws. Its intelligence division actively pursues gamblers, narcotics dealers, and other violators who do not report their illegal financial gains as taxable income.

The Customs Bureau guards points of entry into the United States and prevents smuggling of contraband into or out of the country.

The Secret Service, an arm of the Treasury Department, was originally charged with enforcing laws against counterfeiting. Today it also protects the president and vice president and their families, presidential candidates, and former presidents.

County Law Enforcement

The county police department is an independent agency whose senior officer, the **sheriff,** is usually elected. The county sheriff's role has evolved from that of the early English **shire reeve,** whose main duty was to assist royal judges in trying prisoners and enforcing the law outside cities. From the time of U.S. westward expansion until municipal departments were developed, the sheriff often was the sole legal authority in vast territories.

Today there are about 150,000 full-time officers and 89,000 other employees in about 3,000 sheriff's departments in the United States.[15] Their duties vary according to the size and degree of development of the county. Officials within the department may serve as coroners, tax assessors, tax collectors, overseers of highways and bridges, custodians of the county treasury, keepers of the county jail, court attendants, and executors of criminal and civil processes; in years past, sheriff's offices also conducted executions. Many of the sheriff's law enforcement functions today are carried out only in unincorporated areas within a county or in response to city departments' requests for aid in such matters as patrol or investigation.

State Police

The Texas Rangers, organized in 1835, are considered the first state police force. However, the Rangers were more a quasi-military force that supported the Texas state militia than a law enforcement body. The first true state police forces emerged at the turn of the twentieth century, with Pennsylvania's leading the way.

The impetus for creating state police agencies can be traced both to the low regard of the public for the crime-fighting ability of local police agencies and to the increasingly greater mobility of law violators. Using automobiles, thieves could strike at will and be out of the jurisdiction of local police before an investigation could be mounted. Therefore, a law enforcement agency with statewide jurisdiction was needed. Also, state police gave governors a powerful enforcement arm that was under their personal control and not that of city politicians.

Today there are about 55,000 full-time state police officers and 29,000 other full-time employees in 49 departments (Hawaii has no state police).[16] The major role of state police is controlling traffic on the highway system, tracing stolen automobiles, and aiding in disturbances and crowd control. In states with large, powerful county sheriff's departments, the state police function is usually restricted to highway patrol. In others, where the county sheriff's law enforcement role is limited, state police usually maintain a more active investigative and enforcement role.

Metropolitan Police

Metropolitan police agencies make up the vast majority of the law enforcement community's members. There are approximately 410,000 local police officers and 110,000 other full-time employees in 13,000 departments. They range in size from New York's, which employs around 36,000 sworn officers, and Chicago's, with more than 13,000 officers, to the single police officer

Table 16.2 Local Police Departments by Size of Agency

NUMBER OF FULL-TIME SWORN PERSONNEL	AGENCIES	
	NUMBER	PERCENT
All sizes	13,578	100%
1,000 or more officers	41	.3%
500–999	39	.3
250–499	91	.7
100–249	344	2.5
50–99	698	5.1
25–49	1,350	9.9
10–24	2,662	19.6
5–9	2,616	19.3
2–4	3,058	22.5
1	1,657	12.2
0	1,022	7.5

Source: Brian A. Reaves and Andrew L. Goldberg, *Census of State and Local Law Enforcement Agencies, 1996* (Washington, D.C.: Bureau of Justice Statistics, 1998), p. 5.

Figure 16.1   Organization of a Metropolitan Police Department

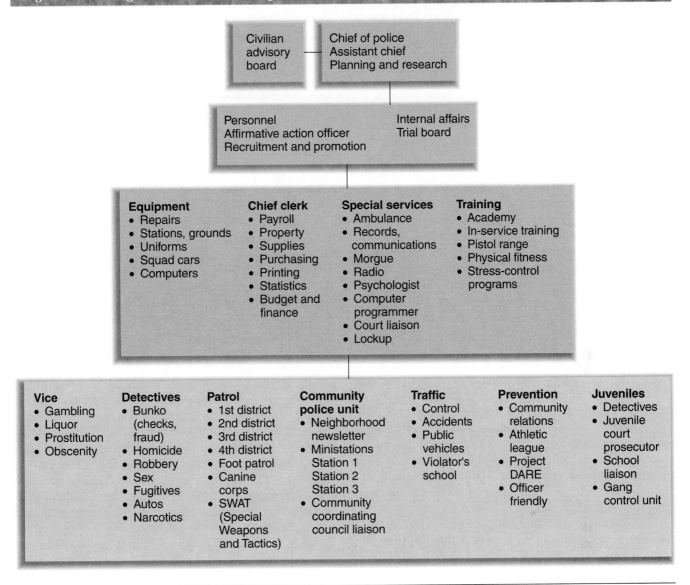

who is a small town's only staff. In all, about 41 departments have more than 1,000 full-time officers, whereas more than 5000 have 4 or fewer (see Table 16.2).

Most larger urban departments are independent agencies operating without specific administrative control from any higher governmental authority. They are organized at the executive level of government. It is therefore common for the city mayor (or the equivalent) to control the hiring and firing of the police chief and, consequently, determine departmental policies.

Most municipal departments are organized in a military way, often using military terms to designate seniority (sergeant, lieutenant, captain).The organization of a typical metropolitan police department is illustrated in Figure 16.1. This complex structure is a function of the multiplicity of roles that police are en-

trusted with. Among the daily activities of police agencies are

- Identifying criminal suspects.
- Investigating crimes.
- Apprehending offenders and participating in their trials.
- Deterring crime through patrol.
- Aiding individuals in danger or in need of assistance; providing emergency services.
- Resolving conflict and keeping the peace.
- Maintaining a sense of community security.
- Keeping vehicular and pedestrian movement efficient.
- Promoting civil order.
- Operating and administering the police department.

The remainder of this chapter examines local policing.

What do local police actually do? What are their major functions, and how well do they perform them? This section discusses these issues.

Patrol Function

Patrol entails police officers' visible presence on the streets and public places of their jurisdiction. The purpose of patrol is to deter crime, maintain order, enforce laws, and aid in service functions, such as emergency medical care. There is a large variety of patrol techniques. In early police forces, **foot patrol** was almost exclusively used. Each officer had a particular area, or *beat,* to walk; the police officer was the symbol of state authority in that area. The beat officer dispensed "street justice," and some became infamous for their use of clubs or nightsticks.

When the old-style beat officer needed assistance, he would pound the pavement with his stick to summon his colleagues from nearby areas. Later call boxes were introduced so the officer could communicate more easily with headquarters. Today patrol cars, motorcycles, helicopters, and other types of mechanized transportation have all but ended *walking the beat.* Although the patrol car allows police to supervise more territory with fewer officers, it has removed and isolated patrol officers from the communities they serve. Some experts argue that this impersonal style of enforcement has worsened relations between police and community. In some communities **aggressive preventive patrol,** designed to deter crime, has heightened tensions between the police and minorities.

Considerable tension is involved in patrolling, especially in high-crime areas where police feel they are open targets. The patrol officer must learn to work the street, taking whatever action is necessary to control the situation and no more. When patrol officers take inappropriate action or when their behavior results in violence or death, they are subject to intense scrutiny by public agencies and may be subject to disciplinary measures from the police department's **internal affairs division.** Patrol officers are expected to make mature, reasoned decisions while facing a constant flow of people in emotional crisis.

A patrol officer's job is extremely demanding and often is unrewarding and unappreciated. It is not surprising that the attitudes of police officers toward the public have been characterized by ambivalence, cynicism, and tension.[17]

How Effective Is Patrol?   Most police departments assign the majority of officers to patrol work; it can be stated that the patrol officer is the backbone of policing. But does police patrol deter crime? Put another way, should police spend so much time and resources keeping a visible presence on the street if their efforts do little to control crime? Research, especially the oft-cited Kansas City patrol study, shows that police presence per se has little influence on crime rates.[18]

> **CONNECTIONS**
>
> As you may recall from Chapter 5, the most comprehensive effort to evaluate the patrol function, the Kansas City study, found that police patrol had little effect on crime patterns. The presence or absence of patrol did not seem to affect residential or business burglaries, auto thefts, larcenies involving auto accessories, robberies, vandalism, or other criminal behavior.

One reason may be that patrol officers rarely make arrests for serious crimes. About 600,000 law enforcement officers make approximately 2 million index crime arrests per year, or four per officer, an average of fewer than one every two months. Although arrests alone cannot be equated with effectiveness, relatively little of a police officer's time is spent confronting and arresting felons.

Although the mere presence of police may not be sufficient to deter crime, the manner in which they approach their task may make a difference. In a classic study, James Q. Wilson and Barbara Boland found that a proactive, aggressive law enforcement style may help reduce crime rates. Jurisdictions that encourage patrol officers to stop motor vehicles to issue citations and to aggressively arrest and detain suspicious persons also experience lower crime rates than jurisdictions that do not follow such proactive policies.[19] Departments that actively enforce public order crimes (such as disorderly conduct) and traffic laws experience lower rates of serious crime.[20]

It is difficult to determine why some experiments in proactive policing work so effectively. Aggressive policing may have a direct deterrent effect: it increases community perception that police arrest a lot of criminals and that most violators get caught. Aggressive police arrest more suspects, and their subsequent conviction gets them off the street; fewer criminals produce lower crime rates. The recent downturn in New York City violent crime has been attributed by some to aggressive police work aimed at lifestyle crimes like vandalism, panhandling, and graffiti. Is it possible that aggressive policing efforts for one type of crime may help reduce the incidence of other serious crime?[21]

> **CONNECTIONS**
>
> *Diffusion of benefits* is a term used by rational choice theorists to describe how efforts to prevent one crime can cause the unintended prevention of another and how crime control efforts in one locale can reduce crime in other, nontarget areas. See Chapter 5 for more on this phenomenon.

Before a general policy of vigorous police work can be adopted, more research is needed on proactive policing. Not all evaluations have found that aggressive patrol efforts actually bring the crime rate down.[22] Aggressive patrol seems to work best when it targets particular offenders (such as gang members) or offenses (such as gun possession).[23]

The downside of aggressive tactics must also be considered. Proactive police strategies breed resentment in minority areas where citizens believe they are the target of police suspicion and reaction.[24] Evidence exists that such aggressive police tactics as random stop-and-frisks and rousting teenagers who congregate on street corners are the seeds from which racial conflict grows.[25]

Investigation Function

The second prominent police role is investigation and crime detection. The detective has been a figure of great romantic appeal since the first independent bureau was established by the London Metropolitan Police in 1841. The detective has been portrayed as the elite of the police force in such films and television shows as *Dirty Harry, NYPD Blue,* and *Lethal Weapon,* to name but a few.

Detective branches are organized on the individual precinct level or out of a central headquarters and perform various functions. Some jurisdictions maintain **morals** or **vice squads,** which are usually staffed by plainclothes officers or detectives specializing in victimless crimes such as prostitution or gambling. Vice squad officers may set themselves up as customers for illicit activities to make arrests. For example, undercover detectives may frequent public men's rooms and make advances toward men; those who respond are arrested for homosexual soliciting. In other instances, female police officers may pose as prostitutes. These covert police activities have often been criticized as violating the personal rights of citizens, and their appropriateness and fairness have been questioned.

Investigators must often enter a case after it has been reported to police and attempt to accumulate enough evidence to identify the perpetrator.[26] Detectives use various investigatory techniques. Sometimes they obtain fingerprints from a crime scene and match them with those on file. Other cases demand the aid of informers to help identify perpetrators. In some instances, victims or witnesses are asked to identify offenders by viewing their pictures, or **mug shots,** or by pulling them out of lineups. It is also possible for detectives to solve a crime by being familiar with the working methods of particular offenders—their *modus operandi* or **MO.** The detective identifies the criminal by matching the facts of the crime with the criminal's peculiar habits or actions. In some cases, stolen property is located, and then the case is cleared. Either the

suspect is arrested on another matter and subsequently found to possess stolen merchandise, or during routine questioning, a person confesses to criminal acts the police did not suspect of him or her.

Finally, detectives can use their own initiative in solving a case. For example, the **sting** type of operation has received widespread publicity.[27] Here detectives pose as fences with thieves interested in selling stolen merchandise. Transactions are videotaped to provide prosecutors with strong cases.

Sting-type undercover operations are controversial because they involve a police officer's becoming involved in illegal activity and encouraging offenders to break the law. Stings may encourage crime when area residents realize that a new group is offering cash for stolen goods.[28] The ethics of these operations have been questioned, especially when the police actively recruit criminals. Nonetheless, sting operations seem to have found a permanent place in the law enforcement repertoire.

Are Investigations Effective? Although detectives in the movies and on television always capture the villains, research indicates that real detectives are much less successful. The Rand Corporation, in a classic 1975 study of 153 detective bureaus, found that a great deal of detectives' time was spent in nonproductive work and that investigative expertise did little to help them solve cases.[29] In more than half of the cases cleared, simple, routine actions solved the case; there was little need for scientific, highly trained investigators. The Rand researchers estimated that half of all detectives could be removed without reducing crime clearance rates.

Replications of the Rand study have found that when a suspect was identified, it usually occurred *before* the case was assigned to a detective. Initial identification of suspects usually took place at the crime scene or through routine follow-up procedures.[30] Similarly, the Police Executive Research Forum found that most solved cases involved data gathered at the crime scene by patrol officers; detectives dropped 75 percent of cases after one day and spent an average of four hours on each case.[31]

Efforts have been made to revamp investigation procedures. Patrol officers have been given greater responsibilities in conducting preliminary investigations at crime scenes. In addition, the precinct detective is being replaced by specialized units, such as homicide or burglary squads, that operate over larger areas and can bring specific expertise to bear on a particular case. Another trend has been the development of regional squads of local, state, and federal officers (called *regional strike forces*) that concentrate on major crimes and organized crime activities and use their wider jurisdiction and expertise to provide services beyond the capabilities of a metropolitan police department. An additional common operation is to focus on the investigation and arrest of hard-core career criminals.[32] Ever more specialized units are being created. For example, Washington, D.C.'s, metropolitan police department has a Cold Case Homicide Squad (CCS), which, in cooperation with FBI agents who work directly with the squad, specializes in unsolved crimes at least a year old. [33]

Other Police Functions

Another important public-contact police task is traffic control. This involves such activities as intersection control (directing traffic), traffic law enforcement, radar operations, parking law enforcement, and accident investigation.[34]

Traffic control is a complex daily task involving thousands, even millions, of motor vehicles within a single police jurisdiction. Consequently, police departments use **selective enforcement** in maintaining traffic laws. Police departments neither expect nor wish to punish all traffic violators. A department may set up traffic control units only at particular intersections, although its traffic coordinators know that violations are occurring in many other areas of the city. Officers may be allocated to the traffic division based on prediction of accident or violation expectancy rates, determined by statistical analysis of previous patterns and incidents.

As the model of the typical police department in Figure 16.1 indicates, various other roles are carried out by police agencies. For example, most departments are responsible for administering and controlling their budgets. This task involves purchasing equipment and services, planning future expenditures, and managing the department's resources.

Many departments maintain separate units that keep records on offenders. Modern data management systems have been used to provide easy access to records for case investigations. Similarly, most larger departments have sophisticated communications networks that process citizen complaints and police calls for assistance and dispatch vehicles to respond to them as efficiently as possible.

To promote citizen cooperation, many police departments have specialized community relations officers. Community relations teams perform such tasks as working with citizen groups, lecturing students on traffic safety, and creating neighborhood programs to prevent crime.

Some police agencies maintain (or have access to) forensic laboratories that enable them to identify substances to be used as evidence, classify fingerprints, and augment investigations in other ways.

Another function often found in larger departments is planning and research. The planning and research division designs new programs to increase police efficiency and develops strategies to test their effectiveness.

Police planners monitor recent technological developments and institute programs to adapt them to ongoing police services.

CHANGING THE POLICE ROLE

If you watch the fictional police officers played by Mel Gibson and Danny Glover in *Lethal Weapon* get involved in shoot-outs with automatic weapons, it is easy to see why many people believe that the major police role is law enforcement. In reality, relatively little of a police officer's time is spent on crime-fighting duties.[35] Instead, most effort is devoted to what has been described as *order maintenance* or *peacekeeping*.[36] James Q. Wilson's pioneering work, *Varieties of Police Behavior*, viewed the major police role as "handling the situation."[37] Wilson found that police encounter many troubling incidents that need some sort of "fixing up." Enforcing the law might be one tool a police officer uses; threat, coercion, sympathy, understanding, and apathy might be others. Most important is "keeping things under control so that there are no complaints that he is doing nothing or that he is doing too much."

The peacekeeping role of the police has been documented by several different studies that find that the police function essentially as order-keeping, dispute-settling agents of public health and safety.[38] Figure 16.2 shows the results of a national survey of police behavior. As many as 45 million Americans have contacts with the police each year; most of these involve noncriminal incidents such as getting assistance or traffic-related issues. The "other reasons" category in Figure 16.2, accounting for 20 million annual contacts, involves such instances as police warning people about shoveling snow into the street, responding to a neighbor's complaint about music being too loud during a party, or warning kids not to shoot fireworks. This survey indicates that the police role is both varied and complex.[39]

The burdens of police work have helped set law enforcement officers outside the mainstream of society and have encouraged the development of a police subculture marked by insulation from the outside world and a code of secrecy.[40]

Community-Oriented Policing (COP)

In a highly regarded article, "Broken Windows: The Police and Neighborhood Safety," criminologists James Q. Wilson and George Kelling called for a return to a nineteenth-century style of **community-oriented policing** in which police maintained a presence in the community, walked beats, got to know citizens, and inspired feelings of public safety.[41] Wilson and Kelling asked police administrators to get their officers out of

Figure 16.2   Number of Residents Age 12 or
Older with Face-to-Face Contact with Police
During 1996, by Reason for Contact

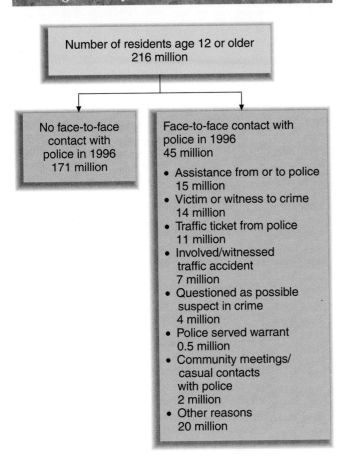

Number of residents age 12 or older
216 million

No face-to-face
contact with
police in 1996
171 million

Face-to-face contact with
police in 1996
45 million

- Assistance from or to police
  15 million
- Victim or witness to crime
  14 million
- Traffic ticket from police
  11 million
- Involved/witnessed
  traffic accident
  7 million
- Questioned as possible
  suspect in crime
  4 million
- Police served warrant
  0.5 million
- Community meetings/
  casual contacts
  with police
  2 million
- Other reasons
  20 million

Source: Lawrence Greenfeld, Patrick Langan, and Steven Smith, *Police Use of Force* (Washington, D.C.: Bureau of Justice Statistics, 1997), p. 2.

depersonalizing patrol cars. Instead of deploying police on the basis of crime rates or in areas where citizens make the most calls for help, police administrators should station their officers where they can do the most to promote public confidence and elicit citizen cooperation. Community preservation, public safety, and order maintenance—not crime fighting—should become the primary focus of police. Implied in the Wilson and Kelling model was a *proactive* police role. Instead of merely responding to calls for help (known as *reactive* policing), police should play an active role in the community, identify neighborhood problems and needs, and set a course of action for an effective response. Wilson and Kelling conclude,

> Just as physicians now recognize the importance of fostering health rather than simply treating illness, so the police—and the rest of us—ought to recognize the importance of maintaining intact communities without broken windows.[42]

The "broken windows" article had an important impact on policing, and since its publication, there has been a continuing reanalysis of the police role.

Implementing COP   A form of COP was first implemented in the 1970s, when **team policing** was instituted around the United States.[43] This concept brought together a group of junior officers and a supervisor who were given constant jurisdiction over a designated neighborhood. The supervisor had complete responsibility for the team area, and the team could patrol the area in the manner it believed would be the most effective. The team determined its own deployment, working hours, assignments, and methods within broad policy guidelines established by the department. The purpose of the team was to create strong ties between the police officers and the community they served and to involve the neighborhood in police operation.[44] When team policing proved less effective than imagined and federal funds dried up, programs were terminated.

The current COP movement began when foot patrols were reintroduced in a limited number of jurisdictions. Foot patrol was believed to be an effective device that could help police monitor community concerns and control drug dealers, vandals, and other petty criminals associated with community decline. Officers on foot are more easily approachable and offer a comforting presence to citizens.. Evaluations of these programs found that although foot patrols had little effect on community crime rates, they did help to improve citizen attitudes toward police.[45]

The success of these early experiments encouraged other cities to implement innovative patrol strategies. These community policing strategies include Neighborhood Watch and other programs in which police organize local citizens to aid them in crime prevention efforts, decentralized command structures in which police operate out of neighborhood ministations, newsletters, and other devices that bring the police and the community closer.[46] These early efforts signaled a change in policing that culminated in a concerted effort to actively pursue citizen involvement in police activities, to orient police strategies toward the neighborhood or block level, and to identify community-level problems and seek their solutions.[47]

CONNECTIONS

By aiming to make it more difficult to commit crimes and by creating clear strategies to reduce area crime rates, the community policing concept borrows ideas from the crime prevention through environmental design and situational crime prevention models. Chapter 5 discusses these ideas in greater detail.

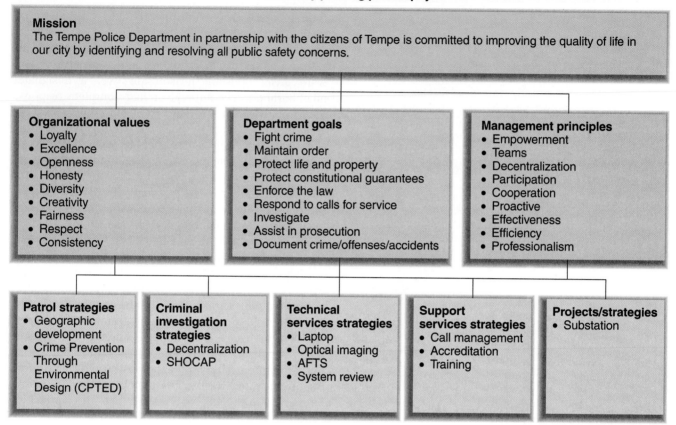

Figure 16.3 Tempe, Arizona, Police Department Planning Model

Community policing philosophy

Mission
The Tempe Police Department in partnership with the citizens of Tempe is committed to improving the quality of life in our city by identifying and resolving all public safety concerns.

Organizational values
- Loyalty
- Excellence
- Openness
- Honesty
- Diversity
- Creativity
- Fairness
- Respect
- Consistency

Department goals
- Fight crime
- Maintain order
- Protect life and property
- Protect constitutional guarantees
- Enforce the law
- Respond to calls for service
- Investigate
- Assist in prosecution
- Document crime/offenses/accidents

Management principles
- Empowerment
- Teams
- Decentralization
- Participation
- Cooperation
- Proactive
- Effectiveness
- Efficiency
- Professionalism

Patrol strategies
- Geographic development
- Crime Prevention Through Environmental Design (CPTED)

Criminal investigation strategies
- Decentralization
- SHOCAP

Technical services strategies
- Laptop
- Optical imaging
- AFTS
- System review

Support services strategies
- Call management
- Accreditation
- Training

Projects/strategies
- Substation

Source: Tempe, Arizona, Police Department.

Community Policing in Action COP programs have been implemented in large cities, suburban areas, and rural communities (see Figure 16.3).[48] Some COP programs assign officers to neighborhoods, organize training programs for community leaders, and feature a bottom-up approach to dealing with community problems: decision making involves the officer on the scene, not a directive from central headquarters. Some departments have created programs for juveniles such as neighborhood cleanup efforts, whereas others contact local businesspeople and community groups to get them involved in planning.[49] In Spokane, Washington, the community police effort created a program called COPY Kids, a summer outreach program for disadvantaged youths that promotes a positive work ethic, emphasizes the values of community involvement, and helps create a positive image of the police departments. Spokane's Neighborhood Investigative Resource Officer (NIRO) program reassigned detectives to patrol sectors based on efforts to detect and prevent crime.[50]

Another example of a successful COP model is Washington, D.C.'s, Howard University Violence Prevention Project. The project, which aims to create a safety net that protects youths against social risk factors, relies on a team approach that involves parents, teachers, mental health professionals, business owners, and local police. The police component of the project, called the Youth Trauma Team, requires that police officers and psychologists respond to violent incidents that occur at night. They talk to children who have been part of or have witnessed violence and afterward link them with needed services. Police officers involved in the project receive training in conflict resolution, cultural sensitivity, and crisis deescalation. They also have networked or partnered extensively with existing community social service providers in a multidisciplinary team effort to provide comprehensive care.[51]

Neighborhood Policing To achieve the goals of COP, some agencies have tried to decentralize, an approach sometimes referred to as **neighborhood policing**. Problems are best solved at the neighborhood level where issues originate, not at a far-off central headquarters. Because each neighborhood has its own particular needs, police decision making must be flexible and adaptive. For example, neighborhoods undergoing change in racial

Some community policing programs assign police officers to outreach programs for disadvantaged youths in order to promote a positive work ethic, emphasize the values of community involvement, and help create a positive image of the police department. Here two police officers assigned to a local substation in New Orleans get involved in a basketball league with neighborhood kids.

composition often experience high levels of racially motivated violence.[52] Police must be able to distinguish these neighborhoods and allocate resources to meet their needs.

Because COP also stresses sharing power with local groups and individuals, neighborhood initiatives may be an ideal way to fight crime. Citizens actively participate with police to fight crime, for example, by providing information in area crime investigations or helping police reach out to troubled area youths. Police in Houston adopted the Positive Interaction Program, in which captains in each of the city's nine (decentralized) substations were required to meet monthly with area business leaders and prominent residents to discuss neighborhood problems. Substation captains were then charged with using available resources to resolve the problems.[53]

Problem-Oriented Policing

Another COP strategy involves the development of **problem-oriented policing.** According to originator Herman Goldstein, police departments have been too concerned with internal efficiency and have therefore given insufficient attention to substantive problems in the work environment.[54] Police have been reactive, responding to calls for help. Instead they should play an active role in identifying particular community problems—street-level drug dealers, prostitution rings, gang

hangouts—and developing strategies to counteract them. Problems are better defined narrowly; for example, the focus would be on reducing larceny from the mall on weekends, not a general reduction in the crime rate. Solutions draw on the creative talents found in two important resources: the community and the line officers who are familiar with community problems. Rather than stifle or control creativity, problem-oriented policing encourages new solutions to old problems.

Problem-oriented policing techniques are used in a number of police departments. For example, the New York City police department has worked with Victim Services in the Domestic Violence Intervention Education Project (DIVIEP), which provides follow-up services to the victims of domestic violence.[55] DIVIEP reduces the risk of repeat victimization by informing victims of their legal rights and making it clear to perpetrators that their behavior is being monitored. An evaluation of the program indicates that it had little significant effect on reducing violence rates but did increase calls to the police; DIVIEP may have increased citizen confidence in law enforcement.[56] In Vancouver, Canada, community police officers assigned to reduce and control street prostitution actually included prostitutes in their planning and were able to reduce neighborhood conflict by mediating between residents and prostitutes. They included both groups to help control collateral problems such as drug dealing and pornography.[57]

Problem-oriented policing strategies are also aimed at reducing community fear levels. Fear reduction is viewed both as an important element of police services to the community and also as a means of increasing citizen cooperation with police officers.[58]

One strategy of crime-specific policing is the **crackdown,** in which particular problem areas in a city are the target of increased police resources.[59]

CONNECTIONS

As you may recall from Chapter 5, Lawrence Sherman found that crackdowns work effectively as a short-term crime reduction strategy, perhaps because they have a shock effect on the local criminal population. In the long term, however, their effect on crime control decays. Sherman finds that this form of problem-oriented policing might be best instituted for short periods and rotated among different problem areas.

Research shows that a significant portion of all police calls emanate from relatively few locations: bars, malls, the bus depot, hotels, certain apartment buildings.[60] By implication, concentrating police resources on these **hot spots** could appreciably reduce crime.[61]

Does Community Policing Work?

Many police experts and administrators have embraced the community and problem-oriented policing concepts as a revolutionary revision of the basic police role. COP efforts have been credited with helping to reduce crime rates in large cities such as New York and Boston. The most professional and highly motivated officers are the ones most likely to support COP efforts.[62]

Not all criminologists agree that a return to the older model of policing is a panacea. For example, justice historian Samuel Walker has criticized the "broken windows" concept on the grounds that it misinterprets and romanticizes police history: old-style police were neither liked nor respected.[63] Police expert Jack Greene has argued that COP strategies fail to accurately define the concept of *community*—an ecological area defined by common norms, shared values, and interpersonal bonds.[64] Community policing often ignores community boundaries for administrative convenience.

It may also be difficult to retrain and reorient police from their traditional roles into more of a social service orientation.[65] Most police officers do not have the social service skills required of effective community agents. Some are reluctant to develop new skills—for example, considering it a waste of time when asked to take courses in cultural diversity to make them more sensitive to community needs.[66] Surveys of police officers involved report that while they are generally favor-

able to COP, they also suffer ridicule from their peers because of the "cushy" assignment that is not "real" police work, that they are often unsure of what to do, and that their program has little effect on the crime rate.[67] If police are in fact mistrustful and cynical, then community police efforts will be difficult to implement. Police administrators, while enjoying the public support created by COP, are reluctant to give up the autonomy and authority that power sharing with the public demands.[68] They may find that the practices demanded by COP conflict with what they consider to be effective, efficient law enforcement. National surveys find that police administrators still consider law enforcement their top priority; providing community and social services is not considered a significant police role.[69] A recent national survey of police organizations found that they had actually undergone relatively little structural change since the advent of the COP movement. Police departments have even become more specialized in the 1990s, an organizational development in opposition to the COP vision of police as informal problem solvers.[70]

These concerns are valid; but a number of research evaluations indicate that COP programs improve community relations, upgrade the image of local police, and reduce levels of community fear.[71] There is also evidence that local police departments can implement community programs without straining or sacrificing their ability to provide emergency services.[72]

Little question exists that community and problem-oriented policing will continue to find support. They fit well with efforts to reduce crime among high-risk populations.[73] It is becoming difficult to separate innovative policing models from more traditional ones, and in the future the norm may be a blend that includes elements of problem solving, community actions, and public security.[74] Some experts are already beginning to combine innovative policing strategies into a unified concept and are using the acronym COPPS to stand for a community-oriented, problem-solving approach to identify, assess, and address crime-related community issues.[75].

POLICE AND THE RULE OF LAW

Like other areas of criminal justice, police behavior is carefully controlled by court action. On the one hand, police want a free hand to enforce the law as they see fit. On the other hand, the courts must balance the needs of efficient law enforcement with the constitutional rights of citizens. Some important legal issues have emerged from this conflict, the most critical being citizen rights during police interrogation and the right to be free from illegal searches and seizures by police officers.

Custodial Interrogation

The Fifth Amendment guarantees people the right to be free from self-incrimination. This has been interpreted as meaning that law enforcement agents cannot use physical or psychological coercion while interrogating suspects under their control to get them to confess or give information.

The federal government has long held that a confession must be made voluntarily if it is to be admissible as evidence in a criminal trial. Confessions obtained from defendants through coercion, force, trickery, or promises of leniency are inadmissible because their trustworthiness is questionable. The rule of voluntariness applies to confessions obtained at any time, whether the defendant was in police custody or not. In the past, one of the major drawbacks to determining the voluntariness of confessions was that the decision was subjective and made case by case.

In 1966 the Supreme Court, in the case of *Miranda v. Arizona,* created objective standards for questioning by police after a defendant has been taken into custody.[76] *Custody* occurs when a person is not free to walk away, as when an individual is arrested. The Court maintained that before the police can question a person who has been arrested or is in custody, they must inform the individual of the Fifth Amendment right to be free from self-incrimination. This is accomplished by the police issuing what is known as the *Miranda warning,* which informs the suspect that

1. He or she has the right to remain silent.
2. If he or she makes a statement, it can be used against him or her in court.
3. He or she has the right to consult an attorney and to have the attorney present at the time of the interrogation.
4. If he or she cannot afford an attorney, one will be appointed by the state.

If the defendant is not given the Miranda warning before the investigation, the evidence obtained from the interrogation cannot be admitted at trial. Finally, the accused can waive his or her Miranda rights at any time. However, for the waiver to be effective, the state must first show that the defendant was aware of all the Miranda rights and must then prove that the waiver was made with the full knowledge of constitutional rights.

The Miranda Rule Today The Supreme Court has used case law to define the boundaries of the Miranda warning since its inception. Important Court rulings on the Miranda warning have created the following guidelines:

1. Evidence obtained in violation of the Miranda warning can be used by the government to impeach a defendant's testimony during trial, if they perjure themselves.[77]
2. At trial, the testimony of a witness is permissible even though his or her identity was revealed by the defendant in violation of the Miranda rule.[78]
3. It is permissible to renew questioning of suspects who had invoked their Miranda right to remain silent if the warning is restated by police.
4. The Miranda warning applies only to the right to have an attorney present; the suspect cannot demand to speak to a priest, probation officer, or any other official.[79]
5. Information provided by a suspect that leads to the seizure of incriminating evidence is permissible if the evidence would have been obtained anyway by other means or sources; this is now referred to as the **inevitable discovery rule.**[80]
6. A suspect can be questioned in the field without a Miranda warning if the information the police seek is needed to protect *public safety;* for example, in an emergency, suspects can be asked where they hid their weapons.[81]
7. Initial errors by police in getting statements do not make subsequent statements inadmissible; a subsequent Miranda warning that is properly given can "cure the condition" that made the initial statements inadmissible.[82]
8. Suspects need not be aware of all the possible outcomes of waiving their rights for the Miranda warning to be considered properly given.[83]
9. The admissions of mentally impaired defendants can be admitted in evidence as long as the police acted properly and there is a "preponderance of the evidence" that they understood the meaning of Miranda.[84]
10. An attorney's request to see the defendant does not affect the validity of the defendant's waiver of the right to counsel; police misinformation to an attorney does not affect waiver of Miranda rights.[85]
11. People who are mentally ill due to clinically diagnosed schizophrenia may voluntarily confess and waive their Miranda rights.[86]
12. Once a criminal suspect has invoked his or her Miranda rights, police officials cannot reinitiate interrogation in the absence of counsel even if the accused has consulted with an attorney in the meantime.[87]
13. The erroneous admission of a coerced confession at trial can be ruled a "harmless error" that would not automatically result in overturning a conviction.[88]
14. A suspect who makes an ambiguous reference to an attorney during questioning, such as "Maybe I should talk to an attorney," is not protected under Miranda; the police may continue their questioning.[89]

It appears that recent case law has narrowed the scope of Miranda and given police greater leeway in their actions. Critics warn that this may encourage police to pressure suspects to confess without benefit of counsel to protect their civil rights. One recent analysis of 60 cases where a confession later proved false showed that police routinely induce confessions from suspects, a practice that imposes substantial deprivations of liberty on the defendants. At trial, these false confessions are considered important evidence in the minds of jurors and criminal justice officials even if they seem inconsistent with the facts of the case.[90] Recording police interrogations would significantly reduce miscarriages of justice that stem from confessions coerced by the police.[91]

Nonetheless, the Miranda rule still protects criminal defendants who are being interrogated by police.

Search and Seizure

In order to conduct investigations, the police may want to search people, their cars, and homes. In order to do so, they must under normal circumstances obtain a **search warrant.**

CONNECTIONS

As you may recall from Chapter 15, the Fourth Amendment protects against unreasonable searches and seizures by police officers. This means that, with some exceptions, police officers must have a search warrant issued by a magistrate to search a person and his or her possessions.

When the police try to obtain search warrants, they usually rely on the word of informers. In the case of *Illinois v. Gates,* the Supreme Court created what is known as the *totality of the circumstances* test for obtaining a search warrant.[92] Loosely interpreted, if judges are presented with sufficient, knowledgeable evidence for issuing a warrant, they may do so even if the source of the information is anonymous or unknown. The *Gates* doctrine makes it significantly easier for police to obtain valid search warrants.

To make it easier for police to conduct investigations and to protect public safety, the Court has ruled that under certain circumstances, a valid search may be conducted without a search warrant. The six major exceptions are search incident to a valid arrest, threshold inquiry (stop-and-frisk), automobile search, consent search, plain-sight search, and seizure of nonphysical evidence.

1. *Search incident to an arrest.* A warrantless search is valid if it is made incident to a lawful arrest. The reason for this exception is that the arresting officer must have the power to disarm the accused, protect him- or herself, preserve the evidence of the crime, and prevent the accused's escape from custody. Because the search

is lawful, the officer retains what he or she finds if it is connected with a crime. The officer is permitted to search only the defendant's person and the areas in the defendant's immediate physical surroundings that are under his or her control.[93]

2. *Threshold inquiry (stop-and-frisk).* Threshold inquiry deals with the situation in which, although the officer does not have probable cause to arrest, his or her suspicions are raised concerning the behavior of an individual. In such a case, the officer has a right to stop and question the individual; if the officer has reason to believe that the person is carrying a concealed weapon, he or she may frisk the suspect. Unlike searching, frisking is a limited procedure; it is a pat-down of the outer clothing for the purpose of finding a concealed weapon. If no weapon is found, the search must stop. However, if an illegal weapon is found, then an arrest can be made and a search incident to the arrest performed.[94] In a threshold inquiry situation, a police officer is permitted to conduct a limited search—that is, one confined to determining whether a suspect is armed.

3. *Automobile search.* An automobile may be searched without a warrant if there is probable cause to believe that the car was involved in a crime.[95] The rationale for allowing a search of an automobile involves the mobility of automobiles, which creates a significant chance that the evidence will be lost if the search is not conducted immediately, and the fact that people should not expect as much privacy in their cars as in their homes.[96] Police officers who have legitimately stopped an automobile and who have probable cause to believe that contraband is concealed somewhere within it may conduct a warrantless search of the vehicle that is as thorough as a magistrate could authorize by warrant. The Supreme Court has ruled that police who have stopped a motorist for a traffic violation can search the vehicle if after they stop the car they see probable cause that the vehicle is involved in a crime; for example, after stopping a car for an illegal U-turn, they spot drug paraphernalia in the front seat. The search is permissible even if the police had been watching the car because they were suspicious that the driver was involved in a drug deal.[97]

4. *Consent search.* In a consent search, individuals waive their constitutional rights; therefore, neither a warrant nor probable cause need exist. However, for the search to be legal, the consent must be given voluntarily; threat or compulsion invalidates the search.[98] Although it has been held that voluntary consent is required, it has also been maintained that the police are under no obligation to inform individuals of their right to refuse the search. For example, police do not have to tell motorists they have stopped for a traffic violation that they are actually free to go before asking permission to search the car.[99]

5. *Plain view.* Even when an object is in a house or other areas involving an expectation of privacy, the ob-

A warrantless search is valid if it is made incident to a lawful arrest. The Supreme Court allows this type of search to preserve the evidence of the crime, prevent the accused's escape from custody, and protect the life of the officer who might be otherwise threatened by hidden weapons. The scope of the search is only within "arm's reach" of the suspect.

ject can be freely inspected if it can be seen by the general public. For example, if a police officer looks through a fence and sees marijuana growing in a suspect's fields, no search warrant is needed for the property to be seized. The articles are considered to be in plain view, and therefore a search warrant need not be obtained to seize them.[100]

6. *Seizure of nonphysical evidence.* Police can seize nonphysical evidence, such as a conversation, if the suspects had no reason to expect privacy—for example, if police overhear and record a conversation in which two people conspire to kill a third party. In *Katz v. United States,* the Supreme Court addressed the issue that the Fourth Amendment protects people and not property.[101] In *Katz* the FBI attached an electronic recording device to a public telephone booth for the purpose of obtaining evidence that the defendant was transmitting wagering information in violation of a federal statute. The Court held that the FBI's action constituted an unreasonable search and seizure. The Court maintained that a search occurs whenever police activity violates a person's privacy. In this case, it was reasonable for the defendant to expect that he would have privacy in a phone booth.

In recent years the Court has given police greater latitude to search for and seize evidence and has eased restrictions on how police operate. The Court's policy has reflected the legal orientation of its more conservative members.

CONNECTIONS

The exclusionary rule (discussed in Chapter 15), once a powerful control on police evidence-gathering procedures, has been substantially weakened by a more conservative Supreme Court but still remains the law of the land.

ISSUES IN POLICING

A number of important issues face police departments today. Although an all-encompassing discussion of each is beyond the scope of this text, a few of the more important aspects of policing are discussed here.

Police Personality and Subculture

It has become commonplace to argue that a majority of U.S. police officers have unique personality traits that place them apart from the average citizen. The typical police personality is thought to include authoritarianism, suspicion, racism, hostility, insecurity, conservatism, and cynicism.[102] These negative values and attitudes are believed to cause police officers to be secretive and isolated from the rest of society, producing what has been described by William Westly as the **blue curtain** subculture.[103] Isolation and conflict may also contribute to the extreme stress that is an occupational hazard of police work.[104] Studies of police officers show that their stress levels increase substantially after urban unrest, when some officers may feel estranged from the community they are forced to control.[105]

There are two opposing viewpoints on the cause of this phenomenon. One position holds that police departments attract recruits who are by nature cynical, authoritarian, secretive, and so on; other experts maintain that socialization and experience on the police force cause these character traits to develop in police officers.[106] Because research evidence supportive of both viewpoints has been produced, neither position dominates on the issue of how the police personality develops; it is not even certain that such a personality actually exists.

The Police Subculture More than 40 years ago, police expert William Westly argued that most police officers develop into cynics because of their daily duties.[107] Westly maintained that police officers learn to mistrust the citizens they protect because they are constantly faced with keeping people in line and come to believe that most people are out to break the law or harm a police officer. As a consequence, most officers band together in a police subculture characterized by clannishness, secrecy, and insulation from others in society. Policing expert John Crank has described how the sources of police culture can be traced to the need to be a moral force on their beat; to the fear of the unknown and hidden dangers; and to the overwhelming need for peer support to cope with adversity. The police culture, then, has its roots in morality, solidarity, and the need for common sense or "street smarts."[108]

Both the daily routines of police work as well as their close peer relations support the subculture. Police officers tend to socialize with each other and believe their occupation cuts them off from relationships with civilians. Joining the police subculture means having to support fellow officers against outsiders; maintaining a tough, macho exterior personality; and mistrusting the motives and behavior of outsiders.[109] Normative behavior might include a tough, almost cold-hearted exterior that makes them immune to the emotional turmoil a civilian might feel when encountering a shooting victim or a body that has been left for a week in a sealed apartment.[110] The police subculture encourages its members to draw a sharp distinction between good and evil. Officers are more than mere enforcers of the law; they are warriors in the "age-old battle between right and wrong."[111] In contrast, criminals are referred to as "terrorists" and "predators"—terms that portray them as evil individuals ready to prey upon the poor and vulnerable. Because the "predators" represent a real danger, police culture demands that its members be both competent and concerned with the safety of their peers and partners. Competence is often translated into respect and authority, and citizens must obey lest they face "payback."[112]

Because many police–citizen encounters involve more than one officer, some sort of cooperative arrangement is necessary between the officers involved. Shared group norms may take precedence over individual style in handling daily activities.[113] Because of this solidarity, strong myths develop about police work that, after becoming institutionalized, help shape the structure and activities of police departments themselves.[114] Some officers may be frustrated by a criminal justice system that seems to favor the rights of the criminal and "handcuffs" the police; others might be sensitive to a perceived lack of support from government officials and the general public. Officers who perceive strain may be less likely to embrace innovative ideas such as community policing.[115] The most serious consequences of the police subculture are police officers' resistance to change and mistrust of the public they serve. Opening the police to change will be a prime task of police officials who seek professionalism and progress in their departments.

Police Style Even if a unique police personality exists, that does not mean that all police officers share a common job orientation or style. Some officers are service-oriented, whereas others take a much more active law enforcement role; some are more concerned about their advancement through the ranks; others enjoy the action of the streets.[116] Departments themselves differ in their orientation toward police activities; some take a more active role in arresting felons, whereas others exhibit a less legalistic orientation.[117] The various styles of policing are illustrated in Figure 16.4.

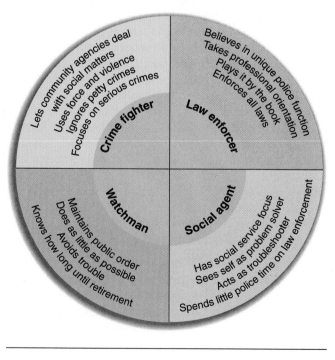

Figure 16.4 Four Styles of Policing

Crime fighter
- Lets community agencies deal with social matters
- Uses force and violence
- Ignores petty crimes
- Focuses on serious crimes

Law enforcer
- Believes in unique police function
- Takes professional orientation
- Plays it by the book
- Enforces all laws

Watchman
- Maintains public order
- Does as little as possible
- Avoids trouble
- Knows how long until retirement

Social agent
- Has social service focus
- Sees self as problem solver
- Acts as troubleshooter
- Spends little police time on law enforcement

Discretion

In one of the most important justice-related papers, Joseph Goldstein argued in 1960 that the law enforcement function of police is not merely a matter of enforcing the rule of law but also involves an enormous amount of personal *discretion* as to whether to invoke the power of arrest.[118] Since then, police discretion has been recognized as a crucial force in all law enforcement decision making.[119]

Police discretion involves the selective enforcement of the law by duly authorized police agents. However, unlike members of almost every other criminal justice agency, police officers are neither regulated in their daily procedures by administrative scrutiny nor subjected to judicial review (except when their behavior clearly violates an offender's constitutional rights). As a result, the exercise of discretion by police may sometimes deteriorate into discrimination, violence, and other abusive practices.[120] The factors that are believed to influence police discretion are illustrated in Figure 16.5.

Environmental and Community Factors Various factors have been associated with the exercise of police discretion.[121] Community crime levels influence police perception and activities. In areas where social problems abound and deviant behavior is the norm, police officers may become cynical and view crime victims as being undeserving of their full attention; the line between criminal and victim becomes blurred.[122] Police are overburdened in these deteriorated neighborhoods and begin to put routine crimes on the back burner. Informal rules among experienced police officers hold that deviant acts in these areas deserve less vigorous reactions than the same acts would generate in a more stable, low-crime area.[123]

Community structure, attitudes, and beliefs also influence the enforcement or nonenforcement of certain laws (for example, obscenity statutes). Conservative communities may demand a higher level of police activity than jurisdictions whose population holds more moderate or tolerant attitudes. The communities' ability to fund treatment and rehabilitation programs may influence an officer's judgment because these programs provide alternatives to official police intervention or processing. A police officer may exercise discretion and arrest an individual in a particular circumstance if it seems that nothing else can be done, even if the officer does not believe that an arrest is good police work. In an environment with abundant social agencies—detoxification units, drug control centers, and child care services, for example—a police officer has more alternatives from which to choose. In fact, referring cases to these agencies saves the officer both time and effort—no records need be made out, and court appearances can be avoided. Thus social agencies provide for greater latitude in police decision making.

Departmental Factors The policies, practices, and customs of the local police department and its administrators also influence discretion. Departments often issue written policies that limit or expand police discretion, spelling out when an arrest should be made and which behaviors can be handled informally.

Organizational behavior may also determine how police deal with different groups in society. Police departments may routinely patrol particular areas of the city while leaving others relatively unattended. Consequently, some residents have a greater chance of experiencing detection and arrest. Although racial profiling in arrest decisions violates constitutional rights, courts have upheld the use of race as a personal identifying factor that helps narrow police searches for suspects. Police manuals also suggest that officers be aware of race when watching for suspicious characters (for example, questioning those who do not "belong" on their beat). Similarly, courts have upheld the government's use of race as a condition of determining probable cause in searches for illegal aliens and in drug courier profiles.[124]

An individual supervisor, such as a sergeant or lieutenant, can influence subordinates' decisions by making known his or her personal preferences and attitudes. Peer pressure also influences decision making. Fellow police officers dictate acceptable responses to street-level problems by displaying or withholding approval in squad room discussions. The officer who takes the job seriously and desires the respect and friendship of others will take their advice, abide by their norms, and seek out the most experienced and most influential patrol officers on the force and follow their behavior models.

Figure 16.5 Influences on Police Discretion

Does Race Influence the Police Use of Discretion?

In the late summer of 1997 New Yorkers were shocked as an astounding case of police brutality began to unfold in the daily newspapers. Abner Louima, 33, a Haitian immigrant, had been arrested outside Club Rendez-Vous, a Brooklyn nightclub, on August 9, 1997, after a fight had broken out. Louima later claimed that the arresting officers had become furious when he protested his arrest, twice stopping the patrol car to beat him with their fists. When they arrived at the station house, two officers, apparently angry because some of the clubgoers had fought with the police, led Louima to the men's room, removed his trousers, and attacked him with the handle of a toilet plunger, first shoving it into his rectum and then into his mouth, breaking teeth, while Louima screamed, "Why are you doing this to me? Why? Why?" The officers also shouted racial slurs at Louima, who was rushed to a hospital for emergency surgery to repair a puncture in his small intestine and injuries to his bladder. Louima, who witnesses said had no bruises or injuries when officers took him into custody, arrived at the hospital three hours later bleeding profusely.

In the aftermath of the case, NYPD investigators granted departmental immunity to nearly 100 officers in order to gain information. By cracking the "blue curtain" of silence they were able to indict four officers in the attack on charges of sexual abuse and first-degree assault.

One often-debated issue is whether police take race, class, and gender into account when making arrest decisions. The question is whether police discretion works against the young, males, the poor, and minority group members and favors the wealthy, the politically connected, and majority group members. Research has uncovered evidence supporting both sides of this argument. For example, Ronald Weitzer found that while police are involved in at least some discrimination against racial minorities, the frequency and scope of police discrimination may be less than anticipated. In contrast, after thoroughly reviewing the literature on police bias, Samuel Walker, Cassia Spohn, and Miriam DeLone conclude that police discriminate against racial minorities and that significant problems persist between the police and racial and ethnic communities in the United States. The

Walker research concludes that despite progress, significant racial and ethnic disparities remain the norm.

The debate over race discrimination by police is reflected in the research literature. A significant body of literature shows that police are more likely to hassle or arrest poor African-American males. Multistate research efforts have found that race and demeanor do in fact play an important role in police discretion. For example, Darlene Conley found evidence that police frequently stop and question youths of color walking down the streets of their neighborhoods or standing on corners. Neighborhood kids told her how suspicion produces crime: if you're going to be harassed and "messed with," you might as well not care and commit crime.

In contrast to these findings, a number of studies have produced data indicating that racial bias does not influence the decision to arrest and process a suspect. According to this view, prior record, crime seriousness, and other legal factors control police decision making, not a suspect's race, ethnicity, or gender. Suspects who are intoxicated and belligerent are more likely to invoke the ire of police

Situational Influences Another discretionary influence is the way that a crime or situation is encountered. If, for example, a police officer stumbles on an altercation or a break-in, the discretionary response may be quite different than if the officer had been summoned by police radio. If official police recognition has been given to an act, action must be taken or an explanation made as to why it was not taken. If a matter is brought to an officer's attention by a citizen observer, the officer can ignore the request and risk a complaint or take discretionary action. When an officer chooses to become involved in a situation without benefit of a summons or complaint, maximum discretion can be used. Even in this circumstance, however, the presence of a crowd or witnesses may contribute to the officer's decision. Police officers may also be influenced by their physical condition, mental state, whether there are other duties to perform, and so on. For example, research by Geoffrey Alpert and his associates finds that when police arrest someone after a car chase they are more likely to use excessive force; the excitement and danger of the pursuit seem to prompt an aggressive response in the subjects they interviewed.[125]

Legal Factors The likelihood of legal action may depend on how officers view offense severity. An altercation between two friends or relatives may be handled quite differently than an assault on a stranger. For example, research shows that at least in some jurisdictions, police are likely to treat domestic violence cases more casually than other assault cases.[126] There is evidence that police intentionally delay responding to domestic disputes, hoping that by the time they arrive the incident will be settled.[127] Research by James Fyfe and his associates found that even in cases involving serious felony incidents, police are more than twice as likely to make arrests (13 percent as compared to 28 percent) in incidents where the parties are unrelated or not involved in a romantic relationship.[128] In contrast, David Klinger found that most cases involving interpersonal violence (including spousal assault) did not re-officers regardless of their race or ethnicity.

One reason for this dilemma is that racial influences on police decision making are often quite subtle and hard to detect. For example, perhaps the *victim's* race, not the criminal's, is the key to racial bias: police officers are more likely to take formal action when the victim of crime is white than when the victim is a minority group member. These data suggest that any valid study of police discretion must take into account both victim and offender characteristics.

It is also possible that police bias is a function of administrative policy, not individual officer bias. Targeting African-Americans who sell drugs in open markets like parks and crack houses produces large numbers of easy arrests. Because drug sweeps and crackdowns often violate civil rights, many cases later get tossed out by prosecutors. However, when the charges stick, offenders usually get long prison sentences. Should one racial group be targeted by police because their modus operandi makes them easier to arrest?

Regardless of which position is correct, not all police officers operate unfairly, nor can all police departments be accused of racial bias. The influence of race on police discretion varies from jurisdiction to jurisdiction

and may be a function of the professionalism of the individual department. Similarly, there is evidence that gender bias has decreased.

CRITICAL THINKING

1. What, if anything, can be done to reduce racial bias on the part of police? Would adding minority officers help? Would it be a form of racism to assign minority officers to minority neighborhoods?

2. Would research showing that police are more likely to make arrests in interracial incidents than intraracial incidents constitute evidence of racism?

 INFOTRAC COLLEGE EDITION RESEARCH

To read more about the police and race relations, see:

Joseph C. Kennedy. Presumed guilty: to racist police, innocence is no defense. *Washington Monthly* March 28 (1996), p. 19.

Jim Impoco, Mike Tharp. Under siege at the LAPD. *U.S. News & World Report* 119 (Oct 16, 1995), p. 44.

Source: David Kocieniewski," Man Says Officers Tortured Him After Arrest," *New York Times,* 13 August 1997, p. 1; Dan Barry, "Second Officer Faces Charges in Torture," *New York Times,* 16 August 1997,

p. 1; Dan Barry, "Officers' Silence Still Thwarting Torture," *New York Times,* 5 September 1997; John Kavanagh, "The Occurrence of Resisting Arrest in Arrest Encounters: A Study of Police–Citizen Violence," *Criminal Justice Review* 22 (1997): 16–29; Ronald Weitzer, "Racial Discrimination in the Criminal Justice System: Findings and Problems in the Literature," *Journal of Criminal Justice* 24 (1996): 309–322; Samuel Walker, Cassia Spohn, and Miriam DeLone, *The Color of Justice: Race, Ethnicity and Crime in America* (Belmont, Calif.: Wadsworth, 1996), p. 115; Sandra Lee Browning, Francis Cullen, Liqun Cao, Renee Kopache, and Thomas Stevenson, "Race and Getting Hassled by the Police: A Research Note," *Police Studies* 17 (1994): 1–10; Dale Dannefer and Russell Schutt, "Race and Juvenile Justice Processing in Court and Police Agencies," *American Journal of Sociology* 87 (1982): 1113–32; Christy Visher, "Arrest Decisions and Notions of Chivalry," *Criminology* 21 (1983): 5–28; Darlene Conley, "Adding Color to a Black and White Picture: Using Qualitative Data to Explain Racial Disproportionality in the Juvenile Justice System," *Journal of Research in Crime and Delinquency* 31 (1994): 135–48. See generally, William Wilbanks, *The Myth of a Racist Criminal Justice System* (Monterey, Calif.: Brooks/Cole, 1987); see also Douglas Smith and Jody Klein, "Police Control of Interpersonal Disputes," *Social Problems* 31 (1984): 368–481; Marvin Krohn, James Curry, and Shirley Nelson-Kilger, "Is Chivalry Dead? An Analysis of Changes in Police Dispositions of Males and Females," *Criminology* 21 (1983): 417–37.

sult in an arrest, suggesting that domestic violence is treated similarly to other types of interpersonal conflict and that a great deal of discretion is used in all police actions.[129] Other legal factors that might influence police are the use of a weapon, seriousness of injury, and the presence of alcohol or drugs.

Extralegal Factors: Race, Class, and Gender The demeanor, attitude, race, age, and gender of the offender may be considered when police officers decide to invoke their arrest powers. This issue is far from settled, but most early empirical studies found that police discretion works against the young, the poor, and members of minority groups and favors the wealthy, the politically well connected, and members of the majority group.[130] Studies confirm that three-quarters of all complaints filed against the police for misconduct tend to concern nonwhite males under the age of 30. Over one-half of the complainants were divorced or single and unemployed or blue-collar workers.[131]

Suspect demeanor has long been thought to influence police discretion: being contrite and remorseful can result in a break; acting defiant is more likely to result in arrest.[132] More recent research has failed to show a clear association between suspect demeanor and arrest outcome. Although suspect attitude may influence police in some encounters, it has little effect in others.[133] One reason may be that experienced officers have learned to ignore verbal taunts and bad attitudes. In his study of police in Dade County, Florida, criminologist David Klinger found that suspect behavior influences discretion only in the event that suspects display "extreme hostility" toward the officer.[134]

The most important extralegal factor in the use of police discretion involves charges that police take race into account when deciding whether to treat a case informally with a warning or arrest a suspect. This issue is discussed in the Race, Culture, Gender, and Criminology feature titled "Does Race Influence the Police Use of Discretion?"

Limiting Police Discretion Numerous efforts have been made to limit police discretion. Police administrators have attempted to establish guidelines for police officers' operating behavior.[135] Most departments have created rules to guide police officers' daily activities. Some departments have established special units to oversee patrol activities; others have created boundaries of police behavior, suggesting that any conduct in excess of these limits, such as racial profiling, will not be tolerated.[136]

Perhaps limiting police discretion can be carried out only by outside review. One approach is to develop civilian review boards that monitor police behavior and tactics and investigate civilian complaints. No two models are alike, but a national study of the 50 largest police departments by Samuel Walker indicates that the review board model is gaining acceptance. About 30 departments have adopted some form of civilian board, most since 1986.[137]

It is possible, as Robert Worden and Robin Shepard suggest, that the changing composition and outlooks of police may be reflected in the way they use their discretion.[138] As police departments embrace COP models, police officers may begin to use their discretion differently, making arrests more selectively and relying less on extralegal issues.[139] Efforts to improve police sensitivity to minority rights may have helped reduce discrimination because some recent studies show that police may be less biased than before.[140] For example, Marvin Krohn and his associates examined almost 20,000 cases in a north-central American city and found that gender bias was a relatively insignificant problem.[141]

In sum, research indicates that the effect of offenders' class, race, and gender characteristics may be diminishing, but it continues to influence police discretion.

Women and Minority Police Officers

For the past decade, U.S. police departments have made a concerted effort to attract women and minority police officers. The latter group includes African-Americans, Asians, Hispanics, Native Americans, and members of other racial minorities. The reasons for recruiting minority and female officers are varied. Viewed in its most positive light, such recruitment reflects police departments' desire to field a more balanced force that truly represents the community it serves. A culturally diverse police force can be instrumental in gaining the public's confidence by helping to dispel the view that police departments are generally bigoted or biased organizations.

Another important reason for recruiting female and minority police officers is the need to comply with various federal guidelines on hiring.[142] Legal actions brought by minority representatives have resulted in local, state, and federal courts ordering police departments to either create hiring quotas to increase minority representation or rewrite entrance exams and requirements to encourage the employment of women and minorities. In one important case, *United States v. Paradise,* the Supreme Court upheld the use of racial quotas to counter the effects of past discrimination. The decision upheld a lower court ruling that ordered the Alabama Department of Public Safety to promote one black trooper for every white candidate elevated in rank as long as qualified black candidates were available, until 25 percent of each rank was filled by minorities; this would represent the actual racial makeup of the labor market.[143] Several such lawsuits have resulted in either court-ordered hiring judgments or voluntary compliance.

Despite court orders, women and minorities are still underrepresented in many police departments. The number of women and minorities in local policing has been increasing, now amounting to about 20 percent of all sworn officers. Minority and female representation is highest in the nation's largest police departments, reflecting both the population of their locale and their sensitivity to affirmative action issues. As might be expected, cities with large minority populations have a higher proportion of minority officers in their municipal police departments.[144] Many cities, such as Los Angeles, have had, or now have, African-American police chiefs, and a few, most notably Houston, have promoted women to command positions, including chief.

Minority Officers African-Americans have served on police forces since the mid-nineteenth century. A Republican mayor appointed the first black police officer in Chicago in 1872; by 1884 there were 23 African-American officers serving in that city.[145] Black officers are still underrepresented on the nation's police forces, but legal and social pressure has been mounting to increase their numbers. Some cities have made great strides in minority recruitment.

As African-Americans were appointed to police forces, it was assumed that they would face numerous challenges. In a classic work published more than 25 years ago, Nicholas Alex found that black police officers suffered "double marginality."[146] On the one hand, African-American officers must deal with the expectation that they will give members of their own race a break. On the other hand, they often experience overt racism from police colleagues.

Alex found that black officers' treatment of other blacks ranged from denying that African-Americans should be treated differently from whites to treating black offenders more harshly than white offenders to prove lack of bias. Alex offered various reasons why some black police officers are tougher on black offenders: they desire acceptance from their white colleagues; they are particularly sensitive to any disrespect shown them by black teenagers; they view themselves as the protectors of the black community.[147] Evidence of this

The number of women and minority officers in the nation's police departments are steadily increasing. A culturally diverse police force can be instrumental in gaining the public's confidence by helping to dispel the view that police departments are generally bigoted or biased organizations.

effect was found by criminologist Kim Michelle Lersch in her 1998 study of complaints against police officers. Lersch found that minority citizens were actually more likely to accuse a minority officer of misconduct than a Caucasian officer.[148]

The problems of black officers can also be exacerbated by the cool reception they are given by their white colleagues, who see them as potential competitors for promotions and special assignments. As James Jacobs and Jay Cohen point out, white police officers view affirmative action hiring and promotion programs as a threat to their job security.[149]

As more minorities join U.S. police forces, their situation appears to be changing. They now appear to be experiencing some of the same problems and issues encountered by white officers. For example, minority police officers report feeling somewhat higher rates of job-related stress and strain than white officers.[150] African-American and white police officers share similar attitudes toward community policing (although minority police report being even more favorable than white officers).[151] Interviews with black police officers in New York City show that they hold much the same attitudes toward policing as white police officers.[152]

Female Police Officers The first female police officers were appointed in New York as early as 1845, but they were designated as "matrons," and their duties were restricted to handling females in custody.[153] In 1893 Chicago hired policewomen but again restricted their activities to making court visitations and assisting male detectives with cases involving women and children. In 1910 Alice Stebbins Wells of the Los Angeles Police Department became the first woman to hold the title of police officer and have full arrest powers. It was not until the 1972 passage of the final version of Title VII of the Civil Rights Act that police departments around the nation began to hire females and assign them to regular patrol duties.

How Effective Are Female Police Officers? In general, evaluations of policewomen show them to be equal or superior to male officers in most areas of police work. In one highly regarded study of policewomen, Catherine Milton found that female officers in Washington, D.C., responded to similar types of calls as their male colleagues, and the arrests they made were as likely to result in conviction.[154] Women were more likely to receive support from the community and less likely to be charged with police misconduct. On the negative side, policewomen made fewer felony and misdemeanor arrests and received lower supervisory ratings than male officers. The generally favorable results obtained by Milton have also been found in other studies assessing policewomen's performance.[155]

Despite their relative proficiency, female police officers have not received general support from their colleagues or the public. Male officers perceive the public to be less cooperative toward them if females are on patrol and report that they receive more insults and threats when patrolling with female partners.[156] Surveys have shown a relatively low acceptance rate for females in police functions, especially those involving hazardous duties.[157] Some male police officers believe that female officers are more likely to use deadly force than males because their smaller stature prevents them from using unarmed techniques to subdue suspects. Females do not do as well as males on strength tests and are much more likely to fail the entrance physical than male recruits; critics contend that many of these tests do not reflect the actual tasks police do on the job.[158] Ironically, research shows that female officers are actually less likely to use firearms than male officers and that when male and female officers are partners, it is the male who is more likely to use a firearm.[159]

Some jurisdictions still assign female officers to secretarial and clerical posts; and in some cities, when budget cutbacks require layoffs, women officers are released in disproportionate numbers.[160]

There is evidence that both male and female officers share many personality traits when they first enter police work; both report a high degree of self-confidence and idealism. Self-perceptions of female officers diminish significantly after their police academy training.[161] Sex-role conflicts produce disillusionment with police work, accompanied by denial, self-doubt, repressed anger, and confusion. Significantly more female than male officers report being the victims of job discrimination. This form of bias is not unique to the United States. Research shows that women police officers working in northern England report being excluded from full membership in the force based on gender inequality. Although policewomen in the U.K. are enthusiastic for crime-related work, their aspirations are frequently frustrated in favor of male officers.[162]

Some male officers allege that they have also experienced gender-based discrimination. However, they typically claim that it comes at the hands of female officers who use their "sexuality" for job-related benefits.[163] It is not surprising, then, that women experience significant levels of job stress.[164] It is likely that as the number of women on police forces increases, so too will their job satisfaction and work experiences. Research by Joanne Belknap and Jill Kastens Shelley shows that women who work in departments with a large proportion of female officers report that they are viewed as more professionally competent and also perceive greater acceptance by fellow officers and police administrators.[165]

Black Female Police Officers Black women, who account for only about 2 percent of police officers, occupy a unique status because of both race and gender issues. A recent study conducted by Susan Martin of black female police serving in five large municipal departments found that they perceive significantly more racial discrimination than either other female officers or black

male officers.[166] White female officers were significantly more likely to perceive sexual discrimination than black female officers.

Martin found that black female officers often incur the hostility of both white women and black men, who feel threatened that they will take their place. On patrol, black female officers were treated differently than white female officers by male officers: although neither group of females was viewed as equals, white female officers were protected and coddled, whereas black females were viewed as passive, lazy, and unequal. In the station house, male officers had very little respect for black females, who faced "widespread racial stereotypes as well as outright racial harassment."[167] Black women also report having difficult relationships with black male officers, their relationships strained by tensions and dilemmas "associated with sexuality and competition for desirable assignments and promotions.[168] Surprisingly, there was little unity among the female officers. Martin concludes,

> Despite changes in the past two decades, the idealized image of the representative of the forces of "law and order" and protector who maintains "the thin blue line" between "them" and "us" remains white and male.[169]

The Police and Violence

Anthony Baez was playing touch football in the street with his brothers in December 1994 when an errantly thrown ball struck New York City Police Officer Francis Livoti's patrol car. The officer tried to stop the game, and Baez, 29, of Orlando, Florida, died in the ensuing struggle. A police department investigation found that Livoti had used an illegal chokehold to subdue Baez. Although Livoti was acquitted in 1996 of negligent homicide, he was fired from the force and in June 1998 was convicted of violating Baez's civil rights in federal court. On October 1, 1998, the city agreed to pay nearly $3 million to settle lawsuits filed by the family of the man choked to death by a police officer.[170]

The Baez case illustrates the persistent problems police departments have in regulating violent contacts with citizens. Police officers are empowered to use force and violence in pursuit of their daily tasks. Some scholars argue that this is the core of the police role:

> The role of the police is best understood as a mechanism for the distribution of non-negotiable coercive force employed in accordance with the dictates of an intuitive group of situational exigencies.[171]

Police violence first became a major topic for discussion in the 1940s, when rioting provoked serious police backlash. Thurgood Marshall, then of the National Association for the Advancement of Colored People, referred to the Detroit police as a "gestapo" after a 1943 race riot left 34 people dead.[172] Twenty-five years later, excessive police force was again an issue when television cameras captured police violence against protesters at the Democratic National Convention in Chicago. However, general day-to-day police brutality against individual citizens seems to be diminishing. In 1967 the President's Commission on Criminal Justice concluded,

> The Commission believes that physical abuse is not as serious a problem as it was in the past. The few statistics which do exist suggest small numbers of cases involving excessive use of force. Although the relatively small number of reported complaints cannot be considered an accurate measurement of the total problem, most persons, including civil rights leaders, believe that verbal abuse and harassment, not excessive use of force, is the major police–community relations problem today.[173]

The diminution of police force was noted in the classic study by Albert Reiss of police–citizen interactions in high-crime areas in Washington, D.C., Chicago, and Boston.[174] Verbal abuse of citizens was quite common, but the excessive use of physical force was relatively rare, occurring in 44 cases out of the 5,360 observations made. There were actually few racial differences in the use of force; when force was used, it was against more selective groups—those who showed disrespect for police authority once they were arrested. Subsequent researchers also found that violent interactions are quite rare; when force is used, it typically involves grabbing and restraining; weapons are rarely used.[175]

How Common Is the Use of Force Today? How much force is being used by the police today? Is it too much?[176] The most recent (1993) national survey, conducted by Anthony Pate and Lorie Fridell, surveyed almost 1700 law enforcement agencies about incidents of force and also about complaints made by citizens during a single year.[177] They found that the least intrusive types of force, like handcuffing, are used much more often than the most intrusive, like lethal violence. A number of interesting conclusions can be drawn from these data. Although the use of weapons is quite rare (for every 1,000 police officers there were about four incidents in which an officer shot at a civilian), about half the officers cuffed someone, and more than one-quarter used bodily force of some kind. Whereas males made up less than half of the population within the jurisdictions of the surveyed departments, they accounted for almost three-quarters of the people making complaints of excessive force. This most likely occurs because males are more often involved in violent crimes and evoke in-kind responses from police. Only about 10 percent of all complaints were sustained after investigation.

Race and Force The routine use of force may be diminishing, but there is still debate over whether police are more likely to get rough with minority suspects. Whether or not police discriminate against minorities in

The danger of violence became a national issue when New York City police officers cut down Amadou Diallo in a barrage of more than 40 bullets. The Diallo killing inspired numerous demonstrations and calls for the creation of an independent civilian commission to oversee complaints of police misconduct. Four of the officers, all white, were later indicted on murder charges.

their use of discretion, minority citizens are much more likely to perceive that police are more likely to "hassle them": stop them or watch them closely when they have done nothing wrong. They are also more likely to know someone who has been mistreated by police. Perceptions of "hassling" may erode an individual's future relations with police and affect police–community relations as a whole.[178]

Who Are Problem-Prone Cops? Are there bad cops or bad departments? One view is that a few violence-prone cops spoil the image of the whole department. Another view is that some departments tolerate problem cops. Recent research by Kim Michelle Lersch and Tom Mieczkowski found that in the Southeastern city they studied, a few officers (7 percent) are chronic offenders who account for a significant portion of all citizen complaints (33 percent). Those officers receiving the bulk of the complaints tend to be younger and less experienced and are accused of harassment or violence after a proactive encounter. Although repeat offenders were more likely to be accused of misconduct by minority citizens, there was little evidence that attacks were racially motivated; complaints were predominantly intraracial.[179]

Deadly Force A more recent area of concern has been the use of deadly force in apprehending fleeing or violent offenders. As commonly used, **deadly force** refers to the actions of a police officer who shoots and kills a suspect who is either fleeing from arrest, assaulting a victim, or attacking the officer.[180]

The justification for the use of deadly force can be traced to English common law, in which almost every criminal offense merited a felony status and subsequent death penalty. Thus execution effected during the arrest of a felon was considered expedient, saving the state from the burden of trial. It is estimated that somewhere between 250 and 1,000 citizens are now killed by police each year, although these figures are highly speculative.[181] The numbers of shooting incidents have been declining, reflecting efforts to control police use of deadly force.

Research indicates that the following factors are related to police violence:[182]

- *Exposure to threat and stress:* Areas with an unusually high incidence of violent crime are likely to experience shootings by police.
- *Police workload:* Violence corresponds to the number of police officers on the street, the number of calls for service, the number and nature of police dispatches, and the number of arrests made in a given jurisdiction.
- *Firearm availability:* Cities that have many crimes committed with firearms are also likely to have high police violence rates. For example, Houston, which ranks first in firearm availability, has many more police shootings per 1,000 arrests than San Francisco, which ranks tenth.
- *Population type and density:* Jurisdictions swollen by large numbers and varied types of transients and nonresidents also experience a disproportionate amount of police shootings. Research findings suggest that many individuals shot by police are nonresidents caught at or near the scenes of robberies or burglaries of commercial establishments.
- *Race and class discrimination:* It is alleged that blacks and other racial minorities are killed at a significantly higher rate than whites. It is common to focus on race as the primary predictive factor in police violence.[183] The poorest areas with high degrees of income inequality and a large percentage of minority citizens experienced the highest levels of police shootings.[184]

Despite the evidence indicating that police shootings are motivated by racial bias, research shows that police officers are most likely to shoot when they are attacked by armed suspects, that many shootings stem from incidents in which police officers are injured or killed, and that minorities are more likely to be involved in weapon assaults on police officers than whites (37 percent of events involving white citizens were gun incidents, whereas the rates for blacks and Hispanics were 58 and 56 percent, respectively).[185]

Research also indicates that minority police officers are responsible for a disproportionate number of police shootings and that they are more likely to shoot other minorities than white officers. James Fyfe found that minority officers were often assigned to inner-city ghetto areas in which violence against police was common; it is therefore not surprising that minority officers' use of violence was relatively more frequent. However, in an analysis of police shootings in Memphis, Tennessee, Fyfe found that white police were more likely to shoot black citizens than white and that "police there did differentiate racially with their trigger fingers, by shooting blacks in circumstances less threatening than those in which they shot whites."[186] Thus the charge that police "have one trigger finger for whites and another for blacks" may have more validity in some areas than in others.

Not all research suggests that personal factors account for police shooting. Some evidence points to the nature of the criminal interaction itself. Police shootings are influenced by the nature of the opponents the officers face; whether the officers are on duty or off duty; the number of officers present; and the nature of the physical environment.[187] In many instances suicidal people challenge police officers in a calculated manner in order to force officers to take their lives; this is sometimes referred to as *death by police.*

Police departments might control the use of deadly force by developing policies that stress containing armed offenders while specially trained backup teams are sent to take charge of the situation. Training might also emphasize the outcome choices available in situations involving violence and conflict. Lorie Fridell and Arnold Binder found that deadly force situations often involve ambiguity and surprise.[188] Officers trained to take advantage of what little information is available to make quick, accurate decisions may be the most likely to avoid a potentially fatal confrontation.

Controlling Force   In 1985 the Supreme Court moved to restrict police use of deadly force when, in *Tennessee v. Garner,* it banned the shooting of unarmed or nondangerous fleeing felons.[189] The Court based its decision on the premise that shooting an unarmed, nondangerous suspect was an illegal seizure of his or her body under the Fourth Amendment. According to the ruling, police could not justifiably use force unless it was "necessary to prevent the escape, and the officer has probable cause to believe that the suspect poses a significant threat of death or serious physical injury to the officers or others—for example, if the suspect threatens the officer or the officer has probable cause to believe that the suspect has committed a crime involving serious physical harm. Before *Garner,* the policy of shooting unarmed fleeing felons had still been used in 17 states.

The Criminological Enterprise

In the Line of Fire: Shootings of Police

Although police officers are often taken to task for being too violent, the public sometimes forgets that police are often injured and killed by armed assailants. This stressful situation has not been improved by the fact that professional criminals and drug dealers are armed with automatic weapons while police officers carry .38-caliber revolvers.

Every year, between 50 and 100 law enforcement and public safety officers are feloniously killed in the line of duty; about two-thirds of these are shooting victims. The most common incidents that result in the death of an officer are arrest situations, disturbance calls, and the aftermath of investigations of suspicious persons and circumstances. In addition, about 70 officers are killed each year in job-related incidents, such as traffic accidents.

What factors predict the shooting of police officers? The majority of incidents are initiated by the officers themselves, as opposed to an unexpected attack by a hidden assailant; black officers have a greater risk of getting killed than white officers, more likely by black assailants. Police officers face the greatest danger when they attempt to arrest armed assailants. Ecological patterns may also be present when a police officer becomes the victim of violent crime: southern cities, with high violence and gun ownership rates, ex-

perience the highest numbers of police officer fatalities.

Research also shows that off-duty police and plainclothes officers are very likely to be shot. One reason is that off-duty officers, who are usually armed, are expected to take appropriate action yet suffer tactical disadvantages, such as a lack of communication and backup. Plainclothes officers are often mistaken for perpetrators or unwanted interveners.

A recent FBI report shows that police officers may get killed because they fail to follow proper procedures, perhaps because they are too trusting and let their guard down: they fail to call for backup; act alone; fail to search suspects completely; and in an effort to make suspects more comfortable, fail to secure handcuffs properly. When interviewed by the FBI, the slain officers' peers describe them as friendly to everyone and quick to look for good in people. In contrast, their slayers suffer personality disorders that render them incapable of obeying social norms, having a conscience, or feeling remorse.

The FBI report, though illuminating, has been criticized by William King and Beth Sanders for being methodologically flawed. It is possible, they suggest, that the difference between fatal and nonfatal incidents can be attributed to use of bullet-proof

vests, near-by medical facilities, or just plain luck!. Clearly more research is needed to understand the circumstances of why police get killed in the line of duty.

CRITICAL THINKING

1. How can the shooting of police be prevented?
2. It is possible that wearing protective equipment and body armor can significantly reduce police fatalities. Would such measures inhibit community policing?

 INFOTRAC COLLEGE EDITION RESEARCH

To read more about the police use of force, see:
Barbara Dority. Established: A Pattern of Abuse. *The Humanist* (59) 1999: p. 5.

Source: Anthony Pinizzotto, Edward F. Davis, and Charles E. Miller III, "In the Line of Fire: Learning from Assaults on Law Enforcement Officers," *The FBI Law Enforcement Bulletin* 67 (1998):15–24; William Wilbanks, "Cops Killed and Cop-Killers: An Historical Perspective," *American Journal of Police* 13 (1994): 31–41; FBI, *Killed in the Line of Duty: A Study of Selected Felonious Killings of Law Enforcement Officers* (Washington, D.C.: U.S. Government Printing Office, 1992); William King and Beth Sanders, "Nice Guys Finish Last: A Critical Review of Killed in the Line of Duty," *Policing* 20 (1997): 392–408.

There are other methods of controlling police shootings. One is through training and counseling sessions that teach police to use less violence. Another is through internal review and policymaking by police departments. For example, the New York City police department established a new firearms policy based on the American Law Institute's Model Penal Code. The policy stated the following:

a. In all cases, only the minimum amount of force will be used which is consistent with the accomplishment of a mission. Every other reasonable means will be utilized for arresting, preventing or terminating a felony or for the defense of oneself or another before a police officer resorts to the use of his firearms.

b. A firearm shall not be discharged under circumstances where lives of innocent persons may be endangered.

c. The firing of a warning shot is prohibited.

d. The discharging of a firearm to summon assistance is prohibited, except where the police officer's safety is endangered.

e. Discharging a firearm at or from a moving vehicle is prohibited unless the occupants of the other vehicle are using deadly force against the officer or another, by means other than the vehicle.[190]

The New York police department also created the Firearm Discharge Review Board to evaluate shooting incidents. In examining the effects of this policy, James Fyfe found that a considerable reduction in the frequency of police shootings followed the policy change.[191]

In addition to state and local policy, the Federal Crime Control Act of 1994 enables the attorney general to obtain a judicial injunction eliminating police practices that encourage excessive force and to obtain damages for injured parties.[192]

Police use of force continues to be an important issue, but there is little question that control measures seem to be working.[193] Fewer people are being killed by police, and fewer officers are being killed than ever before. In 1997, for example, 66 officers were killed in the line of duty, down from the 82 killed in 1995; since 1988, 700 officers have been killed in the line of duty.[194]

Nonlethal Weapons In the last few years, about 1,000 local police forces have started using some sort of less-than-lethal weapon designed to subdue suspects. The most widely used nonlethal weapons are wood, rubber, or polyurethane bullets shot out of modified 37-mm pistols or 12-gauge shotguns. At short distances, officers use pepper spray and tasers, which deliver electric shocks with long wire tentacles, producing intense muscle spasms. Other technologies still in development include guns that shoot giant nets, guns that squirt sticky glue, and lights that can temporarily blind a suspect. For example, Cincinnati police officers now use shotguns that fire bean bags filled with lead pellets; the weapons have a range of 100 feet and pack the wallop of a pro boxer's punch.[195]

Recent research efforts indicate that nonlethal weapons may help reduce police use of force.[196] Greater effort must be made to regulate these nonlethal weapons and create effective policies for their use.[197]

SUMMARY

Police officers are the gatekeepers of the criminal justice process. They use their power of arrest to initiate the justice process.

U.S. police agencies are modeled after their British counterparts. Early in British history, law enforcement was a personal matter. Later constables were appointed to keep peace among groups of 100 families. This rudimentary beginning was the seed of today's police departments. In 1838 the first true U.S. police department was born in Boston.

The first U.S. police departments were created because of the need to control mob violence, which was common during the nineteenth century. The police were viewed as being dominated by political bosses who controlled their hiring practices and policies.

Reform movements begun during the 1920s culminated in the concept of professionalism in the 1950s and 1960s. Police professionalism was interpreted to mean tough, rule-oriented police work featuring advanced technology and hardware. However, the view that these measures would quickly reduce crime proved incorrect.

There are several major law enforcement agencies. On the federal level, the FBI is the premier law enforcement organization. Other agencies include the Drug Enforcement Administration, the U.S. marshals, and the Secret Service. County-level law enforcement is provided by sheriff's departments, and most states maintain state police agencies. However, most law enforcement activities are carried out by local police agencies.

The police role is multilevel. Police officers fight crime, keep the peace, and provide community services. The conflicts and burdens involved in their work insulate them from the community and create great stress that has been linked to burnout.

Some criminologists question whether police patrol is actually effective. One important study conducted in Kansas City found that the extent of patrol had little effect on the crime rate or citizens' satisfaction.

The second prominent police role is investigation. Detectives collect evidence to identify perpetrators. Although detectives use various techniques, including sting operations, studies have shown that detective work is generally ineffective. Other police functions include traffic control, departmental administration and maintenance, and improvement of relations between police and community.

In recent years many police operations have been controlled by court decisions. Most important, the courts have set limits on the extent of police interrogations and search and seizure of evidence.

Police departments face crucial issues today. One involves understanding the police personality and its effect on performance. Another involves police officers' use of discretion and how it can be controlled. Women and minority officers probably will become more prevalent in police departments, and their worth must be more fully appreciated by rank-and-file patrol officers. Police violence has received much attention. There is some debate over whether police officers kill members of minority groups more frequently than white citizens; recent evidence indicates that this may be the case in some cities. Technology is being embraced by police departments and holds the promise of improving police productivity.

See the book-specific web site at www.cj.wadsworth.com for additional chapter links, discussions, and quizzes.

THINKING LIKE A CRIMINOLOGIST

You are a consultant to the local police department. The chief has recently read Malcolm Sparrow, Mark Moore, and David Kennedy's book *Beyond 911: A New Era for Policing,* in which they define the core values of the typical police officer as follows:

1. Police officers are the only real crime fighters. The public wants the police officer to fight crime; other agencies, both public and private, only play at fighting crime.

2. No one else understands the real nature of police work. Lawyers, academics,

politicians, and the public in general have little concept of what it means to be a police officer.

3. Loyalty to colleagues counts above everything else. Police officers have to stick together because everyone is out to get the police and make the job more difficult.

4. It is impossible to win the war against crime without bending the rules. Courts have awarded criminal defendants too many civil rights.

5. Members of the public are basically unsupportive and unreasonably demanding. People are quick to criticize police unless they need an officer themselves.

6. Patrol work is the pits. Detective work is glamorous and exciting.

The chief is planning a major policy initiative that will emphasize community policing. He wants to know if these values will help his initiative or make it more difficult to implement. He wants your opinion on the issue. What would you do to change police values if they conflict with community policing?

KEY TERMS

gatekeepers
Mollen Commission
Knapp Commission
pledge system
watch system
justice of the peace
Sir Robert Peel
Wickersham Commission
August Vollmer
sheriff

shire reeve
foot patrol
aggressive preventive patrol
internal affairs division
morals squad
vice squad
mug shots
modus operandi (MO)
sting
selective enforcement

community-oriented policing
team policing
neighborhood policing
problem-oriented policing
crackdown
hot spots
inevitable discovery rule
search warrant
blue curtain
deadly force

NOTES

1. Deborah Sontag and Dan Barry, "Using Settlements to Measure Police Abuse," *New York Times,* 17 September 1997, p. A5.

2. Bernie Patterson, "Job Experience and Perceived Job Stress Among Police, Correctional, and Probation/Parole Officers," *Criminal Justice and Behavior* 19 (1992): 260–85.

3. John Klofas, "Drugs and Justice: The Impact of Drugs on Criminal Justice in a Metropolitan Community," *Crime and Delinquency* 39 (1993): 204–24.

4. Steven Tuch and Ronald Weitzer, "The Polls—Trends, Racial Differences in Attitudes Toward the Police," *Public Opinion Quarterly* 61 (1997): 642–63.

5. Eric Jefferis, Robert Kaminski, Stephen Homes, and Dena Hanley, "The Effect of a Videotaped Arrest on Public Perceptions of Police Use of Force," *Journal of Criminal Justice* 25 (1997): 381–95.

6. This section relies heavily on Daniel Devlin, *Police Procedure, Administration and Organization* (London: Butterworth, 1966); Robert Fogelson, *Big City Police* (Cambridge: Harvard University Press, 1977); Roger Lane, *Policing the City: Boston 1822–1885* (Cambridge: Harvard University Press, 1967); Roger Lane, "Urban Police and Crime in Nineteenth Century America," in *Crime and Justice,* vol. 2, ed. N. Morris and M. Tonry (Chicago: University of Chicago Press, 1980), pp. 1–45; J. J. Tobias, *Crime and Industrial Society in the Nineteenth Century* (New York: Schoken Books, 1967); Samuel Walker, *A Critical History of Police Reform: The Emergence of Professionalism*

(Lexington, Mass.: Lexington Books, 1977); Samuel Walker, *Popular Justice* (New York: Oxford University Press, 1980); President's Commission on Law Enforcement and the Administration of Justice, *Task Force Report: The Police* (Washington, D.C.: Government Printing Office, 1967), pp. 1–9.

7. Devlin, *Police Procedure, Administration and Organization,* p. 3.

8. Walker, *Popular Justice,* p. 18.

9. Lane, "Urban Police and Crime in Nineteenth Century America," p. 5.

10. Michael Vaughn, "Political Patronage in Law Enforcement: Civil Liability Against Police Supervisors for Violating Their Subordinates' First Amendment Rights," *Journal of Criminal Justice* 25 (1997): 347–66.

11. Walker, *Popular Justice,* p. 61.

12. Preston William Slossom, *A History of American Life,* 12 vols., *The Great Crusade and After, 1914–1929,* vol. 12, ed. Arthur M. Schlesinger and Dixon Ryan Fox (New York: Macmillan, 1931), p. 102.

13. See, generally, Walker, *A Critical History of Police Reform.*

14. This section was adapted from Law Enforcement Assistance Administration, *Two Hundred Years of American Criminal Justice* (Washington, D.C.: Government Printing Office, 1976).

15. Brian A. Reaves and Andrew L. Goldberg, *Census of State and Local Law Enforcement Agencies, 1996* (Washington, D.C.: Bureau of Justice Statistics, 1998).

16. Reaves and Goldberg, *Census of State and Local Law Enforcement Agencies, 1996.*

17. See Harlan Hahn, "A Profile of Urban Police," in *The Ambivalent Force,* ed. A. Niederhoffer and A. Blumberg (Hinsdale, Ill.: Dryden Press, 1967), p. 59.

18. George Kelling, Tony Pate, Duane Dieckman, and Charles Brown, *The Kansas City Preventive Patrol Experiment: A Summary Report* (Washington, D.C.: Police Foundation, 1974).

19. James Q. Wilson and Barbara Boland, "The Effect of Police on Crime," *Law and Society Review* 12 (1978): 367–84.

20. Robert Sampson and Jacqueline Cohen, "Deterrent Effects of the Police on Crime: A Replication and Theoretical Extension," *Law and Society Review* 22 (1988): 163–91.

21. For a thorough review of this issue, see Andrew Karmen, "Why Is New York City's Murder Rate Dropping So Sharply?" (New York: John Jay College, 1996).

22. Alexander Weiss and Sally Freels, "The Effects of Aggressive Policing: The Dayton Traffic Enforcement Experiment," *American Journal of Police* 15 (1996): 45–63.

23. Eric Fritsch, Tory Caeti, and Robert Taylor, "Gang Suppression Through Saturation Patrol, Aggressive Curfew, and Truancy Enforcement: A Quasi-Experimental Test of the Dallas Anti-Gang Initiative," *Crime and Delinquency* 45 (1999): 122–39.

24. Lawrence Sherman, "Policing Communities: What Works," in *Crime and Justice,* vol. 8, ed. Al Reiss and Michael Tonry (Chicago: University of Chicago Press, 1986), pp. 366–79.

25. Sherman, "Policing Communities: What Works," p. 368.

26. See, generally, Peter Greenwood and Joan Petersilia, *The Criminal Investigation Process, Vol. 1: Summary and Policy Implications* (Santa Monica, Calif.: Rand Corporation, 1975); P. Greenwood, J. Chaiken, J. Petersilia, and L. Prusoff, *The Criminal Investigation Process, Vol. 3: Observations and Analysis* (Santa Monica, Calif.: Rand Corporation, 1975).

27. C. Cotter and J. Burrows, *Property Crime Program, a Special Report: Overview of the STING Program and Project Summaries* (Washington, D.C.: Criminal Conspiracies Division, Office of Criminal Justice Programs, Law Enforcement Assistance Administration, U.S. Department of Justice, 1981).

28. Robert Langworthy, "Stings: A Crime Control Tool." Paper presented at the American Society of Criminology, Atlanta, November 1986.

29. Greenwood and Petersilia, *The Criminal Investigation Process.*

30. Mark T. Willman and John R. Snortum, "Detective Work: The Criminal Investigation Process in a Medium-Size Police Department," *Criminal Justice Review* 9 (1984): 33–39.

31. John Eck, *Solving Crimes: The Investigation of Burglary and Robbery* (Washington, D.C.: Police Executive Research Forum, 1984).

32. See, for example, Susan Martin, "Policing Career Criminals: An Examination of an Innovative Crime Control Program," *Journal of Criminal Law and Criminology* 77 (1986): 1159–82.

33. Charles L. Regini, "The Cold Case Concept," *The FBI Law Enforcement Bulletin* 66 (1997): 1.

34. See, generally, Robert Sheehan and Gary Cordner, *Introduction to Police Administration* (Reading, Mass.: Addison-Wesley, 1979).

35. See Clarence Schrag, *Crime and Justice: American Style* (Washington, D.C.: U.S. Government Printing Office, 1970), p. 47.

36. Egon Bittner, *The Functions of Police in Modern Society* (Cambridge, Mass.: Delgeschlager, Gunn and Hain, 1980), p. 149.

37. J. Q. Wilson, *Varieties of Police Behavior: The Management of Law and Order in Eight Communities* (Cambridge: Harvard University Press, 1968).

38. Richard Sykes and Edward Brent, *Policing: A Social Behaviorist Perspective* (New Brunswick, N.J.: Rutgers University Press, 1983).

39. Lawrence A. Greenfeld, Patrick A. Langan, and Steven K. Smith, *Police Use of Force: Collection of National Data* (Washington, D.C.: Bureau of Justice Statistics, 1997).

40. Bittner, *The Functions of Police in Modern Society,* pp. 63–72.

41. James Q. Wilson and George Kelling, "Broken Windows: The Police and Neighborhood Safety," *Atlantic Monthly,* March 1982, pp. 29–38.

42. Wilson and Kelling, "Broken Windows," p. 37.

43. See, generally, Lawrence Sherman, *Team Policing—Seven Case Studies* (Washington, D.C.: Police Foundation, 1973).

44. John Angell, "The Democratic Model Needs a Fair Trial: Angell's Response," *Criminology* 12 (1975): 379–84.

45. "Many Cities Experimenting with Foot Patrol," *Criminal Justice Newsletter* 16 (15 May 1985): 1–2.

46. Jerome Skolnick and David Bayley, "Theme and Variation in Community Policing," in *Crime and Justice, A Review of Research,* vol. 12, ed. Michael Tonry and Norval Morris (Chicago: University of Chicago Press, 1988), pp. 1–38.

47. Edward Maguire and Charles Katz, "The Validity and Reliability of Police Agencies Community Policing Claims." Paper presented at the American Society of Criminology meeting, San Diego, Calif., 1997.

48. Albert Cardarelli, Jack McDevitt, and Katrina Baum, "The Rhetoric and Reality of Community Policing in Small and Medium-Sized Cities and Towns," *Policing* 21 (1998): 397–415.

49. Police Foundation, *The Effects of Police Fear Reduction Strategies: A Summary of Findings from Houston and Newark* (Washington, D.C.: Police Foundation, 1986).

50. Quint Thurman and Phil Bogen, "Research Note: Spokane Community Policing Officers Revisited," *American Journal of Police* 15 (1996): 97–114.

51. Diana Fishbein, "The Comprehensive Care Model," *The FBI Law Enforcement Bulletin* 67 (1998): 1–5.

52. Donald Green, Dara Strolovitch, and Janelle Wong, "Defended Neighborhoods, Integration, and Racially Motivated Crime," *American Journal of Sociology* 104 (1998): 372–403.

53. Lee Brown, "Neighborhood-Oriented Policing," *American Journal of Police* 9 (1990): 197–207.

54. Herman Goldstein, *Problem-Oriented Policing* (New York: McGraw-Hill, 1990).

55. Robert Davis and Bruce Taylor, "A Proactive Response to Family Violence: The Results of a Randomized Experiment," *Criminology* 35 (1997): 307–333.

56. Davis and Taylor, "A Proactive Response to Family Violence."

57. E. Nick Larsen, "Community Policing and the Control of Street Prostitution." Paper presented at the annual meeting of the American Society of Criminology, Chicago, Ill., November, 1996.

58. George Kelling, *What Works—Research and the Police* (Washington, D.C.: National Institute of Justice, 1988), p. 3.

59. Lawrence Sherman, "Police Crackdowns: Initial and Residual Deterrence," in *Crime and Justice, A Review of Research,* vol. 12, ed. Michael Tonry and Norval Morris (Chicago: University of Chicago Press, 1990), pp. 1–48.

60. Lawrence Sherman, Patrick Gartin, and Michael Buerger, "Hot Spots of Predatory Crime: Routine Activities and the Criminology of Place," *Criminology* 27 (1989): 27–55.

61. Dennis Roncek and Pamela Maier, "Bars, Blocks, and Crimes Revisited: Linking the Theory of Routine Activities to the Empiricism of 'Hot Spots,'" *Criminology* 29 (1991): 725–53.

62. L. Thomas Winfree, Gregory Bartku, and George Seibel, "Support for Community Policing Versus Traditional Policing Among Nonmetropolitan Police Officers: A Survey of Four New Mexico Police Departments," *American Journal of Police* 15 (1996): 23–47.

63. Samuel Walker, "Broken Windows and Fractured History: The Use and Misuse of History in Recent Police Patrol Analysis," *Justice Quarterly* 1 (1984): 75–90.

64. Jack R. Greene, "The Effects of Community Policing on American Law Enforcement: A Look at the Evidence." Paper presented at the International Congress on Criminology, Hamburg, Germany, September 1988, p. 19.

65. For a review of how to recruit police officers, see Wesley Skogan and Susan Hartnett, *Community Policing, Chicago Style* (New York: Oxford University Press, 1997), chap. 4.

66. Larry Gould, "Can an Old Dog Be Taught New Tricks? Teaching Cultural Diversity to Police Officers," *Policing* 20 (1997): 339–57.

67. "Community Policing Officers See Benefits in Citizen Relations," *Criminal Justice Newsletter* 27 (15 February 1996), pp. 4–5.

68. Annette Jolin and Charles Moose, "Evaluating a Domestic Violence Program in a Community Policing Environment: Research Implementation Issues," *Crime and Delinquency* 43 (1997): 279–97.

69. Jihong Zhao and Quint Thurman, "Community Policing: Where Are We Now?" *Crime and Delinquency* 43 (1997): 345–57.

70. Edward Maguire, "Structural Change in Large Municipal Police Organizations During the Community Policing Era," *Justice Quarterly* 14 (1997): 547–76.

71. Quint Thurman, Andrew Giacomazzi, and Phil Bogen, "Research Note: Cops, Kids, and Community Policing—An Assessment of a Community Policing Demonstration Project," *Crime and Delinquency* 39 (1993): 554–664; Bonnie Fisher, "What Works: Block Watch Meetings or Crime Prevention Seminars," *Journal of Crime and Justice* 16 (1993): 1–20.

72. David Kessler, "Integrating Calls for Services with Community- and Problem-Oriented Policing: A Case Study," *Crime and Delinquency* 39 (1993) 485–508.

73. Susan Guarino-Ghezzi, "Reintegrative Police Surveillance of Juvenile Offenders: Forging an Urban Model," *Crime and Delinquency* 40 (1994): 131–53.

74. Allan Jiao, "Factoring Police Models," *Policing* 20 (1997): 454–73.

75. Ronald W. Glensor and Ken Peak, "Implementing Change: Community-Oriented Policing and Problem Solving," *The FBI Law Enforcement Bulletin* 65 (1996): 14–22.

76. *Miranda v. Arizona,* 384 U.S. 436 (1966).

77. *Harris v. New York,* 401 U.S. 222 (1971).

78. *Michigan v. Tucker,* 417 U.S. 433 (1974).

79. *Moran v. Burbine,* 106 S.Ct. 1135 (1986); *Michigan v. Mosley,* 423 U.S. 96 (1975); *Fare v. Michael C.,* 442 U.S. 23 (1979).

80. *Nix v. Williams,* 104 S.Ct. 2501 (1984).

81. *New York v. Quarles,* 104 S.Ct. 2626 (1984).

82. *Oregon v. Elstad,* 105 S.Ct. 1285 (1985).

83. *Colorado v. Spring,* 107 S.Ct. 851 (1987).

84. *Colorado v. Connelly,* 107 S.Ct. 515 (1986).

85. *Moran v. Burbine,* 106 S.Ct. 1135 (1986).

86. *Colorado v. Connelly,* 107 S.Ct. 515 (1986).

87. *Minnick v. Miss.,* 498 U.S. 46; 111 S.Ct. 486; 112 L.Ed. 2d. 489 (1990).

88. *Arizona v. Fulminante,* 499 U.S. 279, 111 S.Ct. 1246; 113 L.Ed. 2d. 302 (1991).

89. *Davis v. United States,* 114 S.Ct. 2350 (1994).

90. Richard A. Leo and Richard J. Ofshe, "The Consequences of False Confessions: Deprivations of Liberty and Miscarriages of Justice in the Age of Psychological Interrogation," *Journal of Criminal Law and Criminology* 88 (1998): 429–96.

91. Leo and Ofshe, "The Consequences of False Confessions," p. 490.

92. *Illinois v. Gates,* 104 S.Ct. 2626 (1984).

93. *Chimel v. California,* 395 U.S. 752 (1969).

94. *Terry v. Ohio,* 392 U.S. 1 (1968).

95. *Carroll v. United States,* 267 U.S. 132 (1925).

96. *United States v. Ross,* 102 S.Ct. 2147 (1982).

97. *Whren et al. v. U.S.,* no. 95-5841 (1996).

98. *Bumper v. North Carolina,* 391 U.S. 543 (1960).

99. *Ohio v. Robinette,* 117 S. Ct. 417 (1996).

100. Limitations on the plain view doctrine have been defined in *Arizona v. Hicks,* 107 S.Ct. 1149 (1987); the recording of serial numbers from stereo components in a suspect's apartment could not be justified as being in plain view.

101. *Katz v. United States,* 389 U.S. 347 (1967).

102. Richard Lundman, *Police and Policing* (New York: Holt, Rinehart and Winston, 1980); see also Jerome Skolnick, *Justice Without Trial* (New York: Wiley, 1966).

103. Cited in Authur Neiderhoffer, *Behind the Shield: The Police in Urban Society* (Garden City, N.Y.: Doubleday, 1967), p. 65.

104. For an impressive review, see Peter Finn, "Reducing Stress: An Organization-Centered Approach," *The FBI Law Enforcement Bulletin* 66 (1997): 20.

105. Terri Harvey-Lintz and Romeria Tidwell, "Effects of the 1992 Los Angeles Civil Unrest: Post Traumatic Stress Disorder Symptomatology Among Law Enforcement Officers," *The Social Science Journal* 34 (1997): 171–84.

106. See, for example, Richard Bennett and Theodore Greenstein, "The Police Personality: A Test of the Predispositional Model," *Journal of Police Science and Administration* 3 (1975): 439–45.

107. William Westly, *Violence and the Police: A Sociological Study of Law, Custom and Morality* (Cambridge: MIT Press, 1970); W. Westly, "Violence and the Police," *American Journal of Sociology* 49 (1953): 34–41.

108. John Crank, *Understanding Police Culture* (Cincinnati, Ohio, Anderson, 1997).

109. See, for example, Richard Harris, *The Police Academy: An Inside View* (New York: John Wiley, 1973); John Van Maanen, "Observations on the Making of Policemen," *Human Organization* 32 (1973): 407–18; Jonathan Rubenstein, *City Police* (New York: Ballantine, 1973); John Broderick, *Police in a Time of Change* (Morristown, N.J.: General Learning Press, 1977).

110. Steve Herbert, "Police Subculture Reconsidered," *Criminology* 36 (1998): 343–69.

111. Herbert, "Police Subculture Reconsidered," p. 360.

112. Herbert, "Police Subculture Reconsidered," p. 359.

113. David Klinger, "Negotiating Order in Patrol Work: An Ecological Theory of Police Response to Deviance," *Criminology* 35 (1997): 277–306.

114. John Crank and Robert Langworthy, "An Institutional Perspective of Policing," *Journal of Criminal Law and Criminology* 83 (1992): 338–457.

115. Donald Yates and Vijayan Pillai, "Attitudes Toward Community Policing: A Causal Analysis," *Social Science Journal* 33 (1996): 193–209.

116. Michael Brown, *Working the Street: Police Discretion and the Dilemmas of Reform* (New York: Russell Sage Foundation, 1981); William Muir, *Police: Streetcorner Politicians* (Chicago: University of Chicago Press, 1977).

117. John Crank, "Police Style and Legally Serious Crime: A Contextual Analysis of Municipal Police Departments," *Journal of Criminal Justice* 20 (1992): 401–12.

118. Joseph Goldstein, "Police Discretion Not to Invoke the Criminal Process," *Yale Law Journal* 69 (1960): 543–94.

119. Richard C. Donnelly, "Police Authority and Practices," *Annals of the American Academy of Political and Social Science* 339 (January 1962): 91–92.

120. See, generally, Kenneth C. Davis, *Discretionary Justice—A Preliminary Inquiry* (Baton Rouge: Louisiana State University Press, 1969).

121. Stephen Mastrofski, R. Richard Ritti, and Debra Hoffmaster, "Organizational Determinants of Police Discretion: The Case of Drinking and Driving," *Journal of Criminal Justice* 15 (1987): 387–402.

122. David Klinger, "Negotiating Order in Patrol Work: An Ecological Theory of Police Response to Deviance," *Criminology* 35 (1997): 277–306.

123. Klinger, "Negotiating Order in Patrol Work," p. 296.

124. Sherri Lynn Johnson, "Race and the Decision to Detain a Suspect," *Yale Law Journal* 93 (1983): 214–58.

125. Geoffrey Alpert, Dennis Kenney, and Roger Dunham, "Police Pursuits and the Use of Force: Recognizing and Managing the 'Pucker Factor'—A Research Note," *Justice Quarterly* 14 (1997): 371–86.

126. Helen Eigenberg, Kathryn Scarborough, and Victor Kappeler, "Contributory Factors Affecting Arrest in Domestic and Non-Domestic Assaults," *American Journal of Police* 15 (1996): 27–51.

127. Leonore Simon, "A Therapeutic Jurisprudence Approach to the Legal Processing of Domestic Violence Cases," *Psychology Public Policy and Law* 1 (1995): 43–79.

128. James Fyfe, David Klinger, and Jeanne Flaving, "Differential Police Treatment of Male-on-Female Spousal Violence," *Criminology* 35 (1997): 455–73.

129. David Klinger, "Policing Spousal Assault," *Journal of Research in Crime and Delinquency* 32 (1995): 308–324.

130. See, for example, Nathan Goldman, *The Differential Selection of Juvenile Offenders for Court Appearance* (New York: National Council on Crime and Delinquency, 1963); Aaron Cicourel, *The Social Organization of Juvenile Justice* (New York: John Wiley, 1968); Irving Piliavin and Scott Briar, "Police Encounters with Juveniles," *American Journal of Sociology* 70 (1964): 206.

131. Richard R. Johnson, "Citizen Complaints: What the Police Should Know," *The FBI Law Enforcement Bulletin* 67 (1998): 1–6.

132. Donald Black, "The Social Organization of Arrest," *Stanford Law Review* 23 (1971): 1087–1111.

133. Richard Lundman, "Demeanor or Crime? The Midwest City Police–Citizen Encounters Study," *Criminology* 36 (1994): 631–56.

134. David Klinger, "More on Demeanor and Arrest in Dade County," *Criminology* 34 (1996): 61–82.

135. Jerome Skolnick and J. Richard Woodworth, "Bureaucracy, Information and Social Control: A Study of a Morals Detail," in *The Police, Six Sociological Essays,* ed. David Bordua (New York: John Wiley, 1960).

136. John Gardiner, *Traffic and the Police: Variations in Law Enforcement Policy* (Cambridge: Harvard University Press, 1969).

137. Samuel Walker, *Civilian Review of the Police: A National Survey of the 50 Largest Cities, 1991* (Omaha: University of Nebraska, Department of Criminal Justice, 1991).

138. Robert Worden and Robin Shepard, "Demeanor, Crime and Police Behavior: A Reexamination of the Police Services Study Data," *Criminology* 34 (1996): 83–105.

139. Stephen Mastrofski, Robert Worden, and Jeffrey Snipes, "Law Enforcement in a Time of Community Policing," *Criminology* 33 (1995): 39–563.

140. Gregory Howard Williams, *The Law and Politics of Police Discretion* (Westport, Conn.: Greenwood Press, 1984); Dennis Powell, "Race, Rank, and Police Discretion," *Journal of Police Science and Administration* 9 (1981): 383–89; Douglas Smith and Jody Klein, "Police Control of Interpersonal Disputes," *Social Problems* 31 (1984): 468–81; Goldman, *The Differential Selection of Juvenile Offenders for Court Appearance;* Dale Dannefer and Russell Schutt, "Race and Juvenile Justice Processing in Court and Police Agencies," *American Journal of Sociology* 87 (1982): 1113–32.

141. Marvin Krohn, James Curry, and Shirley Nelson-Kilger, "Is Chivalry Dead? An Analysis of Changes in Police Dispositions of Males and Females," *Criminology* 21 (1983): 417–37.

142. Most important is the Equal Employment Opportunity Act of 1972, amending Title VII of the Civil Rights Act of 1964.

143. *United States v. Paradise,* 55 L.W. 4211 (1987).

144. Jihong Zhao and Nicholas Lovrich, "Determinants of Minority Employment in American Municipal Police Agencies: The Representation of African American Officers," *Journal of Criminal Justice* 26 (1998): 267–78.

145. Walker, *Popular Justice,* p. 61.

146. Nicholas Alex, *Black in Blue: A Study of the Negro Policeman* (New York: Appleton Century Crofts, 1969).

147. Alex, *Black in Blue,* p. 154.

148. Kim Michelle Lersch, "Predicting Citizens' Race in Allegations of Misconduct Against the Police," *Journal of Criminal Justice* 26 (1998): 87–99.

149. James Jacobs and Jay Cohen, "The Impact of Racial Integration on the Police," *Journal of Police Science and Administration* 6 (1978): 182.

150. Donald Yates and Vijayan Pillai, "Frustration and Strain Among Fort Worth Police Officers," *Sociology and Social Research* 76 (1992): 145–49.

151. Donald Yates and Vijayan Pillai, "Race and Police Commitment to Community Policing," *The Journal of Intergroup Relations* 19 (1993): 14–23.

152. Stephen Leinen, *Black Police, White Society* (New York: New York University Press, 1984).

153. See, generally, David J. Bell, "Policewomen: Myths and Reality," *Journal of Police Science and Administration* 10 (1982): 112–20.

154. Catherine Milton, *Women in Policing* (Washington, D.C.: Police Foundation, 1972).

155. See, generally, A. Bouza, "Women in Policing," *FBI Law Enforcement Bulletin* 44 (1975): 2–7; Joyce Sichel, Lucy Friedman, Janet Quint, and Micall Smith, *Women on Patrol: A Pilot Study of Police Performance in New York City* (Washington, D.C.: National Criminal Justice Reference Service, 1978); William Weldy, "Women in Policing: A Positive Step Toward Increased Police Enthusiasm," *Police Chief* 43 (1976): 47.

156. Patricia Marshall, "Policewomen on Patrol," *Manpower* 5 (1973): 14–20.

157. R. Hindman, "A Survey Related to Use of Female Law Enforcement Officers," *Police Chief* 42 (1975): 58–60.

158. Michael Birzer and Delores Craig, "Gender Differences in Police Physical Ability Test Performance," *American Journal of Police* 15 (1996): 93–106.

159. Sean Grennan, "Findings on the Role of Officer Gender in Violent Encounters with Citizens," *Journal of Police Science and Administration* 15 (1987): 79–85.

160. Bell, "Policewomen: Myths and Realities," p. 114.

161. Sally Gross, "Women Becoming Cops: Developmental Issues and Solutions," *Police Chief* 51 (1984): 32–35.

162. Simon Holdaway and Sharon K. Parker, "Policing Women Police: Uniform Patrol, Promotion and Representation in the CID," *British Journal of Criminology* 38 (1998): 40–48.

163. Susan Martin, "'Outsider Within' the Station House: The Impact of Race and Gender on Black Women Police," *Social Problems* 41 (1994): 383–400.

164. Curt Bartol, George Bergen, Julie Seager Volckens, and Kathleen Knoras, "Women in Small-Town Policing," *Criminal Justice and Behavior* 19 (1992): 240–59.

165. Joanne Belknap and Jill Kastens Shelley, "The New Lone Ranger: Policewomen on Patrol," *American Journal of Police* 12 (1993): 47–75.

166. Martin, "'Outsider Within' the Station House," p. 387.

167. Martin, "'Outsider Within' the Station House," p. 392.

168. Martin, "'Outsider Within' the Station House," p. 394.

169. Martin, "'Outsider Within' the Station House," p. 397.

170. Associated Press, "NY Pays $3M to Police Victim Kin," *New York Times,* 2 October 1998, p. A1.

171. Bittner, *The Functions of Police in Modern Society,* p. 46.

172. Walker, *Popular Justice,* p. 197.

173. President's Commission on Law Enforcement and the Administration of Justice, *Task Force Report: The Police,* pp. 181–82.

174. Albert Reiss, The Police and the Public (New Haven: Yale University Press, 1972).

175. David Bayley and James Garofalo, "The Management of Violence by Police Patrol Officers," *Criminology* 27 (1989): 1–27; Lawrence Sherman, "Causes of Police Behavior: The Current State of Quantitative Research," *Journal of Research in Crime and Delinquency* 17 (1980): 80–81.

176. For a general review, see Tom McEwen, *National Data Collection on Police Use of Force* (Washington, D.C.: National Institute of Justice, 1996).

177. Antony Pate and Lorie Fridell, *Police Use of Force: Official Reports, Citizen Complaints, and Legal Consequences* (Washington, D.C.: Police Foundation, 1993).

178. Sandra Lee Browning, Francis Cullen, Liqun Cao, Renee Kopache, and Thomas Stevenson, "Race and Getting Hassled by the Police: A Research Note," *Police Studies* 17 (1994): 1–11.

179. Kim Michelle Lersch and Tom Mieczkowski, "Who Are the Problem-Prone Officers? An Analysis of Citizen Complaints," *American Journal of Police* 15 (1996): 23–42.

180. For a comprehensive view of this issue, see William Geller and Michael Scott, "Deadly Force: What We Know," in *Thinking About Police,* ed. Carl Klockars and Stephen Mastrofski (New York: McGraw-Hill, 1991), pp. 446–77; James Fyfe, "Police Use of Deadly Force: Research and Reform," *Justice Quarterly* 5 (1988): 165–205.

181. Fyfe, "Police Use of Deadly Force: Research and Reform," p. 178; Kenneth Mattulla, *A Balance of Forces* (Washington, D.C.: U.S. Government Printing Office, 1982), p. 17.

182. This discussion is adapted from James Fyfe, "Toward a Typology of Police Shootings." Paper presented at the annual meeting of the Academy of Criminal Justice Sciences, Oklahoma City, March 1980.

183. Betty Jenkins and Adrienne Faison, *An Analysis of 248 Persons Killed by New York City Policemen* (New York: Metropolitan Applied Research Center, 1974).

184. Jonathan Sorensen, James Marquart, and Deon Brock, "Factors Related to Killings of Felons by Police Officers: A Test of the Community Violence and Conflict Hypotheses," *Justice Quarterly* 10 (1993): 417–40.

185. James Fyfe, "Race and Extreme Police–Citizen Violence," in *Race, Crime and Criminal Justice,* ed. R. L. McNeely and Carl Pope (Beverly Hills: Sage, 1981).

186. James Fyfe, "Blind Justice? Police Shooting in Memphis." Paper prepared for the annual meeting of the Academy of Criminal Justice Science, Philadelphia, March 1981, p. 18.

187. Peter Scharf and Arnold Binder, *The Badge and the Bullet: Police Use of Deadly Force* (New York: Praeger, 1983).

188. Lorie Fridell and Arnold Binder, "Police Officer Decisionmaking in Potentially Violent Confrontations," *Journal of Criminal Justice* 20 (1992): 385–99.

189. *Tennessee v. Garner,* 105 S.Ct. 1694 (1985).

190. New York City Police Department, *Temporary Operating Procedure 237,* p. 1.

191. James Fyfe, "Administrative Interventions on Police Shooting Discretion: An Empirical Examination," *Journal of Criminal Justice* 7 (1979): 309–23.

192. Crime Control Act of 1994, Section 210401.

193. Estimate based on Geller and Scott, "Deadly Force: What We Know," p. 452.

194. FBI, *Law Enforcement Officers Killed and Assaulted, 1997* (Washington, D.C.: U.S. Government Printing Office, 1998).

195. Warren Cohen, "When Lethal Force Won't Do," *U.S. News & World Report* 122 (23 June 1997): 12.

196. Richard Lumb and Paul Friday, "Impact of Pepper Spray Availability on Police Officer Use-of-Force Decisions," *Policing* 20 (1997): 136–49.

197. Tom McEwen, "Policies on Less-Than-Lethal Force in Law Enforcement Agencies," *Policing* 20 (1997): 39–60.

The Judicatory Process

INTRODUCTION

On December 2, 1997, Dale E. Mahan, 36, and Ronnie B. Mahan, 50, two Alabama brothers, walked free after spending almost 14 years in a state prison. The two were exonerated after DNA tests conducted by the Alabama Department of Forensic Sciences showed that they were wrongfully convicted in 1983 of raping and kidnapping a woman. "Do you know what it's like to be locked up 14 years and then to be able to come downtown and look around?" Dale Mahan told reporters after his release. "You don't really know what freedoms you have until you've been incarcerated for a while."[1]

The Mahan case illustrates the tremendous burden placed on the court system. It must render fair, impartial justice in deciding the outcome of a conflict between criminal and victim, law enforcement agents and violators of the law, parent and child, federal government and violators of governmental regulations, or other parties. Regardless of the issues involved, the parties' presence in a courtroom should guarantee that they will have a hearing conducted under rules of procedure in an atmosphere of fair play and objectivity and that the outcome of the hearing will be clear. If a party believes that the ground rules have been violated, he or she may take the case to a higher court, where the procedures of the original trial will be examined. If it finds that a violation of legal rights has occurred, the appellate court may deem the findings of the original trial improper and either order a new hearing or hold that some other measure must be carried out; for example, the court may dismiss the charge outright. As the Mahan case shows, an erroneous judgment can devastate people's lives.

The court is a complex social agency with many independent but interrelated subsystems — clerk, prosecutor, defense attorney, judge, and probation department — each having a role in the court's operation. It is also the scene of many important elements of criminal justice decision making — detention, jury selection, trial, and sentencing.

Ideally, the judicatory process operates with absolute fairness and equality. The entire process — from

Dale and Ronnie Mahan were freed from prison on December 2, 1997, after spending more than 14 years in prison for a crime they did not commit. How can such miscarriages of justice be prevented?

Figure 17.1 Structure of a State Judicial System

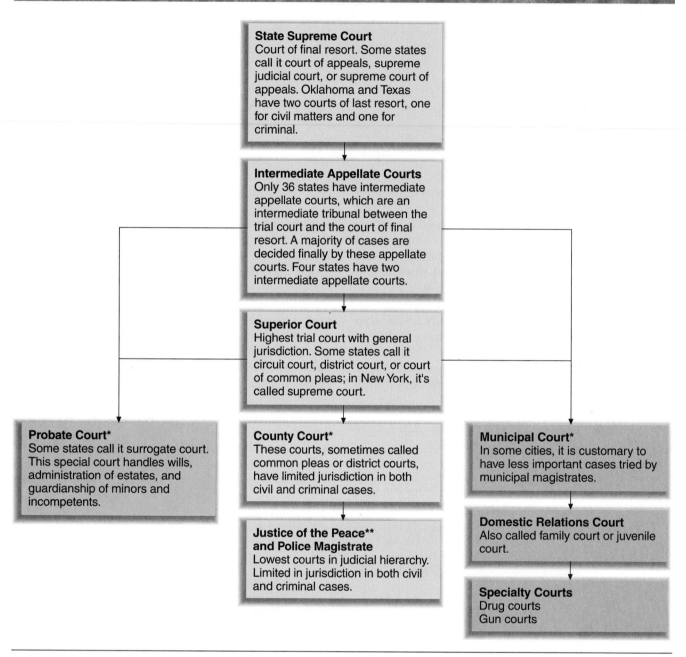

State Supreme Court
Court of final resort. Some states call it court of appeals, supreme judicial court, or supreme court of appeals. Oklahoma and Texas have two courts of last resort, one for civil matters and one for criminal.

Intermediate Appellate Courts
Only 36 states have intermediate appellate courts, which are an intermediate tribunal between the trial court and the court of final resort. A majority of cases are decided finally by these appellate courts. Four states have two intermediate appellate courts.

Superior Court
Highest trial court with general jurisdiction. Some states call it circuit court, district court, or court of common pleas; in New York, it's called supreme court.

Probate Court*
Some states call it surrogate court. This special court handles wills, administration of estates, and guardianship of minors and incompetents.

County Court*
These courts, sometimes called common pleas or district courts, have limited jurisdiction in both civil and criminal cases.

Municipal Court*
In some cities, it is customary to have less important cases tried by municipal magistrates.

Justice of the Peace**
and Police Magistrate
Lowest courts in judicial hierarchy. Limited in jurisdiction in both civil and criminal cases.

Domestic Relations Court
Also called family court or juvenile court.

Specialty Courts
Drug courts
Gun courts

*Courts of special jurisdiction, such as probate, family, or juvenile courts, and the so-called inferior courts, such as common pleas or municipal courts, may be separate courts or part of the trial court of general jurisdiction.

**Justices of the peace do not exist in all states. Where they do exist, their jurisdictions vary greatly from state to state.

Source: American Bar Association, *Law and the Courts* (Chicago: ABA, 1974), 20. Updated information provided by West Publishing, St. Paul, Minnesota.

filing the initial complaint to final sentencing of the defendant — is governed by precise rules of law designed to ensure fairness. No defendant tried before a U.S. court should suffer or benefit because of his or her personal characteristics, beliefs, or affiliations.

However, U.S. criminal justice can be selective. Discretion accompanies defendants through every step of the process, determining what will happen to them and how their cases will be resolved. Discretion means that two people committing similar crimes will receive highly dissimilar treatment; for example, most people convicted of homicide receive a prison sentence, but about 5 percent receive probation as a sole sentence; more murderers get probation than the death penalty.[2]

This chapter reviews some of the institutions and processes involved in adjudication and trial. The chap-

Figure 17.2 The Federal Judicial System

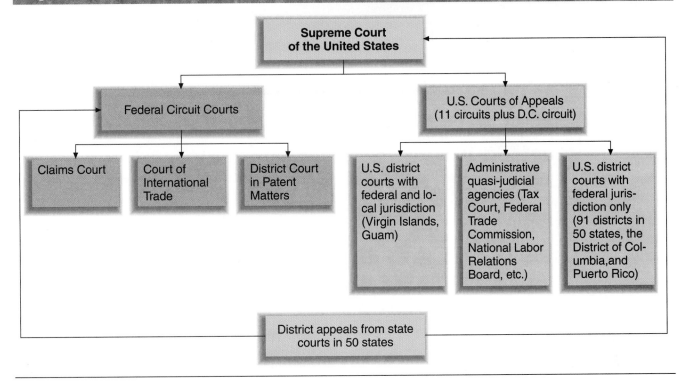

Source: American Bar Association, *Law and the Courts* (Chicago: ABA, 1974), 21. Updated information provided by the Federal Courts Improvement Act of 1982 and West Publishing, St. Paul, Minnesota.

ter briefly describes the court structure and then discusses the actors in the process — prosecution, defense, judges, and juries. The pretrial stage of the justice process is the next focus of attention, as such issues as bail and plea bargaining are described. The criminal trial is then discussed in some detail; finally, sentencing formats are explained.

COURT STRUCTURE

Criminal adjudication is played out within the court system. The nation's 16,000 courts are organized on the municipal, county, state, and federal levels.

State Courts

The typical state court structure is illustrated in Figure 17.1. Most states employ a multitiered court structure. Lower courts try misdemeanors and conduct the preliminary processing of felony offenses. Superior trial courts try felony cases. Appellate courts review the criminal procedures of trial courts to determine whether the offenders were treated fairly. Superior appellate courts or state supreme courts, used in about half the states, review lower appellate court decisions.

Federal Courts

The federal court system has three tiers, as shown in Figure 17.2. The **U.S. district courts** are the trial courts of the system; they have jurisdiction over cases involving violations of federal law, such as interstate transportation of stolen vehicles and racketeering.

Appeals from the district court are heard in one of the intermediate **federal courts of appeal.** However, the highest federal appeals court, the **U.S. Supreme Court,** is the court of last resort for all cases tried in the various federal and state courts.

The Supreme Court is composed of nine members, appointed for lifetime terms by the president with the approval of Congress. In general, the Court hears only cases it deems important and appropriate. When the Court decides to hear a case, it usually grants a **writ of certiorari**, requesting a transcript of the case proceedings for review. The process by which a case gets to the Supreme Court is set out in Figure 17.3.

The Supreme Court can word a decision so that it becomes a **precedent** that must be honored by all lower courts. For example, if the Court grants a particular litigant the right to counsel at a police lineup, then all people in similar situations must be given the same right. This type of ruling is usually referred to as a **landmark decision.** The use of precedent in the legal system

Figure 17.3 Tracing a Case to the U.S. Supreme Court

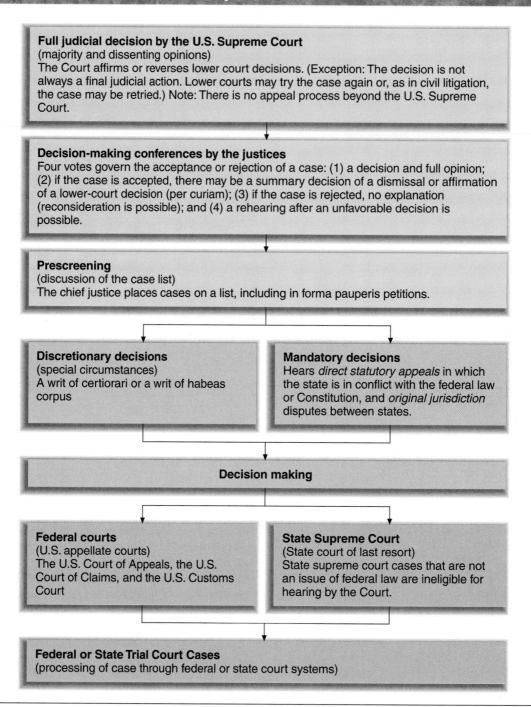

Full judicial decision by the U.S. Supreme Court
(majority and dissenting opinions)
The Court affirms or reverses lower court decisions. (Exception: The decision is not always a final judicial action. Lower courts may try the case again or, as in civil litigation, the case may be retried.) Note: There is no appeal process beyond the U.S. Supreme Court.

Decision-making conferences by the justices
Four votes govern the acceptance or rejection of a case: (1) a decision and full opinion; (2) if the case is accepted, there may be a summary decision of a dismissal or affirmation of a lower-court decision (per curiam); (3) if the case is rejected, no explanation (reconsideration is possible); and (4) a rehearing after an unfavorable decision is possible.

Prescreening
(discussion of the case list)
The chief justice places cases on a list, including in forma pauperis petitions.

Discretionary decisions
(special circumstances)
A writ of certiorari or a writ of habeas corpus

Mandatory decisions
Hears *direct statutory appeals* in which the state is in conflict with the federal law or Constitution, and *original jurisdiction* disputes between states.

Decision making

Federal courts
(U.S. appellate courts)
The U.S. Court of Appeals, the U.S. Court of Claims, and the U.S. Customs Court

State Supreme Court
(State court of last resort)
State supreme court cases that are not an issue of federal law are ineligible for hearing by the Court.

Federal or State Trial Court Cases
(processing of case through federal or state court systems)

gives the Supreme Court power to influence and mold the everyday operating procedures of police agencies, trial courts, and corrections institutions. This influence was quite pronounced during the tenure of Chief Justice Earl Warren, who, during the 1960s, greatly amplified and extended the power of the Court to affect criminal justice policies.

The American court system is a vast enterprise. About 90 million new cases of all kinds and 280,000

appeals are brought before the courts of the 50 states and the District of Columbia.[3] These statistics can be misleading because about 60 percent of all cases (51 million) are traffic violations handled by municipal or traffic court. Nonetheless, about 13 million cases involving criminal actions are handled by the courts each year, as well as 2 million juvenile delinquency cases.

As Figure 17.4 shows, the number of serious cases has trended upward over the past decade in both state

Figure 17.4   Caseload Growth in State and Federal Courts by Type of Case

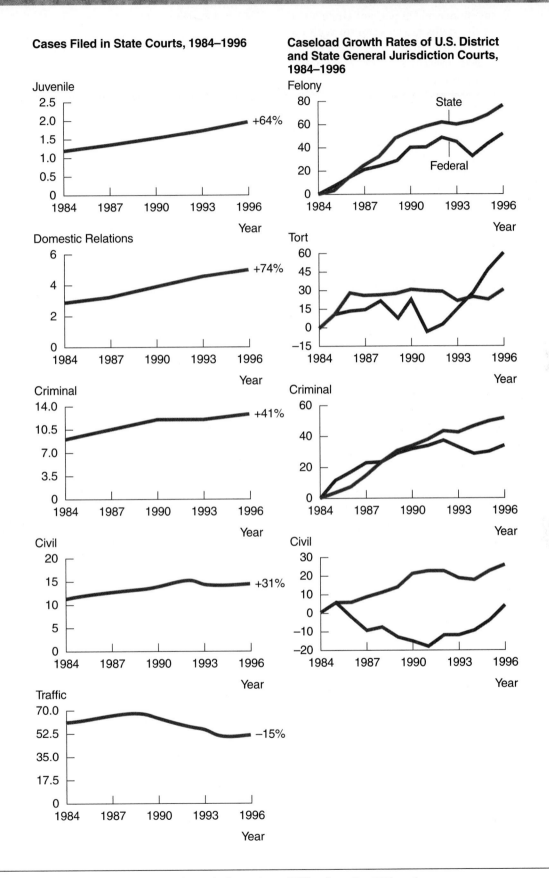

Cases Filed in State Courts, 1984–1996

Caseload Growth Rates of U.S. District and State General Jurisdiction Courts, 1984–1996

Source: National Center for State Courts, *Examining the Work of State Courts* (Williamsburg, Va.: 1998), p. xi.

and federal courts, a movement explained in part by the increases in violent crimes and drug offenses; domestic violence cases increased 99 percent since 1989. Almost two-thirds of the states fail to keep up with the flow of criminal and civil case filings. The extent of this caseload has placed great pressure on the major actors in the pretrial, trial, and sentencing process: the prosecutor, the defense attorney, and the judge.

One reason for the increase in court caseloads is the recent attempt in some communities to lower the crime rate by aggressively prosecuting petty offenses and nuisance crimes such as panhandling or vagrancy. In New York City, for example, the number of felonies has stayed roughly the same since the early 1990s, whereas the number of misdemeanor cases has soared by 85 percent. In 1998, 77 New York City judges handled 275,379 cases—about 3,500 cases each—in the city's lower criminal courts, which handle misdemeanors involving sentences of less than a year in jail. For defendants who want to fight charges, the average waiting time for a misdemeanor trial is 284 days, up from 208 days in 1991.[4]

It is within the confines of this criminal court system that the key action of the entire justice process—the adversary process—takes place.

ACTORS IN THE JUDICATORY PROCESS

The judge, the prosecutor, and the defense attorney are the key players in the adversary process. The prosecution and defense oppose each other in a hotly disputed contest—the criminal trial—in accordance with rules of law and procedure. In every criminal case, the prosecutor represents the state's interests and the defense attorney the criminal defendant's, with each side trying to bring evidence and arguments forward to advance its case. Theoretically, the ultimate objective of the adversary system is to seek the truth, to determine whether the evidence presented at the trial is sufficient to prove the facts of the charge. So that the defendant is given a fair trial, the judge acts as an impartial arbiter of procedure, ensuring that neither side violates the rules of trial conduct.

Prosecutor

The **prosecution** represents the state in criminal matters that come before the courts. At last count, state court prosecutors' offices employed about 71,000 attorneys, investigators, and support staff, an increase of more than 25 percent since 1992.[5] The prosecutor's major duties are listed in Table 17.1.

Prosecutors' jobs are changing with the times as they confront new crime patterns and become more

Table 17.1 The Prosecutor's Most Significant Responsibilities

- *Investigating law violations.* Prosecutors are empowered to conduct their own investigations into alleged violations of the law. In some jurisdictions, they maintain a staff of detectives and investigators; in others they rely on local or state police. In jurisdictions with grand jury systems, the prosecutor can convene the grand jury to collect information and interview witnesses for the purpose of accumulating enough evidence to indict suspects in criminal conspiracies.

- *Cooperating with police.* The prosecutor's office usually works closely with police agencies. Police prepare the investigation report of a crime according to the format desired by the prosecutor's office. Prosecutors also advise police agents about the legal issues in a given case. For example, they supervise the drawing up of requests (**affidavits**) for search warrants and then make sure that the police understand the limitations presented by the warrant. Some prosecutor's offices help train police officers, making them aware of the legal issues involved in securing a warrant or a legal arrest, interrogating a suspect, and so on.

- *Determining charges.* The prosecutor determines the charges to be brought against the suspect. The charge on which defendants are brought to trial may not resemble the original reasons they were arrested. For example, a suspect picked up for disorderly conduct may later be identified at a police lineup as the perpetrator of a string of liquor store robberies. The disorderly conduct charge may then be dropped in favor of prosecution on the more serious robbery charges.

- *Representing the government in pretrial hearings and motions.* The prosecutor brings the case to trial. Prosecutors contact witnesses and prepare them to testify, secure physical evidence, and discuss the victim's testimony. If the defendant attempts to have evidence suppressed at a pretrial hearing (for example, because of violations of the exclusionary rule), the prosecutor represents the state's position on the matter.

- *Plea bargaining.* The prosecutor is empowered to negotiate a guilty plea with the defendant, thereby ending the formal trial process.

- *Trying criminal cases.* The prosecutor acts as the state's attorney at criminal trials. Consequently, another name for the prosecutor is people's attorney.

- *Sentencing.* The prosecutor recommends dispositions at the completion of the trial. Usually, the type of sentence recommended is influenced by plea bargaining cooperation, public opinion, the seriousness of the crime, the offender's prior record, and other factors related to the case.

- *Representing the government at appeals.* If the defendant is found guilty as charged, he or she may appeal the conviction before a higher court. The prosecutor represents the government at these hearings.

- *Conducting special investigations.* Some jurisdictions empower special prosecutors to seek indictments for serious crimes considered important to the public interest. This practice became well known during the Watergate investigation, when first Archibald Cox and then Leon Jaworski were appointed as special prosecutors to investigate the break-ins and subsequent cover-up. In recent years Kenneth Starr has served as an independent counsel investigating the Clinton presidency.

sensitive to old ones. For example, a recent survey found that almost 90 percent of all offices now prosecute felony domestic violence and child abuse cases, and about half the offices prosecute cases involving new kinds of firearms offenses.[6]

Types of Prosecutors In the federal system, the chief prosecuting officer is the U.S. attorney general; his or her assistant prosecutors are known as U.S. attorneys and are appointed by the president. They represent the government in federal district courts. The chief prosecutor is usually an administrator; assistants normally handle the actual preparation and trial work. Federal prosecutors are professional civil service employees with reasonable salaries and job security.

Office titles for state court prosecutors include district attorney, county attorney, prosecuting attorney, commonwealth attorney, and state's attorney. They are typically elected officials. Again, most criminal prosecution and staff work is performed by scores of full-time and part-time attorneys, police investigators, and clerical personnel. Most attorneys who work for prosecutors at state and county levels are political appointees who earn low salaries, handle many cases, and in some jurisdictions, maintain private law practices. Many young lawyers serve in this capacity to gain trial experience, then leave for better-paying positions. In some state, county, and municipal jurisdictions, however, the office of the prosecutor can be described as meeting the highest standards of professional skill, personal integrity, and working conditions.

In urban settings, the structure of the district attorney's office is often specialized, with separate divisions for felonies, misdemeanors, and trial and appeal assignments. In rural offices, chief prosecutors handle many of the criminal cases themselves. Where assistant prosecutors are employed, they often work part-time, have limited professional opportunities, and depend on the political patronage of chief prosecutors for their positions.

The job is stressful because of both work pressure and also the danger of the job. One survey found that 75 percent of the offices provided security or assistance for felony case victims or witnesses who had been threatened; half the offices reported a staff member received a work-related threat or was assaulted; 25 percent of chief prosecutors carried a firearm for personal security.[7] The percentage of all offices receiving threats is on the increase.

Prosecutorial Discretion Prosecutors maintain broad discretion in the exercise of their duties. In fact, for more than 60 years, full enforcement of the law has been so rare that it has been assumed that prosecutors will choose what cases to bring to court.[8]

Prosecutors exercise discretion in a variety of circumstances. One major decision involves the choice of acting on the information brought by police or deciding not to file for an indictment. The prosecutor can also attempt to prosecute and then decide to drop the case; this is known as a *nolle prosequi*.

Figure 17.5 shows the pattern of prosecutor decision making found by one study of case processing in 30 urban jurisdictions.[9] About half of all arrests are dismissed before they reach the trial stage. Some are diverted into treatment programs; others are rejected after being screened by the prosecutor; and another group is dealt with in lower court by either dismissal or misdemeanor conviction. Of those carried forward to trial, the great majority end with a plea bargain.

This research illustrates the significant influence prosecutors have over the criminal process. By effectively screening out cases in which conviction could not reasonably be expected, cases inappropriate for criminal action (such as minor thefts by first offenders), and cases involving offenders with special needs (such as the emotionally disturbed or mentally retarded), the prosecutor can concentrate on bringing to trial those who commit more serious criminal offenses. The relatively few cases that do get to trial are most often settled through plea negotiations conducted by the prosecutor's office.[10]

Factors Influencing Decision Making Research indicates that widely varied factors influence prosecutorial discretion in invoking criminal sanctions, including the characteristics of the crime, the criminal, and the victim. A defendant who is a known drug user, who has a long history of criminal offending, and who causes the victim extensive physical injuries will more likely be prosecuted than one who is a first offender, does not use drugs, and does not seriously injure a victim.[11] The effect of race on prosecutorial decision making is uncertain. Although some research efforts have found that the race of the offender or victim influences prosecutorial discretion, others show that decisions are relatively unbiased.[12]

Numerous attempts have been made to examine the charging decision. In his classic work *Prosecution: The Decision to Charge a Subject with a Crime*, Frank Miller pinpoints the factors influencing prosecutorial discretion, including[13]

- The attitude of the victim.
- The cost of prosecution to the criminal justice system.
- The possibility of undue harm to the suspect.
- The availability of alternative procedures.
- The availability of civil sanctions.
- The willingness of the suspect to cooperate with law enforcement authorities.

In another classic work, Wayne LaFave also identified factors related to prosecutorial discretion.[14] According to LaFave, when acts have been overcriminalized—such as when laws provide stiff sentences for

Figure 17.5 Felony Arrest Typical Outcomes

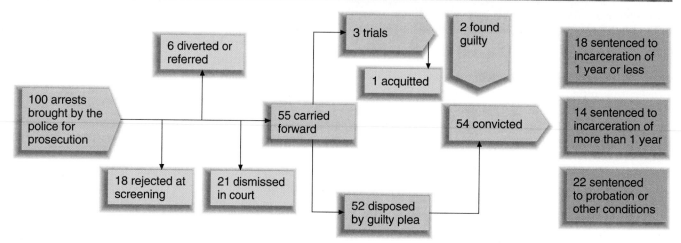

The data collected for this report indicate that for every 100 adult arrests for a felony, 54 will result in conviction of either a felony or a misdemeanor. Of those 54,

- 52 will be guilty pleas.
- 2 will be convictions at trial.

Of the 54 arrests resulting in conviction:

- 32 will lead to a sentence of incarceration.
- 18 will result in a sentence of 1 year or less.
- 14 will result in a sentence of more than 1 year.

Of the 46 arrests that do not result in convictions,

- 6 will result in the defendants' being referred to diversion programs or to other courts for prosecution.
- 18 will be rejected for prosecution at screening, before court charges are filed.
- 21 will be dismissed in court.
- 1 will result in an acquittal at trial.

Source: Barbara Boland, Paul Mahanna, and Ronald Sones, *The Prosecution of Felony Arrests, 1988* (Washington, D.C.: Bureau of Justice Statistics, February 1992), p. 3.

---

possessing small quantities of recreational drugs—they are not prosecuted. Limited resources force the prosecutor to select only the most serious cases. Also, alternatives to prosecution are used whenever possible to spare offenders the stigma of a criminal conviction.

In some instances LaFave found that the prosecutor may decide to take no action; this occurs when the victim expresses the desire not to prosecute, the cost would be excessive, the harm of prosecution outweighs the benefits, or the harm done by the offender can be corrected without a criminal trial. LaFave also points out that prosecutors can invoke obscure statutes to punish unrepentant offenders or refuse leniency to defendants who will not cooperate with them. Thus, to LaFave, prosecutorial discretion is a two-edged sword. Table 17.2 lists some of the other factors that have been identified as influencing prosecutorial discretion.

Case pressure is also considered an important influence on prosecutorial discretion. Although some criminologists dispute whether prosecutors' decisions are based on their work schedule, others say that the prosecutor who is deluged by serious cases is likely to not prosecute or to offer a plea bargain. Prosecutors in large

Table 17.2 Factors Influencing Prosecutorial Discretion

- Evidence problems that result from a failure to find sufficient physical evidence linking the defendant to the offense
- Witness problems that arise, for example, when a witness fails to appear, gives unclear or inconsistent statements, is reluctant to testify, or is unsure of the identity of the offender
- Office policy, wherein the prosecutor decides not to prosecute certain types of offenses, particularly those that violate the letter but not the spirit of the law (for example, offenses involving insignificant amounts of property damage)
- Due process problems that involve violations of the constitutional requirements for seizing evidence and questioning the accused
- Combination with other cases, for example, when the accused is charged in several cases and the prosecutor pursues all of the charges in a single case
- Pretrial diversion, which occurs when the prosecutor and the court agree to drop charges when the accused successfully meets the conditions for diversion, such as completion of a treatment program

Source: Joseph Senna and Larry Siegel, *Introduction to Criminal Justice* (Belmont, Calif.: Wadsworth/West, 1999).

counties are less likely to bring felons to trial than those in smaller, less crime-ridden counties. This is not conclusive proof of the effect of case pressure; an alternative explanation is that police work is sloppier in urban areas, forcing prosecutors to drop cases. However, it shows that jurisdictions in which prosecutors are forced to deal with more serious, violent felonies are also the ones in which the most selectivity is used.[15]

Is prosecutorial discretion inherently harmful? Not necessarily, argues Judge Charles Breitel, who, in a famous statement, asserted that prosecutorial discretion is indispensable to ensure efficiency in the criminal justice system:

> If every policeman, every prosecutor, every court, and every post-sentence agency performed his or its responsibility in strict accordance with rules of law, precisely and narrowly laid down, the criminal law would be ordered but intolerable. Living would be a sterile compliance with soul-killing rules and taboos. By comparison, a primitive tribal society would seem free, indeed.[16]

Although eliminating prosecutorial discretion may not always be desirable, efforts have been made to control its content and direction. For example, national commissions have established guidelines for the exercise of appropriate prosecutorial actions.[17] Other methods of controlling prosecutorial decision making include

- Identification of the reasons for charging decisions.
- Publication of prosecution office policies.
- Review by nonprosecutorial groups.
- Charging conferences.
- Evaluation of charging policies and decisions and development of screening, diversion, and plea negotiation procedures.[18]

Defense Attorney

The defense counsel performs many functions while representing the accused in the criminal process (see Table 17.3). Although prominent criminal defense lawyers are numerous in the United States, the majority of criminal defendants are indigents who cannot afford legal counsel. The Supreme Court has interpreted the Sixth Amendment of the Constitution to mean that people facing trial for offenses that can be punished by incarceration have the right to legal counsel.[19] If they cannot afford counsel, the state must provide an attorney free of charge. Consequently, three systems have been developed to provide legal counsel to the indigent:

- Assigning private attorneys to represent indigent clients on a case-by-case basis (sometimes referred to as an *attorney list system*), with the state paying their fees
- Contracting with a law firm or group of private attorneys to regularly provide defense services to indigents
- Creating a publicly funded defender's office

Table 17.3 The Role of the Defense Attorney

- Investigating the incident
- Interviewing the client, police officers, and other witnesses
- Discussing the matter with the prosecutor
- Representing the defendant at the various pretrial procedures, such as arrest, interrogation, lineup, and arraignment
- Entering into plea negotiations
- Preparing the case for trial, including developing the tactics and strategy to be used
- Filing and arguing legal motions with the court
- Representing the defendant at trial
- Providing assistance at sentencing
- Determining the appropriate basis for appeal

Source: Joseph Senna and Larry Siegel, *Introduction to Criminal Justice* (Belmont, Calif.: Wadsworth/West, 1999), p. 323.

These three systems can be used independently or in combination.[20] In general, the **attorney list/assigned counsel system** is used in less populated areas, where case flow is minimal and a full-time public defender is not needed. **Public defenders** are usually found in larger urban areas with high case flow rates. So although a proportionately larger area of the country is served by the assigned counsel system, a significant proportion of criminal defendants receive public defenders. Public defenders can be part of a statewide agency, county government, the judiciary, or an independent nonprofit organization or other institution.

A survey of the indigent defense system found that it is a vast enterprise supported by billions of dollars in taxpayers' money. About three-fourths of the inmates in state prisons and about half of those in federal prisons received publicly provided legal counsel for the offense for which they were serving time. About 80 percent of defendants charged with felonies in the nation's 75 largest counties relied on a public defender or on assigned counsel for legal representation.[21]

Conflicts of Defense Because of how the U.S. system of justice operates today, criminal defense attorneys face many role conflicts. They are viewed as prime movers in what is essentially an **adversarial process:** the prosecution and the defense fight over the facts of the case at hand, with the prosecutor arguing the case for the state and the defense counsel using all possible means to aid the client.

However, as members of the legal profession, defense attorneys must be aware of their role as officers of the court. As an attorney, the defense counsel is obligated to uphold the integrity of the legal profession and to observe the requirements of the Code of Professional Responsibility of the American Bar Association in the defense of a client. The code makes the following

It is possible for defendants in a criminal case to represent themselves if a judge finds them competent to conduct a trial; this is referred to as a *pro se defense*. That is what "suicide doctor" Jack Kevorkian, shown here questioning a witness, did in his trial on murder charges. The 1999 trial ended with his conviction on a charge of murder in the second degree. Kevorkian was allowed to consult with legal advisors during the trial who helped him present the case.

statement regarding the duties of the lawyer in the adversary system of justice:

> Our legal system provides for the adjudication of disputes governed by the rules of substantive, evidentiary, and procedural law. An adversary presentation counters the natural human tendency to judge too swiftly in terms of the familiar that which is not yet fully known; the advocate, by his zealous preparation of facts and law, enables the tribunal to come to the hearing with an open and neutral mind and to render impartial judgements. The duty of a lawyer to his client and his duty to the legal system are the same: To present his client zealously within the boundaries of the law.[22]

In this dual capacity of being both a defensive advocate and an officer of the court, the attorney often faces conflicting obligations to client and profession. These issues are sometimes so complex that even the Supreme Court has had difficulty setting standards of proper behavior. However, in *Nix v. Whiteside,* the Court sustained an attorney's right to refuse to represent a client whom he suspected would commit perjury. The Court also ruled that an attorney's threat to withdraw from the case and tell the court about the perjury did not violate the client's right to competent assistance of counsel.[23]

Beyond their ethical problems, criminal defense attorneys often find themselves at the bottom of the legal profession's financial hierarchy. In prestigious urban law firms, attorneys begin at about $75,000, average $140,000 by their seventh year, and make between $250,000 and $600,000 when they become partner. In contrast, a public defender averages between $20,000 and $30,000. Consequently, talented criminal attorneys feel pressure to leave the field and enter more lucrative areas of the law.[24]

Judge

The third major participant in the criminal trial is the **judge**—the senior officer in a court of criminal law. Judges' duties are quite varied and are far more extensive than the average citizen might suspect. During trials, the judge rules on the appropriateness of conduct, settles questions of evidence and procedure, and guides the questioning of witnesses. When a jury trial occurs, the judge must instruct jury members on which evidence can be examined and which should be ignored. The judge also formally charges the jury by instructing its members on what points of law and evidence they must consider before reaching a decision of guilty or innocent. When a jury trial is waived, the judge must decide for the complainant or the defendant. Finally, if a defendant is found guilty, the judge decides on the sentence (in some cases the sentence is legislatively determined). This duty includes choosing the type of sentence, its length, and—in the case of probation—the conditions under which it may be revoked. Obviously this decision has a significant effect on an offender's future.[25]

Beyond these stated duties, the trial judge has extensive control and influence over the other service agencies of the court: probation agencies, court clerks, police agencies, and the district attorney's office. Probation and the clerk may be under the judge's explicit control. In some courts, the operations, philosophy, and procedures of these agencies are within the magistrate's administrative domain. In other courts—for example, where a state agency controls the probation department—the attitudes of the county or district court judge still influence how a probation department is run.

Judicial Selection   Several methods are used to select state court judges.[26] In some jurisdictions, the governor simply appoints judges. In others, judicial recommendations must be confirmed by the state senate, the governor's council, a special confirmation committee, an executive council elected by the state assembly, or an elected review board. Some states employ screening bodies that submit names to the governor for approval. Another form of judicial selection is through popular election, either partisan or nonpartisan. This practice is used in a majority of states.

About 16 states have adopted what is known as the **Missouri Plan** to select judges. This three-part approach consists of (1) a judicial nominating commission to nominate candidates for the bench, (2) an elected official (usually from the executive branch) to make appointments from the list submitted by the commission, and (3) subsequent nonpartisan, noncompetitive elections in which incumbent judges run on their records. Some states, such as New York and Texas, use different methods to select judges on the appellate and trial levels. New York appellate court judges are appointed by the governor; trial court judges are elected; and criminal court and family court judges in New York City are appointed by the mayor.[27]

Judicial Overload   There has been great concern about stress placed on judges by case pressure. In most states, people appointed to the bench have had little or no training in the role of judge. Others may have held administrative posts and may not have appeared before a court in years. Once they are appointed to the bench, judges are given an overwhelming amount of work that has risen dramatically over the years. The number of civil and criminal filings per state court judge has increased significantly since 1985; federal judges handle fewer cases, and the number of civil cases in federal court has actually declined. Annually there are about 1,400 civil and criminal case filings per state court judge and 450 per federal judge.[28] State court judges deal with far more cases, but federal cases may be more complex and demand more judicial time. In any event, the number of civil and criminal cases, especially in state courts, seems to be outstripping the ability of states to create new judgeships.

Several agencies have been created to improve the quality of the judiciary. The National Conference of State Court Judges and the National College of Juvenile Justice both operate judicial training seminars and publish manuals and guides on state-of-the-art judicial techniques. Their ongoing efforts are designed to improve the quality of the nation's judges.

Now that the actors in the judicatory process have been introduced and the structure within which they work defined, our attention will turn to the three main stages of the process itself: pretrial procedures, the trial, and sentencing.

PRETRIAL PROCEDURES

After arrest, or if an arrest warrant has been served, a **criminal charge** is drawn up by the appropriate prosecutor's office. The charge is a formal written document identifying the criminal activity, the facts of the case, and the circumstances of the arrest. If the crime is a felony, the charge is called a **bill of indictment** (if it is to be considered by a grand jury) or an **information** (if that particular jurisdiction uses the preliminary hearing system); misdemeanants are charged with a **complaint.**

After an indictment or information is filed, the accused is brought before the trial court for **arraignment,** at which the judge informs the defendant of the charge, ensures that the accused is properly represented by counsel, and determines whether the person should be released on bail or some alternative plan pending a hearing or trial.

The defendant who is arraigned on an indictment or information can ordinarily plead guilty, not guilty, or nolo contendere, which is equivalent to a guilty plea but which cannot be used as evidence in subsequent cases. When a guilty plea is entered, the defendant admits to all the elements of the crime, and the court begins to review the person's background for sentencing purposes. A plea of not guilty sets the stage for a trial or for plea bargaining between the prosecutor and the defense attorney.

This section reviews in detail two important issues related to pretrial procedures: bail and plea bargaining.

Bail

Bail represents money or some other security provided to the court to ensure the appearance of the defendant at trial. The amount of bail is set by a magistrate who reviews the facts of the case and the history of the defendant. Defendants who cannot afford or are denied bail are detained, usually in a county jail or lockup, until their trial date. Those who make bail are free to pursue their defense before trial.

The bail system goes back to English common law. At one time the legal relationship existing in the contract law of bailment even permitted the trying and sentencing of the bailor (the person who posted bail) if the bailee did not appear for trial.[29]

Under the U.S. system of justice, the right to bail comes from the Eighth Amendment of the Constitution, which states that people can expect to be released on reasonable bail in all but capital cases. Thus, in most cases, accused persons have the right to be released on reasonable bail to prepare their defense and continue their life in the community.

Bail Today   The most recent national data available indicate that most defendants (62 percent) made bail; an estimated 38 percent of all defendants were detained until the courts disposed of their cases, including 7 percent who were denied bail. A majority of defendants charged with murder (79 percent), robbery (57 percent), or burglary (53 percent) were detained. Forty-three percent of murder defendants were denied bail, which means that the majority of people charged with killing someone were in fact offered pretrial release.[30] About a third of released defendants committed one or more types of pretrial misconduct that resulted in the revocation of their release. Twenty-four percent failed to appear in court as scheduled, and 15 percent were rearrested for a new offense.

Making Bail   Not all defendants make bail. Some defendants are detained because they cannot afford to make bail; others are denied bail because of the danger they present to the community, a practice called **preventive detention.**

The likelihood of making bail is directly related to the criminal charge: drug and public order offenders are the most likely to be bailed; violent offenders are more likely to be detained. A prior history of absconding before trial is also related to a lower probability of release. More than half of all defendants with an active criminal justice status (such as out on bail or on probation) were detained until case disposition, compared to 30 percent of those without such a status. Defendants on parole (76 percent) were the most likely to be detained, followed by those on probation (57 percent).

The Problems of Bail   Bail is quite controversial because it penalizes the indigent offender who does not have the means to pay the bond. Of concern is the fact that detention centers are dreary, dangerous places, and those who are held in them can be victims of the justice system even if they are innocent of all charges. The bail system is also costly because the state must pay for the detention of offenders who are unable to raise bail and

who might otherwise remain in the community. Legal scholar Caleb Foote, one of the nation's leading experts on bail, once stated,

> The basic problem—poor people and those being locked up before trial—remains. I still think pretrial detention is the most pervasive denial of equal protection and equal rights in American law.[31]

What are the most significant problems associated with bail today?

• **Increases punishment risk:** The significance of bail is further amplified because both the amount of bail ordered and the length of stay in pretrial detention for those who cannot raise bail are associated with a greater likelihood of conviction and a longer prison sentence after conviction.[32] Not making bail increases the risk of punishment. People detained before trial get convicted more often and, when convicted, receive longer and more punitive sentences than those granted pretrial release. Upon conviction, 87 percent of detained defendants were sentenced to incarceration, with 50 percent receiving a prison sentence and 38 percent a jail term. In contrast, 51 percent of the released defendants who were convicted were sentenced to incarceration, with more receiving a jail sentence (32 percent) than a prison sentence (19 percent). Convicted defendants who were detained until case disposition (50 percent) were more than twice as likely as released defendants to receive a state prison sentence. Among defendants who were detained through trial and sentencing, 67 percent were convicted and sentenced to incarceration, compared to 29 percent of those who were released.[33]

• **Bonding and recovery agents:** Another problem of the bail system is the institution of the professional **bail bonding agent.** Normally the bail bonding agent puts up 90 percent of a bond fee and the defendant the remaining 10 percent (this is called a *surety bond*). When the defendant appears at trial, the bail is returned and the bonding agent keeps the entire amount; the defendant's 10 percent serves as the bonding agent's commission. If the defendant does not show up for trial, the bonding agent must pay the entire bail. Usually bonding agents expect defendants, their friends, or their relatives to put up further collateral (such as the deed to their house) to cover the risk; they may also purchase insurance to reduce their risk. If collateral is unavailable or the bonding agent believes the offender presents too great a risk, the bonding agent will refuse to lend bail money, relegating the defendant to a jail stay until the trial date. Bail bonding agents have often been accused of unscrupulous practices, such as bribing police and court personnel to secure referrals. Some judges have been accused of refusing to collect forfeited bail owed from bonding agents.[34]

If a bailee fails to return for trial, the bonding agent may hire *skip tracers* or *recovery agents* to track down the fugitive in order to recover the lost bond. These

Table 17.4 Bail Systems

PROGRAM	DESCRIPTION
Nonfinancial Release	
1. Release on recognizance	The defendant is released on a promise to appear, without any requirement of money bond. This form of release is unconditional—that is, without imposition of special conditions, supervision, or specially provided services. The defendant must simply appear in court for all scheduled hearings.
2. Conditional release	The defendant is released on a promise to fulfill some stated requirements that go beyond those associated with release on recognizance. Four types of conditions are placed on defendants, all of which share the common aims of increasing the defendant's likelihood of returning to court and maintaining community safety: (1) status quo conditions, such as requiring that the defendant maintain residence or employment status; (2) restrictive conditions, such as requiring that the defendant remain in the jurisdiction, stay away from the complainant, or maintain a curfew; (3) contact conditions, such as requiring that the defendant report by telephone or in person to the release program or a third party at various intervals; and (4) problem-oriented conditions, such as requiring that the defendant participate in drug or alcohol treatment programs.
Financial release	
3. Unsecured bail	The defendant is released with no immediate requirement of payment. However, if the defendant fails to appear, he or she is liable for the full amount.
4. Privately secured bail	A private organization or individual posts the bail amount, which is returned when the defendant appears in court. In effect, the organization provides services akin to those of a professional bonding agent, but without cost to the defendant.
5. Property bail	The defendant may post evidence of real property in lieu of money.
6. Deposit bail	The defendant deposits a percentage of the bail amount, typically 10 percent, with the court. When the defendant appears in court, the deposit is returned, sometimes minus an administrative fee. If the defendant fails to appear, he or she is liable for the full amount of the bail.
7. Surety bail	The defendant pays a percentage of the bond, usually 10 percent, to a bonding agent who posts the full bail. The fee paid to the bonding agent is not returned to the defendant if he or she appears in court. The bonding agent is liable for the full amount of the bond should the defendant fail to appear. Bonding agents often require posting of collateral to cover the full bail amount.
8. Cash bail	The defendant pays the entire amount of bail set by the judge in order to secure release. The bail is returned to the defendant when he or she appears in court.

Source: Adapted from Andy Hall, *Pretrial Release Program Options* (Washington, D.C.: National Institute of Justice, 1984), pp. 32–33.

modern bounty hunters receive a share of the recovery. Unlike police, bounty hunters can enter a suspect's home without a warrant in most states, thanks to an 1873 Supreme Court ruling that gives agents of bail bonding agents sweeping powers. Each year bounty hunters catch about 25,000 fugitives, according to the National Institute of Bail Enforcement.[35] However, their brutal tactics sometimes end in tragedy. For example, in September 1997 five bounty hunters wearing black "ninja" clothing, body armor, and ski masks burst into a Phoenix, Arizona, home, held children at gunpoint, and shot and killed a young couple, Christopher Foote, 23, and Spring Wright, 20. They were charged with second-degree murder when it turned out they had entered the wrong house and killed two innocent people.[36]

Bail Reform The bail reform movement was started in 1961 to help alleviate the problems presented by the bail process. In New York the Vera Foundation, set up by philanthropist Louis Schweitzer and later supported by the Ford Foundation, pioneered the concept of **release on recognizance** (ROR).[37] This project found that if the court had sufficient background information about the defendant, it could make a reasonably good judgment about whether the accused would return to court.

The project proved to be a great success. A significant majority of clients returned for trial when released on their own recognizance. The success of ROR in New York prompted its adoption in many other large cities around the country. The Federal Bail Reform Act of 1984 has made release on recognizance an assumption unless the need for greater control can be shown in court.[38]

Abuses by bail bonding agents have prompted a number of jurisdictions, including Wisconsin, Nebraska, Kentucky, Oregon, and Illinois, to set up systems that allow defendants to post a percentage of their bond (usually 10 percent) with the court; the full amount is required only if the defendant fails to show for trial. This **deposit bail** system is designed to replace the bonding agents. The major forms of bail are set out in Table 17.4.

John William King and Lawrence Russell Brewer are escorted from the Jasper County courthouse on June 9, 1998, after being charged in the dragging death of James Byrd. The Eighth Amendment to the Constitution recognizes that people charged with capital offenses should be held in confinement prior to their trial without the possibility of bail.

Bail reform has been considered one of the great successes in criminal justice reform, but some research efforts indicate great disparity in the way judges handle bail decisions. They also show that racial and socioeconomic disparity might be a factor in decision making.[39] If this is so, then the original purposes of reforming bail would be negated by bias in the justice system. One approach to limiting disparity is the use of **bail guidelines,** which set standard bail amounts based on such factors as criminal history and the current charge.[40]

In sum, bail reform movements have encouraged the use of pretrial release. Studies show that most defendants return for trial and most bailees do not commit more crime while in the community.

Preventive Detention   Although only about 14 percent of bailees are rearrested for committing other crimes before trial, the threat they present to the public is dis-

turbing. After all, if 2 million people receive bail each year for serious crimes, about 300,000 crimes are committed by bailees who could have remained in pretrial detention. And assuming a 5-to-1 ratio of crimes to arrests, bailees may be responsible for 1.5 million serious crimes each year.

Because of the concern over defendant misconduct while on bail, about 30 states have limited bail for certain offenses and offenders, such as those who previously absconded, are recidivists, or have violent histories. Similarly, the federal Bail Reform Act of 1984 provides that federal offenders may be detained without bail if "no condition or combination of conditions (of bail) will reasonably assure . . . the safety of any other person and the community."[41]

The issue of preventive detention is particularly vexing because a person who has not been convicted of any crime is incarcerated for an extended period without the chance to participate in his or her own defense. Those supporting preventive detention argue that it helps control witness intimidation and reduces avoidable criminal acts.

In a landmark decision, *United States v. Salerno,* the Supreme Court upheld the Bail Reform Act's preventive detention provision on the grounds that its purpose was public safety, that it was not excessive for its stated purpose, and that it contained no punitive intent but was designed to regulate the behavior of accused criminals in a legally permissible way.[42] Similarly, in the case of *Schall v. Martin,* the court upheld a New York law providing for the preventive detention of a juvenile offender if the judicial authority believes the offender threatens community safety.[43]

An analysis of the federal Bail Reform Act shows that it increased the number of people held before trial. Before the act took effect, about 24 percent of all defendants were detained or did not make bail. After the act took effect, that number rose to 29 percent; 19 percent of the detainees did not qualify for bail consideration under the new guidelines.[44] Most of those held without bail had used firearms, were drug offenders, or had violated immigration laws.

Despite years of reform efforts, bail remains a troubling aspect of the criminal process. It is one of the few areas in which people are seriously penalized because of their economic circumstances. Whereas some defendants are kept in jail for lack of a few hundred dollars, others are released because they can afford bail in the millions. Those who cannot make bail face a greater chance of conviction and a harsher penalty if convicted.

Plea Bargaining

The majority of defendants in criminal trials are convicted by their own pleas of guilty; plea bargains are also common in juvenile court.[45] About 90 percent of all those charged with felonies plead guilty; if misdemeanors are included, the percentage jumps to 98 percent.[46]

Plea bargaining usually occurs between arraignment (or initial appearance, in the case of a misdemeanor) and the onset of trial. The ways a bargain can be struck in exchange for a guilty plea are set out in Table 17.5.

There are a number of different motivations for plea bargaining. Defendants, aware of the prosecutor's strong case, plea-bargain to minimize their sentences and avoid the harmful effects of a criminal conviction. Some may plead guilty to protect accomplices or confederates by "taking the rap" themselves.[47]

The defense attorney may seek a bargain to limit his or her own involvement in the case. In some instances, defense attorneys may wish to increase their operating profits by minimizing the effort they put forth for an obviously guilty client.[48] In other instances, they may

Table 17.5	Methods of Plea Bargaining

- The initial charges may be reduced to those of a lesser offense, thus automatically reducing the sentence imposed. For example, a first-degree murder charge may be reduced to second-degree murder, eliminating the threat of the death penalty.
- The charge may be reduced from a felony to a misdemeanor. For example, a felony burglary charge may be reduced to breaking and entering, a misdemeanor for which time can be served in the local jail.
- In cases where there are multiple offenses or counts (multiple charges for the same crime, such as three rape accusations), only a single charge may be filed. For example, a person is accused of raping five women. By his pleading guilty on one charge, the other four are dropped. People convicted of a single crime are less likely to be given a long sentence than those convicted of several. A defendant who commits armed robbery may plead guilty to unarmed robbery. Possessing a gun during a robbery adds an automatic three years to the sentence, which the defendant can avoid with his or her plea.
- The prosecutor may promise to recommend a lenient sentence, such as probation or a short prison term, in exchange for a plea.
- When the charge imposed has a negative label attached (such as child molester), the prosecutor may alter the charge to a less damaging one (such as assault) in exchange for a plea of guilty.
- Prosecutors may promise to get a defendant into a specific treatment program in exchange for his or her plea. For example, a substance abuser may be promised admission into the state's detoxification unit in exchange for a guilty plea.

simply wish to adapt to the bureaucratic structure favorable to plea bargaining that exists in most U.S. criminal courts.[49] Defense attorneys may wish to secure noncriminal dispositions for their clients, such as placement in a treatment program, and may advise them to plead guilty in exchange for this consideration.

The prosecution also can benefit from a plea bargain. The prosecutor's case may be weaker than hoped for, convincing him or her that a trial is too risky. A prosecutor may also believe that the arresting officers made a serious procedural error in securing evidence that would be brought out during pretrial motions. When a defendant pleads guilty, it voids all prior constitutional errors made in that case. And, of course, no matter how strong the state's case, there is always the chance that a jury will render an unfavorable decision. Prosecutors also bargain to gain the cooperation of informers and codefendants.

Plea Bargaining Issues Those who favor plea bargaining argue that it actually benefits both the state and the defendant:

1. The overall financial costs of criminal prosecution are reduced.

Table 17.6 Sentencing Outcomes for Murder Convictions by Type of Trial

TYPE OF CONVICTION	TYPE OF SENTENCE FOR MURDER OR NONNEGLIGENT MANSLAUGHTER			
	TOTAL	LIFE	DEATH	OTHER
Total	100%	25%	2%	73%
Trial	100	38	3	59
Jury	100	41	4	55
Bench	100	11	0	89
Guilty plea	100	17	1	82

Source: Patrick A. Langan and Jodi M. Brown, *Felony Sentences in State Courts, 1994* (Washington, D.C.: Bureau of Justice Statistics, 1998).

2. The administrative efficiency of the courts is greatly improved.

3. The prosecution is able to devote more time to cases of greater seriousness and importance.

4. The defendant avoids possible detention and extended trial and may receive a reduced sentence.[50]

Thus, those who favor plea bargaining believe it is appropriate to enter into plea discussions where the effective administration of justice will be served.

It has been argued, however, that plea bargaining encourages defendants to waive their constitutional right to a trial. In addition, some experts suggest that sentences tend to be less severe in guilty plea situations than as a result of trials and that plea bargains result in even greater sentencing disparity. For example, Table 17.6 shows the outcome of murder cases based on type of trial. Murderers convicted by a jury were the most likely to have received a life sentence (41 percent) or the death penalty (4 percent). In contrast, those pleading guilty were the least likely to receive these dispositions (18 percent).

Particularly in the eyes of the general public, plea bargaining allows the defendant to beat the system and further tarnishes the criminal justice process. Plea bargaining also raises the danger that an innocent person will be convicted of a crime if the individual is convinced that the lighter treatment resulting from a guilty plea is preferable to the possible risk of a harsher sentence following a formal trial. Some suggest that plea bargaining allows dangerous offenders to get off lightly and therefore weakens the deterrent effect of the criminal law.[51] It may also undermine public confidence in the law.[52]

Control of Plea Bargaining It is unlikely that plea negotiations will be eliminated or severely curtailed in the near future. Those who support their total abolition are in the minority. As a result of abuses, however, efforts are being made to improve plea bargaining operations. Such reforms include the development of uniform plea practices, the presence of counsel during plea negotiations, and the establishment of time limits on plea negotiations.[53]

Some recent efforts have been made to convert plea bargaining into a more visible, understandable, and fair dispositional process. Safeguards and guidelines have been developed in many jurisdictions to prevent violations of due process and to ensure that innocent defendants do not plead guilty under coercion. For example, the judge questions the defendant about the facts of the guilty plea before accepting the plea; the defense counsel is present and able to advise the defendant of his or her rights. Open discussions about the plea occur between the prosecutor and the defense attorney; and full information regarding the offender and the offense is made available at this stage of the process. Judicial supervision is also an effective mechanism to ensure that plea bargaining is undertaken fairly.

The most extreme method of reforming plea bargaining has been to abolish it completely. A ban on plea bargaining has been tried in numerous jurisdictions throughout the country. Alaska eliminated the practice in 1975. In Honolulu, Hawaii, efforts were made to abolish plea bargaining. Jurisdictions in other states, including Iowa, Arizona, and Delaware, along with the District of Columbia, have also sought to limit the use of plea bargaining.[54] These jurisdictions give no consideration or concessions to the defendant in exchange for a guilty plea.

Efforts to control plea bargaining have met with mixed results. Evaluation of the Alaska experiment found that the number of guilty pleas did not change significantly after plea bargaining was eliminated, nor did the ban increase the prison sentences given to the most serious offenders.[55] This and similar efforts indicate that attempts to eliminate plea bargaining most likely move prosecutorial discretion farther up in the system. For example, eliminating felony plea bargaining may cause prosecutors to automatically charge offenders with a misdemeanor so they can retain the option of offering them a "deal" in exchange for their cooperation before trial.

The problem of controlling plea bargaining remains. Despite calls for its abolishment, it flourishes in U.S. trial practice.[56]

THE CRIMINAL TRIAL

Although the jury trial is relatively rare, it is still one of the cornerstones of the criminal justice process. Although most criminal prosecutions result in plea bargains and do not involve the adversary determination of guilt or innocence, the trial process remains vitally important to the criminal justice system. The opportunity to go to trial guards against abuse of informal processing and encourages faith in the criminal justice system.[57] Because of its importance, jury trial stages, critical issues, and associated legal rights are discussed here.

Jury Selection

The first stage of the trial process involves jury selection. Jurors are selected randomly in both civil and criminal cases, usually from voter registration lists within each court's jurisdiction. The initial list of persons chosen, which is called a **venire** or jury array, provides the state with a group of citizens potentially capable of serving on a jury. Many states, by law, review the venire to eliminate unqualified persons and to exempt those who by reason of their professions are not allowed to be jurors; this latter group may include, but is not limited to, physicians, the clergy, and government officials. The actual jury selection process begins with those remaining on the list.

The court clerk, who handles the administrative affairs of the trial — including the processing of the complaint, the evidence, and other documents — randomly selects enough names to supply the required number of jurors. In most cases, a criminal trial jury consists of 12 persons, with two alternate jurors standing by to serve should one of the regular jurors be unable to complete the trial. Once the prospective jurors have been chosen, the process of **voir dire** begins: all persons selected are questioned by both the prosecution and the defense to determine their appropriateness to sit on the jury. They are examined under oath by the government, the defense, and sometimes the judge about their backgrounds, occupations, residences, and possible knowledge about or interest in the case. A juror who acknowledges any bias for or prejudice against the defendant — a juror who is a friend or relative of the defendant, for example, or who has already formed an opinion about the case — is removed for cause and replaced with another. Thus any prospective juror who reveals an inability to be impartial and render a verdict solely on the basis of the evidence presented at the trial may be removed by either the prosecution or the defense. Because normally no limit is placed on the number of challenges for cause that can be offered, it often takes considerable time to select a jury for controversial criminal cases.

In addition to challenges for cause, both the prosecution and the defense are allowed **peremptory challenges,** through which they can excuse jurors for no particular or an undisclosed reason. For example, a prosecutor might not want a bartender as a juror in a drunken driving case, believing that a person in that occupation might be sympathetic to the accused. Or a defense attorney might excuse a male prospective juror to try to obtain a predominantly female jury for the client. The number of peremptory challenges permitted is limited by statute and often varies by case and jurisdiction.

The peremptory challenge has long been criticized by legal experts who question its fairness and propriety.[58] Of particular concern was the challenging of African-American jurors in interracial crimes that resulted in the trying of African-American defendants by all-white juries. In a significant case, *Batson v. Kentucky,* the Supreme Court ruled that the use of peremptory challenges to dismiss all black jurors violated the defendant's right to equal protection of the law.[59] Since *Batson* the Supreme Court has further limited the use of peremptory challenges, including jury selection in civil trials and jury selection on the basis of gender.

Impartial Juries The Sixth Amendment to the Constitution provides for the right to a speedy, public trial by an impartial jury. Throughout the 1960s and 1970s, the Supreme Court sought to ensure compliance with this constitutional mandate of impartiality through decisions eliminating racial discrimination in jury selection. For instance, in *Ham v. South Carolina* in 1973, the Court held that the defense counsel of an African-American civil rights leader was entitled to question each juror on the issue of racial prejudice.[60] In *Turner*

The trial of a criminal case is a formal process conducted in a specific and orderly fashion in accordance with rules of criminal law, procedure, and evidence. Here in the trial of British au pair Louise Woodward, accused of killing a baby left in her care, the presiding judge Hiller Zobel leans from the bench to give a direction to the jury.

v. Murray, the Court ruled that African-American defendants accused of murdering whites are entitled to have jurors questioned about their racial bias.[61] In *Taylor v. Louisiana,* the Court overturned the conviction of a man by an all-male jury because a Louisiana statute allowed women but not men to exempt themselves from jury duty.[62]

These and similar decisions have provided safeguards against jury bias. However, in many instances, potential jury bias is not part of the trial process. For example, while the Supreme Court in *Ham* ruled that bias was a consideration in a trial involving a civil rights worker, it ruled in another case that in "ordinary crimes"—noncapital cases, such as a robbery—defense counsel may not examine the racial bias of jurors even if the crime is interracial.[63]

The Trial Process

The trial of a criminal case is a formal process conducted in a specific, orderly fashion in accordance with rules of criminal law, procedure, and evidence (see Figure 17.6).

Unlike trials in popular television programs, where witnesses are often asked leading and prejudicial questions and where judges go far beyond their supervisory role, the modern criminal trial is a complicated and often time-consuming technical affair. It is a structured adversary proceeding in which both the prosecution and the defense follow specific rules and argue the merits of their cases before the judge and the jury. Each side seeks to present its case in the most favorable light. Where possible, the prosecutor and the defense attorney object to evidence they consider damaging to their individual points of view. The prosecutor uses direct testimony, physical evidence, and a confession, if available, to convince the jury that the accused is guilty beyond a reasonable doubt. The defense attorney rebuts the government's case with his or her own evidence, makes certain that the constitutional rights of the defendant are considered during all phases of the trial, and determines whether an appeal is appropriate if the client is found guilty. Throughout the process, the judge promotes an orderly, fair trial.

The basic steps of the criminal trial proceed as follows:

1. *Opening statements:* As the trial begins, both prosecution and defense address the jury and present their cases. They describe what they will attempt to prove and the major facts of the case. They introduce the witnesses, prepare the jury for their testimony, and tell them what information to listen for. The defense begins to emphasize that any doubts about the guilt of the accused must be translated into an acquittal; the prosecution dwells on civic duty and responsibility.

2. *The prosecution's case:* Following the opening statement, the government begins its case by presenting

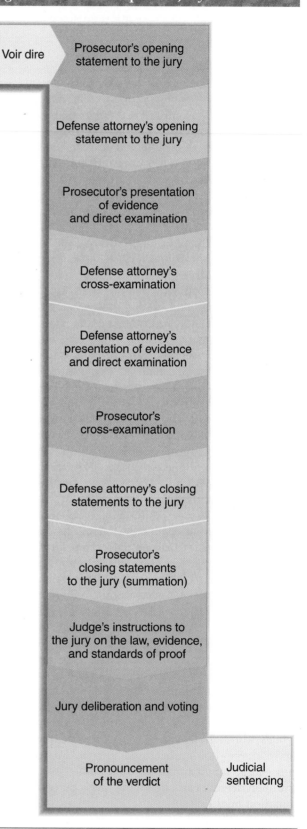

Figure 17.6   The Steps of a Jury Trial

Voir dire

Prosecutor's opening statement to the jury

Defense attorney's opening statement to the jury

Prosecutor's presentation of evidence and direct examination

Defense attorney's cross-examination

Defense attorney's presentation of evidence and direct examination

Prosecutor's cross-examination

Defense attorney's closing statements to the jury

Prosecutor's closing statements to the jury (summation)

Judge's instructions to the jury on the law, evidence, and standards of proof

Jury deliberation and voting

Pronouncement of the verdict

Judicial sentencing

Source: Marvin Zalman and Larry Siegel, *Criminal Procedure: Constitution and Society* (St. Paul, Minn.: West Publishing, 1991), p. 655.

evidence to the court through its witnesses. Those called as witnesses—such as police officers, victims, or expert witnesses—provide testimony via **direct examination,** during which the prosecutor questions the witness to reveal the facts believed pertinent to the government case. Testimony involves what the witness actually saw, heard, or touched; it does not include opinions. However, a witness's opinion can be given in certain situations, such as in describing the motion of a vehicle or indicating whether a defendant appeared to act intoxicated or insane. Witnesses may also give their opinions if they are experts on a particular subject relevant to the case; for example, a psychiatrist may testify as to a defendant's mental capacity at the time of the crime.

3. *Cross-examination:* After the prosecutor finishes questioning a witness, the defense **cross-examines** the same witness by asking questions in an attempt to clarify the defendant's role in the crime. The prosecutor may seek a **redirect examination** after the defense attorney has completed cross-examination; this allows the prosecutor to ask additional questions about information brought out during cross-examination. Finally, the defense attorney may question or cross-examine the witness once again. All witnesses for the trial are sworn in and questioned in the same basic manner.

4. *The defense's case:* At the close of the prosecution's case, the defense may ask the presiding judge to rule on a motion for a **directed verdict.** If this motion is sustained, the judge directs the jury to acquit the defendant, thereby ending the trial. A directed verdict means that the prosecution did not present enough evidence to prove all the elements of the alleged crime. If the judge fails to sustain the motion, the defense presents its case. Witnesses are called to testify in the same manner used by the prosecution.

5. *Rebuttal:* After the defense concludes its case, the government may present **rebuttal** evidence. This normally involves bringing forward evidence that was not used when the prosecution initially presented its case. The defense may examine the rebuttal witnesses and introduce new witnesses in a process called *surrebuttal.* After all the evidence has been presented to the court, the defense attorney may again submit a motion for a directed verdict. If the motion is denied, both the prosecution and the defense prepare to make closing arguments; and the case on the evidence is ready for consideration by the jury.

6. *Closing arguments:* Closing arguments are used by the attorneys to review the facts and evidence of the case in a manner favorable to their positions. At this stage of the trial, both prosecution and defense are permitted to draw reasonable inferences and show how the facts prove or refute the defendant's guilt. Often both attorneys have a free hand in arguing about facts, issues, and evidence, including the applicable law. They cannot comment, however, on matters not in evidence, nor,

where applicable, can they comment on the defendant's failure to testify. Normally, the defense attorney makes a closing statement first, followed by the prosecutor. Either party can elect to forgo the final summation to the jury.

7. *Instructions to the jury:* In a criminal trial, the judge instructs, or *charges,* the jury on the principles of law that ought to guide and control the decision on the defendant's innocence or guilt. Included in the charge is information about the elements of the alleged offense, the type of evidence needed to prove each element, and the burden of proof required to obtain a guilty verdict. Although the judge commonly provides the instructions, he or she may ask the prosecutor and the defense attorney to submit instructions for consideration; the judge then uses discretion in determining whether to use any of their instructions. The instructions that cover the law applicable to the case are extremely important because they may serve as the basis for a subsequent appeal.

One important aspect of instructing the jury is explaining the level of proof needed to find the person guilty of a crime. As mentioned, the U.S. system of justice requires guilt to be proved beyond a reasonable doubt. The judge must inform the jurors that if they have even the slightest suspicion that the defendant is not guilty, then they cannot find for the prosecution. Also, the judge must explain how, in criminal cases, the burden of proof is on the prosecution to prove the defendant guilty; the accused does not have to prove his or her innocence.

8. *Verdict:* Once the charge has been given to the jury, the jurors retire to deliberate on a verdict. The verdict in a criminal case is usually required to be unanimous. A review of the case by the jury may take hours or even days. The jurors are always sequestered during their deliberations; in some lengthy, highly publicized cases, they are kept overnight in a hotel until the verdict is reached. In less sensational cases, the jurors may be allowed to go home but are often cautioned not to discuss the case with anyone. If a verdict cannot be reached, the trial may result in a hung jury; in this case the prosecutor has to bring the defendant to trial again to get a conviction.

9. *Sentence:* If found not guilty, the defendant is released. If the defendant is convicted, the judge normally orders a presentence investigation by the probation department preparatory to imposing a sentence. Before sentencing, the defense attorney often submits a motion for a new trial, alleging that legal errors occurred in the trial proceedings. The judge may deny the motion and impose a sentence immediately, a practice quite common in most misdemeanor offenses. In felony cases, however, the judge sets a date for sentencing, and the defendant is either placed on bail or held in custody until that time. Sentencing usually occurs a short time after trial. At the sentencing hearing, the judge may

consider evidence that is relevant to the case, including victim impact statements.[64] In most jurisdictions, typical criminal penalties include fines, community supervision, incarceration, and the death penalty.

10. *Appeal:* After sentencing, defendants have the right to appeal the case, charging either that the law under which they were tried was unconstitutional (for example, discriminatory or vague) or that the procedures used by agents of the justice system violated their constitutional rights (for example, police did not give them a proper Miranda warning, or improperly obtained evidence was used at trial). If the appeal is granted, a new trial may be ordered. If the appeal is not sustained, the convicted offender begins serving the sentence imposed, thus marking the end of the judicatory process.

Trials and the Rule of Law

Every trial has its constitutional issues, complex legal procedures, rules of court, and interpretations of statutes, all designed to ensure that the accused gets a fair trial. This section discusses the most important constitutional rights of the accused at trial and reviews the legal nature of the trial process.

Right to a Speedy and Public Trial   The Sixth Amendment guarantees a defendant the right to a speedy trial. This means that an accused is entitled to be tried within a reasonable period. If a person's right to a speedy trial is violated, then a complete dismissal of the charges against him or her is required according to *Strunk v. United States.*[65] The right to a speedy trial was made applicable to state courts through the due process clause of the Fourteenth Amendment in the case of *Klopfer v. North Carolina.*[66] It should be noted, however, that a defendant can waive the right to a speedy trial. A waiver of the right is implied when defendants cause the delay or when they do not assert their right when the trial takes too long to get under way.

In determining whether a defendant's right to speedy trial has been violated, several factors are considered; length of delay alone does not constitute a violation. The Supreme Court, in the case of *Barker v. Wingo,* enumerated the factors that should be considered in determining whether the speedy trial requirement has been complied with: (1) the length of the delay, (2) the reason for the delay, (3) the timeliness of the defendant's assertion of his or her right to a speedy trial, and (4) the prejudice to the defendant.[67]

There is no set standard, but the Federal Speedy Trial Act of 1974 mandates 30 days from arrest to indictment and 70 days from indictment to trial. However, the states vary widely in their definitions of a speedy trial. For example, in Louisiana the limit is 730 days (two years) in a noncapital case and 1,095 days (three years) in capital cases; in New York the time limit is 180 days.[68] Recent research on the time trials currently take shows that mean time from arrest to sentencing is just over six months. Median time is slightly under five months. Jury trial cases take the most time — 10 months on average from arrest to sentencing. Cases disposed of by guilty plea take the least time — a little over six months on average.[69]

Right to a Jury Trial   Because a jury trial is considered a fundamental right, the Supreme Court, in the case of *Duncan v. Louisiana,* made the guarantee applicable to the states through the Fourteenth Amendment.[70] However, the question arises as to whether this right extends to all defendants — those charged with misdemeanors as well as felonies. The Supreme Court addressed this issue in the case of *Baldwin v. New York,* in which it decided that defendants are entitled to a jury trial only if they face the possibility of a prison sentence of more than six months.[71] Later, in *Blanton v. City of North Las Vegas,* the Court upheld the six month–plus jail sentence requirement for a jury trial but did not rule out that a lesser term accompanied by the possibility of other punishment, such as a large fine or loss of a driver's license for a year, might warrant a jury trial.[72]

Although most people think of a jury as having 12 members and, historically, most have had 12, the Sixth Amendment does not specify a jury size. In fact, in the case of *Williams v. Florida,* the Supreme Court held that a six-person jury fulfilled a defendant's right to a trial by jury.[73] However, a unanimous verdict is required when a six-person jury is used. When a 12-person jury is used, the Supreme Court has maintained that the Sixth Amendment does not require a unanimous verdict, except in first-degree murder cases. In *Apodica v. Oregon,* the Court found constitutional an Oregon statute that required a finding of guilt by 10 out of 12 jurors in cases of assault with a deadly weapon, burglary, and larceny.[74] However, it should be noted that the majority of states and the federal courts still require a unanimous verdict.

Right to Be Free from Double Jeopardy   The Fifth Amendment provides that no person shall "be subject for the same offense to be twice put in jeopardy of life or limb." This means that a defendant cannot be prosecuted by a jurisdiction more than once for a single offense. For example, if a defendant is tried and convicted of murder in Texas, he cannot be tried again for the same murder in Texas. The right to be protected from double jeopardy was made applicable to the states through the Fourteenth Amendment in the case of *Benton v. Maryland.*[75] However, a person tried in federal court can be tried in state court, and vice versa.[76] And in 1985 the Court ruled in *Heath v. Alabama* that if a single act violates the laws of two states, the offender may be punished for each offense under the *dual sov-*

ereignty doctrine: legal jurisdictions have the right to enforce their own laws, and a single act can violate the laws of two separate jurisdictions.[77]

Right to Legal Counsel Regardless of the legal rights citizens command at trial, without legal counsel to aid them, they would be rendered defenseless before the law. Consequently, the Sixth Amendment provides the right to be represented by an attorney in criminal trials. However, the vast majority of criminal defendants are indigents who cannot afford private legal services. In a series of cases beginning in the 1930s, the U.S. Supreme Court established the defendant's right to be represented by an attorney and, in the event he or she cannot pay for representation, to have the state provide free legal services. First, in *Powell v. Alabama,* the Court held that an attorney was essential in capital cases where the defendant's life was at stake.[78] Then, in the critically important case of *Gideon v. Wainwright,* the Court granted the absolute right to counsel in all felony cases.[79] Finally, in *Argersinger v. Hamlin,* the defendant's right to counsel in misdemeanor cases was established.[80] Today most defendants are represented by attorneys from the time they are in police custody until their final sentencing and appeal.

Right to Competent Legal Representation In the 1984 case of *Strickland v. Washington,* the Supreme Court found that defendants also have the right to reasonably effective assistance of counsel. The Court enumerated the qualities characterizing competent representation:

> Representation of a criminal defendant entails certain basic duties. Counsel's function is to assist the defendant, and hence counsel owes the client a duty of loyalty, a duty to avoid conflicts of interest. From counsel's function as assistant to the defendant derive the overarching duty to advocate the defendant's cause and the more particular duties to consult with the defendant on important decisions and to keep the defendant informed of important developments in the course of the prosecution. Counsel also has a duty to bring to bear such skill and knowledge as will render the trial a reliable adversarial testing process.[81]

If convicted, defendants can have their sentences overturned if they can prove that (1) counsel's performance was so deficient that he or she was not functioning as the counsel guaranteed by the Sixth Amendment and (2) the deficient performance prejudiced the case and deprived them of a fair trial.

Right to Confront Witnesses The accused has the right to confront witnesses to challenge their assertions and perceptions: Did they really hear what they thought they did? Or see what they think they saw? Are they biased? Honest? Trustworthy?

One recent issue involving confrontation is the role of child witnesses in sex abuse cases. Sometimes a court appearance is so traumatic to children that they are unable to give accurate information in court. A number of devices have been used to make the experience less difficult. In one recent case, the Supreme Court overturned the conviction of an alleged sex criminal after the trial judge allowed his two teenage victims to testify behind a screen so as to avoid eye contact.[82] But in *Maryland v. Craig* the Court ruled that child witnesses could testify via closed-circuit television as long as safeguards were set up to protect the defendant's rights.[83] Protections included the defendant being able to view the witness and being in communication with the witness's attorney at all times.

In a 1992 case, *White v. Illinois,* the Court again restricted the confrontation clause by ruling that the state's attorney is required to neither produce victims in child abuse cases nor demonstrate why they are unavailable to serve as witnesses.[84] *White* involved the use as testimony of statements given by a child to the child's baby-sitter, mother, doctor, nurse, and a police officer concerning the facts and identity of the alleged assailant in a sexual assault case. The prosecutor twice tried to call the child to testify, but both times, the 4-year-old experienced emotional difficulty and was unavailable to appear in court. The case outcome then hinged solely on the testimony of the five witnesses who repeated in court the statements made to them by the child. By allowing the use of **hearsay evidence** (second-party statements) in this case, the *White* decision negates the requirement that defendants be allowed to confront their accusers in open court. In both *Craig* and *White,* the Court showed that it is willing to compromise defendants' rights of confrontation to achieve a social objective—the prosecution of child abuse.[85]

SENTENCING

After a defendant has been found guilty of a criminal offense or has pleaded guilty, he or she is brought before the court for imposition of a criminal penalty—**sentencing.** Historically, a full range of punishment has been meted out to criminal offenders: corporal punishment, such as whipping or mutilation; fines; banishment; incarceration; and death.

> CONNECTIONS
>
> The evolution of punishment as a means of correction is discussed in Chapter 18.

In U.S. society, incarceration in a federal, state, or local institution is generally the most serious penalty given out to offenders. In addition, the death penalty remains on the statute books of most jurisdictions and has been used at an increasing rate in recent years.

Purposes of Sentencing

A multiplicity of goals lies behind the imposition of a criminal sentence;[86] no single philosophy of justice governs sentencing decisions. Each jurisdiction employs its own sentencing philosophies, and each individual decision maker views the purpose of sentencing differently. A 23-year-old college student arrested for selling cocaine might be seen as essentially harmless by one judge and granted probation; another judge might see the young drug dealer as a threat to the moral fabric of society and deserving of a prison term. One of the great flaws of the U.S. justice system has been the extraordinary amount of disparity in criminal punishment.[87]

In general, four goals—deterrence, incapacitation, rehabilitation, and desert/retribution—are associated with imposition of a sentence.[88]

1. *Deterrence:* By sentencing the convicted criminal, the court hopes to deter others from committing similar crimes. The validity of deterrence rests on the premise that punishing one offender will convince other potential criminals to abstain from crime.

2. *Incapacitation:* Incapacitation is directed at controlling the behavior of offenders considered a menace to society. At least while the offenders are under correctional control, they will not be able to commit crime. In some instances, incapacitation involves supervising offenders while they remain in the community; in others, it calls for confining them in an institution. Incapacitation involves predicting behavior patterns: offenders are confined not for what they have done but for what it is feared they might do in the future.

3. *Rehabilitation:* Correctional rehabilitation is another goal of sentencing. Its purpose is to reduce future criminality by administering some type of treatment under supervision of correctional agents. Rehabilitation efforts focus on emotional stress, vocational training, education, or substance abuse. Rehabilitation also involves predicting future behavior: unless the offenders receive treatment, they will commit future crimes; treatment reduces the likelihood of their reoffending.

4. *Desert/retribution:* Another goal of sentencing is to punish offenders for their misdeeds. Whereas the goals of deterrence, incapacitation, and rehabilitation are based on what might happen or what the offender might do, desert focuses on the event that led to conviction. Because criminals benefit from their misdeeds, they must now pay society back to make things even. For example, it is only fair that criminals who have committed the worst crime, murder, receive the most severe penalty, death. Those who benefit from illegal business transactions should pay large fines to return their illegal gains.

Each of these goals is in operation when a person is sentenced. Sometimes one policy or goal becomes popular and for a while dominates sentencing considerations. In the 1960s and 1970s rehabilitation became the prime goal of sentencing, and innovative treatment methods were stressed. Today rising violence rates, the supposed failure of rehabilitation, and a generally conservative outlook make desert, deterrence, and incapacitation the primary sentencing goals.

Sentencing Dispositions

Generally, five kinds of sentences or dispositions are available to the court:

1. Fines
2. Probation
3. Alternative or intermediate sanctions
4. Incarceration
5. Capital punishment

A *fine* is usually exacted for a minor crime and may also be combined with other sentencing alternatives, such as probation or confinement.[89] *Probation* allows the offender to live in the community subject to compliance with legally imposed conditions. *Alternative sanctions* involve probation plus some other sanction, such as house arrest, electronic monitoring, or forfeiture of property. The sentence of total confinement, or *incarceration,* is imposed when it has been decided that the general public needs to be protected from further criminal activity by the defendant. *Capital punishment* or the death penalty is reserved for people who commit first-degree murder under aggravated circumstances, such as with extreme cruelty, violence, or torture.

Imposing the Sentence   Sentencing is one of the most crucial functions of judges. Sentencing authority may also be exercised by the jury, an administrative body, or a group of judges, or it may be mandated by statute.

In most felony cases, except where the law dictates **mandatory prison terms,** sentencing is usually based on a variety of information available to the judge. Some jurisdictions allow victims to make impact statements that are considered at sentencing hearings, although these often have little impact on sentencing outcomes.[90] Most judges consider a presentence investigation report by the probation department. This report, which is a social and personal history as well as an evaluation of the defendant, is used by the judge in making a sentencing decision.[91] Some judges heavily weigh the presentence investigation report; others may dismiss it completely or rely on only certain portions.

When an accused is convicted of two or more charges, he or she must be sentenced on each charge. If the sentences are **concurrent,** they begin the same day, and the sentence has been completed after the longest term has been served. For example, a defendant is sentenced to 3 years' imprisonment on a charge of assault and 10 years for burglary, the sentences to be served concurrently. After the offender serves 10 years in prison, the sentences would be completed. Conversely, a **consecutive sentence** means that upon completion of one sentence, the other term of incarceration begins. For example, a defendant sentenced to 10 years' imprisonment on a charge of rape, 3 years for possession of a handgun, and 4 years for drug possession, the sentences to be served consecutively, would serve a total of 17 years. In most instances sentences are given concurrently.

> CONNECTIONS
>
> The following sections discuss incarceration sentences and the death penalty. For purposes of organization, community sentences, such as probation and fines, are discussed in Chapter 18.

Sentencing Structures

When a convicted offender is sentenced to prison, the statutes of the jurisdiction in which the crime was committed determine the penalties that may be imposed by the court. Over the years, a variety of sentencing structures have been used, including determinate sentences, indeterminate sentences, and mandatory sentences.

The Indeterminate Sentence The first U.S. prison sentences were for a fixed period that the offender was forced to serve before release. Harsh prison conditions and rules enforced by physical punishment left inmates with little incentive for rehabilitation or self-improvement. During the latter half of the nineteenth century reformers attempted to apply progressive views of human behavior and change to the penal system and called for modernization in sentencing laws. What developed over the next 50 years was a type of **indeterminate sentence** with very brief minimums and very long maximums, allowing inmates to be released as soon as a parole board concluded they were rehabilitated.

The indeterminate sentence is still used in a majority of states. Under most sentencing models, convicted offenders who are not eligible for community supervision are given a short minimum sentence that must be served and a lengthy maximum sentence that is the outer boundary of the time that can possibly be served. For example, the legislature might set a sentence of a minimum of 1 year and a maximum of 20 years for burglary.

Under this scheme, the actual length of time served is controlled by the corrections agency. The inmate can be paroled after serving the minimum sentence whenever the institution and parole personnel believe that he or she is ready to live in the community. The minimum (or maximum) might also be reduced by inmates earning "time off for good behavior" or for participating in counseling and vocational training programs. In many instances, sentencing reduction programs allow inmates to serve only a fraction of their minimum sentences. Inmates today serve about one-third of their original sentences.

Most jurisdictions that use indeterminate sentences specify minimum and maximum terms but allow judges discretion to fix the actual sentence within those limits. For example, if burglary is punishable by a sentence of 2–20 years, the judge can give one offender 5–10 and another 2–5 years.[92]

The underlying purpose of indeterminate sentencing is to individualize each sentence in the interests of rehabilitating the offender. This type of sentencing allows for flexibility not only in the type of sentence imposed but also in the length of time served.

> CONNECTIONS
>
> The indeterminate sentence is the heart of the rehabilitation model of justice discussed in Chapter 15. Offenders may be released after a relatively short prison stay if they convince correctional authorities that they can forgo a criminal career. Yet because many policymakers believe that the rehabilitation of offenders has generally failed, alternative sentencing schemes are being given more consideration.

The Determinate Sentence Determinate sentences were actually the first kind used in the United States. As originally constructed, the judge could impose a sentence, based on personal and professional judgment, that fell within limits set by statute. For example, a state criminal code could set the sentence for burglary at up to 20 years in prison. After evaluating each case, the judge could impose a sentence of 5 years on a first-time defendant, 10 on a more experienced criminal, and the full 20 on a third who may have been a repeater and carried a weapon to the crime scene. Unlike the indeterminate models in which release dates are controlled by correctional authorities, in a **determinate sentence** the duration of the offender's prison stay is determined by the judiciary when the sentence is imposed.

When the original determinate sentencing statutes were replaced by indeterminate sentences early in the twentieth century, judicial discretion remained quite broad. Both determinate and indeterminate sentences allowed judges to place one defendant on probation while sentencing another to a lengthy prison term for essentially the same crime. Such unbridled discretion allowed disparity and unfairness in the sentencing process. In addition, indeterminate sentences gave correctional authorities quasi-judicial power, allowing them to decide when an inmate was to be returned to society. Correctional discretion could then be used to control the inmate population.

In 1969 Kenneth Culp Davis published *Discretionary Justice,* which was followed in 1972 by Judge Marvin Frankel's landmark study *Criminal Sentences — Law Without Order.*[93] These works exposed the disparity in the justice process and called for reform. Frankel stated, "The almost wholly unchecked and sweeping powers we give to judges in the fashioning of sentences are terrifying and intolerable for a society that professes devotion to the rule of law."[94]

In response to these concerns, a number of jurisdictions replaced indeterminate sentences and discretionary parole with a system of determinate sentencing that featured a single term of years without discretionary parole. Earned good time can reduce sentences, in some cases, by up to one-half. These modern versions of determinate sentencing reflect an orientation toward desert, deterrence, and equality at the expense of treatment and rehabilitation. Most jurisdictions have attempted to structure judicial decision making by suggesting appropriate prison terms for particular crimes.[95]

Guideline Sentencing The federal government and a number of state jurisdictions have legislated guidelines to control sentences. **Guideline sentences** are usually based on the seriousness of a crime and the background of an offender: the more serious the crime and the more extensive the offender's background, the longer the prison term recommended by the guidelines. For example, guidelines might require that all people convicted of robbery who had no prior offense record and who did not use excessive violence be given an average of a five-year sentence; those who used force and had a prior record will have three years added to their sentence.

Sentencing guidelines can be computed for a variety of offense and offender types. Table 17.7 shows the guidelines used in Minnesota. Each case is evaluated on the basis of offense seriousness and the offender's prior record to determine where it fits in the guideline grid. Those that fall above the incarceration line let the judge choose probation or sentence the offender to up to 12 months in jail.[96] In more serious cases that fall below the incarceration line, judges may impose the guideline sentence but are granted discretion to increase or decrease the sentence based on mitigating or aggravating circumstances. The range of sentences in the Minnesota guideline grid has been altered over the years. In 1989 the Minnesota legislature adopted get-tough policies, including mandatory minimum prison terms for certain drug crimes and life without parole

for certain first-degree murders. In the original guidelines, a first-level offense with a criminal history score of 6 was eligible for a probation sentence, whereas offenders falling in that category today get 19 months in prison.

So far 17 states and the federal government have adopted some form of sentencing guidelines; 10 employ presumptive or mandatory guidelines that must be followed by judges; 7 use voluntary, advisory guidelines. Massachusetts, Michigan, and Montana are studying the possible adoption of guidelines. In 1997 the District of Columbia established a sentencing commission as required by Congress.[97]

Future of Structured Sentencing There seems little question that structured sentences will continue to be considered in other jurisdictions now that the federal government has adopted them and the Supreme Court has upheld their use.[98]

Despite the widespread acceptance of guidelines, some nagging problems remain. Research indicates that judges diverge from the guidelines.[99] Legislators have also backtracked on guidelines, creating loopholes that undercut their determinacy, such as allowing for early release from prison by administrative order.[100]

Others suggest that race and economic status continue to influence sentencing.[101] For example, Michael Tonry found that the Minnesota guidelines helped conserve state resources, were resistant to political pressure, and increased overall fairness in the sentencing system.[102] Yet he also found evidence that the federal guidelines have never been accepted by the judiciary and are often circumvented or breached; he calls them "the most controversial and disliked sentencing reform initiative in United States history."[103] In his book *Sentencing Matters,* Tonry offers a prescription to improve structured sentencing guidelines that calls in part for the creation of ongoing sentencing commissions, creation of realistic guidelines, reliance on alternative sanctions, and a sentencing philosophy that stresses the "least punitive and intrusive appropriate sentence."[104]

The federal guidelines have also been criticized because they punish possession of crack cocaine much more heavily than powdered cocaine; the former is a crime associated with African-American offenders and the latter with white offenders.[105] The federal guidelines also require incarceration sentences for minor offenders who in preguideline days would have been

Table 17.7 Sentencing Guidelines Grid (Presumptive Sentence Lengths in Months)

SEVERITY LEVEL OF CONVICTION OFFENSE		CRIMINAL HISTORY SCORE						
		0	1	2	3	4	5	6 OR MORE
Murder, 2nd degree (intentional murder; drive-by-shootings)	X	306 *299–313*	326 *319–333*	346 *339–353*	366 *359–373*	386 *379–393*	406 *399–413*	426 *419–433*
Murder, 3rd degree Murder, 2nd degree (unintentional murder)	IX	150 *144–156*	165 *159–171*	180 *174–186*	195 *189–201*	210 *204–216*	225 *219–231*	240 *234–246*
Criminal sexual conduct, 1st degree Assault, 1st degree	VIII	86 *81–91*	98 *93–103*	110 *105–115*	122 *117–127*	134 *129–139*	146 *141–151*	158 *153–163*
Aggravated robbery, 1st degree	VII	48 *44–52*	58 *54–62*	68 *64–72*	78 *74–82*	88 *84–92*	98 *94–102*	108 *104–112*
Criminal sexual conduct, 2nd degree (a) & (b)	VI	21	26	30	34 *33–35*	44 *42–46*	54 *50–58*	65 *60–70*
Residential burglary Simple robbery	V	18	23	27	30 *29–31*	38 *36–40*	46 *43–49*	54 *50–58*
Nonresidential burglary	IV	12*	15	18	21	25 *24–26*	32 *30–34*	41 *37–45*
Theft crimes (over $2,500)	III	12*	13	15	17	19 *18–20*	22 *21–23*	25 *24–26*
Theft crimes ($2,500 or less) Check forgery ($200–$2,500)	II	12*	12*	13	15	17	19	21 *20–22*
Sale of simulated controlled substance	I	12*	12*	12*	13	15	17	19 *18–20*

Italicized numbers within the grid denote the range within which a judge may sentence without the sentence being deemed a departure. Offenders with nonimprisonment felony sentences are subject to jail time according to law.

*One year and one day.

☐ Presumptive commitment to state imprisonment. First-degree murder is excluded from the guidelines by law and continues to have a mandatory life sentence.

☐ Presumptive stayed sentence; at the discretion of the judge, up to a year in jail and/or other nonjail sanctions can be imposed as conditions of probation. However, certain offenses in this section of the grid always carry a presumptive commitment to a state prison. These offenses include 3rd-degree controlled substance crimes when the offender has a prior felony drug conviction, burglary of an occupied dwelling when the offender has a prior felony burglary conviction, second and subsequent criminal sexual conduct offenses, and offenses carrying a mandatory minimum prison term due to the use of a dangerous weapon (e.g., 2nd-degree assault).

Source: Minnesota Sentencing Guideline Commission, 1996.

given probation; many of these petty offenders might be better served with cheaper alternative sanctions.[106]

Some defense attorneys oppose the use of guidelines because they result in longer prison terms, prevent judges from considering mitigating circumstances, and reduce the use of probation.[107] However, there is little evidence that states using determinate sentences have experienced an above-normal increase in their prison populations, and in at least two states that use guidelines, Minnesota and Washington, prison populations have been reduced.[108]

The ultimate test of guidelines or other determinate sentencing models is whether they can ease crime rates. So far there is little evidence that these laws can alone reduce the incidence of crime.[109]

Mandatory Sentences Another effort to limit judicial discretion has been the development of mandatory (minimum) sentences that require the incarceration of all offenders convicted of specific crimes. Some states, for example, exclude offenders convicted of certain offenses, such as drug trafficking or handgun crimes, from even the possibility of being placed on probation; some exclude recidivists; and others bar certain offenders from being considered for parole. Mandatory sentencing generally limits the judge's discretionary power to impose any disposition but that authorized by the legislature.

Mandatory sentencing legislation may supplement an indeterminate sentencing structure or be a feature of structured sentencing. For example, in Massachusetts, which uses indeterminate sentencing, conviction for possessing an unregistered handgun brings with it a mandatory prison term of at least one year.[110] The Federal Drug Control Acts of 1986 and 1988 mandate long minimum sentences for drug trafficking and double these sentences in the event of a prior conviction.[111]

It is difficult to say if depriving the judiciary of discretion and placing all sentencing power in the hands of the legislature or a sentencing commission will deter the commission of offenses. The use of mandatory minimum sentences can lead to an increase in plea bargaining as offenders seek avenues to escape harsh sentences and prosecutors use the threat of mandatory sentences to force guilty pleas to lesser offenses.[112] Michael Tonry argues mandatory sentencing creates the following results:

1. Lawyers and judges take steps to avoid application of laws they consider unduly harsh.
2. Dismissal rates typically increase at early stages of the criminal justice process after mandatory laws are implemented as practitioners attempt to shield some defendants from the laws' reach.
3. Defendants whose cases are not dismissed or diverted make more vigorous efforts to avoid conviction and delay sentencing.

4. Defendants who are convicted of the target offenses are often sentenced more severely than they would be in the absence of the mandatory law.
5. Because declines in conviction rates for those arrested tend to offset increases in imprisonment rates for those convicted, the overall probability that defendants will be incarcerated remains about the same after enactment of a mandatory sentencing law.[113]

Truth in Sentencing First enacted in 1984, truth-in-sentencing laws require offenders to serve a substantial portion of their prison sentences behind bars.[114] Parole eligibility and good-time credits are restricted or eliminated. The truth-in-sentencing movement has been a response to prison crowding that in some instances has forced the early release of inmates from overcrowded institutions. The Violent Offender Incarceration and Truth-in-Sentencing Incentive Grants Program in the 1994 Crime Act offered the states funds to support the costs of longer sentences.[115] To qualify for federal funds, states must require persons convicted of violent felony crimes to serve not less than 85 percent of their prison sentences. The provision is already having an effect. Violent offenders released from prison in 1996 were sentenced to serve an average of 85 months in prison. Prior to release they served about half of their prison sentences or 45 months. Under truth-in-sentencing laws, violent offenders would serve an average of 88 months in prison based on the average sentence for violent offenders admitted to prison in 1996. By 1998, 27 states and the District of Columbia met the federal Truth-in-Sentencing Incentive Grant Program eligibility criteria. Eleven states adopted truth-in-sentencing laws in 1995.

Three Strikes Laws Public concern over crime has convinced lawmakers to toughen sentences for repeat offenders. One new group of laws mandates lengthy periods of incarceration for repeat offenders, which in some cases can mean a life sentence for a minor felony.[116] The new "three strikes and you're out" laws provide these lengthy terms for any person convicted of three felony offenses even if the third crime is relatively trivial. California's "three strikes" statute is aimed at getting habitual criminals off the street. Anyone convicted of a third felony must do a minimum term of 25 years to life; the third felony does not have to be serious or violent.[117] The Federal Crime Bill of 1994 also adopted a "three strikes and you're out" provision, requiring a mandatory life sentence for any offender convicted of three felony offenses; 22 states have followed suit.

Although welcomed by conservatives looking for a remedy for violent crime, the "three strikes" policy is quite controversial because it can give a life sentence to a person convicted of an extremely minor felony. There

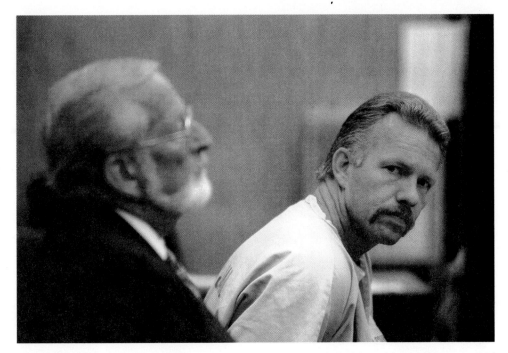

Three-strikes laws provide lengthy terms for any person convicted of three felony offenses, even if the third crime is relatively trivial. California's law is aimed at getting habitual criminals off the street. Anyone convicted of a third serious felony must do a minimum term of 25 years to life. Here heroin addict Lawrence Olin is shown just after receiving a sentence of 25 to life for his third theft—a pair of bluejeans. Some judges are ignoring the three-strike laws because they consider sentences too harsh. The California Supreme Court has ruled that judges do have the discretion to ignore prior convictions when handing out sentences.

are reports that some judges are defying "three strikes" provisions because they consider them unduly harsh.

"Three strikes" laws may in fact help put some chronic offenders behind bars, but can they realistically be expected to lower the crime rate? Marc Mauer of the Sentencing Project, a private group that conducts research on justice-related issues, finds that the "three strikes" approach may satisfy the public's hunger for retribution but makes little practical sense.[118] First, three-time losers are at the brink of aging out of crime; locking them up for life should have little effect on the crime rate. Second, current sentences for chronic violent offenders are already quite severe, yet their punishment seems to have had little influence on reducing national violence rates. Mauer also suggests that a "three strikes" policy will enlarge an already overburdened prison system, driving up costs and, presumably, reducing resources available to house non–"three strikes" inmates. Mauer warns that African-Americans face an increased risk of being sentenced under "three strikes" statutes, expanding the racial disparity in sentencing. More ominous is the fact that police officers may be put at risk because two-time offenders will violently resist arrest, knowing that they face a life sentence.

"Three strikes" laws have undeniable political appeal to legislators being pressed by their constituents to "do something about crime." Yet any effort to deter crim-inal behavior through tough laws is not without costs. Most states that have passed "three strikes" laws rarely invoke the penalty, but California has used it with thousands of offenders. Whereas many are serious offenders, 192 people (as of 1996) were sentenced to life for possessing marijuana![119] A study by the Rand Corporation concluded that the state's "three strikes" law may actually reduce serious felonies by between 22 and 34 percent. However, the price of this reduction is an extra $4.5 billion to $6.5 billion per year in correctional costs in California alone.[120] "Three strikes" laws are now being challenged legally, and their future is uncertain.

CONNECTIONS

Although the Rand study suggests correctional costs may increase because of "three strikes" laws, there are other social savings when the crime rate drops. Chapter 4 discusses the costs of crime to victims.

How People Are Sentenced

What sentences do people actually receive for their criminal behavior? A recent analysis of sentencing practices using data from 300 jurisdictions found that many people convicted of serious felonies are not incarcerated (Table 17.8). For example, about 29 percent

Table 17.8 Who Goes to Prison

| | PERCENTAGE OF CONVICTED FELONS WHO RECEIVED A PRISON SENTENCE | | | | PROBATION-ONLY SENTENCES (1994) |
	1988	1990	1992	1994	
All offenses	44%	46%	44%	45%	29%
Murder	91	91	93	95	3
Rape	69	67	68	71	12
Robbery	75	73	74	77	12
Aggravated assault	45	45	44	48	25
Burglary	54	54	52	53	25
Larceny	39	40	38	38	34
Drug trafficking	41	49	48	48	29

Source: Patrick A. Langan and Jodi M. Brown, *Felony Sentences in State Courts, 1994* (Washington, D.C: Bureau of Justice Statistics, 1997).

Figure 17.7 Key Findings from the National Survey of Sentencing in State Courts

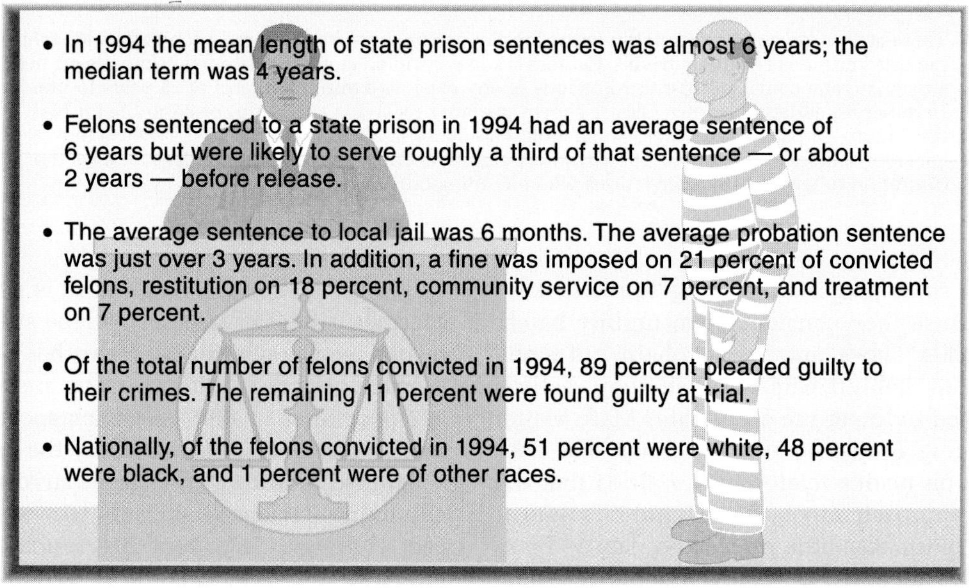

- In 1994 the mean length of state prison sentences was almost 6 years; the median term was 4 years.

- Felons sentenced to a state prison in 1994 had an average sentence of 6 years but were likely to serve roughly a third of that sentence — or about 2 years — before release.

- The average sentence to local jail was 6 months. The average probation sentence was just over 3 years. In addition, a fine was imposed on 21 percent of convicted felons, restitution on 18 percent, community service on 7 percent, and treatment on 7 percent.

- Of the total number of felons convicted in 1994, 89 percent pleaded guilty to their crimes. The remaining 11 percent were found guilty at trial.

- Nationally, of the felons convicted in 1994, 51 percent were white, 48 percent were black, and 1 percent were of other races.

Source: Patrick A. Langan and Jodi M. Brown, *Felony Sentences in State Courts, 1994* (Washington, D.C.: Bureau of Justice Statistics, 1998).

of convicted rapists and 23 percent of convicted robbers did not receive prison sentences. Some of the key findings of the national study are contained in Figure 17.7.

Table 17.8 shows that the likelihood of going to prison upon conviction for crime has been relatively stable since the late 1980s. Table 17.8 also shows that many people convicted of the most serious crimes get a sentence of only probation. For example, 12,000 murderers were convicted in 1994, and 3 percent received a sentence of community supervision. This means that 360 people convicted of killing another person spent no time in prison or jail. Similarly, of the 20,000 people convicted of rape, 12 percent, or 2,400 offenders, avoided

incarceration. How could such serious offenders avoid prison or jail? Most likely they cooperated with the prosecution and were willing to testify against other people.

Sentencing Disparity   Sentencing disparity has long been a problem in the justice system. Simply put, it is common for people convicted of similar criminal acts to receive widely different sentences. For example, one person convicted of burglary receives a three-year prison sentence, whereas another is granted probation. Few defendants actually serve their entire sentences, causing even greater disparity. Such differences seem to violate the constitutional rights of due process and equal protection. State sentencing codes usually include various factors that can legitimately influence the length of prison sentences, including

- How severe the offense is.
- The offender's prior criminal record.
- Whether the offender used violence.
- Whether the offender used weapons.
- Whether the crime was committed for money.

Research in fact shows a strong correlation between these legal variables and the type and length of sentence received. For example, judges seem less willing to use discretion in cases involving the most serious criminal charges, such as terrorism, while employing greater control in minor cases.[121]

The suspicion remains, however, that such extralegal factors as age, race, gender, and economic status influence sentencing outcomes. These extralegal factors appear to influence sentencing because the inmate population is disproportionately male, African-American, young, and lower-class. Although this phenomenon may be a result of discrimination, it could also be simply a function of existing crime patterns — males, minorities, and members of the lower class commit the crimes that are most likely to result in prison sentences (homicide, rape, armed robbery, and so on).

Numerous studies have been conducted to determine the cause of sentencing disparity in the United States.[122] Some have found a pattern of racial discrimination in sentencing, whereas others indicate that class bias exists.[123] There is also considerable evidence being assembled that the race and class of the victim, not the offender, may be the most important factor in sentencing decisions. Crimes involving a white victim seem to be more heavily punished than those in which a minority group member is the target.[124] Sentencing disparity is the topic of the Race, Culture, Gender, and Criminology feature titled "Race and Sentencing."

Because of the lingering problem of racial and class bias in the sentencing process, one primary goal of the criminal justice system in the 1990s was to reduce disparity by creating new forms of criminal sentences that limit judicial discretion and are aimed at uniformity and fairness.

THE DEATH PENALTY

Although the execution of convicted criminals has been common throughout human history, it is a topic that has long perplexed social thinkers. Today the death penalty for murder is used in 38 states and by the federal government with the approval of about 75 percent of the population. After many years of abolition, New York reinstated the death penalty in 1995 and expanded its use to cover numerous acts including serial murder,

contract killing, and the use of torture.[125] There are more than 3,300 people on death row, and each year between 60 and 75 people are executed; before execution the average inmate was on death row for more than 10 years.[126] A growing number of death row inmates are foreign nationals whose execution can cause international ill will. For example, a Paraguayan citizen, Angel Francisco Breard, 32, was executed in April 1998 in Virginia for murder and attempted rape, despite a plea from the International Court of Justice that he be spared and intense efforts by the Paraguayan government to stay the execution.[127]

As of 1999 lethal injection was the predominant method of death, although a number of states use the gas chamber and electric chair. In 1999 the Supreme Court refused to hear a case against Florida's use of the electric chair as the sole means of execution. Even though the chair has malfunctioned several times, sending up smoke and flames, the Court refused to consider whether this amounted to cruel and unusual punishment. Of the 38 death penalty states, only Alabama, Georgia, Nebraska, and Florida still use the electric chair as the only means of execution.[128]

The Death Penalty Debate

The death penalty has long been one of the most controversial aspects of the justice system, and it likely will continue to be a source of significant debate.[129]

Arguments for the Death Penalty Various arguments have been offered in support of the death penalty. Among these rationales are that executions have always been used, that it is inherent in human nature to punish the wicked, and that the death penalty is favored by most Americans and used in three-quarters of the nations of the world, including Japan, which has an extremely low murder rate.[130] (See the Race, Culture, Gender, and Criminology feature titled "The International Use of the Death Penalty.")

The Bible describes methods of executing criminals. Many moral philosophers and religious leaders, such as Thomas More, John Locke, and Immanuel Kant, did not oppose the death penalty; neither did the framers of the U.S. Constitution.

The death penalty also seems to be in keeping with the current mode of dispensing punishment. Criminal law exacts proportionately harsher penalties for crimes based on their seriousness; this practice is testimony to a retributionist philosophy. Therefore, the harshest penalty for the most severe crime represents a logical step in the process.

Some also argue that the death penalty is sometimes the only real threat available to deter crime. For example, prison inmates serving life sentences can be controlled only if they know that further transgressions can lead to death. Or a person committing a crime that

Race and Sentencing

No issue concerning sentencing disparity is more important than the suspicion that race influences sentencing outcomes. One reason is that somewhat surprisingly, research on sentencing has failed to show a definitive pattern of racial discrimination. Although some studies indicate that a defendant's race directly impacts sentencing outcomes, other efforts show that the influence of race on sentencing is less clear than anticipated. Perhaps the disproportionate number of minority inmates results from crime and arrest patterns, not racial bias by judges; racial and ethnic minorities commit more crime, the argument goes, and therefore they are more likely to wind up in prison.

Despite this inconclusive evidence, racial disparity in sentencing has been suspected because a disproportionate number of minority inmates are in state prisons and on death row. Research efforts show that minority defendants suffer discrimination in a variety of court actions: they are more likely to be detained before trial than whites and, upon conviction, are more likely to receive incarceration rather than fines. Prosecutors are less likely to divert minorities from the legal system than whites who commit the same crimes; minorities are also less likely to win appeals than white appellants.

Criminal Incident Effects

The relationship between race and sentencing may be difficult to establish because their association may not be linear: minority defendants may be punished more severely for some crimes, but under some circum-

stances, they are treated more leniently for others. For example, James Nelson studied misdemeanant sentencing in New York State and found that minorities were given more lenient sentences than whites if they had no prior arrest record; in contrast, African-Americans with prior arrests received harsher sentences than whites with similar criminal backgrounds. Alexander Alvarez and Ronet Bachman's study of sentencing in Arizona found that Native Americans received harsher sentences for robbery and burglary, whereas Caucasians were punished more harshly for homicide.

Sociologist Darnell Hawkins explains this phenomenon as a matter of "appropriateness":

> Certain crime types are considered less "appropriate" for blacks than for whites. Blacks who are charged with committing these offenses will be treated more severely than blacks who commit crimes that are considered more "appropriate." Included in the former category are various white-collar offenses and crimes against political and social structures of authority. The latter groups of offenses would include various forms of victimless crimes associated with lower social status (e.g., prostitution, minor drug use, or drunkenness). This may also include various crimes against the person, especially those involving black victims.

Race may impact sentencing because some race-specific crimes are punished more harshly than others. African-Americans receive longer sentences for drug crimes than whites because they are more likely to be arrested for crack possession and sales and because crack dealing is more se-

verely punished by state and federal laws than other drug crimes. Because Caucasians are more likely to use marijuana and methamphetamines, prosecutors are more willing to plea-bargain and offer shorter jail terms for these offenses.

Racial bias has also been linked to victim–offender status. Minority defendants are sanctioned more severely if their victims are white than if their targets are fellow minority group members. Judges may base sentencing decisions on the race of the victim, not the race of the defendant. For example, Charles Crawford, Ted Chiricos, and Gary Kleck found that African-American defendants are more likely to be prosecuted under habitual offender statutes if they commit crimes where there is a greater likelihood of a white victim, such as larceny and burglary, than if they commit violent crimes, which are largely intraracial. Where there is a perceived "racial threat" due to interracial crime, punishments are enhanced.

System Effects

Sentencing disparity may also reflect race-based differences in criminal justice practices and policies associated with sentencing. For example, probation presentence reports may favor white over minority defendants, causing judges to award whites probation more often than minorities. Defendants who can afford bail receive more lenient sentences than those who remain in pretrial detention; minority defendants are less likely to make bail because they earn less. Sentencing outcome is also affected by

carries with it a long prison sentence might be more likely to kill witnesses if the threat of death did not exist.

Death is the ultimate incapacitation. Some offenders are so dangerous that they can never be safely let out in society. The death penalty is a sure way of preventing these people from ever harming others. More than 280 inmates on death row today had prior homicide convictions; if they had been executed for their

first offenses, at least 280 innocent people would still be alive.

The death penalty is believed to be cost-effective. Considering the crowded prison system and the expense of keeping an inmate locked up for many years, an execution makes financial sense.

Finally, although there have been allegations of racism, more whites are on death row than minorities, the defendant's ability to afford a private attorney and expensive expert witnesses. These factors place the poor and minority group members at a disadvantage and result in sentencing disparity. And although considerations of prior record may be legitimate in sentencing, minorities are more likely to have prior records because of organizational and individual bias on the part of police.

Jurisdictional Differences
There are also significant differences in the racial influence on sentencing between jurisdictions. Some states exhibit little racial bias, whereas others demonstrate a great deal. Studies that use multiple-state data in their analysis may therefore miss the effects of race on sentencing within particular states.

In a thorough review of sentencing disparity, Samuel Walker, Cassia Spohn, and Miriam Delone identify what they call **contextual discrimination**. This term refers to how judges in some jurisdictions impose harsher sentences on African-Americans or give racial minorities prison sentences in borderline cases for which whites get probation. Sentencing disparity may also be influenced by regional sentencing practices: the greatest percentage of the African-American population lives in the South, where judges are more punitive to all defendants, regardless of race. According to Walker, Spohn, and Delone, racism is subtle and hard to detect but still exerts an influence in the court setting.

Are Sentencing Practices Changing?
If racial discrepancies exist, new sentencing laws featuring determinate and mandatory sentences may help reduce disparity. For example, Jon'a Meyer and Tara Gray found that California jurisdictions that use mandatory sentences for crimes such as drunk driving also show little racial disparity in sentences between Caucasians and minority group members. Similarly, a national survey of sentencing practices conducted by the Bureau of Justice Statistics found that although white defendants are somewhat more likely to receive probation and other nonincarceration sentences than black defendants (34 percent versus 31 percent), there is little racial disparity in the length of prison sentences. Critics have also called for change in how sentencing guidelines are designed, asking that the provisions that punish crack possession more heavily than powdered cocaine possession be repealed. Outcomes that favor one group over another, regardless of their cause or implementation, cannot be tolerated in a democratic society.

CRITICAL THINKING

1. There is some inconclusive evidence that judges let race factors influence their sentencing decisions. Race seems more directly associated with legal factors that are correlated with sentencing outcomes (such as making bail, plea bargaining, having dependent children, or appearing nondangerous). Does this still amount to racial disparity, or is it income inequality?

 INFOTRAC COLLEGE EDITION RESEARCH

For an interesting case history and analysis of racial effects on sentencing, see:
Jill Neimark. Crime and punishment? *Psychology Today* 28 (July-August 1995) p. 54.

Source: Travis Pratt, "Race and Sentencing: A Meta-Analysis of Conflicting Empirical Research Results," *Journal of Criminal Justice* 26 (1998): 513–25; Charles Crawford, Ted Chiricos, and Gary Kleck, "Race, Racial Threat, and Sentencing of Habitual Offenders," *Criminology* 36 (1998): 481–511; Jon'a Meyer and Tara Gray, "Drunk Drivers in the Courts: Legal and Extra-Legal Factors Affecting Pleas and Sentences," *Journal of Criminal Justice* 25 (1997): 155–63; Alexander Alvarez and Ronet Bachman, "American Indians and Sentencing Disparity: An Arizona Test," *Journal of Criminal Justice* 24 (1996): 549–61; Carole Wolff Barnes and Rodney Kingsworth "Race, Drugs, and Criminal Sentencing: Hidden Effects of the Criminal Law," *Journal of Criminal Justice* 24 (1996): 39–55; Samuel Walker, Cassia Spohn, and Miriam DeLone, *The Color of Justice: Race, Ethnicity and Crime in America* (Belmont, Calif.: Wadsworth, 1996), pp. 145–46; Jo Dixon, "The Organizational Context of Sentencing," *American Journal of Sociology* 100 (1995): 1157–98; Alfred Blumstein, "On the Racial Disproportionality of the United States Prison Population," *Journal of Criminal Law and Criminology* 73 (1982): 1259–81; Celesta Albonetti and John Hepburn, "Prosecutorial Discretion to Defer Criminalization: The Effects of Defendants' Ascribed and Achieved Status Characteristics," *Journal of Quantitative Criminology* 12 (1996): 63–81; Jimmy Williams, "Race of Appellant, Sentencing Guidelines, and Decision Making in Criminal Appeals: A Research Note," *Journal of Criminal Justice* 23 (1995); Joan Petersilia, *Racial Disparities in the Criminal Justice System* (Santa Monica, Calif.: Rand Corp., 1983); Darnell Hawkins, "Race, Crime Type, and Imprisonment," *Justice Quarterly* 3 (1986): 251–69; James Nelson, "A Dollar or a Day: Sentencing Misdemeanants in New York State," *Journal of Research in Crime and Delinquency* 31 (1994): 183–201; Robert Crutchfield, George Bridges, and Susan Pitchford, "Analytical and Aggregation Biases in Analyses of Imprisonment: Reconciling Discrepancies in Studies of Racial Disparity," *Journal of Research in Crime and Delinquency* 31 (1994): 166–82.

and there appears to be little racial difference in the rate of capital sentencing over the past 30 years.

In summary, supporters view capital punishment as the ultimate deterrent to crime. They believe that so serious a sanction prevents many potential criminals from taking the lives of innocent victims. The justification for the death penalty, therefore, relies on the premise that sacrificing the lives of a few evil people is a cost-effective way to save the lives of many innocent ones.

Arguments Against the Death Penalty   Even if the general public voices approval of the death penalty, abolitionists argue that "social vengeance by death is a primitive way of revenge which stands in the way of moral progress."[131] People who support the death penalty may

The International Use of the Death Penalty

The United States is not alone in using the death penalty. Many nations use capital punishment, proof that it has universal appeal. For example, nations that operate under Islamic law, such as Saudi Arabia, routinely employ the death penalty and publicly execute convicted criminals. In 1997 the Saudi government beheaded more than 100 criminals, including more than 50 drug smugglers; 68 people were beheaded in 1996 and 192 in 1995.

What is the state of capital punishment around the world? According to Amnesty International, about 57 countries and territories have abolished the death penalty for all crimes, 15 countries have abolished the death penalty for all but exceptional crimes, and another 26 countries can be considered abolitionist de facto: they retain the death penalty in law but have not carried out any executions for at least 10 years. In all, 98 countries have abolished the death penalty in law or practice. In contrast, 95 other countries retain and use the death penalty.

Amnesty International believes that use of capital punishment will be further curtailed. More than two countries a year on average have abolished the death penalty since 1976. Over 20 countries and territories have abolished the death penalty for ordinary crimes or for all crimes since 1989. They include countries in Africa (examples include Angola, Mauritius, Mozambique, and South Africa), Latin America (Paraguay), Asia (Cambodia and Hong Kong), Eastern Europe (Hungary, Moldova, and Romania), Western Europe (Belgium, Greece, Italy, Spain, and Switzerland), and the Pacific (New Zealand). In contrast, during the same period only four abolitionist countries reintroduced the death penalty. One of them—Nepal—has since abol-

ished the death penalty again, and there have been no executions in the other three (Gambia, Papua New Guinea, and the Philippines).

Although opposition to executions is growing in some areas, in others, such as the Caribbean, the public is demanding increased use of the death penalty. In 1998 the governments of Jamaica, Guyana, and Barbados all expressed interest in speeding the use of the death penalty. More than 250 prisoners are currently on death row across the English-speaking Caribbean. Trinidad tops the list, with 107 prisoners convicted of capital crimes and awaiting execution, followed by Jamaica, with 47, and the Bahamas, with an estimated 40. In July 1998 the twin-island federation of St. Kitts and Nevis executed its first prisoner since becoming independent in 1983. Jamaica has ordered its first execution in a decade, that of a 29-year-old hitchhiker convicted of strangling a business executive who gave him a ride.

How many people are executed each year? During 1997 an estimated 2,375 prisoners were executed in 41 countries, and 3,707 defendants were sentenced to death in 69 countries. The true total amount may be higher because of undocumented cases. As in previous years, a small number of countries accounted for the vast majority of executions recorded: 1800 executions in China, 143 in Iran, and 122 in Saudi Arabia.

Execution of Juveniles

International human rights treaties prohibit anyone under 18 years old at the time of the crime being sentenced to death. The International Covenant on Civil and Political Rights, the American Convention on Human Rights, and the U.N. Convention on the Rights of the Child all have provisions to this effect. More than 100

countries have laws specifically excluding the execution of juvenile offenders or may be presumed to exclude such executions by being parties to one or another of the above treaties. A small number of countries, however, continue to execute juvenile offenders. Five countries since 1990 are known to have executed prisoners who were under 18 years old at the time of the crime—Iran, Pakistan, Saudi Arabia, the United States, and Yemen. However, the United States leads the world in juvenile executions. Since 1976 there have been 12 U.S. executions of those who were under 18 at the time of their crimes; 9 of the 12 occurred in the 1990s. Seventy-two additional juveniles are on death row.

CRITICAL THINKING

The movement toward abolition in the United States is encouraged by the fact that so many nations have abandoned the death penalty. Should we model our system of punishment after other nations, or is our crime problem so unique that it requires the use of capital punishment?

 INFOTRAC COLLEGE EDITION RESEARCH

To read more about the death penalty abroad, see:
Caroline Moorehead. Tinkering with death. *World Press Review* 42 (July 1995), p. 38.

Source: Larry Rohter, "In Caribbean, Support Growing for Death Penalty," *New York Times,* 4 October 1998, p. B1; Associated Press, "Chechen Pair Executed in Public," *Boston Globe,* 19 September 1997, p. 9; Reuters, "Saudi Beheadings over 100 for 1997," *Boston Globe.* 28 September 1997, p. A29; List of Abolitionist and Retentionist Countries, Amnesty International Index: ACT 05/07/97.

be motivated by racial prejudice.[132] Its inherent brutality places it in violation of the Eighth Amendment of the U.S. Constitution, which prohibits cruel and unusual punishment. Deborah Denno has documented the cruel nature of the existing means of execution. For example, electrocution is often accompanied by charring of the skin and severe external burns; some condemned criminals literally burst into flames during botched executions.[133] Although the current application of the death penalty seems to fall outside the Eighth Amendment's "cruel and unusual" standard, Denno finds that many legislators and judges want to keep the death penalty and therefore are reluctant to question its legality.

Critics also question whether the general public gives blanket approval to the application of capital punishment. Research suggests that most people may accept capital punishment in principle but also believe it should be used less.[134] Surveys show that the general public is usually willing to forgo use of the death penalty when given choices of other penalties, such as life in prison without parole and compensation to the victim's family.[135]

The death penalty is very costly. For example, in 1998 there were 508 men and 9 women on death row in California. Because of numerous appeals, the median time between sentencing and execution was 14 years. Processing appeals is expensive: currently an annual budget of $5 million pays for California's public defender staff of 45 lawyers who represent inmates in death penalty cases.[136] Inmates may also be represented by private attorneys, and the California legislature recently increased the hourly pay from $98 to $125 for private lawyers who agree to appeal death penalties.

Opponents also object to the finality of the death penalty. It of course precludes any possibility of rehabilitation. Studies indicate that death row inmates released because of legal changes rarely recidivate and present little threat to the community.[137] It is also quite possible for an innocent person to be convicted of crime; once the person is executed, the mistake can never be rectified.[138] Many people convicted of murder are later released because of mistaken identity or perjured testimony. For example, Rolando Cruz and Alejandro Hernandez, wrongfully convicted of murder, were released in 1995 after spending more than a decade on death row in the Illinois prison system; three former prosecutors and four deputy sheriffs who worked on the case were later charged with fabricating evidence against the pair.[139]

"It is better that a thousand guilty go free than one innocent man be executed" is a statement abolitionists often make. This point has been convincingly made by Michael Radelet and Hugo Bedeau, who claim that there have been about 350 wrongful convictions this century, of which 23 led to executions. They estimate that about three death sentences are returned every two years in cases where the defendants have been falsely accused. More than half the errors stem from perjured testimony, false identification, coerced confessions, and suppression of evidence. In addition to the 23 who were executed, 128 of the falsely convicted served more than six years in prison; 39 served more than 16 years; and eight died while serving their sentences.[140] Even though the system attempts to be especially cautious in capital cases, it is evident that unacceptable mistakes can occur.

The discretionary nature of the death penalty also draws criticism from its opponents. Legal scholar Charles Black argues that "arbitrary discretion pervades every road to the chair."[141] The beliefs and personal background of judges, including their age and political affiliation, can determine whether they uphold the death penalty (not surprisingly, younger Democrats seem more liberal than older Republicans).[142] Because discretion and personal beliefs influence decision making, the death penalty can be employed in a discriminatory fashion. Between 1930 and 1967, 3,859 alleged criminals were executed in the United States. Of those executed, 53.5 percent were African-American and 45.4 percent were white. A moratorium was then put on executions, during which the legality of capital punishment was debated (discussed next). During the 22-year period (1977–1999) since executions resumed, more than 450 executions have taken place in 26 states.

Research indicates that white defendants convicted of murder actually have a greater probability of receiving the death penalty than African-Americans.[143] One reason is that the victim's race controls death penalty decisions, not the offender's.[144] People who kill whites are significantly more likely to be sentenced to death than people who kill blacks.[145] Because murder is essentially intraracial, whites are more likely to receive capital sentences because their victims are most often white. Nonetheless, the likelihood of receiving the death penalty is greatest in the relatively infrequent instance where a black criminal kills a white victim.[146]

Abolitionists claim that capital punishment has never proven to be a deterrent, any more than has life in prison. In fact, capital punishment may encourage murder because it sets an example of violence and brutality.[147]

CONNECTIONS

Advocates of the due process model of justice warn of this danger and demand that the justice system take steps to reduce the threat of mistaken convictions. See Chapter 15 for a discussion of this perspective of justice.

CONNECTIONS

As you may recall from Chapter 5, there is little hard evidence that the threat of capital punishment is related to murder rates.

Abolitionists also point out that such nations as Denmark and Sweden have long abandoned the death penalty and that 40 percent of the countries with a death penalty have active abolitionist movements.[148]

The death penalty is capricious; receiving death is similar to losing a lottery.[149] Each year about 10,000 people are convicted of murder; more receive probation as a sole sentence than get the death penalty. Is it fair to release one person who has taken a life into the community and execute another?

Legality of the Death Penalty

For most of this country's history, capital punishment was used in a discretionary, haphazard manner without strict legal controls. As a result, its application was marked by extreme racial disparity; more than half the executions conducted in America involved African-Americans. Then, in 1972, the U.S. Supreme Court, in *Furman v. Georgia,* ruled that the discretionary imposition of the death penalty was cruel and unusual punishment under the Eighth and Fourteenth Amendments of the Constitution.[150] The Court did not rule out the use of capital punishment as a penalty; rather, it objected to the arbitrary and capricious manner in which it was imposed. After *Furman,* many states changed statutes that had allowed juries discretion in imposing the death penalty. Some states enacted guidelines that spelled out specific conditions of aggravation that must be met for the death penalty to be considered.

Despite these changes, no further executions were carried out while the Supreme Court pondered additional cases concerning the death penalty. In July 1976 the Supreme Court ruled on the constitutionality of five states' death penalty statutes. In the first case, *Gregg v. Georgia,* the Court found valid the Georgia statute that held that a jury must find at least one "aggravating circumstance" before the death penalty can be imposed in murder cases.[151] In the *Gregg* case, for example, the jury imposed the death penalty after establishing beyond a reasonable doubt the presence of two aggravating circumstances:

1. The murder was committed while the offender was committing two other capital felonies.
2. The offender committed the murder for the purpose of receiving money and other financial gain (an automobile).

The Court also upheld the constitutionality of a Texas statute on capital punishment in *Jurek v. Texas*[152] and of a Florida statute in *Proffitt v. Florida.*[153] These statutes are similar to Georgia's in that they limit sentencing discretion not only by specifying the crimes for which capital punishment can be handed down but also by stipulating criteria concerning the circumstances surrounding the crimes. However, the Supreme Court declared that mandatory death sentences were unconstitutional.

In the late 1970s and early 1980s, a more conservative Supreme Court eased the way for executions by lifting some of the legal roadblocks to capital punishment, such as allowing the removal of jurors who are opposed to the death penalty.[154] In a 1987 case, *Tison v. Arizona,* the Court permitted executions of people who were major participants in a murder case and displayed reckless indifference to human life but did not actually kill anybody.[155]

In what may have been the last major challenge to the death penalty, *McCleskey v. Kemp,* the Supreme Court upheld the capital sentence of an African-American man in Georgia despite social science evidence that a black criminal who kills a white victim has a much greater chance of receiving the death penalty than a white criminal who kills a black victim.[156] Many observers felt that this case was the last legal obstacle the death penalty had to overcome to become a standard mode of punishment in the American justice system. The Court subsequently upheld the states' right to execute youthful offenders who killed after reaching the age of 16.[157] Ironically, when McCleskey reappealed his case on other procedural grounds, the Court used that case as a vehicle to limit the access of death row inmates to the appeals process; Warren McCleskey was executed in 1993.[158]

SUMMARY

The judicatory process provides a forum for deciding the outcome of a conflict between two or more parties. Unfortunately, discretion and personal decision making interfere with the equality that should be built into the law.

The judicatory process is played out in the nation's court system. State courts usually involve a multitiered system — lower trial courts, superior trial courts, appellate courts, and supreme court. The federal system is similar; it contains trial courts, appellate courts, and the Supreme Court. The U.S. Supreme Court is the final court of appeals for all state and federal cases.

There are three main actors in the judicatory process. The prosecutor brings charges against the offender and then represents the state in all criminal matters. The defense attorney represents the accused at all stages of the judicatory process. Some defendants can afford to hire private attorneys for their defense, but the majority are represented by defense counsel appointed and paid for by the state. The judge controls the trial, rules on issues of evidence, charges the jury, and in some cases can choose the type and length of sentence.

The pretrial stage of the justice process involves such issues as bail and plea bargaining. Bail is a money bond the defendant puts up to secure freedom before trial. It is controversial because those who cannot make bail must spend their time in detention. Critics charge that bail discriminates against the poor, who can neither afford bond nor borrow it from bonding agents. Consequently, reform programs, such as release on recognizance, have been started.

Plea bargaining involves the prosecutor's allowing defendants to plead guilty as charged in return for some consideration—for example, a reduced sentence or dropped charges. Plea bargaining has been criticized because it represents the unchecked use of discretion by prosecutors. Often serious criminals can receive light sentences by bargaining, and some people may be coerced into pleading guilty because they fear a harsh sentence if they go to trial. An effort has been made to control plea bargains, but they are still frequently used.

The second stage of the judicatory process is the criminal trial. The trial has a number of distinct stages, including jury selection, opening statements, presentation of evidence by prosecution and defense, closing arguments, instructions to the jury, verdict, sentence, and appeal. The rule of law also affects criminal trials. The Supreme Court has required that trials be speedy, public, and fair and has ruled that people have a right to be free from double jeopardy and to be represented by competent counsel.

After a conviction, sentencing occurs. Each state, as well as the federal government, has its own types of sentences and punishments. Fines, suspended sentences, community supervision, and prison are the most common forms of punishment. Prison sentences are divided into determinate and indeterminate types. There are also mandatory sentences that must be served upon conviction and carry no hope of probation. Efforts to control sentencing disparity include the use of sentencing guidelines, as well as determinate and mandatory sentences.

See the book-specific web site at www.cj.wadsworth.com for additional chapter links, discussions, and quizzes.

THINKING LIKE A CRIMINOLOGIST

The director of the American Civil Liberties Union has contacted you, asking for your professional opinion. She has read a paper by criminologists William Bowers and Glenn Pierce, who argue that far from being a deterrent, capital punishment actually produces more violence than it prevents; they label this the brutalization effect. Executions, they say, actually increase murder rates because they raise the general violence level in society and because violence-prone people identify with the executioner, not with the target of the death penalty. Consequently, when someone gets in a conflict with them or challenges their authority, they execute them in the same manner that the state executes people who violate its rules.

Assuming that Bowers and Pierce are correct, the ACLU director asks, does this mean that the death penalty violates the general public's civil rights? She asks whether it might be possible to turn public opinion against the death penalty on the basis that it actually does more harm than good, thereby endangering their lives. How would you respond?

KEY TERMS

U.S. district courts
federal courts of appeal
U.S. Supreme Court
writ of certiorari
precedent
landmark decision
prosecution
affidavits
attorney list/assigned counsel system
public defenders
adversarial process
judge
Missouri Plan
criminal charge
bill of indictment

information
complaint
arraignment
bail
preventive detention
bail bonding agent
release on recognizance
deposit bail
bail guidelines
plea bargaining
venire
voir dire
peremptory challenge
direct examination
cross-examination

redirect examination
directed verdict
rebuttal
hearsay evidence
sentencing
mandatory prison term
concurrent sentence
consecutive sentence
indeterminate sentence
determinate sentence
guideline sentences
sentencing disparity
contextual discrimination

NOTES

1. Kevin Sack, "DNA Tests Free Two Men Convicted of Rape in '83," *New York Times,* 4 December 1997, p. A1.

2. Patrick A. Langan and Jodi M. Brown, *Felony Sentences in State Courts, 1994* (Washington, D.C: Bureau of Justice Statistics, 1997).

3. The data in these sections are taken from National Center for State Courts, *Examining the Work of State Courts, 1996: A National Perspective from the Court Statistics Project* (Williamsburg, Va.: National Center for State Courts, 1998). Herein cited as *Examining the Work of State Courts, 1996.*

4. David Rohde, "Arrests Soar in Giuliani Crackdown," *New York Times,* 2 February 1999.

5. Carol J. DeFrances and Greg W. Steadman, *Prosecutors in State Courts, 1996* (Washington: D.C.: Bureau of Justice Statistics, 1998).

6. DeFrances and Steadman, *Prosecutors in State Courts, 1996.*

7. Carol J. DeFrances, Steven K. Smith, and Louise van der Does, *Prosecutors in State Courts, 1994* (Washington, D.C.: Bureau of Justice Statistics, 1996).

8. Newman Baker, "The Prosecutor Initiation of Prosecution," *Journal of Criminal Law, Criminology and Police Science* 23 (1933): 770–71.

9. Barbara Boland, Paul Mahanna, and Ronald Sones, *The Prosecution of Felony Arrests, 1988* (Washington, D.C.: Bureau of Justice Statistics, 1993), p. 3.

10. Edward Lisefski and Donald Manson, *Tracking Offenders, 1984* (Washington, D.C.: Bureau of Justice Statistics, 1988), p. 1.

11. Janell Schmidt and Ellen Hochstedler Steury, "Prosecutorial Discretion in Filing Charges in Domestic Violence Cases," *Criminology* 27 (1989): 487–510.

12. Rodney Kingsworth, John Lopez, Jennifer Wentworth, and Debra Cummings, "Adult Sexual Assault: The Role of Racial/Ethnic Composition in Prosecution and Sentencing," *Journal of Criminal Justice* 26 (1998): 359–72.

13. Frank W. Miller, *Prosecution: The Decision to Charge a Suspect with a Crime* (Boston: Little, Brown, 1970).

14. Wayne LaFave, "The Prosecutor's Discretion in the United States," *American Journal of Comparative Law* 18 (1970): 532–48.

15. DeFrances, Smith, and van der Does, *Prosecutors in State Courts, 1994;* Patrick Langan, *State Felony Courts and Felony Laws* (Washington, D.C.: Bureau of Justice Statistics, 1987), pp. 1–3.

16. Charles Breitel, "Controls in Criminal Law Enforcement," *University of Chicago Law Review* 27 (1960): 427–35.

17. See, generally, "A Symposium on Prosecutorial Discretion," *American Criminal Law Review* (1976): 379–99.

18. George Cole, "The Decision to Prosecute," *Law and Society Review* 4 (1970): 331–43.

19. *Gideon v. Wainwright,* 372 U.S. 335 (1963); *Argersinger v. Hamlin,* 407 U.S. 25 (1972).

20. Steven K. Smith and Carol J. DeFrances, *Indigent Defense* (Washington, D.C: Bureau of Justice Statistics, 1996).

21. Smith and DeFrances, *Indigent Defense.*

22. See American Bar Association, Special Committee on Evaluation of Ethical Standards, *Code of Professional Responsibility* (Chicago: American Bar Association 1968), p. 81.

23. *Nix v. Whiteside,* 106 S.Ct. 988 (1986).

24. James Eisenstein and Jacob Herbert, *Felony Justice* (Boston: Little, Brown, 1977); see, generally, Malcolm Feeley, *The Process Is the Punishment* (New York: Russell Sage Foundation, 1979).

25. William Lineberry, ed., *Justice in America: Law, Order and the Courts* (New York: H. W. Wilson, 1972).

26. Sari Escovitz, with Fred Kurland and Nan Gold, *Judicial Selection and Tenure* (Chicago: American Judicature Society, 1974), pp. 3–16.

27. *Examining the Work of State Courts, 1996.*

28. *Examining the Work of State Courts, 1996.*

29. M. Ozanne, R. Wilson, and D. Gedney, Jr., "Toward a Theory of Bail Risk," *Criminology* 18 (1980): 149.

30. Brian A. Reaves, *Felony Defendants in Large Urban Counties, 1994* (Washington, D.C.: Bureau of Justice Statistics, 1998).

31. Caleb Foote, "A Study of the Administration of Bail in New York," *University of Pennsylvania Law Review* 106 (1960): 693–730; William Rhodes, *Pretrial Release and Misconduct* (Washington, D.C.: Bureau of Justice Statistics, 1985).

32. John Goldkamp, *Two Classes of Accused* (Cambridge, Mass.: Ballinger, 1979).

33. Brian A. Reaves and Jacob Perez, *Pretrial Release of Felony Defendants, 1992: National Pretrial Reporting Program* (Washington: D.C.: Bureau of Justice Statistics, 1994).

34. Goldkamp, *Two Classes of Accused.*

35. Timothy M. Ito, "Wild West Saga: Have Gun, Will Shoot," *U.S. News & World Report* 123 (15 September 1997), p. 7.

36. Ito, "Wild West Saga: Have Gun, Will Shoot."

37. Vera Institute of Justice, *Programs in Criminal Justice* (New York: Vera Institute, 1972).

38. Reaves and Perez, *Pretrial Release of Felony Defendants, 1992,* p. 5.

39. Malcolm Feeley, *Court Reform on Trial* (New York: Basic Books, 1983); John Goldkamp, "Judicial Reform of Bail Practices: The Philadelphia Experiment," *Court Management Journal* (1983): 16–20.

40. John Goldkamp and Michael Gottfredson, *Judicial Decision Guidelines for Bail: The Philadelphia Experiment* (Washington, D.C.: National Institute of Justice, 1983).

41. 18 U.S.C. Sec. 3142 (e) (1985).

42. *United States v. Salerno,* 107 S.Ct. 2095 (1987).

43. *Schall v. Martin,* 104 S.Ct. 2403 (1984).

44. Stephen Kennedy and Kenneth Carlson, *Pretrial Release and Detention: The Bail Reform Act of 1984* (Washington, D.C.: Bureau of Justice Statistics, 1988).

45. Joseph Sanborn, "Philosophical, Legal, and Systemic Aspects of Juvenile Court Plea Bargaining," *Crime and Delinquency* 39 (1993): 509–27.

46. Carla Gaskins, *Felony Case Processing in State Courts, 1986* (Washington, D.C.: Bureau of Justice Statistics, 1990), p. 1. See also Donald Newman, "Making a Deal," in *Legal Process and Corrections,* ed. N. Johnston and L. Savitz (New York: John Wiley, 1982), p. 93.

47. Newman, "Making a Deal," pp. 96–97.

48. These sentiments are similar to those expressed by Abraham Blumberg in "The Practice of Law as a Confidence Game: Organizational Co-optation of a Profession," *Law and Society Review* 1 (1967): 15–39.

49. Again, these thoughts are similar to Blumberg's views as expressed in "The Practice of Law as a Confidence Game."

50. National Advisory Commission on Criminal Justice Standards and Goals, *Courts* (Washington, D.C.: U.S. Government Printing Office, 1976).

51. Richard Kuh, "Plea Copping," *Bar Bulletin* 24 (1966–1967): 160.

52. Alan Alschuler, "The Defense Counsel's Role in Plea Bargaining," *Yale Law Journal* 84 (1975): 1179.

53. See, generally, Milton Heumann, "A Note on Plea Bargaining and Case Pressure," *Law and Society Review* 9 (1975): 515.

54. National Institute of Law Enforcement and Criminal Justice, *Plea Bargaining in the United States* (Washington, D.C.: Georgetown University, 1978), p. 8.

55. Michael Rubenstein, Stevens Clarke, and Teresa White, *Alaska Bans Plea Bargaining* (Washington, D.C.: U.S. Department of Justice, 1980).

56. Newman, "Making a Deal," p. 102.

57. National Advisory Commission on Criminal Justice Standards and Goals, *Courts,* p. 66.

58. See, for example, "Limiting the Peremptory Challenge: Representation of Groups on Petit Juries," *Yale Law Journal* 86 (1977): 1715.

59. *Batson v. Kentucky,* 476 U.S. 79 (1986).

60. *Ham v. South Carolina,* 409 U.S. 524, 93 S.Ct. 848, 35 L.Ed.2d 46 (1973).

61. *Turner v. Murray,* 106 S.Ct. 1683 (1986).

62. *Taylor v. Louisiana,* 419 U.S. 522, 42 L.Ed.2d 690, 95 S.Ct. 692 (1975).

63. In *Ristaino v. Ross* [424 U.S. 589 (1976)], the Court said questioning the jury on racial issues was not automatic in all interracial crimes.

64. Edna Erez, "Victim Participation in Sentencing: Rhetoric and Reality," *Journal of Criminal Justice* 18 (1990): 19–31.

65. *Strunk v. United States,* 412 U.S. 434 (1973).

66. *Klopfer v. North Carolina,* 38 U.S. 213 (1967).

67. *Barker v. Wingo,* 404 U.S. 307 (1971).

68. Bureau of Justice Statistics, *Report to the Nation on Crime and Justice* (Washington, D.C.: U.S. Department of Justice, 1983), p. 66.

69. Patrick A. Langan and Jodi M. Brown, *Felony Sentences in State Courts, 1994* (Washington, D.C: Bureau of Justice Statistics, 1997).

70. *Duncan v. Louisiana,* 391 U.S. 145 (1968).

71. *Baldwin v. New York,* 399 U.S. 66 (1970).

72. *Blanton v. City of North Las Vegas,* 489 U.S. 538, 109 S.Ct. 1289, 103 L.Ed.2d 550 (1989).

73. *Williams v. Florida,* 399 U.S. 78 (1970).

74. *Apodica v. Oregon,* 406 U.S. 404 (1972).

75. *Benton v. Maryland,* 395 U.S. 784 (1969).

76. *United States v. Lanza,* 260 U.S. 377 (1922); *Bartkus v. Illinois,* 359 U.S. 121 (1959); *Abbate v. U.S.,* 359 U.S. 187 (1959).

77. *Heath v. Alabama,* 106 S.Ct. 433 (1985).

78. *Powell v. Alabama,* 287 U.S. 45 (1932).

79. *Gideon v. Wainwright,* 372 U.S. 335 (1963).

80. *Argersinger v. Hamlin,* 407 U.S. 25 (1972).

81. *Strickland v. Washington,* 104 S.Ct. 2052 (1984).

82. *Coy v. Iowa,* 48 U.S. 1012, 108 S.Ct. 2798, 101 L.Ed.2d. 857 (1988).

83. *Maryland v. Craig,* 110 S.Ct. 3157, 111 L.Ed.2d 666 (1990).

84. *White v. Illinois,* 112 S.Ct. 736 (1992).

85. Myrna Raeder, "*White*'s Effect on Right to Confront One's Accuser," *Criminal Justice* (Winter 1993): 2–7.

86. For a general review, see Candace McCoy, "Sentencing (and) the Underclass," *Law and Society Review* 31 (1997): 589–612.

87. See, generally, Norval Morris, *Equal Justice Under the Law* (Washington, D.C.: U.S. Government Printing Office, 1977).

88. See V. O'Leary, M. Gottfredson, and A. Gelman, "Contemporary Sentencing Proposals," *Criminal Law Bulletin* 11 (1975): 558–60.

89. Sally Hillsman, Barry Mahoney, George Cole, and Bernard Auchter, *Fines as Criminal Sanctions* (Washington, D.C.: National Institute of Justice, 1987).

90. Edna Erez and Pamela Tontodonato, "The Effect of Victim Participation in Sentencing on Sentencing Outcome," *Criminology* 28 (1990): 451–74.

91. Kriss Drass and J. William Spencer, "Accounting for Presentencing Recommendations: Typologies and Probation Officers' Theory of Office," *Social Problems* 34 (1987): 277–93.

92. Patrick Langan, *State Felony Courts and Felony Laws* (Washington, D.C.: Bureau of Justice Statistics, 1987), p. 6.

93. Kenneth Culp Davis, *Discretionary Justice: A Preliminary Inquiry* (Baton Rouge: Louisiana State University Press, 1969).

94. See Marvin Frankel, *Criminal Sentences—Law Without Order* (New York: Hill and Wang, 1972), p. 5.

95. Thomas Marvell and Carlisle Moody, "Determinate Sentencing and Abolishing Parole: The Long-Term Impacts on Prisons and Crime," *Criminology* 34 (1996): 105–128.

96. John Kramer, Robin Lubitz, and Cynthia Kempinen, "Sentencing Guidelines: A Quantitative Comparison of Sentencing Policies in Minnesota, Pennsylvania, and Washington," *Justice Quarterly* 6 (1989): 565–87.

97. James Austin, *1996 National Survey of State Sentencing Structures* (Washington, D.C: National Institute of Justice, 1998).

98. *Mistretta v. United States,* 44 Cr.L. 3061 (1989).

99. David Griswold, "Deviation from Sentencing Guidelines: The Issue of Unwarranted Disparity," *Journal of Criminal Justice* 16 (1988): 317–29; Minnesota Sentencing Guidelines Commission, *The Impact of the Minnesota Sentencing Guidelines: Three-Year Evaluation* (St. Paul: Minnesota Sentencing Guidelines Commission, 1984), p. 162.

100. Pamala Griset, "Determinate Sentencing and Administrative over Time Served in Prison: A Case Study of Florida," *Crime and Delinquency* 42 (1996): 127–43.

101. Terence Miethe and Charles Moore, "Socioeconomic Disparities Under Determinate Sentencing Systems: A Comparison of Preguideline and Postguideline Practices in Minnesota," *Criminology* 23 (1985): 337–63; Richard Frase, "Implementing Commission-Based Sentencing Guidelines: The Lessons of the First Ten Years in Minnesota" (paper presented at the annual meeting of the American Society of Criminology, San Francisco, November 1991), p. 5.

102. Michael Tonry, "The Politics and Process of Sentencing Commissions," *Crime and Delinquency* 37 (1991): 307–29.

103. Michael Tonry, "The Failure of the U.S. Sentencing Commission's Guidelines," *Crime and Delinquency* 39 (1993): 131–49 at 131.

104. Michael Tonry, *Sentencing Matters* (New York: Oxford University Press, 1996), p. 5.

105. Samuel Walker, Cassia Spohn, and Miriam DeLone, *The Color of Justice: Race, Ethnicity and Crime in America* (Belmont, Calif.: Wadsworth, 1996), p. 159.

106. Elaine Wolf and Marsha Weissman, "Revising Federal Sentencing Policy: Some Consequences of Expanding Eligibility for Alternative Sanctions," *Crime and Delinquency* 42 (1996): 192–205.

107. Chris Eskridge, "Sentencing Guidelines: To Be or Not to Be," *Federal Probation* 50 (1986): 70–76.

108. Marvell and Moody, "Determinate Sentencing and Abolishing Parole," p. 123.

109. Marvell and Moody, "Determinate Sentencing and Abolishing Parole," p. 122.

110. Michael Tonry, *Sentencing Reform Impacts* (Washington, D.C.: U.S. Government Printing Office, 1987), pp. 26–27.

111. Timothy Bynum, "Prosecutorial Discretion and the Implementation of a Legislative Mandate," in *Implementing Criminal Justice Policies,* ed. Merry Morash (Beverly Hills: Sage, 1982).

112. Alan Dershowitz, *Fair and Certain Punishment: Report of the Twentieth Century Task Force on Criminal Sentencing* (New York: Twentieth Century Fund, 1976).

113. Tonry, *Sentencing Reform Impacts,* pp. 26–30.

114. This section is based on Paula M. Ditton and Doris James Wilson, *Truth in Sentencing in State Prisons* (Washington: D.C.: Bureau of Justice Statistics, 1999).

115. Pub.L. No. 103-322, 108 Stat. 1796 (1994).

116. Michael Vitiello, "Three Strikes: Can We Return to Rationality?" *Journal of Criminal Law and Criminology* 87 (1997): 395–481.

117. "California Passes a Tough Three-Strikes-You're-Out Law," *Criminal Justice Newsletter* 24 (4 April 1993), p. 4.

118. Marc Mauer, "Testimony Before the U.S. Congress House Judiciary Committee on 'Three Strikes and You're Out,'" 1 March 1994 (Washington, D.C.: The Sentencing Project, 1994).

119. "Three-Strikes Laws Rarely Used, Except California's, Study Finds," *Criminal Justice Newsletter* 27: (17 September 1996), p. 4.

120. Rand Research Brief, *California's New Three-Strikes Law: Benefits, Costs, and Alternatives* (Santa Monica, Calif.: Rand Corp., 1994).

121. Brent Smith and Kelly Damphouse, "Terrorism, Politics, and Punishment: A Test of Structural-Contextual Theory and the 'Liberation Hypothesis,'" *Criminology* 36 (1998): 67–92.

122. For a general review of this issue, see Florence Ferguson, "Sentencing Guidelines: Are (Black) Offenders Given Just Treatment?" Paper presented at the American Society of Criminology meeting, Montreal, November 1987.

123. Alfred Blumstein, "On the Racial Disproportionality of the United States Prison Population," *Journal of Criminal Law and Criminology* 73 (1982): 1259–81; Darnell Hawkins, "Race, Crime Type, and Imprisonment," *Justice Quarterly* 3 (1986): 251–69; Martha Myers, "Offended Parties and Official Reactions: Victims and the Sentencing of Criminal Defendants," *Sociological Quarterly* 20 (1979): 529–40.

124. Raymond Paternoster, "Race of the Victim and Location of the Crime: The Decision to Seek the Death Penalty in South Carolina," *Journal of Criminal Law and Criminology* 74 (1983): 754–85.

125. "Many State Legislatures Focused on Crime in 1995, Study Finds," *Criminal Justice Newsletter* 27 (2 January 1996), p. 2.

126. Tracy Snell, *Capital Punishment, 1997* (Washington, D.C: Bureau of Justice Statistics, 1998, revised, 1999).

127. David Stout, "Clemency Denied, Paraguayan Is Executed," *New York Times,* 15 April 1998.

128. *Lopez v. Singletary,* No. 98-6065.

129. For two impressive views on the death penalty, see Robert Bohm, "Humanism and the Death Penalty with Special Emphasis on the Post-*Furman* Experience," *Justice Quarterly* 6 (1989): 173–96; and David Friedrichs, "Comment—Humanism and the Death Penalty: An Alternative Perspective," *Justice Quarterly* 6 (1989): 197–211.

130. Dennis Wiechman, Jerry Kendall, and Ronald Bae, "International Use of the Death Penalty," *International Journal of Comparative and Applied Criminal Justice* 14 (1990): 239–59.

131. See, for example, Ernest Van Den Haag, *Punishing Criminals: Concerning a Very Old and Painful Question* (New York:

Basic Books, 1975), pp. 209–11; Walter Berns, "Defending the Death Penalty," *Crime and Delinquency* 26 (1980): 503–11.

132. Marian Borg, "The Southern Subculture of Punitiveness? Regional Variation in Support for Capital Punishment," *Journal of Research in Crime and Delinquency* 34 (1997): 24–45.

133. Deborah Denno, "Getting to Death: Are Executions Constitutional?" *Iowa Law Review* 82 (1997): 319–464.

134. Norman Finkel and Stefanie Smith, "Principals and Accessories in Capital Felony-Murder: The Proportionality Principle Reigns Supreme," *Law and Society Review* 27 (1993): 129–46.

135. Marla Sandys and Edmund McGarrell, "Attitudes Toward Capital Punishment: Preference for the Penalty or Mere Acceptance?" *Journal of Research in Crime and Delinquency* 32 (1995): 191–213.

136. Don Terry, "California Prepares for Faster Execution Pace," *New York Times,* 17 October 1998, p. A7.

137. James Marquart and Jonathan Sorensen, "Institutional and Postrelease Behavior of *Furman*-Commuted Inmates in Texas," *Justice Quarterly* 26 (1988): 677–93.

138. Kilman Shin, *Death Penalty and Crime* (Fairfax, Va.: George Mason University, 1978), p. 1.

139. "Illinois Ex-Prosecutors Charged with Framing Murder Defendants," *Criminal Justice Newsletter* 28 (2 January 1997), p. 3.

140. Michael Radelet and Hugo Bedeau, "Miscarriages of Justice in Potentially Capital Cases," *Stanford Law Review* 40 (1987): 21–181. For an opposing view, see Stephen Markman and Paul Cassell, "Protecting the Innocent: A Response to the Bedeau-Radelet Study," *Stanford Law Review* 41 (1988): 121–70; for their response, see Hugo Adam Bedeau and Michael Radelet, "The Myth of Infallibility: A Reply to Markman and Cassell," *Stanford Law Review* 42 (1988): 161–70.

141. Charles Black, "Objections to S. 1382, a Bill to Establish Rational Criteria for the Imposition of Capital Punishment," *Crime and Delinquency* 26 (1980): 441–53.

142. Melinda Gann Hall and Paul Brace, "The Vicissitudes of Death by Decree: Forces Influencing Capital Punishment Decision Making in State Supreme Courts," *Social Science Quarterly* 75 (1994): 138–48.

143. Hall and Brace, "The Vicissitudes of Death by Decree."

144. Thomas Keil and Gennaro Vito, "Race, Homicide Severity, and Application of the Death Penalty: A Consideration of the Barnett Scale," *Criminology* 27 (1989): 511–31; Thomas Keil and Gennaro Vito, "Capital Sentencing in Kentucky: An Analysis of Factors Influencing Decision Making in the Post-*Gregg* Period," *Journal of Criminal Law and Criminology* 79 (1988): 483–503.

145. David Baldus, C. Pulaski, and G. Woodworth, "Comparative Review of Death Sentences: An Empirical Study of the Georgia Experience," *Journal of Criminal Law and Criminology* 74 (1983): 661–93.

146. D. Dwayne Smith, "Patterns of Discrimination in Assessments of the Death Penalty: The Case of Louisiana," *Journal of Criminal Justice* 15 (1987): 279–86; S. Gross and R. Mauro, "Patterns of Death: An Analysis of Racial Disparities in Capital Sentencing and Homicide Victimization," *Stanford Law Review* 37 (1984): 27–153.

147. William Bowers and Glenn Pierce, "Deterrence or Brutalization: What Is the Effect of Executions?" *Crime and Delinquency* 26 (1980): 453–84.

148. Joseph Schumacher, "An International Look at the Death Penalty," *International Journal of Comparative and Applied Criminal Justice* 14 (1990): 307–15.

149. Richard Berk, Robert Weiss, and Jack Boger, "Chance and the Death Penalty," *Law and Society Review* 27 (1993): 89–108. For an opposing view, see Raymond Paternoster, "Assessing Capriciousness in Capital Cases," *Law and Society Review* 27 (1993): 111–22.

150. *Furman v. Georgia,* 408 U.S. 238, 92 S.Ct. 2726, 33 L.Ed.2d 346 (1972).

151. *Gregg v. Georgia,* 428 U.S. 153, 96 S.Ct. 2909, 49 L.Ed.2d 859 (1976).

152. *Jurek v. Texas,* 428 U.S. 262, 96 S.Ct. 2950, 49 L.Ed.2d 929 (1976).

153. *Proffitt v. Florida,* 428 U.S. 325, 96 S.Ct. 3001, 49 L.Ed.2d 944 (1976).

154. *Witherspoon v. Illinois,* 391 U.S. 510 (1968); *Wainwright v. Witt,* 469 U.S. 412 (1985).

155. *Tison v. Arizona,* 481 U.S. 137 (1987).

156. *McCleskey v. Kemp,* 106 S.Ct. 1331 (1986).

157. *Stanford v. Kentucky* and *Wilkins v. Missouri,* 109 S.Ct. 2969 (1989).

158. *McCleskey v. Zant,* 49 Cr.L. 2031 (1991).

Corrections

INTRODUCTION

When a person is convicted for a criminal offense, society exercises the right to punish or *correct* his or her behavior. Equating crime and punishment is certainly not a new practice. Criminal offenders have been punished by governmental authorities throughout recorded history. Over the centuries, there has been significant debate as to why people should be punished and what type of punishment is most appropriate to correct, treat, or deter criminal offenders. The style and purpose of criminal correction have gone through many stages and have featured a variety of penal sanctions.

The correctional system provides many services in programs differentiated by level of security and intrusiveness. The least secure and intrusive programs involve community supervision by probation officers. Some offenders who need more secure treatment or control are placed under house arrest or held in community correctional centers. Those who require the most secure settings are placed in an incarceration facility. Felons are usually incarcerated in a state or federal *prison;* misdemeanants are housed in county *jails* or reformatories.

The entire correctional system has been a source of great controversy. Probation is viewed as a slap on the wrist for people convicted of serious crimes. Jails have been the scene of suicides and rapes. Prisons have been viewed as warehouses that, far from helping rehabilitate inmates, are places of violence and degradation. There is evidence that prison populations are highest in states with large minority populations, reinforcing conflict theory's charge that the justice system is biased.[1] Some critics call for tearing down prisons, whereas others argue that new ones should be built and sentences lengthened. They fear the inmate population, whom they regard as dangerous and unrepentant. Their fears may be valid: at last count, a total of 314 federal, state, and local correctional officers have been killed in the line of duty by inmates, including 306 men and 8 women.[2]

One goal of the correctional system is to provide punishment strict enough to convince offenders that the pains of correctional treatment outweigh any possible benefit of criminal gain. The punishment goal of corrections may interfere with its efforts to treat and rehabilitate criminals.

This chapter considers some of the basic elements of U.S. correctional treatment. First the history of corrections is reviewed to show how our current system evolved. Then modern correctional institutions are explored, including such issues as penal institutions, the prisoner's social world, correctional treatment, and prisoners' rights.

HISTORY OF PUNISHMENT AND CORRECTIONS

Throughout history, punishment has been present in all major institutions.[3] The punishment of criminals has undergone many noteworthy changes, reflecting custom, economic conditions, and religious and political ideals.[4]

In ancient times, the most common state-administered punishment was banishment or exile. Only slaves were commonly subject to harsh physical punishment for their misdeeds. In Rome, for example, the only crime for which capital punishment could be administered was *furtum manifestum*—a thief caught in the act was executed on the spot. More common were economic sanctions and fines, levied for such crimes as assault on a slave, arson, or housebreaking.

In both ancient Greece and Rome, interpersonal violence, even murder, was viewed as a private matter. Neither Greek nor Roman (until quite late in its history) state laws punished violent crime. Execution of an offender was a prerogative of the deceased's family.

The Middle Ages

Little law or governmental control existed during the early Middle Ages (fifth century to eleventh century A.D.). Offenses were settled by blood feuds between the families of the injured parties. When possible, the Roman custom of settling disputes by fine or an exchange of property was adopted as a means of resolving interpersonal conflicts with a minimum of bloodshed.

CONNECTIONS

The earliest legal codes still exist. As noted in Chapter 2, the formation of laws can be traced to early Hebraic and Sumerian societies. The first criminal punishments are contained in these codes.

After the eleventh century, during the feudal period, forfeiture of land and property was common punishment for people who violated law and customs or who failed in the feudal obligations to their lord. The word *felony* comes from the twelfth century, when the term *felonia* referred to a breach of faith with one's feudal lord.

During this period, the main emphasis of criminal law and punishment lay in maintaining public order.[5] If in the heat of passion or in a state of intoxication, a person severely injured or killed a neighbor, free men in the area would gather to pronounce judgment and make the culprit do penance or make a payment to the injured party called *wergild*.

CONNECTIONS

The origins of wergild and the development of money damages are discussed more fully in Chapter 2.

The purpose of the wergild was to pacify the injured party and ensure that the conflict would not develop into a blood feud and anarchy. The inability of lower-class offenders to pay a fine led to the development of corporal punishment, such as whipping or branding, as a substitute penalty.

By the fifteenth century, changing social conditions influenced the relationship between crime and punishment. First the population of England and Europe began to increase after a century of decimation by constant warfare and plague. At the same time the developing commercial system caused large tracts of agricultural fields to be converted to grazing lands. Soon unemployed peasants and landless noblemen began flocking to newly developing urban centers, such as London and Paris, or taking to the roads as highwaymen, beggars, or vagabonds.

The later Middle Ages also saw the rise of strong monarchs, such as Henry VIII and Elizabeth I of England, who were determined to keep a powerful grip on their realm. The administration of the "King's Peace" under the shire reeve and constable became stronger.

These developments led to the increased use of **capital** and **corporal punishment** to control the criminal poor. Whereas the wealthy could buy their way out of punishment and into exile, the poor were executed and mutilated at ever-increasing rates. It is estimated that 72,000 thieves were hanged during the reign of Henry VIII alone.[6] Execution, banishment, mutilation, branding, and flogging were used on a wide range of offenders, from murderers and robbers to vagrants and gypsies. Punishments became unmatched in their cruelty, featuring a gruesome variety of physical tortures. Also during this period, punishment became a public spectacle, presumably so the sadistic sanctions would act as a deterrent. But the variety and imagination of the tortures inflicted on even minor criminals before their death suggest that sadism and spectacle were more important than any presumed deterrent effect.

Although criminologists generally view the rise of the prison as an eighteenth-century phenomenon, Marvin Wolfgang has written about Le Stinche, a prison in Florence, Italy, which was used to punish offenders as early as 1301. Prisoners were enclosed in separate cells and classified on the basis of gender, age, mental state, and crime seriousness. Furloughs and conditional release were permitted, and perhaps for the first time, a period of incarceration replaced corporal punishment for some offenses. Le Stinche existed for 500 years, but relatively little is known about its administration or whether this early example of incarceration is unique to Florence.[7]

Punishment in the Seventeenth and Eighteenth Centuries

By the end of the sixteenth century, the rise of the city and overseas colonization provided tremendous markets for manufactured goods. In England and France, population growth was checked by constant warfare and internal disturbances. Labor was scarce in many manufacturing areas of England, Germany, and Holland. The Thirty Years War in Germany and the constant warfare among England, France, and Spain helped drain the population.

The punishment of criminals changed to meet the demands created by these social conditions. Instead of the wholesale use of capital and corporal punishment, many offenders were forced to labor for their crimes. **Poor laws** developed in the early seventeenth century required that the poor, vagrants, and vagabonds be put to work in public or private enterprise. Houses of correction were developed to make it convenient for petty law violators to be assigned to work details. Many convicted offenders were pressed into sea duty as galley slaves, a fate considered so loathsome that many convicts mutilated themselves rather than submit to it.

The constant labor shortage in the colonies also prompted the authorities to transport convicts overseas. In England the Vagrancy Act of 1597 legalized deportation for the first time. An Order in Council of 1617 granted a reprieve and stay of execution to people convicted of robbery and other felonies who were strong enough to be employed overseas. Similar measures were used in France and Italy to recruit galley slaves and workers.

Transportation to the colonies became popular; it supplied labor, cost little, and was actually profitable for the government because manufacturers and plantation owners paid for convicts' services. The Old Bailey Court in London supplied at least 10,000 convicts between 1717 and 1775.[8] Convicts would serve a period as workers and then become free again.

Transportation to the colonies waned as a method of punishment with the increase in colonial population, the further development of the land, and the increasing importation of African slaves in the eighteenth century. The American Revolution ended transportation of felons to North America; the remaining areas used were Australia, New Zealand, and African colonies.

Corrections in the Late Eighteenth and Nineteenth Centuries

Between the American Revolution in 1776 and the first decades of the nineteenth century, the population of Europe and America increased rapidly. The gulf between poor workers and wealthy landowners and merchants widened. The crime rate rose significantly, prompting a return to physical punishment and the increased use of the death penalty. During the last part of the eighteenth century, 350 types of crime in England were punishable by death.[9] Although many people sentenced to death for trivial offenses were spared the gallows, there is little question that the use of capital punishment rose significantly between 1750 and 1800.[10]

CONNECTIONS

Prompted by these excesses, legal philosophers, such as Jeremy Bentham and Cesare Beccaria, argued that physical punishment should be replaced by periods of confinement and incapacitation in prison. See Chapter 1 for more on the history of penal philosophy.

Correctional reform in the United States was first instituted in Pennsylvania under the leadership of William Penn.[11] At the end of the seventeenth century, Penn revised Pennsylvania's criminal code to forbid torture and the capricious use of mutilation and physical punishment. These devices were replaced by the penalties of imprisonment at hard labor, moderate flogging, fines, and forfeiture of property. All lands and goods belonging to felons were used to make restitution to the victims of crimes, with restitution limited to twice the value of the damages. Felons who owned no property were required by law to labor in the prison workhouse until the victim was compensated.

Penn ordered that a new type of institution be built to replace the widely used public forms of punishment — stocks, pillories, the gallows, and the branding iron. Each county was instructed to build a house of corrections similar to today's jails. These measures remained in effect until Penn's death in 1718, when the penal code reverted to its earlier emphasis on open public punishment and harsh brutality.

In 1776 postrevolutionary Pennsylvania again adopted William Penn's code, and in 1787 a group of Quakers led by Dr. Benjamin Rush formed the Philadelphia Society for Alleviating the Miseries of Public Prisons. The aim of the society was to bring humane and orderly treatment to the growing penal system. The Quakers' influence on the legislature resulted in limiting the use of the death penalty to cases involving treason, murder, rape, and arson.

Under pressure from the Quakers, the Pennsylvania Legislature in 1790 called for the renovation of the prison system. The ultimate result was the creation of Philadelphia's **Walnut Street Prison.** At this institution, most prisoners were placed in solitary cells, where they remained in isolation and did not have the right to work.[12] Quarters that contained the solitary or separate cells were called the *penitentiary house,* as was already the custom in England.

The new Pennsylvania prison system took credit for a rapid decrease in the crime rate — from 131 convictions in 1789 to 45 in 1793.[13] The prison became known as a school for reform. The Walnut Street Prison's equitable conditions were credited with reducing escapes to none in the first four years of its existence (except for 14 on opening day).

However, the Walnut Street Prison was not a total success. Overcrowding undermined the goal of solitary confinement of serious offenders, and soon more than one inmate was placed in each cell. Despite these difficulties, similar institutions were erected in New York (Newgate in 1791), New Jersey (Trenton in 1798), Virginia (1800), Massachusetts (Castle Island in 1785), and Kentucky (1800). Alexis Durham III has described the Newgate prison of Connecticut, which was constructed in an old copper mine in 1773, as the first "prison" in America.[14]

The Auburn System   In the early 1800s both the Pennsylvania and New York prison systems were experiencing difficulties maintaining the ever-increasing numbers of convicted criminals. Initially administrators dealt with the problem by increasing the use of pardons, relaxing prison discipline, and limiting supervision.

In 1816 New York built a new prison at Auburn, hoping to alleviate some of the overcrowding at Newgate. The Auburn prison design became known as the *tier system* because cells were built vertically on five floors of the structure. It was sometimes also referred to as the *congregate system* because most prisoners ate and worked in groups. In 1819 construction was started on a wing of solitary cells to house unruly prisoners. Three classes of prisoners were then created: one group remained continually in solitary confinement as a result of breaches of prison discipline; the second group was allowed labor as an occasional form of recreation; and the third and largest class worked and ate together during the days and went into seclusion only at night.

The philosophy of the **Auburn system** was crime prevention through fear of punishment and silent confinement. The worst felons were cut off from all contact with other prisoners; and although they were treated and fed relatively well, they had no hope of pardon to relieve their isolation. For a time, some of the worst convicts were forced to remain totally alone and silent during the entire day; this practice caused many prisoners to have mental breakdowns, resulting in many suicides and self-mutilations. This practice was abolished in 1823.[15]

The combination of silence and solitude as a method of punishment was not abandoned easily. Prison officials sought to overcome the side effects of total isolation while maintaining the penitentiary system. The solution Auburn adopted was to keep convicts in separate cells at night but allow them to work together during the day under enforced silence. Hard work and silence became the foundation of the Auburn system wherever it was adopted. Silence was the key to prison discipline; it prevented the formulation of escape plans, averted plots and riots, and allowed prisoners to contemplate their infractions.

When discipline was breached in the Auburn system, punishment was applied in the form of a rawhide whip on the inmate's back. Immediate and effective, Auburn discipline was so successful that when 100 inmates were chosen to build the famous Sing-Sing prison in 1825, not one dared escape, although they were housed in an open field with only minimal supervision.[16]

The New Pennsylvania System   In 1818 Pennsylvania took the radical step of establishing a prison that placed each inmate in a single cell with no work to do. Classifications were abolished because each cell was intended as a miniature prison that would prevent the inmates from contaminating one another.

The new Pennsylvania prison, called the Western Penitentiary, had an unusual architectural design. It was built in a semicircle, with the cells positioned along its circumference. Built back-to-back, some cells faced the boundary wall while others faced the internal area of the circle. Its inmates were kept in solitary confinement almost constantly, being allowed about an hour a day for exercise. In 1820 a second, similar penitentiary using the isolate system was built in Philadelphia and called the Eastern Penitentiary.

The supporters of the Pennsylvania system believed that the penitentiary was truly a place to do penance. By advocating totally removing the sinner from society and allowing the prisoner a period of isolation in which to reflect alone upon the evils of crime, the supporters of the Pennsylvania system reflected the influence of religious philosophy on corrections. In fact, its advocates believed that solitary confinement (with in-cell labor as a recreation) would eventually make working so attractive that upon release the inmate would be well suited to resume a productive existence in society. The Pennsylvania system eliminated the need for large numbers of guards or disciplinary measures. Isolated from each other, inmates could not plan escapes or collectively break rules. When discipline was a problem, whips and iron gags were used (iron gags were jammed in inmates' mouths so they could not speak, causing great discomfort).

The congregate system eventually prevailed, however, and spread throughout the United States; many of its features are still used today. Its innovations included congregate working conditions, the use of solitary confinement to punish unruly inmates, military regimentation, and discipline. In Auburn-like institutions, prisoners were marched from place to place; their time was regulated by bells telling them to sleep, wake up, and work. The system was so like the military that many of its early administrators were recruited from the armed services.

Although the prison was viewed as an improvement over capital and corporal punishment, it quickly became the scene of depressed conditions; inmates were treated harshly and routinely whipped and tortured. As historian Samuel Walker notes,

> Prison brutality flourished. It was ironic that the prison had been devised as a more humane alternative to corporal and capital punishment. Instead, it simply moved corporal punishment indoors where, hidden from public view, it became even more savage.[17]

Yet in the midst of such savagery some inmates were able to adjust to institutional living and even improve their lives through prison-administered literacy programs.[18]

Post–Civil War Developments The prison of the late nineteenth century was remarkably similar to that of today. The congregate system was adopted in all states except Pennsylvania. Prisons experienced overcrowding, and the single-cell principle was often ignored. The prison, like the police department, became the scene of political intrigue and efforts by political administrators to control the hiring of personnel and dispensing of patronage.

Prison industry developed and became the predominant theme around which institutions were organized. Some prisons used the **contract system,** in which officials sold the labor of inmates to private businesses. Sometimes the contractor supervised the inmates inside the prison itself. Under the **convict-lease system,** the state leased its prisoners to a business for a fixed annual fee and gave up supervision and control. Finally, the **state account system** had prisoners produce goods in prison for state use.[19]

The development of prison industry quickly led to abuse of inmates, who were forced to work for almost no wages, and to profiteering by dishonest administrators and businessmen. During the Civil War era, prisons were major manufacturers of clothes, shoes, boots, furniture, and the like. During the 1880s, opposition by trade unions sparked restrictions on interstate commerce in prison goods and ended their profitability.

There were also reforms in prison operations. **Z. R. Brockway,** warden at the Elmira Reformatory in New York, advocated individualized treatment, indeterminate sentences, and parole. The reformatory program initiated by Brockway included elementary education for illiterates, designated library hours, lectures by local college faculty members, and a group of vocational training shops. The cost to the state of the institution's operations was to be held to a minimum. Although Brockway proclaimed Elmira an ideal reformatory, his actual achievements were limited. The greatest significance of his contribution was the injection of a degree of humanitarianism into the industrial prisons of that day. Although many institutions were constructed across the country and labeled reformatories as a result of the Elmira model, most of them continued to be industrially oriented.[20]

Corrections in the Twentieth Century

The early twentieth century was a time of contrasts in the U.S. prison system.[21] At one extreme were those who advocated reform, such as the Mutual Welfare League, led by Thomas Mott Osborne. Prison reform groups proposed better treatment for inmates, an end to harsh corporal punishment, and the creation of meaningful prison industries and educational programs. Reformers argued that prisoners should not be isolated from society; rather, the best elements of society—education, religion, meaningful work, self-governance—should be brought to the prison. Osborne even spent one week in New York's notorious Sing-Sing Prison to learn about its conditions firsthand.

Opposed to the reformers were conservative prison administrators and state officials, who believed that stern discipline was needed to control dangerous prison inmates. They continued the time-honored system of regimentation. Although the whip was eventually abolished, solitary confinement in dark, bare cells became a common penal practice.

In time, some of the more rigid prison rules gave way to liberal reform. By the mid-1930s few prisons required inmates to wear the red-and-white-striped convict suit and substituted nondescript gray uniforms. The code of silence ended, as did the lockstep shuffle. Prisoners were allowed to mingle and exercise an hour or two each day.[22] Movies and radio appeared in the prisons in the 1930s. Visiting policies and mail privileges were liberalized.

A more important trend was the development of specialized prisons designed to treat particular types of offenders. For example, in New York, the prisons at Clinton and Auburn were viewed as industrial facilities for hard-core inmates, Great Meadow as an agricultural center to house nondangerous offenders, and Dannemora as a facility for the criminally insane. In California, San Quentin housed inmates considered salvageable by correctional authorities, whereas Folsom was reserved for hard-core offenders.[23]

Prison industry also evolved. Opposition by organized labor helped end the convict-lease system and forced inmate labor. Although some vestiges of private prison industry existed into the 1920s, most convict labor was devoted to state-use items, such as license plates and laundry.

Despite these changes and reforms, the prison in the mid-twentieth century remained a destructive total institution. Although some aspects of inmate life improved, severe discipline, harsh rules, and solitary confinement were the way of life in prison.

Prisoner in the Alfred Hughes prison in Texas. State and federal prisons are used to incarcerate felons for extended periods of time and more than one million people are currently behind bars.

The Modern Era

The modern era has witnessed change and turmoil in the nation's correctional system. Three trends stand out. First, between 1960 and 1980, a great deal of litigation was brought by inmates seeking greater rights and privileges. State and federal court rulings gave inmates rights to freedom of religion and speech, medical care, due process, and proper living conditions. Since 1980, the "prisoners' rights" movement has slowed as judicial activism waned during the Reagan–Bush era.

Second, violence within the correctional system became a national scandal. Well-publicized riots at New York's Attica Prison and the New Mexico State Penitentiary have drawn attention to the potential for death and destruction that lurks in every prison. One reaction has been to improve conditions and provide innovative programs that give inmates a voice in running the institution. Another has been to tighten discipline and build maximum-security prisons to control dangerous offenders.

Third, the alleged failure of correctional rehabilitation has prompted many penologists to reconsider the purpose of incapacitating criminals. Today it is more common to view the correctional system as a mechanism for control and punishment than as a device for rehabilitation and reform.

The inability of the prison to reduce recidivism has prompted the development of alternatives to incarceration, including diversion, restitution, and community-based corrections. The nation's correctional policy seems to keep as many nonthreatening offenders out of the correctional system as possible by means of community-based programs and, conversely, to incarcerate dangerous, violent offenders for long periods.[24] Unfortunately, despite the development of alternatives to incarceration, the number of people under lock and key has skyrocketed.

Corrections Today Correctional treatment can be divided today into community-based programs and secure confinement. Community-based corrections include **probation,** which involves supervision under the control of the sentencing court, and an array of **intermediate sanctions,** which provide greater supervision and treatment than traditional probation but are less intrusive than incarceration.

Treatment in the community is viewed as a viable alternative to traditional correctional practices.[25] First, it is significantly less expensive to supervise inmates in the community than to house them in secure institutional facilities. Second, community-based corrections are necessary if the prison system is not to be overwhelmed by an influx of offenders. Third, community-based treatment is designed so that first-time or non-serious offenders can avoid the stigma and pain of imprisonment and be rehabilitated in the community.

In secure confinement, the jail houses misdemeanants (and some felons) serving their sentences, as well as felons and misdemeanants awaiting trial who have not been released on bail. State and federal prisons incarcerate felons for extended periods. Parole and aftercare agencies supervise prisoners who have been given early release from their sentences. Although parolees are actually in the community, parole is usually considered both organizationally and philosophically part of the secure correctional system.

These institutions are discussed in the next sections.

PROBATION

Probation usually involves the suspension of the offender's sentence in return for the promise of good behavior in the community under the supervision of the probation department. It usually replaces a term in an institution, although minors can be placed on probation without the threat of detention. In some cases the offender is first sentenced to a prison term, and then the sentence is suspended and the defendant placed on probation. In others, the imposition of a prison sentence is delayed or suspended while the offender is put on probation. Probation is not limited to minor or petty criminals. As Table 18.1 shows, a significant proportion of people convicted of felony offenses receive probation.

As practiced in all 50 states and by the federal government, probation implies a contract between the court and the offender in which the former promises to hold a prison term in abeyance while the latter promises to adhere to a set of rules or conditions required by the court. If the rules are violated, and especially if the probationer commits another criminal offense, probation may be **revoked;** this means that the contract is terminated and the original sentence enforced. If an offender on probation commits a second offense that is more severe than the first, he or she may be indicted, tried, and sentenced on that second offense. Probation may also be revoked simply because its rules and conditions have not been met, even if the offender has not committed another crime. In a series of cases, most importantly *Gagnon v. Scarpelli*,[26] the Supreme Court ruled that before probation can be revoked, the offender must (1) be given a hearing before the sentencing court and (2) be provided with counsel if there is a substantial reason for him or her to require legal assistance.

Each probationary sentence is for a fixed period, depending on the seriousness of the offense and the statutory law of the jurisdiction. Probation is considered served when the offender fulfills the conditions set by the court for that period; after that, he or she can live without interference from the state.

Probationary Sentences

Probationary sentences may be granted by state and federal district courts and state superior (felony) courts. Probation has become an accepted, widely used sentence for adult felons and misdemeanants and juvenile delinquents.

In most jurisdictions, juries can recommend probation, but the judge has the final say in the matter. In nonjury trials, probation is granted solely by judicial mandate. Except where state law expressly prohibits a community supervision option, almost all offenders are eligible for probation, even those convicted of violent felonies, such as rape and homicide. Only mandatory sentencing laws that require incarceration preclude the probation option.

The term of the probationary sentence may extend to the limit of the suspended prison term. Misdemeanor probation usually extends for the entire period of the jail sentence. Felony probationary periods are likely to be shorter than the prison sentences would have been.

Probation Organizations

About 2,000 agencies nationwide list adult probation as their major function; at last count there were more than 3,200,000 adults under federal, state, or local jurisdiction.[27] Half of all offenders on probation had been convicted of a felony; one-quarter were on probation for a misdemeanor. One in every six probationers had been convicted of driving while intoxicated.

During any given year, about 1.5 million people are placed on probation and somewhat fewer (1.3 million) complete their probationary sentences; this imbalance has resulted in a steadily increasing probation population. In 1980, 1.1 million people were on probation; the number of probationers has almost tripled in 15 years. In all, almost two-thirds of the correctional population is on probation.

Table 18.1 Percentage of Serious Felons Receiving Probation-Only Sentences									
MURDER	**RAPE**	**ROBBERY**	**ASSAULT**	**BURGLARY**	**LARCENY**	**FRAUD**	**DRUG POSSESSION**	**DRUG DEALING**	**WEAPONS**
3%	12%	12%	25%	25%	34%	40%	34%	29%	31%

Source: Patrick Langan and Jodi Brown, *Felony Sentences in State Courts, 1994* (Washington, D.C: Bureau of Justice Statistics, 1998), p. 3.

Most probation agencies function at the state level; the remainder are organized at the county or municipal level. About 30 states combine probation and parole supervision into a single state agency.[28]

There are arguments for both placing probation services under the supervision of individual courts and creating statewide agencies. Local supervision makes probation more responsive to court discretion and helps judges get better information on the effectiveness of their decisions. Because the bulk of the probation department's work is in the local courts, it seems appropriate that the agencies should be organized at the county level.

Those who advocate large state probation agencies argue that probation is a correctional service and therefore should be part of the executive level of government.[29] Larger agencies can coordinate programs and staff, establish training programs, and distribute funds.

Probation Services

After a person is convicted of a crime, the probation department investigates the case to determine the factors related to the criminality of the offender. Based on this presentence investigation, the department recommends to the sentencing judge whether the offender is eligible for community release. In the event the offender is placed on probation, the investigation findings will be used as the basis for treatment and supervision. If the offender is placed on probation, the department diagnoses his or her personality and treatment needs; this is referred to as **offender classification.** Based on this evaluation, offenders classified as minimal risks will be given little supervision, perhaps a monthly phone call or visit, whereas those classified as high risks will receive close supervision and intensive care and treatment. Developing accurate risk classification methods is a major goal of probation.[30] Some studies show these methods to be effective predictors of probationer success in the community.[31]

Probation officers once commonly supervised treatment. Today clients are more commonly placed in community mental health, substance abuse, and family counseling clinics. There has also been an explosion of privately run community-based treatment programs that provide comprehensive for-profit correctional treatment. Probation officers can mandate that offenders attend biweekly treatment sessions, attend support groups, report for polygraph testing and urinalysis, and complete homework assignments.[32]

The treatment function is a product of both the investigative and the diagnostic aspects of probation. A probation officer who discovers that a client has a drinking problem may help find a detoxification center willing to accept the case; a chronically underemployed offender may be placed with a job counseling

center. Or, in the case of juvenile delinquency, a probation officer may work with teachers and other school officials to help a young offender stay in school. Although outside treatment placements are the norm, it is not unknown for probation officers to provide direct treatment to offenders who have substance abuse problems in communities that lack adequate, effective community-based programs.[33] Probation officers also conduct special programs for clients, such as teaching child-rearing skills to parents of juvenile offenders in their caseloads.[34] Of course, most cases do not (or cannot) receive such individualized treatment; some treatment mechanisms merely involve a yearly phone call to determine whether the offender is maintaining a job or attending school.[35] Regardless of how it is handled, probationers who complete their treatment plans are less likely to recidivate than offenders who fail at treatment.[36]

Probation Rules and Revocation

Each offender granted probation is given a set of rules to guide his or her behavior. Most jurisdictions have a standard set of rules that includes

- Maintaining steady employment
- Making restitution for loss or damage
- Cooperating with the probation officer
- Obeying all laws
- Meeting family responsibilities

Sometimes an individual probationer is given specific rules that relate to his or her particular circumstances, such as the requirement to enroll in a drug treatment program.

If rules are violated, a person's probation may be revoked by the court, and the person either begins serving the sentence or, if he or she has not yet been sentenced, receives a prison sentence from the court. Revocation for violation of probation rules is called a **technical violation;** probation also can be revoked if the offender commits another offense.

A 1991 federally sponsored survey of prison inmates found that there were more than 162,000 probation violators in prison. Of these, 74 percent had been convicted of a new offense and the remaining 26 percent had violated a technical condition.[37] What type of acts caused their probation to be terminated? Most (87 percent) had been arrested for new offenses (but not charged or convicted). Others had tested positive for drug use, failed to report for drug testing or treatment, failed to report for counseling, left their jurisdictions without telling their probation officers, neglected to make restitution payments, made contact with known offenders, or failed to report changes in address.

Success of Probation

How successful is probation? How often do probationers commit new crimes while they are under supervision? Some research studies have found that probation is not as successful as hoped. In an often-cited 1985 study, Joan Petersilia and her colleagues at the Rand Corporation followed the careers of 1,672 California men granted probation for felony offenses.[38] They found that 1,087 (65 percent) were rearrested, 853 (51 percent) were convicted, and 568 (34 percent) were incarcerated. The researchers uncovered the disturbing fact that 75 percent of the new arrests were for serious crimes, including larceny, burglary, and robbery; 18 percent of the probationers were convicted of serious violent crimes. They also found that about 25 percent of felons granted probation had personal and legal characteristics indistinguishable from people put in prison for the same original charges. The Petersilia research was an early indication that felons often qualified for and later failed on probation.

Similarly disturbing results were found in the 1991 federal study of probationers serving prison time after their community sentences had been revoked. The 162,000 probation violators in state prison committed at least 6,400 murders, 7,400 rapes, 10,400 assaults, and 17,000 robberies while under supervision in the community.[39] Unfortunately, these findings are not a fluke. Of the more than 1.6 million probationers released on supervision in 1997 (the most recent data available), 18 percent (211,800) were subsequently incarcerated because of rule violations or new offenses.

CONNECTIONS

Crime control advocates are appalled that so many people are killed and injured by people who have been convicted of crime and then returned once again to the community. They are referred to as *avertable recidivists* because their crimes could have been avoided had they been incarcerated. See Chapter 15 for more on the crime control philosophy.

Although the recidivism rate of probationers seems high, it is lower than the recidivism rate of prison inmates.[40] And some studies have found a lower recidivism rate among particular classes of probationers (such as young, non–drug-using property offenders), indicating that probation may be a relatively effective correctional alternative for large groups of offenders.[41]

Probation remains the sentence of choice in almost half of all felony cases, including 5 percent of murder cases, 14 percent of rapes, and more than half of felony drug cases. Because it costs far less to maintain an offender in the community than in prison, and because prison overcrowding continues, there is constant economic pressure to grant probation to serious felony offenders. Even if probation is no more successful than prison, it costs less and is therefore extremely attractive to policymakers. However, some believe that the risk of probation failure is too high and that judges should think carefully before sentencing felons to probation. This topic is discussed in the Policy and Practice in Criminology feature titled "The Risk of Probation Failure."

INTERMEDIATE SANCTIONS

At a time when overcrowding has produced a crisis in the nation's prison system, alternative sanctions are viewed as a new form of corrections that falls somewhere between probation and incarceration.[42] Alternative sanctions include fines, forfeiture, home confinement, electronic monitoring, intensive probation supervision, restitution, community corrections, and boot camps.

The development of these intermediate sanctions can be tied to a number of different sources. Primary is the need to develop alternatives to prisons, which have proved both ineffective and injurious. Research indicates that about half of all prison inmates are likely to be rearrested and returned to prison, many soon after their release from an institution.[43] High revocation rates indicate that probation alone may not be an effective solution to the prison crowding problem. Therefore, a sanction that falls somewhere between prison and probation might be a more effective alternative to traditional forms of correction.

Intermediate sanctions also meet the need to develop punishments that are fair, equitable, and proportional. It seems unfair to treat both a rapist and a shoplifter with the same type of sentence, considering the differences in their criminal acts. Intermediate sanctions can provide the successive steps for a meaningful "ladder" of scaled punishments outside prison (see Figure 18.1), thereby restoring fairness and equity to nonincarceration sentences.[44] For example, a forger may be ordered to make restitution to the victim, and an abusive husband can be ordered to reside in a community correctional center, whereas a rapist would be sent to state prison. This feature of intermediate sanctions allows judges to fit the punishment to the crime without resorting to a prison sentence. Intermediate sanctions can be designed to be punitive by increasing punishments for people whose serious or repeat crimes make straight probation sentences inappropriate yet for whom prison sentences would be unduly harsh and dysfunctional.[45] In fact, the punitive nature of intermediate sanctions is not lost on offenders, some of whom prefer prison to the new, tougher forms of probation.[46]

The most likely candidates are convicted criminals who would normally be sent to prison but either have a low risk of recidivating or pose little threat to society

Figure 18.1 The Punishment Ladder

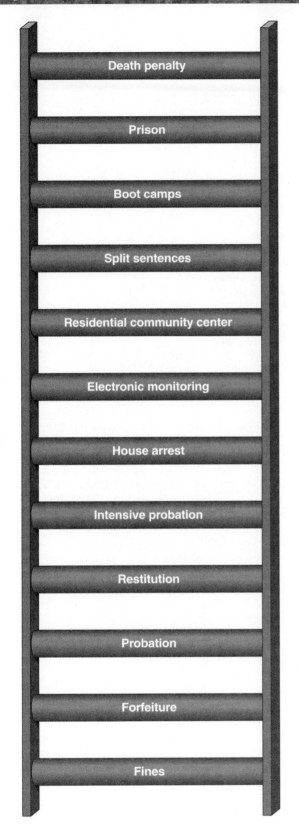

Death penalty

Prison

Boot camps

Split sentences

Residential community center

Electronic monitoring

House arrest

Intensive probation

Restitution

Probation

Forfeiture

Fines

(such as nonviolent property offenders). Used in this sense, intermediate sanctions are a viable solution to the critical problem of prison overcrowding.

The following sections more thoroughly discuss the forms of intermediate sanctions in use.

Fines

Fines are monetary payments imposed on an offender as an intermediate punishment for criminal acts. They are a direct offshoot of the early common-law practice requiring compensation to the victim and the state for criminal acts. Although fines are most commonly used in misdemeanors, they are also frequently employed in felonies where the offender benefited financially. Investor Ivan Boesky paid over $100 million in fines for violating insider stock trading rules; the firm of Drexel, Burnham Lambert paid $650 million in 1988 for securities violations.[47] Fines may be used as a sole sanction or combined with other punishment, such as probation or confinement. Quite commonly judges levy other monetary sanctions along with fines, such as court costs, public defender fees, probation and treatment fees, and victim restitution, to increase the force of the financial punishment.[48]

Some jurisdictions, such as New York City, are experimenting with **day fines,** a concept originated in Europe that gears fines to an offender's net daily income in an effort to make them more equitable. In contrast to the traditional fixed-sum fining system, in which the fine amount is governed principally by the nature of the crime, the day-fine approach tailors the fine amount to the defendant's ability to pay. Thus, for a given crime, the day fine is larger for a high-income offender than for an irregularly employed or low-paid offender. The impact of the fine on each should be approximately equal. Under the traditional approach, a given fine amount could be relatively severe for a low-income offender but trivial for a person of substantial means. A pilot day-fine project conducted on Staten Island demonstrated that a typical American court could implement day fines successfully, substituting day for fixed fines.[49]

Although it is far from certain that fines are an effective sanction, either alone or in combination with other penalties, they remain one of the most commonly used criminal penalties. Research sponsored by the federal government found that lower-court judges impose fines alone or in tandem with other penalties in 86 percent of their cases, whereas superior court judges impose fines in 42 percent of their cases.[50]

Forfeiture

Another financially based alternative sanction is criminal (*in personam*) and civil (*in rem*) **forfeiture.** Both involve the seizure of goods and instrumentalities related

The Risk of Probation Failure

Does the threat of new crimes being committed by probationers present an unacceptable risk to the general public? Is probation a failure? Correctional expert John DiIulio, Jr., thinks so. He claims that a half-dozen studies prove what every veteran police officer knows: most convicts are not petty, nonviolent thieves or mere first-time, low-level drug offenders. Yet most of these hardened criminals are still out on the street. On any given day in America three convicted adult criminals are out on probation or parole for every one in prison, and many of these are indistinguishable (in terms of their violent criminal histories) from those who remain in prison. Dozens of careful studies document that probation and parole are failing to protect the public. Nearly half of all state prisoners committed their latest crimes while out on probation or parole. While formally under supervision in the community, they were responsible for more than 13,000 murders, some 39,000 robberies, and tens of thousands of other crimes. More than a quarter of all felons charged with gun crimes were out on probation and parole. Here, too, what's true for the revolving-door adult system is even more true for the no-fault juvenile system. In many cities, for example, most cases involving violent older teen thugs who get referred to adult court result in probation because they plea-bargain to lighter sentences.

Why are the adult and juvenile probation systems so poor, and what, realistically, can be done to improve them? DiIulio thinks that a big part of the answer is that we spend next to nothing on probation and get about what we pay for. We currently spend about $200 per year on each probationer's supervision. More than 90 percent of probationers are supposed to get substance abuse counseling, pay victim restitution, or meet other requirements, but only about half comply with the terms of their probation. Probation sanctions are not rigorously enforced. But how can these criminals be properly supervised by overworked, underpaid probation officers with scores of cases to manage? Even probationers who are categorized as high-risk offenders receive little direct, face-to-face supervision. Over half of street-level juvenile probation officers earn less than $30,000 a year. In big cities, the probation caseload of serious, violent juvenile cases has increased rapidly. In a national survey, probation officers admitted that their average urban caseloads were at least 25 percent higher than they should be.

To "reinvent probation," DiIulio thinks we will need to reinvest in it. More money, more agents, and closer supervision are just the first phase. Equally important is creative, critical thinking like that in the Boston project that has teamed local probation officers with local police officers. Patrolling the streets together, they have cut crime. Probation officers now work with inner-city clergy on a wide range of crime control and prevention initiatives.

Other probation experts suggest that probation be supplemented with more stringent rules, such as curfews, and closer supervision. Even though such measures can dramatically increase the cost of probation, they would still be far less expensive than incarceration.

CRITICAL THINKING

1. A significant percentage of all criminal acts are committed by avertable recidivists. Considering this, should we try to hold suspected and convicted criminals as long as possible, toughening bail requirements, restricting probation to the most deserving, and eliminating parole?

2. Would the cost of such a get-tough policy outweigh the benefits of a lowered crime rate?

 INFOTRAC COLLEGE EDITION RESEARCH

Community release might be improved by observing what is being done abroad. To find out about the English experience, read:
Judith Rumgay, Mary Brewster. Restructuring probation in England and Wales: lessons from an American experience. *Prison Journal* Sep 76 (1996): p. 331.
Mike Maguire, Pete Raynor. The revival of throughcare: rhetoric and reality in automatic conditional release. *British Journal of Criminology* 37 (1997): p. 1.

Source: John J. DiIulio, Jr., "Reinventing parole and probation," *Brookings Review* 15 (1997): 40–43.

to the commission or outcome of a criminal act. For example, federal law provides that after arresting drug traffickers, the government may seize the boat they used to import the narcotics, the car they used to carry them overland, the warehouse in which they were stored, and the home paid for with drug money; upon conviction, the drug dealers permanently lose ownership of these instrumentalities of crime.

Forfeiture is not a new sanction. During the Middle Ages forfeiture of estate was a mandatory result of most felony convictions. The Crown could seize all of a felon's real and personal property. Forfeiture derived from the common-law concept of "corruption of blood" or "attaint," which prohibited a felon's family from receiving his or her estate. Common law mandated that descendants could not inherit property from a relative who may have attained the property illegally: "(T)he Corruption of Blood stops the Course of Regular Descent, as to Estates, over which the Criminal could have no Power, because he never enjoyed them."[51]

The use of forfeiture was reintroduced in American law with the passage of the Racketeer Influenced and Corrupt Organizations (RICO) and the Continuing Criminal Enterprises acts, both of which allow the seizure of any property derived from illegal enterprises or conspiracies.

Restitution

Another popular intermediate sanction is restitution, which can take the form of requiring convicted defendants to either repay the victims of crime (**monetary restitution**) or serve the community to compensate for their criminal acts (**community service restitution**).[52]

CONNECTIONS

Restitution programs are typically included within the framework of restorative justice because they involve offenders' interaction with their victims, they are community based, and successful restitution allows the offender to be reintegrated into society. For more on restorative justice, see Chapters 9 and 15.

Restitution programs offer convicted offenders a chance to avoid jail or prison sentences or lengthy probation. Restitution may also be used as a diversionary device that allows some offenders to avoid a criminal record altogether. In this instance, a judge continues the case "without a finding" while the defendant completes the restitution order; after the probation department determines that restitution has been made, the case is dismissed.[53]

Because restitution appears to benefit the crime victim, the offender, the criminal justice system, and society as a whole, national interest in the concept has been tremendous. Restitution is inexpensive, avoids stigma, and helps compensate crime victims. Offenders doing community service have worked in schools, hospitals, and nursing homes. Helping them avoid jail can save the public thousands of dollars that would have maintained them in secure institutions, free needed resources, and give the community the feeling that equity has been returned to the justice system.

Does restitution work? Most reviews give it a qualified success rating. It is estimated that almost 90 percent of eligible offenders successfully complete their restitution orders and that restitutioners have equal or lower recidivism rates when compared to control groups of various kinds.[54]

Shock Probation and Split Sentencing

Split sentences and shock probation are alternative sanctions that allow judges to grant offenders community release only after they have sampled prison life.

These sanctions are based on the premise that if offenders are given a taste of incarceration sufficient to "shock" them into law-abiding behavior, they will be reluctant to violate the rules of probation or commit other criminal acts.

In a number of states and in the federal criminal code, a jail term can actually be a condition of probation; this is known as **split sentencing.** Under current federal practices, about 25 percent of all convicted federal offenders receive some form of split sentence, including both prison and jail as a condition of probation.[55]

Another approach, known as **shock probation,** involves resentencing an offender after a short prison stay. The shock comes because the offender originally receives a long maximum sentence but is then eligible for release to community supervision at the discretion of the judge (usually within 90 days of incarceration). About one-third of all probationers in the 14 states that use the program, including Ohio, Kentucky, Idaho, New Jersey, Tennessee, Utah, and Vermont, receive periods of confinement.[56] Evaluations of shock probation have indicated that it is between 78 percent and 91 percent effective.[57]

Shock probation has been praised as a program that limits prison time and allows offenders to be quickly integrated into the community, a mechanism that can maintain family ties, and a way of reducing prison populations and the costs of corrections.[58]

Intensive Probation Supervision

Intensive probation supervision (IPS) programs are another important form of intermediate sanction. IPS programs, which have been implemented in some form in about 45 states, involve small caseloads of 15 to 40 clients who are kept under close watch by probation officers.[59] The primary goal of IPS is *diversion:* without intensive supervision, clients would normally have been sent to already overcrowded prisons or jails.[60] The second goal is *control:* high-risk offenders can stay in the community under much closer security than traditional probation efforts can provide. A third goal is *reintegration:* offenders can maintain community ties and be reoriented toward a more productive life while avoiding the pain of imprisonment.

Who is eligible for IPS? Most programs have admissions criteria based on the nature of the offense and the offender's criminal background. Some programs, such as New Jersey's, exclude violent offenders; others will not consider substance abusers. In contrast, some jurisdictions, such as Massachusetts, do not exclude offenders based on their prior criminal history. About 60 percent of IPS programs exclude offenders who have already violated probation orders or otherwise failed on probation.

The form and structure of IPS programs vary a great deal. The typical model requires clients to meet with their supervisors almost every day. However, a national survey discovered significant variations between programs.[61] Although 16 percent demanded almost daily contacts, 13 percent required only one to four contacts with clients per month. There are also significant differences in the length and types of contacts. For example, most IPS programs are divided into treatment phases, with the number of contacts diminishing as the client progresses between program stages. In some programs the most intensive stage, in which clients are seen daily, lasts almost six months; in others daily contact is terminated after 90 days. Some programs demand face-to-face contacts at home, at work, or in the probation office, whereas others rely on telephone contacts, curfew checks, or collateral contacts (with family, friends or employers); most employ routine drug testing.[62]

Despite its promise, the failure rate in IPS caseloads is quite high, approaching 50 percent.[63] Younger offenders who commit petty crimes are the most likely to fail on IPS; ironically, people with these characteristics are the most likely to be included in IPS programs.[64] It is possible that closer supervision "produces" failures because supervisors are better able to detect technical and legal violations. Continuous drug testing alone should produce a higher failure rate among IPS clients than traditional probationers.

These failure rates seem high, but IPS is designed for clients who have more serious prior records and histories of drug abuse than regular probationers. However, in an important analysis of IPS in three California counties, Joan Petersilia found that IPS clients were actually less dangerous than those sent to prison and just as likely to recidivate as clients in traditional probation caseloads.[65] IPS is a waste of taxpayers' money if it works no better than traditional probation while serving a similar clientele.

Home Confinement/Electronic Monitoring

A number of states, including Florida, Oklahoma, Oregon, Kentucky, and California, have developed **home confinement** (HC) programs (also called *house arrest* or *home detention*) as an intermediate sanction. The HC concept requires convicted offenders to spend extended periods in their own homes as an alternative to incarceration. For example, an individual convicted of drunk driving might be sentenced to spend the period between 6 P.M. Friday and 8 A.M. Monday and every weekday after 5:30 P.M. in his or her home for the next six months. Current estimates indicate that as many as 10,000 people are placed under HC yearly.[66]

Like IPS programs, there is a great deal of variation in HC initiatives: some are administered by probation departments, whereas others are simply judicial sentences monitored by *surveillance officers;* some check clients 10 or more times a month, whereas others make only a few curfew checks; some use 24-hour confinement, whereas others allow offenders to attend work or school. Regardless of the model used, house arrest programs are designed to be more punitive than IPS and

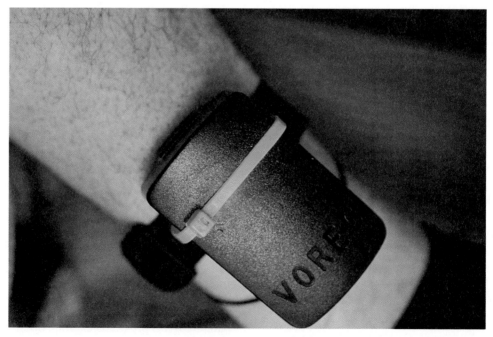

Electronically monitored offenders wear devices attached to their ankles, to their wrists, or around their necks that send signals back to a control office. Active systems constantly monitor the offender by continuously sending a signal back to the central office. Passive systems usually involve random phone calls generated by computers to which the offender has to respond within a particular time.

Figure 18.2 Key Decision Points Where Electronic Monitoring Programs Are Used

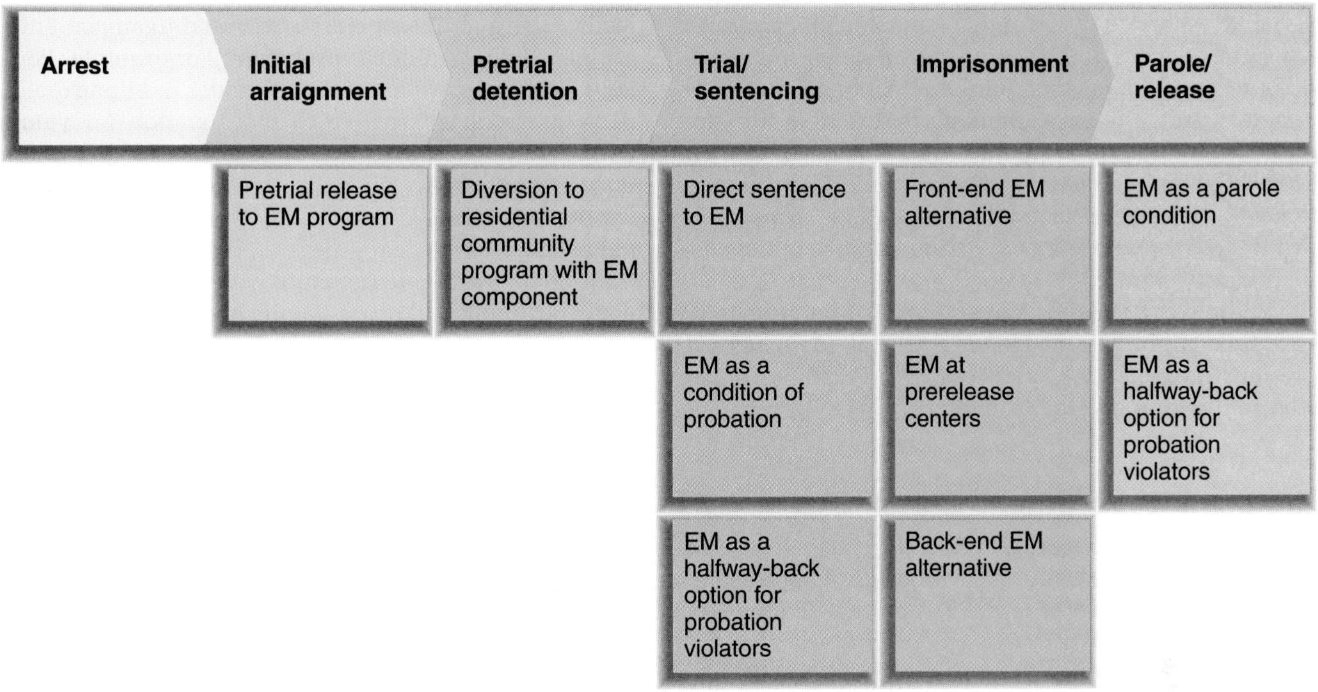

Arrest	Initial arraignment	Pretrial detention	Trial/ sentencing	Imprisonment	Parole/ release
	Pretrial release to EM program	Diversion to residential community program with EM component	Direct sentence to EM	Front-end EM alternative	EM as a parole condition
			EM as a condition of probation	EM at prerelease centers	EM as a halfway-back option for probation violators
			EM as a halfway-back option for probation violators	Back-end EM alternative	

Source: James Byrne, Arthur Lurigio, and Christopher Baird, *The Effectiveness of the New Intensive Supervision Programs, Research in Corrections Series*, vol. 2, no. 2 (preliminary unpublished draft; Washington, D.C.: National Institute of Corrections, 1989), p. 8.

are considered a "last chance" before prison: if you are caught violating a house arrest order, the next logical stop is a secure correctional facility.[67]

As yet, no definitive data indicates that HC effectively deters crime, nor is there sufficient evidence to conclude that it lowers recidivism rates. Nonetheless, considering its cost advantages and the overcrowded status of prisons and jails, it is evident that house arrest will continue to grow in the new millenium.

For house arrest to work, sentencing authorities must be assured that arrestees are actually at home during their assigned times. Random calls and visits are one way to check on compliance with house arrest orders. However, a more advanced method of control has been the introduction of **electronic monitoring** (EM) devices to manage offender obedience to home confinement orders. Electronically monitored offenders wear devices attached to their ankles, wrists, or necks that send signals back to a control office. Two basic types of systems are used: active and passive. *Active systems* constantly monitor the offender by continuously sending a signal back to the central office. If the offender leaves his or her home at an unauthorized time, the signal is broken and the "failure" recorded. In some cases the control officer is automatically notified electronically through a beeper. In contrast, *passive systems* usually involve random phone calls generated by computers to which the offender has to respond within a

particular time (such as 30 seconds). Some passive systems require the offender to place the monitoring device into a verifier box, which then sends a signal back to the control computer; another approach is to have the arrestee repeat words that are analyzed by a voice verifier. Most electronic surveillance systems use telephone lines, but some employ radio transmitters that receive a signal from a device worn by the offender and relay it back to a computer monitoring system.

Growth in the number of electronically monitored offenders has been explosive. Up to 1 million people may eventually be monitored electronically in the United States.[68] EM is being hailed as one of the most important developments in correctional policy.[69] It has the benefits of relatively low cost and high security while at the same time helping offenders avoid imprisonment in overcrowded, dangerous state facilities. Electronic monitoring is capital- rather than labor-intensive. Because offenders are monitored by computers, an initial investment in hardware rules out the need for hiring many more supervisory officers to handle large numbers of clients. It can also be used at many stages of the justice process, including at the front end as a condition of pretrial release and at the back end as part of parole (see Figure 18.2).

A general review of EM programs indicates that recidivism rates are lower than recorded for comparable groups of probationers or parolees.[70] There are variations in the success rates of programs, and EM may be more effective with some offenders than others and at certain stages of the justice process than at others. EM seems to work much more efficiently with convicted offenders than as a pretrial detention; juveniles respond better than adults.[71] Among those convicted, serious felony offenders, substance abusers, and repeat offenders are the most likely to fail on EM.[72] EM may effectively reduce recidivism among targeted groups of nonviolent offenders, especially drunk drivers, whose incarceration helps clog the correctional system.[73]

Although EM holds the promise of being a low-cost, less painful alternative to incarceration, to some it presents the potential for excessive government intrusion in the lives of American citizens.[74]

Residential Community Corrections

A more secure intermediate sanction is a sentence to a residential community corrections (RCC) program. These programs have been defined by the National Institute of Corrections as

> a freestanding nonsecure building that is not part of a prison or jail and houses pre-trial and adjudicated adults. The residents regularly depart to work, to attend school, and/or participate in community corrections activities and programs.[75]

The traditional role of community corrections was to provide a nonsecure "halfway house" environment designed to reintegrate soon-to-be-paroled prison inmates into the community. Inmates spend the last few months of their sentences in halfway houses acquiring suitable employment, building up cash reserves, obtaining apartments, and developing job-related wardrobes. These facilities often look like residential homes because many were originally private residences. In urban centers, small apartment buildings have been used to house clients. Usually these facilities have a central treatment theme — such as group therapy or reality therapy — for rehabilitating and reintegrating clients. Another popular approach in community-based corrections is the use of ex-offenders as staff members. These individuals have experienced making the transition between the closed institution and society and can be invaluable in helping residents overcome the many hurdles to proper readjustment. Clients learn how to reestablish family and friendship ties, and the shock of sudden reentry into society is considerably reduced.

The traditional concept of community corrections has expanded recently. Today the community correctional facility provides intermediate sanctions as well as a prerelease center for those about to be paroled from prison. For example, RCC has been used as a direct sentencing option for judges who believe particular offenders need a correctional alternative halfway between traditional probation and a stay in prison. Placement in a RCC center can be used as a condition of probation for offenders who need a nonsecure community facility that provides a more structured treatment environment than traditional probation. For example, Portland House, a private residential center in Minneapolis, operates as an alternative to incarceration for young adult felony offenders. The 25 residents receive group therapy and regular financial, vocational, educational, family, and personal counseling. Residents may earn a high-school equivalency degree. With funds withheld from their work-release employment earnings, residents pay room and board, family and self support, and income taxes. Portland House appears to be successful. It is significantly cheaper to run than a state institution, and the recidivism rate of clients is much lower than that of convicts who have gone through traditional correctional programs.[76]

In addition to being a sole sentence and a halfway house, RCC programs have also been used as a residential pretrial release center for offenders who need immediate social services before their trial and as a halfway-back alternative for both parole and probation violators who might otherwise have to be imprisoned. In this capacity, RCC programs serve as a base from which offenders can be placed in outpatient psychiatric facilities, drug and alcohol treatment programs, job training, and so on.

Boot Camps/Shock Incarceration

Another intermediate sanction gaining popularity around the United States is **shock incarceration** (SI) or **boot camps.** These programs typically include youthful, first-time offenders and feature military discipline and physical training. The concept is that short periods (90 to 180 days) of high-intensity exercise and work will shock young criminals into going straight. (Figure 18.3 describes the day in a typical boot camp.) Tough physical training is designed to promote responsibility and improve decision-making skills, build self-confidence, and teach socialization skills. Inmates are treated with rough intensity by drill masters, who may call them names and punish the entire group for the failure of one of its members.

There is wide variety in the more than 75 programs now operating around the United States.[77] Some programs include educational and training components, counseling sessions, and treatment for special-needs populations; others devote little or no time to therapeutic activities. Some receive program participants directly from court sentencing, whereas others choose potential candidates from the general inmate population. Some allow voluntary participation and others voluntary termination.[78]

Is shock incarceration a correctional panacea or another fad doomed to failure? The results so far are

Rita finishes 50 sit-ups and springs to her feet. At 6 A.M. her platoon begins a 5-mile run, the last portion of this morning's physical training. After five months in New York's Lakeview Shock Incarceration Correctional Facility, the morning workout is easy. Rita even enjoys it, taking pride in her physical conditioning.

When Rita graduates and returns to New York City, she will face six months of intensive supervision before moving to regular parole. More than two-fifths of Rita's platoon did not make it this far; some withdrew voluntarily, and the rest were removed for misconduct or failure to participate satisfactorily. By completing shock incarceration, she will enter parole 11 months before her minimum release date.

The requirements for completing shock incarceration are the same for male and female inmates. The women live in a separate housing area of Lakeview. Otherwise, men and women participate in the same education, physical training, drill and ceremony, drug education, and counseling programs. Men and women are assigned to separate work details and attend network group meetings held in inmates' living units.

Daily schedule

A.M.
5:30	Wake up and standing count
5:45–6:30	Calisthenics and drill
6:30–7:00	Run
7:00–8:00	Mandatory breakfast/cleanup
8:15	Standing count and company formation
8:30–11:55	Work/school schedules

P.M.
12:00–12:30	Mandatory lunch and standing count
12:30–3:30	Afternoon work/school schedule
3:30–4:00	Shower
4:00–4:45	Network community meeting
4:45–5:45	Mandatory dinner, prepare for evening
6:00–9:00	School, group counseling, drug counseling, prerelease counseling, decision-making classes
8:00	Count while in programs
9:15–9:30	Squad bay, prepare for bed
9:30	Standing count, lights out

Source: Cherie Clark, David Aziz, and Doris MacKenzie, *Shock Incarceration in New York: Focus on Treatment* (Washington, D.C.: National Institute of Justice, 1994), p. 5.

mixed. The costs of boot camps are no lower than those of traditional prisons, but because sentences are shorter, boot camps provide long-term savings. Some programs suffer high failure-to-complete rates, which makes program evaluations difficult (even if "graduates" are successful, it is possible that success is achieved because troublesome cases drop out and are placed in the general inmate population). What evaluations exist indicate that the recidivism rates of inmates who attend shock programs are in some cases no lower than those released from traditional prisons.[79] Many of these evaluations have been conducted by Doris Layton Mackenzie and her associates. One study with James Shaw found that although boot camp inmates may have lower recidivism rates than probationers and parolees, they have higher rates of technical violations and revocations.[80] These results are disappointing, but Mackenzie reports that both staff and inmates seem excited by the programs, and even those who fail on parole report they felt SI was a valuable experience.[81] She also finds, with Alex Piquero, that carefully managed boot camp programs can make a major dent in prison overcrowding.[82] Nonetheless, Mackenzie's extensive evaluations of the boot camp experience generate little evidence that they can significantly lower recidivism rates. Programs that seem to work, such as those in New York, stress treatment and therapeutic activities, are voluntary, and are longer in duration.[83] Perhaps the therapeutic aspect of the programs, not the military part, provides any achieved benefits.

Can Alternatives Work?

There is little evidence that alternative sanctions can prevent crime, reduce recidivism, or work much better than traditional probation or prison. Those who favor this approach argue that even without conclusive evidence that alternative sanctions are better than prison, they are certainly cheaper. Yet this rationale is valid only if the client population served would have been placed in more restrictive, costly secure confinement absent the opportunity for alternative sentencing. If, as some critics contend, placement is restricted to people who would have ordinarily been granted straight probation, then alternative sanctions are actually a more expensive method to achieve about the same result.

In a careful analysis of alternative sanctions, Frank Cullen finds that although they often produce some "small victories," they "have not shown the general ability to defeat the powerful forces fueling the [corrections] crisis."[84] Despite such cautions, alternative sanctions seem an attractive correctional alternative, and a number of states have in the past few years expanded their programs, including adding restitution (Alabama) and community service (Maine) sentencing options.[85]

JAILS

The **jail** is a secure institution used to (1) detain offenders before trial if they cannot afford or are not eligible for bail and (2) house misdemeanants sentenced to terms of one year or less, as well as some nonserious felons. The

Table 18.2 Jail Functions and Services

- Receive individuals pending arraignment and hold them awaiting trial, conviction, or sentencing
- Readmit probation, parole, and bail-bond violators and absconders
- Temporarily detain juveniles pending transfer to juvenile authorities
- Hold mentally ill persons pending their movement to appropriate health facilities
- Hold individuals for the military, for protective custody, for contempt, and for the courts as witnesses
- Release convicted inmates to the community upon completion of sentence
- Transfer inmates to federal, state, or other authorities
- House inmates for federal, state, or other authorities because of crowding of their facilities
- Relinquish custody of temporary detainees to juvenile and medical authorities
- Sometimes operate community-based programs as alternatives to incarceration
- Hold inmates sentenced to short terms (generally under one year)

Source: Darrell K. Gilliard and Allen J. Beck, *Prison and Jail Inmates at Midyear 1996* (Washington, D.C: Bureau of Justice Statistics, 1997), p. 3.

jail is a multipurpose correctional institution whose other main functions are set out in Table 18.2.

The jail originated in Europe in the sixteenth century and was used to house those awaiting trial and punishment. Jails were not used to house sentenced criminals because at that time punishment was achieved by fine, exile, corporal punishment, or death. Throughout their history, jails have been considered hellholes of pestilence and cruelty. In early English history, they housed offenders awaiting trial, as well as vagabonds, debtors, the mentally ill, and assorted others.[86] The early colonists adopted the European custom of detaining prisoners in jail. As noted previously, William Penn instituted the first jails to house convicted offenders while they worked off their sentences. The Walnut Street Prison, built in 1790, is considered the first modern jail.

Jail Populations

There has been a national effort to remove as many people from local jails as possible through bail reform measures and pretrial diversion. Nonetheless, jail populations have been steadily increasing, due in part to the increased use of mandatory jail sentences for such common crimes as drunk driving and the use of local jails to house inmates for whom there is no room in state prisons.

How many people are in jail today? In 1997, the last data available, an estimated 567,079 inmates were held in the nation's local jails, up 9.4 percent from the previous year. Since 1990 the number of jail inmates per 100,000 U.S. residents has risen from 163 to 212.[87]

Whereas the number of jails has declined from a high of 4,037 in 1970 to about 3,500 today, the number of inmates has increased more than 300 percent (from 160,683); there is a trend toward fewer but larger jails. In 1997 the 25 largest jail jurisdictions held 27 percent of all jail inmates. Los Angeles County and New York City, the largest jurisdictions, accounted for 7 percent of the national total.

Who Are Jail Inmates? Although removing juveniles from adult jails has long been a national priority, it is likely that over 50,000 youths are admitted to adult jails each year. More than 8,000 persons under age 18 are housed in adult jails on a given day. Over two-thirds of these young inmates have been convicted or are being held for trial as adults in criminal court.

Male inmates make up about 90 percent of the local jail inmate population. However, the female population, like the crime rate, has been growing at a faster pace. On average, the female jail population has grown 10.2 percent annually since 1985, while the male inmate population has grown annually by 6.1 percent.

A majority of local jail inmates are either black or Hispanic. White non-Hispanics make up 41.6 percent of the jail population; black non-Hispanics, 41.1 percent; Hispanics, 15.6 percent; and other races (Asians, Pacific Islanders, American Indians, and Alaska Natives), 1.7 percent. Relative to their number of U.S. residents, black non-Hispanics are six times as likely as white non-Hispanics, over twice as likely as Hispanics, and over eight times as likely as persons of other races to have been held in a local jail.

Jail Conditions

Jail conditions have become a national scandal. Throughout the United States, jails are marked by violence, overcrowding, deteriorated physical conditions, and lack of treatment or rehabilitation efforts. Suicides are common, as are fires and other natural calamities.[88] Another problem is the housing together of convicted offenders and detainees. And, despite government efforts to end the practice, many juvenile offenders occupy cells in adult jail facilities. About one-quarter of jails with large populations are under court order to improve. The most common grievances are overcrowding, inadequate recreational facilities and services, insufficient libraries, and deficient medical services and facilities.[89]

Some effort has been made to ameliorate jail conditions. The American Correctional Association has set up the Commission on Accreditation for Corrections, which has defined standards for health care, treatment, and visitations. A multistate pilot project has helped local facilities improve conditions so they may be accredited by the commission.[90]

In a similar vein, a number of states have enacted minimum standards to force counties to improve their jail conditions. State funding is made available to counties that cannot comply with conditions because of budgetary problems.[91] When state efforts have not been sufficient, national agencies have sometimes helped. The National Institute of Corrections has established a national jail center in Boulder, Colorado, to train jail personnel.

PRISONS

State and federal governments maintain closed correctional facilities to house convicted felons. Usually called **prisons** or **penitentiaries,** these institutions have become familiar to most people as harsh, frightening places filled with dangerous men and women. San Quentin (California), Attica (New York), Joliet (Illinois), and Marion (Illinois) are but a few of the large state and federal prisons made well known by films, books, or other media.

This section discusses types of correctional institutions, life and treatment in prison, and the prisoners' rights movement.

Types of Institutions

Of the more than 500 U.S. adult prisons, the overwhelming majority are state institutions.[92] These prisons are usually categorized according to their level of security and inmate populations as maximum-, medium-, and minimum-security institutions. Large maximum-security prisons are surrounded by high walls, have elaborate security measures and armed guards, and house inmates classified as potentially dangerous. High security and stone walls give the inmates the sense that the facility is impregnable and reassure citizens that convicts will be completely incapacitated. During the day, the inmates engage in closely controlled activities: meals, workshops, education, and so on. Rule violators may be confined to their cells; working and other shared recreational activities are viewed as privileges. Some inmates are considered so dangerous that they are housed in new prisons that are described in the Policy and Practice in Criminology feature titled "Ultra-Maximum-Security Prisons."

Medium-security prisons have similar protective measures but usually contain less violent inmates. Consequently, they are more likely to offer a variety of treatment and educational programs to their residents. They may be similar in appearance to the maximum-security prison; however, security and atmosphere are neither so tense nor so vigilant. Medium-security prisons are also surrounded by walls, but there may be fewer guard towers or other security precautions. For example, visitor privileges may be more extensive, and personal contact may be allowed; in a maximum-security prison, visitors may be separated from inmates by Plexiglas or other barriers (to prohibit the passing of contraband). Although most prisoners are housed in cells, individual honor rooms in medium-security prisons are used to reward those who make exemplary rehabilitation efforts. Finally, medium-security prisons promote greater treatment efforts, and the relaxed atmosphere allows freedom of movement for rehabilitation workers and other therapeutic personnel.

Minimum-security prisons operate without armed guards or walls; usually they are constructed in compounds surrounded by chain-link fences. Minimum-security prisons house the most trustworthy and least violent offenders; white-collar criminals may be their most common occupants. Inmates may be transferred to these nonrestrictive institutions as a reward for good behavior prior to their release. A great deal of personal freedom is allowed inmates. Instead of being marched to activities by guards, they are summoned by bells or loudspeaker announcements and assemble on their own. Work furloughs and educational releases are encouraged, and vocational training is of the highest level. Minimum-security prisons have been scoffed at for being too much like country clubs; some federal facilities catering to white-collar criminals even have tennis courts and pools. Yet they remain prisons, and the isolation and loneliness of prison life deeply affects the inmates at these facilities. And, of course, if an inmate cannot adjust to the relaxed security or if attempts escape, he or she will be transferred to a higher-security institution.

Farms and Camps   In addition to closed institutions, prison farms and camps are used to detain offenders. This type of facility is found primarily in the South and the West. Today about 40 farms, 40 forest camps, 80 road camps, and 67 similar facilities (vocational training centers, ranches, and so on) exist in the nation. Prisoners on farms produce dairy products, grain, and vegetable crops that are used in the state correctional system and other government facilities, such as hospitals and schools. Forestry camp inmates maintain state parks, fight forest fires, and do reforestation work. Ranches, primarily a western phenomenon, employ inmates in cattle raising and horse breeding, among other activities. Road gangs repair roads and state highways.

One controversial aspect of these open institutions has been the use of stun belts to control inmates while they work outdoors. Once confined in a stun belt, the inmate can receive a shock of 50,000 volts and three to four milliamps for a period of eight seconds. Although not fatal, the shock is very painful, and victims are immediately incapacitated. Burns may develop where the electrodes touch the skin above the left kidney, which may take months to heal. Critics charge that stun guns are brutal and can be used to terrorize or torture inmates.[93]

Ultra-Maximum-Security Prisons

Timothy McVeigh, the convicted Oklahoma City bomber, is being held in the super-maximum-security federal prison in Florence, Colorado. For McVeigh's protection, he lives in a 7-by-12-foot cell, isolated from the 407 other prisoners, who include some of the nation's most violent convicts.

Florence is the nation's most dramatic example of the *consolidation model* of corrections, which places all highly dangerous inmates at one location and controls them through heightened security procedures. As of 1998, approximately 20 percent of the Florence inmates are there for the murder or attempted murder of a fellow inmate, 18 percent for assaulting another inmate with a weapon, 16 percent for serious assault on a staff member, 10 percent for a serious escape attempt, and 5 percent for rioting. Others have been sent to Florence for attempted murder of a staff member, taking a staff member hostage, leading a work or food strike, introducing narcotics into an institution, and leading a prison gang. Only about 3 percent of Florence inmates were sent there directly from court.

For security reasons, there is no group dining, exercise, work, or religious services. Each inmate has an in-cell shower stall with floodproof plumbing controlled by guards. The bed, desk, stool, and bookcase are made of reinforced concrete, anchored in place. Meals are served through a slot in the cell door (see Figure A).

Florence prison has the most sophisticated security measures in the United States, including 168 video cameras and 1,400 electronically controlled gates. Inside the cells all furniture is unmovable; the desk, bed, and TV stand are made of cement. All potential weapons, including soap dishes, toilet seats, and toilet handles, have been removed. The cement walls are 5,000-pound quality, and steel bars are placed so they crisscross every eight inches inside the walls. Cells are angled so that inmates can see neither each other nor the outside scenery. This cuts down on communication and denies inmates a sense of location in order to prevent escapes. Inmates are handcuffed whenever they come in contact with staff to prevent violent offenders from assaulting staff and other inmates; this eliminates the possibility that escape-prone inmates will attempt to take a hostage or access an area of the institution that will facilitate an escape. Inmates eat and recreate individually or in small, carefully screened, supervised groups.

Getting out of the prison seems impossible. There are six guard towers at different heights to prevent air attacks. To get out, the inmates would have to pass through seven three-inch-thick steel doors, each of which can be opened only after the others have closed. If a guard tower is ever seized, all controls are switched to the next station. If the whole prison is seized, it can be controlled from the outside. It appears the only way out is through good works and behavior, through which an inmate can earn transfer to another prison within three years.

Although security is extremely tight, inmates are offered a range of programs and services, most delivered at the inmate's cell. On- and off-unit recreation, visiting medical care, in-cell television, religious activities, education, and other self-improvement programs are available from the day of arrival at Florence.

A number of states have constructed ultra-maximum or "maxi-maxi" prisons to house the most dangerous predatory criminals. Some maxi-maxi prisons lock inmates in their cells 22–24 hours a day, never allowing them out unless they are shackled. Threat of transfer to the maxi-maxi institution is used to deter inmate misbehavior in less restrictive institutions. The threat may work. Most inmates at Florence demonstrate that they can be returned to traditional prisons. Once in regular penitentiaries, fewer than 20 percent of the former maxi- inmates are returned for security reasons.

CRITICAL THINKING

1. Civil rights groups charge that maxi-maxi prisons violate the United Nations standards for the treatment of inmates. Is it inhumane to place even the most violent offenders within such harsh penal surroundings?

INFOTRAC COLLEGE EDITION RESEARCH

To read about other methods of improving prison security, see: Stephen Donohoe, Anthony Greloch. Keeping it simple. *Corrections Today* 59 (July 1997): 90.

Source: Gregory L. Hershberger, "To the Max: Supermax Facilities Provide Prison Administrators with More Security Options," *Corrections Today* 60 (February 1998): 54–58; Dennis Cauchon, "The Alcatraz of the Rockies," *USA Today,* 16 November 1994, p. 6a.

Few parts are movable or can be used as weapons. For example, buttons replace switches or levers; furniture and appliances are secured to the floor or walls.

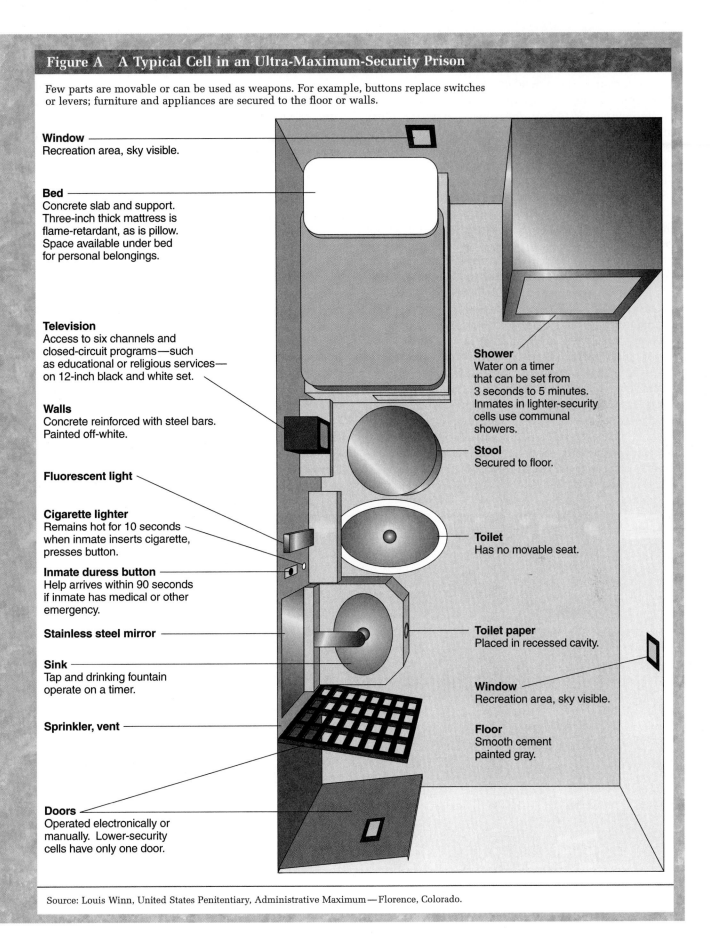

Window
Recreation area, sky visible.

Bed
Concrete slab and support.
Three-inch thick mattress is
flame-retardant, as is pillow.
Space available under bed
for personal belongings.

Television
Access to six channels and
closed-circuit programs—such
as educational or religious services—
on 12-inch black and white set.

Walls
Concrete reinforced with steel bars.
Painted off-white.

Fluorescent light

Cigarette lighter
Remains hot for 10 seconds
when inmate inserts cigarette,
presses button.

Inmate duress button
Help arrives within 90 seconds
if inmate has medical or other
emergency.

Stainless steel mirror

Sink
Tap and drinking fountain
operate on a timer.

Sprinkler, vent

Doors
Operated electronically or
manually. Lower-security
cells have only one door.

Shower
Water on a timer
that can be set from
3 seconds to 5 minutes.
Inmates in lighter-security
cells use communal
showers.

Stool
Secured to floor.

Toilet
Has no movable seat.

Toilet paper
Placed in recessed cavity.

Window
Recreation area, sky visible.

Floor
Smooth cement
painted gray.

Source: Louis Winn, United States Penitentiary, Administrative Maximum—Florence, Colorado.

Private Prisons   A current development in corrections is the increased use of privately run correctional institutions.[94] For-profit incarceration has grown from a sole 350-bed lockup in 1983 to 90,000 inmates in more than 100 prisons in 1997.[95] The federal government has used private companies to run detention centers for aliens who are being held for trial or deportation. One firm, the Corrections Corporation of America, runs a federal halfway house, two detention centers, and a 370-bed jail in Bay County, Florida. On January 6, 1986, the U.S. Corrections Corporation opened the first privately run state prison in Marion, Kentucky—a 300-bed minimum-security facility for inmates who are within three years of parole. Today more than 20 companies are trying to enter the private prison market, 5 states are contracting with private companies to operate facilities, and more than 10 others, including Oregon, New Mexico, and Florida, have recently passed laws authorizing or expanding the use of private prison contractors.[96] Fully privatized prisons will soon have a capacity of over 100,000 beds.[97]

Although privately run institutions have been around for a few years, their increased use may present a number of problems. For example, will private providers be able to effectively evaluate programs knowing that a negative evaluation might cause them to lose their contracts? Will they skimp on services and programs to reduce costs? Might they not skim off the easy cases and leave the hard-core inmates for state care?

And will the need to keep business booming require "widening the net" to fill empty cells? The notion of running prisons for profit may be unpalatable to large segments of the population. However, is this much different from a private hospital or college, both of which offer services also provided by the state?

The issues that determine the future of private corrections may be efficiency and cost-effectiveness, not fairness and morality. Privately run correctional institutions have been found to provide better services at lower cost than public facilities.[98] They may experience some of the same problems as state-run institutions, but there is little conclusive evidence that they cannot operate as or even more efficiently than traditional institutions.[99] And, importantly, a 1999 evaluation of recidivism among inmates released from private and public facilities found that recidivism rates were actually lower among the private prison group than the state prison inmates.[100] Inmates released from private prisons who did reoffend committed less serious offenses than those released from public institutions.

Prisoners in the United States

One of the most significant problems in the criminal justice system has been the meteoric rise in the prison population; today over 1,100,000 people are in prisons (see Figure 18.4).[101] Like the jail population, the prison incarceration has increased sharply. There are today an es-

Figure 18.4   Prison Population Trends

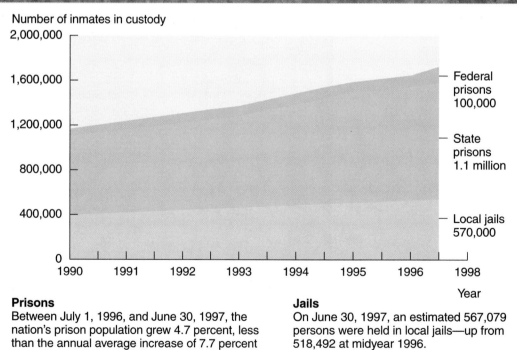

Prisons
Between July 1, 1996, and June 30, 1997, the nation's prison population grew 4.7 percent, less than the annual average increase of 7.7 percent since 1990.

Jails
On June 30, 1997, an estimated 567,079 persons were held in local jails—up from 518,492 at midyear 1996.

Source: Darrell Gilliard and Allen Beck, *Prison and Jail Inmates at Midyear 1997* (Washington, D.C.: Bureau of Justice Statistics, 1998; updated, 1999), p. 1.

timated 420 prison inmates per 100,000 U.S. residents— up from 292 at the end of 1990. Average growth in the prison population between 1990 and 1997 was about 7 percent per year.[102] This number represents a dramatic increase since 1925, when fewer than 100,000 people were in prison, and the incarceration rate was 79 per 100,000! The number of prisoners has grown by more than 200 percent since 1980, when 329,000 were incarcerated in state prisons. Because of this influx of offenders, many of the nation's prisons are operating at over 100 percent of capacity, even though thousands of prisoners are held in local jails because of overcrowding.

Recognizing the dangers associated with overcrowding, courts have ordered a number of state jurisdictions to reduce their inmate populations. To address the situation, various state correctional authorities have adopted plans to reduce the inmate population; others have called for the removal of less dangerous older inmates from secure facilities to less expensive community alternatives.[103] Some states, such as Texas, are building thousands more cells in the coming decade. Despite these measures, and while spending on corrections is growing faster than any other state expenditure, prison capacity is not keeping pace with the number of inmates.

Why Has the Prison Population Skyrocketed? Why has the prison population grown so much? One reason is that although the crime rate has declined, the conviction rate is increasing. Table 18.3 shows the growing conviction rates for crimes that are traditionally punished with prison sentences.

Although the *incarceration rate* has remained stable for the past decade at about 45 percent for all felony convictions, the increased *conviction rate* has helped drive up prison populations.

The growth of the correctional population may also be linked to changing public opinion, which has demanded a more punitive response to criminal offenders. Public concern about drugs and violent crime has not been lost on state lawmakers. Both mandatory sentencing and truth-in-sentencing laws have been implemented by a majority of states and the federal government; they increase eligibility for incarceration and limit the availability of parole.[104] It is ironic that the United States is embracing these extremely punitive sentencing policies at the same time many other Western nations are moving in the opposite direction by employing more humane, moderate criminal punishments such as fines and community sentencing orders.[105]

CONNECTIONS

As you may recall, Chapter 17 discussed truth in sentencing and mandatory sentencing, two policy initiatives that have helped drive up correctional populations.

As Figure 18.5 shows, violent offenders released from prison in 1996 served about 45 months; those sentenced in 1998 in one of the 27 truth-in-sentencing states will serve about 88 months before their release.[106] Although the number of people admitted to prison has stabilized, the time they are expected to serve has increased.

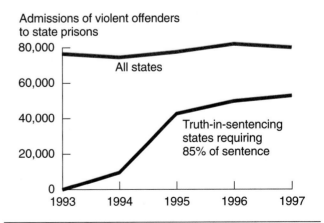

Figure 18.5 Truth-in-Sentencing Laws Require Inmates to Serve More of Their Sentences

State prisons, 1996

First releases

All offenders — 62 month sentence / 30 month time served

Violent offenders — 85 month / 45 month

New admissions

Violent offenders — 104 month sentence / 88 month time to serve

— 85% —

Admissions of violent offenders to state prisons

All states

Truth-in-sentencing states requiring 85% of sentence

1993 1994 1995 1996 1997

Source: Paula Ditton and Doris James Wilson, *Truth in Sentencing in State Prisons* (Washington, D.C.: Bureau of Justice Statistics, 1999), p. 1.

Table 18.3 Approximate Likelihood of Felony Arrest Leading to Felony Conviction

	1988	1990	1992	1994
Murder	48%	55%	65%	65%
Robbery	32	37	41	39
Aggravated assault	10	13	14	14
Burglary	33	38	41	39
Drug trafficking	39	53	55	52

Source: Patrick A. Langan and Jodi M. Brown, *Felony Sentences in State Courts, 1994* (Washington, D.C.: Bureau of Justice Statistics, 1998), p. 3.

Table 18.4 The Lifetime Likelihood of Serving a Prison Sentence

- If recent incarceration rates remain unchanged, an estimated 1 of every 20 persons (5.1 percent) will serve time in a prison.
- Men (9.0 percent) are over eight times as likely as women (1.1 percent) to be incarcerated at least once during their lives.
- Among men, blacks (28.5 percent) are about twice as likely as Hispanics (16.0 percent) and six times as likely as whites (4.4 percent) to be admitted to prison during their lives.
- Among women, 3.6 percent of blacks, 1.5 percent of Hispanics, and 0.5 percent of whites will enter prison at least once.
- The chance of going to prison for the first time declines with age.

Source: Thomas P. Bonczar and Allen J. Beck, *Lifetime Likelihood of Going to State or Federal Prison* (Washington, D.C: Bureau of Justice Statistics, 1997), p. 1.

Table 18.5 Middle-Aged Inmates Comprise a Growing Part of the Nation's Prison Population

	PERCENTAGE OF INMATES HELD IN STATE OR FEDERAL PRISON	
	1991	1997
Total	100%	100%
17 or younger	0.6	0.4
18–19	2.9	2.7
20–24	17.4	15.8
25–29	23.6	18.7
30–34	21.3	19.2
35–39	14.4	17.5
40–44	9.1	12.1
45–54	7.2	10.3
55 or older	3.4	3.3

Source: Darrell K. Gilliard and Allen J. Beck, *Prisoners in 1997* (Washington, D.C.: Bureau of Justice Statistics, 1998), p. 7.

The rise in the prison population has also been fueled in part by an increase in inmates serving time for drug offenses. The number of arrests for drug offenses has increased more than 60 percent in the past decade, and today over 1 million people per year are arrested on drug-related charges. This increase is magnified by the fact that between 1988 and 1999 many states and the federal government adopted mandatory minimum sentences for drug crimes. The number of drug arrestees who are later convicted has increased by more than 30 percent; and the number of convicted drug offenders who are sent to prison has increased by about 20 percent.[107] As a result, an increasing portion of the inmate population is incarcerated for drug law violations.

If current trends continue, the prison population will continue to climb; and as Table 18.4 shows, a significant number of all Americans (5 percent, or more than 12 million people) will have served a prison sentence during their lives.

Profile of Prison Inmates

What are the personal characteristics of U.S. prison inmates?[108] As expected, prisoners reflect the same qualities that are found in samples of arrestees. Inmates of state prisons are predominantly poor, young adult males with less than a high school education. However, although inmates tend to be young, longer sentences have dictated an aging inmate population. As Table 18.5 shows, there is a growing pool of inmates aged 35 plus; the number of inmates under age 35 has actually declined. Prison inmates who are aged 51 and beyond will make up 33 percent of the total prison population by the year 2010, placing pressure on prison administrators to devise ways of keeping aged inmates in the prison workforce, helping them maintain family ties, and assuring them access to medical and mental health specialists.[109]

Prison is not a new experience for many inmates: over 60 percent have been incarcerated before. About 80 percent of all inmates have had prior sentences to either probation or incarceration; about 5 percent have had 100 or more prior sentences!

In years past, most inmates did time for robbery or burglary. Today drug trafficking has risen to the number two spot, behind robbery and just ahead of burglary.

The profile of inmates reinforces the presumed association between criminal behavior and social problems. Many inmates grew up in single-parent households. More than a quarter say their parents abused drugs or alcohol; the great majority (80 percent) have been substance abusers themselves; more than 60 percent were regular drug users. For example, one study of 400 Texas inmates found that almost 75 percent suffer from lifetime substance abuse or dependence disorder, which is characterized by psychologists as abuse of drugs for at least one continuous month (or repeated symptoms occurring over a longer period), "failure to fulfill major role obligations," and "substance-related legal problems."[110] Considering this background, it should come as no surprise that more inmates die from HIV-related disease than from prison violence.[111]

Males and minorities are overrepresented in the prison population. About 94 percent of inmates are males, and about half of the population is white. Hispanic inmates, who may be of any race, totaled an estimated 200,400 at year-end 1996—increasing 54 percent from 1990. In 1996, the rate of inmates among the population of black males totaled 3,098 prisoners per 100,000 residents, compared to 1,278 per 100,000 Hispanic males and 370 per 100,000 white males in the United States.

Inmates are educational and vocational underachievers. Only one-third graduated from high school, and about one-half were employed full-time before their incarceration; about half earned under $10,000 per year. Only 18 percent were married, far below the standard rate for adult Americans.

The profile of the prison inmate supports the reality of a problem behavior syndrome. From birth, the path that led the inmate to prison was littered with insurmountable family, economic, and social problems.

Prison Life: Males

Inmates in large, inaccessible prisons find themselves physically cut off from families, friends, and former associates. Those who are fathers may become depressed because they are anxious about their kids.[112] Their families and friends may find it difficult to travel great distances to visit them; mail is censored and sometimes destroyed. The prison is a "total institution," regulating dress, work, sleep, and eating habits.[113]

Inmates soon find themselves in a totally new world with its own logic, behavior, rules, and language. They must learn to live with the stress of prison life. According to Gresham Sykes, the major losses are goods and services, liberty, heterosexual relationships, autonomy, and security.[114] Prisoners find they have no privacy; even when locked in their own cells, they are surrounded and observed by others.

Inmates must adjust to the incentives prison administrators have created to promote security and control behavior.[115] One type of incentive involves the level of comfort provided the inmate. Those obeying rules are given choice work assignments, privileges, and educational opportunities. Those who flout prison rules may be segregated, locked in their cells, or put in solitary confinement (**the hole**).

Administrators can also control the amount of time spent in prison. Furloughs can be dispensed to allow prisoners the opportunity to work or visit outside prison walls. Good-time credit can be extended to lessen sentences. Parole decisions can be influenced by reports on inmates' behavior.

The inmate must learn to deal with sexual exploitation and violence in the prison. One position says that this phenomenon is a function of racial conflict; another holds that inmates who become victims are physically weaker and less likely to form cohesive defensive groups.[116] In one study, criminologist Daniel Lockwood found that inmate aggressors come from a street culture that stresses violence and continue to behave violently while in prison.[117] Young males may be raped and kept as sexual slaves by older, more aggressive inmates. When these "slave holders" are released, they often sell their "prison wives" to other inmates.[118]

To avoid victimization, inmates must learn to adopt a lifestyle that shields them from victimization.[119] They must discover areas of safety and danger, whom to trust and whom to avoid. Some learn how to fight back to prove they are not people who can be taken advantage of. Whereas some kill their attackers and get even longer sentences, others join cliques and gangs that provide protection and the ability to acquire power within the institution. Gangs are powerful in the larger prison systems, especially in California. Some inmates seek transfers to a different cell block or prison, ask for protective custody, or simply remain in their cells all the time.

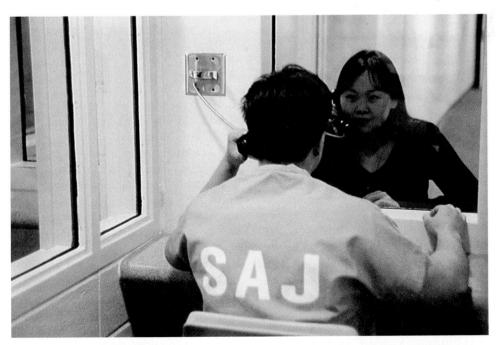

Prison life is an alienating experience broken by occasional visits from family and friends. Very often personal visits are limited, and family and friends are separated by a glass partition and can only communicate by phone.

Part of inmates' early adjustment involves their becoming familiar with and perhaps participating in the hidden, black-market economy of the prison—the *hustle*. Hustling provides inmates with a source of steady income and the satisfaction of believing they are beating the system.[120] Hustling involves the sale of such illegal commodities as drugs (uppers, downers, pot), alcohol, weapons, and illegally obtained food and supplies. When prison officials crack down on hustled goods, it merely drives the price up—giving hustlers a greater incentive to promote their black-market activities.[121]

Inmates must also learn to deal with daily racial conflict. Prisoners tend to segregate themselves and, if peace is to reign in the institution, stay out of each other's way. Often racial groupings are quite exact; for example, Hispanics may separate themselves according to their national origin (Mexicans, Puerto Ricans, Colombians, and so on). In large California prisons, segregation and power struggles create even narrower divisions. For example, Hispanic gangs are now organized by area of origin: northern California (Nortenos), southern California (Surenos), and Mexican-born (Border Brothers).[122] Prisons represent one area in which minorities often hold power; as sociologist James B. Jacobs observed, "Prison may be the one institution in American society that blacks control."[123]

Prisoners must learn to deal with their frustrations over getting a "rotten deal." They may find that some other inmates received far lower sentences for similar crimes. They may be turned down for parole and then observe that others with similar records are granted early release. There is some evidence that perceived discrimination in the distribution of rewards and treatment may contribute to dissatisfaction, maladjustment, and prison violence.[124]

Finally, as the inmates' sentences wind down and their parole dates near, they must learn to cope with the anxiety of being released into the outside world. During this period, inmates may question their ability to make it in an environment in which they have failed before. Have their families stood by them? Are they outcasts? Facing release, these inmates often experience low self-esteem, become depressed, and suffer anxiety.[125]

Inmate Society   A significant element of the inmate's adjustment to prison is the encounter with what is commonly known as the **inmate subculture**.[126] One major aspect of the inmate subculture is a unique **social code**—unwritten guidelines that express the values, attitudes, and types of behavior that the older inmates demand of younger inmates. Passed on from one generation of inmates to another, the inmate social code represents the values of interpersonal relations within the prison.

National attention was first drawn to the inmate social code and subculture by Donald Clemmer. In *The Prison Community,* Clemmer presented a detailed sociological study of life in a maximum-security prison.[127]

Clemmer was able to identify a unique language (*argot*) of prisoners. In addition, Clemmer found that prisoners tend to group themselves into cliques on the basis of such personal criteria as sexual preference, political beliefs, and offense history. He found that there were complex sexual relationships in prison and concluded that many heterosexual men will turn to homosexual relationships when faced with long sentences and the loneliness of prison life.

Clemmer's most important contribution may have been his identification of the **prisonization** process. This he defined as the inmate's assimilation into the prison culture through acceptance of its language, sexual code, and norms of behavior. Those who become the most prisonized will be the least likely to reform on the outside.

Not all prison experts believe that the prison culture is a function of the harsh conditions in a total institution. In 1962 John Irwin and Donald Cressey published a paper in which they conceded that a prison culture exists but claimed that its principles are actually imported from the outside world.[128] In their **importation model,** Irwin and Cressey conclude that inmate culture is affected by the values of newcomers: many inmates come to prison with a record of many terms in correctional institutions. These men, some of whom have institutional records dating back to early childhood, bring with them a ready-made set of patterns they apply to the new situation, taking control of the prison culture's content.

The New Inmate Culture   Although the "old" inmate subculture may have been harmful because its norms and values insulated the inmate from change efforts, it also helped create order within the institution and prevented violence among the inmates. People who violated the code and victimized others were sanctioned by their peers. An understanding developed between guards and inmate leaders: the guards would let the inmates have things their own way, and the inmates would not let things get out of hand and draw the attention of the administration.

The old system may be dying or already dead in most institutions. The change seems to have been precipitated by the black power movement in the 1960s and 1970s. Black inmates were no longer content to fill a subservient role and challenged the power of established white inmates. As the black power movement gained prominence, racial tension in prisons created divisions that severely altered the inmate subculture. Older, respected inmates could no longer cross racial lines to mediate disputes. Predatory inmates could victimize others without fear of retaliation.[129] Consequently, more inmates than ever are assigned for their safety to protective custody.

Sociologist James B. Jacobs is perhaps the most influential expert on the changing inmate subculture. His research has helped him to conclude that the development of "black (and Latino) power" in the 1960s, spurred by the Black Muslim movement, significantly influenced the nature of prison life.[130]

According to Jacobs, black and Latin inmates are much more cohesively organized than whites. Their groups are sometimes rooted in religious and political affiliations, such as the Black Muslims; are created specifically to combat discrimination in prison, such as the Latin group *La Familia;* or are reformations of street gangs, such as the Vice Lords, Disciples, or Blackstone Rangers in the Illinois prison system and the Crips in California. Only in California have white inmates successfully organized, and there it is in the form of neo-Nazi groups, such as the *Aryan Brotherhood.* Racially homogeneous gangs are so cohesive and powerful that they are able to supplant the original inmate code with their own. Consider the oath taken by new members of *Nuestra Familia* (Our Family), a Latin gang operating in California prisons: "If I go forward, follow me. If I hesitate, push me. If they kill me, avenge me. If I am a traitor, kill me."

Racial conflict prompted Jacobs to suggest that it may be humane and appropriate to segregate inmates along racial lines to maintain order and protect individual rights. Jacobs believes that in some prisons, administrators use integration as a threat to keep inmates in line; to be transferred to a racially mixed setting may mean beatings or death.

Although Jacobs paints the new prison culture as one of danger and chaos, in some areas, prison life has become even more disorganized, with new gangs forming and engaging in ever-increasing violent confrontations. The new breed of inmate is younger, more dangerous, and disdainful of older gang members.[131] As the prison population expands, the violence and danger of the streets will be imported into the prison culture.

Prison Life: Females

Women make up about 6 percent of the adult prison population. Usually they are housed in minimum-security institutions more likely to resemble college dormitories than high-security male prisons.

Women in prison tend to be of three basic types, described by Esther Heffernan as "the square," who is

Female inmates first go through a period in which they deny the reality of their situation. Then comes a period of anger over the circumstances that led to their incarceration; during this phase, they begin to accept the circumstances of their imprisonment. A third stage finds female inmates greatly depressed because they can no longer deny that they are in prison to stay. Many female inmates eventually find reason to hope that their lives will improve.

basically a noncriminal but who, in a fit of rage, may have shot or stabbed a husband or boyfriend; "the life," who is a repeat offender (shoplifter, prostitute, drug user, or pusher); and "the cool," who is part of the sophisticated criminal underworld. The square usually espouses conventional values and wants to follow the rules; the life rejects prison authority and is a rebel; the cool is aloof, manipulates the environment, and does not participate in prison life.[132]

Like men, female inmates must adjust to the prison experience. Female inmates first go through a period in which they deny the reality of their situation. Then comes a period of anger over the circumstances that led to their incarceration; during this phase, they begin to accept the circumstances of their imprisonment. A third stage finds female inmates greatly depressed because they can no longer deny that they are in prison to stay. Many female inmates eventually find reason to hope that their lives will improve.[133]

Daily life in the women's prison community is also somewhat different from that in male institutions. For one thing, women usually do not present the immediate physical danger to staff and fellow inmates that many male prisoners do. For another, the rigid, antiauthority inmate social code found in many male institutions does not exist in female prisons. Despite the fact that they present less threat, female inmates are more often controlled with mood-altering drugs than male inmates.[134]

Confinement for women, however, may produce severe anxiety and anger because they are separated from families and loved ones and unable to function in normal female roles. Low self-esteem is a major problem among female inmates.[135] Unlike men, who direct their anger outward, female prisoners may revert to more self-destructive acts to cope with their problems. Female inmates are perhaps more likely than males to mutilate their own bodies and attempt suicide. It is not surprising, considering these circumstances, that female inmates are more likely to be treated with mood-altering drugs and placed in psychiatric care, whereas male inmates' adjustment difficulties are viewed as disciplinary problems.[136]

One common form of adaptation to prison employed by women is the surrogate family. This group contains masculine and feminine figures acting as fathers and mothers; some even act as children and take on the role of either brother or sister. Formalized marriages and divorces may be conducted. Sometimes multiple roles are held by one inmate, so that a "sister" in one family may "marry" and become the "wife" in another.[137]

The special needs of female inmates must be addressed by correctional authorities. Health care is an issue. Many institutions have inadequate facilities to care for women who are pregnant when they enter prison or become pregnant during their prison stay.[138] There is a growing problem of HIV-related illnesses as the ongoing war on drugs increases the number of substance-abusing female inmates who are at risk for AIDS.[139]

Helping women to adjust after they leave the institution is another goal. Surveys indicate that the prison experience does little to prepare women to reenter the workforce after their sentences have been completed. Gender stereotypes still shape vocational opportunities.[140] Female inmates are still being trained for "women's roles," such as child rearing, and are not given the programming to make successful adjustments in the community.[141]

Correctional Treatment

Correctional treatment has been an integral part of prison life since Z. R. Brockway introduced it as part of the daily regimen at the Elmira Reformatory. Today more than 90 percent of all prison inmates participate in some form of program or activity after admission.[142] There are many approaches to treatment. Some, based on a medical model, rely heavily on counseling and clinical therapy. Others attempt to prepare inmates for reintegration into the community; they rely on work release, vocational training, and educational opportunities. Others stress self-help through 12-step or Alcoholics Anonymous programs. The most popular programs have a religious theme and involve Bible clubs and other pious activities. Although it is beyond the scope of this book to describe the vast number of correctional treatment programs, a few important types will be discussed.

Therapy and Counseling The most traditional type of treatment in prison involves psychological counseling and therapy. Counseling programs exist in almost every major institution. Some stress individual treatment with psychotherapy or other techniques. However, because of lack of resources, it is more common for group methods to be used. Some groups are led by trained social workers, counselors, or therapists; others rely on lay personnel as leaders.

Group counseling in prison usually tries to stimulate inmates' self-awareness and their ability to deal with everyday problems.[143] Various innovative psychological treatment approaches have been used in the prison system:

- *Behavior therapy* uses tokens to reward conformity and help develop positive behavior traits.
- *Reality therapy* is meant to help satisfy individuals' needs to feel worthwhile to themselves and others.
- *Transactional analysis* encourages inmates to identify the different aspects of their personalities and to be their own therapists.
- *Milieu therapy* uses the social structure and processes of the institution to influence the behavior patterns of offenders.[144]

Educational Programs The first prison treatment programs were educational. A prison school was opened at the Walnut Street Prison in 1784. Elementary courses were offered in New York's prison system in 1801 and in Pennsylvania's in 1844. An actual school system was established in Detroit's House of Corrections in 1870, and Elmira Reformatory opened a vocational trade school in 1876.

Today most institutions provide some type of education. Some prisons allow inmates to obtain a high school diploma through equivalency exams or general educational development (GED) certificates. Some prisons provide college courses, usually staffed by teachers who work at nearby institutions. Nearly one-half of all inmates have received some form of academic education, and about one-third have had vocational training since entering prison.[145]

Vocational Rehabilitation Most prisons operate numerous vocational training programs designed to help inmates develop skills for securing employment on their release. In the past, the traditional prison industries of laundry and license plate manufacture failed to provide these skills. Today programs stress such marketable skills as dental laboratory work, computer programming, auto repair, and radio and television work.

Unfortunately, prisons often have difficulty obtaining the necessary equipment to run meaningful programs. Therefore, many have adopted *work furlough* programs that allow inmates to work in the community during the day and return to the institution at night.

Several state correctional departments also have instituted prerelease and postrelease employment services. Employment program staff members assess inmates' backgrounds to determine their abilities, interests, goals, and capabilities. They also help them create job plans (which are essential to their receiving early parole) and help them obtain placements in sheltered environments so that inmates can bridge the gap between the institution and the outside world; services include job placement, skill development, family counseling, and legal and medical attention.

Private Industry in Prisons A new version of vocational rehabilitation is the development of private industry in prison. This can take many different forms, including private citizens sitting on prison industry boards, private vendors marketing goods from prison industry, inmates manufacturing and marketing their own goods, private management of state-owned prison industry, franchising within the prison system in which manufactured goods are marketed under license from a private firm, and privately owned industries on prison grounds employing inmate labor.

Another approach is the **free-venture programs** developed in the 1980s in Minnesota, Kansas, and other areas with the aid of the federal government.[146] The programs involve businesses set up by private entrepreneurs off prison grounds that contract with state officials to hire inmates at free-market wages and produce goods that are competitively marketed. Inmates can be fired by being sent back to the general prison population.

On paper, private industry in prison is quite attractive. It teaches inmates skills in usually desirable commercial areas, such as data processing. It increases employment opportunities on the outside in areas where the ex-offender can earn enough to forgo a life of crime. Various evaluations of the programs have given them high marks. However, private industry programs have so far used relatively few inmates. It is questionable whether they could be applied to the general prison population, which contains many people with educational deficiencies and a history of substance abuse. Yet a policy of full employment in prison may be one way of reducing future recidivism.[147]

Inmate Self-Help Recognizing that the probability of failure on the outside is acute, inmates have attempted to organize self-help groups to provide the psychological tools needed to prevent recidivism.[148] Some are chapters of common national organizations such as Alcoholics Anonymous. Membership in these programs is designed to improve inmates' self-esteem and help them cope with common problems such as alcoholism, narcotics abuse, or depression. Special-needs inmates at the Kentucky State Reformatory outside Louisville have taken the unusual step of forming a Boy Scout Troop within prison walls to serve as a vehicle for self-help and group solidarity.[149]

Other groups are organized along racial and ethnic lines. For example, there are chapters of the Chicanos Organizados Pintos Aztlan (COPA), the Afro-American Coalition, and the Native American Brotherhood in prisons stretching from California to Massachusetts. These groups try to establish a sense of brotherhood in order to work together for individual betterment. Members hold literacy, language, and religious classes as well as offering counseling, legal advice, and prerelease support. Ethnic groups seek ties with outside minority organizations such as the NAACP, Urban League, La Raza, and American Indian Movement as well as the religious and university communities.

A third type of self-help group includes those developed specifically to help inmates find the strength to make it on the outside. The most well known are the Fortune society, which claims 30,000 members, and the Seventh Step organization, which was developed by ex-offender Bill Sands. The Prison Fellowship is a religiously oriented group that sponsors seminars and Bible studies. Inmates who frequently attend services and seminars appear to have lower recidivism rates than other inmates.[150]

Does Rehabilitation Work? Despite the variety and number of treatment programs in operation, some question their effectiveness. In their often-cited research, Robert Martinson and his associates found that a majority of treatment programs were failures.[151] Martinson found in a national study that, with few exceptions, rehabilitative efforts seemed to have no appreciable effect on recidivism.

Martinson's work was followed by efforts that found, embarrassingly, that some high-risk offenders were more likely to commit crimes after they had been placed in treatment programs than before the onset of rehabilitation efforts.[152] Even California's highly touted community treatment program, which matched youthful offenders and counselors on the basis of their psychological profiles, was found by Paul Lerman to exert negligible influence on its clients.[153] Recent analysis of correctional treatment programs has reaffirmed the inadequacy of correctional treatment efforts.[154]

These less-than-enthusiastic reviews of correctional rehabilitation helped develop a more conservative view of corrections, which, according to such advocates as Charles Logan, means that prisons are viewed as places of incapacitation and confinement; their purpose is punishment, not treatment.[155] Current social policy stresses eliminating the nonserious offender from the correctional system while increasing the sentences of serious, violent offenders. The development of lengthy mandatory and determinate sentences to punish serious offenders and the simultaneous evolution of alternative sanctions to limit the nonserious offender's interface with the system are manifestations of this view.

Some criminologists continue to challenge the "nothing works" philosophy.[156] D. A. Andrews and his associates have suggested that treatment can be effective if treatment modalities are matched with the needs of inmates.[157] For example, inmates who have completed higher levels of education find it easier to gain employment upon release and consequently are less likely to recidivate over long periods.[158] Among the characteristics associated with the most successful programs are these:

- Services are intensive, lasting only a few months.
- Programs are cognitive, aimed at helping inmates learn new skills in order to better cope with personality problems such as impulsivity.
- Program goals are reinforced firmly and fairly, using positive rewards rather than negative punishment.
- Therapists relate to clients sensitively and positively. Therapists are trained and supervised appropriately.
- Clients are insulated from disruptive interpersonal networks and placed in environments where prosocial activities predominate.[159]

So although the concept of correctional treatment is often questioned, many criminologists still believe that it is possible to help some inmates within prison walls.

Prison Violence

One of the more significant problems facing prison administrators is the constant fear of interpersonal and collective violence. Hans Toch, an expert on violence, has said,

> Jails and prisons . . . have a climate of violence which has no free-world counterpart. Inmates are terrorized by other inmates and spend years in fear of harm. Some inmates request segregation, others lock themselves in and some are hermits by choice. Many inmates injure themselves.[160]

What are the causes of prison violence? There is no single explanation for either collective or individual violence, but theories abound. One position holds that inmates are often violence-prone individuals who have always used force to get their own way. In the crowded, dehumanizing world of the prison, it is not surprising that they resort to force to dominate others.[161]

A second view is that prisons convert people to violence by their inhumane conditions, including overcrowding, depersonalization, and threats of homosexual rape. One social scientist, Charles Silberman, suggests that even in the most humane prisons, life is a constant put-down, and prison conditions threaten the inmates' sense of self-worth; violence is a consequence of these conditions.[162]

Still another view is that prison violence stems from mismanagement, lack of strong security, and inadequate control by prison officials.[163] This view has contributed to the escalated use of solitary confinement in recent years as a means of control. Also contributing to prison violence is the changing prison population. Younger, more violent inmates, who often have been members of teenage gangs, now dominate prison life. The old code of "do your own time" and "be a right guy" may be giving way to a prison culture dominated by gangs, whose very nature breeds violence.

Prison violence may also be associated with the overcrowding caused by rapid increases in the prison population. Data from Texas indicate that a large increase in the inmate population, unmatched by creation of new space, was associated with increases in suicide, violent death, and disciplinary action rates. The largest prisons in Texas (with populations of over 1,600) demonstrated violence rates higher than the smaller prisons (800 or less).[164]

Prison Riots Sometimes prison violence takes the form of large-scale rioting. The American Correctional Association gives these reasons for such prison flare-ups:

- Unnatural institutional environment
- Antisocial characteristics of inmates
- Inept management
- Inadequate personnel practices
- Inadequate facilities
- Insufficient constructive, meaningful activity
- Insufficient legitimate rewards
- Basic social values and unrest in the larger community
- Inadequate finances
- Inequities and complexities in the criminal justice system[165]

In a more recent analysis, Randy Martin and Sherwood Zimmerman have identified the following causes of prison riots:

- *Environmental conditions:* Poor physical conditions make the prison a time bomb waiting to explode.
- *Spontaneity:* Some spark, such as a fight between gangs, escalates into a general prison disturbance.
- *Conflict:* A repressive administration denies inmate rights, which leads to violence.
- *Collective behavior and social control:* Informal social control mechanisms, such as inmate leaders and councils, break down and violence escalates.
- *Power vacuum:* A conflict between guards and the administration creates an anomic condition exploited by the inmates.
- *Rising expectations:* Inmates expect increased freedom and better conditions. When these expectations are not met, inmates' frustration leads to collective violence.[166]

Each of these conditions can trigger collective prison disturbances.

Corrections and the Rule of Law

For many years, the nation's courts did not interfere in prison operations, maintaining what is called the **hands-off doctrine.** The judiciary's reluctance to interfere in prison matters was based on the belief that it lacked technical competence in prison administration, society's general apathy toward prisons, and the belief that prisoners' complaints involved privileges rather than rights.[167] Consequently, prisoners had no legal rights and were "slaves of the state."

The hands-off doctrine was lifted in the 1960s. General concern with civil and human rights, increasing militancy in the prison population, and the reformist nature of the Warren Court created a climate conducive to reform. The first area of change came in the First Amendment right of freedom of religion. The Black Muslims, a politically active religious organization led by Elijah Muhammed of Chicago, recruited many members in the prison system (including Malcolm X). Using their legal and financial clout, the Muslims litigated claims that their followers were being denied the right to worship according to their faith. A series of Supreme Court cases upheld the Muslims' freedom of religion and opened the door to other issues of inmates' rights.[168]

Today most litigation is brought under the federal Civil Rights Act (28 U.S.C. 1982), which states,

> Every person who, under color of any statute, ordinance, regulation, custom, or usage of any State or Territory subjects, or causes to be subjected, any citizen of the United States or other person within the jurisdiction thereof to the deprivation of any rights, privileges, or immunities secured by the Constitution and laws shall be liable to the party injured in an action at law, suit in equity or other proper proceeding for redress.

For many years the Supreme Court upheld inmates' rights, granting them access to the courts to seek legal redress for improper or damaging prison conditions. Recently claims that prisoner-inspired lawsuits were clogging the courts swayed a more conservative Court to limit the methods by which inmates can seek release or redress, for example by discouraging inmates from filing "frivolous" lawsuits.[169] Nonetheless, some of the gains won by inmates continue in force, including the following:

- *Freedom of press and speech:* The courts have ruled that inmates retain freedom of speech and press unless correctional authorities can show that it interferes with or threatens institutional freedom. For example, in *Procunier v. Martinez,* a court ruled that an inmate's mail could be censored only if there existed substantial belief that its contents would threaten security. However, in *Saxbe v. Washington Post,* the right of an inmate to grant press interviews was limited; the Supreme Court argued that such interviews would enhance the reputations of particular inmates and jeopardize authorities' desire to treat everyone equally.[170]
- *Medical rights:* After many years of indifference, inmates have only recently been given the right to secure proper medical attention. To gain their medical rights, prisoners have generally resorted to class action suits to ask courts to require adequate medical care.[171] In 1976, after reviewing the legal principles established over the preceding 20 years, the Supreme Court in *Estelle v. Gamble* clearly stated the inmate's right to medical care:[172]

> Deliberate indifference to serious medical needs of prisoners constitutes the "unnecessary and wanton infliction of pain," . . . proscribed by the Eighth Amendment. This is true whether the indifference is manifested by prison doctors in their response to the prisoner's needs or by prison guards in intentionally denying or delaying access to medical care or intentionally interfering with the treatment once prescribed.[173]

Lower courts will now decide, case by case, whether "deliberate indifference" has actually occurred.

Cruel and Unusual Punishment and Overall Conditions Prisoners have long suffered severe physical punishment in prison, ranging from whipping to extended periods of solitary confinement. The courts have held that such treatment is unconstitutional when it

- Degrades the dignity of human beings.[174]
- Is more severe than the offense for which it has been given.[175]
- Shocks the general conscience and is fundamentally unfair.[176]

The courts have also ruled on the necessity for maintaining the general prison system in a humane manner. For example, in 1970, the entire prison system in Arkansas was declared unconstitutional because its practices of overt physical punishment were ruled to violate the Eighth Amendment.[177]

In *Rhodes v. Chapman*[178] the Supreme Court upheld the practice of double-bunking two or more inmates in a small cell (50 square feet). "Conditions of confinement," the court argued, "must not involve the wanton and unnecessary infliction of pain nor may they be grossly disproportionate to the severity of the crime warranting imprisonment," but "conditions that cannot be said to be cruel and unusual under contemporary standards are not unconstitutional. To the extent that such conditions are restrictive and even harsh, they are part of the penalty that criminal offenders pay for their offenses against society."[179]

Although *Rhodes* limited inmates' rights to better living conditions, a number of state cases, especially *Estelle v. Ruiz,* have put corrections departments on notice that overcrowding will not be tolerated, and no new inmates can be admitted to prison unless the number of inmates is reduced.[180]

PAROLE

Parole is the planned release and community supervision of incarcerated offenders before the expiration of their prison sentences. It is usually considered a way of completing a prison sentence in the community and is not the same as a pardon; the paroled offender can be legally recalled to serve the remainder of his or her sentence in an institution if parole authorities deem the offender's adjustment inadequate or if the offender commits another crime while on parole.

The decision to parole is determined by statutory requirement and usually involves the completion of a minimum sentence. Parole is granted by a state *parole board,* a body of men and women who review cases and determine whether an offender has been rehabilitated sufficiently to deal with the outside world. The board

also dictates the specific parole rules a parolee must obey. Some states with determinate sentencing statutes, such as Indiana and California, do not use parole boards but release inmates at the conclusion of their maximum terms less accumulated good time. This form of *mandatory* parole release has been increasing rapidly as states adopt various forms of determinate sentencing.

In states where discretionary parole is used, the decision is made at a **parole grant hearing.** There the full board or a subcommittee reviews information, may meet with the offender, and then decides whether the parole applicant has a reasonable chance of succeeding outside prison. Candidates for parole may be chosen by statutory eligibility on the basis of time served in relation to their sentences. In most jurisdictions, good time reduces the minimum sentence and therefore hastens eligibility for parole. In making its decision, the board considers the inmate's offense, time served, evidence of adjustment, and opportunities on the outside.

To help these parole decision makers, parole prediction tables have been developed.[181] These tables correlate personal information on inmates who were released in the past with their rates of rearrest. The best known predictive device is the Salient Factor Score Index. The salient factor score includes age, type of offense, prior parole revocations, history of heroin use, and employment background.[182]

The Parolee in the Community

Once community release has begun, the offender is supervised by a trained staff of parole officers who help the offender adjust to the community and search for employment as they monitor behavior and activities to ensure that the offender conforms to the conditions of parole.

Parolees are subject to strict standardized or personalized rules that guide their behavior and limit their activities. If at any time these rules are violated, the offender can be returned to the institution to serve the remainder of the sentence; this is known as a *technical parole violation.* Inmates released in determinate sentencing states can have part or all of their good time revoked if they violate the conditions of their release.

Parole can also be revoked if the offender commits a second offense; the offender may be tried and sentenced for this crime. The Supreme Court has granted parolees due process rights similar to those of probationers at revocation hearings.

Parole is viewed as an act of grace on the part of the criminal justice system. It is a manifestation of the policy of returning the offender to the community. There are two conflicting sides to parole, however: the paroled offender is given a break and allowed to serve part of the sentence in the community; on the other hand, the sentiment exists that parole is a privilege, not a right, and that the parolee is in reality a dangerous criminal who must be carefully watched and supervised. The conflict between the treatment and enforcement aspects of parole has not been reconciled by the criminal justice system, and the parole process still contains elements of both orientations.

More than 700,000 criminals are now on parole; the parole population has tripled since 1980.[183]

How Effective Is Parole?

Conservative thinkers criticize parole because it allows possibly dangerous offenders into the community before the completion of their sentences. Parole decision making relies on human judgment, so it is quite possible that dangerous offenders, who should actually have remained inside a secure facility, are released into society while others who would probably make a good adjustment to the community are denied release.

The evaluation of parole effectiveness has produced some disturbing results. A federal study of 16,000 men and women released in 11 states in 1983 found that within three years, 63 percent had been rearrested for a felony or serious misdemeanor, 47 percent had been convicted of a new crime, and 41 percent had been sent back to prison.[184] The inmates most likely to fail on parole have extensive prior arrests; the study found that 5 percent of the inmates released on parole had 45 or more prior arrests! The inmates most likely to be rearrested shared the following characteristics: released at age 24 or younger; more than seven prior arrests; prior escape attempt; prior parole revoca-tion; committed robbery, burglary, or property offenses; first arrested at a relatively young age; prior drug and violent crime arrests.

A 1991 federal survey of prisons found that 156,000 inmates were released on parole and reinstitutionalized because of violations. Based on the offenses that brought parolees back to prison, these offenders committed at least 6,800 murders, 5,500 rapes, 8,800 assaults, and 22,500 robberies while under supervision in the community an average of 13 months.[185]

What factors predict parole failure? Most research efforts indicate that a long history of criminal behavior, an antisocial personality, a record of substance abuse, and childhood experiences with family dysfunction are all correlated with postrelease recidivism.[186] Parolees who have had a good employment record in the past and who maintain jobs after their release are the most likely to avoid recidivating.[187]

The specter of recidivism is especially frustrating to the American public: it is so difficult to apprehend and successfully prosecute criminal offenders that it seems foolish to grant them early release so they can prey on more victims. This problem is exacerbated when the parolee is a chronic, frequent offender.

In sum, many parolees are returned to prison for technical violations. It is therefore likely that one of the reasons for prison overcrowding is the large number of technical parole violators who are returned within three years of their release. If overcrowding is to be successfully dealt with, a more realistic parole violation policy may have to be developed in areas where the correctional system is under stress.

SUMMARY

Corrections involve the punishment, treatment, and incapacitation of convicted criminal offenders. Methods of punishing offenders have undergone many changes through history. At first fines were levied to compensate the victims and their families for losses. Then cruel corporal and capital punishments were developed. The mercantile system and the development of overseas colonies created the need for labor, so slavery and forced labor began to replace physical punishment. In the late eighteenth century, the death penalty began to be used once again.

Reformers pushed for alternatives to harsh, physical punishment. The prison developed as an alternative that promised to reform and rehabilitate offenders. However, early institutions were brutal places featuring silence, corporal punishment, work details, and warehousing of prisoners. Around the turn of the century, reformers began to introduce such measures as educational training and counseling for inmates. Today corrections can be divided into four components—community-based corrections, jails, prisons, and parole programs.

Many convicted offenders are treated in the community. Some are put on probation under the supervision of local probation departments. If they obey the rules of probation, they are allowed to serve their sentences in the community. A new development is intermediate sanctions, including fines, forfeiture, intensive probation supervision, house arrest, electronic monitoring, and community-based correction facilities. These programs fall somewhere between placement in a closed correctional institution and the freedom of probation. Despite their promise, the effectiveness of alternative corrections methods has not been adequately tested.

The jail is the second element of corrections. It houses misdemeanant offenders serving their sentences and both felons and misdemeanants awaiting trial. The jail is a sore spot in the criminal justice system because jails are usually old and dilapidated and lack rehabilitation programs.

Prisons house convicted felony offenders. Recent shifts in criminal justice philosophy and the passage of laws requiring mandatory sentences have caused a large increase in the U.S. prison population and consequent overcrowding. Prisons are total institutions. Inmates must adjust to a new regimen that controls every aspect of their lives. Prison is a violent, stressful place with its own unique subculture and language. Various rehabilitation devices are used in the prison system, including counseling, educational programs, and vocational training. However, critics charge that these methods do not work. Consequently, the most recent philosophy to dominate the justice system holds that prisons are places of punishment and incapacitation, not treatment.

In the past 20 years, prisoners have been awarded some legal rights by the nation's courts, including rights to medical treatment, freedom of religion, procedural due process, and correspondence with the media.

The fourth component of corrections is aftercare or parole. Parole officers supervise inmates in the community while they complete their sentences. There is little evidence that corrections and parole actually work, and a significant number of released inmates recidivate.

See the book-specific web site at www.cj.wadsworth.com for additional chapter links, discussions, and quizzes.

THINKING LIKE A CRIMINOLOGIST

You are a corrections expert, and the governor has asked for your opinion on a proposed program that will allow prisoners to have completely private regular meetings with their families. The explicit purpose of this visitation program is to grant inmates access to normal family and sexual outlets and thereby counteract the pain of imprisonment.

Those who favor family visitation argue that, if properly administered, it could provide a number of important benefits: inmate frustration levels would diminish, family ties would be strengthened, and normal sexual patterns would continue. Those opposed argue that such visits can serve only the minority of inmates who are married; appropriate facilities are almost universally lacking; family visits can create jealousy among the unmarried inmates; spouses may feel embarrassment at openly sexual visits; and children may be born to parents who cannot support them.

Given the controversy surrounding the issue of family visits, would you recommend the program to the governor?

KEY TERMS

capital punishment
corporal punishment
poor laws
Walnut Street Prison
Auburn system
contract system
convict-lease system
state account system
Z. R. Brockway
probation
intermediate sanction
revoke
offender classification

technical violation
day fines
forfeiture
monetary restitution
community service restitution
split sentencing
shock probation
intensive probation supervision
home confinement
electronic monitoring
shock incarceration
boot camps
jail

prison
penitentiary
the hole
inmate subculture
social code
prisonization
importation model
free-venture programs
hands-off doctrine
parole
parole grant hearing

NOTES

1. Edmund McGarrell, "Institutional Theory and the Stability of a Conflict Model of Incarceration Rate," *Justice Quarterly* 10 (1993): 7–28.

2. Craig W. Floyd, "Violence Behind Bars," *Corrections Today*, 59 (1997): 64.

3. Graeme Newman, *The Punishment Response* (Philadelphia: J. B. Lippincott, 1978), p. 13.

4. Among the most helpful sources for this section are Benedict Alper, *Prisons Inside-Out* (Cambridge, Mass.: Ballinger, 1974); Gustave de Beaumont and Alexis de Tocqueville, *On the Penitentiary System in the United States and Its Application in France* (Carbondale: Southern Illinois University Press, 1964); Orlando Lewis, *The Development of American Prisons and Prison Customs 1776–1845* (Montclair, N.J.: Patterson-Smith, 1967); Leonard Orland, ed., *Justice, Punishment and Treatment* (New York: Free Press, 1973); J. Goebel, *Felony and Misdemeanor* (Philadelphia: University of Pennsylvania Press, 1976); Georg Rusche and Otto Kircheimer, *Punishment and Social Structure* (New York: Russell and Russell, 1939); Samuel Walker, *Popular Justice* (New York: Oxford University Press, 1980); Newman, *The Punishment Response.*

5. Rusche and Kircheimer, *Punishment and Social Structure*, p. 9.

6. Rusche and Kircheimer, *Punishment and Social Structure*, p. 19.

7. Marvin Wolfgang, "Crime and Punishment in Renaissance Florence," *Journal of Criminal Law and Criminology* 81 (1990): 567–84.

8. G. Ives, *A History of Penal Methods* (Montclair, N.J.: Patterson-Smith, 1970).

9. Leon Radzinowicz, *A History of English Criminal Law*, vol. 1 (London: Stevens, 1943), p. 5.

10. Newman, *The Punishment Response*, p. 139.

11. Walker, *Popular Justice*, p. 34.

12. Lewis, *The Development of American Prisons and Prison Customs*, p. 17.

13. Lewis, *The Development of American Prisons and Prison Customs*, p. 29.

14. Alexis Durham III, "Social Control and Imprisonment During the American Revolution: Newgate of Connecticut," *Justice Quarterly* 7 (1990): 293–324.

15. De Beaumont and de Tocqueville, *On the Penitentiary System in the United States*, p. 49.

16. Orland, *Justice, Punishment and Treatment*, p. 143.

17. Walker, *Popular Justice*, p. 70.

18. Larry Goldsmith, "History from the Inside Out: Prison Life in Nineteenth-Century Massachusetts," *Journal of Social History* 31 (1997): 109–136.

19. Walker, *Popular Justice*, p. 71.

20. See Z. R. Brockway, "The Ideal of a True Prison System for a State," in *Transactions of the National Congress on Penitentiary and Reformatory Discipline*, reprint ed. (Washington, D.C.: American Correctional Association, 1970), pp. 38–65.

21. This section relies heavily on David Rothman, *Conscience and Convenience* (Boston: Little, Brown, 1980). See also David Rothman, *The Discovery of the Asylum* (Boston: Little, Brown, 1970).

22. Rothman, *Conscience and Convenience*, p. 23.

23. Rothman, *Conscience and Convenience*, p. 133.

24. See, generally, Jameson Doig, *Criminal Corrections: Ideals and Realities* (Lexington, Mass.: Lexington Books, 1983).

25. See, generally, Chris Eskridge, Richard Seiter, and Eric Carlson, "Community Based Corrections: From the Community to the Community," in *Critical Issues in Corrections*, ed. V. Webb and R. Roberg (St. Paul: West Publishing, 1981), pp. 171–203.

26. *Gagnon v. Scarpelli*, 411 U.S. 778, 93 S.Ct. 1756, 36 L.Ed.2d 655 (1973).

27. Bureau of Justice Statistics, "Nation's Probation and Parole Population Reached New High Last Year," (news release, 16 August 1998).

28. H. Allen, E. Carlson, and E. Parks, *Critical Issues in Adult Probation* (Washington, D.C.: U.S. Government Printing Office, 1979), p. 47.

29. Allen, Carlson, and Parks, *Critical Issues in Adult Probation*.

30. Patricia Harris, "Client Management Classification and Prediction of Probation Outcomes," *Crime and Delinquency* 40 (1994): 154–74.

31. Barbara Sims and Mark Jones, "Predicting Success or Failure on Probation: Factors Associated with Felony Probation Outcomes," *Crime and Delinquency* 43 (1997): 314–27.

32. Karol Lucken, "Privatizing Discretion: 'Rehabilitating' Treatment in Community Corrections," *Crime and Delinquency* 43 (1997): 243–59.

33. David Duffee and Bonnie Carlson, "Competing Value Premises for the Provision of Drug Treatment to Probationers," *Crime and Delinquency* 42 (1996): 574–92.

34. Laurie Schaffner, "Families on Probation: Court-Ordered Parenting Skills Classes for Parents of Juvenile Offenders," *Crime and Delinquency* 43 (1997): 412–37.

35. See, generally, Patrick McAnany, Doug Thomson, and David Fogel, *Probation and Justice: Reconsideration of Mission* (Cambridge, Mass.: Oelgeschlager, Gunn and Hain, 1984).

36. Kit Van Stelle, Elizabeth Mauser, and D. Paul Moberg, "Recidivism to the Criminal Justice System of Substance-Abusing Offenders Diverted into Treatment," *Crime and Delinquency* 40 (1994): 175–96.

37. Robyn L. Cohen, *Probation and Parole Violators in State Prison, 1991* (Washington, D.C.: Bureau of Justice Statistics, 1995).

38. Joan Petersilia, Susan Turner, James Kahan, and Joyce Peterson, *Granting Felons Probation: Public Risks and Alternatives* (Santa Monica, Calif.: Rand Corporation, 1985).

39. Cohen, *Probation and Parole Violators in State Prison, 1991*.

40. Cohen, *Probation and Parole Violators in State Prison, 1991*.

41. W. Reed Benedict and Lin Huff-Corzine, "Return to the Scene of the Punishment: Recidivism of Adult Male Property Offenders on Felony Probation, 1986–1989," *Journal of Research in Crime and Delinquency* 34 (1997): 237–52.

42. For a thorough review, see James Byrne, Arthur Lurigio, and Joan Petersilia, eds., *Smart Sentencing: The Emergence of Intermediate Sanctions* (Newbury Park, Calif.: Sage, 1992).

43. Allen Beck, *Recidivism of Prisoners Released in 1983* (Washington, D.C.: Bureau of Justice Statistics, 1989).

44. Michael Tonry and Richard Will, *Intermediate Sanctions*, Preliminary Report to the National Institute of Justice (Washington, D.C.: National Institute of Justice, 1988), p. 6.

45. Tonry and Will, *Intermediate Sanctions*, p. 8.

46. Ben Crouch, "Is Incarceration Really Worse? Analysis of Offenders' Preferences for Prison over Probation," *Justice Quarterly* 10 (1993): 67–88.

47. David Pauly and Carolyn Friday, "Drexel's Crumbling Defense," *Newsweek*, 19 December 1988, p. 44.

48. George Cole, Barry Mahoney, Marlene Thorton, and Roger Hanson, *The Practices and Attitudes of Trial Court Judges Regarding Fines as a Criminal Sanction* (Washington, D.C.: U.S. Government Printing Office, 1987).

49. Voncile Gowdy, *Intermediate Sanctions* (Washington, D.C.: National Institute of Justice, 1993); "'Day Fines' Being Tested in a New York City Court," *Criminal Justice Newsletter*, 1 September 1988, pp. 4–5.

50. Cole, Mahoney, Thorton, and Hanson, *The Practices and Attitudes of Trial Court Judges Regarding Fines as a Criminal Sanction*.

51. C. Yorke, *Some Consideration on the Law of Forfeiture for High Treason* 26 (2d ed. 1746), cited in David Freid, "Rationalizing Criminal Forfeiture," *Journal of Criminal Law and Criminology* 79 (1988): 328–436 at 329.

52. For a general review, see Robert Carter, Jay Cocks, and Daniel Glazer, "Community Service: A Review of the Basic Issues," *Federal Probation* 51 (1987): 4–11.

53. For a further analysis of restitution, see Larry Siegel, "Court Ordered Victim-Restitution: An Overview of Theory and Action," *New England Journal of Prison Law* 5 (1979): 135–50.

54. Peter Schneider, Anne Schneider, and William Griffith, *Two-Year Report on the National Evaluation of the Juvenile Restitution Initiative: An Overview of Program Performance* (Eugene, Ore.: Institute of Policy Analysis, 1982); Anne Schneider, "Restitution and Recidivism Rates of Juvenile Offenders: Four Experimental Studies," *Criminology* 24 (1936): 533–52.

55. Michael Block and William Rhodes, *The Impact of Federal Sentencing Guidelines* (Washington, D.C.: National Institute of Justice, 1987).

56. Lawrence Greenfeld, *Probation and Parole 1984* (Washington, D.C.: Bureau of Justice Statistics, 1985), p. 2.

57. Harry Allen, Chris Eskridge, Edward Latessa, and Gennaro Vito, *Probation and Parole in America* (New York: Free Press, 1985), p. 88.

58. Joan Petersilia, *The Influence of Criminal Justice Research* (Santa Monica, Calif.: Rand Corp, 1987).

59. James Byrne, Arthur Lurigio, and Christopher Baird, *The Effectiveness of the New Intensive Supervision Programs*, Research in Corrections Series, vol. 2, no. 2 (preliminary unpublished draft; Washington, D.C.: National Institute of Corrections, 1989), p. 16.

60. Stephen Gettinger, "Intensive Supervision: Can It Rehabilitate Probation?" *Corrections* 9 (April 1983): 7–18.

61. James Byrne, "The Control Controversy: A Preliminary Examination of Intensive Probation Supervision Programs in the United States," *Federal Probation* 50 (1986): 4–16.

62. Billie Erwin and Lawrence Bennett, *New Dimensions in Probation: Georgia's Experience with Intensive Probation Supervision (IPS)* (Washington, D.C.: National Institute of Justice, 1987).

63. Michael Agopian, "The Impact of Intensive Supervision Probation on Gang-Drug Offenders," *Criminal Justice Policy Review* 4 (1990): 214–22; Peter Jones, "Expanding the Use of Non-Custodial Sentencing Options: An Evaluation of the Kansas Community Corrections Act," *Howard Journal* 29 (1990): 114–29; Patrick Langan and Mark Cuniff, *Recidivism of Felons on Probation, 1986–1989*, (Washington, D.C.: Bureau of Justice Statistics, 1992), pp. 1–4.

64. James Ryan, "Who Gets Revoked? A Comparison of Intensive Supervision Successes and Failures in Vermont," *Crime and Delinquency* 43 (1997): 104–118.

65. Joan Petersilia, "An Evaluation of Intensive Probation in California," *Journal of Criminal Law and Criminology* 82 (1992): 610–58; Joan Petersilia, "Comparing

Intensive and Regular Supervision for High-Risk Probationers: Early Results from an Experiment in California," *Crime and Delinquency* 36 (1990): 87–111; see also Joan Petersilia, "Conditions That Permit Intensive Supervision Programs to Survive," *Crime and Delinquency* 36 (1990): 126–45.

66. Joan Petersilia, *Expanding Options for Criminal Sentencing* (Santa Monica, Calif.: Rand Corporation, 1987), p. 32.

67. Joan Petersilia, *Expanding Options for Criminal Sentencing*, p. 28.

68. Joan Petersilia, *Expanding Options for Criminal Sentencing*, p. 13.

69. Kenneth Moran and Charles Lindner, "Probation and the Hi-Technology Revolution: Is Reconceptualization of the Traditional Probation Officer Role Model Inevitable?" *Criminal Justice Review* 3 (1987): 25–32.

70. For an extensive review, see Frank Cullen, "Control in the Community: The Limits of Reform" (paper presented at the annual meeting of the International Association of Residential and Community Alternatives, Philadelphia, 1993).

71. Terry Baumer, Michael Maxfield, and Robert Mendelsohn, "A Comparative Analysis of Three Electronically Monitored Home Detention Programs," *Justice Quarterly* 10 (1993): 121–42.

72. Sudipto Roy, "Five Years of Electronic Monitoring of Adults and Juveniles in Lake County, Indiana: A Comparative Study on Factors Related to Failure," *Journal of Crime and Justice* 20 (1997): 141–57.

73. J. Robert Lilly, Richard Ball, G. David Curry, and John McMullen, "Electronic Monitoring of the Drunk Driver: A Seven-Year Study of the Home Confinement Alternative," *Crime and Delinquency* 39 (1993): 462–84.

74. Alexander Esteves, "Electronic Incarceration in Massachusetts: A Critical Analysis," *Social Justice* 17 (1991): 76–90.

75. James Byrne and Linda Kelly, *Restructuring Probation as an Intermediate Sanction: An Evaluation of the Massachusetts Intensive Probation Supervision Program* (Final Report to the National Institute of Justice, Research Program on the Punishment and Control of Offenders, 1989), p. 33.

76. Phone conversation, Scott Hughes, Portland House, October 28, 1997.

77. Doris Layton Mackenzie, Robert Brame, David McDowall, and Claire Souryal, "Boot Camp Prisons and Recidivism in Eight States," *Criminology* 33 (1995): 327–57.

78. Mackenzie, Brame, McDowall, and Souryal, "Boot Camp Prisons and Recidivism in Eight States," pp. 328–29.

79. See, for example, Dale Sechrest, "Prison 'Boot Camps' Do Not Measure Up," *Federal Probation* 53 (1989): 15–20.

80. Doris Layton Mackenzie and James Shaw, "The Impact of Shock Incarceration on Technical Violations and New Criminal Activities," *Justice Quarterly* 10 (1993): 463–87.

81. Doris Layton Mackenzie, "Boot Camp Prisons: Components, Evaluations, and Empirical Issues," *Federal Probation* 54 (1990): 44–52.

82. Doris Layton MacKenzie and Alex Piquero, "The Impact of Shock Incarceration Programs on Prison Crowding," *Crime and Delinquency* 40 (1994): 222–49.

83. Mackenzie, Brame, McDowall, and Souryal, "Boot Camp Prisons and Recidivism in Eight States." pp. 352–53.

84. Cullen, "Control in the Community: The Limits of Reform," p. 28.

85. "Many State Legislatures Focused on Crime in 1995, Study Finds," *Criminal Justice Newsletter* 27 (1 January 1996), p. 2.

86. Margaret Wilson, *The Crime of Punishment*, Life and Letter Series no. 64 (London: Jonathan Cape Ltd., 1934), p. 186.

87. Darrell K. Gilliard and Allen J. Beck, *Prison and Jail Inmates at Midyear 1997* (Washington: D.C.: Bureau of Justice Statistics, 1998), p. 1.

88. See, generally, Daniel Kennedy, "A Theory of Suicide While in Police Custody," *Journal of Police Science and Administration* 12 (1984): 191–200.

89. Allen Beck, Thomas Bonczar, and Darrell Gilliard, *Jail Inmates 1992* (Washington, D.C.: Bureau of Justice Statistics, 1993), p. 3.

90. Note, *Jail Administration Digest* 3 (1980): 4.

91. See Note, *Jail Administration Digest* 2 (1979): 6.

92. Bureau of Justice Statistics, *Prisons and Prisoners* (Washington, D.C.: U.S. Government Printing Office, 1982).

93. Lawrence Hinman, "Stunning Morality: The Moral Dimensions of Stun Belts," *Criminal Justice Ethics* 17 (1998): 3–6.

94. John DiIulio, *Private Prisons* (Washington, D.C.: U.S. Government Printing Office, 1988); Joan Mullen, *Corrections and the Private Sector* (Washington, D.C.: National Institute of Justice, 1984).

95. Vince Beiser. "The New Growth Industry: 'Jailing for Dollars,'" *The New Leader* 80 (1997): 10–12.

96. "Many State Legislatures Focused on Crime in 1995, Study Finds," *Criminal Justice Newsletter* 27 (2 January 1996), p. 2.

97. Lonn Lanza-Kaduce, Karen Parker, and Charles Thomas, "A Comparative Recidivism Analysis of Releases from Private and Public Prisons," *Crime and Delinquency* 45 (1999): 28–47.

98. Charles Logan and Bill McGriff, "Comparing Costs of Public and Private Prisons: A Case Study," *NIJ Reports* (September/October 1989): 2–8.

99. Philip Ethridge and James Marquart, "Private Prisons in Texas: The New Penology for Profit," *Justice Quarterly* 10 (1993): 29–48.

100. Lanza-Kaduce, Parker, and Thomas, "A Comparative Recidivism Analysis of Releases from Private and Public Prisons," pp. 42–43.

101. Darrell K. Gilliard and Allen J. Beck, *Prison and Jail Inmates at Midyear 1997*.

102. Paula Ditton and Doris James Wilson, *Truth in Sentencing in State Prisons* (Washington, D.C.: Bureau of Justice Statistics, 1999).

103. Julia G. Hall, "Why Not Free Older Prisoners?" *Philadelphia Inquirer*, 11 January 1991, p. 19A.

104. Ditton and Wilson, *Truth in Sentencing in State Prisons;* Todd Clear, *Harm in American Penology: Offenders, Victims and Their Communities* (Albany: State University of New York Press, 1994).

105. Michael Tonry, "Parochialism in U.S. Sentencing Policy," *Crime and Delinquency* 45 (1999): 48–65.

106. Ditton and Wilson, *Truth in Sentencing in State Prisons*, p. 1.

107. Patrick A. Langan and Jodi M. Brown, *Felony Sentences in State Courts, 1994*, updated ed. (Washington, D.C.: Bureau of Justice Statistics, 1998).

108. Data here are taken from a variety of sources, including Darrell K. Gilliard and Allen J. Beck, *Prisoners in 1997* (Washington, D.C.: Bureau of Justice Statistics, 1998); Bureau of Justice Statistics, *National Corrections Reporting Program, 1992* (Washington, D.C: Bureau of Justice Statistics, 1994); and Allen Beck, Darrell Gilliard, Lawrence Greenfeld, Caroline Harlow, Thomas Hester, Louis Jankowski, Tracy Snell, James Stephan, and Danielle Morton, *Survey of State Prison Inmates, 1991* (Washington, D.C.: Bureau of Justice Statistics, 1993).

109. Connie L. Neeley, Laura Addison, and Delores Craig-Moreland, "Addressing the Needs of Elderly Offenders," *Corrections Today* 59 (1997): 120–24.

110. Roger Peters, Paul Greenbaum, John Edens, Chris Carter, and Madeline Ortiz, "Prevalence of DSM-IV Substance Abuse and Dependence Disorders Among Prison Inmates," *American Journal of Drug and Alcohol Abuse* 24 (1998): 573–80.

111. Craig Hemmens and James Marquart, "Fear and Loathing in the Joint: The Impact of Race and Age on Inmate Support for Prison AIDS Policies," *Prison Journal* 78 (1998): 133–52.

112. C. S. Lanier, "Affective States of Fathers in Prison," *Justice Quarterly* 10 (1993): 48–65.

113. See E. Goffman, "Characteristics of Total Institutions," in *Justice, Punishment and Treatment*, ed. Leonard Orland (New York: Free Press, 1973), pp. 153–58.

114. Gresham Sykes, *The Society of Captives* (Princeton, N.J.: Princeton University Press, 1958), pp. 79–82.

115. Nicolette Parisi, "The Prisoner's Pressures and Responses," in *Coping with Imprisonment*, ed. N. Parisi (Beverly Hills: Sage, 1982), pp. 9–16.

116. Daniel Lockwood, "The Contribution of Sexual Harassment to Stress and Coping in Confinement," in *Coping with Imprisonment,* ed. N. Parisi (Beverly Hills: Sage, 1982), p. 47.

117. Lockwood, "The Contribution of Sexual Harassment to Stress and Coping in Confinement."

118. Wilbert Rideau and Ron Wikberg, *Life Sentences: Rage and Survival Behind Bars* (New York: Times Books, 1992), pp. 78–80.

119. John Wooldredge, "Inmate Lifestyles and Opportunities for Victimization," *Journal of Research in Crime and Delinquency* 35 (1998): 480–502.

120. Sandra Gleason, "Hustling: The 'Inside' Economy of a Prison," *Federal Probation* 42 (1978): 32–39.

121. Gleason, "Hustling: The 'Inside' Economy of a Prison," p. 39.

122. Geoffrey Hunt, Stephanie Riegel, Tomas Morales, and Dan Waldorf, "Changes in Prison Culture: Prison Gangs and the Case of the 'Pepsi Generation,'" *Social Problems* 40 (1993): 398–407.

123. James B. Jacobs, "The Killing Ground," *Newsweek,* 18 February 1980, p. 75.

124. Parisi, "The Prisoner's Pressures and Responses."

125. Thomas Castellano and Irina Soderstrom, "Self-Esteem, Depression, and Anxiety Evidenced by a Prison Inmate Sample: Interrelationships and Consequences for Prison Programming," *Prison Journal* 77 (1997): 259–71.

126. John Irwin, "Adaptation to Being Corrected: Corrections from the Convict's Perspective," in *Handbook of Criminology,* ed. Daniel Glazer (Chicago: Rand McNally, 1974), pp. 971–93.

127. Donald Clemmer, *The Prison Community* (New York: Holt, Rinehart & Winston, 1958).

128. John Irwin and Donald Cressey, "Thieves, Convicts, and the Inmate Culture," *Social Problems* 10 (1962): 142–55.

129. Paul Gendreau, Marie-Claude Tellier, and J. Stephen Wormith, "Protective Custody: The Emerging Crisis Within Our Prisons," *Federal Probation* 69 (1985): 55–64.

130. James B. Jacobs, *New Perspectives on Prisons and Imprisonment* (Ithaca, N.Y.: Cornell University Press, 1983); James B. Jacobs, "Street Gangs Behind Bars," *Social Problems* 21 (1974): 395–409; James B. Jacobs, "Race Relations and the Prison Subculture," in *Crime and Justice,* ed. N. Morris and M. Tonry (Chicago: University of Chicago Press, 1979), pp. 1–28.

131. Hunt, Riegel, Morales, and Waldorf, "Changes in Prison Culture," pp. 405–408.

132. Esther Heffernan, *Making It in Prison: The Square, the Cool and the Life* (New York: John Wiley, 1972).

133. Christina Jose-Kampfner, "Coming to Terms with Existential Death: An Analysis of Women's Adaptation to Life in Prison," *Social Justice* 17 (1991): 110–20.

134. Merry Morash, Robin Harr, and Lila Rucker, "A Comparison of Programming for Women and Men in U.S. Prison in the 1980's," *Crime and Delinquency* 40 (1994): 197–221.

135. Beverly Fletcher, Lynda Dixon Shaver, and Dreama Moon, *Women Prisoners: A Forgotten Population* (Westport, Conn.: Greenwood Press, 1993), chap. 3.

136. Ira Sommers and Deborah Baskin, "The Prescription of Psychiatric Medications in Prison: Psychiatric Versus Labeling Perspectives," *Justice Quarterly* 7 (1990): 739–55.

137. Rose Giallombardo, *Society of Women: A Study of a Women's Prison* (New York: John Wiley, 1966), pp. 165–89.

138. John Wooldredge and Kimberly Masters, "Confronting Problems Faced by Pregnant Inmates in State Prisons," *Crime and Delinquency* 39 (1993): 195–203.

139. James Marquart, Victoria Brewer, Janet Mullings, and Ben Crouch, "The Implications of Crime Control Policy on HIV/AIDS-Related Risk Among Women Prisoners," *Crime and Delinquency* 45 (1999): 82–98.

140. Pamela Schram, "Stereotypes About Vocational Programming for Female Inmates," *Prison Journal* 78 (1998): 244–71.

141. Morash, Harr, and Rucker, "A Comparison of Programming for Women and Men in U.S. Prison in the 1980's," pp. 214–17.

142. Allen Beck, *Survey of State Prison Inmates, 1991* (Washington, D.C.: Bureau of Justice Statistics, 1993), p. 27.

143. See, generally, G. Kassebaum, D. Ward, and D. Wilner, "Group Counseling," in *Legal Process and Corrections,* ed. N. Johnston and L. Savitz (New York: John Wiley, 1982), pp. 255–70.

144. See William Glasser, *Reality Therapy* (New York: Harper & Row, 1965).

145. Beck, *Survey of State Prison Inmates, 1991,* p. 27.

146. See, generally, Michael Fedo, "Free Enterprise Goes to Prison," *Corrections* 7 (1981): 11–18.

147. Timothy Flanagan and Kathleen Maguire, "A Full Employment Policy for Prisons in the United States: Some Arguments, Estimates and Implications," *Journal of Criminal Justice* 21 (1993): 117–30.

148. This section leans heavily on Mark Hamm, "Current Perspectives on the Prisoner Self-Help Movement," *Federal Probation* 52 (1988): 49–56.

149. Al Parke, "Bringing the Boy Scouts of America into Prison," *Corrections Today* 53 (1991): 154–57.

150. Byron Johnson, David Larson, and Timothy Pitts, "Religious Programs, Institutional Adjustment, and Recidivism Among Former Inmates in Prison Fellowship Programs," *Justice Quarterly* 14 (1997): 145–66.

151. D. Lipton, R. Martinson, and J. Wilks, *The Effectiveness of Correctional Treatment: A Survey of Treatment Evaluation Studies* (New York: Praeger, 1975).

152. Charles Murray and Louis Cox, *Beyond Probation: Juvenile Corrections and the Chronic Delinquent* (Beverly Hills: Sage, 1979).

153. Paul Lerman, *Community Treatment and Social Control* (Chicago: University of Chicago Press, 1975).

154. John Whitehead and Steven Lab, "A Meta-Analysis of Juvenile Correctional Treatment," *Journal of Research in Crime and Delinquency* 26 (1989): 276–95.

155. Charles Logan, *Well Kept: Comparing the Quality of Confinement in a Public and Private Prison* (Washington, D.C.: National Institute of Justice, 1991).

156. Francis Cullen and Karen Gilbert, *Reaffirming Rehabilitation* (Cincinnati: Anderson Publications, 1982).

157. D. A. Andrews, Ivan Zinger, Robert Hoge, James Bonta, Paul Gendreau, and Francis Cullen, "Does Correctional Treatment Work? A Clinically Relevant and Psychologically Informed Meta-Analysis," *Criminology* 28 (1990): 369–405; for an alternative view, see Steven Lab and John Whitehead, "From Nothing Works to the Appropriate Works: The Latest Stop on the Search for the Secular Grail," *Criminology* 28 (1990): 405–19.

158. Mary Ellen Batiuk, Paul Moke, and Pamela Wilcox Rountree, "Crime and Rehabilitation: Correctional Education as an Agent of Change—A Research Note," *Justice Quarterly* 14 (1997): 167–80.

159. Paul Gendreau and Claire Goffin, "Principles of Effective Correctional Programming," *Forum on Correctional Research* 2 (1996): 38–41.

160. Hans Toch, *Police, Prisons and the Problems of Violence* (Washington, D.C.: U.S. Government Printing Office, 1977), p. 53.

161. For a series of papers on the position, see A. Cohen, G. Cole, and R. Baily, eds., *Prison Violence* (Lexington, Mass.: Lexington Books, 1976).

162. Charles Silberman, *Criminal Violence, Criminal Justice* (New York: Vintage Books, 1978).

163. See Hans Toch, "Social Climate and Prison Violence," *Federal Probation* 42 (1978): 21–23.

164. Cited in G. McCain, V. Cox, and P. Paulus, *The Effect of Prison Crowding on Inmate Behavior* (Washington, D.C.: U.S. Government Printing Office, 1981), p. vi.

165. American Correctional Association, *Riots and Disturbances in Correctional Institutions* (Washington, D.C.: American Correctional Association, 1970), p. 1.

166. Randy Martin and Sherwood Zimmerman, "A Typology of the Causes of Prison Riots and an Analytical Extension to the 1986 West Virginia Riot," *Justice Quarterly* 7 (1990): 711–37.

167. National Advisory Commission on Criminal Justice Standards and Goals, *Volume on Corrections* (Washington, D.C.: U.S. Government Printing Office, 1973), p. 18.

168. See, for example, *Cooper v. Pate,* 378 U.S. 546 (1964).

169. *Lewis v. Casey,* 94.1511 (1996).

170. *Procunier v. Martinez,* 416 U.S. 396 (1974); *Saxbe v. Washington Post,* 41 L.Ed.2d 514 (1974).

171. *Newman v. Alabama,* 349 F.Supp. 278 (M.D.Ala., 1974).

172. *Estelle v. Gamble,* 429 U.S. 97 (1976).

173. 97 S.Ct. 291 (1976).

174. See, for example, *Trop v. Dulles,* 356 U.S. 86, 78 S.Ct. 590 (1958); see also *Furman v. Georgia,* 408 U.S. 238, 92 S.Ct. 2726, 33 L.Ed.2d 346 (1972).

175. See, for example, *Weems v. United States,* 217 U.S. 349, 30 S.Ct. 544, 54 L.Ed. 793 (1910).

176. See, for example, *Lee v. Tahash,* 352 F.2d 970 (8th Cir., 1965).

177. 309 F. Supp. 362 (E.D. Ark. 1970); aff'd 442 F.2d 304 (Ninth Cir., 1971).

178. *Rhodes v. Chapman,* 452 U.S. 337 (1981).

179. *Rhodes v. Chapman,* 337.

180. *Estelle v. Ruiz,* 74-329 (E.D. Texas, 1980).

181. See Peter Hoffman and Lucille DeGostin, "Parole Decision-Making: Structuring Discretion," *Federal Probation* 38 (1974): 19–21.

182. Peter Hoffman and Barbara Stone-Meierhoefer, "Post-Release Arrest Experiences of Federal Prisoners: A Six Year Follow-Up," *Journal of Criminal Justice* 7 (1979): 193–216.

183. Bureau of Justice Statistics News Release, "Probation and Parole Population Reaches Almost 3.8 Million" (news release, 30 June 1996).

184. Allen Beck and Bernard Shipley, *Recidivism of Prisoners Released in 1983* (Washington, D.C.: Bureau of Justice Statistics, 1989).

185. Robyn L. Cohen, *Probation and Parole Violators in State Prison, 1991: Survey of State Prison Inmates, 1991* (Washington, D.C: Bureau of Justice Statistics, 1995).

186. James Bonta, Moira Law, and Karl Hanson, "The Prediction of Criminal and Violent Recidivism Among Mentally Disordered Offenders: A Meta-Analysis," *Psychological Bulletin* 123 (1998): 123–42.

187. Thomas Hanlon, David Nurco, Richard Bateman, and Kevin O'Grady, "The Response of Drug Abuser Parolees to a Combination of Treatment and Intensive Supervision," *Prison Journal* 78 (1998): 31–45.

GLOSSARY

absolute deterrent A legal control measure designed to totally eliminate a particular criminal act.

Academy of Criminal Justice Sciences The society that serves to further the development of the criminal justice profession; its membership includes academics and practitioners involved in criminal justice.

access control A crime prevention technique that stresses target hardening through security measures, such as alarm systems, that make it more difficult for criminals to attack a target.

accountability system A way of dealing with police corruption by making superiors responsible for the behavior of their subordinates.

acquittal Release or discharge, especially by verdict of a jury.

active precipitation The view that the source of many criminal incidents is the aggressive or provocative behavior of victims.

actus reus An illegal act. The *actus reus* can be an affirmative act, such as taking money or shooting someone, or a failure to act, such as failing to take proper precautions while driving a car.

addict A person with an overpowering physical and psychological need to continue taking a particular substance or drug by any means possible.

addiction-prone personality The view that the cause of substance abuse can be traced to a personality with a compulsion for mood-altering drugs.

adjudication The determination of guilt or innocence; a judgment concerning criminal charges. Most offenders plead guilty as charged. The remainder are adjudicated by a judge and a jury or by a judge alone, and others are dismissed.

adversary system The procedure used to determine truth in the adjudication of guilt or innocence in which the defense (advocate for the accused) is pitted against the prosecution (advocate for the state), with the judge acting as arbiter of the legal rules. Under the adversary system, the burden is on the state to prove the charges beyond a reasonable doubt. This system of having the two parties publicly debate has proved to be the most effective method of achieving the truth regarding a set of circumstances. (Under the accusatory, or inquisitorial, system, which is used in continental Europe, the charge is evidence of guilt that the accused must disprove, and the judge takes an active part in the proceedings.)

affidavit A written statement of fact, signed and sworn to before a person having authority to administer an oath.

age of onset Age at which youths begin their delinquent careers. Early onset of delinquency is believed to be linked with chronic offending patterns.

aging out The process by which individuals reduce the frequency of their offending behavior as they age. It is also known as spontaneous remission, because people are believed to spontaneously reduce the rate of their criminal behavior as they mature. Aging out is thought to occur among all groups of offenders.

aggregate data Data collected on groups of people rather than individuals. A good example of aggregate data is the Uniform Crime Reports index crimes; although the number of criminal incidents that occur in a given area can be counted, little data are provided on the offenders who commit the crimes or the circumstances in which they occurred. Self-report surveys are usually considered individual-level data, since subjects' responses can be examined on a case-by-case basis.

aggressive preventive patrol A patrol technique designed to suppress crime before it occurs.

alien conspiracy theory The view that organized crime was imported to the United States by Europeans and that crime cartels have a policy of restricting their membership to people of their own ethnic background.

alienation A mental condition marked by normlessness and role confusion.

alternative sanctions The group of punishments falling between probation and prison; "probation plus." Community-based sanctions, including house arrest and intensive supervision, serve as alternatives to incarceration.

American Society of Criminology The professional society of criminology that is devoted to enhancing the status of the discipline.

androgens Male sex hormones.

anesthetics Drugs used as nervous system depressants. Local anesthetics block nervous system transmissions; general anesthetics act on the brain to produce a generalized loss of sensation, stupor, or unconsciousness.

anger rape A rape motivated by the rapist's desire to release pent-up anger and rage.

anomie A condition produced by normlessness. Because of rapidly shifting moral values, the individual has few guides to what is socially acceptable. According to Merton, anomie is a condition that occurs when personal goals cannot be achieved by available means. In Agnew's revision anomie can occur when positive or valued stimuli are removed or negative or painful ones applied.

antisocial personality Synonymous with psychopath, the antisocial personality is characterized by a lack of normal responses to life situations, the inability to learn from punishment, and violent reactions to non-threatening events.

appeal A review of lower-court proceedings by a higher court. Appellate courts do not retry the case under review. Rather, the transcript of the lower-court case is read by the appellate judges, who determine the legality of lower-court proceedings. When appellate courts reverse lower-court judgments, it is usually because of "prejudicial error" (deprivation of rights), and the case is remanded for retrial.

appellate courts Courts that reconsider a case that has already been tried to determine whether the measures used complied with accepted rules of criminal procedure and were in line with constitutional doctrines.

arbitrage The practice of buying large blocks of stock in companies that are believed to be the target of corporate buyouts or takeovers.

argot The unique language that influences the prison culture.

arousal theory A view of crime suggesting that people who have a high arousal level seek powerful stimuli in their environment to maintain an optimal level of arousal. These stimuli are often associated with violence and aggression. Sociopaths may need greater than average stimulation to bring them up to comfortable levels of living; this need explains their criminal tendencies.

arraignment The step in the criminal justice process at which the accused are read the charges against them, asked how they plead, and advised of their rights. Possible pleas are guilty, not guilty, *nolo contendere,* and not guilty by reason of insanity.

arrest The taking of a person into the custody of the law, the legal purpose of which is to restrain the accused until he or she can be held accountable for the offense at court proceedings. The legal requirement for an arrest is probable cause. Arrests for investigation, suspicion, or harassment are improper and of doubtful legality. The police have the responsibility to use only the reasonable physical force necessary to make an arrest. The summons has been used as a substitute for arrest.

arrest warrant A written court order by a magistrate authorizing and directing that an individual be taken into custody to answer criminal charges.

arson The intentional or negligent burning of a home, structure, or vehicle for criminal purposes such as profit, revenge, fraud, or crime concealment.

Aryan Brotherhood A white supremacist prison gang.

assembly-line justice The view that the justice process resembles an endless production line that handles most cases in a routine and perfunctory fashion.

atavistic traits According to Lombroso, the physical characteristics that distinguish born criminals from the general population and are throwbacks to animals or primitive people.

attainder The loss of all civil rights because of a conviction for a felony offense.

attention deficit/hyperactive disorder (ADHD) A psychological disorder in which a child shows a developmentally inappropriate impulsivity, hyperactivity, and lack of attention.

attorney general The senior federal prosecutor and cabinet member who heads the Justice Department.

Auburn system The prison system developed in New York during the 19th century that stressed congregate working conditions.

authoritarian A personality type that revolves around blind obedience to authority.

authority conflict pathway The path to a criminal career that begins with early stubborn behavior and defiance of parents.

bail The monetary amount for or condition of pretrial release, normally set by a judge at the initial appearance. The purpose of bail is to ensure the return of the accused at subsequent proceedings. If the accused is unable to make bail, he or she is detained in jail. The Eighth Amendment provides that excessive bail shall not be required.

bail bonding The business of providing bail to needy offenders, usually at an exorbitant rate of interest.

Bail Reform Act of 1984 Federal legislation that provides for both greater emphasis on release on recognizance for nondangerous offenders and preventive detention for those who present a menace to the community.

base penalty The model sentence in a structured sentencing state, which can be enhanced or diminished to reflect aggravating or mitigating circumstances.

behaviorism The branch of psychology concerned with the study of observable behavior rather than unconscious motives. It focuses on the relationship between particular stimuli and people's responses to them.

beyond a reasonable doubt Degree of proof required for conviction of a defendant in criminal and juvenile delinquency proceedings. It is less than absolute certainty but more than high probability. If there is doubt based on reason, the accused is entitled to the benefit of that doubt by acquittal.

bill of indictment A document submitted to a grand jury by the prosecutor asking it to take action and indict a suspect.

Bill of Rights The first ten amendments to the U.S. Constitution.

blameworthiness The amount of culpability or guilt a person maintains for participating in a particular criminal offense.

blue curtain According to William Westly, the secretive, insulated police culture that isolates the officer from the rest of society.

booking The administrative record of an arrest listing the offender's name, address, physical description, date of birth, and employer; the time of arrest; the offense; and the name of arresting officer. Photographing and fingerprinting of the offender are also part of booking.

boot camp A short-term militaristic correctional facility in which inmates undergo intensive physical conditioning and discipline.

bot Under Anglo-Saxon law, the restitution paid for killing someone in an open fight.

bourgeoisie In Marxist theory, the owners of the means of production; the capitalist ruling class.

broken windows The term used to describe the role of the police as maintainers of community order and safety.

brothel A house of prostitution, typically run by a madam who sets prices and handles "business" arrangements.

brutalization effect The belief that capital punishment creates an atmosphere of brutality that enhances rather than deters the level of violence in society. The death penalty reinforces the view that violence is an appropriate response to provocation.

brutalization process According to Athens, the first stage in a violent career during which parents victimize children, causing them to develop a belligerent, angry demeanor.

burden of proof Duty of proving disputed facts on the trial of a case. The duty commonly lies on the person who asserts the affirmative of an issue and is sometimes said to shift when sufficient evidence is furnished to raise a presumption that what is alleged is true.

burglary Breaking into and entering a home or structure for the purposes of committing a felony.

call girls Prostitutes who make dates via the phone and then service customers in hotel rooms or apartments. Call girls typically have a steady clientele who are repeat customers.

capital punishment The use of the death penalty to punish transgressors.

career criminal A person who repeatedly violates the law and organizes his or her lifestyle around criminality.

Carriers case A 15th-century case that defined the law of theft and reformulated the concept of taking the possessions of another.

cerebral allergies A physical condition that causes brain malfunction due to exposure to some environmental or biochemical irritant.

certiorari Literally, "to be informed of, to be made certain in regard to." *See* writ of certiorari

challenge for cause Removing a juror because he or she is biased, has prior knowledge about a case, or otherwise is unable to render a fair and impartial judgment in a case.

chancery court A court created in 15th-century England to oversee the lives of high-born minors who were orphaned or otherwise could not care for themselves.

charge In a criminal case, the specific crime the defendant is accused of committing.

cheater theory A theory suggesting that a sub-population of men has evolved with genes that incline them toward extremely low parental involvement. Sexually aggressive, they use their cunning to gain sexual conquests with as many females as possible.

Chicago Crime Commission A citizen action group set up in Chicago to investigate problems in the criminal justice system and explore avenues for positive change; the fore-runner of many such groups around the country.

child abuse Any physical, emotional, or sexual trauma to a child for which no reasonable explanation, such as an accident, can be found. Child abuse can also be a function of neglecting to give proper care and attention to a young child.

chivalry hypothesis The idea that low female crime and delinquency rates are a reflection of the leniency with which police treat female offenders.

choice theory The school of thought holding that people will engage in delinquent and criminal behavior after weighing the consequences and benefits of their actions. Delinquent behavior is a rational choice made by a motivated offender who perceives that the chances of gain outweigh any perceived punishment or loss.

Christopher Commission An investigatory group led by Warren Christopher that investigated the Los Angeles Police Department in the wake of the Rodney King beating.

chronic offender According to Wolfgang, a delinquent offender who is arrested five or more times before he or she is 18 and who stands a good chance of becoming an adult criminal; such offenders are responsible for more than half of all serious crimes.

chronicity State of being a chronic recidivist.

churning A white-collar crime in which a stockbroker makes repeated trades to fraudulently increase his or her commissions.

civil death The custom of terminating the civil rights of convicted felons, such as forbidding them the right to vote or marry. No state uses civil death today.

civil law All law that is not criminal, including torts (personal wrongs), contract, property, maritime, and commercial law.

Civil Rights Division That part of the U.S. Justice Department that handles cases involving violations of civil rights guaranteed by the Constitution and federal law.

classical theory The theoretical perspective suggesting that (1) people have free will to choose criminal or conventional behaviors; (2) people choose to commit crime for reasons of greed or personal need; and (3) crime can be controlled only by the fear of criminal sanctions.

classification The procedure in which prisoners are categorized on the basis of their personal characteristics and criminal history and then assigned to an appropriate institution.

cocaine The most powerful natural stimulant. Its use produces euphoria, laughter, restlessness, and excitement. Overdoses can cause delirium, increased reflexes, violent manic behavior, and possible respiratory failure.

Code of Hammurabi The first written criminal code developed in Babylonia about 2000 B.C.

coeducational prison An institution that houses both male and female inmates who share work and recreational facilities.

cognitive theory The study of the perception of reality and of the mental processes required to understand the world we live in.

cohort study A study using a sample of subjects whose behavior is followed over a period of time.

common law Early English law, developed by judges, that incorporated Anglo-Saxon tribal custom, feudal rules and practices, and the everyday rules of behavior of local villages. Common law became the standardized law of the land in England and eventually formed the basis of the criminal law in the United States.

community notification laws Recent legislative efforts that require convicted sex offenders to register with local police when they move into an area or neighborhood.

community policing A police strategy that emphasizes fear reduction, community organization, and order maintenance rather than crime fighting.

community service restitution An alternative sanction that requires an offender to work in the community at such tasks as cleaning public parks or helping handicapped children in lieu of an incarceration sentence.

community treatment The actions of correctional agencies that attempt to maintain the convicted offender in the community, instead of a secure facility; includes probation, parole, and residential programs.

compensation Financial aid awarded to the victims of crime to repay them for their loss and injuries.

complaint A sworn allegation made in writing to a court or judge that an individual is guilty of some designated (complained of) offense. This is often the first legal document filed regarding a criminal offense. The complaint can be "taken out" by the victim, the police officer, the district attorney, or another interested party. Although the complaint charges an offense, an indictment or information may be the formal charging document.

compliance A white-collar enforcement strategy that encourages law-abiding behavior through both the threat of economic sanctions and the promise of rewards for conformity.

concurrent sentences Literally, running sentences together. Someone who is convicted of two or more charges must be sentenced on each charge. If the sentences are concurrent, they begin the same day and are completed after the longest term has been served.

conduct disorder A psychological condition marked by repeated and severe episodes of antisocial behaviors.

conduct norms Behaviors expected of social group members. If group norms conflict with those of the general culture, members of the group may find themselves described as outcasts or criminals.

conflict view The view that human behavior is shaped by interpersonal conflict and that those who maintain social power will use it to further their own needs.

conjugal visit A prison program that allows inmates to receive private visits from their spouses for the purpose of maintaining normal interpersonal relationships.

consecutive sentences Prison sentences for two or more criminal acts that are served one after the other.

consensus view of crime The belief that the majority of citizens in a society share common ideals and work toward a common good and that crimes are acts that are outlawed because they conflict with the rules of the majority and are harmful to society.

consent decree Decree entered by consent of the parties. Not properly a judicial sentence but in the nature of a solemn contract or agreement of the parties that the decree is a just determination of their rights based on the real facts of the case, if such facts are proved.

constable The peacekeeper in early English towns. The constable organized citizens to protect his territory and supervised the night watch.

constructive intent The finding of criminal liability for an unintentional act that is the result of negligence or recklessness.

constructive possession In the crime of larceny, willingly giving up temporary physical possession of property but retaining legal ownership.

containments According to Reckless, internal and external factors and conditions that help insulate youths from delinquency-promoting situations. Most important of the internal containments is a strong self-concept, while external containments include positive support from parents and teachers.

continuance A judicial order to continue a case without a finding, to gather more information or allow the defendant to begin a community-based treatment program.

continuity of crime The view that crime begins early in life and continues throughout the life course. Thus, the best predictor of future criminality is past criminality.

contract system (attorney) Providing counsel to indigent offenders by having attorneys under contract to the county to handle all (or some) such cases.

contract system (convict) The system used earlier in the century in which inmates were leased out to private industry to work.

convict subculture The separate culture in the prison that has its own set of rewards and behaviors. The traditional culture is now being replaced by a violent gang culture.

conviction A judgment of guilt; a verdict by a jury, a plea by a defendant, or a judgment by a court that the accused is guilty as charged.

co-offending Committing criminal acts in groups. It is believed that a significant number of delinquent and criminal acts involve more than one offender.

corner boy According to Cohen, a role in the lower-class culture in which young men remain in their birth neighborhood, acquire families and menial jobs, and adjust to the demands of their environment.

corporal punishment The use of physical chastisement, such as whipping or electroshock, to punish criminals.

corporate crime White-collar crime involving a legal violation by a corporate entity, such as price fixing, restraint of trade, or hazardous waste dumping.

corpus delicti The body of the crime, made up of the *actus reus* and *mens rea*.

corrections The agencies of justice that take custody of offenders after their conviction and are entrusted with their treatment and control.

court administrator The individual who controls the operations of the courts system in a particular jurisdiction; he or she may be in charge of scheduling, juries, judicial assignment, and so on.

court-leet During the Middle Ages, the local hundred or manor court that dealt with most secular violations.

court of last resort A court that handles the final appeal on a matter. The U.S. Supreme Court is the official court of last resort for criminal matters.

courtroom work group The phrase used to denote that all parties in the adversary process work together to settle cases with the least amount of effort and conflict.

courts of limited jurisdiction Courts that handle misdemeanors and minor civil complaints.

covert pathway A path to a criminal career that begins with minor underhanded behavior and progresses to fire starting and theft.

crack A smokable form of purified cocaine that provides an immediate and powerful high.

crackdown The concentration of police resources on a particular problem area, such as street-level drug dealing, to eradicate or displace criminal activity.

crime A violation of societal rules of behavior as interpreted and expressed by a criminal legal code created by people holding social and political power. Individuals who violate these rules are subject to sanctions by state authority, social stigma, and loss of status.

crime control A model of criminal justice that emphasizes the control of dangerous offenders and the protection of society. Its advocates call for harsh punishments, such as the death penalty, as a deterrent to crime.

crime displacement An effect of crime prevention efforts in which efforts to control crime in one area shift illegal activities to another.

crime fighter A police style that stresses dealing with hard crimes and arresting dangerous criminals.

criminal anthropology Early efforts to discover a biological basis of crime through measurement of physical and mental processes.

Criminal Division The branch of the U.S. Justice Department that prosecutes federal criminal violations.

criminal justice process The decision-making points from the initial investigation or arrest by police to the eventual release of the offender and his or her reentry into society; the various sequential criminal justice stages through which the offender passes.

criminal law The body of rules that define crimes, set out their punishments, and mandate the procedures in carrying out the criminal justice process.

criminal sanction The right of the state to punish people if they violate the rules set down in the criminal code; the punishment connected to commission of a specific crime.

criminological enterprise The areas of study and research that taken together make up the field of criminology. Criminologists typically specialize in one of the subareas of criminology, such as victimology or the sociology of law.

criminology The scientific study of the nature, extent, cause, and control of criminal behavior.

cross-examination The process in which the defense and the prosecution interrogate witnesses during a trial.

cross-sectional data Survey data that derive from all age, race, gender, and income segments of the population being measured simultaneously. Since people from every age group are represented, age-specific crime rates can be determined. Proponents believe that this is a sufficient substitute for the more expensive longitudinal approach that follows a group of subjects over time in order to measure crime rate changes.

cruel and unusual punishment Physical punishment that is far in excess of that given to people under similar circumstances and is therefore banned by the Eighth Amendment. The death penalty has so far not been considered cruel and unusual if it is administered in a fair and nondiscriminatory fashion.

culpable Referring to a wrongful act that does not involve malice. It connotes fault rather than guilt.

cultural transmission The concept that conduct norms are passed down from one generation to the next so that they become stable within the boundaries of a culture. Cultural transmission guarantees that group lifestyle and behavior are stable and predictable.

culture conflict According to Sellin, a condition brought about when the rules and norms of an individual's subcultural affiliation conflict with the role demands of conventional society.

culture of poverty The view that people in the lower class of society form a separate culture with its own values and norms that are in conflict with conventional society; the culture is self-maintaining and ongoing.

curtilage The fields attached to a house.

custodial convenience The principle of giving jailed inmates the minimum comforts required by law to contain the costs of incarceration.

cynicism The belief that most peoples' actions are motivated solely by personal needs and selfishness.

DARE Drug Abuse Resistance Education, a school-based antidrug program initiated by the Los Angeles police and now adopted around the United States.

day fines Fines geared to the average daily income of the convicted offender in an effort to bring equity to the sentencing process.

day reporting centers Nonresidential, community-based treatment programs.

deadly force The ability of the police to kill suspects if they resist arrest or present a danger to an officer or the community. The police cannot use deadly force against an unarmed fleeing felon.

decarceration A correctional philosophy that stresses the "least restrictive alternative possible" for removing as many people from secure detention as possible and making use of community alternatives.

decriminalization Reducing the penalty for a criminal act but not actually legalizing it.

defeminization The process by which policewomen become enculturated into the police profession at the expense of their feminine identity.

defendant The accused in criminal proceedings; he or she has the right to be present at each stage of the criminal justice process, except grand jury proceedings.

defense attorney The counsel for the defendant in a criminal trial who represents the individual from arrest to final appeal.

defensible space The principle that crime prevention can be achieved through modifying the physical environment to reduce the opportunity individuals have to commit crime.

degenerate anomalies According to Lombroso, the primitive physical characteristics that make criminals animalistic and savage.

deinstitutionalization The movement to remove as many offenders as possible from secure confinement and treat them in the community.

demeanor The way in which a person outwardly manifests his or her personality.

demystify The process by which Marxists unmask the true purpose of the capitalist system's rules and laws.

desert-based sentences Sentences in which the length is based on the seriousness of the criminal act and not the personal characteristics of the defendant or the deterrent impact of the law; punishment is based on what people have done and not on what they or others may do in the future.

desistance The process in which crime rate declines with the perpetrator's age; synonymous with the aging-out process.

detective The police personnel assigned to investigate crimes after they have been reported, to gather evidence, and to identify the perpetrator.

detention Holding an offender in secure confinement before trial.

determinate sentence A fixed term of incarceration, such as three years' imprisonment. Determinate sentences are felt by many to be too restrictive for rehabilitative purposes; the advantage is that offenders know how much time they have to serve—that is, when they will be released. *See also* indeterminate sentence

deterrence The act of preventing crime before it occurs by means of the threat of criminal sanctions. Deterrence involves the perception that the pain of apprehension and punishment outweighs any chances of criminal gain or profit.

developmental criminology A branch of criminology that examines change in a criminal career over the life course. Developmental factors include biological, social, and psychological change. Among the topics of developmental criminology are desistance, resistance, escalation, and specialization.

deviance Behavior that departs from the social norm.

differential association According to Sutherland, the principle that criminal acts are related to a person's exposure to an excess amount of antisocial attitudes and values.

diffusion of benefits An effect that occurs when an effort to control one type of crime has the unexpected benefit of reducing the incidence of another.

direct examination The questioning of one's own (prosecution or defense) witness during a trial.

directed verdict The right of a judge to direct a jury to acquit a defendant because the state has not proven the elements of the crime or otherwise has not established guilt according to law.

disaggregate Analyzing the relationship between two or more independent variables while controlling for the influence of a third dependent variable. For example, looking at the relationship between conviction for murder and the likelihood of a death sentence disaggregated by race would entail separate analysis of the sentencing outcomes of whites and African Americans convicted of first-degree murder.

discouragement An effect that occurs when an effort made to eliminate one type of crime also controls others, because it reduces the value of criminal activity by limiting access to desirable targets.

discretion The use of personal decision making and choice in carrying out operations in the criminal justice system. For example, police discretion can involve the decision to make an arrest, while prosecutorial discretion can involve the decision to accept a plea bargain.

disposition For juvenile offenders, the equivalent of sentencing for adult offenders. The theory is that disposition is more rehabilitative than retributive. Possible dispositions may be to dismiss the case, release the youth to the custody of his or her parents, place the offender on probation, or send him or her to a correctional institution.

disputatiousness In the subculture of violence, it is considered appropriate behavior for a person who has been offended to seek satisfaction through violent means.

district attorney The county prosecutor who is charged with bringing offenders to justice and enforcing the laws of the state.

diversion An alternative to criminal trial usually featuring counseling, job training, and educational opportunities.

DNA profiling The identification of criminal suspects by matching DNA samples taken from them with specimens found at crime scenes.

double bunking The practice of holding two or more inmates in a single cell because of prison overcrowding; upheld in *Rhodes v. Chapman*.

double marginality According to Alex, the social burden African American police officers carry by being both minority group members and law enforcement officers.

drift According to Matza, the view that youths move in and out of delinquency and that their lifestyles can embrace both conventional and deviant values.

drug courier profile A way of identifying drug runners based on their personal characteristics; police may stop and question individuals based on the way they fit the characteristics contained in the profile.

Drug Enforcement Administration (DEA) The federal agency that enforces federal drug control laws.

due process The constitutional principle based on the concept of the primacy of the individual and the complementary concept of limitation on governmental power; a safeguard against arbitrary and unfair state procedures in judicial or administrative proceedings. Embodied in the due process concept are the basic rights of a defendant in criminal proceedings and the requisites for a fair trial. These rights and requirements have been expanded by appellate court decisions and include (1) timely notice of a hearing or trial that informs the accused of the charges against him or her; (2) the opportunity to confront accusers and to present evidence on the accused's own behalf before an impartial jury or judge; (3) the presumption of innocence under which guilt must be proven by legally obtained evidence and the verdict must be supported by the evidence presented; (4) the right of an accused to be warned of constitu-

tional rights at the earliest stage of the criminal process; (5) protection against self-incrimination; (6) assistance of counsel at every critical stage of the criminal process; and (7) the guarantee that an individual will not be tried more than once for the same offense (double jeopardy).

Durham rule A definition of insanity used in New Hampshire that required that the crime be excused if it was a product of a mental illness.

early onset A term that refers to the assumption that a criminal career begins early in life and that people who are deviant at a very young age are the ones most likely to persist in crime.

economic compulsive behavior Behavior that occurs when drug users resort to violence to gain funds to support their habit.

economic crime An act in violation of the criminal law that is designed to bring financial gain to the offender.

economism The policy of controlling white-collar crime through monetary incentives and sanctions.

egalitarian family A family structure in which both parents share equal authority and power.

ego identity According to Erikson, ego identity is formed when persons develop a firm sense of who they are and what they stand for.

electroencephalogram (EEG) A device that can record the electronic impulses given off by the brain, commonly called brain waves.

embedded Becoming entrenched in a delinquent way of life, thereby reducing any chances of future success in the marketplace.

embezzlement A type of larceny that involves taking the possessions of another (fraudulent conversion) that have been placed in the thief's lawful possession for safekeeping, such as a bank teller misappropriating deposits or a stockbroker making off with a customer's account.

enterprise syndicate An organized crime group that profits from the sale of illegal goods and services, such as narcotics, pornography, and prostitution.

entrapment A criminal defense maintaining that the police originated the criminal idea or initiated the criminal action.

entrepreneur One willing to take risks for profit in the marketplace.

equipotentiality View that all individuals are equal at birth and are thereafter influenced by their environment.

equity The action or practice of awarding each his or her just due; sanctions based on equity seek to compensate individual victims and the general society for their losses due to crime.

ex post facto **laws** Laws that make an act criminal after it was committed or that retroactively increase the penalty for a crime; for example, an *ex post facto* law could change shoplifting from a misdemeanor to a felony and penalize offenders with a prison term, even though they had been apprehended six months prior. Such laws are unconstitutional.

exceptional circumstances doctrine Under this policy, courts would hear only those cases brought by inmates in which the circumstances indicated a total disregard for human dignity, while denying hearings on less serious crimes. Cases allowed access to the courts usually involve a situation of total denial of medical care.

exclusionary rule The principle that prohibits using evidence illegally obtained in a trial. Based on the Fourth Amendment "right of the people to be secure in their persons, houses, papers, and effects, against unreasonable searches and seizures," the rule is not a bar to prosecution, as legally obtained evidence may be available that may be used in a trial.

excuse A defense to a criminal charge in which the accused maintains he or she lacked the intent to commit the crime (*mens rea*).

expressive crime A crime that has no purpose except to accomplish the behavior at hand, such as shooting someone.

expressive violence Violence that is designed not for profit or gain but to vent rage, anger, or frustration.

extinction The phenomenon in which a crime prevention effort has an immediate impact that then dissipates as criminals adjust to new conditions.

extraversion a personality trait marked by impulsivity and the inability to examine motives and behavior.

false pretenses Illegally obtaining money, goods, or merchandise from another by fraud or misrepresentation.

Federal Bureau of Investigation (FBI) The arm of the U.S. Justice Department that investigates violations of federal law, gathers crime statistics, runs a comprehensive crime laboratory, and helps train local law enforcement officers.

felony A serious offense that carries a penalty of incarceration in a state prison, usually for one year or more. Persons convicted of felony offenses lose such rights as the rights to vote, hold elective office, or maintain certain licenses.

fence A buyer and seller of stolen merchandise.

field training officer A senior police officer who trains recruits in the field.

fixed time rule A policy in which people must be tried within a stated period after their arrest; overruled in *Barker v. Wingo,* which created a balancing test.

flat or fixed sentencing A sentencing model mandating that all people who are convicted of a specific offense and who are sent to prison must receive the same length of incarceration.

focal concerns According to Miller, the value orientations of lower-class cultures; features include the needs for excitement, trouble, smartness, fate, and personal autonomy.

folkways Generally followed customs that do not have moral values attached to them, such as not interrupting people when they are speaking.

foot patrols Police patrols that take officers out of cars and put them on a walking beat to strengthen ties with the community.

forfeiture The seizure of personal property by the state as a civil or criminal penalty.

fraud Taking the possessions of another through deception or cheating, such as selling a person a desk that is represented as an antique but is known to be a copy.

free venture Privately run industries in a prison setting in which the inmates work for wages and the goods are sold for profit.

free will The idea that people are in charge of their own destinies and are free to make personal behavior choices unencumbered by environmental controls; the opposite of determinism. Choice theories are based on the concept of free will.

functionalism The sociological perspective that suggests that each part of society makes a contribution to the maintenance of the whole. Functionalism stresses social cooperation and consensus of values and beliefs among a majority of society's members.

fundamental fairness The legal principle that all people should be equal before the law and treated so.

furlough A correctional policy that allows inmates to leave the institution for vocational or educational training, for employment, or to maintain family ties.

gay bashing Violent hate crimes directed toward people because of their sexual orientation.

general deterrence A crime control policy that depends on the fear of criminal penalties. General deterrence measures, such as long prison sentences for violent crimes, are aimed at convincing the potential law violator that the pains associated with crime outweigh its benefits.

general intent Actions that on their face indicate a criminal purpose, such as breaking into a locked building or trespassing on someone's property.

gentrification A process of reclaiming and reconditioning deteriorated neighborhoods by refurbishing depressed real estate and then renting or selling the properties to upper-middle-class professionals.

good faith exception The principle of law holding that evidence may be used in a criminal trial even though the search warrant used to obtain it is technically faulty, if the police acted in good faith and to the best of their ability when they sought to obtain it from a judge.

good-time credit Time taken off a prison sentence in exchange for good behavior within the institution, such as ten days per month. The device is used to limit disciplinary problems within the prison.

graffiti Inscription or drawing made on a wall or structure. Used by delinquents for gang messages and turf definition.

grand jury A group (usually consisting of 23 citizens) chosen to hear testimony in secret and to issue formal criminal accusations (indictments). It also serves an investigatory function.

grass eaters A term used for police officers who accept payoffs when their everyday duties place them in a position to be solicited by the public.

greenmail The process by which an arbitrager buys large blocks of a company's stock and threatens to take over the company and replace the management. To ward off the threat to their positions, members of management use company funds to repurchase the shares at a much higher price, creating huge profits for the corporate raiders.

guardian *ad litem* A court-appointed attorney who protects the interests of a child in cases involving the child's welfare.

habeas corpus *See* writ of habeas corpus

habitual criminal statutes Laws that require long-term or life sentences for offenders who have multiple felony convictions.

halfway house A community-based correctional facility that houses inmates before their outright release so that they can become gradually acclimated to conventional society.

Hallcrest Report A government-sponsored national survey of the private security industry conducted by the Hallcrest Corporation.

hallucinogens Drugs, either natural or synthetic, that produce vivid distortions of the senses without greatly disturbing the viewer's consciousness. Some produce hallucinations, and others cause psychotic behavior in otherwise normal people.

hands-off doctrine The judicial policy of not interfering in the administrative affairs of a prison.

hate crimes Acts of violence or intimidation designed to terrorize or frighten people considered undesirable because of their race, religion, ethnic origin, or sexual orientation.

hearsay evidence Testimony that is not firsthand but relates information told by a second party.

heroin The most dangerous commonly used drug made from the poppy plant. Users rapidly build a tolerance for it, fueling the need for increased doses in order to feel a desired effect.

hot spots of crime The locations of a significant portion of all police calls. These hot spots include taverns and housing projects.

house of correction A county correctional institution generally used for the incarceration of more serious misdemeanants, whose sentences are usually less than one year.

hue and cry In medieval England, the policy of self-help used in villages demanding that all respond if a citizen raised a hue and cry to get their aid.

hulks Mothballed ships that were used to house prisoners in 18th-century England.

hundred In medieval England, a group of 100 families who were responsible for maintaining the order and trying minor offenses.

hung jury A jury that cannot reach a decision in a criminal case. If a jury is hung, the prosecution can retry the case.

hustle The underground prison economy.

hypoglycemia A condition that occurs when glucose (sugar) in the blood falls below levels necessary for normal and efficient brain functioning.

identity crisis A psychological state, identified by Erikson, in which youth face inner turmoil and uncertainty about life roles.

importation model The view that the violent prison culture reflects the criminal culture of the outside world and is neither developed in nor unique to prisons.

impulsivity According to Gottfredson and Hirschi's general theory, the trait that produces criminal behavior; impulsive people lack self-control.

incapacitation The policy of keeping dangerous criminals in confinement to eliminate the risk of their repeating their offense in society.

inchoate crimes Incomplete or contemplated crimes such as criminal solicitation or criminal attempts.

indeterminate sentence A term of incarceration with a stated minimum and maximum length, such as a sentence to prison for a period of from three to ten years. The prisoner would be eligible for parole after the minimum sentence had been served. Based on the belief that sentences should fit the criminal, indeterminate sentences allow individualized sentences and provide for sentencing flexibility. Judges can set a high minimum to override the purpose of the indeterminate sentence. *See also* determinate sentence

index crimes The eight crimes that, because of their seriousness and frequency, the FBI reports the incidence of in the annual Uniform Crime Reports. Index crimes include murder, rape, assault, robbery, burglary, arson, larceny, and motor vehicle theft.

indictment A written accusation returned by a grand jury charging an individual with a specified crime after determination of probable cause; the prosecutor presents enough evidence (a *prima facie* case) to establish probable cause.

indigent Needy and poor or lacking the means to provide a living.

inevitable discovery A rule of law stating that evidence that almost assuredly would be independently discovered can be used in a court of law, even though it was obtained in violation of legal rules and practices.

information Like an indictment, a formal charging document. The prosecuting attorney makes out the information and files it in court. Probable cause is determined at the preliminary hearing, which, unlike grand jury proceedings, is public and attended by the accused and his or her attorney.

inhalants Vapors from lighter fluid, paint thinner, cleaning fluid, and model airplane glue sniffed to reach a drowsy, dizzy state, sometimes accompanied by hallucinations.

initial appearance The stage in the justice process during which the suspect is brought before a magistrate for consideration of bail. The suspect must be taken for initial appearance within a "reasonable time" after arrest. For petty offenses, this step often serves as the final criminal proceeding, either through adjudication by a judge or the offering of a guilty plea.

inmate social code The informal set of rules that govern inmates.

inmate subculture The loosely defined culture that pervades prisons and has its own norms, rules, and language.

insanity A legal defense maintaining that a defendant was incapable of forming criminal intent because he or she suffered from a defect of reason or mental illness.

insider trading Illegal buying of stock in a company based on information provided by someone who has a fiduciary interest in the company, such as an employee or an attorney or accountant retained by the firm. Federal laws and the rules of the Securities and Exchange Commission require that all profits from such trading be returned and provide for both fines and a prison sentence.

instrumental Marxist theory The view that capitalist institutions, such as the criminal justice system, have as their main purpose the control of the poor to maintain the hegemony of the wealthy.

instrumental violence Violence designed to improve the financial or social position of the criminal.

intensive probation supervision A type of intermediate sanction involving small probation caseloads and strict daily or weekly monitoring.

interactional theory The idea that interaction with institutions and events during the life course determines criminal behavior patterns; crimogenic influences evolve over time.

interactionist perspective The view that one's perception of reality is significantly influenced by one's interpretations of the reactions of others to similar events and stimuli.

interrogation The method of accumulating evidence in the form of information or confessions from suspects; questioning that has been restricted because of concern about the use of brutal and coercive methods and to protect against self-incrimination.

interstitial area In criminology, a space or separation in the social fabric; an interstitial area encourages the formation of gangs.

investigation An inquiry concerning suspected criminal behavior for the purpose of identifying offenders or gathering further evidence to assist the prosecution of apprehended offenders.

jail A place to detain people awaiting trial, hold drunks and disorderly individuals, and confine convicted misdemeanants serving sentences of less than one year.

jailhouse lawyer An inmate trained in law or otherwise educated who helps other inmates prepare legal briefs and appeals.

just desert The philosophy of justice that asserts that those who violate the rights of others deserve to be punished. The severity of punishment should be commensurate with the seriousness of the crime.

justice model A philosophy of corrections that stresses determinate sentences, abolition of parole, and the view that prisons are places of punishment and not rehabilitation.

justification A defense to a criminal charge in which the accused maintains that his or her actions were justified by the circumstances and therefore he or she should not be held criminally liable.

juvenile delinquency Participation in illegal behavior by a minor who falls under a statutory age limit.

juvenile justice process Court proceedings for youths within the juvenile age group. Under the paternal (*parens patriae*) philosophy, juvenile procedures are informal and nonadversary, invoked *for* the juvenile of-

fender rather than against him or her; a petition instead of a complaint is filed; courts make findings of involvement or adjudication of delinquency instead of convictions; and juvenile offenders receive dispositions instead of sentences. Court decisions (*In re Kent* and *In re Gault*) have increased the adversarial nature of juvenile court proceedings. However, the philosophy remains one of diminishing the stigma of delinquency and providing for the youth's well-being and rehabilitation rather than seeking retribution.

Kansas City study An experimental program that evaluated the effectiveness of patrol. The Kansas City study found that the presence of patrol officers had little deterrent effect.

Knapp Commission A public body that led an investigation into police corruption in New York and uncovered a widespread network of payoffs and bribes.

labeling The process by which a person becomes fixed with a negative identity, such as "criminal" or "ex-con," and is forced to suffer the consequences of outcast status.

labeling theory Theory that views society as creating deviance through a system of social control agencies that designate certain individuals as deviants. The stigmatized individual is made to feel unwanted in the normal social order. Eventually, the individual begins to believe that the label is accurate, assumes it as a personal identity, and enters into a deviant or criminal career.

landmark decision A decision handed down by the Supreme Court that becomes the law of the land and serves as a precedent for similar legal issues.

latent trait A stable feature, characteristic, property, or condition, present at birth or soon after, that makes some people crime-prone over the life course.

learning disabilities Neurological dysfunctions that prevent people from learning up to their potential.

left realism A branch of conflict theory that holds that crime is a "real" social problem experienced by the lower classes and that lower-class

concerns about crime must be addressed by radical scholars.

legalization The removal of all criminal penalties from a previously outlawed act.

life course The study of changes in criminal offending patterns over a person's entire life. Are there conditions or events that occur later in life that influence the way people behave, or is behavior predetermined by social or personal conditions at birth?

life history A research method that uses the experiences of an individual as the unit of analysis, such as using the life experience of an individual gang member to understand the natural history of gang membership.

longitudinal (cohort) research Research that tracks the development of a group of subjects over time.

lower courts A generic term referring to those courts that have jurisdiction over misdemeanors and conduct preliminary investigations of felony charges.

make-believe families Peer units, with mother and father figures, formed by women in prison to compensate for the loss of family and loved ones.

mala in se **crimes** Acts that are outlawed because they violate basic moral values, such as rape, murder, assault, and robbery.

mala prohibitum **crimes** Acts that are outlawed because they clash with current norms and public opinion, such as tax, traffic, and drug laws.

mandamus *See* writ of mandamus

mandatory sentence A statutory requirement that a certain penalty shall be set and carried out in all cases on conviction for a specified offense or series of offenses.

Manhattan Bail Project The innovative experiment in bail reform that introduced and successfully tested the concept of release on recognizance.

Mann Act Federal legislation that made it a crime to transport women across state lines for the purpose of prostitution.

marijuana (*Cannabis sativa*) A hemp plant grown throughout the world. Its main active ingredient is tetrahydrocannabinol (THC), a mild hallucinogen that alters sensory impressions and can cause drastic distortion in auditory and visual perception, even producing hallucinatory effects.

marital exemption The practice in some states of prohibiting the prosecution of husbands for the rape of their wives.

masculinity hypothesis The view that women who commit crimes have biological and psychological traits similar to those of men.

mass murder The killing of a large number of people in a single incident by an offender who typically does not seek concealment or escape.

matricide The murder of a mother by her son or daughter.

maxi-maxi prisons High-security prisons, based on the federal prison in Marion, Illinois, that house the most dangerous inmates in around-the-clock solitary confinement.

maximum-security prisons Correctional institutions that house dangerous felons and maintain strict security measures, high walls, and limited contact with the outside world.

meat eaters A term used to describe police officers who actively solicit bribes and vigorously engage in corrupt practices.

medical model A view of corrections holding that convicted offenders are victims of their environment who need care and treatment to be transformed into valuable members of society.

medium-security prisons Less secure institutions that house nonviolent offenders and provide more opportunities for contact with the outside world.

mens rea "Guilty mind." The mental element of a crime or the intent to commit a criminal act.

methadone A synthetic narcotic used as a substitute for heroin in drug-control efforts.

middle-class measuring rods According to Cohen, the standards by which teachers and other representatives of state authority evaluate lower-class youths. Because they cannot live up to middle-class standards, lower-class youths are bound for failure, which gives rise to frustration and anger at conventional society.

minimum-security prisons The least secure institutions that house white-collar and nonviolent offenders, maintain few security measures, and have liberal furlough and visitation policies.

Miranda **warning** The result of two U.S. Supreme Court decisions (*Escobedo v. Illinois* [378 U.S. 478] and *Miranda v. Arizona* [384 U.S. 436]) that require police officers to inform individuals under arrest of their constitutional right to remain silent and to know that their statements can later be used against them in court, that they can have an attorney present to help them, and that the state will pay for an attorney if they cannot afford to hire one. Although aimed at protecting an individual during in-custody interrogation, the warning must also be given when the investigation shifts from the investigatory to the accusatory stage — that is, when suspicion begins to focus on an individual.

misdemeanor A minor crime usually punished by less than one year's imprisonment in a local institution, such as a county jail.

Missouri Plan A way of picking judges through nonpartisan elections as a means of ensuring judicial performance standards.

Mollen Commission An investigative unit set up to inquire into police corruption in New York in the 1990s.

monetary restitution A sanction requiring that convicted offenders compensate crime victims by reimbursing them for out-of-pocket losses caused by the crime. Losses can include property damage, lost wages, and medical costs.

moonlighting The practice of police officers holding after-hours jobs in private security or other related professions.

moral crusades Efforts by interest-group members to stamp out behavior they find objectionable. Typically, moral crusades are directed at public order crimes, such as drug abuse or pornography.

moral entrepreneurs Interest groups that attempt to control social life and the legal order in order to promote their own personal set of moral values. People who use their influence to shape the legal process in ways they see fit.

motion An oral or written request asking the court to make a specified finding, decision, or order.

motivated offenders The potential offenders in a population. According to rational choice theory, crime rates will vary according to the number of motivated offenders.

murder transaction The concept that murder is usually a result of behavior interactions between the victim and the offender.

National Crime Survey The ongoing victimization study conducted jointly by the Justice Department and the U.S. Census Bureau that surveys victims about their experiences with law violation.

negative affective states According to Agnew, the anger, depression, disappointment, fear, and other adverse emotions that derive from strain.

neighborhood policing A style of police management that emphasizes community-level crime-fighting programs and initiatives.

neocortex A part of the human brain; the left side of the neocortex controls sympathetic feelings toward others.

neurological Pertaining to the brain and central nervous system.

neuroticism A personality trait marked by unfounded anxiety, tension, and emotional instability.

neurotics People who fear that their primitive id impulses will dominate their personality.

neutralization The ability to overcome social norms and controls. Neutralization theory holds that offenders adhere to conventional values while "drifting" into periods of illegal behavior. In order to drift, people must first neutralize legal and moral values.

niche A way of adapting to the prison community that stresses finding one's place (niche) in the system rather than fighting for one's individual rights.

no bill A decision by a grand jury not to indict a criminal suspect.

nolle prosequi The term used when a prosecutor decides to drop a case after a complaint has been formally made. Reasons for a *nolle prosequi* include insufficient evidence, reluctance of witnesses to testify, police error, and office policy.

nolo contendere No contest. An admission of guilt in a criminal case with the condition that the finding cannot be used against the defendant in any subsequent civil cases.

nonintervention A justice philosophy that emphasizes the least intrusive treatment possible. Among its central policies are decarceration, diversion, and decriminalization. Less is better.

oath-helpers During the Middle Ages, groups of 12 to 25 people who would support the accused's innocence.

obitiatry According to Jack Kevorkian, the practice of helping people take their own lives.

obscenity According to current legal theory, sexually explicit material that lacks a serious purpose and appeals solely to the prurient interest of the viewer. While nudity per se is not usually considered obscene, open sexual behavior, masturbation, and exhibition of the genitals is banned in most communities.

official crime Criminal behavior that has been recorded by the police.

opportunist robber Someone who steals small amounts when a vulnerable target presents itself.

organizational crime Crime that involves large corporations and their efforts to control the marketplace and earn huge profits through unlawful bidding, unfair advertising, monopolistic practices, or other illegal means.

paraphilias Bizarre or abnormal sexual practices that may involve recurrent sexual urges focused on objects, humiliation, or children.

parens patriae Power of the state to act in behalf of the child and provide care and protection equivalent to that of a parent.

parole The early release of a prisoner subject to conditions set by a parole board. Depending on the jurisdiction, inmates must serve a certain proportion of their sentences before becoming eligible for parole. If an inmate is granted parole, the conditions may require him or her to report regularly to a parole officer, refrain from criminal conduct, maintain and support his or her family, avoid contact with other convicted criminals, abstain from using alcohol and drugs, remain within the jurisdiction, and so on. Violations of the conditions of parole may result in revocation of parole, in which case the individual will be returned to prison. The concept behind parole is to allow the release of the offender to community supervision, where rehabilitation and readjustment will be facilitated.

parricide The killing of a close relative by a child.

Part I offenses Another term for index crimes.

Part II offenses All crimes other than index and minor traffic offenses. The FBI records annual arrest information for Part II offenses.

partial deterrent A legal measure designed to restrict or control rather than eliminate an undesirable act.

particularity The requirement that a search warrant state precisely where the search is to take place and what items are to be seized.

passive precipitation The view that some people become victims because of personal and social characteristics that make them "attractive" targets for predatory criminals.

paternalism An approach to government or organizations in which leaders are seen as father figures and others are treated as "children."

pathways The view that the path to a criminal career may have more than one route, beginning with mild misconduct and escalating to serious crimes.

patriarchy A male-dominated system. The patriarchal family is one dominated by the father.

patricide The murder of a father by his son or daughter.

peacemaking A branch of conflict theory that stresses humanism, mediation, and conflict resolution as a means to end crime.

Pennsylvania system The prison system developed in Pennsylvania during the 19th century that stressed total isolation and individual penitence as a means of reform.

peremptory challenge The dismissal of a potential juror by either the prosecution or the defense for unexplained, discretionary reasons.

persisters Those criminals who do not age out of crime; chronic delinquents who continue offending into their adulthood.

pilferage Theft by employees through stealth or deception.

plain view The doctrine that evidence that is in plain view to police officers may be seized without a search warrant.

plea An answer to formal charges by an accused. Possible pleas are guilty, not guilty, *nolo contendere,* and not guilty by reason of insanity. A guilty plea is a confession of the offense as charged. A not guilty plea is a denial of the charge and places the burden on the prosecution to prove the elements of the offense.

plea bargaining The discussion between the defense counsel and the prosecution by which the accused agrees to plead guilty for certain considerations. The advantage to the defendant may be a reduction of the charges, a lenient sentence, or (in the case of multiple charges) dropped charges. The advantage to the prosecution is that a conviction is obtained without the time and expense of lengthy trial proceedings.

pleasure principle According to Freud, a theory in which id-dominated people are driven to increase their personal pleasure without regard to consequences.

pledge system An early method of law enforcement that relied on self-help and mutual aid.

police discretion The ability of police officers to enforce the law selectively. Police officers in the field have great latitude to use their discretion in deciding whether to invoke their arrest powers.

police officer style The belief that the bulk of police officers can be classified into ideal personality types. Popular style types include supercops, who desire to enforce only serious crimes, such as robbery and rape; professionals, who use a broad definition of police work; service-oriented officers, who see their job as a helping profession; and avoiders, who do as little as possible. The actual existence of ideal police officer types has been much debated.

poor laws Seventeenth-century laws that bound out vagrants and abandoned children to masters as indentured servants.

population All people who share a particular personal characteristic, such as all high school students or all police officers.

positivism The branch of social science that uses the scientific method of the natural sciences and suggests that human behavior is a product of social, biological, psychological, or economic forces.

power control According to Hagan, the power and standing each parent has in the economic structure, which determines the manner in which the parents exert control over their families and, in particular, adolescent behavior.

power groups Criminal organizations that do not provide services or illegal goods but trade exclusively in violence and extortion.

power rape A rape motivated by the need for sexual conquest.

power syndicates Organized crime groups that use force and violence to extort money from legitimate businesses and other criminal groups engaged in illegal business enterprises.

praxis The application of theory in action; in Marxist criminology, applying theory to promote revolution.

precocious sexuality Sexual experimentation in early adolescence.

preliminary hearings The step at which criminal charges initiated by an information are tested for probable cause; the prosecution presents enough evidence to establish probable cause—that is, a *prima facie* case. The hearing is public and may be attended by the accused and his or her attorney.

premenstrual syndrome The stereotype that several days prior to and during menstruation females are beset by irritability and poor judgment as a result of hormonal changes.

preponderance of the evidence The level of proof in civil cases; more than half the evidence supports the allegations of one side.

presentence report An investigation performed by a probation officer attached to a trial court after the conviction of a defendant. The report contains information about the defendant's background, education, previous employment, and family; his or her own statement concerning the offense; the person's prior criminal record; interviews with neighbors or acquaintances; and his or her mental and physical condition (that is, information that would not be made record in the case of a guilty plea or that would be inadmissible as evidence at a trial but could be influential and important at the sentencing stage). After conviction, a judge sets a date for sentencing (usually ten days to two weeks from the date of conviction), during which time the presentence report is made. The report is required in felony cases in federal courts and in many states, is optional with the judge in some states, and in others is mandatory before convicted offenders can be placed on probation. In the case of juvenile offenders, the presentence report is also known as a social history report.

presumptive sentences Sentencing structures that provide an average sentence that should be served along with the option of extending or decreasing the punishment because of aggravating or mitigating circumstances.

preventive detention The practice of holding dangerous suspects before trial without bail.

primary deviance According to Lemert, deviant acts that do not help redefine the self and public image of the offender.

primary sociopaths People with an inherited trait that predisposes them to antisocial behavior.

prison A state or federal correctional institution for incarceration of felony offenders for terms of one year or more.

pro bono The practice by private attorneys of taking the cases of indigent offenders without fee as a service to the profession and the community.

probability sample A randomly drawn sample in which each member of the population being tapped has an equal chance of being selected.

probable cause The evidentiary criterion necessary to sustain an arrest or the issuance of an arrest or search warrant; less than absolute certainty or "beyond a reasonable doubt" but greater than mere suspicion or "hunch." A set of facts, information, circumstances, or conditions that would lead a reasonable person to believe that an offense was committed and that the accused committed that offense. An arrest made without probable cause may be susceptible to prosecution as an illegal arrest under "false imprisonment" statutes.

probation A sentence entailing the conditional release of a convicted offender into the community under the supervision of the court (in the form of a probation officer), subject to certain conditions for a specified time. The conditions are usually similar to those of parole. (Probation is a sentence, an alternative to incarceration; parole is administrative release from incarceration.) Violation of the conditions of probation may result in revocation of probation.

problem-oriented policing A style of police management that stresses proactive problem solving rather than reactive crime fighting.

procedural law The rules that define the operation of criminal proceedings. Procedural law describes the methods that must be followed in obtaining warrants, investigating offenses, effecting lawful arrests, using force, conducting trials, introducing evidence, sentencing convicted offenders, and reviewing cases by appellate courts (in general, legislatures have ignored postsentencing procedures). While the substantive law defines criminal offenses, procedural law delineates how the substantive offenses are to be enforced.

progressives Early 20th-century reformers who believed that state action could relieve human ills.

proletariat A term used by Marx to refer to the working class members of society who produce goods and services but who do not own the means of production.

proof beyond a reasonable doubt The standard of proof needed to convict in a criminal case. The evidence offered in court does not have to amount to absolute certainty, but it should leave no reasonable doubt that the defendant committed the alleged crime.

property in service The 18th-century practice of selling control of inmates to shipmasters who would then transport them to colonies for sale as indentured servants.

prosecutor Representative of the state (executive branch) in criminal proceedings; advocate for the state's case—the charge—in the adversary trial; for example, the attorney general of the United States, U.S. attorneys, attorneys general of the states, district attorneys, and police prosecutors. The prosecutor participates in investigations both before and after arrest, prepares legal documents, participates in obtaining arrest or search warrants, decides whether to charge a suspect and, if so, with which offense. The prosecutor argues the state's case at trial, advises the police, participates in plea negotiations, and makes sentencing recommendations.

prosecutorial agency A federal, state, or local criminal justice agency whose principal function is the prosecution of alleged offenders.

proximity hypothesis The view that people become crime victims because they live or work in areas with large criminal populations.

psychoanalytic (psychodynamic) approach Branch of psychology holding that the human personality is controlled by unconscious mental processes developed early in childhood.

psychopath A person whose personality is characterized by a lack of warmth and feeling, inappropriate behavior responses, and an inability to learn from experience. While some psychologists view psychopa-thy as a result of childhood trauma, others see it as a result of biological abnormality.

psychotics In Freudian theory, people whose id has broken free and now dominates their personality. Psychotics suffer from delusions and experience hallucinations and sudden mood shifts.

public order crimes Acts that are considered illegal because they threaten the general well-being of society and challenge its accepted moral principles. Prostitution, drug use, and the sale of pornography are considered public order crimes.

Racketeer Influenced and Corrupt Organizations Act (RICO) Federal legislation that enables prosecutors to bring additional criminal or civil charges against people whose multiple criminal acts constitute a conspiracy. RICO features monetary penalties that allow the government to confiscate all profits derived from criminal activities. Originally intended to be used against organized criminals, RICO has also been used against white-collar criminals.

random sample A sample selected on the basis of chance so that each person in the population has an equal opportunity to be selected.

rational choice The view that crime is a function of a decision-making process in which the potential offender weighs the potential costs and benefits of an illegal act.

reaction formation According to Cohen, rejecting goals and standards that seem impossible to achieve. Because a boy cannot hope to get into college, for example, he considers higher education a waste of time.

reality principle According to Freud, the ability to learn about the consequences of one's actions through experience.

reasonable competence The standard by which legal representation is judged: Did the defendant receive a reasonable level of legal aid?

reasonable doubt The possibility that a defendant did not commit the crime. A jury cannot find the defendant guilty if a reasonable doubt exists that he or she committed the crime. The level of proof needed to convict in a criminal trial is "beyond a reasonable doubt."

recidivism Repetition of criminal behavior; habitual criminality. Recidivism is measured by (1) criminal acts that result in conviction by a court when committed by individuals who are under correctional supervision or who had been released from correctional supervision within the previous three years, and (2) technical violations of probation or parole in which a sentencing or paroling authority has taken action resulting in an adverse change in the offender's legal status.

reciprocal altruism According to sociobiology, acts that are outwardly designed to help others but that have at their core benefits to the self.

recoupment Forcing indigents to repay the state for at least part of their legal costs.

reflected appraisal According to Matsueda and Heimer, a youth's self-evaluation based on his or her perceptions of how others evaluate him or her.

reflective role-taking According to Matsueda and Heimer, the phenomenon that occurs when youths who view themselves as delinquents are giving an inner-voice to their perceptions how significant others feel about them.

reintegration The correctional philosophy that stresses reintroducing the inmate into the community.

reintegrative shaming A method of correction that encourages offenders to confront their misdeeds, experience shame because of the harm they caused, and then be reincluded in society.

relative deprivation The condition that exists when people of wealth and poverty live in close proximity to one another. Some criminologists attribute crime rate differentials to relative deprivation.

release on recognizance A nonmonetary condition for the pretrial release of an accused individual; an alternative to monetary bail that is granted after the court determines that the accused has ties in the community, has no prior record of default, and is likely to appear at subsequent proceedings.

restitution A condition of probation in which the offender repays society or the victim of crime for the trouble the offender caused. Monetary restitution involves a direct payment to the victim as a form of compensation. Community service restitution may be used in victimless crimes and involves work in the community in lieu of more severe criminal penalties.

revocation An administrative act performed by a parole authority that removes a person from parole or a judicial order by a court removing a person from parole or probation, in response to a violation on the part of the parolee or probationer.

right to counsel The right of the accused to the assistance of defense counsel in all criminal prosecutions.

right to treatment The philosophy espoused by many courts that offenders have a statutory right to treatment. A federal constitutional right to treatment has not been established.

rights of defendant Powers and privileges that are constitutionally guaranteed to every defendant in a criminal trial.

R/k **selection theory** *R/k* theory holds that all organisms can be located along a continuum based on their reproductive drives. Those along the *r*- end reproduce rapidly whenever they can and invest little in their offspring; those along the *k*-end reproduce slowly and cautiously and take care in raising their offspring.

role diffusion According to Erikson, a phenomenon that occurs when youths spread themselves too thin, experience personal uncertainty, and place themselves at the mercy of leaders who promise to give them a sense of identity they cannot develop for themselves.

routine activities The view that crime is a "normal" function of the routine activities of modern living. Offenses can be expected if there is a suitable target that is not protected by capable guardians.

sadistic rape A rape motivated by the offender's desire to torment and abuse the victim.

sample A limited number of people selected for study from a population.

schizophrenia A type of psychosis often marked by bizarre behavior, hallucinations, loss of thought control, and inappropriate emotional responses. Schizophrenic types include catatonic, which characteristically involves impairment of motor activity; paranoid, which is characterized by delusions of persecution; and hebephrenic, which is characterized by immature behavior and giddiness.

search and seizure The legal term, contained in the Fourth Amendment to the U.S. Constitution, that refers to the searching for and carrying away of evidence by police during a criminal investigation.

secondary deviance According to Lemert, accepting deviant labels as a personal identity. Acts become secondary when they form a basis for self-concept, as when a drug experimenter becomes an "addict."

secondary sociopaths People who are constitutionally normal but whose life experiences influence their antisocial behavior. Suspected influences include poor parenting, racial segregation, and social conflict.

seductions of crime According to Katz, the visceral and emotional appeal that the situation of crime has for those who engage in illegal acts.

selective incapacitation The policy of creating enhanced prison sentences for the relatively small group of dangerous chronic offenders.

self-control theory According to Gottfredson and Hirschi, the view that the cause of delinquent behavior is an impulsive personality. Kids who are impulsive may find that their bond to society is weak.

self-fulfilling prophecy Deviant behavior patterns that are a response to an earlier labeling experience. People act in synch with social labels, even if the labels are falsely bestowed.

self-report study A research approach that requires subjects to reveal their own participation in delinquent or criminal acts.

sentence The criminal sanction imposed by the court on a convicted defendant, usually in the form of a fine, incarceration, or probation. Sentencing may be carried out by a judge, jury, or sentencing council (panel of judges), depending on the statutes of the jurisdiction. *See also* determinate sentence; indeterminate sentence

sequester The insulation of jurors from the outside world so that their decision making cannot be influenced or affected by extralegal events.

serial murder The killing of a large number of people over time by an offender who seeks to escape detection.

sheriff The chief law enforcement officer in a county.

shield laws Laws designed to protect rape victims by prohibiting the defense attorney from inquiring about their previous sexual relationships.

shire-gemot During the Middle Ages, an assemblage of local landholders who heard more serious and important criminal cases.

shire reeve In early England, the senior law enforcement figure in a county, the forerunner of today's sheriff.

shock incarceration A short prison sentence served in boot camp–type facilities.

shock probation A sentence in which offenders serve a short prison term to impress them with the pains of imprisonment before they begin probation.

short-run hedonism According to Cohen, the desire of lower-class gang youths to engage in behavior that will give them immediate gratification and excitement but in the long run will be dysfunctional and negative.

situational crime prevention A method of crime prevention that stresses tactics and strategies to eliminate or reduce particular crimes in narrow settings, such as reducing burglaries in a housing project by increasing lighting and installing security alarms.

skeezers Prostitutes who trade sex for drugs, usually crack.

skinhead Member of a white supremacist gang, identified by a shaved skull and Nazi or Ku Klux Klan markings.

social bond Ties a person has to the institutions and processes of society. According to Hirschi, elements of the social bond include commitment, attachment, involvement, and belief.

social capital Positive relations with individuals and institutions that are life sustaining.

social control The ability of society and its institutions to control, manage, restrain, or direct human behavior.

social disorganization A neighborhood or area marked by culture conflict, lack of cohesiveness, transient population, insufficient social organizations, and anomie.

social ecology Environmental forces that have a direct influence on human behavior.

social learning theory The view that human behavior is modeled through observation of human social interactions, either directly from observing those who are close and from intimate contact, or indirectly through the media. Interactions that are rewarded are copied, while those that are punished are avoided.

social process Operations of formal and informal social institutions. Elements of the social process include socialization within family and peer groups, the educational process, and the justice system.

social structure The various stratifications that characterize the fabric of postindustrial society. Within the social structure are the various classes, institutions, and groups of society.

socialization Process of human development and enculturation. Socialization is influenced by key social processes and institutions.

sociobiology Branch of science that views human behavior as being motivated by inborn biological urges and desires. The urge to survive and preserve the species motivates human behavior.

sociopath Person whose personality is characterized by lack of warmth and affection, inappropriate responses, and an inability to learn from experience. The term is used interchangeably with *psychopath* and *antisocial personality disorder.*

sodomy Illegal sexual intercourse. Sodomy has no single definition, and acts included within its scope are usually defined by state statute.

somatotyping A system developed for categorizing people on the basis of their body build.

special (specific) deterrence A crime control policy suggesting that punishment be severe enough to convince convicted offenders never to repeat their criminal activity.

specific intent The intent to accomplish a specific purpose as an element of crime, such as breaking into someone's house for the express purpose of stealing jewels.

spontaneous remission Another term for the aging-out process.

stalking laws Laws that make it a criminal offense to stalk or harass a victim even though no actual assault or battery has occurred.

standard of proof The level of proof needed to process a person at various stages of the justice system; the standard of proof for an arrest to be made is "probable cause." The Supreme Court has made the "beyond a reasonable doubt" standard a due process and constitutional requirement for conviction at trial.

stare decisis To stand by decided cases; the legal principle by which the decision or holding in an earlier case becomes the standard by which subsequent similar cases are judged.

statutory law Laws created by legislative bodies to meet changing social conditions, public opinion, and custom.

steroids Drugs used to gain muscle bulk and strength for athletics and body building.

stigma An enduring label that taints a person's identity and changes him or her in the eyes of others.

stimulants Synthetic drugs that stimulate action in the central nervous system. They produce an intense physical reaction: increased blood pressure, increased breathing rate, increased bodily activity, and elevated mood. One widely used set of stimulants, amphetamines, produce psychological effects such as increased confidence, euphoria, fearlessness, talkativeness, impulsive behavior, and loss of appetite.

sting An undercover police operation in which police pose as criminals to trap law violators.

stoopers Petty criminals who earn their living by retrieving winning tickets that are accidentally discarded by racetrack patrons.

stop and frisk The situation where police officers who are suspicious of an individual run their hands lightly over the suspect's outer garments to determine whether the person is carrying a concealed weapon. Also called a "patdown" or "threshold inquiry," a stop and frisk is intended to stop short of any activity that could be considered a violation of Fourth Amendment rights.

strain The emotional turmoil and conflict caused when people believe they cannot achieve their desires and goals through legitimate means. Members of the lower-class might feel strain because they are denied access to adequate educational opportunities and social support.

stratification Grouping according to social strata or levels. American society is considered stratified on the basis of economic class and wealth.

street crime Illegal acts designed to prey on the public through theft, damage, and violence.

strict-liability crimes Illegal acts whose elements do not contain the need for intent, or *mens rea;* they are usually acts that endanger the public welfare, such as illegal dumping of toxic wastes.

structural Marxist theory The view that the law and the justice system are designed to maintain the capitalist system and that members of both the owner and worker classes whose behavior threatens the stability of the system will be sanctioned.

subculture A group that is loosely part of the dominant culture but maintains a unique set of values, beliefs, and traditions.

subpoena A court order requiring the recipient to appear in court on an indicated time and date.

substantive criminal laws A body of specific rules that declare what conduct is criminal and prescribe the punishment to be imposed for such conduct.

suitable target According to routine activities theory, a target for crime that is relatively valuable, easily transportable, and not capably guarded.

summons An alternative to arrest usually used for petty or traffic offenses; a written order notifying an individual that he or she has been charged with an offense. A summons directs the person to appear in court to answer the charge. It is used primarily in instances of low risk, where the person will not be required to appear at a later date. The summons is advantageous to police officers in that they are freed from having to spend time on arrest and booking procedures; it is advantageous to the accused in that he or she is spared time in jail.

sureties During the Middle Ages, people who made themselves responsible for the behavior of offenders released in their care.

surplus value The Marxist view that the laboring classes produce wealth that far exceeds their wages and goes to the capitalist class as profits.

surrebuttal Introducing witnesses during a criminal trial to disprove damaging testimony by other witnesses.

suspended sentence A prison term that is delayed while the defendant undergoes a period of community treatment. If the treatment is successful, the prison sentence is terminated.

symbolic interaction The sociological view that people communicate through symbols. People interpret symbolic communication and incorporate it within their personality. A person's view of reality, then, depends on his or her interpretation of symbolic gestures.

systemic link Violent behavior that results from the conflict inherent in the drug trade.

team policing An experimental police technique in which groups of officers are assigned to a particular area of the city on a 24-hour basis.

technical parole violation Revocation of parole because conditions set by correctional authorities have been violated.

technique of neutralization According to neutralization theory, the ability of delinquent youth to neutralize moral constraints so they may drift into criminal acts.

temperance movement An effort to prohibit the sale of liquor in the United States that resulted in the passage of the Eighteenth Amendment to the Constitution in 1919, which prohibited the sale of alcoholic beverages.

testosterone The principal male steroid hormone. Testosterone levels decline during the life cycle and may explain why violence rates diminish over time.

thanatos According to Freud, the instinctual drive toward aggression and violence.

threshold inquiry A term used to describe a stop and frisk.

tithings During the Middle Ages, groups of about ten families who were responsible for maintaining order among themselves and dealing with disturbances, fires, wild animals, and so on.

tort The law of personal wrongs and damage. Tort actions include negligence, libel, slander, assault, and trespass.

totality of the circumstances A legal doctrine mandating that a decision maker consider all the issues and circumstances of a case before judging the outcome. For example, before concluding whether a suspect understood a *Miranda* warning, a judge must consider the totality of the circumstances under which the warning was given. The suspect's age, intelligence, and competency may influence his or her understanding and judgment.

transferred intent The principle that if an illegal yet unintended act results from the intent to commit a crime, that act is also considered illegal.

transitional neighborhood An area undergoing a shift in population and structure, usually from middle-class residential to lower-class mixed use.

turning points According to Laub and Sampson, the life events that alter the development of a criminal career.

venire The group called for jury duty from which jury panels are selected.

vice squad Police officers assigned to enforce morally tinged laws, such as those governing prostitution, gambling, and pornography.

victim-precipitated crime A crime in which the victim's behavior was the spark that ignited the subsequent offense, as when the victim abused the offender verbally or physically.

victimization survey A crime measurement technique that surveys citizens to measure their experiences as victims of crime.

victimless crimes Crimes that violate the moral order but in which there is no actual victim or target. In these crimes, which include drug abuse and sex offenses, it is society as a whole and not an individual who is considered the victim.

victimology The study of the victim's role in criminal transactions.

virulency According to Athens, a stage in a violent career in which criminals develop a violent identity that makes them feared. They consequently enjoy hurting others.

voir dire The process in which a potential jury panel is questioned by the prosecution and the defense to select jurors who are unbiased and objective.

waiver The act of voluntarily relinquishing a right or advantage; often used in the context of waiving one's right to counsel (for example, the *Miranda* warning) or waiving certain steps in the criminal justice process (such as the preliminary hearing). Essential to waiver is the voluntary consent of the individual.

warrant A written court order issued by a magistrate authorizing and directing that an individual be taken into custody to answer criminal charges.

watch system In medieval England, men organized in church parishes to guard against disturbances and breaches of the peace at night; they were under the direction of the local constable.

watchman A style of policing that stresses reacting to calls for service rather than aggressively pursuing crime.

wergild Under medieval law, the money paid by the offender to compensate the victim and the state for a criminal offense.

white-collar crime Illegal acts that capitalize on a person's status in the marketplace. White-collar crimes can involve theft, embezzlement, fraud, market manipulation, restraint of trade, and false advertising.

Wickersham Commission Created in 1931 by President Herbert Hoover to investigate the state of the nation's police forces, a commission that found police training to be inadequate and the average officer incapable of effectively carrying out his duties.

widening the net The charge that programs designed to divert offenders from the justice system actually enmesh them further in the process by substituting more intrusive treatment programs for less intrusive punishment-oriented outcomes.

wite The portion of the wergild that went to the victim's family.

work furlough A prison treatment program that allows inmates to leave during the day to work in the community and return to prison at night.

writ of certiorari An order of a superior court requesting that the record of an inferior court (or administrative body) be brought forward for review or inspection.

writ of habeas corpus A judicial order requesting that a person detaining another produce the body of the prisoner and give reasons for his or her capture and detention. Habeas corpus is a legal device used to request that a judicial body review the reasons for a person's confinement and the conditions of confinement. Habeas corpus is known as "the great writ."

writ of mandamus An order of a superior court commanding that a lower court, administrative body, or executive body perform a specific function. It is commonly used to restore rights and privileges lost to a defendant through illegal means.

TABLE OF CASES

NAME INDEX

Giordano, Peggy, 80, 215, 250, 252, 253, 383
Giroux, Bruce, 314
Glasser, William, 609
Glazer, Daniel, 178, 282, 287, 311, 466, 607, 609
Gleason, Sandra, 609
Gleason, Walter, 107
Glensor, Ronald W., 531
Glick, Barry, 80
Glueck, Eleanor, 171, 182, 249, 286, 295–296, 313
Glueck, Sheldon, 170–171, 182, 249, 286, 295–296, 313
Goddard, Henry, 173, 182
Goebel, J., 606
Goetting, Ann, 249
Goffin, Clare, 609
Goffman, E., 608
Gold, Martin, 80, 82
Gold, Nan, 570
Gold, Steven, 358
Goldberg, Andrew L., 506, 529
Goldberg, Carey, 359
Golden, Reid, 218
Goldkamp, John, 469, 570
Goldman, David, 180
Goldman, M. S., 467
Goldman, Nathan, 531, 532
Goldsmith, Larry, 607
Goldsmith, M., 422
Goldstein, Herman, 513, 530
Goldstein, Joseph, 519, 531
Goldstein, Michael, 466
Goldstein, Paul, 357, 433, 465, 466, 467, 468
Golub, Andrew Lang, 61, 445, 452, 467, 468
Goodstein, Laurie, 253, 465
Goodwin, D. W., 467
Gordon, Robert, 182, 183, 251
Gornick, Janet, 109
Gottfredson, Denise, 108, 217
Gottfredson, Gary, 108, 217
Gottfredson, Michael, 25, 69, 70, 81, 82, 141, 239, 289–294, 307, 312, 313, 405, 421, 469, 570, 571
Gottfredson, Stephen, 141
Gottschalk, Earl, 419
Gould, Larry, 530
Gould, Leroy, 74, 82
Gove, Walter, 82, 142, 178, 180, 253
Gowdy, Voncile, 607
Goyer, P. F., 179
Graham, Hugh Davis, 496
Grandison, Terry, 107
Grasmick, Harold, 142, 143, 144, 217, 312, 313
Gray, Gregory, 178
Gray, Lewis, Jr., 356
Gray, Tara, 565

Gray, Thomas, 80, 467
Gray, Wayne, 421
Greeley, A., 466
Green, Donald, 143, 144, 530
Green, Gary, 129, 143, 420
Green, Lorraine, 126, 142
Green, Stephanie, 82
Green, William, 357
Greenbaum, Paul, 608
Greenberg, David, 81, 144, 260, 281, 282, 283
Greenberg, Stephanie, 217
Greenburg, Robyn J., 410
Greene, Jack R., 514, 530
Greene, Michael, 357
Greenfeld, Lawrence, 107, 108, 144, 431, 468, 511, 530, 607, 608
Greenhouse, Joel, 179
Greenleaf, Richard, 281
Greenstein, Theodore, 531
Greenwood, Peter, 82, 137, 145, 469, 530
Greloch, Anthony, 592
Grennan, Sean, 532
Griffith, William, 607
Griset, Pamala, 571
Griswold, David, 252, 571
Groff, M., 182, 183
Gross, Michael Joseph, 465
Gross, S., 572
Gross, Sally, 532
Groth, A. Nicholas, 328, 329, 358
Grove, H., 420
Groves, W. Byron, 25, 216, 217, 265, 281, 282, 283, 421
Guarino-Ghezzi, Susan, 530
Guerry, Andre-Michel, 7
Guest, Avery, 189
Guijarro, Margarita, 313
Gulley, Bill, 180
Gundry, Gwen, 180
Gurr, Theodore Robert, 361, 496
Gusfield, Joseph, 466
Gussfield, Joseph, 426, 464

Hackler, James, 380
Hagan, John, 82, 141, 142, 217, 219, 253, 275, 281, 282, 283, 315
Hagedorn, John M., 61, 250
Hahn, Harlan, 529
Hakim, Simon, 109, 141, 383
Halbfinger, David M., 420
Hale, Chris, 82
Hale, Matthew, 329
Hall, Andy, 547
Hallet, Amanda, 313
Hall, Jerome, 49, 383
Hall, Joseph S., 420
Hall, Julia G., 608
Hall, Melinda Gann, 572
Hallam, J., 466
Halleck, Seymour, 181
Haller, Mark, 385–386, 418

Halperin, William, 141
Hamburg, Beatrix, 467
Hamlin, John, 251
Hamm, Mark, 609
Hammett, Theodore, 421
Hammock, Georgina, 108
Hamparian, Donna, 82
Hanley, Dena, 529
Hanlon, Thomas, 610
Hansell, Stephen, 301, 468
Hansen, David, 25
Hanson, Karl, 182, 610
Hanson, Roger, 607
Harbinger, Bonny, 420
Harden, Philip, 179, 180
Hardt, Robert, 80
Harer, Miles, 62, 81, 82, 218
Hargarten, Stephen W., 66
Harlow, Caroline Wolf, 109, 360, 468, 608
Harr, Robin, 609
Harries, Keith, 216, 357, 359
Harring, Sidney, 283
Harris, Judith Rich, 150–151, 159
Harris, Patricia, 119, 141, 383, 607
Harris, Richard, 531
Harrison, Lana, 468
Harrison, Wilfred, 140
Harry, Joseph, 143, 218
Hart, Elizabeth, 180
Hart, H. L. A., 426, 464
Hartman, Carl, 420
Hartnagel, Timothy, 143, 252
Hartnett, Susan, 530
Hartstone, Eliot, 216
Harvey-Lintz, Terri, 531
Hatfield, E., 464
Hathaway, R. Starke, 171, 182
Hawke, W., 178
Hawkins, Darnell, 564, 565
Hawkins, J. David, 250, 293, 300, 312, 314
Hawkins, Keith, 421
Hawley, C., 179
Hawley, F. Frederick, 357
Hay, Dale, 182, 356
Hay, Douglas, 49
Hayeslip, David, 468
Hazelbaker, Kim, 383
Hazlett, Michael, 359
Hazlewood, Robert, 142, 358
Heald, F. P., 180
Healy, William, 173, 182
Heath, James, 49
Heath, Linda, 169
Heaviside, Sheila, 250
Heffernan, Esther, 599–600, 609
Hefler, Gerd, 217
Hegel, Georg W. F., 258
Heide, Kathleen, 95, 337, 357, 359
Heimer, Karen, 142, 251, 253
Heinzelmann, Fred, 468
Heitgerd, Janet, 217
Helfer, R., 359

SUBJECT INDEX

COP (community-oriented policing), 212, 503, 510–514, 522
COPA (Chicanos Organizados Pintos Aztlan), 601
COPY Kids, 512
Corallo, Tony, 416
Corill, Dean, 337
Corner boy role, 209
Corporal punishment, 14–15, 133–134, 134
Corporate crime, 386, 387, 398–401, 410
  law enforcement, 405, 406
  and organized crime, 412
Corporate culture theory, 404–405
Correctionalism, 269
Corrections, 14–15, 477–478, 574–605
  community-based, 493, 494, 579–580, 588
  and criminal justice process, 482
  history of, 575–580, 590, 601
  jails, 35, 589–591
  parole, 478, 482, 557, 597, 604–605
  See also Criminal justice system; Incarceration; Intermediate sanctions; Probation; Punishment; Sentencing
Corruption, 387, 391
  in criminal justice system, 392–393, 499
Costello, Frank, 414
Counseling. *See* Therapy
Counterfeit Active Device and Computer Fraud and Abuse Act, 403
County law enforcement, 506
Courtroom work group, 486
Courts. *See* Judicatory process
Covert pathway to crime, 297
Cox, Archibald, 540
CPI (California Personality Inventory), 171
Crack, 99, 444, 445
Crackdowns, 129, 514
Credit card theft, 373, 395
Crime Act, 560
Crime and Everyday Life (Felson), 100
Crime and Human Nature (Wilson & Herrnstein), 174, 288, 289
Crime and Punishment in America (Currie), 494
Crime Commission, 475
Crime control model of criminal justice, 490–491, 582
Crime, defined, 19–20, 39–41
Crime discouragers, 125
Crime displacement, 115, 125–126
Crime in the Making (Sampson & Laub), 307
Crime patterns, 63–75
  and age, 69–71
  and biological trait theories, 161
  and cartographic school, 7
  ecological factors, 63–64
  and firearm availability, 64–67
  and gender, 69, 71–74, 340

and general theory of crime, 292
and labeling theory, 245–246
and race, 74–75
rape, 327–328
and social class, 67–69
Crime Prevention Through Environmental Design (Jeffery), 123–124
Crime rates, 12, 14–15. *See also* Criminal statistics
Crime, Shame and Reintegration (Braithwaite), 134
Crimes of reduction, 270
Crimes of repression, 270
Crime trends, 59–63. *See also specific trends*
Crime typology, 13–14
Criminal anthropology, 7, 9, 148–149
Criminal attempts (inchoate crimes), 33, 36
Criminal behavior systems, 13–14
Criminal careers, 75–79
  and developmental theories, 295
  and general strain theory, 205
  and integrated theories, 286–287
  and labeling theory, 239, 240, 244
  property crimes, 366–369, 377–379
  and rational choice theory, 115–116, 117
  and selective incapacitation, 137–138
  and substance abuse, 453–454
Criminal charge. *See* Charging
Criminal Copyright Infringement Act, 403
Criminal courts. *See* Judicatory process
Criminal defenses. *See* Defenses
Criminal gangs, 210
Criminal justice, 10, 12
Criminal justice system, 473–495
  components of, 475–478
  concepts, 490–495
  corruption in, 392–393
  history of, 473–475
  juvenile justice system, 274–275, 478, 480–481, 490, 493, 566, 568
  and labeling theory, 240, 246
  and law, 486–490
  process of, 478–479, 482–486
  sexism in, 274–275
  See also Corrections; Judicatory process; Law enforcement; Police
Criminal law. *See* Law
Criminal Sentences-Law Without Order (Frankel), 558
Criminal statistics, 12
  international perspective, 14–15
  self-report surveys, 20, 55–57, 59
  trends, 59–63
  victim surveys, 57–59
  See also Crime patterns; Uniform Crime Report; *specific crimes*
Criminal Violence, Criminal Justice (Silberman), 74

Criminology field:
  vs. criminal justice, 10, 12
  defined, 4
  vs. deviance, 10–11, 12
  ethical issues, 23
  history of, 5–9
  major perspectives, 10
  research methods, 20–23
  subareas of, 12–16
Crisis intervention, 103
Cross-examination, 553
Cross-national studies. *See* International perspectives
Cross-sectional research, 20
Crowds, 224
Crush, The, 87, 147
Crusted-over children, 324
Cruz, Rolando, 567
Cult killings, 336
Cultural deviance theory, 190–191, 207–211
  and differential association theory, 230
  and lack of opportunity, 117
  and substance abuse, 450
  and violent crimes, 324–325
  and white-collar crime, 404–405
Cultural transmission, 191
Culture conflict, 207, 228
Culture Conflict and Crime (Sellin), 207
Culture of poverty, 188
Curfew laws, 493
Custodial interrogation, 515–516
Custody, 478–479, 515
Customary courts, 34
Customs Bureau, 506
Cycle of violence hypothesis, 88

DA (differential association) theory, 226–231, 378, 404
Dahmer, Jeffrey, 42, 337
Dalkon Shield case, 407
Dangerous classes, 263
DARE (Drug Abuse Resistance Education), 460–461
Dark Ages, 29–30
Darvon, 446
Data leakage, 403
Date rape, 95, 167, 170, 329
Davis, Richard Allen, 37
Day fines, 583
DEA (Drug Enforcement Administration), 503
Deadly force, 525–526
Death penalty. *See* Capital punishment
Death squads, 354
DeBartolo, Eddie, Jr., 391
Deceptive pricing, 399
Deconstructionist analysis, 276
Decriminalization, 11, 33, 46, 435, 493
Deer Hunter, The, 168
Defective intelligence, 162
Defense attorneys, 543–544, 549, 553, 555

rape, 327
spousal abuse, 343
substance abuse, 11, 441–442, 443–444
terrorism, 350–351
violence, 321, 473
HIV. *See* AIDS
Hizballah group, 351
Hoffa, Johnny, 414
Hole, 597
Holy-motes, 30
Home confinement (HC), 586–587
Homicide. *See* Murder
Homicide networks, 335
Homophobia, 429
Homosexuality, 240, 241, 427–430
Honduran Anti-Communist Liberation
    Army, 352
Honduras, 352
Hormones, 46, 153–154
Hot spots, 93, 514
Hoult, Jennifer, 34
House Is Not a Home, A (Adler), 432
Houses of correction. *See* Jails
Housing and Urban Development (HUD),
    U.S. Department of, 392
Huberty, James, 338
Humanistic psychology, 166
Human nature theory, 288–289
Humiliation. *See* Shame
Hundred-gemot, 30
Hundreds, 30, 500
Hung jury, 482
Huntington's chorea, 157
Husband battering, 343
Hush, 147
Hustling, 598
Hyperactivity (ADHD), 154, 156, 298
Hyperarousal, 86
Hypermasculinity, 330
Hypoglycemia, 153

Id, 163
Identical bidding, 398
Identity crisis, 164
Ignorance defense, 41
Iheduru, Chris Ahamefule, 41
I Know What You Did Last Summer, 147
Illegal enterprise crimes, 385–386. *See
    also* Organized crime; White-collar
    crime
IMC Fertilizer, 410
Imitation theory, 162, 226
Immigration, 14, 18, 41
Immigration and Naturalization Service,
    503, 506
Imperatively coordinated associations,
    259
Imperial Food Products, 410
Impersonation, 403
Implied (constructive) malice, 333
Importation model, 598

Impulsivity, 290–294
Incapacitation effect, 136–138, 556, 564,
    579
Incarceration, 555–556, 591–604
    classification of inmates, 477–478
    history of, 575, 576–577
    and incapacitation effect, 136–138
    inmate profile, 596–597
    institution types, 591–594
    and law, 603–604
    prisoners' rights, 492, 579, 603–604
    prison life, 597–600
    prison overcrowding, 136, 459, 490,
        594–596
    prison violence, 579, 597, 602–603
    and treatment, 579–580, 600–602
Inchoate crimes (criminal attempts), 33
Increasers, 328
Indeterminate sentences, 557
Index crimes, 51, 52
India, terrorism, 352
Indictment, 479
Indirect costs, 85
Inevitable discovery rule, 515
Inferiority complex, 164
Influence peddling, 391–394
Informal sanctions, 131, 167
Information (charging), 479, 545
Information-processing theory, 166, 167,
    170
Inheritance school, 148–149
Inmate subculture, 598
Inner cities:
    and Chicago School, 8, 185, 191
    and crime patterns, 64, 67, 74, 75
    crime trends, 60
    poverty in, 189
    and relative deprivation theory, 202
    social disorganization theory, 190,
        191–198
    and victimization, 89–90, 92, 98
    See also Gangs
Innovation, 199
Inquisition, 4
Insanity defense, 42–43, 44, 176, 490
Insider trading, 390–391
Instinct, 152
Institute for Social Research, 56
Institutional anomie theory, 200–202
Instrumental crimes, 67, 319–320
Instrumental Marxism, 267–268
Insurance fraud, 395
Integrated structural Marxist theory, 271
Integrated theories, 286–310, 311
    latent trait theories, 161, 206, 287–294
    multifactor, 286, 287
    See also Developmental theories
Integrative-constitutive theory, 270
Intelligence, 154, 172–175, 247, 289
Intensive probation supervision (IPS),
    585–586

Intent, 39, 40–41
Interactional theory, 306–307
Interactionist theory, 18–19, 161
Interdiction strategies, 459
Interdisciplinary nature of criminology, 4
Intermediate sanctions, 556, 579,
    582–589
    electronic monitoring, 587–588
    fines, 30, 556, 583
    forfeiture, 30, 583–585
    home confinement, 586–587
    intensive probation supervision,
        585–586
    residential community corrections, 588
    restitution, 246, 494, 585
    shock incarceration, 588–589
    shock probation, 585
    split sentencing, 585
Internal affairs divisions, 508
Internal Revenue Service, 506
International perspectives:
    capital punishment, 566, 568
    common law, 34
    criminal careers, 77, 78
    criminal statistics, 14–15
    drug dealing/trafficking, 15, 458–459
    general theory of crime, 293
    hate crimes, 347
    incarceration, 595
    intelligence, 174
    morality, 425–426
    organized crime, 415–416
    restorative justice, 278–279
    substance abuse, 441, 463
    terrorism, 351–354
    white-collar crime, 387–388
    See also History
Internet crime, 373, 401–402, 411, 440
Interstate and Foreign Travel or
    Transportation in Aid of Racketeering
    Enterprises Act, 416
Interview research, 22
Intoxication defense, 43
Investigation, 478, 509–510, 540
Involuntary (negligent) manslaughter, 333
Involvement, 237
IPS (intensive probation supervision),
    585–586
Iran, 354–355, 463
Iran and Libya Sanctions Act, 354–355
Irresistible Impulse Test, 43
Irvin, Michael, 331
Italy, 15

Jahnke, Richard and Deborah, 96
Jails, 35, 477, 589–591
Japan, 14, 415–416
Jaworski, Leon, 540
J.C. Penney, 391
Jeans, Sam, 501
Joyriding, 373

Littleton shooting, 320
Lockheed Aircraft Corporation, 393, 394, 399
Logic bombs, 402–403
Lojack auto protection system, 126, 374
Lombrosian theory, 6–7
Longitudinal research, 20–21
Lord, Steven, 95
Louima, Abner, 520
Love serial killers, 338
Lower class. *See* Social class; Social structure theories
"Lower-Class Culture as a Generating Milieu of Gang Delinquency" (Miller), 207
LSD, 443
Luciano, Lucky, 409, 414
Lumpen proletariat, 257

Madams, 432
Mafia, 411, 412, 413, 417
Maggadino, Stefano, 414
Magoto, Marita, 16
Mahan, Dale and Ronnie, 535
Mala in se crimes, 35–36, 37
Mala prohibitum crimes, 35–36, 37
Malcolm X, 603
Malice, 333
Malls, 100
Management fraud, 394
Managers, 125
Mandatory sentencing, 15, 473, 556, 560
    and criminal careers, 79
    and gun control, 66, 129
    and prison overcrowding, 136, 595, 596
Maniac Cop, 147
Mann Act, 435, 503
Manorial courts, 31
Manslaughter, 36, 333. *See also* Violent crimes
MAO (monoamine oxidase), 157
Ma, Po Chieng, 375
Mapplethorpe, Robert, 425, 438
Marginalization, 266
Marijuana, 11, 443, 446, 447, 449, 457
Marijuana Tax Act, 33, 456
Marital rape, 329–330
Marital status, 91–92, 307
Marks, 375
Marxist criminology, 264–272
    critique of, 272
    development of, 264–265
    formal theories, 270–271
    fundamentals of, 265–267
    instrumental, 267–268
    research on, 269–272
    structural, 268–269
    See also Marxist theory
Marxist feminism, 273–274
Marxist theory, 9, 255–258. *See also* Marxist criminology

Marxist theory of deviance, 270–271
Masculinities and Crime (Messerschmidt), 274
Masculinity hypothesis, 72
Mask of Love, The (Sullivan), 277
Massage parlors, 434
Mass murderers, 337
Mating habits, 293
Maximum-security prisons, 591, 592, 593
MBD (Minimal brain dysfunction), 155
McCarthy, Carolyn, 16
McCleskey, Warren, 568
McDonnell-Douglas Aircraft Corporation, 393, 407
McDougal, Jim, 396
McDougal, Susan, 396
McVeigh, Timothy, 40, 430, 592
MDMA (ecstasy), 446
Mechanical solidarity, 199
Medellin drug cartel, 415
Media:
    and criminal justice system, 473
    and differential association theory, 227
    economic crimes, 363
    police in, 509, 510
    prostitution in, 432, 433
    rape in, 327, 330, 331
    and social structure, 187, 188
    stalking in, 94
    and trait theories, 147–148
    victimization in, 87
    violence in, 166, 168–169
Mediation, 278, 349, 493, 494
Medical model. *See* Rehabilitation model of criminal justice
Medium-security prisons, 591
Megan's Law, 47
Menendez, Eric and Lyle, 96
Mens rea, 39, 40–41, 44
Mental illness, 96, 170, 331. *See also* Biological trait theories
Merritt, Andrew, 336
Mescaline, 443
Mesomorphs, 149
Methadone, 445, 461, 462
Methedrine, 442–443
Metropolitan police agencies, 506–507
Mexico, 459
MFY (Mobilization for Youth), 212
Microsoft, 267, 268
Middle Ages, 4–5
Middle-class measuring rods, 208
Middle East, 350, 351, 354
Milieu therapy, 600
Military:
    and homosexuality, 429–430
    and rape, 327
    and spouse abuse, 343
    white-collar crime in, 392, 407
Milken, Michael, 119, 390–391, 403
Milk, Harvey, 152

Miltown, 442
Minimal brain dysfunction (MBD), 155
Minimum-security prisons, 591
Minnesota Multiphasic Personality Inventory (MMPI), 171
Miranda, Ernesto, 484
Miranda rule, 490, 515–516
Misdemeanors, 35
Misery, 147
Mission hate crimes, 347
Misson-oriented serial killers, 337
Missouri Plan, 545
MMPI (Minnesota Multiphasic Personality Inventory), 171
M'Naghten Rule, 42, 43
MO (*modus operandi*), 509
Mobilization for Youth (MFY), 212
Moceanu, Dominique, 27
Modus operandi (MO), 509
Mollen Commission, 393, 499
Monetary restitution, 585
Money Train, 168
Monitoring the Future, 56
Monoamine oxidase (MAO), 157
Monroe Parker Securities Inc., 390
Moral crusades, 426–427
Moral development theory, 166, 167
Moral entrepreneurs, 18, 240–241, 427
Morality, 37–38, 424–427
Moral Sense, The (Wilson), 153
Morals squads, 509
Moran, Bugs, 412
Mores, 28, 36
Morning glory seeds, 443
Morphine, 444
Morris, Robert, 403
Morton Thiokol, Inc., 387
Mosaic Code, 28
Moscone, George, 152
Motivated offenders, 98, 117
Movies. *See* Media
MPQ (Multidimensional Personality Questionnaire), 171–172
Muckrakers, 398
Mug shots, 509
Multidimensional Personality Questionnaire (MPQ), 171–172
Multifactor theories, 286, 287
Multistage sampling technique, 58
Munoz Talavera, Rafael, 459
Murder, 332–339
    defined, 32–33, 36, 332–333
    degrees of, 333
    and general deterrence theory, 130
    parricide, 96
    and rational choice theory, 122
    serial killers, 87, 122, 164, 336–339
    trends, 62, 63
    See also Violent crimes
Mutual societies, 121
Mutual Welfare League, 578
Mysoped, 337

Sting operations, 509
Stings, 388
Stokes, Edward Harvey, 491
STP, 443
Strain theories, 198–206
    anomie theory, 8, 198–200
    cultural deviance theory, 117, 190–191,
        207–211, 230, 324–325, 404–405, 450
    general strain theory, 203–206
    institutional anomie theory, 200–202
    and lack of opportunity, 117
    relative deprivation theory, 75, 186,
        202–203, 272
Stranger-to-stranger rape, 329
Stratified society, 186
Strawder, Jonathan, 388
Street Corner Society (Whyte), 22
Street crimes, 364. *See also* Auto theft;
    Prostitution
Street junkies, 453
Streetwalkers, 432, 436
Strict-liability crimes, 41
Structural Criminology (Hagan), 275
Structural locations, 266
Structural Marxism, 268–269
Stun belts, 591
Sturges, Jock, 424
Subculture of violence theory, 75,
    324–325
Subcultures, 191
    corporate, 404–405
    police, 517–518, 520
    prison, 598
    and violence, 75, 324–325
    See also Cultural deviance theory
Substance abuse, 441–463
    and AIDS, 446, 448–449, 450, 454, 463
    and burglary, 99, 379
    causation, 450–452
    common drugs, 442–446
    control strategies, 11, 460–463
    and crime trends, 61
    and desistance, 71
    and differential association theory, 229
    extent of, 446–449
    and feticide, 333
    history of, 11, 33–34, 441–442
    international perspectives, 15
    and law, 11, 33–34, 456–458
    and law enforcement, 458–460
    and prostitution, 433–434, 436, 450
    and rational choice theory, 120,
        451–452
    and self-report surveys, 57
    types of, 452–454
    and victimization, 93, 99
    and violent crimes, 99, 325–326, 343,
        445, 454–456, 457
    See also Drug dealing/trafficking
Substantial Capacity Test, 43
Substantive criminal law, 17, 36
Subterranean values, 232

Subway crime, 127
Sufferance, 349
Sugar, 152
Suicide, 8, 34, 326
    assisted, 12, 46, 426
Suitable targets, 98, 116–117
Superconducting interference device
    (SQUID), 155
Superego, 163
Superfund, 401
Super-zapping, 402
Supreme Court. *See* U.S. Supreme Court
Surety bail, 546, 547
Surplus value, 257–258, 266–267
Surveillance officers, 586
Survey research, 20
Swindles, 388–389
Symbolic interaction school of sociology,
    18
Symbolic interaction theory, 239
Syndicated pornography rings, 437
Systematic check forgers, 372–373
Systemic link, 326

Tamalio, Jesus Antonio, 122
Tangible direct costs, 85
Target hardening strategies, 104–105, 124,
    372
Target reduction strategies, 124
Target removal strategies, 372
Task Force on Victims of Crime, 101
Tate, Christopher, 409
Tax evasion, 396–398
Taxi Driver, 168
Team policing, 511
Teamsters Union, 414
Technical violations, 581, 604
Teen crime. *See* Juvenile crime
Television. *See* Media
Temperance movement, 441–442
Temperature, 64
Temp, The, 147
Terrorism, 349–355. *See also* Violent
    crimes
Terrorist serial killers, 338
Teslac, 446
Testosterone, 153
Testosterone defense, 46
Texas Rangers, 506
Thailand, 387, 441, 463
Thanatos, 322–323
Theft. *See* Property crimes
Thematic Apperception Test, 171
Therapy, 170, 175–176, 600–601. *See also*
    Rehabilitation; Treatment
Thief takers, 365
Thinking About Crime (Wilson), 115
Thomasson, Paul, 429
Thorazine, 442
Three-strikes laws, 79, 137–138, 473,
    560–561. *See also* Mandatory
    sentencing

Threshold inquiry, 516
Thrill killing, 335
Thrill seeking, 122, 123, 157–158
Thrill-seeking hate crimes, 347
Tier system, 577
Time-series research design, 21–22
Tithings, 30, 500
Torrio, Johnny, 412, 414
Tort law, 34–35
Torture, Middle Ages, 5
Totality of circumstances test, 516
Toxic Substance Control Act, 401
Track system, 224
Traffic control, 510
Train robbery, 368
Trait theories:
    and media violence, 147–148
    policy implications, 175–176
    See also Biological trait theories; Latent
        trait theories; Psychological trait
        theories
Tranquilizers, 442
Transactional analysis, 600
Transferred intent, 40
Transitional neighborhoods, 192
Transition pornography rings, 437
Treason, history of, 30
Treasury, U.S. Department of the, 506
Treatment:
    and age-graded theory, 294
    and biological trait theories, 175–176
    and incarceration, 579–580, 600–602
    and information-processing theory,
        170
    and juvenile justice system, 480
    and probation, 581
    and rehabilitation model, 492–493
    and residential community corrections,
        588
    and social process theories, 246
    and substance abuse, 461
    See also Rehabilitation
Trial by combat, 29
Trials, 31, 32, 550–555
Trojan horse, 402
Truly disadvantaged, 189
Truth-in-sentencing laws, 560, 595
Tucker, Karla Faye, 38
Tumors, 155, 156–157
Turbulence, 147
Turning points, 307–308
Twelve Tables, 28
"Twinkie defense," 152
Twin studies, 159
2 Live Crew, 438
Tying arrangement, 398
Tyson, Mike, 484

UCR. *See* Uniform Crime Report
Unabomber, 302, 478
Underclass, 132, 188, 189
Undeserving poor concept, 188, 190

PHOTO CREDITS

attn: Rotary
for Tracy

Fax # 747-3562